NTC's Multilingual Dictionary of AMERICAN SIGN LANGUAGE

NTC's Multilingual Dictionary of AMERICAN SIGN LANGUAGE

Claude O. Proctor, Ph.D.

Illustrated by Tony Landon McGregor

Printed on recyclable paper

National Textbook Company
a division of *NTC Publishing Group* • Lincolnwood, Illinois USA

1996 Printing

©1995 National Textbook Company, a division of NTC Publishing Group, 4255 West Touhy Avenue, Lincolnwood (Chicago), Illinois, 60646-1975 U.S.A.

6 7 8 9 ML 9 8 7 6 5 4 3 2

For Edwin deSteiguer (Ned) Snead
a true Renaissance man

Contents

Introduction

The dictionary contains approximately 2,500 entries in Arabic, Chinese, Dutch, English, French, German, Italian, Japanese, Korean, Portuguese, Russian, Spanish, and Swedish—each illustrated with an appropriate representation of the word in American Sign Language. Romanized spellings are given for the Chinese, Japanese, Korean, and Russian words in each entry, along with the traditional non-Roman writing systems of these languages.

In its totality, this reference work is unique in its breadth of major world languages and accompanying ASL signs, comprehensiveness of lexical items, and convenient cross-indexing feature for each dictionary entry. Functionality and simplicity were the major guiding principles in compiling and designing the dictionary. For the most part, pronunciation of the romanized forms is fairly conventional with the following notable exceptions in the Pinyin system of romanizing Chinese. The letter **c** is pronounced "ts," the letter **q** is pronounced "ch," and the letter **x** is pronounced "sh."

This comprehensive work should prove to be a valuable reference volume for libraries, academic institutions, language-training centers, government agencies, international organizations for the deaf, international companies, travelers, translators, researchers, teachers, students, and professional businesspeople.

Preface and Acknowledgments

A plaque on my office wall offers a sobering reminder of the somewhat capricious nature of lexicography, or any attempt at translation for that matter: *Traduttore—Traditore* 'the translator is a traitor.' Indeed, the compilation of a dictionary—albeit one in fourteen languages—is not unlike the risk involved in Russian roulette! As a professional linguist and translator I am all too aware of the pitfalls of striving for linguistic equivalence among natural languages. Of course, in an endeavor of this kind, both the challenges and the rewards are magnified many times over by the number of languages.

The prodigious task of producing a multilingual dictionary grew out of a project begun by the Rotary Club of Georgetown, Texas, to promote the idea of improving communication and understanding among the speakers of the different languages of the world. This idea, which has intrigued humankind for centuries, strongly reflects Rotary's goal of advancing international understanding, good will, and peace through a world fellowship of business and professional people united in the ideal of service. For the compiler and editor, this book has been a labor of love. I hope it is evident.

Needless to say, a publication of this scope would never have become the realization of a dream without the encouragement, support, and assistance of a multitude of people. Unfortunately, it is impossible to acknowledge them all here, but fellow Rotarian Ned Snead merits a special expression of gratitude for his inspirational and significant support of the project. The following people also deserve a distinct measure of recognition: Richard "Andy" Anderson, Larry Bingham, John Hall, Dale Illig, Tom Locke, Maurice "Mo" McKinney, Lou Markwith, Robert "Skip" Morse, Bill Smith, and Paul Williams; our talented illustrator Tony Landon McGregor; Stephen G. Brown and his staff, Javier and Gloria Galdeano, Kay Fabricio, Dr. Mohamed F. Ghanayem, Marcello Guercini, Lev Gutman, Carl E. Moncrief, Len Palmgren, Anneke Phillips, and Arlette Quervel at International Translating & Typesetting Company of Dallas; Laurel K. Kao and her staff, Steve and Hyun-Sook Choi, Kuenja C. Chung, Mieko Dotson and Mei-Yun Lee at Far East Language Service of Dallas; Consuelo Arteaga, Wouter Barendregt, Clelia Benjamin, Lena Hoegfeldt, Poong-Ja Toyoko Kang, Jocelyn Liu, Henry and Miyuki Nakagawa, Regine Reynolds-Cornell, Charles Robertson, Jutta Sharpe, Suk-soon Suh, Michael Thomas, and Chiaki Watanabe; and finally, my dear wife Doris and sons Chris and Gabe for their love and support. In addition to the specific assistance mentioned above, this dictionary would not have been printed without the financial commitment of Rotarians Jim Albers, Ken Anderson, Richard "Andy" Anderson, Richard "Rich" Anderson, Nelson Barrett, Alan Battersby, Larry Bingham, Howard Burt, Bill Bryce, Virgil Carlson, Hank Carver, James A. Davidson, R. Mark Dietz, Jim Donovan,

Lloyd Evans, Wallace Evans, Ken Ewan, Wallace Giddings, Art Goethe, Tom Guyton, Jeff Hallett, Don Hewlett, Dale Illig, John T. King, Brian Lambeth, Carl Lidell, Bill Ludwig, Dan Mansour, Mo McKinney, Mike McMaster, John Overton, Norm Peters, Glenn Pittsford, Claude O. Proctor, Fred Sellers, Jay C. Sloan, Billy Smith, Ned Snead, Chuck Starnes, Ken Stubblefield, William R. Stump, Clark Thurmond, Wade Todd, Charles Turner, and Paul Williams.

Claude O. Proctor
Georgetown, Texas

American Sign Language

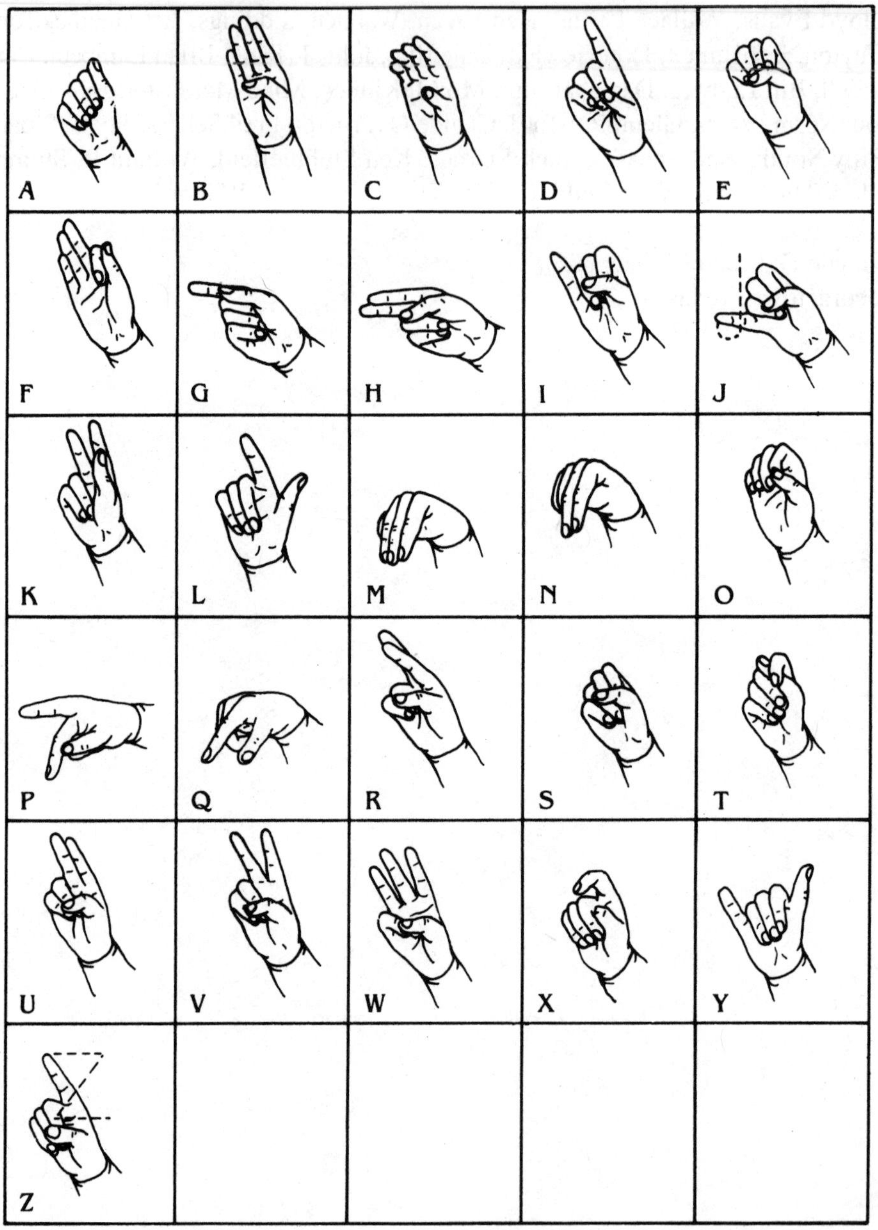

A	B	C	D	E
F	G	H	I	J
K	L	M	N	O
P	Q	R	S	T
U	V	W	X	Y
Z				

International Sign Language

A	B	C	D	E
F	G	H	I	J
K	L	M	N	O
P	Q	R	S	T
U	V	W	X	Y
Z				

NTC's Multilingual Dictionary of AMERICAN SIGN LANGUAGE

1. abandon [v.]

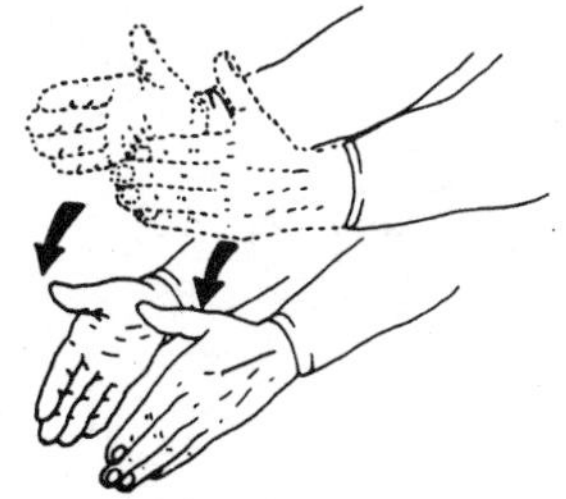

Arabic: táraka ترك
Chinese: líqì 離棄
Dutch: verlaten
French: abandonner
German: verlassen
Italian: abbandonare
Japanese: misuteru 見捨てる
Korean: bŏrida 버리다
Portuguese: abandonar
Russian: pokidát' покидать
Spanish: abandonar
Swedish: överge

2. abbreviate [v.]

Arabic: ikhtásara إختصر
Chinese: suō lüè 縮略
Dutch: afkorten
French: abréger
German: abkürzen
Italian: abbreviare
Japanese: shōryaku suru 省略する
Korean: saengnyakhada 생략하다
Portuguese: abreviar
Russian: sokrashchát' сокращать
Spanish: abreviar
Swedish: förkorta

3. ability [n.]

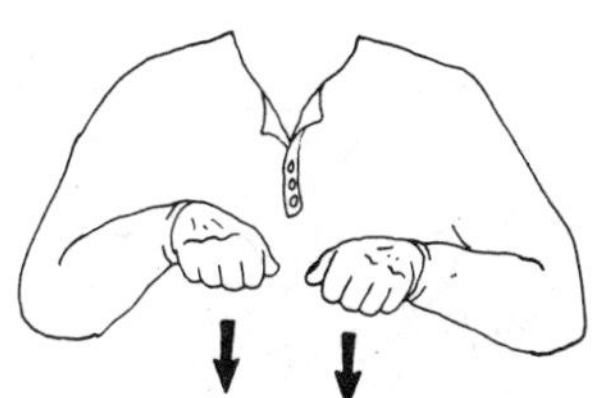

Arabic: máqdira مقدرة
Chinese: nénglì 能力
Dutch: vermogen
French: capacité
German: Fähigkeit
Italian: capacità
Japanese: nōryoku 能力
Korean: nŭngnyŏk 능력
Portuguese: capacidade
Russian: sposóbnost' способность
Spanish: habilidad
Swedish: förmåga

4. abolish [v.]

Arabic: lágha لغى
Chinese: fèichú 廢除
Dutch: afschaffen
French: abolir
German: abschaffen
Italian: abolire
Japanese: haishi suru 廃止する
Korean: p'yejihada 포기하다
Portuguese: abolir
Russian: otmenyát' отменять
Spanish: abolir
Swedish: avskaffa

5. about (concerning) [prep.]

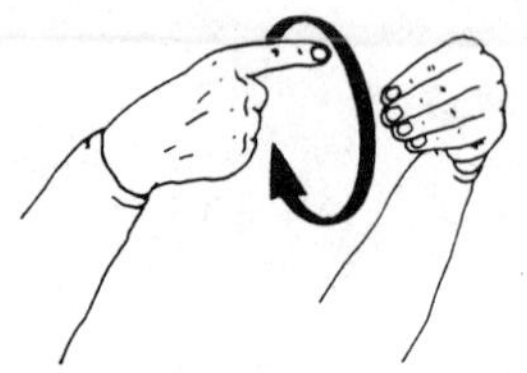

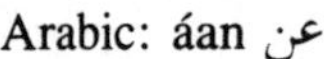

Arabic: áan عن
Chinese: guānyú 關於
Dutch: betreffende
French: au sujet de
German: um
Italian: riguardo a
Japanese: ...ni tsuite …に就いて
Korean: ...e kwanhayŏ ~에 관하여.
Portuguese: a respeito de
Russian: o о
Spanish: con respecto a
Swedish: om

6. above [adv./prep.]

Arabic: fauq فوق
Chinese: zài...shàngmiàn 在 … 上面
Dutch: boven
French: au-dessus
German: über
Italian: sopra
Japanese: ...no ueni …の上に
Korean: ...boda wie ~보다 위
Portuguese: sôbre
Russian: nad над
Spanish: sobre
Swedish: ovanför

7. abroad [adv.]

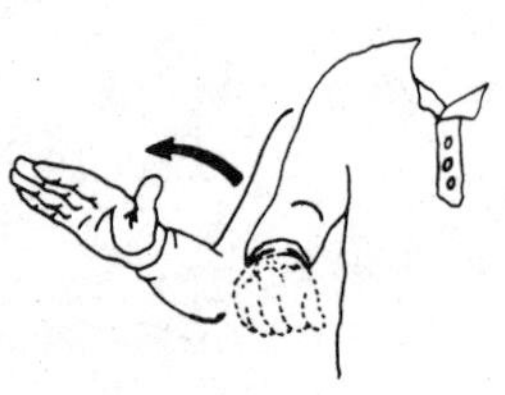

Arabic: fil-khárij في الخارج
Chinese: zài guówài 在 … 國外
Dutch: in het buitenland
French: à l'étranger
German: im Ausland
Italian: all'estero
Japanese: hiroku 広く
Korean: haeoee 해외
Portuguese: no estrangeiro
Russian: za granítsey за границей
Spanish: al extranjero
Swedish: utomlands

8. absence [n.]

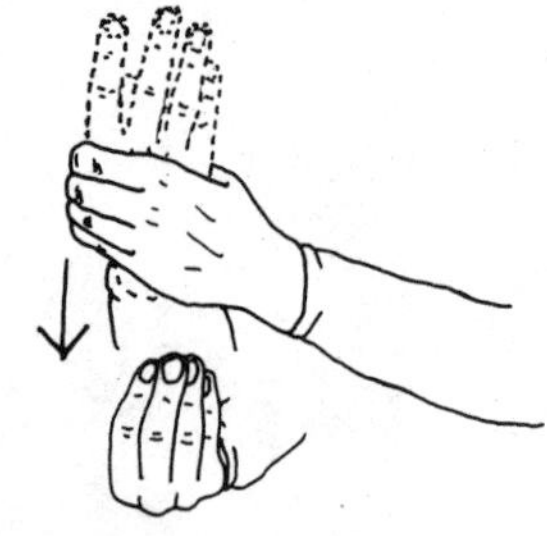

Arabic: ghiyáb غياب
Chinese: quēxí 缺席
Dutch: afwezigheid
French: absence
German: Abwesenheit
Italian: assenza
Japanese: kesseki 欠席
Korean: bujae 부재
Portuguese: ausência
Russian: otsútstviye отсутствие
Spanish: ausencia
Swedish: frånvaro

9. absurd [adj.]

Arabic: muhál محال
Chinese: huāngtáng 荒唐
Dutch: absurd
French: absurde
German: absurd
Italian: assurdo
Japanese: bakarashii 馬鹿らしい
Korean: t'ŏmuniŏmnŭn 터무니 없는
Portuguese: absurdo
Russian: absúrdnyy абсурдный
Spanish: absurdo
Swedish: absurd

10. accept [v.]

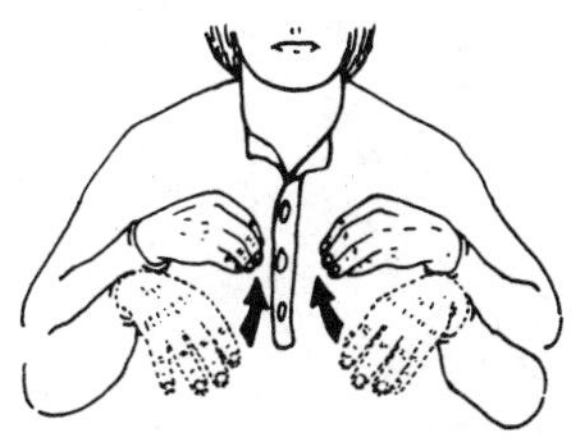

Arabic: qábila قبل
Chinese: jiēshòu 接受
Dutch: accepteren
French: accepter
German: akzeptieren
Italian: accettare
Japanese: ukeru 受ける
Korean: badadŭrida 받아 들이다
Portuguese: aceitar
Russian: prinimát' принимать
Spanish: aceptar
Swedish: acceptera

11. accident [n.]

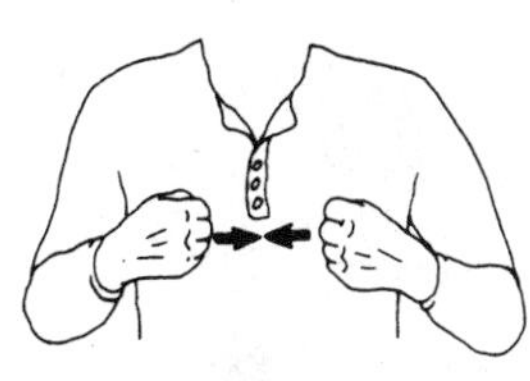

Arabic: hádith حادث
Chinese: shìgù 事故
Dutch: ongeluk
French: accident
German: Unfall
Italian: incidente
Japanese: jiko 事故
Korean: sago 사고
Portuguese: acidente
Russian: aváriya авария
Spanish: accidente
Swedish: olycka

12. accompany [v.]

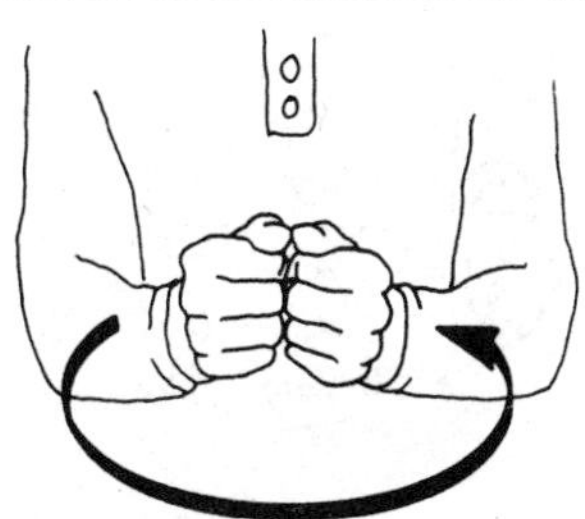

Arabic: ráafaqa رافق
Chinese: péitóng 陪同
Dutch: begeleiden
French: accompagner
German: begleiten
Italian: accompagnare
Japanese: dohan suru 同伴する
Korean: dongban'hada 동반하다
Portuguese: acompanhar
Russian: soprovozhdát' сопровождать
Spanish: acompañar
Swedish: följa

13. accomplish [v.]

Arabic: ánjaza انجز
Chinese: wánchéng 完成
Dutch: volbrengen
French: accomplir
German: vollbringen
Italian: realizzare
Japanese: nashitogeru 成し遂げる
Korean: iruda 이루다
Portuguese: realizar
Russian: sovershát' совершать
Spanish: realizar
Swedish: fullborda

14. account [n.]

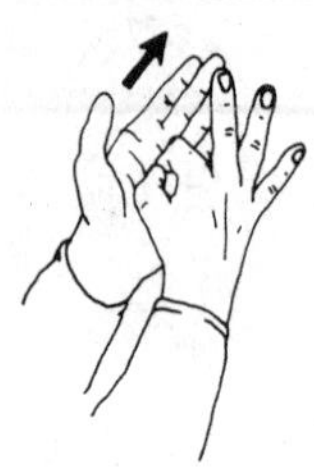

Arabic: hisáb حساب
Chinese: zhàngmù 賬目
Dutch: rekening
French: compte
German: Konto
Italian: conto
Japanese: kaikei 会計
Korean: kyesansŏ 계산서
Portuguese: conta
Russian: schyót счёт
Spanish: cuenta
Swedish: konto

15. accumulate [v.]

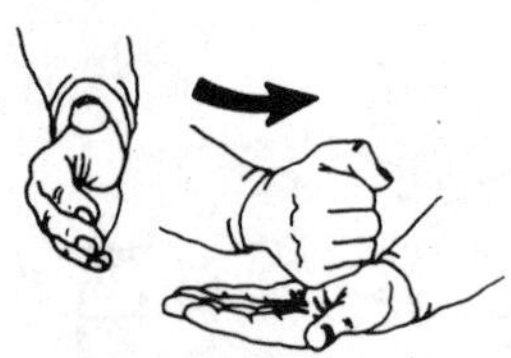

Arabic: jámaa جمع
Chinese: lěijī 累積
Dutch: verzamelen
French: accumuler
German: ansammeln
Italian: accumulare
Japanese: tameru ためる
Korean: moŭda 모으다
Portuguese: acumular
Russian: nakáplivat' накапливать
Spanish: acumular
Swedish: ackumulera

16. accurate [adj.]

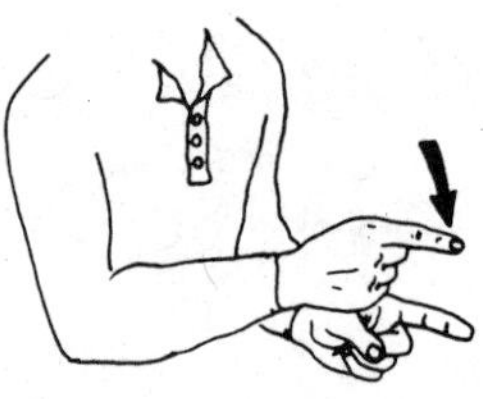

Arabic: madbút مضبوط
Chinese: zhǔn què 準確
Dutch: precies
French: précis
German: genau
Italian: esatto
Japanese: seikakuna 正確な
Korean: chŏnghwak'an 정확한
Portuguese: exato
Russian: tóchnyy точный
Spanish: exacto
Swedish: noggrann

17. accuse [v.]

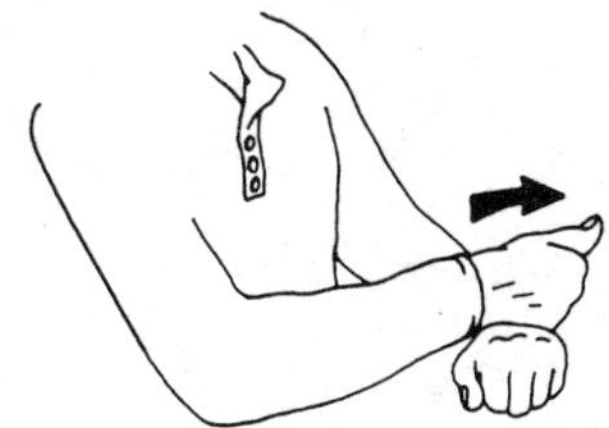

Arabic: itáhama إتهم
Chinese: qiǎnzé 譴責
Dutch: beschuldigen
French: accuser
German: beschuldigen
Italian: accusare
Japanese: togameru とがめる
Korean: binanhada 비난하다
Portuguese: acusar
Russian: obvinyát' обвинять
Spanish: acusar
Swedish: anklaga

18. accustom (to) [v.]

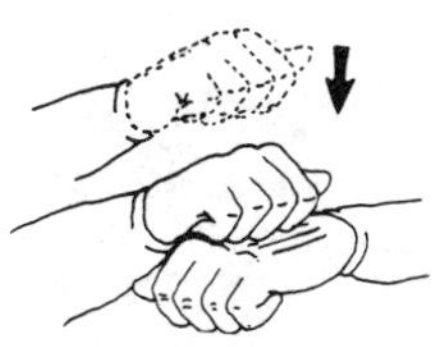

Arabic: iaatáda إعتاد
Chinese: shǐ xíguàn 使習慣
Dutch: aanwennen
French: habituer
German: gewöhnen
Italian: abituare
Japanese: narasu 慣らす
Korean: iksukk'e hada 익숙하다
Portuguese: acostumar
Russian: priuchát' приучать
Spanish: acostumbrar
Swedish: vänja

19. ache [n.]

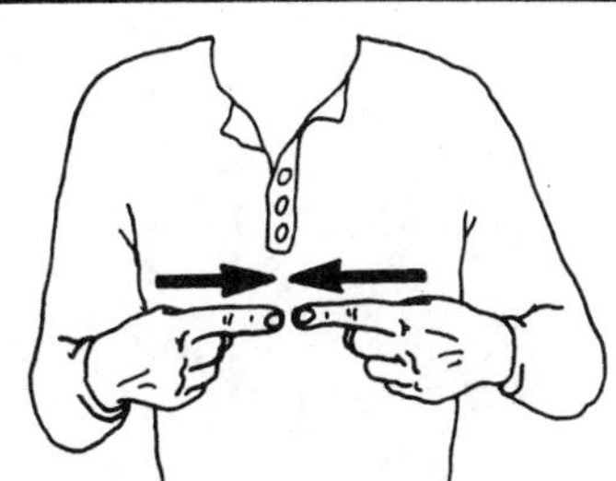

Arabic: álam ألم
Chinese: téngtòng 疼痛
Dutch: pijn
French: douleur
German: Schmerz
Italian: dolore
Japanese: itami 痛み
Korean: ap'ŭm 아픔
Portuguese: dor
Russian: bol' боль
Spanish: dolor
Swedish: värk

20. achieve [v.]

Arabic: ánjaza انجز
Chinese: chéngjiòu 成就
Dutch: presteren
French: accomplir
German: erreichen
Italian: raggiungere
Japanese: tassei suru 達成する
Korean: sŏngch'wihada 성취하다
Portuguese: alcançar
Russian: dostigát' достигать
Spanish: lograr
Swedish: uppnå

21. acquire [v.]

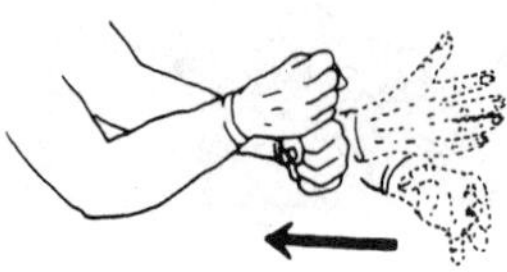

Arabic: náala نال
Chinese: huòdé 獲得
Dutch: verwerven
French: acquérir
German: erwerben
Italian: acquistare
Japanese: shūtoku suru 習得する
Korean: ŭt'nŭnda 얻는다
Portuguese: adquirir
Russian: priobretát' приобретать
Spanish: adquirir
Swedish: skaffa sig

22. across [prep.]

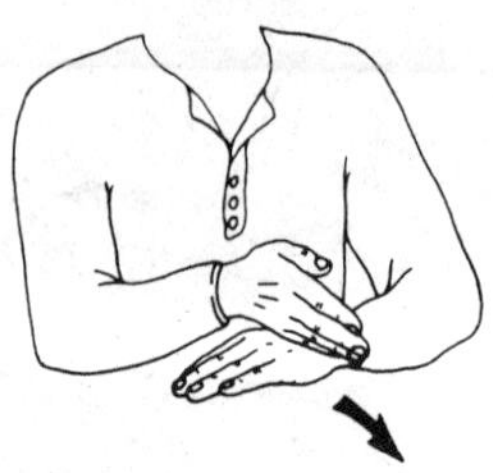

Arabic: áabr عبر
Chinese: yuè guò 越過
Dutch: overheen
French: à travers
German: quer über
Italian: attraverso
Japanese: . . . o yokogitte を横切って
Korean: kŏnnŏsŏ 건너서
Portuguese: através de
Russian: chérez через
Spanish: a través de
Swedish: tvärs över

23. act [v.]

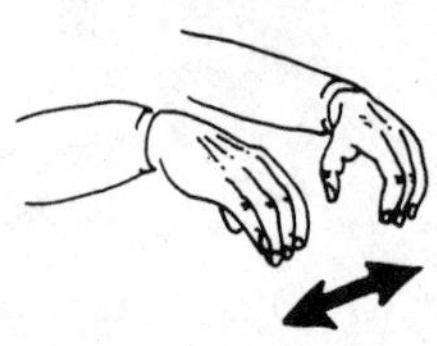

Arabic: tasárafa تصرف
Chinese: xíngdòng 行動
Dutch: handelen
French: agir
German: handeln
Italian: agire
Japanese: kōdō suru 行動する
Korean: haenghada 행하다
Portuguese: agir
Russian: déystvovat' действовать
Spanish: obrar
Swedish: handla

24. action [n.]

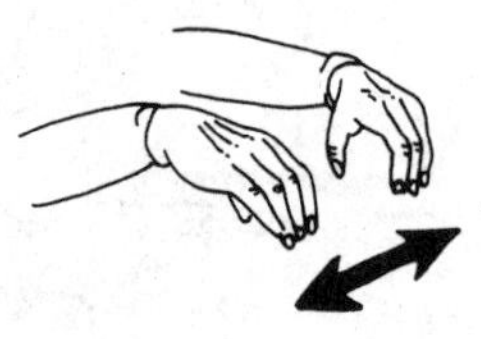

Arabic: áamal عمل
Chinese: xíngwéi 行爲
Dutch: handeling
French: action
German: Handlung
Italian: azione
Japanese: katsudō 活動
Korean: haengwi 행위
Portuguese: ação
Russian: déystviye действие
Spanish: acción
Swedish: handling

25. active [adj.]

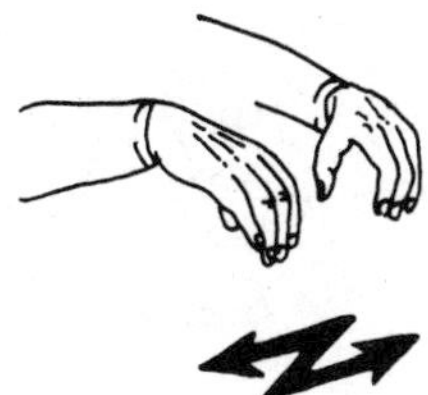

Arabic: nashíit نشيط
Chinese: huódòngde 活動的
Dutch: aktief
French: actif
German: aktiv
Italian: attivo
Japanese: katsudo teki na 活動的な
Korean: hwalbarhan 활발한
Portuguese: ativo
Russian: aktívnyy активный
Spanish: activo
Swedish: aktiv

26. activity [n.]

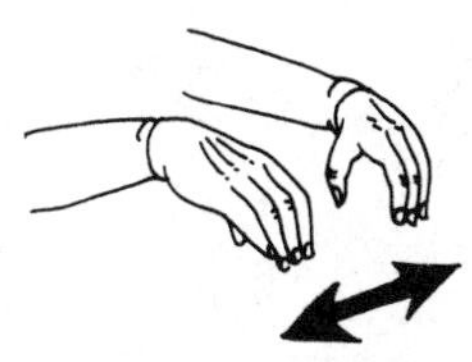

Arabic: nasháat نشاط
Chinese: huódòng 活動
Dutch: aktiviteit
French: activité
German: Tätigkeit
Italian: attività
Japanese: katsudō 活動
Korean: hwaldong 활동
Portuguese: atividade
Russian: déyatel'nost' деятельность
Spanish: actividad
Swedish: aktivitet

27. actor [n.]

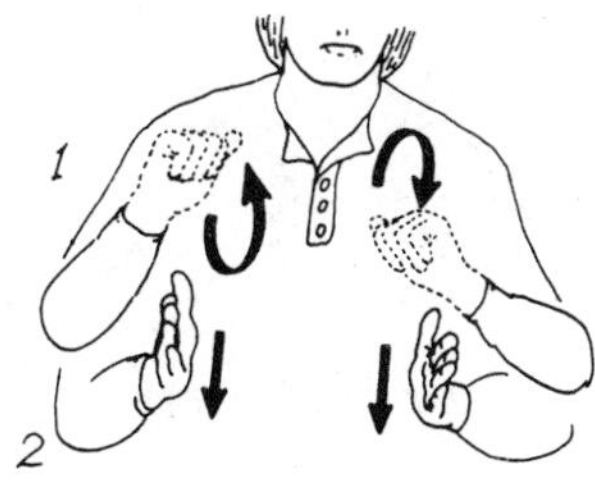

Arabic: mométhil ممثل
Chinese: nán yǎnyuán 男演員
Dutch: acteur
French: acteur
German: Schauspieler
Italian: attore
Japanese: haiyū 男優
Korean: baeu 배우
Portuguese: ator
Russian: aktyór актëр
Spanish: actor
Swedish: skådespelare

28. actress [n.]

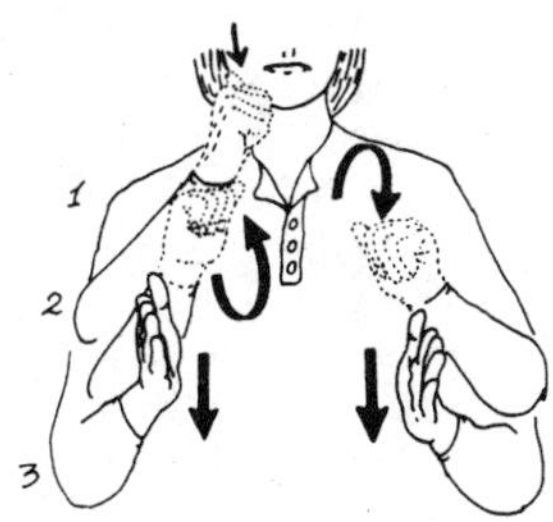

Arabic: mométhila ممثلة
Chinese: nǚ yǎnyuán 女演員
Dutch: actrice
French: actrice
German: Schauspielerin
Italian: attrice
Japanese: joyū 女優
Korean: yŏbaeu 여배우
Portuguese: atriz
Russian: aktrísa актриса
Spanish: actriz
Swedish: skådespelerska

29. actual(ly) [adj./adv.]

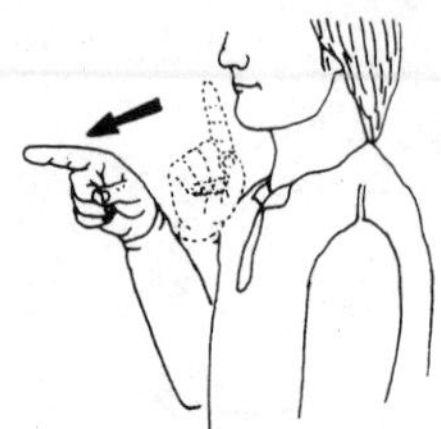

Arabic: haqíeqi حقيقي
Chinese: shíjìde 實際的
Dutch: werkelijk
French: réel
German: tatsächlich
Italian: reale
Japanese: jissai no 実際の
Korean: siljaeui 실제의
Portuguese: real
Russian: deystvítel'nyy действительный
Spanish: real
Swedish: faktisk

30. add (increase) [v.]

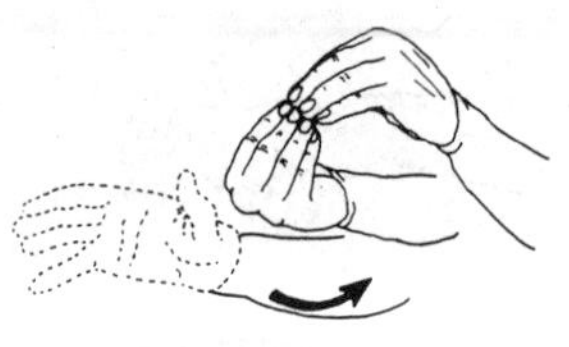

Arabic: adáafa اضاف
Chinese: jiā 加
Dutch: toevoegen
French: ajouter
German: hinzufügen
Italian: aggiungere
Japanese: kuwaeru 加える
Korean: tŏhada 더하다
Portuguese: adicionar
Russian: pribavlyát' прибавлять
Spanish: añadir
Swedish: tillägga

31. address [n.]

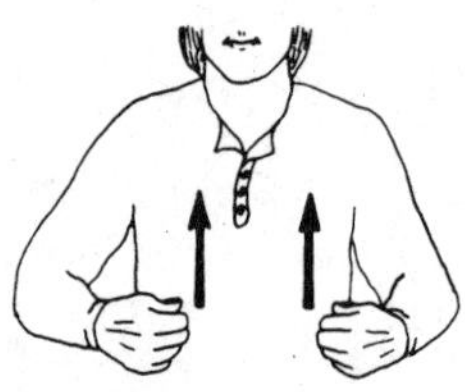

Arabic: anwán عنوان
Chinese: dìzhǐ 地址
Dutch: adres
French: adresse
German: Adresse
Italian: indirizzo
Japanese: jūsho 住所
Korean: juso 주소
Portuguese: endereço
Russian: ádres адрес
Spanish: dirección
Swedish: adress

32. administration [n.]

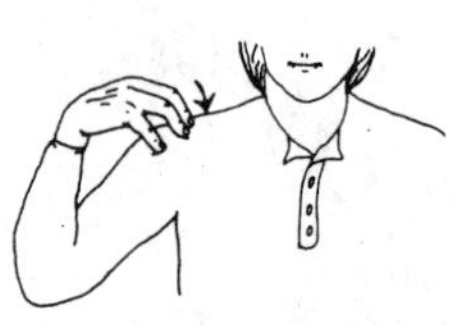

Arabic: idára ادارة
Chinese: xíngzhèng 行政
Dutch: administratie
French: administration
German: Verwaltung
Italian: amministrazione
Japanese: kanri 管理
Korean: haengjŏng 행정
Portuguese: administração
Russian: administrátsiya администрация
Spanish: administración
Swedish: administration

33. admire [v.]

Arabic: áajaba اعجب
Chinese: xīn shǎng 欣賞
Dutch: bewonderen
French: admirer
German: bewundern
Italian: ammirare
Japanese: shōsan suru 称賛する
Korean: kamt'anhada 감탄하다
Portuguese: admirar
Russian: lyubovát'sya любоваться
Spanish: admirar
Swedish: beundra

34. admit [v.]

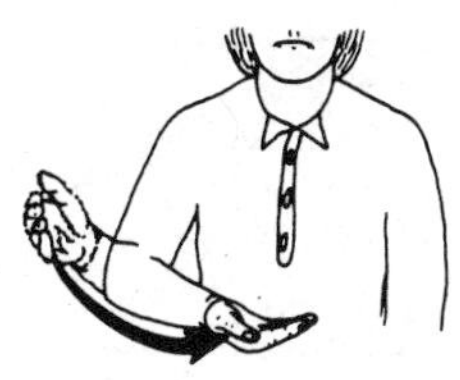

Arabic: sámaha bi سمح بـ
Chinese: chéngrèn 承認
Dutch: toelaten
French: admettre
German: zulassen
Italian: ammettere
Japanese: mitomeru 認める
Korean: injŏnghada 인정하다
Portuguese: admitir
Russian: dopuskát' допускать
Spanish: admitir
Swedish: släppa in

35. advance [v.]

Arabic: taqáddama تقدم
Chinese: qiánjìn 前進
Dutch: vorderen
French: avancer
German: vorgehen
Italian: avanzare
Japanese: susumeru 進める
Korean: jŏnjinhada 전진하다
Portuguese: avançar
Russian: prodvigát'sya продвигаться
Spanish: avanzar
Swedish: göra framsteg

36. advantage [n.]

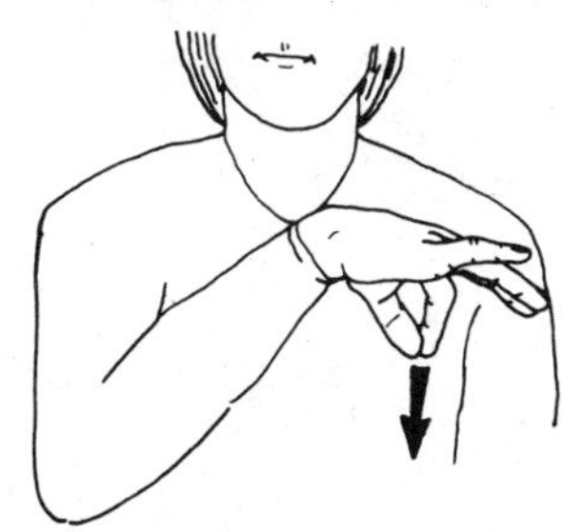

Arabic: mízza ميزة
Chinese: yǒulì tiáojiàn 有利條件
Dutch: voordeel
French: avantage
German: Vorteil
Italian: vantaggio
Japanese: yūri 有利
Korean: iik 이익
Portuguese: vantagem
Russian: preimúshchestvo преимущество
Spanish: ventaja
Swedish: fördel

37. adventure [n.]

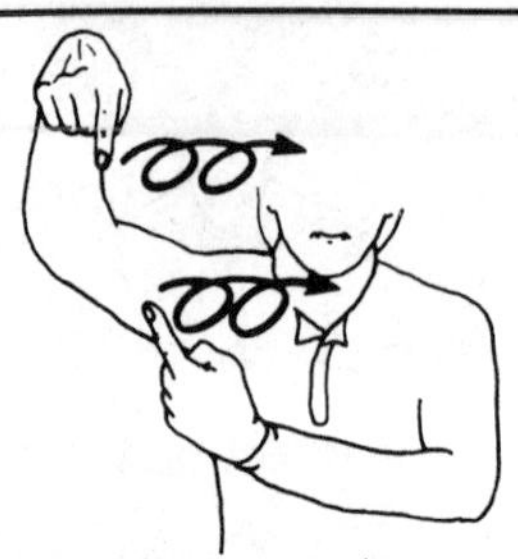

Arabic: mughámara مغامرة
Chinese: màoxiǎn 冒險
Dutch: avontuur
French: aventure
German: Abenteuer
Italian: avventura
Japanese: bōken 冒険
Korean: mohŏm 모험
Portuguese: aventura
Russian: priklyuchéniye приключение
Spanish: aventura
Swedish: äventyr

38. advertisement [n.]

Arabic: iaalán اعلان
Chinese: guǎnggào 廣告
Dutch: advertentie
French: publicité
German: Anzeige
Italian: inserzione pubblicitaria
Japanese: kōkoku 広告
Korean: kwanggo 광고
Portuguese: anúncio
Russian: rekláma реклама
Spanish: anuncio
Swedish: annons

39. advice [n.]

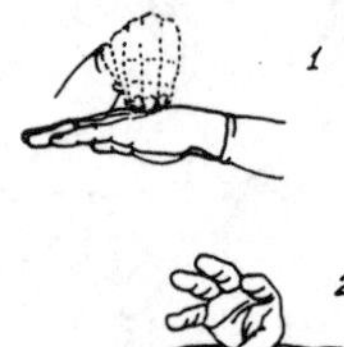

Arabic: nasíha نصيحة
Chinese: zhōnggào 忠告
Dutch: advies
French: conseil
German: Rat
Italian: consiglio
Japanese: chūkoku 忠告
Korean: ch'unggo 충고
Portuguese: conselho
Russian: sovét совет
Spanish: consejo
Swedish: råd

40. advise [v.]

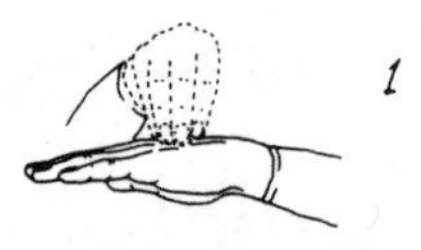

Arabic: násaha نصح
Chinese: zhōnggào 忠告
Dutch: adviseren
French: conseiller
German: raten
Italian: consigliare
Japanese: chūkoku suru 忠告する
Korean: ch'unggohada 충고하다
Portuguese: aconselhar
Russian: sovétovat' советовать
Spanish: aconsejar
Swedish: råda

41. affect [v.]

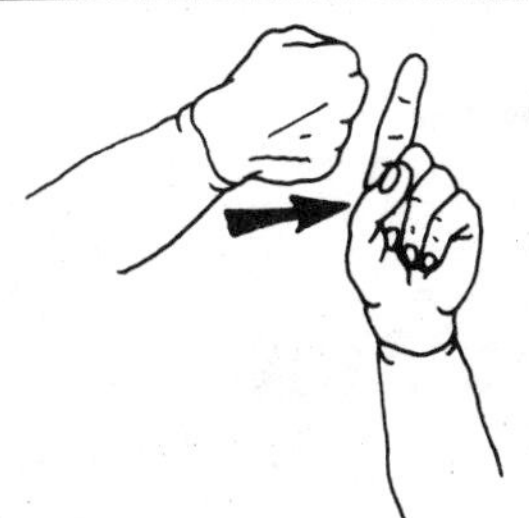

Arabic: áththara أثر
Chinese: yǐngxiǎng 影響
Dutch: beïnvloeden
French: affecter
German: betreffen
Italian: influire su
Japanese: eikyō suru 影響する
Korean: yŭnghyangjuda 영향주다
Portuguese: afetar
Russian: déystvovat' na действовать на
Spanish: afectar
Swedish: inverka

42. afraid [adj.]

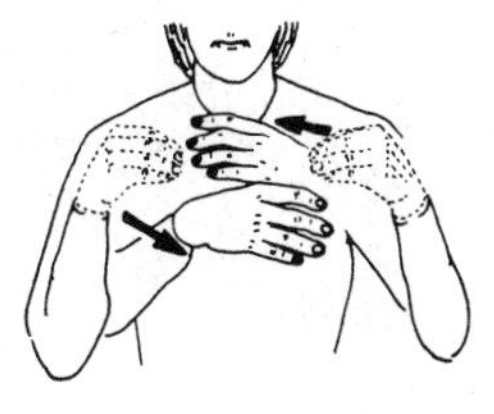

Arabic: khá'if خائف
Chinese: hàipà 害怕
Dutch: bang
French: effrayé
German: ängstlich
Italian: spaventato
Japanese: osorete 恐れて
Korean: musŏwŏ 무서워
Portuguese: com mêdo
Russian: ispúgannyy испуганный
Spanish: miedoso
Swedish: rädd

43. Africa [n.]

Arabic: afríqia افريقيا
Chinese: fēizhōu 非洲
Dutch: Afrika
French: Afrique
German: Afrika
Italian: Africa
Japanese: Afurika アフリカ
Korean: Apŭrika 아프리카
Portuguese: África
Russian: Áfrika Африка
Spanish: África
Swedish: Afrika

44. after [adv./prep.]

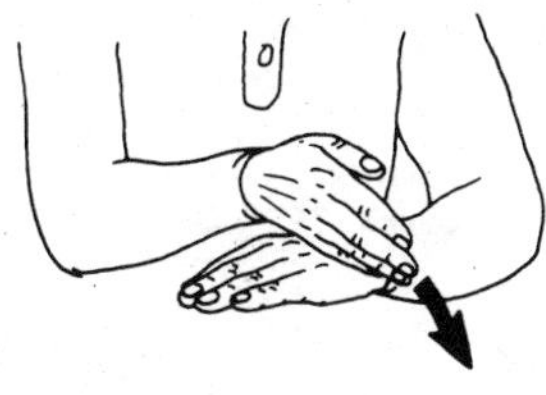

Arabic: báad بعد
Chinese: zàihòu 在後
Dutch: na
French: après
German: nach
Italian: dopo
Japanese: . . . no atoni 後に
Korean: dwie 뒤에
Portuguese: depois
Russian: pósle после
Spanish: después
Swedish: efter

45. afternoon [n.]

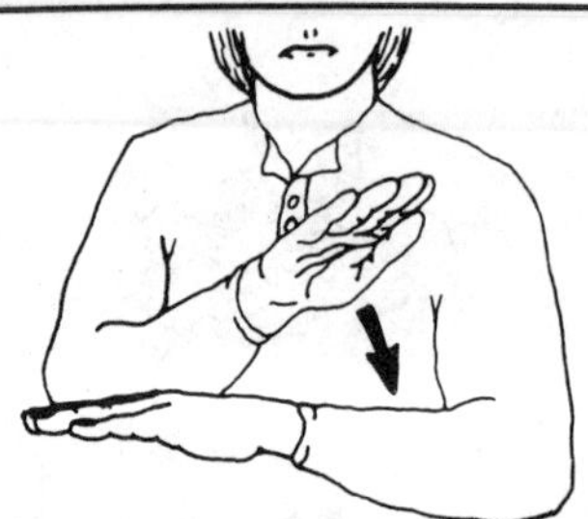

Arabic: báad az-zúher بعد الظهر
Chinese: xiàwǔ 下午
Dutch: namiddag
French: après-midi
German: Nachmittag
Italian: pomeriggio
Japanese: gogo 午後
Korean: ohu 오후
Portuguese: tarde
Russian: vrémya pósle polúdnya время после полудня
Spanish: tarde
Swedish: eftermiddag

46. again [adv.]

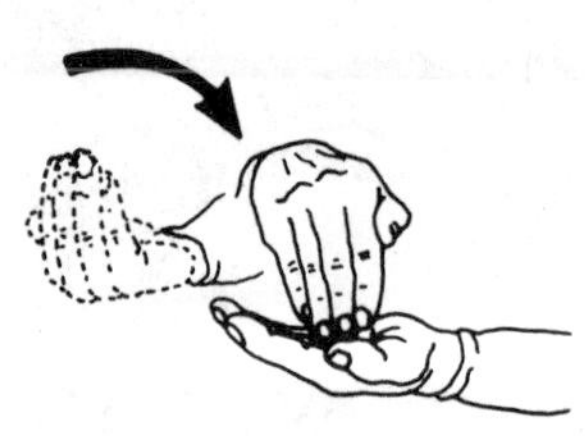

Arabic: mára úkhra مرة اخرى
Chinese: zài 再
Dutch: weer
French: encore
German: wieder
Italian: di nuovo
Japanese: futatabi 再び
Korean: dashi 다시
Portuguese: outra vez
Russian: opyát' опять
Spanish: otra vez
Swedish: igen

47. against [prep.]

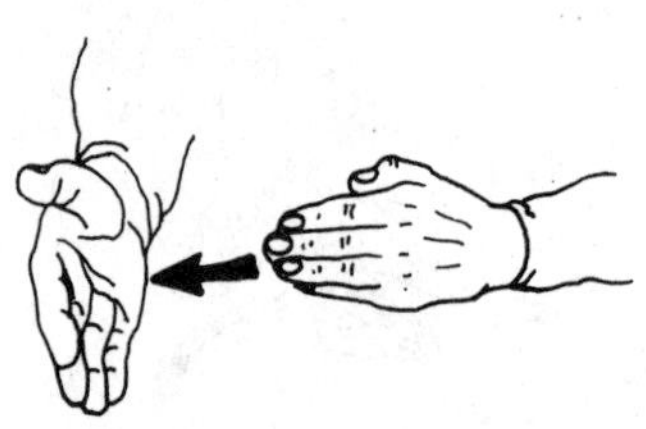

Arabic: dod ضد
Chinese: nì 逆
Dutch: tegen
French: contre
German: gegen
Italian: contro
Japanese: . . .ni taishite …に対して
Korean: bandae 반대의
Portuguese: contra
Russian: prótiv против
Spanish: contra
Swedish: emot

48. age [n.]

Arabic: ómur عمر
Chinese: niánlíng 年齢
Dutch: leeftijd
French: âge
German: Alter
Italian: età
Japanese: toshi 年
Korean: nai 나이
Portuguese: idade
Russian: vózrast возраст
Spanish: edad
Swedish: ålder

49. ago [adv.]

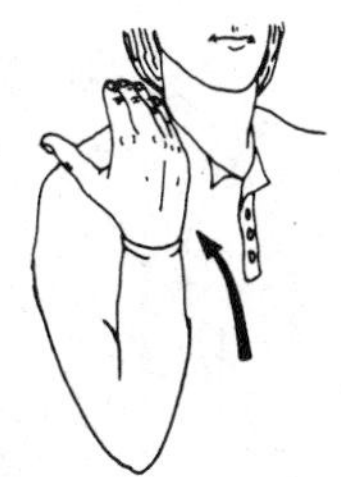

Arabic: qábl قبل
Chinese: yǐqián 以前
Dutch: geleden
French: il y a
German: vor
Italian: fa
Japanese: izen ni 以前に
Korean: jŏne 전에
Portuguese: há
Russian: tomú nazád тому назад
Spanish: hace
Swedish: för. . .sedan

50. agree [v.]

Arabic: wáafaqa وافق
Chinese: tóngyì 同意
Dutch: instemmen
French: s'accorder
German: übereinstimmen
Italian: accordarsi
Japanese: dōi suru 同意する
Korean: dongŭihada 동의하다
Portuguese: concordar
Russian: soglashát'sya соглашаться
Spanish: convenir
Swedish: instämma

51. agriculture [n.]

Arabic: ziráa زراعة
Chinese: nóngyè 農業
Dutch: landbouw
French: agriculture
German: Landwirtschaft
Italian: agricoltura
Japanese: nōgyō 農業
Korean: nongŏp 농업
Portuguese: agricultura
Russian: sél'skoye khozyáystvo сельское хозяйство
Spanish: agricultura
Swedish: jordbruk

52. ahead [adv.]

Arabic: íla al-amám الى الامام
Chinese: zài qián 在 前
Dutch: vooruit
French: en avant
German: vorwärts
Italian: avanti
Japanese: saki ni 先に
Korean: mŏnjŏ 먼저
Portuguese: adiante
Russian: vperyód вперёд
Spanish: delante
Swedish: före

53. aid [n.]

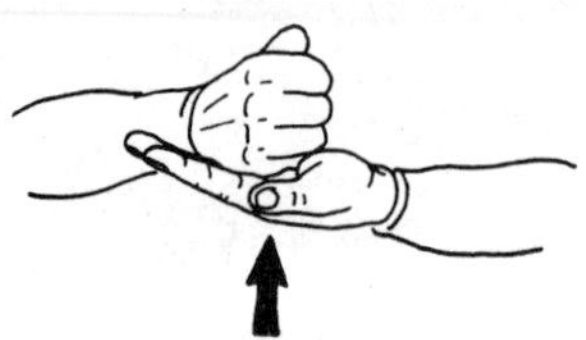

Arabic: musáada مساعدة
Chinese: yuánzhù 援助
Dutch: hulp
French: secours
German: Hilfe
Italian: soccorso
Japanese: enjo 援助
Korean: wŏnjo 원조
Portuguese: socorro
Russian: pómoshch' помощь
Spanish: ayuda
Swedish: hjälp

54. aim [v.]

Arabic: sáwwaba صوب
Chinese: zhēndùi 針對
Dutch: mikken
French: viser
German: zielen
Italian: puntare
Japanese: nerau ねらう
Korean: kyŏnyanghada 겨냥하다
Portuguese: apontar
Russian: stremít'sya стремиться
Spanish: apuntar
Swedish: sikta

55. air [n.]

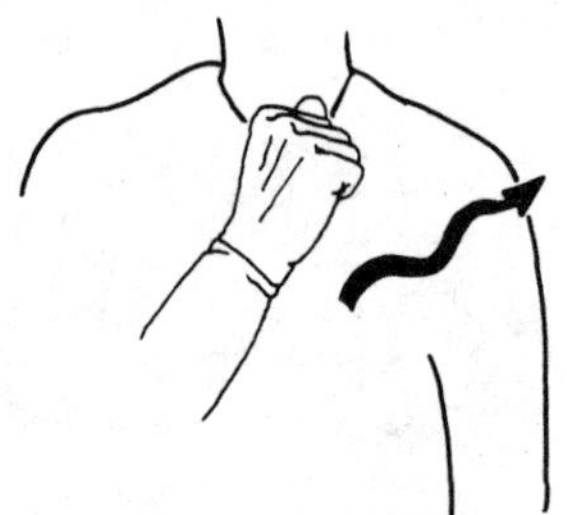

Arabic: hawwá' هواء
Chinese: kōngqì 空氣
Dutch: lucht
French: air
German: Luft
Italian: aria
Japanese: kūki 空気
Korean: konggi 공기
Portuguese: ar
Russian: vózdukh воздух
Spanish: aire
Swedish: luft

56. airplane [n.]

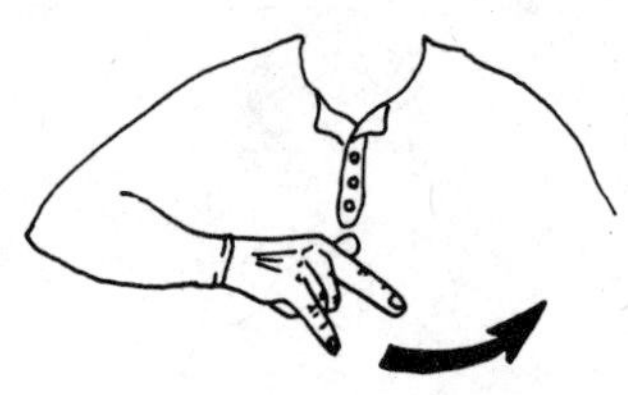

Arabic: tá'era طائرة
Chinese: fēijī 飛機
Dutch: vliegtuig
French: avion
German: Flugzeug
Italian: aeroplano
Japanese: hikōki 飛行機
Korean: bihaenggi 비행기
Portuguese: avião
Russian: samolyót самолёт
Spanish: avión
Swedish: flygplan

57. airport [n.]

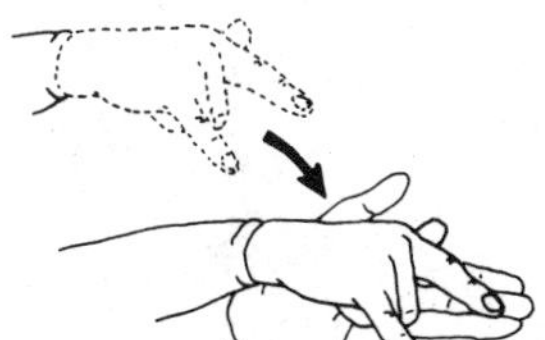

Arabic: matár مطار
Chinese: fēijīchǎng 飛機場
Dutch: luchthaven
French: aéroport
German: Flughafen
Italian: aeroporto
Japanese: kūkō 空港
Korean: konghang 공항
Portuguese: aeroporto
Russian: aeropórt аэропорт
Spanish: aeropuerto
Swedish: flygplats

58. air force [n.]

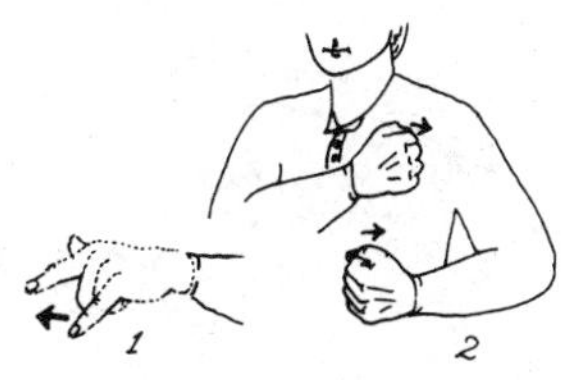

Arabic: al-quwát al-jauwíya القوات الجوية
Chinese: kōngjūn 空軍
Dutch: luchtmacht
French: force aérienne
German: Luftwaffe
Italian: forza aerea
Japanese: kūgun 空軍
Korean: konggun 공군
Portuguese: força aérea
Russian: voyénno-vozdúshnyye síly военно-воздушные силы
Spanish: fuerza aérea
Swedish: flygvapen

59. alarm [n.]

Arabic: ínthar انذار
Chinese: jǐngbào 警報
Dutch: alarm
French: alarme
German: Alarm
Italian: allarme
Japanese: keihō 警報
Korean: kyŏngbo 경보
Portuguese: alarme
Russian: trevóga тревога
Spanish: alarma
Swedish: alarm

60. Albania [n.]

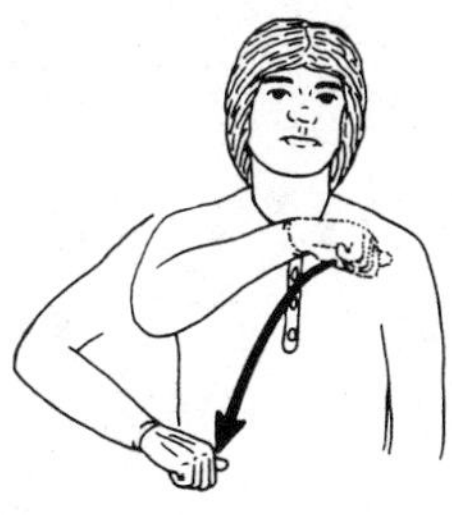

Arabic: albániya البانيا
Chinese: āěrbāníyǎ 阿爾巴尼亞
Dutch: Albanië
French: Albanie
German: Albanien
Italian: Albania
Japanese: Arubania アルバニア
Korean: Albania 알바니아
Portuguese: Albânia
Russian: Albániya Албания
Spanish: Albania
Swedish: Albanien

61. alert [v.]

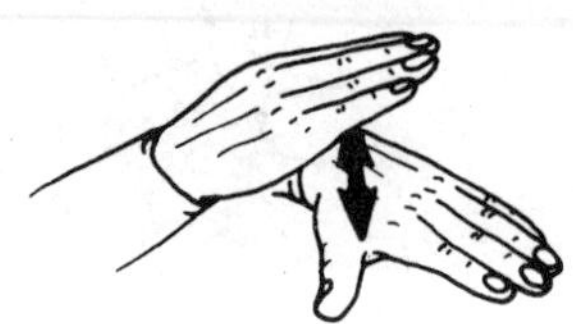

Arabic: nábbaha نبه
Chinese: jǐngjuéde 警覺的
Dutch: waarschuwen
French: alerter
German: aufmerksam machen
Italian: allarmare
Japanese: keikaisaseru 警戒させる
Korean: kyŭnggyehada 경계하다
Portuguese: alertar
Russian: nastorázhivat' настораживать
Spanish: alertar
Swedish: alarmera

62. alike [adj./adv.]

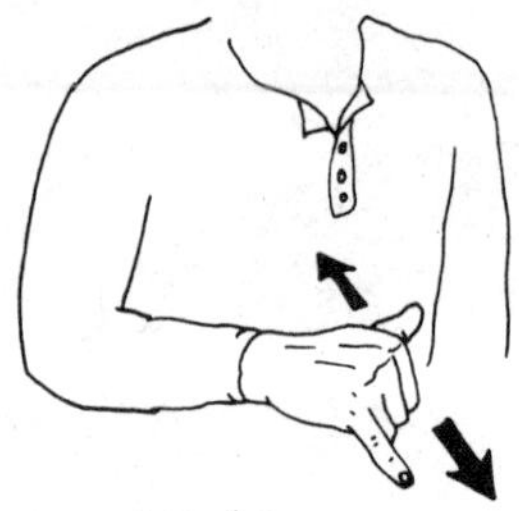

Arabic: mathíl مثيل
Chinese: xiāngsìde 相似的
Dutch: eender
French: égal
German: gleich
Italian: uguale
Japanese: dō yō na 同様な
Korean: bisut'han 비슷한
Portuguese: igual
Russian: odinákovyy одинаковый
Spanish: igual
Swedish: lik

63. alive [adj.]

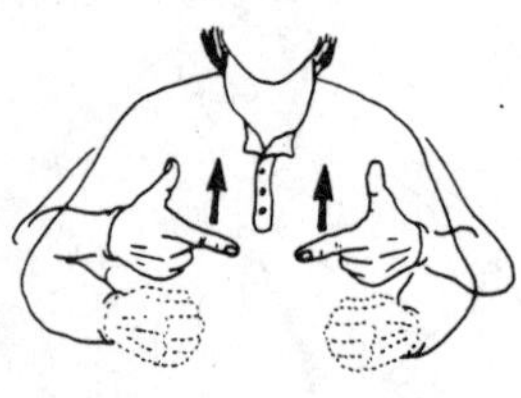

Arabic: háee حي
Chinese: huózhede 活着的
Dutch: levend
French: vivant
German: lebendig
Italian: vivo
Japanese: ikiikishite いまいまして
Korean: sara innŭn 살아있는
Portuguese: vivo
Russian: zhivóy живой
Spanish: vivo
Swedish: levande

64. all [adj.]

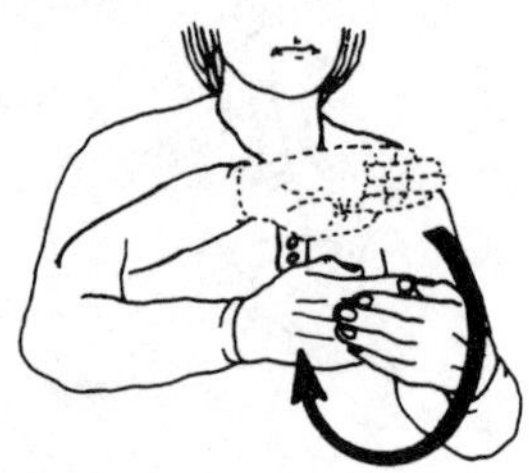

Arabic: kull كل
Chinese: suǒyǒude 所有的
Dutch: allen
French: tout
German: alle
Italian: tutto
Japanese: subete no すべての
Korean: modŭn 모든
Portuguese: tôdo
Russian: vse все
Spanish: todo
Swedish: all

65. allow [v.]

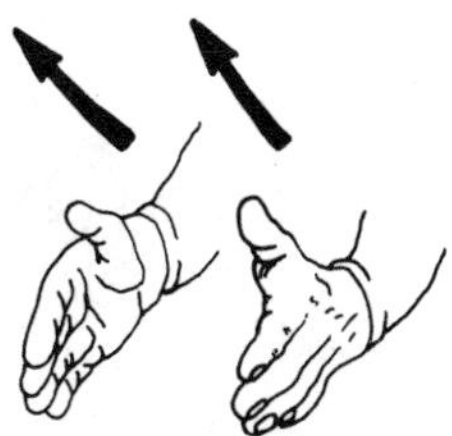

Arabic: sámaha سمح
Chinese: zhǔnxǔ 准許
Dutch: toelaten
French: permettre
German: erlauben
Italian: permettere
Japanese: yurusu 許す
Korean: hŏrakhada 허락하다
Portuguese: permitir
Russian: pozvolyát' позволять
Spanish: permitir
Swedish: tillåta

66. ally [n.]

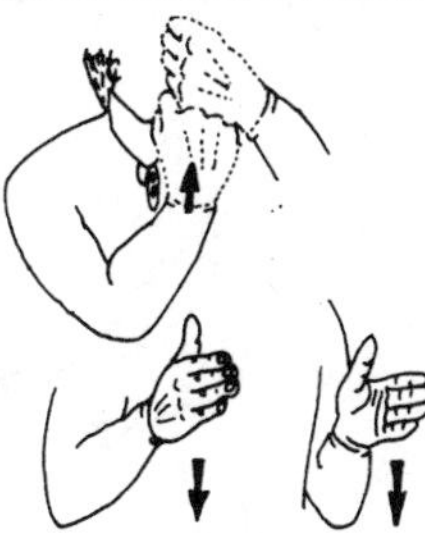

Arabic: halíf حليف
Chinese: tóngméng 同盟
Dutch: bondgenoot
French: allié
German: Verbündeter
Italian: alleato
Japanese: dōmeisha 同盟者
Korean: dongmaengguk 동맹국
Portuguese: aliado
Russian: soyúznik союзник
Spanish: aliado
Swedish: bundsförvant

67. almost [adv.]

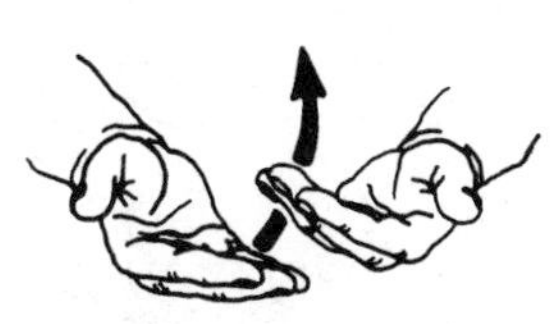

Arabic: taqríban تقريباً
Chinese: jīhū 幾乎
Dutch: bijna
French: presque
German: fast
Italian: quasi
Japanese: hotondo 殆ど
Korean: kŏŭi 거의
Portuguese: quase
Russian: pochtí почти
Spanish: casi
Swedish: nästan

68. alone [adj.]

Arabic: wahíd وحيد
Chinese: dāndúde 單獨的
Dutch: alleen
French: seul
German: allein
Italian: solo
Japanese: tandoku de 単独で
Korean: hollo 홀로
Portuguese: só
Russian: odinókiy одинокий
Spanish: solo
Swedish: ensam

69. along (alongside) [prep.]

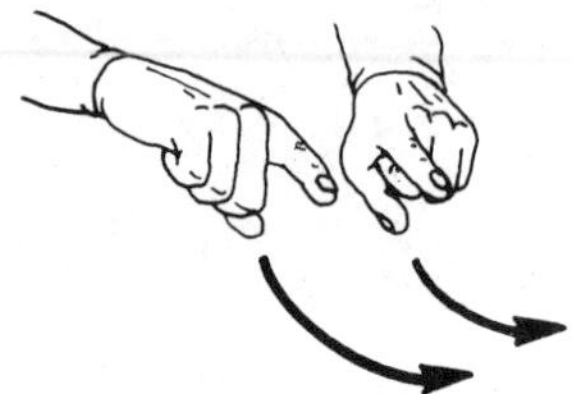

Arabic: bijánib بجانب
Chinese: yánje 沿著
Dutch: langs
French: le long de
German: entlang
Italian: lungo
Japanese: . . .ni sotte …に沿って
Korean: ttarasŏ 따라서
Portuguese: ao longo de
Russian: vdól' вдоль
Spanish: a lo largo de
Swedish: längs

70. alphabet [n.]

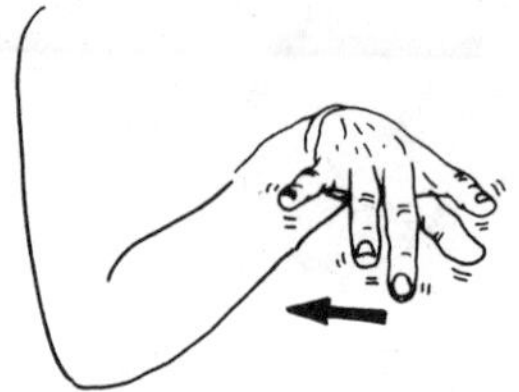

Arabic: hurúf al-hijá' حروف الهجاء
Chinese: zìmŭbiăo 字母表
Dutch: alfabet
French: alphabet
German: Alphabet
Italian: alfabeto
Japanese: arufabetto アルファベット
Korean: alp'abet 알파벧
Portuguese: alfabeto
Russian: ázbuka азбука
Spanish: alfabeto
Swedish: alfabet

71. already [adv.]

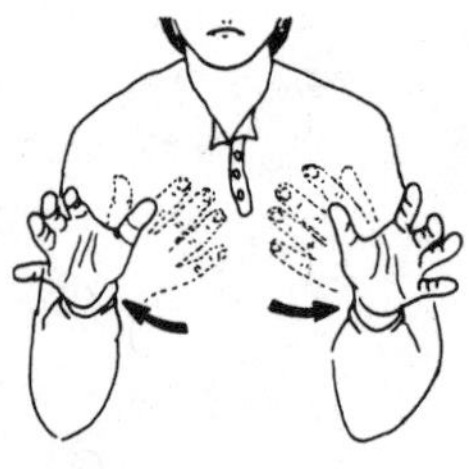

Arabic: al-áan الآن
Chinese: yĭjīng 已經
Dutch: al
French: déjà
German: schon
Italian: già
Japanese: sudeni 既に
Korean: bŏlssŏ 벌써
Portuguese: já
Russian: uzhé уже
Spanish: ya
Swedish: redan

72. also [adv.]

Arabic: áidan ايضاً
Chinese: yě 也
Dutch: ook
French: aussi
German: auch
Italian: anche
Japanese: mata また
Korean: yŏkshi 역시
Portuguese: também
Russian: tózhe тоже
Spanish: también
Swedish: också

73. altogether [adv.]

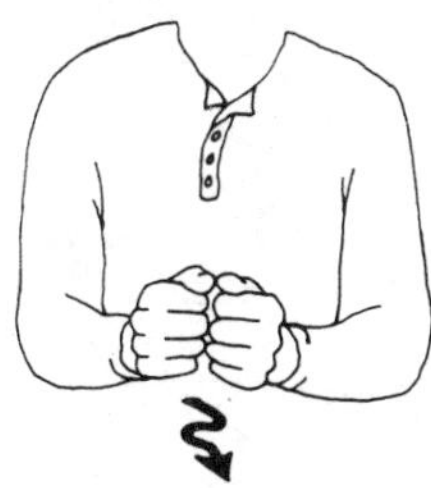

Arabic: bil-ijmál بالاجمال
Chinese: yígòng 一共
Dutch: helemaal
French: entièrement
German: alles in allem
Italian: tutti insieme
Japanese: mattaku 全く
Korean: modu 모두
Portuguese: inteiramente
Russian: vsevó всего
Spanish: enteramente
Swedish: helt och hållet

74. always [adv.]

Arabic: dá'iman دائماً
Chinese: zǒngshì 總是
Dutch: altijd
French: toujours
German: immer
Italian: sempre
Japanese: tsune ni 常に
Korean: ŏnjena 언제나
Portuguese: sempre
Russian: vsegdá всегда
Spanish: siempre
Swedish: alltid

75. amaze [v.]

Arabic: dháhala ذهل
Chinese: shǐ jīngqí 使驚奇
Dutch: verbazen
French: étonner
German: erstaunen
Italian: sbalordire
Japanese: odorokasu 驚かす
Korean: nollage hada 놀라게하다
Portuguese: espantar
Russian: izumlyát' изумлять
Spanish: asombrar
Swedish: förvåna

76. ambassador [n.]

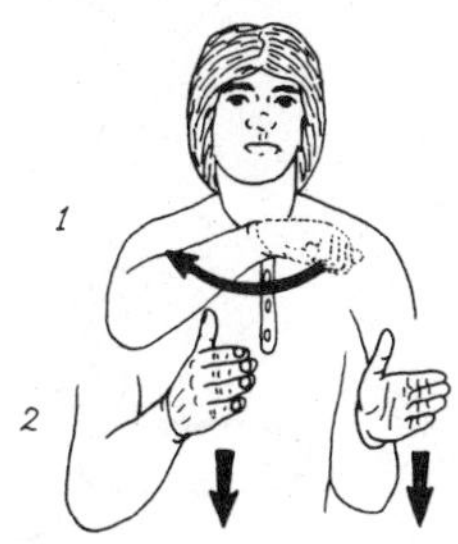

Arabic: safír سفير
Chinese: dàshǐ 大使
Dutch: ambassadeur
French: ambassadeur
German: Botschafter
Italian: ambasciatore
Japanese: taishi 大使
Korean: daesa 대사
Portuguese: embaixador
Russian: posól посол
Spanish: embajador
Swedish: ambassadör

77. ambition [n.]

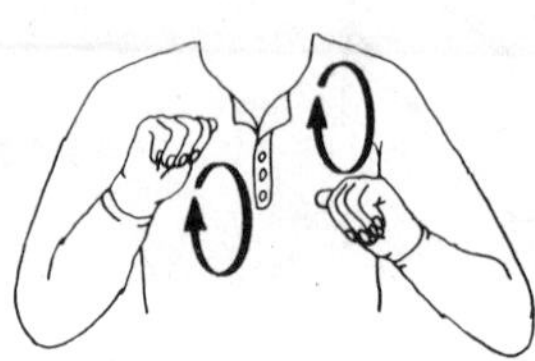

Arabic: tumúuhun طموح
Chinese: yěxīn 野心
Dutch: ambitie
French: ambition
German: Ehrgeiz
Italian: ambizione
Japanese: yashin 野心
Korean: yamang 야망
Portuguese: ambição
Russian: chestolyúbiye честолюбие
Spanish: ambición
Swedish: ambition

78. ambulance [n.]

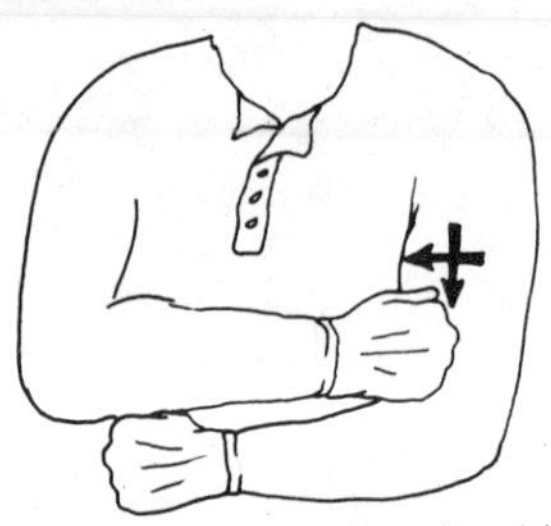

Arabic: sayyárit al-isáaf سيارة الاسعاف
Chinese: jiùhùchē 救護車
Dutch: ambulance
French: ambulance
German: Krankenwagen
Italian: ambulanza
Japanese: kyūkyūsha 救急車
Korean: kugŭpch'a 구급차
Portuguese: ambulância
Russian: karéta skóroy pómoshchi карета скорой помощи
Spanish: ambulancia
Swedish: ambulans

79. America [n.]

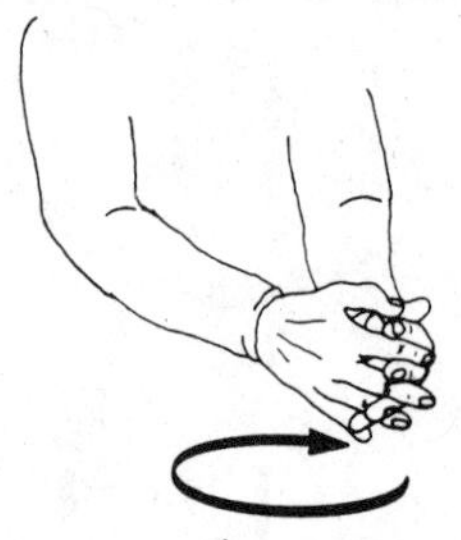

Arabic: amríka امريكا
Chinese: měiguó 美國
Dutch: Amerika
French: Amérique
German: Amerika
Italian: America
Japanese: Amerika アメリカ
Korean: Amerik'a 미국
Portuguese: América
Russian: Amérika Америка
Spanish: América
Swedish: Amerika

80. American [adj.]

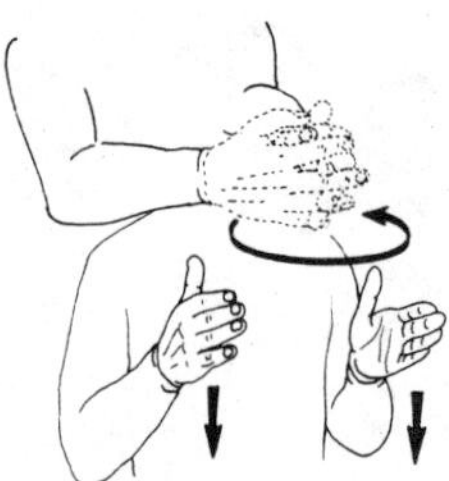

Arabic: amríki امريكي
Chinese: měiguóde 美國的
Dutch: amerikaans
French: américain
German: amerikanisch
Italian: americano
Japanese: Amerika no アメリカの
Korean: Migukŭi 미국의
Portuguese: americano
Russian: amerikánskiy американский
Spanish: americano
Swedish: amerikansk

81. among [prep.]

Arabic: báina بين
Chinese: qízhōng 其中
Dutch: tussen
French: parmi
German: zwischen
Italian: fra
Japanese: . . .no nakade …の中で
Korean: gaundae 가운데
Portuguese: entre
Russian: sredí среди
Spanish: entre
Swedish: bland

82. amount [n.]

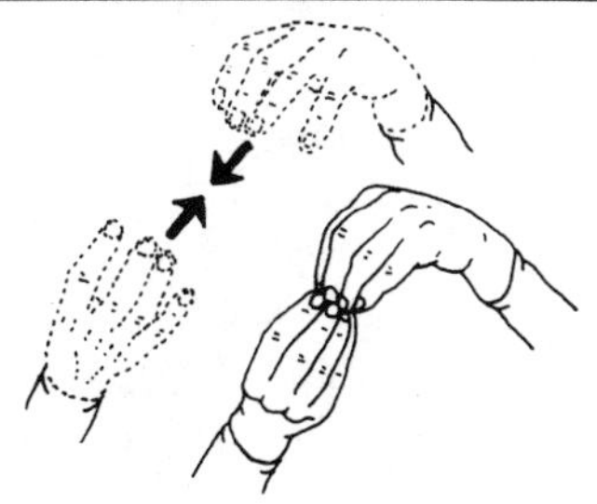

Arabic: miqdár مقدار
Chinese: zǒngshù 總數
Dutch: bedrag
French: somme
German: Betrag
Italian: quantità
Japanese: gōkei 合計
Korean: yang 양
Portuguese: quantidade
Russian: kolíchestvo количество
Spanish: cantidad
Swedish: belopp

83. amusing [adj.]

Arabic: musálli مسلي
Chinese: yǒuqùde 有趣的
Dutch: grappig
French: amusant
German: amüsant
Italian: divertente
Japanese: omoshiroi 面白い
Korean: jaeminan 재미난
Portuguese: divertido
Russian: zabávnyy забавный
Spanish: divertido
Swedish: lustig

84. analyze [v.]

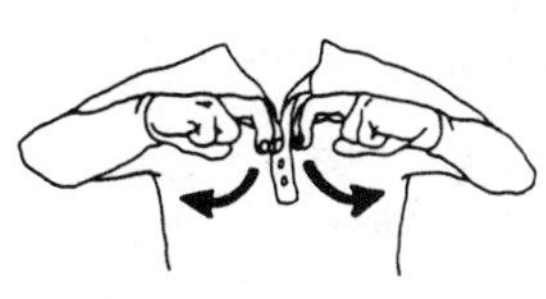

Arabic: hállala حلل
Chinese: fēnxī 分析
Dutch: analyseren
French: analyser
German: analysieren
Italian: analizzare
Japanese: bunseki suru 分析する
Korean: bunsŏk'hada 분석하다
Portuguese: analisar
Russian: analizírovat' анализировать
Spanish: analizar
Swedish: analysera

85. ancestor [n.]

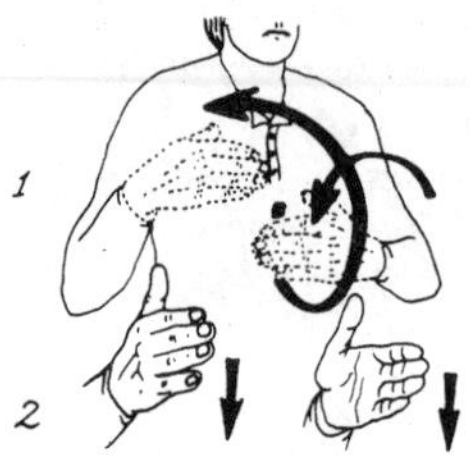

Arabic: sálaf سلف
Chinese: zǔxiān 祖先
Dutch: voorvaderen
French: ancêtre
German: Vorfahre
Italian: antenato
Japanese: senzo 先祖
Korean: sŏnjo 선조
Portuguese: antepassado
Russian: prédok предок
Spanish: antepasado
Swedish: förfader

86. ancient [adj.]

Arabic: qadím قديم
Chinese: gǔdàide 古代的
Dutch: oud
French: ancien
German: antik
Italian: antico
Japanese: kodai no 古代の
Korean: yennarŭi 옛날의
Portuguese: antigo
Russian: drévniy древний
Spanish: antiguo
Swedish: forntids

87. and [conj.]

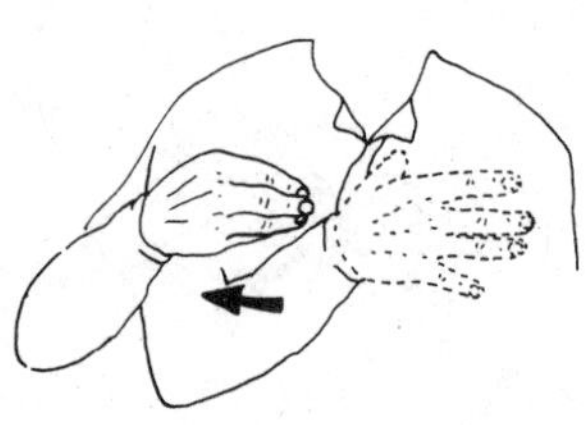

Arabic: wa و
Chinese: hé 和
Dutch: en
French: et
German: und
Italian: e
Japanese: soshite そして
Korean: gwa ~와
Portuguese: e
Russian: i и
Spanish: y
Swedish: och

88. angel [n.]

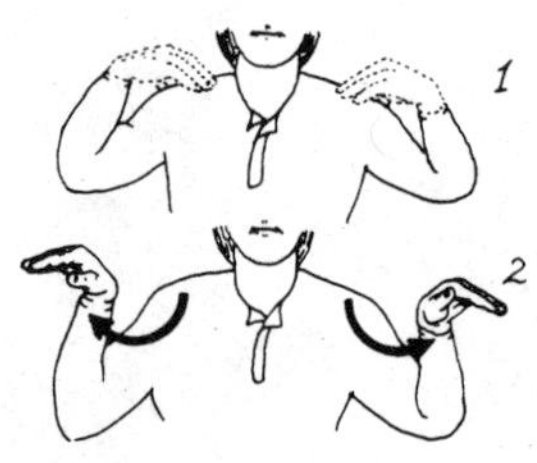

Arabic: maláak ملاك
Chinese: tiānshǐ 天使
Dutch: engel
French: ange
German: Engel
Italian: angelo
Japanese: tenshi 天使
Korean: ch'ŏnsa 천사
Portuguese: anjo
Russian: ángel ангел
Spanish: ángel
Swedish: ängel

89. anger [n.]

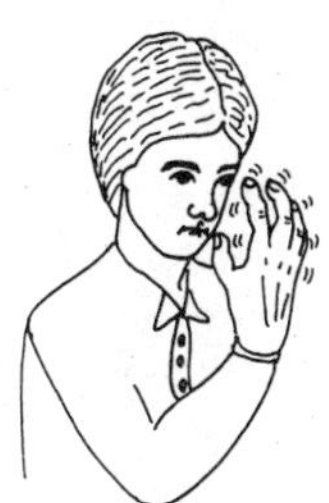

Arabic: ghádab غضب
Chinese: fènnù 憤怒
Dutch: toorn
French: colère
German: Zorn
Italian: collera
Japanese: ikari 怒り
Korean: noyŏum 노여움
Portuguese: raiva
Russian: gnev гнев
Spanish: enojo
Swedish: ilska

90. angry [adj.]

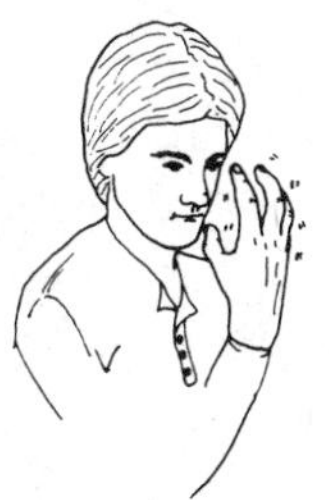

Arabic: ghadbán غضبان
Chinese: shēngqìde 生氣的
Dutch: boos
French: fâché
German: wütend
Italian: arrabbiato
Japanese: okotta 怒った
Korean: sŏngnan 성난
Portuguese: zangado
Russian: serdítyy сердитый
Spanish: enojado
Swedish: vred

91. animal [n.]

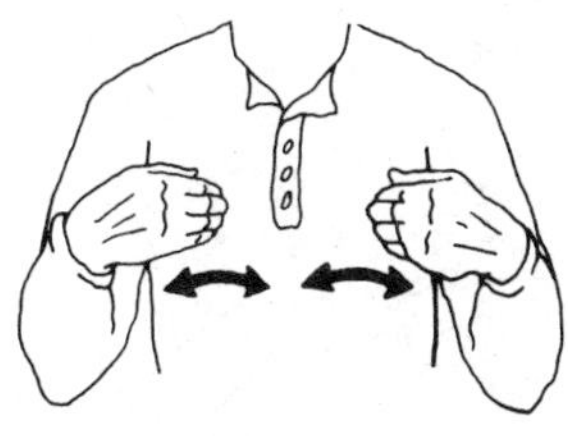

Arabic: háyawan حيوان
Chinese: dòngwù 動物
Dutch: dier
French: animal
German: Tier
Italian: animale
Japanese: dōbutsu 動物
Korean: jimsŭng 짐승
Portuguese: animal
Russian: zhivótnoye животное
Spanish: animal
Swedish: djur

92. announce [v.]

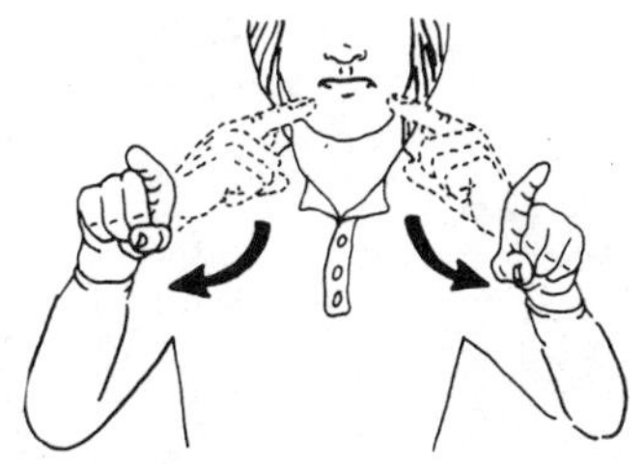

Arabic: áalana اعلن
Chinese: xuānbù 宣佈
Dutch: aankondigen
French: annoncer
German: ankündigen
Italian: annunciare
Japanese: shiraseru 知らせる
Korean: balp'yohada 발표하다
Portuguese: anunciar
Russian: ob''yavlyát' объявлять
Spanish: anunciar
Swedish: tillkännage

93. annoy [v.]

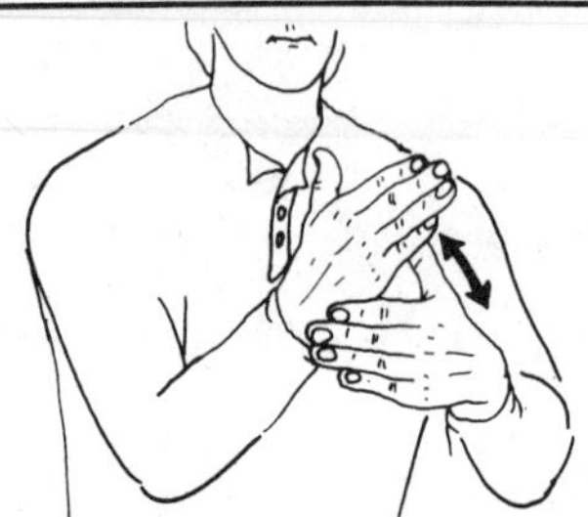

Arabic: azáaja ازعج
Chinese: fánrén 烦人
Dutch: irriteren
French: ennuyer
German: ärgern
Italian: molestare
Japanese: . . . o iraira saseru いらいらさせる
Korean: koerop'ida 괴롭히다
Portuguese: aborrecer
Russian: razdrazhát' раздражать
Spanish: fastidiar
Swedish: förarga

94. annual [adj.]

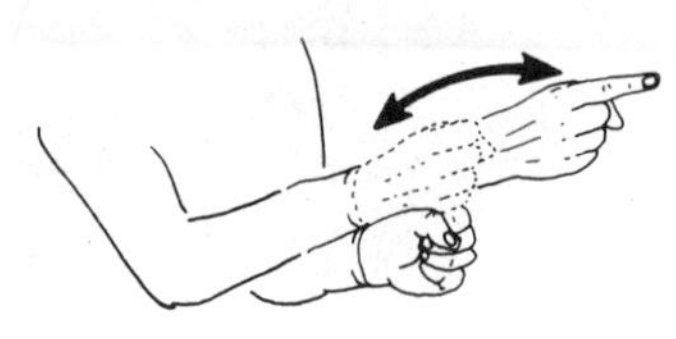

Arabic: sánawi سنوي
Chinese: měiniánde 每年的
Dutch: jaarlijks
French: annuel
German: jährlich
Italian: annuale
Japanese: ichinengoto no 一年ごとの
Korean: illyonŭi 일년의
Portuguese: anual
Russian: yezhegódnyy ежегодный
Spanish: anual
Swedish: årlig

95. another [adj./pron.]

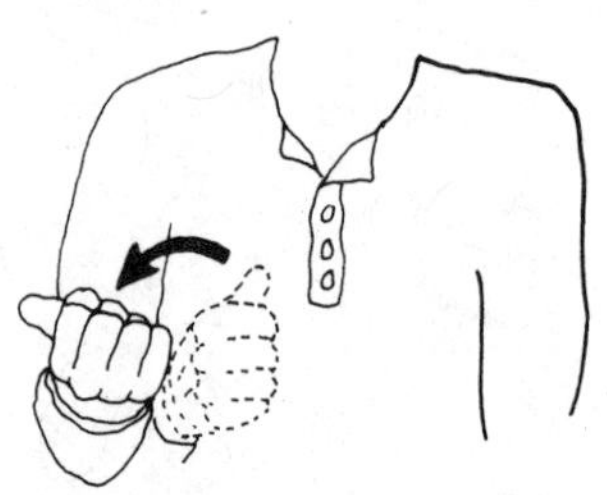

Arabic: ákhar اخر
Chinese: biéde 别的
Dutch: een ander
French: un autre
German: ein anderer
Italian: un altro
Japanese: mō hitotsu no もう一つの
Korean: tto hanaŭi 또 하나의
Portuguese: um outro
Russian: drugóy другой
Spanish: otro
Swedish: en annan

96. answer [n.]

Arabic: jawáb جواب
Chinese: huídá 回答
Dutch: antwoord
French: réponse
German: Antwort
Italian: risposta
Japanese: kotae 答え
Korean: daedap 대답
Portuguese: resposta
Russian: otvét ответ
Spanish: respuesta
Swedish: svar

97. anxiety [n.]

Arabic: qálaq قلق
Chinese: yōulù 憂慮
Dutch: ongerustheid
French: anxiété
German: Sorge
Italian: ansia
Japanese: shimpai 心配
Korean: gŭnshim 근심
Portuguese: ansiedade
Russian: bespokóystvo беспокойство
Spanish: ansiedad
Swedish: ängslan

98. any [adj./pron.]

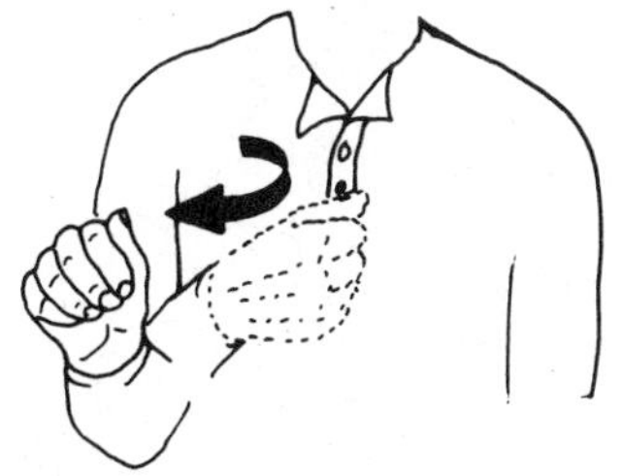

Arabic: áee أي
Chinese: rènhé 任何
Dutch: elk
French: tout
German: jeder
Italian: qualche
Japanese: ikuraka いくらか
Korean: ŏddŏn 어떤
Portuguese: qualquer
Russian: vsyákiy всякий
Spanish: cualquier
Swedish: någon

99. anyone (anybody) [pron.]

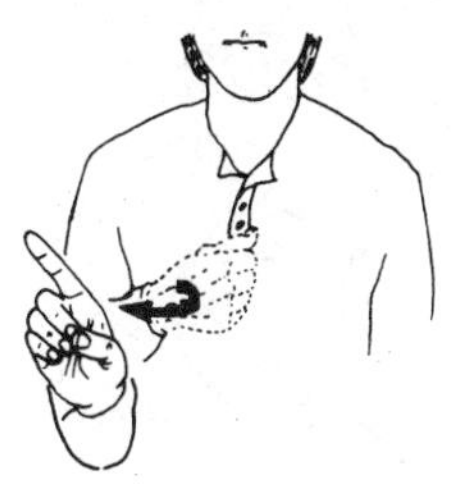

Arabic: áee wáhad أي واحد
Chinese: rènhé rén 任何人
Dutch: iedereen
French: quelqu'un
German: ein jeder
Italian: chiunque
Japanese: daremo 誰も
Korean: nugun-ga 누군가
Portuguese: qualquer pessoa
Russian: któ-nibud' кто-нибудь
Spanish: cualquiera
Swedish: vem som helst

100. anything [pron.]

Arabic: áee shaee أي شيء
Chinese: rènhé shìwù 任何事物
Dutch: iets
French: quelque chose
German: irgend etwas
Italian: qualunque cosa
Japanese: nandemo なんでも
Korean: muŏshidŭn 무엇이든
Portuguese: qualquer coisa
Russian: chtó-nibud' что-нибудь
Spanish: cualquier cosa
Swedish: vad som helst

101. anywhere [adv.]

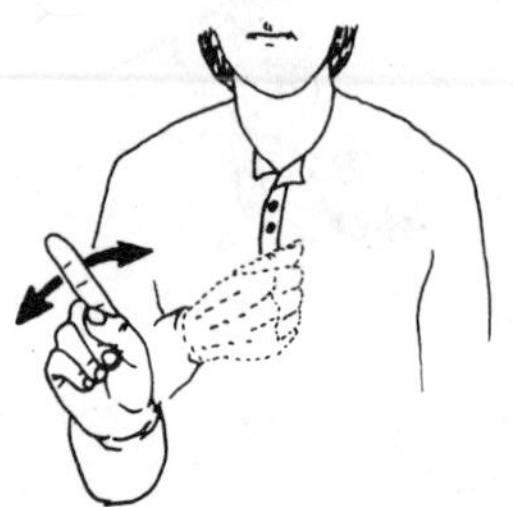

Arabic: áee makán أي مكان
Chinese: wúlùn héchù 無論何處
Dutch: ergens
French: quelque part
German: irgendwo
Italian: dovunque
Japanese: dokonidemo どこにでも
Korean: ŏdedŭnji 어디든지
Portuguese: qualquer parte
Russian: gdé-nibud'/kudá-nibud' где-нибудь/куда-нибудь
Spanish: dondequiera
Swedish: var som helst

102. apart [adv.]

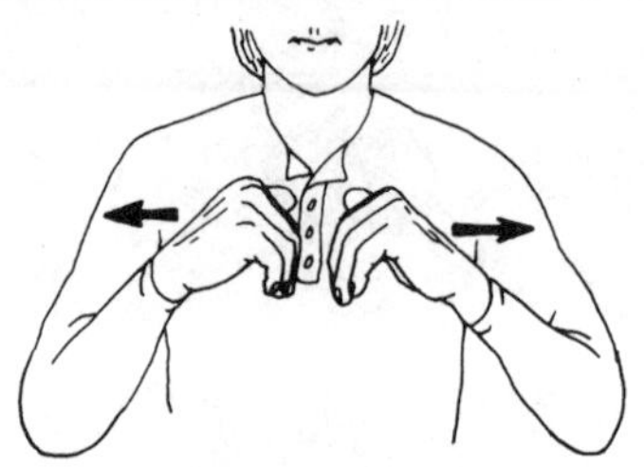

Arabic: múnfared منفرد
Chinese: fēnbié 分別
Dutch: afzonderlijk
French: à part
German: getrennt
Italian: a parte
Japanese: betsubetsu ni 別々に
Korean: ttŏrŏjin 떨어진
Portuguese: à parte
Russian: otdél'no отдельно
Spanish: aparte
Swedish: isär

103. apartment [n.]

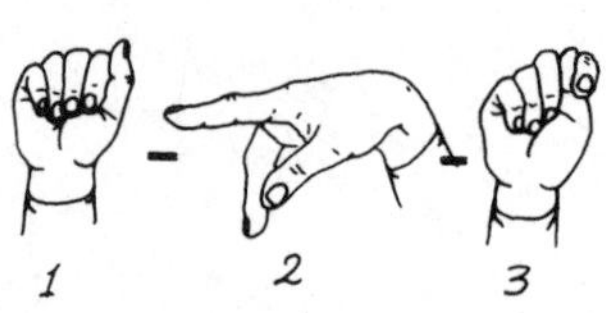

Arabic: shóqqa شقة
Chinese: gōngyù 公寓
Dutch: appartement
French: appartement
German: Wohnung
Italian: appartamento
Japanese: apāto アパート
Korean: ap'at'ŭ 아파트
Portuguese: apartamento
Russian: kvartíra квартира
Spanish: apartamento
Swedish: lägenhet

104. apologize [v.]

Arabic: iaatádhara اعتذر
Chinese: dàoqiàn 道歉
Dutch: verontschuldigen
French: faire des excuses
German: sich entschuldigen
Italian: scusarsi
Japanese: ayamaru あやまる
Korean: sagwahada 사과하다
Portuguese: desculpar-se
Russian: izvinyát'sya извиняться
Spanish: disculparse
Swedish: be om ursäkt

105. apparent(ly) [adj./adv.]

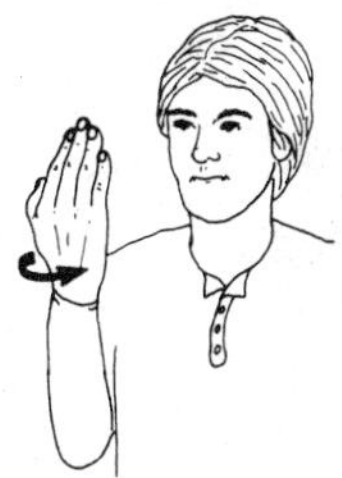

Arabic: dháher ظاهر
Chinese: míngxiǎnde 明顯的
Dutch: duidelijk
French: apparemment
German: anscheinend
Italian: apparentemente
Japanese: meihaku na 明白な
Korean: bunmyong'hi 분명히
Portuguese: aparentemente
Russian: ochevídno очевидно
Spanish: aparentemente
Swedish: tydligen

106. appear [v.]

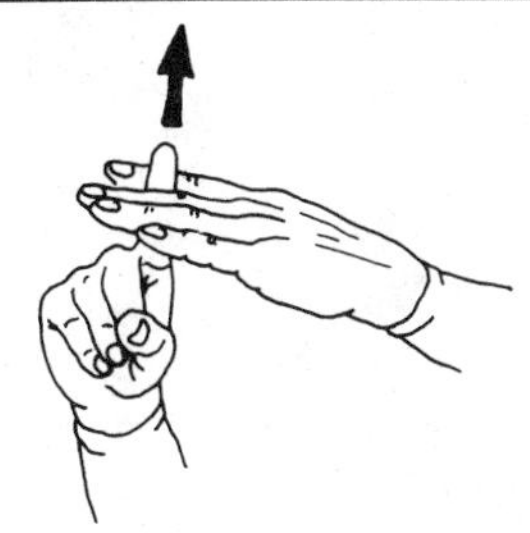

Arabic: dháhara ظهر
Chinese: chūxiàn 出現
Dutch: verschijnen
French: apparaître
German: erscheinen
Italian: apparire
Japanese: arawareru 現われる
Korean: nat'anada 나타나다
Portuguese: aparecer
Russian: poyavlyát'sya появляться
Spanish: aparecer
Swedish: framträda

107. applaud [v.]

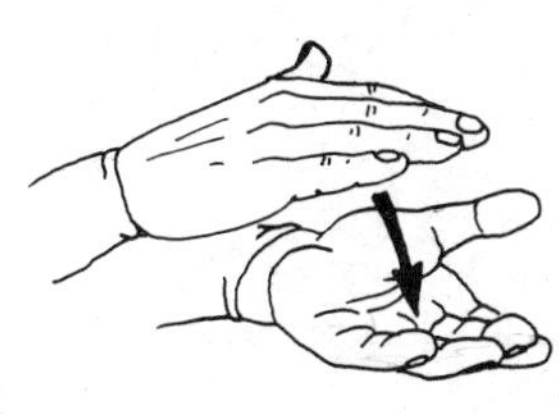

Arabic: sáffaqa صفق
Chinese: gǔzhǎng 鼓掌
Dutch: applaudisseren
French: applaudir
German: applaudieren
Italian: applaudire
Japanese: hakushu kassai suru 拍手かっさいする
Korean: baksu chida 박수치다
Portuguese: aplaudir
Russian: aplodírovat' аплодировать
Spanish: aplaudir
Swedish: applådera

108. apple [n.]

Arabic: tufáh تفاح
Chinese: píngguǒ 蘋果
Dutch: appel
French: pomme
German: Apfel
Italian: mela
Japanese: ringo リンゴ
Korean: sagwa 사과
Portuguese: maçã
Russian: yábloko яблоко
Spanish: manzana
Swedish: äpple

109. apply (put/lay on) [v.]

Arabic: tábbaqa طبق
Chinese: yìngyòng 應用
Dutch: aanbrengen
French: appliquer
German: auftragen
Italian: applicare
Japanese: tsukeru 付ける
Korean: jŭgyong hada 적용하다
Portuguese: aplicar
Russian: nanosít' наносить
Spanish: aplicar
Swedish: tillämpa

110. appoint [v.]

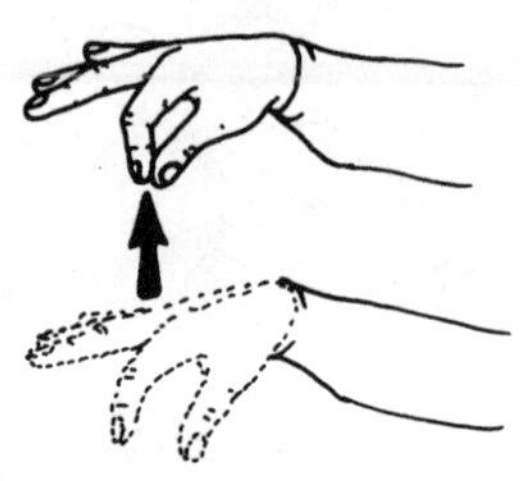

Arabic: áayyana عين
Chinese: rènmìng 任命
Dutch: aanstellen
French: nommer
German: ernennen
Italian: nominare
Japanese: mējiru 命じる
Korean: immyŏnghada 임명하다
Portuguese: nomear
Russian: naznachát' назначать
Spanish: nombrar
Swedish: utnämna

111. appointment (engagement) [n.]

Arabic: máwaad موعد
Chinese: yuēdìng 約定
Dutch: afspraak
French: rendez-vous
German: Verabredung
Italian: appuntamento
Japanese: yakusoku 約束
Korean: yaksok 약속
Portuguese: encontro marcado
Russian: svidániye свидание
Spanish: cita
Swedish: avtalat möte

112. appreciate [v.]

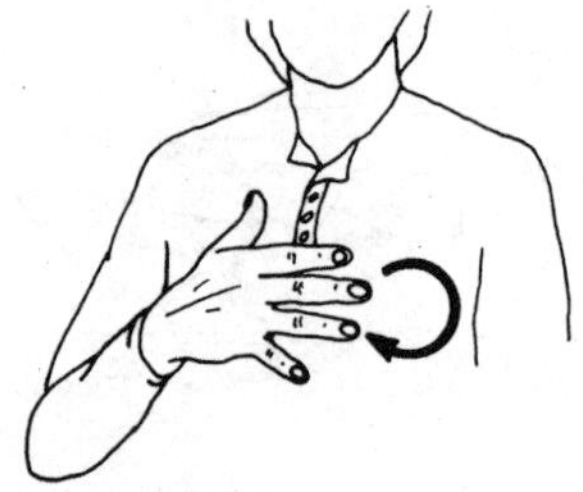

Arabic: qáddara قدر
Chinese: zhēnxí 珍惜
Dutch: waarderen
French: apprécier
German: schätzen
Italian: apprezzare
Japanese: kansha suru 感謝する
Korean: gamsahada 감사하다
Portuguese: apreciar
Russian: tsenít' ценить
Spanish: apreciar
Swedish: värdesätta

113. approach [v.]

Arabic: iqtáraba اقترب
Chinese: jiējìn 接近
Dutch: naderen
French: s'approcher
German: sich nähern
Italian: avvicinarsi
Japanese: chikazuku 近づく
Korean: jŏbkŭnhada 접근하다
Portuguese: aproximar-se
Russian: priblizhát'sya приближаться
Spanish: acercarse
Swedish: närma sig

114. approve [v.]

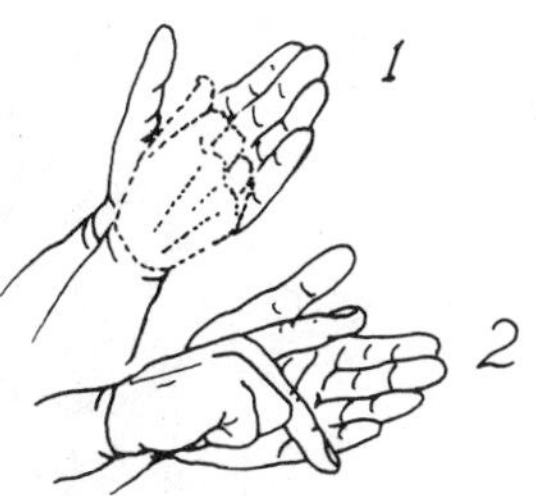

Arabic: wáfaqa وافق
Chinese: pīzhŭn 批准
Dutch: goedkeuren
French: approuver
German: anerkennen
Italian: approvare
Japanese: shōnin suru 承認する
Korean: ch'ansŏnghada 찬성하다
Portuguese: aprovar
Russian: odobryát' одобрять
Spanish: aprobar
Swedish: gilla

115. approximate(ly) [adj./adv.]

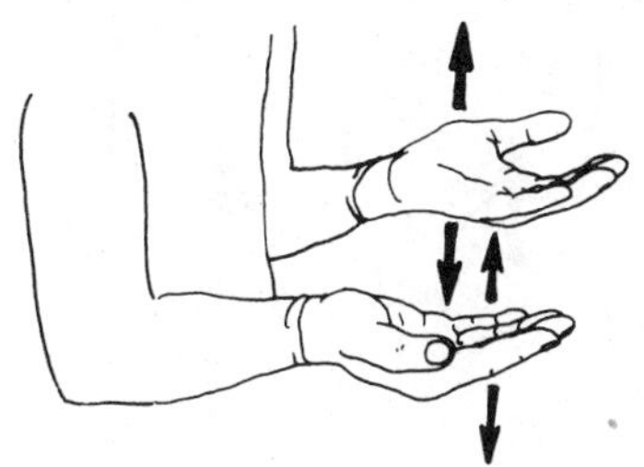

Arabic: taqríban تقريباً
Chinese: dàgài 大概
Dutch: ongeveer
French: environ
German: ungefähr
Italian: approssimativamente
Japanese: daitai no だいたいの
Korean: daeryak 대략
Portuguese: aproximadamente
Russian: priblizítel'no приблизительно
Spanish: aproximadamente
Swedish: ungefär

116. April [n.]

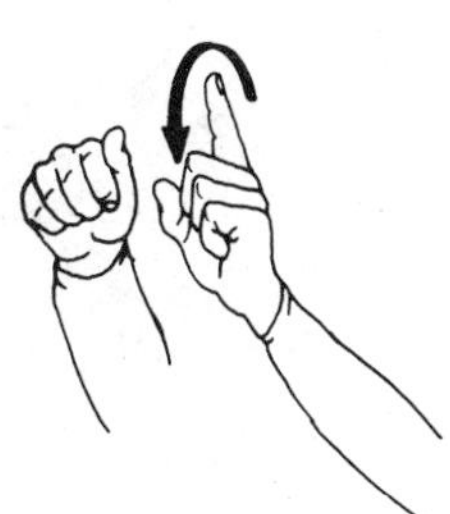

Arabic: abríl ابريل
Chinese: sìyuè 四月
Dutch: april
French: avril
German: April
Italian: aprile
Japanese: shigatsu 四月
Korean: sawŏl 사월
Portuguese: abril
Russian: aprél' апрель
Spanish: abril
Swedish: april

117. area [n.]

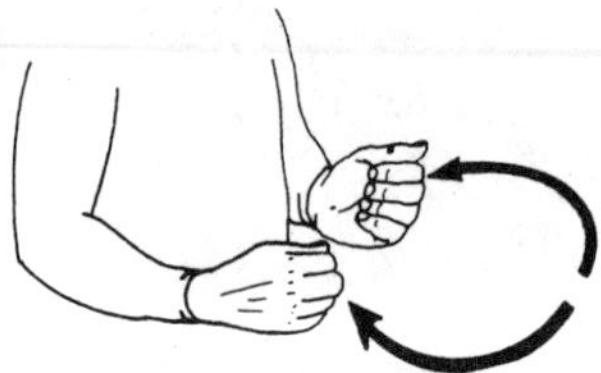

Arabic: misáha مساحة
Chinese: dìqū 地區
Dutch: gebied
French: région
German: Gebiet
Italian: regione
Japanese: chiiki 地域
Korean: jigyŏk 지역
Portuguese: região
Russian: rayón район
Spanish: región
Swedish: område

118. Argentina [n.]

Arabic: al-arjantín الارجنتين
Chinese: āgēntíng 阿根廷
Dutch: Argentinië
French: Argentine
German: Argentinien
Italian: Argentina
Japanese: Aruzenchin アルゼンチン
Korean: Arjentina 알젠티나
Portuguese: Argentina
Russian: Argentína Аргентина
Spanish: Argentina
Swedish: Argentina

119. argue (quarrel) [v.]

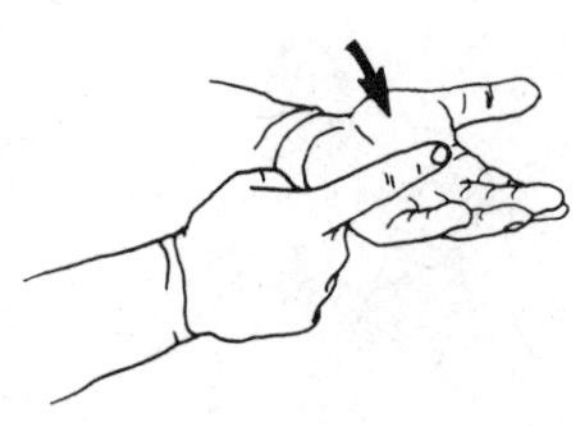

Arabic: jáadala جادل
Chinese: zhēnglùn 爭論
Dutch: redetwisten
French: se disputer
German: streiten
Italian: disputare
Japanese: giron suru 議論する
Korean: tat'uda 다투다
Portuguese: disputar
Russian: spórit' спорить
Spanish: disputar
Swedish: gräla

120. arise (originate) [v.]

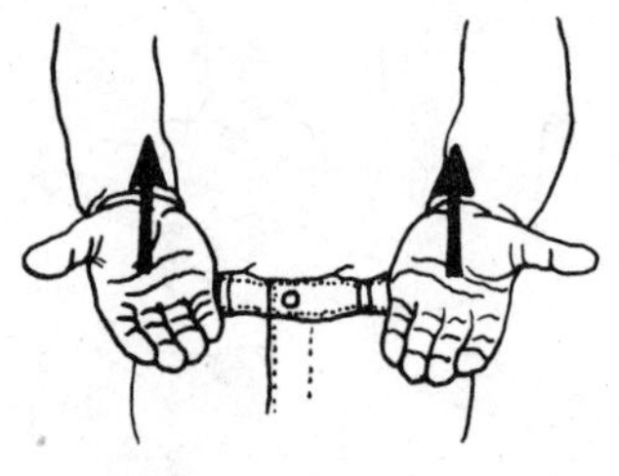

Arabic: náhada نهض
Chinese: qǐlái 起來
Dutch: ontstaan
French: surgir
German: entstehen
Italian: sorgere
Japanese: okoru 起る
Korean: irŏnada 일어나다
Portuguese: surgir
Russian: voznikát' возникать
Spanish: surgir
Swedish: uppstå

121. arm [n.]

Arabic: dhiráa ذراع
Chinese: shǒubì 手臂
Dutch: arm
French: bras
German: Arm
Italian: braccio
Japanese: ude 腕
Korean: p'al 팔
Portuguese: braço
Russian: ruká рука
Spanish: brazo
Swedish: arm

122. armament [n.]

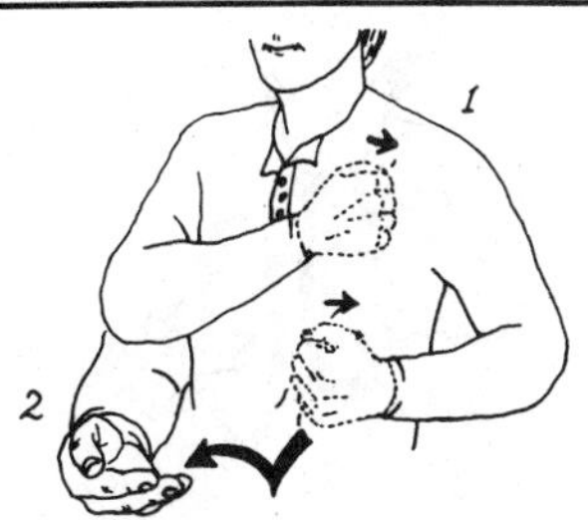

Arabic: tásaluh تسلح
Chinese: wǔzhuāng 武裝
Dutch: bewapening
French: armement
German: Bewaffnung
Italian: armamento
Japanese: gumbi 軍備
Korean: kunbi 군비
Portuguese: armamento
Russian: vooruzhéniye вооружение
Spanish: armamento
Swedish: rustning

123. army [n.]

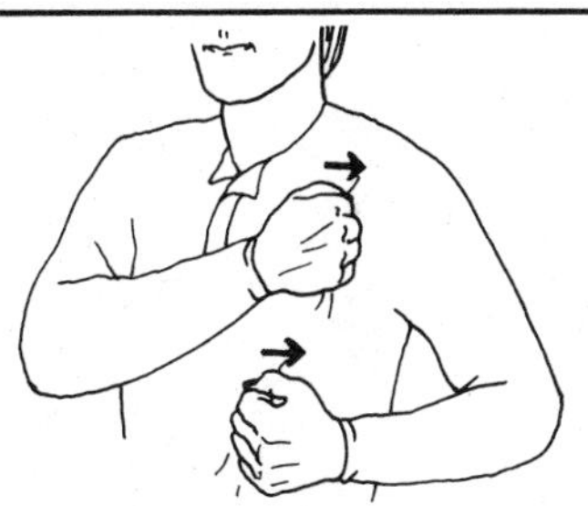

Arabic: jáeesh جيش
Chinese: jūnduì 軍隊
Dutch: leger
French: armée
German: Armee
Italian: esercito
Japanese: rikugun 陸軍
Korean: yukkun 육군
Portuguese: exército
Russian: ármiya армия
Spanish: ejército
Swedish: armé

124. around (on all sides) [adv./prep.]

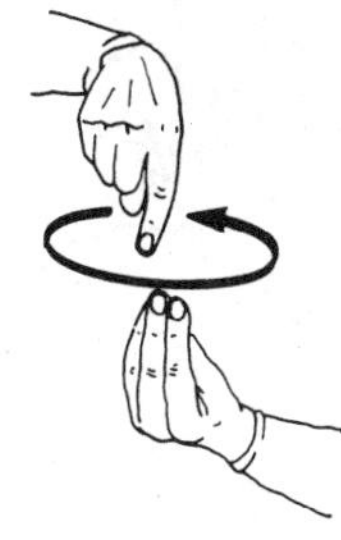

Arabic: hawl حول
Chinese: zhōuwéi 周圍
Dutch: rondom
French: autour de
German: rundherum
Italian: intorno a
Japanese: mawari ni まわりに
Korean: sabange 사방의
Portuguese: à volta de
Russian: vokrúg вокруг
Spanish: alrededor de
Swedish: omkring

125. arouse [v.]

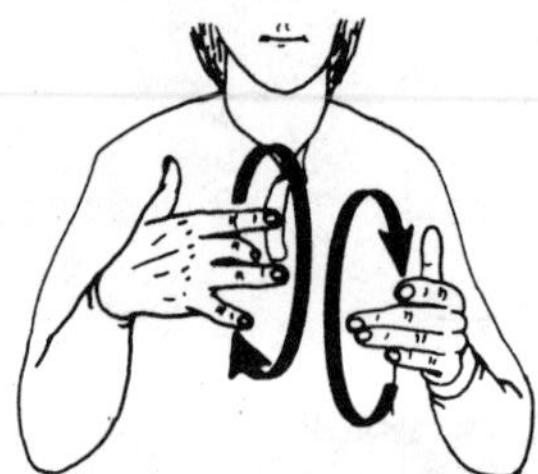

Arabic: atháara اثار
Chinese: huànxǐng 唤起
Dutch: opwekken
French: éveiller
German: aufrütteln
Italian: svegliare
Japanese: okosu 起こす
Korean: irŏnagehada 일어나게 하다
Portuguese: despertar
Russian: vozbuzhdát' возбуждать
Spanish: excitar
Swedish: väcka

126. arrange [v.]

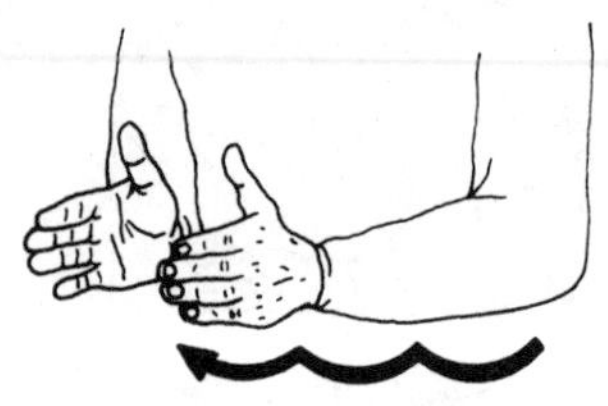

Arabic: ráttaba رتب
Chinese: ānpái 安排
Dutch: regelen
French: arranger
German: arrangieren
Italian: disporre
Japanese: totonoeru 整える
Korean: jojŏnghada 조정하다
Portuguese: arranjar
Russian: ustráivat' устраивать
Spanish: disponer
Swedish: ordna

127. arrest [v.]

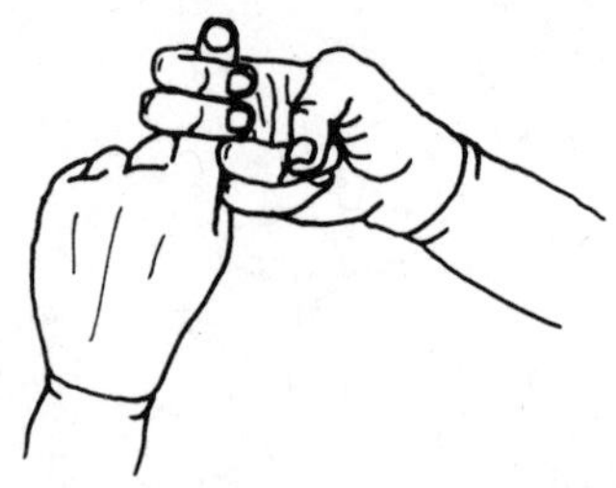

Arabic: iaatáqala اعتقل
Chinese: dàibǔ 逮捕
Dutch: arresteren
French: arrêter
German: verhaften
Italian: arrestare
Japanese: taiho suru 逮捕する
Korean: ch'ep'ohada 체포하다
Portuguese: prender
Russian: arestóvyvat' арестовывать
Spanish: arrestar
Swedish: arrestera

128. arrival [n.]

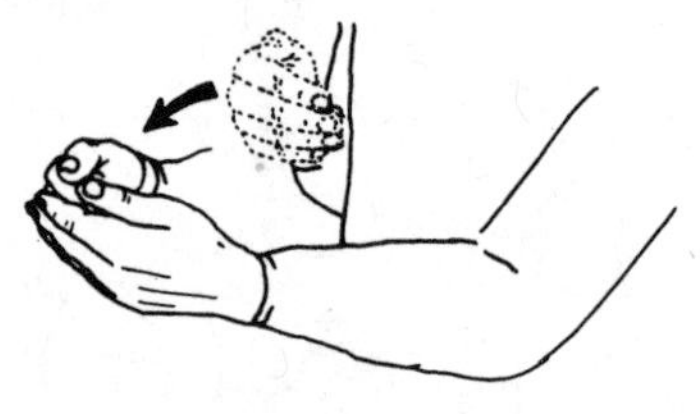

Arabic: wusúul وصول
Chinese: dàodá 到達
Dutch: aankomst
French: arrivée
German: Ankunft
Italian: arrivo
Japanese: tōchaku 到着
Korean: doch'ak 도착
Portuguese: chegada
Russian: pribýtiye прибытие
Spanish: llegada
Swedish: ankomst

129. art [n.]

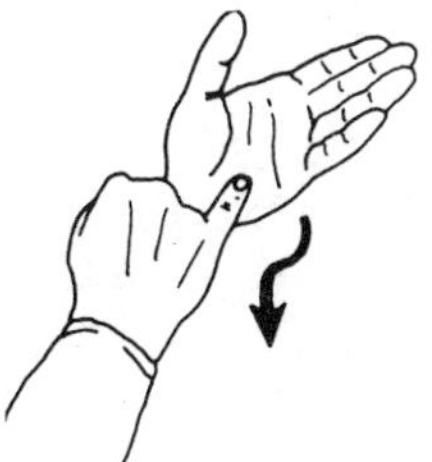

Arabic: fan فن
Chinese: yìshù 藝術
Dutch: kunst
French: art
German: Kunst
Italian: arte
Japanese: geijutsu 芸術
Korean: yesul 예술
Portuguese: arte
Russian: iskússtvo искусство
Spanish: arte
Swedish: konst

130. article (item) [n.]

Arabic: sháee' شيء
Chinese: wùjiàn 物件
Dutch: artikel
French: article
German: Gegenstand
Italian: articolo
Japanese: buppin 物品
Korean: mulpum 물품
Portuguese: artigo
Russian: stat'yá статья
Spanish: artículo
Swedish: artikel

131. artificial [adj.]

Arabic: musánnaa مصنع
Chinese: rénzàode 人造的
Dutch: kunstmatig
French: artificiel
German: künstlich
Italian: artificiale
Japanese: jinkō no 人工の
Korean: ingongjŏgin 인공적인
Portuguese: artificial
Russian: iskússtvennyy искусственный
Spanish: artificial
Swedish: konstgjord

132. artist [n.]

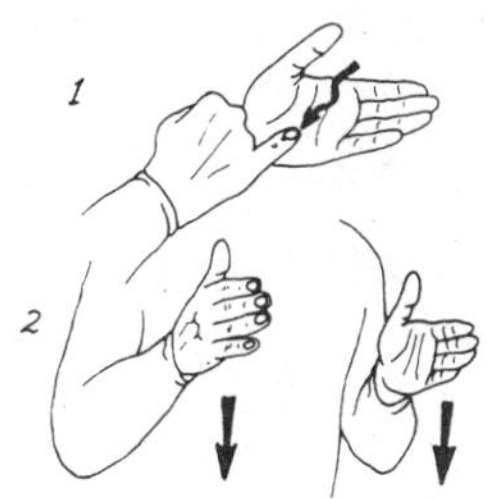

Arabic: fannán فنان
Chinese: yìshùjiā 藝術家
Dutch: artiest
French: artiste
German: Künstler
Italian: artista
Japanese: geijutsuka 芸術家
Korean: yesulga 예술가
Portuguese: artista
Russian: khudózhnik художник
Spanish: artista
Swedish: kontsnär

133. as [adv./conj.]

Arabic: káma كما
Chinese: dāng...shíhòu 當…時候
Dutch: als
French: comme
German: so
Italian: come
Japanese: ...to onajikurai
…と同じくらい
Korean: ...mank'ŭm ~만큼
Portuguese: como
Russian: kak как
Spanish: como
Swedish: så

134. ashamed [adj.]

Arabic: khajláan خجلان
Chinese: cánkuì 慚愧
Dutch: beschaamd
French: honteux
German: beschämt
Italian: vergognoso
Japanese: hajite 恥じて
Korean: bukkŭrŏun 부끄러운
Portuguese: envergonhado
Russian: pristýzhennyy
пристыженный
Spanish: avergonzado
Swedish: skamsen

135. Asia [n.]

Arabic: ásiya اسيا
Chinese: yàzhōu 亞洲
Dutch: Azië
French: Asie
German: Asien
Italian: Asia
Japanese: Ajia アジア
Korean: Asia 아시아
Portuguese: Ásia
Russian: Áziya Азия
Spanish: Asia
Swedish: Asien

136. ask [v.]

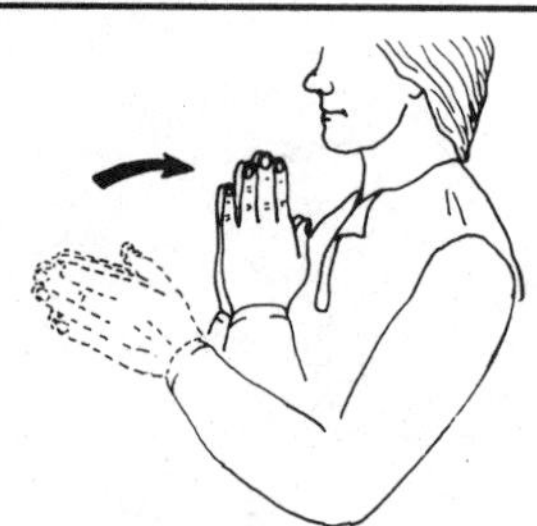

Arabic: sá'ala سأل
Chinese: wèn 問
Dutch: vragen
French: demander
German: fragen
Italian: domandare
Japanese: tazuneru 尋ねる
Korean: murŏ boda 물어보다
Portuguese: perguntar
Russian: prosít' просить
Spanish: preguntar
Swedish: fråga

137. asleep [adj.]

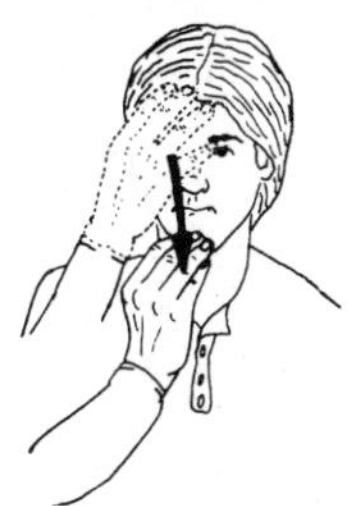

Arabic: ná'im نائم
Chinese: shuìzháo 睡着
Dutch: in slaap
French: endormi
German: eingeschlafen
Italian: addormentato
Japanese: nemutte 眠って
Korean: jamdŭrŭn 잠들은
Portuguese: adormecido
Russian: spyáshchiy спящий
Spanish: dormido
Swedish: sovande

138. aspire [v.]

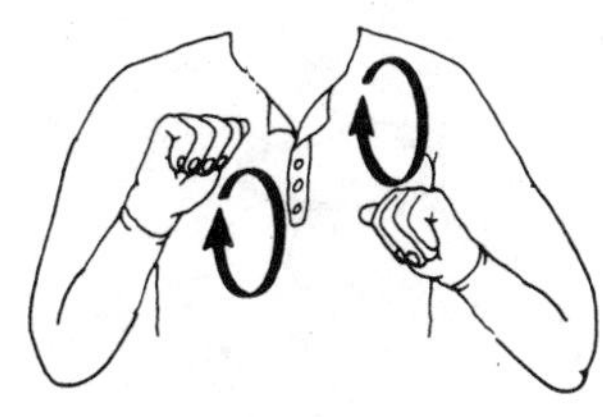

Arabic: támaha íla طمح الى
Chinese: rèwàng 熱望
Dutch: streven
French: aspirer
German: streben
Italian: aspirare
Japanese: netsubō suru 熱望する
Korean: yŏlmanghada 열망하다
Portuguese: aspirar
Russian: stremít'sya стремиться
Spanish: aspirar
Swedish: sträva

139. assemble (gather) [v.]

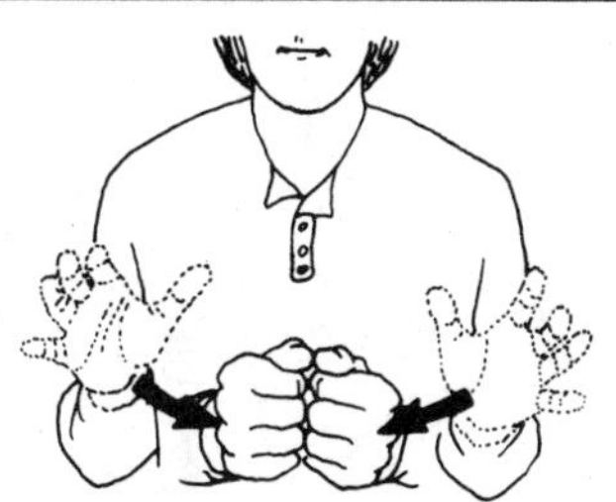

Arabic: jámaa جمع
Chinese: jùjí 聚集
Dutch: verzamelen
French: assembler
German: versammeln
Italian: riunire
Japanese: . . .o atsumeru 集める
Korean: moŭda 모으다
Portuguese: reunir
Russian: sobirát' собирать
Spanish: reunir
Swedish: samla

140. assist [v.]

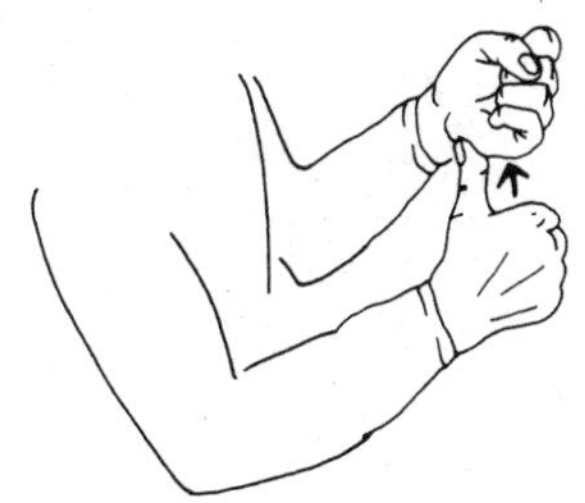

Arabic: sáada ساعد
Chinese: bāngzhù 幫助
Dutch: assisteren
French: aider
German: beistehen
Italian: aiutare
Japanese: tasukeru 助ける
Korean: topnŭnda 돕는다
Portuguese: ajudar
Russian: pomogát' помогать
Spanish: ayudar
Swedish: hjälpa

141. associate [v.]

Arabic: dhámma ضم
Chinese: liánhé 聯合
Dutch: associeren
French: associer
German: vereinigen
Italian: associare
Japanese: rengō saseru 連合させる
Korean: kyojehada 교제하다
Portuguese: associar
Russian: obshchát'sya общаться
Spanish: asociar
Swedish: associera

142. assume (suppose) [v.]

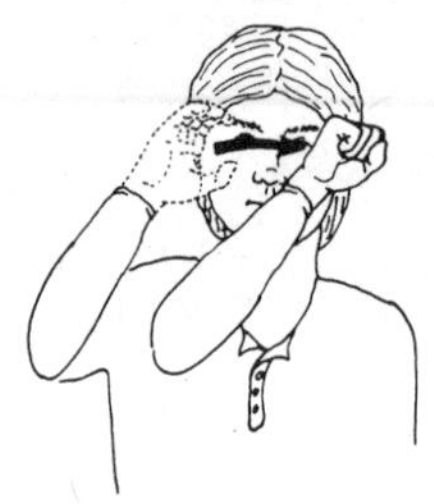

Arabic: iftárada افترض
Chinese: jiǎdìng 假定
Dutch: aannemen
French: supposer
German: annehmen
Italian: supporre
Japanese: okusokusuru 憶測する
Korean: kajŏnghada 가정하다
Portuguese: supor
Russian: predpolagát' предполагать
Spanish: suponer
Swedish: antaga

143. astonish [v.]

Arabic: ád-hasha ادهش
Chinese: shǐ. . . jīngyà 使驚訝
Dutch: verbijsteren
French: étonner
German: erstaunen
Italian: stupire
Japanese: . . . o odorokasu 驚かす
Korean: nollage hada 놀라게하다
Portuguese: espantar
Russian: udivlyát' удивлять
Spanish: asombrar
Swedish: förvåna

144. astronaut [n.]

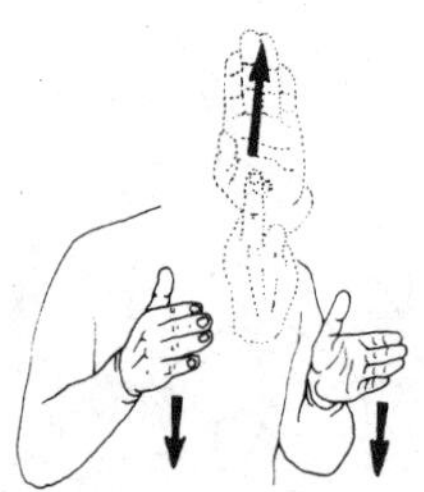

Arabic: fadháa'i فضائي
Chinese: tàikōngrén 太空人
Dutch: ruimtevaarder
French: astronaute
German: Astronaut
Italian: astronauta
Japanese: uchūhikōka 宇宙飛行家
Korean: ujuin 우주인
Portuguese: astronauta
Russian: kosmonávt космонавт
Spanish: astronauta
Swedish: astronaut

145. at [prep.]

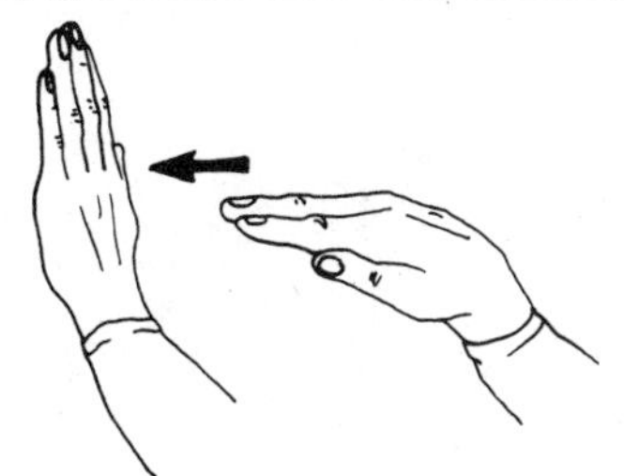

Arabic: fi في
Chinese: zài 在
Dutch: bij
French: à/en
German: in/an/bei
Italian: a/in
Japanese: . . . de/. . . ni …で/…に
Korean: . . . esŏ ~에서
Portuguese: a/em
Russian: v/na в/на
Spanish: a/en
Swedish: på/hos/i

146. athlete [n.]

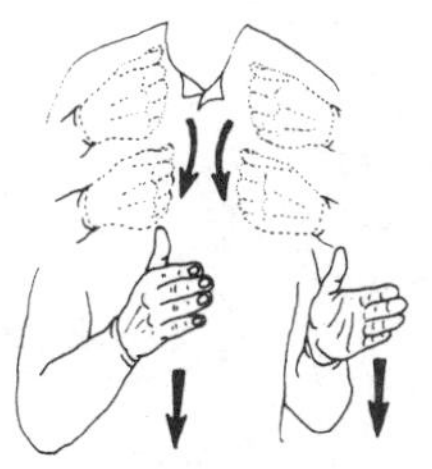

Arabic: riyáada رياضة
Chinese: yùndòngyuán 運動員
Dutch: atleet
French: athlète
German: Athlet
Italian: atleta
Japanese: undōka 運動家
Korean: undongga 운동가
Portuguese: atleta
Russian: atlét атлет
Spanish: atleta
Swedish: atlet

147. attach (fasten) [v.]

1

2

Arabic: álhaqa ألحق
Chinese: liángjiē 連接
Dutch: vastmaken
French: attacher
German: festmachen
Italian: attaccare
Japanese: toritsukeru 取り付ける
Korean: buch'ida 부치다
Portuguese: prender
Russian: prikreplyát' прикреплять
Spanish: sujetar
Swedish: fästa

148. attack [n.]

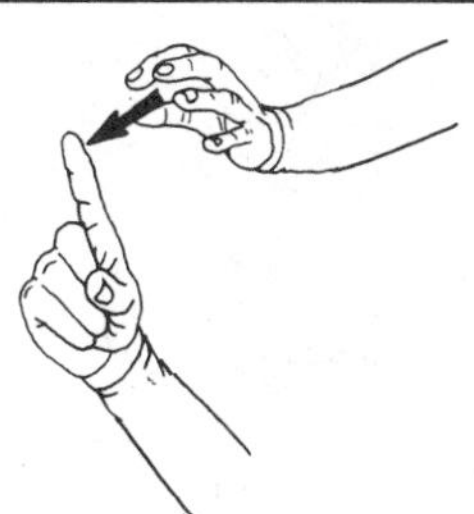

Arabic: hujúum هجوم
Chinese: gōngjí 攻擊
Dutch: aanval
French: attaquer
German: Angriff
Italian: attacco
Japanese: kōgeki 攻撃する
Korean: gongkyŏk 공격
Portuguese: ataque
Russian: atáka атака
Spanish: ataque
Swedish: anfall

149. attempt [v.]

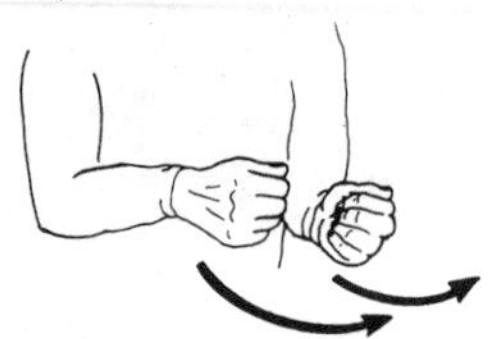

Arabic: háawala حاول
Chinese: qìtú 企圖
Dutch: proberen
French: tenter
German: versuchen
Italian: tentare
Japanese: kokoromiru 試みる
Korean: shidohada 시도하다
Portuguese: tentar
Russian: pytát'sya пытаться
Spanish: intentar
Swedish: försöka

150. attention [n.]

Arabic: intibá انتباه
Chinese: zhùyì 注意
Dutch: attentie
French: attention
German: Achtung
Italian: attenzione
Japanese: chūi 注意
Korean: ju'i 주의
Portuguese: atenção
Russian: vnimániye внимание
Spanish: atención
Swedish: uppmärksamhet

151. attitude [n.]

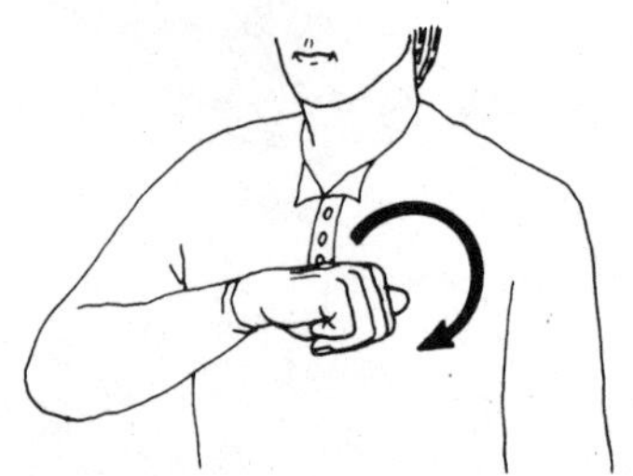

Arabic: máwqif موقف
Chinese: tàidù 態度
Dutch: houding
French: attitude
German: Haltung
Italian: attitudine
Japanese: taido 態度
Korean: t'aedo 태도
Portuguese: atitude
Russian: otnoshéniye отношение
Spanish: actitud
Swedish: hållning

152. attract [v.]

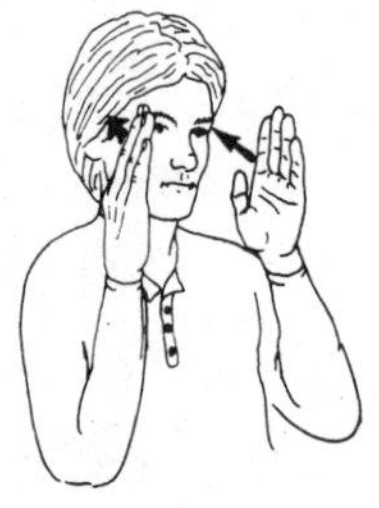

Arabic: jádhaba جذب
Chinese: xīyǐn 吸引
Dutch: aantrekken
French: attirer
German: anziehen
Italian: attrarre
Japanese: hikitsukeru 引きつける
Korean: kkŭlda 끌다
Portuguese: atrair
Russian: privlekát' привлекать
Spanish: atraer
Swedish: tilldra sig

153. attractive [adj.]

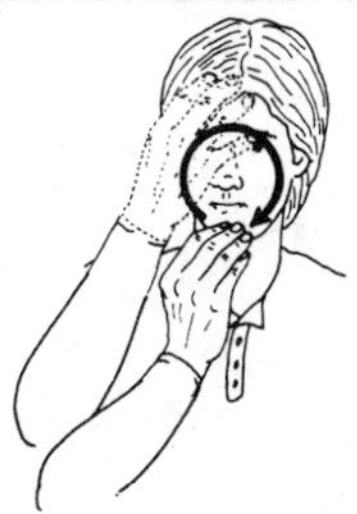

Arabic: jádhab جذاب
Chinese: yǒu xīyǐnglì de 有吸引力的
Dutch: aantrekkelijk
French: attrayant
German: anziehend
Italian: attraente
Japanese: miryoku no aru 魅力のある
Korean: maeryŏkjŏkin 매력적인
Portuguese: atraente
Russian: privlekátel'nyy привлекательный
Spanish: atractivo
Swedish: tilldragande

154. audience [n.]

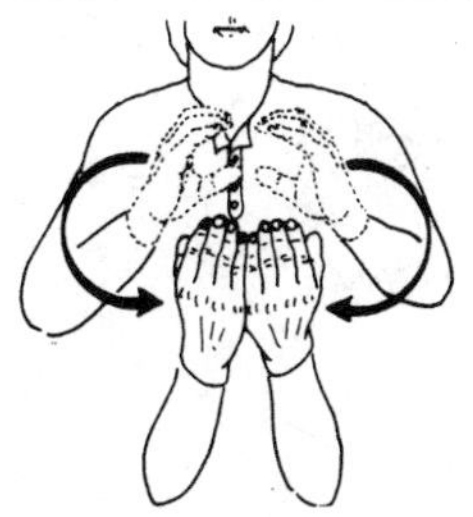

Arabic: al-hodóur الحضور
Chinese: guānzhòng 觀衆
Dutch: audiëntie
French: audience
German: Zuhörer
Italian: udienza
Japanese: kankyaku 観客
Korean: gwanjung 관중
Portuguese: audiência
Russian: slúshateli слушатели
Spanish: audiencia
Swedish: publik

155. August [n.]

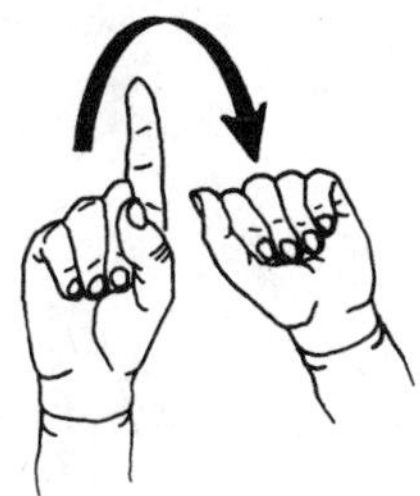

Arabic: óghostos اغسطس
Chinese: bāyuè 八月
Dutch: augustus
French: août
German: August
Italian: agosto
Japanese: hachigatsu 八月
Korean: p'arwŏl 팔월
Portuguese: agôsto
Russian: ávgust август
Spanish: agosto
Swedish: augusti

156. aunt [n.]

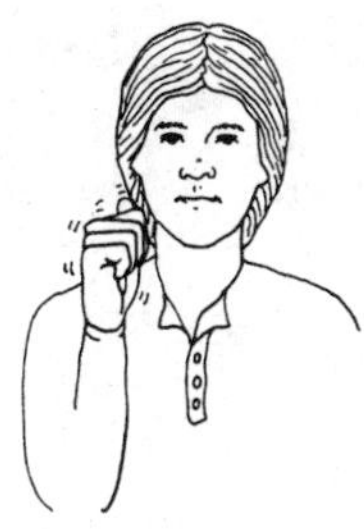

Arabic: áama/kháala خالة / عمة
Chinese: gūmā 姑媽
Dutch: tante
French: tante
German: Tante
Italian: zia
Japanese: oba おば
Korean: ajumŏni 아주머니
Portuguese: tia
Russian: tyótya тётя
Spanish: tía
Swedish: tant

157. Australia [n.]

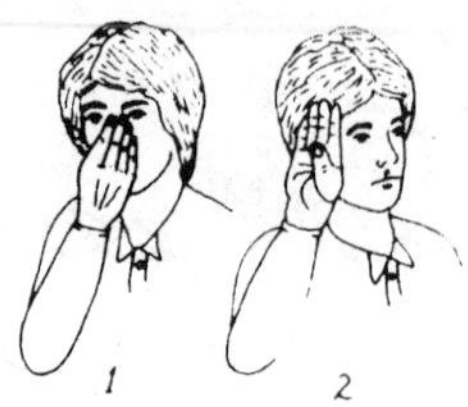

Arabic: osturália استراليا
Chinese: àodàlìyà 澳大利亞
Dutch: Australië
French: Australie
German: Australien
Italian: Australia
Japanese: Osutoraria オーストラリア
Korean: Osŭt'ŭreillia 오스트렐리아
Portuguese: Austrália
Russian: Avstráliya Австралия
Spanish: Australia
Swedish: Australien

158. Austria [n.]

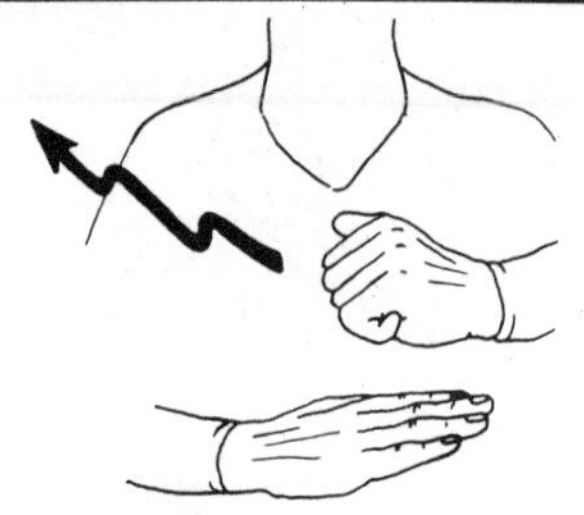

Arabic: án-namsa النمسا
Chinese: àodìlì 奧地利
Dutch: Oostenrijk
French: Autriche
German: Österreich
Italian: Austria
Japanese: Osutoria オーストリア
Korean: Osŭtŭria 오스트리아
Portuguese: Áustria
Russian: Ávstriya Австрия
Spanish: Austria
Swedish: Österrike

159. author [n.]

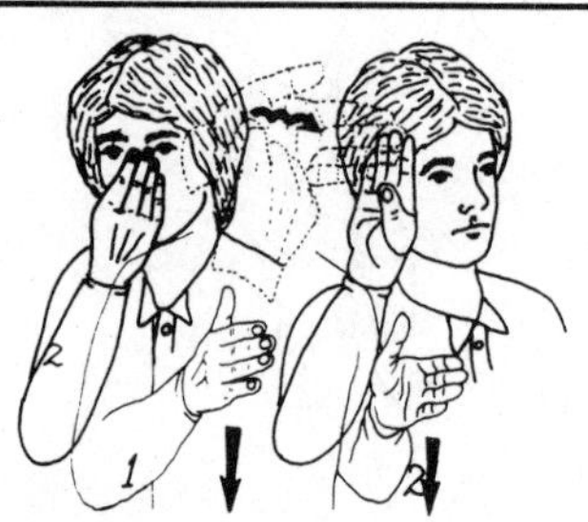

Arabic: mu'állef مؤلف
Chinese: zuòzhě 作者
Dutch: auteur
French: auteur
German: Autor
Italian: autore
Japanese: sakka 作家
Korean: jakka 작가
Portuguese: autor
Russian: ávtor автор
Spanish: autor
Swedish: författare

160. authority [n.]

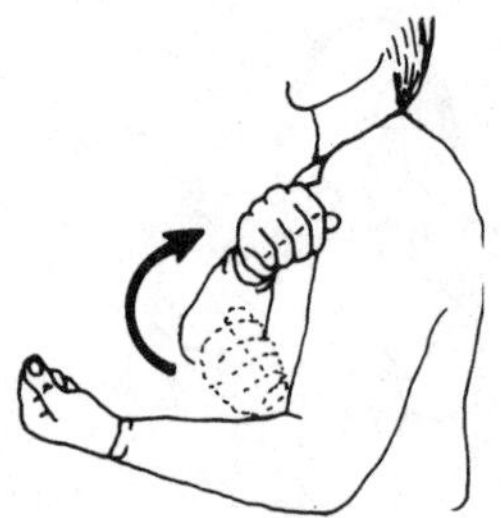

Arabic: súlta سلطة
Chinese: quánwēi 權威
Dutch: autoriteit
French: autorité
German: Autorität
Italian: autorità
Japanese: kenryoku 権力
Korean: kwŏnwi 권위
Portuguese: autoridade
Russian: avtoritét авторитет
Spanish: autoridad
Swedish: autoritet

161. autumn [n.]

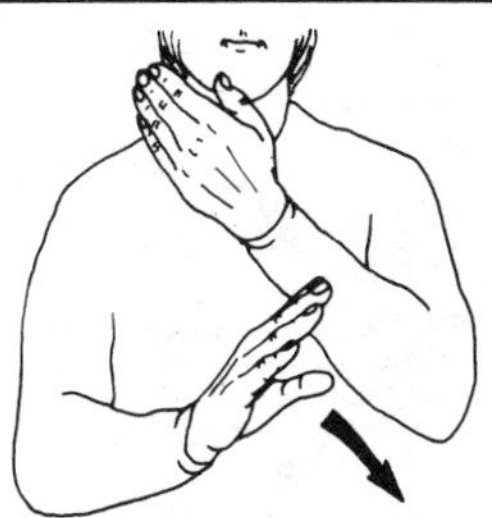

Arabic: al-kharíf الخريف
Chinese: qiūtiān 秋天
Dutch: herfst
French: automne
German: Herbst
Italian: autunno
Japanese: aki 秋
Korean: kaŭl 가을
Portuguese: outono
Russian: ósen' осень
Spanish: otoño
Swedish: höst

162. avenue [n.]

Arabic: sháarea' شارع
Chinese: jiē 街
Dutch: laan
French: avenue
German: Allee
Italian: viale
Japanese: ōdōri 大通り
Korean: gil 길
Portuguese: avenida
Russian: prospékt проспект
Spanish: avenida
Swedish: aveny

163. average [adj.]

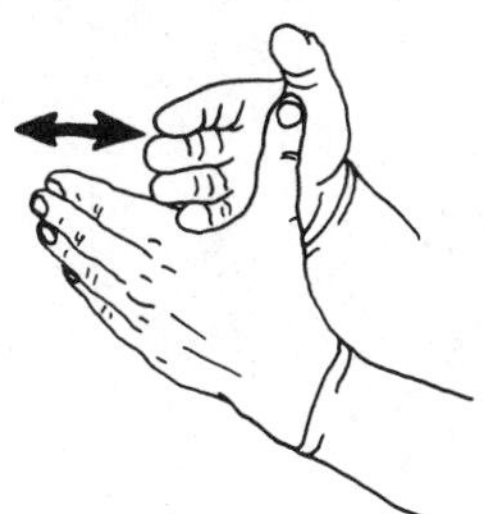

Arabic: mutawwássit متوسط
Chinese: píngjūn 平均
Dutch: gemiddeld
French: moyen
German: durchschnittlich
Italian: medio
Japanese: heikin no 平均の
Korean: p'yŏnggyun 평균
Portuguese: médio
Russian: srédniy средний
Spanish: promedio
Swedish: genomsnittlig

164. avoid [v.]

Arabic: tajánnaba تجنب
Chinese: bìmiǎn 避免
Dutch: vermijden
French: éviter
German: vermeiden
Italian: evitare
Japanese: . . . o sakeru 避ける
Korean: p'ihada 피하다
Portuguese: evitar
Russian: izbegát' избегать
Spanish: evitar
Swedish: undvika

165. awake(n) [v.]

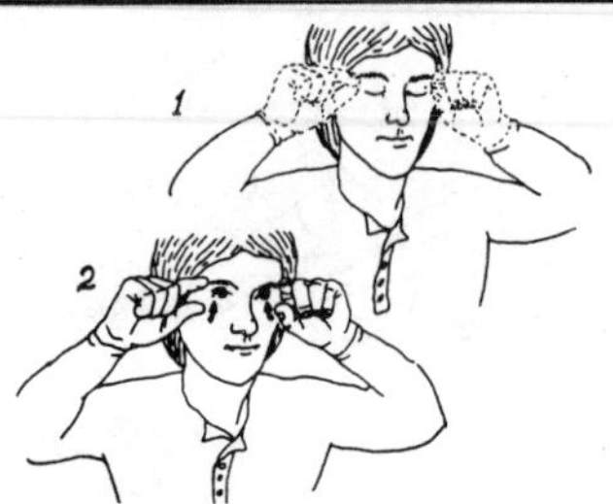

Arabic: sáha صحى
Chinese: huànxǐng 喚醒
Dutch: wekken
French: réveiller
German: wecken
Italian: svegliare
Japanese: me o samasaseru 目をさまさせる
Korean: irŏnada 일어나다
Portuguese: acordar
Russian: razbudít' разбудить
Spanish: despertar
Swedish: väcka

166. award [n.]

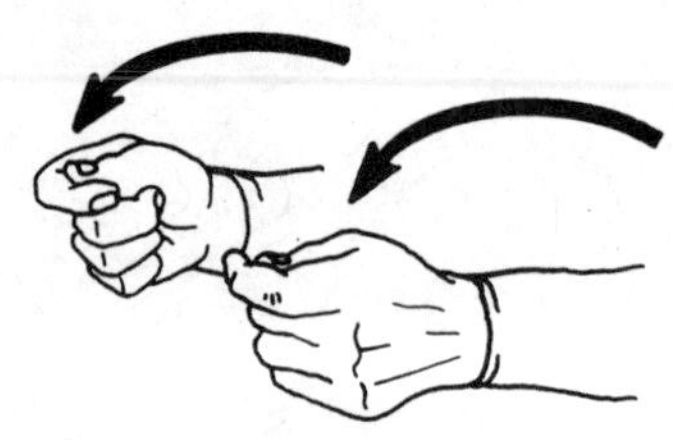

Arabic: já'iza جائزة
Chinese: jiǎng 獎
Dutch: onderscheiding
French: récompense
German: Preis
Italian: premio
Japanese: shōhin 賞品
Korean: sangp'um 상품
Portuguese: prêmio
Russian: nagráda награда
Spanish: premio
Swedish: pris

167. aware (of) [adj.]

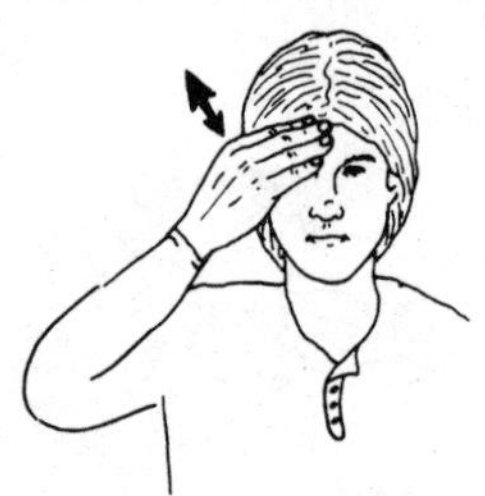

Arabic: múdrik مدرك
Chinese: zhīdàode 知道的
Dutch: bewust van
French: conscient de
German: sich bewußt sein
Italian: conscio
Japanese: kizuite 気づいて
Korean: alda 알다
Portuguese: ciente
Russian: soznayúshchiy сознающий
Spanish: consciente de
Swedish: medveten om

168. away [adv.]

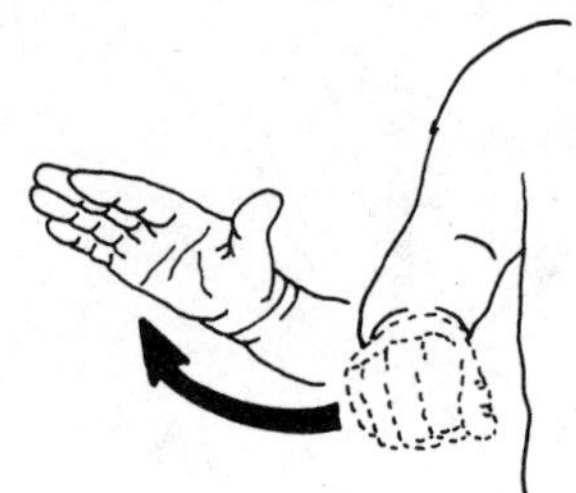

Arabic: ba-íd بعيد
Chinese: líkāi 離開
Dutch: weg
French: loin
German: weg
Italian: via
Japanese: hanarete 離れて
Korean: mŏlli 멀리
Portuguese: fora
Russian: proch' прочь
Spanish: lejos
Swedish: bort

169. awful [adj.]

Arabic: baghídh بغيض
Chinese: kěpàde 可怕的
Dutch: verschrikkelijk
French: terrible
German: schrecklich
Italian: terribile
Japanese: osoroshii 恐ろしい
Korean: turyŏun 두려운
Portuguese: terrível
Russian: uzhásnyy ужасный
Spanish: terrible
Swedish: fruktsanvärd

170. awkward (clumsy) [adj.]

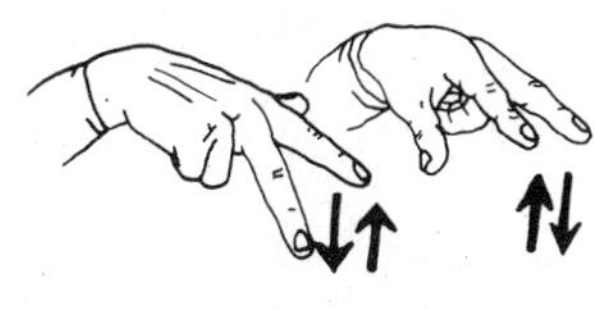

Arabic: ákhraq اخرق
Chinese: bènzhuóde 笨拙的
Dutch: onhandig
French: maladroit
German: ungeschickt
Italian: goffo
Japanese: bukiyo na 無器用な
Korean: ŏsaekhan 어색한
Portuguese: desajeitado
Russian: nelóvkiy неловкий
Spanish: torpe
Swedish: klumpig

171. axe [n.]

Arabic: fa's فأس
Chinese: fŭtóu 斧頭
Dutch: bijl
French: hache
German: Axt
Italian: scure
Japanese: ono 斧
Korean: dokki 도끼
Portuguese: machado
Russian: topór топор
Spanish: hacha
Swedish: yxa

172. baby [n.]

Arabic: tifl طفل
Chinese: yīng-ér 嬰兒
Dutch: baby
French: bébé
German: Baby
Italian: bambino
Japanese: akambō 赤ん坊
Korean: agi 아기
Portuguese: bebê
Russian: rebyónok ребёнок
Spanish: bebé
Swedish: baby

173. bachelor (unmarried) [n.]

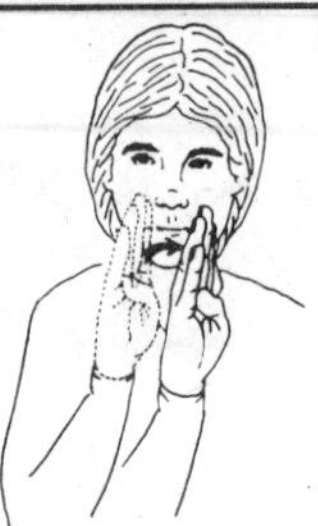

Arabic: áa'zab اعزب
Chinese: dānshēnhàn 單身漢
Dutch: vrijgezel
French: célibataire
German: Junggeselle
Italian: scapolo
Japanese: dokushin 独身
Korean: dokshinja 독신자
Portuguese: solteiro
Russian: kholostyák холостяк
Spanish: soltero
Swedish: ungkarl

174. back [n.]

Arabic: dháher ظهر
Chinese: bèi 背
Dutch: rug
French: dos
German: Rücken
Italian: dorso
Japanese: senaka 背中
Korean: dwi 뒤
Portuguese: costas
Russian: spiná спина
Spanish: espalda
Swedish: rygg

175. background [n.]

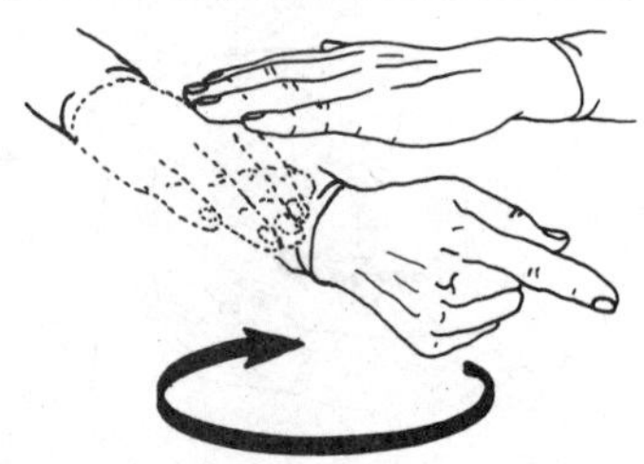

Arabic: khalfía خلفية
Chinese: bèijǐng 背景
Dutch: achtergrond
French: arrière-plan
German: Hintergrund
Italian: sfondo
Japanese: keireki 経歴
Korean: baekyŏng 배경
Portuguese: fundo
Russian: fon фон
Spanish: fondo
Swedish: bakgrund

176. backward(s) [adj./adv.]

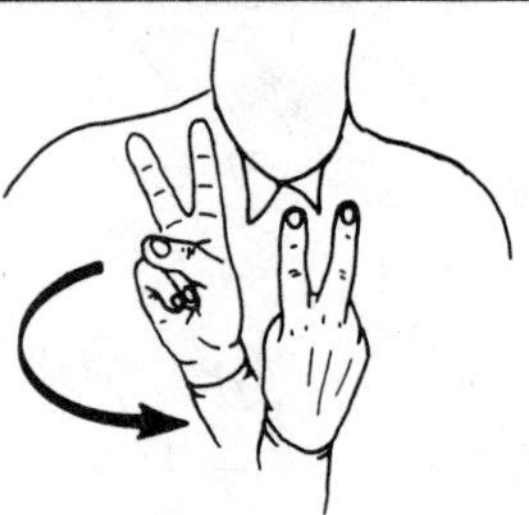

Arabic: mutakhállif متخلف
Chinese: dàotuìde 倒退的
Dutch: achteruit
French: en arrière
German: rückwärts
Italian: dietro
Japanese: ushiro e 後ろへ
Korean: hujin 후진
Portuguese: para trás
Russian: nazád назад
Spanish: al revés
Swedish: bakåt

177. bad [adj.]

Arabic: séyya' سيّ
Chinese: huàide 壞的
Dutch: slecht
French: mauvais
German: schlecht
Italian: cattivo
Japanese: warui 悪い
Korean: nabbŭn 나쁜
Portuguese: mau
Russian: plokhóy плохой
Spanish: malo
Swedish: dålig

178. bag [n.]

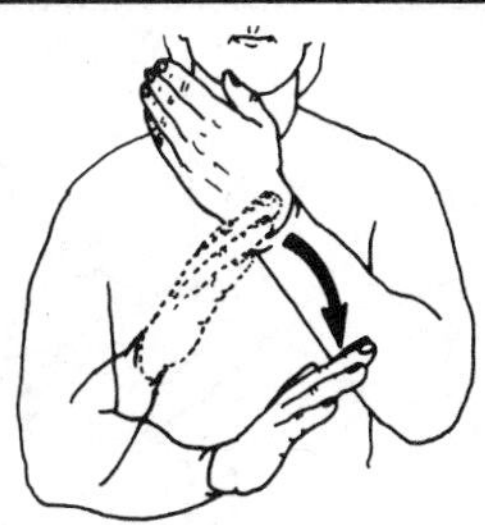

Arabic: kís كيس
Chinese: dàizi 袋子
Dutch: zak
French: sac
German: Beutel
Italian: sacco
Japanese: fukuro 袋
Korean: baek 백
Portuguese: saco
Russian: meshók мешок
Spanish: bolsa
Swedish: väska

179. baggage [n.]

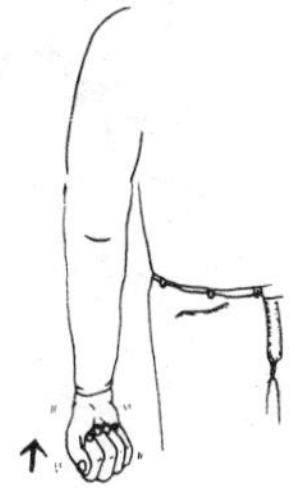

Arabic: amtia'a امتعة
Chinese: xínglǐ 行李
Dutch: bagage
French: bagage
German: Gepäck
Italian: bagaglio
Japanese: tenimotsu 手荷物
Korean: suhamul 수하물
Portuguese: bagagem
Russian: bagázh багаж
Spanish: equipaje
Swedish: bagage

180. bake [v.]

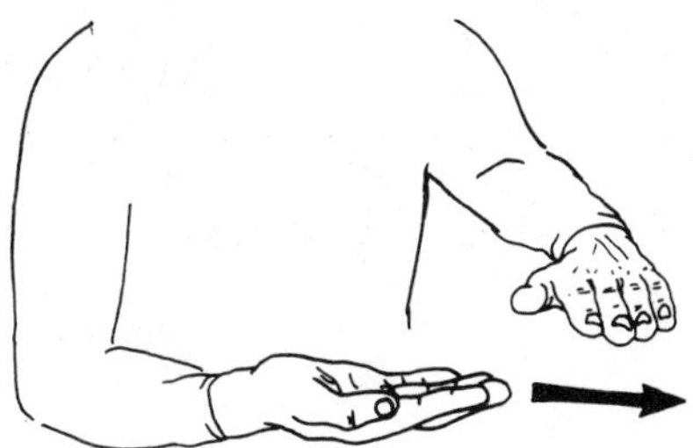

Arabic: khábaza خبز
Chinese: hōng 烘
Dutch: bakken
French: cuire au four
German: backen
Italian: cuocere al forno
Japanese: yaku 焼く
Korean: kupta 굽다
Portuguese: cozinhar
Russian: pech' печь
Spanish: cocer al horno
Swedish: baka

181. balance (equilibrium) [n.]

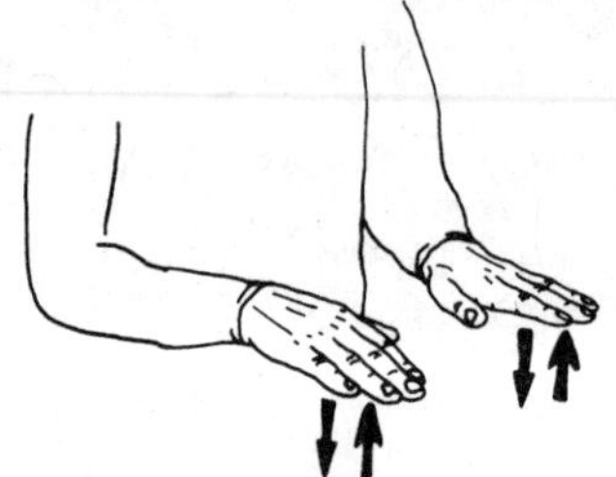

Arabic: tawázun توازن
Chinese: pínghéng 平衡
Dutch: evenwicht
French: équilibre
German: Gleichgewicht
Italian: equilibrio
Japanese: tsuriai 釣合
Korean: jŏul 저울
Portuguese: equilíbrio
Russian: ravnovésiye равновесие
Spanish: equilibrio
Swedish: jämvikt

182. bald [adj.]

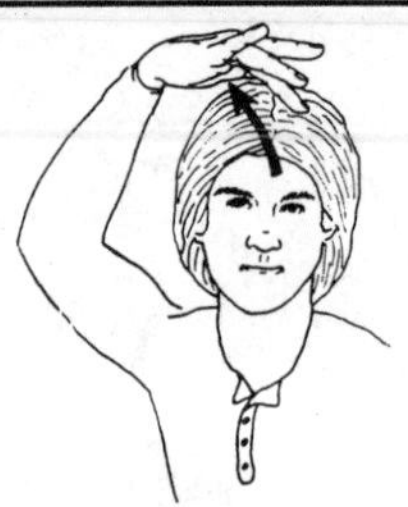

Arabic: asláa' اصلع
Chinese: tūde 秃的
Dutch: kaal
French: chauve
German: kahl
Italian: calvo
Japanese: hageta はげた
Korean: bŏsŏjin 벗어진
Portuguese: careca
Russian: lýsyy лысый
Spanish: calvo
Swedish: flintskalllig

183. ball (game) [n.]

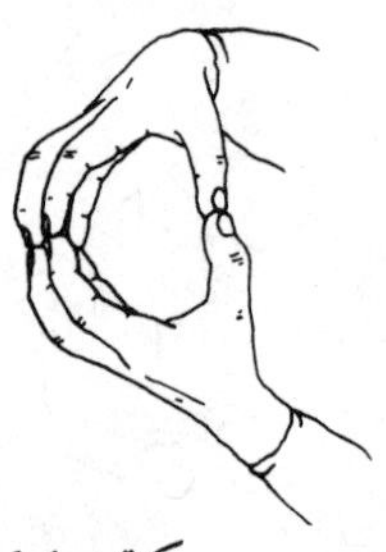

Arabic: kóra كرة
Chinese: qiú 球
Dutch: bal
French: balle
German: Ball
Italian: palla
Japanese: tama 球
Korean: kong 공
Portuguese: bola
Russian: myách мяч
Spanish: pelota
Swedish: boll

184. banana [n.]

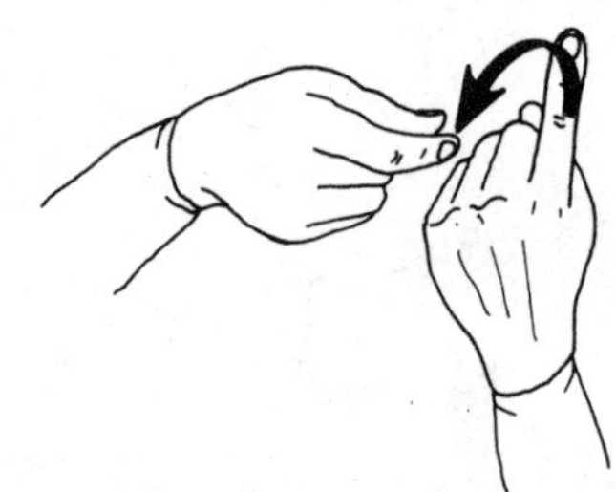

Arabic: moz موز
Chinese: xiāngjiāo 香蕉
Dutch: banaan
French: banane
German: Banane
Italian: banana
Japanese: banana バナナ
Korean: banana 바나나
Portuguese: banana
Russian: banán банан
Spanish: banana
Swedish: banan

185. bandage [n.]

Arabic: dhammáda ضمادة
Chinese: bēngdài 繃帶
Dutch: verband
French: bandage
German: Verband
Italian: bendaggio
Japanese: hōtai 包帯
Korean: bungdae 붕대
Portuguese: bandagem
Russian: bint бинт
Spanish: venda
Swedish: förband

186. bank (money) [n.]

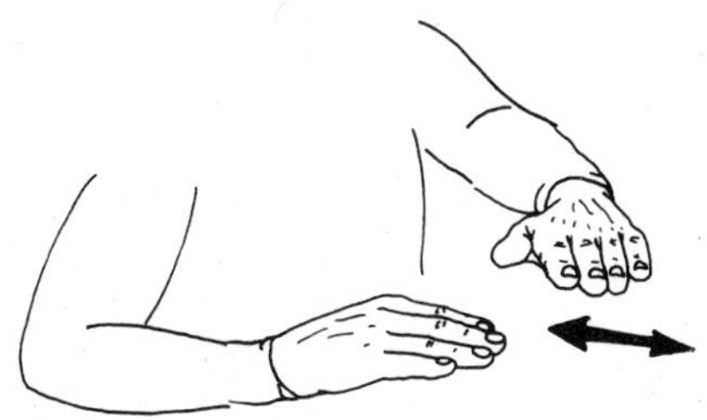

Arabic: bank بنك
Chinese: yínháng 銀行
Dutch: bank
French: banque
German: Bank
Italian: banca
Japanese: ginkō 銀行
Korean: ŭnhaeng 은행
Portuguese: banco
Russian: bank банк
Spanish: banco
Swedish: bank

187. banquet [n.]

Arabic: walíma وليمة
Chinese: yànhuì 宴會
Dutch: feestmaal
French: banquet
German: Bankett
Italian: banchetto
Japanese: enkai 宴会
Korean: yŏnhoe 연회
Portuguese: banquête
Russian: bankét банкет
Spanish: banquete
Swedish: bankett

188. baptism [n.]

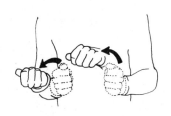

Arabic: máamada معمدة
Chinese: jìnlǐ 浸禮
Dutch: doop
French: baptême
German: Taufe
Italian: battesimo
Japanese: senrei 洗礼
Korean: serye 세례
Portuguese: batismo
Russian: kreshchéniye крещение
Spanish: bautismo
Swedish: dop

189. barber(shop) [n.]

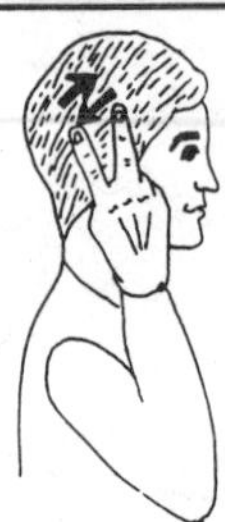

Arabic: halláq حلاق
Chinese: lĭfă 理髮
Dutch: kapper
French: coiffeur
German: Friseur
Italian: barbiere
Japanese: tokoya 床屋
Korean: ibalsa 이발사
Portuguese: barbeiro
Russian: parikmákher парикмахер
Spanish: barbero
Swedish: herrfrisör

190. bare (naked) [adj.]

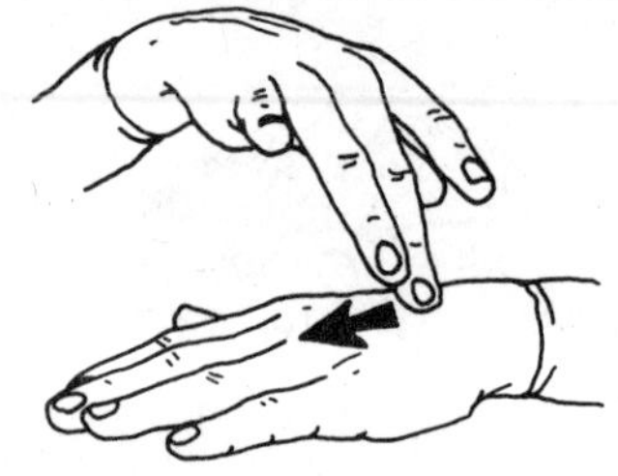

Arabic: aarín عارٍ
Chinese: chìluŏde 赤裸的
Dutch: naakt
French: nu
German: nackt
Italian: nudo
Japanese: hadakano 裸の
Korean: bŏlgŏbŏsŭn 발가벗은
Portuguese: nu
Russian: gólyy голый
Spanish: desnudo
Swedish: naken

191. barn [n.]

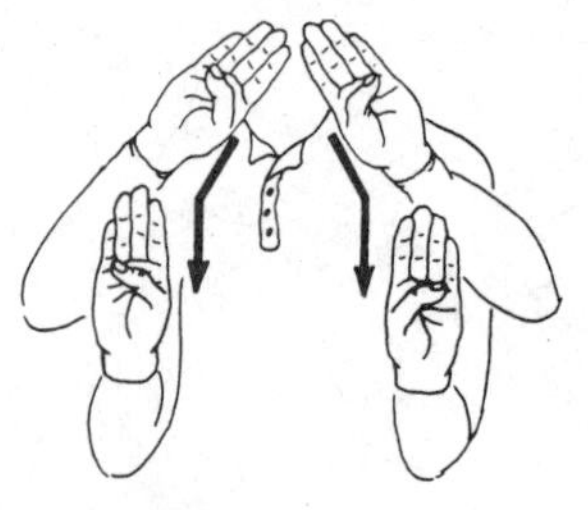

Arabic: hadhíra حظيرة
Chinese: gŭcāng 穀倉
Dutch: schuur
French: grange
German: Scheune
Italian: granaio
Japanese: naya 納屋
Korean: gwang 광
Portuguese: celeiro
Russian: ambár амбар
Spanish: establo
Swedish: lada

192. barrel [n.]

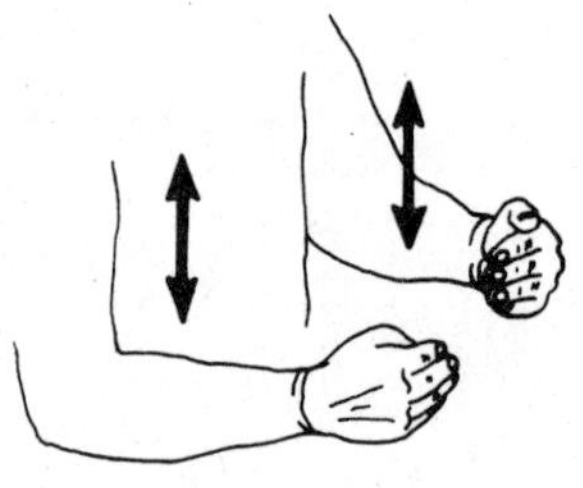

Arabic: bermíl برميل
Chinese: tŏng 桶
Dutch: vat
French: baril
German: Faß
Italian: barile
Japanese: taru たる
Korean: t'ong 통
Portuguese: barril
Russian: bóchka бочка
Spanish: barril
Swedish: tunna

193. base [n.]

Arabic: qáeda قاعدة
Chinese: gēnjī 根基
Dutch: basis
French: base
German: Grundlage
Italian: base
Japanese: kiso 基礎
Korean: kich'o 기초
Portuguese: base
Russian: bázis базис
Spanish: base
Swedish: bas

194. baseball [n.]

Arabic: beis-ból بيسبول
Chinese: bàngqiú 棒球
Dutch: honkbal
French: base-ball
German: Baseball
Italian: baseball
Japanese: yakyū 野球
Korean: yagu 야구
Portuguese: beisebol
Russian: beysból бейсбол
Spanish: béisbol
Swedish: baseboll

195. bashful [adj.]

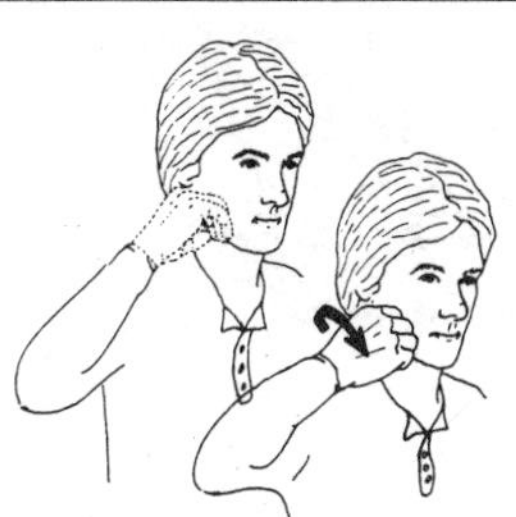

Arabic: khajúul خجول
Chinese: miăntiănde 腼腆的
Dutch: verlegen
French: timide
German: schüchtern
Italian: timido
Japanese: hazukashigariano はずかしがりの
Korean: sujubŭn 수줍은
Portuguese: tímido
Russian: zasténchivyy застенчивый
Spanish: tímido
Swedish: blyg

196. basis [n.]

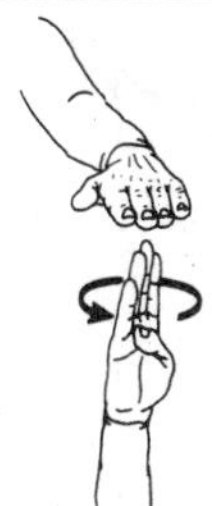

Arabic: qawáad قواعد
Chinese: jīchŭ 基礎
Dutch: basis
French: base
German: Basis
Italian: base
Japanese: kiso 基礎
Korean: todae 토대
Portuguese: base
Russian: osnovániye основание
Spanish: base
Swedish: basis

197. basket [n.]

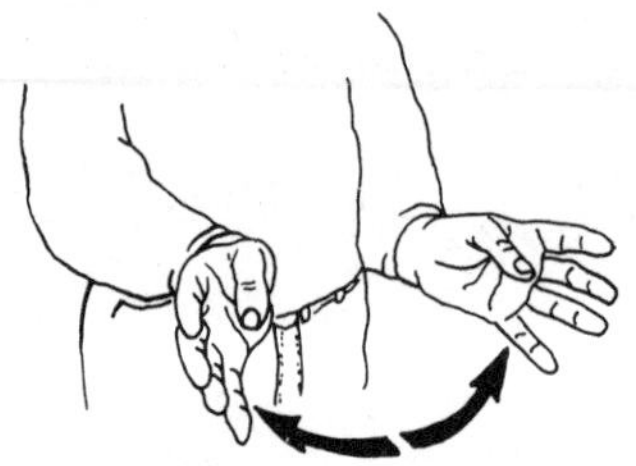

Arabic: sálla سلة
Chinese: lánzi 籃子
Dutch: mand
French: corbeille
German: Korb
Italian: paniere
Japanese: kago かご
Korean: baguni 바구니
Portuguese: cêsto
Russian: korzína корзина
Spanish: cesto
Swedish: korg

198. basketball [n.]

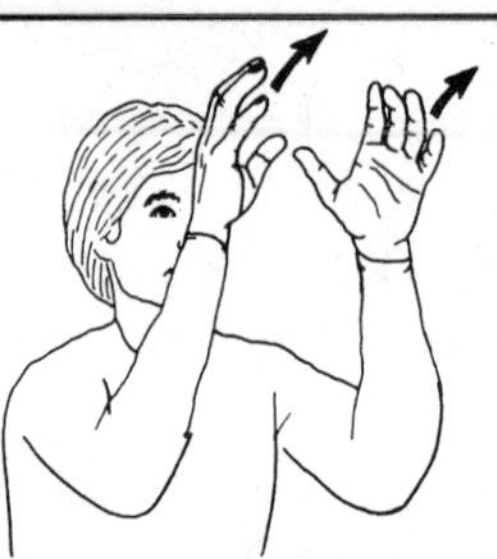

Arabic: kórat as-sálla كرة السلة
Chinese: lánqiú 籃球
Dutch: basketbal
French: basket-ball
German: Basketball
Italian: pallacanestro
Japanese: basuketto bōru バスケツトボール
Korean: nonggu 농구
Portuguese: basquetebol
Russian: basketból баскетбол
Spanish: baloncesto
Swedish: basketboll

199. bath [n.]

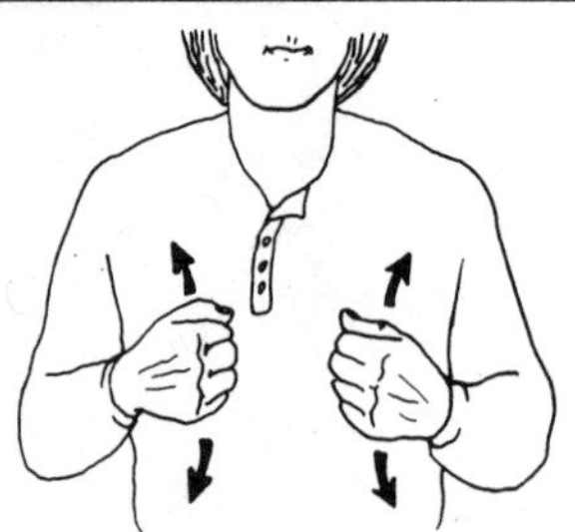

Arabic: hámmam حمام
Chinese: mùyù 沐浴
Dutch: bad
French: bain
German: Bad
Italian: bagno
Japanese: furo 風呂
Korean: mogyok 목욕
Portuguese: banho
Russian: vánna ванна
Spanish: baño
Swedish: bad

200. battle [n.]

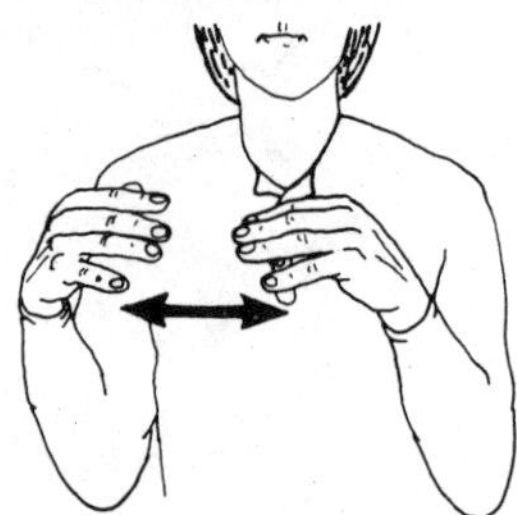

Arabic: máaraka معركة
Chinese: zhànyì 戰役
Dutch: veldslag
French: bataille
German: Schlacht
Italian: battaglia
Japanese: sentō 戦闘
Korean: jŏnjaeng 전쟁
Portuguese: batalha
Russian: bítva битва
Spanish: batalla
Swedish: slag

201. be [v.]

Arabic: kána كان
Chinese: shì 是
Dutch: zijn
French: être
German: sein
Italian: essere
Japanese: . . .de aru …である
Korean: . . .mnida ~입니다
Portuguese: ser
Russian: byt' быть
Spanish: ser/estar
Swedish: vara

202. beach [n.]

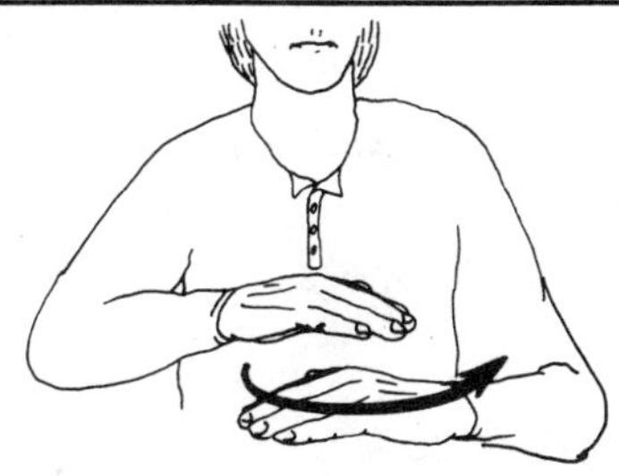

Arabic: sháaty شاطئ
Chinese: shātān 沙灘
Dutch: strand
French: plage
German: Strand
Italian: spiaggia
Japanese: kaigan 海岸
Korean: haebyŏn 해변
Portuguese: praia
Russian: plyázh пляж
Spanish: playa
Swedish: strand

203. bean(s) [n.]

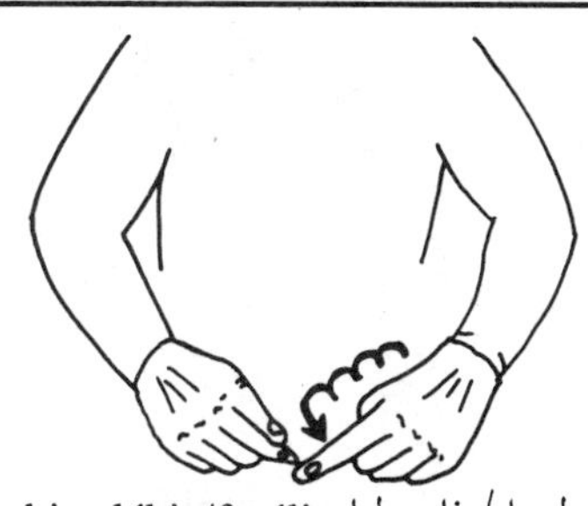

Arabic: lábia/fasúlia لوبيا / فاصوليا
Chinese: dòu 豆
Dutch: boon
French: haricot
German: Bohne
Italian: fagiolo
Japanese: mame 豆
Korean: k'ong 콩
Portuguese: feijão
Russian: bob боб
Spanish: frijol
Swedish: böna

204. bear (carry) [v.]

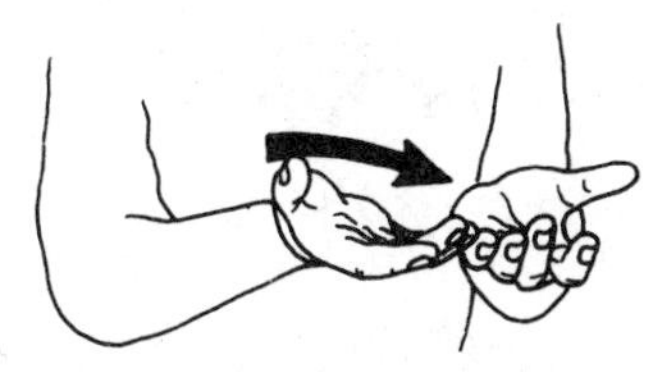

Arabic: hámala حمل
Chinese: xīdài 攜帶
Dutch: dragen
French: porter
German: tragen
Italian: portare
Japanese: motsu 持つ
Korean: narŭda 나르다
Portuguese: carregar
Russian: nosít' носить
Spanish: llevar
Swedish: bära

205. beard [n.]

Arabic: léhia لحية
Chinese: húzi 鬍子
Dutch: baard
French: barbe
German: Bart
Italian: barba
Japanese: agohige あごひげ
Korean: suyŏm 수염
Portuguese: barba
Russian: borodá борода
Spanish: barba
Swedish: skägg

206. beat (hit) [v.]

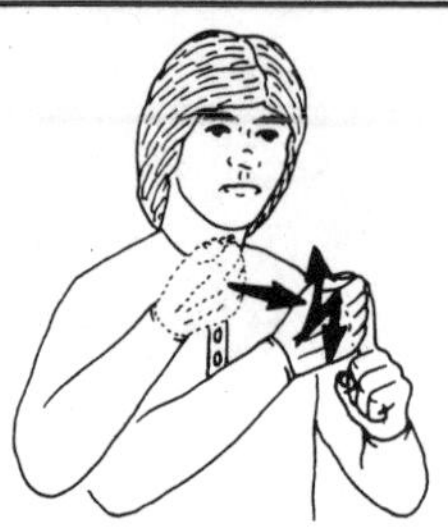

Arabic: dháraba ضرب
Chinese: dǎ 打
Dutch: slaan
French: battre
German: schlagen
Italian: battere
Japanese: tataku たたく
Korean: ttaerida 때리다
Portuguese: bater
Russian: bit' бить
Spanish: batir
Swedish: slå

207. beautiful [adj.]

Arabic: jamíl جميل
Chinese: mĕilìde 美麗的
Dutch: mooi
French: beau
German: schön
Italian: bello
Japanese: utsukushii 美しい
Korean: yeppŭn 예쁜
Portuguese: belo
Russian: krasívyy красивый
Spanish: bello
Swedish: vacker

208. because [conj.]

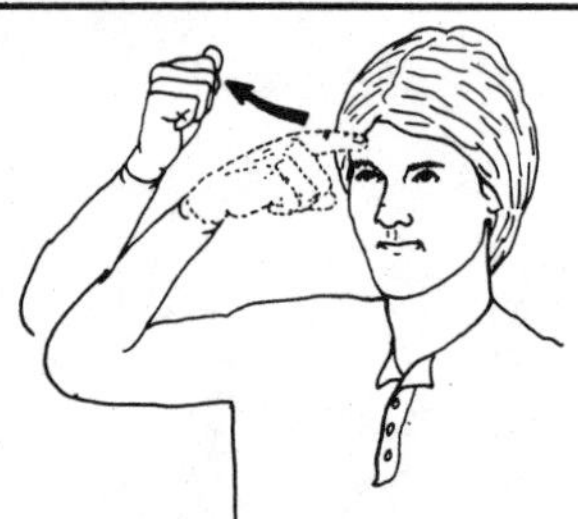

Arabic: li'anna لأن
Chinese: yīnwèi 因爲
Dutch: omdat
French: parce que
German: weil
Italian: perchè
Japanese: nazenaraba なぜならば
Korean: ttaemune 때문에
Portuguese: porque
Russian: potomú chto потому что
Spanish: porque
Swedish: därför att

209. become [v.]

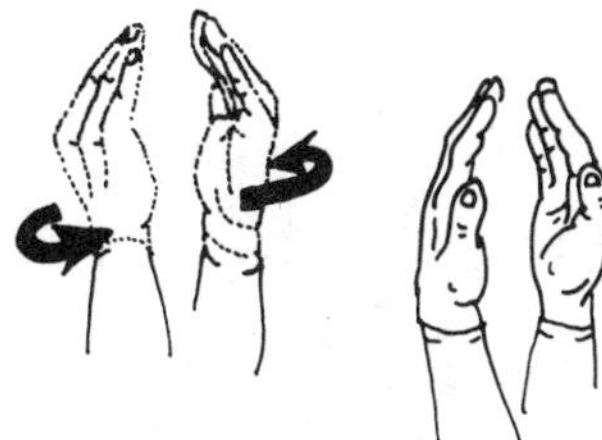

Arabic: ásbaha اصبح
Chinese: biànchéng 變成
Dutch: worden
French: devenir
German: werden
Italian: divenire
Japanese: . . . ni naru …になる
Korean: doeda ~이 되다
Portuguese: tornar-se
Russian: stanovít'sya становиться
Spanish: volverse
Swedish: bli

210. bed [n.]

Arabic: ferásh فراش
Chinese: chuáng 床
Dutch: bed
French: lit
German: Bett
Italian: letto
Japanese: shindai 寝台
Korean: ch'imdae 침대
Portuguese: cama
Russian: krovát' кровать
Spanish: cama
Swedish: säng

211. bedroom [n.]

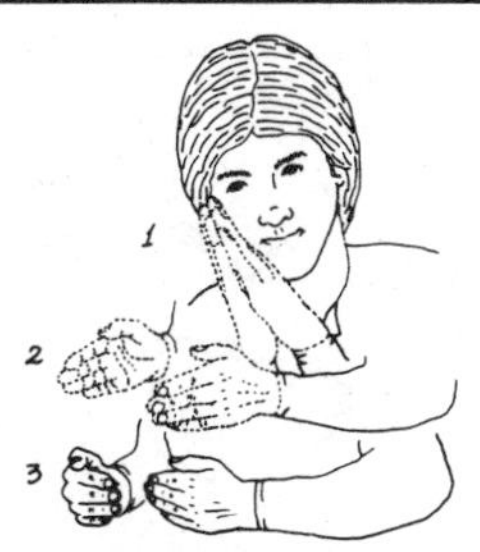

Arabic: ghórfat an-naum غرفة النوم
Chinese: wòshì 卧房
Dutch: slaapkamer
French: chambre à coucher
German: Schlafzimmer
Italian: camera da letto
Japanese: shinshitsu 寝室
Korean: ch'imshil 침실
Portuguese: quarto de dormir
Russian: spál'nya спальня
Spanish: alcoba
Swedish: sovrum

212. bee [n.]

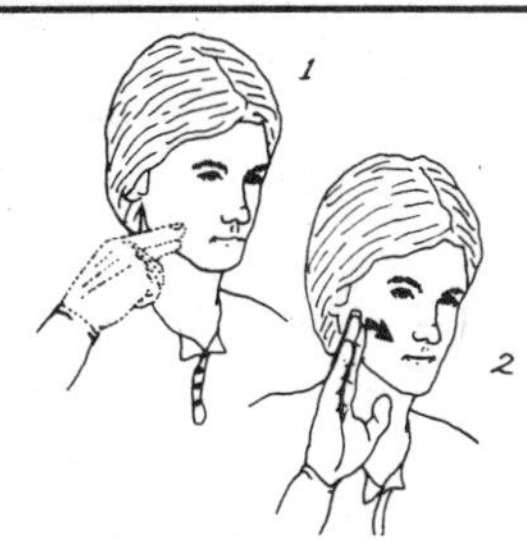

Arabic: náhla نحلة
Chinese: mìfēng 蜜蜂
Dutch: bij
French: abeille
German: Biene
Italian: ape
Japanese: mitsubachi ミツバチ
Korean: bŏl 벌
Portuguese: abelha
Russian: pchelá пчела
Spanish: abeja
Swedish: bi

213. beef [n.]

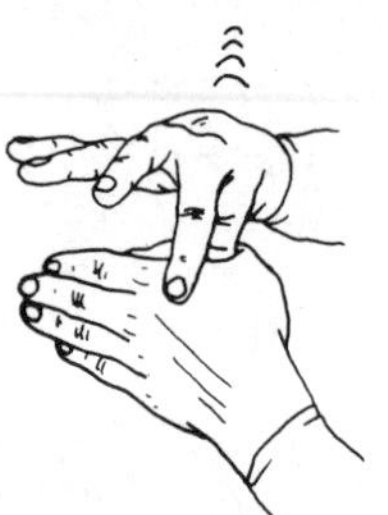

Arabic: láhem al-báqar لحم البقر
Chinese: niúròu 牛肉
Dutch: rundvlees
French: boeuf
German: Rindfleisch
Italian: manzo
Japanese: gyūniku 牛肉
Korean: soegogi 쇠고기
Portuguese: carne de vaca
Russian: govyádina говядина
Spanish: carne de res
Swedish: oxkött

214. beer [n.]

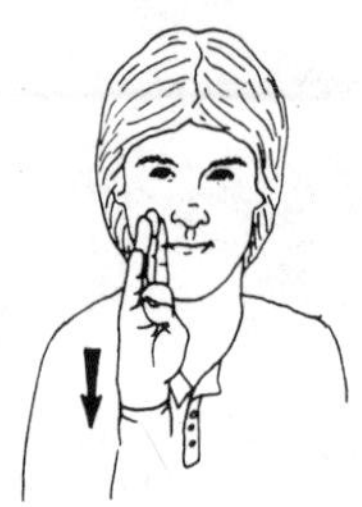

Arabic: bíra بيره
Chinese: píjiǔ 啤酒
Dutch: bier
French: bière
German: Bier
Italian: birra
Japanese: biiru ビール
Korean: maekju 맥주
Portuguese: cerveja
Russian: pívo пиво
Spanish: cerveza
Swedish: öl

215. before [adv./conj./prep.]

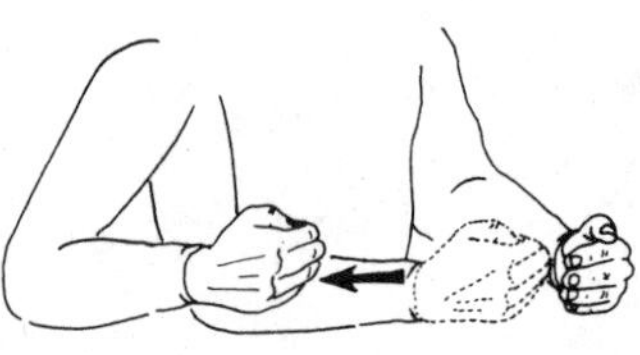

Arabic: qábla قبل
Chinese: yǐqián 以前
Dutch: vóór
French: avant
German: vorher
Italian: prima
Japanese: maeni 前に
Korean: ab'pe ~앞에
Portuguese: antes
Russian: péred перед
Spanish: antes
Swedish: före

216. beg (request) [v.]

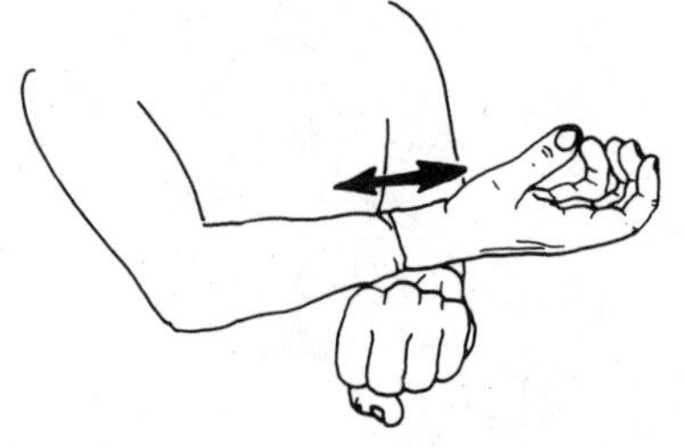

Arabic: istájda استجدى
Chinese: qǐngqiú 乞求
Dutch: verzoeken
French: demander
German: bitten
Italian: pregare
Japanese: negau 願う
Korean: butakhada 부탁하다
Portuguese: pedir
Russian: prosít' просить
Spanish: pedir
Swedish: begära

217. begin [v.]

Arabic: báda'a بدأ
Chinese: kāishǐ 開始
Dutch: beginnen
French: commencer
German: anfangen
Italian: cominciare
Japanese: hajimeru 始める
Korean: shijak'hada 시작하다
Portuguese: começar
Russian: nachinát' начинать
Spanish: comenzar
Swedish: börja

218. behavior [n.]

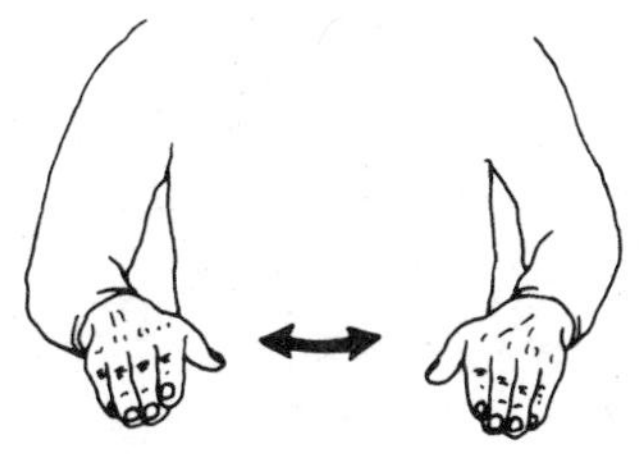

Arabic: sulúk سلوك
Chinese: xíngwéi 行爲
Dutch: gedrag
French: conduite
German: Betragen
Italian: comportamento
Japanese: kōi 行為
Korean: hyangdong 행동
Portuguese: comportamento
Russian: povedéniye поведение
Spanish: comportamiento
Swedish: uppförande

219. behind [adv./prep.]

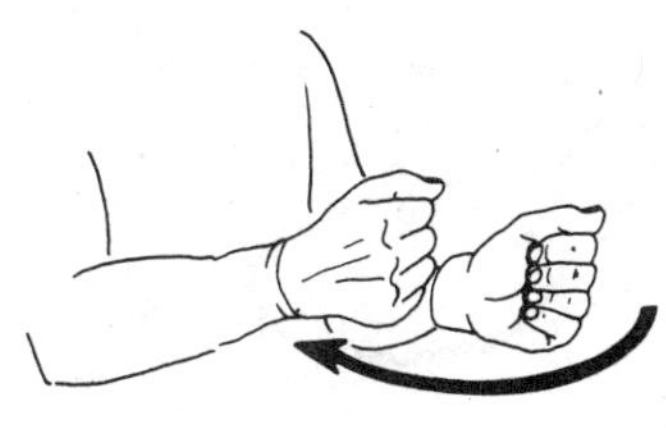

Arabic: khalf خلف
Chinese: zài...hòumiàn 在…後面
Dutch: achter
French: derrière
German: hinter
Italian: dietro
Japanese: ushironi 後ろに
Korean: twie ~뒤에
Portuguese: atrás
Russian: za за
Spanish: detrás de
Swedish: bakom

220. Belgium [n.]

Arabic: baljíka بلجيكا
Chinese: bǐlìshí 比利時
Dutch: België
French: Belgique
German: Belgien
Italian: Belgio
Japanese: Berugii ベルギー
Korean: Belgŭm 벨지움
Portuguese: Bélgica
Russian: Bél'giya Бельгия
Spanish: Bélgica
Swedish: Belgien

221. belief [n.]

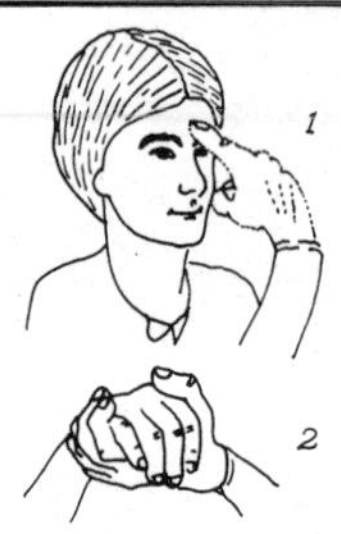

Arabic: iimán ايمان
Chinese: xìnyǎng 信仰
Dutch: geloof
French: croyance
German: Glaube
Italian: fede
Japanese: shinnen 信念
Korean: shinyŭm 신념
Portuguese: crença
Russian: véra вера
Spanish: creencia
Swedish: tro

222. bell [n.]

Arabic: járas جرس
Chinese: zhōng 鐘
Dutch: bel
French: cloche
German: Glocke
Italian: campana
Japanese: kane 鐘
Korean: jong 종
Portuguese: campainha
Russian: kólokol колокол
Spanish: campana
Swedish: klocka

223. belong [v.]

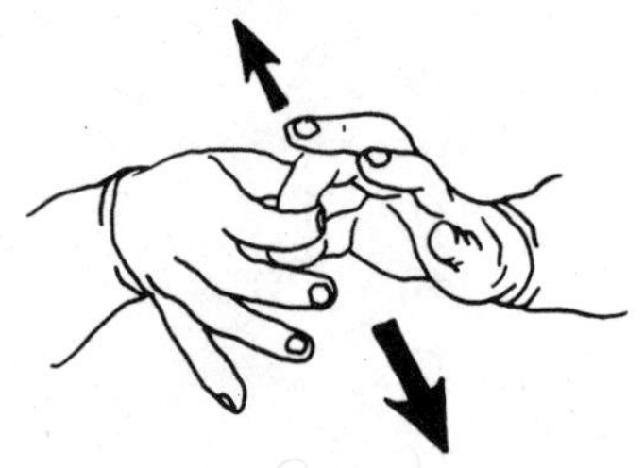

Arabic: khássa خص
Chinese: shǔyú 屬於
Dutch: toebehoren aan
French: appartenir
German: gehören
Italian: appartenere
Japanese: zokusuru 属する
Korean: . . .e sok'hada ~에 속하다
Portuguese: pertencer
Russian: prinadlezhát' принадлежать
Spanish: pertenecer
Swedish: tillhöra

224. below [adv./prep.]

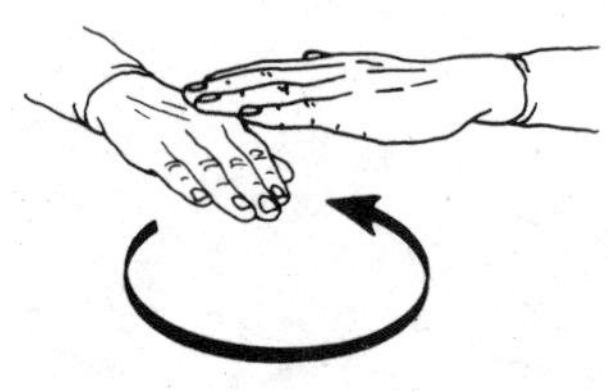

Arabic: táhta تحت
Chinese: zài. . .xiàmiàn 在…下面
Dutch: beneden
French: sous
German: unten
Italian: sotto
Japanese: . . .yori shitani …より下に
Korean: mit'e 밑에
Portuguese: abaixo
Russian: vnizú внизу
Spanish: abajo
Swedish: nedan

225. belt (waist) [n.]

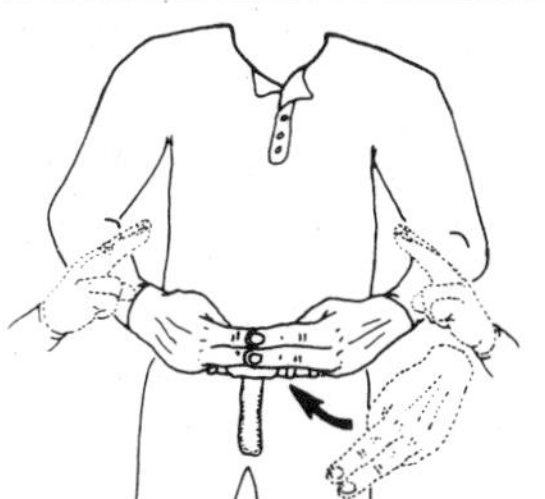

Arabic: hezám حزام
Chinese: yāodài 腰帶
Dutch: gordel
French: ceinture
German: Gürtel
Italian: cintura
Japanese: beruto ベルト
Korean: belt'ŭ 벨트
Portuguese: cinto
Russian: póyas пояс
Spanish: cinturón
Swedish: bälte

226. bench [n.]

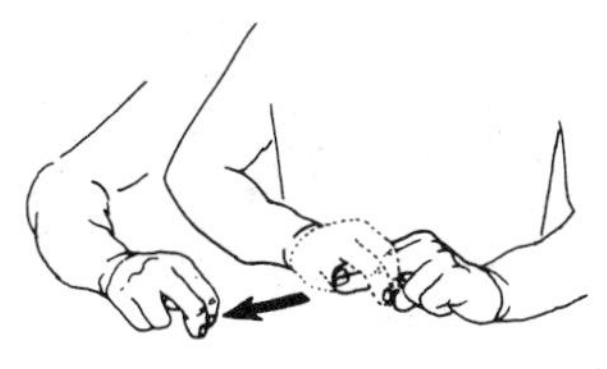

Arabic: bank بنك
Chinese: chángdèng 長櫈
Dutch: bank
French: banc
German: Bank
Italian: banco
Japanese: benchi ベンチ
Korean: benchi 벤치
Portuguese: banco
Russian: skam'yá скамья
Spanish: banco
Swedish: bänk

227. bend [v.]

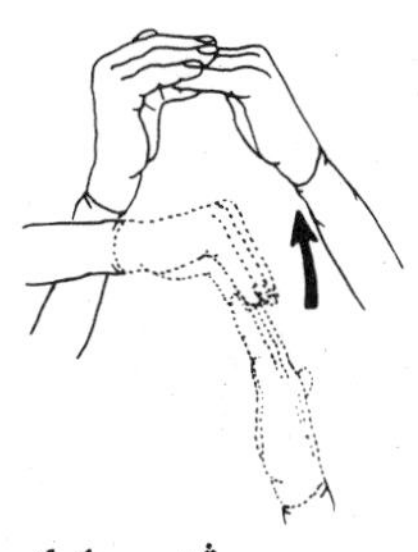

Arabic: thána ثنى
Chinese: nòngwān 弄彎
Dutch: buigen
French: fléchir
German: biegen
Italian: piegare
Japanese: mageru 曲げる
Korean: kuburida 구부리다
Portuguese: dobrar
Russian: nagibát' нагибать
Spanish: doblar
Swedish: böja

228. beneath [adv./prep.]

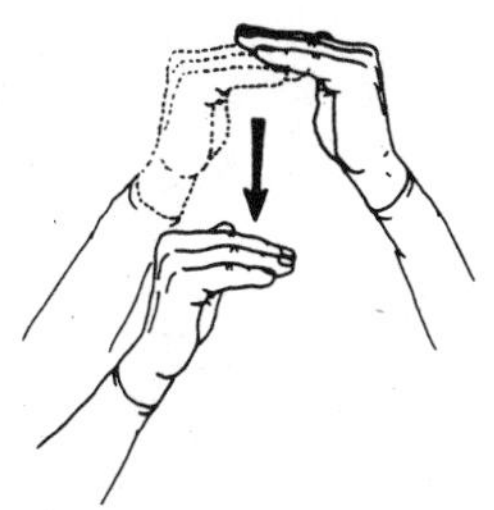

Arabic: táht تحت
Chinese: zài...xiàfāng 在 … 下方
Dutch: onder
French: sous
German: unter
Italian: sotto
Japanese: shitani 下に
Korean: mit'e 밑에
Portuguese: debaixo
Russian: pod под
Spanish: debajo
Swedish: nedanför

229. benefit [n.]

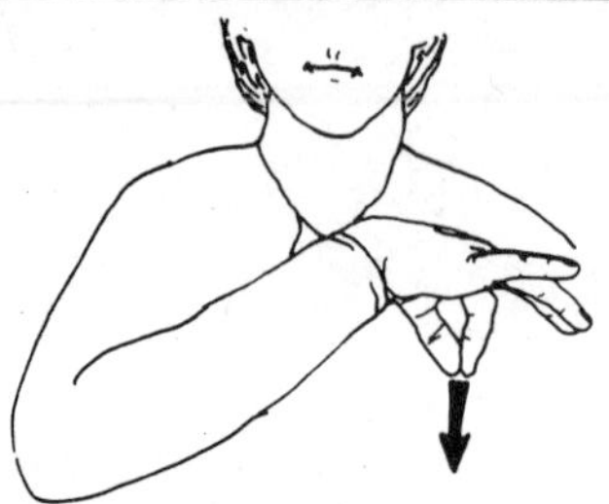

Arabic: fá'ida فائدة
Chinese: lìyì 利益
Dutch: voordeel
French: profit
German: Vorteil
Italian: beneficio
Japanese: rieki 利益
Korean: iik 밑에
Portuguese: benefício
Russian: výgoda выгода
Spanish: beneficio
Swedish: fördel

230. berry [n.]

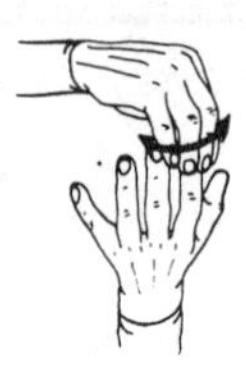

Arabic: tút توت
Chinese: jiāngguǒ 漿果
Dutch: bes
French: baie
German: Beere
Italian: bacca
Japanese: mi 実
Korean: ddalgi 이익
Portuguese: baga
Russian: yágoda ягода
Spanish: baya
Swedish: bär

231. beside [prep.]

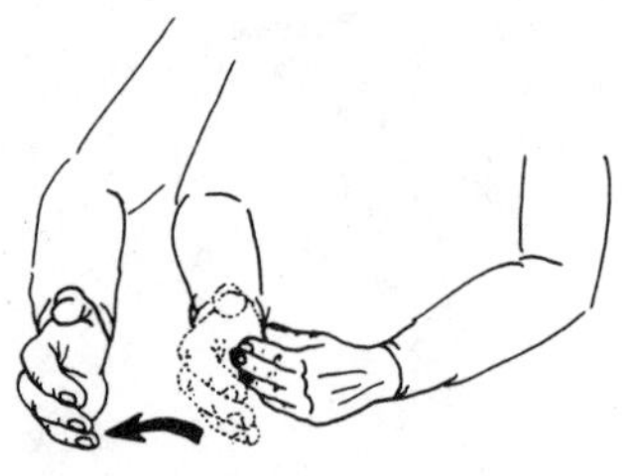

Arabic: bijánib بجانب
Chinese: zài...pángbiān 在…旁邊
Dutch: naast
French: hormis
German: neben
Italian: accanto a
Japanese: ...no sobani …のそばに
Korean: kyŏt'e ~곁에
Portuguese: ao lado de
Russian: ryádom s рядом с
Spanish: al lado de
Swedish: bredvid

232. besides [adv./prep.]

Arabic: bil-idháfa íla بالاضافة الى
Chinese: lìngwài 另外
Dutch: bovendien
French: en outre
German: außerdem
Italian: inoltre
Japanese: ...no hokani …の他に
Korean: ...oee ~외에
Portuguese: além de
Russian: króme кроме
Spanish: además
Swedish: dessutom

233. best [adj.]

Arabic: al-áhsan الأحسن
Chinese: zuìhăode 最好的
Dutch: beste
French: le meilleur
German: best
Italian: migliore
Japanese: saijō no 最上の
Korean: kajang joŭn 가장 좋은
Portuguese: o melhor
Russian: lúchshiy лучший
Spanish: el mejor
Swedish: bäst

234. bet [n.]

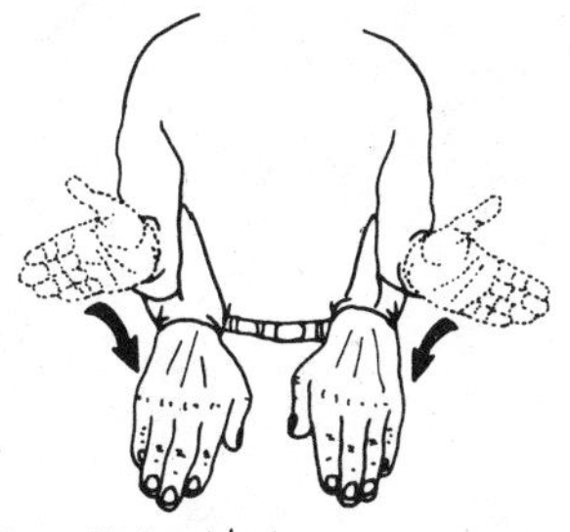

Arabic: rihán رهان
Chinese: dădŭ 打賭
Dutch: weddenschap
French: pari
German: Wette
Italian: scommessa
Japanese: kake 賭
Korean: naegi 내기
Portuguese: aposta
Russian: parí пари
Spanish: apuesta
Swedish: vad

235. betray [v.]

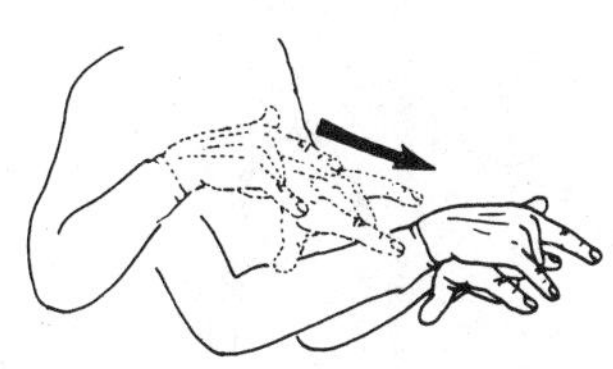

Arabic: khána خان
Chinese: bèipàn 背叛
Dutch: verraden
French: trahir
German: verraten
Italian: tradire
Japanese: uragiru 裏切る
Korean: baebanhada 배반하다
Portuguese: trair
Russian: predavát' предавать
Spanish: traicionar
Swedish: förråda

236. better [adj./adv.]

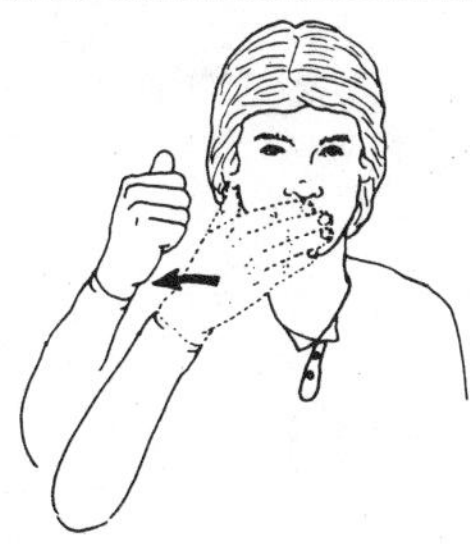

Arabic: áhsan احسن
Chinese: bĭjiào hăode 比較好的
Dutch: beter
French: mieux
German: besser
Italian: meglio
Japanese: yoriyoi より良い
Korean: dŏjohŭn 더 좋은
Portuguese: melhor
Russian: lúchshe лучше
Spanish: mejor
Swedish: bättre

237. between [prep.]

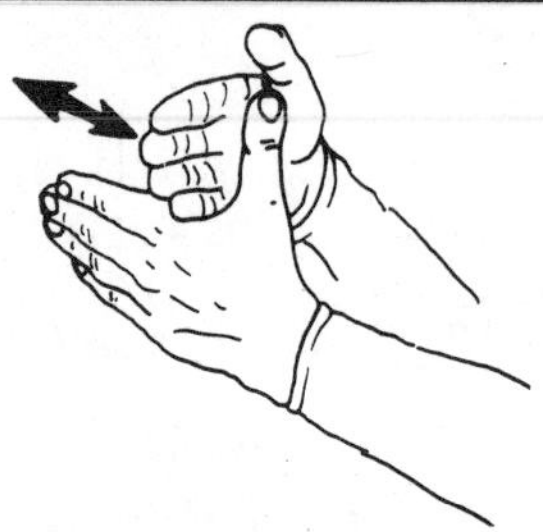

Arabic: béiin بين
Chinese: zài...zhījiān 在… 中間
Dutch: tussen
French: entre
German: dazwischen
Italian: fra
Japanese: ...no aidani …の間に
Korean: sai 사이
Portuguese: entre
Russian: mézhdu между
Spanish: entre
Swedish: mellan

238. beyond [adv./prep.]

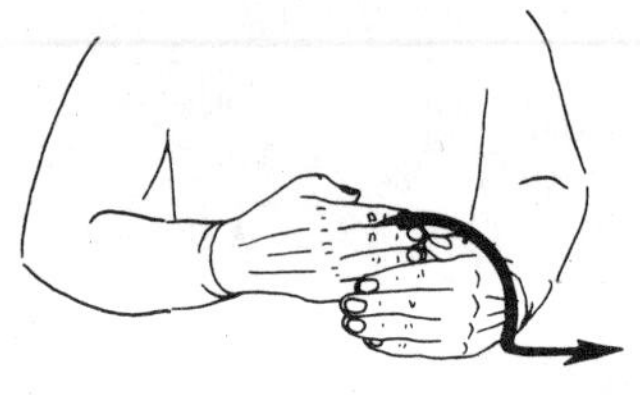

Arabic: khalf خلف
Chinese: chāoguò 超過
Dutch: voorbij
French: au-delà
German: jenseits
Italian: al di là
Japanese: ...no mukō ni …の向こうに
Korean: jŏtchoge 저쪽에
Portuguese: além
Russian: za за
Spanish: más allá de
Swedish: bortom

239. bible [n.]

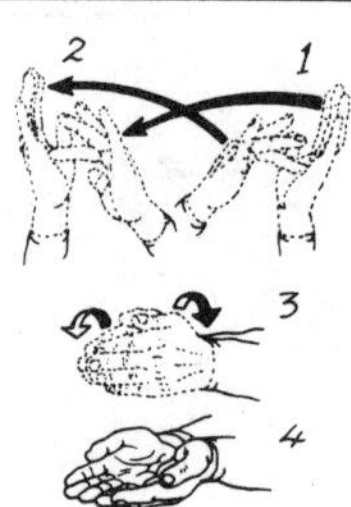

Arabic: al-injíl الأنجيل
Chinese: shèngjīng 聖經
Dutch: bijbel
French: Bible
German: Bibel
Italian: Bibbia
Japanese: Seisho 聖書
Korean: Sŏnggyŏng 성경
Portuguese: Bíblia
Russian: bíbliya библия
Spanish: Biblia
Swedish: Bibel

240. bicycle [n.]

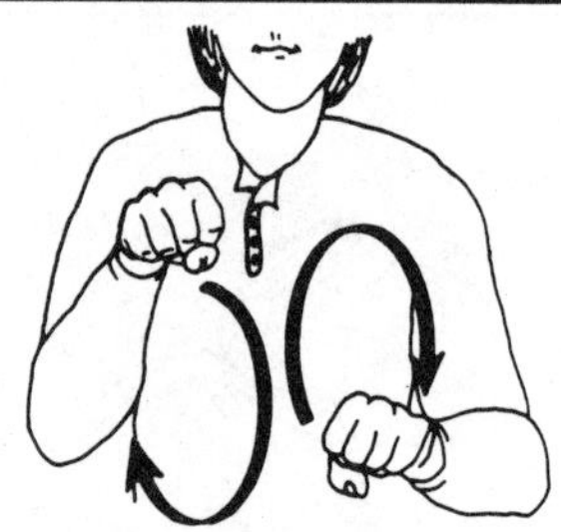

Arabic: darája دراجة
Chinese: zìxíngchē 自行車
Dutch: fiets
French: bicyclette
German: Fahrrad
Italian: bicicletta
Japanese: jitensha 自転車
Korean: jajŏngŏ 자전거
Portuguese: bicicleta
Russian: velosipéd велосипед
Spanish: bicicleta
Swedish: cykel

241. big [adj.]

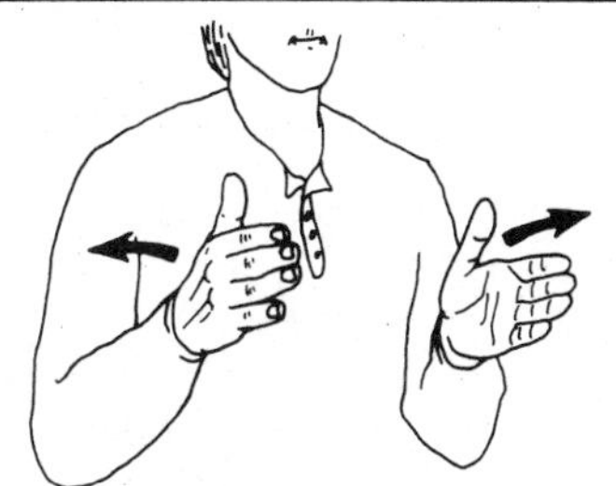

Arabic: kabír كبير
Chinese: dà 大
Dutch: groot
French: grand
German: groß
Italian: grande
Japanese: ōkii 大きい
Korean: k'ŭn 큰
Portuguese: grande
Russian: bol'shóy большой
Spanish: grande
Swedish: stor

242. billion [n.]

Arabic: bilión بليون
Chinese: wànwàn 萬萬
Dutch: miljard
French: milliard
German: Milliarde
Italian: miliardo
Japanese: jūoku 十億
Korean: shibŏk 십억
Portuguese: bilhão
Russian: milliárd миллиард
Spanish: mil millones
Swedish: miljard

243. bind (join/connect) [v.]

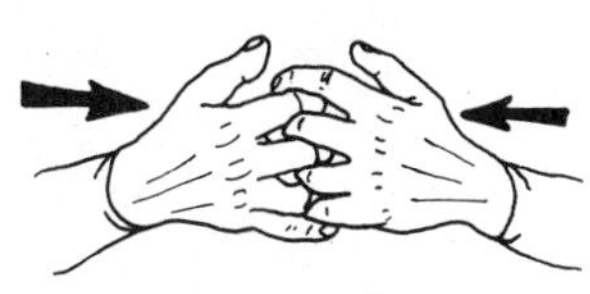

Arabic: rábata ربط
Chinese: kŭnbăng 捆綁
Dutch: binden
French: lier
German: binden
Italian: legare
Japanese: shibaru 縛る
Korean: maeda 매다
Portuguese: juntar
Russian: svyázyvat' связывать
Spanish: ligar
Swedish: binda

244. bird [n.]

Arabic: táyer طير
Chinese: niǎo 鳥
Dutch: vogel
French: oiseau
German: Vogel
Italian: uccello
Japanese: tori 鳥
Korean: sae 새
Portuguese: pássaro
Russian: ptítsa птица
Spanish: pájaro
Swedish: fågel

245. birth [n.]

Arabic: milád ميلاد
Chinese: chūshēng 出生
Dutch: geboorte
French: naissance
German: Geburt
Italian: nascita
Japanese: tanjō 誕生
Korean: ch'ulsaeng 출생
Portuguese: nascimento
Russian: rozhdéniye рождение
Spanish: nacimiento
Swedish: födelse

246. birthday [n.]

Arabic: yom al-milád يوم الميلاد
Chinese: shēngrì 生日
Dutch: verjaardag
French: anniversaire
German: Geburtstag
Italian: compleanno
Japanese: tanjōbi 誕生日
Korean: saengil 생일
Portuguese: aniversário
Russian: den' rozhdéniya день рождения
Spanish: cumpleaños
Swedish: födelsedag

247. bite [v.]

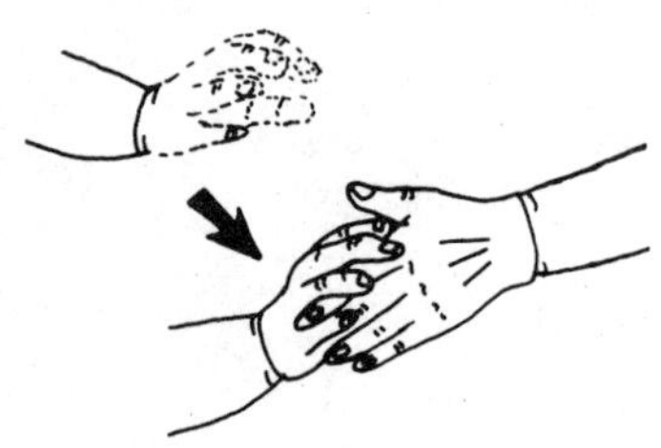

Arabic: áadha عض
Chinese: yǎo 咬
Dutch: bijten
French: mordre
German: beißen
Italian: mordere
Japanese: kamu かむ
Korean: mulda 물다
Portuguese: morder
Russian: kusát' кусать
Spanish: morder
Swedish: bita

248. bitter [adj.]

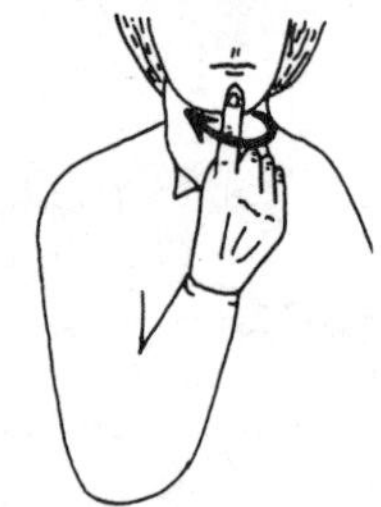

Arabic: morr مر
Chinese: kǔde 苦的
Dutch: bitter
French: amer
German: bitter
Italian: amaro
Japanese: nigai にがい
Korean: tsŭn 쓴
Portuguese: amargo
Russian: gór'kiy горький
Spanish: amargo
Swedish: bitter

249. black [adj.]

Arabic: áswad اسود
Chinese: hēide 黑的
Dutch: zwart
French: noir
German: schwarz
Italian: nero
Japanese: kuroi 黒い
Korean: kŏmŭn 까만
Portuguese: preto
Russian: chyórnyy чёрный
Spanish: negro
Swedish: svart

250. blackboard [n.]

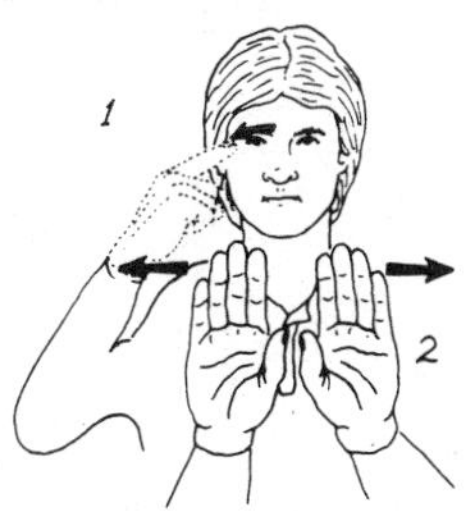

Arabic: subbúra سبورة
Chinese: hēibǎn 黑板
Dutch: bord
French: tableau
German: Wandtafel
Italian: lavagna
Japanese: kokuban 黒板
Korean: hŭkp'an 흑판
Portuguese: quadro negro
Russian: doská доска
Spanish: pizarra
Swedish: svart tavla

251. blame [v.]

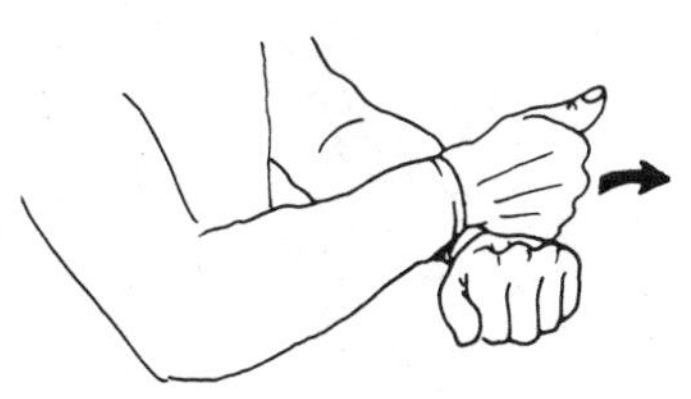

Arabic: láma لام
Chinese: zébèi 責備
Dutch: beschuldigen
French: reprocher
German: beschuldigen
Italian: biasimare
Japanese: hinan suru 非難する
Korean: namurada 나무래다
Portuguese: culpar
Russian: poritsát' порицать
Spanish: culpar
Swedish: klandra

252. blanket [n.]

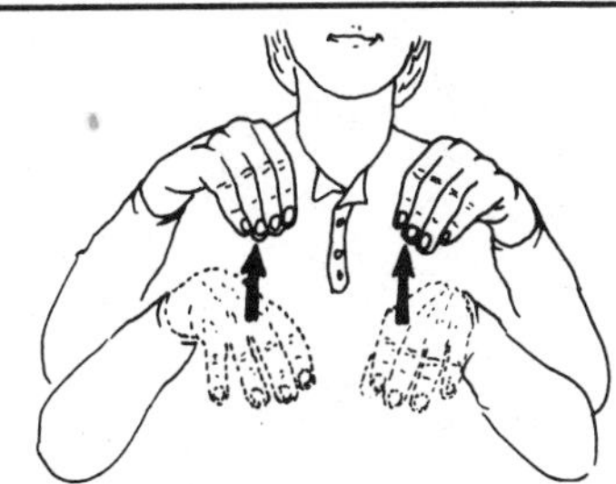

Arabic: battanía بطانية
Chinese: tǎnzi 毯子
Dutch: deken
French: couverture
German: Decke
Italian: coperta
Japanese: mōfu 毛布
Korean: tamnyo 담요
Portuguese: cobertor
Russian: odeyálo одеяло
Spanish: manta
Swedish: filt

253. blind [adj.]

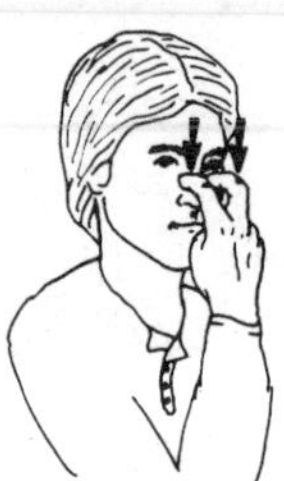

Arabic: kafíf كفيف
Chinese: mángmùde 盲目的
Dutch: blind
French: aveugle
German: blind
Italian: cieco
Japanese: mekura no めくらの
Korean: nunmŏn 눈먼
Portuguese: cego
Russian: slepóy слепой
Spanish: ciego
Swedish: blind

254. block (form/shape) [n.]

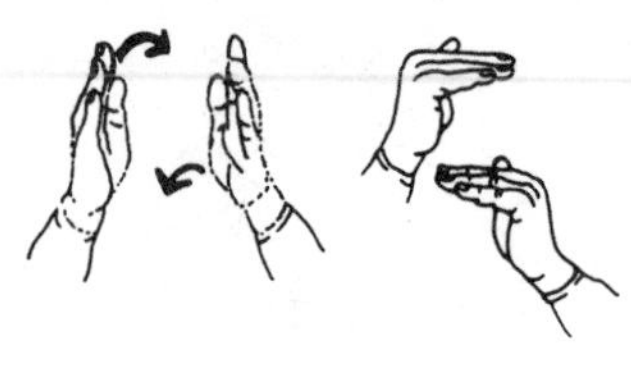

Arabic: kútla كتلة
Chinese: kuài 塊
Dutch: blok
French: bloc
German: Block
Italian: blocco
Japanese: katamari 塊
Korean: tŏngŏri 덩어리
Portuguese: bloco
Russian: blok блок
Spanish: bloque
Swedish: block

255. blood [n.]

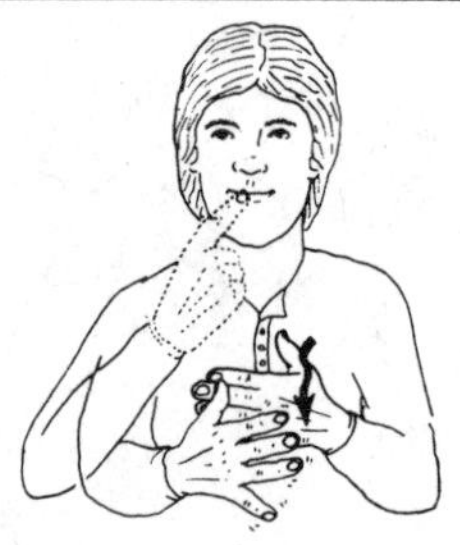

Arabic: damm دم
Chinese: xuě 血
Dutch: bloed
French: sang
German: Blut
Italian: sangue
Japanese: ketsueki 血液
Korean: p'i 피
Portuguese: sangue
Russian: krov' кровь
Spanish: sangre
Swedish: blod

256. blossom [n.]

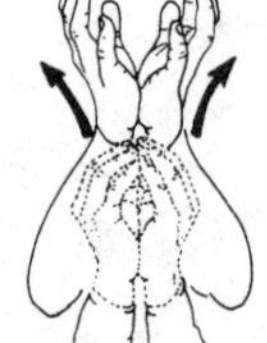

Arabic: záhara زهرة
Chinese: huā 花
Dutch: bloesem
French: fleur
German: Blüte
Italian: fiore
Japanese: hana 花
Korean: kkot 꽃
Portuguese: flor
Russian: tsvetók цветок
Spanish: flor
Swedish: blomma

257. blow [v.]

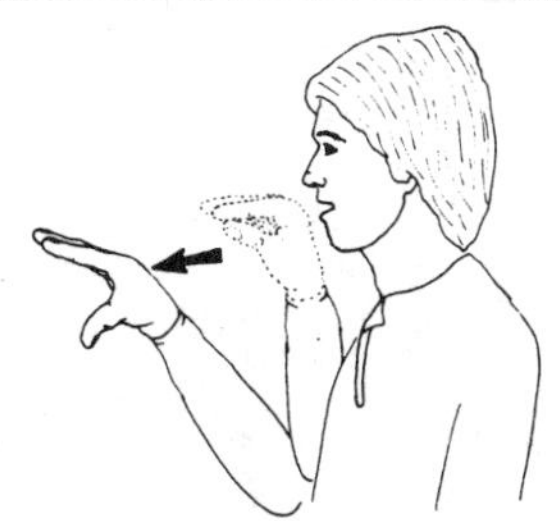

Arabic: hábba هب
Chinese: chūi 吹
Dutch: blazen
French: souffler
German: blasen
Italian: soffiare
Japanese: fuku 吹く
Korean: pulda 불다
Portuguese: soprar
Russian: dut' дуть
Spanish: soplar
Swedish: blåsa

258. blue [adj.]

Arabic: ázraq ازرق
Chinese: lánde 藍的
Dutch: blauw
French: bleu
German: blau
Italian: blu
Japanese: aoi 青い
Korean: p'urŭn 파란
Portuguese: azul
Russian: síniy синий
Spanish: azul
Swedish: blå

259. blush [v.]

Arabic: istáhaa استحى
Chinese: liǎnhóng 臉紅
Dutch: blozen
French: rougir
German: erröten
Italian: arrossire
Japanese: akaku naru 赤くなる
Korean: nach'ŭl bulk'ida 낯을 붉히다
Portuguese: corar
Russian: krasnét' краснеть
Spanish: ruborizarse
Swedish: rodna

260. boast [v.]

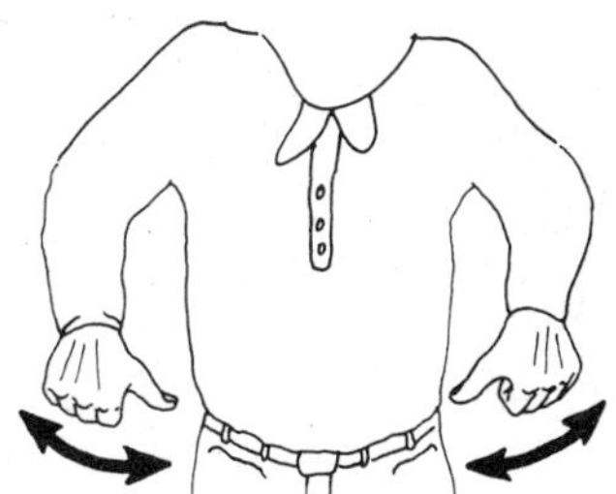

Arabic: iftákhara افتخر
Chinese: zìkuā 自誇
Dutch: opscheppen
French: se vanter
German: prahlen
Italian: vantarsi
Japanese: jiman suru 自慢する
Korean: jaranghada 자랑하다
Portuguese: gabar-se
Russian: khvástat'sya хвастаться
Spanish: jactarse
Swedish: skryta

261. boat [n.]

Arabic: qáreb قارب
Chinese: chuán 船
Dutch: boot
French: bateau
German: Boot
Italian: barca
Japanese: bōto ボート
Korean: bot'ŭ 보트
Portuguese: barco
Russian: lódka лодка
Spanish: barco
Swedish: båt

262. body [n.]

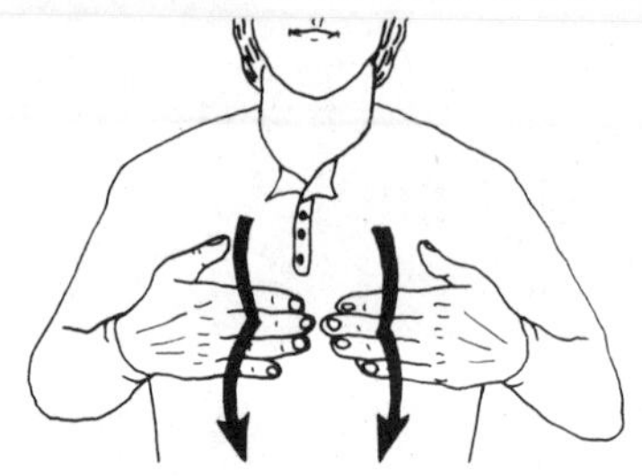

Arabic: jism جسم
Chinese: shēntǐ 身體
Dutch: lichaam
French: corps
German: Körper
Italian: corpo
Japanese: karada 体
Korean: mom 몸
Portuguese: corpo
Russian: télo тело
Spanish: cuerpo
Swedish: kropp

263. boil [v.]

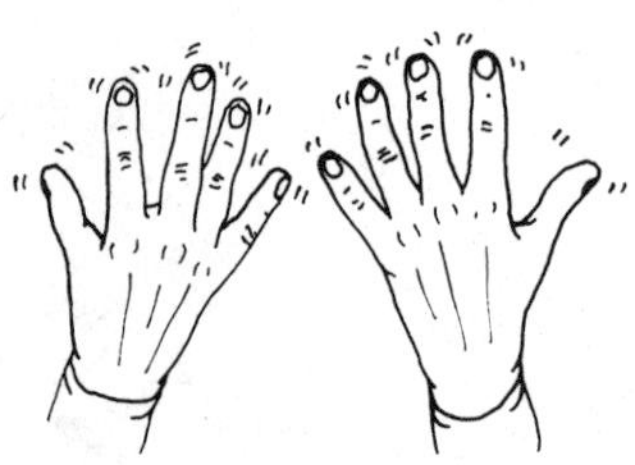

Arabic: ghála غلى
Chinese: zhǔkāi 煮開
Dutch: koken
French: bouillir
German: kochen
Italian: bollire
Japanese: futtosuru 沸騰する
Korean: kkurida 끓이다
Portuguese: ferver
Russian: kipét' кипеть
Spanish: hervir
Swedish: koka

264. bold (daring) [adj.]

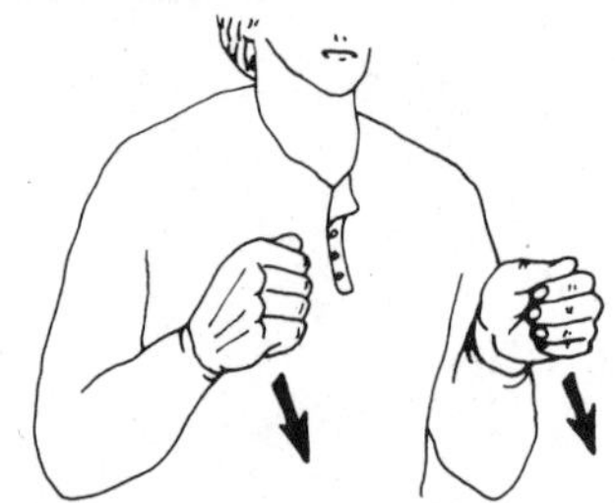

Arabic: shujeáa شجاع
Chinese: dàdǎnde 大膽的
Dutch: stoutmoedig
French: téméraire
German: mutig
Italian: temerario
Japanese: daitan na 大胆な
Korean: daedamhan 대담한
Portuguese: atrevido
Russian: smélyy смелый
Spanish: atrevido
Swedish: djärv

265. Bolivia [n.]

Arabic: bolívia بوليفيا
Chinese: pōlìwéiyǎ 玻利維亞
Dutch: Bolivië
French: Bolivie
German: Bolivien
Italian: Bolivia
Japanese: Boribia ボリビア
Korean: Bolibia 볼리비아
Portuguese: Bolívia
Russian: Bolíviya Боливия
Spanish: Bolivia
Swedish: Bolivia

266. bone [n.]

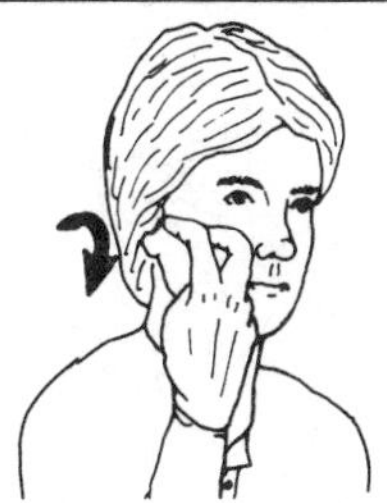

Arabic: áathem عظم
Chinese: gǔtóu 骨頭
Dutch: been
French: os
German: Knochen
Italian: osso
Japanese: hone 骨
Korean: bpyŏ 뼈
Portuguese: osso
Russian: kost' кость
Spanish: hueso
Swedish: ben

267. book [n.]

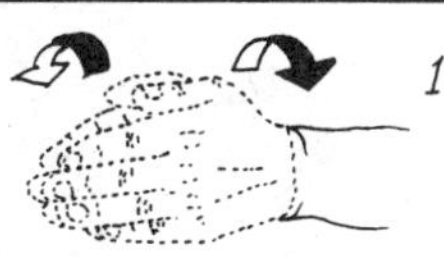

Arabic: kitáb كتاب
Chinese: shū 書
Dutch: boek
French: livre
German: Buch
Italian: libro
Japanese: hon 本
Korean: ch'aek 책
Portuguese: livro
Russian: kníga книга
Spanish: libro
Swedish: bok

268. boot(s) [n.]

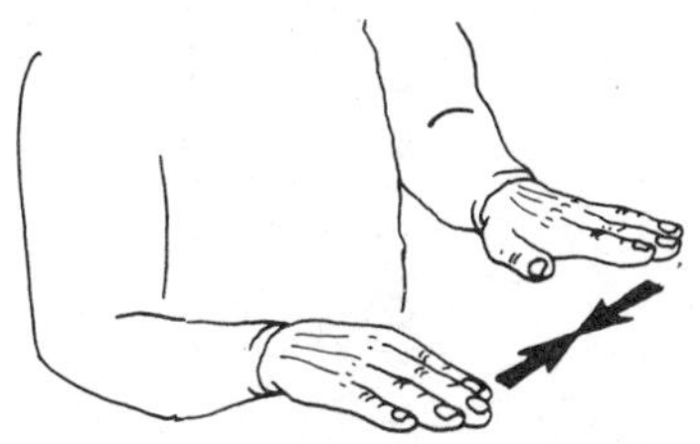

Arabic: hithá' حذاء
Chinese: xuēzi 靴子
Dutch: laars
French: botte
German: Stiefel
Italian: stivale
Japanese: nagagutsu 長靴
Korean: janghwa 장화
Portuguese: bota
Russian: sapóg сапог
Spanish: bota
Swedish: stövel

269. boring [adj.]

Arabic: mumíl ممل
Chinese: wú liaǒ 無聊
Dutch: vervelend
French: ennuyeux
German: langweilig
Italian: noioso
Japanese: taikutsu na 退屈な
Korean: shinggŏun 싱거운
Portuguese: maçante
Russian: skúchnyy скучный
Spanish: aburrido
Swedish: tråkig

270. born (to be) [v.]

Arabic: wúlida ولد
Chinese: chūshēng 出生
Dutch: geboren
French: naître
German: geboren
Italian: nascere
Japanese: umare ni 生れに
Korean: t'aeŏnat'da 태어나다
Portuguese: nascer
Russian: rodít'sya родиться
Spanish: nacer
Swedish: född

271. borrow [v.]

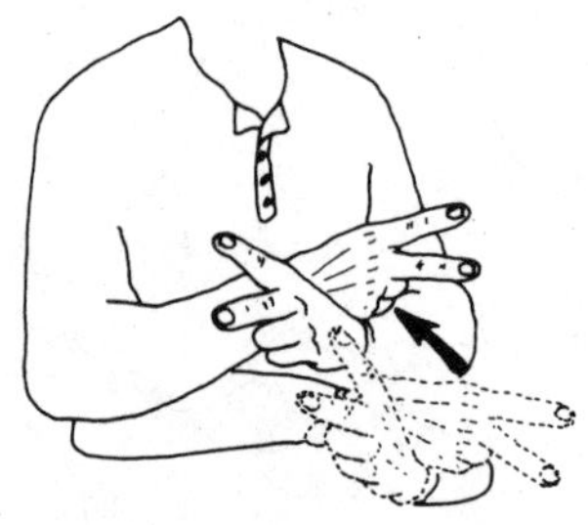

Arabic: istadána استدان
Chinese: jiè 借
Dutch: lenen
French: emprunter
German: borgen
Italian: prendere a prestito
Japanese: kariru 借りる
Korean: bilda 빌다
Portuguese: pedir emprestado
Russian: brat' vzaymý брать взаймы
Spanish: pedir prestado
Swedish: låna

272. both [adj./pron.]

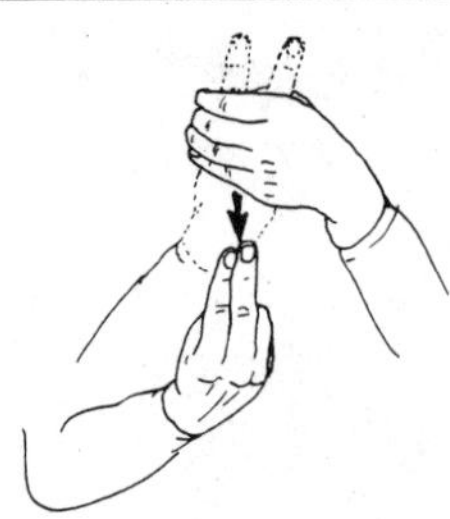

Arabic: kilahóma كلاهما
Chinese: shuāngfāng 雙方
Dutch: beide
French: tous deux
German: beide
Italian: ambedue
Japanese: ryōhō no 両方の
Korean: dul da 둘 다, 양쪽
Portuguese: ambos
Russian: óba оба
Spanish: ambos
Swedish: båda

273. bother (annoy) [v.]

Arabic: ázaaja ازعج
Chinese: dărăo 打攪
Dutch: hinderen
French: tracasser
German: plagen
Italian: molestare
Japanese: jama suru 邪魔する
Korean: koerop'ida 괴롭히다
Portuguese: aborrecer
Russian: nadoyedát' надоедать
Spanish: molestar
Swedish: besvära

274. bottle [n.]

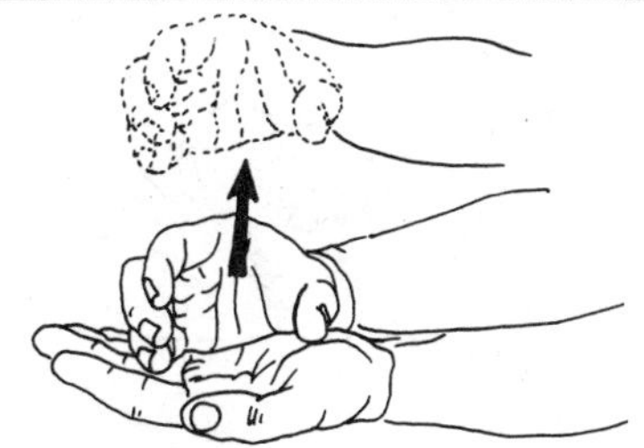

Arabic: qennína قنينة
Chinese: píngzi 瓶子
Dutch: fles
French: bouteille
German: Flasche
Italian: bottiglia
Japanese: bin 瓶
Korean: byŏng 병
Portuguese: garrafa
Russian: butýlka бутылка
Spanish: botella
Swedish: flaska

275. bottom [n.]

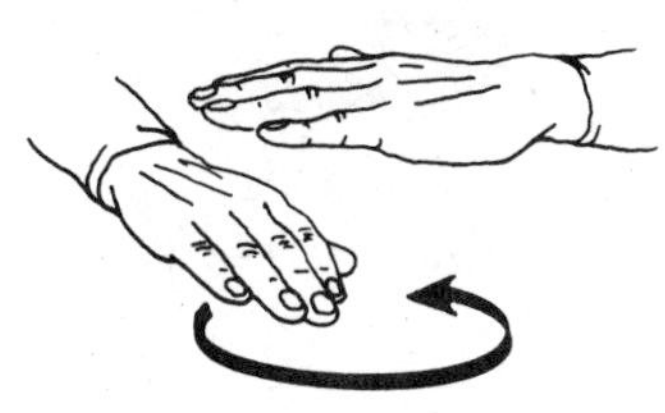

Arabic: qaa قاع
Chinese: dĭ 底
Dutch: bodem
French: fond
German: Boden
Italian: fondo
Japanese: soko 底
Korean: mitbadak 밑바닥
Portuguese: fundo
Russian: dno дно
Spanish: fondo
Swedish: botten

276. bow (greet) [v.]

Arabic: inhána lil-tahía انحنى للتحية
Chinese: júgōng 鞠躬
Dutch: zich buigen
French: s'incliner
German: sich verbeugen
Italian: inchinarsi
Japanese: ojigi suru おじぎする
Korean: mŏrirŭl sugida 머리를 숙이다
Portuguese: curvar-se
Russian: klányat'sya кланяться
Spanish: inclinarse
Swedish: buga

277. bowl [n.]

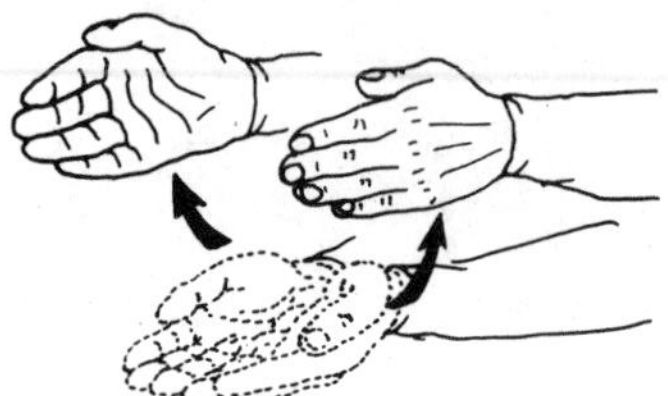

Arabic: zebdía زبدية
Chinese: wăn 碗
Dutch: schaal
French: bol
German: Schüssel
Italian: scodella
Japanese: hachi 鉢
Korean: sabal 사발
Portuguese: tijela
Russian: chásha чаша
Spanish: tazón
Swedish: skål

278. box [n.]

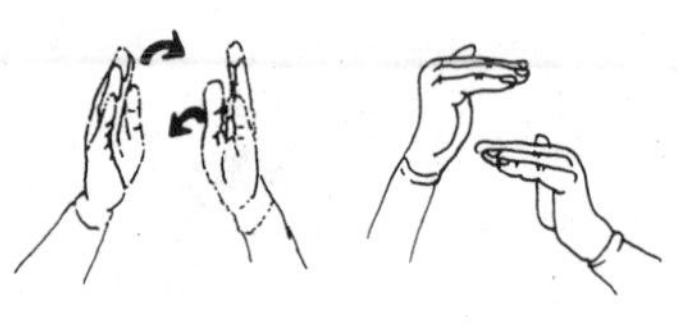

Arabic: sundúq صندوق
Chinese: hézi 盒子
Dutch: doos
French: boîte
German: Schachtel
Italian: scatola
Japanese: hako 箱
Korean: sangja 상자
Portuguese: caixa
Russian: koróbka коробка
Spanish: caja
Swedish: ask

279. boxing [n.]

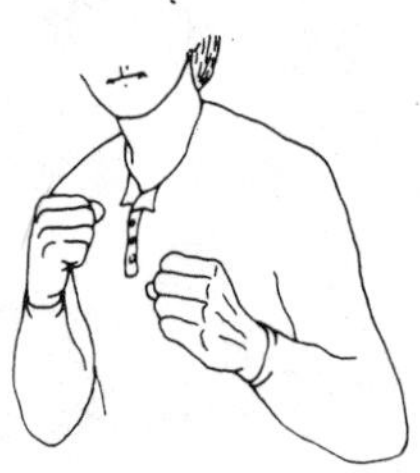

Arabic: mulákama ملاكمة
Chinese: quánjí 拳擊
Dutch: boksen
French: boxe
German: Boxsport
Italian: pugilato
Japanese: kentō 拳闘
Korean: gwŏnt'u 권투
Portuguese: boxe
Russian: boks бокс
Spanish: boxeo
Swedish: boxning

280. boy [n.]

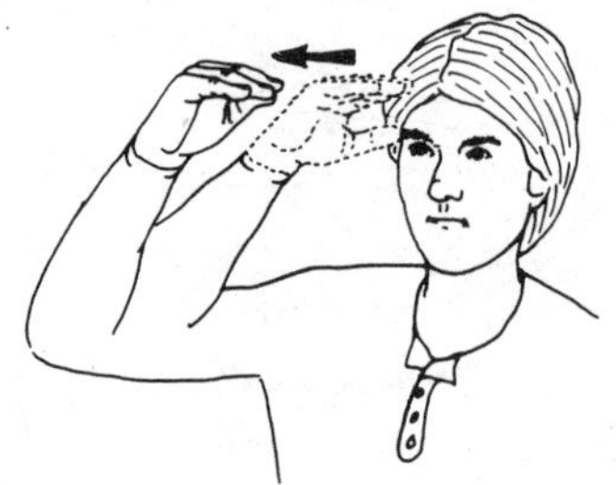

Arabic: wálad ولد
Chinese: nánhái 男孩
Dutch: jongen
French: garçon
German: Junge
Italian: ragazzo
Japanese: shōnen 少年
Korean: sonyŏn 소년
Portuguese: môço
Russian: mál'chik мальчик
Spanish: muchacho
Swedish: pojke

281. brain(s) [n.]

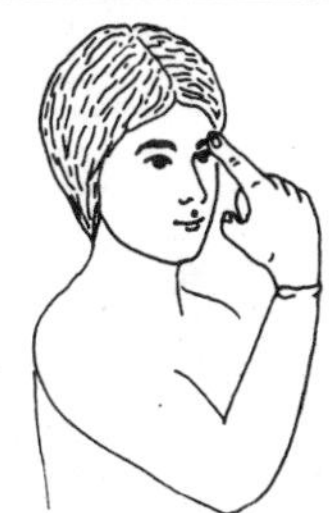

Arabic: mukh مخ
Chinese: nǎo 脑
Dutch: hersenen
French: cerveau
German: Gehirn
Italian: cervello
Japanese: nō 脳
Korean: noe 뇌
Portuguese: cérebro
Russian: mozg мозг
Spanish: cerebro
Swedish: hjärna

282. branch [n.]

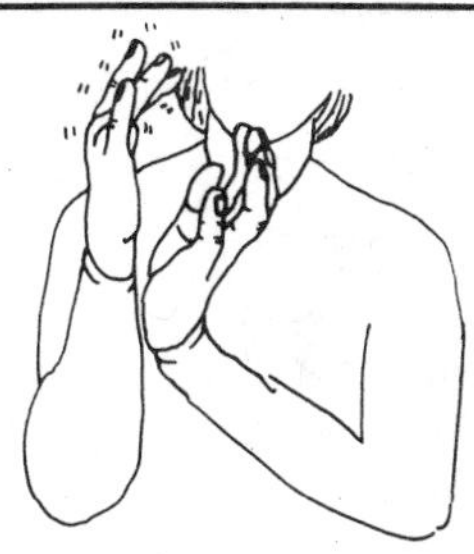

Arabic: fára' فرع
Chinese: fēnzhī 分枝
Dutch: tak
French: branche
German: Zweig
Italian: ramo
Japanese: eda 枝
Korean: gaji 가지
Portuguese: ramo
Russian: vetv' ветвь
Spanish: rama
Swedish: gren

283. brave [adj.]

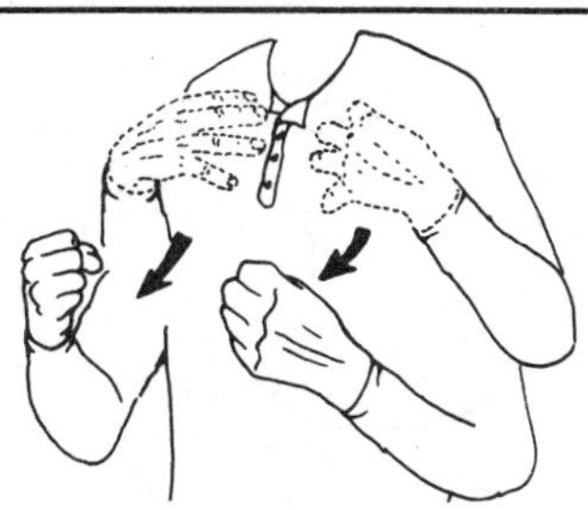

Arabic: shujéaa شجاع
Chinese: yǒnggǎn 勇敢
Dutch: dapper
French: courageux
German: tapfer
Italian: coraggioso
Japanese: yūkan na 勇敢な
Korean: yonggamhan 용감한
Portuguese: corajoso
Russian: khrábryy храбрый
Spanish: valiente
Swedish: tapper

284. Brazil [n.]

Arabic: al-barazíl البرازيل
Chinese: bāxī 巴西
Dutch: Brazilië
French: Brésil
German: Brasilien
Italian: Brasile
Japanese: Burajiru ブラジル
Korean: Burajil 브라질
Portuguese: Brasil
Russian: Brazíliya Бразилия
Spanish: Brasil
Swedish: Brasilien

285. bread [n.]

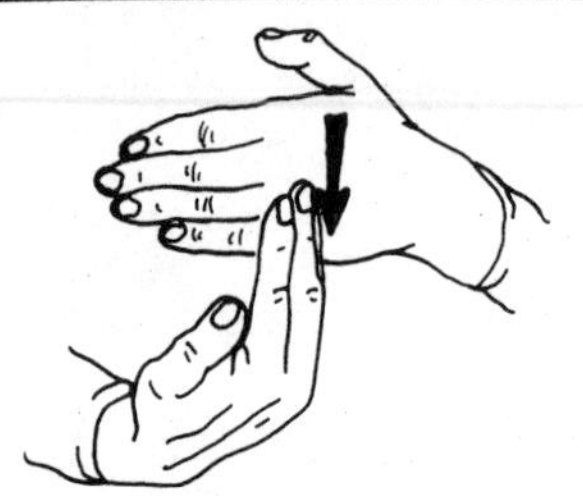

Arabic: khubz/áeesh خبز / عيش
Chinese: miànbāo 麵包
Dutch: brood
French: pain
German: Brot
Italian: pane
Japanese: pan パン
Korean: pbang 빵
Portuguese: pão
Russian: khleb хлеб
Spanish: pan
Swedish: bröd

286. break [v.]

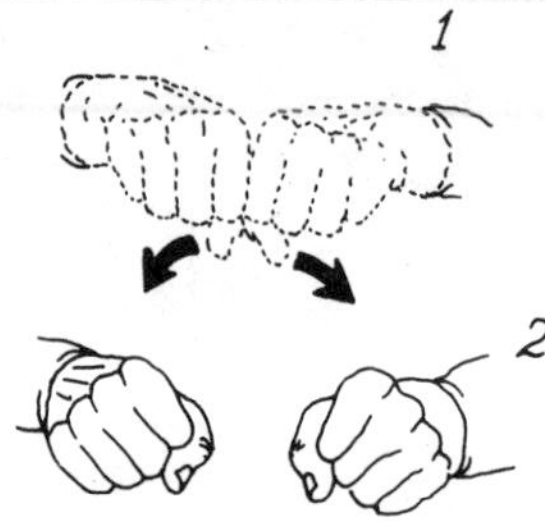

Arabic: kásara كسر
Chinese: dăpò 打破
Dutch: breken
French: rompre
German: brechen
Italian: rompere
Japanese: . . . o kowasu こわす
Korean: kkaettŭrida 깨트리다
Portuguese: romper
Russian: lomát' ломать
Spanish: romper
Swedish: bryta

287. breakfast [n.]

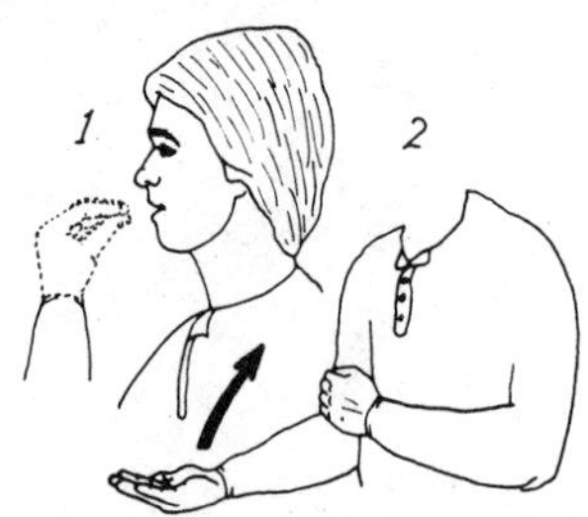

Arabic: iftár افطار
Chinese: zăofàn 早飯
Dutch: ontbijt
French: petit déjeuner
German: Frühstück
Italian: prima colazione
Japanese: chōshoku 朝食
Korean: joban 조반
Portuguese: café da manhã
Russian: závtrak завтрак
Spanish: desayuno
Swedish: frukost

288. breast [n.]

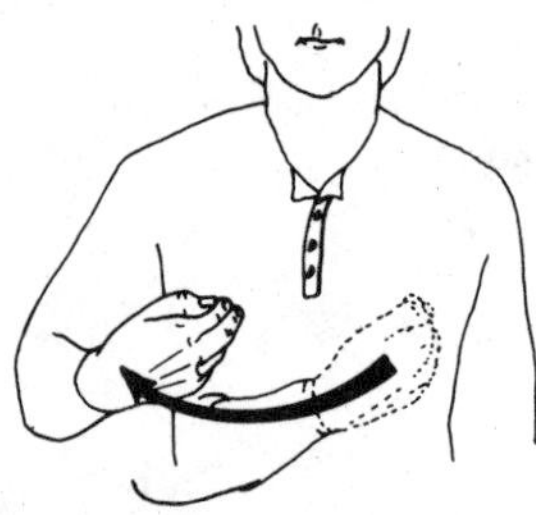

Arabic: sadr صدر
Chinese: rŭfáng 乳房
Dutch: borst
French: poitrine
German: Brust
Italian: seno
Japanese: mune 胸
Korean: kasŭm 가슴
Portuguese: seio
Russian: grud' грудь
Spanish: seno
Swedish: bröst

289. breath [n.]

Arabic: náfas نفس
Chinese: hūxī 呼吸
Dutch: adem
French: souffle
German: Atem
Italian: respiro
Japanese: kokyū 呼吸
Korean: sum 숨
Portuguese: respiração
Russian: dykhániye дыхание
Spanish: aliento
Swedish: anda

290. breeze [n.]

Arabic: nasím نسيم
Chinese: wéifēng 微風
Dutch: bries
French: brise
German: Brise
Italian: brezza
Japanese: bifū 微風
Korean: sandŭlbaram 산들바람
Portuguese: brisa
Russian: briz бриз
Spanish: brisa
Swedish: bris

291. bribe [n.]

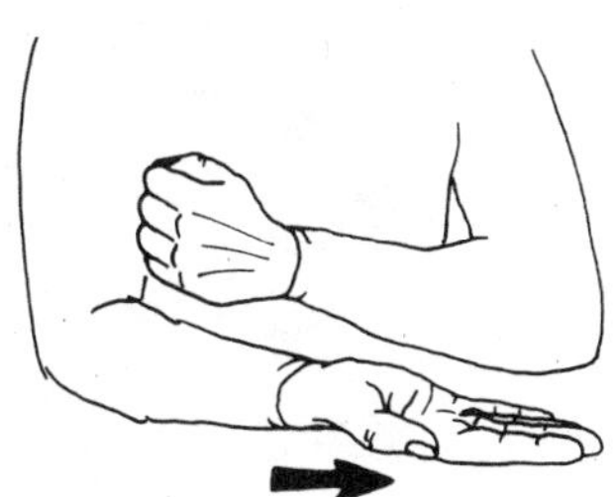

Arabic: ráshwa رشوة
Chinese: huìlù 賄賂
Dutch: omkoopgeld
French: pot-de-vin
German: Bestechung
Italian: dono (per corrompere)
Japanese: wairo 賄賂
Korean: noemul 뇌물
Portuguese: subôrno
Russian: vzyátka взятка
Spanish: soborno
Swedish: mutor

292. brick [n.]

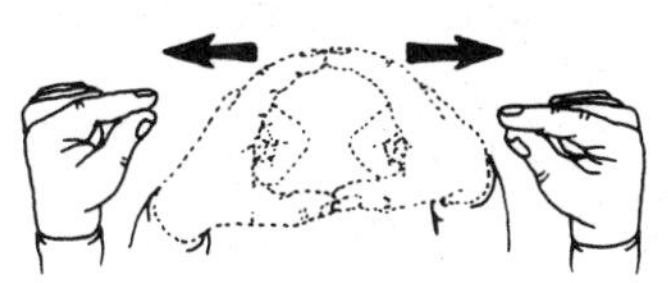

Arabic: túba طوبة
Chinese: zhuān 甎
Dutch: baksteen
French: brique
German: Ziegel
Italian: mattone
Japanese: renga 煉瓦
Korean: byŏkdol 벽돌
Portuguese: tijolo
Russian: kirpích кирпич
Spanish: ladrillo
Swedish: tegelsten

293. bride [n.]

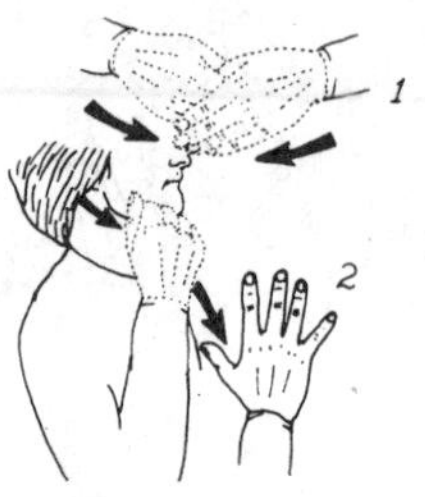

Arabic: arúss عروس
Chinese: xīnniáng 新娘
Dutch: bruid
French: mariée
German: Braut
Italian: sposa
Japanese: hanayome 花嫁
Korean: shinbu 신부
Portuguese: noiva
Russian: nevésta невеста
Spanish: novia
Swedish: brud

294. bridegroom [n.]

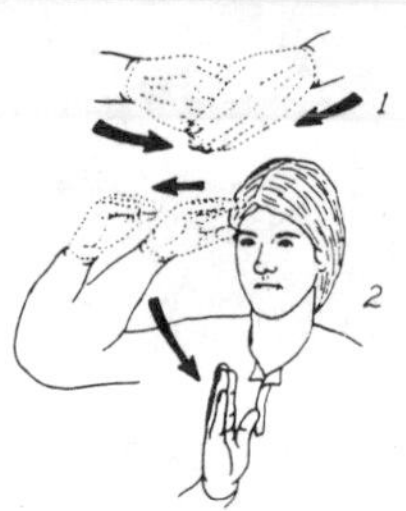

Arabic: aarís عريس
Chinese: xīnláng 新郎
Dutch: bruidegom
French: marié
German: Bräutigam
Italian: sposo
Japanese: hanamuko 花婿
Korean: shillang 신랑
Portuguese: noivo
Russian: zheníkh жених
Spanish: novio
Swedish: brudgum

295. bridge [n.]

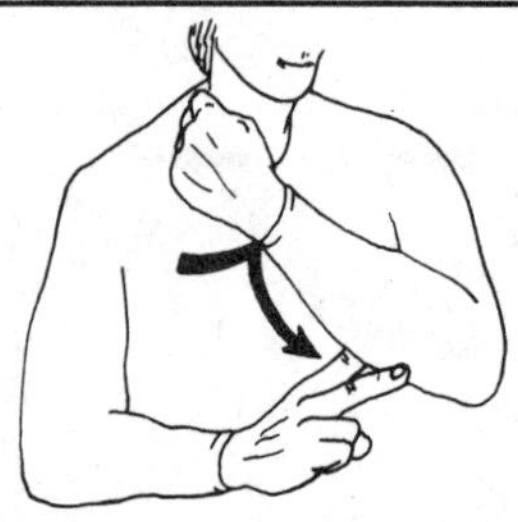

Arabic: jisr/kúbri كوبري / جسر
Chinese: qiáoliáng 橋樑
Dutch: brug
French: pont
German: Brücke
Italian: ponte
Japanese: hashi 橋
Korean: dari 다리
Portuguese: ponte
Russian: most мост
Spanish: puente
Swedish: bro

296. brief [adj.]

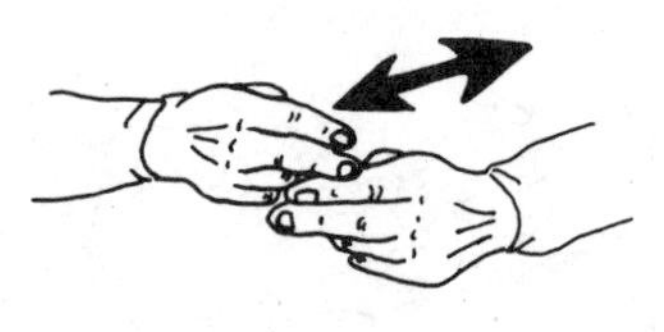

Arabic: mukhtásar مختصر
Chinese: jiǎnduǎnde 簡短的
Dutch: kort
French: bref
German: kurz
Italian: breve
Japanese: tanjikan no 短時間の
Korean: gandanhan 간단한
Portuguese: breve
Russian: krátkiy краткий
Spanish: breve
Swedish: kort

297. bright (light) [adj.]

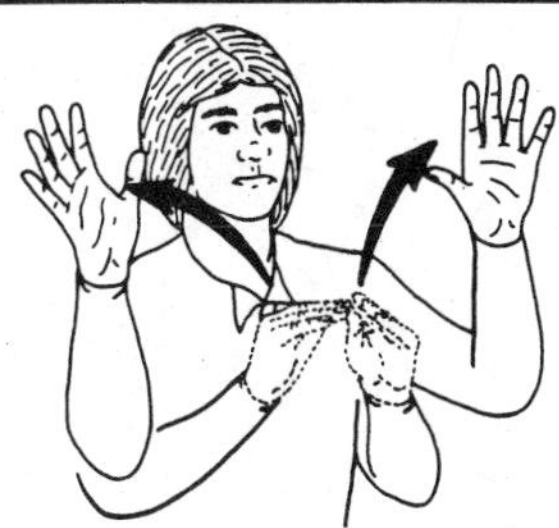

Arabic: lámeaa لامع
Chinese: míngliàngde 明亮的
Dutch: helder
French: brillant
German: hell
Italian: brillante
Japanese: akarui 明るい
Korean: balgŭn 밝은
Portuguese: brilhante
Russian: yárkiy яркий
Spanish: brillante
Swedish: glänsande

298. bring [v.]

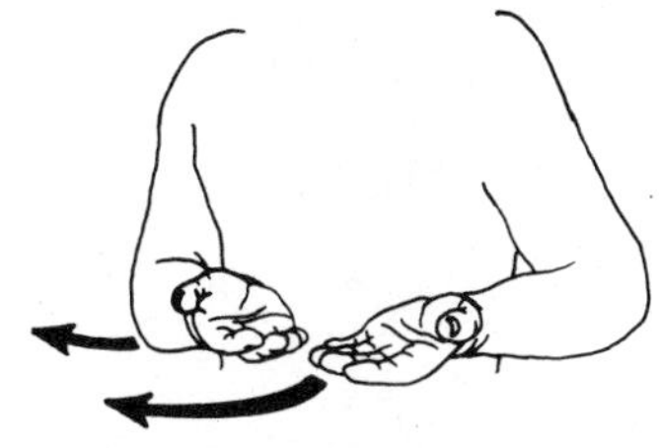

Arabic: ákhdara احضر
Chinese: dàilái 帶來
Dutch: brengen
French: apporter
German: bringen
Italian: portare
Japanese: motte kuru 持ってくる
Korean: gajŏoda 가져오다
Portuguese: trazer
Russian: prinosít' приносить
Spanish: traer
Swedish: medföra

299. broad [adj.]

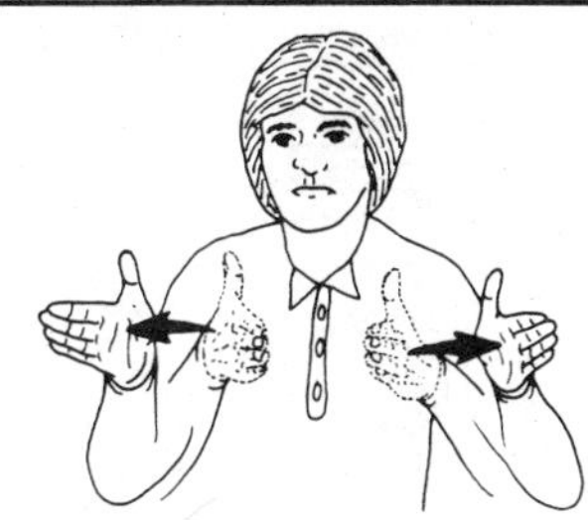

Arabic: wásea' واسع
Chinese: kuānhóngde 寬宏的
Dutch: breed
French: large
German: breit
Italian: largo
Japanese: hiroi 広い
Korean: nŏlbŭn 넓은
Portuguese: largo
Russian: shirókiy широкий
Spanish: ancho
Swedish: bred

300. brother [n.]

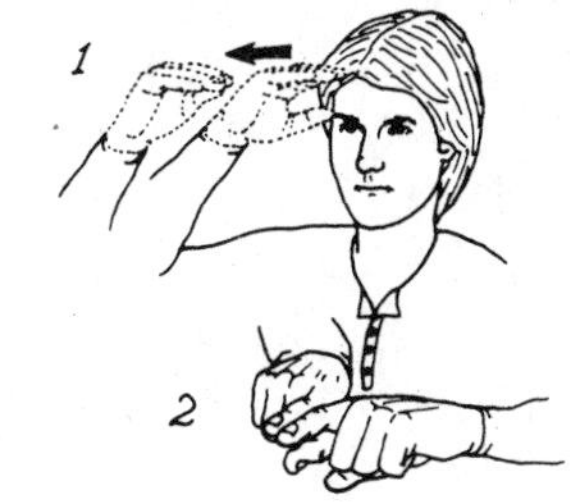

Arabic: akh اخ
Chinese: xiōngdì 兄弟
Dutch: broer
French: frère
German: Bruder
Italian: fratello
Japanese: kyōdai 兄弟
Korean: hyŏngje 형제
Portuguese: irmão
Russian: brat брат
Spanish: hermano
Swedish: broder

301. brown [adj.]

Arabic: búnni بني
Chinese: zōngsè 棕色
Dutch: bruin
French: brun
German: braun
Italian: marrone
Japanese: chairo no 茶色の
Korean: galsaekŭi 갈색의
Portuguese: castanho
Russian: koríchnevyy коричневый
Spanish: castaño
Swedish: brun

302. brush [n.]

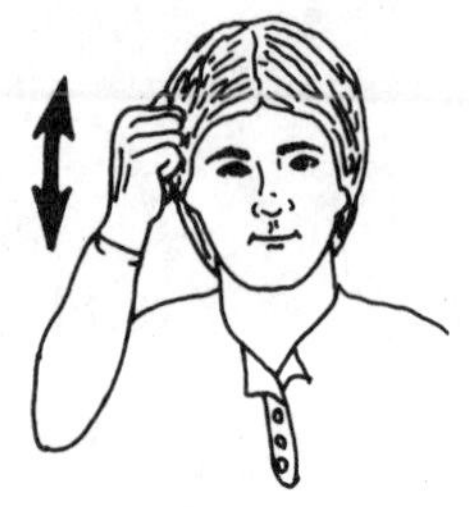

Arabic: fursháa فرشاه
Chinese: shuāzi 刷子
Dutch: borstel
French: brosse
German: Bürste
Italian: spazzola
Japanese: hake 刷毛
Korean: sol 솔
Portuguese: escôva
Russian: shchyótka щётка
Spanish: cepillo
Swedish: borste

303. bug (insect) [n.]

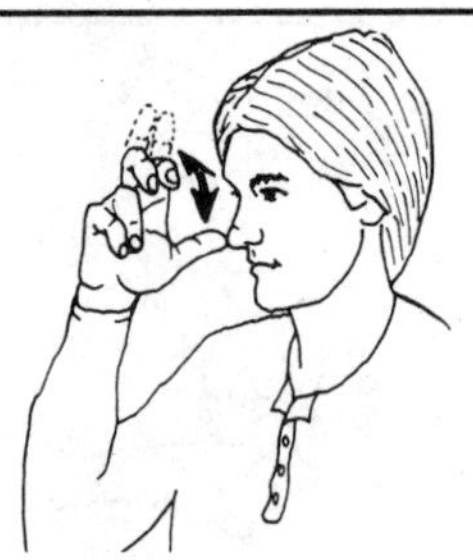

Arabic: háshara حشرة
Chinese: chóng 蟲
Dutch: insekt
French: insecte
German: Käfer
Italian: insetto
Japanese: mushi 虫
Korean: bŏlle 벌레
Portuguese: inseto
Russian: nasekómoye насекомое
Spanish: insecto
Swedish: vägglus

304. build [v.]

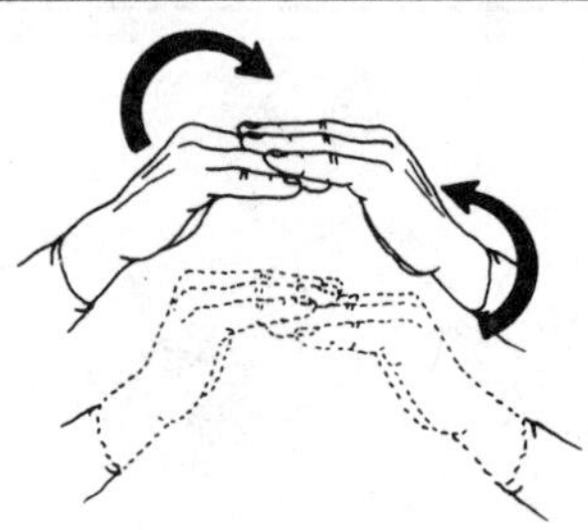

Arabic: bánaa بنى
Chinese: jiànzào 建造
Dutch: bouwen
French: construire
German: bauen
Italian: costruire
Japanese: kenchiku suru 建築する
Korean: seuda 세우다
Portuguese: construir
Russian: stroít' строить
Spanish: construir
Swedish: bygga

305. building [n.]

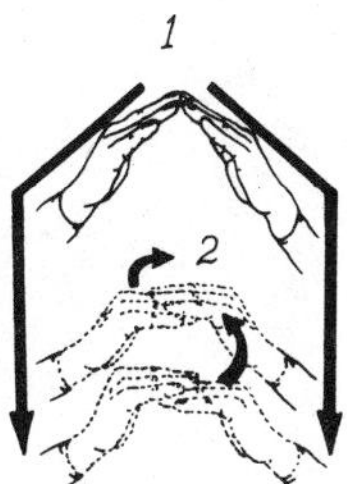

Arabic: mábna مبنى
Chinese: jiànzhúwù 建築物
Dutch: gebouw
French: construction
German: Gebäude
Italian: edificio
Japanese: tatemono 建物
Korean: gŏnmul 건물
Portuguese: edifício
Russian: zdániye здание
Spanish: edificio
Swedish: byggnad

306. Bulgaria [n.]

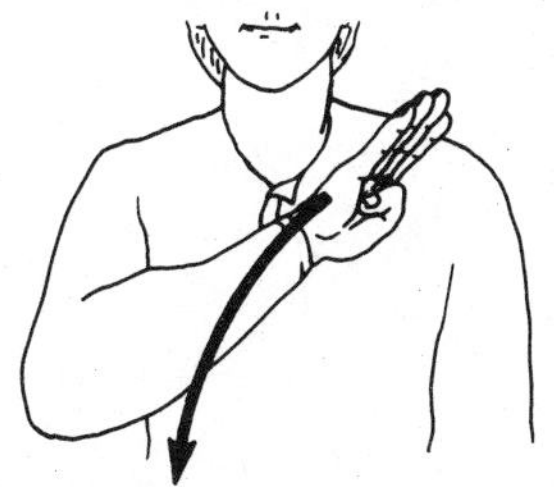

Arabic: bulghária بلغاريا
Chinese: bǎojiālìyǎ 保加利亞
Dutch: Bulgarije
French: Bulgarie
German: Bulgarien
Italian: Bulgaria
Japanese: Burugaria ブルガリア
Korean: Bulgaria 불가리아
Portuguese: Bulgária
Russian: Bolgáriya Болгария
Spanish: Bulgaria
Swedish: Bulgarien

307. bull [n.]

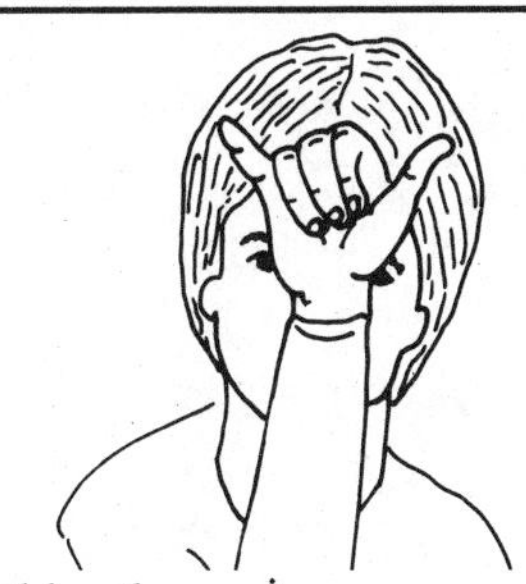

Arabic: thor ثور
Chinese: gōngniú 公牛
Dutch: stier
French: taureau
German: Stier
Italian: toro
Japanese: oushi 雄牛
Korean: hwangso 황소
Portuguese: touro
Russian: byk бык
Spanish: toro
Swedish: tjur

308. bullet [n.]

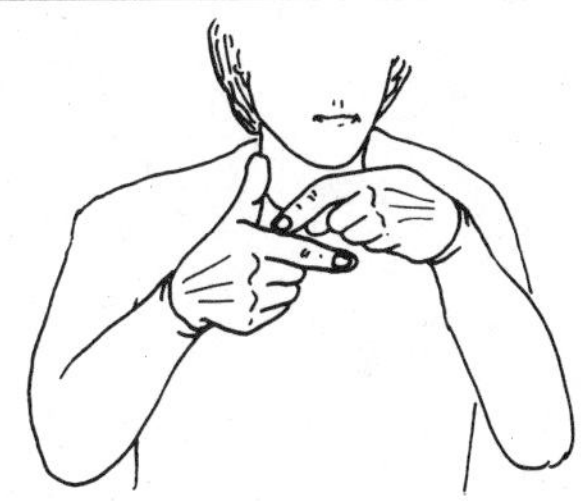

Arabic: rasáasa رصاصة
Chinese: zǐdàn 子弹
Dutch: kogel
French: balle
German: Kugel
Italian: pallottola
Japanese: dangan 弾丸
Korean: ch'ongal 총알
Portuguese: bala
Russian: púlya пуля
Spanish: bala
Swedish: kula

309. bulletin [n.]

Arabic: náshra نشرة
Chinese: gōngbào 公報
Dutch: bulletin
French: bulletin
German: Bekanntmachung
Italian: bollettino
Japanese: keiji 掲示
Korean: keshi 게시
Portuguese: boletim
Russian: byulletén' бюллетень
Spanish: boletín
Swedish: bulletin

310. burden [n.]

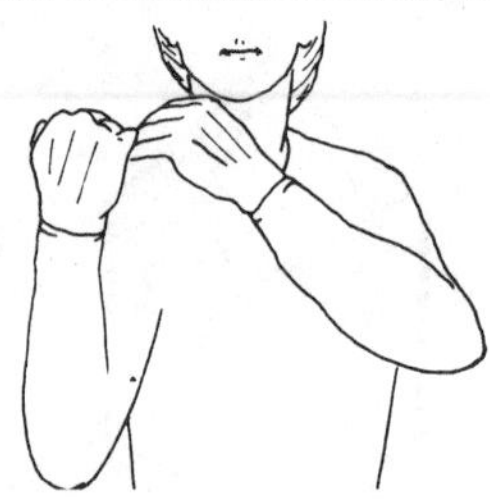

Arabic: hímmel حمل
Chinese: fùdān 負擔
Dutch: last
French: charge
German: Bürde
Italian: fardello
Japanese: futan 負担
Korean: mugŏun jim 무거운 짐
Portuguese: fardo
Russian: nósha ноша
Spanish: carga
Swedish: börda

311. burn [v.]

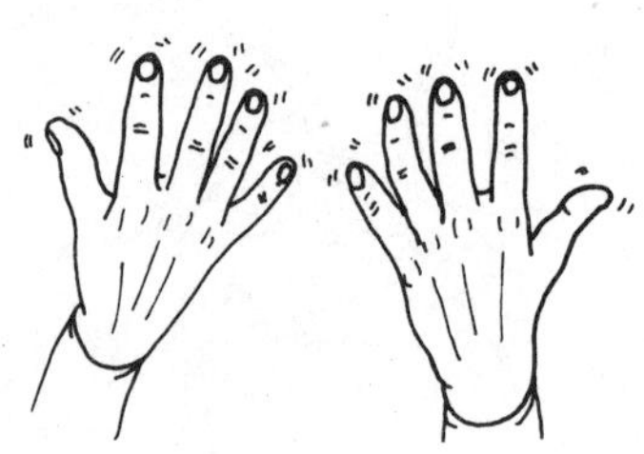

Arabic: háraqa حرَق
Chinese: shāo 燒
Dutch: branden
French: brûler
German: brennen
Italian: bruciare
Japanese: moeru 燃える
Korean: pult'ada 불타다
Portuguese: queimar
Russian: gorét' гореть
Spanish: quemar
Swedish: bränna

312. burst [v.]

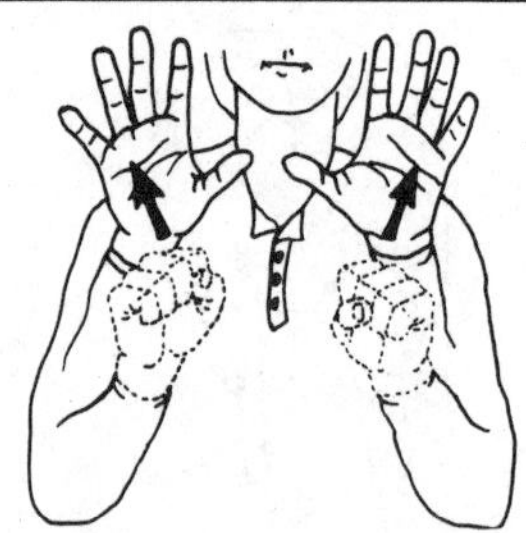

Arabic: infájara انفجر
Chinese: bàozhà 爆炸
Dutch: barsten
French: éclater
German: bersten
Italian: scoppiare
Japanese: bakuhatsu suru 爆発する
Korean: t'ŏjida 터지다
Portuguese: rebentar
Russian: vzryvát'sya взрываться
Spanish: reventar
Swedish: brista

313. bury [v.]

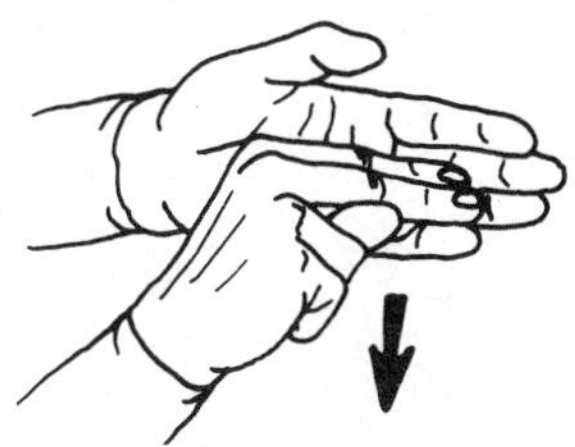

Arabic: défina دفن
Chinese: máizàng 埋葬
Dutch: begraven
French: enterrer
German: begraben
Italian: sotterrare
Japanese: maisō suru 埋葬する
Korean: mutnŭnda 묻는다
Portuguese: enterrar
Russian: khoronít' хоронить
Spanish: enterrar
Swedish: begrava

314. bus [n.]

Arabic: baas باص
Chinese: gōnggòng qìchē 公共汽車
Dutch: bus
French: autobus
German: Bus
Italian: autobus
Japanese: basu バス
Korean: bŏs 뻐스
Portuguese: ônibus
Russian: avtóbus автобус
Spanish: autobús
Swedish: buss

315. bush [n.]

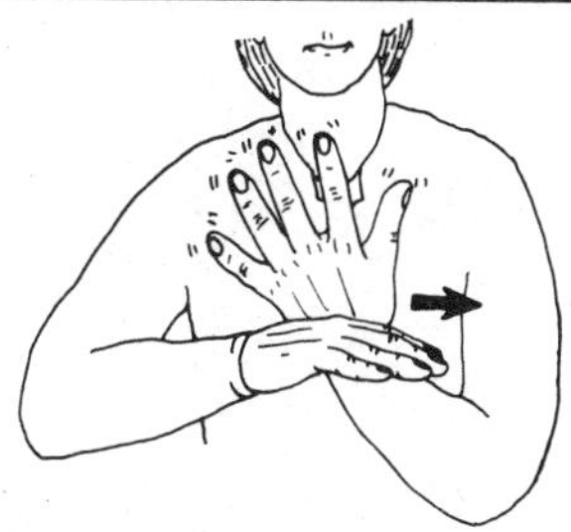

Arabic: shujéira شجيرة
Chinese: ǎi shùcóng 矮樹叢
Dutch: struik
French: buisson
German: Busch
Italian: cespuglio
Japanese: kamboku 潅木
Korean: sup'ul 수풀
Portuguese: arbusto
Russian: kust куст
Spanish: arbusto
Swedish: buske

316. business (affair/matter) [n.]

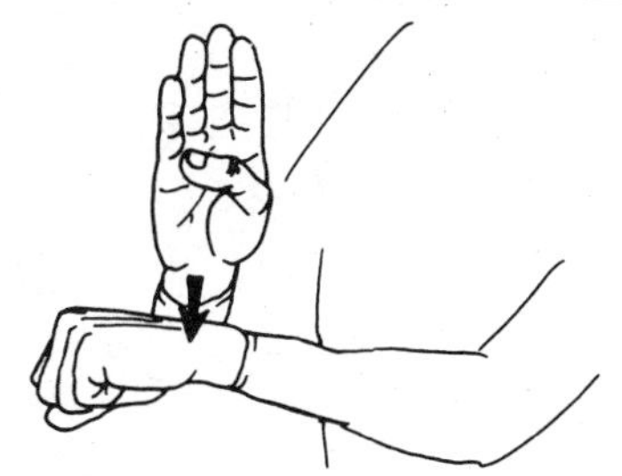

Arabic: tijára تجارة
Chinese: shēngyì 生意
Dutch: zaak
French: affaire
German: Geschäft
Italian: affare
Japanese: shigoto 仕事
Korean: yongmu 업무
Portuguese: negócio
Russian: délo дело
Spanish: negocio
Swedish: affärer

317. busy [adj.]

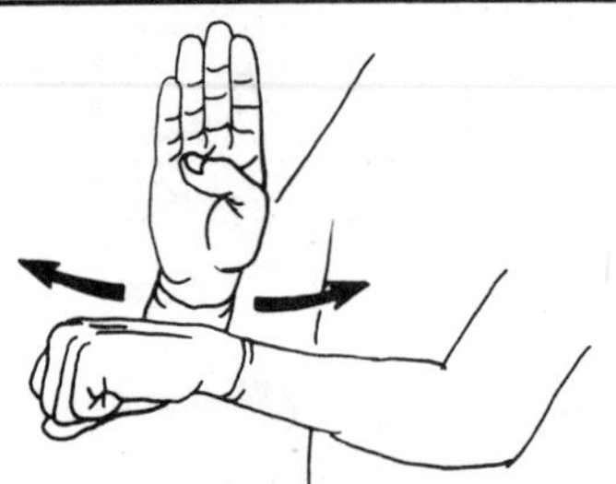

Arabic: mashghúul مشغول
Chinese: máng 忙
Dutch: druk
French: occupé
German: geschäftig
Italian: occupato
Japanese: isogashii 忙しい
Korean: bappŭn 바쁜
Portuguese: ocupado
Russian: zányatyy занятый
Spanish: ocupado
Swedish: upptagen

318. but [conj.]

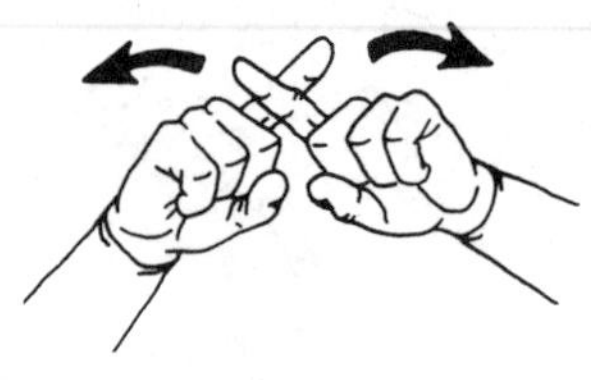

Arabic: lakínna لكن
Chinese: dànshì 但是
Dutch: maar
French: mais
German: aber
Italian: ma
Japanese: shikashi しかし
Korean: gŭrŏna 그러나
Portuguese: mas
Russian: no но
Spanish: pero
Swedish: men

319. butter [n.]

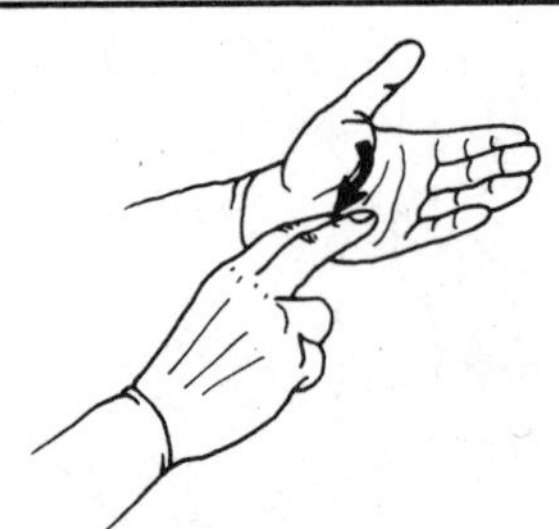

Arabic: zúbda زبدة
Chinese: huángyóu 黄油
Dutch: boter
French: beurre
German: Butter
Italian: burro
Japanese: batā バター
Korean: bŏt'ŏ 뻐터
Portuguese: manteiga
Russian: máslo масло
Spanish: mantequilla
Swedish: smör

320. butterfly [n.]

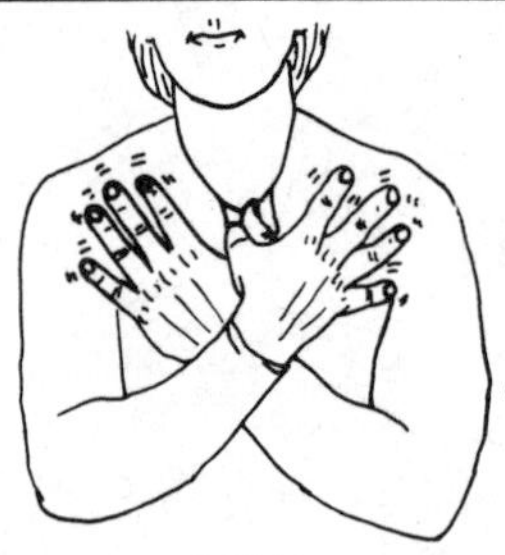

Arabic: farásha فراشة
Chinese: húdié 蝴蝶
Dutch: vlinder
French: papillon
German: Schmetterling
Italian: farfalla
Japanese: chō チョウ
Korean: nabi 나비
Portuguese: borboleta
Russian: bábochka бабочка
Spanish: mariposa
Swedish: fjäril

321. button [n.]

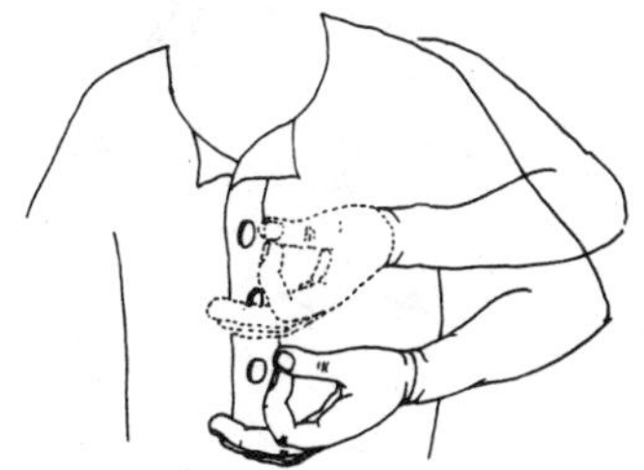

Arabic: zir زر
Chinese: niŭkòu 鈕扣
Dutch: knoop
French: bouton
German: Knopf
Italian: bottone
Japanese: botan ボタン
Korean: danch'u 단추
Portuguese: botão
Russian: púgovitsa пуговица
Spanish: botón
Swedish: knapp

322. buy [v.]

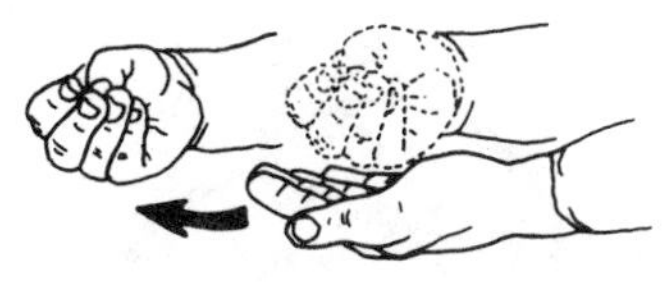

Arabic: ishtára اشترى
Chinese: măi 買
Dutch: kopen
French: acheter
German: kaufen
Italian: comprare
Japanese: kau 買う
Korean: sada 사다
Portuguese: comprar
Russian: pokupát' покупать
Spanish: comprar
Swedish: köpa

323. cabbage [n.]

Arabic: malfúf/korónb ملفوف / كرنب
Chinese: gānláncài 甘籃菜
Dutch: kool
French: chou
German: Kohl
Italian: cavolo
Japanese: kyabetsu キャベツ
Korean: yangbaech'u 양배추
Portuguese: couve
Russian: kapústa капуста
Spanish: berza
Swedish: kål

324. cake [n.]

Arabic: káaka كعكة
Chinese: dàngāo 蛋糕
Dutch: gebak
French: gâteau
German: Kuchen
Italian: torta
Japanese: kēki ケーキ
Korean: keikŭ 케이크
Portuguese: bôlo
Russian: tort торт
Spanish: tarta
Swedish: kaka

325. calculate [v.]

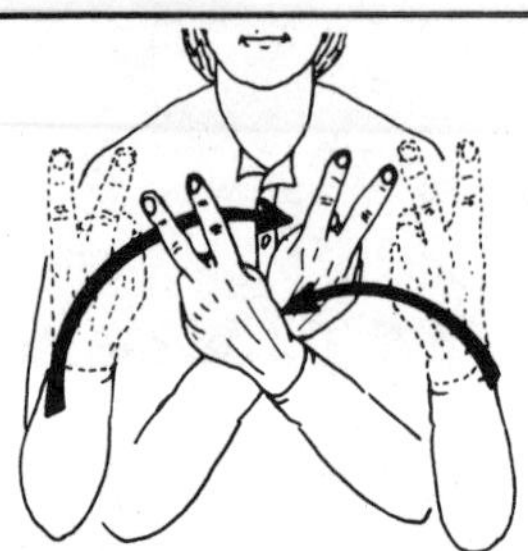

Arabic: hásaba حسب
Chinese: jìsuàn 計算
Dutch: berekenen
French: calculer
German: rechnen
Italian: calcolare
Japanese: keisan suru 計算する
Korean: kyesanhada 계산하다
Portuguese: calcular
Russian: vychislyát' вычислять
Spanish: calcular
Swedish: beräkna

326. calendar [n.]

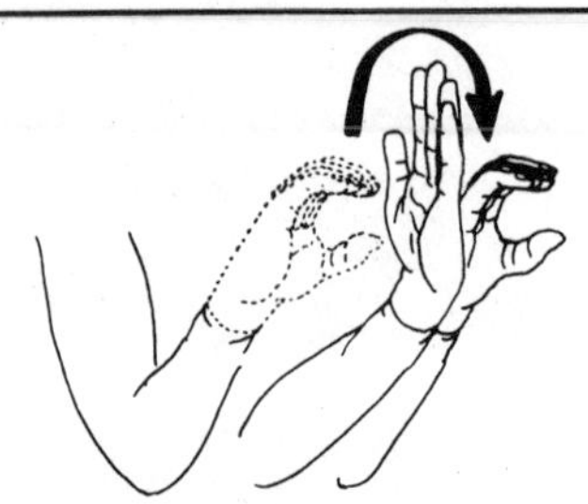

Arabic: taqwím تقويم
Chinese: rìlì 日曆
Dutch: kalender
French: calendrier
German: Kalender
Italian: calendario
Japanese: karendā カレンダー
Korean: dallyŏk 달력
Portuguese: calendário
Russian: kalendár' календарь
Spanish: calendario
Swedish: kalender

327. calf (animal) [n.]

Arabic: éjl عجل
Chinese: xiǎo niú 小牛
Dutch: kalf
French: veau
German: Kalb
Italian: vitello
Japanese: koushi 子牛
Korean: songaji 송아지
Portuguese: vitela
Russian: telyónok телёнок
Spanish: ternero
Swedish: kalv

328. call [v.]

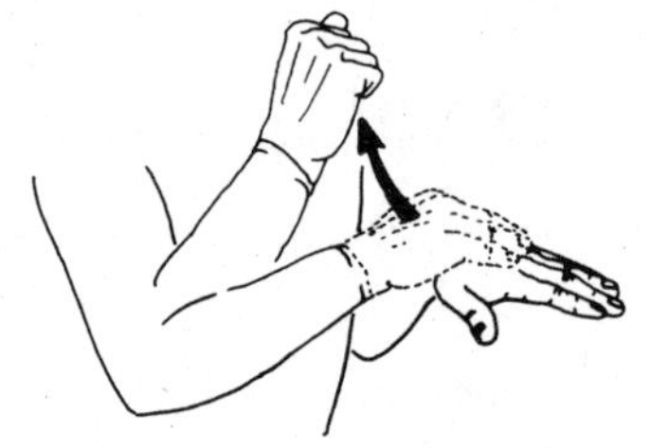

Arabic: náada نادى
Chinese: jiào 叫
Dutch: roepen
French: appeler
German: rufen
Italian: chiamare
Japanese: yobu 呼ぶ
Korean: burŭda 부르다
Portuguese: chamar
Russian: zvat' звать
Spanish: llamar
Swedish: ropa

329. calm [adj.]

Arabic: sákin ساكن
Chinese: píngjìngde 平靜的
Dutch: kalm
French: calme
German: ruhig
Italian: calmo
Japanese: shizukana 静かな
Korean: joyonghan 조용한
Portuguese: calmo
Russian: spokóynyy спокойный
Spanish: calmado
Swedish: lugn

330. camera [n.]

Arabic: kámera كاميرا
Chinese: zhàoxiàngjī 照相機
Dutch: camera
French: appareil photo
German: Kamera
Italian: macchina fotografica
Japanese: kamera カメラ
Korean: k'amera 카메라
Portuguese: máquina fotográfica
Russian: fotoapparát фотоаппарат
Spanish: cámara fotográfica
Swedish: kamera

331. camp [n.]

Arabic: moáskar معسكر
Chinese: lùyíng 露營
Dutch: kamp
French: camp
German: Lager
Italian: accampamento
Japanese: kyampu キャンプ
Korean: k'aemp'u 캠프
Portuguese: acampamento
Russian: láger' лагерь
Spanish: campamento
Swedish: läger

332. can (tin) [n.]

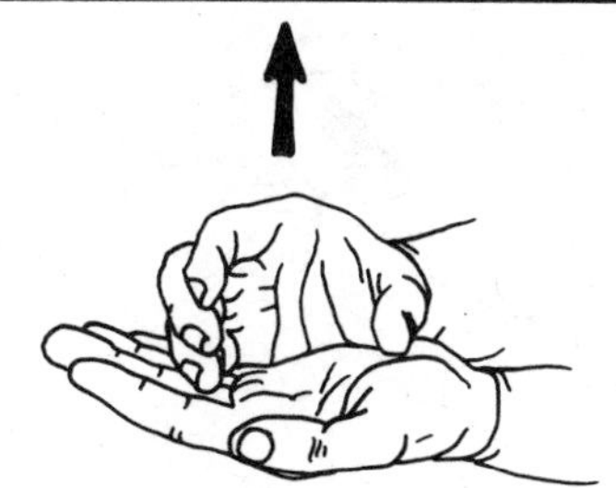

Arabic: safíha صفيحة
Chinese: guàntóu 罐頭
Dutch: blik
French: bidon
German: Büchse
Italian: lattina
Japanese: kan かん
Korean: kkangt'ong 깡통
Portuguese: lata
Russian: bánka банка
Spanish: lata
Swedish: burk

333. can (be able) [v.]

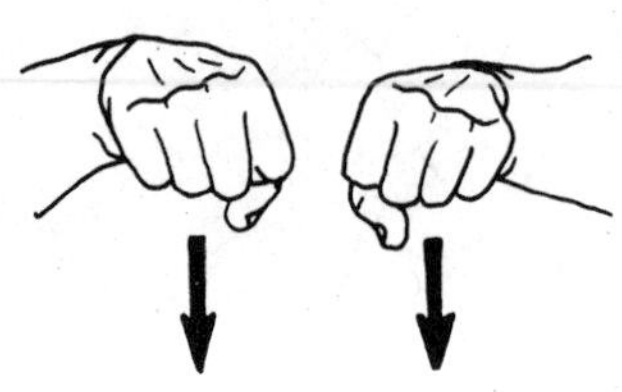

Arabic: qádira قدر
Chinese: néng 能
Dutch: kunnen
French: pouvoir
German: können
Italian: potere
Japanese: . . .suru koto ga dekiru することが出来る
Korean: hal su itta ~할 수 있다
Portuguese: poder
Russian: moch' мочь
Spanish: poder
Swedish: kunna

334. Canada [n.]

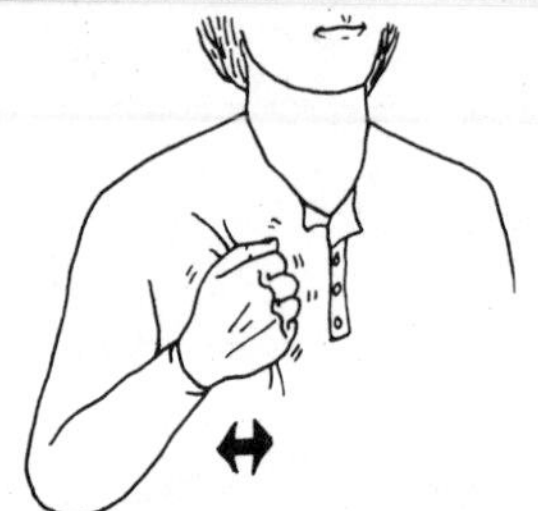

Arabic: kánada كندا
Chinese: jiānádà 加拿大
Dutch: Canada
French: Canada
German: Kanada
Italian: Canadà
Japanese: Kanada カナダ
Korean: Kanada 카나다
Portuguese: Canadá
Russian: Kanáda Канада
Spanish: Canadá
Swedish: Kanada

335. cancel [v.]

Arabic: lághaa لغى
Chinese: qǔxiāo 取消
Dutch: annuleren
French: annuler
German: absagen
Italian: annullare
Japanese: torikesu 取り消す
Korean: ch'wisohada 취소하다
Portuguese: cancelar
Russian: annulírovat' аннулировать
Spanish: cancelar
Swedish: annullera

336. candidate [n.]

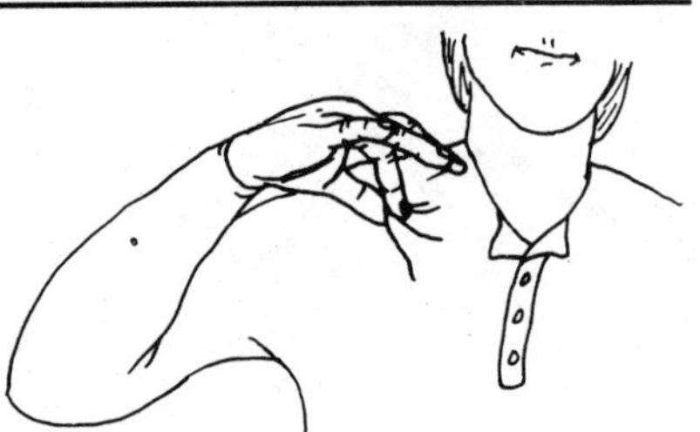

Arabic: muráshah مرشح
Chinese: hòuxuǎnrén 候選人
Dutch: kandidaat
French: candidat
German: Kandidat
Italian: candidato
Japanese: kōhosha 候補者
Korean: huboja 후보자
Portuguese: candidato
Russian: kandidát кандидат
Spanish: candidato
Swedish: kandidat

337. candle [n.]

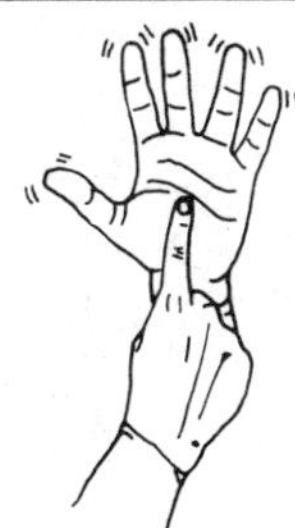

Arabic: qendíl قنديل
Chinese: làzhú 臘燭
Dutch: kaars
French: bougie
German: Kerze
Italian: candela
Japanese: rōsoku ろうそく
Korean: yangch'o 양초
Portuguese: vela
Russian: svechá свеча
Spanish: vela
Swedish: stearinljus

338. candy [n.]

Arabic: hálwa حلوى
Chinese: tángguǒ 糖菓
Dutch: snoep
French: bonbon
German: Bonbon
Italian: candito
Japanese: kyandē キャンディー
Korean: sat'ang 사탕
Portuguese: bombom
Russian: konféta конфета
Spanish: bombón
Swedish: konfekt

339. cap [n.]

Arabic: qúbaa قبعة
Chinese: màozi 帽子
Dutch: pet
French: bonnet
German: Mütze
Italian: berretto
Japanese: bōshi 帽子
Korean: moja 모자
Portuguese: gôrro
Russian: képka кепка
Spanish: gorra
Swedish: mössa

340. capable [adj.]

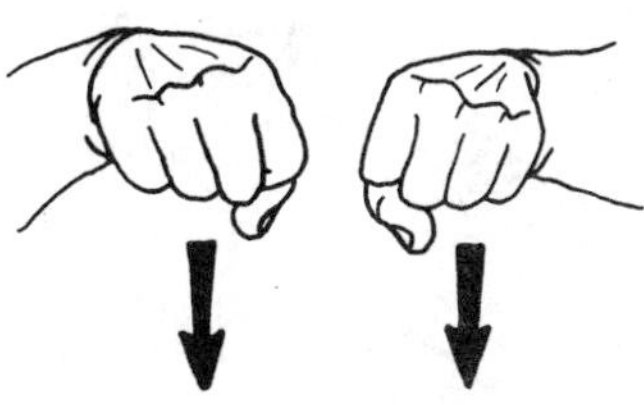

Arabic: qáader قادر
Chinese: yǒu nénglì 有能力的
Dutch: bekwaam
French: capable
German: fähig
Italian: capace
Japanese: yūnō na 有能な
Korean: nŭngyŏkitnŭn 능력있는
Portuguese: capaz
Russian: sposóbnyy способный
Spanish: capaz
Swedish: duglig

341. capacity [n.]

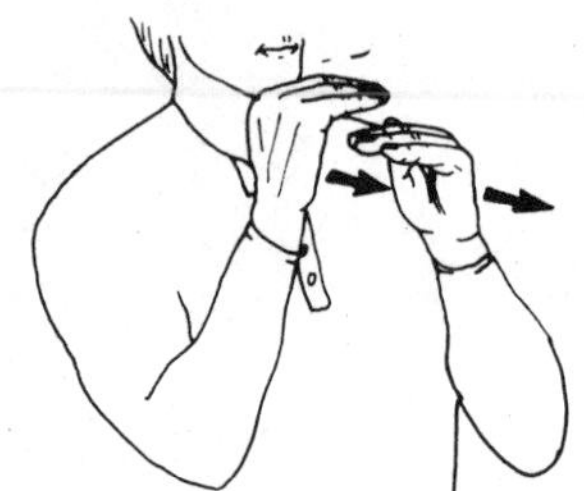

Arabic: seaa سعة
Chinese: nénglì 能力
Dutch: capaciteit
French: capacité
German: Inhalt
Italian: capacità
Japanese: shūyōryoku 収容力
Korean: nŭngyŏk 능력
Portuguese: capacidade
Russian: ob"yóm объём
Spanish: capacidad
Swedish: kapacitet

342. capital (city) [n.]

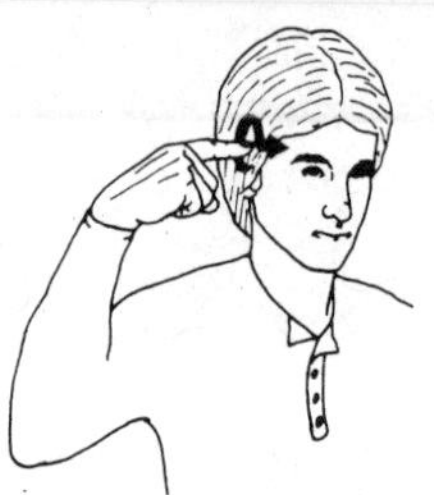

Arabic: aásima عاصمة
Chinese: shǒudū 首都
Dutch: hoofdstad
French: capitale
German: Hauptstadt
Italian: capitale
Japanese: shuto 主都
Korean: sudo 수도
Portuguese: capital
Russian: stolítsa столица
Spanish: capital
Swedish: huvudstad

343. capitalist [n.]

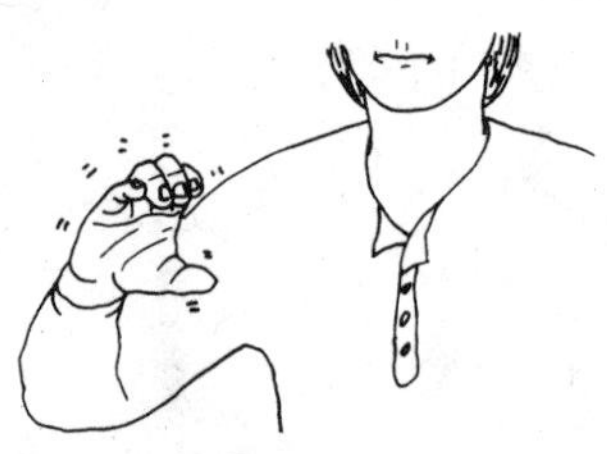

Arabic: ra's-malía رأسمالية
Chinese: zīběnjiā 資本家
Dutch: kapitalist
French: capitaliste
German: Kapitalist
Italian: capitalista
Japanese: shihonshugisha 資本主義者
Korean: jabonga 자본가
Portuguese: capitalista
Russian: kapitalíst капиталист
Spanish: capitalista
Swedish: kapitalist

344. captain [n.]

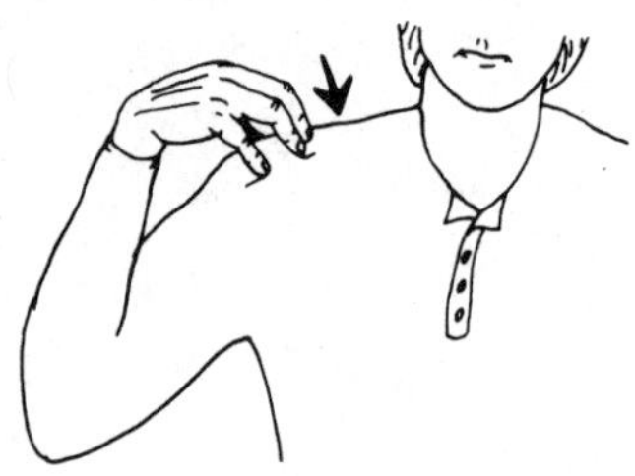

Arabic: naqíb نقيب
Chinese: shàngwèi 上尉
Dutch: kapitein
French: capitaine
German: Kapitän
Italian: capitano
Japanese: sencho 船長
Korean: sŏnjang 선장
Portuguese: capitão
Russian: kapitán капитан
Spanish: capitán
Swedish: kapten

345. capture [v.]

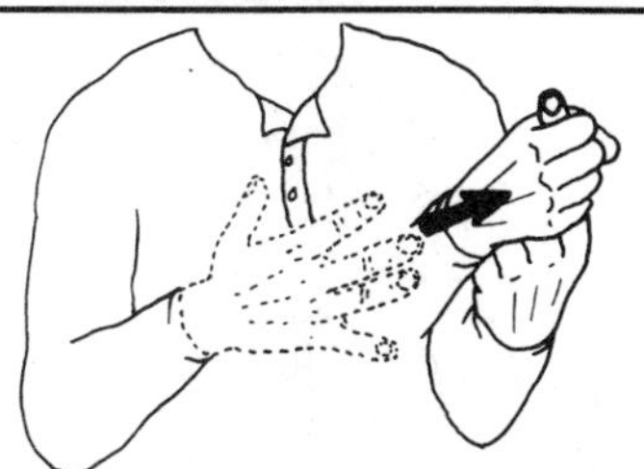

Arabic: qábada aala قبض على
Chinese: bǔhuò 捕獲
Dutch: vangen
French: capturer
German: einfangen
Italian: catturare
Japanese: toraeru 捕える
Korean: japta 잡다
Portuguese: capturar
Russian: zakhvátyvat' захватывать
Spanish: capturar
Swedish: tillfångata

346. car [n.]

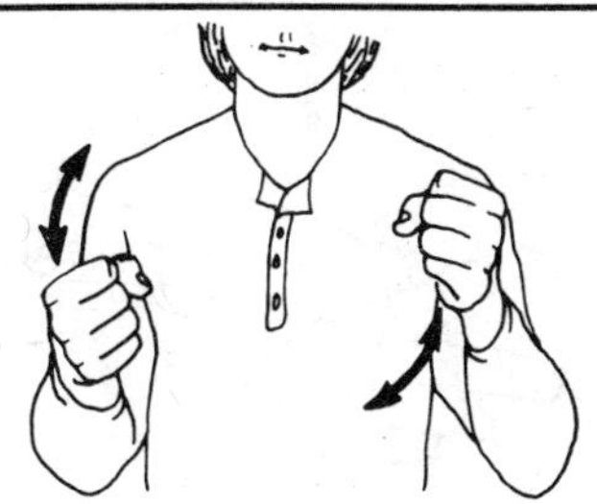

Arabic: sayyára سيارة
Chinese: chēzi 汽車
Dutch: auto
French: voiture
German: Auto
Italian: auto
Japanese: jidosha 自動車
Korean: jadongch'a 자동차
Portuguese: carro
Russian: mashína машина
Spanish: coche
Swedish: bil

347. card [n.]

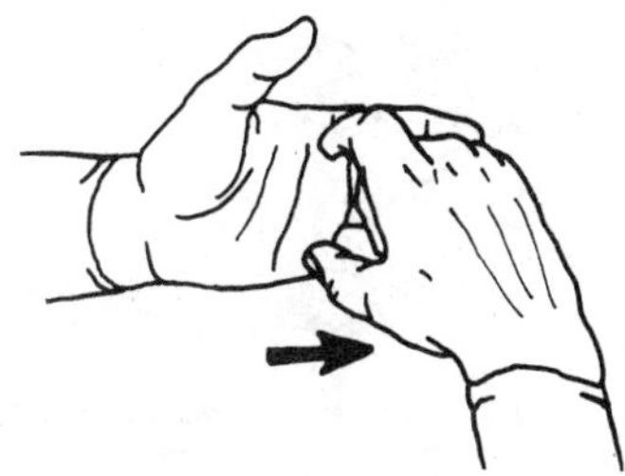

Arabic: bitáaqa بطاقة
Chinese: kǎpiàn 卡片
Dutch: kaart
French: carte
German: Karte
Italian: tessera
Japanese: kādo カード
Korean: k'adŭ 카드
Portuguese: cartão
Russian: kárta карта
Spanish: tarjeta
Swedish: kort

348. care [n.]

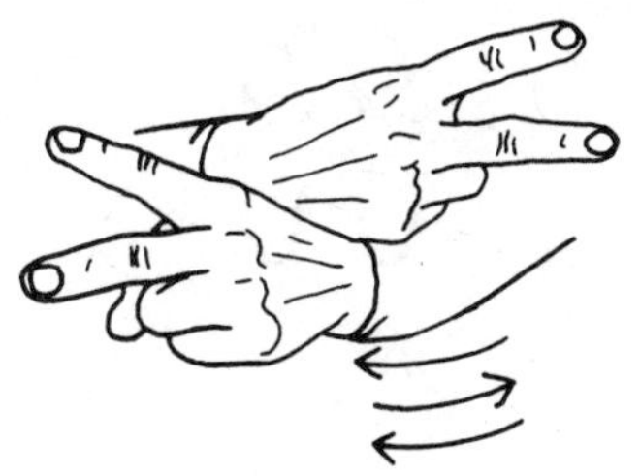

Arabic: ihtimám اهتمام
Chinese: zhàoliào 照料
Dutch: zorg
French: souci
German: Sorge
Italian: cura
Japanese: kitzukai 気づかい
Korean: kŏkjŏng 걱정
Portuguese: cuidado
Russian: zabóta забота
Spanish: cuidado
Swedish: bekymmer

349. careful [adj.]

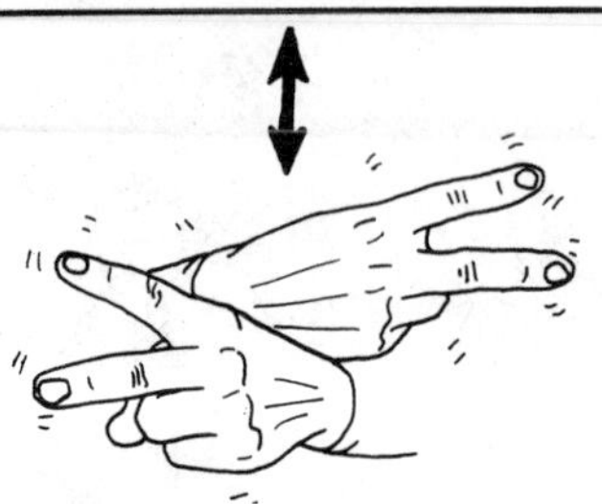

Arabic: muntábi منتبه
Chinese: xiǎoxīnde 小心的
Dutch: voorzichtig
French: prudent
German: sorgsam
Italian: attento
Japanese: chūibukai 注意深い
Korean: juui kip'ŭn 주의깊은
Portuguese: cuidadoso
Russian: ostorózhnyy осторожный
Spanish: cuidadoso
Swedish: försiktig

350. careless [adj.]

Arabic: múhmil مهمل
Chinese: cūxīnde 粗心
Dutch: zorgeloos
French: négligent
German: sorglos
Italian: negligente
Japanese: fuchūi na 不注意な
Korean: bujuihan 부주의한
Portuguese: descuidado
Russian: nebrézhnyy небрежный
Spanish: descuidado
Swedish: vårdslös

351. carnival [n.]

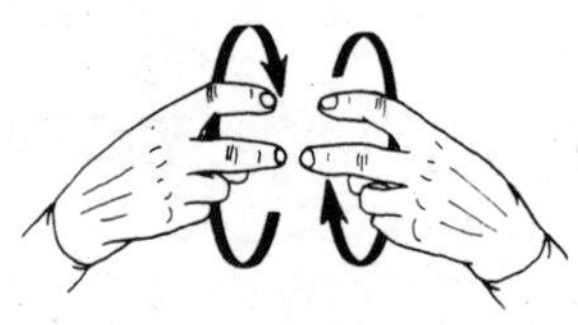

Arabic: karnavál كرنفال
Chinese: kuánghuānjié 狂歡節
Dutch: carnaval
French: carnaval
German: Karneval
Italian: carnevale
Japanese: kānibaru カーニバル
Korean: ka'aanibal 카니발
Portuguese: carnaval
Russian: karnavál карнавал
Spanish: carnaval
Swedish: karneval

352. carpenter [n.]

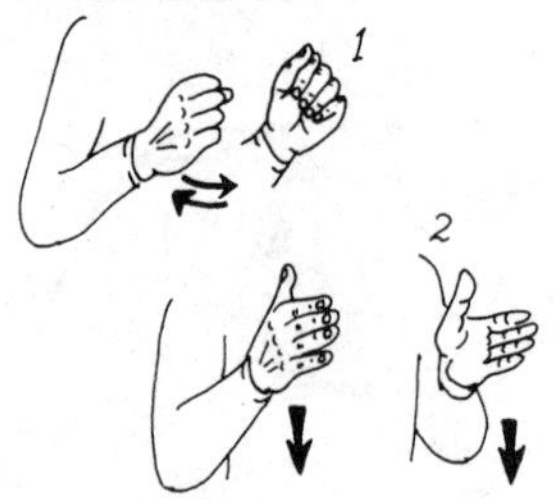

Arabic: najár نجار
Chinese: mùjiàng 木匠
Dutch: timmerman
French: menuisier
German: Tischler
Italian: falegname
Japanese: daiku 大工
Korean: moksu 목수
Portuguese: carpinteiro
Russian: plótnik плотник
Spanish: carpintero
Swedish: snickare

353. carry [v.]

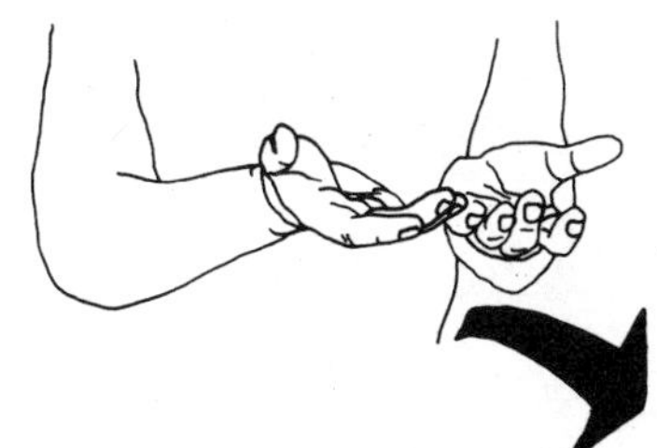

Arabic: hámala حمل
Chinese: xīdài 攜帶
Dutch: dragen
French: porter
German: tragen
Italian: portare
Japanese: hakobu 運ぶ
Korean: unbanhada 운반하다
Portuguese: carregar
Russian: nosít' носить
Spanish: llevar
Swedish: bära

354. cart [n.]

Arabic: áaraba عربة
Chinese: shǒutuīchē 手推車
Dutch: wagen
French: charrette
German: Karren
Italian: carretto
Japanese: niguruma 荷車
Korean: jimmach'a 짐마차
Portuguese: carreta
Russian: teléga телега
Spanish: carreta
Swedish: kärra

355. cat [n.]

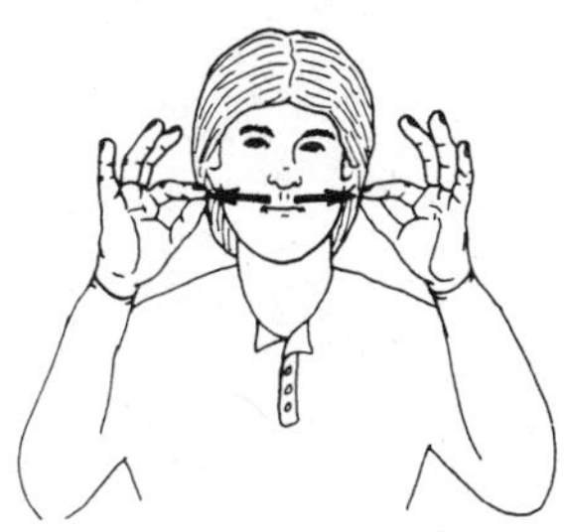

Arabic: qétta قطة
Chinese: māo 貓
Dutch: kat
French: chat
German: Katze
Italian: gatto
Japanese: neko ネコ
Korean: goyangi 고양이
Portuguese: gato
Russian: kóshka кошка
Spanish: gato
Swedish: katt

356. catalog [n.]

Arabic: beyán بيان
Chinese: mùlù 目錄
Dutch: catalogus
French: catalogue
German: Katalog
Italian: catalogo
Japanese: katarogu カタログ
Korean: mongnok 목록
Portuguese: catálogo
Russian: katalóg каталог
Spanish: catálogo
Swedish: katalog

357. catch [v.]

Arabic: másaka مسك
Chinese: zhuāzhù 抓住
Dutch: vangen
French: attraper
German: fangen
Italian: afferrare
Japanese: . . . o tsukamu …をつかむ
Korean: jabta 잡다
Portuguese: agarrar
Russian: lovít' ловить
Spanish: coger
Swedish: fånga

358. catholic [n.]

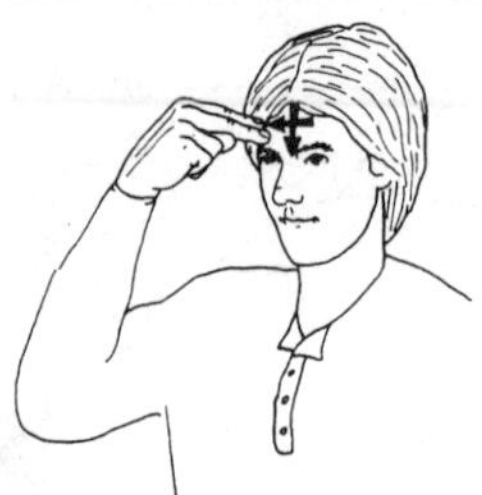

Arabic: kathulíki كاثوليكي
Chinese: tiānzhŭjiào 天主教
Dutch: katholiek
French: catholique
German: Katholik
Italian: cattolico
Japanese: katorikku カトリック
Korean: ch'ŏnjukyodo 천주교도
Portuguese: católico
Russian: katólik католик
Spanish: católico
Swedish: katolik

359. cattle [n.]

Arabic: al-máshia الماشية
Chinese: niú 牛
Dutch: vee
French: bétail
German: Vieh
Italian: bestiame
Japanese: ushi 牛
Korean: gach'uk 가축
Portuguese: gado
Russian: skot скот
Spanish: ganado
Swedish: boskap

360. cause [v.]

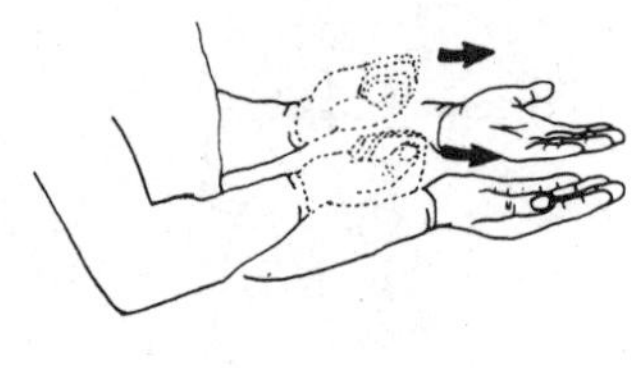

Arabic: sábbaba سبب
Chinese: yĭngĭ 引起
Dutch: veroorzaken
French: causer
German: verursachen
Italian: causare
Japanese: saseru …させる
Korean: irŭk'ida 일으키다
Portuguese: causar
Russian: vyzyvát' вызывать
Spanish: causar
Swedish: orsaka

361. caution [n.]

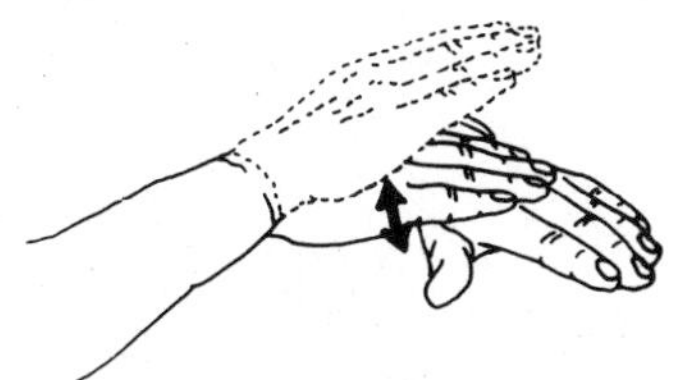

Arabic: tahdhír تحذير
Chinese: jǐnshèn 謹慎
Dutch: voorzichtigheid
French: précaution
German: Vorsicht
Italian: cautela
Japanese: chūi 注意
Korean: joshim 조심
Portuguese: cautela
Russian: ostorózhnost' осторожность
Spanish: advertencia
Swedish: försiktighet

362. cease [v.]

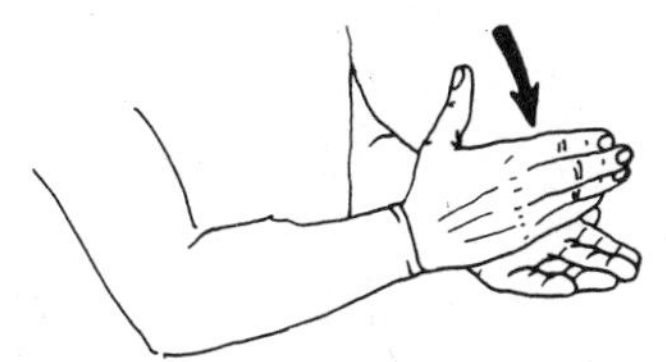

Arabic: áuqafa وقف
Chinese: tíngzhǐ 停止
Dutch: ophouden
French: cesser
German: aufhören
Italian: cessare
Japanese: . . .o yameru をやめる
Korean: kkŭtch'ida 끝치다
Portuguese: cessar
Russian: perestát' перестать
Spanish: cesar
Swedish: upphöra

363. celebrate [v.]

Arabic: ihtáfala احتفل
Chinese: qìngzhù 慶祝
Dutch: vieren
French: célébrer
German: feiern
Italian: celebrare
Japanese: . . .o iwau …を祝う
Korean: ch'uk'hahada 축하하다
Portuguese: celebrar
Russian: prázdnovat' праздновать
Spanish: celebrar
Swedish: fira

364. cemetery [n.]

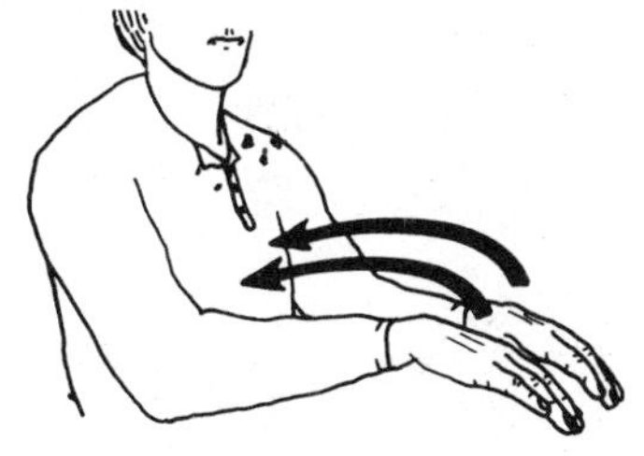

Arabic: máqbara مقبرة
Chinese: mùdì 基地
Dutch: begraafplaats
French: cimetière
German: Friedhof
Italian: cimitero
Japanese: bochi 墓地
Korean: myoji 묘지
Portuguese: cemitério
Russian: kládbishche кладбище
Spanish: cementerio
Swedish: kyrkogård

365. cent [n.]

Arabic: sint سنت
Chinese: fēn 分
Dutch: cent
French: centime
German: Cent
Italian: centesimo
Japanese: sento セント
Korean: sent'ŭ 센트
Portuguese: centavo
Russian: tsent цент
Spanish: centavo
Swedish: cent

366. center [n.]

Arabic: márkaz مركز
Chinese: zhōngxīn 中心
Dutch: centrum
French: centre
German: Zentrum
Italian: centro
Japanese: chūō 中央
Korean: jungang 중앙
Portuguese: centro
Russian: tséntr центр
Spanish: centro
Swedish: center

367. centimeter [n.]

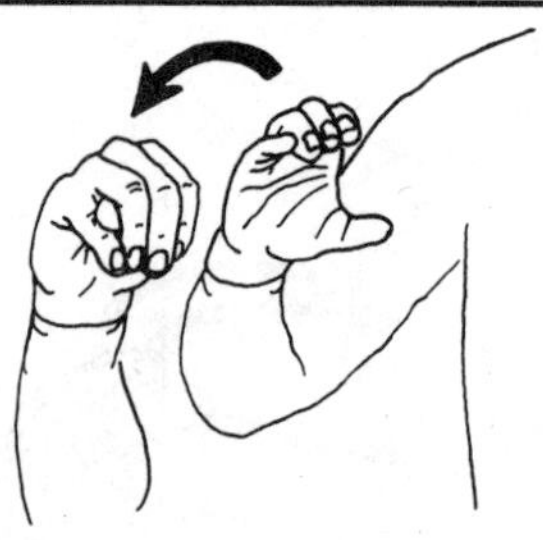

Arabic: santimíter سنتميتر
Chinese: gōngfēn 公分
Dutch: centimeter
French: centimètre
German: Zentimeter
Italian: centimetro
Japanese: senchimētoru センチメーター
Korean: sentimita 센티미터
Portuguese: centímetro
Russian: santimétr сантиметр
Spanish: centímetro
Swedish: centimeter

368. century [n.]

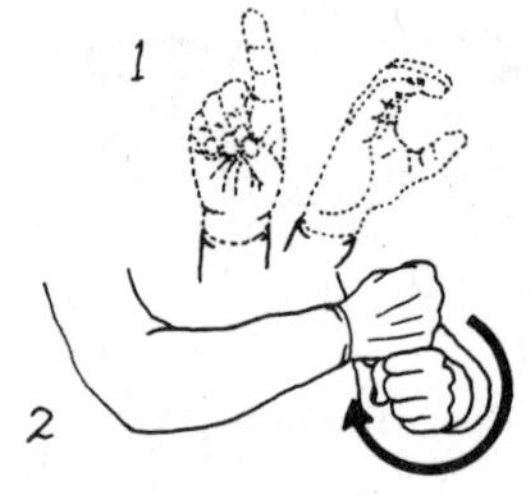

Arabic: qarn قرن
Chinese: shìjì 世紀
Dutch: eeuw
French: siècle
German: Jahrhundert
Italian: secolo
Japanese: seiki 世紀
Korean: ilsegi 일세기
Portuguese: século
Russian: vek век
Spanish: siglo
Swedish: sekel

369. certain [adj./adv.]

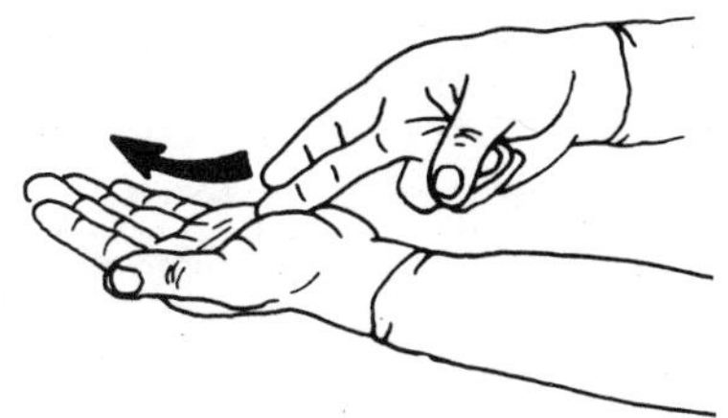

Arabic: muta'ákid متأكد
Chinese: quèshíde 確實
Dutch: zeker
French: certain
German: sicher
Italian: certo
Japanese: kakujitsuna 確実な
Korean: hwaksilhan 확실한
Portuguese: certo
Russian: opredelyónyy определёный
Spanish: cierto
Swedish: säker

370. certificate [n.]

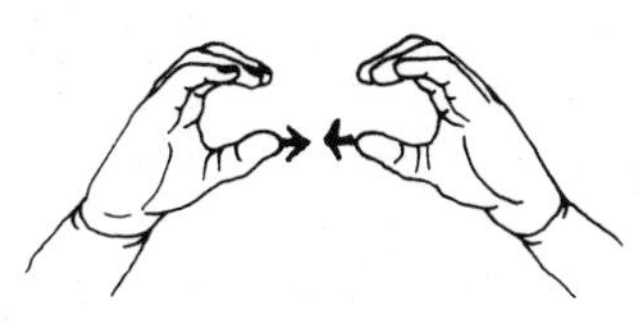

Arabic: shaháda شهادة
Chinese: zhèngshū 證書
Dutch: certificaat
French: certificat
German: Zeugnis
Italian: certificato
Japanese: shōmei sho 証明書
Korean: jŭngmyŏngsŏ 증명서
Portuguese: certificado
Russian: svidétel'stvo свидетельство
Spanish: certificado
Swedish: certifikat

371. chain [n.]

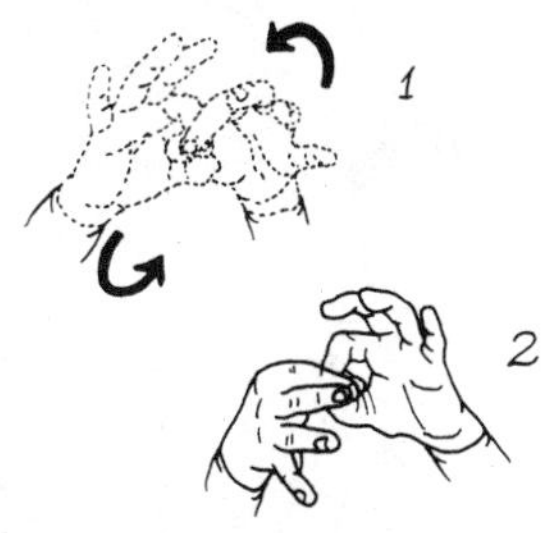

Arabic: sílsila سلسلة
Chinese: liànzi 鏈子
Dutch: ketting
French: chaîne
German: Kette
Italian: catena
Japanese: kusari 鎖
Korean: sasŭl 사슬
Portuguese: cadeia
Russian: tsep' цепь
Spanish: cadena
Swedish: kedja

372. chair [n.]

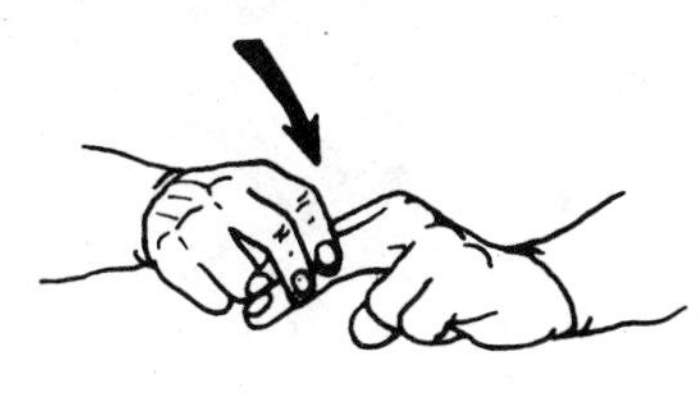

Arabic: kúrsi كرسي
Chinese: yǐzi 椅子
Dutch: stoel
French: chaise
German: Stuhl
Italian: sedia
Japanese: isu 椅子
Korean: ŭija 의자
Portuguese: cadeira
Russian: stul стул
Spanish: silla
Swedish: stol

373. chairman [n.]

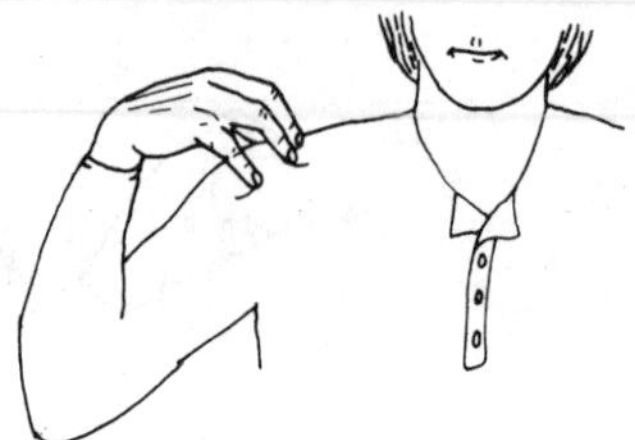

Arabic: ra'ís al-májlis رئيس المجلس
Chinese: zhǔxí 主席
Dutch: voorzitter
French: président
German: Vorsitzender
Italian: presidente
Japanese: gichō 議長
Korean: ŭijang 의장
Portuguese: presidente
Russian: predsedátel' председатель
Spanish: presidente
Swedish: ordförande

374. chalk [n.]

Arabic: tabashír طباشير
Chinese: fěnbǐ 粉筆
Dutch: krijt
French: craie
German: Kreide
Italian: gesso
Japanese: chōku チョーク
Korean: bunp'il 분필
Portuguese: giz
Russian: mel мел
Spanish: tiza
Swedish: krita

375. challenge [n.]

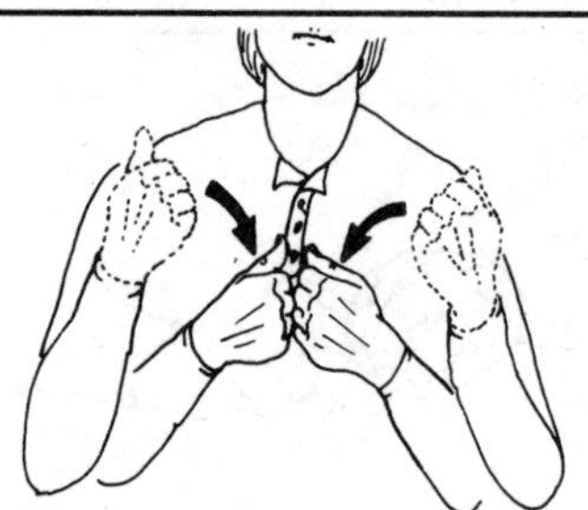

Arabic: taháddii تحدي
Chinese: tiǎozhàn 挑戰
Dutch: uitdaging
French: défi
German: Herausforderung
Italian: sfida
Japanese: chōsen 挑戦
Korean: dojŏn 도전
Portuguese: desafio
Russian: výzov вызов
Spanish: desafío
Swedish: utmaning

376. champion [n.]

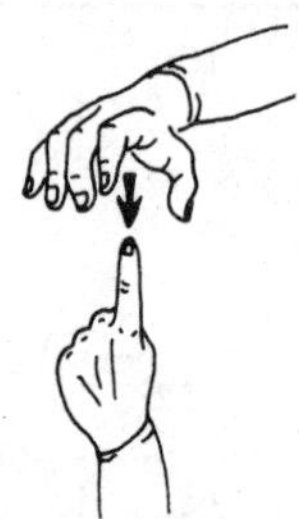

Arabic: al-bátal البطل
Chinese: guànjūn 冠軍
Dutch: kampioen
French: champion
German: Meister
Italian: campione
Japanese: champion チャンピオン
Korean: usŭngja 우승자
Portuguese: campeão
Russian: chempión чемпион
Spanish: campeón
Swedish: mästare

377. chance (occasion) [n.]

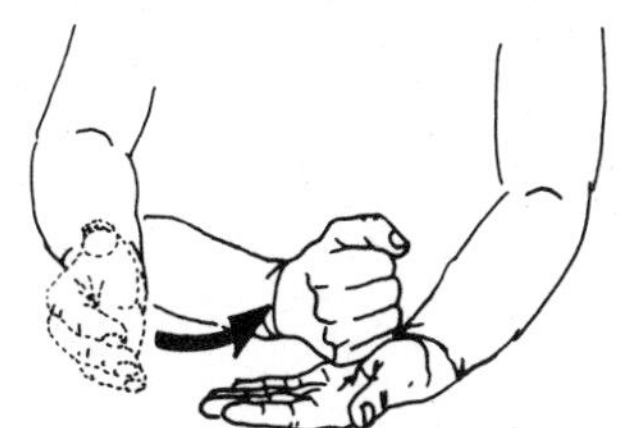

Arabic: fúrsa فرصة
Chinese: jīhuì 機會
Dutch: gelegenheid
French: occasion
German: Gelegenheit
Italian: occasione
Japanese: kikai 機会
Korean: kihoe 기회
Portuguese: ocasião
Russian: slúchay случай
Spanish: oportunidad
Swedish: tillfällighet

378. change [v.]

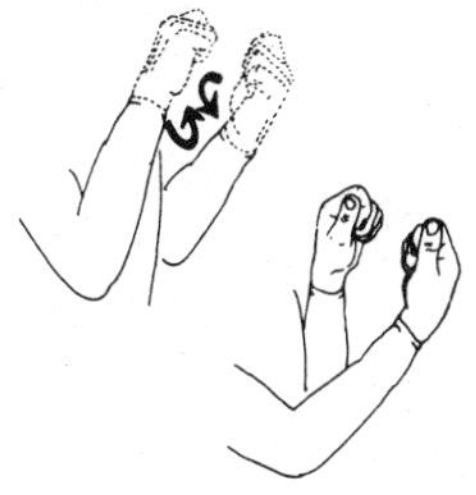

Arabic: gháyyara غير
Chinese: gǎibiàn 改變
Dutch: veranderen
French: changer
German: verändern
Italian: cambiare
Japanese: ...o kaeru を変える
Korean: byŏnhada 변하다
Portuguese: mudar
Russian: izmenyát' изменять
Spanish: cambiar
Swedish: förändra

379. chapter [n.]

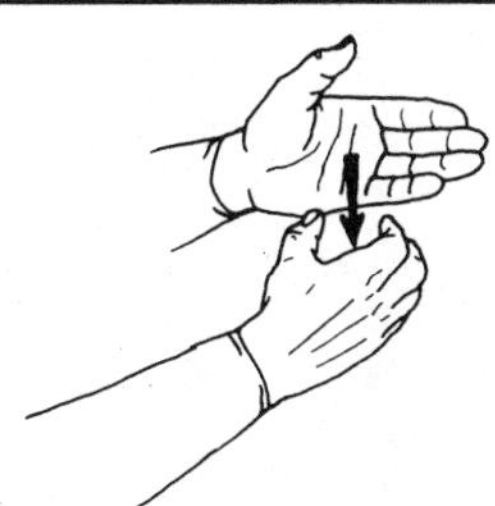

Arabic: fasl فصل
Chinese: zhāng 章
Dutch: hoofdstuk
French: chapitre
German: Kapitel
Italian: capitolo
Japanese: shō 章
Korean: jang 장
Portuguese: capítulo
Russian: glavá глава
Spanish: capítulo
Swedish: kapitel

380. character [n.]

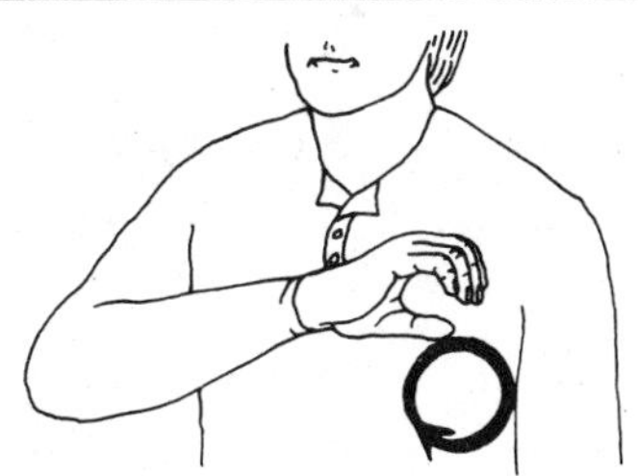

Arabic: sífa صفة
Chinese: tèxìng 特性
Dutch: karakter
French: caractère
German: Charakter
Italian: carattere
Japanese: seikaku 性格
Korean: sŏngkyŏk 성격
Portuguese: caráter
Russian: kharákter характер
Spanish: carácter
Swedish: karaktär

381. chase [v.]

Arabic: tárada طارد
Chinese: zhuī 追
Dutch: achtervolgen
French: chasser
German: jagen
Italian: inseguire
Japanese: . . . o oikakeru ...を追いかける
Korean: twirŭl jjotda 뒤를 쫓다
Portuguese: caçar
Russian: gonyát'sya гоняться
Spanish: perseguir
Swedish: jaga

382. chat [v.]

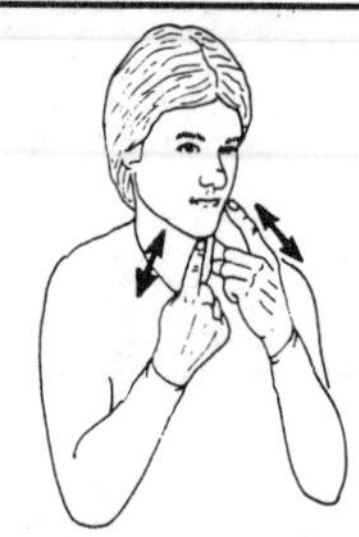

Arabic: taháadatha تحادث
Chinese: tántiān 談天
Dutch: keuvelen
French: bavarder
German: plaudern
Italian: chiacchierare
Japanese: zatsudan suru 談笑する
Korean: jabtamhada 잡담하다
Portuguese: conversar
Russian: boltát' болтать
Spanish: charlar
Swedish: prata

383. cheap [adj.]

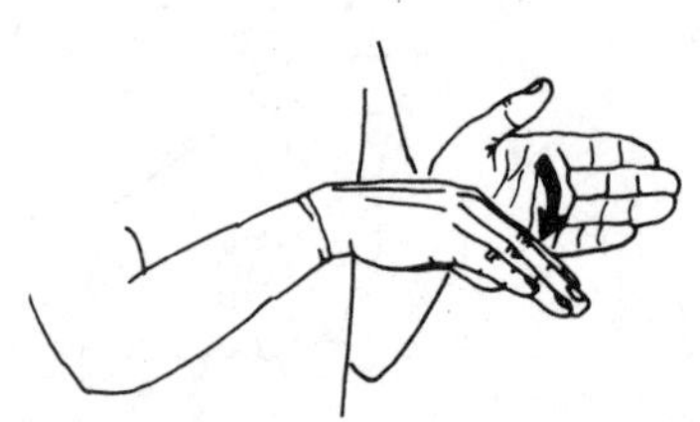

Arabic: rakhís رخيص
Chinese: piányide 便宜的
Dutch: goedkoop
French: peu coûteux
German: billig
Italian: economico
Japanese: yasui 安い
Korean: ssan 싼
Portuguese: barato
Russian: deshyóvyy дешёвый
Spanish: barato
Swedish: billig

384. cheat [v.]

Arabic: gháshsha غش
Chinese: qīpiàn 欺騙
Dutch: bedriegen
French: duper
German: betrügen
Italian: ingannare
Japanese: . . . o damasu だます
Korean: sogida 속이다
Portuguese: enganar
Russian: obmányvat' обманывать
Spanish: estafar
Swedish: fuska

385. check (verification) [n.]

Arabic: fahs فحص
Chinese: jiǎnchá 檢查
Dutch: controle
French: contrôle
German: Kontrolle
Italian: verifica
Japanese: kensa 検査
Korean: gŏmsa 검사
Portuguese: verificação
Russian: provérka проверка
Spanish: verificación
Swedish: kontroll

386. check (verify) [v.]

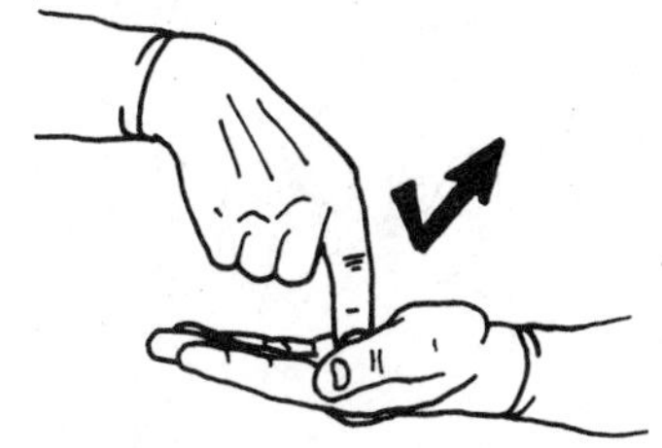

Arabic: fáhasa فحص
Chinese: jiǎnchá 檢查
Dutch: controleren
French: vérifier
German: kontrollieren
Italian: verificare
Japanese: kensa suru 検査する
Korean: hwakinhada 확인하다
Portuguese: verificar
Russian: proveryat' проверять
Spanish: verificar
Swedish: kontrollera

387. cheerful [adj.]

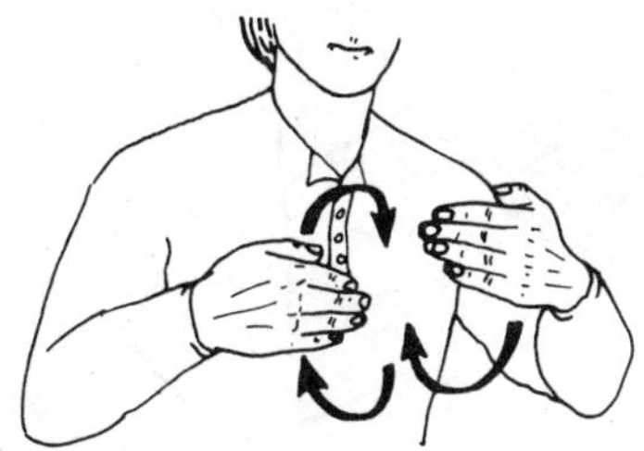

Arabic: mubtáhij مبتهج
Chinese: gāoxìngde 高興的
Dutch: opgewekt
French: joyeux
German: fröhlich
Italian: allegro
Japanese: kigen no yoi 機嫌がよい
Korean: jŭlgŏun 즐거운
Portuguese: alegre
Russian: vesyólyy весёлый
Spanish: alegre
Swedish: glad

388. cheese [n.]

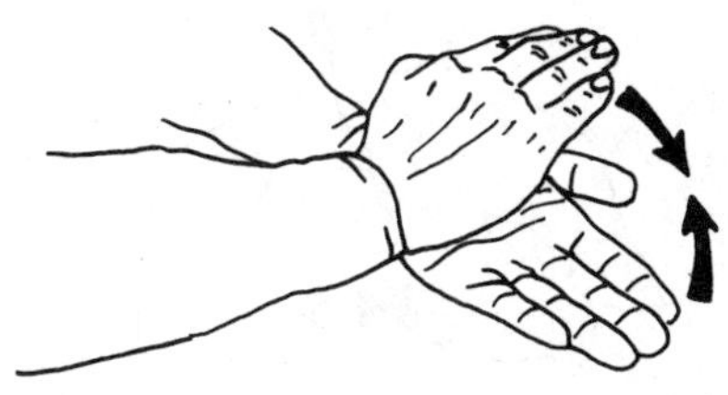

Arabic: júbna جبنة
Chinese: rŭlào 乳酪
Dutch: kaas
French: fromage
German: Käse
Italian: formaggio
Japanese: chiizu チーズ
Korean: ch'iju 치즈
Portuguese: queijo
Russian: syr сыр
Spanish: queso
Swedish: ost

389. cherry [n.]

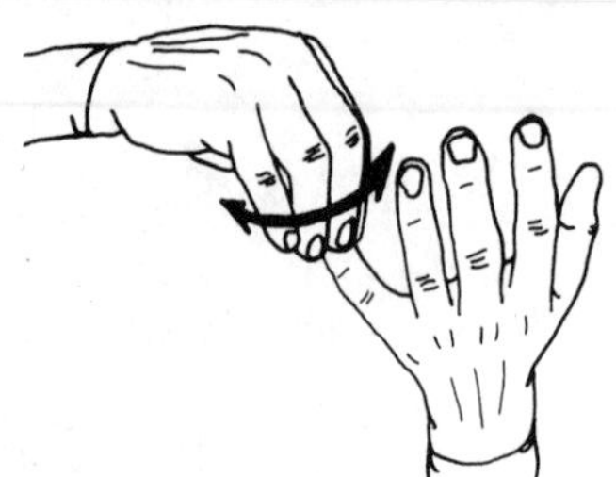

Arabic: káraz كرز
Chinese: yīngtáo 樱桃
Dutch: kers
French: cerise
German: Kirsche
Italian: ciliegia
Japanese: sakurambo さくらんぼ
Korean: bŏtchi 뻐찌
Portuguese: cereja
Russian: víshnya вишня
Spanish: cereza
Swedish: körsbär

390. chess [n.]

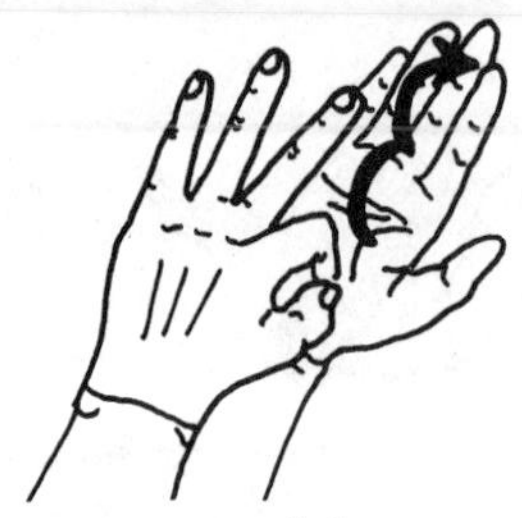

Arabic: shataránj شطرنج
Chinese: guójì xiàngqí 國際象棋
Dutch: schaakspel
French: échecs
German: Schach
Italian: scacchi
Japanese: chesu チェス
Korean: ch'esŭ 체스
Portuguese: xadrez
Russian: shákhmaty шахматы
Spanish: ajedrez
Swedish: schack

391. chest (anatomy) [n.]

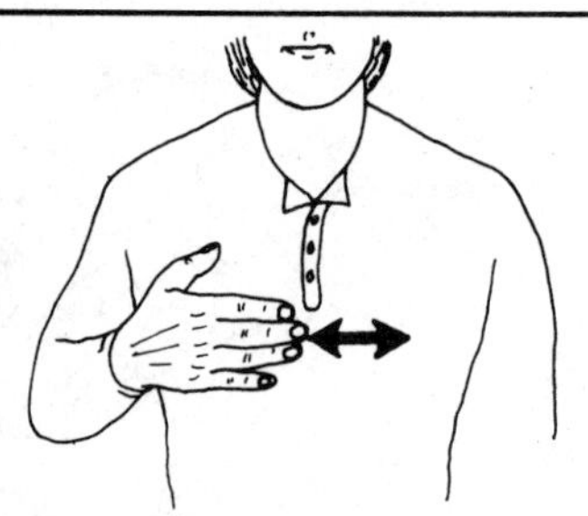

Arabic: sadr صدر
Chinese: xiōngbù 胸部
Dutch: borst
French: poitrine
German: Brust
Italian: petto
Japanese: mune 胸
Korean: gasŭm 가슴
Portuguese: peito
Russian: grudnáya klétka грудная клетка
Spanish: pecho
Swedish: brost

392. chew [v.]

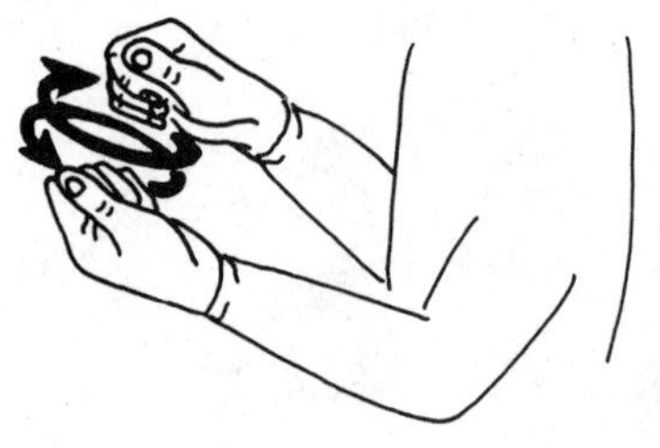

Arabic: mádagha مضغ
Chinese: jiáo 嚼
Dutch: kauwen
French: mâcher
German: kauen
Italian: masticare
Japanese: kamu かむ
Korean: ssipda 씹다
Portuguese: mastigar
Russian: zhevát' жевать
Spanish: masticar
Swedish: tugga

393. chicken [n.]

Arabic: dajáj دجاج
Chinese: jī 鷄
Dutch: lip
French: poulet
German: Huhn
Italian: pollo
Japanese: niwatori 鶏
Korean: tak 닭
Portuguese: frango
Russian: kúritsa курица
Spanish: pollo
Swedish: kyckling

394. chief [n.]

Arabic: ra'ís رئيس
Chinese: shǒulǐng 首領
Dutch: chef
French: chef
German: Leiter
Italian: capo
Japanese: kashira かしら
Korean: jang 장
Portuguese: chefe
Russian: rukovodítel' руководитель
Spanish: jefe
Swedish: chef

395. child [n.]

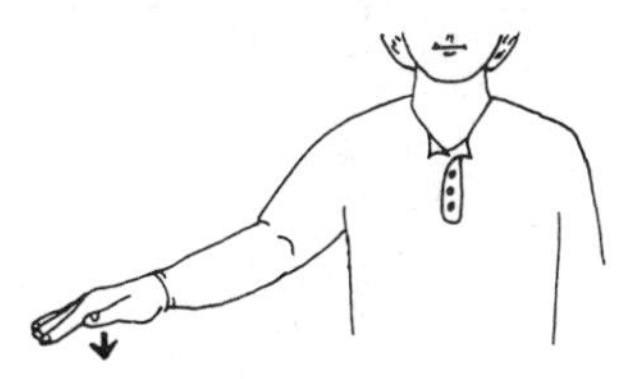

Arabic: tifl طفل
Chinese: háizi 孩子
Dutch: kind
French: enfant
German: Kind
Italian: bambino
Japanese: kodomo 子供
Korean: ai 아이
Portuguese: criança
Russian: dityá дитя
Spanish: niño
Swedish: barn

396. children [n.]

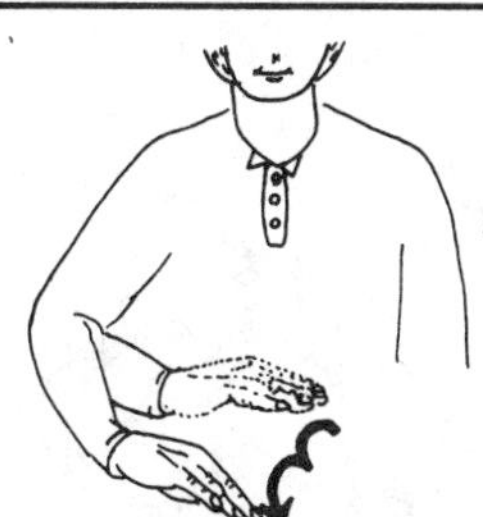

Arabic: atfáal اطفال
Chinese: háizimen 孩子们
Dutch: kinderen
French: enfants
German: Kinder
Italian: bambini
Japanese: kodomotachi 子供達
Korean: aidŭl 아이들
Portuguese: crianças
Russian: déti дети
Spanish: niños
Swedish: barn

397. Chile [n.]

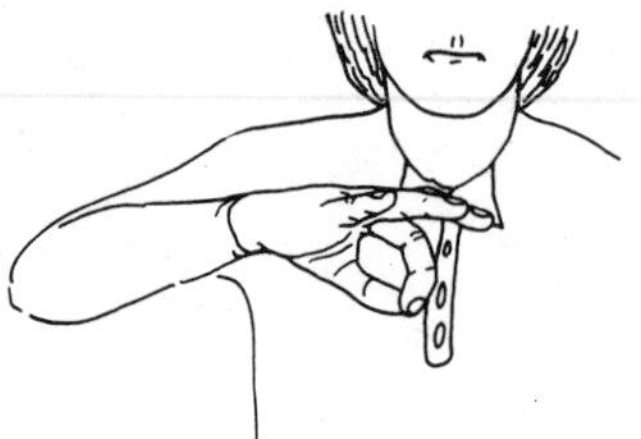

Arabic: chíli تشيلي
Chinese: zhìlì 智利
Dutch: Chile
French: Chili
German: Chile
Italian: Cile
Japanese: Chiri チリ
Korean: Chili 칠리
Portuguese: Chile
Russian: Chíli Чили
Spanish: Chile
Swedish: Chile

398. chilly [adj.]

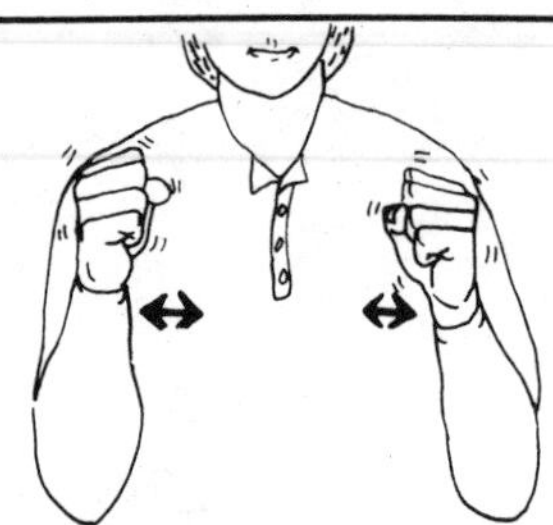

Arabic: báred بارد
Chinese: hánlěngde 寒冷的
Dutch: kil
French: froid
German: kühl
Italian: freddo
Japanese: hiebie suru 冷え冷えする
Korean: ch'agaun 차거운
Portuguese: friorento
Russian: zyábkiy зябкий
Spanish: fresco
Swedish: kylig

399. chimney [n.]

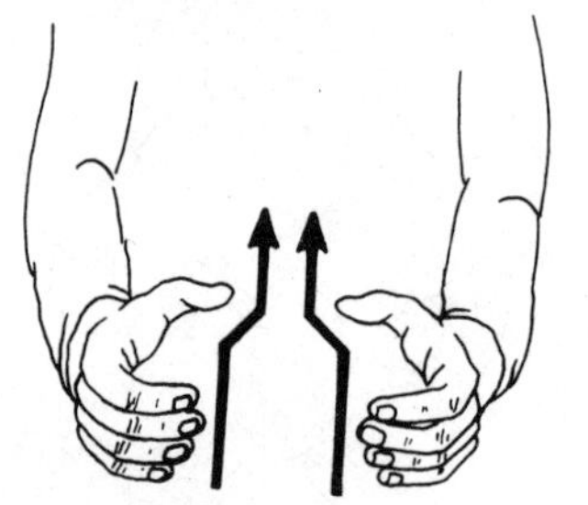

Arabic: mádkhana مدخنة
Chinese: yāncōng 煙囪
Dutch: schoorsteen
French: cheminée
German: Schornstein
Italian: camino
Japanese: entotsu 煙突
Korean: gulttuk 굴뚝
Portuguese: chaminé
Russian: dymováya trubá дымовая труба
Spanish: chimenea
Swedish: skorsten

400. chin [n.]

Arabic: dhaqn ذقن
Chinese: xiàbā 下巴
Dutch: kin
French: menton
German: Kinn
Italian: mento
Japanese: ago 顎(あご)
Korean: t'ŏk 턱
Portuguese: queixo
Russian: podboródok подбородок
Spanish: barbilla
Swedish: haka

401. China [n.]

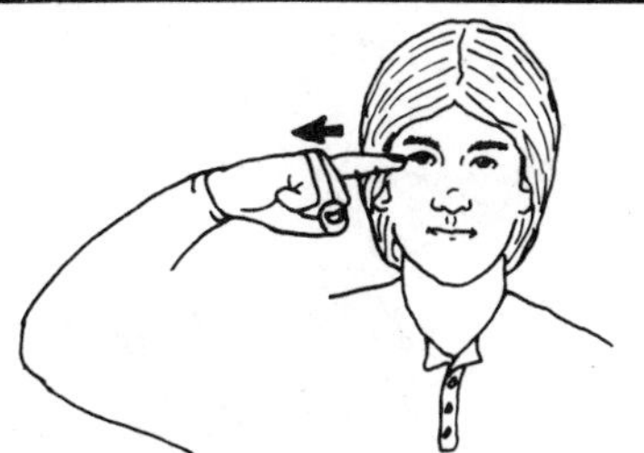

Arabic: as-sín الصين
Chinese: zhōngguó 中國
Dutch: China
French: Chine
German: China
Italian: Cina
Japanese: Chūgoku 中国
Korean: Chungguk 중국
Portuguese: China
Russian: Kitáy Китай
Spanish: China
Swedish: Kina

402. chocolate [n.]

Arabic: shokoláta شيكولاتا
Chinese: qiǎokèlì 巧克力
Dutch: chocolade
French: chocolat
German: Schokolade
Italian: cioccolata
Japanese: chokorēto チョコレート
Korean: chokolaet 초콜렛
Portuguese: chocolate
Russian: shokolád шоколад
Spanish: chocolate
Swedish: choklad

403. choice [n.]

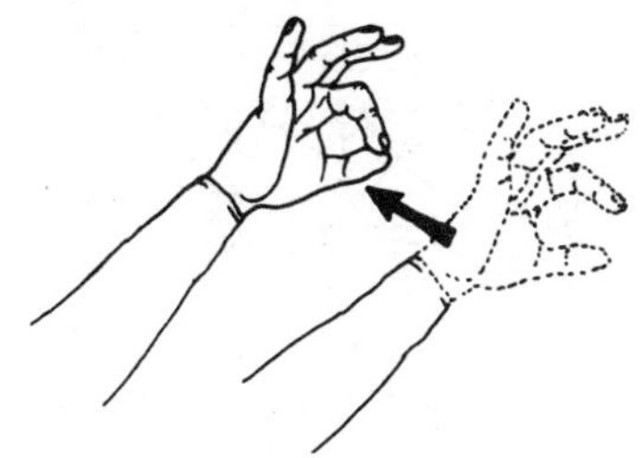

Arabic: ikhtiár اختيار
Chinese: xuǎnzé 選擇
Dutch: keus
French: choix
German: Wahl
Italian: scelta
Japanese: sentaku 選択
Korean: sŏnt'aek 선택
Portuguese: escolha
Russian: výbor выбор
Spanish: selección
Swedish: val

404. choke [v.]

Arabic: khánaqa خنق
Chinese: zhìxí 窒息
Dutch: stikken
French: étouffer
German: ersticken
Italian: soffocare
Japanese: chissoku saseru 窒息させる
Korean: chilshikshik'ida 질식시키다
Portuguese: sufocar
Russian: dushít' душить
Spanish: ahogar
Swedish: strypa

405. choose [v.]

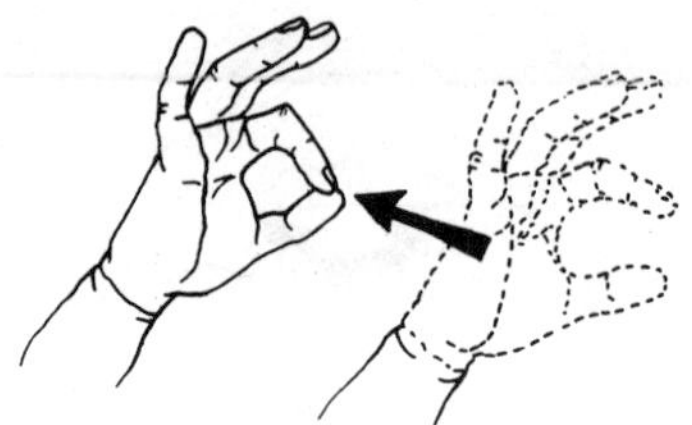

Arabic: ikhtára اختار
Chinese: xuǎnzé 選擇
Dutch: kiezen
French: choisir
German: wählen
Italian: scegliere
Japanese: erabu 選ぶ
Korean: korŭda 고르다
Portuguese: escolher
Russian: vybirát' выбирать
Spanish: escoger
Swedish: välja

406. christian [n.]

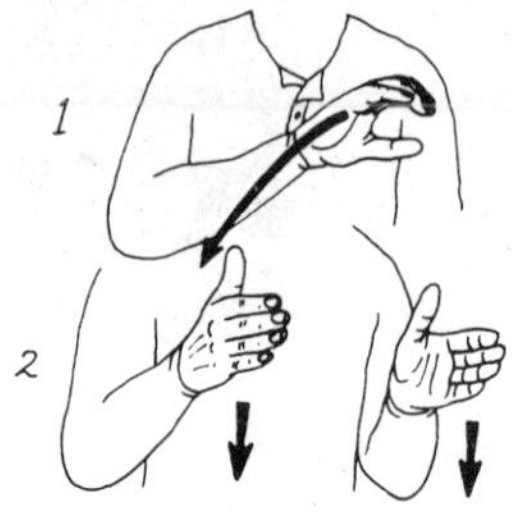

Arabic: masíhi مسيحي
Chinese: jīdū jiàotú 基督教徒
Dutch: christen
French: chrétien
German: Christ
Italian: cristiano
Japanese: kirisutokyōto キリスト教徒
Korean: kŭrischian 크리스챤
Portuguese: cristão
Russian: khristianín христианин
Spanish: cristiano
Swedish: kristen

407. Christmas [n.]

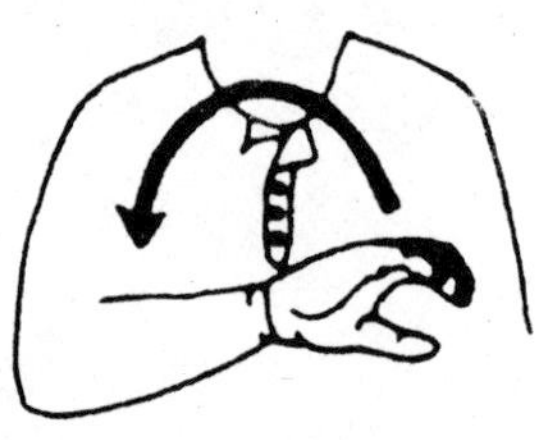

Arabic: eíd al-milád عيد الميلاد
Chinese: shèngdànjié 聖誕節
Dutch: Kerstmis
French: Noël
German: Weihnachten
Italian: Natale
Japanese: Kurisumasu クリスマス
Korean: K'ŭrisŭmasŭ 크리스마스
Portuguese: Natal
Russian: Rozhdestvó Рождество
Spanish: Navidad
Swedish: Jul

408. church [n.]

Arabic: kanísa كنيسة
Chinese: jiàohuì 教會
Dutch: kerk
French: église
German: Kirche
Italian: chiesa
Japanese: kyōkai 教会
Korean: kyohoe 교회
Portuguese: igreja
Russian: tsérkov' церковь
Spanish: iglesia
Swedish: kyrka

409. cigarette [n.]

Arabic: sajáyir سجاير
Chinese: xiāngyān 香烟
Dutch: sigaret
French: cigarette
German: Zigarette
Italian: sigaretta
Japanese: tabako タバコ
Korean: dambae 담배
Portuguese: cigarro
Russian: sigaréta сигарета
Spanish: cigarrillo
Swedish: cigarrett

410. circle [n.]

Arabic: dá'ira دائرة
Chinese: yuánquān 圓圈
Dutch: cirkel
French: cercle
German: Kreis
Italian: circolo
Japanese: en 円
Korean: wŏn 원
Portuguese: círculo
Russian: krug круг
Spanish: círculo
Swedish: cirkel

411. circus [n.]

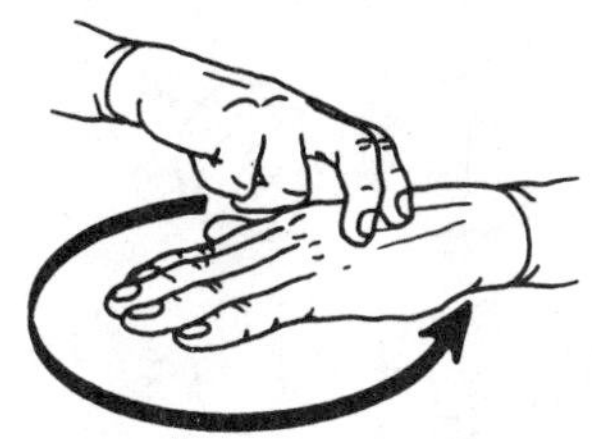

Arabic: serk سيرك
Chinese: mǎxìtuán 馬戲團
Dutch: circus
French: cirque
German: Zirkus
Italian: circo
Japanese: sākasu サーカス
Korean: ssŏk'ŏsŭ 써커스
Portuguese: circo
Russian: tsirk цирк
Spanish: circo
Swedish: cirkus

412. citizen [n.]

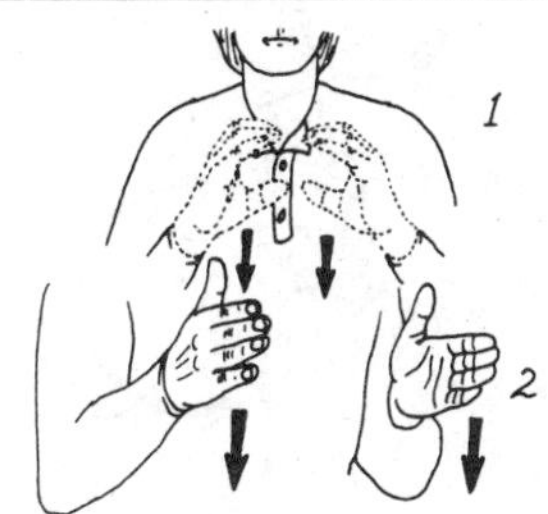

Arabic: muwáaten مواطن
Chinese: gōngmín 公民
Dutch: burger
French: citoyen
German: Bürger
Italian: cittadino
Japanese: kokumin 市民
Korean: shimin 시민
Portuguese: cidadão
Russian: grazhdanín гражданин
Spanish: ciudadano
Swedish: borgare

413. city [n.]

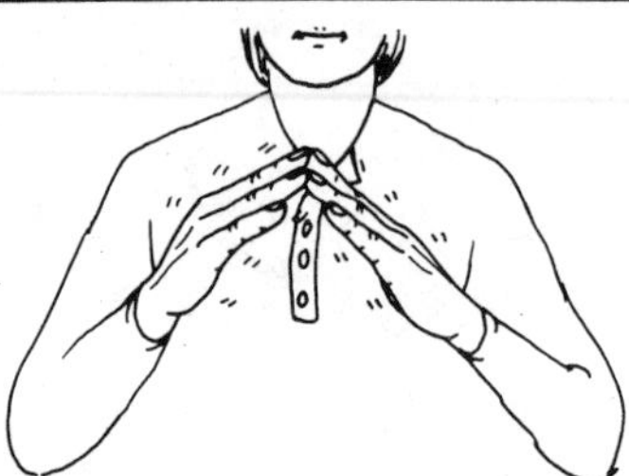

Arabic: madína مدينة
Chinese: chéngshì 城市
Dutch: stad
French: ville
German: Stadt
Italian: città
Japanese: shi 市
Korean: doshi 도시
Portuguese: cidade
Russian: górod город
Spanish: ciudad
Swedish: stad

414. civic/civil [adj.]

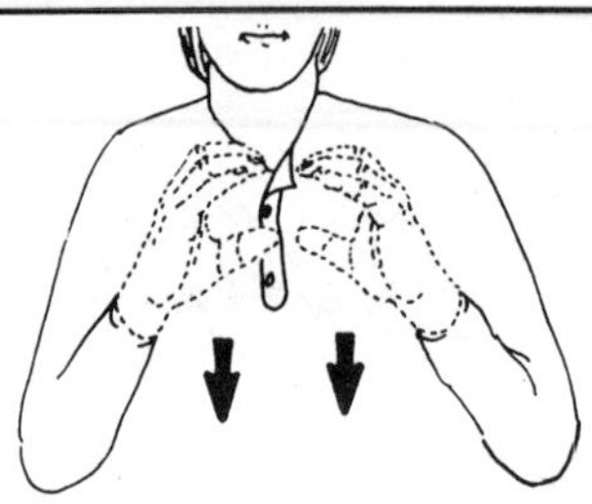

Arabic: mádani مدني
Chinese: chéngshìde 城市的
Dutch: burgerlijk
French: civil
German: zivil
Italian: civile
Japanese: shimin no 市民の
Korean: minkanui 민간의
Portuguese: civil
Russian: grazhdánskiy гражданский
Spanish: civil
Swedish: medborgerlig

415. class (sort) [n.]

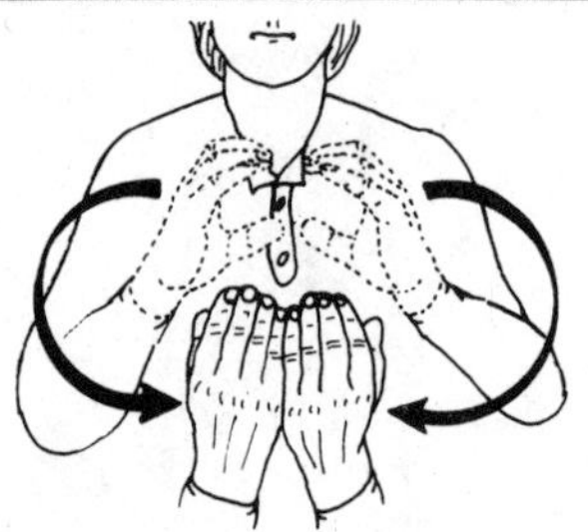

Arabic: tábaqa طبقة
Chinese: děngjí 等級
Dutch: klas
French: classe
German: Klasse
Italian: classe
Japanese: shurui 種類
Korean: jongnyu 종류
Portuguese: classe
Russian: klass класс
Spanish: clase
Swedish: klass

416. classroom [n.]

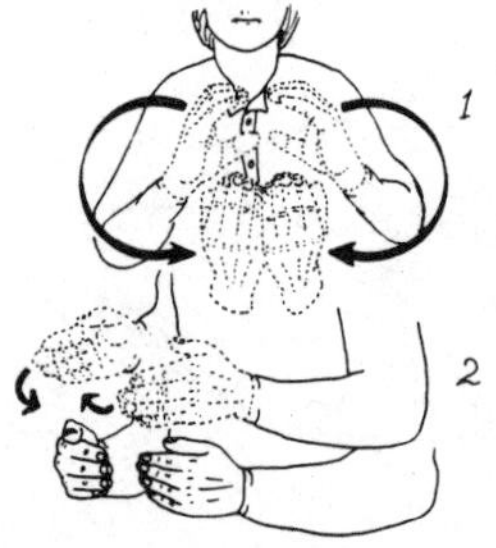

Arabic: ghórfat at-tadrís غرفة التدريس
Chinese: jiàoshì 教室
Dutch: klas
French: salle de classe
German: Klassenzimmer
Italian: aula
Japanese: kyōshitsu 教室
Korean: kyoshil 교실
Portuguese: sala de aula
Russian: klass класс
Spanish: aula
Swedish: klassrum

417. clean [adj.]

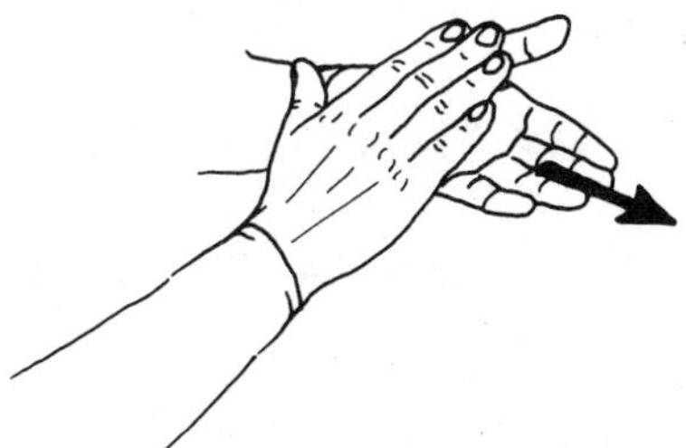

Arabic: nadhíf نظيف
Chinese: gānjìngde 乾淨的
Dutch: schoon
French: propre
German: sauber
Italian: pulito
Japanese: kirei na 綺麗な
Korean: kkaekkŭt'han 깨끗한
Portuguese: limpo
Russian: chístyy чистый
Spanish: limpio
Swedish: ren

418. clear [adj.]

Arabic: wádeh واضح
Chinese: qīngchǔde 清楚的
Dutch: helder
French: clair
German: klar
Italian: chiaro
Japanese: sunda 澄んだ
Korean: malgŭn 맑은
Portuguese: claro
Russian: yásnyy ясный
Spanish: claro
Swedish: klar

419. clever [adj.]

Arabic: fatn فطن
Chinese: cōngmíngde 聰明的
Dutch: handig
French: habile
German: klug
Italian: abile
Japanese: kashikoi 賢い
Korean: yŏngnihan 영리한
Portuguese: esperto
Russian: úmnyy умный
Spanish: inteligente
Swedish: skicklig

420. climb [v.]

Arabic: sáada صعد
Chinese: pá 爬
Dutch: klimmen
French: grimper
German: klettern
Italian: arrampicarsi
Japanese: noboru 登る
Korean: orŭda 오르다
Portuguese: trepar
Russian: podnimát'sya подниматься
Spanish: trepar
Swedish: klättra

421. clock [n.]

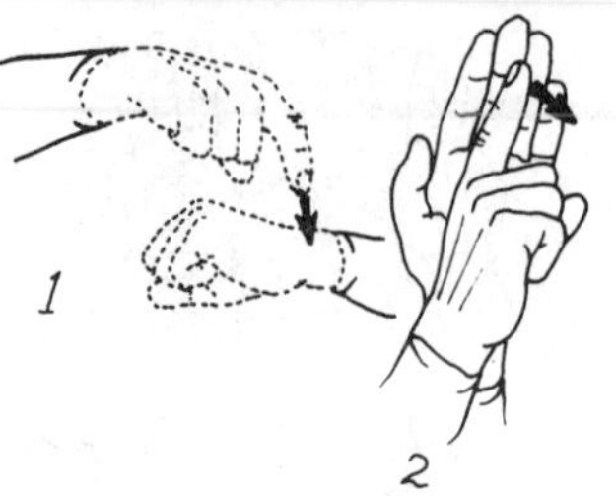

Arabic: séaa ساعة
Chinese: zhōng 鐘
Dutch: klok
French: pendule
German: Uhr
Italian: orologio
Japanese: tokei 時計
Korean: shikye 시계
Portuguese: relógio
Russian: chasý часы
Spanish: reloj
Swedish: ur

422. close [v.]

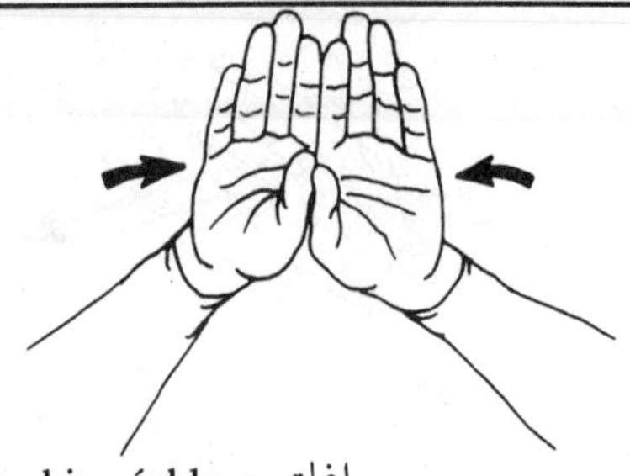

Arabic: ághlaqa اغلق
Chinese: guān 關
Dutch: sluiten
French: fermer
German: schließen
Italian: chiudere
Japanese: . . . o tojiru …を閉じる
Korean: datnŭnda 닫는다
Portuguese: fechar
Russian: zakryvát' закрывать
Spanish: cerrar
Swedish: sluta

423. cloth [n.]

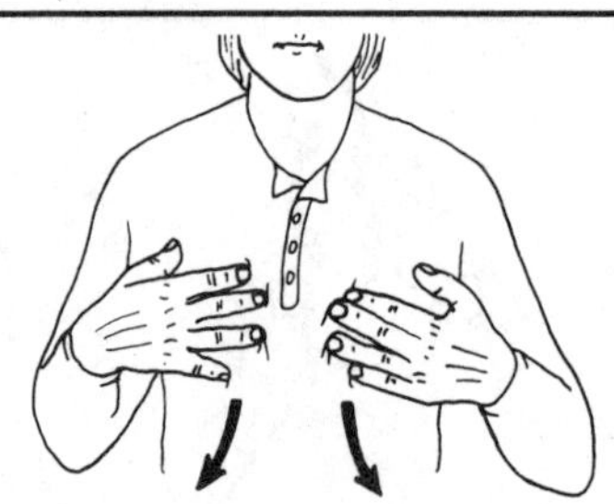

Arabic: qemásh قماش
Chinese: bù 布
Dutch: doek
French: tissu
German: Tuch
Italian: stoffa
Japanese: nuno 布
Korean: ch'ŏn 천
Portuguese: pano
Russian: suknó сукно
Spanish: paño
Swedish: tyg

424. clothes [n.]

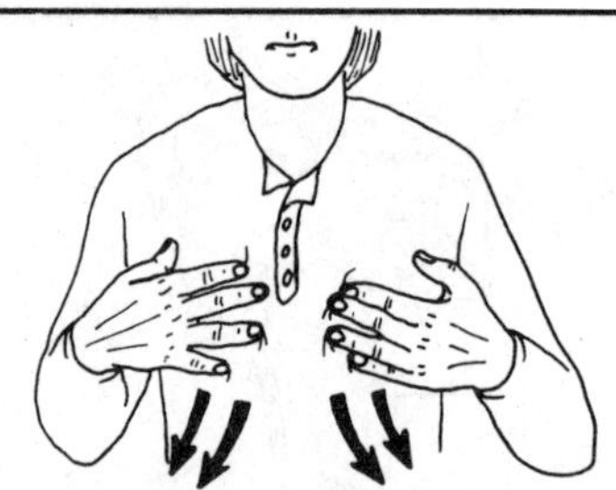

Arabic: malábis ملابس
Chinese: yīfú 衣服
Dutch: kleren
French: vêtements
German: Kleidung
Italian: vestiti
Japanese: irui 衣類
Korean: ot 옷
Portuguese: roupas
Russian: odézhda одежда
Spanish: ropa
Swedish: kläder

425. cloud [n.]

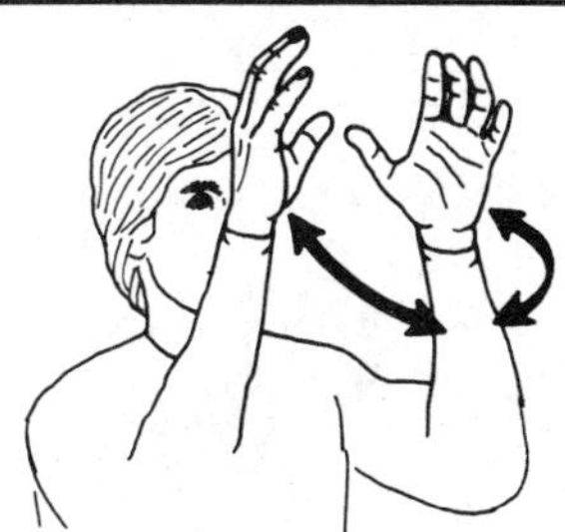

Arabic: sahâb سحاب
Chinese: yún 雲
Dutch: wolk
French: nuage
German: Wolke
Italian: nuvola
Japanese: kumo 雲
Korean: kurŭm 구름
Portuguese: nuvem
Russian: óblako облако
Spanish: nube
Swedish: moln

426. club (group) [n.]

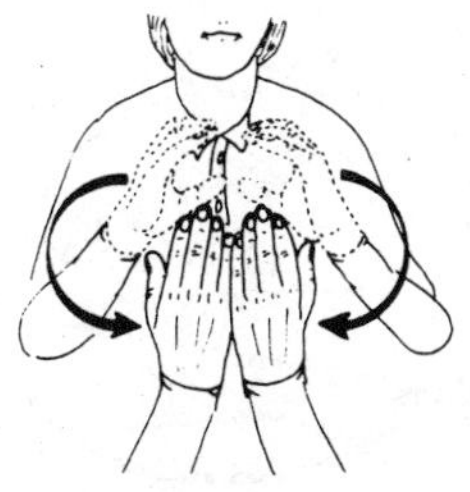

Arabic: nádi نادي
Chinese: jùlèbù 俱樂部
Dutch: club
French: club
German: Klub
Italian: circolo
Japanese: kurabu クラブ
Korean: k'ŭllŏp 클럽
Portuguese: clube
Russian: klub клуб
Spanish: club
Swedish: klubb

427. clumsy (awkward) [adj.]

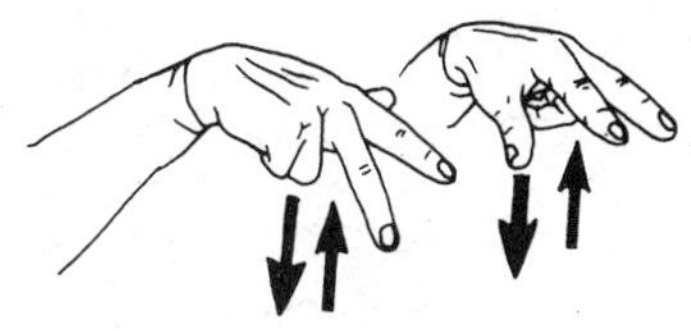

Arabic: ákhraq اخرق
Chinese: bènzhuóde 笨拙的
Dutch: onhandig
French: maladroit
German: ungeschickt
Italian: goffo
Japanese: bukiyō na 無器用な
Korean: sŏt'urŭn 서투른
Portuguese: desajeitado
Russian: neuklyúzhiy неуклюжий
Spanish: torpe
Swedish: klumpig

428. coal [n.]

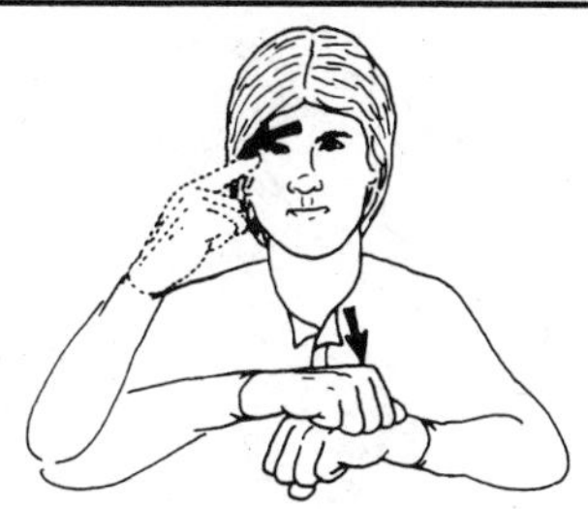

Arabic: fáhem فحم
Chinese: méi 煤
Dutch: kool
French: charbon
German: Kohle
Italian: carbone
Japanese: sekitan 石炭
Korean: sŏkt'an 석탄
Portuguese: carvão
Russian: úgol' уголь
Spanish: carbón
Swedish: kol

429. coast [n.]

Arabic: sáhel ساحل
Chinese: hǎi-àn 海岸
Dutch: kust
French: côte
German: Küste
Italian: costa
Japanese: kaigan 海岸
Korean: haebyŏn 해변
Portuguese: costa
Russian: poberézh'ye побережье
Spanish: costa
Swedish: kust

430. coat (clothing) [n.]

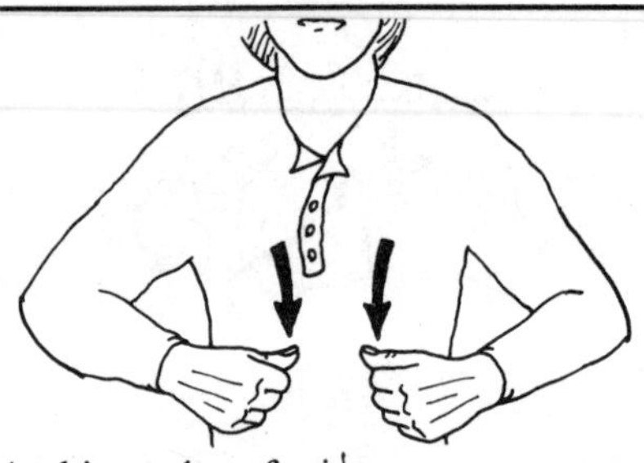

Arabic: méaatof معطف
Chinese: wàiyī 外衣
Dutch: jas
French: manteau
German: Mantel
Italian: cappotto
Japanese: kōto コート
Korean: chŏgori 저고리
Portuguese: casaco
Russian: pal'tó пальто
Spanish: abrigo
Swedish: rock

431. coffee [n.]

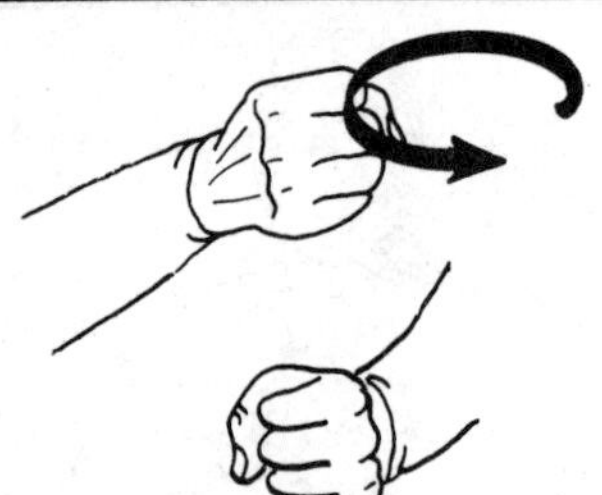

Arabic: qáhwa قهوة
Chinese: kāfēi 咖啡
Dutch: koffie
French: café
German: Kaffee
Italian: caffè
Japanese: kōhii コーヒー
Korean: k'op'i 커피
Portuguese: café
Russian: kófe кофе
Spanish: café
Swedish: kaffe

432. coin [n.]

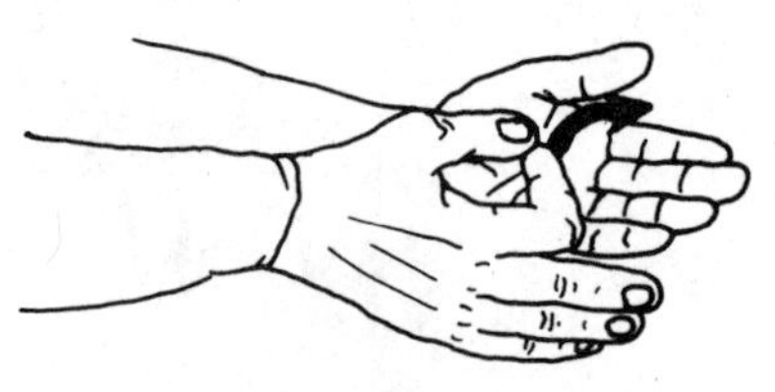

Arabic: qétaa núqdia maadanía
قطعة نقدية معدنية
Chinese: tóngbǎn 銅板
Dutch: munt
French: pièce de monnaie
German: Münze
Italian: moneta
Japanese: kōka 硬貨
Korean: don 돈
Portuguese: moeda
Russian: monéta монета
Spanish: moneda
Swedish: mynt

433. coincide [v.]

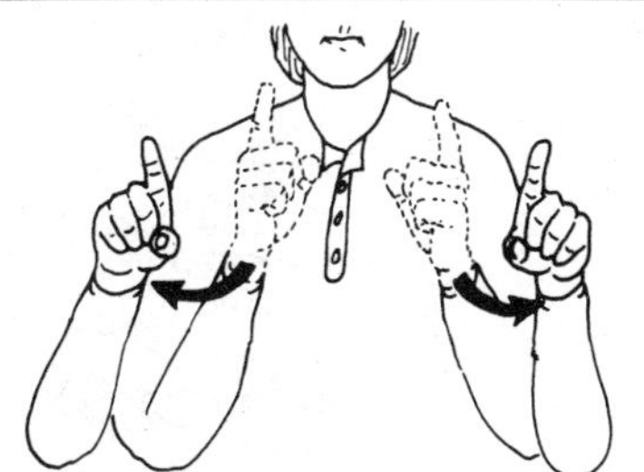

Arabic: tazámmana تزامن
Chinese: fúhé 符合
Dutch: samenvallen
French: coïncider
German: zusammentreffen
Italian: coincidere
Japanese: icchi suru 一致する
Korean: ilchihada 일치하다
Portuguese: coincidir
Russian: sovpadát' совпадать
Spanish: coincidir
Swedish: sammanfalla

434. cold [adj.]

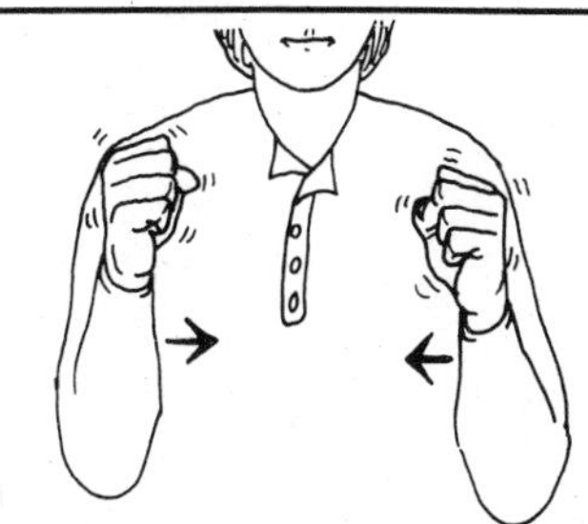

Arabic: bárid بارد
Chinese: lěng 冷
Dutch: koud
French: froid
German: kalt
Italian: freddo
Japanese: tsumetai 冷めたい
Korean: ch'uun 추운
Portuguese: frio
Russian: kholódnyy холодный
Spanish: frío
Swedish: kall

435. collapse [v.]

Arabic: inhára انهار
Chinese: bēngkuì 崩潰
Dutch: instorten
French: s'effondrer
German: zusammenbrechen
Italian: crollare
Japanese: hōkai suru 崩壊する
Korean: munŏjida 무너지다
Portuguese: desmoronar-se
Russian: rúshit'sya рушиться
Spanish: desplomarse
Swedish: kollapsa

436. collar [n.]

Arabic: qábba/yáaqa قبة / ياقة
Chinese: lǐngzi 領子
Dutch: kraag
French: col
German: Kragen
Italian: colletto
Japanese: eri えり
Korean: k'alla 칼라
Portuguese: colarinho
Russian: vorotník воротник
Spanish: collar
Swedish: krage

437. collect (gather) [v.]

Arabic: jámaa جمع
Chinese: shōují 收集
Dutch: verzamelen
French: recueillir
German: sammeln
Italian: raccogliere
Japanese: . . . o atsumeru を集める
Korean: sujip'ada 수집하다
Portuguese: coletar
Russian: sobirát' собирать
Spanish: recoger
Swedish: samla

438. college [n.]

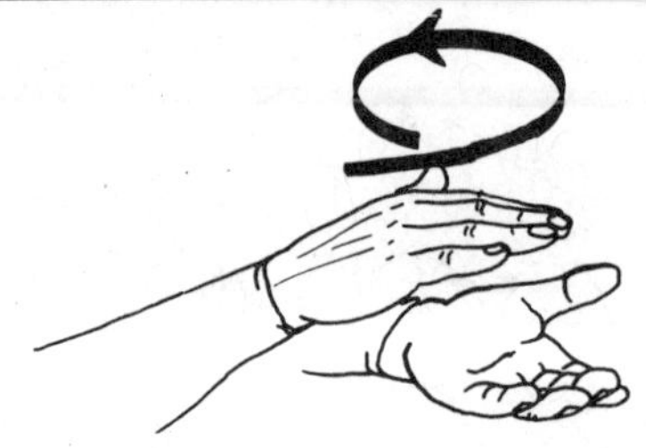

Arabic: kullíya كلية
Chinese: dàxué 大學
Dutch: college
French: université
German: Hochschule
Italian: collegio
Japanese: daigaku 大学
Korean: daehak 대학
Portuguese: colégio
Russian: kollédzh колледж
Spanish: universidad
Swedish: college

439. collide [v.]

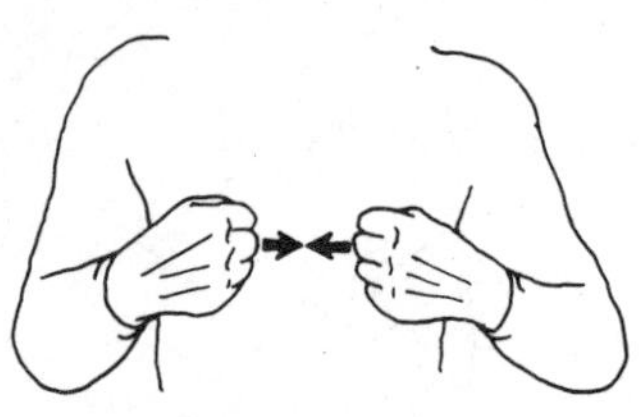

Arabic: tasáadama تصادم
Chinese: pèngzhuàng 碰撞
Dutch: botsen
French: entrer en collision
German: zusammenstoßen
Italian: scontrarsi
Japanese: shōtotsu suru 衝突する
Korean: budich'ida 부딪히다
Portuguese: chocar
Russian: stálkivat'sya сталкиваться
Spanish: chocar
Swedish: kollidera

440. color [n.]

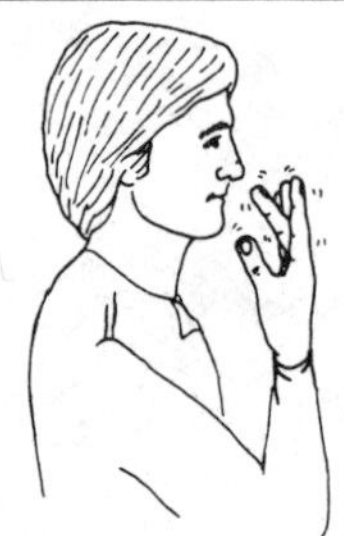

Arabic: laun لون
Chinese: yánsè 顏色
Dutch: kleur
French: couleur
German: Farbe
Italian: colore
Japanese: iro 色
Korean: saek 색
Portuguese: côr
Russian: tsvet цвет
Spanish: color
Swedish: färg

441. comb [n.]

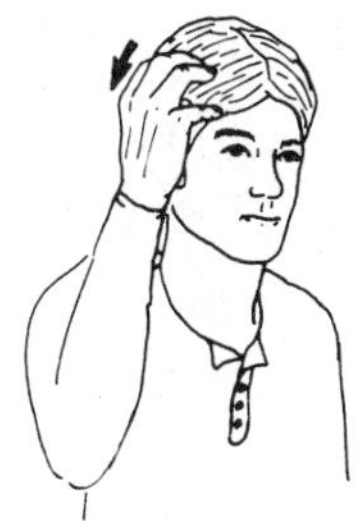

Arabic: misht مشط
Chinese: shūzi 梳子
Dutch: kam
French: peigne
German: Kamm
Italian: pettine
Japanese: kushi 櫛
Korean: bit 빗
Portuguese: pente
Russian: grebyónka гребёнка
Spanish: peine
Swedish: kamm

442. combat [n.]

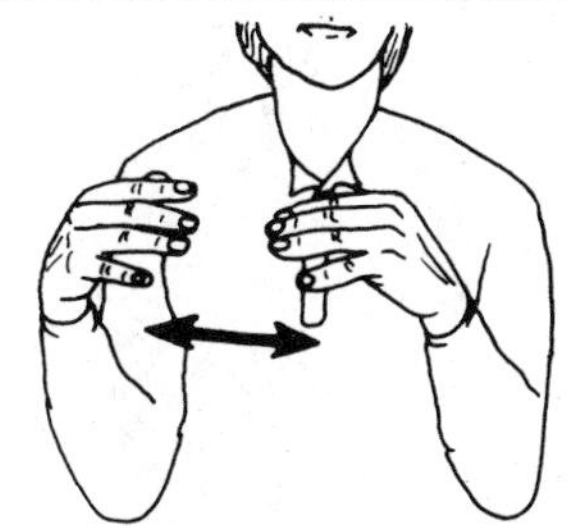

Arabic: qetál قتال
Chinese: zhàndòu 戰鬥
Dutch: gevecht
French: combat
German: Kampf
Italian: combattimento
Japanese: sentō 戦闘
Korean: ssaum 싸움
Portuguese: combate
Russian: boy бой
Spanish: combate
Swedish: kamp

443. combine [v.]

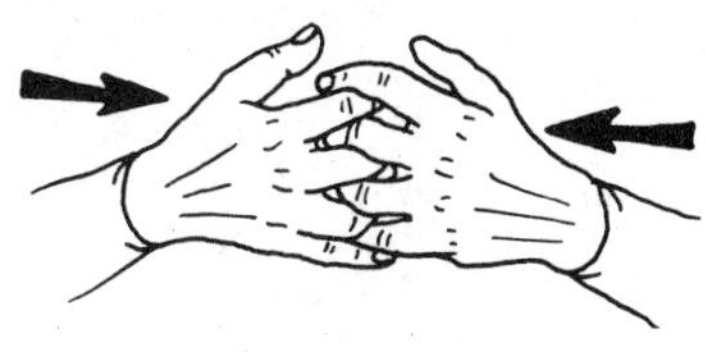

Arabic: jámaa جمع
Chinese: hùnhé 混合
Dutch: combineren
French: combiner
German: kombinieren
Italian: combinare
Japanese: kumiawaseru 組み合わせる
Korean: habxh'ida 합치다
Portuguese: combinar
Russian: sochetát' сочетать
Spanish: combinar
Swedish: kombinera

444. come [v.]

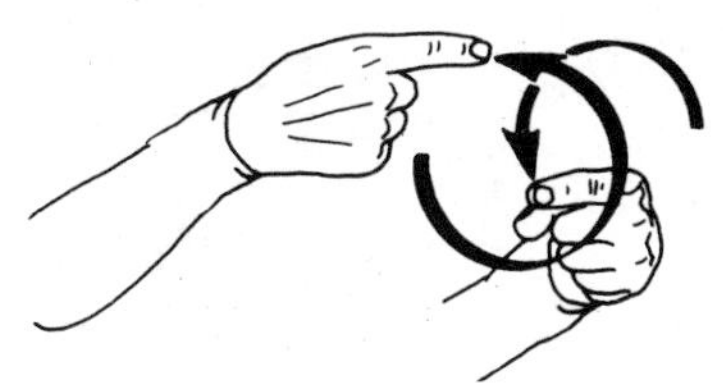

Arabic: já'a جاء
Chinese: lái 來
Dutch: komen
French: venir
German: kommen
Italian: venire
Japanese: kuru 来る
Korean: oda 오다
Portuguese: vir
Russian: prikhodít' приходить
Spanish: venir
Swedish: komma

445. comfort [n.]

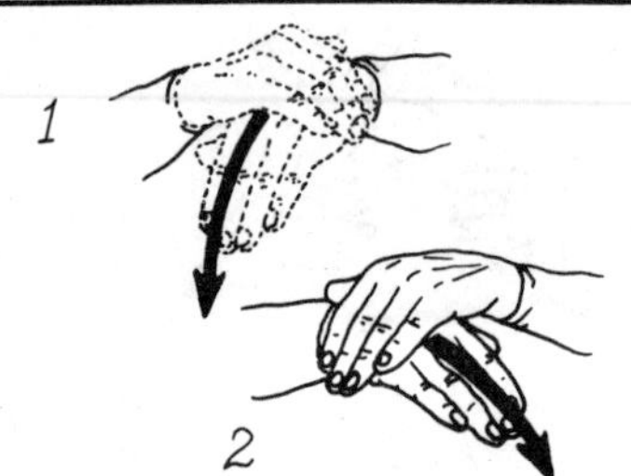

Arabic: ráha راحة
Chinese: shūshì 舒适
Dutch: komfort
French: confort
German: Komfort
Italian: comodità
Japanese: nagusame 慰め
Korean: p'yŏnan 편안
Portuguese: comodidade
Russian: komfórt комфорт
Spanish: comodidad
Swedish: komfort

446. command (order) [n.]

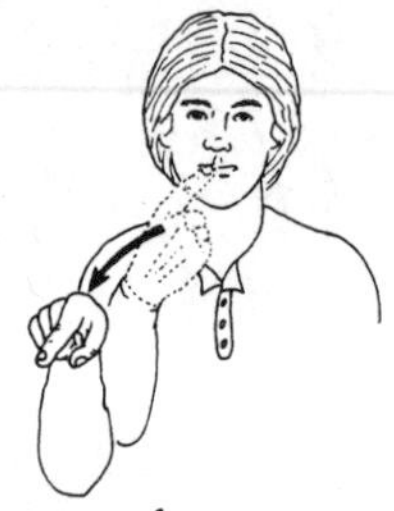

Arabic: amr أمر
Chinese: mìnglìng 命令
Dutch: bevel
French: ordre
German: Befehl
Italian: ordine
Japanese: meirei 命令
Korean: myŏngnyŏng 명령
Portuguese: ordem
Russian: kománda команда
Spanish: orden
Swedish: befallning

447. commend [v.]

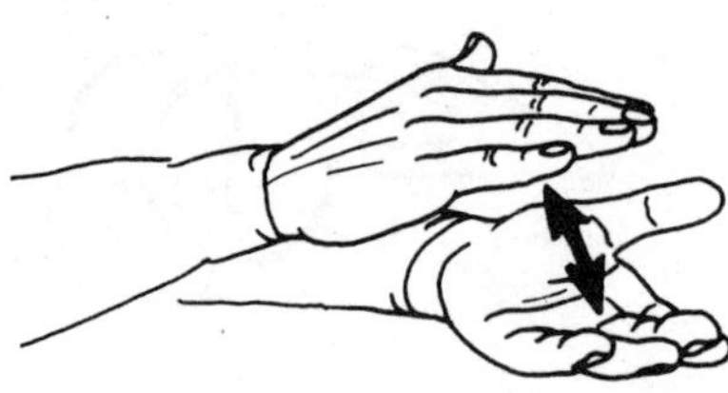

Arabic: áussa/mádaha اوصى / مدح
Chinese: tuījiàn 推薦
Dutch: aanbevelen
French: louer
German: belobigen
Italian: lodare
Japanese: suisho suru 推奨する
Korean: ch'uch'ŏnhada 추천하다
Portuguese: elogiar
Russian: khvalít' хвалить
Spanish: encomendar
Swedish: anförtro

448. committee [n.]

Arabic: lájna لجنة
Chinese: wĕiyuánhuì 委員會
Dutch: commissie
French: comité
German: Kommitee
Italian: comitato
Japanese: iinkai 委員会
Korean: wiwŏnhoe 위원회
Portuguese: comitê
Russian: komitét комитет
Spanish: comité
Swedish: kommitté

449. common (joint/universal) [adj.]

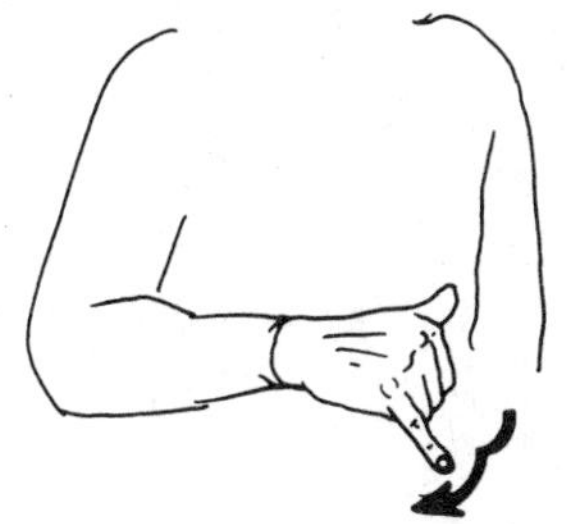

Arabic: aam عام
Chinese: gòngtóngde 共同的
Dutch: algemeen
French: commun
German: allgemein
Italian: comune
Japanese: kyōtsū no 共通の
Korean: kongdongŭi 공동의
Portuguese: comum
Russian: óbshchiy общий
Spanish: común
Swedish: allmän

450. communication (correspondence) [n.]

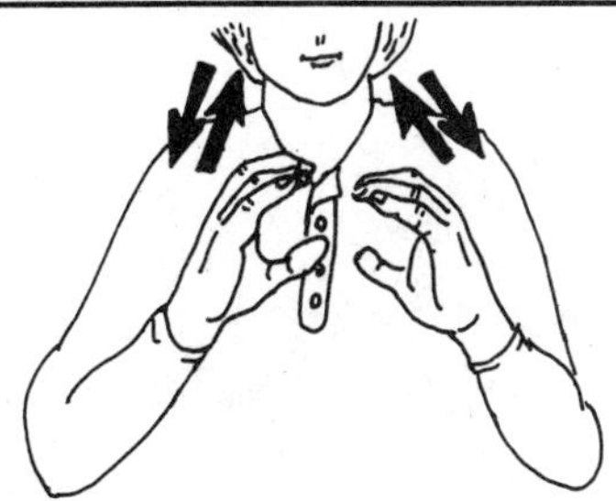

Arabic: murasalát مراسلات
Chinese: tōngxùn 通訊
Dutch: mededeling
French: communication
German: Mitteilung
Italian: comunicazione
Japanese: tsūshin 通信
Korean: t'ongshin 통신
Portuguese: comunicação
Russian: soobshchéniye сообщение
Spanish: comunicación
Swedish: meddelande

451. communism [n.]

Arabic: shiyuaíya شيوعية
Chinese: gòngchăn zhŭyì 共產主義
Dutch: communisme
French: communisme
German: Kommunismus
Italian: comunismo
Japanese: kyōsanshugi 共産主義
Korean: kongsanjuui 공산주의
Portuguese: comunismo
Russian: kommunízm коммунизм
Spanish: comunismo
Swedish: kommunism

452. community [n.]

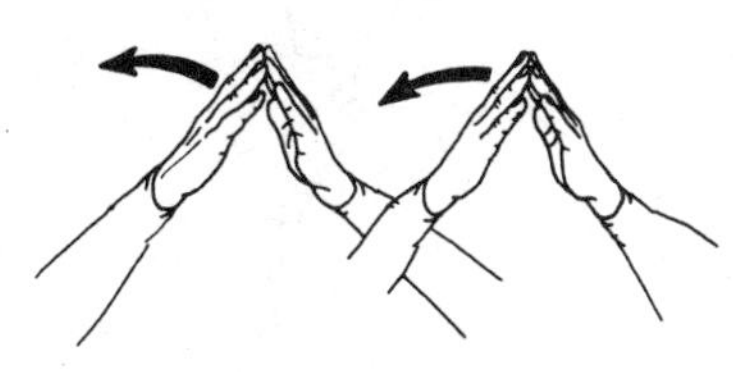

Arabic: jália جالية
Chinese: shèqū 社區
Dutch: gemeenschap
French: communauté
German: Gemeinschaft
Italian: comunità
Japanese: kyōdō seikatsutai 共同生活体
Korean: danch'e 단체
Portuguese: comunidade
Russian: obshchína община
Spanish: comunidad
Swedish: gemenskap

453. company (business) [n.]

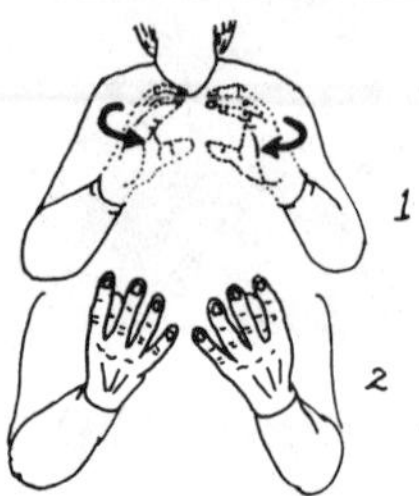

Arabic: shárika شركة
Chinese: gōngsī 公司
Dutch: gezelschap
French: compagnie
German: Firma
Italian: compagnia
Japanese: kaisha 会社
Korean: hoesa 회사
Portuguese: companhia
Russian: fírma фирма
Spanish: compañía
Swedish: sällskap

454. compare [v.]

Arabic: qárana قارن
Chinese: bǐjiào 比較
Dutch: vergelijken
French: comparer
German: vergleichen
Italian: confrontare
Japanese: hikaku suru を比較する
Korean: bikyohada 비교하다
Portuguese: comparar
Russian: srávnivat' сравнивать
Spanish: comparar
Swedish: jämföra

455. compel [v.]

Arabic: álzama الزم
Chinese: qiángpò 強迫
Dutch: dwingen
French: contraindre
German: zwingen
Italian: costringere
Japanese: kyōyō suru 強要する
Korean: kangyohada 강요하다
Portuguese: compelir
Russian: zastavlyát' заставлять
Spanish: compeler
Swedish: framtvinga

456. compete [v.]

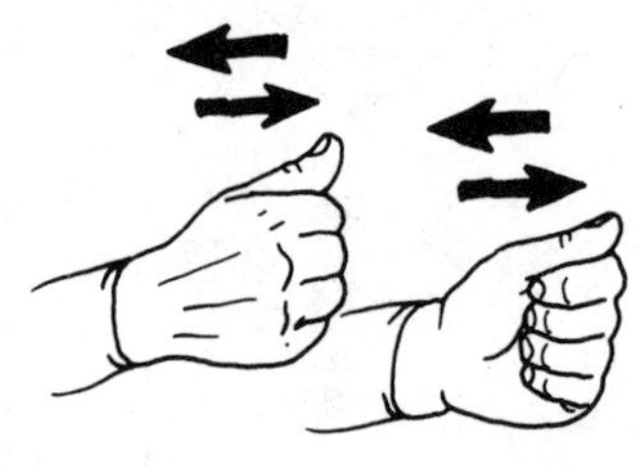

Arabic: náfasa نافس
Chinese: jìngzhēng 競爭
Dutch: mededingen
French: rivaliser
German: konkurrieren
Italian: competere
Japanese: kyōsō suru 競争する
Korean: kyŏngjaenghada 경쟁하다
Portuguese: competir
Russian: konkurírovat' конкурировать
Spanish: competir
Swedish: tävla

457. competent [adj.]

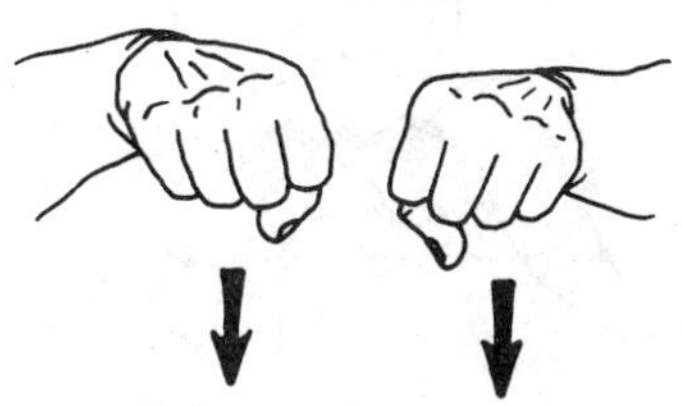

Arabic: káafi كاف
Chinese: shēngrènde 勝任的
Dutch: bevoegd
French: compétent
German: kompetent
Italian: competente
Japanese: nōryoku no aru 能力のある
Korean: nŭngnyŏkitnŭn 능력있는
Portuguese: competente
Russian: kompeténtnyy компетентный
Spanish: competente
Swedish: kompetent

458. complain [v.]

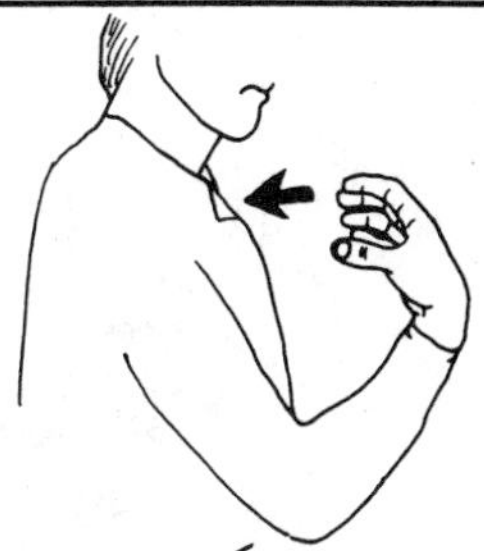

Arabic: shakáa شكى
Chinese: bàoyuàn 抱怨
Dutch: klagen
French: se plaindre
German: sich beklagen
Italian: lagnarsi
Japanese: fuhei o iu 不平を言う
Korean: bulp'yŏnghada 불평하다
Portuguese: reclamar
Russian: zhálovat'sya жаловаться
Spanish: quejarse
Swedish: beklaga sig

459. complete [v.]

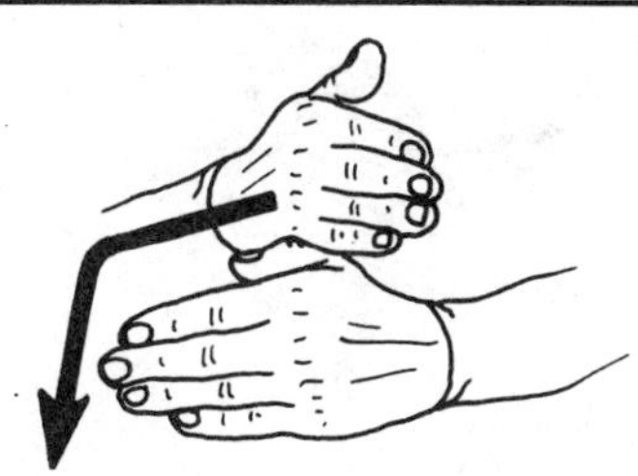

Arabic: ákmala اكمل
Chinese: wánzhěngde 完整的
Dutch: voltooien
French: compléter
German: vollenden
Italian: completare
Japanese: kansei suru 完成する
Korean: wansŏngshikida 완성하다
Portuguese: completar
Russian: zakánchivat' заканчивать
Spanish: completar
Swedish: komplettera

460. complicate [v.]

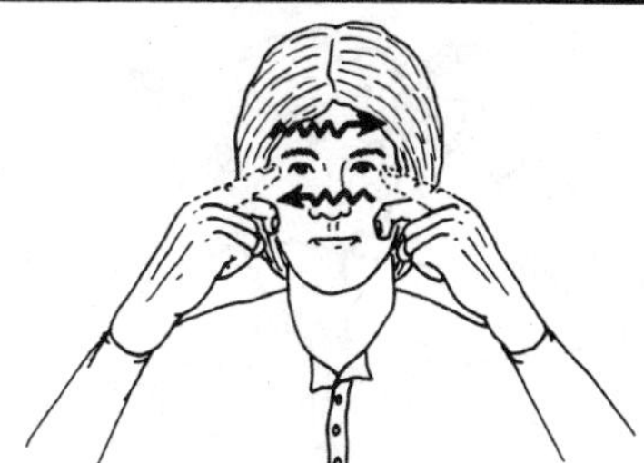

Arabic: aáqada عقد
Chinese: fùzá...shǐ 使 … 複雜
Dutch: ingewikkeld maken
French: compliquer
German: komplizieren
Italian: complicare
Japanese: fukuzatsu ni suru 複雑にする
Korean: bokjabhakemandŭnda 복잡하게 만들다
Portuguese: complicar
Russian: uslozhnyát' усложнять
Spanish: complicar
Swedish: komplicera

461. compose (put together) [v.]

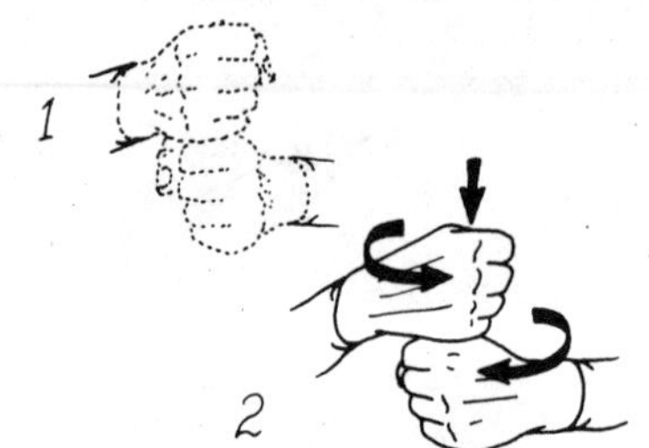

Arabic: jámaa جمع
Chinese: chuàngzuò 創作
Dutch: samenstellen
French: composer
German: zusammenstellen
Italian: comporre
Japanese: kumitateru 組み立てる
Korean: jorip'hada 조립하다
Portuguese: compor
Russian: sostavlyát' составлять
Spanish: componer
Swedish: sammanställa

462. computer [n.]

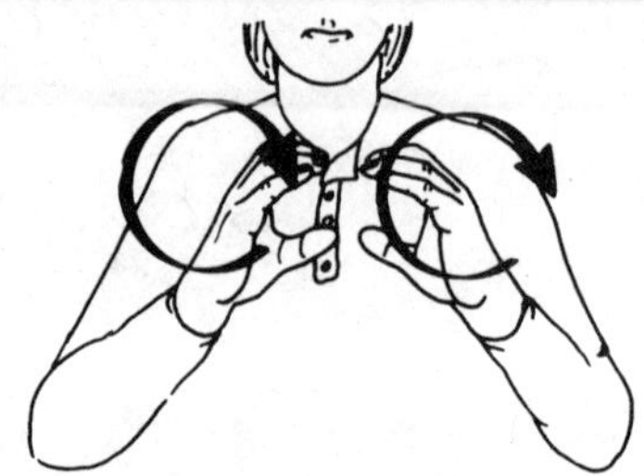

Arabic: kombyúter كمبيوتر
Chinese: jìsuànjī 電腦
Dutch: computer
French: ordinateur
German: Computer
Italian: computer
Japanese: kompyūtā コンピューター
Korean: kompyuta 컴퓨터
Portuguese: computador
Russian: komp'yúter компьютер
Spanish: computadora
Swedish: data-maskin

463. conceit [n.]

Arabic: ghurúr غرور
Chinese: zìfù 自負
Dutch: verwaandheid
French: vanité
German: Eitelkeit
Italian: presunzione
Japanese: jifushin 自負心
Korean: jabushim 자부심
Portuguese: vaidade
Russian: samomnéniye самомнение
Spanish: presunción
Swedish: inbilskhet

464. conceive [v.]

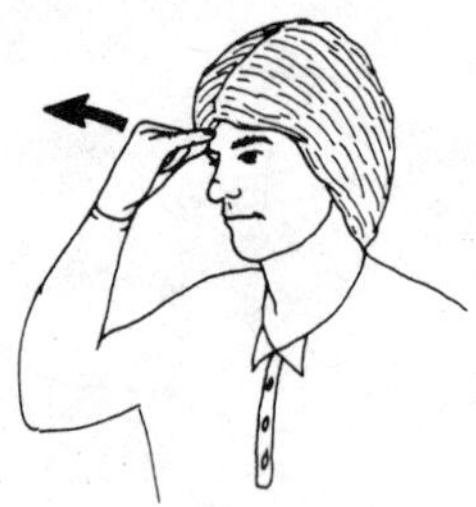

Arabic: takhéiala تخيل
Chinese: xiǎngchū 想出
Dutch: opvatten
French: concevoir
German: begreifen
Italian: concepire
Japanese: kokoro ni idaku 心に抱く
Korean: p'umta 품다
Portuguese: conceber
Russian: zadúmyvat' задумывать
Spanish: concebir
Swedish: avfatta

465. concentrate(consolidate/focus)[v.]

Arabic: rákkaza ركز
Chinese: quán shén guàn zhù 全神貫注
Dutch: concentreren
French: concentrer
German: konzentrieren
Italian: concentrare
Japanese: . . .o shūchū suru …を集中する
Korean: jibjunghada 집중하다
Portuguese: concentrar
Russian: sosredotóchit' сосредоточить
Spanish: concentrar
Swedish: koncentrera

466. concept [n.]

Arabic: fíkra فكرة
Chinese: guānniàn 觀念
Dutch: begrip
French: concept
German: Begriff
Italian: concetto
Japanese: gainen 概念
Korean: kaenyŏm 개념
Portuguese: conceito
Russian: ponyátiye понятие
Spanish: concepto
Swedish: begrepp

467. concern (care) [n.]

Arabic: ihtimám اهتمام
Chinese: guānqiè 關切
Dutch: bezorgdheid
French: souci
German: Sorge
Italian: preoccupazione
Japanese: kanshin 関心
Korean: kwanshim 관심
Portuguese: preocupação
Russian: zabóta забота
Spanish: preocupación
Swedish: bekymmer

468. conclusion (termination) [n.]

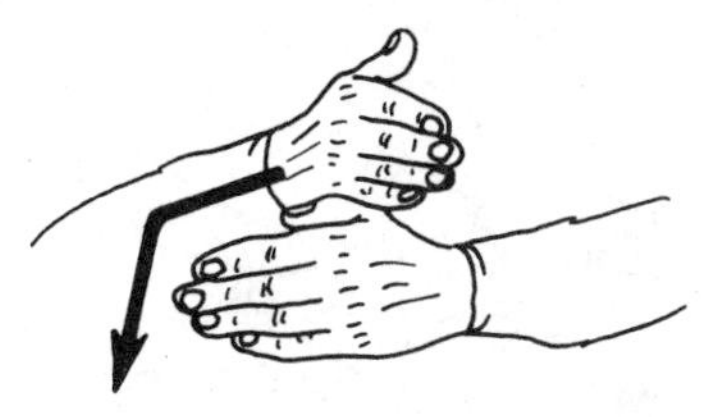

Arabic: istintáj استنتاج
Chinese: jiélùn 結論
Dutch: conclusie
French: conclusion
German: Schluß
Italian: conclusione
Japanese: ketsumatsu 結末
Korean: chonggyŏl 종결
Portuguese: conclusão
Russian: okonchániye окончание
Spanish: conclusión
Swedish: slutsats

469. condemn [v.]

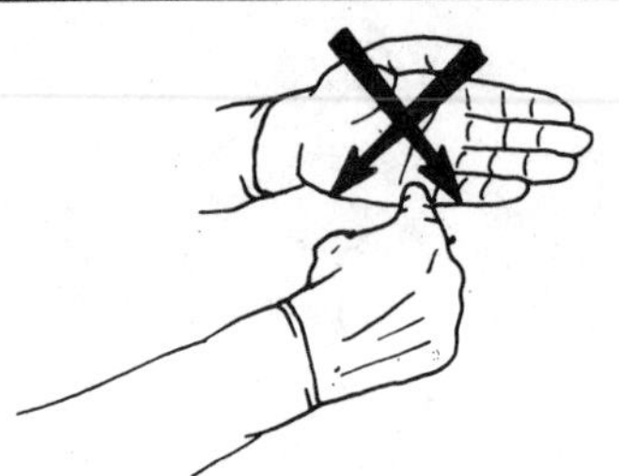

Arabic: shájaba شجب
Chinese: qiǎnzé 譴責
Dutch: veroordelen
French: condamner
German: verurteilen
Italian: condannare
Japanese: hinan suru 非難する
Korean: ch'aekmanghada 책망하다
Portuguese: condenar
Russian: osuzhdát' осуждать
Spanish: condenar
Swedish: fördöma

470. condition [n.]

Arabic: háala حالة
Chinese: tiáojiàn 條件
Dutch: voorwaarde
French: condition
German: Zustand
Italian: condizione
Japanese: jōtai 状態
Korean: jokŏn 조건
Portuguese: condição
Russian: uslóviye условие
Spanish: condición
Swedish: villkor

471. conduct [v.]

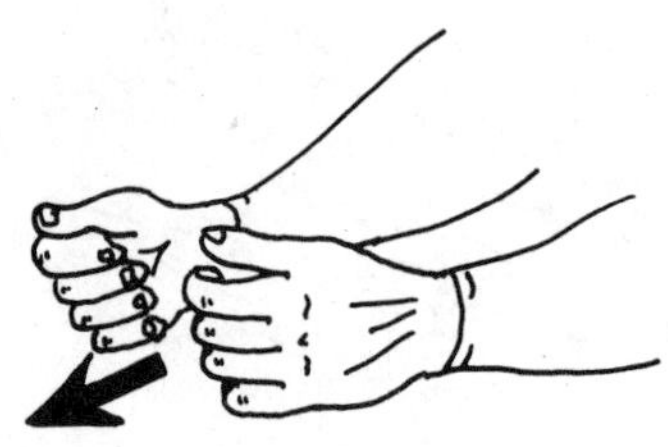

Arabic: wássala وصل
Chinese: zhǐhuī 指揮
Dutch: leiden
French: conduire
German: leiten
Italian: condurre
Japanese: shiki suru 指揮する
Korean: haengdonghada 행동하다
Portuguese: conduzir
Russian: vodít' водить
Spanish: conducir
Swedish: föra

472. conference [n.]

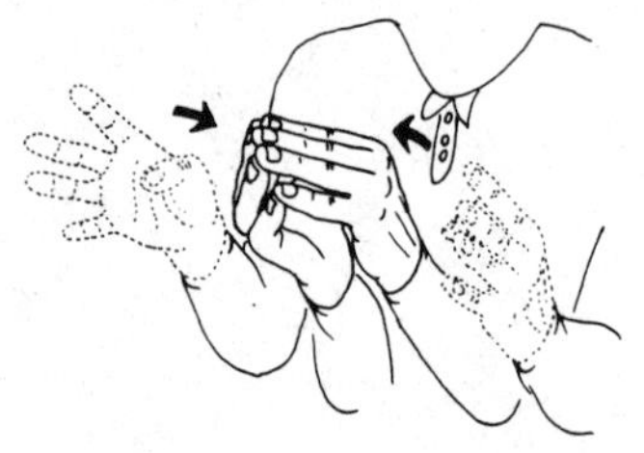

Arabic: mu'támar مؤتمر
Chinese: tǎolùnhuì 討論會
Dutch: conferentie
French: conférence
German: Konferenz
Italian: conferenza
Japanese: kaigi 会議
Korean: hoeŭi 회의
Portuguese: conferência
Russian: konferéntsiya конференция
Spanish: conferencia
Swedish: konferens

473. confess [v.]

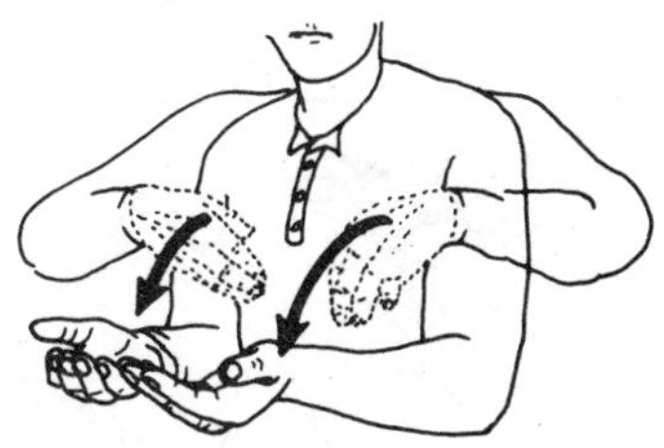

Arabic: iaatárafa اعترف
Chinese: chéngrèn 承認
Dutch: bekennen
French: avouer
German: bekennen
Italian: confessare
Japanese: hakujō suru 白状する
Korean: jabaek'hada 자백하다
Portuguese: confessar
Russian: ispovédovat' исповедовать
Spanish: confesar
Swedish: bekänna

474. confidence [n.]

Arabic: thíqa ثقة
Chinese: xìnrèn 信任
Dutch: vertrouwen
French: confiance
German: Vertrauen
Italian: fiducia
Japanese: jishin 自信
Korean: hwakshin 확신
Portuguese: confiança
Russian: dovériye доверие
Spanish: confidencia
Swedish: förtroende

475. confirmation [n.]

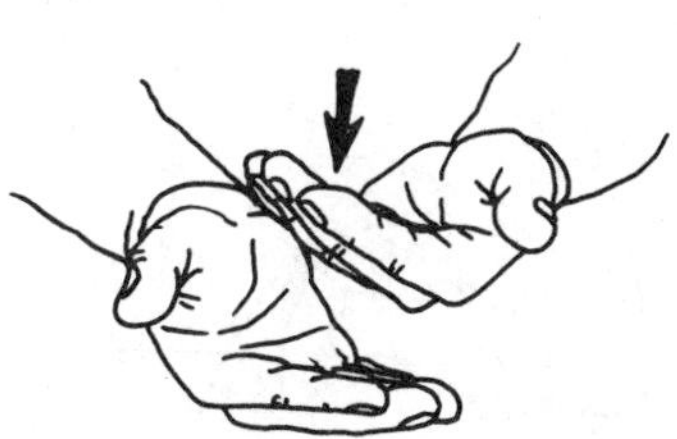

Arabic: tá'kid تأكيد
Chinese: quèdìng 確定
Dutch: bevestiging
French: confirmation
German: Bestätigung
Italian: conferma
Japanese: kakunin 確認
Korean: hwakin 확인
Portuguese: confirmação
Russian: podtverzhdéniye подтверждение
Spanish: confirmación
Swedish: bekräftelse

476. confusion [n.]

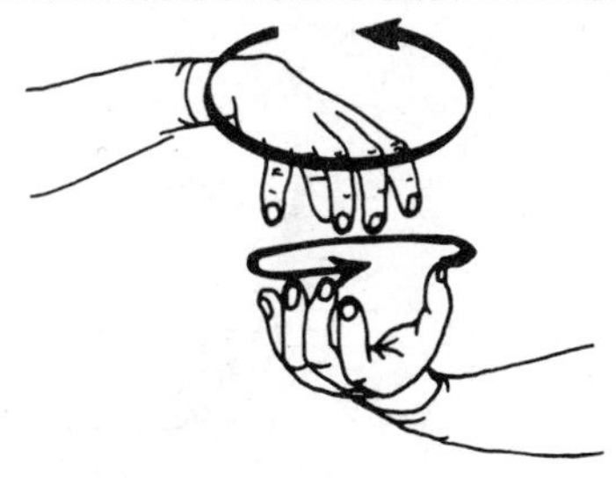

Arabic: iltibás التباس
Chinese: hùnluàn 混淆
Dutch: verwarring
French: confusion
German: Verwirrung
Italian: confusione
Japanese: konran 混乱
Korean: hollan 혼란
Portuguese: confusão
Russian: smushchéniye смущение
Spanish: confusión
Swedish: förvirring

477. congratulate [v.]

Arabic: hánna'a هنئ
Chinese: gōngxǐ 恭喜
Dutch: feliciteren
French: féliciter
German: gratulieren
Italian: congratularsi con
Japanese: iwau 祝う
Korean: ch'uk'hahada 축하하다
Portuguese: parabenizar
Russian: pozdravlyát' поздравлять
Spanish: felicitar
Swedish: gratulera

478. congress [n.]

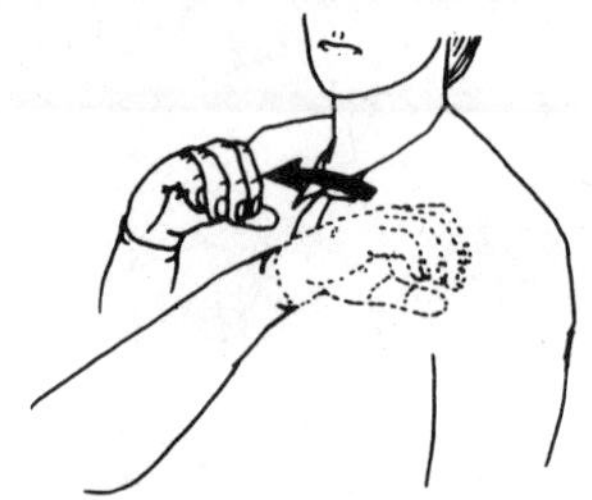

Arabic: al-kóngres الكونجرس
Chinese: guóhuì 國會
Dutch: congres
French: congrès
German: Kongress
Italian: congresso
Japanese: gikai 議会
Korean: hoeŭi 회의
Portuguese: congresso
Russian: kongréss конгресс
Spanish: congreso
Swedish: kongress

479. connection [n.]

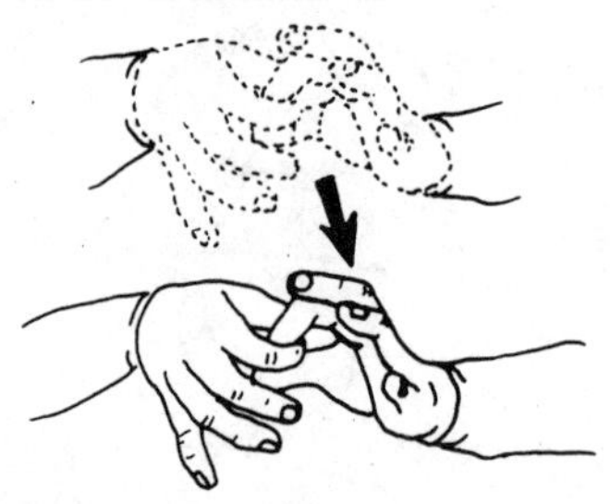

Arabic: wásla وصلة
Chinese: guān lián 關聯
Dutch: verbinding
French: relation
German: Verbindung
Italian: connessione
Japanese: kankei 関係
Korean: kwangye 관계
Portuguese: conexão
Russian: svyaz' связь
Spanish: conexión
Swedish: förbindelse

480. conquer [v.]

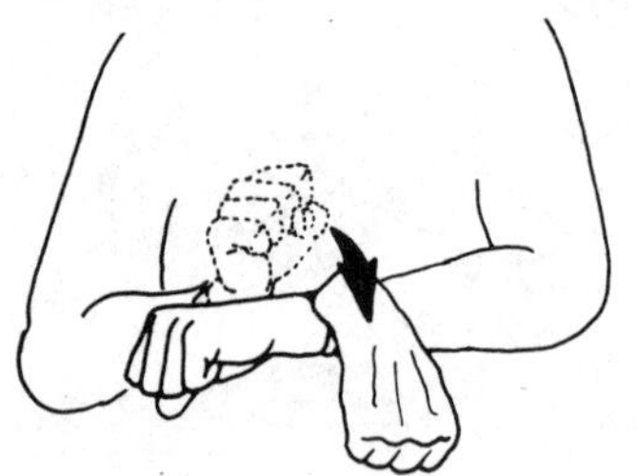

Arabic: ákhdaa اخضع
Chinese: zhēngfú 征服
Dutch: veroveren
French: vaincre
German: besiegen
Italian: conquistare
Japanese: seifuku suru 征服する
Korean: jŏngbok'hada 정복하다
Portuguese: conquistar
Russian: zavoyóvyvat' завоёвывать
Spanish: conquistar
Swedish: erövra

481. conscience [n.]

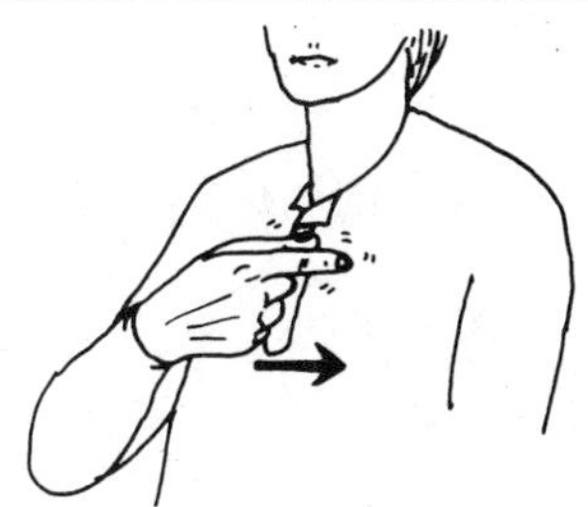

Arabic: damír ضمير
Chinese: liángxīn 良心
Dutch: geweten
French: conscience
German: Gewissen
Italian: coscienza
Japanese: ryōshin 良心
Korean: yangshim 양심
Portuguese: consciência
Russian: sóvest' совесть
Spanish: conciencia
Swedish: samvete

482. conscious [adj.]

Arabic: múdrik مدرك
Chinese: zìjuéde 自覺的
Dutch: bewust
French: conscient
German: bewußt
Italian: conscio
Japanese: ishiki shite iru 意識している
Korean: ŭishikiitnŭn 의식있는
Portuguese: cônscio
Russian: soznátel'nyy сознательный
Spanish: consciente
Swedish: medveten

483. consequence [n.]

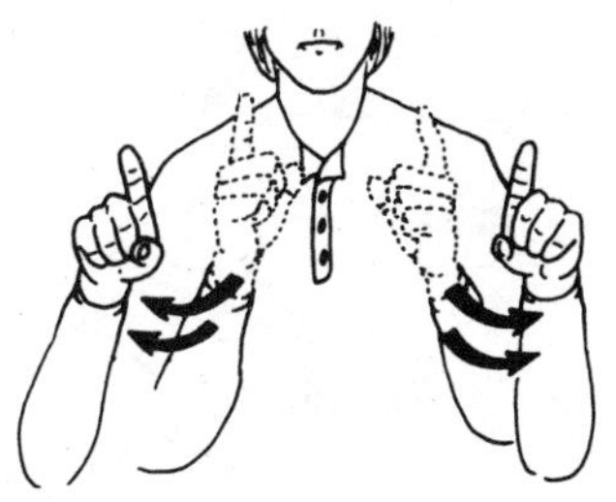

Arabic: natíja نتيجة
Chinese: jiéguǒ 結果
Dutch: gevolg
French: conséquence
German: Konsequenz
Italian: conseguenza
Japanese: kekka 結果
Korean: kyŏlkwa 결과
Portuguese: conseqüência
Russian: slédstviye следствие
Spanish: consecuencia
Swedish: följd

484. consider [v.]

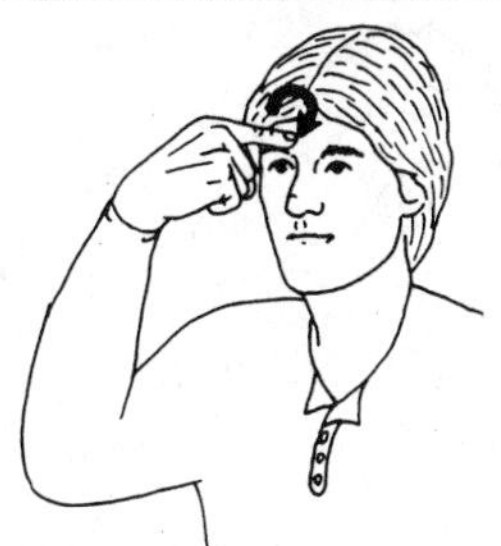

Arabic: iaatábara اعتبر
Chinese: kǎolǜ 考慮
Dutch: overwegen
French: considérer
German: erwägen
Italian: considerare
Japanese: kōryo suru 考慮する
Korean: koryŏhada 고려하다
Portuguese: considerar
Russian: schitát' считать
Spanish: considerar
Swedish: överväga

485. constant [adj.]

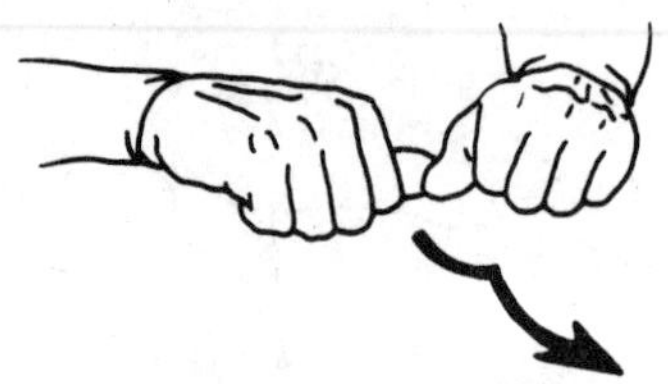

Arabic: thábit ثابت
Chinese: héngjiǔ 恒久
Dutch: standvastig
French: constant
German: beständig
Italian: costante
Japanese: taezu 絶えず
Korean: bulbyŏnŭi 불변의
Portuguese: constante
Russian: postoyánnyy постоянный
Spanish: constante
Swedish: beständig

486. constitution (document) [n.]

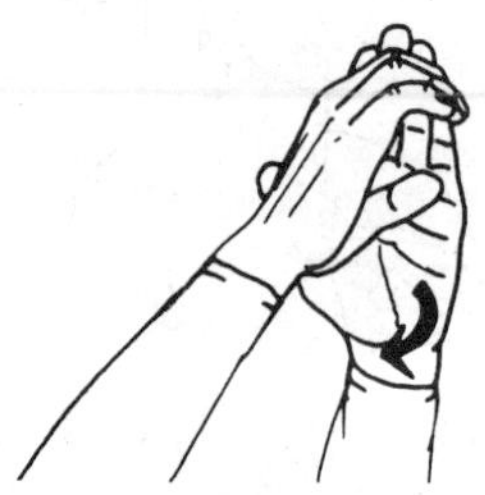

Arabic: distúr دستور
Chinese: xiànfǎ 憲法
Dutch: constitutie
French: constitution
German: Verfassung
Italian: costituzione
Japanese: kempō 憲法
Korean: hŏnbop 헌법
Portuguese: constituição
Russian: konstitútsiya конституция
Spanish: constitución
Swedish: konstitution

487. construct [v.]

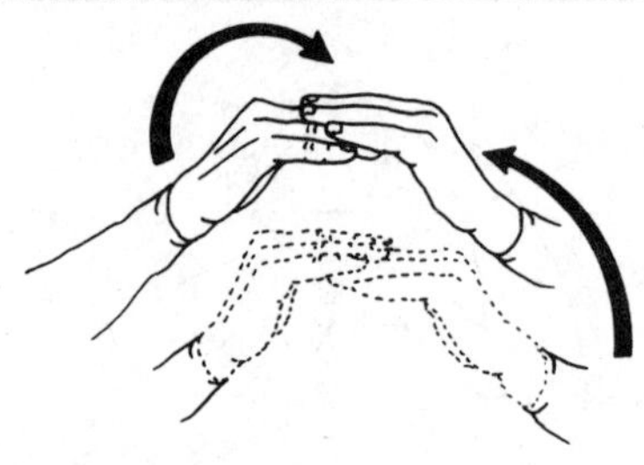

Arabic: bána بنى
Chinese: jiànzào 建造
Dutch: bouwen
French: bâtir
German: erbauen
Italian: costruire
Japanese: kensetsu suru 建築する
Korean: seuda 세우다
Portuguese: construir
Russian: stróit' строить
Spanish: construir
Swedish: konstruera

488. contact [n.]

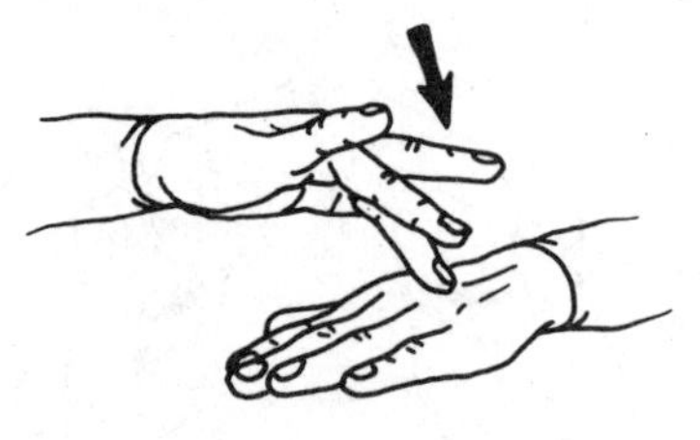

Arabic: talámus تلامس
Chinese: jiēchù 接觸
Dutch: contact
French: contact
German: Kontakt
Italian: contatto
Japanese: sesshoku 接触
Korean: jŏpchok 접촉
Portuguese: contato
Russian: kontákt контакт
Spanish: contacto
Swedish: kontakt

489. contempt [n.]

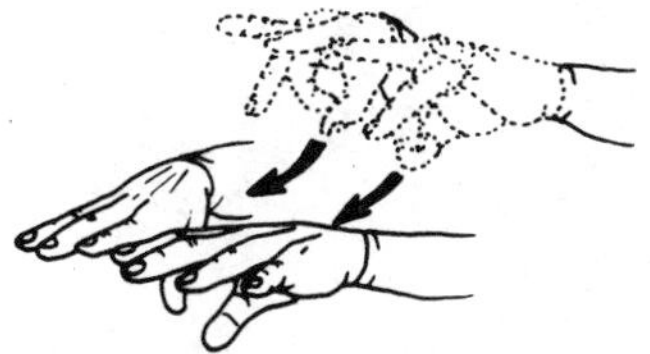

Arabic: ehtiqár احتقار
Chinese: miǎoshì 藐視
Dutch: minachting
French: mépris
German: Verachtung
Italian: disprezzo
Japanese: keibetsu 軽蔑
Korean: myŏlshi 멸시
Portuguese: desprêzo
Russian: prezréniye презрение
Spanish: desprecio
Swedish: förakt

490. content (to feel) [v.]

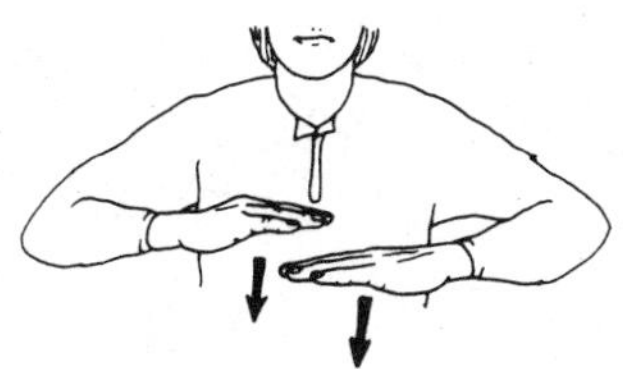

Arabic: rádaa رضى
Chinese: mǎnyìde 满意的
Dutch: tevredenstellen
French: contenter
German: zufriedenstellen
Italian: accontentare
Japanese: manzoku suru 満足する
Korean: manjokhada 만족하다
Portuguese: contentar
Russian: udovletvoryát' удовлетворять
Spanish: contentar
Swedish: belåten

491. content(s) [n.]

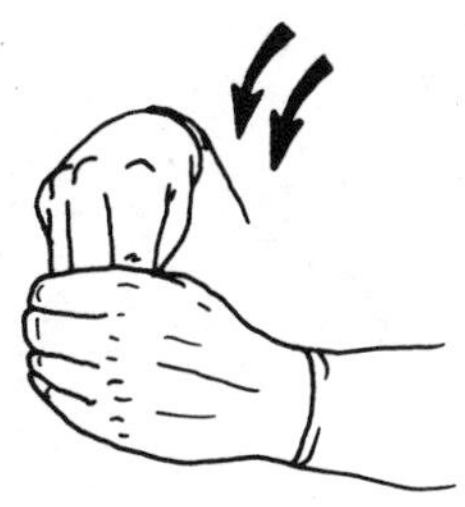

Arabic: muhtáwa محتوى
Chinese: nèiróng 内容
Dutch: inhoud
French: contenu
German: Inhalt
Italian: contenuto
Japanese: naiyō 内容
Korean: naeyong 내용
Portuguese: conteúdo
Russian: soderzhániye содержание
Spanish: contenido
Swedish: innehåll

492. continent [n.]

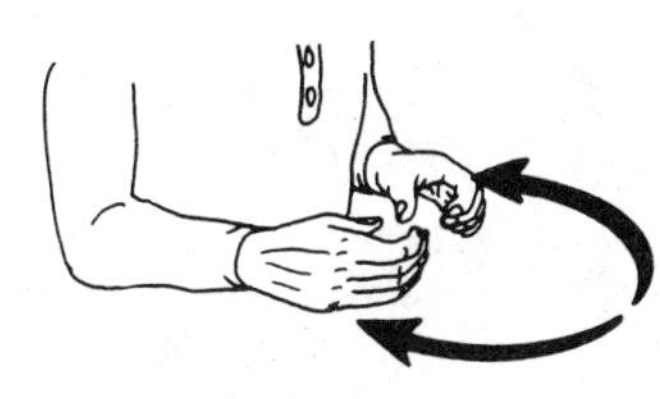

Arabic: qárra قارة
Chinese: dàlù 大陸
Dutch: continent
French: continent
German: Kontinent
Italian: continente
Japanese: tairiku 大陸
Korean: daeryuk 대륙
Portuguese: continente
Russian: kontinént континент
Spanish: continente
Swedish: kontinent

493. continue [v.]

Arabic: istamára استمر
Chinese: jìxù 繼續
Dutch: vervolgen
French: continuer
German: weiterführen
Italian: continuare
Japanese: tsuzuku 続く
Korean: kyesok'hada 계속하다
Portuguese: continuar
Russian: prodolzhát' продолжать
Spanish: continuar
Swedish: fortsätta

494. contradict [v.]

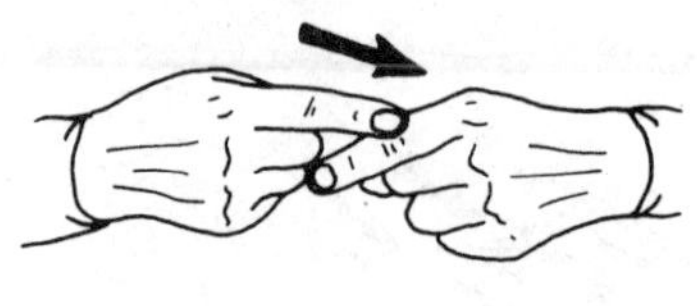

Arabic: khálafa خالف
Chinese: wéifǎn 違反
Dutch: tegenspreken
French: contredire
German: widersprechen
Italian: contraddire
Japanese: hantai suru 反対する
Korean: banbak'hada 반박하다
Portuguese: contradizer
Russian: protivoréchit' противоречить
Spanish: contradecir
Swedish: motsäga

495. contribute [v.]

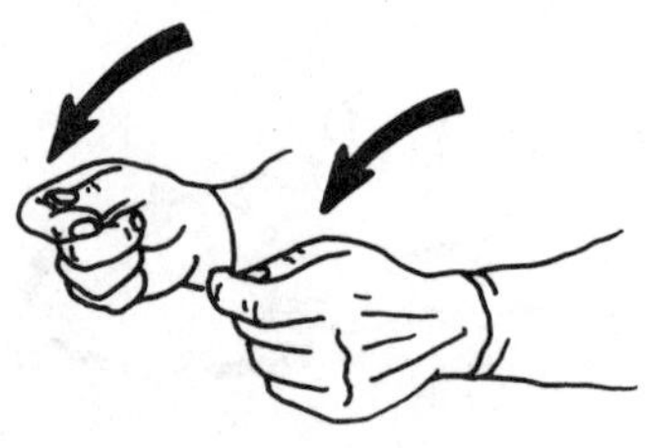

Arabic: tabaráa تبرع
Chinese: gòngxiàn 貢獻
Dutch: bijdragen
French: contribuer
German: beitragen
Italian: contribuire
Japanese: kōken suru 貢献する
Korean: konghŏnhada 공헌하다
Portuguese: contribuir
Russian: sdélat' vklad
сделать вклад
Spanish: contribuir
Swedish: bidraga

496. control [n.]

Arabic: tahákum تحكم
Chinese: kòngzhì 控制
Dutch: controle
French: contrôle
German: Kontrolle
Italian: controllo
Japanese: shihai 支配
Korean: jibae 지배
Portuguese: contrôle
Russian: kontról' контроль
Spanish: control
Swedish: kontroll

497. convenient [adj.]

Arabic: munásib مناسب
Chinese: fāngbiànde 方便的
Dutch: gemakkelijk
French: commode
German: bequem
Italian: conveniente
Japanese: benrina 便利な
Korean: p'yŏllihan 편리한
Portuguese: conveniente
Russian: udóbnyy удобный
Spanish: conveniente
Swedish: bekväm

498. conversation [n.]

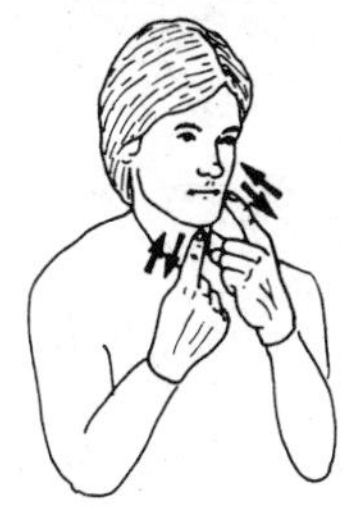

Arabic: muháadatha محادثة
Chinese: huìhuà 會話
Dutch: gesprek
French: conversation
German: Gespräch
Italian: conversazione
Japanese: kaiwa 会話
Korean: hoehwa 회화
Portuguese: conversação
Russian: razgovór разговор
Spanish: conversación
Swedish: konversation

499. convince [v.]

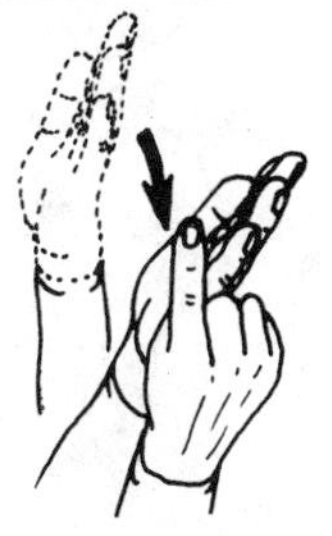

Arabic: áqnaa'a اقنع
Chinese: shǐ xìnfú 使信服
Dutch: overtuigen
French: convaincre
German: überzeugen
Italian: convincere
Japanese: nattoku saseru 納得させる
Korean: napdŭkshik'ida 납득시키다
Portuguese: convencer
Russian: ubezhdát' убеждать
Spanish: convencer
Swedish: övertyga

500. cook [v.]

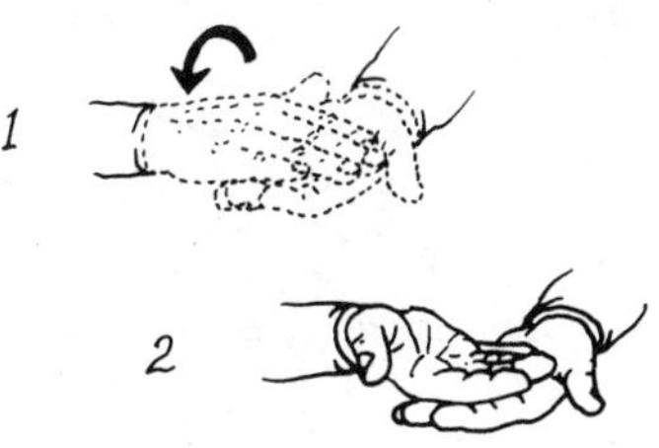

Arabic: tábakha طبخ
Chinese: zhǔ 煮
Dutch: koken
French: cuire
German: kochen
Italian: cucinare
Japanese: ryōri suru 料理する
Korean: yorihada 요리하다
Portuguese: cozinhar
Russian: gotóvit' готовить
Spanish: cocinar
Swedish: koka

501. cool [adj.]

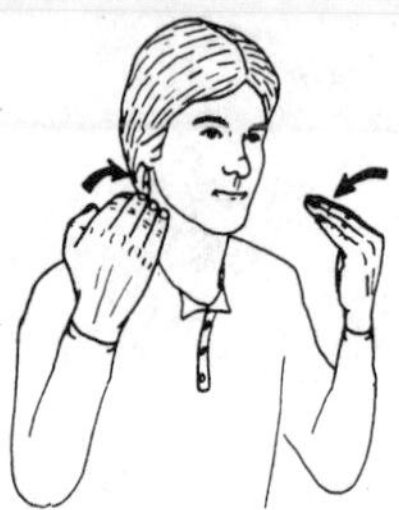

Arabic: bárid بارد
Chinese: liángde 凉的
Dutch: koel
French: frais
German: kühl
Italian: fresco
Japanese: suzushii 涼しい
Korean: sŏnŭrhan 서늘한
Portuguese: fresco
Russian: prokhládnyy прохладный
Spanish: fresco
Swedish: sval

502. cooperate [v.]

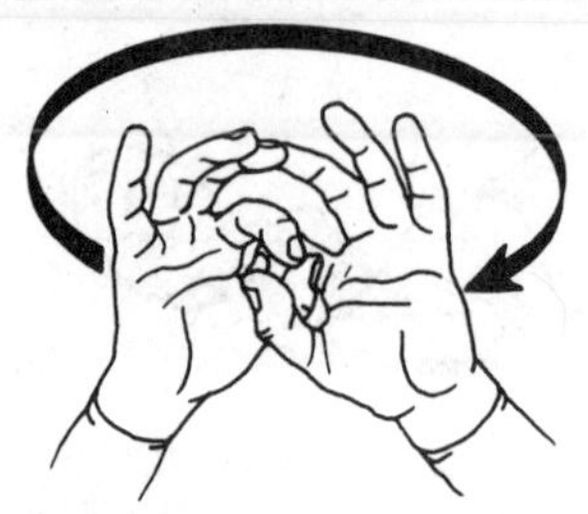

Arabic: taáwana تعاون
Chinese: hézuò 合作
Dutch: samenwerken
French: coopérer
German: mitwirken
Italian: cooperare
Japanese: kyōryoku suru 協力する
Korean: hyŏmnyŏk'hada 협력하다
Portuguese: cooperar
Russian: sotrúdnichat' сотрудничать
Spanish: cooperar
Swedish: samarbeta

503. copy [n.]

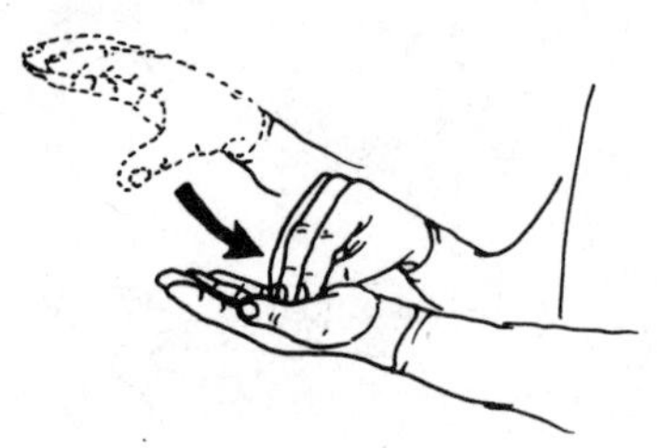

Arabic: núskha نسخة
Chinese: fùběn 副本
Dutch: kopie
French: copie
German: Kopie
Italian: copia
Japanese: kopii コピー
Korean: sabon 사본
Portuguese: cópia
Russian: kópiya копия
Spanish: copia
Swedish: kopia

504. corn (grain) [n.]

Arabic: dhúra ذرة
Chinese: yùmǐ 玉米
Dutch: maïs
French: maïs
German: Mais
Italian: granoturco
Japanese: tōmorokoshi トーモロコシ
Korean: oksusu 옥수수
Portuguese: milho
Russian: kukurúza кукуруза
Spanish: maíz
Swedish: majs

505. corner [n.]

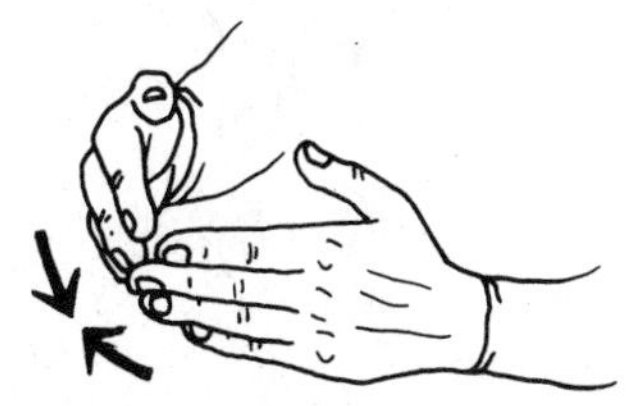

Arabic: rokn ركن
Chinese: jiǎoluò 角落
Dutch: hoek
French: coin
German: Ecke
Italian: angolo
Japanese: kado 角(かど)
Korean: mot'ungi 모퉁이
Portuguese: esquina
Russian: úgol угол
Spanish: esquina
Swedish: hörn

506. correct [v.]

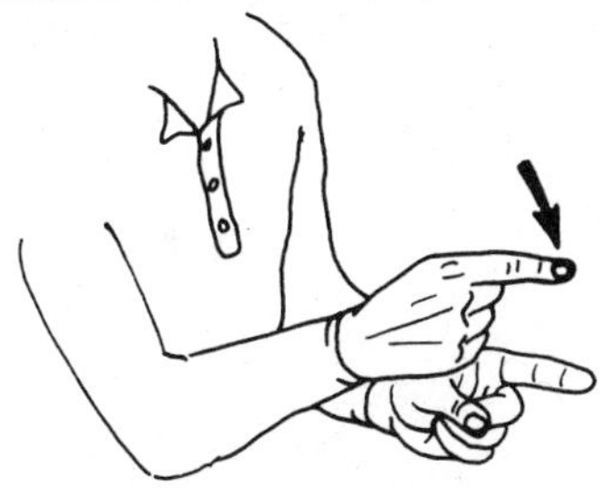

Arabic: sáhhaha صحح
Chinese: gǎizhèng 改正
Dutch: verbeteren
French: corriger
German: berichtigen
Italian: correggere
Japanese: naosu 直す
Korean: gochita 고치다
Portuguese: corrigir
Russian: ispravlyát' исправлять
Spanish: corregir
Swedish: korrigera

507. cost [n.]

Arabic: takalíf تكاليف
Chinese: huāfèi 花費
Dutch: prijs
French: coût
German: Preis
Italian: costo
Japanese: nedan 値段
Korean: kap 값
Portuguese: custo
Russian: tsená цена
Spanish: costo
Swedish: pris

508. cotton [n.]

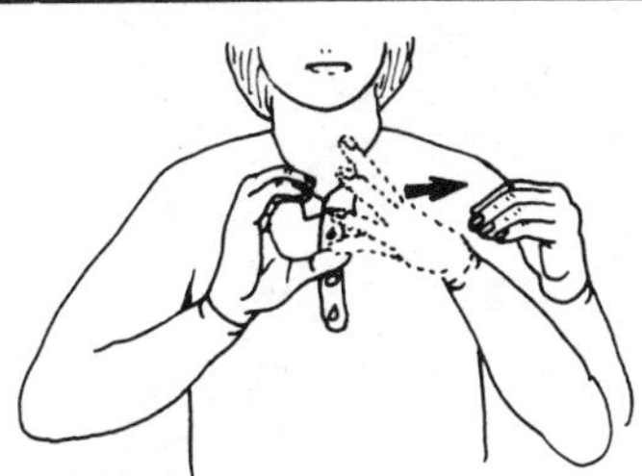

Arabic: qotn قطن
Chinese: miánhuā 棉花
Dutch: katoen
French: coton
German: Baumwolle
Italian: cotone
Japanese: men 綿
Korean: som 솜
Portuguese: algodão
Russian: khlópok хлопок
Spanish: algodón
Swedish: bomull

509. cough [n.]

Arabic: qáhha قحة
Chinese: késòu 咳嗽
Dutch: hoest
French: toux
German: Husten
Italian: tosse
Japanese: seki 咳
Korean: gich'im 기침
Portuguese: tosse
Russian: káshel' кашель
Spanish: tos
Swedish: hosta

510. count [v.]

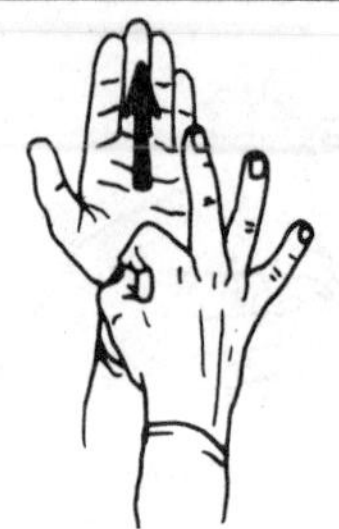

Arabic: áadda عد
Chinese: jìsuàn 計算
Dutch: tellen
French: compter
German: zählen
Italian: contare
Japanese: kazoeru 数える
Korean: gyesanhada 계산하다
Portuguese: contar
Russian: schitát' считать
Spanish: contar
Swedish: räkna

511. country (nation) [n.]

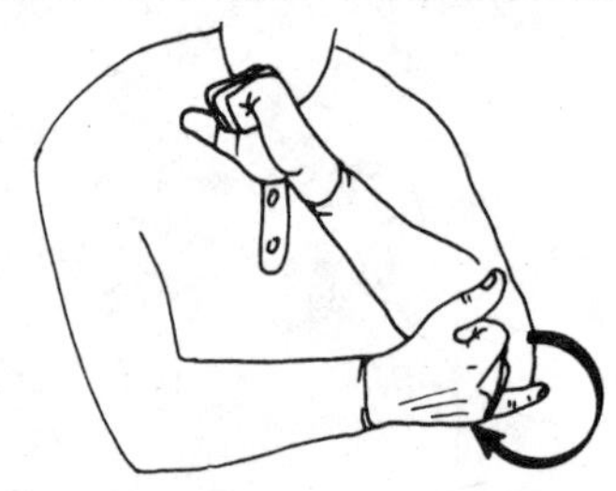

Arabic: bálad بلد
Chinese: guójiā 國家
Dutch: land
French: pays
German: Land
Italian: paese
Japanese: kuni 国
Korean: shigol 시골
Portuguese: país
Russian: straná страна
Spanish: país
Swedish: land

512. courage [n.]

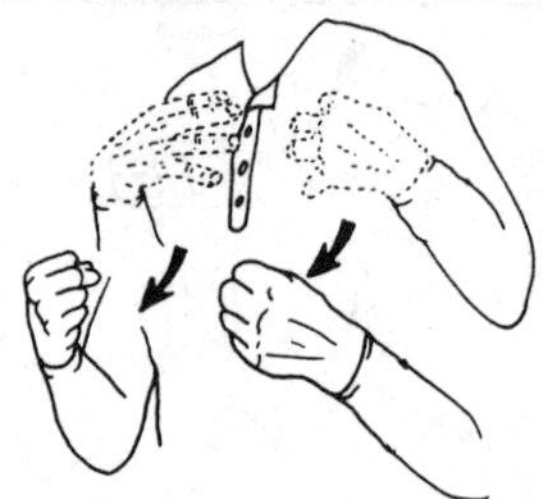

Arabic: shajaá شجاعة
Chinese: yǒngqì 勇氣
Dutch: moed
French: courage
German: Mut
Italian: coraggio
Japanese: yūki 勇気
Korean: yonggi 용기
Portuguese: coragem
Russian: múzhestvo мужество
Spanish: valor
Swedish: mod

513. course (duration/progress) [n.]

Arabic: athná' اثناء
Chinese: fāngxiàng 方向
Dutch: koers
French: cours
German: Verlauf
Italian: corso
Japanese: shinkō 進行
Korean: kwajŏng 과정
Portuguese: curso
Russian: kurs курс
Spanish: curso
Swedish: kurs

514. court (judicial) [n.]

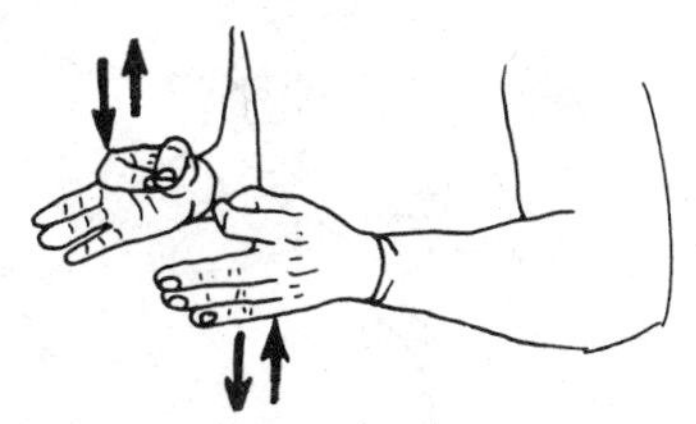

Arabic: máhkama محكمة
Chinese: fǎyuàn 法院
Dutch: gerechtshof
French: tribunal
German: Gericht
Italian: tribunale
Japanese: saibansho 裁判所
Korean: jaep'anso 재판소
Portuguese: tribunal
Russian: sud суд
Spanish: tribunal
Swedish: domstol

515. cousin [n.]

Arabic: íbnil-áam/íbnil-khál/
bint il-áam/bint il-khál / ابن العم / ابن الخال / بنت العم / بنت الخال
Chinese: tángxiōngdì 唐兄弟
Dutch: neef
French: cousin
German: Vetter/Kousine
Italian: cugino
Japanese: itoko いとこ
Korean: sachon 사촌
Portuguese: primo
Russian: kuzén кузен
Spanish: primo

516. cover [v.]

Arabic: gháttaa غطى
Chinese: zhēgài 遮蓋
Dutch: bedekken
French: couvrir
German: bedecken
Italian: coprire
Japanese: kabuseru 被せる
Korean: dŏpda 덮다
Portuguese: cobrir
Russian: pokryvát' покрывать
Spanish: cubrir
Swedish: betäcka

517. cow [n.]

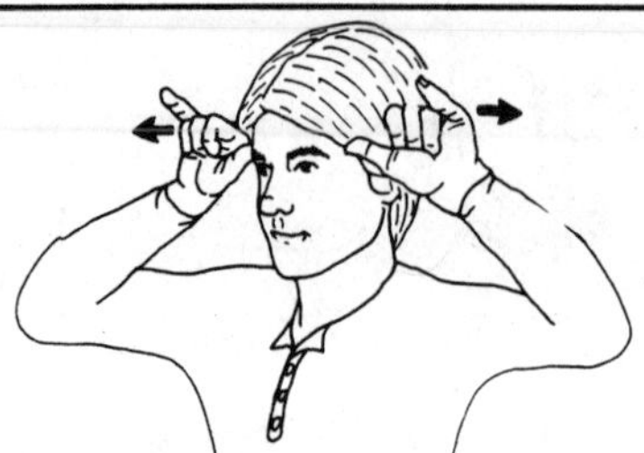

Arabic: báqara بقرة
Chinese: mǔ niú 母牛
Dutch: koe
French: vache
German: Kuh
Italian: vacca
Japanese: ushi 牛
Korean: amso 암소
Portuguese: vaca
Russian: koróva корова
Spanish: vaca
Swedish: ko

518. coward [n.]

Arabic: jabán جبان
Chinese: nuòfū 懦夫
Dutch: lafaard
French: poltron
German: Feigling
Italian: codardo
Japanese: okubyōmono 臆病者
Korean: gŏbjangi 겁쟁이
Portuguese: covarde
Russian: trus трус
Spanish: cobarde
Swedish: feg

519. crack (chink) [n.]

Arabic: shaq شق
Chinese: liè hén 裂痕
Dutch: spleet
French: fente
German: Riß
Italian: crepa
Japanese: hibi ひび
Korean: t'ŭm 틈
Portuguese: fenda
Russian: tréshchina трещина
Spanish: grieta
Swedish: spricka

520. crash (collision) [n.]

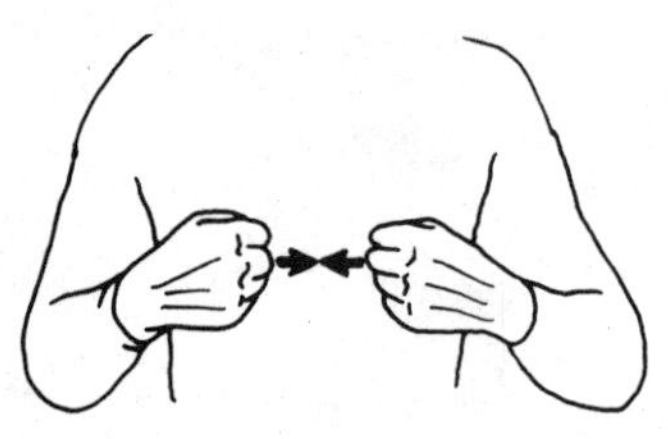

Arabic: tasádum تصادم
Chinese: zhuàngjí 撞擊
Dutch: botsing
French: collision
German: Zusammenstoß
Italian: scontro
Japanese: shōtotsu 衝突する
Korean: ch'ungdol 충돌
Portuguese: choque
Russian: stolknovéniye столкновение
Spanish: choque
Swedish: kollision

521. crawl [v.]

Arabic: záhafa زحف
Chinese: páxíng 爬行
Dutch: kruipen
French: ramper
German: kriechen
Italian: strisciare
Japanese: hau はう
Korean: giŏgada 기어가다
Portuguese: engatinhar
Russian: pólzat' ползать
Spanish: arrastrarse
Swedish: kräla

522. crazy (insane) [adj.]

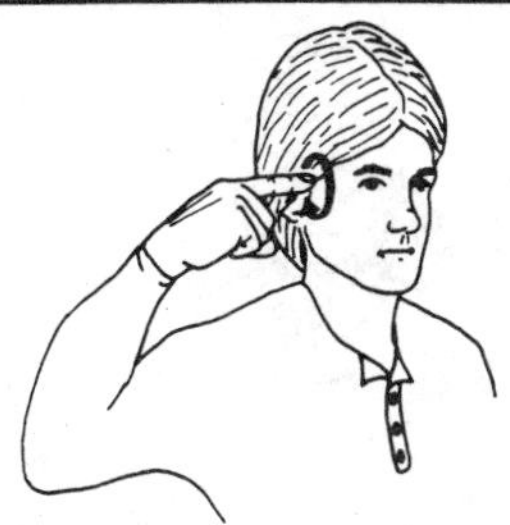

Arabic: majnún مجنون
Chinese: fēng 瘋
Dutch: gek
French: fou
German: verrückt
Italian: pazzo
Japanese: kyōkino 狂気の
Korean: mich'in 크림
Portuguese: louco
Russian: bezúmnyy безумный
Spanish: loco
Swedish: galen

523. cream (dairy) [n.]

Arabic: qíshta قشطة
Chinese: nǎiyóu 奶油
Dutch: room
French: crème
German: Sahne
Italian: panna
Japanese: kuriimu クリーム
Korean: k'ŭrim 미친
Portuguese: nata
Russian: slívki сливки
Spanish: nata
Swedish: grädde

524. create [v.]

Arabic: khálaqa خلق
Chinese: chuàngzào 創造
Dutch: scheppen
French: créer
German: erschaffen
Italian: creare
Japanese: sōzōsuru 創造する
Korean: ch'angjohada 창조하다
Portuguese: criar
Russian: sozdavát' создавать
Spanish: crear
Swedish: skapa

525. crime [n.]

Arabic: jaríma جريمة
Chinese: zuì-è 罪惡
Dutch: misdaad
French: crime
German: Verbrechen
Italian: crimine
Japanese: hanzai 犯罪
Korean: bŏmjoe 범죄
Portuguese: crime
Russian: prestupléniye преступление
Spanish: crimen
Swedish: brott

526. criticism [n.]

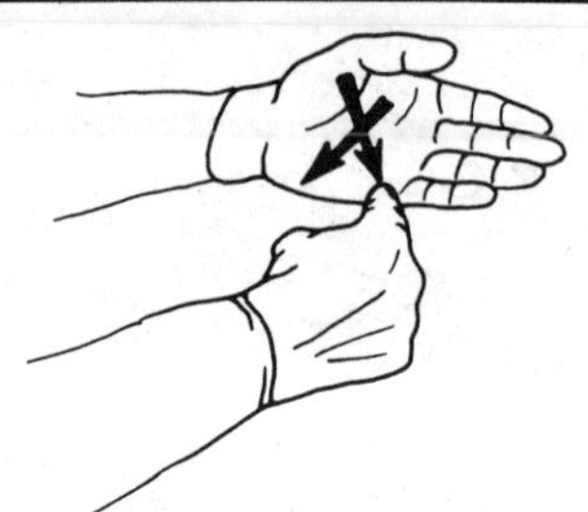

Arabic: náqed نقد
Chinese: pínglùn 評論
Dutch: kritiek
French: critique
German: Kritik
Italian: critica
Japanese: hihyō 批評
Korean: bip'yŏng 비평
Portuguese: crítica
Russian: krítika критика
Spanish: crítica
Swedish: kritik

527. crooked (curved) [adj.]

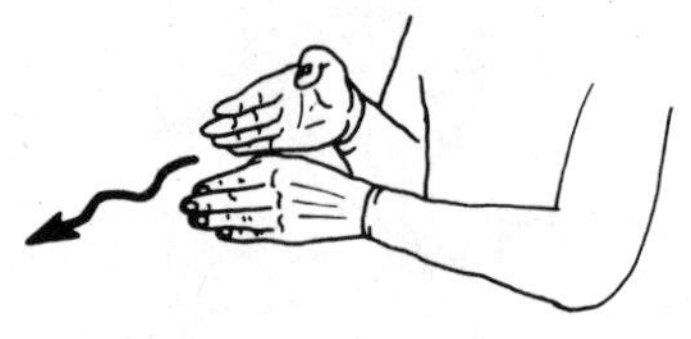

Arabic: méaawaj معوج
Chinese: wānqṻ 彎曲
Dutch: krom
French: courbé
German: krumm
Italian: curvo
Japanese: magatta 曲がった
Korean: guburŏjin 구부러진
Portuguese: curvo
Russian: krivóy кривой
Spanish: torcido
Swedish: krokig

528. cross (traverse) [v.]

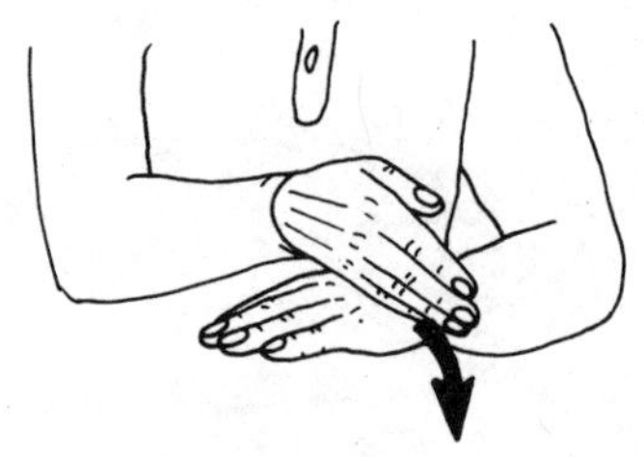

Arabic: aábara عبر
Chinese: yuèguò 越過
Dutch: doorkruisen
French: traverser
German: durchqueren
Italian: attraversare
Japanese: wataru 渡る
Korean: gŏnnŏgada 건너가다
Portuguese: atravessar
Russian: perekhodít' переходить
Spanish: cruzar
Swedish: korsa

529. crowd (throng) [n.]

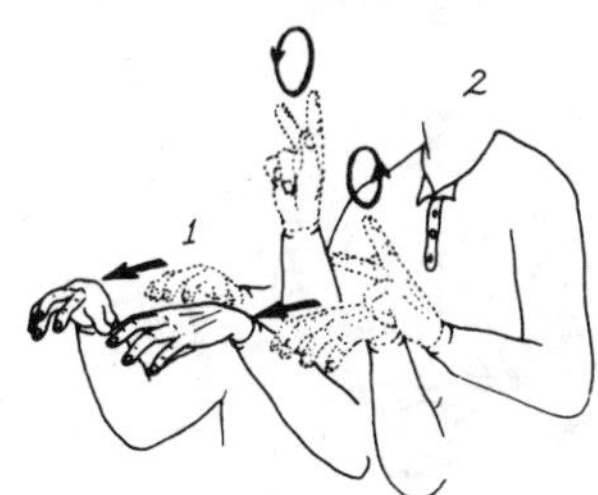

Arabic: háshid (min an-nás)
حشد (من الناس)
Chinese: qúnzhòng 羣衆
Dutch: menigte
French: foule
German: Gedränge
Italian: folla
Japanese: hitogomi 人込み
Korean: gunjung 군중
Portuguese: multidão
Russian: tolpá толпа
Spanish: muchedumbre
Swedish: folkmassa

530. crown [n.]

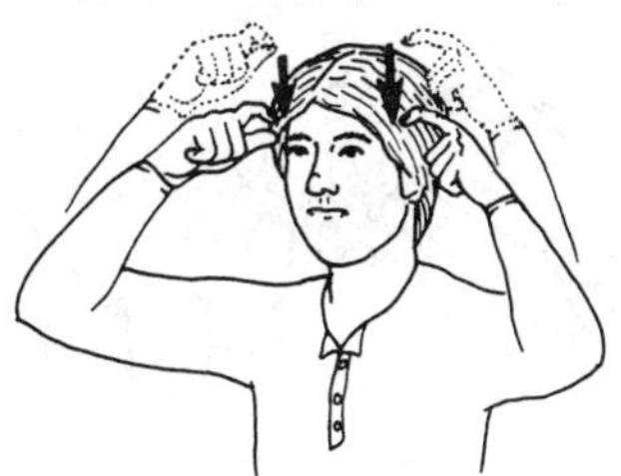

Arabic: tajj تاج
Chinese: huángguàn 皇冠
Dutch: kroon
French: couronne
German: Krone
Italian: corona
Japanese: ōkan 王冠
Korean: wanggwan 왕관
Portuguese: coroa
Russian: venéts венец
Spanish: corona
Swedish: krona

531. cruel [adj.]

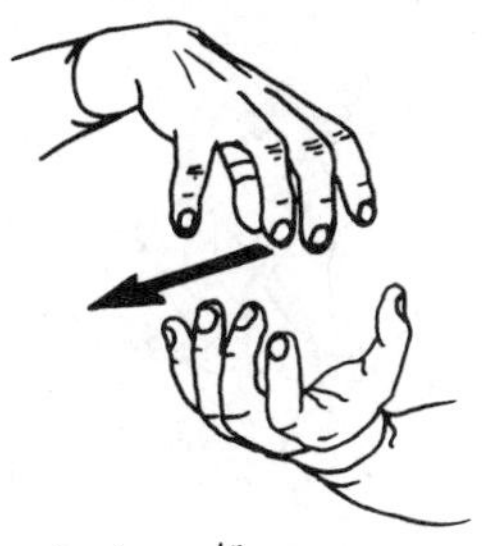

Arabic: qáasi قاسي
Chinese: cánrěnde 殘忍的
Dutch: wreed
French: cruel
German: grausam
Italian: crudele
Japanese: zankokuna 残酷な
Korean: janinhan 잔인한
Portuguese: cruel
Russian: zhestókiy жестокий
Spanish: cruel
Swedish: grym

532. cry (weep) [v.]

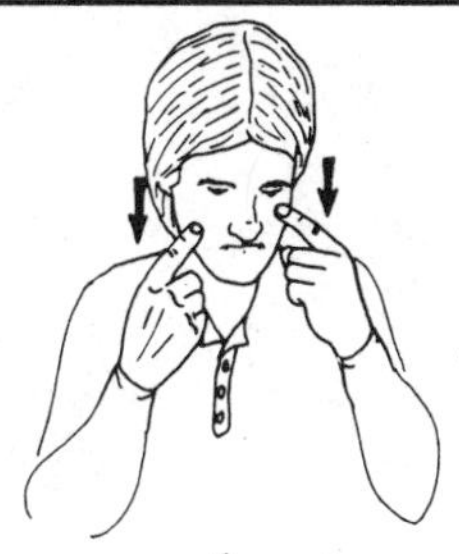

Arabic: báka بكى
Chinese: kū 哭
Dutch: huilen
French: pleurer
German: weinen
Italian: piangere
Japanese: naku 泣く
Korean: ulda 울다
Portuguese: chorar
Russian: plákat' плакать
Spanish: llorar
Swedish: gråta

533. Cuba [n.]

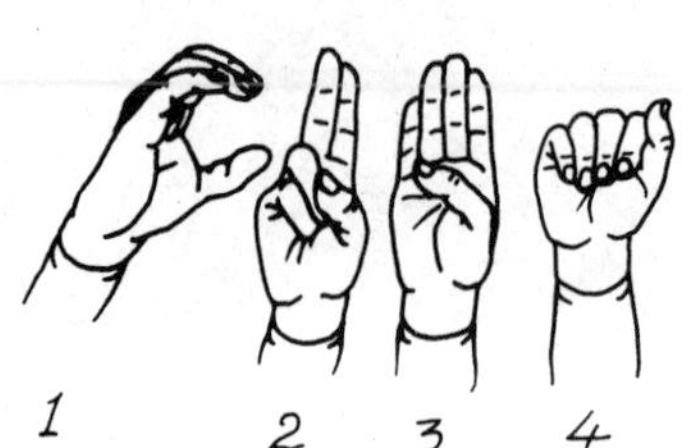

Arabic: kúba كوبا
Chinese: gǔbā 古巴
Dutch: Cuba
French: Cuba
German: Kuba
Italian: Cuba
Japanese: Kyūba キューバ
Korean: Kuba 큐바
Portuguese: Cuba
Russian: Kúba Куба
Spanish: Cuba
Swedish: Kuba

534. cup [n.]

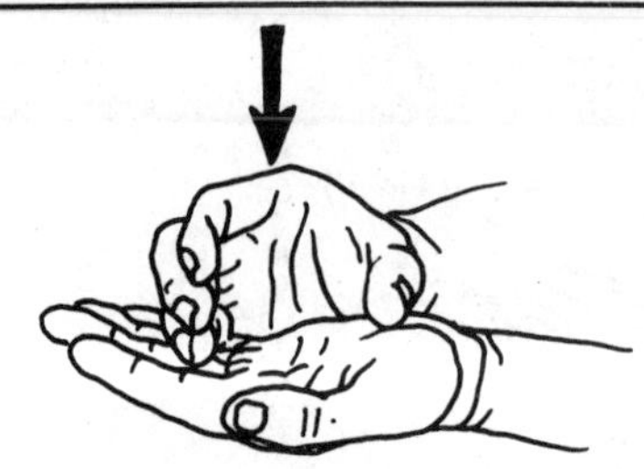

Arabic: finján فنجان
Chinese: bēizi 杯子
Dutch: kop
French: tasse
German: Tasse
Italian: tazza
Japanese: koppu コップ
Korean: k'ŏp 컵
Portuguese: taça
Russian: cháshka чашка
Spanish: taza
Swedish: kopp

535. cure (heal) [v.]

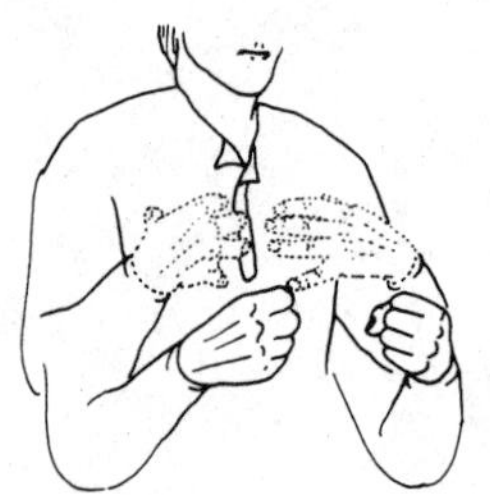

Arabic: áalaja عالج
Chinese: zhìliáo 治療
Dutch: genezen
French: guérir
German: kurieren
Italian: curare
Japanese: chiryō suru 治療する
Korean: ch'iryohada 치료하다
Portuguese: curar
Russian: izléchivat' излечивать
Spanish: curar
Swedish: läka

536. curious (inquisitive) [adj.]

Arabic: fudhúli فضولي
Chinese: hàoqíde 好奇的
Dutch: nieuwsgierig
French: curieux
German: neugierig
Italian: curioso
Japanese: kōkishin no aru
好奇心のある
Korean: hogishimi kanghan
호기심이 강한
Portuguese: curioso
Russian: lyubopýtnyy любопытный
Spanish: curioso
Swedish: nyfiken

537. curl [v.]

Arabic: láffa لف
Chinese: nòngjuǎn 弄卷
Dutch: krullen
French: friser
German: kräuseln
Italian: arricciare
Japanese: maku 巻く
Korean: k'ŏlhanda 곱슬하게하다
Portuguese: encaracolar
Russian: vít'sya виться
Spanish: rizar
Swedish: locka

538. current (present) [adj.]

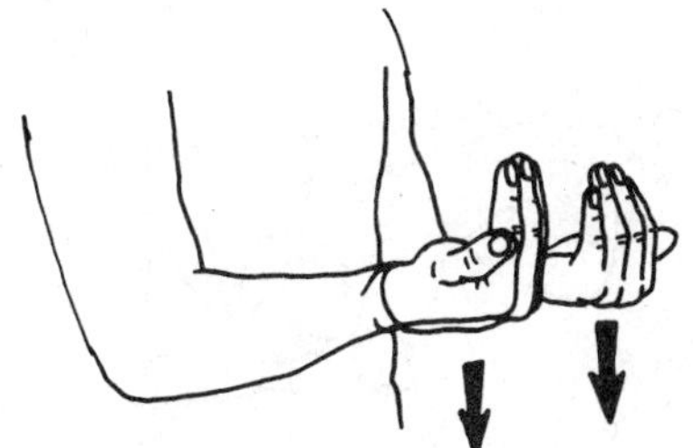

Arabic: háli حالي
Chinese: dāngshíde 當時的
Dutch: huidig
French: en cours
German: gegenwärtig
Italian: corrente
Japanese: genzai no 現在の
Korean: hyŏnjaeui 현제의
Portuguese: corrente
Russian: tekúshchiy текущий
Spanish: corriente
Swedish: nuvarande

539. curtain [n.]

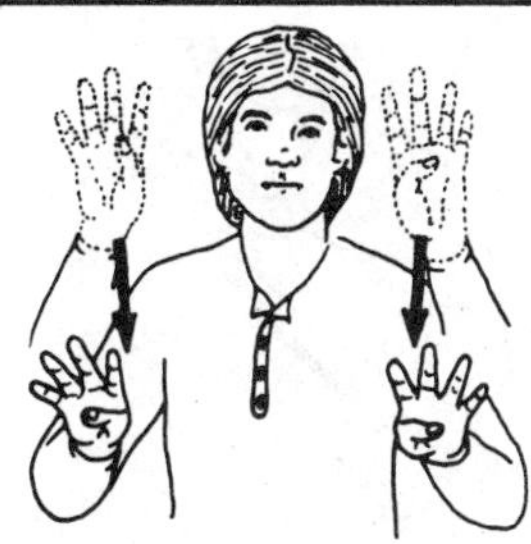

Arabic: sitára ستارة
Chinese: chuānglián 窗簾
Dutch: gordijn
French: rideau
German: Vorhang
Italian: cortina
Japanese: kāten カーテン
Korean: k'ŏt'ŭn 커텐
Portuguese: cortina
Russian: zánaves занавес
Spanish: cortina
Swedish: gardin

540. curve [n.]

Arabic: munhána منحنى
Chinese: wānqǖ 彎曲
Dutch: bocht
French: courbe
German: Kurve
Italian: curva
Japanese: kyokusen 曲線
Korean: kŏbu 커브
Portuguese: curva
Russian: izgíb изгиб
Spanish: curva
Swedish: kurva

541. custom [n.]

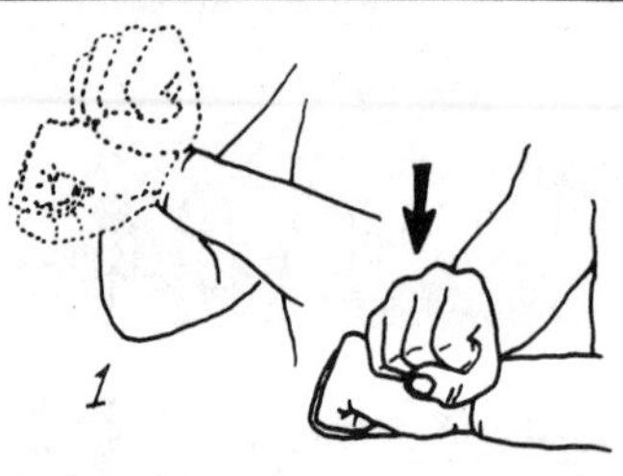

Arabic: áada عادة
Chinese: fēngsú 風俗
Dutch: gewoonte
French: coutume
German: Sitte
Italian: costume
Japanese: shūkan 習慣
Korean: sŭpkwan 습관
Portuguese: costume
Russian: obýchay обычай
Spanish: costumbre
Swedish: vana

542. customer [n.]

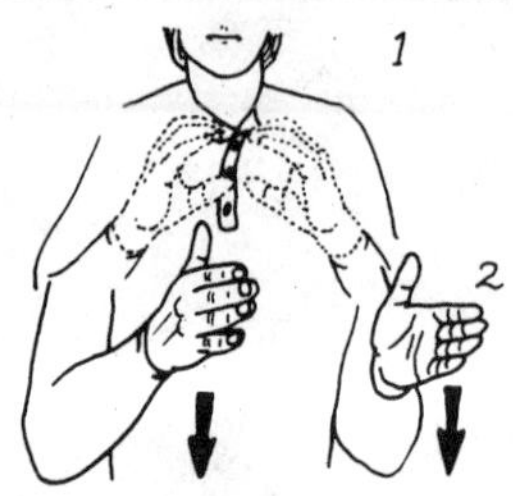

Arabic: zubún زبون
Chinese: gùkè 顧客
Dutch: klant
French: client
German: Kunde
Italian: cliente
Japanese: kyaku 客
Korean: sonnim 손님
Portuguese: cliente
Russian: pokupátel' покупатель
Spanish: cliente
Swedish: kund

543. cut [v.]

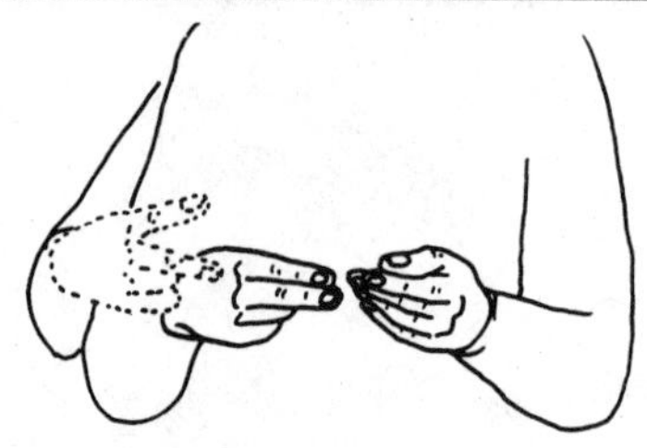

Arabic: qátaa قطع
Chinese: qiē 切
Dutch: snijden
French: couper
German: schneiden
Italian: tagliare
Japanese: kiru 切る
Korean: jarŭda 짜르다
Portuguese: cortar
Russian: rézat' резать
Spanish: cortar
Swedish: skära

544. Czechoslovakia [n.]

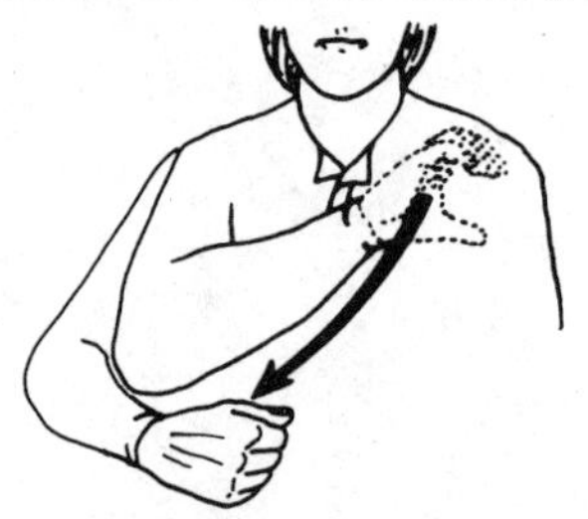

Arabic: chikoslofákia تشيكوسلوفاكيا
Chinese: jiékè 捷克
Dutch: Tsjechoslowakije
French: Tchécoslovaquie
German: Tschechoslowakei
Italian: Cecoslovacchia
Japanese: Chekosurobakia チェコスロバキア
Korean: Chekoslobakia 체코슬로바키아
Portuguese: Checoslováquia
Russian: Chekhoslovákiya Чехословакия
Spanish: Checoslovaquia
Swedish: Tjeckoslovakien

545. daily [adj.]

Arabic: yáumi يومي
Chinese: tiāntiān 天天
Dutch: dagelijks
French: quotidien
German: täglich
Italian: quotidiano
Japanese: mainichi no 毎日の
Korean: maeirŭi 매일의
Portuguese: diário
Russian: yezhednévnyy ежедневный
Spanish: diario
Swedish: daglig

546. damage [n.]

Arabic: dhárar ضرر
Chinese: sŭnhài 損害
Dutch: schade
French: dommage
German: Schaden
Italian: danno
Japanese: songai 損害
Korean: p'ihae 피해
Portuguese: dano
Russian: povrezhdéniye повреждение
Spanish: daño
Swedish: skada

547. damp [adj.]

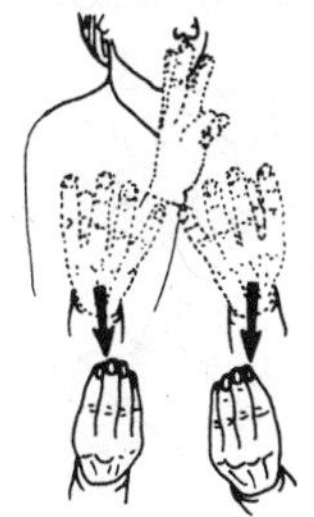

Arabic: ráteb رطب
Chinese: cháoshīde 潮濕的
Dutch: vochtig
French: humide
German: feucht
Italian: umido
Japanese: shikke no aru 湿気のある
Korean: sŭp'han 습한
Portuguese: úmido
Russian: syróy сырой
Spanish: húmedo
Swedish: fuktig

548. dance [v.]

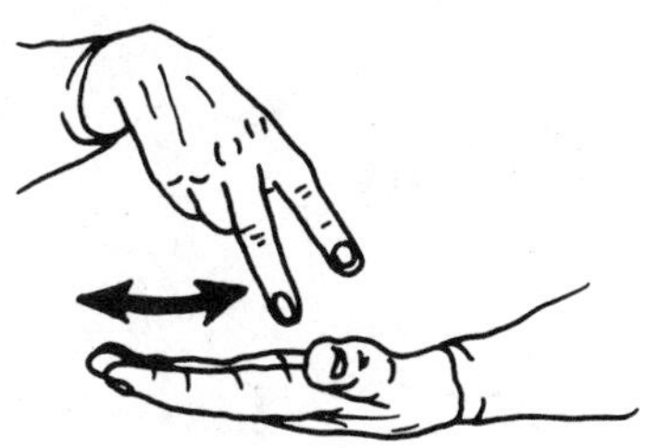

Arabic: ráqasa رقص
Chinese: tiàowŭ 跳舞
Dutch: dansen
French: danser
German: tanzen
Italian: ballare
Japanese: odoru 踊る
Korean: ch'umch'uda 춤추다
Portuguese: dançar
Russian: tantsevát' танцевать
Spanish: bailar
Swedish: dansa

549. danger [n.]

Arabic: khátar خطر
Chinese: wéixiǎn 危險
Dutch: gevaar
French: danger
German: Gefahr
Italian: pericolo
Japanese: kiken 危険
Korean: wihŏm 위험
Portuguese: perigo
Russian: opásnost' опасность
Spanish: peligro
Swedish: fara

550. dark [adj.]

Arabic: múdhlem مظلم
Chinese: ànde 暗的
Dutch: donker
French: sombre
German: dunkel
Italian: oscuro
Japanese: kurai 暗い
Korean: ŏduun 어두운
Portuguese: escuro
Russian: tyómnyy тёмный
Spanish: obscuro
Swedish: mörk

551. date (calendar) [n.]

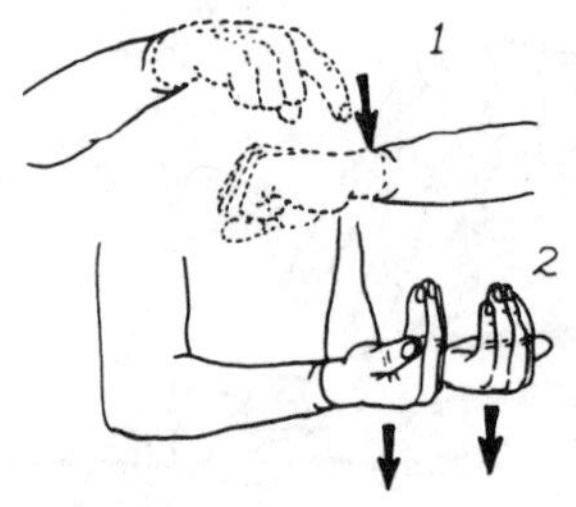

Arabic: at-taríkh التاريخ
Chinese: rìqí 日期
Dutch: datum
French: date
German: Datum
Italian: data
Japanese: hizuke 日付
Korean: naltja 날자
Portuguese: data
Russian: dáta дата
Spanish: fecha
Swedish: datum

552. daughter [n.]

Arabic: bint بنت
Chinese: nǚ-ér 女兒
Dutch: dochter
French: fille
German: Tochter
Italian: figlia
Japanese: musume 娘
Korean: ttal 딸
Portuguese: filha
Russian: doch' дочь
Spanish: hija
Swedish: dotter

553. day [n.]

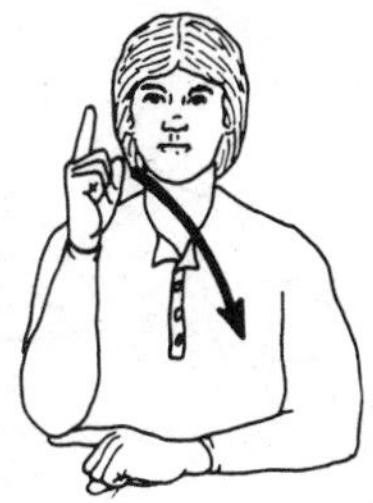

Arabic: yum يوم
Chinese: tiān 天
Dutch: dag
French: jour
German: Tag
Italian: giorno
Japanese: hi 日
Korean: nal 날
Portuguese: dia
Russian: den' день
Spanish: día
Swedish: dag

554. dead [adj.]

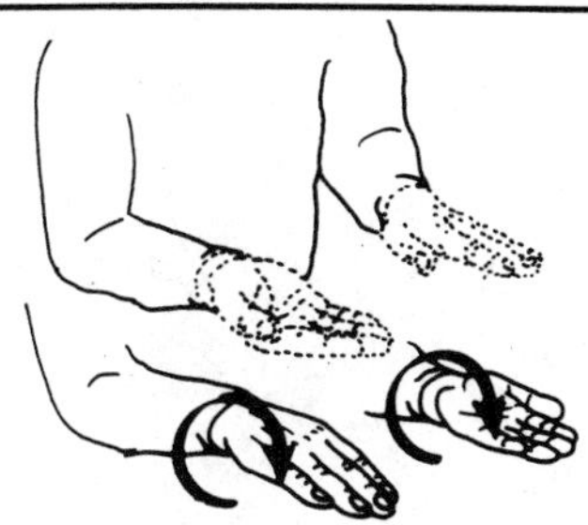

Arabic: méyet ميت
Chinese: sǐde 死的
Dutch: dood
French: décédé
German: tot
Italian: morto
Japanese: shinda 死んだ
Korean: jugŭn 죽은
Portuguese: morto
Russian: myórtvyy мёртвый
Spanish: muerto
Swedish: död

555. deaf [adj.]

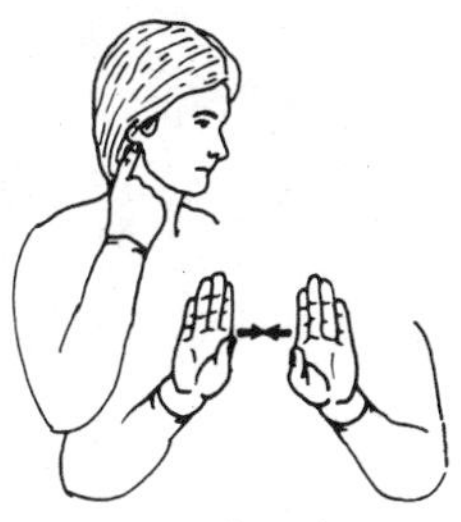

Arabic: asám أصم
Chinese: lóngde 聾的
Dutch: doof
French: sourd
German: taub
Italian: sordo
Japanese: tsumbo no つんぼの
Korean: kwimŏgŭn 귀먹은
Portuguese: surdo
Russian: glukhóy глухой
Spanish: sordo
Swedish: döv

556. dear (beloved) [adj.]

Arabic: aazíz عزيز
Chinese: qīn-àide 親愛的
Dutch: lief
French: cher
German: lieber
Italian: caro
Japanese: shin aina 親愛な
Korean: chinaehanŭn 친애하는
Portuguese: caro
Russian: dorogóy дорогой
Spanish: querido
Swedish: kär

557. death [n.]

Arabic: maut موت
Chinese: sǐwáng 死亡
Dutch: dood
French: mort
German: Tod
Italian: morte
Japanese: shi 死
Korean: jugŭm 죽음
Portuguese: morte
Russian: smert' смерть
Spanish: muerte
Swedish: död

558. debt [n.]

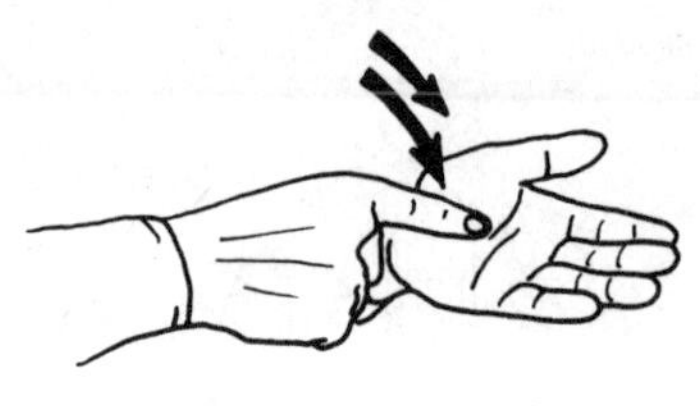

Arabic: deyn دين
Chinese: zhàiwù 債物
Dutch: schuld
French: dette
German: Schuld
Italian: debito
Japanese: shakkin 借金
Korean: bit 빚
Portuguese: dívida
Russian: dolg долг
Spanish: deuda
Swedish: skuld

559. decay (rot) [v.]

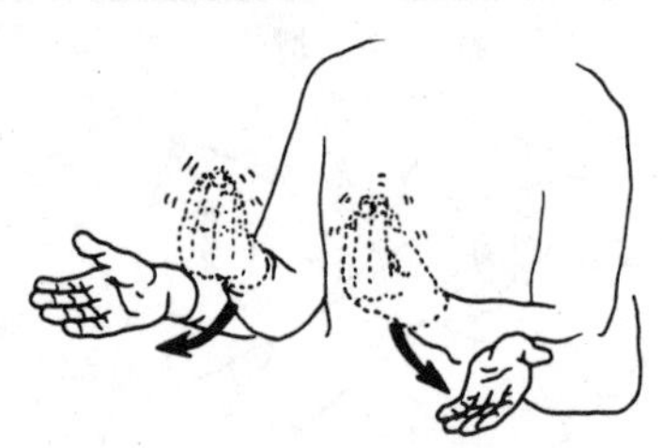

Arabic: tahállala تحلل
Chinese: fŭlàn 腐爛
Dutch: verrotten
French: pourrir
German: faulen
Italian: imputridire
Japanese: kuchiru 朽ちる
Korean: ssŏkta 썩다
Portuguese: apodrecer
Russian: gnit' гнить
Spanish: pudrirse
Swedish: ruttna

560. deceit [n.]

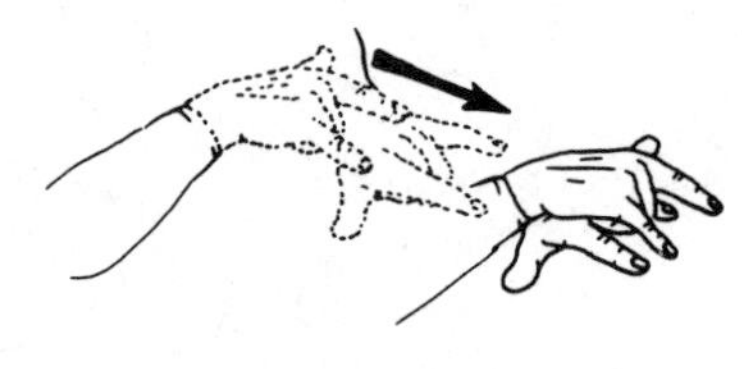

Arabic: ghush غش
Chinese: qīpiàn 欺騙
Dutch: bedrog
French: tromperie
German: Betrug
Italian: inganno
Japanese: sagi 詐欺
Korean: sogim 속임
Portuguese: engano
Russian: obmán обман
Spanish: engaño
Swedish: bedrägeri

561. December [n.]

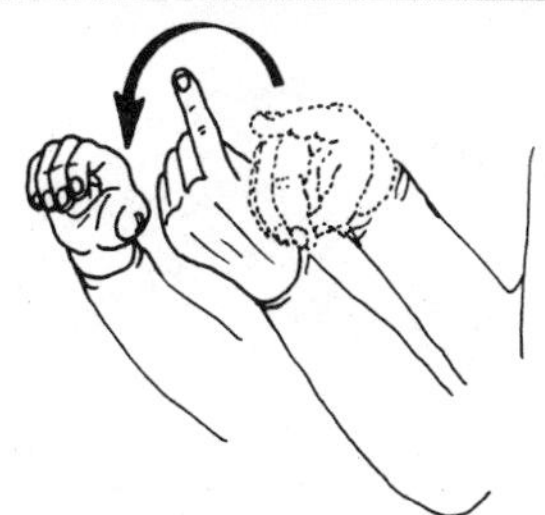

Arabic: disémber ديسمبر
Chinese: shí-èryuè 十二月
Dutch: december
French: décembre
German: Dezember
Italian: dicembre
Japanese: jūnigatsu 十二月
Korean: shibiwŏl 십이월
Portuguese: dezembro
Russian: dekábr' декабрь
Spanish: diciembre
Swedish: december

562. decide [v.]

Arabic: qárara قرر
Chinese: juédìng 决定
Dutch: beslissen
French: décider
German: entscheiden
Italian: decidere
Japanese: kimeru 決める
Korean: kyŏljŏnghada 결정하다
Portuguese: decidir
Russian: reshát' решать
Spanish: decidir
Swedish: bestämma

563. declare [v.]

Arabic: áalana اعلن
Chinese: xuānbù 宣佈
Dutch: verklaren
French: déclarer
German: erklären
Italian: dichiarare
Japanese: sengen suru 宣言する
Korean: sŏnŏnhada 선언하다
Portuguese: declarar
Russian: ob''yavlyát' объявлять
Spanish: declarar
Swedish: uppgiva

564. decorate (adorn) [v.]

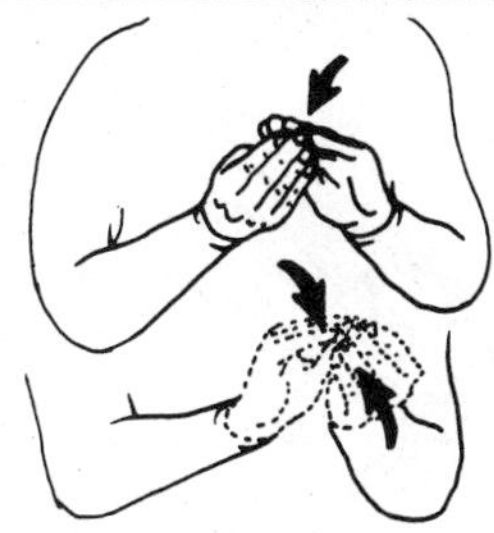

Arabic: zéyana زين
Chinese: zhuāngshì 裝飾
Dutch: versieren
French: décorer
German: schmücken
Italian: decorare
Japanese: kazaru 飾る
Korean: jangshik'hada 장식하다
Portuguese: decorar
Russian: ukrashát' украшать
Spanish: decorar
Swedish: dekorera

565. decrease [v.]

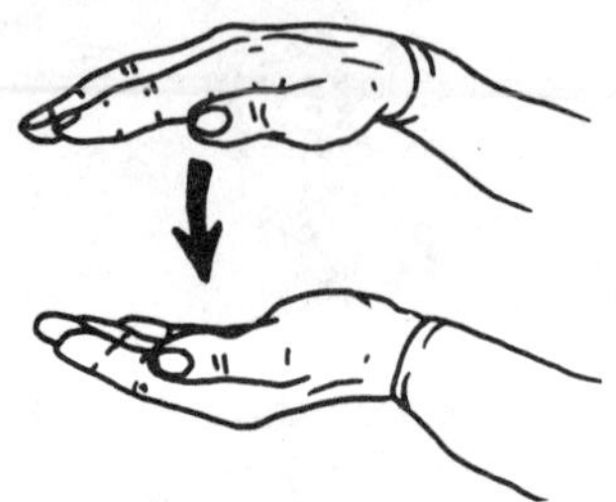

Arabic: náqasa نقص
Chinese: jiǎnshǎo 減少
Dutch: verminderen
French: diminuer
German: abnehmen
Italian: diminuire
Japanese: genshō suru 減少する
Korean: julda 줄다
Portuguese: diminuir
Russian: umen'shát' уменьшать
Spanish: disminuir
Swedish: förminska

566. deed (feat) [n.]

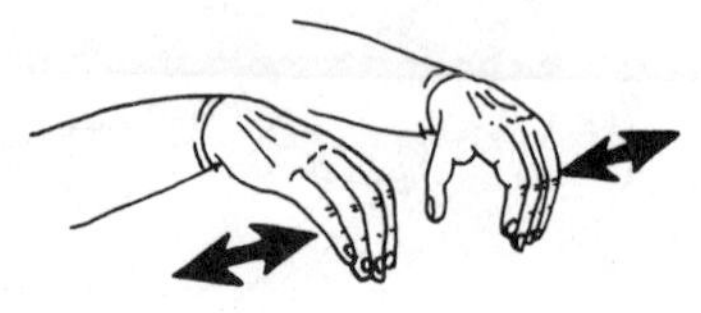

Arabic: áamal عمل
Chinese: xíngwéi 行爲
Dutch: daad
French: exploit
German: Tat
Italian: fatto
Japanese: kōi 行為
Korean: haengwi 행위
Portuguese: ação
Russian: postúpok поступок
Spanish: hazaña
Swedish: gärning

567. deep [adj.]

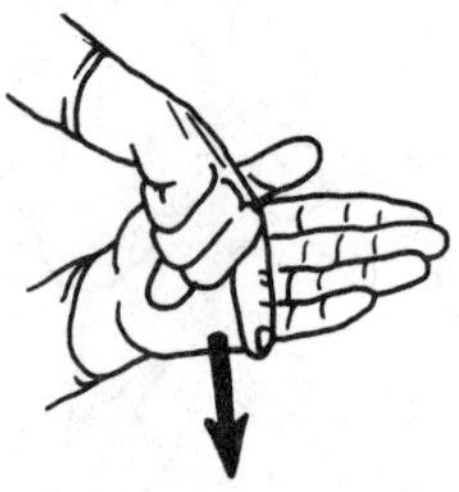

Arabic: aamíyuq عميق
Chinese: shēnde 深的
Dutch: diep
French: profond
German: tief
Italian: profondo
Japanese: fukai 深い
Korean: gip'ŭn 깊은
Portuguese: profundo
Russian: glubókiy глубокий
Spanish: profundo
Swedish: djup

568. deer [n.]

Arabic: ghazáal غزال
Chinese: lù 鹿
Dutch: hert
French: cerf
German: Wild
Italian: cervo
Japanese: shika 鹿
Korean: sasŭm 사슴
Portuguese: veado
Russian: olén' олень
Spanish: ciervo
Swedish: hjort

569. defeat [v.]

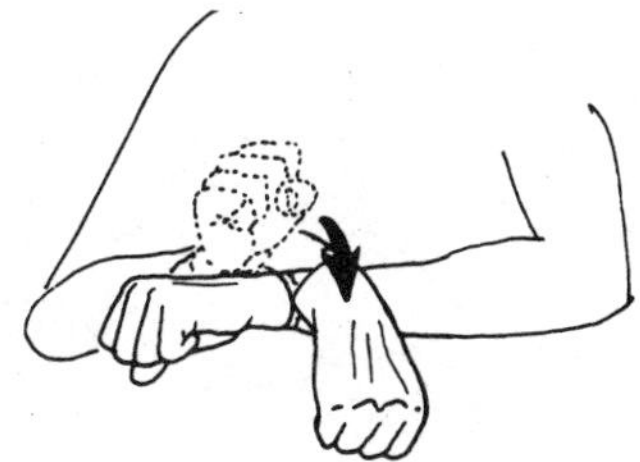

Arabic: házama هزم
Chinese: dǎbài 打敗
Dutch: verslaan
French: vaincre
German: schlagen
Italian: sconfiggere
Japanese: makasu 負かす
Korean: jiuda 지우다
Portuguese: derrotar
Russian: pobezhdát' побеждать
Spanish: derrotar
Swedish: besegra

570. defend [v.]

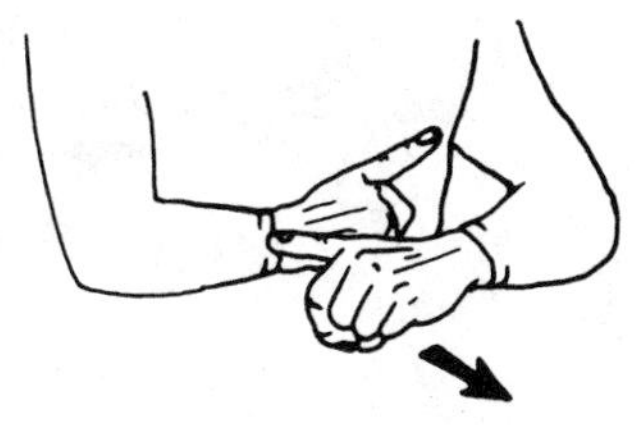

Arabic: dáfaa دافع
Chinese: bǎowèi 保衛
Dutch: verdedigen
French: défendre
German: verteidigen
Italian: difendere
Japanese: mamoru 守る
Korean: bangwihada 방위하다
Portuguese: defender
Russian: zashchishchát' защищать
Spanish: defender
Swedish: försvara

571. deficiency [n.]

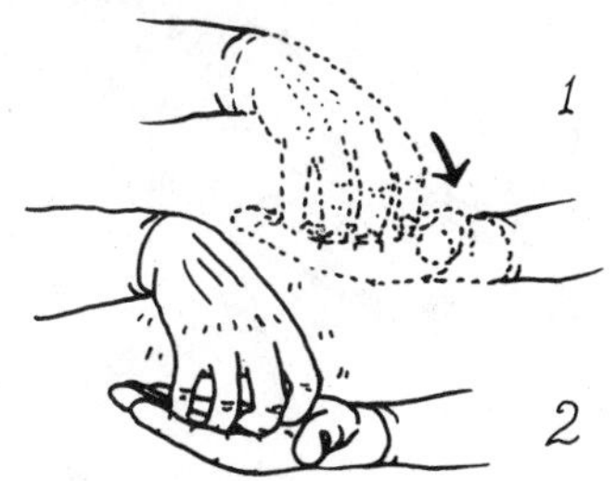

Arabic: áajiz عجز
Chinese: quēxiàn 缺陷
Dutch: gebrek
French: insuffisance
German: Mangel
Italian: deficienza
Japanese: fusoku 不足
Korean: kyŏlham 결함
Portuguese: deficiência
Russian: nedostátok недостаток
Spanish: deficiencia
Swedish: bristfällighet

572. define [v.]

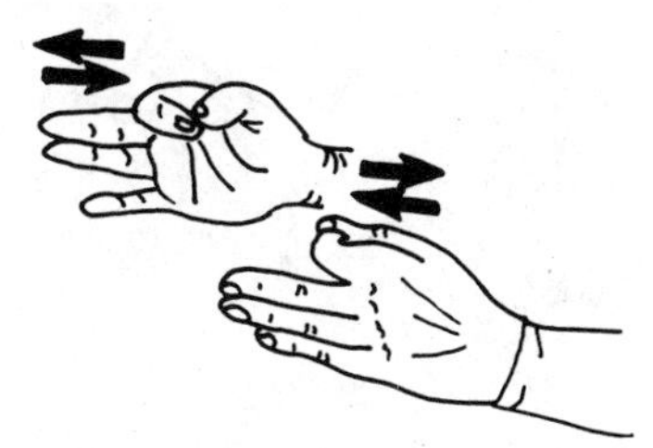

Arabic: áarafa عرف
Chinese: xià dìngyì 下定義
Dutch: bepalen
French: définir
German: definieren
Italian: definire
Japanese: teigi suru 定義する
Korean: jŏnghada 정하다
Portuguese: definir
Russian: opredelyát' определять
Spanish: definir
Swedish: definiera

573. degree (extent) [n.]

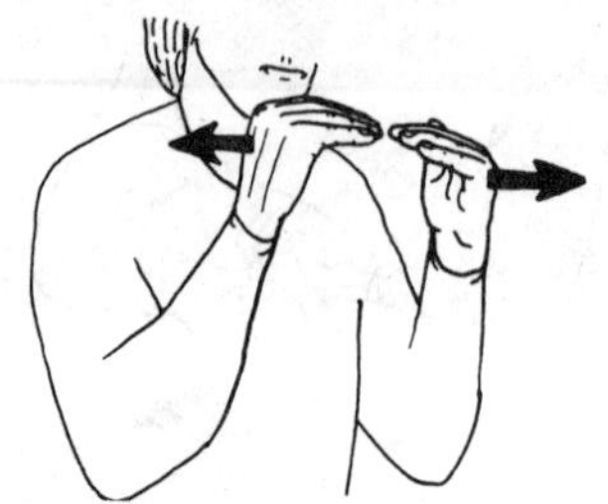

Arabic: dáraja درجة
Chinese: chéngdù 程度
Dutch: graad
French: degré
German: Grad
Italian: grado
Japanese: teido 程度
Korean: jŏngdo 정도
Portuguese: grau
Russian: stépen' степень
Spanish: grado
Swedish: grad

574. delay [v.]

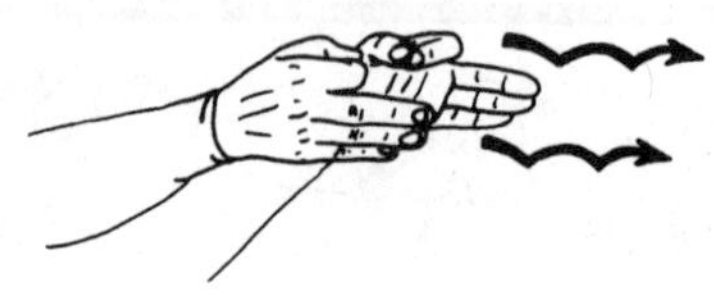

Arabic: ákhara أخر
Chinese: yánwù 延誤
Dutch: vertragen
French: retarder
German: verzögern
Italian: ritardare
Japanese: okuraseru 遅らせる
Korean: jiyŏnshik'ida 지연시키다
Portuguese: atrasar
Russian: zadérzhivat' задерживать
Spanish: retrasar
Swedish: fördröja

575. delicate [adj.]

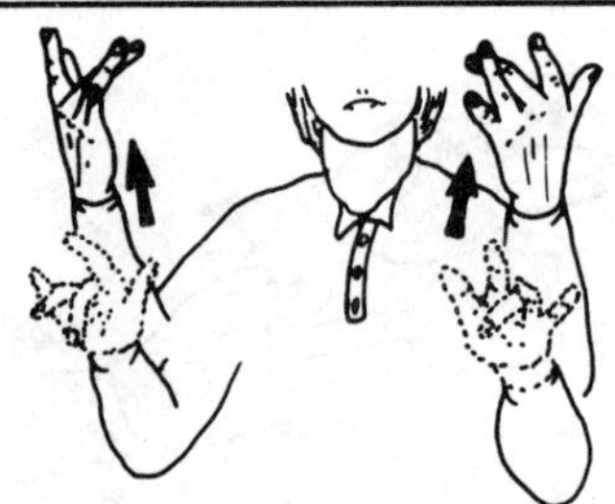

Arabic: raqíeq رقيق
Chinese: jīng zhì 精緻
Dutch: fijn
French: délicat
German: zart
Italian: delicato
Japanese: sensai na 繊細な
Korean: mimyohan 미묘한
Portuguese: delicado
Russian: delikátnyy деликатный
Spanish: delicado
Swedish: fin

576. delicious [adj.]

Arabic: ladhídh لذيذ
Chinese: hǎochī 好吃
Dutch: lekker
French: délicieux
German: köstlich
Italian: delizioso
Japanese: totemo oishii とてもおいしい
Korean: madinnŭn 맛있는
Portuguese: delicioso
Russian: vkúsnyy вкусный
Spanish: delicioso
Swedish: läcker

577. delight [n.]

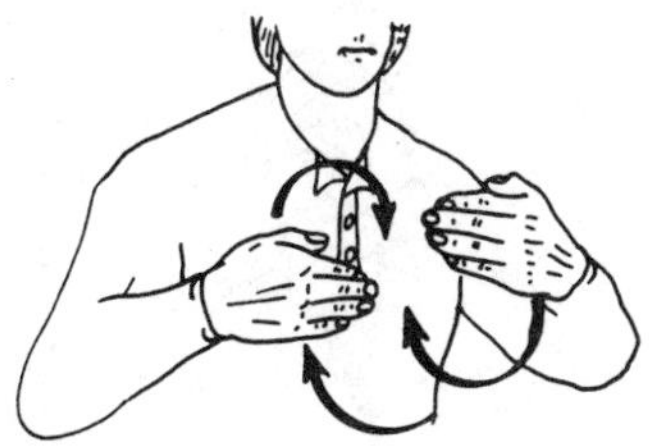

Arabic: surúr سرور
Chinese: huānxǐ 歡喜
Dutch: genot
French: délice
German: Entzücken
Italian: diletto
Japanese: yorokobi 喜び
Korean: gibbŭm 기쁨
Portuguese: deleite
Russian: vostórg восторг
Spanish: deleite
Swedish: glädje

578. deliver [v.]

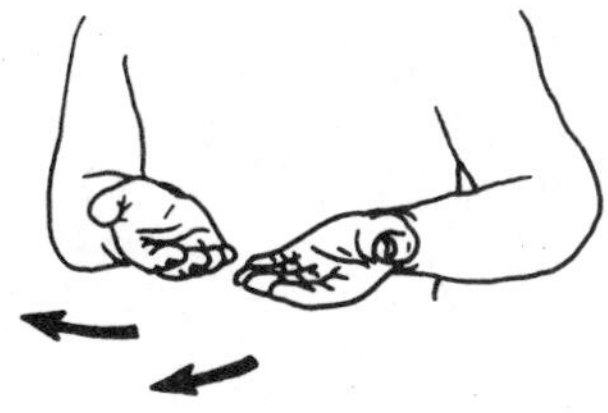

Arabic: wassála وصل
Chinese: dìsòng 遞送
Dutch: afleveren
French: livrer
German: liefern
Italian: consegnare
Japanese: haitatsu suru 配達する
Korean: jŏnhada 전하다
Portuguese: entregar
Russian: dostavlyát' доставлять
Spanish: entregar
Swedish: leverera

579. demand (requirement) [n.]

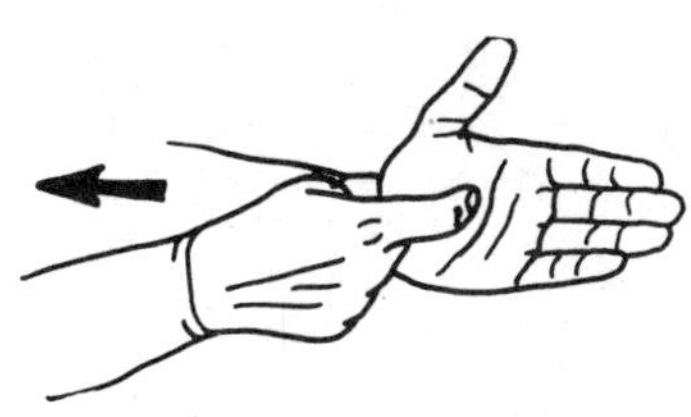

Arabic: tálab طلب
Chinese: yāoqiú 要求
Dutch: vraag
French: exigence
German: Erfordernis
Italian: esigenza
Japanese: yōkyū 要求
Korean: yogu 요구
Portuguese: exigência
Russian: trébovaniye требование
Spanish: exigencia
Swedish: krav

580. democracy [n.]

Arabic: dimoqratía ديمقراطية
Chinese: mínzhŭ zhŭyì 民主主義
Dutch: democratie
French: démocratie
German: Demokratie
Italian: democrazia
Japanese: minshu-shugi 民主主義
Korean: minjujuui 민주주의
Portuguese: democracia
Russian: demokrátiya демократия
Spanish: democracia
Swedish: demokrati

581. demonstrate [v.]

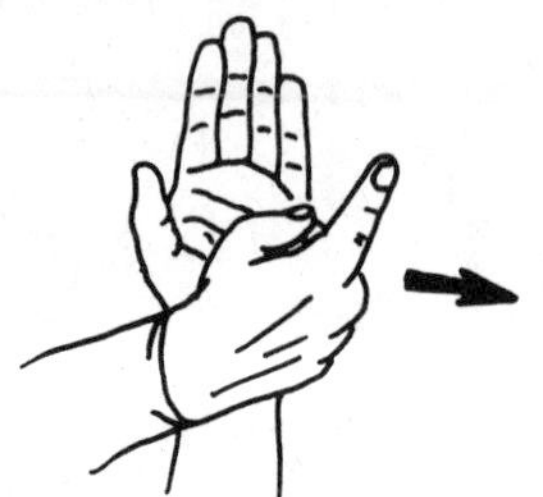

Arabic: áarada عرض
Chinese: shìfàn 示範
Dutch: demonstreren
French: démontrer
German: demonstrieren
Italian: dimostrare
Japanese: setsumei suru 説明する
Korean: shiwihada 시위하다
Portuguese: demonstrar
Russian: demonstrírovat' демонстрировать
Spanish: demostrar
Swedish: demonstrera

582. Denmark [n.]

Arabic: ad-dénimark الدانمارك
Chinese: dānmài 丹麥
Dutch: Denemarken
French: Danemark
German: Dänemark
Italian: Danimarca
Japanese: Denmāku デンマーク
Korean: Denma'k 덴막
Portuguese: Dinamarca
Russian: Dániya Дания
Spanish: Dinamarca
Swedish: Danmark

583. dentist [n.]

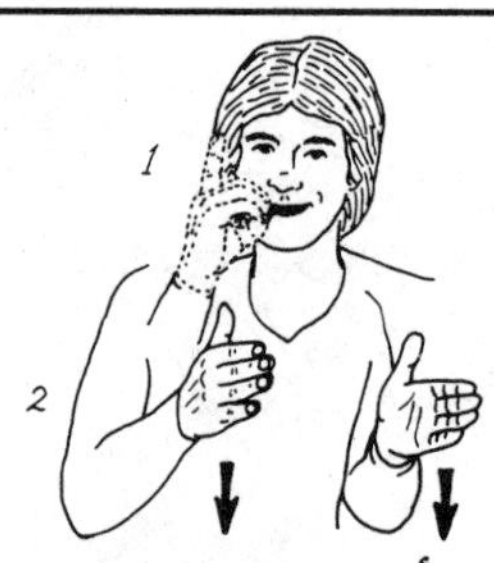

Arabic: tabíb asnán طبيب أسنان
Chinese: yákē yīshēng 牙科醫生
Dutch: tandarts
French: dentiste
German: Zahnarzt
Italian: dentista
Japanese: haisha 歯医者
Korean: ch'ikwa ŭisa 치과의사
Portuguese: dentista
Russian: zubnóy vrach зубной врач
Spanish: dentista
Swedish: tandläkare

584. deny [v.]

Arabic: ráfada رفض
Chinese: fǒurèn 否認
Dutch: ontkennen
French: démentir
German: verweigern
Italian: negare
Japanese: hinin suru 否認する
Korean: bujŏnghada 부정하다
Portuguese: negar
Russian: otritsát' отрицать
Spanish: negar
Swedish: förneka

585. department (branch) [n.]

Arabic: qism قسم
Chinese: bùmén 部門
Dutch: afdeling
French: département
German: Abteilung
Italian: dipartimento
Japanese: bu 部
Korean: bu 부
Portuguese: departamento
Russian: otdél отдел
Spanish: departamento
Swedish: avdelning

586. depend (on) [v.]

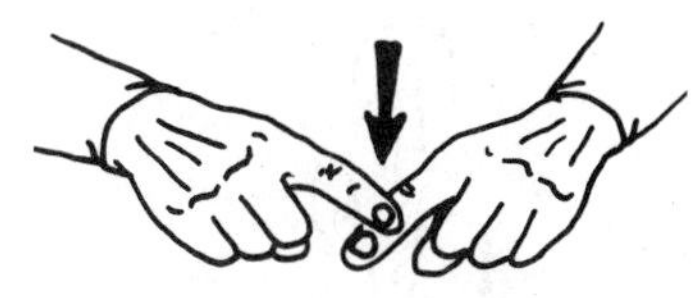

Arabic: iaatámada áala اعتمد على
Chinese: yīkào 依靠
Dutch: afhangen
French: dépendre
German: abhängen
Italian: dipendere
Japanese: . . . ni yoru …による
Korean: ŭijonhada 의존하다
Portuguese: depender
Russian: zavíset' ot зависеть от
Spanish: depender
Swedish: vara beroende

587. deposit [v.]

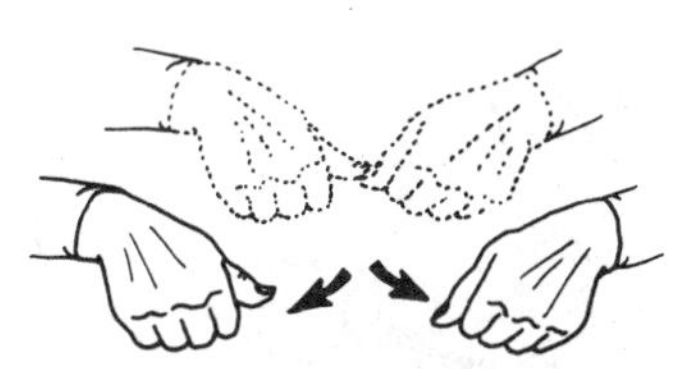

Arabic: áudaa اودع
Chinese: jīcún 積存
Dutch: storten
French: déposer
German: deponieren
Italian: depositare
Japanese: azukeru 預ける
Korean: nŏt'a 넣다
Portuguese: depositar
Russian: klast' класть
Spanish: depositar
Swedish: deponera

588. deprive [v.]

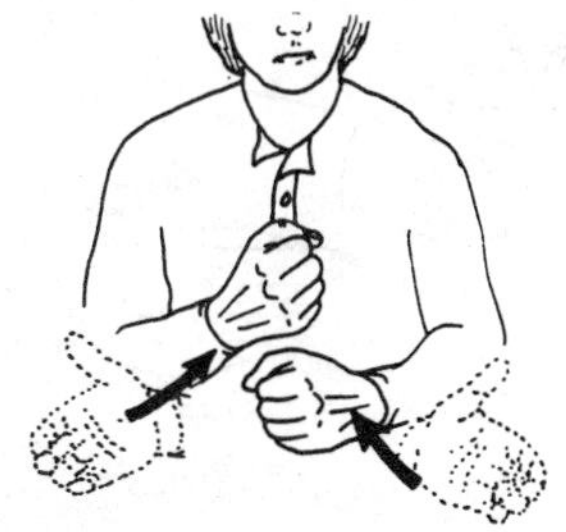

Arabic: hárama حرم
Chinese: bōduó 剝奪
Dutch: beroven
French: priver
German: berauben
Italian: privare
Japanese: ubau 奪う
Korean: ppaeat'nŭnda 빼앗는다
Portuguese: privar
Russian: lishát' лишать
Spanish: privar
Swedish: beröva

589. descend [v.]

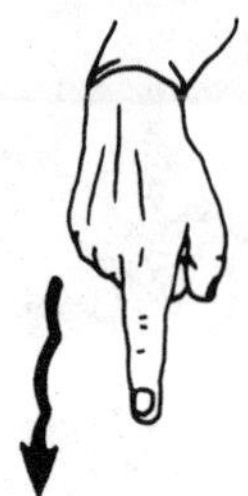

Arabic: inhádara انحدر
Chinese: chuánxià 降下
Dutch: neerdalen
French: descendre
German: inabsteigen
Italian: discendere
Japanese: sagaru 下がる
Korean: naeryŏoda 내려오다
Portuguese: descender
Russian: spuskát'sya спускаться
Spanish: descender
Swedish: gå ned

590. descendant [n.]

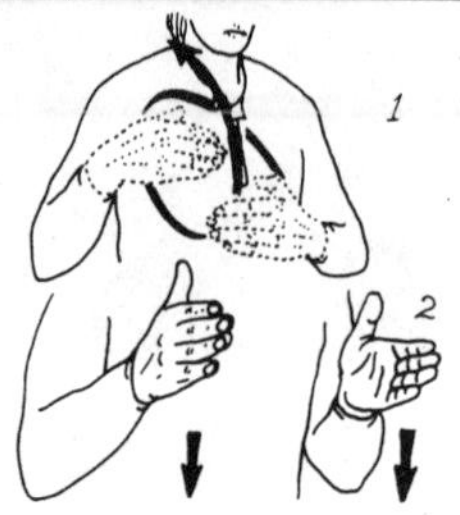

Arabic: salíl سليل
Chinese: hòudài 後代
Dutch: nakomeling
French: descendant
German: Abkömmling
Italian: discendente
Japanese: shison 子孫
Korean: jason 자손
Portuguese: descendente
Russian: potómok потомок
Spanish: descendiente
Swedish: avkomling

591. describe [v.]

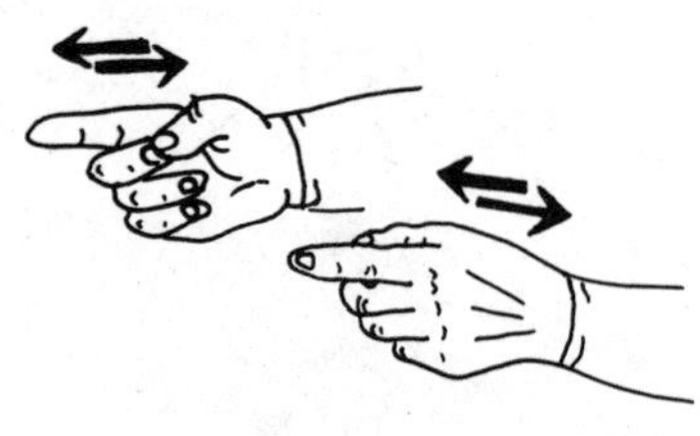

Arabic: wásafa وصف
Chinese: miáoxiě 描述
Dutch: beschrijven
French: décrire
German: beschreiben
Italian: descrivere
Japanese: kijutsu suru 記述する
Korean: malhada 말하다
Portuguese: descrever
Russian: opísyvat' описывать
Spanish: describir
Swedish: beskriva

592. deserve [v.]

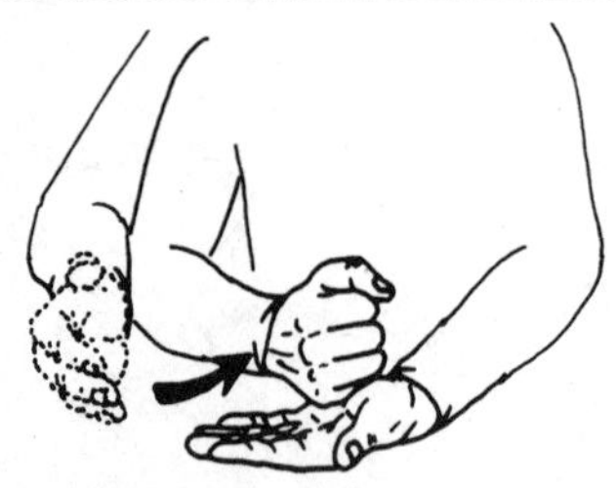

Arabic: istaháqa استحق
Chinese: gāidé 該得
Dutch: verdienen
French: mériter
German: verdienen
Italian: meritare
Japanese: . . .o ukeru ni atai suru
…を受けるに値する
Korean: kach'iga itda 가치가 있다
Portuguese: merecer
Russian: zaslúzhivat' заслуживать
Spanish: merecer
Swedish: förtjäna

593. desire [n.]

Arabic: rághba رغبة
Chinese: yùwàng 慾望
Dutch: wens
French: désir
German: Verlangen
Italian: desiderio
Japanese: gambō 願望
Korean: sowŏn 소원
Portuguese: desejo
Russian: zhelániye желание
Spanish: deseo
Swedish: önskan

594. despise [v.]

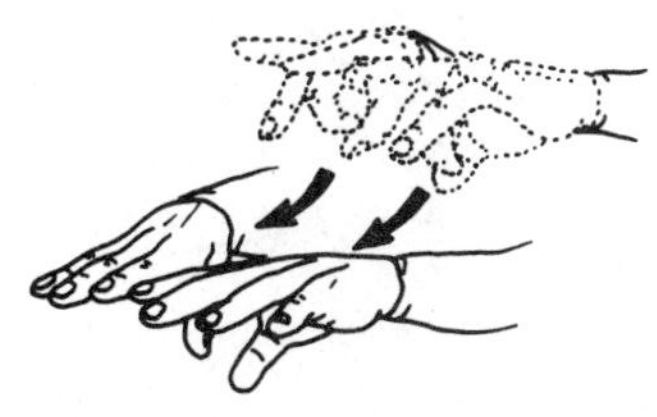

Arabic: ihtáqara احتقر
Chinese: qīngshì 輕視
Dutch: verachten
French: mépriser
German: verachten
Italian: disprezzare
Japanese: . . . o keibetsu suru
…を軽蔑する
Korean: kyŏngmyŏrhada 경멸하다
Portuguese: desprezar
Russian: prezirát' презирать
Spanish: despreciar
Swedish: förakta

595. despite (in spite of) [prep.]

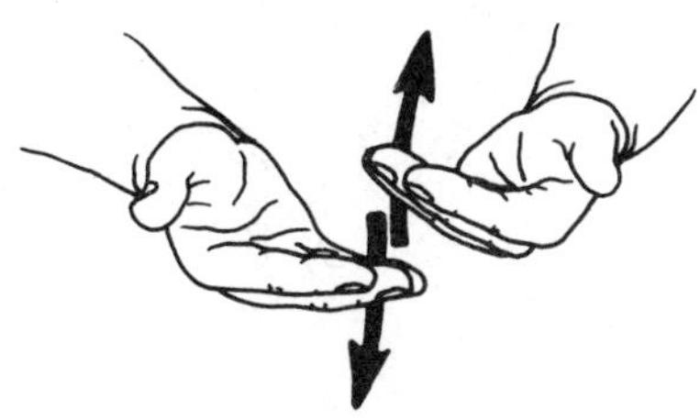

Arabic: áala arrágham min
على الرغم من
Chinese: bùguǎn 不管
Dutch: ondanks
French: malgré
German: trotz
Italian: malgrado
Japanese: . . . nimo kakawarazu
…にもかかわらず
Korean: bulguhago 불구하고
Portuguese: apesar de
Russian: nesmotryá na несмотря на
Spanish: a pesar de
Swedish: trots

596. destroy [v.]

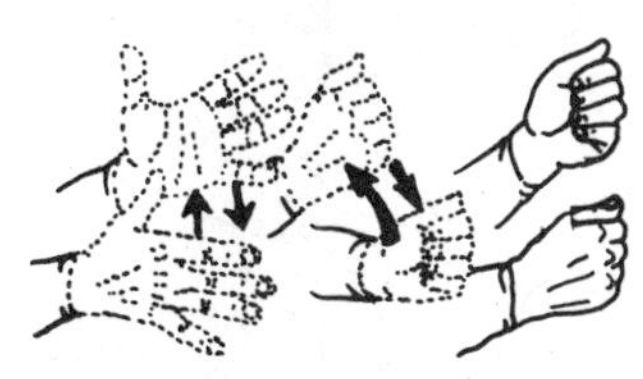

Arabic: háttama حطم
Chinese: huǐhuài 毀壞
Dutch: vernietigen
French: détruire
German: zerstören
Italian: distruggere
Japanese: hōkai suru 崩壊する
Korean: p'agoehada 파괴하다
Portuguese: destruir
Russian: unichtozhát' уничтожать
Spanish: destruir
Swedish: förstöra

597. detect [v.]

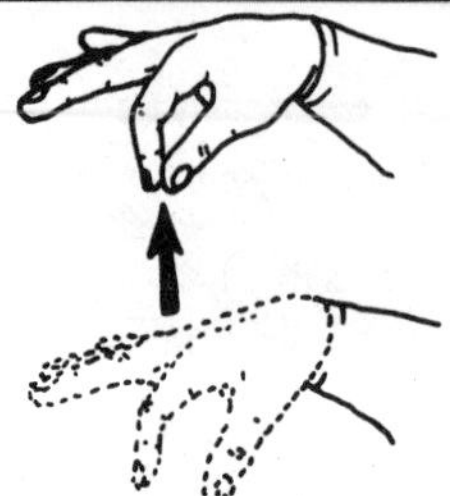

Arabic: iktáshafa اكتشف
Chinese: zhēn chá 偵査
Dutch: ontdekken
French: détecter
German: entdecken
Italian: scoprire
Japanese: miyaburu 見破る
Korean: t'amjihada 탐지하다
Portuguese: detectar
Russian: obnarúzhivat' обнаруживать
Spanish: detectar
Swedish: upptäcka

598. determine [v.]

Arabic: qárara قرر
Chinese: juédìng 决定
Dutch: bepalen
French: déterminer
German: bestimmen
Italian: determinare
Japanese: kesshin suru 決心する
Korean: gyŏlshimhada 결심하다
Portuguese: determinar
Russian: opredelyát' определять
Spanish: determinar
Swedish: bestämma

599. develop [v.]

Arabic: táwwara طور
Chinese: fāzhǎng 發展
Dutch: ontwikkelen
French: développer
German: entwicklen
Italian: sviluppare
Japanese: . . .o hattatsu saseru …を発達させる
Korean: baldalsikida 발달시키다
Portuguese: desenvolver
Russian: razvivát' развивать
Spanish: desarrollar
Swedish: utveckla

600. development [n.]

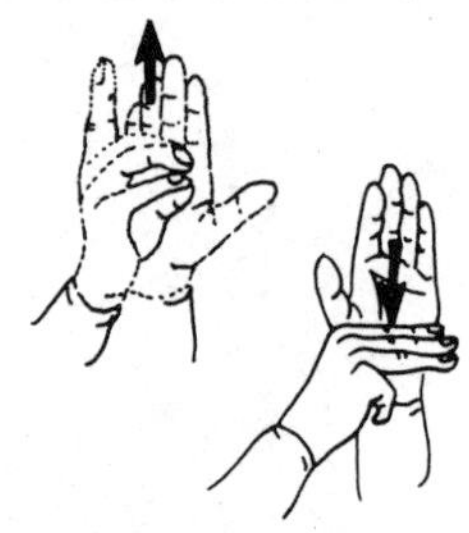

Arabic: tatwír تطوير
Chinese: fāzhǎng 發展
Dutch: ontwikkeling
French: développement
German: Entwicklung
Italian: sviluppo
Japanese: hattatsu 発達
Korean: baldal 발달
Portuguese: desenvolvimento
Russian: razvítiye рфзвитие
Spanish: desarrollo
Swedish: utveckling

601. deviate [v.]

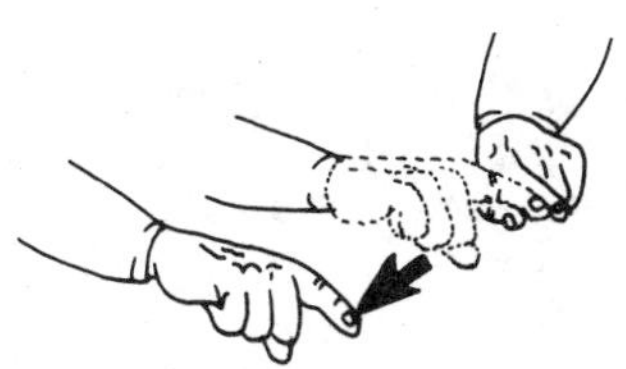

Arabic: inhárafa انحرف
Chinese: piānlí 偏離
Dutch: afwijken
French: dévier
German: abweichen
Italian: deviare
Japanese: hanareru 離れる
Korean: bitnagada 빗나가다
Portuguese: desviar-se
Russian: otklonyát'sya отклоняться
Spanish: desviar
Swedish: avvika

602. devil [n.]

Arabic: shaytán شيطان
Chinese: móguǐ 魔鬼
Dutch: duivel
French: diable
German: Teufel
Italian: diavolo
Japanese: akuma 悪魔
Korean: angma 악마
Portuguese: diabo
Russian: chyórt чёрт
Spanish: diablo
Swedish: djävul

603. diamond [n.]

Arabic: al-más الماس
Chinese: zuànshí 鑽石
Dutch: diamant
French: diamant
German: Diamant
Italian: diamante
Japanese: daiamondo ダイヤモンド
Korean: daiamondŭ 다이아몬드
Portuguese: diamante
Russian: almáz алмаз
Spanish: diamante
Swedish: diamant

604. dictionary [n.]

Arabic: moájam معجم
Chinese: zìdiǎn 字典
Dutch: woordenboek
French: dictionnaire
German: Wörterbuch
Italian: dizionario
Japanese: jisho 辞書
Korean: sajŏn 사전
Portuguese: dicionário
Russian: slovár' словарь
Spanish: diccionario
Swedish: ordbok

605. die [v.]

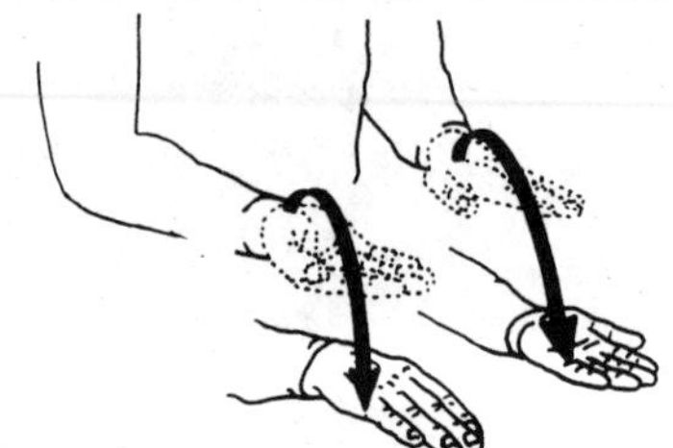

Arabic: máata مات
Chinese: sǐ 死
Dutch: sterven
French: mourir
German: sterben
Italian: morire
Japanese: shinu 死ぬ
Korean: juknŭnda 죽는다
Portuguese: morrer
Russian: umirát' умирать
Spanish: morir
Swedish: dö

606. difference [n.]

Arabic: farq فرق
Chinese: chābié 差别
Dutch: verschil
French: différence
German: Unterschied
Italian: differenza
Japanese: chigai 違い
Korean: ch'ai 차이
Portuguese: diferença
Russian: ráznitsa разница
Spanish: diferencia
Swedish: skillnad

607. difficult [adj.]

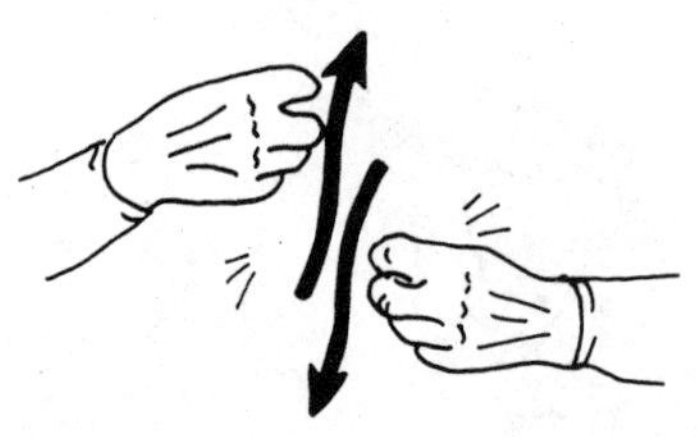

Arabic: sáab صعب
Chinese: kùn nán de 困難的
Dutch: moeilijk
French: difficile
German: schwer
Italian: difficile
Japanese: muzukashii むずかしい
Korean: ŏryŏun 어려운
Portuguese: difícil
Russian: trúdnyy трудный
Spanish: difícil
Swedish: svår

608. dig [v.]

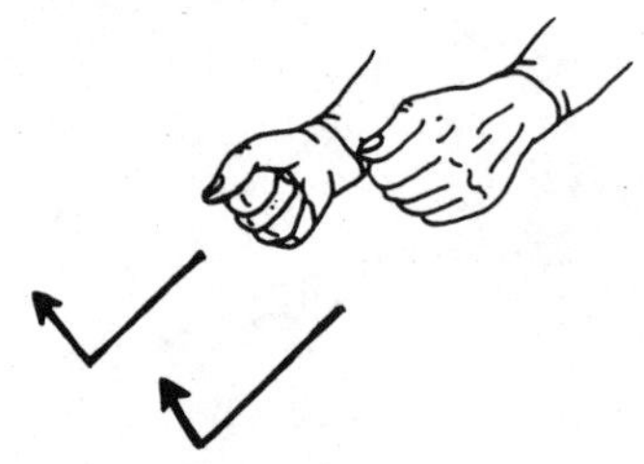

Arabic: háfara حفر
Chinese: wājué 挖掘
Dutch: graven
French: creuser
German: graben
Italian: scavare
Japanese: horu 掘る
Korean: p'ada 파다
Portuguese: cavar
Russian: kopát'sya копаться
Spanish: cavar
Swedish: gräva

609. diligence [n.]

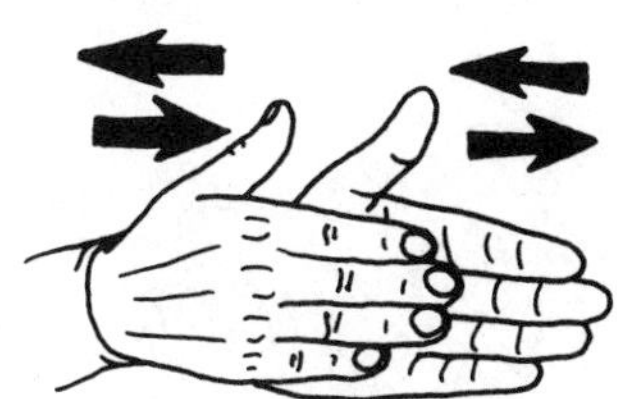

Arabic: nasháat نشاط
Chinese: qínfèn 勤奮
Dutch: ijver
French: diligence
German: Fleiß
Italian: diligenza
Japanese: kimben 勤勉な
Korean: gŭnmyŏn 근면
Portuguese: zêlo
Russian: usérdiye усердие
Spanish: diligencia
Swedish: flit

610. dinner (midday meal) [n.]

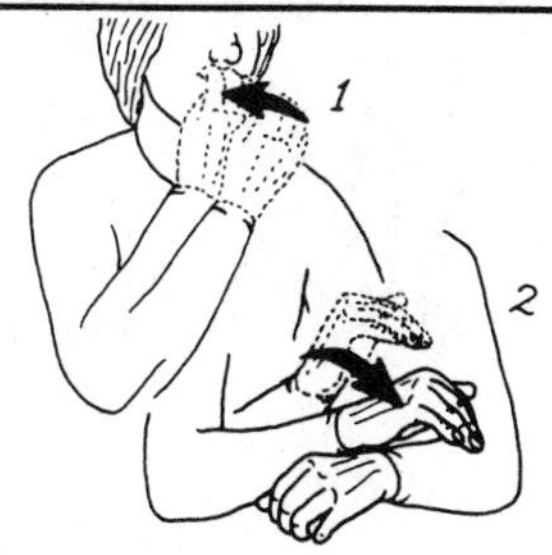

Arabic: ghidhá' غذاء
Chinese: zhōngfàn 中飯
Dutch: middagmaal
French: déjeuner
German: Mittagessen
Italian: pranzo
Japanese: chūshoku 昼食
Korean: jŏngshiksa 정 식사
Portuguese: almôço
Russian: obéd обед
Spanish: almuerzo
Swedish: middag

611. diploma [n.]

Arabic: diblóma ديبلوما
Chinese: zhèngshū 證書
Dutch: diploma
French: diplôme
German: Diplom
Italian: diploma
Japanese: sotsugyō shōsho 卒業証書
Korean: jorŏbjang 졸업장
Portuguese: diploma
Russian: diplóm диплом
Spanish: diploma
Swedish: diplom

612. direct [v.]

Arabic: wájjaha وجه
Chinese: zhǐhuī 指揮
Dutch: leiden
French: diriger
German: leiten
Italian: dirigere
Japanese: shiki suru 指揮する
Korean: garik'ida 가리키다
Portuguese: dirigir
Russian: napravlyát' направлять
Spanish: dirigir
Swedish: rikta

613. direction [n.]

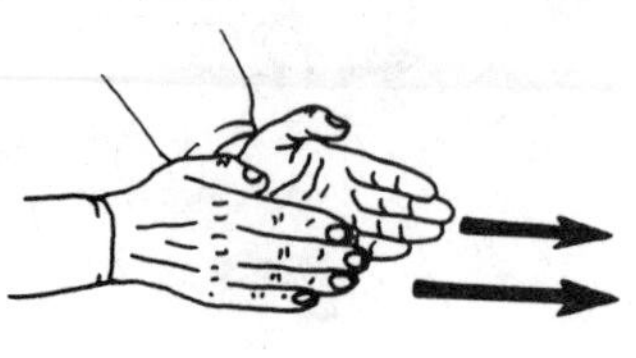

Arabic: itijá اتجاه
Chinese: fāngxiàng 方向
Dutch: richting
French: direction
German: Richtung
Italian: direzione
Japanese: hōgaku 方角
Korean: banghyang 방향
Portuguese: direção
Russian: napravléniye направление
Spanish: dirección
Swedish: riktning

614. director [n.]

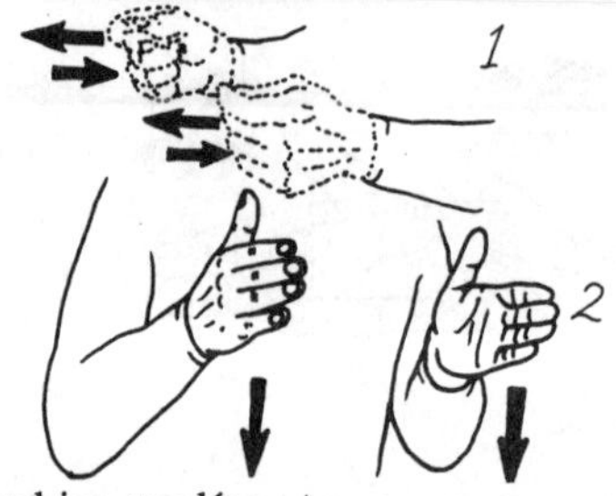

Arabic: mudír مدير
Chinese: zhǐdǎorén 指導人
Dutch: directeur
French: directeur
German: Direktor
Italian: direttore
Japanese: shidōsha 指導者
Korean: jibaein 지배인
Portuguese: diretor
Russian: rukovodítel' руководитель
Spanish: director
Swedish: direktör

615. dirt [n.]

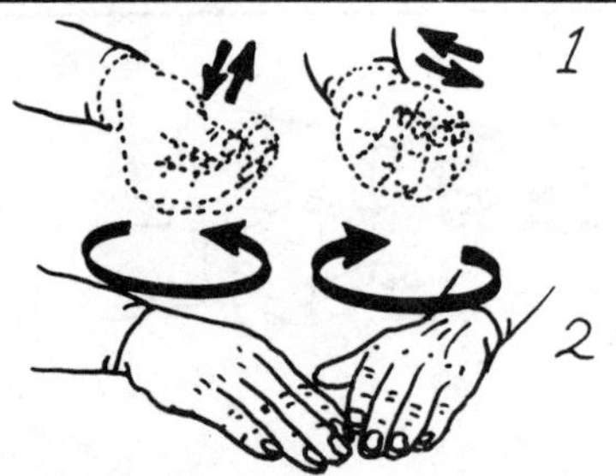

Arabic: qadhurát قاذورات
Chinese: wū wù 污物
Dutch: vuil
French: saleté
German: Schmutz
Italian: sudiciume
Japanese: hokori ほこり
Korean: ssŭregi 쓰레기
Portuguese: sujeira
Russian: gryáz' грязь
Spanish: suciedad
Swedish: smuts

616. dirty [adj.]

Arabic: qádher قذر
Chinese: āng zāng 骯髒
Dutch: vuil
French: sale
German: schmutzig
Italian: sudicio
Japanese: kitanai 汚ない
Korean: dŏrŏun 더러운
Portuguese: sujo
Russian: gryáznyy грязный
Spanish: sucio
Swedish: smutsig

617. disagree [v.]

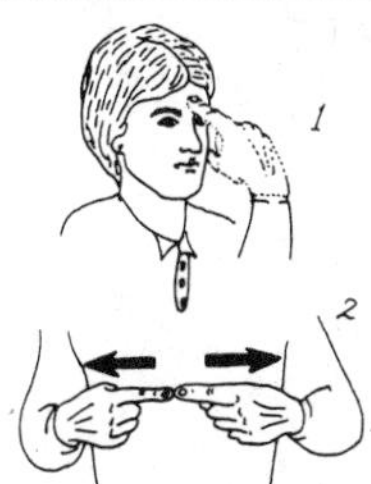

Arabic: khálafa خالف
Chinese: bùtóngyì 不同意
Dutch: het oneens zijn
French: différer
German: nicht übereinstimmen
Italian: dissentire
Japanese: icchi shinai 一致しない
Korean: chansŏnganhanda 찬성안하다
Portuguese: discordar
Russian: ne soglashát'sya не соглашаться
Spanish: discordar
Swedish: vara oense

618. disappear [v.]

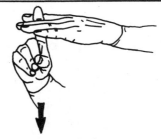

Arabic: ikhtáfa اختفى
Chinese: xiāoshī 消失
Dutch: verdwijnen
French: disparaître
German: verschwinden
Italian: sparire
Japanese: mienaku naru 見えなくなる
Korean: sarajida 사라지다
Portuguese: desaparacer
Russian: ischezát' исчезать
Spanish: desaparecer
Swedish: försvinna

619. disappoint [v.]

Arabic: kháyeba al-amál خيب الآمال
Chinese: shǐ shīwàng 使失望
Dutch: teleurstellen
French: décevoir
German: enttäuschen
Italian: deludere
Japanese: shitsubō saseru 失望させる
Korean: shilmanghada 실망하다
Portuguese: desapontar
Russian: razocharovát' разочаровать
Spanish: decepcionar
Swedish: besvika

620. discipline [n.]

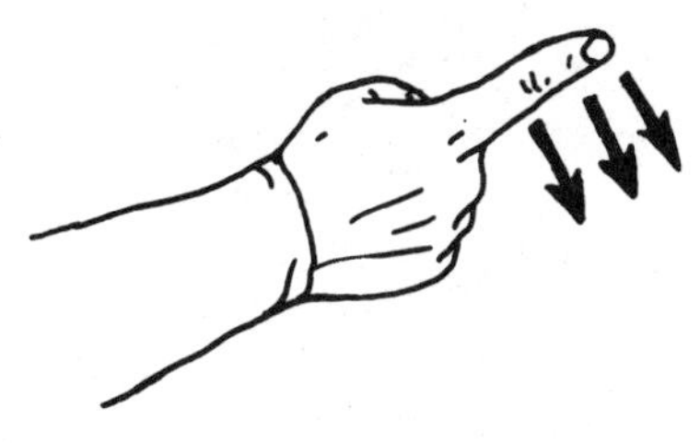

Arabic: ta'adíb تأديب
Chinese: jìlǜ 紀律
Dutch: discipline
French: discipline
German: Disziplin
Italian: disciplina
Japanese: kiritsu 規律
Korean: kyuyul 규율
Portuguese: disciplina
Russian: distsiplína дисциплина
Spanish: disciplina
Swedish: disciplin

621. discourage [v.]

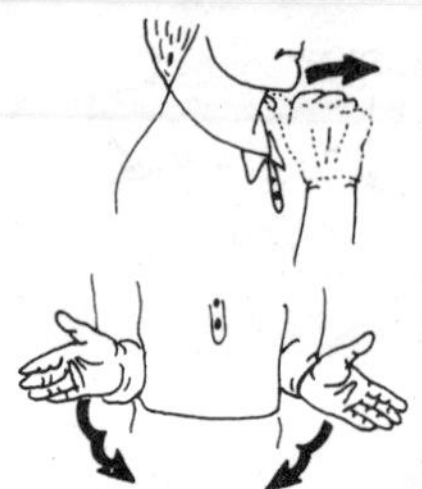

Arabic: áhbata احبط
Chinese: shǐqìněi 使氣餒
Dutch: ontmoedigen
French: décourager
German: entmutigen
Italian: scoraggiare
Japanese: rakutan saseru 落胆させる
Korean: mot'hagehada 못하게 하다
Portuguese: desanimar
Russian: obeskurázhivat' обескураживать
Spanish: desanimar
Swedish: avskräcka

622. discover [v.]

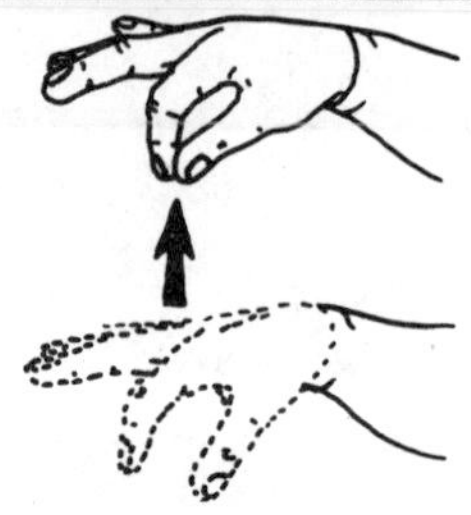

Arabic: iktáshafa اكتشف
Chinese: fāxiàn 發現
Dutch: ontdekken
French: découvrir
German: entdecken
Italian: scoprire
Japanese: hakken suru 発見する
Korean: balgyŏnhada 발견하다
Portuguese: descobrir
Russian: otkryvát' открывать
Spanish: descubrir
Swedish: upptäcka

623. discuss [v.]

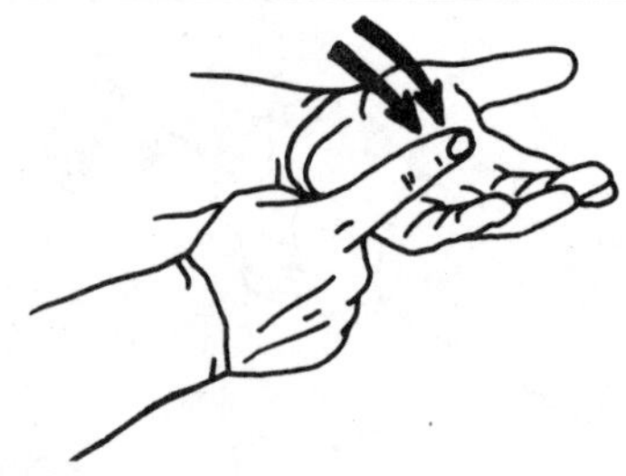

Arabic: náaqasha ناقش
Chinese: tǎolùn 討論
Dutch: bespreken
French: discuter
German: diskutieren
Italian: discutere
Japanese: tōron suru 討論する
Korean: t'oronhada 토론하다
Portuguese: discutir
Russian: obsuzhdát' обсуждать
Spanish: discutir
Swedish: diskutera

624. disease [n.]

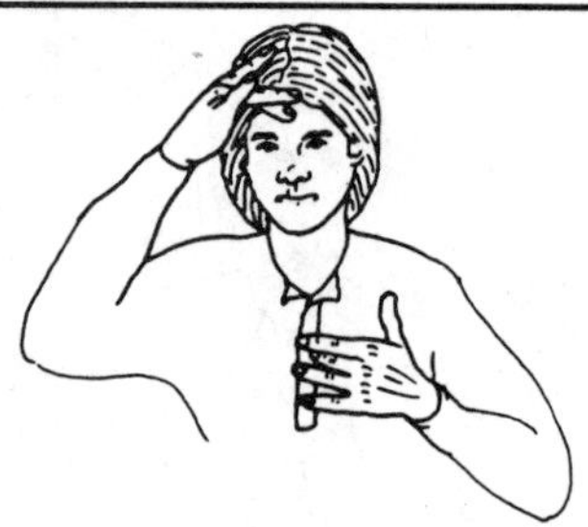

Arabic: márad مرض
Chinese: jíbìng 疾病
Dutch: ziekte
French: maladie
German: Krankheit
Italian: malattia
Japanese: byōki 病気
Korean: byŏng 병
Portuguese: doença
Russian: bolézn' болезнь
Spanish: enfermedad
Swedish: sjukdom

625. disgust [n.]

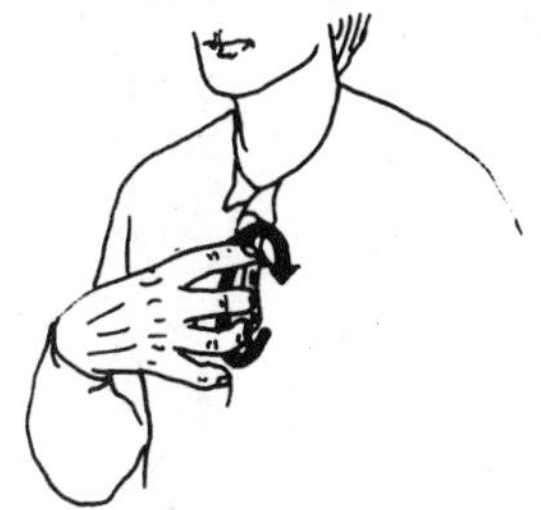

Arabic: ishmí'izaz اشمئزاز
Chinese: yànwù 厭惡
Dutch: walging
French: dégoût
German: Ekel
Italian: disgusto
Japanese: fukai ni suru 不快にする
Korean: shiltjŭng 실증
Portuguese: desgôsto
Russian: otvrashchéniye отвращение
Spanish: disgusto
Swedish: avsmak

626. dish(es) [n.]

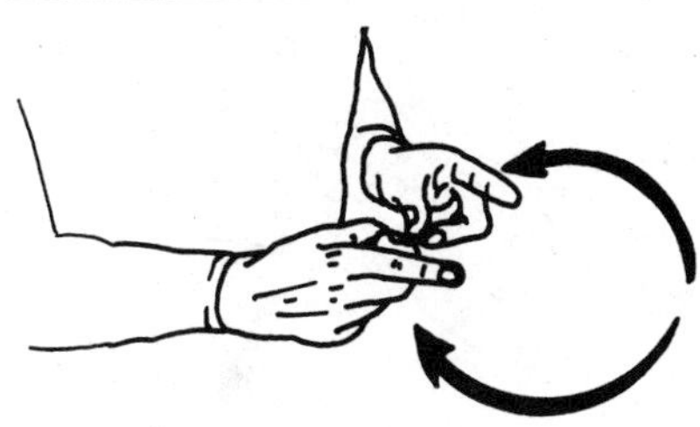

Arabic: sáhun صحن
Chinese: wǎnpán 碗盤
Dutch: schotel
French: plat
German: Geschirr
Italian: piatto
Japanese: sara 皿
Korean: jŏbshi 접시
Portuguese: prato
Russian: posúda посуда
Spanish: plato
Swedish: fat

627. dishonest [adj.]

Arabic: kádheb كاذب
Chinese: bù chéngshí de 不誠實的
Dutch: oneerlijk
French: malhonnête
German: unehrlich
Italian: disonesto
Japanese: fushōjiki na 不正直な
Korean: jŏngjig'haji mot'han
정직하지 못한
Portuguese: desonesto
Russian: nechéstnyy нечестный
Spanish: deshonesto
Swedish: oärlig

628. dislike [v.]

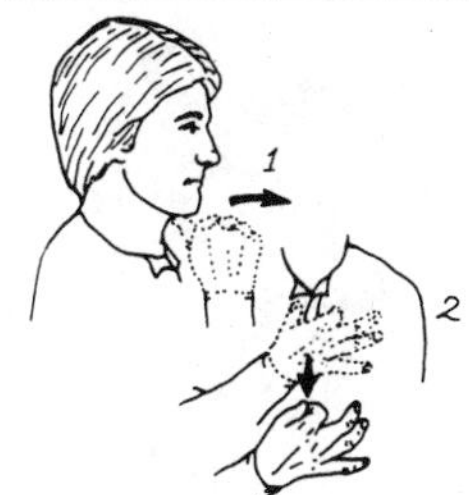

Arabic: káriha كره
Chinese: bù xǐ-aì 不喜爱
Dutch: niet houden van
French: ne pas aimer
German: nicht gerne haben
Italian: non amare
Japanese: kirau 嫌う
Korean: shirŏhada 싫어하다
Portuguese: desgostar
Russian: ne lyubít' не любить
Spanish: desagradar
Swedish: tycka illa om

629. dismiss [v.]

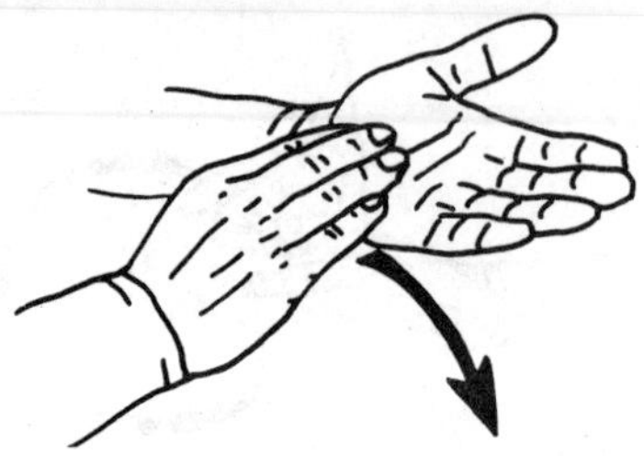

Arabic: tárada طرد
Chinese: jiěsàn 解散
Dutch: ontslaan
French: congédier
German: entlassen
Italian: licenziare
Japanese: kaiko suru 解雇する
Korean: haegohada 해고하다
Portuguese: rejeitar
Russian: otpuskát' отпускать
Spanish: despedir
Swedish: skicka bort

630. disobey [v.]

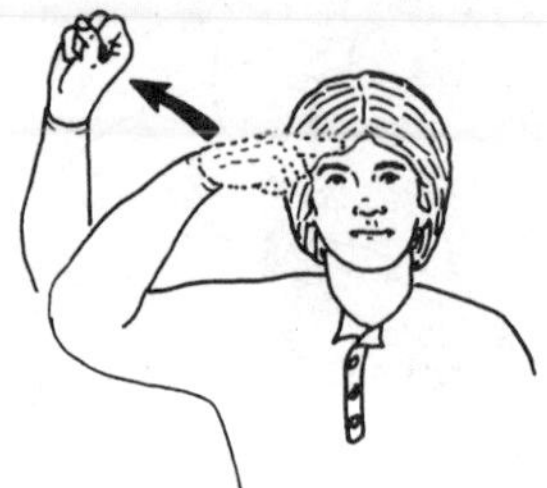

Arabic: áassa عصى
Chinese: bùfúcóng 不服從
Dutch: niet gehoorzamen
French: désobéir
German: nicht gehorchen
Italian: disobbedire
Japanese: shitagawanai 従わない
Korean: ŏgida 어기다
Portuguese: desobedecer
Russian: oslúshat'sya ослушаться
Spanish: desobedecer
Swedish: vara olydig

631. disorder [n.]

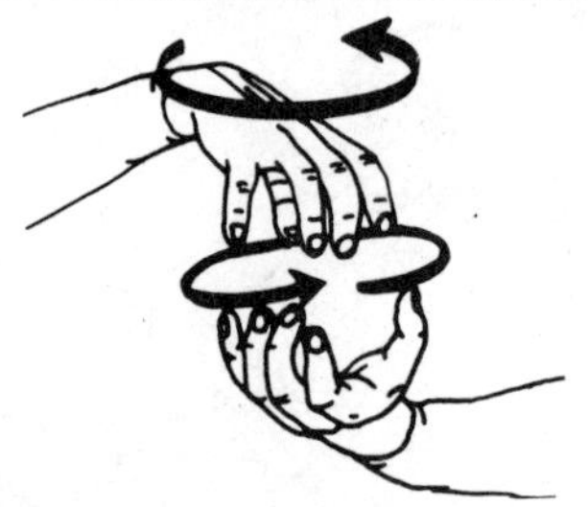

Arabic: itteráb اضطراب
Chinese: hŭnluàn 混亂
Dutch: wanorde
French: désordre
German: Unordnung
Italian: disordine
Japanese: fuseiton 不整頓
Korean: mujilsŏ 무질서
Portuguese: desordem
Russian: besporyádok беспорядок
Spanish: desorden
Swedish: oordning

632. display [v.]

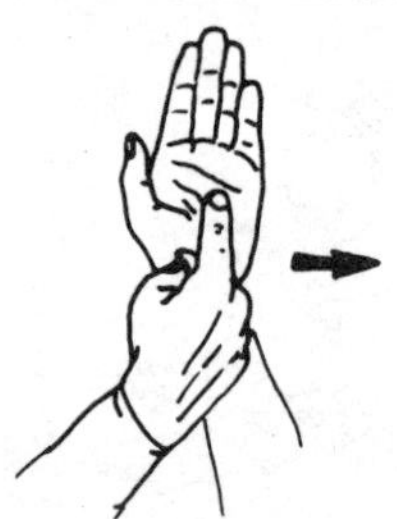

Arabic: áarada عرض
Chinese: zhănshì 展示
Dutch: tentoonstellen
French: étaler
German: ausstellen
Italian: esibire
Japanese: chinretsu suru 陳列する
Korean: jinyŏrhada 진열하다
Portuguese: exibir
Russian: vystavlyát' выставлять
Spanish: exhibir
Swedish: utställa

633. dissatisfaction [n.]

Arabic: istiá' استياء
Chinese: bùmǎnyì 不满意
Dutch: ontevredenheid
French: mécontentement
German: Unzufriedenheit
Italian: malcontento
Japanese: fuman 不満
Korean: bulman 불만
Portuguese: desagrado
Russian: nedovól'stvo недовольство
Spanish: descontento
Swedish: missnöje

634. dissolve [v.]

Arabic: dhába ذاب
Chinese: rónghuà 溶化
Dutch: oplossen
French: dissoudre
German: auflösen
Italian: dissolvere
Japanese: tokasu 溶かす
Korean: nogida 녹이다
Portuguese: dissolver
Russian: rastvoryát' растворять
Spanish: disolver
Swedish: upplösa

635. distance [n.]

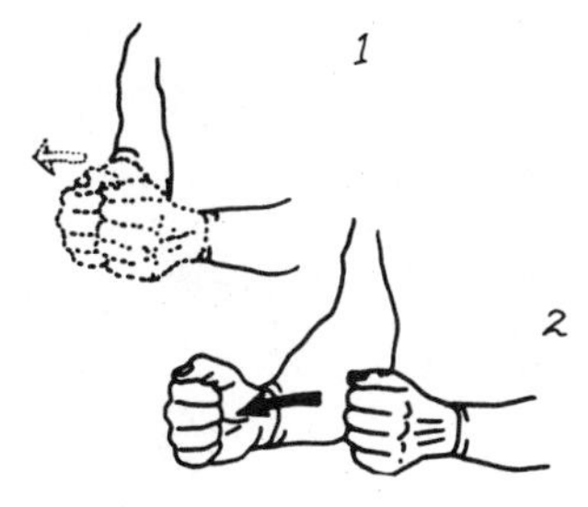

Arabic: masáfa مسافة
Chinese: jùlí 距離
Dutch: afstand
French: distance
German: Entfernung
Italian: distanza
Japanese: kyori 距離
Korean: kŏri 거리
Portuguese: distância
Russian: rasstoyániye расстояние
Spanish: distancia
Swedish: avstånd

636. distribute [v.]

Arabic: wazzáa وزع
Chinese: fēnpèi 分配
Dutch: verdelen
French: distribuer
German: verteilen
Italian: distribuire
Japanese: bumpai suru 分配する
Korean: nanuŏ juda 나누어주다
Portuguese: distribuir
Russian: raspredelyát' распределять
Spanish: distribuir
Swedish: utdela

637. disturb [v.]

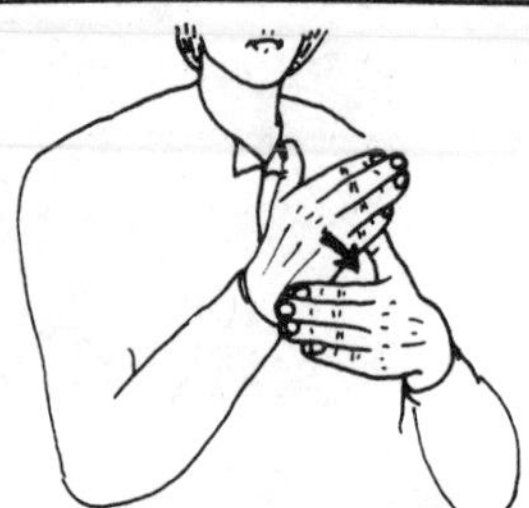

Arabic: sháwwasha شوش
Chinese: dărăo 打攪
Dutch: storen
French: déranger
German: stören
Italian: disturbare
Japanese: jama suru 邪魔する
Korean: banghaehada 방해하다
Portuguese: incomodar
Russian: bespokóit' беспокоить
Spanish: perturbar
Swedish: störa

638. dive [v.]

Arabic: ghátasa غطس
Chinese: qiánshuǐ 潛水
Dutch: duiken
French: plonger
German: tauchen
Italian: tuffare
Japanese: tobikomu 飛び込む
Korean: ttwiŏdŭlda 뛰어들다
Portuguese: mergulhar
Russian: nyryát' нырять
Spanish: bucear
Swedish: dyka

639. divide [v.]

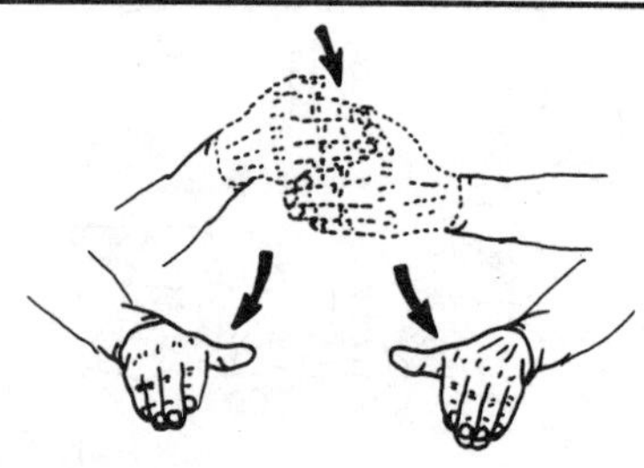

Arabic: qássema قسم
Chinese: fēnkāi 分開
Dutch: delen
French: diviser
German: aufteilen
Italian: dividere
Japanese: wakeru 分ける
Korean: nanuda 나누다
Portuguese: dividir
Russian: delít' делить
Spanish: dividir
Swedish: dela

640. divorce [n.]

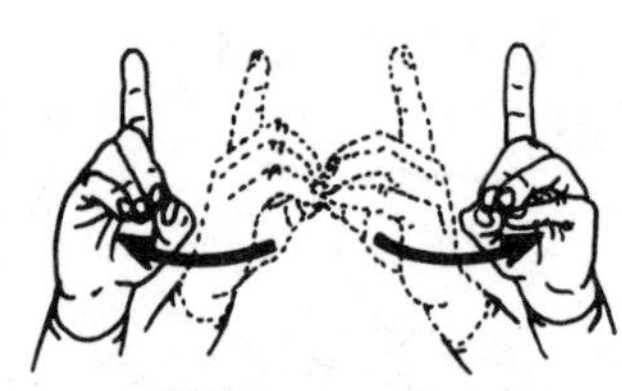

Arabic: taláaq طلاق
Chinese: líhūn 離婚
Dutch: scheiding
French: divorce
German: Scheidung
Italian: divorzio
Japanese: rikon 離婚
Korean: ihon 이혼
Portuguese: divórcio
Russian: razvód развод
Spanish: divorcio
Swedish: skilsmässa

641. dizzy [adj.]

Arabic: musáb bid-dawár
مصاب بالدوار
Chinese: tóuhūn 頭昏
Dutch: duizelig
French: étourdi
German: schwindlig
Italian: vertiginoso
Japanese: memai ga suru 目まいがする
Korean: ŏjlǰilhan 어질어질한
Portuguese: vertiginoso
Russian: golovokruzhítel'nyy
головокружительный
Spanish: mareado
Swedish: yr

642. do [v.]

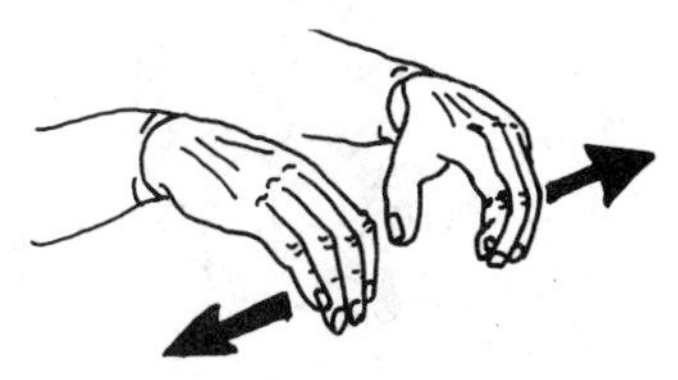

Arabic: aámila عمل
Chinese: zuò 做
Dutch: doen
French: faire
German: tun
Italian: fare
Japanese: suru する
Korean: hada 하다
Portuguese: fazer
Russian: délat' делать
Spanish: hacer
Swedish: göra

643. doctor (medical) [n.]

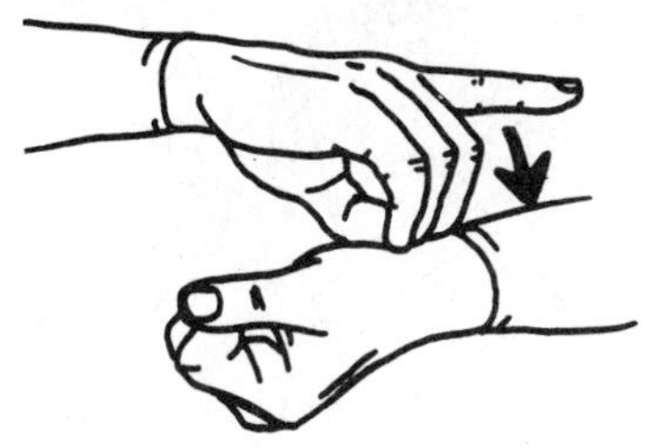

Arabic: tabíb طبيب
Chinese: yīshēng 醫生
Dutch: dokter
French: médecin
German: Doktor
Italian: medico
Japanese: isha 医者
Korean: ŭisa 의사
Portuguese: médico
Russian: vrach врач
Spanish: médico
Swedish: doktor

644. dog [n.]

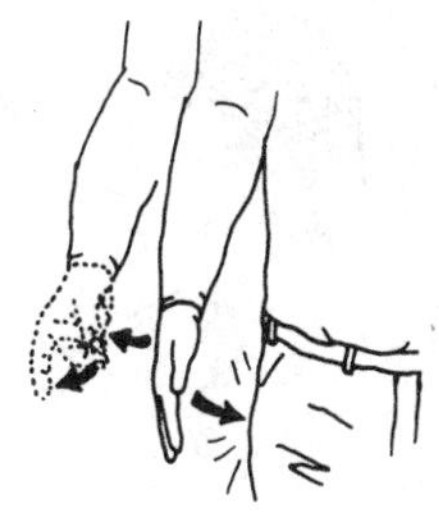

Arabic: kalb كلب
Chinese: gǒu 狗
Dutch: hond
French: chien
German: Hund
Italian: cane
Japanese: inu 犬
Korean: gae 개
Portuguese: cão
Russian: sobáka собака
Spanish: perro
Swedish: hund

645. doll [n.]

Arabic: dómia دمية
Chinese: wán-ǒu 玩偶
Dutch: pop
French: poupée
German: Puppe
Italian: bambola
Japanese: ningyō 人形
Korean: inhyŏng 인형
Portuguese: boneca
Russian: kúkla кукла
Spanish: muñeca
Swedish: docka

646. dollar [n.]

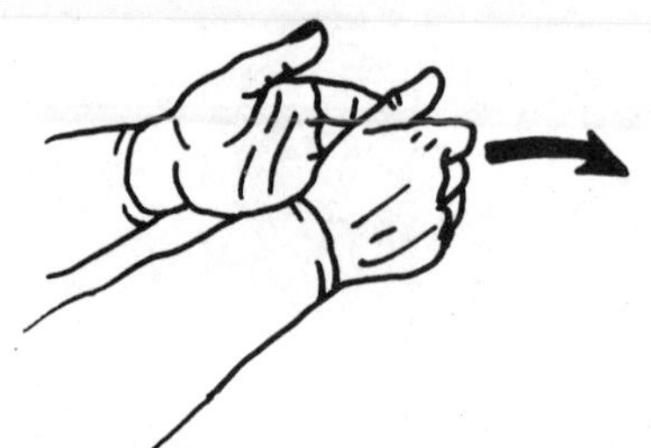

Arabic: dulár دولار
Chinese: yuán 元
Dutch: dollar
French: dollar
German: Dollar
Italian: dollaro
Japanese: doru ドル
Korean: dallo 달러
Portuguese: dólar
Russian: dóllar доллар
Spanish: dólar
Swedish: dollar

647. donkey [n.]

Arabic: hemár حمار
Chinese: lúzi 驢子
Dutch: ezel
French: âne
German: Esel
Italian: asino
Japanese: roba ロバ
Korean: dangnakwi 당나귀
Portuguese: burro
Russian: osyól осёл
Spanish: burro
Swedish: åsna

648. door [n.]

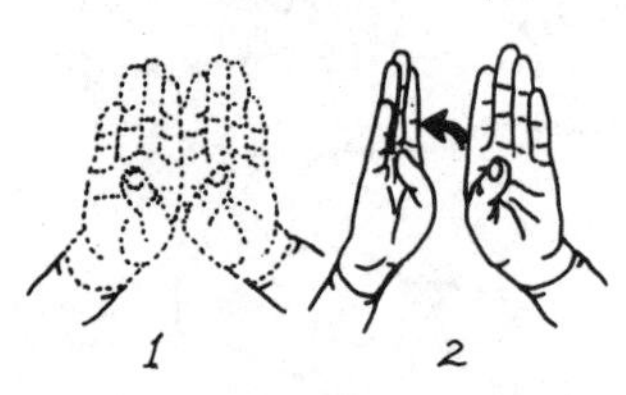

Arabic: bab باب
Chinese: mén 門
Dutch: deur
French: porte
German: Tür
Italian: porta
Japanese: to 戸
Korean: mun 문
Portuguese: porta
Russian: dver' дверь
Spanish: puerta
Swedish: dörr

649. double [adj.]

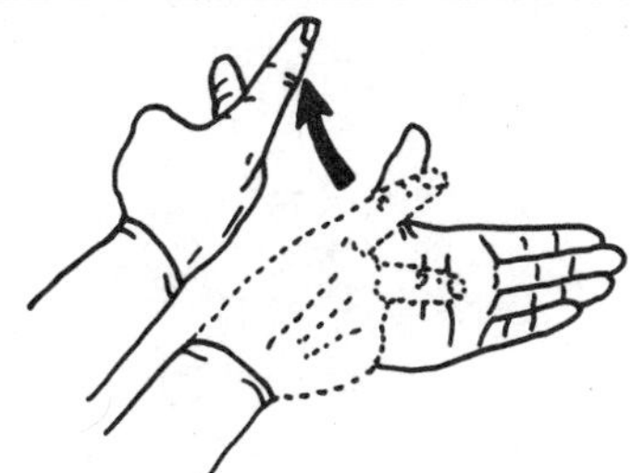

Arabic: mudháaf مضاعف
Chinese: liǎngbèide 兩倍的
Dutch: dubbel
French: double
German: doppelt
Italian: doppio
Japanese: ni bai no 二倍の
Korean: du baeŭi 두배의
Portuguese: duplo
Russian: dvoynóy двойной
Spanish: doble
Swedish: dubbel

650. doubt [n.]

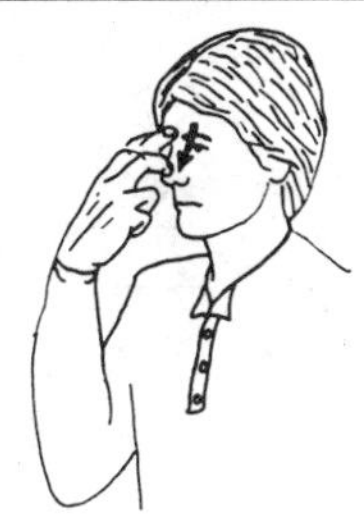

Arabic: shik شك
Chinese: huáiyí 懷疑
Dutch: twijfel
French: doute
German: Zweifel
Italian: dubbio
Japanese: utagai 疑い
Korean: ŭishim 의심
Portuguese: dúvida
Russian: somnéniye сомнение
Spanish: duda
Swedish: tvivel

651. down [adv./prep.]

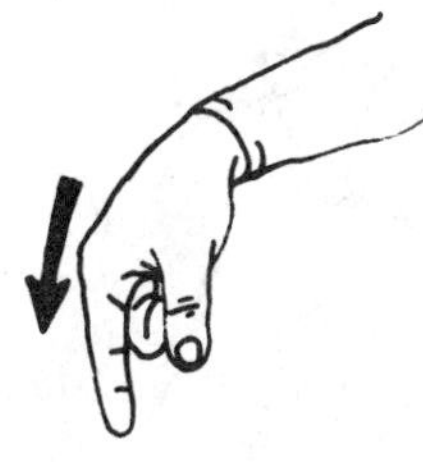

Arabic: taht تحت
Chinese: wǎngxià 往下
Dutch: beneden
French: en bas
German: hinunter
Italian: giù
Japanese: shita e 下へ
Korean: arae 아래
Portuguese: abaixo
Russian: vniz вниз
Spanish: abajo
Swedish: ned

652. drag [v.]

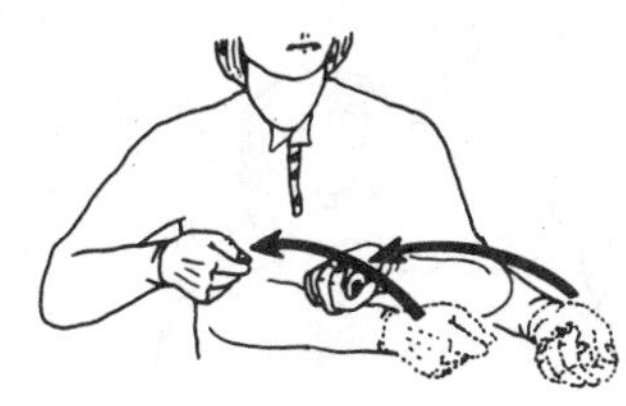

Arabic: járra جر
Chinese: tuō 拖
Dutch: slepen
French: traîner
German: schleppen
Italian: trascinare
Japanese: hiku 引く
Korean: kkŭlda 끌다
Portuguese: arrastar
Russian: tyanút' тянуть
Spanish: arrastrar
Swedish: släpa

653. draw (sketch) [v.]

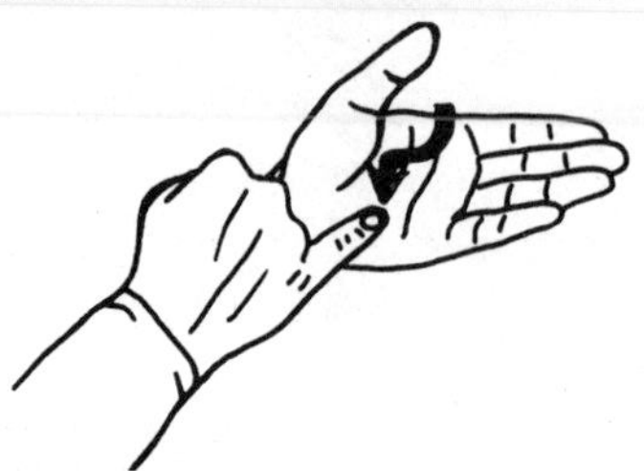

Arabic: rásama رسم
Chinese: huà 畫
Dutch: tekenen
French: dessiner
German: zeichnen
Italian: disegnare
Japanese: egaku 描ん
Korean: gŭrida 그리다
Portuguese: desenhar
Russian: risovát' рисовать
Spanish: dibujar
Swedish: rita

654. dreadful [adj.]

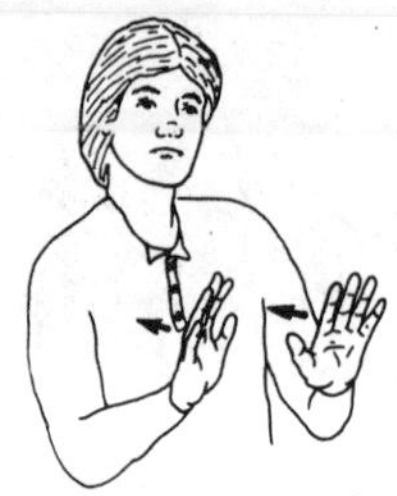

Arabic: múfzeaa مفزع
Chinese: kěpàde 可怕的
Dutch: vreselijk
French: affreux
German: schrecklich
Italian: terribile
Japanese: osoroshii 恐ろしい
Korean: musŏun 무서운
Portuguese: terrível
Russian: uzhásnyy ужасный
Spanish: terrible
Swedish: förskräcklig

655. dream [n.]

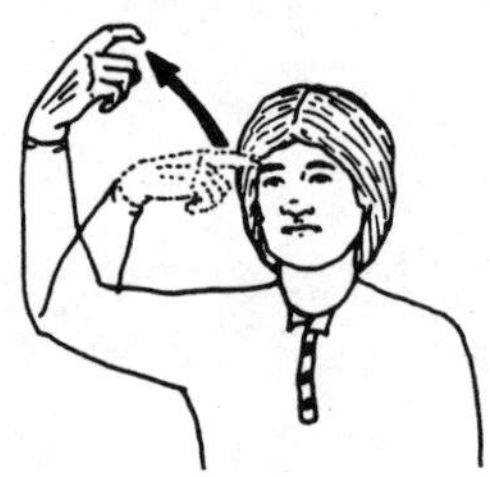

Arabic: hulm حلم
Chinese: mèng 夢
Dutch: droom
French: rêve
German: Traum
Italian: sogno
Japanese: yume 夢
Korean: kkum 꿈
Portuguese: sonho
Russian: son сон
Spanish: sueño
Swedish: dröm

656. dress [v.]

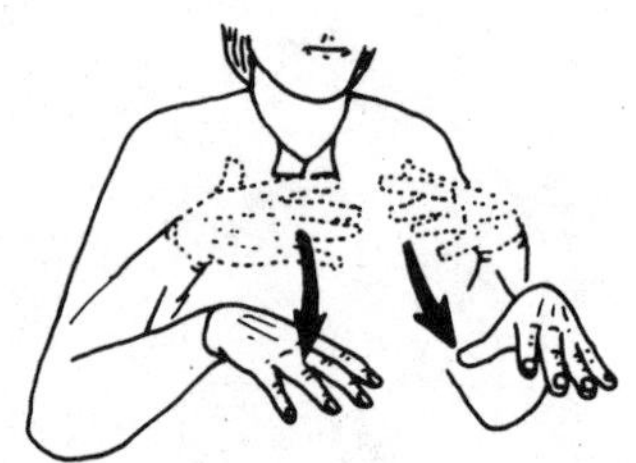

Arabic: lábesa لبس
Chinese: chuān 穿
Dutch: zich aankleden
French: s'habiller
German: sich ankleiden
Italian: vestirsi
Japanese: kiseru 着せる
Korean: ibnŭnda 입는다
Portuguese: vestir-se
Russian: odevát'sya одеваться
Spanish: vestir(se)
Swedish: klä sig

657. drink [v.]

Arabic: shábreba شرب
Chinese: hē 喝
Dutch: drinken
French: boire
German: trinken
Italian: bere
Japanese: nomu 飲む
Korean: mashida 마시다
Portuguese: beber
Russian: pit' пить
Spanish: beber
Swedish: dricka

658. drive (vehicle) [v.]

Arabic: sáaqa ساق
Chinese: kāichē 開車
Dutch: rijden
French: conduire
German: fahren
Italian: guidare
Japanese: unten suru 運転する
Korean: unjŏnhada 운전하다
Portuguese: dirigir
Russian: upravlyát' управлять
Spanish: conducir
Swedish: köra

659. drop [v.]

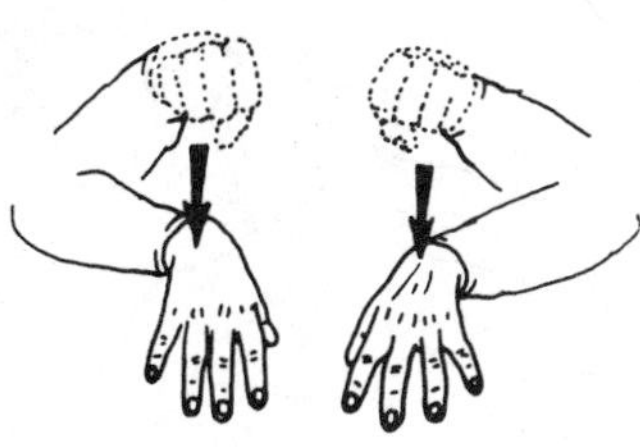

Arabic: hábata هبط
Chinese: diào 掉
Dutch: laten vallen
French: laisser tomber
German: fallen lassen
Italian: far cadere
Japanese: ochiru 落ちる
Korean: ttŏrŏttŭrida 떨어뜨리다
Portuguese: deixar cair
Russian: pádat' падать
Spanish: dejar caer
Swedish: falla

660. drown [v.]

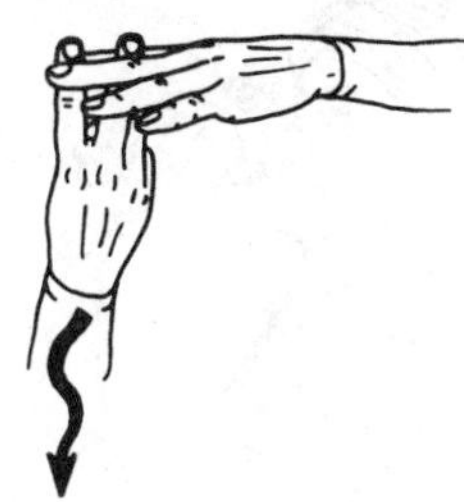

Arabic: ghareqa غرق
Chinese: yānsǐ 淹死
Dutch: verdrinken
French: se noyer
German: ertrinken
Italian: annegare
Japanese: oboreru 溺れる
Korean: ppajida 빠지다
Portuguese: afogar
Russian: zatoplyát' затоплять
Spanish: ahogar
Swedish: drunkna

661. drug (narcotic) [n.]

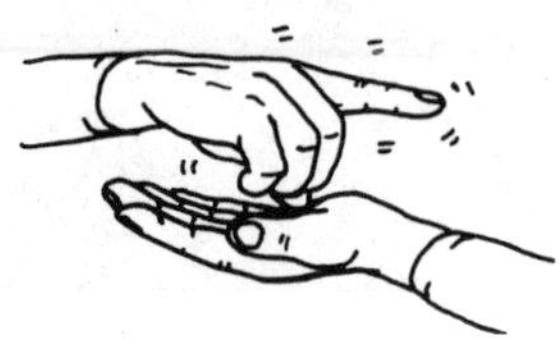

Arabic: mukhádder مخدر
Chinese: má zuì yiào 麻醉藥
Dutch: verdovend middel
French: narcotique
German: Rauschgift
Italian: narcotico
Japanese: mayaku 麻薬
Korean: mach'wiyak 마취약
Portuguese: droga
Russian: narkótik наркотик
Spanish: narcótico
Swedish: narkotiskt medel

662. drum [n.]

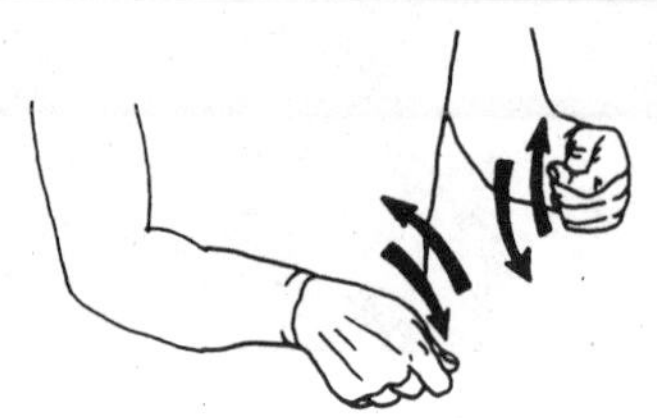

Arabic: tábla طبلة
Chinese: gŭ 鼓
Dutch: trommel
French: tambour
German: Trommel
Italian: tamburo
Japanese: taiko 太鼓
Korean: bug 북
Portuguese: tambor
Russian: barabán барабан
Spanish: tambor
Swedish: trumma

663. drunk [adj.]

Arabic: sakrán سكران
Chinese: zuì jiŏu 醉酒
Dutch: dronken
French: ivre
German: betrunken
Italian: ubriaco
Japanese: yotta 酔った
Korean: sulch'wihan 술취한
Portuguese: bêbado
Russian: p'yányy пьяный
Spanish: borracho
Swedish: berusad

664. dry [adj.]

Arabic: jáaf جاف
Chinese: gānzàode 甘燥的
Dutch: droog
French: sec
German: trocken
Italian: secco
Japanese: kansō shita 乾燥した
Korean: marŭn 마른
Portuguese: sêco
Russian: sukhóy сухой
Spanish: seco
Swedish: torr

665. duck [n.]

Arabic: bátta بطة
Chinese: yāzi 鴨子
Dutch: eend
French: canard
German: Ente
Italian: anitra
Japanese: kamo カモ
Korean: ori 오리
Portuguese: pato
Russian: útka утка
Spanish: pato
Swedish: anka

666. due (owing) [adj.]

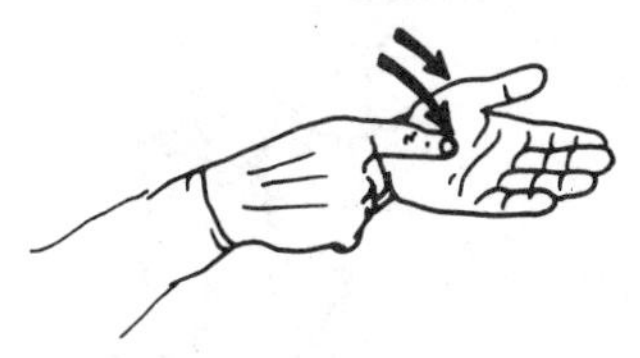

Arabic: wájeb واجب
Chinese: dào qí de 到期的
Dutch: schuldig
French: dû
German: schuldig
Italian: debito
Japanese: shiharaikijitsu ni natte 支払期日になって
Korean: ttaemune 때문에
Portuguese: devido
Russian: dólzhnyy должный
Spanish: debido
Swedish: skyldig

667. dull (blunt) [adj.]

Arabic: ghir hadd غير حاد
Chinese: dùnde 鈍的
Dutch: bot
French: émoussé
German: stumpf
Italian: smussato
Japanese: nibui 鈍い
Korean: mudin 무딘
Portuguese: enfadonho
Russian: tupóy тупой
Spanish: embotado
Swedish: slö

668. dumb (stupid) [adj.]

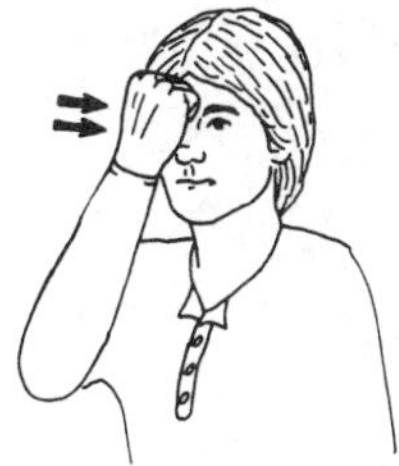

Arabic: ghábi غبي
Chinese: yǘchǔnde 愚蠢的
Dutch: stom
French: stupide
German: dumm
Italian: stupido
Japanese: bakana 馬鹿な
Korean: udunhan 우둔한
Portuguese: estúpido
Russian: glúpyy глупый
Spanish: estúpido
Swedish: dum

669. during [prep.]

Arabic: khilál خلال
Chinese: dāng...shíhòu 當...時候
Dutch: tijdens
French: pendant
German: während
Italian: durante
Japanese: ...no aidajū …の間じゅう
Korean: dongane 동안에
Portuguese: durante
Russian: vo vrémya во время
Spanish: durante
Swedish: under

670. duty [n.]

Arabic: wájeb واجب
Chinese: zhíwù 職務
Dutch: plicht
French: devoir
German: Pflicht
Italian: dovere
Japanese: gimu 義務
Korean: ŭimu 의무
Portuguese: dever
Russian: dolg долг
Spanish: deber
Swedish: plikt

671. each [adj.]

Arabic: kull كل
Chinese: měige 每個
Dutch: elk
French: chaque
German: jeder
Italian: ogni
Japanese: sorezoreno それぞれの
Korean: kakkagŭi 각각의
Portuguese: cada
Russian: kázhdyy каждый
Spanish: cada
Swedish: varje

672. eager [adj.]

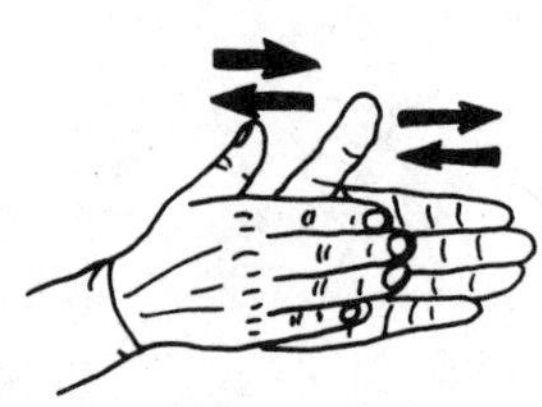

Arabic: tawáq íla تواق الى
Chinese: kěwàngde 渴望的
Dutch: begerig
French: désireux
German: eifrig
Italian: impaziente
Japanese: nesshinna 熱心な
Korean: yŏlmanghanŭn 열망하다
Portuguese: desejoso
Russian: stremyáshchiysya стремящийся
Spanish: ávido
Swedish: ivrig

673. ear [n.]

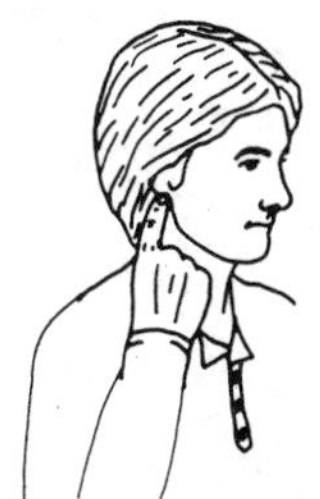

Arabic: ódhun أذن
Chinese: ěrduō 耳朵
Dutch: oor
French: oreille
German: Ohr
Italian: orecchio
Japanese: mimi 耳
Korean: kwi 귀
Portuguese: orelha
Russian: úkho ухо
Spanish: oreja
Swedish: öra

674. early [adj.]

Arabic: mubákkir مبكر
Chinese: zǎode 早的
Dutch: vroeg
French: tôt
German: früh
Italian: sollecito
Japanese: hayai 早い
Korean: irŭn 이른
Portuguese: cedo
Russian: ránniy ранний
Spanish: temprano
Swedish: tidig

675. earn [v.]

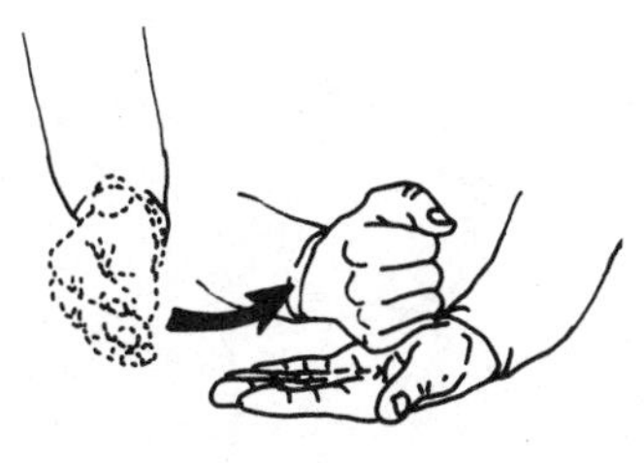

Arabic: káseba كسب
Chinese: zhuàn 賺
Dutch: verdienen
French: gagner
German: verdienen
Italian: guadagnare
Japanese: mōkeru 儲ける
Korean: bŏlda 벌다
Portuguese: ganhar
Russian: zarabátyvat' зарабатывать
Spanish: ganar
Swedish: tjäna

676. earnest [adj.]

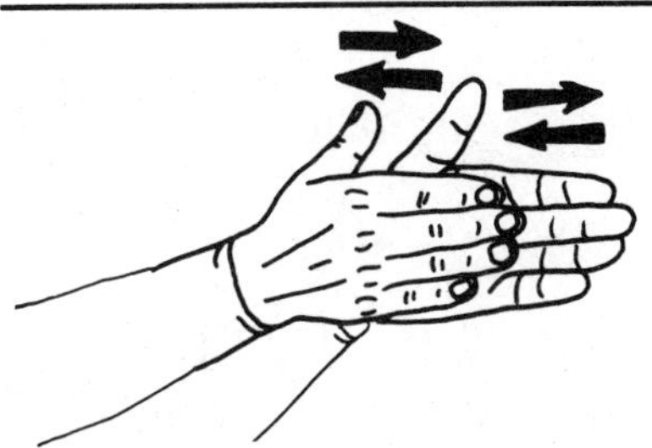

Arabic: jad جاد
Chinese: chéngzhìde 誠摯的
Dutch: ijverig
French: sincère
German: ernst
Italian: serio
Japanese: nesshina 熱心な
Korean: jinjihan 진지한
Portuguese: sério
Russian: ser'yóznyy серьёзный
Spanish: serio
Swedish: allvarlig

677. earth [n.]

Arabic: al-áard الارض
Chinese: dìqiú 地球
Dutch: aarde
French: terre
German: Erde
Italian: terra
Japanese: chikyū 地球
Korean: jiku 지구
Portuguese: terra
Russian: zemlyá земля
Spanish: tierra
Swedish: jord

678. earthquake [n.]

Arabic: zilzál زلزال
Chinese: dìzhèn 地震
Dutch: aardbeving
French: tremblement de terre
German: Erdbeben
Italian: terremoto
Japanese: jishin 地震
Korean: jijin 지진
Portuguese: terremoto
Russian: zemletryaséniye землетрясение
Spanish: terremoto
Swedish: jordbävning

679. east [n.]

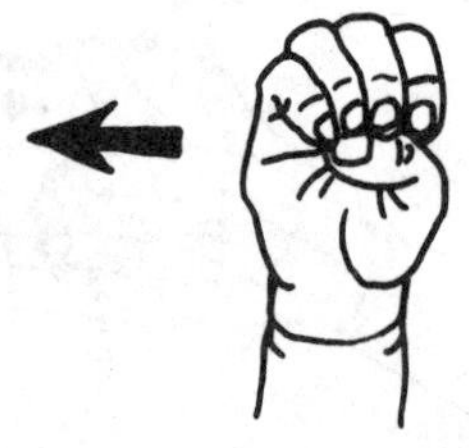

Arabic: sharq شرق
Chinese: dōng 東
Dutch: oosten
French: est
German: Osten
Italian: est
Japanese: higashi 東
Korean: dongtchok 동쪽
Portuguese: este
Russian: vostók восток
Spanish: este
Swedish: öst

680. easy [adj.]

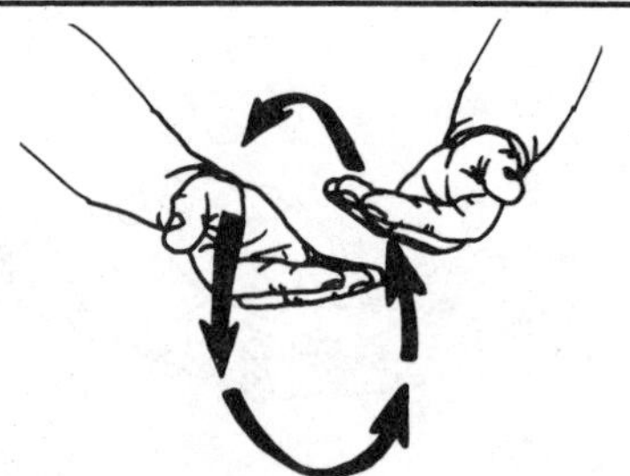

Arabic: sáhel سهل
Chinese: róngyìde 容易的
Dutch: gemakkelijk
French: facile
German: leicht
Italian: facile
Japanese: kantanna 簡単な
Korean: shwiun 쉬운
Portuguese: fácil
Russian: lyógkiy лёгкий
Spanish: fácil
Swedish: lätt

681. eat [v.]

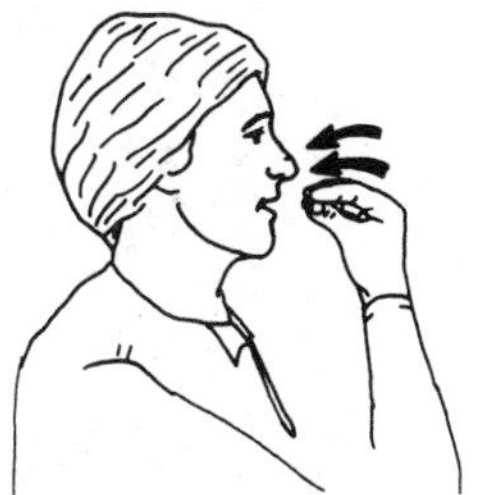

Arabic: ákala اكل
Chinese: chī 吃
Dutch: eten
French: manger
German: essen
Italian: mangiare
Japanese: taberu 食べる
Korean: mokda 먹다
Portuguese: comer
Russian: yést' есть
Spanish: comer
Swedish: äta

682. education [n.]

Arabic: taalím تعليم
Chinese: jiàoyù 教育
Dutch: opvoeding
French: éducation
German: Bildung
Italian: educazione
Japanese: kyōiku 教育
Korean: kyoyuk 교육
Portuguese: educação
Russian: obrazovániye образование
Spanish: educación
Swedish: utbildning

683. effect [n.]

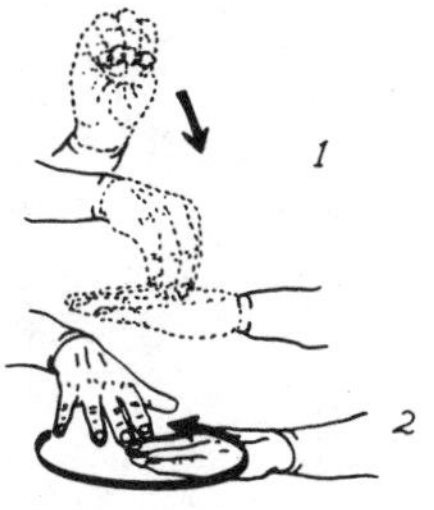

Arabic: ta'thír تأثير
Chinese: xiàoguǒ 效果
Dutch: uitwerking
French: effet
German: Wirkung
Italian: effetto
Japanese: kekka 結果
Korean: kyŏlgwa 결과
Portuguese: efeito
Russian: effékt эффект
Spanish: efecto
Swedish: effekt

684. effort [n.]

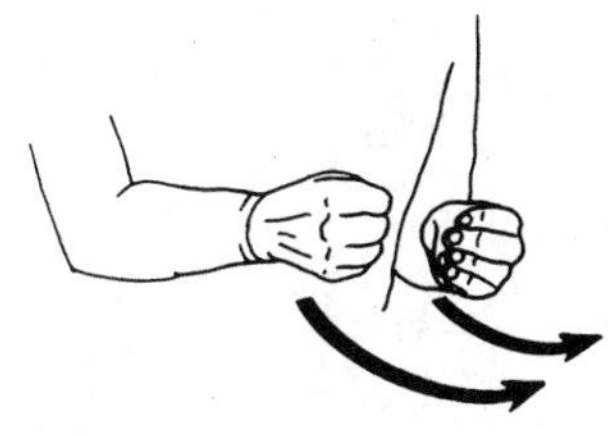

Arabic: júhud جهد
Chinese: nǔlì 努力
Dutch: poging
French: effort
German: Anstrengung
Italian: sforzo
Japanese: doryoku 努力
Korean: noryŏg 노력
Portuguese: esfôrço
Russian: usíliye усилие
Spanish: esfuerzo
Swedish: ansträngning

685. egg [n.]

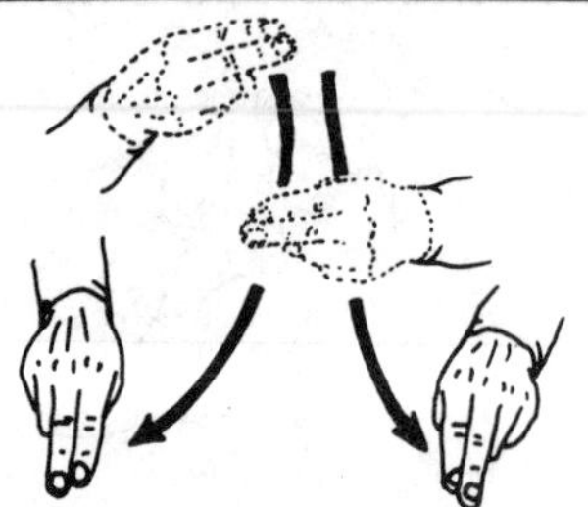

Arabic: beyd بيض
Chinese: dàn 蛋
Dutch: ei
French: oeuf
German: Ei
Italian: uovo
Japanese: tamago 玉
Korean: al 알
Portuguese: ovo
Russian: yaytsó яйцо
Spanish: huevo
Swedish: ägg

686. Egypt [n.]

Arabic: misr مصر
Chinese: āijí 埃及
Dutch: Egypte
French: Égypte
German: Ägypten
Italian: Egitto
Japanese: Ejiputo エジプト
Korean: Iijib't 이집트
Portuguese: Egito
Russian: Yegípet Египет
Spanish: Egipto
Swedish: Egypten

687. eight [adj.]

Arabic: thamánia ثمانية
Chinese: bā 八
Dutch: acht
French: huit
German: acht
Italian: otto
Japanese: hachi 八
Korean: yŏdŏl 여덟
Portuguese: oito
Russian: vósem' восемь
Spanish: ocho
Swedish: åtta

688. eighteen [adj.]

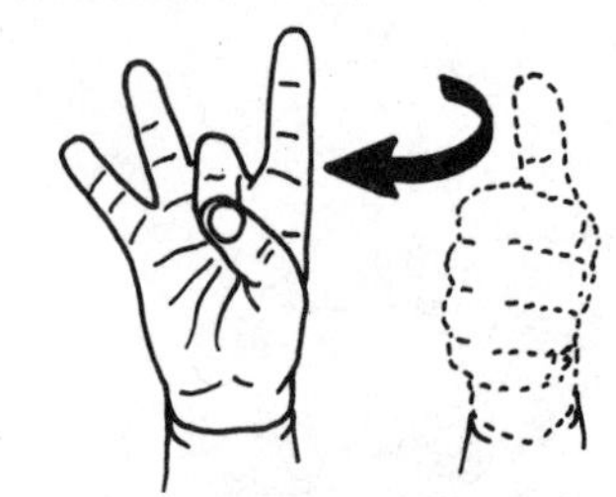

Arabic: thamániat áashar ثمانية عشر
Chinese: shíbā 十八
Dutch: achttien
French: dix-huit
German: achtzehn
Italian: diciotto
Japanese: jūhachi 18
Korean: yŏl yŏdŏl 열여덟
Portuguese: dezoito
Russian: vosemnádtsat' восемнадцать
Spanish: dieciocho
Swedish: aderton

689. eighty [adj.]

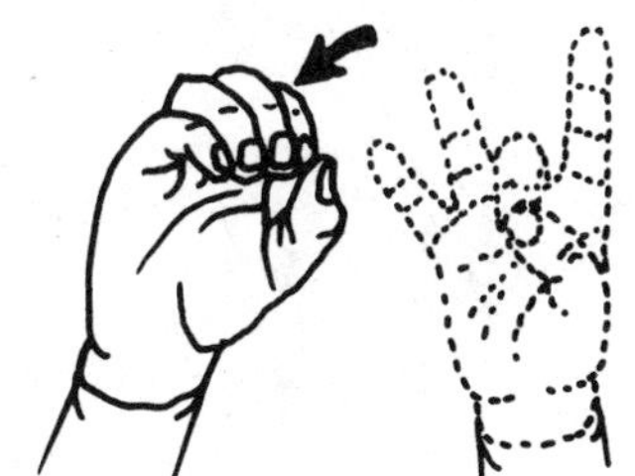

Arabic: thamanín ثمانين
Chinese: bāshí 八十
Dutch: tachtig
French: quatre-vingt
German: achtzig
Italian: ottanta
Japanese: hachijū 80
Korean: yŏdŭn 여든
Portuguese: oitenta
Russian: vósem'desyat восемьдесят
Spanish: ochenta
Swedish: åttio

690. either [adj./pron.]

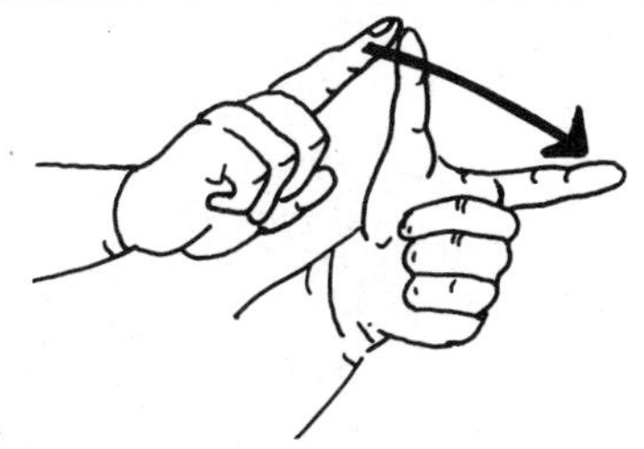

Arabic: ímma اما
Chinese: liǎngzhě zhī yī 兩者之一
Dutch: één van beide
French: l'un ou l'autre
German: einer von beiden
Italian: l'uno o l'altro
Japanese: izureka いずれか
Korean: ŏnŭ hanaŭi 어느 하나의
Portuguese: um ou outro
Russian: tot ili drugóy тот или другой
Spanish: cualquiera de los dos
Swedish: endera

691. elect [v.]

Arabic: intákhaba انتخب
Chinese: xuǎnjǚ 選舉
Dutch: kiezen
French: élire
German: wählen
Italian: eleggere
Japanese: erabu 選ぶ
Korean: ppobta 뽑다
Portuguese: eleger
Russian: izbirát' избирать
Spanish: elegir
Swedish: välja

692. electric [adj.]

Arabic: kahrubá'i كهربائي
Chinese: diànde 電的
Dutch: electrisch
French: électrique
German: elektrisch
Italian: elettrico
Japanese: denki no 電気の
Korean: jŏnkiŭi 전기의
Portuguese: elétrico
Russian: elektrícheskiy электрический
Spanish: eléctrico
Swedish: elektriskt

693. elephant [n.]

Arabic: fíl فيل
Chinese: xiàng 象
Dutch: olifant
French: éléphant
German: Elefant
Italian: elefante
Japanese: zō ゾウ
Korean: k'okkiri 코끼리
Portuguese: elefante
Russian: slon слон
Spanish: elefante
Swedish: elefant

694. elevator [n.]

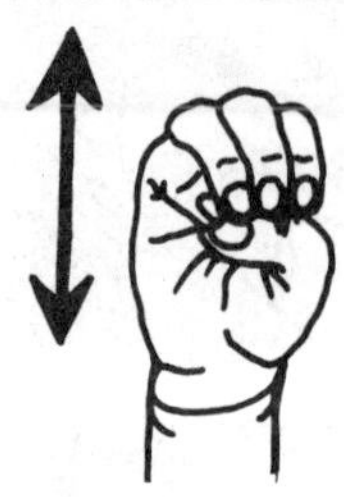

Arabic: mísaad مصعد
Chinese: diàntī 電梯
Dutch: lift
French: ascenseur
German: Fahrstuhl
Italian: ascensore
Japanese: erebētā エレベーター
Korean: sŭngganggi 승강기
Portuguese: elevador
Russian: lift лифт
Spanish: ascensor
Swedish: hiss

695. eleven [adj.]

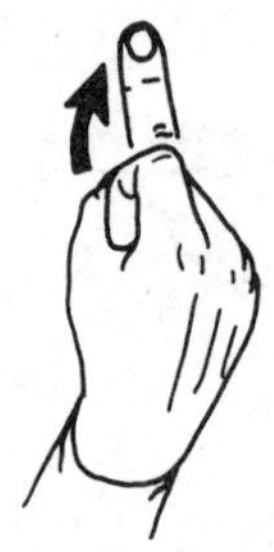

Arabic: éhda áashar احدى عشر
Chinese: shíyī 十一
Dutch: elf
French: onze
German: elf
Italian: undici
Japanese: jūichi 11
Korean: yŏl hana 열하나
Portuguese: onze
Russian: odínnadtsat' одиннадцать
Spanish: once
Swedish: elva

696. eliminate [v.]

Arabic: takhállasa min تخلص من
Chinese: fèichú 廢除
Dutch: uitschakelen
French: éliminer
German: eliminieren
Italian: eliminare
Japanese: torinozoku 取り除く
Korean: jekŏhada 제거하다
Portuguese: eliminar
Russian: ustranyát' устранять
Spanish: eliminar
Swedish: eliminera

697. embarrass [v.]

Arabic: ákhjala اخجل
Chinese: shǐ jiǒngpò 使窘迫
Dutch: verlegen maken
French: embarrasser
German: verlegen machen
Italian: imbarazzare
Japanese: komaraseru 困らせる
Korean: nanch'ŏhada 난처하다
Portuguese: embaraçar
Russian: smushchát' смущать
Spanish: avergonzar
Swedish: genera

698. embrace [v.]

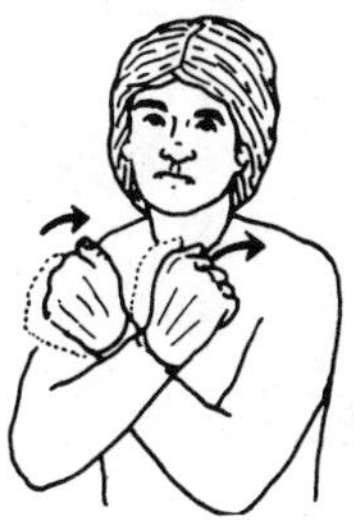

Arabic: aánaqa عانق
Chinese: yōngbào 擁抱
Dutch: omhelzen
French: étreindre
German: umarmen
Italian: abbracciare
Japanese: dakishimeru 抱きしめる
Korean: p'oonghada 포옹하다
Portuguese: abraçar
Russian: obnimát' обнимать
Spanish: abrazar
Swedish: omfamna

699. emphasize [v.]

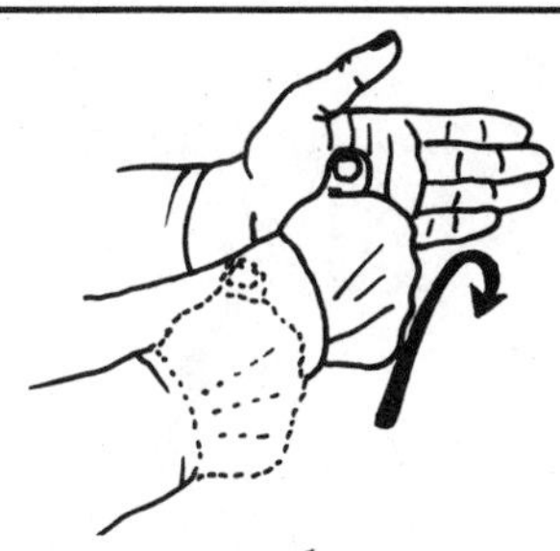

Arabic: ákada اكد
Chinese: qiángdiào 強調
Dutch: benadrukken
French: souligner
German: betonen
Italian: mettere in relievo
Japanese: kyōchō suru 強調する
Korean: gangjohada 강조하다
Portuguese: enfatizar
Russian: podchyórkivat' подчёркивать
Spanish: recalcar
Swedish: betona

700. employment (work) [n.]

Arabic: taudhíf توظيف
Chinese: gùyòng 雇用
Dutch: beroep
French: emploi
German: Anstellung
Italian: impiego
Japanese: koyō 雇用
Korean: koyong 고용
Portuguese: emprêgo
Russian: zanyátiye занятие
Spanish: empleo
Swedish: anställning

701. empty [adj.]

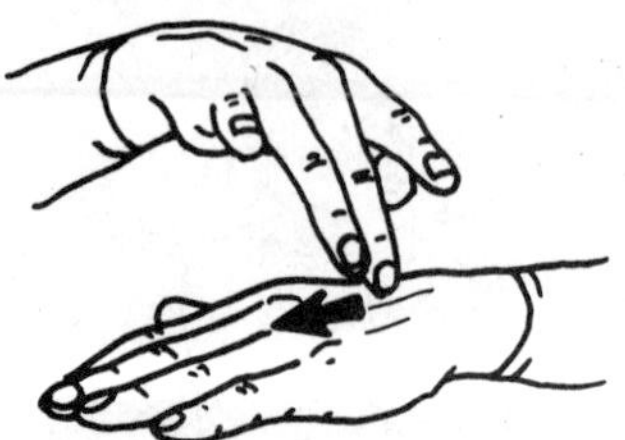

Arabic: farégh فارغ
Chinese: kōngde 空的
Dutch: leeg
French: vide
German: leer
Italian: vuoto
Japanese: kara no 空の（からの）
Korean: bin 빈
Portuguese: vazio
Russian: pustóy пустой
Spanish: vacío
Swedish: tom

702. encourage [v.]

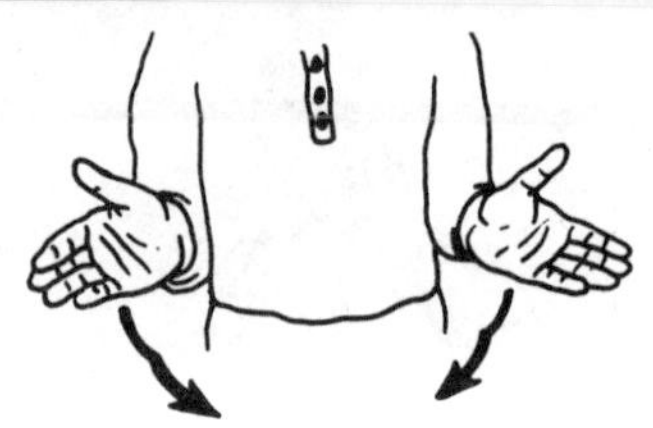

Arabic: shajeáa شجع
Chinese: gŭlì 鼓勵
Dutch: aanmoedigen
French: encourager
German: ermutigen
Italian: incoraggiare
Japanese: yūki zukeru 勇気づける
Korean: kyŏngnyŏhada 격려하다
Portuguese: encorajar
Russian: obodryát' ободрять
Spanish: animar
Swedish: uppmuntra

703. end [n.]

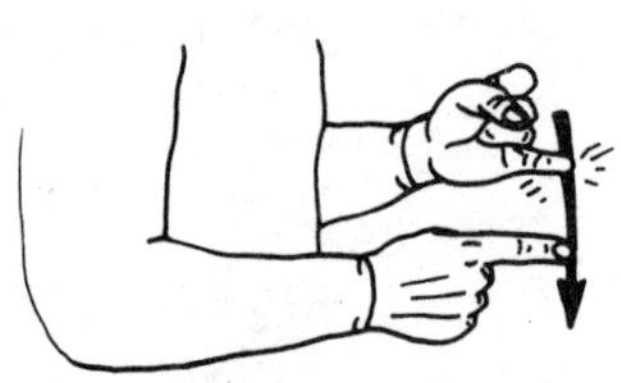

Arabic: niháya نهاية
Chinese: jiéshù 結束
Dutch: einde
French: fin
German: Ende
Italian: fine
Japanese: owari 終り
Korean: kkŭt 끝
Portuguese: fim
Russian: konéts конец
Spanish: fin
Swedish: slut

704. endure [v.]

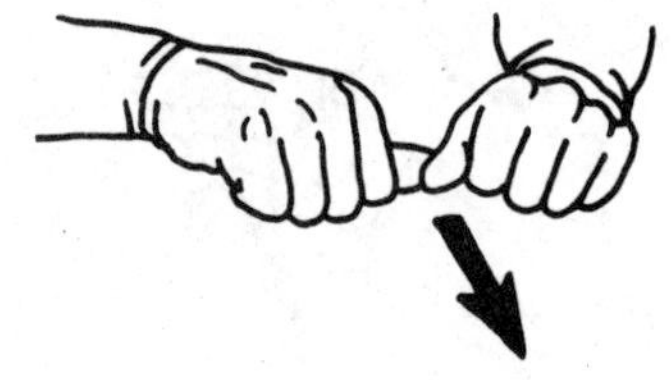

Arabic: tahámmala تحمل
Chinese: rĕnshòu 忍受
Dutch: verdragen
French: supporter
German: ertragen
Italian: sopportare
Japanese: mochikotaeru 持ちこたえる
Korean: kyŏndida 견디다
Portuguese: suportar
Russian: vynosít' выносить
Spanish: soportar
Swedish: uthärda

705. enemy [n.]

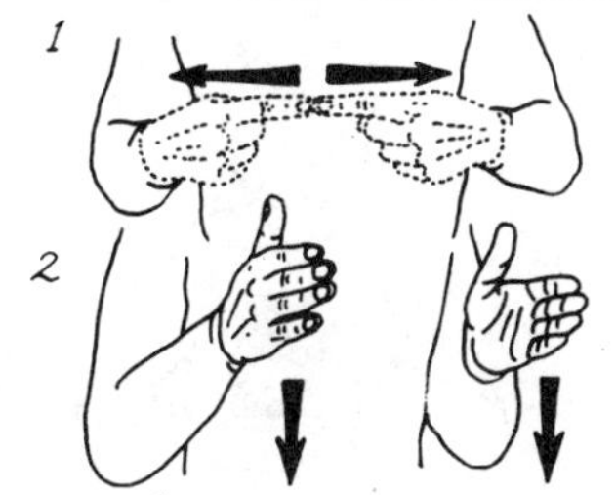

Arabic: aadú عدو
Chinese: dírén 敵人
Dutch: vijand
French: ennemi
German: Feind
Italian: nemico
Japanese: teki 敵
Korean: jŏk 적
Portuguese: inimigo
Russian: vrag враг
Spanish: enemigo
Swedish: fiende

706. engine [n.]

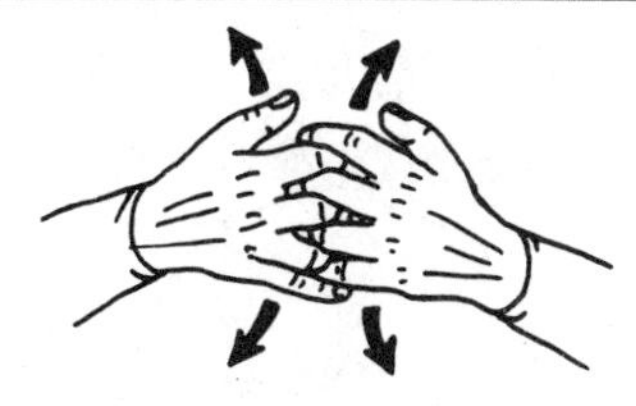

Arabic: makína ماكينة
Chinese: fādòngjī 發動機
Dutch: motor
French: moteur
German: Motor
Italian: motore
Japanese: enjin エンジン
Korean: kigye 기계
Portuguese: motor
Russian: dvígatel' двигатель
Spanish: motor
Swedish: motor

707. engineer [n.]

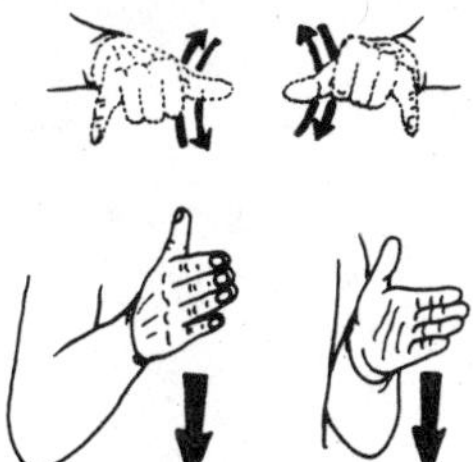

Arabic: muhándis مهندس
Chinese: gōngchéngshī 工程師
Dutch: ingenieur
French: ingénieur
German: Ingenieur
Italian: ingegnere
Japanese: gishi 技師
Korean: kisa 기사
Portuguese: engenheiro
Russian: inzhenér инженер
Spanish: ingeniero
Swedish: ingenjör

708. England [n.]

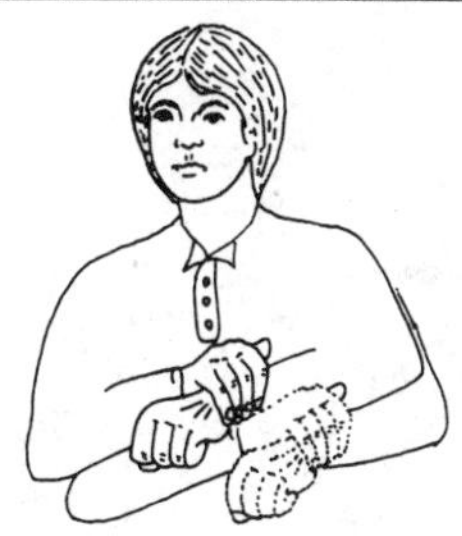

Arabic: ingéltra انجلترا
Chinese: yīngguó 英國
Dutch: Engeland
French: Angleterre
German: England
Italian: Inghilterra
Japanese: Igirisu イギリス
Korean: Yŏngkug 영국
Portuguese: Inglaterra
Russian: Ángliya Англия
Spanish: Inglaterra
Swedish: England

709. English [adj.]

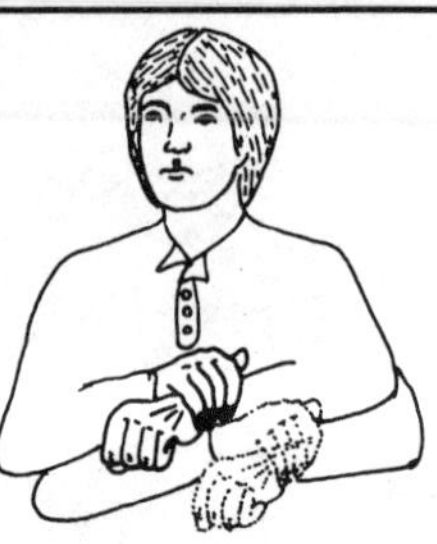

Arabic: ingilízi انجليزي
Chinese: yīngguóde 英國的
Dutch: engels
French: anglais
German: englisch
Italian: inglese
Japanese: Eigo 英語
Korean: Yŏngkugŭi 영어
Portuguese: inglês
Russian: anglíyskiy английский
Spanish: inglés
Swedish: engelsk

710. enjoy [v.]

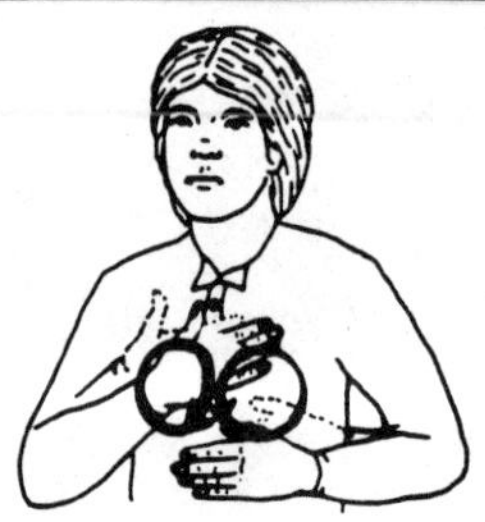

Arabic: tamátaa تمتع
Chinese: xiǎngshòu 享受
Dutch: genieten
French: jouir de
German: genießen
Italian: godere
Japanese: tanoshimu 楽しむ
Korean: jŭlgida 즐기다
Portuguese: aproveitar
Russian: naslazhdát'sya наслаждаться
Spanish: gozar
Swedish: njuta

711. enormous [adj.]

Arabic: dákhem ضخم
Chinese: jùdàde 巨大的
Dutch: enorm
French: énorme
German: enorm
Italian: enorme
Japanese: kyodai na 巨大な
Korean: kŏdaehan 거대한
Portuguese: enorme
Russian: ogrómnyy огромный
Spanish: enorme
Swedish: enorm

712. enough [adj./adv.]

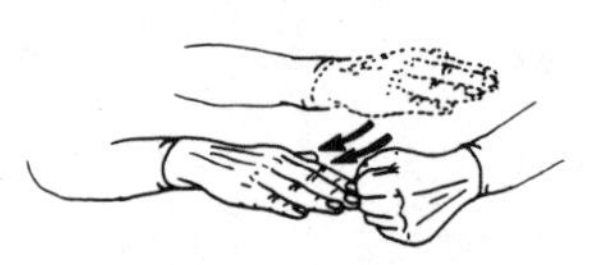

Arabic: káfi كافي
Chinese: gòude 夠的
Dutch: genoeg
French: assez
German: genug
Italian: abbastanza
Japanese: jūbun na 充分な
Korean: ch'ungbunhan 충분한
Portuguese: bastante
Russian: dostátochnyy достаточный
Spanish: bastante
Swedish: tillräcklig

713. enter [v.]

Arabic: dákhala دخل
Chinese: jìnrù 進入
Dutch: binnengaan
French: entrer
German: eintreten
Italian: entrare
Japanese: . . .ni hairu …にはいる
Korean: dŭrŏgada 들어가다
Portuguese: entrar
Russian: vkhodít' входить
Spanish: entrar
Swedish: inträda

714. enthusiasm [n.]

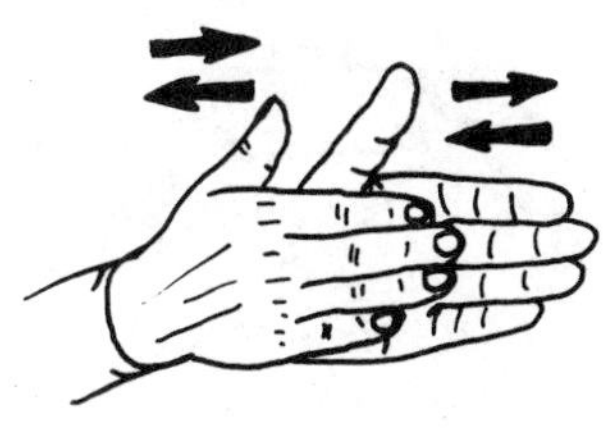

Arabic: hamás حماس
Chinese: rèqíng 熱情
Dutch: enthousiasme
French: enthousiasme
German: Begeisterung
Italian: entusiasmo
Japanese: netsui 熱意
Korean: yŏlshim 열심
Portuguese: entusiasmo
Russian: entuziázm энтузиазм
Spanish: entusiasmo
Swedish: entusiasm

715. entire [adj.]

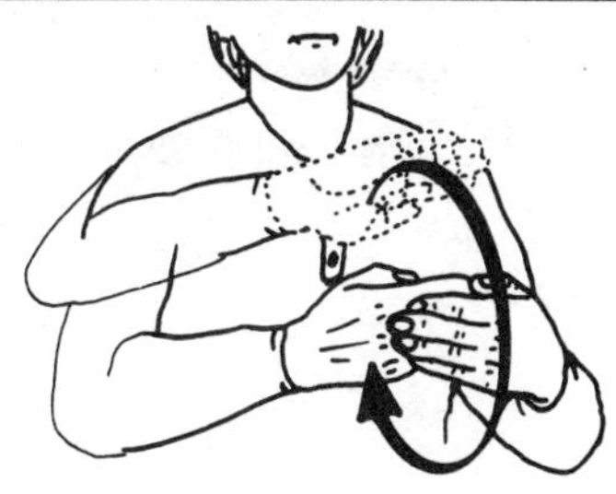

Arabic: kámel كامل
Chinese: quánbùde 全部的
Dutch: gans
French: entier
German: ganz
Italian: intero
Japanese: zentai no 全体の
Korean: jŏnch'eŭi 전체의
Portuguese: inteiro
Russian: tsélyy целый
Spanish: entero
Swedish: hel

716. entrance [n.]

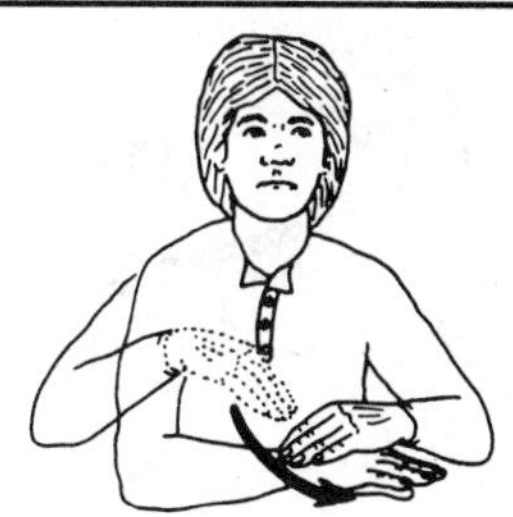

Arabic: médkhel مدخل
Chinese: rùkŏu 入口
Dutch: ingang
French: entrée
German: Eingang
Italian: entrata
Japanese: iriguchi 入口
Korean: ibku 입구
Portuguese: entrada
Russian: vkhód вход
Spanish: entrada
Swedish: ingäng

717. envelope [n.]

Arabic: dharf jawáb ظرف جواب
Chinese: xìnfēng 信封
Dutch: envelop
French: enveloppe
German: Briefumschlag
Italian: busta
Japanese: fūtō 封筒
Korean: bongt'u 봉투
Portuguese: envelope
Russian: konvért конверт
Spanish: sobre
Swedish: kuvert

718. envious [adj.]

Arabic: hasúd حسود
Chinese: xiànmù 羡慕
Dutch: jaloers
French: jaloux
German: neidisch
Italian: invidioso
Japanese: urayamashisōna うらやましそうな
Korean: burŏun 부러운
Portuguese: invejoso
Russian: zavístlivyy завистливый
Spanish: envidioso
Swedish: avundsjuk

719. environment [n.]

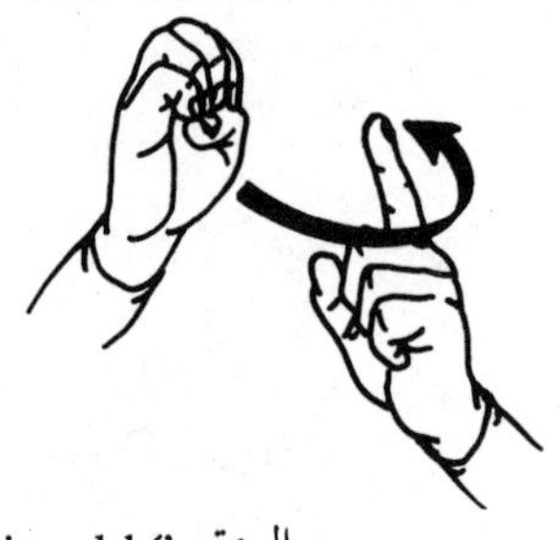

Arabic: al-bí'a البيئة
Chinese: huánjìng 環境
Dutch: omgeving
French: milieu
German: Umgebung
Italian: ambiente
Japanese: kankyō 環境
Korean: hwankyŏng 환경
Portuguese: meio ambiente
Russian: okruzháyushchaya sredá окружающая среда
Spanish: ambiente
Swedish: omgivning

720. equal [adj.]

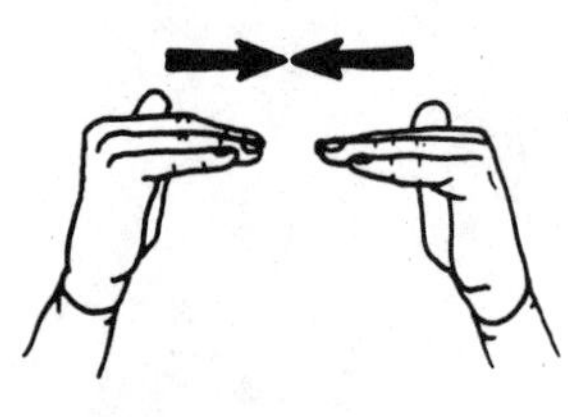

Arabic: musáwi مساوي
Chinese: píngděngde 平等的
Dutch: gelijk
French: égal
German: gleich
Italian: uguale
Japanese: byōdō na 平等な
Korean: dongdŭnghan 동등한
Portuguese: igual
Russian: rávnyy равный
Spanish: igual
Swedish: lika

721. equipment [n.]

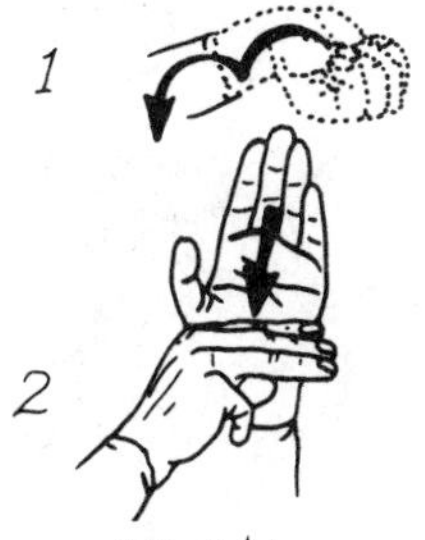

Arabic: moaadát معدات
Chinese: shèbèi 設備
Dutch: uitrusting
French: équipement
German: Ausstattung
Italian: equipaggiamento
Japanese: sōchi 装置
Korean: jangbi 장비
Portuguese: equipamento
Russian: oborúdovaniye оборудование
Spanish: equipo
Swedish: utrustning

722. erase [v.]

Arabic: máha محى
Chinese: cādiào 擦掉
Dutch: uitwissen
French: effacer
German: ausradieren
Italian: cancellare
Japanese: keshitoru 消しとる
Korean: jiuda 지우다
Portuguese: apagar
Russian: stirát' стирать
Spanish: borrar
Swedish: radera

723. error [n.]

Arabic: khatá' خطأ
Chinese: cuòwù 錯誤
Dutch: fout
French: erreur
German: Fehler
Italian: errore
Japanese: ayamari 誤り
Korean: jalmot 잘못
Portuguese: êrro
Russian: oshíbka ошибка
Spanish: error
Swedish: fel

724. escape [v.]

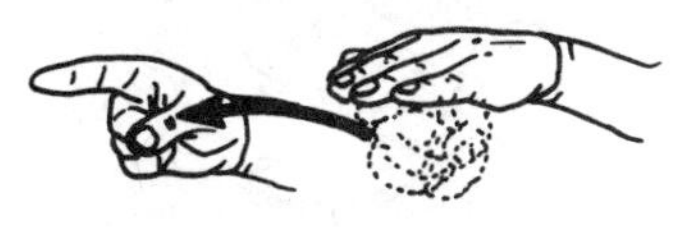

Arabic: háraba هرب
Chinese: táotuō 逃脱
Dutch: ontsnappen
French: échapper
German: entkommen
Italian: fuggire
Japanese: nigeru 逃げる
Korean: domanghada 도망하다
Portuguese: escapar
Russian: ubegát' убегать
Spanish: escapar
Swedish: fly

725. especially [adv.]

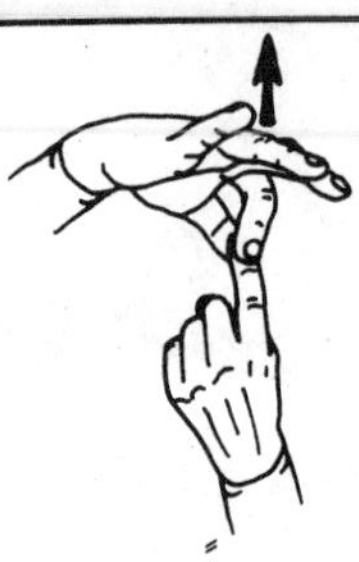

Arabic: khusúsan خصوصاً
Chinese: tèbiéde 特别的
Dutch: speciaal
French: spécialement
German: besonders
Italian: specialmente
Japanese: tokubetsu ni 特別に
Korean: tŭkhi 특기
Portuguese: especialmente
Russian: osóbenno особенно
Spanish: especialmente
Swedish: särsjuktsynnerhet

726. essential [adj.]

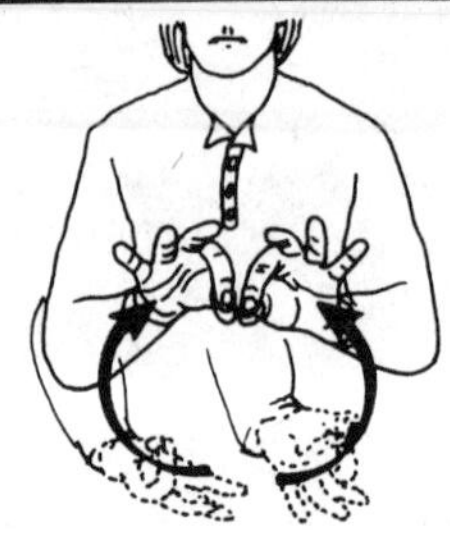

Arabic: asási اساسي
Chinese: jīběnde 基本的
Dutch: essentieel
French: essentiel
German: wesentlich
Italian: essenziale
Japanese: honshitsu tekina 本質的な
Korean: kkogpilyohan 꼭 필요한
Portuguese: essencial
Russian: sushchéstvennyy существенный
Spanish: esencial
Swedish: väsentlig

727. establish [v.]

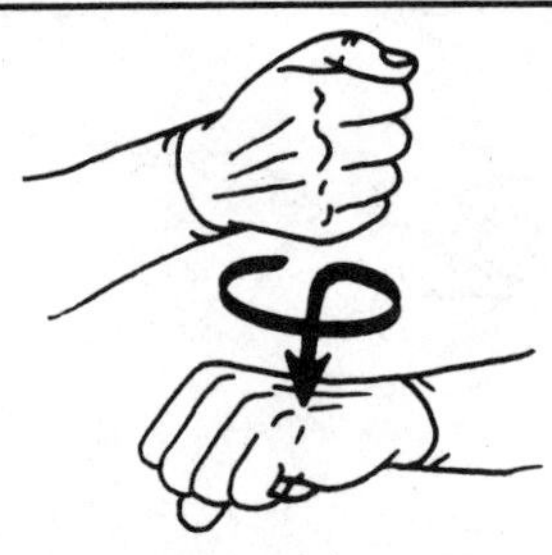

Arabic: ássasa اسس
Chinese: jiànlì 建立
Dutch: vestigen
French: établir
German: feststellen
Italian: stabilire
Japanese: kakuritsu suru 確立する
Korean: sŏllip'hada 설립하다
Portuguese: estabelecer
Russian: ustanávlivat' устанавливать
Spanish: establecer
Swedish: etablera

728. estimate [n.]

Arabic: taqdír تقدير
Chinese: gūjì 估計
Dutch: schatting
French: évaluation
German: Schätzung
Italian: valutazione
Japanese: mitsumori 見積もり
Korean: kyŏnjŏg 견적
Portuguese: estimativa
Russian: otsénka оценка
Spanish: estimación
Swedish: beräkning

729. Ethiopia [n.]

Arabic: al-hábasha الحبشة
Chinese: yīsuōpīyǎ 依索匹亞
Dutch: Ethiopië
French: Éthiopie
German: Äthiopien
Italian: Etiopia
Japanese: Echiopia エチオピア
Korean: Itiopia 이디오피아
Portuguese: Etiópia
Russian: Efiópiya Эфиопия
Spanish: Etiopía
Swedish: Etiopien

730. Europe [n.]

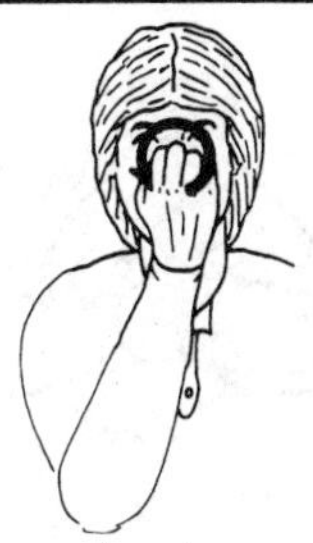

Arabic: oróba اوروبا
Chinese: ōuzhōu 歐洲
Dutch: Europa
French: Europe
German: Europa
Italian: Europa
Japanese: Yōroppa ヨーロッパ
Korean: Yurŏp 유럽
Portuguese: Europa
Russian: Yevrópa Европа
Spanish: Europa
Swedish: Europa

731. evaluate [v.]

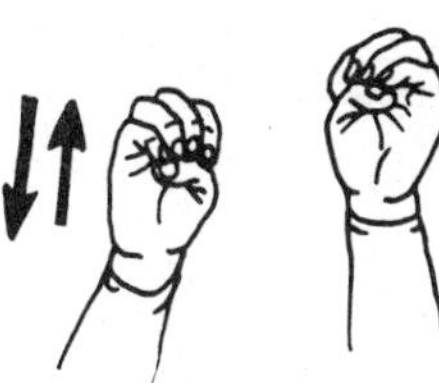

Arabic: qáyyema قيم
Chinese: pínggū 評估
Dutch: schatten
French: évaluer
German: abschätzen
Italian: valutare
Japanese: hyōka suru 評価する
Korean: pyŏngkahada 평가하다
Portuguese: avaliar
Russian: otsénivat' оценивать
Spanish: evaluar
Swedish: evaluera

732. even (level/smooth) [adj.]

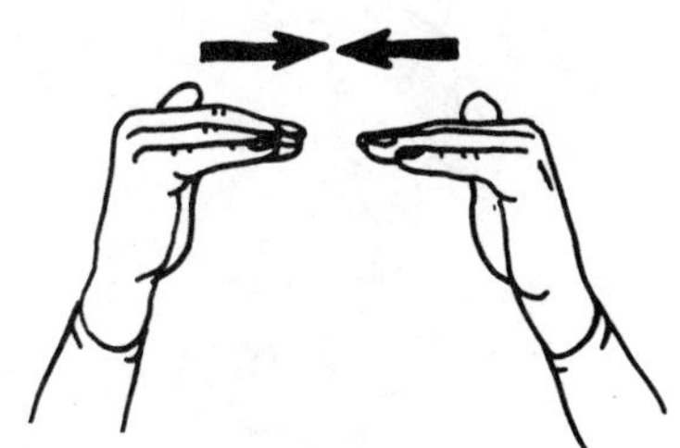

Arabic: mustáwi مستوي
Chinese: shuǐpíngde 水平的
Dutch: plat
French: plan
German: platt
Italian: uguale
Japanese: taira na 平らな
Korean: p'yŏngp'yŏnghan 평등한
Portuguese: plano
Russian: róvnyy ровный
Spanish: plano
Swedish: jämn

733. evening [n.]

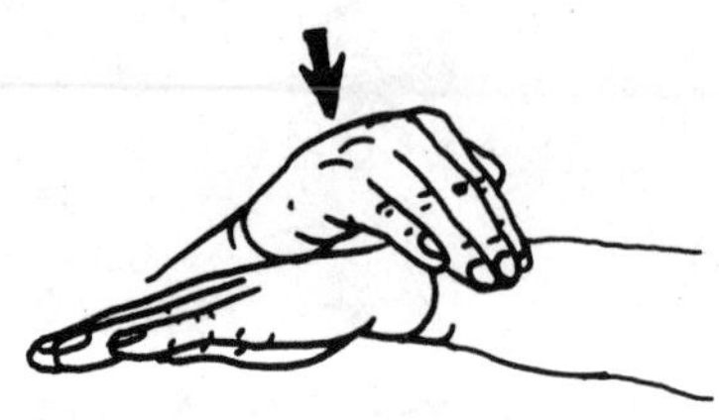

Arabic: masáa' مساء
Chinese: wǎnshàng 晚上
Dutch: avond
French: soir
German: Abend
Italian: sera
Japanese: yūgata 夕方
Korean: jŏnyŏg 저녁
Portuguese: noite
Russian: vécher вечер
Spanish: tarde
Swedish: kväll

734. event [n.]

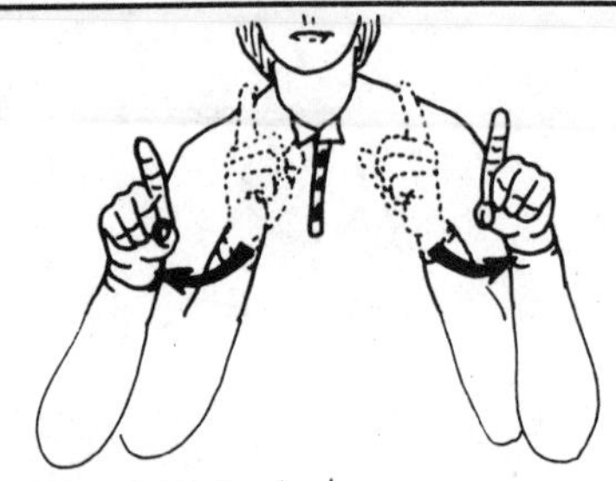

Arabic: hádeth حادث
Chinese: shìjiàn 事件
Dutch: gebeurtenis
French: événement
German: Ereignis
Italian: evento
Japanese: dekigoto 出来事
Korean: sakŏn 사건
Portuguese: acontecimento
Russian: sobýtiye событие
Spanish: acontecimiento
Swedish: händelse

735. every [adj.]

Arabic: kull كل
Chinese: měigede 每個的
Dutch: elk
French: tout
German: jeder
Italian: ogni
Japanese: arayuru あらゆる
Korean: modŭn 모든
Portuguese: cada
Russian: kázhdyy каждый
Spanish: cada
Swedish: varje

736. everybody (everyone) [pron.]

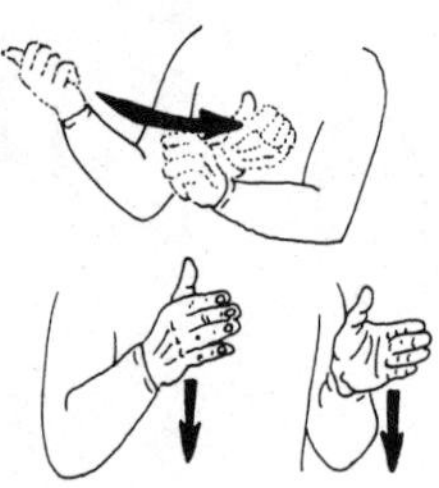

Arabic: kull shakhs كل شخص
Chinese: měirén 每人
Dutch: iedereen
French: tout le monde
German: jedermann
Italian: tutti
Japanese: daremo 誰も
Korean: nuguna da 누구나
Portuguese: todos
Russian: vse все
Spanish: todos
Swedish: alla

737. everything [pron.]

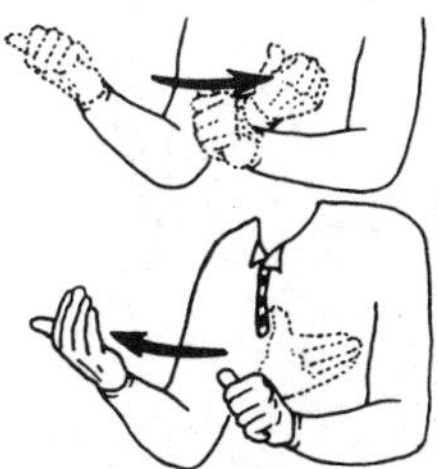

Arabic: kull sháee' كل شيء
Chinese: yīqiè 一切
Dutch: alles
French: tout
German: alles
Italian: tutto
Japanese: nanimokamo なにもかも
Korean: muŏsidŭnji 무엇이든지
Portuguese: tudo
Russian: vsyó всё
Spanish: todo
Swedish: allting

738. everywhere [adv.]

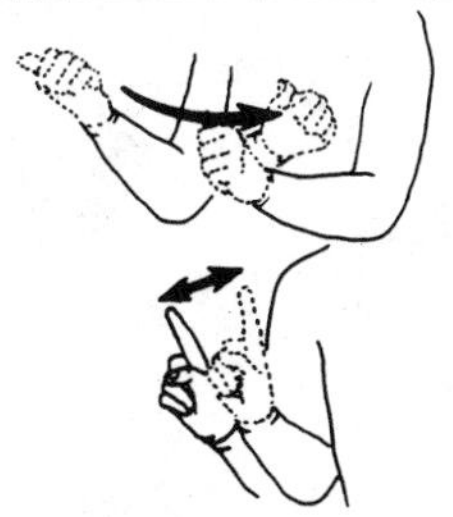

Arabic: fi kúlli makán في كل مكان
Chinese: dàochù 到處
Dutch: overal
French: partout
German: überall
Italian: dovunque
Japanese: dokonimo どこにも
Korean: ŏdina 어디나
Portuguese: por tôda parte
Russian: vezdé везде
Spanish: por todas partes
Swedish: överallt

739. evidence (proof) [n.]

Arabic: dalíl دليل
Chinese: zhèngjù 證據
Dutch: bewijs
French: preuve
German: Beweis
Italian: prova
Japanese: shōko 証拠
Korean: jŭnggŏ 증거
Portuguese: prova
Russian: dokazátel'stvo доказательство
Spanish: prueba
Swedish: bevis

740. evil [n.]

Arabic: sharr شر
Chinese: xié-è 邪惡
Dutch: kwaad
French: mal
German: Übel
Italian: male
Japanese: jaaku 邪悪
Korean: akma 악마
Portuguese: mal
Russian: zloy злой
Spanish: malo
Swedish: ondska

741. exact [adj.]

Arabic: madhbút مضبوط
Chinese: zhèngquède 正確的
Dutch: juist
French: exact
German: genau
Italian: esatto
Japanese: sēkakuna 正確な
Korean: jŏnghwak'han 정확한
Portuguese: exato
Russian: tóchnyy точный
Spanish: exacto
Swedish: exakt

742. exaggerate [v.]

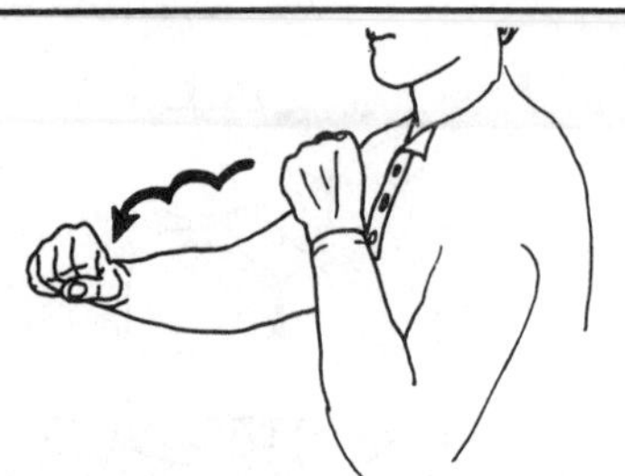

Arabic: bálagha بالغ
Chinese: kuāzhāng 誇張
Dutch: overdrijven
French: exagérer
German: übertreiben
Italian: esagerare
Japanese: kochō suru 誇張する
Korean: kwajanghada 과장하다
Portuguese: exagerar
Russian: preuvelíchivat' преувеличивать
Spanish: exagerar
Swedish: överdriva

743. examination [n.]

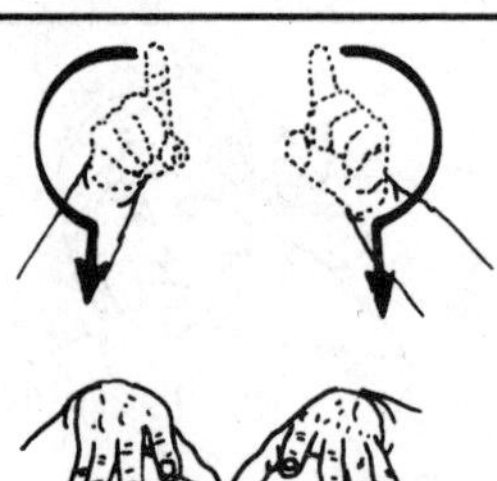

Arabic: ikhtibár اختبار
Chinese: shìyàn 試驗
Dutch: examen
French: examen
German: Examen
Italian: esame
Japanese: shiken 試験
Korean: shihŏm 시험
Portuguese: exame
Russian: ekzámen экзамен
Spanish: examen
Swedish: examen

744. examine [v.]

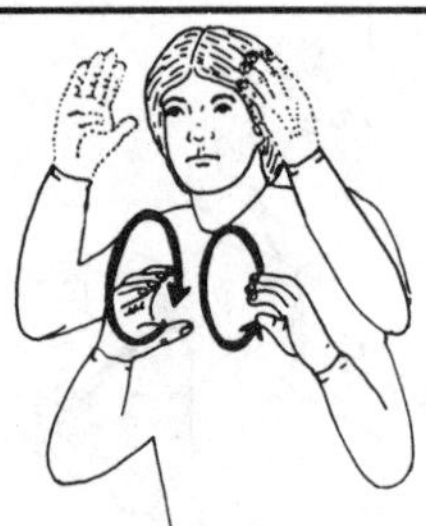

Arabic: akhtábara اختبر
Chinese: jiǎnchá 檢查
Dutch: onderzoeken
French: examiner
German: untersuchen
Italian: esaminare
Japanese: shiraberu 調べる
Korean: shihŏmhada 시험하다
Portuguese: examinar
Russian: osmátrivat' осматривать
Spanish: examinar
Swedish: undersöka

745. example [n.]

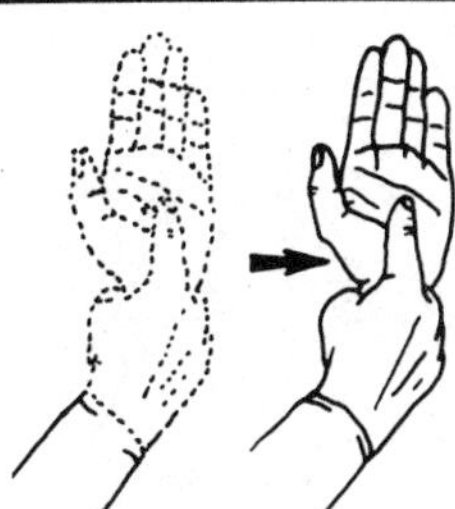

Arabic: mithál مثال
Chinese: lìzi 例子
Dutch: voorbeeld
French: exemple
German: Beispiel
Italian: esempio
Japanese: mihon 見本
Korean: ye 예
Portuguese: exemplo
Russian: primér пример
Spanish: ejemplo
Swedish: exempel

746. exceed [v.]

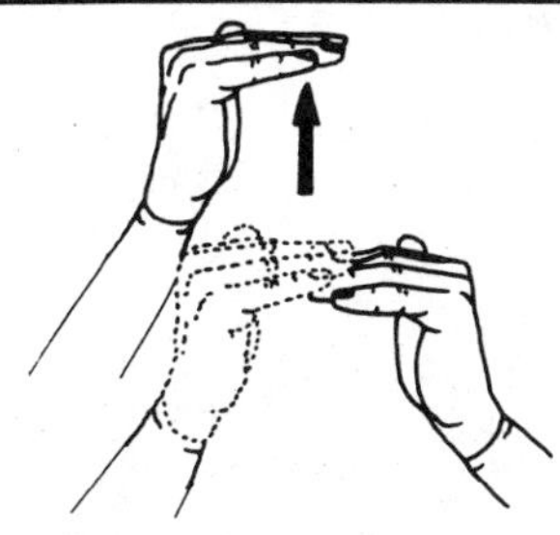

Arabic: táada تعدى
Chinese: chāoguò 超過
Dutch: overschrijden
French: excéder
German: überschreiten
Italian: eccedere
Japanese: koeru 越える
Korean: jinach'ida 지나치다
Portuguese: exceder
Russian: prevyshát' превышать
Spanish: exceder
Swedish: överskrida

747. excellent [adj.]

Arabic: momtáz ممتاز
Chinese: yōuxiùde 優秀的
Dutch: uitstekend
French: excellent
German: ausgezeichnet
Italian: eccellente
Japanese: yūshū na 優秀な
Korean: usuhan 우수한
Portuguese: excelente
Russian: otlíchnyy отличный
Spanish: excelente
Swedish: utmärkt

748. except [prep.]

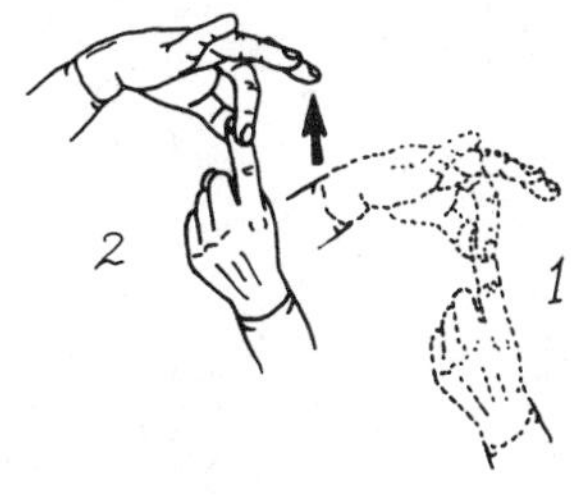

Arabic: fíma áada فيما عدا
Chinese: chúle 除了
Dutch: behalve
French: sauf
German: außer
Italian: eccetto
Japanese: . . .o nozoite …を除いて
Korean: jeoehago 제하고
Portuguese: exceto
Russian: króme кроме
Spanish: excepto
Swedish: utom

749. exchange [v.]

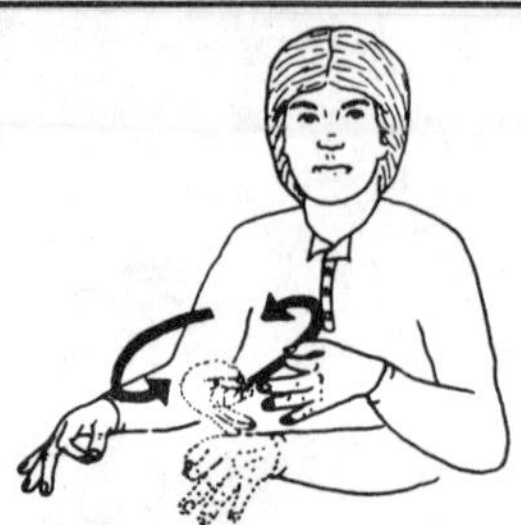

Arabic: báddala بدل
Chinese: jiāohuàn 交換
Dutch: verruilen
French: échanger
German: wechseln
Italian: scambiare
Japanese: kōkan suru 交換する
Korean: bakkuda 바꾸다
Portuguese: trocar
Russian: obménivat' обменивать
Spanish: cambiar
Swedish: utbyda

750. excite [v.]

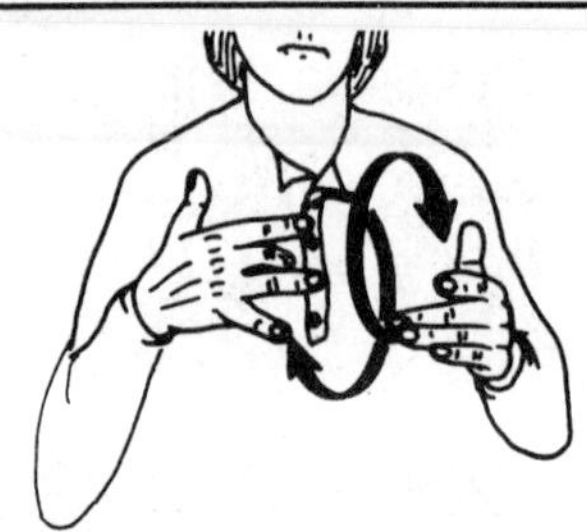

Arabic: athára اثار
Chinese: cìjī 刺激
Dutch: opwinden
French: inciter
German: erregen
Italian: eccitare
Japanese: kōfun suru 興奮する
Korean: hŭngbunshik'ida 흥분시키다
Portuguese: excitar
Russian: vozbuzhdát' возбуждать
Spanish: excitar
Swedish: upphetsa

751. exclude [v.]

Arabic: abaáda ابعد
Chinese: páichú 排除
Dutch: uitsluiten
French: exclure
German: ausschließen
Italian: escludere
Japanese: jogai suru 除外する
Korean: jeoehada 제하다
Portuguese: excluir
Russian: isklyuchát' исключать
Spanish: excluir
Swedish: utesluta

752. excuse [v.]

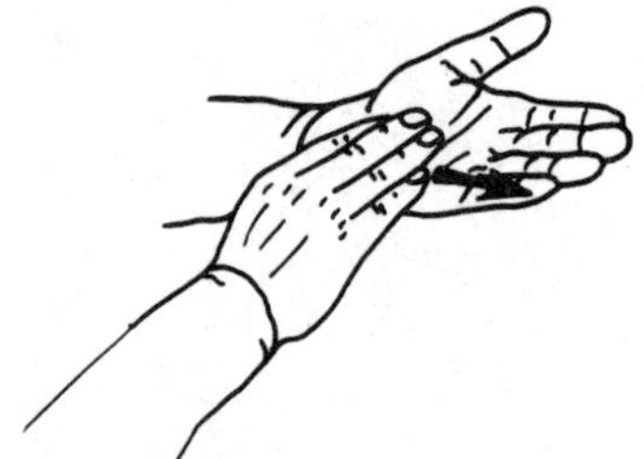

Arabic: bárara برر
Chinese: yuánliàng 原諒
Dutch: verontschuldigen
French: excuser
German: entschuldigen
Italian: scusare
Japanese: yurusu 許す
Korean: yongsŏhada 용서하다
Portuguese: desculpar
Russian: izvinyát' извинять
Spanish: excusar
Swedish: ursäkta

753. exercise (physical) [n.]

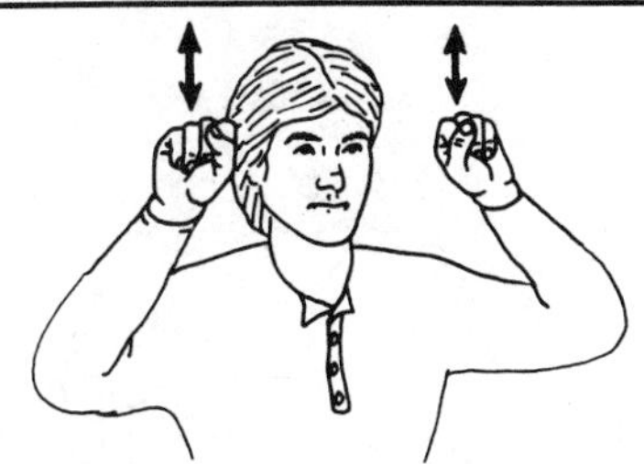

Arabic: tadríb تدريب
Chinese: yùndòng 運動
Dutch: oefening
French: exercice
German: Übung
Italian: esercizio
Japanese: undō 運動
Korean: undong 운동
Portuguese: exercício
Russian: uprazhnéniye упражнение
Spanish: ejercicio
Swedish: exercis

754. exhaust (use up) [v.]

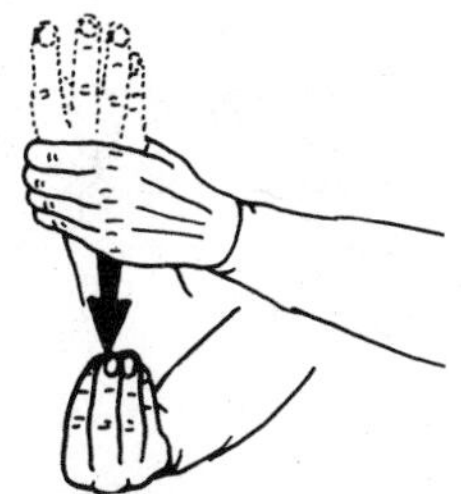

Arabic: istánfadha استنفذ
Chinese: hàojìn 耗盡
Dutch: uitputten
French: épuiser
German: erschöpfen
Italian: esaurire
Japanese: tsukai tsukusu 使い尽くす
Korean: da ssŏbŏrida 다 써버리다
Portuguese: esgotar
Russian: istoshchát' истощать
Spanish: agotar
Swedish: utmatta

755. exist [v.]

Arabic: wájada وجد
Chinese: cúnzài 存在
Dutch: bestaan
French: exister
German: existieren
Italian: esistere
Japanese: jitsuzon suru 実存する
Korean: chonjaehada 존재하다
Portuguese: existir
Russian: sushchestvovát' существовать
Spanish: existir
Swedish: existera

756. exit [n.]

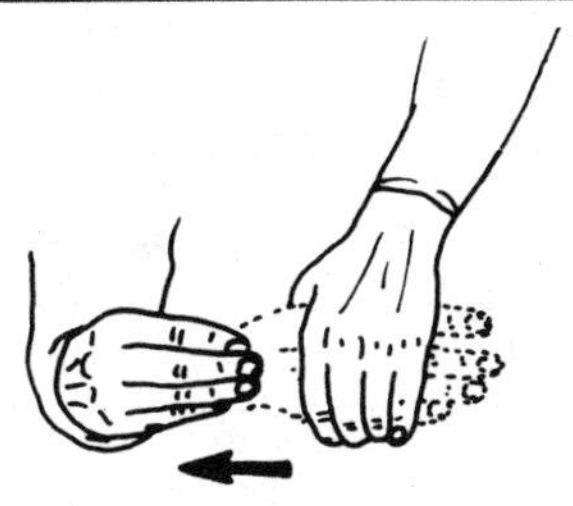

Arabic: mákhraj مخرج
Chinese: chūkǒu 出口
Dutch: uitgang
French: sortie
German: Ausgang
Italian: uscita
Japanese: deguchi 出口
Korean: ch'ulgu 출구
Portuguese: saída
Russian: výkhod выход
Spanish: salida
Swedish: utgång

757. expand [v.]

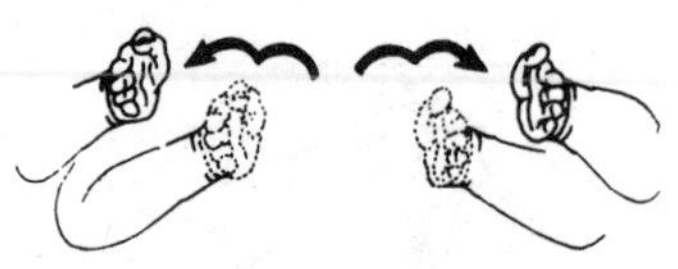

Arabic: tawássaa توسع
Chinese: kuòzhāng 擴張
Dutch: uitbreiden
French: étendre
German: erweitern
Italian: espandere
Japanese: hirogeru 広げる
Korean: hwagchanghada 확장하다
Portuguese: expandir
Russian: rasshiryát' расширять
Spanish: ampliar
Swedish: utbreda

758. expect [v.]

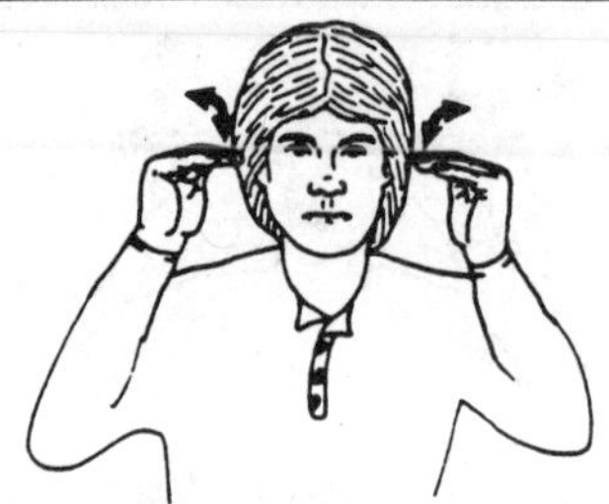

Arabic: tawáqqaa توقع
Chinese: qíwàng 期望
Dutch: verwachten
French: s'attendre
German: erwarten
Italian: presumere
Japanese: kitai suru 期待する
Korean: kidaehada 기대하다
Portuguese: esperar
Russian: ozhidát' ожидать
Spanish: esperar
Swedish: förvänta

759. expel [v.]

Arabic: tárada طرد
Chinese: qūzhú 驅逐
Dutch: verbannen
French: expulser
German: vertreiben
Italian: espellere
Japanese: oidasu 追い出す
Korean: ch'ubanghada 추방하다
Portuguese: expulsar
Russian: isklyuchát' исключать
Spanish: expulsar
Swedish: driva ut

760. expense [n.]

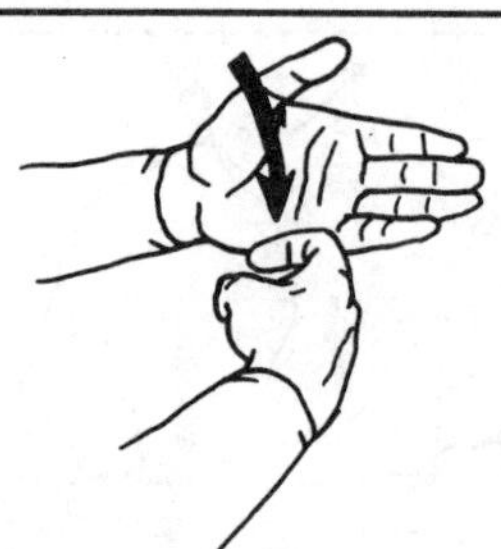

Arabic: taklúfa تكلفة
Chinese: huāfèi 花費
Dutch: kosten
French: dépense
German: Kosten
Italian: spesa
Japanese: shuppi 出費
Korean: biyong 비용
Portuguese: despesa
Russian: raskhód расход
Spanish: gasto
Swedish: utgift

761. expensive [adj.]

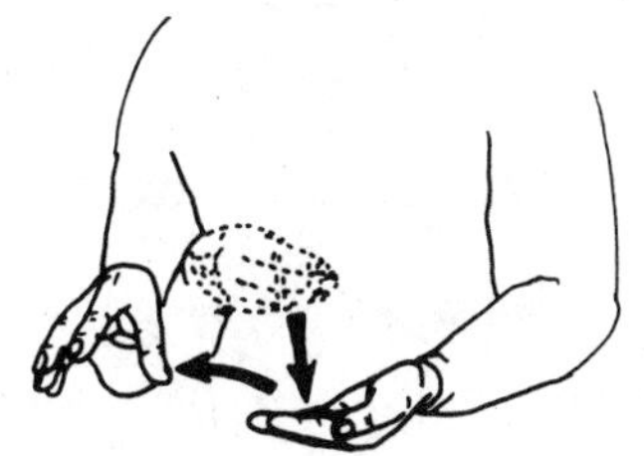

Arabic: mukállef مكلف
Chinese: guì 貴
Dutch: duur
French: coûteux
German: teuer
Italian: costoso
Japanese: kōkana 高価な
Korean: bissan 비싼
Portuguese: caro
Russian: dorogóy дорогой
Spanish: caro
Swedish: dyr

762. experience [n.]

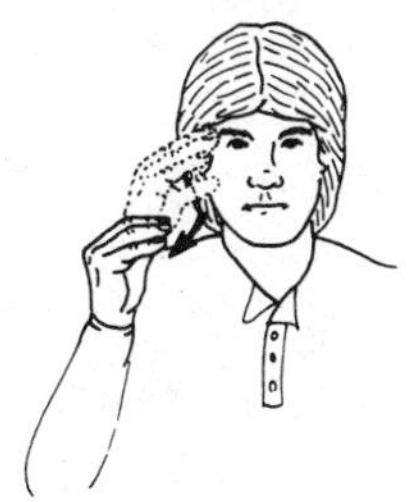

Arabic: khébra خبرة
Chinese: jīngyàn 經驗
Dutch: ervaring
French: expérience
German: Erfahrung
Italian: esperienza
Japanese: keiken 経験
Korean: kyŏnghŏm 경험
Portuguese: experiência
Russian: ópyt опыт
Spanish: experiencia
Swedish: erfarenhet

763. experiment [n.]

Arabic: tájroba تجربة
Chinese: shíyàn 實驗
Dutch: experiment
French: expérience
German: Experiment
Italian: esperimento
Japanese: jikken 実験
Korean: silhŏm 실험
Portuguese: experiência
Russian: eksperimént эксперимент
Spanish: experimento
Swedish: experiment

764. expert [n.]

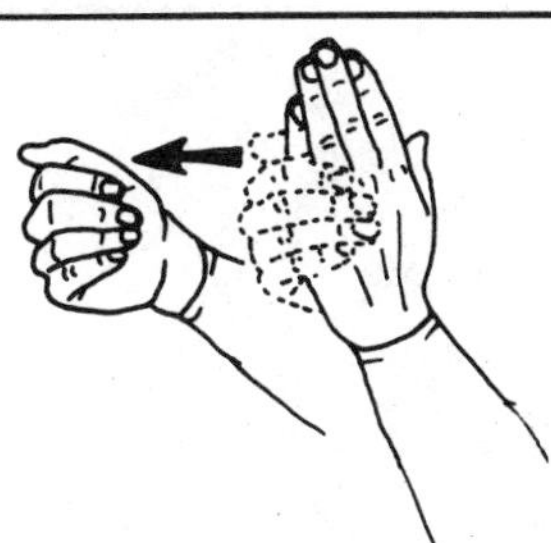

Arabic: khabír خبير
Chinese: zhuānjiā 專家
Dutch: expert
French: expert
German: Fachmann
Italian: esperto
Japanese: semmonka 専門家
Korean: jŏnmunga 전문가
Portuguese: perito
Russian: ekspért эксперт
Spanish: experto
Swedish: expert

765. explain [v.]

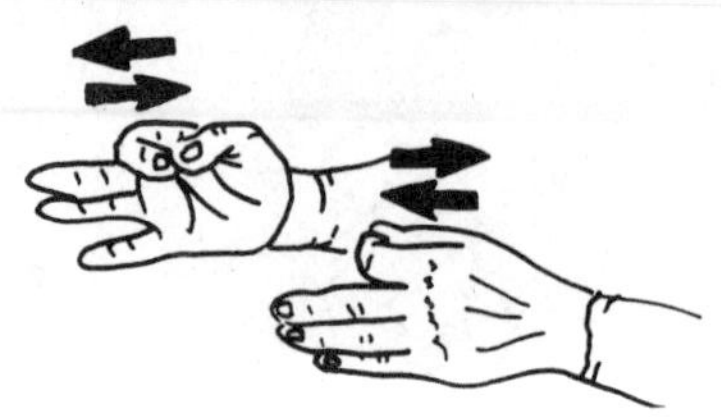

Arabic: sháraha شرح
Chinese: jiěshì 解釋
Dutch: uitleggen
French: expliquer
German: erklären
Italian: spiegare
Japanese: setsumei suru 説明する
Korean: sŏlmyŏnghada 설명하다
Portuguese: explicar
Russian: ob''yasnyát' объяснять
Spanish: explicar
Swedish: förklara

766. explode [v.]

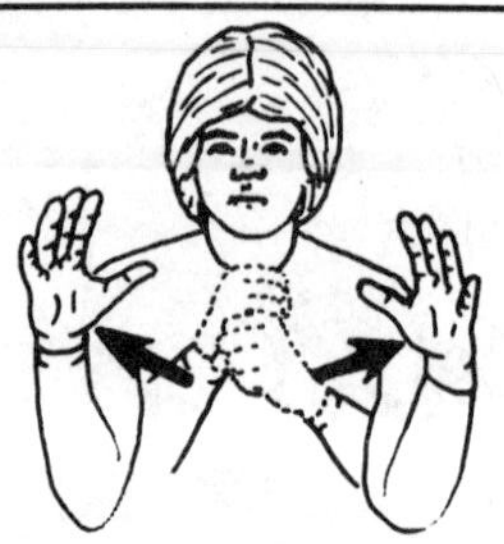

Arabic: infájara انفجر
Chinese: bàozhà 爆炸
Dutch: exploderen
French: exploser
German: explodieren
Italian: esplodere
Japanese: bakuhatsu suru 爆発する
Korean: p'okparhada 폭발하다
Portuguese: explodir
Russian: vzryvát' взрывать
Spanish: explotar
Swedish: explodera

767. explore [v.]

Arabic: istákshafa استكشف
Chinese: tànchá 探査
Dutch: onderzoeken
French: explorer
German: untersuchen
Italian: esplorare
Japanese: tanken suru 探検する
Korean: t'amhŏmhada 탐험하다
Portuguese: explorar
Russian: isslédovat' исследовать
Spanish: explorar
Swedish: utforska

768. expression (phrase/saying) [n.]

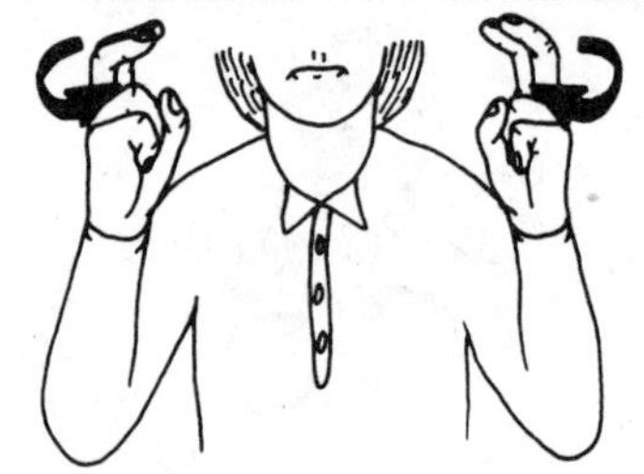

Arabic: taabír تعبير
Chinese: biǎoxiàn 表現
Dutch: uitdrukking
French: expression
German: Ausdruck
Italian: espressione
Japanese: iimawashi 言いまわし
Korean: p'yohyŏn 표현
Portuguese: expressão
Russian: vyrazhéniye выражение
Spanish: expresión
Swedish: uttryck

769. extend [v.]

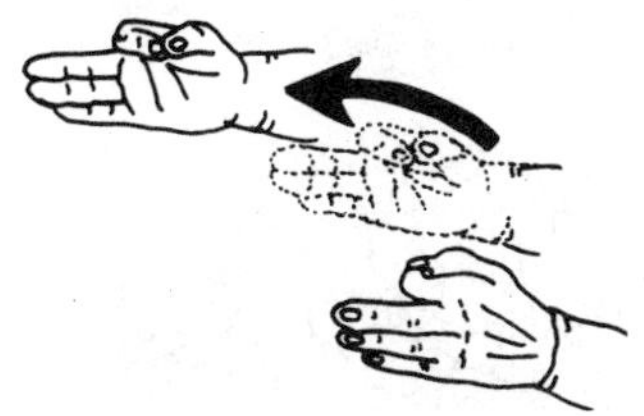

Arabic: mádda مد
Chinese: shēncháng 擴展
Dutch: uitstrekken
French: étendre
German: ausdehnen
Italian: estendere
Japanese: enchō suru 延長する
Korean: nŏlp'ida 넓히다
Portuguese: estender
Russian: vytyágivat' вытягивать
Spanish: extender
Swedish: förlänga

770. eye [n.]

Arabic: áayn عين
Chinese: yǎnjing 眼睛
Dutch: oog
French: oeil
German: Auge
Italian: occhio
Japanese: me 目
Korean: nun 눈
Portuguese: olho
Russian: glaz глаз
Spanish: ojo
Swedish: öga

771. eyeglasses [n.]

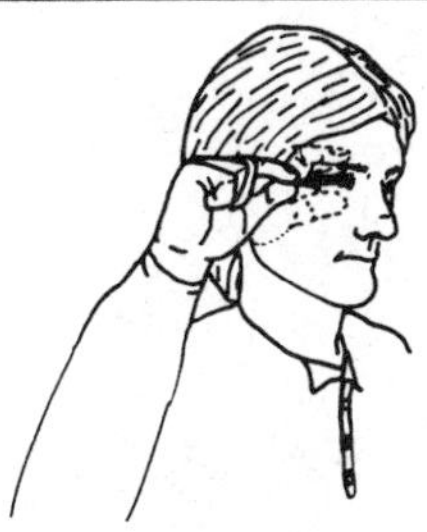

Arabic: nadhára نظارة
Chinese: yǎnjìng 眼鏡
Dutch: bril
French: lunettes
German: Brille
Italian: occhiali
Japanese: megane 眼鏡
Korean: angyŏng 안경
Portuguese: óculos
Russian: ochkí очки
Spanish: anteojos
Swedish: glasögon

772. face [n.]

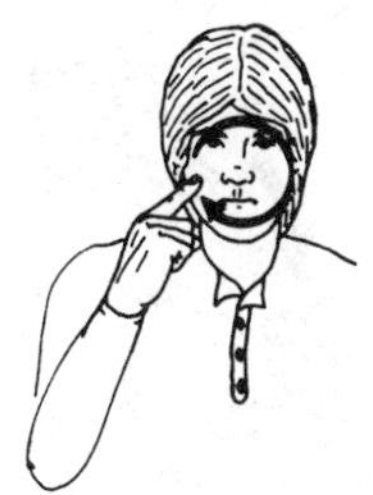

Arabic: wájih وجه
Chinese: liǎn 臉
Dutch: gezicht
French: visage
German: Gesicht
Italian: faccia
Japanese: kao 顔
Korean: ŏlgul 얼굴
Portuguese: cara
Russian: litsó лицо
Spanish: cara
Swedish: ansikte

773. factory [n.]

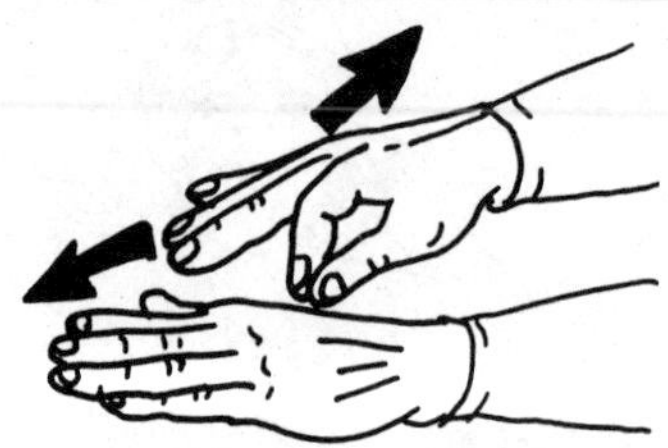

Arabic: masná' مصنع
Chinese: gōngchǎng 工廠
Dutch: fabriek
French: fabrique
German: Fabrik
Italian: fabbrica
Japanese: kōjō 工場
Korean: kongjang 공장
Portuguese: fábrica
Russian: fábrika фабрика
Spanish: fábrica
Swedish: fabrik

774. fade [v.]

Arabic: báhata بهت
Chinese: tuìsè 褪色
Dutch: verschieten
French: pâlir
German: verschießen
Italian: sbiadire
Japanese: iro aseru 色あせる
Korean: baraeda 바래다
Portuguese: desbotar
Russian: uvyadát' увядать
Spanish: desteñirse
Swedish: vissna

775. fail (not succeed) [v.]

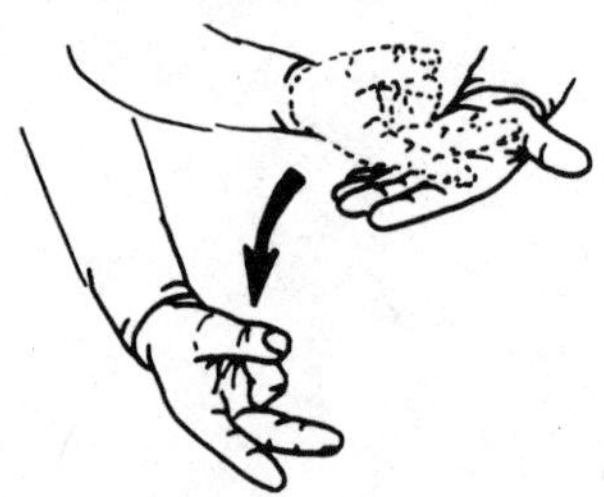

Arabic: sáqata سقط
Chinese: shībài 失敗
Dutch: mislukken
French: échouer
German: mißlingen
Italian: mancare
Japanese: shippai suru 失敗する
Korean: shilp'aehada 실패하다
Portuguese: fracassar
Russian: nedostavát' недоставать
Spanish: fracasar
Swedish: misslyckas

776. faint [v.]

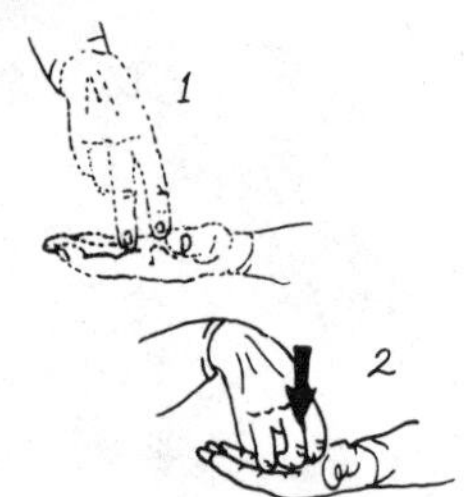

Arabic: yusáb bil-ighmá يصاب بالاغماء
Chinese: yūn 暈
Dutch: flauw vallen
French: défaillir
German: in Ohnmacht fallen
Italian: svenire
Japanese: kizetsu suru 気絶する
Korean: gijŏrhada 기절하다
Portuguese: desmaiar
Russian: pádat' v óbmorok падать в обморок
Spanish: desmayarse
Swedish: svimma

777. fair (just) [adj.]

Arabic: áadel عادل
Chinese: měihǎo 正好
Dutch: rechtvaardig
French: juste
German: gerecht
Italian: giusto
Japanese: kōhei na 公平な
Korean: gongp'yŏnghan 공평한
Portuguese: justo
Russian: spravedlívyy справедливый
Spanish: justo
Swedish: just

778. faith [n.]

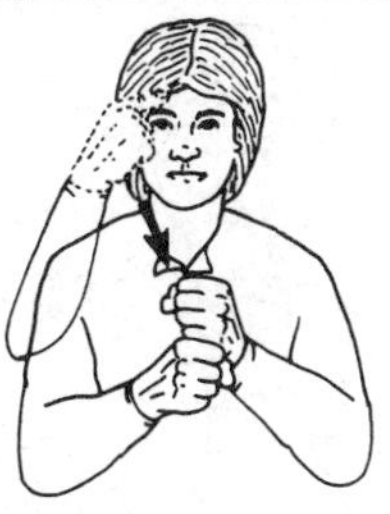

Arabic: eaatiqád اعتقاد
Chinese: xìnxīn 信心
Dutch: geloof
French: foi
German: Glaube
Italian: fede
Japanese: shinrai 信頼
Korean: shinyŏm 신념
Portuguese: fé
Russian: véra вера
Spanish: fe
Swedish: tro

779. faithful [adj.]

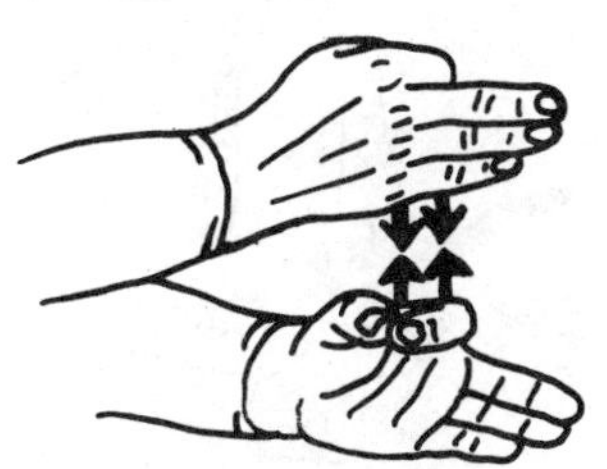

Arabic: mó'min مؤمن
Chinese: zhōngxīnde 忠心的
Dutch: trouw
French: fidèle
German: treu
Italian: fedele
Japanese: seijitsuna 誠実な
Korean: chungshirhan 충실한
Portuguese: fiel
Russian: vérnyy верный
Spanish: fiel
Swedish: trogen

780. fall [v.]

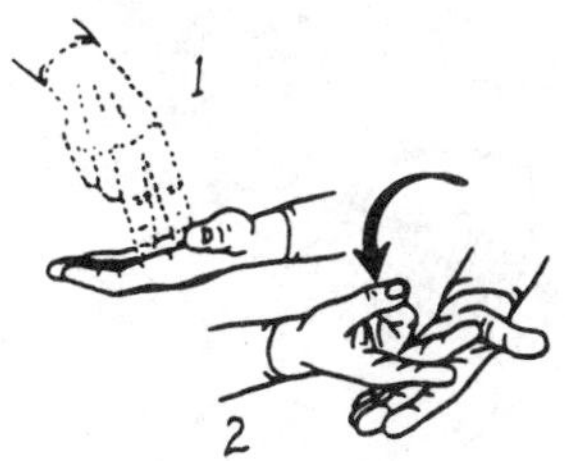

Arabic: sáqata سقط
Chinese: luòxià 落下
Dutch: vallen
French: tomber
German: fallen
Italian: cadere
Japanese: ochiru 落ちる
Korean: nŏmŏjida 넘어지다
Portuguese: cair
Russian: pádat' падать
Spanish: caer
Swedish: falla

781. false [adj.]

Arabic: muzéyyef مزيف
Chinese: xūjiǎ 虛假
Dutch: vals
French: faux
German: falsch
Italian: falso
Japanese: usono 嘘の
Korean: gatchaŭi 가짜의
Portuguese: falso
Russian: lózhnyy ложный
Spanish: falso
Swedish: falsk

782. fame [n.]

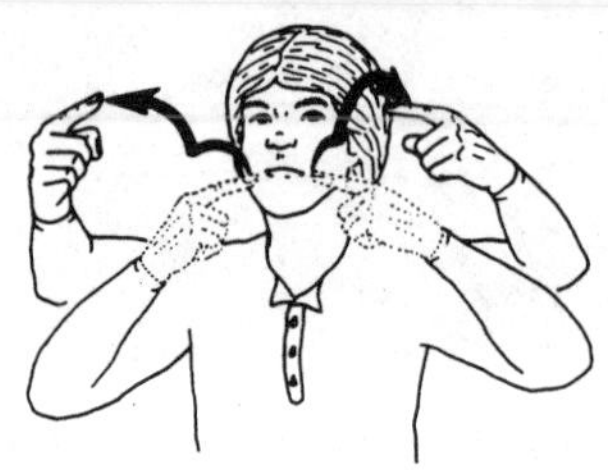

Arabic: shúhra شهرة
Chinese: míngshēng 名聲
Dutch: roem
French: renom
German: Ruhm
Italian: fama
Japanese: meisei 名声
Korean: myŏngsŏng 명성
Portuguese: fama
Russian: izvéstnost' известность
Spanish: fama
Swedish: berömmelse

783. family [n.]

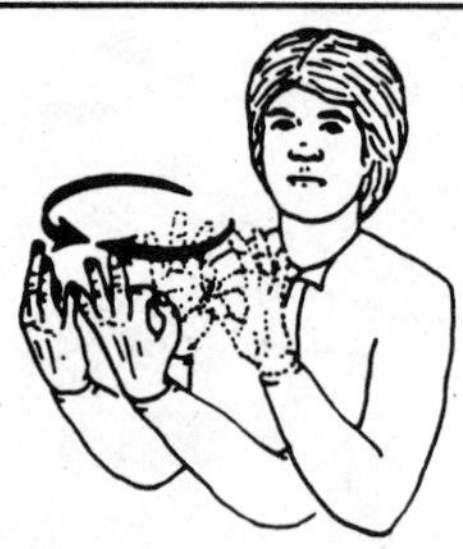

Arabic: aá'ila عائلة
Chinese: jiātíng 家庭
Dutch: familie
French: famille
German: Familie
Italian: famiglia
Japanese: kazoku 家族
Korean: kajok 가족
Portuguese: família
Russian: sem'yá семья
Spanish: familia
Swedish: familj

784. far [adj./adv.]

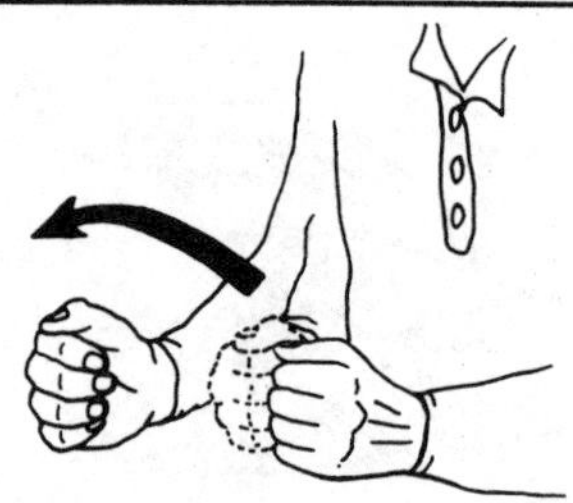

Arabic: ba'íd بعيد
Chinese: yuǎn 遠
Dutch: ver
French: lointain
German: fern
Italian: lontano
Japanese: tōkuni 遠くに
Korean: mŏn 먼
Portuguese: longe
Russian: dál'niy дальний
Spanish: lejano
Swedish: långt

785. farewell [n.]

Arabic: wadeáa' وداع
Chinese: gàobié 告别
Dutch: afscheid
French: adieu
German: Abschied
Italian: addio
Japanese: wakare 別れ
Korean: jakbyŏl 작별
Portuguese: despedida
Russian: proshchániye прощание
Spanish: despedida
Swedish: farväl

786. farm [n.]

Arabic: mazráa مزرعة
Chinese: nóngchăng 農場
Dutch: boerderij
French: ferme
German: Bauernhof
Italian: fattoria
Japanese: nōjō 農場
Korean: nongjang 농장
Portuguese: fazenda
Russian: férma ферма
Spanish: granja
Swedish: lantbruk

787. farmer [n.]

Arabic: muzárea' مزارع
Chinese: nóngfū 農夫
Dutch: boer
French: fermier
German: Bauer
Italian: colono
Japanese: nōfu 農夫
Korean: nongbu 농부
Portuguese: fazendeiro
Russian: férmer фермер
Spanish: granjero
Swedish: lantbrukare

788. farther [adj./adv.]

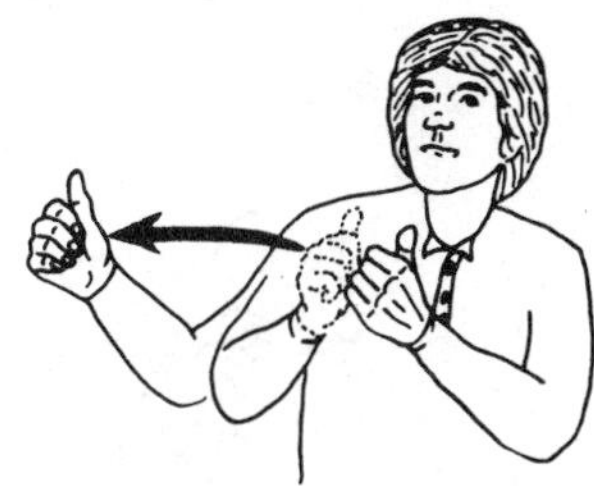

Arabic: abaád ابعد
Chinese: gèng yuăn de 更遠的
Dutch: verder
French: plus loin
German: weiter
Italian: più lontano
Japanese: motto tōku もっと遠く
Korean: dŏ mŏn 더 먼
Portuguese: mais longe
Russian: dál'she дальше
Spanish: más lejos
Swedish: längre

789. fashion [n.]

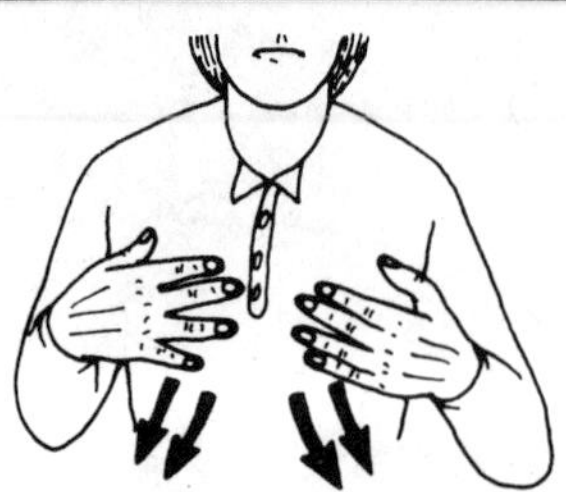

Arabic: zey زي
Chinese: shíshàng 時尚
Dutch: mode
French: mode
German: Mode
Italian: moda
Japanese: ryūkō 流行
Korean: yuhaeng 유행
Portuguese: moda
Russian: móda мода
Spanish: moda
Swedish: mode

790. fast [adj.]

Arabic: sária' سريع
Chinese: kuàide 快的
Dutch: snel
French: rapide
German: schnell
Italian: veloce
Japanese: hayaku 速く
Korean: jaepparŭn 재빠른
Portuguese: rápido
Russian: býstryy быстрый
Spanish: rápido
Swedish: snabb

791. fasten (attach) [v.]

Arabic: rábata ربط
Chinese: jìjǐn 繫緊
Dutch: vastmaken
French: attacher
German: festmachen
Italian: fissare
Japanese: shikkari tomeru
しっかり留める
Korean: dongyŏmaeda 동여매다
Portuguese: fixar
Russian: prikreplyát' прикреплять
Spanish: fijar
Swedish: fästa

792. fat [adj.]

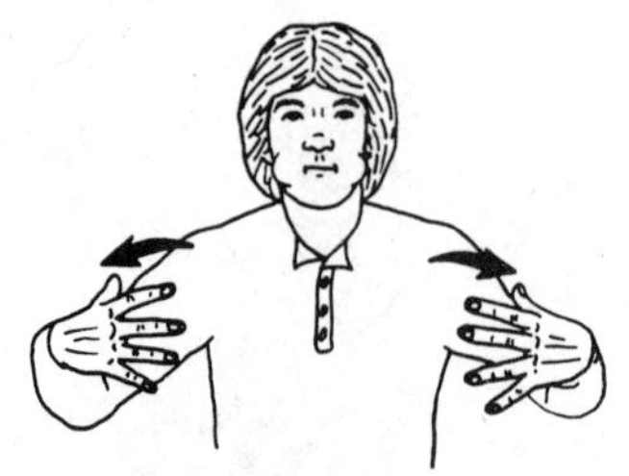

Arabic: samín سمين
Chinese: féipàng 肥胖
Dutch: vet
French: gras
German: fett
Italian: grasso
Japanese: futotta 太った
Korean: saltchin 살찐
Portuguese: gordo
Russian: zhírnyy жирный
Spanish: gordo
Swedish: fet

793. fate [n.]

Arabic: masír مصير
Chinese: mìngyùn 命運
Dutch: lot
French: destin
German: Schicksal
Italian: fato
Japanese: ummei 運命
Korean: unmyŏng 운명
Portuguese: destino
Russian: sud'bá судьба
Spanish: destino
Swedish: ödet

794. father [n.]

Arabic: ab أب
Chinese: fùqīn 父親
Dutch: vader
French: père
German: Vater
Italian: padre
Japanese: chichi 父
Korean: abŏji 아버지
Portuguese: pai
Russian: otéts отец
Spanish: padre
Swedish: fader

795. fault (blame) [n.]

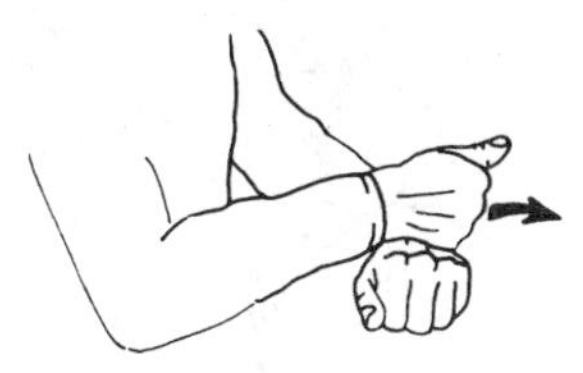

Arabic: lom لوم
Chinese: guòshī 過失
Dutch: schuld
French: faute
German: Schuld
Italian: colpa
Japanese: ketten 欠点
Korean: chalmot 잘못
Portuguese: culpa
Russian: viná вина
Spanish: culpa
Swedish: skuld

796. favor [n.]

Arabic: maarúf معروف
Chinese: ēnhuì 恩惠
Dutch: gunst
French: faveur
German: Gunst
Italian: favore
Japanese: kōi 好意
Korean: but'ak 부탁
Portuguese: favor
Russian: mílost' милость
Spanish: favor
Swedish: tjänst

797. favorite [adj.]

Arabic: mufáddal مفضل
Chinese: xīnàide 心愛的
Dutch: favoriet
French: favori
German: Lieblings-
Italian: favorito
Japanese: okini iri no お気に入りの
Korean: joahanŭn 좋아하는
Portuguese: favorito
Russian: lyubímyy любимый
Spanish: favorito
Swedish: favorit

798. fear [n.]

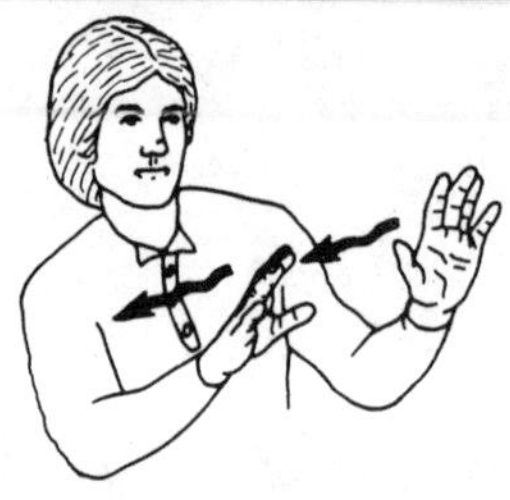

Arabic: khauf خوف
Chinese: hàipà 害怕
Dutch: angst
French: peur
German: Angst
Italian: paura
Japanese: kyōfu 恐怖
Korean: duryŏum 두려운
Portuguese: mêdo
Russian: strakh страх
Spanish: miedo
Swedish: fruktan

799. February [n.]

Arabic: febráer فبراير
Chinese: èryuè 二月
Dutch: februari
French: février
German: Februar
Italian: febbraio
Japanese: nigatsu 二月
Korean: iwŏl 이월
Portuguese: fevereiro
Russian: fevrál' февраль
Spanish: febrero
Swedish: februari

800. fee (honorarium) [n.]

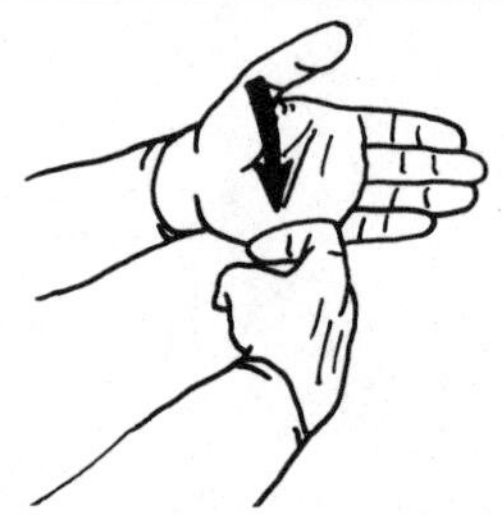

Arabic: ajr اجر
Chinese: fèiyòng 費用
Dutch: honorarium
French: honoraires
German: Honorar
Italian: onorario
Japanese: hōshu 報酬
Korean: susuryo 수수료
Portuguese: honorário
Russian: gonorár гонорар
Spanish: honorario
Swedish: honorer

801. feeble [adj.]

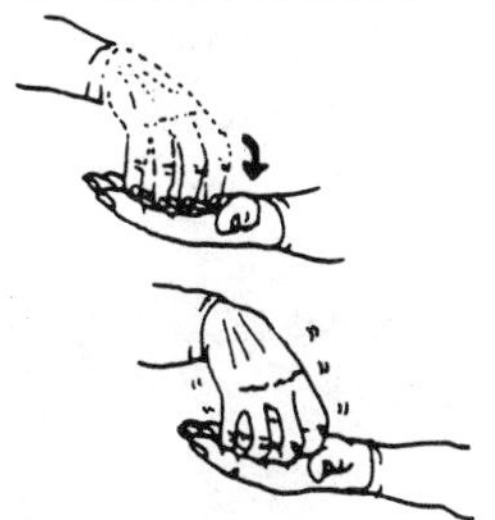

Arabic: dhaíf ضعيف
Chinese: ruǎnruò 軟弱
Dutch: zwak
French: faible
German: schwach
Italian: debole
Japanese: kayowai か弱い
Korean: yak'han 약한
Portuguese: fraco
Russian: bessíl'nyy бессильный
Spanish: débil
Swedish: svag

802. feed [v.]

Arabic: ghádha غذى
Chinese: wèi 餵
Dutch: voeden
French: nourrir
German: füttern
Italian: alimentare
Japanese: tabemono o ataeru 食べ物を与える
Korean: mŏg'ida 먹이다
Portuguese: alimentar
Russian: pitát' питать
Spanish: alimentar
Swedish: mata

803. feeling (sense) [n.]

Arabic: shu'úr شعور
Chinese: gǎnjué 感覺
Dutch: gevoel
French: sentiment
German: Gefühl
Italian: sentimento
Japanese: kimochi 気持
Korean: gamgak 감각
Portuguese: sentimento
Russian: chúvstvo чувство
Spanish: sentimiento
Swedish: känsla

804. feet (anatomy) [n.]

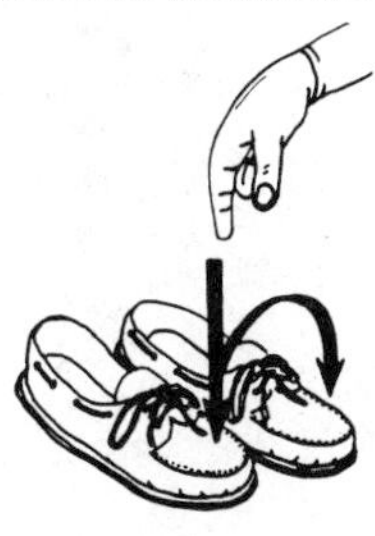

Arabic: qadaméin قدمين
Chinese: jiǎo 腳
Dutch: voet
French: pieds
German: Füße
Italian: piedi
Japanese: ashi 足
Korean: bal 발
Portuguese: pés
Russian: nógi ноги
Spanish: pies
Swedish: fötter

805. female [n.]

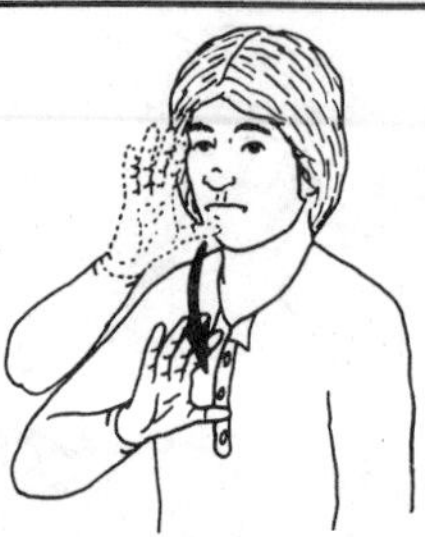

Arabic: úntha انثى
Chinese: nǚzìng 女性
Dutch: vrouwelijk
French: féminin
German: Weib
Italian: femmina
Japanese: josē 女性
Korean: yŏja 여자
Portuguese: fêmea
Russian: zhénshchina женщина
Spanish: hembra
Swedish: hona

806. fence [n.]

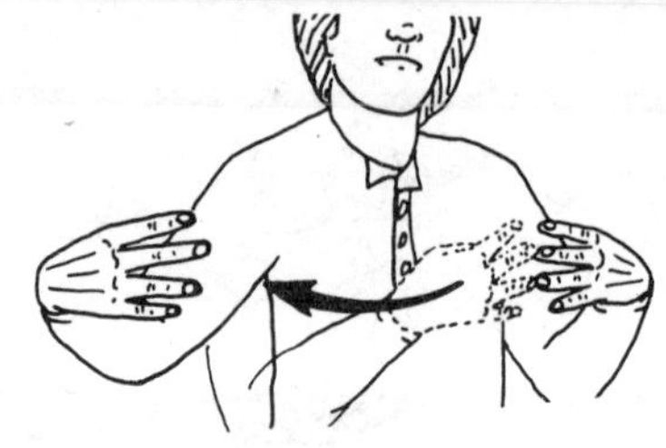

Arabic: síaj سياج
Chinese: líbā 籬笆
Dutch: omheining
French: clôture
German: Zaun
Italian: recinto
Japanese: hei 塀
Korean: ult'ari 울타리
Portuguese: cêrca
Russian: zabór забор
Spanish: cerca
Swedish: stängsel

807. festival [n.]

Arabic: áayd عيد
Chinese: jiérì 節日
Dutch: festival
French: festival
German: Fest
Italian: festival
Japanese: matsuri 祭り
Korean: janch'i 잔치
Portuguese: festival
Russian: festivál' фестиваль
Spanish: fiesta
Swedish: festival

808. fever [n.]

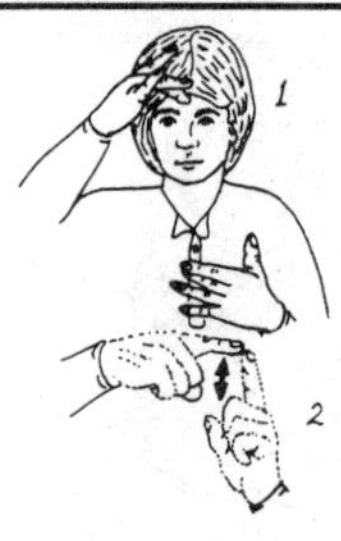

Arabic: húmma حمى
Chinese: fāshāo 發燒
Dutch: koorts
French: fièvre
German: Fieber
Italian: febbre
Japanese: netsu 熱
Korean: yŏl 열
Portuguese: febre
Russian: zhar жар
Spanish: fiebre
Swedish: feber

809. few [adj.]

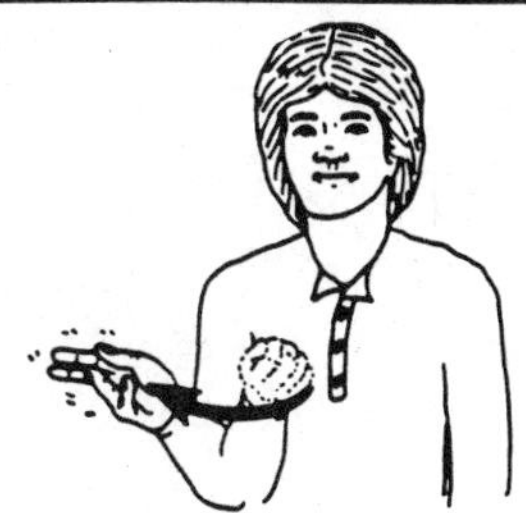

Arabic: qalíl قليل
Chinese: shǎo 少
Dutch: weinig
French: peu
German: wenige
Italian: pochi
Japanese: sukunai 少ない
Korean: sosuŭi 소수의
Portuguese: poucos
Russian: nemnógiy немногий
Spanish: poco
Swedish: få

810. fiction [n.]

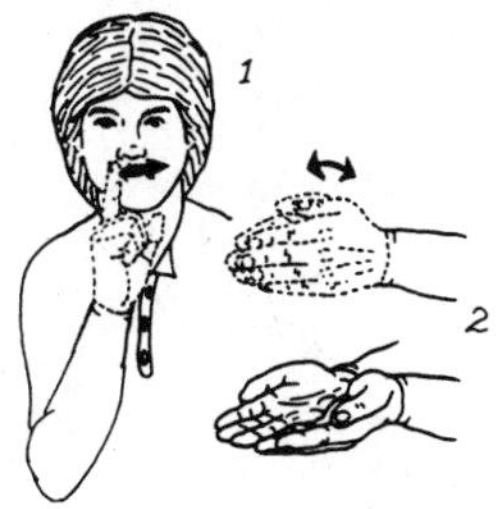

Arabic: ruáia رواية
Chinese: xiǎoshuō 小說
Dutch: fictie
French: fiction
German: Romanliteratur
Italian: finzione
Japanese: shōsetsu 小説
Korean: gagong 가공
Portuguese: ficção
Russian: belletrístika беллетристика
Spanish: ficción
Swedish: skonliteratur

811. field [n.]

Arabic: haql حقل
Chinese: kuàngyě 曠野
Dutch: veld
French: champ
German: Feld
Italian: campo
Japanese: nohara 野原
Korean: tŭl 들
Portuguese: campo
Russian: póle поле
Spanish: campo
Swedish: fält

812. fierce [adj.]

Arabic: muftáris مفترس
Chinese: xiōngměngde 兇猛的
Dutch: woest
French: brutal
German: wild
Italian: feroce
Japanese: mōretsu na 猛烈な
Korean: sanaun 사나운
Portuguese: feroz
Russian: zhestókiy жестокий
Spanish: feroz
Swedish: våldsam

813. fifteen [adj.]

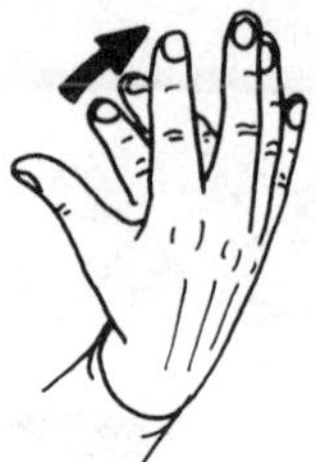

Arabic: khámsat aáshar خمسة عشر
Chinese: shíwŭ 十五
Dutch: vijftien
French: quinze
German: fünfzehn
Italian: quindici
Japanese: jūgo 15
Korean: yŏl tasŏt 열다섯
Portuguese: quinze
Russian: pyatnádtsat' пятнадцать
Spanish: quince
Swedish: femton

814. fifty [adj.]

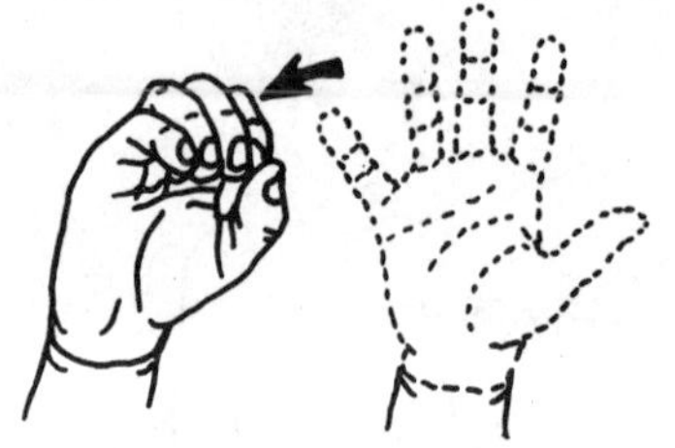

Arabic: khamsún خمسون
Chinese: wŭshí 五十
Dutch: vijftig
French: cinquante
German: fünfzig
Italian: cinquanta
Japanese: gojū 50
Korean: shwin saship 오십
Portuguese: cinquenta
Russian: pyat'desyát пятьдесят
Spanish: cincuenta
Swedish: femtio

815. fight (struggle) [v.]

Arabic: qátala قاتل
Chinese: dòuzhēng 打鬥
Dutch: strijden
French: se battre
German: kämpfen
Italian: lottare
Japanese: tatakau 戦う
Korean: dat'uda 다투다
Portuguese: lutar
Russian: borót'sya бороться
Spanish: luchar
Swedish: strida

816. figure (people) [n.]

Arabic: shakhsía báreza شخصية بارزة
Chinese: shēncái 身材
Dutch: figuur
French: figure
German: Figur
Italian: figura
Japanese: yōshi 容姿
Korean: moyang 모양
Portuguese: figura
Russian: figúra фигура
Spanish: figura
Swedish: figur

817. fill [v.]

Arabic: mála'a ملأ
Chinese: zhuāngmǎn 裝滿
Dutch: vullen
French: emplir
German: füllen
Italian: riempire
Japanese: mitasu 満たす
Korean: ch'aeuda 채우다
Portuguese: encher
Russian: napolnyát' наполнять
Spanish: llenar
Swedish: fylla

818. film (photographic) [n.]

Arabic: felm فيلم
Chinese: yǐngpiàn 影片
Dutch: film
French: pellicule
German: Film
Italian: pellicola
Japanese: fuirumu フィルム
Korean: p'illŭm 필름
Portuguese: filme
Russian: plyónka плёнка
Spanish: película
Swedish: film

819. final [adj.]

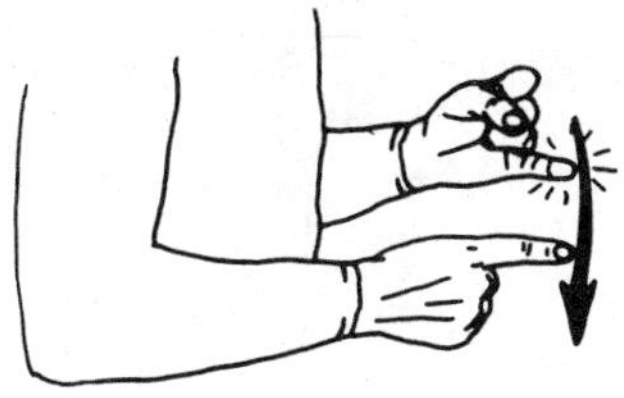

Arabic: nihá'i نهائي
Chinese: zuìhòude 最後的
Dutch: laatst
French: final
German: letzt
Italian: finale
Japanese: saigo no 最後の
Korean: ch'oehuŭi 최후의
Portuguese: final
Russian: okonchátel'nyy окончательный
Spanish: final
Swedish: slutlig

820. find [v.]

Arabic: wájada وجد
Chinese: zhǎodào 找到
Dutch: vinden
French: trouver
German: finden
Italian: trovare
Japanese: mitsukeru 見つける
Korean: balkyŏnhada 발견하다
Portuguese: encontrar
Russian: nakhodít' находить
Spanish: encontrar
Swedish: finna

821. fine (nice/splendid) [adj.]

Arabic: latíf لطيف
Chinese: mĕihăode 美好的
Dutch: fijn
French: fin
German: fein
Italian: bello
Japanese: rippa-na 立派な
Korean: johŭn 좋은
Portuguese: fino
Russian: prekrásnyy прекрасный
Spanish: fino
Swedish: fin

822. finger [n.]

Arabic: úsba' اصبع
Chinese: zhŏuzhĭ 手指
Dutch: vinger
French: doigt
German: Finger
Italian: dito
Japanese: yubi 指
Korean: sonkarak 손가락
Portuguese: dedo
Russian: pálets палец
Spanish: dedo
Swedish: finger

823. finish [v.]

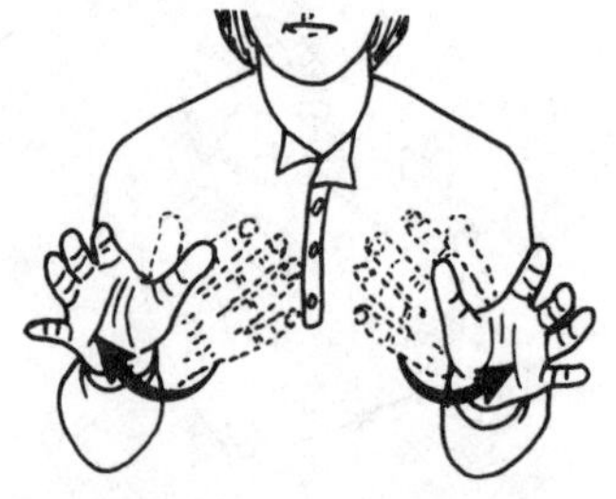

Arabic: ánha انهى
Chinese: zuòwán 做完
Dutch: eindigen
French: finir
German: enden
Italian: finire
Japanese: oeru 終える
Korean: kkŭnnaeda 끝내다
Portuguese: acabar
Russian: konchát' кончать
Spanish: acabar
Swedish: avsluta

824. Finland [n.]

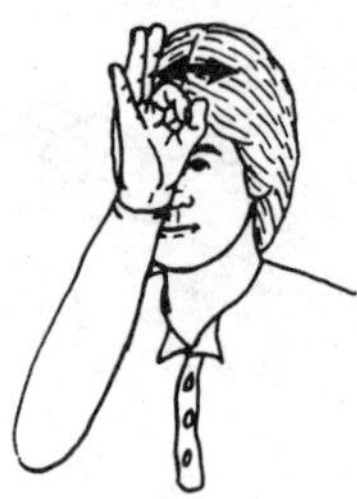

Arabic: finlánda فنلندا
Chinese: fēnlán 芬蘭
Dutch: Finland
French: Finlande
German: Finnland
Italian: Finlandia
Japanese: Finrando フィンランド
Korean: Pinlaend 핀랜드
Portuguese: Finlândia
Russian: Finlyándiya Финляндия
Spanish: Finlandia
Swedish: Finland

825. fire [n.]

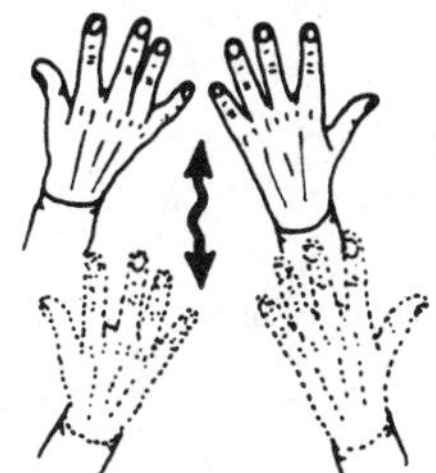

Arabic: haríeq حريق
Chinese: huǒ 火
Dutch: vuur
French: feu
German: Feuer
Italian: fuoco
Japanese: hi 火
Korean: bul 불
Portuguese: fogo
Russian: ogón' огонь
Spanish: fuego
Swedish: eld

826. first [adj.]

Arabic: áwwal اول
Chinese: dìyī 第一
Dutch: eerst
French: premier
German: erst
Italian: primo
Japanese: saisho no 最初の
Korean: ch'otchaeŭi 첫째의
Portuguese: primeiro
Russian: pérvyy первый
Spanish: primero
Swedish: först

827. fish [n.]

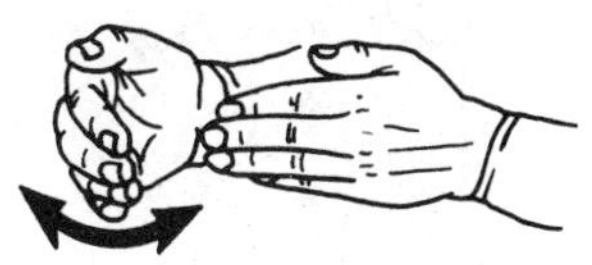

Arabic: sámak سمك
Chinese: yǘ 魚
Dutch: vis
French: poisson
German: Fisch
Italian: pesce
Japanese: sakana 魚
Korean: saengsŏn 생선
Portuguese: peixe
Russian: rýba рыба
Spanish: pescado
Swedish: fisk

828. fish [v.]

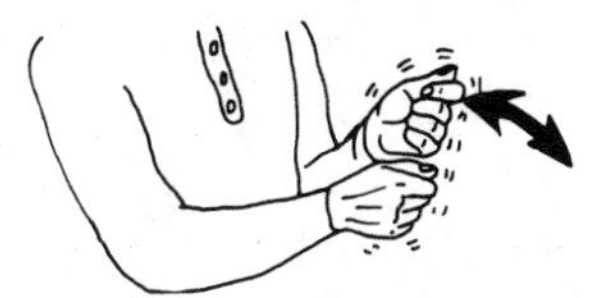

Arabic: sáada صاد
Chinese: diào yǘ 釣魚
Dutch: vissen
French: pêcher
German: angeln
Italian: pescare
Japanese: sakana o toru 魚を釣る
Korean: mulkogijabnŭnda 물고기 잡는다
Portuguese: pescar
Russian: lovít' rýbu ловить рыбу
Spanish: pescar
Swedish: fiska

829. five [adj.]

Arabic: khámsa خمسة
Chinese: wŭ 五
Dutch: vijf
French: cinq
German: fünf
Italian: cinque
Japanese: go 五
Korean: dasŏt 다섯
Portuguese: cinco
Russian: pyát' пять
Spanish: cinco
Swedish: fem

830. fix (make firm/fasten) [v.]

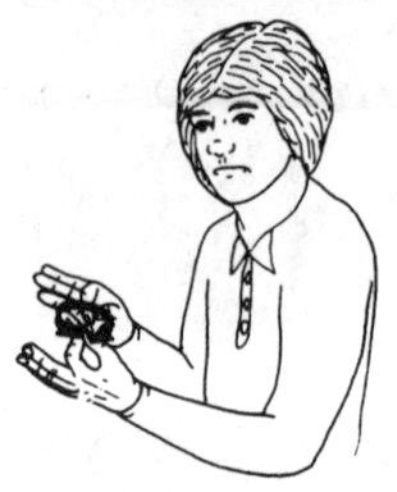

Arabic: thábbata ثبت
Chinese: ānzhuāng 安裝
Dutch: vastmaken
French: fixer
German: festmachen
Italian: fermare
Japanese: kotei saseru 固定させる
Korean: kojŏngshik'ida 고정시키다
Portuguese: fixar
Russian: zakreplyát' закреплять
Spanish: fijar
Swedish: laga

831. flag [n.]

Arabic: áalam علم
Chinese: qí 旗
Dutch: vlag
French: drapeau
German: Flagge
Italian: bandiera
Japanese: hata 旗
Korean: ki 기
Portuguese: bandeira
Russian: flag флаг
Spanish: bandera
Swedish: flagga

832. flame [n.]

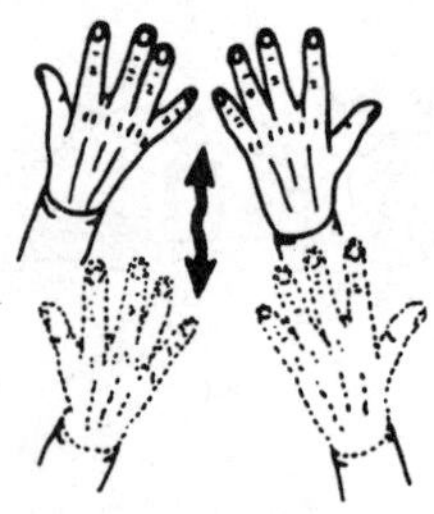

Arabic: láhab لهب
Chinese: huŏyàn 火焰
Dutch: vlam
French: flamme
German: Flamme
Italian: fiamma
Japanese: honoo 炎
Korean: bulkkot 불꽃
Portuguese: chama
Russian: plámya пламя
Spanish: llama
Swedish: låga

833. flash [v.]

Arabic: tawáhaja توهج
Chinese: shǎnshuò 閃爍
Dutch: flitsen
French: étinceler
German: blitzen
Italian: lampeggiare
Japanese: patto terasu ぱっと照らす
Korean: bulbŏntchŏkkŏrida 번쩍거리다
Portuguese: relampejar
Russian: mel'kát' мелькать
Spanish: destellar
Swedish: blixtra

834. flashlight [n.]

Arabic: míshaal kahrubá'i مشعل كهربائي
Chinese: shŏudiàntŏng 手電筒
Dutch: zaklamp
French: lampe de poche
German: Taschenlampe
Italian: lampadina tascabile
Japanese: kaichū dentō 懐中電灯
Korean: sonjŏnji 손전지
Portuguese: lanterna
Russian: karmánnyy fonár' карманный фонарь
Spanish: lámpara de bolsillo
Swedish: ficklampa

835. flat (level) [adj.]

Arabic: musátta مسطح
Chinese: píngtǎnde 平坦的
Dutch: plat
French: plat
German: flach
Italian: piano
Japanese: taira na 平らな
Korean: p'yŏngtanhan 평탄한
Portuguese: plano
Russian: plóskiy плоский
Spanish: plano
Swedish: jämn

836. flatter [v.]

Arabic: tamállaqa تملق
Chinese: fèngchéng 奉承
Dutch: vleien
French: flatter
German: schmeicheln
Italian: lusingare
Japanese: oseji o iu お世辞を言う
Korean: ach'ŏmhada 아첨하다
Portuguese: lisonjear
Russian: l'stít' льстить
Spanish: halagar
Swedish: smickra

837. flee [v.]

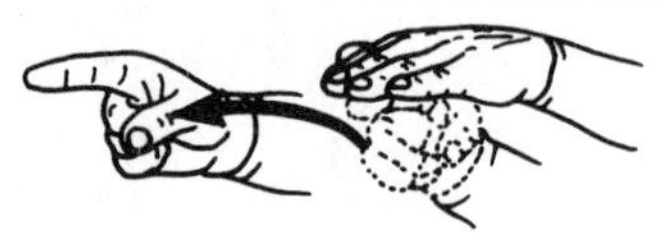

Arabic: fárra فر
Chinese: táo 逃
Dutch: vluchten
French: fuir
German: fliehen
Italian: fuggire
Japanese: nigeru 逃げる
Korean: domanghada 도망하다
Portuguese: fugir
Russian: bezhát' бежать
Spanish: huir
Swedish: fly

838. float [v.]

Arabic: áma عام
Chinese: fú 浮
Dutch: drijven
French: flotter
German: schwimmen
Italian: galleggiare
Japanese: ukabu 浮ぶ
Korean: ttŭda 뜨다
Portuguese: flutuar
Russian: plávat' плавать
Spanish: flotar
Swedish: flyta

839. flood [n.]

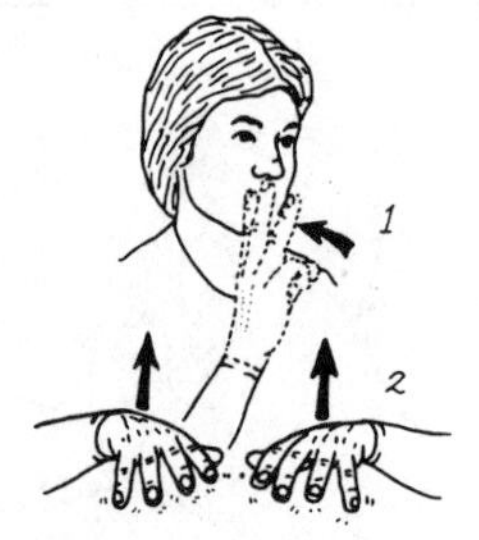

Arabic: tawafán طوفان
Chinese: hóngshuǐ 洪水
Dutch: vloed
French: inondation
German: Flut
Italian: inondazione
Japanese: kōzui 洪水
Korean: hongsu 홍수
Portuguese: inundação
Russian: navodnéniye наводнение
Spanish: inundación
Swedish: flod

840. floor [n.]

Arabic: ardhía ارضية
Chinese: dìbǎn 地板
Dutch: vloer
French: plancher
German: Fußboden
Italian: pavimento
Japanese: yuka 床
Korean: maru 마루
Portuguese: chão
Russian: pol пол
Spanish: suelo
Swedish: golv

841. flour [n.]

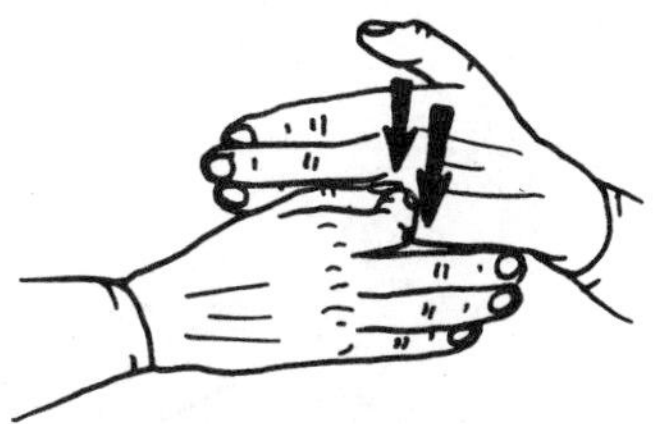

Arabic: tahín طحين
Chinese: miànfěn 麵粉
Dutch: meel
French: farine
German: Mehl
Italian: farina
Japanese: komugiko 小麦粉
Korean: karu 가루
Portuguese: farinha
Russian: muká мука
Spanish: harina
Swedish: vetemjöl

842. flow [v.]

Arabic: tadáffaqa تدفق
Chinese: liú 流
Dutch: vloeien
French: couler
German: fließen
Italian: scorrere
Japanese: nagareru 流れる
Korean: hŭrŭda 흐르다
Portuguese: fluir
Russian: tech' течь
Spanish: fluir
Swedish: flyta

843. flower [n.]

Arabic: záhra زهرة
Chinese: huā 花
Dutch: bloem
French: fleur
German: Blume
Italian: fiore
Japanese: hana 花
Korean: kkot 꽃
Portuguese: flor
Russian: tsvetók цветок
Spanish: flor
Swedish: blomma

844. fly [v.]

Arabic: tára طار
Chinese: fēi 飛
Dutch: vliegen
French: voler
German: fliegen
Italian: volare
Japanese: tobu 飛ぶ
Korean: nalda 날다
Portuguese: voar
Russian: letát' летать
Spanish: volar
Swedish: flyga

845. fog [n.]

Arabic: dhabáb ضباب
Chinese: wù 雾
Dutch: mist
French: brouillard
German: Nebel
Italian: nebbia
Japanese: kiri 霧
Korean: angae 안개
Portuguese: nevoeiro
Russian: tumán туман
Spanish: niebla
Swedish: dimma

846. fold [v.]

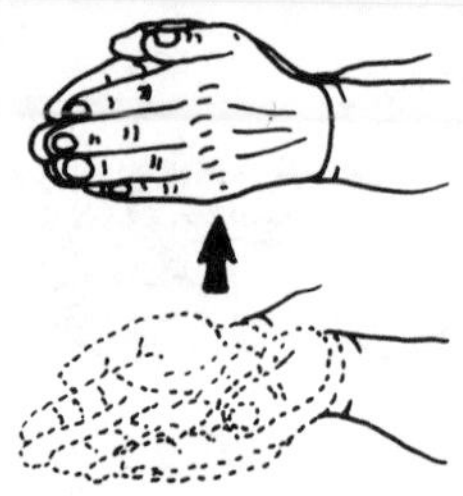

Arabic: áthna اثنى
Chinese: zhédié 折叠
Dutch: vouwen
French: plier
German: falten
Italian: piegare
Japanese: tatamu たたむ
Korean: jŏbda 접다
Portuguese: dobrar
Russian: skládyvat' складывать
Spanish: doblar
Swedish: vika

847. follow [v.]

Arabic: ettábaa يتبع
Chinese: gēnsuí 跟随
Dutch: volgen
French: suivre
German: folgen
Italian: seguire
Japanese: tsuite iku ついて行く
Korean: ttarŭda 따르다
Portuguese: seguir
Russian: sledít' следить
Spanish: seguir
Swedish: följa

848. food [n.]

Arabic: táam طعام
Chinese: shíwù 食物
Dutch: voedsel
French: nourriture
German: Nahrung
Italian: cibo
Japanese: tabemono 食べ物
Korean: ŭmshik 음식
Portuguese: comida
Russian: píshcha пища
Spanish: comida
Swedish: mat

849. fool [n.]

Arabic: mugháffal مغفل
Chinese: shăguā 傻瓜
Dutch: dwaas
French: sot
German: Narr
Italian: sciocco
Japanese: bakamono 馬鹿者
Korean: babo 바보
Portuguese: tolo
Russian: durák дурак
Spanish: tonto
Swedish: dåre

850. foolish [adj.]

Arabic: áhmaq احمق
Chinese: bènde 笨的
Dutch: dwaas
French: sot
German: töricht
Italian: sciocco
Japanese: bakana 馬鹿な
Korean: ŏrisŏgŭn 어리석은
Portuguese: tolice
Russian: glúpyy глупый
Spanish: tonto
Swedish: löjlig

851. foot (anatomy) [n.]

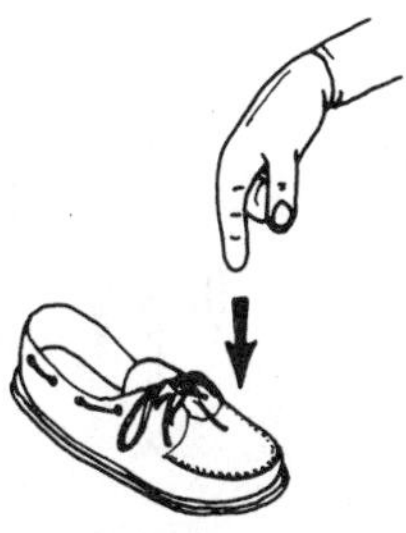

Arabic: qádam قدم
Chinese: jiăo 脚
Dutch: voet
French: pied
German: Fuß
Italian: piede
Japanese: ashi 足
Korean: bal 발
Portuguese: pé
Russian: nogá нога
Spanish: pie
Swedish: fot

852. foot (measurement) [n.]

Arabic: qádam قدم
Chinese: yīngchĭ 呎
Dutch: voet
French: pied
German: Fuß
Italian: piede
Japanese: fiito フィート
Korean: ja 자
Portuguese: pé
Russian: fut фут
Spanish: pie
Swedish: fot

853. football [n.]

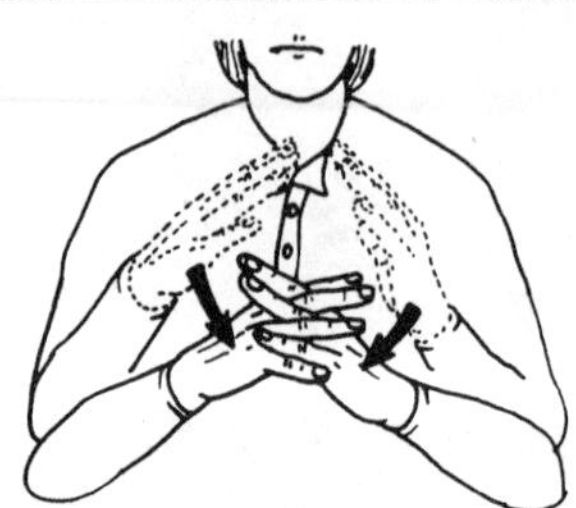

Arabic: kórat al-qádam كرة القدم
Chinese: zúqiú 足球
Dutch: amerikaanse voetbal
French: football américain
German: Football
Italian: pallone
Japanese: futtobōru フットボール
Korean: putbol 풋볼
Portuguese: futebol
Russian: futból футбол
Spanish: fútbol americano
Swedish: fotboll

854. for [prep./conj.]

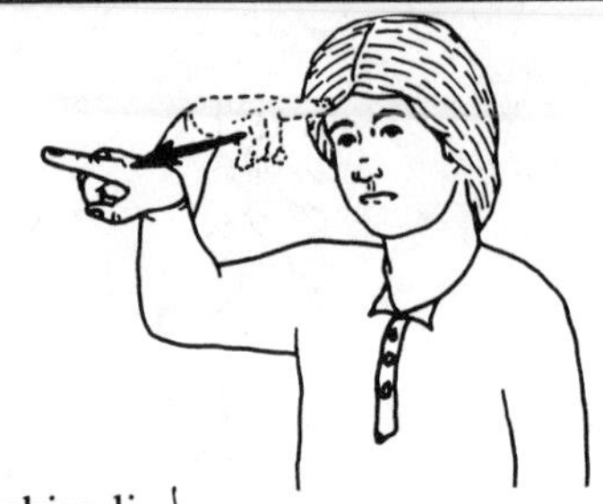

Arabic: li لـ
Chinese: wèile 為了
Dutch: voor
French: pour
German: für
Italian: per
Japanese: . . . no tameni …のために
Korean: wihayŏ ~위하여
Portuguese: para/por
Russian: dlyá для
Spanish: para/por
Swedish: för

855. forbid [v.]

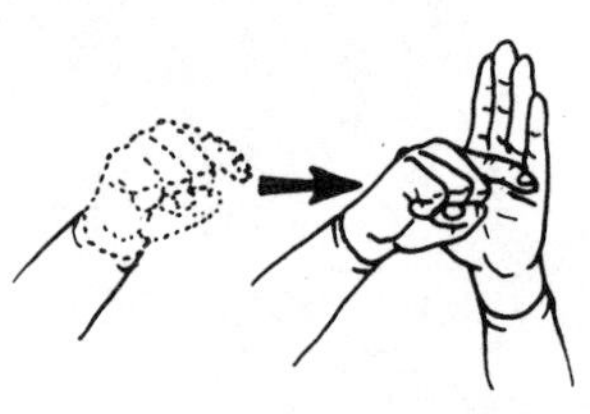

Arabic: manaá منع
Chinese: jìnzhǐ 禁止
Dutch: verbieden
French: interdire
German: verbieten
Italian: proibire
Japanese: kinjiru 禁じる
Korean: kŭmhada 금하다
Portuguese: proibir
Russian: zapreshchát' запрещать
Spanish: prohibir
Swedish: förbjuda

856. force [v.]

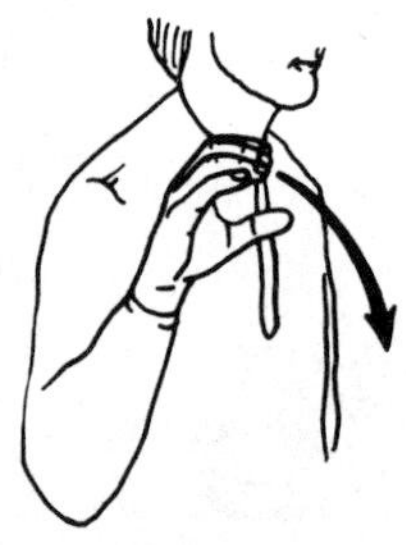

Arabic: ajbára اجبر
Chinese: qiángpò 強迫
Dutch: dwingen
French: forcer
German: zwingen
Italian: costringere
Japanese: muri ni saseru 無理にさせる
Korean: kangyohada 강요하다
Portuguese: forçar
Russian: zastavlyát' заставлять
Spanish: forzar
Swedish: tvinga

857. foreign [adj.]

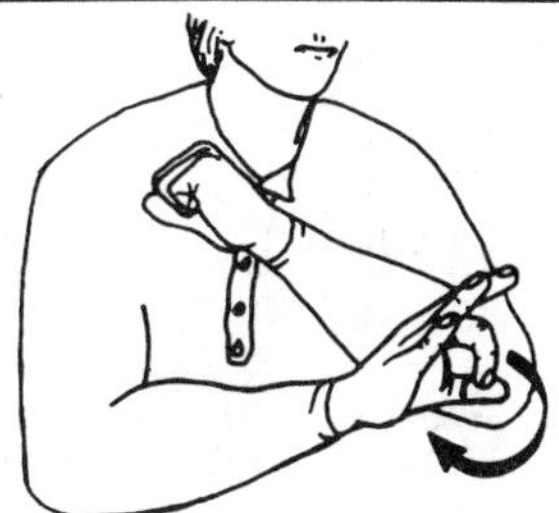

Arabic: gharíb غريب
Chinese: wàiguóde 外國的
Dutch: buitenlands
French: étranger
German: fremd
Italian: straniero
Japanese: gaikoku no 外国の
Korean: oegugŭi 외국의
Portuguese: estranho
Russian: inostránnyy иностранный
Spanish: extranjero
Swedish: utländsk

858. forest [n.]

Arabic: ghába غابة
Chinese: sēnlín 森林
Dutch: woud
French: forêt
German: Wald
Italian: foresta
Japanese: mori 森
Korean: sup 숲
Portuguese: floresta
Russian: les лес
Spanish: bosque
Swedish: skog

859. forever [adv.]

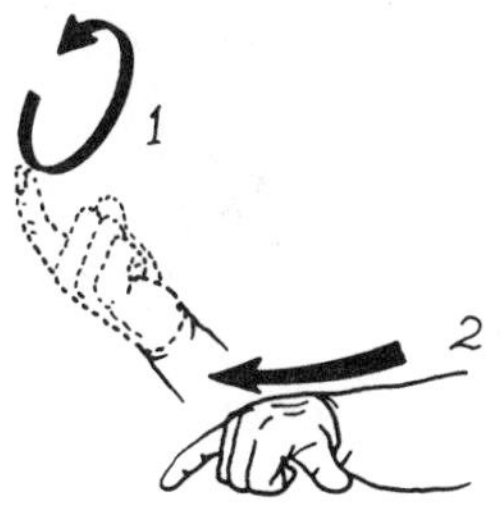

Arabic: lil-ábad للابد
Chinese: yǒngyuǎn 永遠
Dutch: voor altijd
French: à jamais
German: für immer
Italian: per sempre
Japanese: eien ni 永遠に
Korean: yŏngguhi 영구히
Portuguese: para sempre
Russian: navsegdá навсегда
Spanish: por siempre
Swedish: för alltid

860. forget [v.]

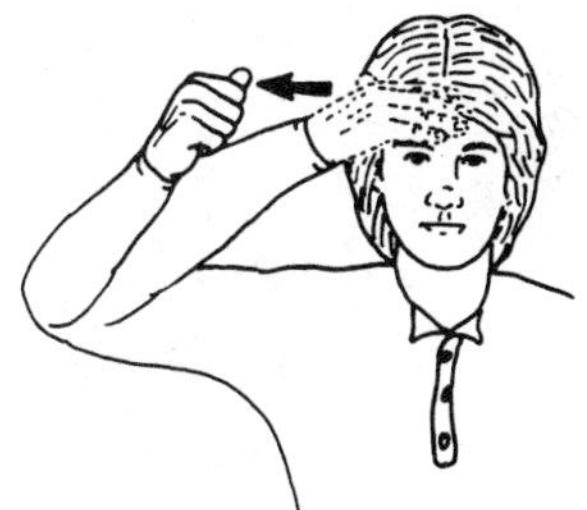

Arabic: nása نسى
Chinese: wàngjì 忘記
Dutch: vergeten
French: oublier
German: vergessen
Italian: dimenticare
Japanese: wasureru 忘れる
Korean: itta 잊다
Portuguese: esquecer
Russian: zabyvát' забывать
Spanish: olvidar
Swedish: glömma

861. forgive [v.]

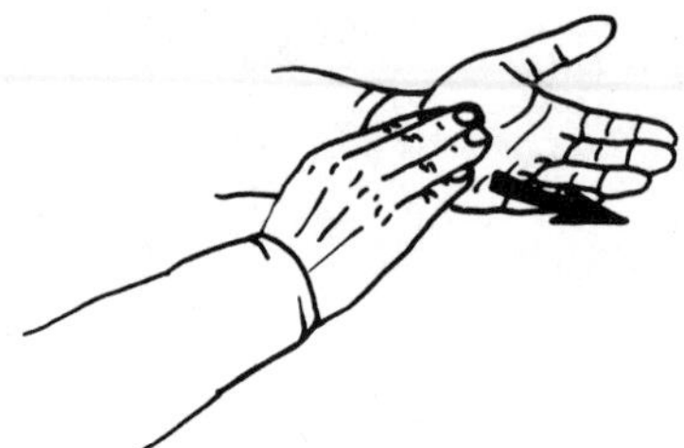

Arabic: sámaha سامح
Chinese: yuánliàng 原諒
Dutch: vergeven
French: pardonner
German: vergeben
Italian: perdonare
Japanese: yurusu 許す
Korean: yongsŏhada 용서하다
Portuguese: perdoar
Russian: proshchát' прощать
Spanish: perdonar
Swedish: förlåta

862. fork [n.]

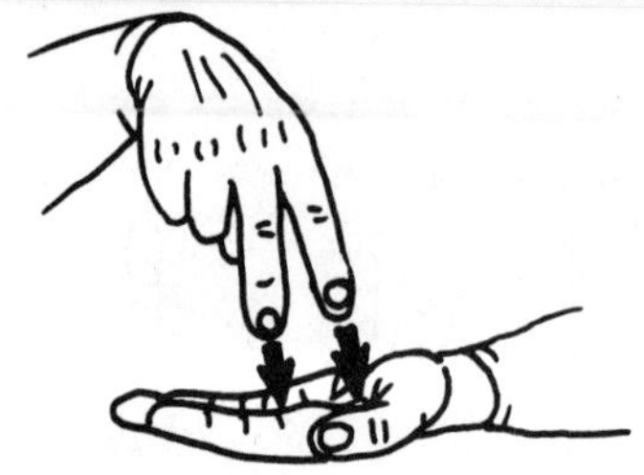

Arabic: sháuka شوكة
Chinese: chāzi 叉子
Dutch: vork
French: fourchette
German: Gabel
Italian: forchetta
Japanese: fōku フォーク
Korean: p'ok'ŭ 포크
Portuguese: garfo
Russian: vílka вилка
Spanish: tenedor
Swedish: gaffel

863. form [v.]

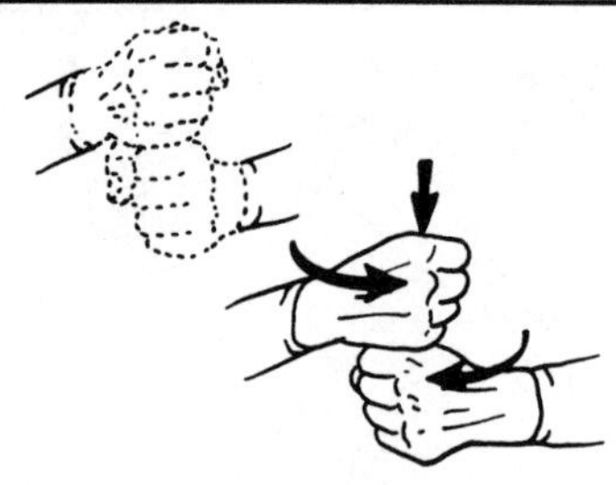

Arabic: shákkala شكل
Chinese: xíngchéng 形成
Dutch: vormen
French: forme
German: formen
Italian: forma
Japanese: katachizukuru 形づくる
Korean: moyangiruda 모양이루다
Portuguese: formar
Russian: formirovát' формировать
Spanish: forma
Swedish: forma

864. formerly [adv.]

Arabic: sáabiqan سابقاً
Chinese: yǐqián 以前
Dutch: voormalig
French: précédemment
German: vormals
Italian: precedentemente
Japanese: izen wa 以前は
Korean: ijŏnŭi 이전의
Portuguese: antigamente
Russian: prézhde прежде
Spanish: anteriormente
Swedish: förr

865. forty [adj.]

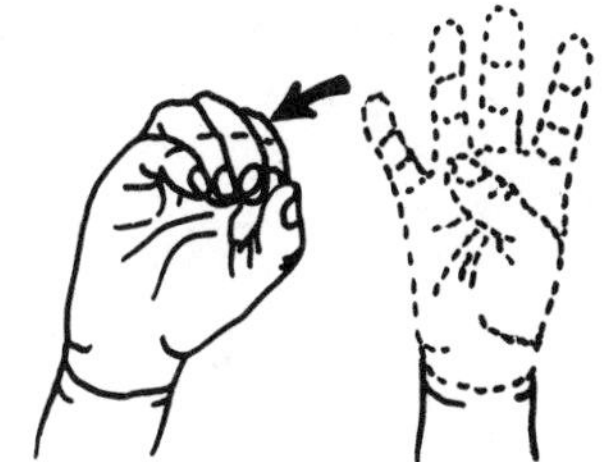

Arabic: árba'un اربعون
Chinese: sìshí 四十
Dutch: veertig
French: quarante
German: vierzig
Italian: quaranta
Japanese: yonjū 40
Korean: mahŭn 사십
Portuguese: quarenta
Russian: sórok сорок
Spanish: cuarenta
Swedish: fyrtio

866. forward [adv.]

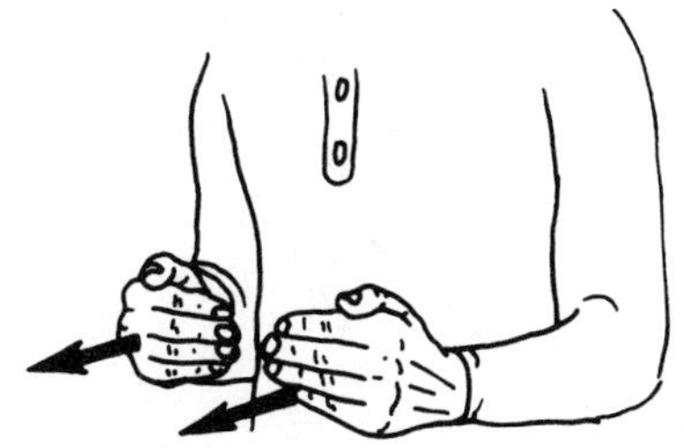

Arabic: lil-amám للامام
Chinese: xiàng qián 向前
Dutch: voorwaarts
French: en avant
German: vorwärts
Italian: avanti
Japanese: zempō ni 前方に
Korean: ap'ŭro 앞으로
Portuguese: adiante
Russian: vperyód вперёд
Spanish: adelante
Swedish: framåt

867. foundation [n.]

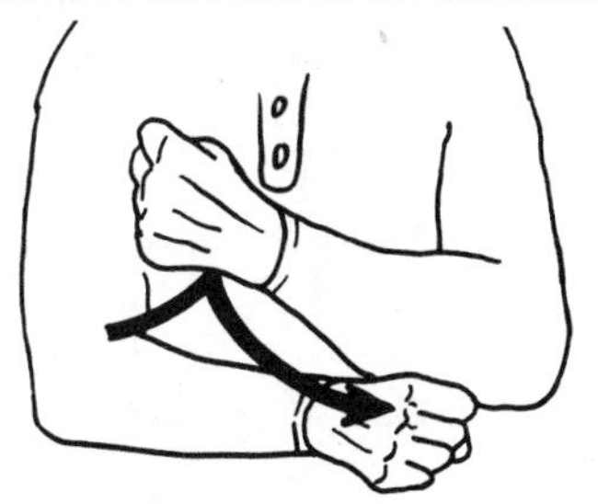

Arabic: asás اساس
Chinese: jīchǔ 基礎
Dutch: basis
French: base
German: Fundament
Italian: fondazione
Japanese: kiso 基礎
Korean: t'odae 토대
Portuguese: fundação
Russian: fundáment фундамент
Spanish: fundamento
Swedish: stiftelse

868. four [adj.]

Arabic: árbaa اربعة
Chinese: sì 四
Dutch: vier
French: quatre
German: vier
Italian: quattro
Japanese: yon 4
Korean: net 넷
Portuguese: quatro
Russian: chetýre четыре
Spanish: cuatro
Swedish: fyra

869. fourteen [adj.]

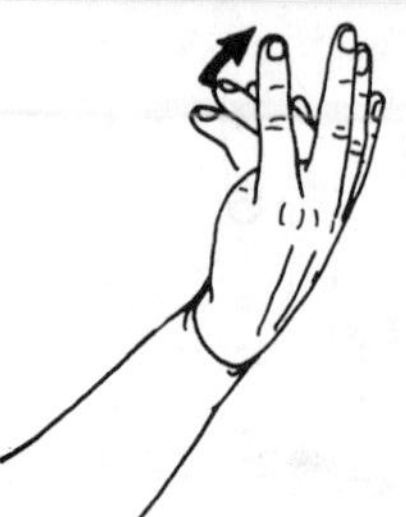

Arabic: arbaáta áashar اربعة عشر
Chinese: shísì 十四
Dutch: veertien
French: quatorze
German: vierzehn
Italian: quattordici
Japanese: jūyon 14
Korean: yŏl net 열넷
Portuguese: catorze
Russian: chetýrnadtsat' четырнадцать
Spanish: catorce
Swedish: fjorton

870. fox [n.]

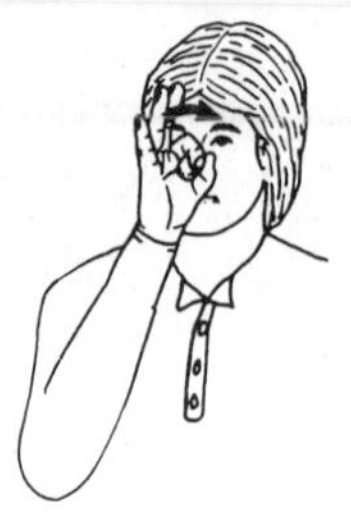

Arabic: tháalab ثعلب
Chinese: húlí 狐狸
Dutch: vos
French: renard
German: Fuchs
Italian: volpe
Japanese: kitsune キツネ
Korean: yŏu 여우
Portuguese: rapôsa
Russian: lisá лиса
Spanish: zorro
Swedish: räv

871. fragrant [adj.]

Arabic: étri عطري
Chinese: fāngxiāng 芳香
Dutch: geurig
French: parfumé
German: wohlriechend
Italian: fragrante
Japanese: kaori no yoi 香りの良い
Korean: hyanggiroŭn 향기로운
Portuguese: fragrante
Russian: aromátnyy ароматный
Spanish: fragante
Swedish: doftande

872. frame [n.]

Arabic: itár اطار
Chinese: kuàng 框
Dutch: omlijsting
French: cadre
German: Rahmen
Italian: cornice
Japanese: honegumi 骨組み
Korean: kujo 구조
Portuguese: moldura
Russian: ráma рама
Spanish: marco
Swedish: ram

873. France [n.]

Arabic: faránsa فرنسا
Chinese: fàguó 法國
Dutch: Frankrijk
French: France
German: Frankreich
Italian: Francia
Japanese: Furansu フランス
Korean: P'ŭrangsŭ 불란서
Portuguese: França
Russian: Frántsiya Франция
Spanish: Francia
Swedish: Frankrike

874. frank [adj.]

Arabic: saríh صريح
Chinese: tănbáide 坦白的
Dutch: openhartig
French: franc
German: freimütig
Italian: franco
Japanese: socchoku na 率直な
Korean: solchik'an 솔직한
Portuguese: franco
Russian: ískrenniy искренний
Spanish: franco
Swedish: öppenhjärtig

875. free [v.]

Arabic: hárara حرر
Chinese: shìfàng 釋放
Dutch: vrijlaten
French: libérer
German: befreien
Italian: liberare
Japanese: jiyū ni suru 自由にする
Korean: sŏkbanghada 석방하다
Portuguese: libertar
Russian: osvobozhdát' освобождать
Spanish: libertar
Swedish: befria

876. freedom [n.]

Arabic: huría حرية
Chinese: zìyóu 自由
Dutch: vrijheid
French: liberté
German: Freiheit
Italian: libertà
Japanese: jiyū 自由
Korean: jayu 자유
Portuguese: liberdade
Russian: svobóda свобода
Spanish: libertad
Swedish: frihet

877. freeze [v.]

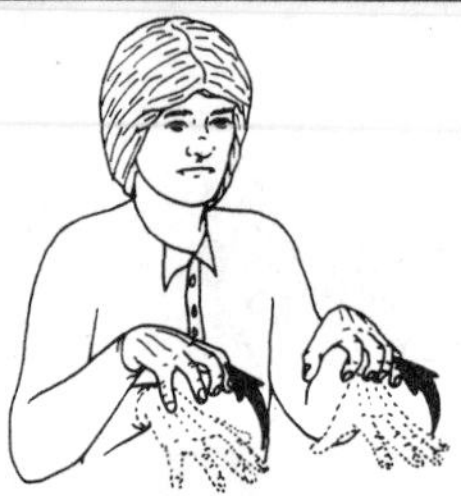

Arabic: jámmada جمد
Chinese: bīngdòng 冰凍
Dutch: bevriezen
French: geler
German: frieren
Italian: congelare
Japanese: kōru 凍る
Korean: ŏlda 얼다
Portuguese: congelar
Russian: zamerzát' замерзать
Spanish: congelar
Swedish: frysa

878. French [adj.]

Arabic: faránsi فرنسي
Chinese: fàguóde 法國的
Dutch: frans
French: français
German: französisch
Italian: francese
Japanese: Furansu no フランスの
Korean: P'ŭrangsŭŭi 불란서
Portuguese: francês
Russian: frantsúzskiy французский
Spanish: francés
Swedish: fransk

879. frequent [adj.]

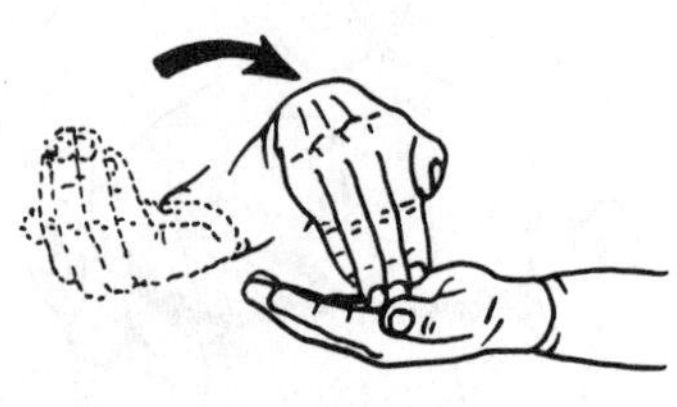

Arabic: mutakárrer متكرر
Chinese: jīngcháng 經常
Dutch: veelvuldig
French: fréquent
German: häufig
Italian: frequente
Japanese: tabitabi no たびたびの
Korean: binbŏnhan 빈번한
Portuguese: frequente
Russian: chástnyy частный
Spanish: frecuente
Swedish: vanlig

880. fresh [adj.]

Arabic: tázij طازج
Chinese: xīnxiānde 新鮮的
Dutch: fris
French: frais
German: frisch
Italian: fresco
Japanese: shinsen na 新鮮な
Korean: saeroun 새로운
Portuguese: fresco
Russian: svézhiy свежий
Spanish: fresco
Swedish: färsk

881. Friday [n.]

Arabic: al-júmaa الجمعة
Chinese: xīngqí wǔ 星期五
Dutch: vrijdag
French: vendredi
German: Freitag
Italian: venerdì
Japanese: kinyō bi 金曜日
Korean: kŭmyoil 금요일
Portuguese: sexta-feira
Russian: pyátnitsa пятница
Spanish: viernes
Swedish: fredag

882. friend [n.]

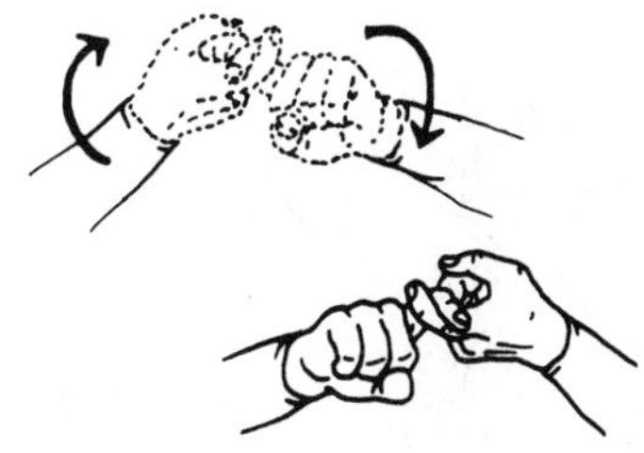

Arabic: sadíeq صديق
Chinese: péngyǒu 朋友
Dutch: vriend
French: ami
German: Freund
Italian: amico
Japanese: tomodachi 友達
Korean: ch'ingu 친구
Portuguese: amigo
Russian: drug друг
Spanish: amigo
Swedish: vän

883. friendly [adj.]

Arabic: wúddi ودي
Chinese: yǒushàn 友善
Dutch: vriendelijk
French: amical
German: freundlich
Italian: amichevole
Japanese: hitonatsukkoi 人なつっこい
Korean: ch'injŏlhan 친절한
Portuguese: amigável
Russian: drúzheskiy дружеский
Spanish: amistoso
Swedish: vänlig

884. fright [n.]

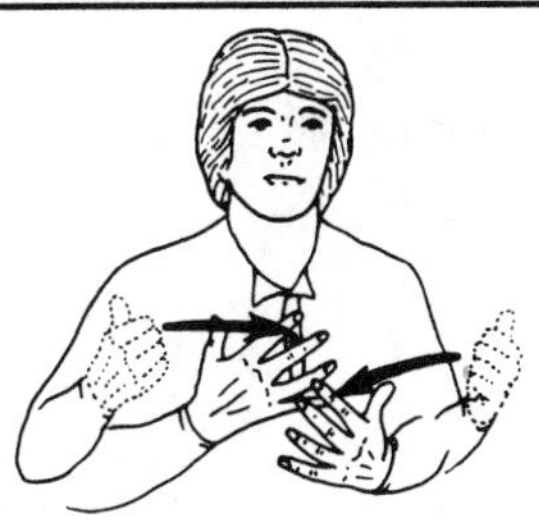

Arabic: khauf خوف
Chinese: kǒngbù 恐怖
Dutch: schrik
French: frayeur
German: Schreck
Italian: spavento
Japanese: kyōfu 恐怖
Korean: kongp'o 공포
Portuguese: espanto
Russian: ispúg испуг
Spanish: miedo
Swedish: skräck

885. frog [n.]

Arabic: dhúfdaa ضفدعة
Chinese: qīngwā 青蛙
Dutch: kikker
French: grenouille
German: Frosch
Italian: rana
Japanese: kaeru カエル
Korean: kaeguri 개구리
Portuguese: rã
Russian: lyagúshka лягушка
Spanish: rana
Swedish: groda

886. from [prep.]

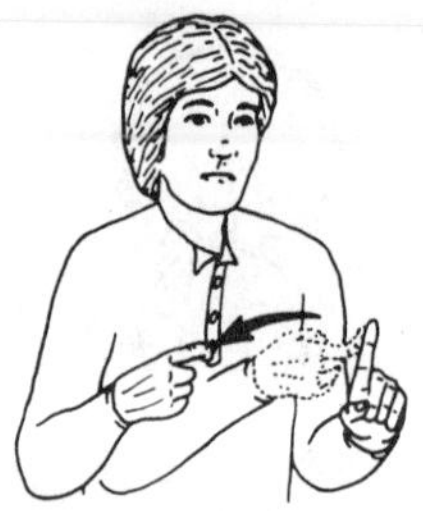

Arabic: min من
Chinese: cóng 從
Dutch: van
French: de
German: von
Italian: da
Japanese: . . . kara …から
Korean: esŏ ~에서
Portuguese: de
Russian: ot от
Spanish: de
Swedish: från

887. front [n.]

Arabic: amám امام
Chinese: qiánmiàn 前面
Dutch: voorkant
French: façade
German: Vorderseite
Italian: facciata
Japanese: shōmen 正面
Korean: ap ~앞에
Portuguese: frente
Russian: fasád фасад
Spanish: frente
Swedish: framsida

888. frost [n.]

Arabic: tijámmud تجمد
Chinese: shuāng 霜
Dutch: vorst
French: gel
German: Frost
Italian: gelo
Japanese: shimo 霜
Korean: sŏri 서리
Portuguese: geada
Russian: moróz мороз
Spanish: escarcha
Swedish: frost

889. frown [v.]

Arabic: tajáhhama تجهم
Chinese: zhòu méi 皺眉
Dutch: het voorhoofd fronsen
French: froncer les sourcils
German: Stirn runzeln
Italian: accigliarsi
Japanese: kao o shikameru 顔をしかめる
Korean: sang tchip'urida 상 찌푸리다
Portuguese: franzir as sobrancelhas
Russian: khmúrit'sya хмуриться
Spanish: fruncir
Swedish: rynka pannan

890. frozen [adj.]

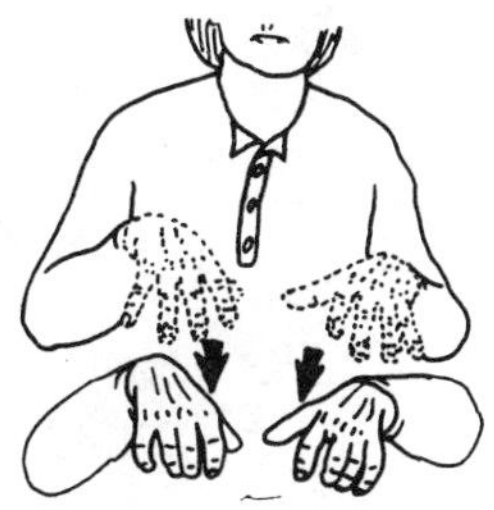

Arabic: mujámmad مجمد
Chinese: bīngdòngde 冰凍的
Dutch: bevroren
French: gelé
German: gefroren
Italian: congelato
Japanese: kōtta 凍った
Korean: ŏn 언
Portuguese: congelado
Russian: zamorózhennyy замороженный
Spanish: congelado
Swedish: frusen

891. fruit [n.]

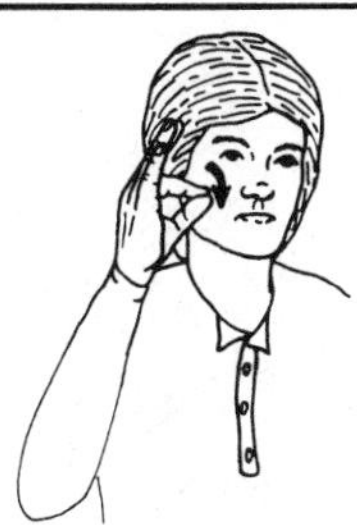

Arabic: fawwáki فواكه
Chinese: shuǐguǒ 水果
Dutch: fruit
French: fruit
German: Frucht
Italian: frutta
Japanese: kudamono 果物
Korean: kwail 과일
Portuguese: fruta
Russian: frúkty фрукты
Spanish: fruta
Swedish: frukt

892. frustration [n.]

Arabic: ihbáat احباط
Chinese: cuòzhé 挫折
Dutch: frustratie
French: frustration
German: Entäuschung
Italian: frustrazione
Japanese: yokkyū fuman 欲求不満
Korean: chwajŏl 좌절
Portuguese: frustração
Russian: rasstróystvo расстройство
Spanish: frustración
Swedish: gäckande

893. fry [v.]

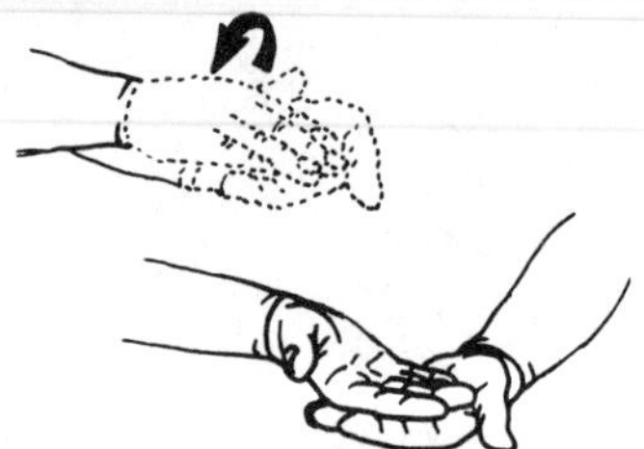

Arabic: qálaa قلى
Chinese: yióuzhà 油炸
Dutch: bakken
French: frire
German: braten
Italian: friggere
Japanese: abura de ageru 油で揚げる
Korean: kirŭme t'wigida 기름에 튀기다
Portuguese: fritar
Russian: zhárit' жарить
Spanish: freír
Swedish: steka

894. fuel [n.]

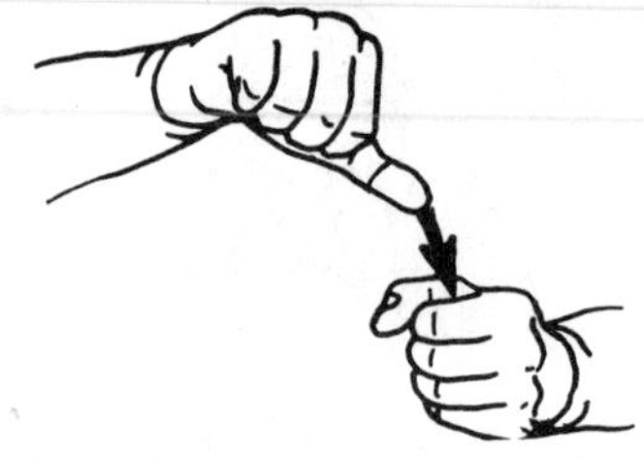

Arabic: wuqúd وقود
Chinese: ránliào 燃料
Dutch: brandstof
French: combustible
German: Brennstoff
Italian: combustibile
Japanese: nenryō 燃料
Korean: yŏllyo 연료
Portuguese: combustível
Russian: tóplivo топливо
Spanish: combustible
Swedish: bränsle

895. full [adj.]

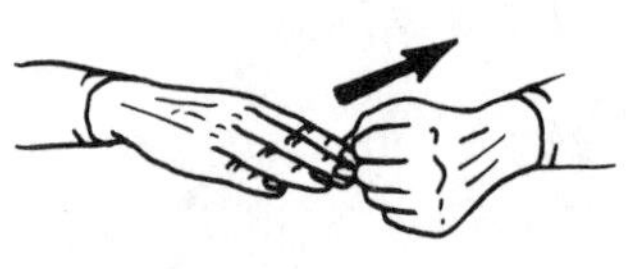

Arabic: mumtáli' ممتلئ
Chinese: mănde 满的
Dutch: vol
French: plein
German: voll
Italian: pieno
Japanese: ippai no いっぱいの
Korean: kadŭk ch'an 가득찬
Portuguese: cheio
Russian: pólnyy полный
Spanish: lleno
Swedish: full

896. fun [n.]

Arabic: házal هزل
Chinese: wánxiào 玩笑
Dutch: pret
French: amusement
German: Spaß
Italian: divertimento
Japanese: omoshirosa 面白さ
Korean: chaemi 재미
Portuguese: divertimento
Russian: vesél'ye веселье
Spanish: diversión
Swedish: nöje

897. function [n.]

Arabic: áamal عمل
Chinese: gōngnéng 功能
Dutch: functie
French: fonction
German: Funktion
Italian: funzione
Japanese: kinō 機能
Korean: kinŭng 기능
Portuguese: função
Russian: fúnktsiya функция
Spanish: función
Swedish: funktion

898. fund(s) [n.]

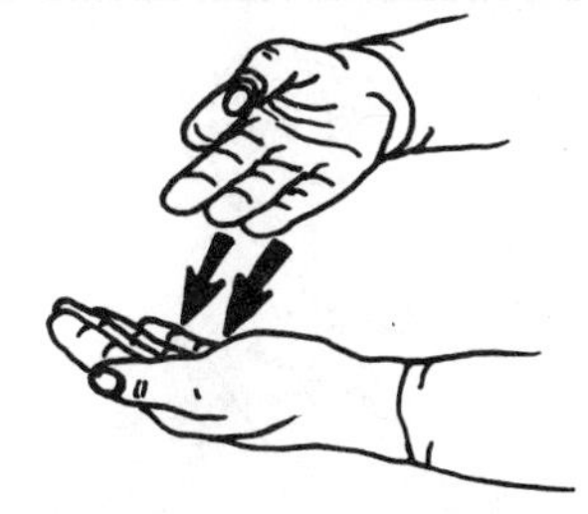

Arabic: tamwíl تمويل
Chinese: jījīn 基金
Dutch: fonds
French: fonds
German: Fonds
Italian: fondo
Japanese: zaigen 財源
Korean: jakŭm 자금
Portuguese: fundos
Russian: fóndy фонды
Spanish: fondos
Swedish: fonder

899. funeral [n.]

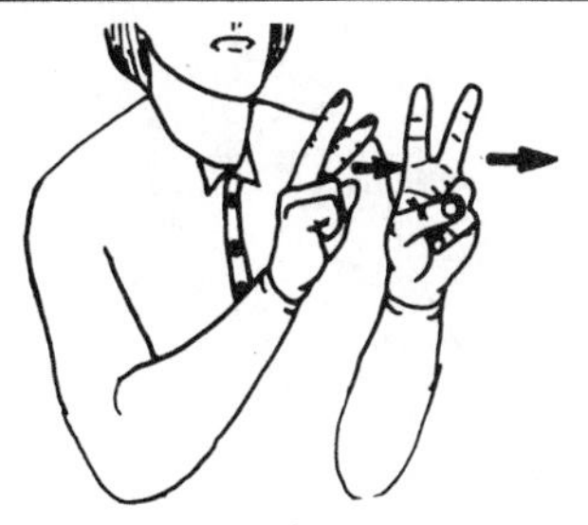

Arabic: janázza جنازة
Chinese: zànglǐ 葬禮
Dutch: begrafenis
French: funérailles
German: Beerdigung
Italian: funerale
Japanese: sōshiki 葬式
Korean: jangnyeshik 장례식
Portuguese: funeral
Russian: pókhorony похороны
Spanish: funeral
Swedish: begravning

900. funny (amusing) [adj.]

Arabic: múdhek مضحك
Chinese: gŭjī 滑稽
Dutch: grappig
French: amusant
German: lustig
Italian: divertente
Japanese: omoshiroi 面白い
Korean: usŭun 우스운
Portuguese: engraçado
Russian: smeshnóy смешной
Spanish: cómico
Swedish: lustig

901. fur [n.]

Arabic: fáru فرو
Chinese: máopí 毛皮
Dutch: bont
French: fourrure
German: Pelz
Italian: pelliccia
Japanese: kegawa 毛皮
Korean: mop'i 모피
Portuguese: pele
Russian: mekh мех
Spanish: piel
Swedish: päls

902. furniture [n.]

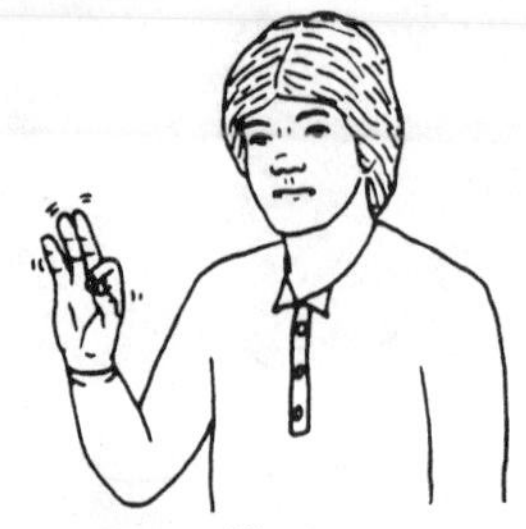

Arabic: atháth اثاث
Chinese: jiājù 傢俱
Dutch: meubelen
French: meubles
German: Möbel
Italian: mobilia
Japanese: kagu 家具
Korean: gagu 가구
Portuguese: mobília
Russian: mébel' мебель
Spanish: muebles
Swedish: möbler

903. further [adj./adv.]

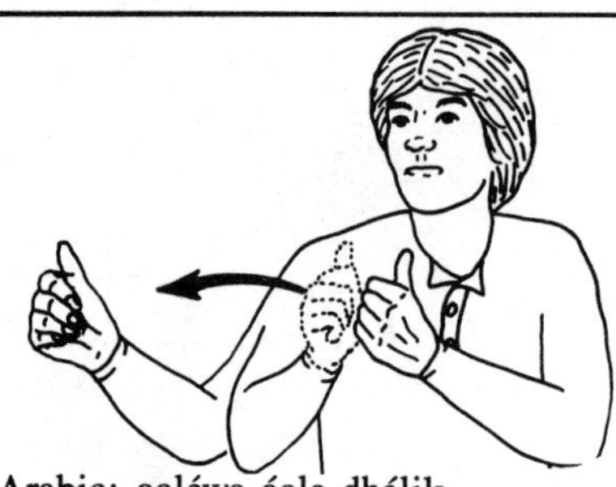

Arabic: aaléwa áala dhálik
علاوة على ذلك
Chinese: gèng yuǎn de 更遠的
Dutch: verder
French: plus loin
German: weiter
Italian: più lontano
Japanese: issō tōku いっそう遠く
Korean: dŏ mŏlli 더 멀리
Portuguese: mais adiante
Russian: dál'she дальше
Spanish: más lejos
Swedish: avlägsnare

904. future [n.]

Arabic: mustáqbal مستقبل
Chinese: jiānglái 將來
Dutch: toekomst
French: avenir
German: Zukunft
Italian: futuro
Japanese: shōrai 将来
Korean: jangnae 장래
Portuguese: futuro
Russian: búdushchiy будущий
Spanish: futuro
Swedish: framtid

905. gain [v.]

Arabic: káseba كسب
Chinese: huòdé 獲得
Dutch: winnen
French: gagner
German: gewinnen
Italian: guadagnare
Japanese: eru 得る
Korean: ŏtta 얻다
Portuguese: ganhar
Russian: vyígryvat' выигрывать
Spanish: ganar
Swedish: öka

906. gallon [n.]

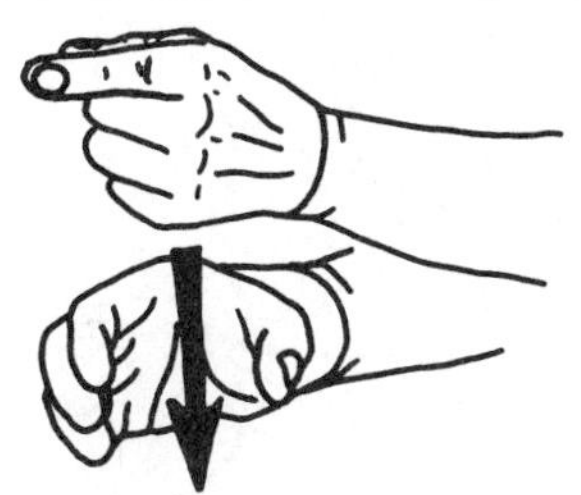

Arabic: galón جالون
Chinese: jiālún 加侖
Dutch: gallon
French: gallon
German: Gallone
Italian: gallone
Japanese: garon ガロン
Korean: gaellon 갈론
Portuguese: galão
Russian: gallón галлон
Spanish: galón
Swedish: gallon

907. gamble [v.]

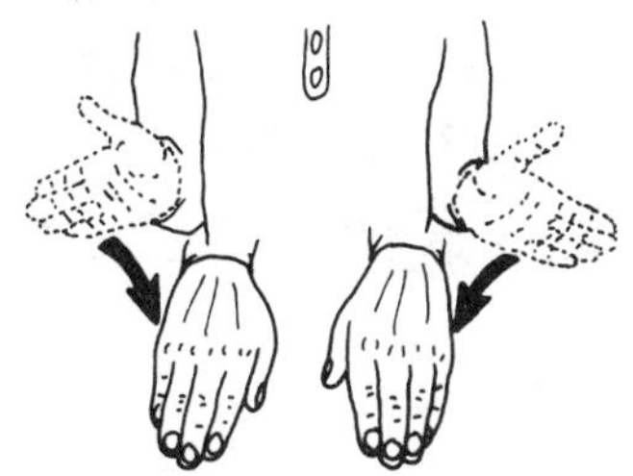

Arabic: qámara قامر
Chinese: dǔbó 賭博
Dutch: gokken
French: jouer de l'argent
German: um Geld spielen
Italian: giocare d'azzardo
Japanese: kakegoto o suru 賭け事をする
Korean: dobaghada 도박하다
Portuguese: jogar à dinheiro
Russian: igrát' v azártnyye ígry играть в азартные игры
Spanish: jugar
Swedish: spela

908. game (play) [n.]

Arabic: lú'ba لعبة
Chinese: bǐsài 遊戲
Dutch: spel
French: jeu
German: Spiel
Italian: gioco
Japanese: gēmu ゲーム
Korean: nori 노리
Portuguese: jôgo
Russian: igrá игра
Spanish: juego
Swedish: spel

909. garden [n.]

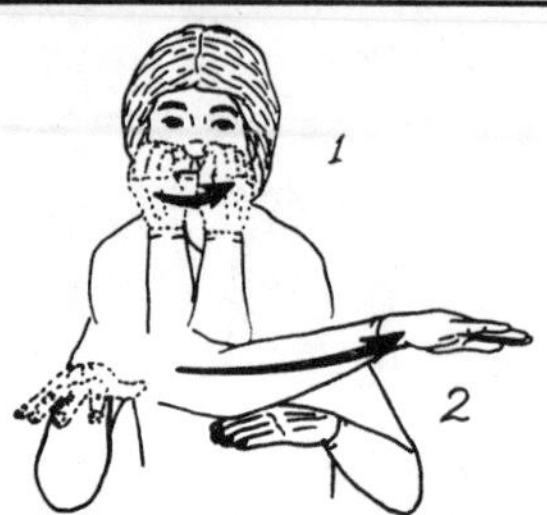

Arabic: hadíeqa حديقة
Chinese: huāyuán 花園
Dutch: tuin
French: jardin
German: Garten
Italian: giardino
Japanese: niwa 庭
Korean: jŏngwŏn 정원
Portuguese: jardim
Russian: sad сад
Spanish: jardín
Swedish: trädgård

910. gas (natural) [n.]

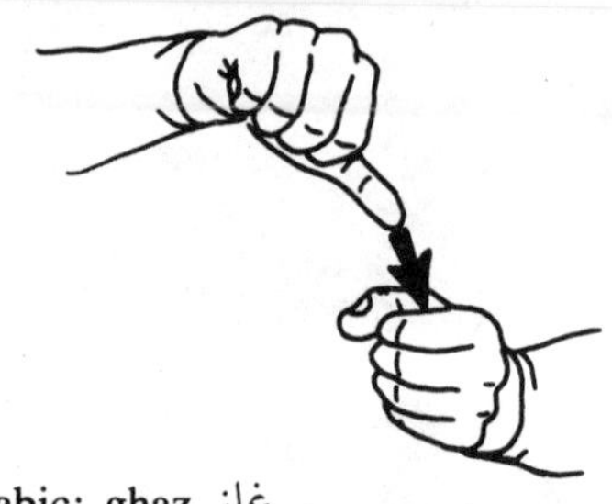

Arabic: ghaz غاز
Chinese: méiqì 煤氣
Dutch: gas
French: gaz
German: Gas
Italian: gas
Japanese: gasu ガス
Korean: gas 가스
Portuguese: gás
Russian: gaz газ
Spanish: gas
Swedish: gas

911. gasoline [n.]

Arabic: benzín بنزين
Chinese: qìyóu 汽油
Dutch: benzine
French: essence
German: Benzin
Italian: benzina
Japanese: gasorin ガソリン
Korean: hwiballyu 휘발유
Portuguese: gasolina
Russian: benzín бензин
Spanish: gasolina
Swedish: bensin

912. gate [n.]

Arabic: bawába بوابة
Chinese: ménkǒu 門口
Dutch: poort
French: porte
German: Tor
Italian: cancello
Japanese: mon 門
Korean: mun 문
Portuguese: portão
Russian: voróta ворота
Spanish: puerta
Swedish: port

913. gather (collect) [v.]

Arabic: jámaa جمع
Chinese: sōují 收集
Dutch: verzamelen
French: amasser
German: sammeln
Italian: raccogliere
Japanese: atsumeru 集める
Korean: sujip'ada 수집하다
Portuguese: coletar
Russian: sobirát' собирать
Spanish: recoger
Swedish: samla

914. generation (of descendants) [n.]

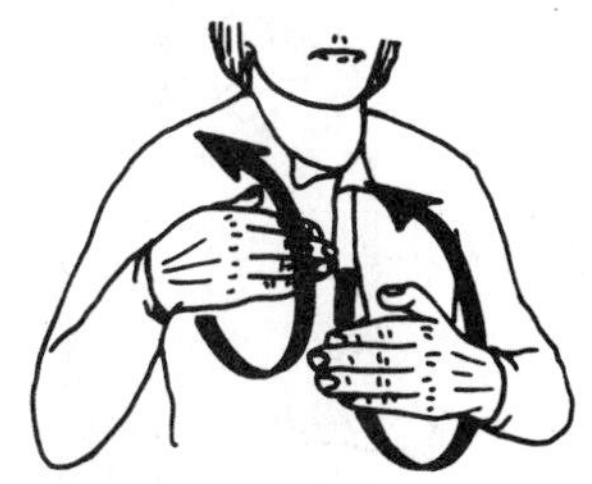

Arabic: jil جيل
Chinese: shìdài 世代
Dutch: geslacht
French: génération
German: Generation
Italian: generazione
Japanese: sedai 世代
Korean: sedae 세대
Portuguese: geração
Russian: pokoléniye поколение
Spanish: generación
Swedish: generation

915. generous [adj.]

Arabic: karím كريم
Chinese: kāngkǎide 慷慨的
Dutch: vrijgevig
French: généreux
German: großmütig
Italian: generoso
Japanese: kandai na 寛大な
Korean: nŏgŭrŏun 너그러운
Portuguese: generoso
Russian: shchédryy щедрый
Spanish: generoso
Swedish: generös

916. gentle [adj.]

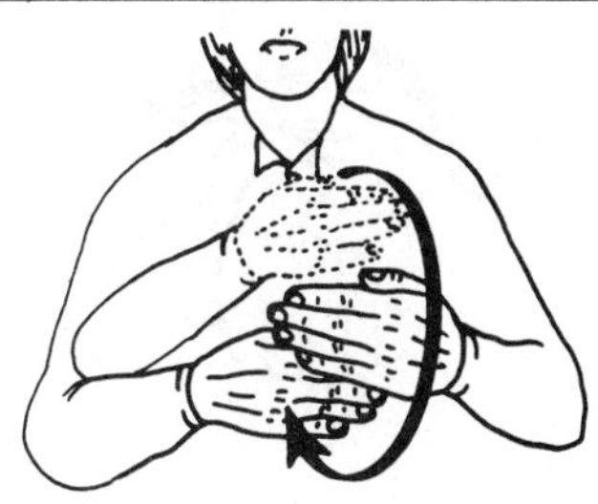

Arabic: latíf لطيف
Chinese: wēnhéde 温和的
Dutch: zacht
French: doux
German: sanft
Italian: gentile
Japanese: yasashi i 優しい
Korean: jŏmjanŭn 점잖은
Portuguese: suave
Russian: myágkiy мягкий
Spanish: suave
Swedish: mild

917. gentleman [n.]

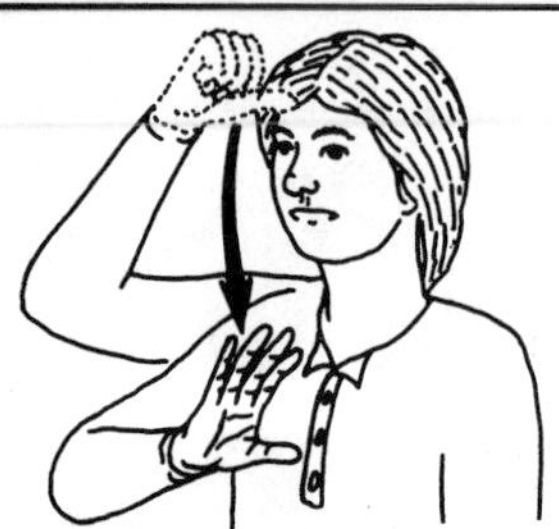

Arabic: séyyid سيد
Chinese: shēnshì 紳士
Dutch: heer
French: gentilhomme
German: Herr
Italian: gentiluomo
Japanese: shin-shi 紳士
Korean: shinsa 신사
Portuguese: cavalheiro
Russian: dzhentl'mén джентльмен
Spanish: caballero
Swedish: herre

918. genuine [adj.]

Arabic: haqíeqi حقيقي
Chinese: zhēnzhèngde 真正的
Dutch: echt
French: authentique
German: echt
Italian: genuino
Japanese: hommono-no 本物の
Korean: jintchaŭi 진짜의
Portuguese: verdadeiro
Russian: nastoyáshchiy настоящий
Spanish: genuino
Swedish: äkta

919. geography [n.]

Arabic: jaghráfia جغرافيا
Chinese: dìlǐ 地理
Dutch: geografie
French: géographie
German: Geographie
Italian: geografia
Japanese: chirigaku 地理学
Korean: jiri 지리
Portuguese: geografia
Russian: geográfiya география
Spanish: geografía
Swedish: geografi

920. Germany [n.]

Arabic: almánia المانيا
Chinese: déguó 德國
Dutch: Duitsland
French: Allemagne
German: Deutschland
Italian: Germania
Japanese: Doitsu ドイツ
Korean: Dogil 독일
Portuguese: Alemanha
Russian: Germániya Германия
Spanish: Alemania
Swedish: Tyskland

921. get [v.]

Arabic: nála نال
Chinese: qǔdé 取得
Dutch: krijgen
French: obtenir
German: bekommen
Italian: ottenere
Japanese: eru 得る
Korean: ŏtta 얻다
Portuguese: obter
Russian: dostavát' доставать
Spanish: obtener
Swedish: få

922. ghost [n.]

Arabic: shábah شبح
Chinese: guǐ 鬼
Dutch: spook
French: fantôme
German: Geist
Italian: fantasma
Japanese: yūrei 幽霊
Korean: yuryŏng 유령
Portuguese: fantasma
Russian: privideniye привидение
Spanish: fantasma
Swedish: spöke

923. giant [n.]

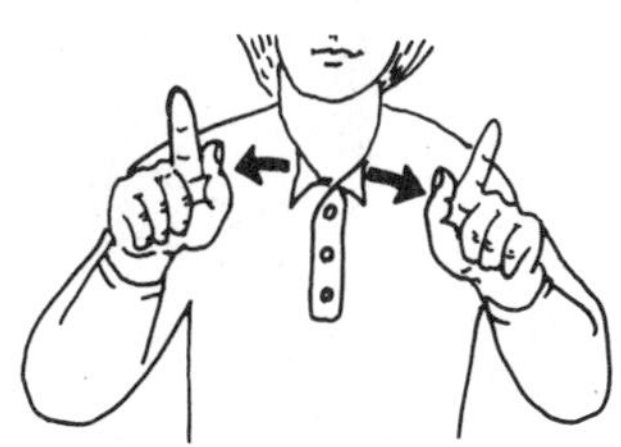

Arabic: eamláq عملاق
Chinese: jùrén 巨人
Dutch: reus
French: géant
German: Riese
Italian: gigante
Japanese: kyojin 巨人
Korean: gŏin 거인
Portuguese: gigante
Russian: velikán великан
Spanish: gigante
Swedish: jätte

924. gift [n.]

Arabic: hadía هدية
Chinese: lǐwù 禮物
Dutch: geschenk
French: cadeau
German: Geschenk
Italian: regalo
Japanese: okurimono 贈物
Korean: sŏnmul 선물
Portuguese: presente
Russian: podárok подарок
Spanish: regalo
Swedish: gåva

925. girl [n.]

Arabic: bint بنت
Chinese: nǚháizi 女孩子
Dutch: meisje
French: fille
German: Mädchen
Italian: ragazza
Japanese: shōjo 少女
Korean: sonyŏ 소녀
Portuguese: môça
Russian: dévushka девушка
Spanish: muchacha
Swedish: flicka

926. give [v.]

Arabic: áata اعطى
Chinese: gěi 給
Dutch: geven
French: donner
German: geben
Italian: dare
Japanese: ataeru 与える
Korean: juda 주다
Portuguese: dar
Russian: davát' давать
Spanish: dar
Swedish: ge

927. glad [adj.]

Arabic: masrúr مسرور
Chinese: gāoxìngde 高興的
Dutch: blij
French: content
German: froh
Italian: contento
Japanese: ureshi i うれしい
Korean: kippŭn 기쁜다
Portuguese: alegre
Russian: rádostnyy радостный
Spanish: alegre
Swedish: glad

928. glass (drinking) [n.]

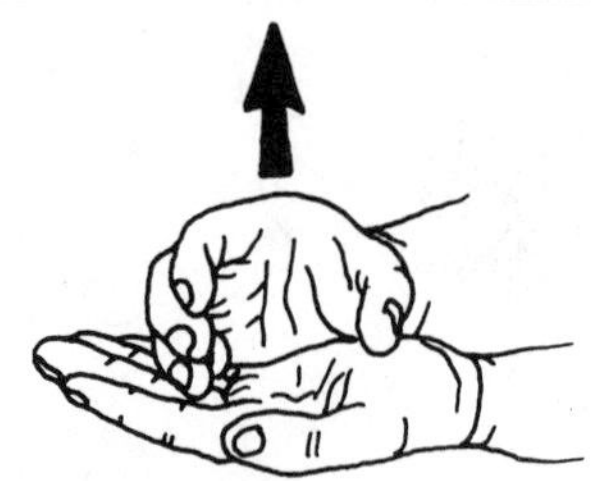

Arabic: ka's كأس
Chinese: bēizi 杯子
Dutch: glas
French: verre
German: Glas
Italian: bicchiere
Japanese: gurasu グラス
Korean: gŭrasŭ 글라스
Portuguese: copo
Russian: stakán стакан
Spanish: vaso
Swedish: glas

929. globe [n.]

Arabic: al-kóra al-ardía الكرة الارضية
Chinese: dìqiúyí 地球
Dutch: aardbol
French: globe
German: Erdball
Italian: globo
Japanese: chikyū 地球
Korean: jigubon 지구
Portuguese: globo
Russian: zemnóy shar земной шар
Spanish: globo
Swedish: glob

930. gloom [n.]

Arabic: dhalám ظلام
Chinese: yōuàn 幽暗
Dutch: duisternis
French: obscurité
German: Dunkelheit
Italian: oscurità
Japanese: yūtsu 憂うつ
Korean: ŏdum 우울
Portuguese: obscuridade
Russian: mrak мрак
Spanish: obscuridad
Swedish: dysterhet

931. glory [n.]

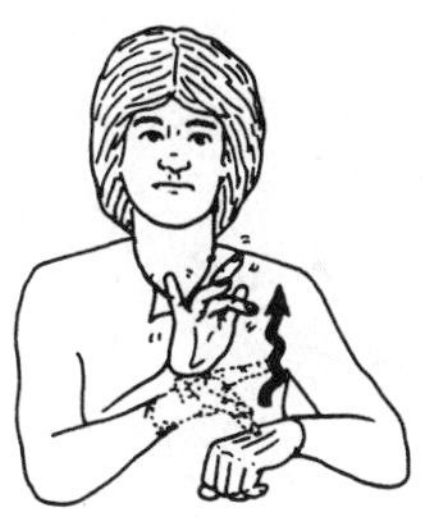

Arabic: majd مجد
Chinese: róngyào 栄耀
Dutch: roem
French: gloire
German: Ruhm
Italian: gloria
Japanese: meiyo 名誉
Korean: yŏngkwang 영광
Portuguese: glória
Russian: sláva слава
Spanish: gloria
Swedish: ära

932. glove(s) [n.]

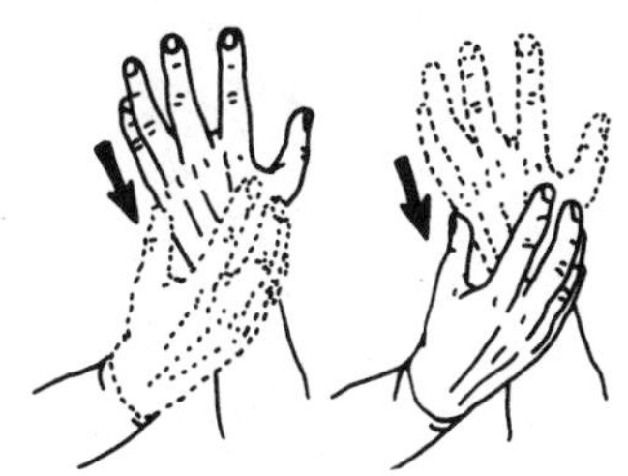

Arabic: qufáz قفاز
Chinese: shŏutào 手套
Dutch: handschoen
French: gant
German: Handschuh
Italian: guanto
Japanese: tebukuro 手袋
Korean: jangkap 장갑
Portuguese: luva
Russian: perchátki перчатки
Spanish: guante
Swedish: handskar

933. glue [n.]

Arabic: sámgha صمغ
Chinese: jiāo 膠
Dutch: lijm
French: colle
German: Leim
Italian: colla
Japanese: nikawa にかわ
Korean: agyo 아교
Portuguese: cola
Russian: kley клей
Spanish: cola
Swedish: lim

934. go [v.]

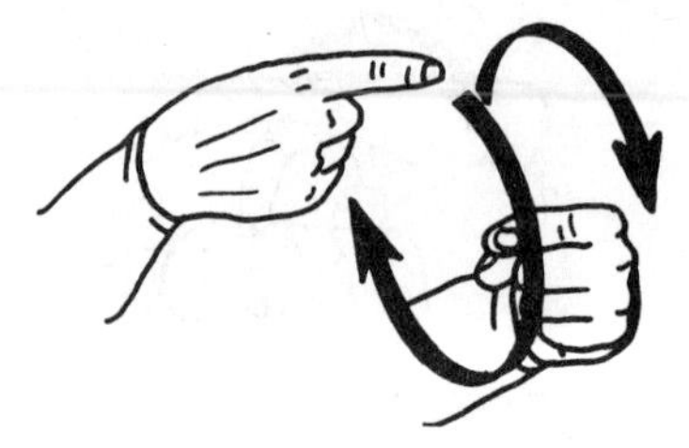

Arabic: dháhaba ذهب
Chinese: qù 去
Dutch: gaan
French: aller
German: gehen
Italian: andare
Japanese: iku 行く
Korean: gada 가다
Portuguese: ir
Russian: idtí/yékhat' идти/ехать
Spanish: ir
Swedish: gå

935. goal (aim) [n.]

Arabic: hádaf هدف
Chinese: mùbiāo 目標
Dutch: doel
French: but
German: Ziel
Italian: meta
Japanese: mokuhyō 目標
Korean: mokjŏk 목적
Portuguese: meta
Russian: tsel' цель
Spanish: meta
Swedish: mål

936. goat [n.]

Arabic: máaz ماعز
Chinese: shānyáng 山羊
Dutch: geit
French: chèvre
German: Ziege
Italian: capra
Japanese: yagi ヤギ
Korean: yŏmso 염소
Portuguese: cabra
Russian: kozyól козёл
Spanish: cabra
Swedish: get

937. God [n.]

Arabic: alláh الله
Chinese: shàngdì 上帝
Dutch: God
French: Dieu
German: Gott
Italian: Dio
Japanese: Kami 神
Korean: Hanŭnim 하느님
Portuguese: Deus
Russian: Bog Бог
Spanish: Dios
Swedish: Gud

938. gold [n.]

Arabic: tháhab ذهب
Chinese: jīnzi 金子
Dutch: goud
French: or
German: Gold
Italian: oro
Japanese: kin 金
Korean: kŭm 금
Portuguese: ouro
Russian: zóloto золото
Spanish: oro
Swedish: guld

939. golf [n.]

Arabic: lú'bet al-ghólf لعبة الغولف
Chinese: gāo-ěrfūqiú 高爾夫球
Dutch: golf
French: golf
German: Golf
Italian: golf
Japanese: gorufu ゴルフ
Korean: golp'u 골프
Portuguese: golfe
Russian: gól'f гольф
Spanish: golf
Swedish: golf

940. good [adj.]

Arabic: jéyyid جيد
Chinese: hǎo 好
Dutch: goed
French: bon
German: gut
Italian: buono
Japanese: yoi 良い
Korean: joŭn 좋은
Portuguese: bom
Russian: khoróshiy хороший
Spanish: bueno
Swedish: god

941. goodbye! [interj.]

Arabic: maa as-saláma مع السلامة
Chinese: zàijiàn 再見
Dutch: tot ziens
French: au revoir
German: auf Wiedersehen
Italian: arrivederci
Japanese: sayōnara さようなら
Korean: anny'ong 안녕
Portuguese: adeus
Russian: do svidániya до свидания
Spanish: adiós
Swedish: adjö

942. goose [n.]

Arabic: wázza وزة
Chinese: é 鵝
Dutch: gans
French: oie
German: Gans
Italian: oca
Japanese: gachō ガチョウ
Korean: kŏwi 거위
Portuguese: ganso
Russian: gus' гусь
Spanish: ganso
Swedish: gås

943. gossip [n.]

Arabic: isheáa اشاعة
Chinese: xiánhuà 閒話
Dutch: kletspraat
French: commérage
German: Geschwätz
Italian: pettegolezzo
Japanese: uwasabanashi うわさ話
Korean: jabdam 잡담
Portuguese: fofoca
Russian: splétni сплетни
Spanish: chismes
Swedish: skvaller

944. government [n.]

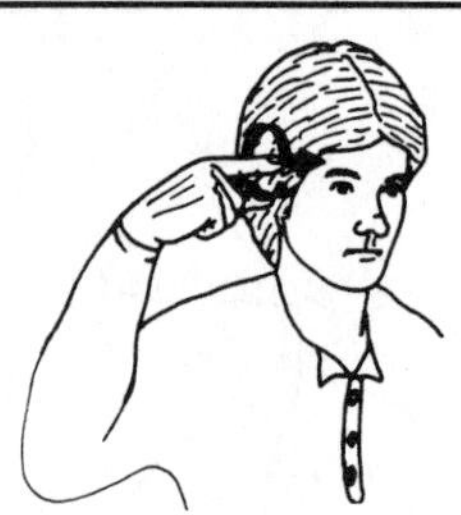

Arabic: hukúma حكومة
Chinese: zhèngfŭ 政府
Dutch: regering
French: gouvernement
German: Regierung
Italian: governo
Japanese: seifu 政府
Korean: jŏngbu 정부
Portuguese: govêrno
Russian: pravítel'stvo правительство
Spanish: gobierno
Swedish: regering

945. graduate [n.]

Arabic: takhárraja تخرج
Chinese: bìyèshēng 畢業生
Dutch: gediplomeerde
French: gradué
German: Graduierter
Italian: laureato
Japanese: sotsugyōsei 卒業生
Korean: jolŏpsaeng 졸업생
Portuguese: graduado
Russian: okónchivshiy окончивший
Spanish: graduado
Swedish: graduerad

946. grain [n.]

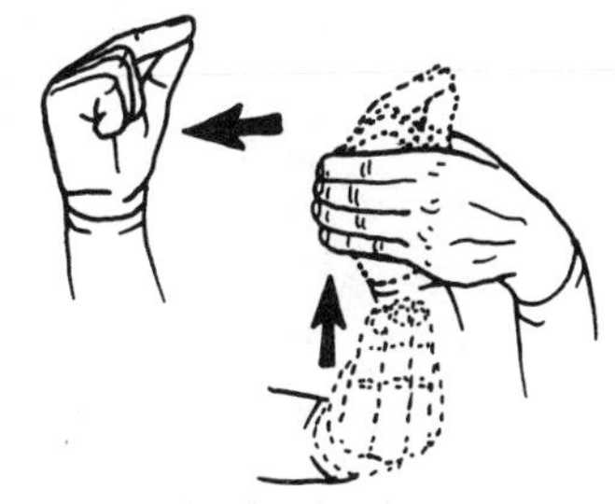

Arabic: hábba حبة
Chinese: gǔwù 穀物
Dutch: graan
French: grain
German: Getreide
Italian: grano
Japanese: kokumotsu 穀物
Korean: kongmul 곡물
Portuguese: grão
Russian: zernó зерно
Spanish: grano
Swedish: korn

947. grammar [n.]

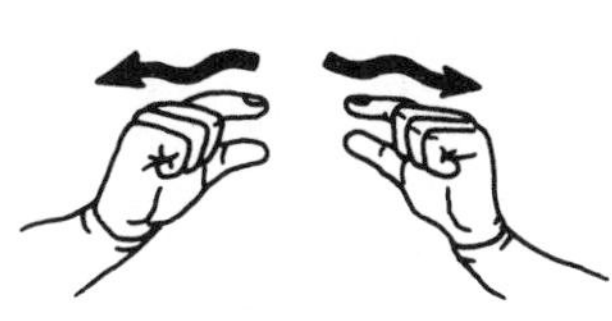

Arabic: qawáaed قواعد
Chinese: wénfǎ 文法
Dutch: grammatica
French: grammaire
German: Grammatik
Italian: grammatica
Japanese: bumpō 文法
Korean: munbŏp 문법
Portuguese: gramática
Russian: grammátika грамматика
Spanish: gramática
Swedish: grammatik

948. grand [adj.]

Arabic: dakhm ضخم
Chinese: shèngdà 盛大
Dutch: groots
French: grandiose
German: großartig
Italian: grande
Japanese: yūdaina 雄大な
Korean: ungdaehan 웅대한
Portuguese: grandioso
Russian: grandióznyy грандиозный
Spanish: grandioso
Swedish: storartad

949. granddaughter [n.]

Arabic: hafída حفيدة
Chinese: sūnnǚ 孫女
Dutch: kleindochter
French: petite-fille
German: Enkelin
Italian: nipote
Japanese: magomusume 孫娘
Korean: sonnyŏ 손녀
Portuguese: neta
Russian: vnúchka внучка
Spanish: nieta
Swedish: sondotter/dotterdotter

950. grandfather [n.]

Arabic: jadd جد
Chinese: zǔfù 祖父
Dutch: grootvader
French: grand-père
German: Großvater
Italian: nonno
Japanese: sofu 祖父
Korean: harabŏji 할아버지
Portuguese: avô
Russian: dédushka дедушка
Spanish: abuelo
Swedish: farfar/morfar

951. grandmother [n.]

Arabic: jádda جدة
Chinese: zǔmǔ 祖母
Dutch: grootmoeder
French: grand-mère
German: Großmutter
Italian: nonna
Japanese: sobo 祖母
Korean: halmŏni 할머니
Portuguese: avó
Russian: bábushka бабушка
Spanish: abuela
Swedish: farmor/mormor

952. grandson [n.]

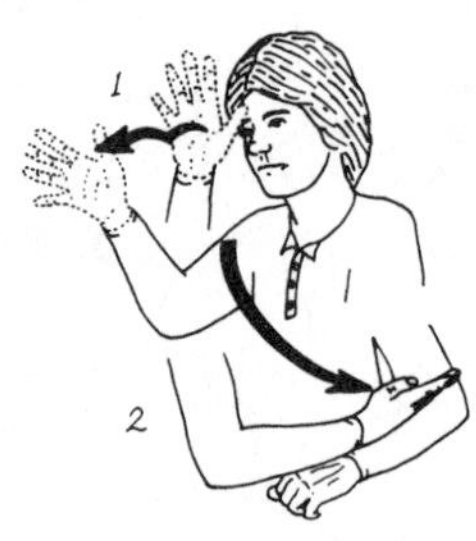

Arabic: hafíd حفيد
Chinese: sūnzi 孫子
Dutch: kleinzoon
French: petit-fils
German: Enkel
Italian: nipote
Japanese: mago 孫(男の)
Korean: sonja 손자
Portuguese: neto
Russian: vnúk внук
Spanish: nieto
Swedish: sonson/dotterson

953. grant [v.]

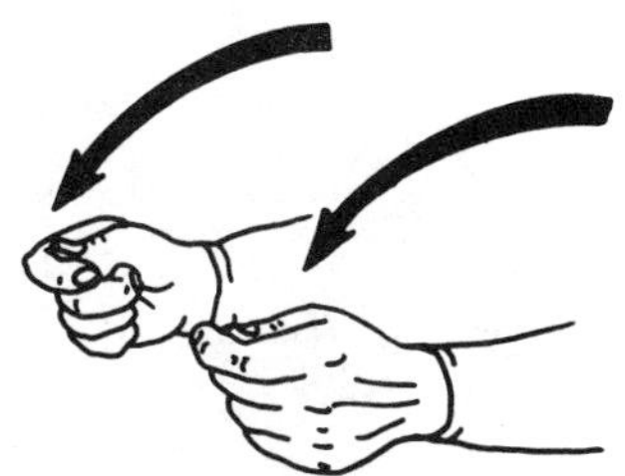

Arabic: mánaha منح
Chinese: shòuyǔ 授予
Dutch: toestaan
French: concéder
German: bewilligen
Italian: concedere
Japanese: kyoka suru 許可する
Korean: hŏrak'hada 허락하다
Portuguese: conceder
Russian: predostavlyát' предоставлять
Spanish: conceder
Swedish: bevilja

954. grape(s) [n.]

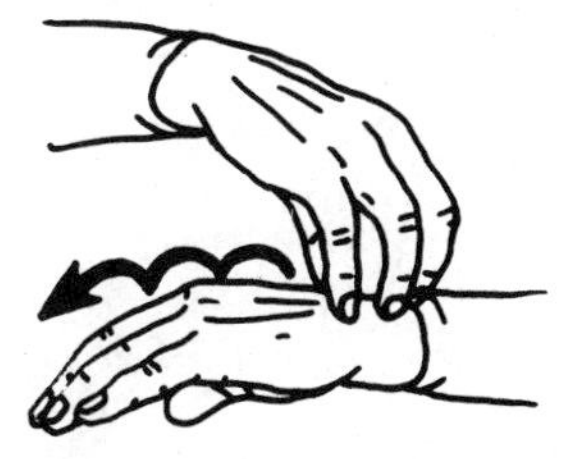

Arabic: énab عنب
Chinese: pútáo 葡萄
Dutch: druif
French: raisin
German: Weintraube
Italian: uva
Japanese: budō ブドウ
Korean: p'odo 포도
Portuguese: uvas
Russian: vinográd виноград
Spanish: uva
Swedish: vindruvor

955. grass [n.]

Arabic: hashísh حشيش
Chinese: cǎo 草
Dutch: gras
French: herbe
German: Gras
Italian: erba
Japanese: kusa 草
Korean: p'ul 풀
Portuguese: grama
Russian: travá трава
Spanish: césped
Swedish: gräs

956. grateful [adj.]

Arabic: muqér bil-jamíl مقر بالجميل
Chinese: gǎnxiède 感謝的
Dutch: dankbaar
French: reconnaissant
German: dankbar
Italian: grato
Japanese: kansha no 感謝の
Korean: gamsahanŭn 감사하는
Portuguese: grato
Russian: blagodárnyy благодарный
Spanish: agradecido
Swedish: tacksam

957. grave [n.]

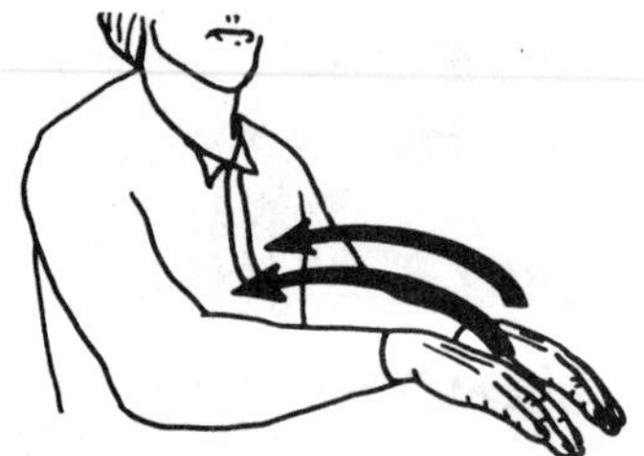

Arabic: qabr قبر
Chinese: fénmù 墳墓
Dutch: graf
French: tombe
German: Grab
Italian: tomba
Japanese: haka 墓
Korean: mudŏm 무덤
Portuguese: sepultura
Russian: mogíla могила
Spanish: sepultura
Swedish: grav

958. gray [adj.]

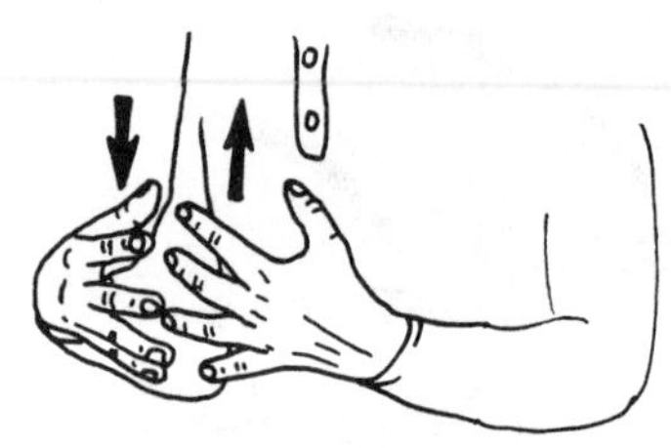

Arabic: ramádi رمادي
Chinese: huīde 灰的
Dutch: grijs
French: gris
German: grau
Italian: grigio
Japanese: haiiro no 灰色の
Korean: hoesaegŭi 회색의
Portuguese: cinzento
Russian: séryy серый
Spanish: gris
Swedish: grå

959. grease [n.]

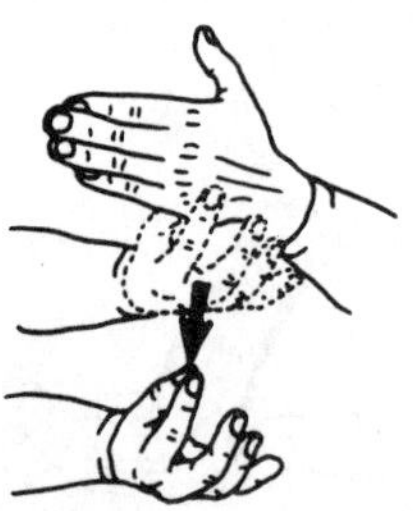

Arabic: sháhem شحم
Chinese: yóuzhǐ 油脂
Dutch: vet
French: graisse
German: Fett
Italian: grasso
Japanese: abura 油
Korean: kirŭm 기름
Portuguese: gordura
Russian: sálo сало
Spanish: grasa
Swedish: fett

960. great [adj.]

Arabic: dakhm ضخم
Chinese: wěidàde 偉大的
Dutch: groot
French: grand
German: groß
Italian: grande
Japanese: ōkina 大きな
Korean: widaehan 위대한
Portuguese: grande
Russian: velíkiy великий
Spanish: grande
Swedish: stor

961. Great Britain [n.]

Arabic: beritánia al-ózma بريطانيا العظمى
Chinese: dàbúlièdiān 大不列巔
Dutch: Groot-Brittanië
French: Grande Bretagne
German: Großbritannien
Italian: Gran Bretagna
Japanese: Dai Buriten 大ブリテン
Korean: Yŏngguk 영국
Portuguese: Grã-Bretanha
Russian: Velikobritániya Великобритания
Spanish: Gran Bretaña
Swedish: Storbritannien

962. Greece [n.]

Arabic: al-yunán اليونان
Chinese: xīlà 希臘
Dutch: Griekenland
French: Grèce
German: Griechenland
Italian: Grecia
Japanese: Girisha ギリシャ
Korean: Gŭrisŭ 그리이스
Portuguese: Grécia
Russian: Grétsiya Греция
Spanish: Grecia
Swedish: Grekland

963. greedy (money) [adj.]

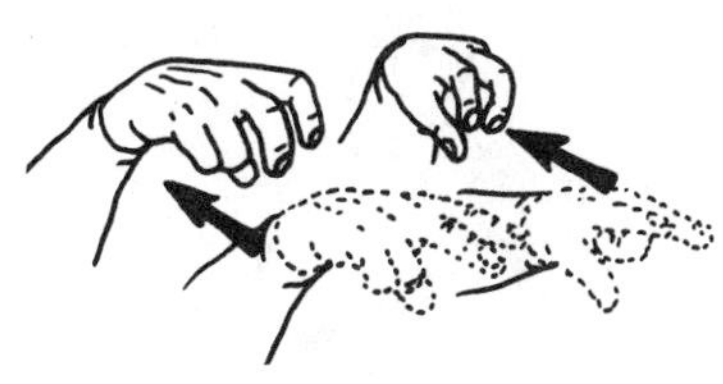

Arabic: támmaa طماع
Chinese: tānxīnde 貪心的
Dutch: hebzuchtig
French: cupide
German: habgierig
Italian: avido
Japanese: yokufukai 欲深い
Korean: yogshim manŭn 욕심 많은
Portuguese: ganancioso
Russian: zhádnyy жадный
Spanish: codicioso
Swedish: girig

964. green [adj.]

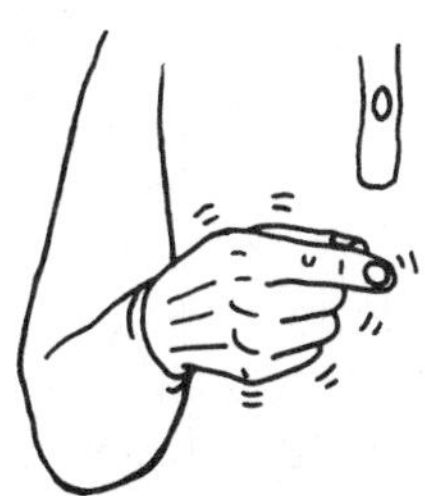

Arabic: ákhdar اخضر
Chinese: lǜde 綠的
Dutch: groen
French: vert
German: grün
Italian: verde
Japanese: midori no 緑の
Korean: noksaegŭi 녹색의
Portuguese: verde
Russian: zelyónyy зелёный
Spanish: verde
Swedish: grön

965. grief [n.]

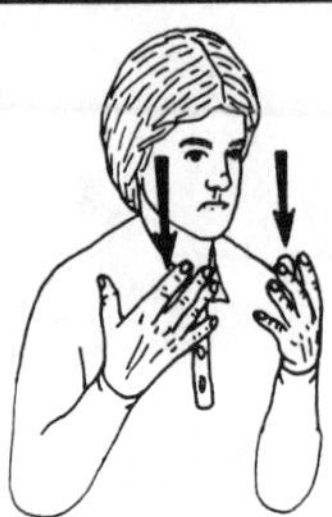

Arabic: huzn حزن
Chinese: bēishāng 悲傷
Dutch: leed
French: affliction
German: Betrübnis
Italian: afflizione
Japanese: fukai kanashimi 深い悲しみ
Korean: sŭlp'ŭm 슬픔
Portuguese: aflição
Russian: góre горе
Spanish: aflicción
Swedish: bedrövelse

966. grind [v.]

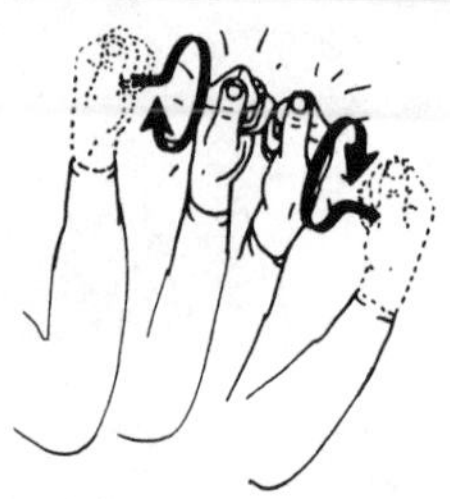

Arabic: tahána طحن
Chinese: muó 磨
Dutch: malen
French: broyer
German: mahlen
Italian: macinare
Japanese: hiku 挽く
Korean: galda 갈다
Portuguese: moer
Russian: molót' молоть
Spanish: moler
Swedish: mala

967. ground (earth) [n.]

Arabic: al-árdh الارض
Chinese: dìmiàn 地面
Dutch: grond
French: terre
German: Grund
Italian: terra
Japanese: jimen 地面
Korean: ttang 땅
Portuguese: terra
Russian: zemlyá земля
Spanish: tierra
Swedish: grund

968. group [n.]

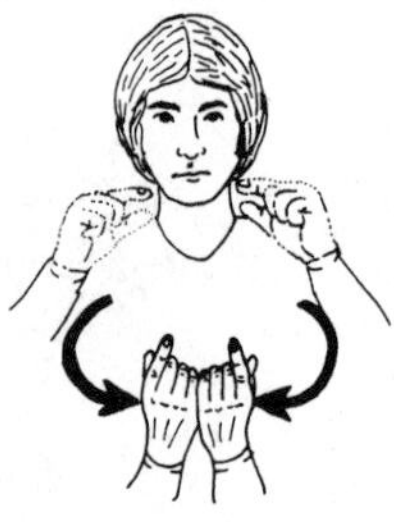

Arabic: jamáa جماعة
Chinese: qún 羣
Dutch: groep
French: groupe
German: Gruppe
Italian: gruppo
Japanese: shūdan 集団
Korean: jibdan 집단
Portuguese: grupo
Russian: grúppa группа
Spanish: grupo
Swedish: grupp

969. grow [v.]

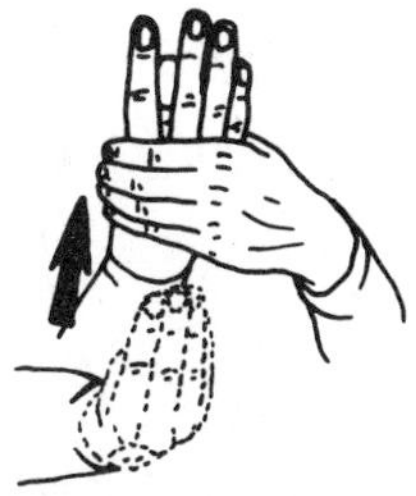

Arabic: náma نمى
Chinese: shēngzhǎng 生長
Dutch: groeien
French: croître
German: wachsen
Italian: crescere
Japanese: sēchō suru 成長する
Korean: sŏngjanghada 성장하다
Portuguese: crescer
Russian: rastí расти
Spanish: crecer
Swedish: växa

970. guarantee [v.]

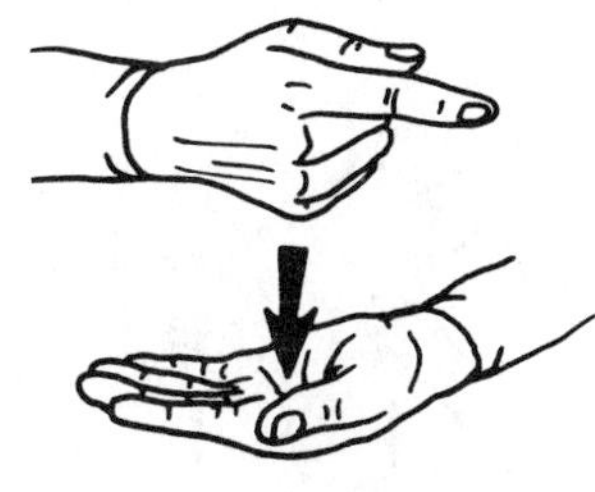

Arabic: dhámena ضمن
Chinese: bǎozhèng 保證
Dutch: garanderen
French: garantir
German: garantieren
Italian: garantire
Japanese: hoshō suru 保証する
Korean: bojŭnghada 보증하다
Portuguese: garantir
Russian: garantírovat' гарантировать
Spanish: garantizar
Swedish: garantera

971. guard [n.]

Arabic: háris حارس
Chinese: jǐngwèi 警衛
Dutch: wacht
French: garde
German: Wächter
Italian: guardia
Japanese: mihari 見張り
Korean: suwi 수위
Portuguese: guarda
Russian: stórozh сторож
Spanish: guarda
Swedish: vakt

972. guess [n.]

Arabic: takhmín تخمين
Chinese: cāixiǎng 猜想
Dutch: gis
French: conjecture
German: Vermutung
Italian: congettura
Japanese: suiryō 推量
Korean: ch'uch'ŭk 추측
Portuguese: conjetura
Russian: dogádka догадка
Spanish: conjetura
Swedish: gissning

973. guest [n.]

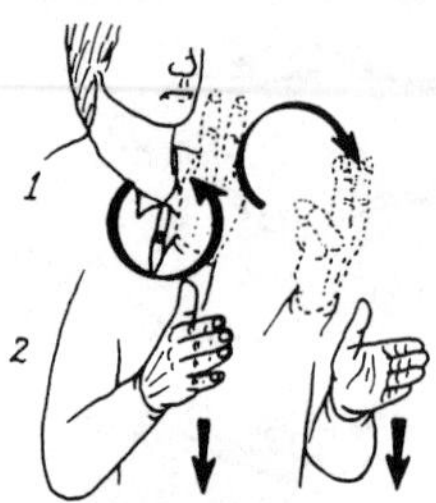

Arabic: dhaíf ضيف
Chinese: kèrén 客人
Dutch: gast
French: invité
German: Gast
Italian: ospite
Japanese: raikyaku 来客
Korean: sonnim 손님
Portuguese: hóspede
Russian: gost' гость
Spanish: huésped
Swedish: gäst

974. guide [n.]

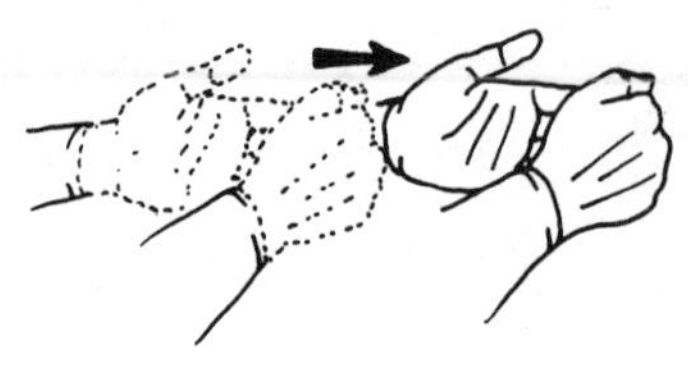

Arabic: dalíl دليل
Chinese: xiàngdǎo 嚮導
Dutch: gids
French: guide
German: Führer
Italian: guida
Japanese: an-nainin 案内人
Korean: annaewŏn 안내원
Portuguese: guia
Russian: gid гид
Spanish: guía
Swedish: ledare

975. guilty [adj.]

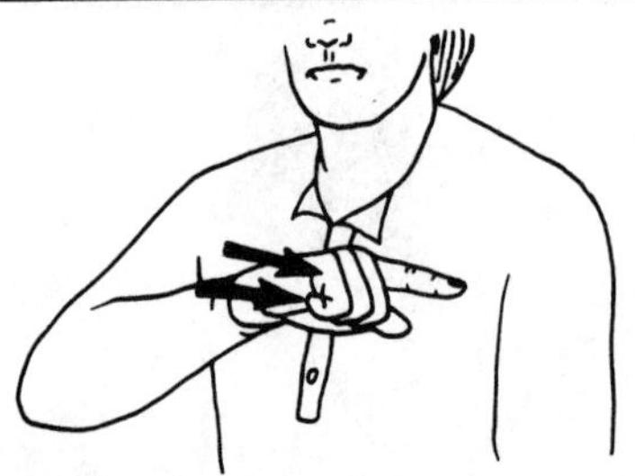

Arabic: múdhneb مذنب
Chinese: yǒu zuì de 有罪的
Dutch: schuldig
French: coupable
German: schuldig
Italian: colpevole
Japanese: yūzai no 有罪の
Korean: yujoeŭi 유죄의
Portuguese: culpado
Russian: vinovátyy виноватый
Spanish: culpable
Swedish: skyldig

976. gun [n.]

Arabic: bundoqía بندقية
Chinese: qiāng 鎗
Dutch: geweer
French: fusil
German: Gewehr
Italian: fucile
Japanese: teppō 鉄砲
Korean: tch'ong 총
Portuguese: espingarda
Russian: ruzh'yó ружьё
Spanish: fusil
Swedish: gevär

977. habit [n.]

Arabic: aáda عادة
Chinese: xíguàn 習慣
Dutch: gewoonte
French: habitude
German: Gewohnheit
Italian: abitudine
Japanese: shūkan 習慣
Korean: subkwan 습관
Portuguese: hábito
Russian: privýchka привычка
Spanish: hábito
Swedish: vana

978. hail [n.]

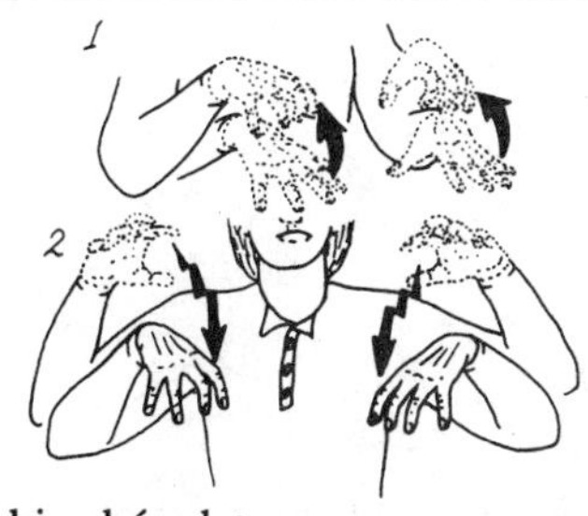

Arabic: bárad برد
Chinese: bīngbào 冰雹
Dutch: hagel
French: grêle
German: Hagel
Italian: grandine
Japanese: hyō 雹
Korean: ubag 우박
Portuguese: granizo
Russian: grad град
Spanish: granizo
Swedish: hagel

979. hair [n.]

Arabic: sháar شعر
Chinese: tóufǎ 頭髮
Dutch: haar
French: cheveu
German: Haar
Italian: capello
Japanese: kami 髪
Korean: t'ŏl 털
Portuguese: cabelo
Russian: vólos волос
Spanish: pelo
Swedish: hår

980. half [n.]

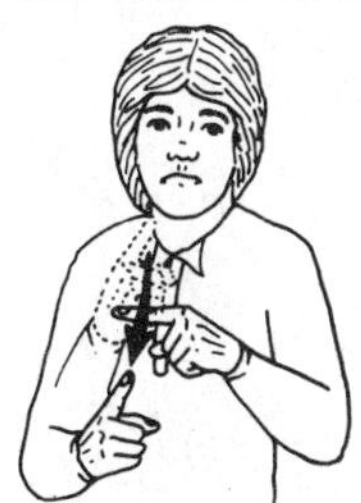

Arabic: nusf نصف
Chinese: yíbàn 一半
Dutch: helft
French: moitié
German: Hälfte
Italian: metà
Japanese: hambun 半分
Korean: ban 반
Portuguese: metade
Russian: polovína половина
Spanish: mitad
Swedish: hälft

981. hall [n.]

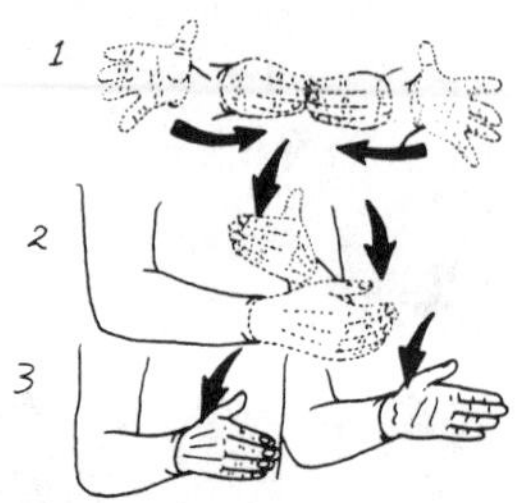

Arabic: qáa قاعة
Chinese: huìtáng 會堂
Dutch: zaal
French: hall
German: Halle
Italian: sala
Japanese: kaikan 会館
Korean: hol 홀
Portuguese: salão
Russian: zal зал
Spanish: sala
Swedish: hall

982. hammer [n.]

Arabic: métraqa مطرقة
Chinese: tiěchuí 鐵鎚
Dutch: hamer
French: marteau
German: Hammer
Italian: martello
Japanese: kanazuchi 金づち
Korean: mangch'i 망치
Portuguese: martelo
Russian: molotók молоток
Spanish: martillo
Swedish: hammare

983. hand [n.]

Arabic: yad يد
Chinese: shǒu 手
Dutch: hand
French: main
German: Hand
Italian: mano
Japanese: te 手
Korean: son 손
Portuguese: mão
Russian: ruká рука
Spanish: mano
Swedish: hand

984. handkerchief [n.]

Arabic: mandíl منديل
Chinese: shǒupà 手帕
Dutch: zakdoek
French: mouchoir
German: Taschentuch
Italian: fazzoletto
Japanese: hankachiifu ハンカチーフ
Korean: sonsugŏn 손수건
Portuguese: lenço
Russian: nosovóy platók
носовой платок
Spanish: pañuelo
Swedish: näsduk

985. handsome [adj.]

Arabic: aníeq انيق
Chinese: yīngjùn 英俊
Dutch: knap
French: beau
German: hübsch
Italian: bello
Japanese: hansamu na ハンサムな
Korean: jal saenggin 잘 생긴
Portuguese: bonito
Russian: krasívyy красивый
Spanish: guapo
Swedish: vacker

986. hang (suspend) [v.]

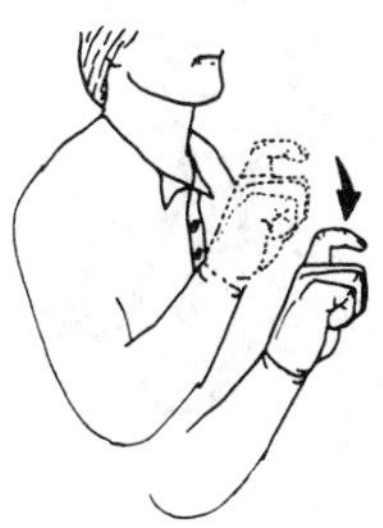

Arabic: áalaqa علق
Chinese: diào 吊
Dutch: hangen
French: suspendre
German: hängen
Italian: appendere
Japanese: kakeru 掛ける
Korean: maedalda 매달다
Portuguese: pendurar
Russian: véshat' вешать
Spanish: colgar
Swedish: hänga

987. happen [v.]

Arabic: hádatha حدث
Chinese: fāshēng 發生
Dutch: gebeuren
French: advenir
German: geschehen
Italian: accadere
Japanese: okoru 起る
Korean: irŏnada 일어나다
Portuguese: acontecer
Russian: proiskhodít' происходить
Spanish: suceder
Swedish: hända

988. happiness [n.]

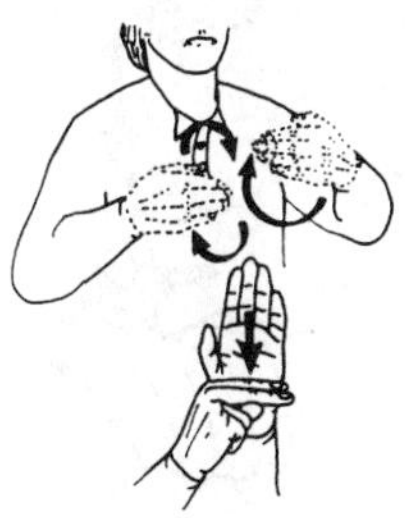

Arabic: sáada سعادة
Chinese: xìngfú 幸福
Dutch: geluk
French: bonheur
German: Glück
Italian: felicità
Japanese: kōfuku 幸福
Korean: haengbog 행복
Portuguese: felicidade
Russian: schást'ye счастье
Spanish: felicidad
Swedish: lycka

989. happy [adj.]

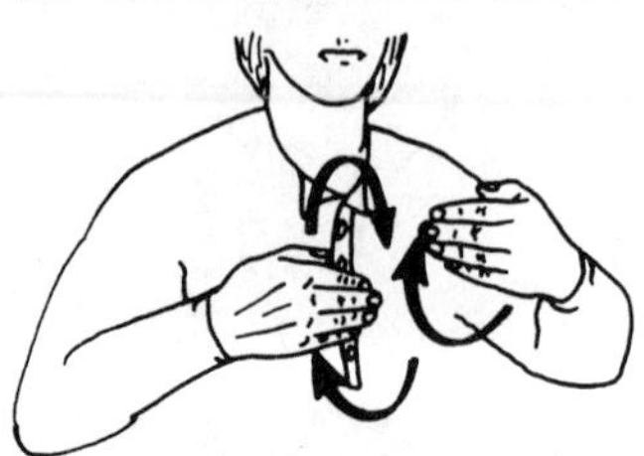

Arabic: saíd سعيد
Chinese: kuàilè 快樂
Dutch: gelukkig
French: heureux
German: glücklich
Italian: felice
Japanese: kōfukuna 幸福な
Korean: haengbog'han 행복한
Portuguese: feliz
Russian: schastlívyy счастливый
Spanish: feliz
Swedish: lycklig

990. harbor [n.]

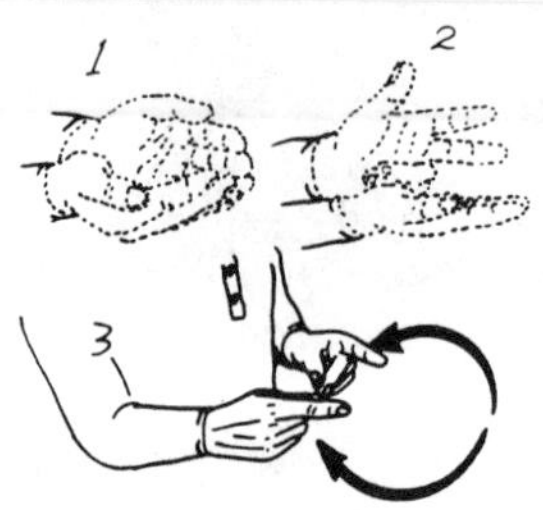

Arabic: mína' ميناء
Chinese: mătóu 碼頭
Dutch: haven
French: port
German: Hafen
Italian: porto
Japanese: minato 港
Korean: hangku 항구
Portuguese: porto
Russian: gávan' гавань
Spanish: puerto
Swedish: hamn

991. hard [adj.]

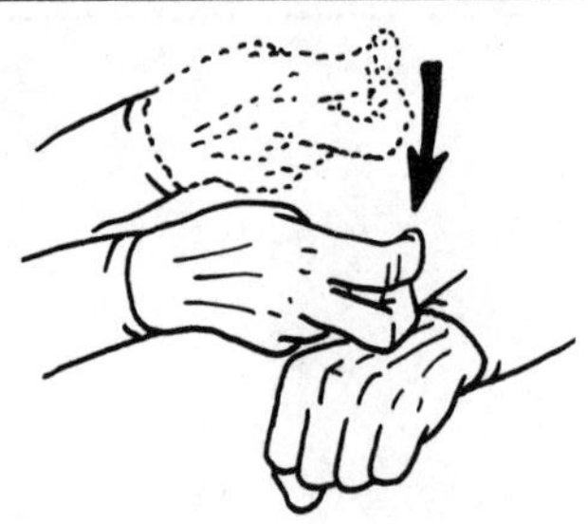

Arabic: salb صلب
Chinese: yìngde 硬的
Dutch: hard
French: dur
German: hart
Italian: duro
Japanese: katai 堅い
Korean: ttagttag'an 딱딱한
Portuguese: duro
Russian: tvyórdyy твёрдый
Spanish: duro
Swedish: hård

992. harm [n.]

Arabic: dhárar ضرر
Chinese: shānghài 傷害
Dutch: schade
French: dommage
German: Schaden
Italian: danno
Japanese: gai 害
Korean: sonhae 손해
Portuguese: dano
Russian: vred вред
Spanish: daño
Swedish: skada

993. harvest [n.]

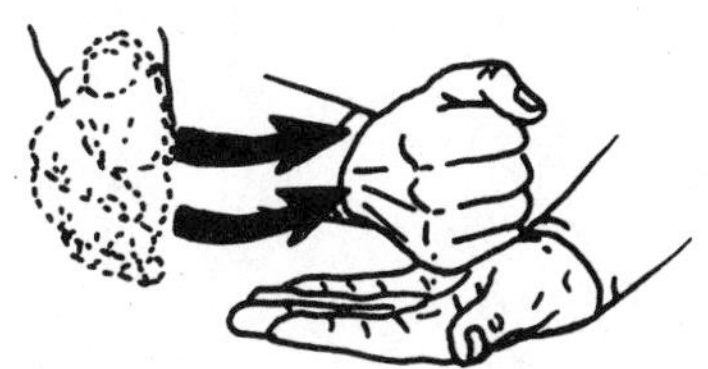

Arabic: hasád حصاد
Chinese: shōuchéng 收成
Dutch: oogst
French: moisson
German: Ernte
Italian: raccolto
Japanese: shukaku 収穫
Korean: suhwak 수확
Portuguese: colheita
Russian: urozháy урожай
Spanish: cosecha
Swedish: skörd

994. haste [n.]

Arabic: taháwwur تهور
Chinese: jípuò 急迫
Dutch: haast
French: hâte
German: Hast
Italian: fretta
Japanese: isogi 急ぎ
Korean: sŏdurŭm 서두름
Portuguese: pressa
Russian: toroplívost' торопливость
Spanish: prisa
Swedish: hast

995. hat [n.]

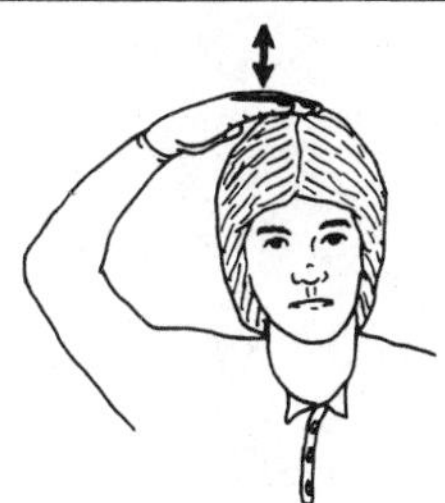

Arabic: qúbaa قبعة
Chinese: màozi 帽子
Dutch: hoed
French: chapeau
German: Hut
Italian: cappello
Japanese: bōshi 帽子
Korean: moja 모자
Portuguese: chapéu
Russian: shlyápa шляпа
Spanish: sombrero
Swedish: hatt

996. hate [v.]

Arabic: káriha كره
Chinese: hèn 恨
Dutch: haten
French: haïr
German: hassen
Italian: odiare
Japanese: nikumu 憎む
Korean: miwŏhada 미워하다
Portuguese: odiar
Russian: nenavídet' ненавидеть
Spanish: odiar
Swedish: hata

997. haughty [adj.]

Arabic: mutaghátris متغطرس
Chinese: àomànde 傲慢的
Dutch: hoogmoedig
French: hautain
German: hochmutig
Italian: altezzoso
Japanese: gōman na 傲慢な
Korean: gŏmanhan 교만한
Portuguese: soberbo
Russian: vysokomérnyy высокомерный
Spanish: altivo
Swedish: högdragen

998. have [v.]

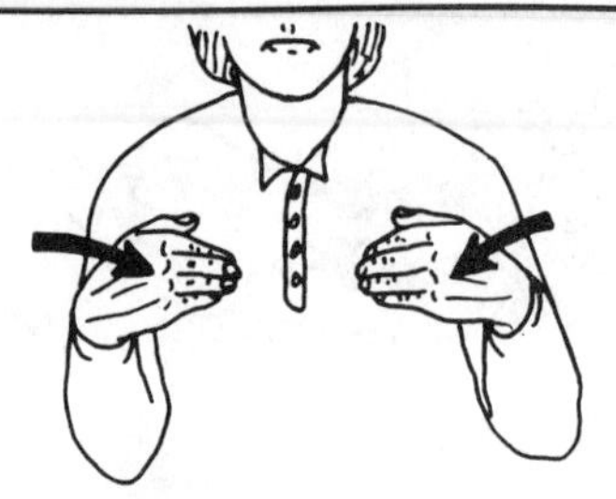

Arabic: málaka ملك
Chinese: yǒu 有
Dutch: hebben
French: avoir
German: haben
Italian: avere
Japanese: motsu 持つ
Korean: gajida 가지다
Portuguese: ter
Russian: imét' иметь
Spanish: tener
Swedish: ha

999. hay [n.]

Arabic: qash قش
Chinese: gāncǎo 乾草
Dutch: hooi
French: foin
German: Heu
Italian: fieno
Japanese: hoshikusa 干し草
Korean: kŏnch'o 건초
Portuguese: feno
Russian: séno сено
Spanish: heno
Swedish: hö

1000. he [pron.]

Arabic: húwa هو
Chinese: tā 他
Dutch: hij
French: il
German: er
Italian: egli
Japanese: kare wa 彼は
Korean: kunamja 그 남자
Portuguese: ele
Russian: on он
Spanish: él
Swedish: han

1001. head [n.]

Arabic: ra'ís رئيس
Chinese: tóu 頭
Dutch: hoofd
French: tête
German: Kopf
Italian: capo
Japanese: atama 頭
Korean: mŏri 머리
Portuguese: cabeça
Russian: golová голова
Spanish: cabeza
Swedish: huvud

1002. headache [n.]

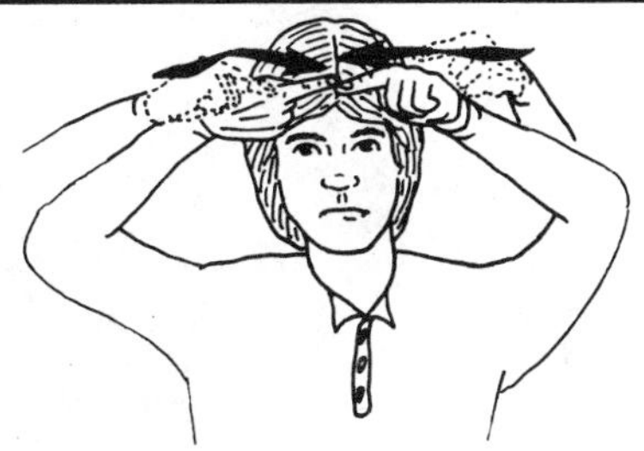

Arabic: súdaa صداع
Chinese: tóuténg 頭疼
Dutch: hoofdpijn
French: mal de tête
German: Kopfschmerzen
Italian: mal di capo
Japanese: zutsū 頭痛
Korean: dut'ong 두통
Portuguese: dor de cabeça
Russian: golovnáya bol' головная боль
Spanish: dolor de cabeza
Swedish: huvudvärk

1003. health [n.]

Arabic: sáhha صحة
Chinese: jiànkāng 健康
Dutch: gezondheid
French: santé
German: Gesundheit
Italian: salute
Japanese: kenko 健康
Korean: kŏngang 건강
Portuguese: saúde
Russian: zdoróv'ye здоровье
Spanish: salud
Swedish: hälsa

1004. hear [v.]

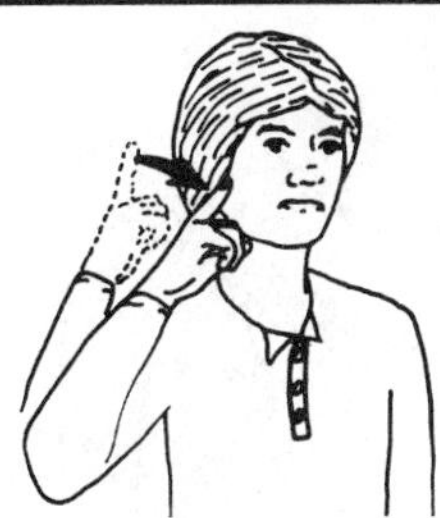

Arabic: sámeaa سمع
Chinese: tīng 聽
Dutch: horen
French: entendre
German: hören
Italian: sentire
Japanese: kiku 聞く
Korean: dŭdda 듣다
Portuguese: ouvir
Russian: slýshat' слышать
Spanish: oír
Swedish: höra

1005. hearing (sense) [n.]

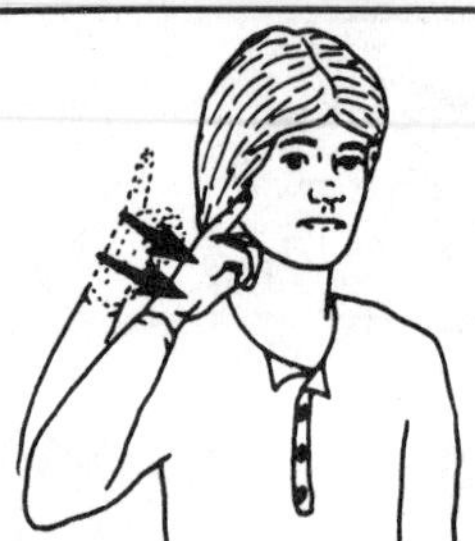

Arabic: samáa سماع
Chinese: tīnglì 聽力
Dutch: gehoor
French: ouïe
German: Gehör
Italian: udito
Japanese: chōryoku 聴力
Korean: dŭllim 들림
Portuguese: ouvido
Russian: slukh слух
Spanish: oído
Swedish: hörsel

1006. heart [n.]

Arabic: qalb قلب
Chinese: xīn 心
Dutch: hart
French: coeur
German: Herz
Italian: cuore
Japanese: shinzō 心臓
Korean: shimjang 심장
Portuguese: coração
Russian: sérdtse сердце
Spanish: corazón
Swedish: hjärta

1007. heat [n.]

Arabic: harára حرارة
Chinese: rè 熱
Dutch: hitte
French: chaleur
German: Hitze
Italian: caldo
Japanese: netsu 熱
Korean: yŏl 더위
Portuguese: calor
Russian: zhará жара
Spanish: calor
Swedish: hetta

1008. heaven [n.]

Arabic: jánna جنة
Chinese: tiāntáng 天堂
Dutch: hemel
French: ciel
German: Himmel
Italian: cielo
Japanese: tengoku 天国
Korean: hanŭl 하늘
Portuguese: céu
Russian: nebesá небеса
Spanish: cielo
Swedish: himmel

1009. heavy [adj.]

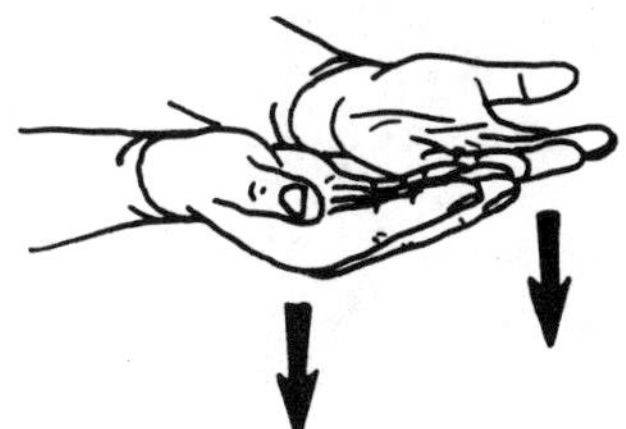

Arabic: thaqíl ثقيل
Chinese: zhòngde 重的
Dutch: zwaar
French: lourd
German: schwer
Italian: pesante
Japanese: omoi 重い
Korean: mugŏun 무거운
Portuguese: pesado
Russian: tyazhyólyy тяжёлый
Spanish: pesado
Swedish: tung

1010. height [n.]

Arabic: tull طول
Chinese: gāodù 高度
Dutch: hoogte
French: hauteur
German: Höhe
Italian: altezza
Japanese: takasa 高さ
Korean: nop'i 높이
Portuguese: altura
Russian: vysotá высота
Spanish: altura
Swedish: höjd

1011. helicopter [n.]

Arabic: hélikobtar هليكوبتر
Chinese: zhíshēng fēijī 直升飛機
Dutch: helicopter
French: hélicoptère
German: Hubschrauber
Italian: elicottero
Japanese: hericoputā ヘリコプター
Korean: helikoptŏ 헬리콥터
Portuguese: helicóptero
Russian: vertolyót вертолёт
Spanish: helicóptero
Swedish: helikopter

1012. hell [n.]

Arabic: jahánnam جهنم
Chinese: dìyǜ 地獄
Dutch: hel
French: enfer
German: Hölle
Italian: inferno
Japanese: jigoku 地獄
Korean: jiog 지옥
Portuguese: inferno
Russian: ad ад
Spanish: infierno
Swedish: helvete

1013. hello/good day (greeting) [interj.]

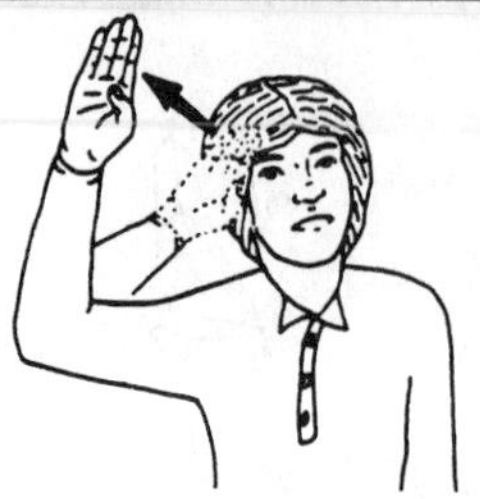

Arabic: márhaban مرحباً
Chinese: nǐhǎo 你好
Dutch: goedendag
French: bonjour
German: guten Tag
Italian: buongiorno
Japanese: konnichi wa 今日は！
Korean: yŏboseyo 여보세요
Portuguese: bom dia
Russian: dóbryy den' добрый день
Spanish: buenos días
Swedish: god dag

1014. help [v.]

Arabic: saáda ساعد
Chinese: bāngzhù 幫助
Dutch: helpen
French: aider
German: helfen
Italian: aiutare
Japanese: tasukeru 助ける
Korean: dopta 돕다
Portuguese: ajudar
Russian: pomogat' помогать
Spanish: ayudar
Swedish: hjälpa

1015. her [pron.]

Arabic: láha لها
Chinese: tā 她
Dutch: haar
French: elle
German: ihr
Italian: lei
Japanese: kanojo no 彼女の
Korean: gŭ yŏja 그 여자
Portuguese: ela/lhe
Russian: yeyó/yey её/ей
Spanish: ella
Swedish: henne

1016. here [adv.]

Arabic: húna هنا
Chinese: zhèr 這兒
Dutch: hier
French: ici
German: hier
Italian: qui
Japanese: koko ni ここに
Korean: yŏgi 여기
Portuguese: aqui
Russian: zdes' здесь
Spanish: aquí
Swedish: här

1017. hero [n.]

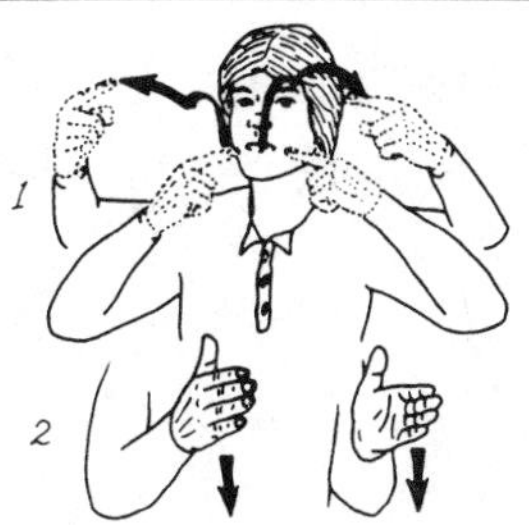

Arabic: bátal بطل
Chinese: yīngxióng 英雄
Dutch: held
French: héros
German: Held
Italian: eroe
Japanese: eiyū 英雄
Korean: yŏngung 영웅
Portuguese: herói
Russian: geróy герой
Spanish: héroe
Swedish: hjälte

1018. herself [pron.]

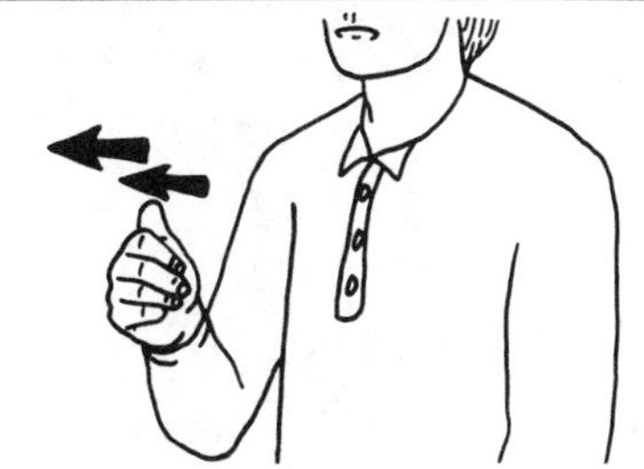

Arabic: nafsúha نفسها
Chinese: tāzìjǐ 她自己
Dutch: zijzelf
French: elle-même
German: sie selbst
Italian: lei stessa
Japanese: kanojo-jishin 彼女自身
Korean: gŭ yŏja jashin 그 여자 자신
Portuguese: ela mesma
Russian: samá сама
Spanish: ella misma
Swedish: henne själv

1019. hesitate [v.]

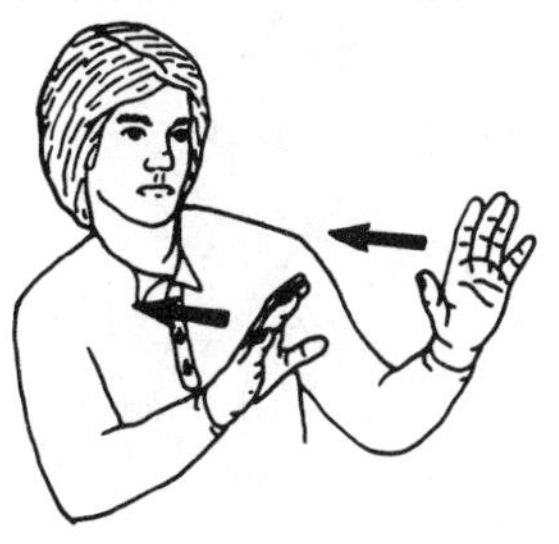

Arabic: taráddada تردد
Chinese: chíyí 犹豫
Dutch: aarzelen
French: hésiter
German: zögern
Italian: esitare
Japanese: tamerau ためらう
Korean: jujŏhada 주저하다
Portuguese: hesitar
Russian: kolebát'sya колебаться
Spanish: vacilar
Swedish: tveka

1020. hide [v.]

Arabic: ákhfa اخفى
Chinese: duǒcáng 躲藏
Dutch: verbergen
French: cacher
German: verbergen
Italian: nascondere
Japanese: kakusu 隠す
Korean: gamch'uda 감추다
Portuguese: esconder
Russian: skryvát' скрывать
Spanish: esconder
Swedish: gömma

1021. high [adj.]

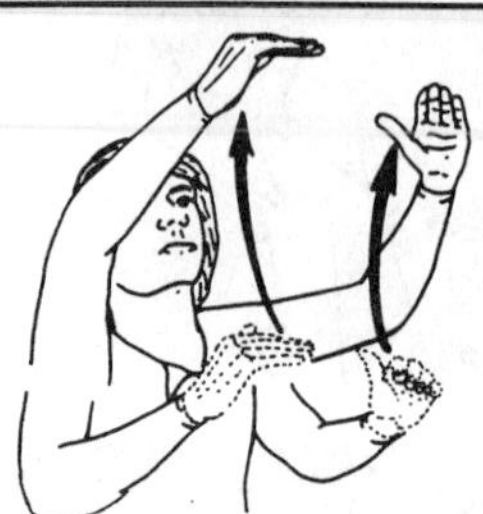

Arabic: murtáfiaa مرتفع
Chinese: gāode 高的
Dutch: hoog
French: haut
German: hoch
Italian: alto
Japanese: takai 高い
Korean: nop'ŭn 높은
Portuguese: alto
Russian: vysókiy высокий
Spanish: alto
Swedish: hög

1022. highway [n.]

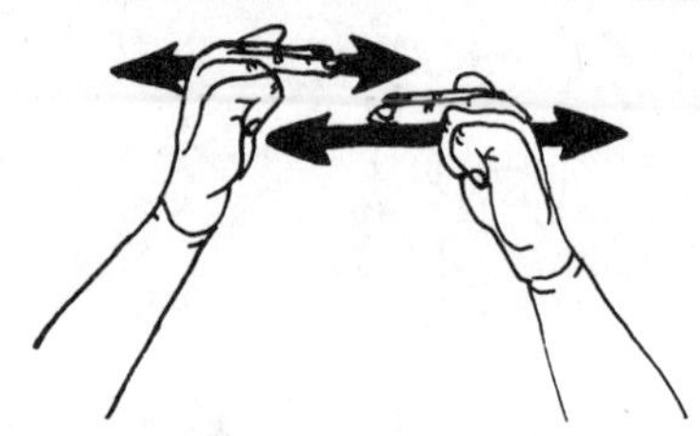

Arabic: taríeq طريق
Chinese: gōnglù 高速公路
Dutch: straatweg
French: grande route
German: Hauptstraße
Italian: strada maestra
Japanese: kōdō 公道
Korean: kansŏn doro 간선도로
Portuguese: estrada
Russian: shossé шоссе
Spanish: carretera
Swedish: motorväg

1023. hill [n.]

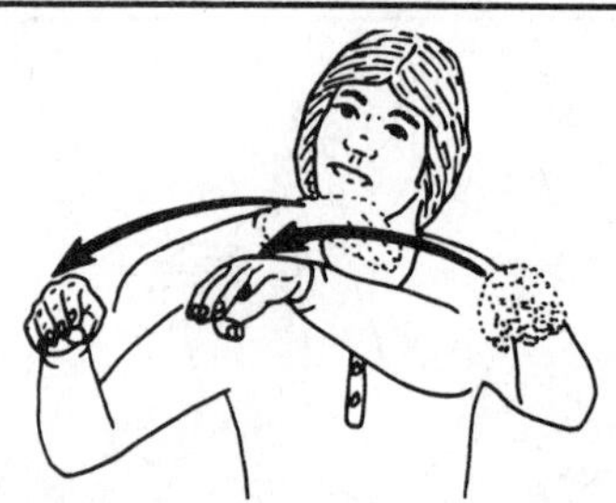

Arabic: háddaba هضبة
Chinese: shānqiū 山丘
Dutch: heuvel
French: colline
German: Hügel
Italian: collina
Japanese: oka 丘
Korean: ŏndŏk 높은
Portuguese: colina
Russian: kholm холм
Spanish: colina
Swedish: backe

1024. him [pron.]

Arabic: lahú له
Chinese: tā 他
Dutch: hem
French: lui
German: ihn
Italian: lui
Japanese: kareo 彼を
Korean: gŭ namja ege 언덕
Portuguese: ele/lhe
Russian: yevó/yemú/im его/ему/им
Spanish: él
Swedish: honom

1025. himself [pron.]

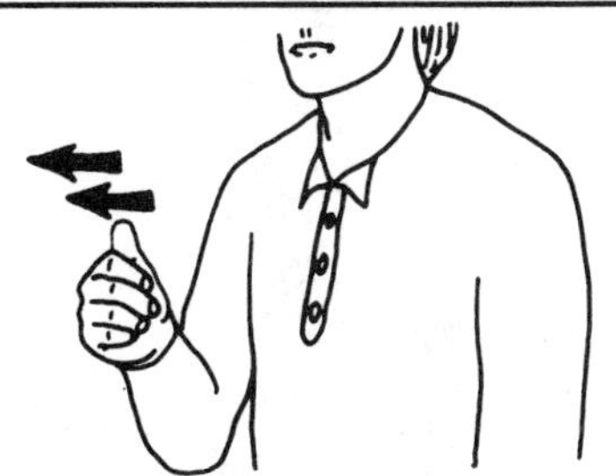

Arabic: nafsáhu نفسه
Chinese: tāzìjǐ 他自己
Dutch: hijzelf
French: lui-même
German: er selbst
Italian: lui stesso
Japanese: kare-jishin 彼自身
Korean: gŭ namja jashin그 남자 자신
Portuguese: ele mesmo
Russian: sam сам
Spanish: él mismo
Swedish: honom själv

1026. history [n.]

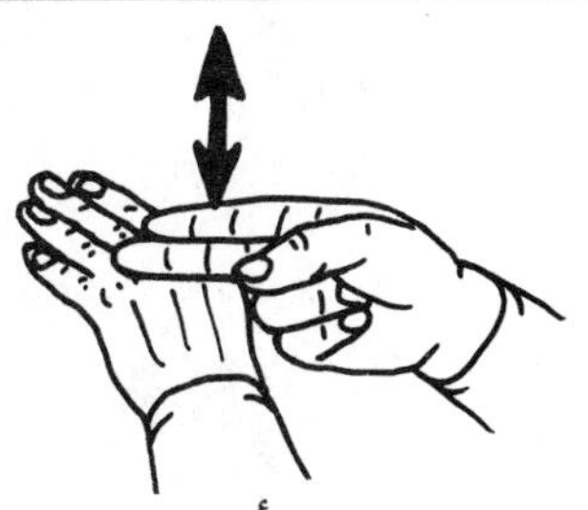

Arabic: taríkh تأريخ
Chinese: lìshǐ 歷史
Dutch: geschiedenis
French: histoire
German: Geschichte
Italian: storia
Japanese: rekishi 歴史
Korean: yŏksa 역사
Portuguese: história
Russian: istóriya история
Spanish: historia
Swedish: historia

1027. hit (strike) [v.]

Arabic: dháraba ضرب
Chinese: dǎ 擊打
Dutch: slaan
French: frapper
German: schlagen
Italian: colpire
Japanese: utsu 打つ
Korean: ch'ida 치다
Portuguese: bater
Russian: udaryát' ударять
Spanish: golpear
Swedish: slå

1028. hold (keep) [v.]

Arabic: ihtáfadha bi احتفظ ب
Chinese: bǎochí 把持
Dutch: houden
French: tenir
German: halten
Italian: tenere
Japanese: te ni motte iru 手に持っている
Korean: jinida 지니다
Portuguese: manter
Russian: derzhát' держать
Spanish: tener
Swedish: hålla

1029. hole [n.]

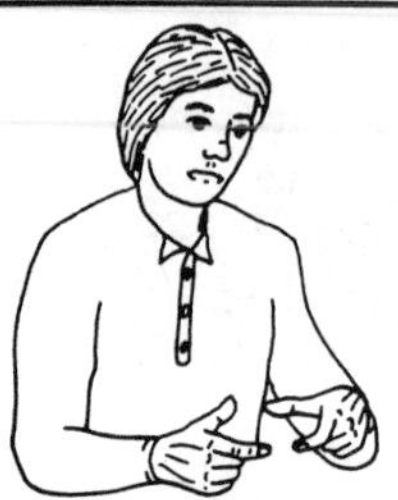

Arabic: húfra حفرة
Chinese: dòng 洞
Dutch: gat
French: trou
German: Loch
Italian: buco
Japanese: ana 穴
Korean: gumŏng 구멍
Portuguese: buraco
Russian: dyrá дыра
Spanish: agujero
Swedish: hål

1030. holiday [n.]

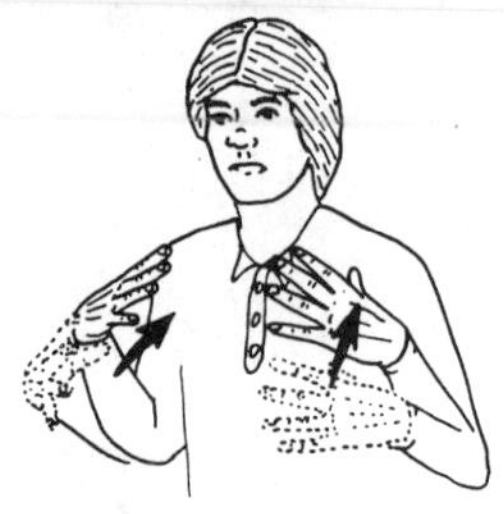

Arabic: ótla عطلة
Chinese: jiàrì 假日
Dutch: feestdag
French: jour de fête
German: Feiertag
Italian: festa
Japanese: shukujitsu 祝日
Korean: myŏngjŏl 명절
Portuguese: feriado
Russian: prázdnik праздник
Spanish: día festivo
Swedish: helgdag

1031. Holland [n.]

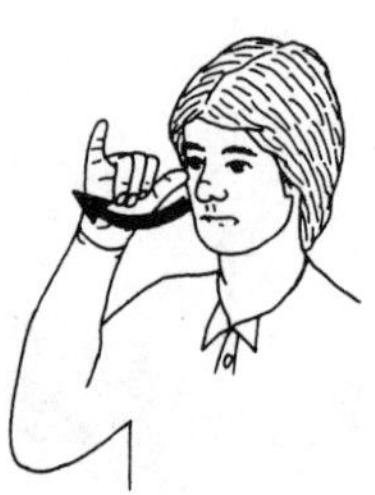

Arabic: holánda هولندا
Chinese: hélán 荷蘭
Dutch: Holland
French: Hollande
German: Holland
Italian: Olanda
Japanese: Oranda オランダ
Korean: Nedŏllandŭ 네덜란드
Portuguese: Holanda
Russian: Gollándiya Голландия
Spanish: Holanda
Swedish: Holland

1032. holy [adj.]

Arabic: muqáddas مقدس
Chinese: shéngshèngde 神聖的
Dutch: heilig
French: saint
German: heilig
Italian: santo
Japanese: shinseina 神聖な
Korean: shinsŏnghan 신성한
Portuguese: sagrado
Russian: svyatóy святой
Spanish: santo
Swedish: helig

1033. home (house) [n.]

Arabic: beyt بيت
Chinese: jiā 家
Dutch: huis
French: maison
German: Heim
Italian: casa
Japanese: jūkyo 住居
Korean: jib 집
Portuguese: lar
Russian: dom дом
Spanish: casa
Swedish: hus

1034. honest [adj.]

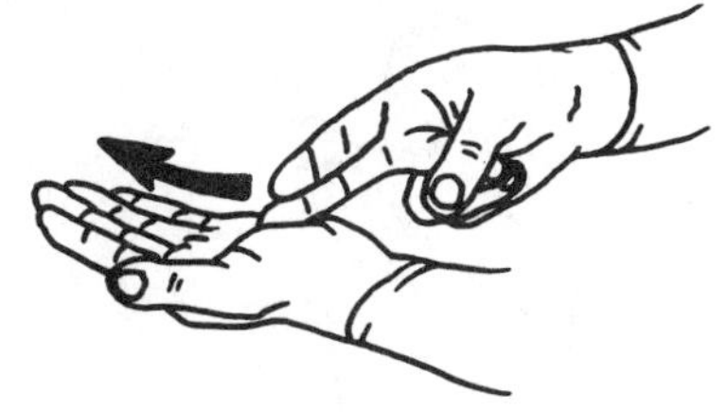

Arabic: amín امين
Chinese: chéngshíde 誠實的
Dutch: eerlijk
French: honnête
German: ehrlich
Italian: onesto
Japanese: shōjiki na 正直な
Korean: jŏngjik'han 정직한
Portuguese: honesto
Russian: chéstnyy честный
Spanish: honesto
Swedish: ärlig

1035. honor [n.]

Arabic: sháraf شرف
Chinese: róngyù 榮譽
Dutch: eer
French: honneur
German: Ehre
Italian: onore
Japanese: meiyo 名誉
Korean: myŏngye 명예
Portuguese: honra
Russian: chest' честь
Spanish: honor
Swedish: ära

1036. hook [n.]

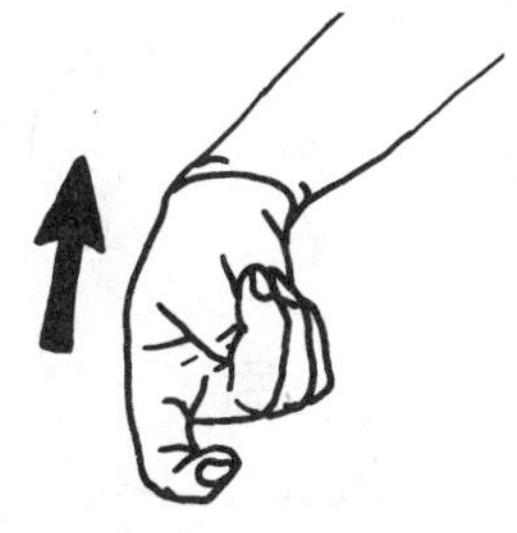

Arabic: khóttaaf خطاف
Chinese: gōuzi 鈎子
Dutch: haak
French: crochet
German: Haken
Italian: gancio
Japanese: kagi かぎ(フック)
Korean: galgori 갈고리
Portuguese: gancho
Russian: kryúk крюк
Spanish: gancho
Swedish: krok

1037. hope [n.]

Arabic: ámal امل
Chinese: xīwàng 希望
Dutch: hoop
French: espoir
German: Hoffnung
Italian: speranza
Japanese: kibō 希望
Korean: hŭimang 희망
Portuguese: esperança
Russian: nadézhda надежда
Spanish: esperanza
Swedish: hopp

1038. horse [n.]

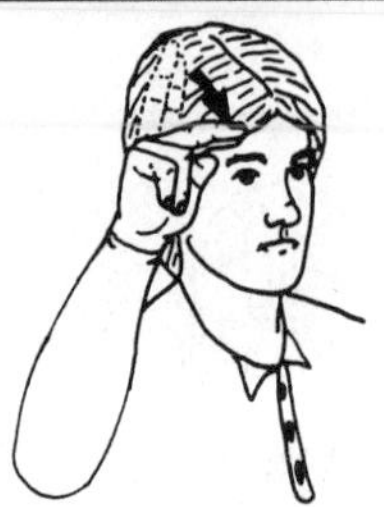

Arabic: hesán حصان
Chinese: mǎ 馬
Dutch: paard
French: cheval
German: Pferd
Italian: cavallo
Japanese: uma 馬
Korean: mal 말
Portuguese: cavalo
Russian: lóshad' лошадь
Spanish: caballo
Swedish: häst

1039. hospital [n.]

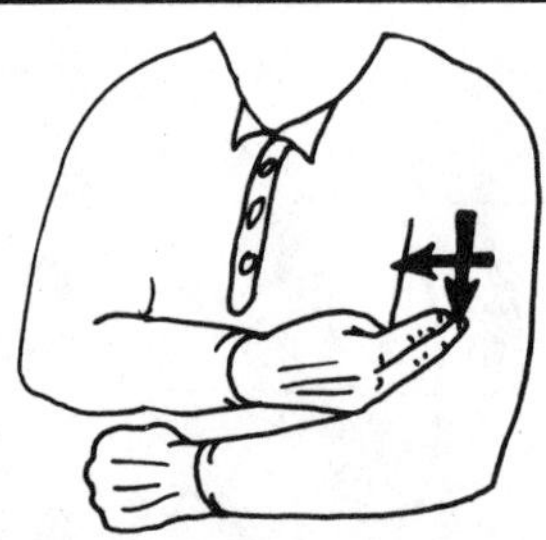

Arabic: mustáshfa مستشفى
Chinese: yīyuàn 醫院
Dutch: ziekenhuis
French: hôpital
German: Krankenhaus
Italian: ospedale
Japanese: byōin 病院
Korean: byŏngwŏn 병원
Portuguese: hospital
Russian: bol'nítsa больница
Spanish: hospital
Swedish: sjukhus

1040. hot [adj.]

Arabic: sákhen ساخن
Chinese: rède 熱的
Dutch: heet
French: très chaud
German: heiß
Italian: caldo
Japanese: atsui 熱い
Korean: dŏun 더운
Portuguese: quente
Russian: goryáchiy горячий
Spanish: caliente
Swedish: het

1041. hotel [n.]

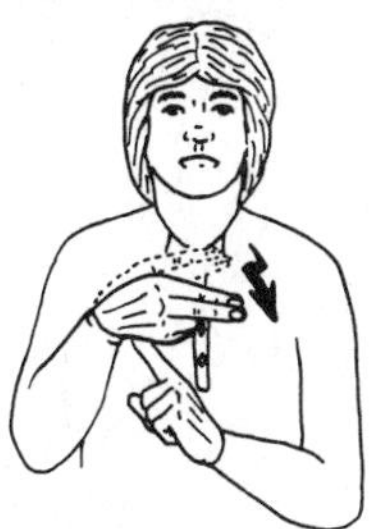

Arabic: fúnduq فندق
Chinese: lǚguǎn 旅舘
Dutch: hotel
French: hôtel
German: Hotel
Italian: albergo
Japanese: hoteru ホテル
Korean: hot'el 호텔
Portuguese: hotel
Russian: gostínitsa гостиница
Spanish: hotel
Swedish: hotell

1042. hour [n.]

Arabic: sáa ساعة
Chinese: xiǎoshí 小時
Dutch: uur
French: heure
German: Stunde
Italian: ora
Japanese: jikan 時間
Korean: shigan 시간
Portuguese: hora
Russian: chas час
Spanish: hora
Swedish: timme

1043. house [n.]

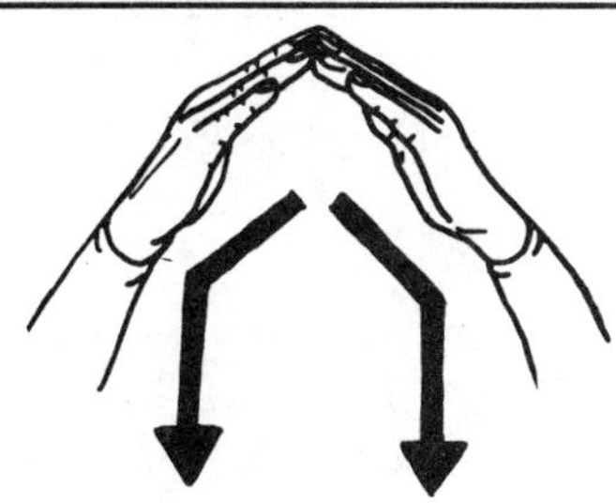

Arabic: beyt بيت
Chinese: fángzi 房子
Dutch: huis
French: maison
German: Haus
Italian: casa
Japanese: uchi 家
Korean: jib 집
Portuguese: casa
Russian: dom дом
Spanish: casa
Swedish: hus

1044. how [adv.]

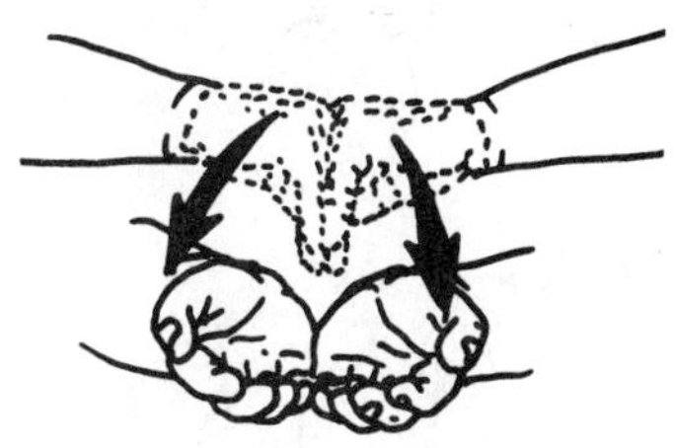

Arabic: kéifa كيف
Chinese: rúhé 如何
Dutch: hoe
French: comment
German: wie
Italian: come
Japanese: dō yatte どうやって
Korean: ŏttŏk'e 어떻게
Portuguese: como
Russian: kak как
Spanish: cómo
Swedish: hur

1045. however [adv./conj.]

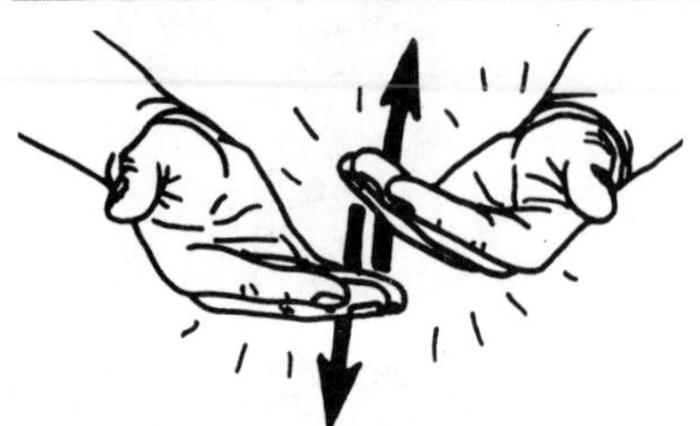

Arabic: áala éyeti hal على اية حال
Chinese: wúlùn rúhé 無論如何
Dutch: echter
French: cependant
German: jedoch
Italian: eppure
Japanese: shikashi-nagara しかしながら
Korean: amuri...haedo 아무리 해도
Portuguese: contudo
Russian: odnáko однако
Spanish: sin embargo
Swedish: emellertid

1046. how many/much? [interr.]

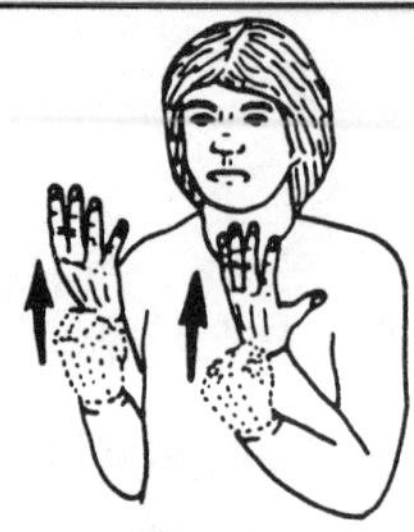

Arabic: kam كم
Chinese: duōshǎo 多少
Dutch: hoeveel
French: combien
German: wie viele/viel
Italian: quanto
Japanese: ikura いくら
Korean: ǒlma 얼마
Portuguese: quanto
Russian: skól'ko сколько
Spanish: cuánto
Swedish: hur många/mycket

1047. huge [adj.]

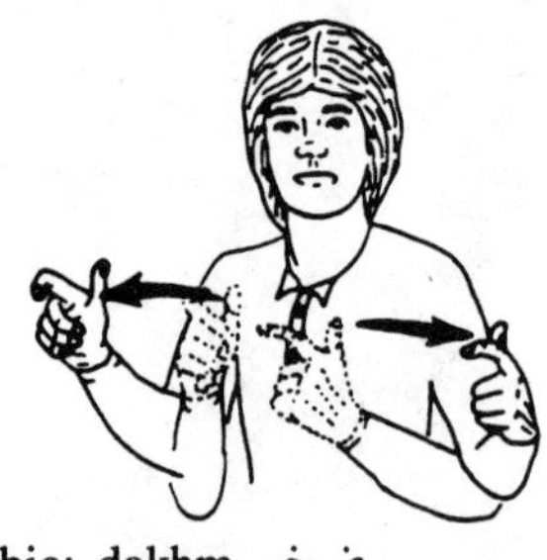

Arabic: dakhm ضخم
Chinese: jùdà 巨大
Dutch: reusachtig
French: énorme
German: riesig
Italian: enorme
Japanese: kyodai na 巨大な
Korean: gǒdaehan 거대한
Portuguese: enorme
Russian: ogrómnyy огромный
Spanish: enorme
Swedish: väldig

1048. human (being) [n.]

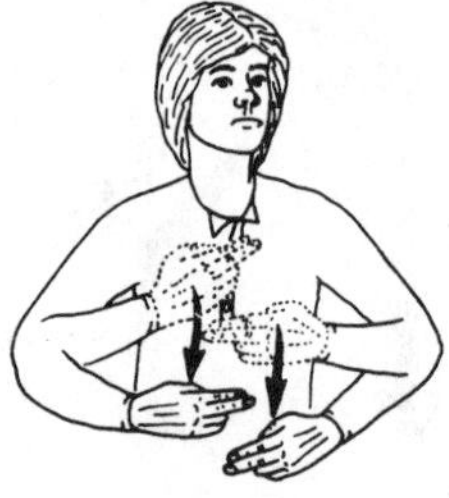

Arabic: insán انسان
Chinese: rénlèi 人類
Dutch: mens
French: être humain
German: Mensch
Italian: essere umano
Japanese: ningen 人間
Korean: ingan 인간
Portuguese: ser humano
Russian: chelovék человек
Spanish: ser humano
Swedish: människa

1049. humanity (mankind) [n.]

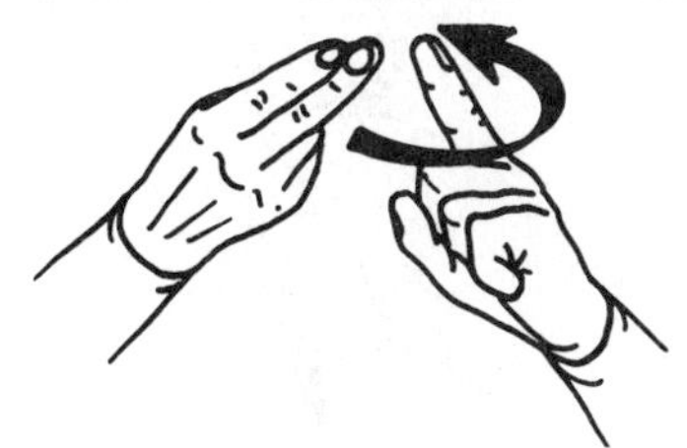

Arabic: insanía انسانية
Chinese: rénxìng 人性
Dutch: mensheid
French: humanité
German: Menschheit
Italian: umanità
Japanese: ningen sei 人間性
Korean: ingansŏng 인간성
Portuguese: humanidade
Russian: chelovéchestvo человечество
Spanish: humanidad
Swedish: mänsklighet

1050. humble [adj.]

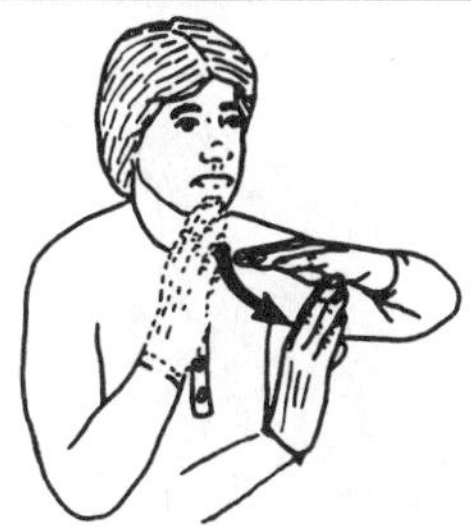

Arabic: mutawádea' متواضع
Chinese: qiānxūde 謙虛
Dutch: nederig
French: humble
German: demütig
Italian: umile
Japanese: kenson na 謙遜な
Korean: gyŏmsonhan 겸손한
Portuguese: humilde
Russian: pokórnyy покорный
Spanish: humilde
Swedish: ödmjuk

1051. humor [n.]

Arabic: fukáha فكاهة
Chinese: yōumò 幽默
Dutch: humor
French: humour
German: Humor
Italian: umore
Japanese: yūmoa ユーモア
Korean: yumŏ 유머
Portuguese: humor
Russian: yúmor юмор
Spanish: humor
Swedish: humör

1052. hundred [adh.]

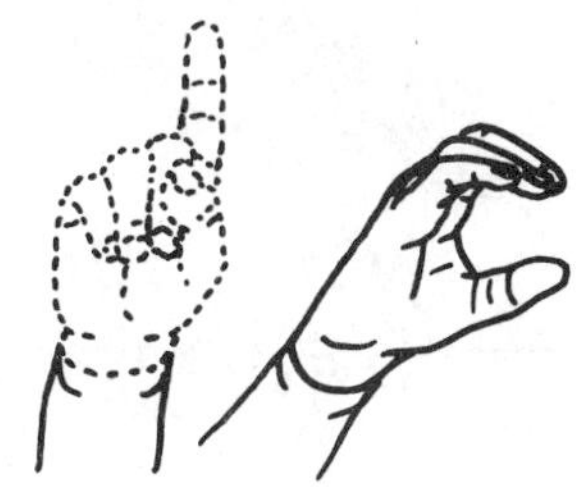

Arabic: mé'a مئة
Chinese: bǎi 百
Dutch: honderd
French: cent
German: hundert
Italian: centro
Japanese: hyaku 百
Korean: baeg 백
Portuguese: cem
Russian: sto сто
Spanish: ciento
Swedish: hundra

1053. Hungary [n.]

Arabic: hanghária هنغاريا
Chinese: xiōngyálì 匈牙利
Dutch: Hongarije
French: Hongrie
German: Ungarn
Italian: Ungheria
Japanese: Hangarii ハンガリー
Korean: Hŏnggari 항가리
Portuguese: Hungria
Russian: Véngriya Венгрия
Spanish: Hungría
Swedish: Ungern

1054. hunger [n.]

Arabic: júa' جوع
Chinese: jī-è 饑餓
Dutch: honger
French: faim
German: Hunger
Italian: fame
Japanese: kūfuku 空腹
Korean: gumjurim 굶주림
Portuguese: fome
Russian: gólod голод
Spanish: hambre
Swedish: hunger

1055. hunting [n.]

Arabic: sáyed صيد
Chinese: dăliè 打獵
Dutch: jacht
French: chasse
German: Jagen
Italian: caccia
Japanese: shuryō 狩猟
Korean: sanyang 사냥
Portuguese: caça
Russian: okhóta охота
Spanish: caza
Swedish: jakt

1056. hurry [v.]

Arabic: ásraa اسرع
Chinese: gănkuài 趕快
Dutch: zich haasten
French: se hâter
German: sich beeilen
Italian: affrettarsi
Japanese: isogu 急ぐ
Korean: sŏdurŭda 서두르다
Portuguese: apressar-se
Russian: toropít'sya торопиться
Spanish: apresurarse
Swedish: skynda sig

1057. hurt (ache) [v.]

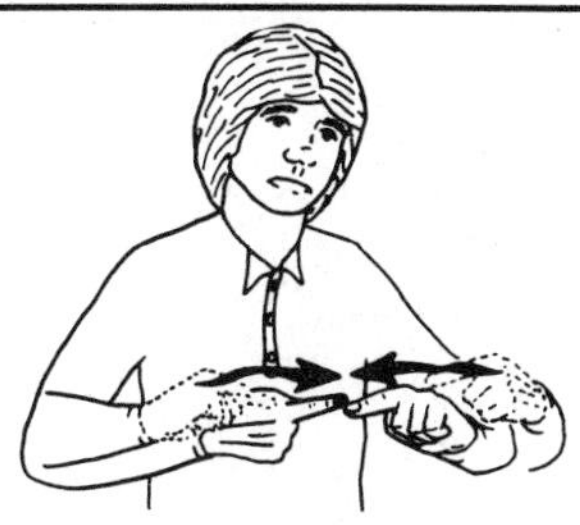

Arabic: álama آلم
Chinese: shānghài 傷害
Dutch: pijn doen
French: faire mal
German: schmerzen
Italian: dolere
Japanese: . . . o kizutsukeru
…を傷つける
Korean: ap'ŭda 아프다
Portuguese: doer
Russian: bolét' болеть
Spanish: doler
Swedish: värka

1058. husband [n.]

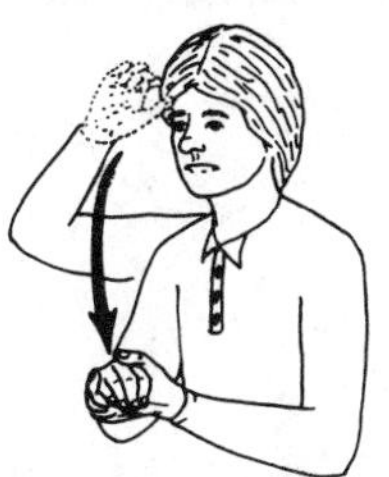

Arabic: zauj زوج
Chinese: zhàngfū 丈夫
Dutch: echtgenoot
French: époux
German: Ehemann
Italian: marito
Japanese: otto 夫
Korean: namp'yŏn 남편
Portuguese: marido
Russian: muzh муж
Spanish: esposo
Swedish: äkta man

1059. I [pron.]

Arabic: ána انا
Chinese: wǒ 我
Dutch: ik
French: je
German: ich
Italian: io
Japanese: watashi wa 私は
Korean: na 나
Portuguese: eu
Russian: ya я
Spanish: yo
Swedish: jag

1060. ice [n.]

Arabic: thalj ثلج
Chinese: bīng 冰
Dutch: ijs
French: glace
German: Eis
Italian: ghiaccio
Japanese: kōri 氷
Korean: ŏrŭm 어름
Portuguese: gelo
Russian: lyód лёд
Spanish: hielo
Swedish: is

1061. ice cream [n.]

Arabic: jeláti جيلاتي
Chinese: bīngqílín 冰淇淋
Dutch: roomijs
French: glace
German: Eiskreme
Italian: gelato
Japanese: aisukuriimu アイスクリーム
Korean: aisŭk'ŭrim 아이스크림
Portuguese: sorvete
Russian: morózhenoye мороженое
Spanish: helado
Swedish: glass

1062. idea [n.]

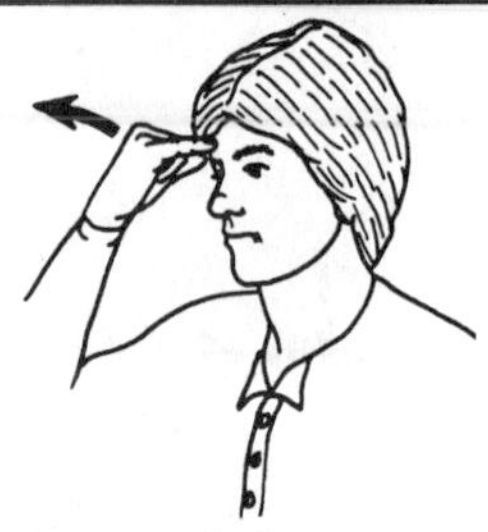

Arabic: fíkra فكرة
Chinese: zhŭyì 主意
Dutch: idee
French: idée
German: Idee
Italian: idea
Japanese: kangae 考え
Korean: ŭigyŏn 의견
Portuguese: idéia
Russian: idéya идея
Spanish: idea
Swedish: idé

1063. idle (inactive) [adj.]

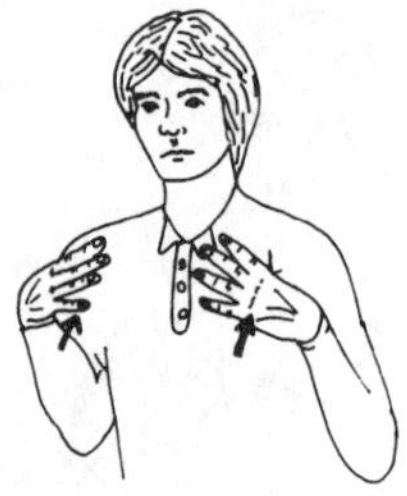

Arabic: áatel áan al-áamal
عاطل عن العمل
Chinese: kòngxiánde 空閒的
Dutch: nietsdoend
French: oisif
German: müßig
Italian: ozioso
Japanese: hima na 暇な
Korean: geŭrŭn 게으른
Portuguese: ocioso
Russian: nezányatyy незанятый
Spanish: ocioso
Swedish: overksam

1064. if [conj.]

Arabic: low لو
Chinese: rúguŏ 假如
Dutch: indien
French: si
German: wenn
Italian: se
Japanese: moshi . . . naraba
もし‥ならば
Korean: manyage 만약에
Portuguese: se
Russian: yésli если
Spanish: si
Swedish: om

1065. ignorant [adj.]

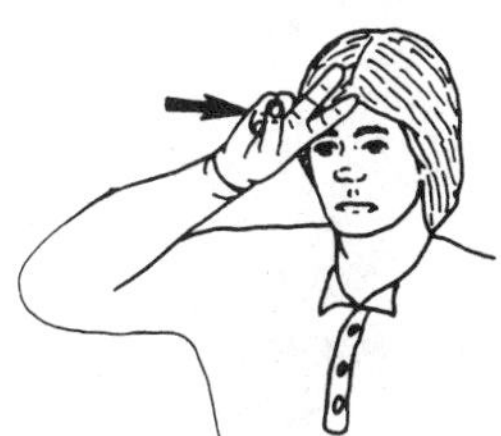

Arabic: jáhel جاهل
Chinese: wúzhīde 無知的
Dutch: onwetend
French: ignorant
German: unwissend
Italian: ignorante
Japanese: muchina 無知な
Korean: mushik'han 무식한
Portuguese: ignorante
Russian: nevézhestvennyy невежественный
Spanish: ignorante
Swedish: okunnig

1066. illegal [adj.]

Arabic: ghér qanúni غير قانوني
Chinese: fēifǎ 非法
Dutch: onwettelijk
French: illégal
German: ungesetzlich
Italian: illegale
Japanese: fuho no 不法の
Korean: bulbŏbŭi 불법의
Portuguese: ilegal
Russian: nezakónnyy незаконный
Spanish: ilegal
Swedish: olaglig

1067. illness [n.]

Arabic: márad مرض
Chinese: jíbìng 疾病
Dutch: ziekte
French: maladie
German: Krankheit
Italian: malattia
Japanese: byōki 病気
Korean: byŏng 병
Portuguese: doença
Russian: bolézn' болезнь
Spanish: enfermedad
Swedish: sjukdom

1068. image [n.]

Arabic: súrra صورة
Chinese: yǐngxiàng 影像
Dutch: beeld
French: image
German: Bild
Italian: immagine
Japanese: imēji イメージ
Korean: moyang 모양
Portuguese: imagem
Russian: óbraz образ
Spanish: imagen
Swedish: bild

1069. imagination [n.]

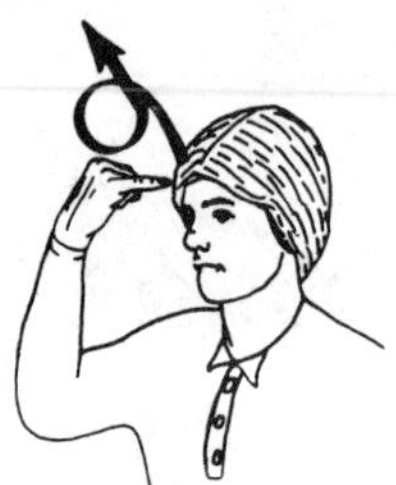

Arabic: kheyál خيال
Chinese: xiǎngxiàng 想像
Dutch: verbeelding
French: imagination
German: Einbildung
Italian: immaginazione
Japanese: sōzō 想像
Korean: sangsang 상상
Portuguese: imaginação
Russian: voobrazhéniye воображение
Spanish: imaginación
Swedish: inbillning

1070. imitate [v.]

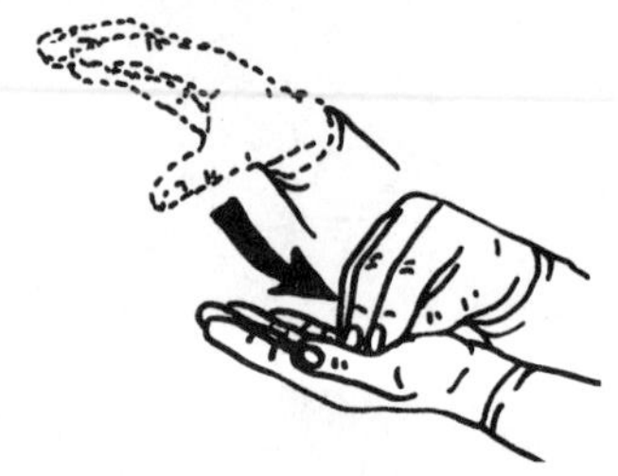

Arabic: qállada قلد
Chinese: mófǎng 摹仿
Dutch: nadoen
French: imiter
German: nachahmen
Italian: imitare
Japanese: maneru をまねる
Korean: mobanghada 모방하다
Portuguese: imitar
Russian: podrazhát' подражать
Spanish: imitar
Swedish: imitera

1071. immediate [adj.]

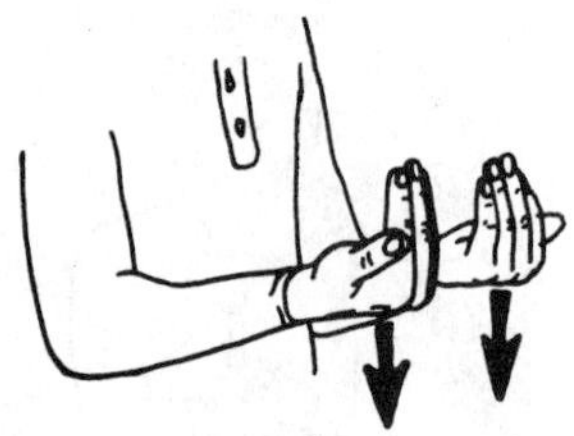

Arabic: háli حالي
Chinese: lìjíde 立即的
Dutch: naaste
French: immédiat
German: unverzüglich
Italian: immediato
Japanese: sokuza no 即座の
Korean: jikjŏbŭi 직접의
Portuguese: imediato
Russian: neposrédstvennyy непосредственный
Spanish: inmediato
Swedish: omedelbar

1072. immediately [adv.]

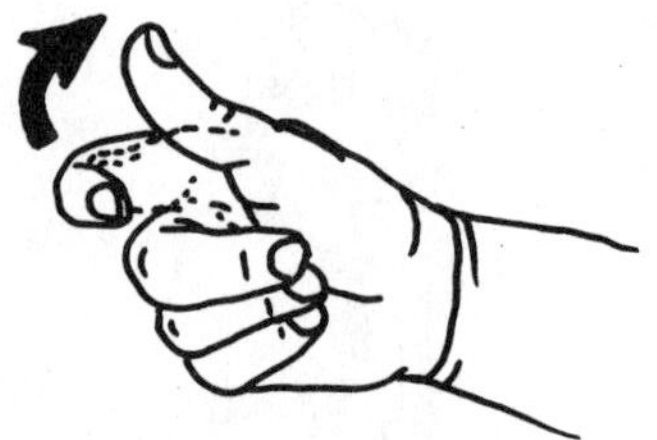

Arabic: hálan حالاً
Chinese: lìkè 立刻
Dutch: onmiddelijk
French: immédiatement
German: sofort
Italian: immediatamente
Japanese: suguni すぐい
Korean: jikjŏb 직접
Portuguese: imediatamente
Russian: neposrédstvenno непосредственно
Spanish: inmediatamente
Swedish: genast

1073. important [adj.]

Arabic: muhím مهم
Chinese: zhòngyàode 重要的
Dutch: belangrijk
French: important
German: wichtig
Italian: importante
Japanese: jūyo na 重要な
Korean: jungyohan 중요한
Portuguese: importante
Russian: vázhnyy важный
Spanish: importante
Swedish: viktig

1074. impossible [adj.]

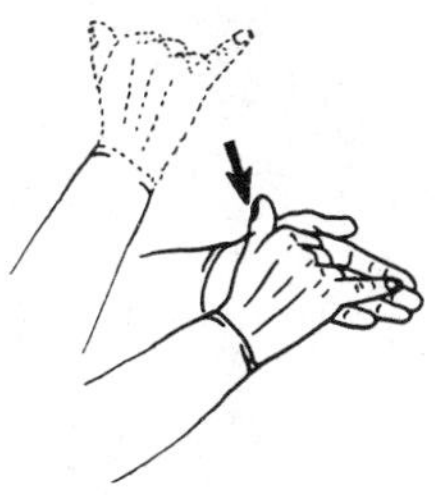

Arabic: mustahíl مستحيل
Chinese: bù kěnéng de 不可能的
Dutch: onmogelijk
French: impossible
German: unmöglich
Italian: impossible
Japanese: fukanō na 不可能な
Korean: bulganŭnghan 불가능한
Portuguese: impossível
Russian: nevozmózhnyy невозможный
Spanish: imposible
Swedish: omöjlig

1075. impression [n.]

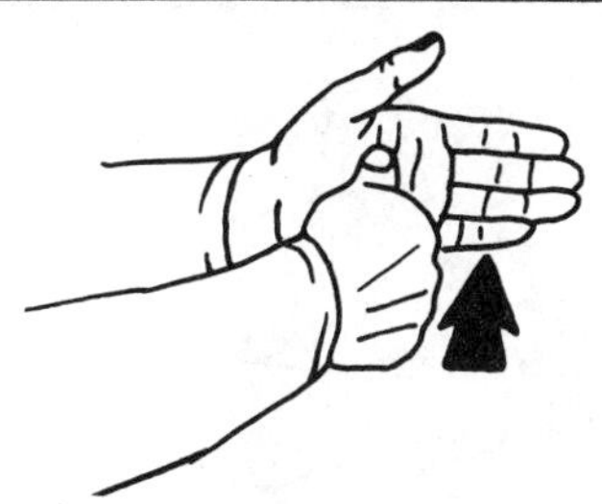

Arabic: intibaa انطباع
Chinese: yìnxiàng 印象
Dutch: indruk
French: impression
German: Eindruck
Italian: impressione
Japanese: inshō 印象
Korean: insang 인상
Portuguese: impressão
Russian: vpechatléniye впечатление
Spanish: impresión
Swedish: intryck

1076. improve [v.]

Arabic: hássana حسن
Chinese: gǎijìn 改進
Dutch: verbeteren
French: améliorer
German: verbessern
Italian: migliorare
Japanese: kaizen suru 改善する
Korean: kaeryanghada 개량하다
Portuguese: melhorar
Russian: uluchshát' улучшать
Spanish: mejorar
Swedish: förbättra

1077. in [adv./prep.]

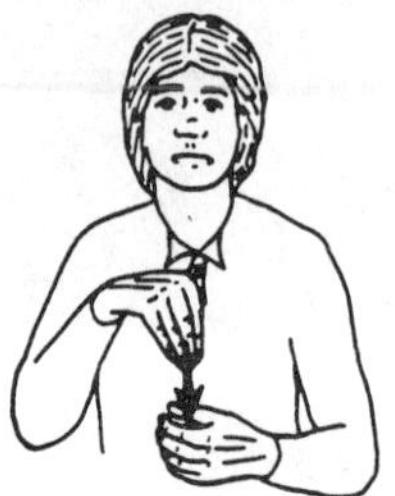

Arabic: fi في
Chinese: zài...lǐmiàn 在…裏面
Dutch: in
French: en
German: in/im
Italian: in
Japanese: ...no naka ni …の中に
Korean: an'e 안의
Portuguese: em
Russian: v/na в/на
Spanish: en
Swedish: in/i/på

1078. inch [n.]

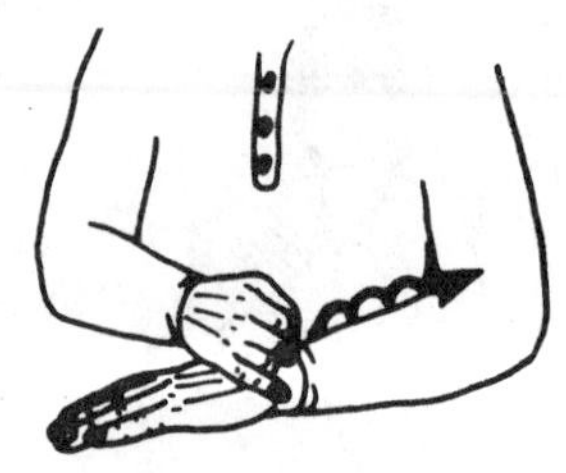

Arabic: búsa بوصة
Chinese: yīngcùn 吋
Dutch: engelse duim
French: pouce
German: Zoll
Italian: pollice
Japanese: inchi インチ
Korean: inch'i 인치
Portuguese: polegada
Russian: dyúym дюйм
Spanish: pulgada
Swedish: tum

1079. include [v.]

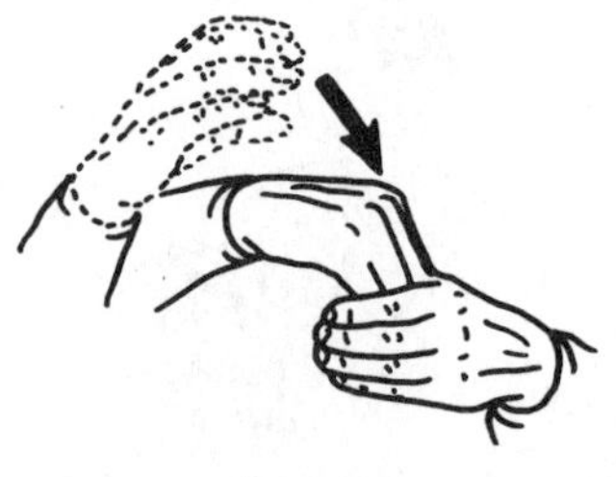

Arabic: tadhámmana تضمن
Chinese: bāoguā 包括
Dutch: insluiten
French: inclure
German: einschließen
Italian: includere
Japanese: ...o fukumu …を含む
Korean: p'ohamhada 포함하다
Portuguese: incluir
Russian: vklyuchát' включать
Spanish: incluir
Swedish: omfatta

1080. income [n.]

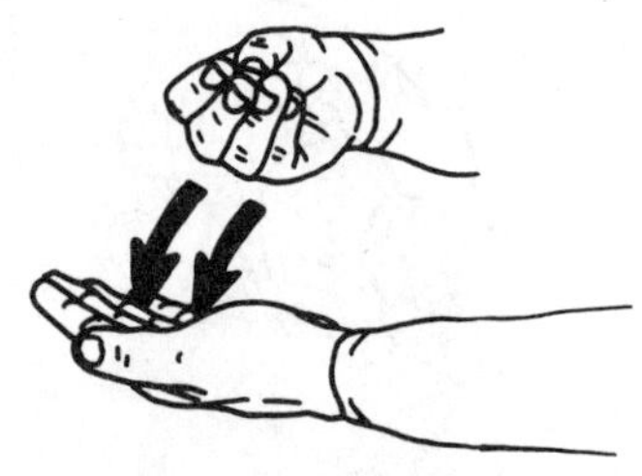

Arabic: dakhl دخل
Chinese: shōurù 收入
Dutch: inkomen
French: revenu
German: Einkommen
Italian: reddito
Japanese: shūnyū 収入（年間）
Korean: suib 수입
Portuguese: renda
Russian: dokhód доход
Spanish: ingresos
Swedish: inkomst

1081. increase [v.]

Arabic: záda زاد
Chinese: zēngjiā 增加
Dutch: toenemen
French: augmenter
German: vermehren
Italian: aumentare
Japanese: fueru 増える
Korean: nŭllida 늘리다
Portuguese: aumentar
Russian: uvelíchivat' увеличивать
Spanish: aumentar
Swedish: öka

1082. indeed [adv.]

Arabic: sahíh صحيح
Chinese: díquè 的確
Dutch: inderdaad
French: vraiment
German: in der Tat
Italian: veramente
Japanese: mattaku 全く
Korean: ch'amŭro 참으로
Portuguese: realmente
Russian: deystvítel'no действительно
Spanish: verdaderamente
Swedish: verkligen

1083. independence [n.]

Arabic: istiqlál استقلال
Chinese: dúlì 獨立
Dutch: onafhankelijkheid
French: indépendance
German: Unabhängigkeit
Italian: indipendenza
Japanese: dokuritsu 独立
Korean: dongnib 독립
Portuguese: independência
Russian: nezavísimost' независимость
Spanish: independencia
Swedish: självständighet

1084. India [n.]

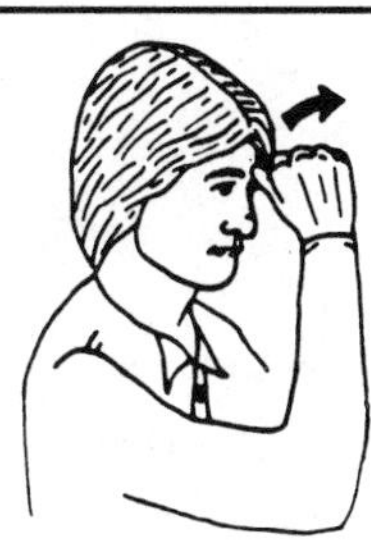

Arabic: al-hínd الهند
Chinese: yìndù 印度
Dutch: India
French: Inde
German: Indien
Italian: India
Japanese: Indo インド
Korean: Indo 인도
Portuguese: India
Russian: Índiya Индия
Spanish: India
Swedish: Indien

1085. indicate [v.]

Arabic: dálla دل
Chinese: zhǐshì 指示
Dutch: aanduiden
French: indiquer
German: anzeigen
Italian: indicare
Japanese: shimesu 示す
Korean: jijŏg'hada 지적하다
Portuguese: indicar
Russian: ukázyvat' указывать
Spanish: indicar
Swedish: visa

1086. indifference [n.]

Arabic: áadam ahamía عدم اهمية
Chinese: lěngdàn 冷淡
Dutch: onverschilligheid
French: indifférence
German: Gleichgültigkeit
Italian: indifferenza
Japanese: mukanshin 無関心
Korean: mugwanshim 무관심
Portuguese: indiferença
Russian: ravnodúshiye равнодушие
Spanish: indiferencia
Swedish: likgiltighet

1087. influence [n.]

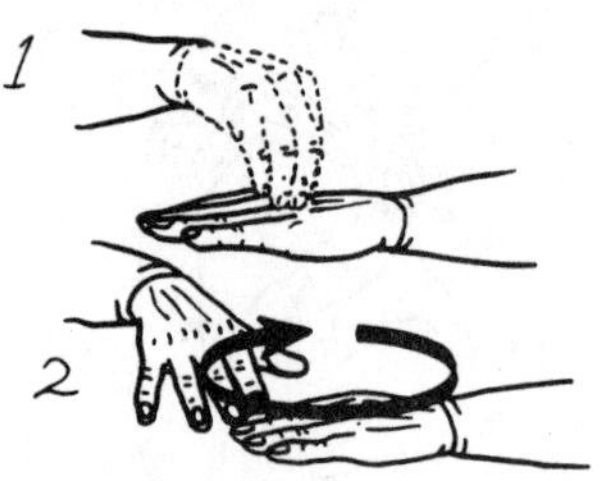

Arabic: ta'thír تأثير
Chinese: yǐngxiǎng 影響
Dutch: invloed
French: influence
German: Einfluß
Italian: influenza
Japanese: eikyō 影響
Korean: yŏnghyang 영향
Portuguese: influência
Russian: vliyániye влияние
Spanish: influencia
Swedish: inflytande

1088. inform [v.]

Arabic: ákhbara اخبر
Chinese: tōngzhī 通知
Dutch: informeren
French: informer
German: benachrichtigen
Italian: informare
Japanese: shiraseru 知らせる
Korean: allida 알리다
Portuguese: informar
Russian: informírovat' информировать
Spanish: informar
Swedish: informera

1089. information [n.]

Arabic: maalumát معلومات
Chinese: xiāoxí 消息
Dutch: informatie
French: information
German: Information
Italian: informazione
Japanese: jōhō 情報
Korean: jŏngbo 정보
Portuguese: informação
Russian: informátsiya информация
Spanish: información
Swedish: information

1090. inheritance [n.]

Arabic: irth ارث
Chinese: yíchăn 遺產
Dutch: erfenis
French: héritage
German: Erbschaft
Italian: eredità
Japanese: sōzoku zaisan 相続財産
Korean: sangsok 상속
Portuguese: herança
Russian: naslédstvo наследство
Spanish: herencia
Swedish: arv

1091. injection (medical) [n.]

Arabic: haqn حقن
Chinese: zhùshè 注射
Dutch: injectie
French: piqûre
German: Injektion
Italian: iniezione
Japanese: chūsha 注射
Korean: jusa 주사
Portuguese: injeção
Russian: in"yéktsiya инъекция
Spanish: inyección
Swedish: injektion

1092. injure [v.]

Arabic: járaha جرح
Chinese: shānghài 傷害
Dutch: kwetsen
French: blesser
German: verletzen
Italian: ferire
Japanese: kegasaseru 怪我させる
Korean: tach'ida 다치다
Portuguese: ferir
Russian: povrezhdát' повреждать
Spanish: herir
Swedish: skada

1093. ink [n.]

Arabic: hebr حبر
Chinese: mòsŭi 墨水
Dutch: inkt
French: encre
German: Tinte
Italian: inchiostro
Japanese: inku インク
Korean: ingk'ŭ 잉크
Portuguese: tinta
Russian: cherníla чернила
Spanish: tinta
Swedish: bläck

1094. innocence [n.]

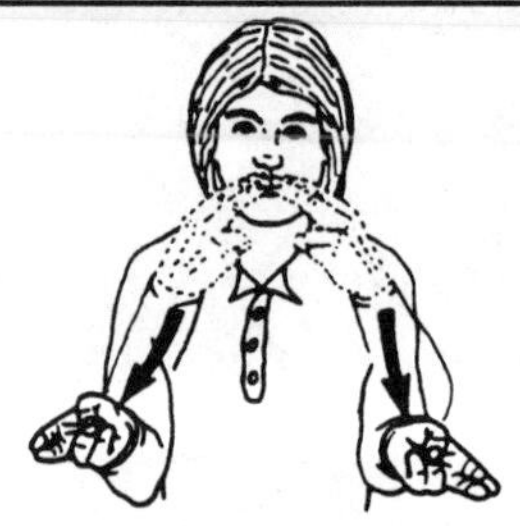

Arabic: bará'a (min al-jaríma) براءة (من الجريمة)
Chinese: tiānzhēn 天真
Dutch: onschuld
French: innocence
German: Unschuld
Italian: innocenza
Japanese: mujaki 無邪気
Korean: kyŏlbaeg 결백
Portuguese: inocência
Russian: nevinóvnost' невиновность
Spanish: inocencia
Swedish: oskuld

1095. insect [n.]

Arabic: háshara حشرة
Chinese: chóng 蟲
Dutch: insect
French: insecte
German: Insekt
Italian: insetto
Japanese: konchū 昆虫
Korean: gonch'ung 곤충
Portuguese: inseto
Russian: nasekómoye насекомое
Spanish: insecto
Swedish: insekt

1096. inside (within) [adv./prep.]

Arabic: dákhil داخل
Chinese: zài nèibù 在内部
Dutch: binnen
French: dans
German: drinnen
Italian: dentro
Japanese: uchi ni 内に
Korean: naebuŭi 내부의
Portuguese: dentro
Russian: vnutrí внутри
Spanish: dentro
Swedish: inuti

1097. insist [v.]

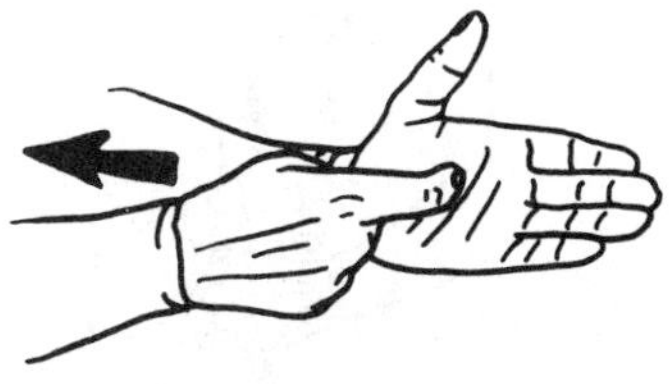

Arabic: asára áala اصر على
Chinese: jiānchí 堅持
Dutch: aandringen
French: insister
German: bestehen auf
Italian: insistere
Japanese: shuchō suru 強く主張する
Korean: chujanghada 주장하다
Portuguese: insistir
Russian: nastáivat' настаивать
Spanish: insistir
Swedish: insistera

1098. inspect [v.]

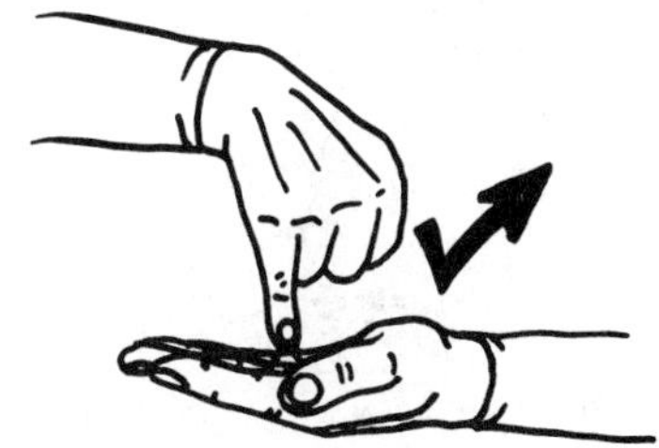

Arabic: fáhasa فحص
Chinese: jiǎnyàn 檢驗
Dutch: inspecteren
French: inspecter
German: inspizieren
Italian: ispezionare
Japanese: kensa suru 検査する
Korean: gǒmsahada 검사하다
Portuguese: inspecionar
Russian: osmátrivat' осматривать
Spanish: inspeccionar
Swedish: inspektera

1099. inspiration [n.]

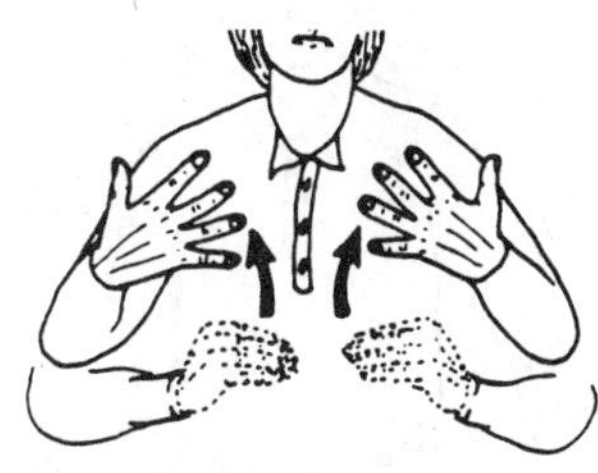

Arabic: ilhám الهام
Chinese: línggǎn 靈感
Dutch: inspiratie
French: inspiration
German: Inspiration
Italian: ispirazione
Japanese: reikan 霊感
Korean: yǒnggam 영감
Portuguese: inspiração
Russian: vdokhnovéniye вдохновение
Spanish: inspiración
Swedish: inspiration

1100. install [v.]

Arabic: rákkaba ركب
Chinese: zhuāng 裝
Dutch: installeren
French: installer
German: installieren
Italian: installare
Japanese: suetsukeru 据えつける
Korean: jangch'ihada 장치하다
Portuguese: instalar
Russian: ustanávlivat' устанавливать
Spanish: instalar
Swedish: installera

1101. instead (of) [prep.]

Arabic: bádalan min بدلاً من
Chinese: dàitì 代替
Dutch: in plaats van
French: au lieu de
German: anstatt
Italian: in luogo di
Japanese: . . . no kawari ni …の代りに
Korean: daeshin e 대신에
Portuguese: em vez de
Russian: vmésto вместо
Spanish: en vez de
Swedish: i stället för

1102. institute [n.]

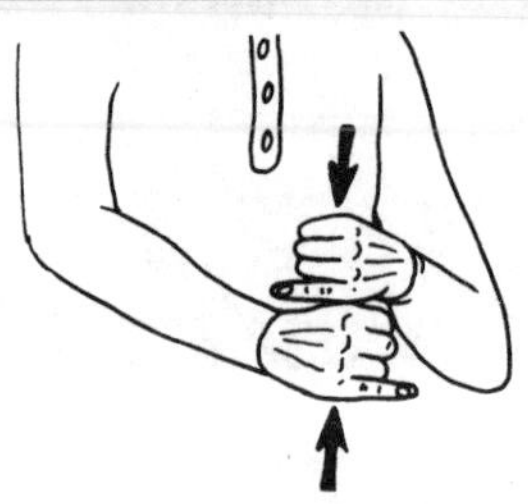

Arabic: máahad معهد
Chinese: jīgòu 機構
Dutch: instituut
French: institut
German: Institut
Italian: istituto
Japanese: gakkai 学会
Korean: hakhoe 학회
Portuguese: instituto
Russian: institút институт
Spanish: instituto
Swedish: institut

1103. instruct (teach) [v.]

Arabic: dárasa درس
Chinese: jiãodăo 教導
Dutch: onderrichten
French: instruire
German: unterrichten
Italian: istruire
Japanese: oshieru 教える
Korean: garŭch'ida 가르치다
Portuguese: instruir
Russian: obuchát' обучать
Spanish: instruir
Swedish: instruera

1104. instrument (tool) [n.]

Arabic: jiház جهاز
Chinese: yíqì 儀器
Dutch: instrument
French: instrument
German: Instrument
Italian: strumento
Japanese: dōgu 道具
Korean: kigu 기구
Portuguese: instrumento
Russian: instrumént инструмент
Spanish: instrumento
Swedish: instrument

1105. insult [n.]

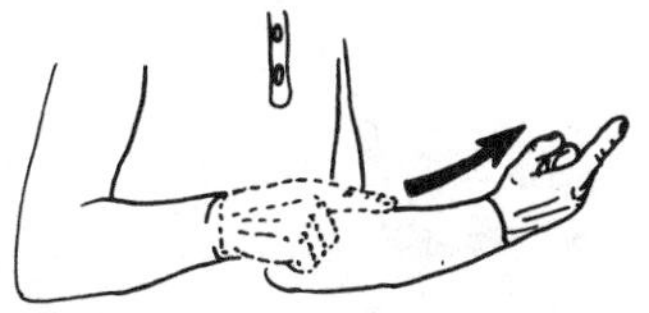

Arabic: ehtiqár احتقار
Chinese: wŭrŭ 侮辱
Dutch: belediging
French: insulte
German: Beleidigung
Italian: insulto
Japanese: bujoku 侮辱
Korean: moyog 모욕
Portuguese: insulto
Russian: oskorbléniye оскорбление
Spanish: insulto
Swedish: förolämpning

1106. insurance [n.]

Arabic: ta'mín تأمين
Chinese: băoxiăn 保險
Dutch: verzekering
French: assurance
German: Versicherung
Italian: assicurazione
Japanese: hoken 保険
Korean: bohŏm 보험
Portuguese: seguro
Russian: strakhovániye страхование
Spanish: seguro
Swedish: försäkring

1107. intelligent [adj.]

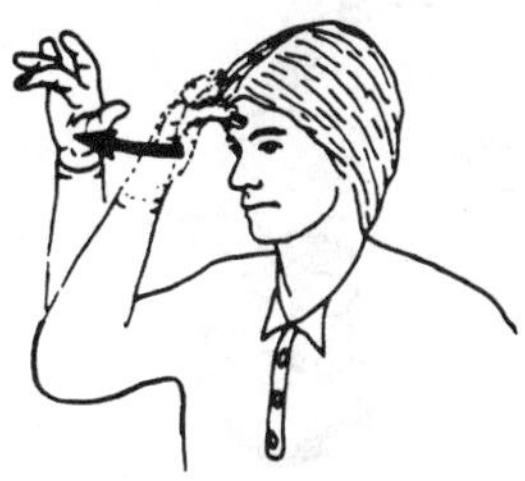

Arabic: dháki ذكي
Chinese: cōngmíng 聰明
Dutch: intelligent
French: intelligent
German: intelligent
Italian: intelligente
Japanese: chinō ga takai 知能が高い
Korean: jichŏgin 지적인
Portuguese: inteligente
Russian: úmnyy умный
Spanish: inteligente
Swedish: intelligent

1108. intend [v.]

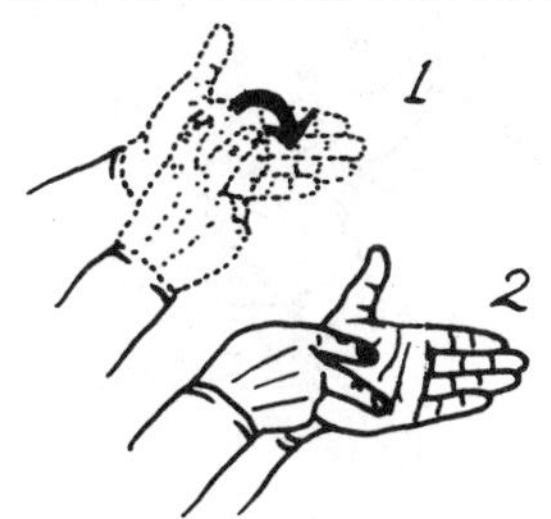

Arabic: náwa نوى
Chinese: dăsuàn 打算
Dutch: van plan zijn
French: avoir l'intention de
German: beabsichtigen
Italian: intendere
Japanese: . . .suru tsumori de aru …するつもりである
Korean: . . .hal jagchŏngida 할 작정이다
Portuguese: intencionar
Russian: namerevát'sya намереваться
Spanish: tener intención de
Swedish: ämna

1109. intensity [n.]

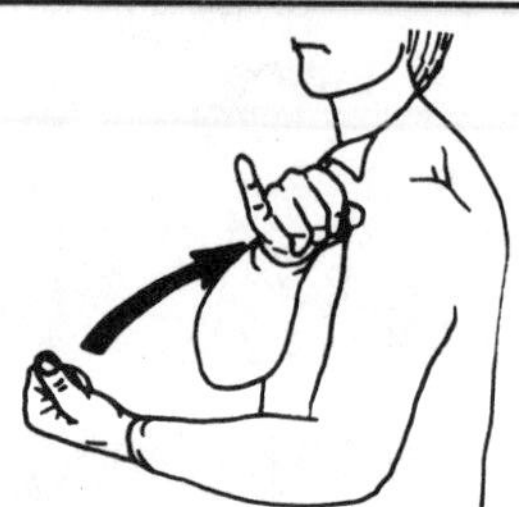

Arabic: shídda شدة
Chinese: qiángdù 強度
Dutch: intensiteit
French: intensité
German: Intensität
Italian: intensità
Japanese: kyōretsu 強烈
Korean: kyŏkryŏl 격렬
Portuguese: intensidade
Russian: intensívnost' интенсивность
Spanish: intensidad
Swedish: intensitet

1110. interest [n.]

Arabic: máslaha مصلحة
Chinese: xìngqù 興趣
Dutch: interesse
French: intérêt
German: Interesse
Italian: interesse
Japanese: kyōmi 興味
Korean: hŭngmi 흥미
Portuguese: interêsse
Russian: interés интерес
Spanish: interés
Swedish: intresse

1111. interfere [v.]

Arabic: tadákhkhala تدخل
Chinese: gānshè 干涉
Dutch: tussenbeide komen
French: intervenir
German: eingreifen
Italian: interferire
Japanese: jamasuru 邪魔する
Korean: gansŏb'hada 간섭하다
Portuguese: interferir
Russian: vméshivat'sya вмешиваться
Spanish: interferir
Swedish: ingripa

1112. international [adj.]

Arabic: dáuli دولي
Chinese: guójìde 國際的
Dutch: internationaal
French: international
German: international
Italian: internazionale
Japanese: kokusaiteki na 国際的な
Korean: gukjejŏgin 국제적인
Portuguese: internacional
Russian: mezhdunaródnyy международный
Spanish: internacional
Swedish: internationell

1113. interpret [v.]

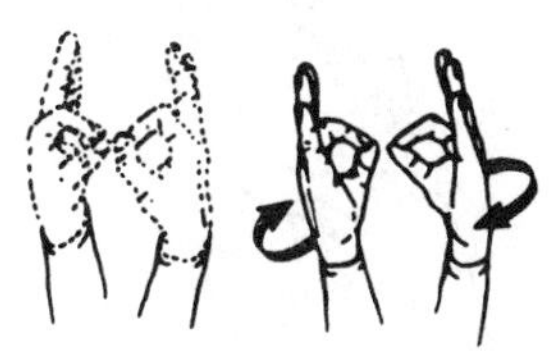

Arabic: tárjama ترجم
Chinese: fānyì 翻譯
Dutch: interpreteren
French: interpréter
German: interpretieren
Italian: interpretare
Japanese: tsūyaku o suru 通訳をする
Korean: t'ongyŏg'hada 통역하다
Portuguese: interpretar
Russian: perevodít' переводить
Spanish: interpretar
Swedish: tolka

1114. interrupt [v.]

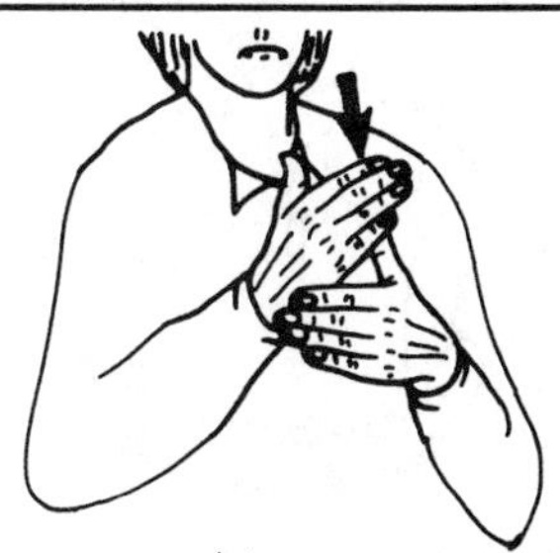

Arabic: qátaa قاطع
Chinese: zhōngduàn 中斷
Dutch: onderbreken
French: interrompre
German: unterbrechen
Italian: interrompere
Japanese: jamasuru 邪魔する
Korean: banghaehada 방해하다
Portuguese: interromper
Russian: preryvát' прерывать
Spanish: interrumpir
Swedish: avbryta

1115. interval [n.]

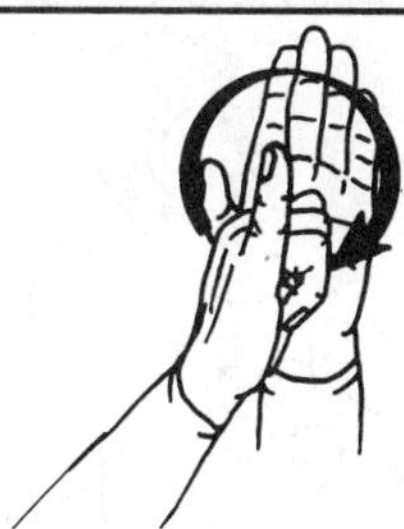

Arabic: fátra فترة
Chinese: jiàngé 間隔
Dutch: interval
French: intervalle
German: Interval
Italian: intervallo
Japanese: kankaku 間隔
Korean: gangyŏg 간격
Portuguese: intervalo
Russian: intervál интервал
Spanish: intervalo
Swedish: intervall

1116. into [prep.]

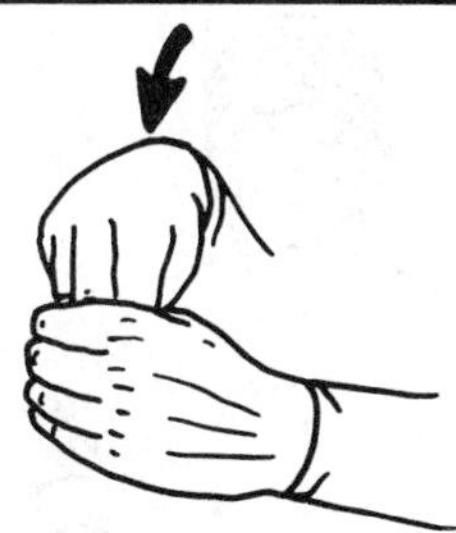

Arabic: fi في
Chinese: dào...lǐmiàn 到…裏面
Dutch: in
French: dans
German: hinein
Italian: in
Japanese: ...no naka e …の中へ
Korean: anŭro 안으로
Portuguese: dentro de
Russian: v/na в/на
Spanish: dentro de
Swedish: in i

1117. introduce [v.]

Arabic: qáddama قدم
Chinese: jièshào 介紹
Dutch: voorstellen
French: présenter
German: vorstellen
Italian: presentare
Japanese: shōkai suru 紹介する
Korean: sogaehada 소개하다
Portuguese: apresentar
Russian: predstavlyát' представлять
Spanish: presentar
Swedish: presentera

1118. invent [v.]

Arabic: ikhtaráa اخترع
Chinese: fāmíng 發明
Dutch: uitvinden
French: inventer
German: erfinden
Italian: inventare
Japanese: hatsumei suru 発明する
Korean: balmyŏnghada 발명하다
Portuguese: inventar
Russian: izobretát' изобретать
Spanish: inventar
Swedish: uppfinna

1119. investigate [v.]

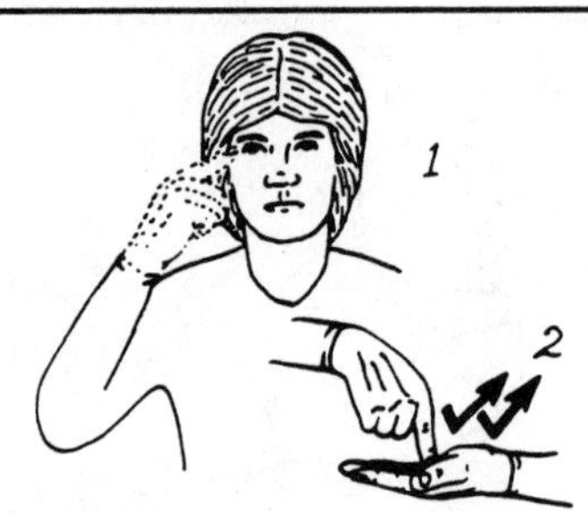

Arabic: báhatha بحث
Chinese: diàochá 調查
Dutch: onderzoeken
French: enquêter
German: untersuchen
Italian: investigare
Japanese: chōsa suru 調査する
Korean: josahada 조사하다
Portuguese: investigar
Russian: rasslédovat' расследовать
Spanish: investigar
Swedish: undersöka

1120. invite [v.]

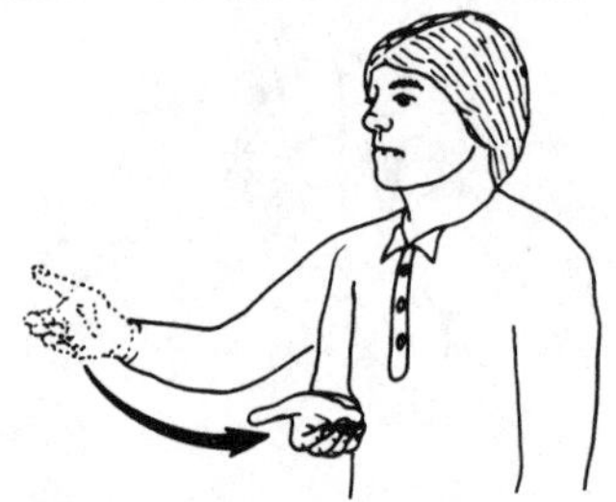

Arabic: dáa دعى
Chinese: yāoqǐ 邀請
Dutch: uitnodigen
French: inviter
German: einladen
Italian: invitare
Japanese: shōtai suru 招待する
Korean: ch'odaehada 초대하다
Portuguese: convidar
Russian: priglashát' приглашать
Spanish: invitar
Swedish: inbjuda

1121. involve [v.]

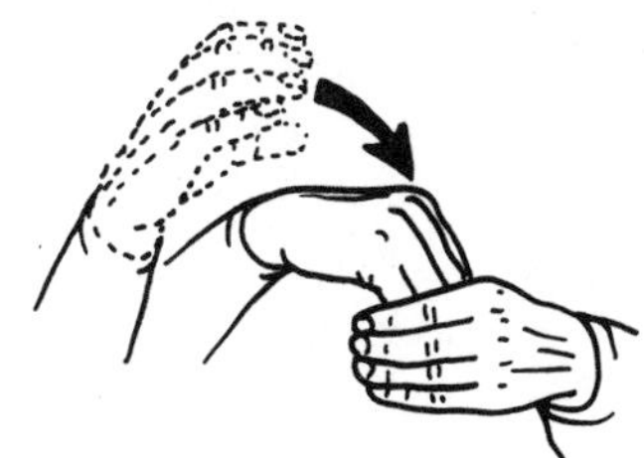

Arabic: tadhámmana تضمن
Chinese: bāohán 包含
Dutch: betrekken
French: impliquer
German: verwickeln
Italian: coinvolgere
Japanese: makikomu 巻きこむ
Korean: gwanyŏhada 광여하다
Portuguese: envolver
Russian: vovlekát' вовлекать
Spanish: envolver
Swedish: inveckla

1122. Iran [n.]

Arabic: irán ايران
Chinese: yīlăng 伊朗
Dutch: Iran
French: Iran
German: Iran
Italian: Iran
Japanese: Iran イラン
Korean: Iran 이란
Portuguese: Irã
Russian: Irán Иран
Spanish: Irán
Swedish: Iran

1123. Ireland [n.]

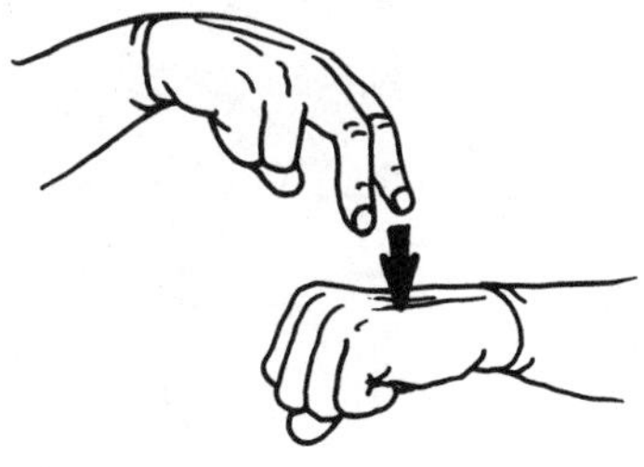

Arabic: erlánda ايرلندا
Chinese: ài-ĕrlán 愛爾蘭
Dutch: Ierland
French: Irlande
German: Irland
Italian: Irlanda
Japanese: Airurando アイルランド
Korean: Aillaendu 아일랜드
Portuguese: Irlanda
Russian: Irlándiya Ирландия
Spanish: Irlanda
Swedish: Irland

1124. iron (metal) [n.]

Arabic: hadíd حديد
Chinese: tiĕ 鐵
Dutch: ijzer
French: fer
German: Eisen
Italian: ferro
Japanese: tetsu 鉄
Korean: ch'ŏl 철
Portuguese: ferro
Russian: zhelézo железо
Spanish: hierro
Swedish: järn

1125. irresponsible [adj.]

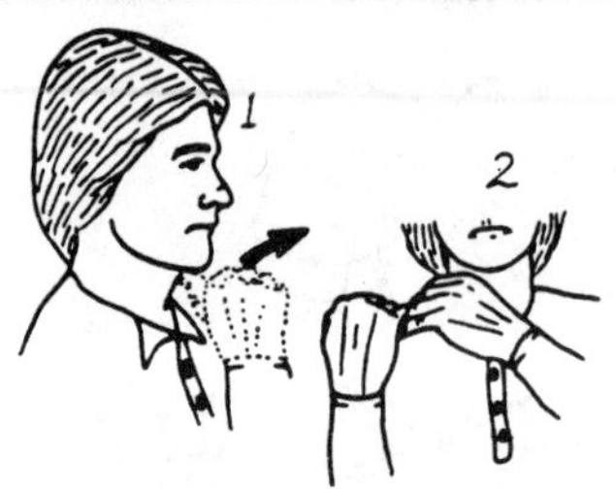

Arabic: gher mas'úl غير مسئول
Chinese: búfùzérèn 不負責任
Dutch: onverantwoordelijk
French: irresponsable
German: unverantwortlich
Italian: irresponsabile
Japanese: musekinin na 無責任な
Korean: much'aegimhan 무책임한
Portuguese: irresponsável
Russian: bezotvétstvennyy безответственный
Spanish: irresponsable
Swedish: oansvarig

1126. island [n.]

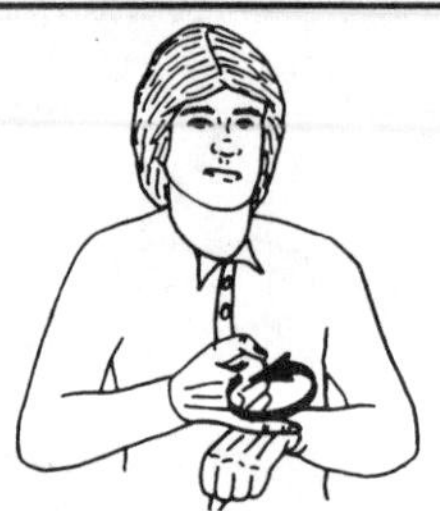

Arabic: jazíra جزيرة
Chinese: bīngdǎo 冰島
Dutch: eiland
French: île
German: Insel
Italian: isola
Japanese: shima 島
Korean: sŏm 섬
Portuguese: ilha
Russian: óstrov остров
Spanish: isla
Swedish: ö

1127. Israel [n.]

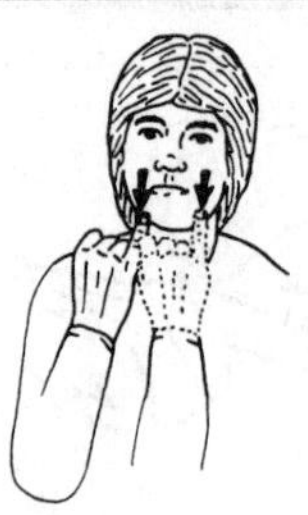

Arabic: israíl اسرائيل
Chinese: yǐsèliè 以色列
Dutch: Israël
French: Israël
German: Israel
Italian: Israele
Japanese: Isuraeru イスラエル
Korean: Isŭra'el 이스라엘
Portuguese: Israel
Russian: Izráil' Израиль
Spanish: Israel
Swedish: Israel

1128. it [pron.]

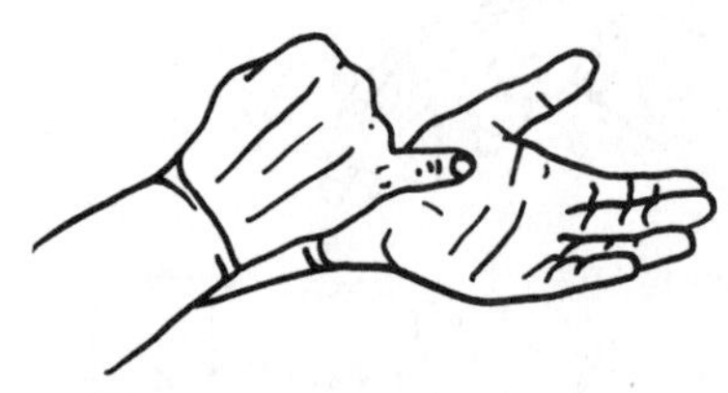

Arabic: húwa/híya هو / هي
Chinese: tā 它
Dutch: het
French: il/ce/c'
German: es
Italian: esso/essa/lo/la
Japanese: sore wa それは
Korean: gŭgŏt 그것
Portuguese: ele/ela/o/a
Russian: on/oná/onó он/она/оно
Spanish: ello
Swedish: den/det

1129. Italy [n.]

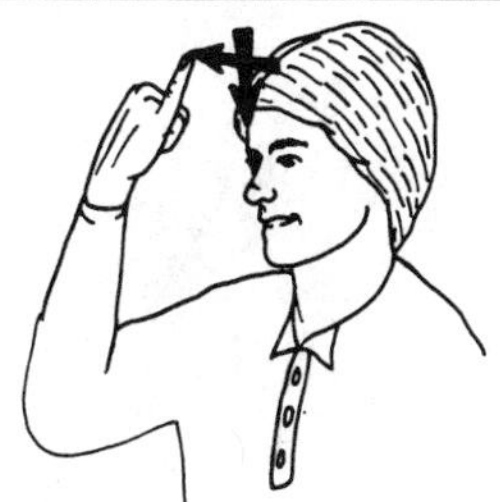

Arabic: itália ايطاليا
Chinese: yìdàlì 義大利
Dutch: Italië
French: Italie
German: Italien
Italian: Italia
Japanese: Itaria イタリア
Korean: It'allia 이태리
Portuguese: Itália
Russian: Itáliya Италия
Spanish: Italia
Swedish: Italien

1130. its [adj./pron.]

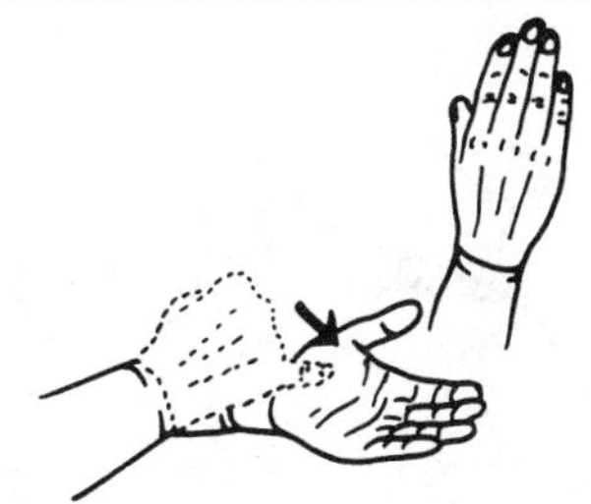

Arabic: láhu/láha لها / له
Chinese: tāde 它的
Dutch: zijn
French: son/sa
German: sein
Italian: suo/sua
Japanese: sore no それの
Korean: gŭgŏtŭi 그것의
Portuguese: seu/sua
Russian: yevó/yeyó/svoy его/её/свой
Spanish: su/sus
Swedish: sinn

1131. itself [pron.]

Arabic: náfsuha نفسها
Chinese: tāzìjǐ 它自己
Dutch: zichzelf
French: soi-même
German: sich selbst
Italian: se stesso
Japanese: sorejishin それ自身
Korean: gŭgŏt jach'e 그것 자체
Portuguese: si mesmo
Russian: sebyá себя
Spanish: sí mismo
Swedish: sigsjälvt

1132. jail [n.]

Arabic: sijn سجن
Chinese: jiānláo 監牢
Dutch: gevangenis
French: prison
German: Gefängnis
Italian: carcere
Japanese: keimusho 刑務所
Korean: gamok 감옥
Portuguese: prisão
Russian: tyur'má тюрьма
Spanish: cárcel
Swedish: fängelse

1133. jam (jelly) [n.]

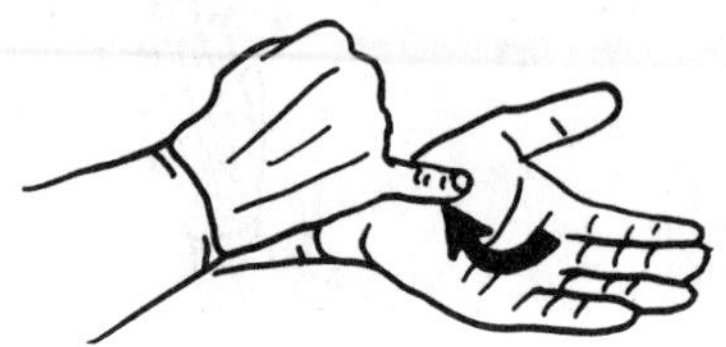

Arabic: murábba مربى
Chinese: guǒjiàng 果醬
Dutch: jam
French: confiture
German: Marmelade
Italian: marmellata
Japanese: jamu ジャム
Korean: jaem 잼
Portuguese: geléia
Russian: varén'ye варенье
Spanish: mermelada
Swedish: marmelad

1134. January [n.]

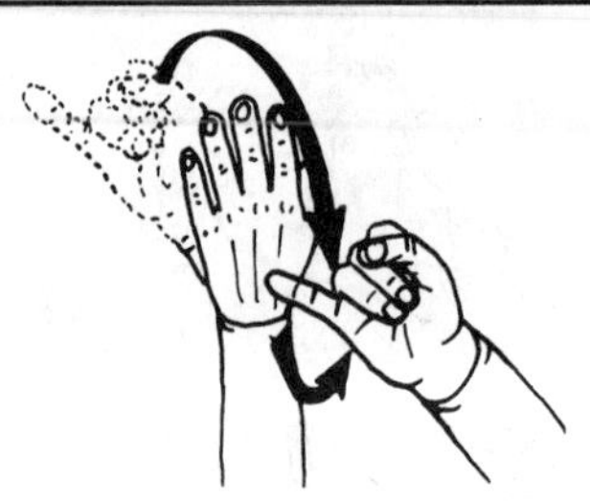

Arabic: yanáyer يناير
Chinese: yīyuè 一月
Dutch: januari
French: janvier
German: Januar
Italian: gennaio
Japanese: ichigatsu 一月
Korean: jŏngwŏl 정월
Portuguese: janeiro
Russian: yanvár' январь
Spanish: enero
Swedish: januari

1135. Japan [n.]

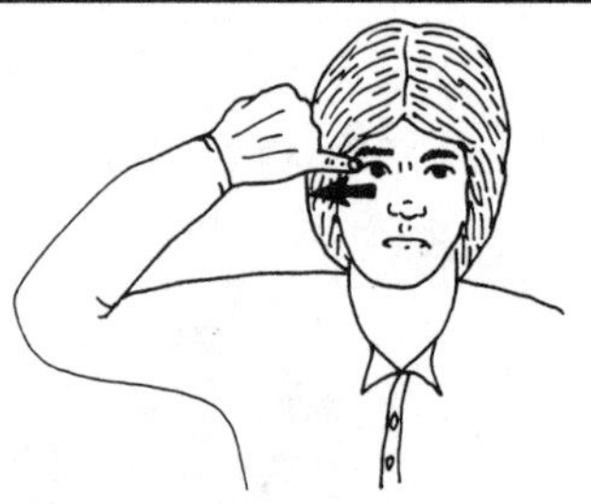

Arabic: aliabán اليابان
Chinese: rìběn 日本
Dutch: Japan
French: Japon
German: Japan
Italian: Giappone
Japanese: Nihon 日本
Korean: Ilbon 일본
Portuguese: Japão
Russian: Yapóniya Япония
Spanish: Japón
Swedish: Japan

1136. jar (glass container) [n.]

Arabic: martabán مرطبان
Chinese: guànzi 罐子
Dutch: pot
French: bocal
German: Krug
Italian: vaso
Japanese: hirokuchi bin 広口びん
Korean: hangari 항아리
Portuguese: jarra
Russian: bánka банка
Spanish: frasco
Swedish: kruka

1137. jealous [adj.]

Arabic: ghayúr غيور
Chinese: jìdùde 嫉妒的
Dutch: jaloers
French: jaloux
German: eifersüchtig
Italian: geloso
Japanese: yakimochi yaki no
やきもちやきの
Korean: jiltuhanŭn 질투하는
Portuguese: ciumento
Russian: revnívyy ревнивый
Spanish: celoso
Swedish: svartsjuk

1138. Jesus [n.]

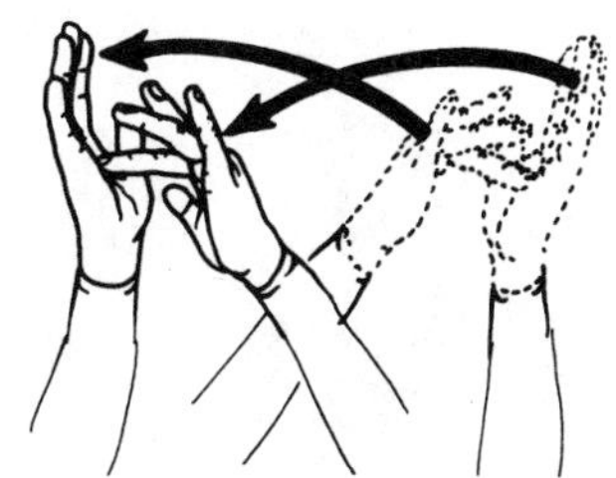

Arabic: éisa عيسى
Chinese: yēsū 耶穌
Dutch: Jezus
French: Jésus
German: Jesus
Italian: Gesù
Japanese: Iesu イエス
Korean: Yesu 예수
Portuguese: Jesus
Russian: Iisús Иисус
Spanish: Jesús
Swedish: Jesus

1139. jet (plane) [n.]

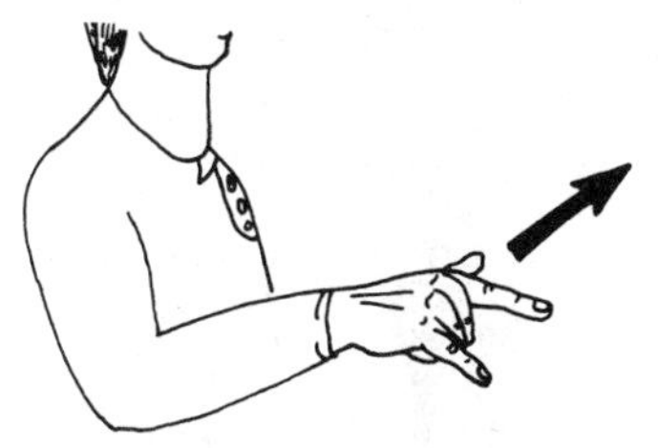

Arabic: tá'ira nafátha طائرة نفاثة
Chinese: pēnshèjī 噴射機
Dutch: straalvliegtuig
French: avion à réaction
German: Düsenflugzeug
Italian: aeroplano a reazione
Japanese: jetto ジェット
Korean: jet'ŭgi 제트기
Portuguese: avião a jato
Russian: reaktívnyy samolyót
реактивный самолёт
Spanish: avión a reacción
Swedish: jet

1140. jewel [n.]

Arabic: héli حلي
Chinese: bǎoshí 寶石
Dutch: juweel
French: joyau
German: Juwel
Italian: gioiello
Japanese: hōseki 宝石
Korean: bosŏk 보석
Portuguese: jóia
Russian: dragotsénnyy kámen'
драгоценный камень
Spanish: joya
Swedish: juvel

1141. job [n.]

Arabic: wadhífa وظيفة
Chinese: gōngzuò 工作
Dutch: karwei
French: travail
German: Arbeit
Italian: lavoro
Japanese: shigoto 仕事
Korean: il 일
Portuguese: trabalho
Russian: rabóta работа
Spanish: trabajo
Swedish: jobb

1142. join (unite) [v.]

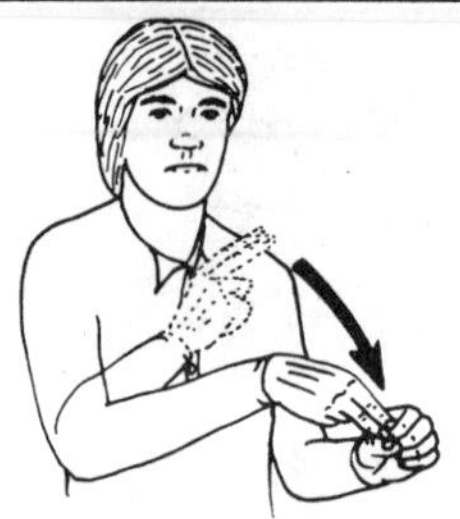

Arabic: indámaja fi اندمج في
Chinese: jiéhé 結合
Dutch: verenigen
French: joindre
German: verbinden
Italian: unire
Japanese: kuwawaru 加わる
Korean: kyŏrhap'hada 결합하다
Portuguese: juntar
Russian: soyedinyát' соединять
Spanish: juntar
Swedish: förena

1143. joke [n.]

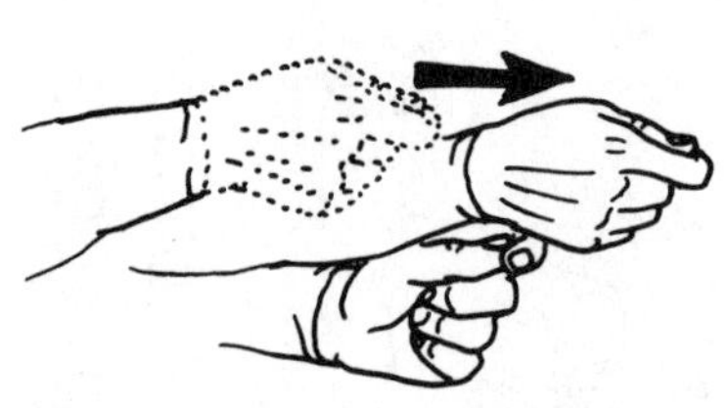

Arabic: núkta نكتة
Chinese: xiàohuà 笑話
Dutch: grap
French: plaisanterie
German: Scherz
Italian: scherzo
Japanese: jōdan 冗談
Korean: nongdam 농담
Portuguese: piada
Russian: shútka шутка
Spanish: chiste
Swedish: skämt

1144. journalist [n.]

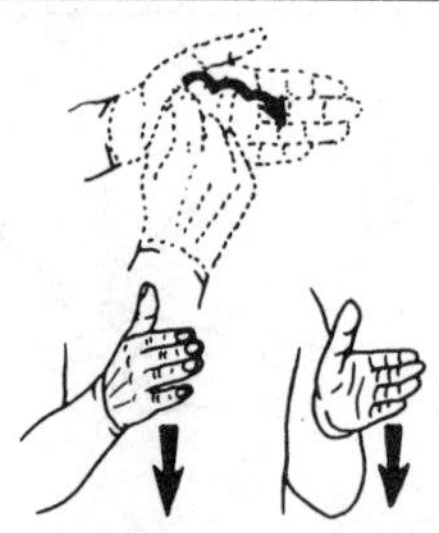

Arabic: sáhafi صحفي
Chinese: jìzhě 記者
Dutch: journalist
French: journaliste
German: Journalist
Italian: giornalista
Japanese: jānarisuto ジャーナリスト
Korean: shinmun kija 신문기자
Portuguese: jornalista
Russian: zhurnalíst журналист
Spanish: periodista
Swedish: journalist

1145. journey [n.]

Arabic: réhla رحلة
Chinese: lǚchéng 旅程
Dutch: reis
French: voyage
German: Reise
Italian: viaggio
Japanese: ryokō 旅行
Korean: yŏhaeng 여행
Portuguese: viagem
Russian: puteshéstviye путешествие
Spanish: viaje
Swedish: resa

1146. joy [n.]

Arabic: faráh فرح
Chinese: kuàilè 快樂
Dutch: vreugde
French: joie
German: Freude
Italian: gioia
Japanese: yorokobi 喜び
Korean: gippŭm 기쁨
Portuguese: alegria
Russian: rádost' радость
Spanish: alegría
Swedish: glädje

1147. Judaism [n.]

Arabic: al-yahudía اليهودية
Chinese: yútàijiào 猶太教
Dutch: jodendom
French: judaïsme
German: Judentum
Italian: ebreismo
Japanese: Yudaya-kyo ユダヤ教
Korean: yudaegyo 유대교
Portuguese: judaísmo
Russian: iudaízm иудаизм
Spanish: judaísmo
Swedish: Judendom

1148. judge [v.]

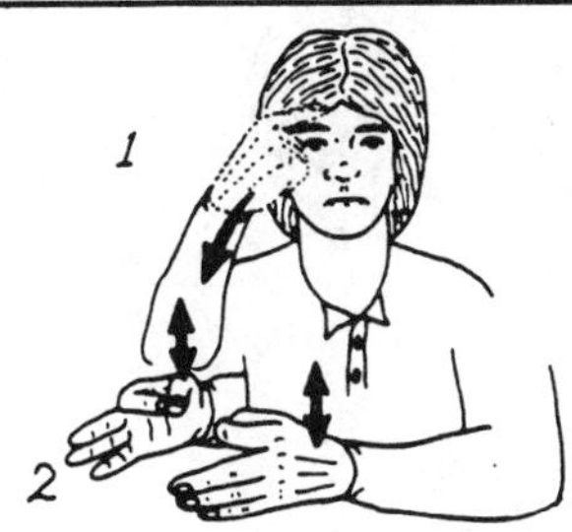

Arabic: qádi قاضي
Chinese: pànduàn 判斷
Dutch: oordelen
French: juger
German: richten
Italian: giudicare
Japanese: handan suru 判断する
Korean: shimp'anhada 심판하다
Portuguese: julgar
Russian: sudít' судить
Spanish: juzgar
Swedish: döma

1149. juice [n.]

Arabic: aasír عصير
Chinese: zhī 汁
Dutch: sap
French: jus
German: Saft
Italian: succo
Japanese: jūsu ジュース
Korean: jusŭ 쥬스
Portuguese: suco
Russian: sok сок
Spanish: jugo
Swedish: saft

1150. July [n.]

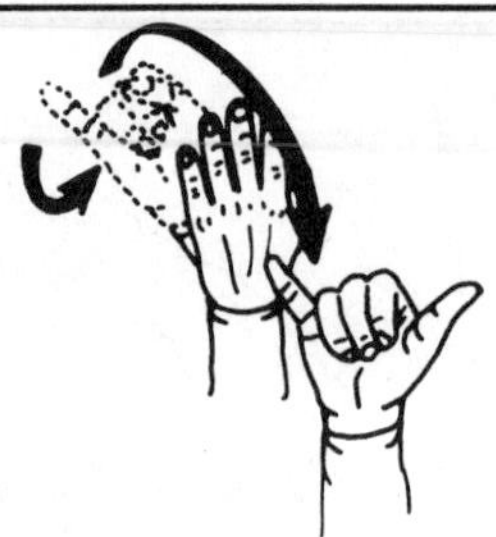

Arabic: yúliu يوليو
Chinese: qīyuè 七月
Dutch: juli
French: juillet
German: Juli
Italian: luglio
Japanese: shichigatsu 七月
Korean: ch'irwŏl 칠월
Portuguese: julho
Russian: iyúl' июль
Spanish: julio
Swedish: juli

1151. jump [v.]

Arabic: qáfaza قفز
Chinese: tiào 跳
Dutch: springen
French: sauter
German: springen
Italian: saltare
Japanese: tobu 跳ぶ
Korean: ttwida 뛰다
Portuguese: pular
Russian: prýgat' прыгать
Spanish: saltar
Swedish: hoppa

1152. June [n.]

Arabic: yúniu يونيو
Chinese: liùyuè 六月
Dutch: juni
French: juin
German: Juni
Italian: giugno
Japanese: rokugatsu 六月
Korean: yuwŏl 유월
Portuguese: junho
Russian: iyún' июнь
Spanish: junio
Swedish: juni

1153. justice [n.]

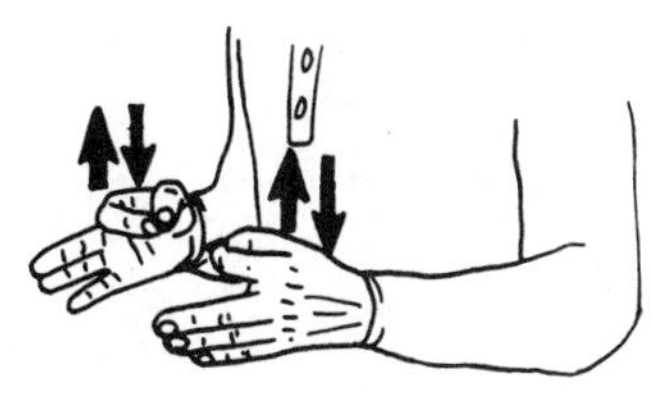

Arabic: aadála عدالة
Chinese: zhèngyì 正義
Dutch: gerechtigheid
French: justice
German: Gerechtigkeit
Italian: giustizia
Japanese: kōhei 公平
Korean: jŏngŭi 정의
Portuguese: justiça
Russian: spravedlívost' справедливость
Spanish: justicia
Swedish: rättvisa

1154. keep (hold) [v.]

Arabic: ihtáfadha bi احتفظ بـ
Chinese: bǎochí 保持
Dutch: houden
French: tenir
German: halten
Italian: tenere
Japanese: tamotsu 保つ
Korean: jinida 지니다
Portuguese: manter
Russian: derzhát' держать
Spanish: guardar
Swedish: hålla

1155. key [n.]

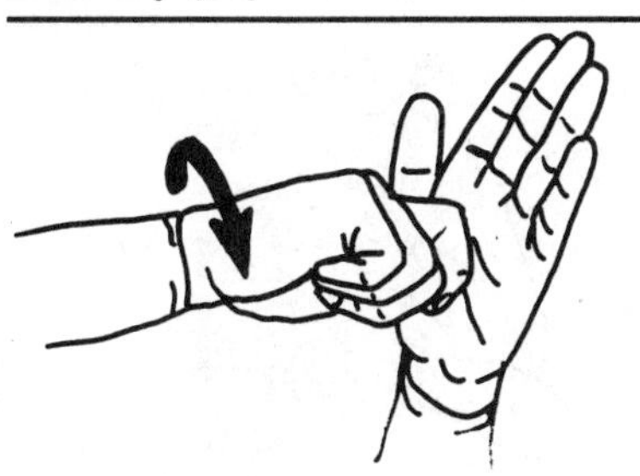

Arabic: muftáh مفتاح
Chinese: yàoshi 鑰匙
Dutch: sleutel
French: clé
German: Schlüssel
Italian: chiave
Japanese: kagi 鍵
Korean: yŏlsoe 열쇠
Portuguese: chave
Russian: klyúch ключ
Spanish: llave
Swedish: nyckel

1156. kick [v.]

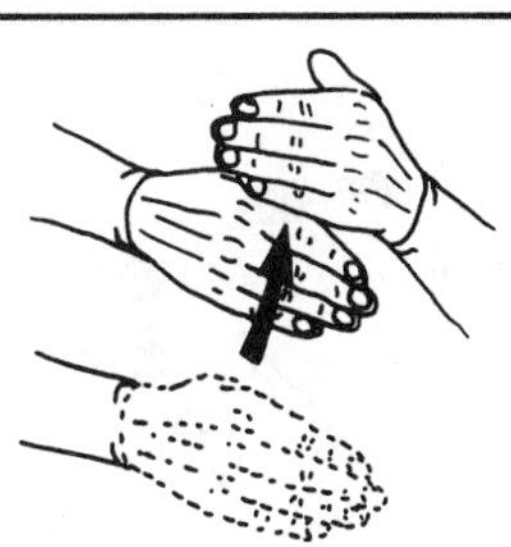

Arabic: ráfada رفض
Chinese: tī 踢
Dutch: schoppen
French: donner un coup de pied
German: stoßen
Italian: calciare
Japanese: keru 蹴る
Korean: ch'ada 차다
Portuguese: dar pontapés
Russian: udaryát' nogóy ударять ногой
Spanish: dar una patada
Swedish: sparka

1157. kill [v.]

Arabic: qátala قتل
Chinese: shāsǐ 殺死
Dutch: doden
French: tuer
German: töten
Italian: uccidere
Japanese: korosu 殺す
Korean: jugida 죽이다
Portuguese: matar
Russian: ubít' убить
Spanish: matar
Swedish: döda

1158. kilogram [n.]

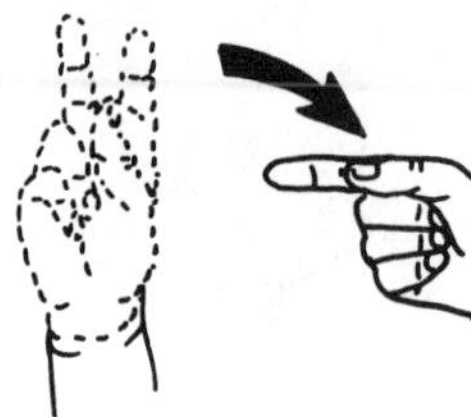

Arabic: kilográm كيلوجرام
Chinese: gōngkè 公克
Dutch: kilogram
French: kilogramme
German: Kilogramm
Italian: chilogrammo
Japanese: kiroguramu キログラム
Korean: kilogram 킬로그람
Portuguese: quilograma
Russian: kilográmm килограмм
Spanish: kilogramo
Swedish: kilogram

1159. kilometer [n.]

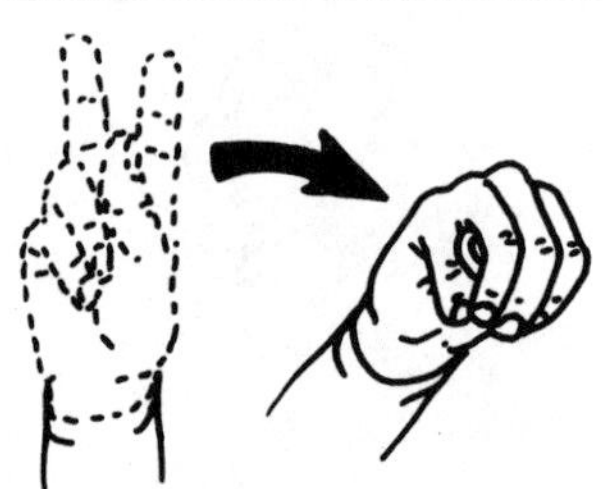

Arabic: kilomítr كيلومتر
Chinese: gōnglǐ 公里
Dutch: kilometer
French: kilomètre
German: Kilometer
Italian: chilometro
Japanese: kiromētā キロメーター
Korean: kilomitŏ 킬로미터
Portuguese: quilômetro
Russian: kilométr километр
Spanish: kilómetro
Swedish: kilometer

1160. kind [adj.]

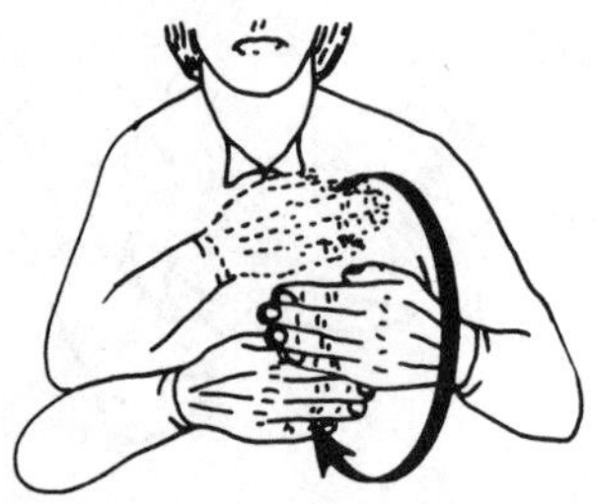

Arabic: hanún حنون
Chinese: réncíde 仁慈的
Dutch: vriendelijk
French: bienveillant
German: gütig
Italian: gentile
Japanese: shinsetsu na 親切な
Korean: ch'injŏrhan 친절한
Portuguese: bondoso
Russian: dóbryy добрый
Spanish: bondadosa
Swedish: vänlig

1161. kind (sort) [n.]

Arabic: nuaa نوع
Chinese: zhǒnglèi 種類
Dutch: soort
French: genre
German: Sorte
Italian: genere
Japanese: shurui 種類
Korean: chongnyu 종류
Portuguese: gênero
Russian: rod род
Spanish: género
Swedish: sort

1162. king [n.]

Arabic: málek ملك
Chinese: wáng 王
Dutch: koning
French: roi
German: König
Italian: re
Japanese: kokuō 国王
Korean: wang 왕
Portuguese: rei
Russian: koról' король
Spanish: rey
Swedish: kung

1163. kingdom [n.]

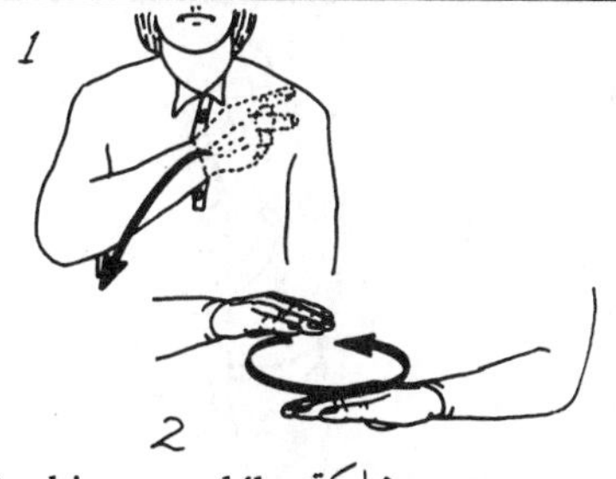

Arabic: mamláka مملكة
Chinese: wángguó 王國
Dutch: koninkrijk
French: royaume
German: Königreich
Italian: regno
Japanese: ōkoku 王国
Korean: wangguk 왕국
Portuguese: reino
Russian: korolévstvo королевство
Spanish: reino
Swedish: kungarike

1164. kiss [v.]

Arabic: qábbala قبل
Chinese: jiēwěn 接吻
Dutch: kussen
French: embrasser
German: küssen
Italian: baciare
Japanese: kisu suru キスする
Korean: k'isŭhada 키스하다
Portuguese: beijar
Russian: tselovát' целовать
Spanish: besar
Swedish: kyssa

1165. kitchen [n.]

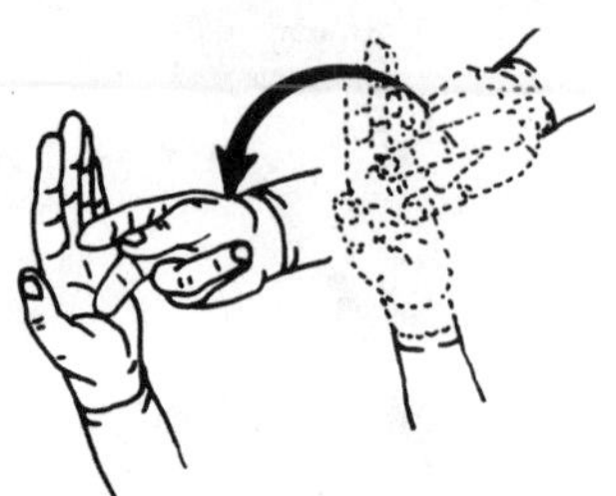

Arabic: mátbakh مطبخ
Chinese: chúfáng 厨房
Dutch: keuken
French: cuisine
German: Küche
Italian: cucina
Japanese: daidokoro 台所
Korean: buŏk 부엌
Portuguese: cozinha
Russian: kúkhnya кухня
Spanish: cocina
Swedish: kök

1166. kneel [v.]

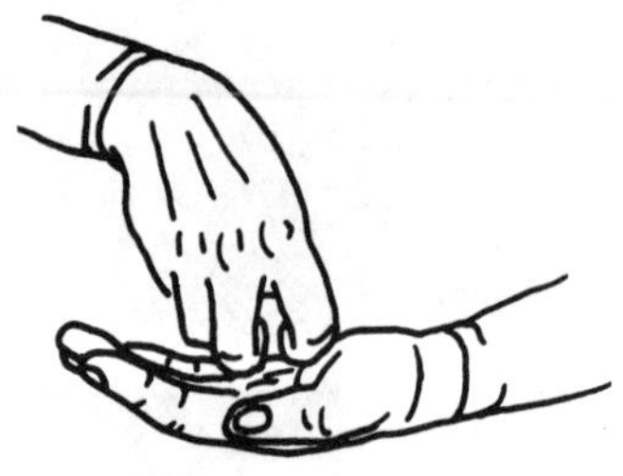

Arabic: rakáa ركع
Chinese: guìxià 跪下
Dutch: knielen
French: s'agenouiller
German: knieen
Italian: inginocchiarsi
Japanese: hizamazuku ひざまずく
Korean: murŭpŭl kkuld'a 무릎을 꿇다
Portuguese: ajoelhar-se
Russian: stoyát' na kolényakh стоять на коленях
Spanish: arrodillarse
Swedish: knäböja

1167. knife [n.]

Arabic: sikína سكينة
Chinese: dāozi 刀子
Dutch: mes
French: couteau
German: Messer
Italian: coltello
Japanese: naifu ナイフ
Korean: k'al 칼
Portuguese: faca
Russian: nozh нож
Spanish: cuchillo
Swedish: kniv

1168. knock [v.]

Arabic: táraqa طرق
Chinese: qiāo 敲
Dutch: kloppen
French: frapper
German: klopfen
Italian: bussare
Japanese: utsu 打つ
Korean: dudŭrida 두드리다
Portuguese: bater
Russian: stuchát'sya стучаться
Spanish: golpear
Swedish: knacka

1169. knot [n.]

Arabic: áuqda عقدة
Chinese: jié 結
Dutch: knoop
French: noeud
German: Knoten
Italian: nodo
Japanese: musubime 結び目
Korean: maedŭp 매듭
Portuguese: nó
Russian: úzel узел
Spanish: nudo
Swedish: knut

1170. know [v.]

Arabic: áarifa عرف
Chinese: zhīdào 知道
Dutch: weten
French: savoir
German: wissen
Italian: sapere
Japanese: shiru 知る
Korean: alda 알다
Portuguese: saber
Russian: znát' знать
Spanish: saber
Swedish: veta

1171. Korea [n.]

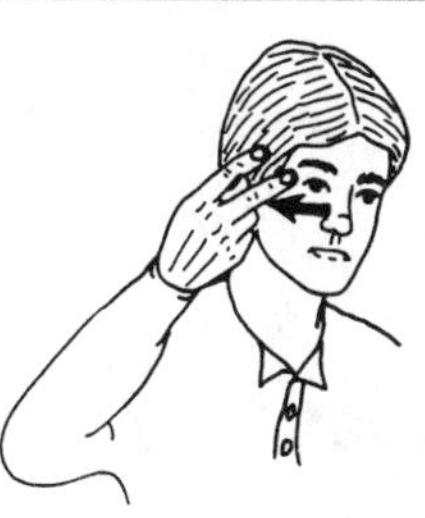

Arabic: kuría كوريا
Chinese: hánguó 韓國
Dutch: Korea
French: Corée
German: Korea
Italian: Corea
Japanese: Kankoku 韓国
Korean: Hanguk 한국
Portuguese: Coréia
Russian: Koréya Корея
Spanish: Corea
Swedish: Korea

1172. labor [n.]

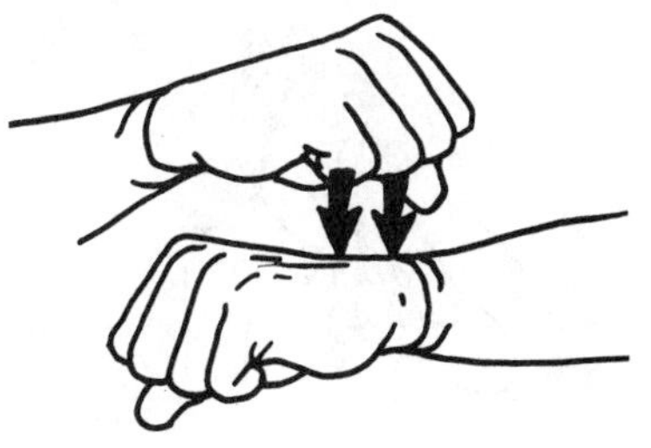

Arabic: áamal عمل
Chinese: láolì 劳力
Dutch: werk
French: travail
German: Arbeit
Italian: lavoro
Japanese: rōdō 労働
Korean: nodong 노동
Portuguese: trabalho
Russian: trud труд
Spanish: trabajo
Swedish: arbete

1173. lack [n.]

Arabic: áadam عدم
Chinese: quēfá 缺乏
Dutch: gebrek
French: manque
German: Mangel
Italian: mancanza
Japanese: fusoku 不足
Korean: gyŏlp'ip 결핍
Portuguese: carência
Russian: nedostátok недостаток
Spanish: carencia
Swedish: brist

1174. ladder [n.]

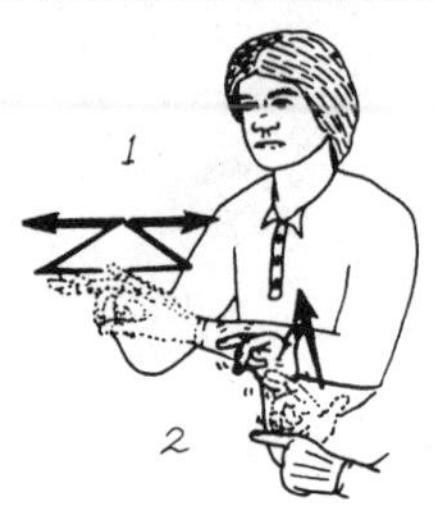

Arabic: súllam سلم
Chinese: tīzi 梯子
Dutch: ladder
French: échelle
German: Leiter
Italian: scala
Japanese: hashigo 梯子
Korean: sadaktari 사닥다리
Portuguese: escada
Russian: léstnitsa лестница
Spanish: escalera
Swedish: stege

1175. lady [n.]

Arabic: séyyida سيدة
Chinese: nǚshì 女士
Dutch: dame
French: dame
German: Dame
Italian: signora
Japanese: shukujo 淑女
Korean: sungnyŏ 숙녀
Portuguese: senhora
Russian: dáma дама
Spanish: señora
Swedish: dam

1176. lag [v.]

Arabic: takhállafa تخلف
Chinese: luòhòu 落後
Dutch: achterblijven
French: rester en arrière
German: zurückbleiben
Italian: restare indietro
Japanese: okureru 遅れる
Korean: dwittŏlŏjida 뒤떨어지다
Portuguese: ficar atrás
Russian: otstavát' отставать
Spanish: quedarse atrás
Swedish: bli efter

1177. lake [n.]

Arabic: buháira بحيرة
Chinese: hú 湖
Dutch: meer
French: lac
German: See
Italian: lago
Japanese: mizuumi 湖
Korean: hosu 호수
Portuguese: lago
Russian: ózero озеро
Spanish: lago
Swedish: sjö

1178. lame [adj.]

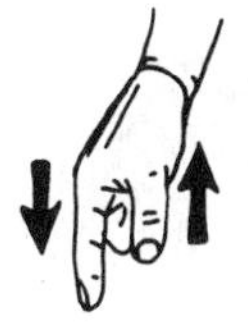

Arabic: múqaad مقعد
Chinese: bǒde 跛的
Dutch: mank
French: boiteux
German: lahm
Italian: zoppo
Japanese: bikko no びっこの
Korean: jŏllŭmbari 절름바리
Portuguese: côxo
Russian: khromóy хромой
Spanish: cojo
Swedish: lam

1179. land [n.]

Arabic: ardh ارض
Chinese: tǔdì 土地
Dutch: land
French: terre
German: Land
Italian: terra
Japanese: tochi 土地
Korean: ttang 땅
Portuguese: terra
Russian: zemlyá земля
Spanish: tierra
Swedish: land

1180. language [n.]

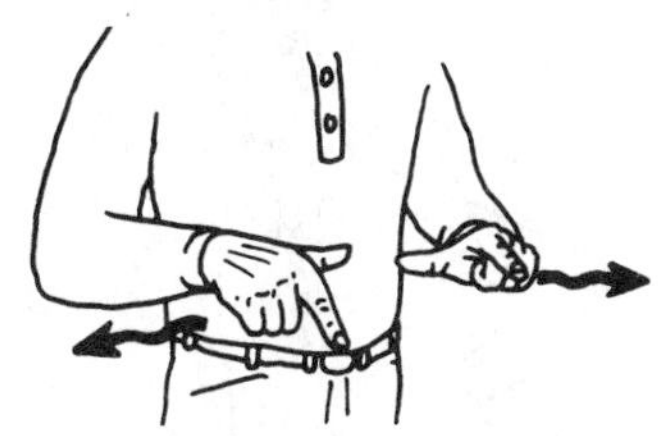

Arabic: lúgha لغة
Chinese: yǔyán 語言
Dutch: taal
French: langue
German: Sprache
Italian: lingua
Japanese: kokugo 国語
Korean: ŏnŏ 언어
Portuguese: língua
Russian: yazýk язык
Spanish: lengua
Swedish: språk

1181. large [adj.]

Arabic: kabír كبير
Chinese: dàde 大的
Dutch: groot
French: grand
German: groß
Italian: grosso
Japanese: ōkina 大きな
Korean: k'ŭn 큰
Portuguese: grande
Russian: bol'shóy большой
Spanish: grande
Swedish: stor

1182. last [adj.]

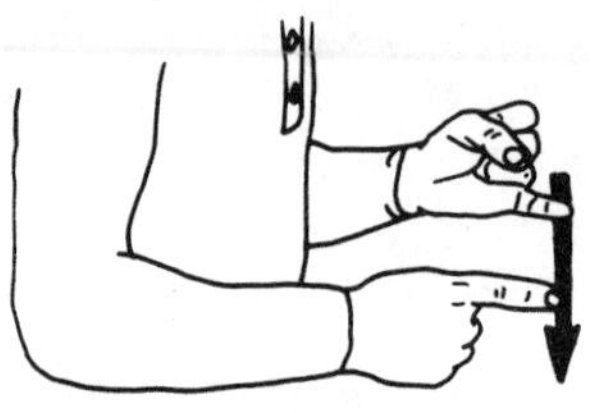

Arabic: ákher اخر
Chinese: zuìhòude 最後的
Dutch: laatst
French: dernier
German: letzt
Italian: ultimo
Japanese: saigo no 最後の
Korean: majimagŭi 마지막의
Portuguese: último
Russian: poslédniy последний
Spanish: último
Swedish: sist

1183. late [adj.]

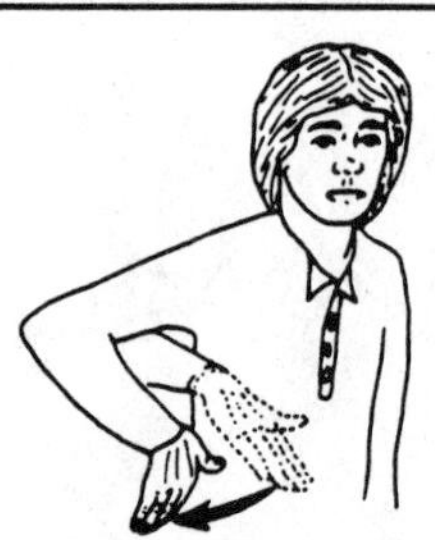

Arabic: muta'ákher متأخر
Chinese: wǎn 晚
Dutch: laat
French: tardif
German: spät
Italian: tardi
Japanese: osoi 遅い
Korean: nŭjŭn 늦은
Portuguese: tardio
Russian: pózdniy поздний
Spanish: tardío
Swedish: sen

1184. later [adj./adv.]

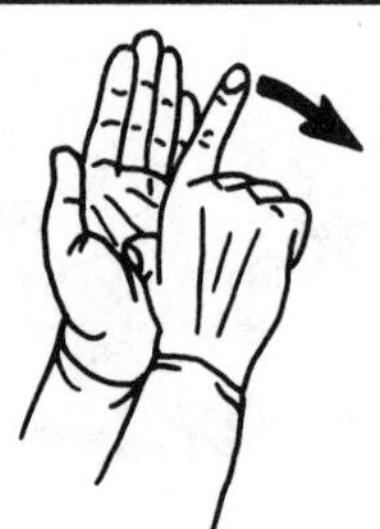

Arabic: fíma baad فيما بعد
Chinese: yǐhòu 以後
Dutch: later
French: plus tard
German: später
Italian: più tardi
Japanese: atode 後で
Korean: tŏ nŭjŭn 더늦은
Portuguese: mais tarde
Russian: pózzhe позже
Spanish: más tarde
Swedish: senare

1185. laugh [v.]

Arabic: dáheka ضحك
Chinese: xiào 笑
Dutch: lachen
French: rire
German: lachen
Italian: ridere
Japanese: warau 笑う
Korean: utta 웃다
Portuguese: rir
Russian: smeyát'sya смеяться
Spanish: reír
Swedish: skratta

1186. laughter [n.]

Arabic: dáhek ضحك
Chinese: xiàoshēng 笑聲
Dutch: gelach
French: rire
German: Gelächter
Italian: risata
Japanese: warai 笑い
Korean: usŭm 웃음
Portuguese: risada
Russian: smekh смех
Spanish: risa
Swedish: skratt

1187. law [n.]

Arabic: qanún قانون
Chinese: fǎlǜ 法律
Dutch: wet
French: loi
German: Gesetz
Italian: legge
Japanese: hōritsu 法律
Korean: bŏb 법
Portuguese: lei
Russian: zakón закон
Spanish: ley
Swedish: lag

1188. lawyer [n.]

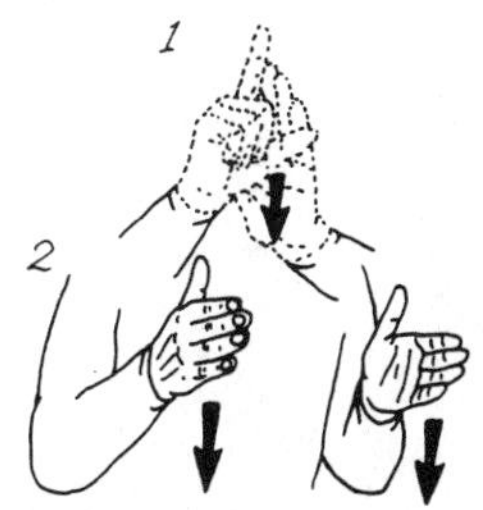

Arabic: muhámi محامي
Chinese: lǜshī 律師
Dutch: advocaat
French: homme de loi
German: Rechtsanwalt
Italian: avvocato
Japanese: bengoshi 弁護士
Korean: bŏmnyulga 법률가
Portuguese: advogado
Russian: yuríst юрист
Spanish: abogado
Swedish: advokat

1189. layer [n.]

Arabic: tábaqa طبقة
Chinese: céngcì 層次
Dutch: laag
French: couche
German: Schicht
Italian: strato
Japanese: kasane 重ね
Korean: chŭng 층
Portuguese: camada
Russian: sloy слой
Spanish: capa
Swedish: lager

1190. laziness [n.]

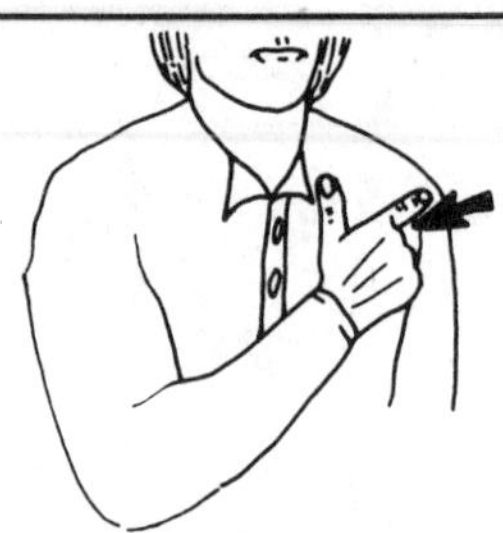

Arabic: kásal كسل
Chinese: lănduò 懶惰
Dutch: luiheid
French: paresse
German: Faulheit
Italian: pigrizia
Japanese: bushō 無精
Korean: geŭrŭm 게으름
Portuguese: preguiça
Russian: len' лень
Spanish: pereza
Swedish: lättja

1191. lead (guide) [v.]

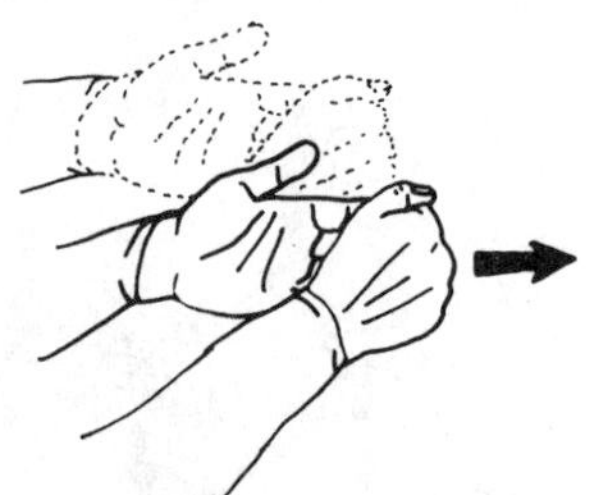

Arabic: qáda قاد
Chinese: yĭndăo 引導
Dutch: leiden
French: guider
German: führen
Italian: guidare
Japanese: annai suru 案内する
Korean: annaehada 안내하다
Portuguese: guiar
Russian: vodít' водить
Spanish: guiar
Swedish: leda

1192. leader [n.]

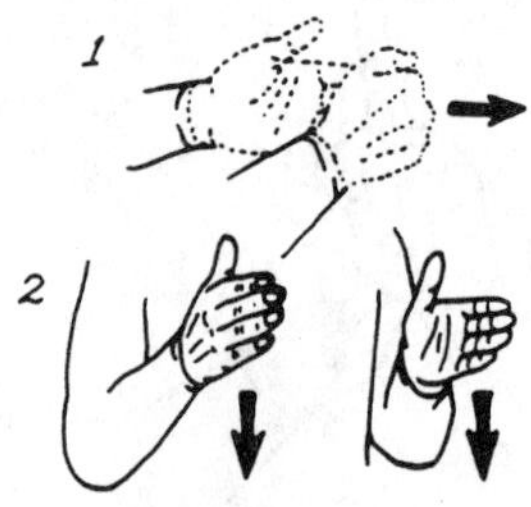

Arabic: qá'ed قائد
Chinese: lĭngdăorén 領導人
Dutch: leider
French: dirigeant
German: Führer
Italian: capo
Japanese: shidōsha 指導者
Korean: jidoja 지도자
Portuguese: líder
Russian: rukovodítel' руководитель
Spanish: líder
Swedish: ledare

1193. leaf [n.]

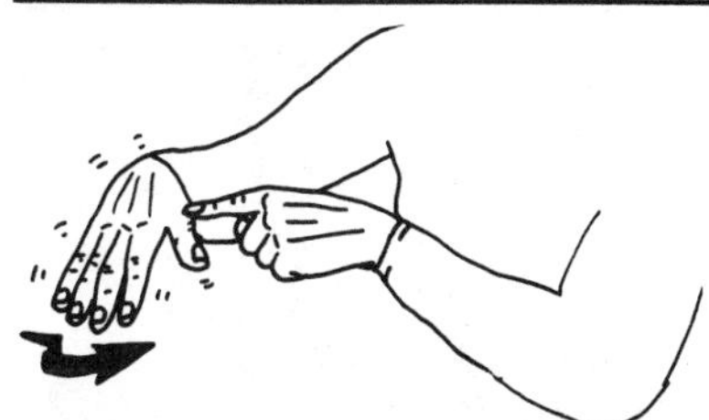

Arabic: wáraqet shájar ورقة شجر
Chinese: yèzi 葉子
Dutch: blad
French: feuille
German: Blatt
Italian: foglia
Japanese: ha 葉
Korean: ip 잎
Portuguese: folha
Russian: list лист
Spanish: hoja
Swedish: löv

1194. leak [v.]

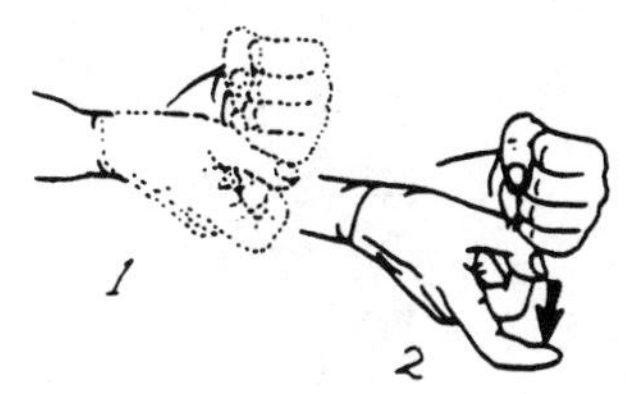

Arabic: tasáraba تسرب
Chinese: lòu 漏
Dutch: lekken
French: fuir
German: lecken
Italian: perdere
Japanese: moreru 漏れる
Korean: saeda 새다
Portuguese: vazar
Russian: tech' течь
Spanish: gotear
Swedish: läcka

1195. learn [v.]

Arabic: taálama تعلم
Chinese: xué 學
Dutch: leren
French: apprendre
German: lernen
Italian: imparare
Japanese: manabu 学ぶ
Korean: baeuda 배우다
Portuguese: aprender
Russian: uchít'sya учиться
Spanish: aprender
Swedish: lära sig

1196. least [adj.]

Arabic: aqálla اقل
Chinese: zhuìshǎo 最少
Dutch: minst
French: moindre
German: geringst
Italian: minimo
Japanese: saishō no 最小の
Korean: gajang jŏkke 가장 적은
Portuguese: o mínimo
Russian: naimén'shiy наименьший
Spanish: mínimo
Swedish: minst

1197. leather [n.]

Arabic: jild جلد
Chinese: pí 皮
Dutch: leer
French: cuir
German: Leder
Italian: cuoio
Japanese: kawa 皮
Korean: gajuk 가죽
Portuguese: couro
Russian: kózha кожа
Spanish: cuero
Swedish: läder

1198. leave (depart) [v.]

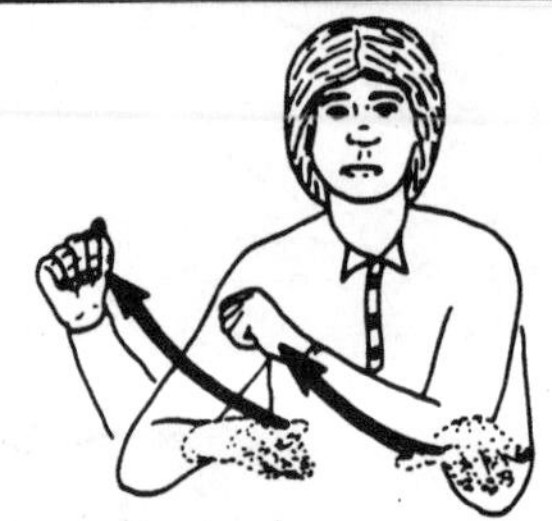

Arabic: táraka ترك
Chinese: líkāi 離開
Dutch: vertrekken
French: partir
German: weggehen
Italian: partire
Japanese: shuppatsu suru 出発する
Korean: ttŏnada 떠나다
Portuguese: partir
Russian: ukhodít' уходить
Spanish: partir
Swedish: avresa

1199. lecture [n.]

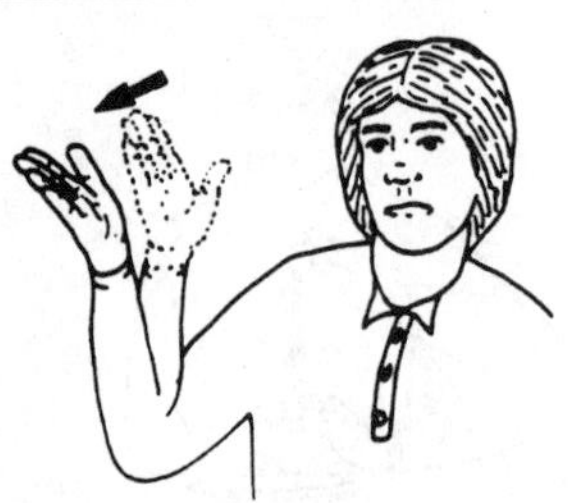

Arabic: muhádara محاضرة
Chinese: yǎnjiǎng 演講
Dutch: lezing
French: conférence
German: Vortrag
Italian: conferenza
Japanese: kōgi 講義
Korean: gangŭi 강의
Portuguese: conferência
Russian: léktsiya лекция
Spanish: conferencia
Swedish: föreläsning

1200. left [adj.]

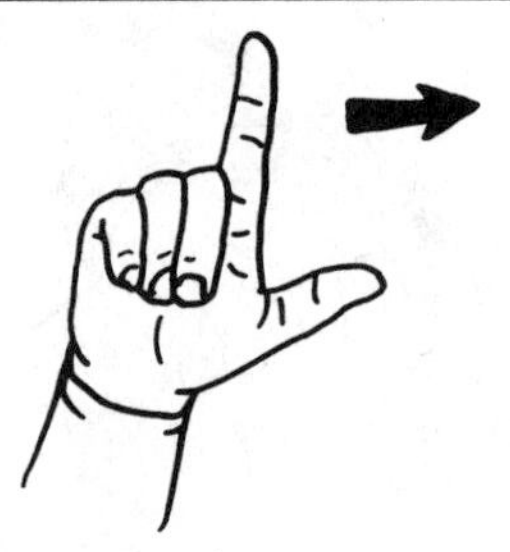

Arabic: yesára يسار
Chinese: zuǒ 左
Dutch: links
French: gauche
German: links
Italian: sinistro
Japanese: hidari no 左の
Korean: oentchogŭi 왼쪽의
Portuguese: esquerdo
Russian: lévyy левый
Spanish: izquierdo
Swedish: vänster

1201. leg [n.]

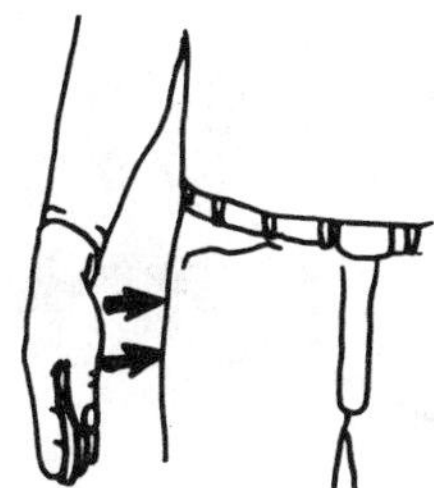

Arabic: rájul رجل
Chinese: tuǐ 腿
Dutch: been
French: jambe
German: Bein
Italian: gamba
Japanese: ashi 足
Korean: dari 다리
Portuguese: perna
Russian: nogá нога
Spanish: pierna
Swedish: ben

1202. legal [adj.]

Arabic: qanúni قانوني
Chinese: héfǎde 合法的
Dutch: wettig
French: légal
German: gesetzlich
Italian: legale
Japanese: hōritsu no 法律の
Korean: habbŏbchŏgin 합법적인
Portuguese: legal
Russian: zakónnyy законный
Spanish: legal
Swedish: laglig

1203. leisure [n.]

Arabic: kholú min al-áamal
خلو من العمل
Chinese: kòngxián 空閒
Dutch: vrije tijd
French: loisir
German: Muße
Italian: svago
Japanese: rejā レジャー
Korean: yŏga 여가
Portuguese: ócio
Russian: dosúg досуг
Spanish: ocio
Swedish: ledighet

1204. lemon [n.]

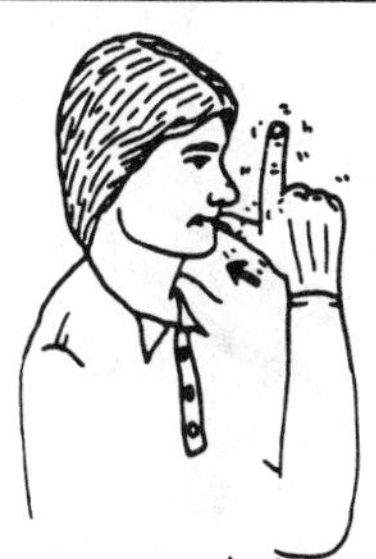

Arabic: leimún ليمون
Chinese: níngméng 檸檬
Dutch: citroen
French: citron
German: Zitrone
Italian: limone
Japanese: remon レモン
Korean: lemon 레몬
Portuguese: limão
Russian: limón лимон
Spanish: limón
Swedish: citron

1205. less [adj./adv.]

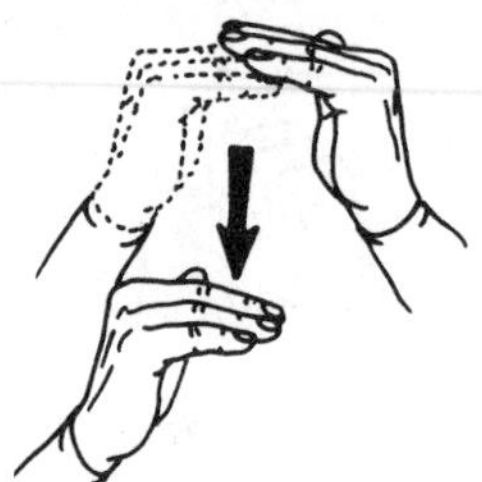

Arabic: aqáll اقل
Chinese: jiào shǎo 較少
Dutch: minder
French: moins
German: weniger
Italian: meno
Japanese: yori chiisai より小さい
Korean: boda jagŭn 보다 적은
Portuguese: menos
Russian: mén'shiy меньший
Spanish: menos
Swedish: mindre

1206. lesson [n.]

Arabic: dars درس
Chinese: gōngkè 功課
Dutch: les
French: leçon
German: Lehrstunde
Italian: lezione
Japanese: jugyō 授業
Korean: suŏp 수업
Portuguese: lição
Russian: urók урок
Spanish: lección
Swedish: lektion

1207. let [v.]

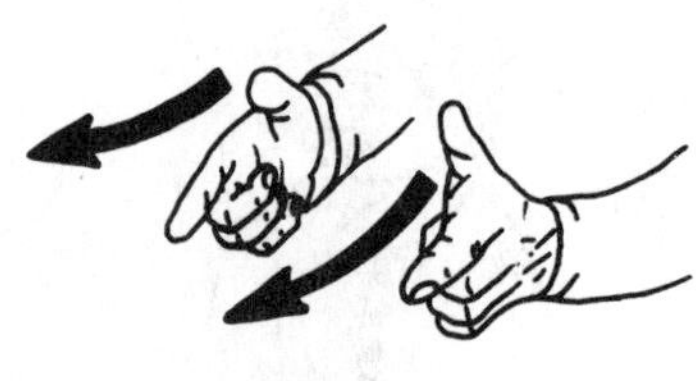

Arabic: sámaha سمح
Chinese: ràng 讓
Dutch: laten
French: laisser
German: lassen
Italian: lasciare
Japanese: . . . saseru …させる
Korean: shik'ida 시키다
Portuguese: deixar
Russian: puskát' пускать
Spanish: dejar
Swedish: låta

1208. letter (correspondence) [n.]

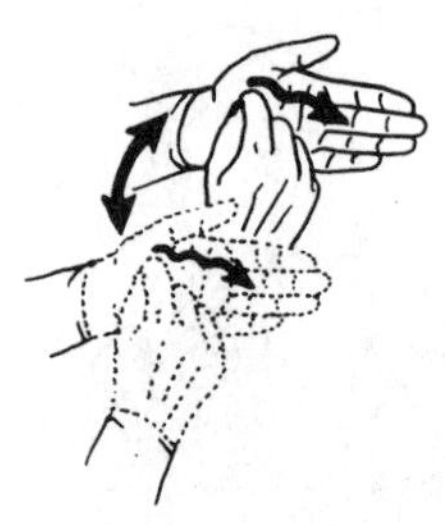

Arabic: risála رسالة
Chinese: xìn 信
Dutch: brief
French: lettre
German: Brief
Italian: lettera
Japanese: tegami 手紙
Korean: p'yŏnji 편지
Portuguese: carta
Russian: pis'mó письмо
Spanish: carta
Swedish: brev

1209. lettuce [n.]

Arabic: khass خس
Chinese: wōjù 萵苣
Dutch: sla
French: laitue
German: Kopfsalat
Italian: lattuga
Japanese: retasu レタス
Korean: sangch'i 상치
Portuguese: alface
Russian: salát салат
Spanish: lechuga
Swedish: sallat

1210. level [n.]

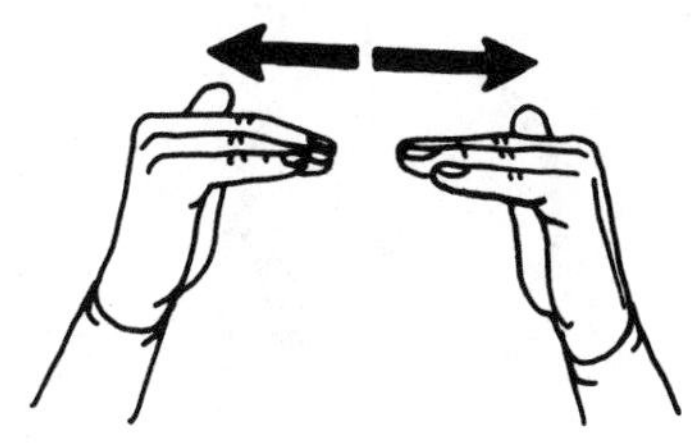

Arabic: mustáwa مستوى
Chinese: shuǐpíng 水平
Dutch: niveau
French: niveau
German: Niveau
Italian: livello
Japanese: hyōjun 標準
Korean: sup'yŏng 수평
Portuguese: nível
Russian: úroven' уровень
Spanish: nivel
Swedish: nivå

1211. liar [n.]

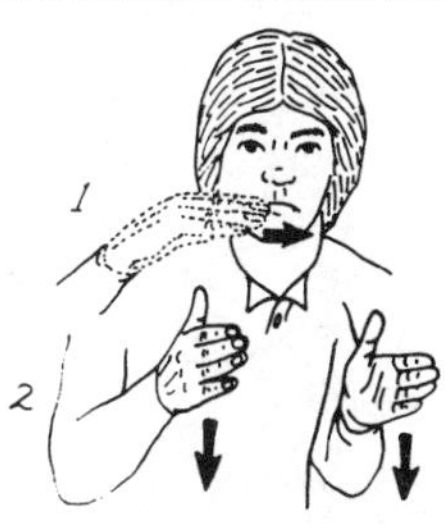

Arabic: kadhdháb كذاب
Chinese: shuōhuǎngderén 説謊的人
Dutch: leugenaar
French: menteur
German: Lügner
Italian: bugiardo
Japanese: usotsuki 嘘つき
Korean: gŏjinmaljangi 거짓말쟁이
Portuguese: mentiroso
Russian: lgún лгун
Spanish: mentiroso
Swedish: lögnare

1212. liberty [n.]

Arabic: horía حرية
Chinese: zìyóu 自由
Dutch: vrijheid
French: liberté
German: Freiheit
Italian: libertà
Japanese: jiyū 自由
Korean: jayu 자유
Portuguese: liberdade
Russian: svobóda свобода
Spanish: libertad
Swedish: frihet

1213. library [n.]

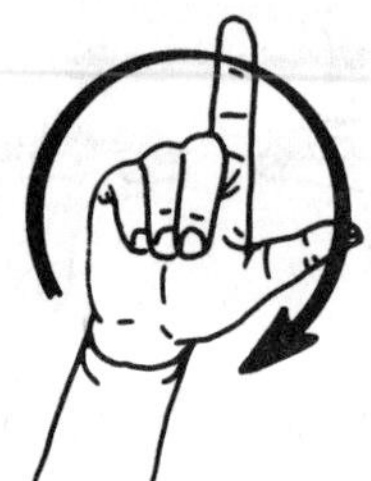

Arabic: máktaba مكتبة
Chinese: túshūguǎn 圖書館
Dutch: bibliotheek
French: bibliothèque
German: Bibliothek
Italian: biblioteca
Japanese: toshokan 図書館
Korean: dosŏkwan 도서관
Portuguese: biblioteca
Russian: bibliotéka библиотека
Spanish: biblioteca
Swedish: bibliotek

1214. license [n.]

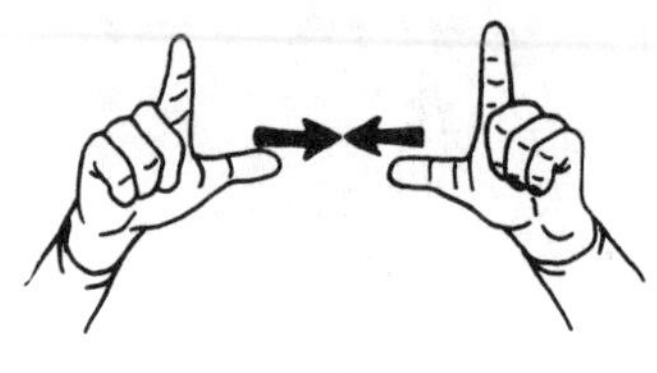

Arabic: rúkhsa رخصة
Chinese: zhízhào 執照
Dutch: vergunning
French: licence
German: Lizenz
Italian: licenza
Japanese: menkyo 免許
Korean: myŏnhŏ 면허
Portuguese: licença
Russian: litsénziya лицензия
Spanish: licencia
Swedish: licens

1215. lie (falsehood) [n.]

Arabic: kádheb كذب
Chinese: huǎnghuà 謊話
Dutch: leugen
French: mensonge
German: Lüge
Italian: menzogna
Japanese: uso 嘘
Korean: gŏjinmal 거짓말
Portuguese: mentira
Russian: lozh' ложь
Spanish: mentira
Swedish: lögn

1216. lie down (prone position) [v.]

Arabic: istálqa استلقى
Chinese: tǎngxià 躺下
Dutch: gaan liggen
French: se coucher
German: sich legen
Italian: coricarsi
Japanese: yokoni natte yasumu 横になって休む
Korean: nupta 눕다
Portuguese: deitar-se
Russian: lozhít'sya ложиться
Spanish: acostarse
Swedish: lägga sig

1217. life [n.]

Arabic: hayáa حياة
Chinese: shēngmìng 生命
Dutch: leven
French: vie
German: Leben
Italian: vita
Japanese: inochi 命
Korean: saengmyŏng 생명
Portuguese: vida
Russian: zhízn' жизнь
Spanish: vida
Swedish: liv

1218. light [n.]

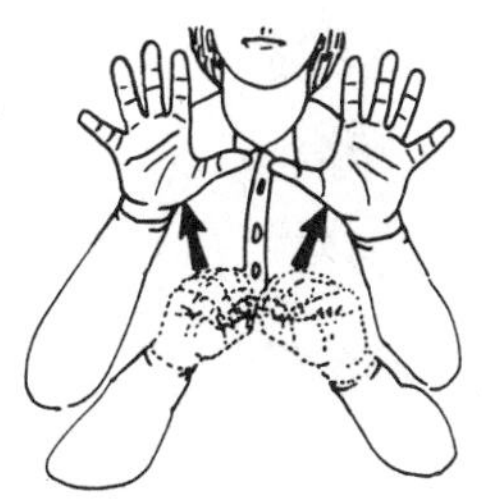

Arabic: dhu' ضوء
Chinese: dēng 燈
Dutch: licht
French: lumière
German: Licht
Italian: luce
Japanese: hikari 光
Korean: bit 빛
Portuguese: luz
Russian: svet свет
Spanish: luz
Swedish: ljus

1219. lightning [n.]

Arabic: barq برق
Chinese: shǎndiàn 閃電
Dutch: bliksem
French: éclair
German: Blitz
Italian: fulmine
Japanese: shōmei 照明
Korean: bŏngae 번개
Portuguese: relâmpago
Russian: mólniya молния
Spanish: relámpago
Swedish: blixt

1220. like [adj./prep.]

Arabic: míthl مثل
Chinese: xiāngxiàngde 相像的
Dutch: zoals
French: pareil
German: gleich
Italian: simile
Japanese: . . . no yō ni …のように
Korean: bisŭt'han 비슷한
Portuguese: semelhante
Russian: pokhózhiy похожий
Spanish: semejante
Swedish: lik

1221. like [v.]

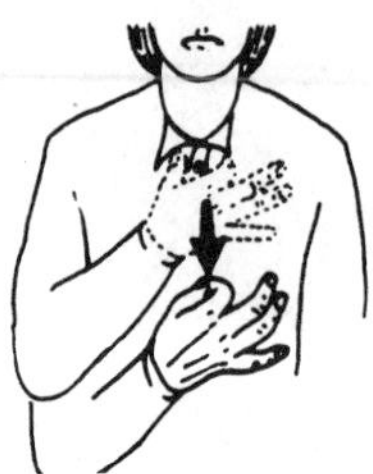

Arabic: hábba حب
Chinese: xǐhuān 喜歡
Dutch: houden van
French: bien aimer
German: gern mögen
Italian: piacere
Japanese: konomu 好む
Korean: joahada 좋아하다
Portuguese: gostar de
Russian: lyubít' любить
Spanish: gustar
Swedish: tycka om

1222. limit [n.]

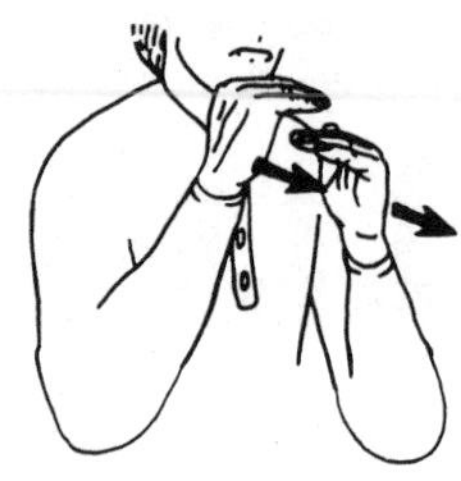

Arabic: had حد
Chinese: jíxiàn 極限
Dutch: grens
French: limite
German: Grenze
Italian: limite
Japanese: gendo 限度
Korean: jehan 제한
Portuguese: limite
Russian: predél предел
Spanish: límite
Swedish: gräns

1223. line [n.]

Arabic: khat خط
Chinese: hángliè 行列
Dutch: lijn
French: ligne
German: Linie
Italian: linea
Japanese: sen 線
Korean: jul 줄
Portuguese: linha
Russian: líniya линия
Spanish: línea
Swedish: lina

1224. lion [n.]

Arabic: ásad اسد
Chinese: shīzi 獅子
Dutch: leeuw
French: lion
German: Löwe
Italian: leone
Japanese: raion ライオン
Korean: saja 사자
Portuguese: leão
Russian: lev лев
Spanish: león
Swedish: lejon

1225. lip [n.]

Arabic: shíffa شفة
Chinese: zuǐcún 嘴唇
Dutch: lip
French: lèvre
German: Lippe
Italian: labbro
Japanese: kuchibiru くちびる
Korean: ibsul 입술
Portuguese: lábio
Russian: gubá губа
Spanish: labio
Swedish: läpp

1226. liquid [n.]

Arabic: mahlúl محلول
Chinese: yètǐ 液體
Dutch: vloeistof
French: liquide
German: Flüssigkeit
Italian: liquido
Japanese: ekitai 液体
Korean: aegch'e 액체
Portuguese: líquido
Russian: zhídkost' жидкость
Spanish: líquido
Swedish: vätska

1227. liquor (alcoholic beverage) [n.]

Arabic: al-kuhúl الكحول
Chinese: lièjiǔ 烈酒
Dutch: sterke drank
French: spiritueux
German: alkoholisches Getränk
Italian: liquore
Japanese: arukōru iṅryō アルコール飲料
Korean: sul 술
Portuguese: bebidas alcoólicas
Russian: spirtnóy napítok спиртной напиток
Spanish: licor
Swedish: sprit

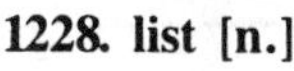

1228. list [n.]

Arabic: qá'ima قائمة
Chinese: dānzi 單子
Dutch: lijst
French: liste
German: Liste
Italian: lista
Japanese: risuto リスト
Korean: myŏngbu 명부
Portuguese: lista
Russian: spísok список
Spanish: lista
Swedish: lista

1229. listen [v.]

Arabic: sámeaa سمع
Chinese: tīng 聽
Dutch: luisteren
French: écouter
German: zuhören
Italian: ascoltare
Japanese: kiku 聞く
Korean: dŭt'da 듣다
Portuguese: escutar
Russian: slúshat' слушать
Spanish: escuchar
Swedish: lyssna

1230. liter [n.]

Arabic: litr لتر
Chinese: gōngshēng 公升
Dutch: liter
French: litre
German: Liter
Italian: litro
Japanese: littoru リットル
Korean: dyoe 되
Portuguese: litro
Russian: lítr литр
Spanish: litro
Swedish: liter

1231. a little [adv.]

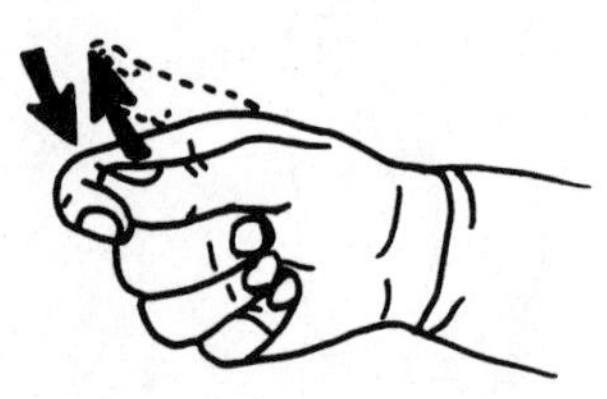

Arabic: qalíl قليل
Chinese: yìdiǎn 一點
Dutch: een beetje
French: un peu
German: ein bißchen
Italian: piccolo
Japanese: sukoshi 少し
Korean: jagŭn 작은
Portuguese: pouco
Russian: nemnógo немного
Spanish: un poco
Swedish: liten

1232. live [v.]

Arabic: áasha عاش
Chinese: zhù 住
Dutch: leven
French: vivre
German: leben
Italian: vivere
Japanese: sumu 住む
Korean: salda 살다
Portuguese: viver
Russian: zhit' жить
Spanish: vivir
Swedish: leva

1233. loan [n.]

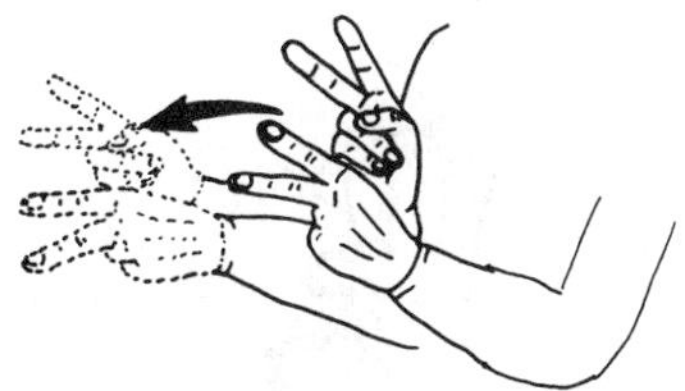

Arabic: qard قرض
Chinese: dàikuǎn 貸款
Dutch: lening
French: prêt
German: Anleihe
Italian: prestito
Japanese: kashitsuke 貸付け
Korean: daebu 대부
Portuguese: empréstimo
Russian: zayóm заём
Spanish: préstamo
Swedish: lån

1234. location (place/position) [n.]

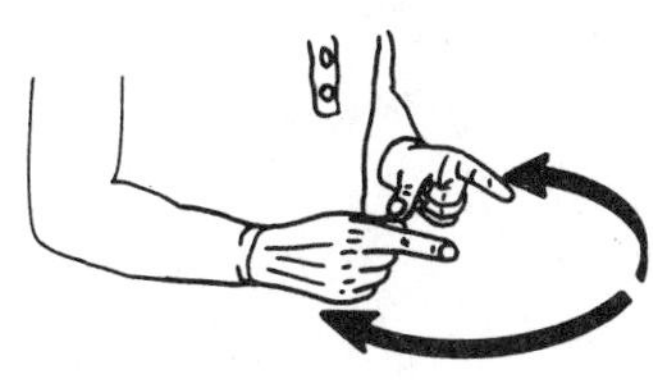

Arabic: máuqea موقع
Chinese: wèizhì 位置
Dutch: plaats
French: emplacement
German: Lage
Italian: posizione
Japanese: ichi 位置
Korean: wich'i 위치
Portuguese: localização
Russian: mestonakhozhdéniye местонахождение
Spanish: ubicación
Swedish: läge

1235. lock (securing device) [n.]

Arabic: qiffl قفل
Chinese: suǒ 鎖
Dutch: slot
French: serrure
German: Schloß
Italian: serrare
Japanese: jō 錠
Korean: jamulsoe 자물쇠
Portuguese: fechadura
Russian: zamók замок
Spanish: cerradura
Swedish: lås

1236. log (wood) [n.]

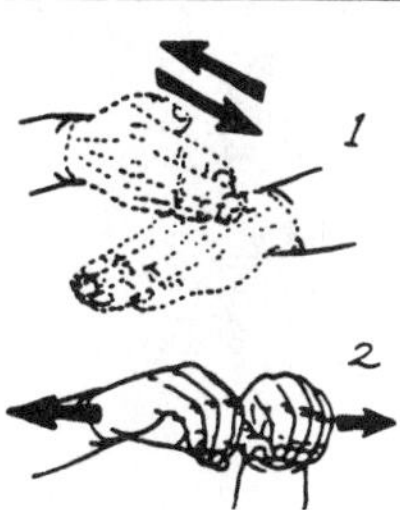

Arabic: zánad al-kháshab زند الخشب
Chinese: mùtóu 木頭
Dutch: houtblok
French: bûche
German: Holzklotz
Italian: ceppo
Japanese: maruta 丸太
Korean: t'ong'namu 통나무
Portuguese: lenha
Russian: brevnó бревно
Spanish: leño
Swedish: stock

1237. logic [n.]

Arabic: mántaq منطق
Chinese: luójí 邏輯
Dutch: logica
French: logique
German: Logik
Italian: logica
Japanese: ronrigaku 論理学
Korean: nolli 논리
Portuguese: lógica
Russian: lógika логика
Spanish: lógica
Swedish: logik

1238. lone [adj.]

Arabic: munáazil منعزل
Chinese: gūdúde 孤獨的
Dutch: alleen
French: seul
German: einzeln
Italian: solo
Japanese: hitori no ひとりの
Korean: godok'ŭi 고독의
Portuguese: só
Russian: odinókiy одинокий
Spanish: solo
Swedish: ensam

1239. lonely [adj.]

Arabic: wahíd وحيد
Chinese: jímòde 寂寞的
Dutch: eenzaam
French: solitaire
German: einsam
Italian: solitario
Japanese: sabishii さびしい
Korean: godok'han 고독한
Portuguese: solitário
Russian: odinókiy одинокий
Spanish: solitario
Swedish: ensam

1240. long [adj.]

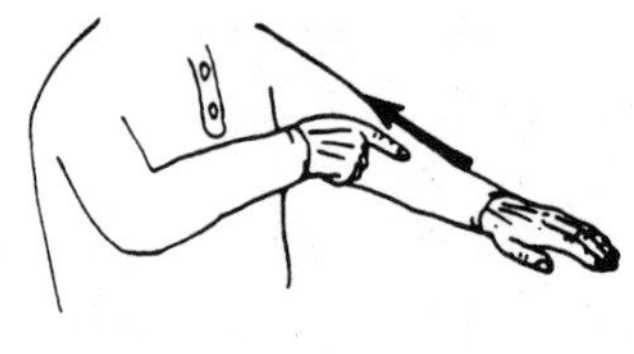

Arabic: tawíl طويل
Chinese: chángde 長的
Dutch: lang
French: long
German: lang
Italian: lungo
Japanese: nagai 長い
Korean: gin 긴
Portuguese: longo
Russian: dlínnyy длинный
Spanish: largo
Swedish: lång

1241. look [v.]

Arabic: nádhara íla نظر الى
Chinese: kàn 看
Dutch: kijken
French: regarder
German: schauen
Italian: guardare
Japanese: miru 見る
Korean: boda 보다
Portuguese: olhar
Russian: smotrét' смотреть
Spanish: mirar
Swedish: titta

1242. loose [adj.]

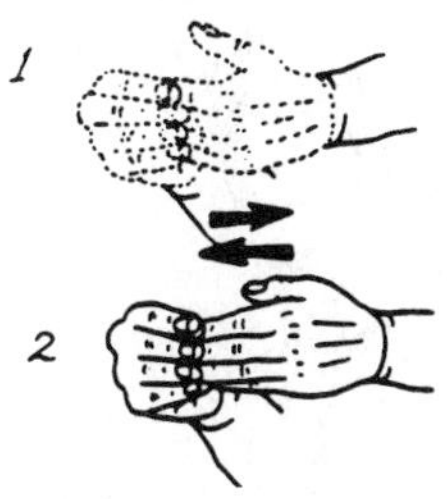

Arabic: fadfád فضفاض
Chinese: sōngchíde 松弛的
Dutch: los
French: lâche
German: lose
Italian: sciolto
Japanese: yurunda ゆるんだ
Korean: hŏlgŏun 헐거운
Portuguese: solto
Russian: razvyázannyy развязанный
Spanish: suelto
Swedish: lös

1243. lose [v.]

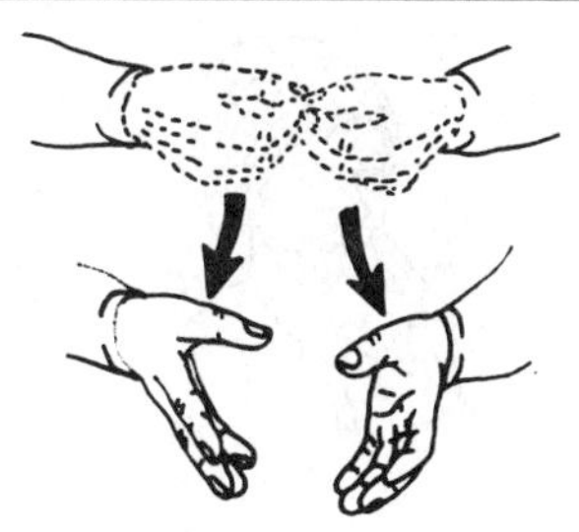

Arabic: fáqada فقد
Chinese: shīqù 失去
Dutch: verliezen
French: perdre
German: verlieren
Italian: perdere
Japanese: nakusuru なくす
Korean: ilt'a 잃다
Portuguese: perder
Russian: teryát' терять
Spanish: perder
Swedish: förlora

1244. a lot [adv.]

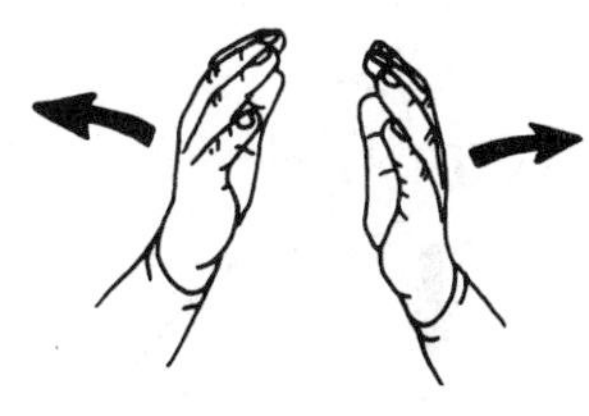

Arabic: kathíran كثيراً
Chinese: hěnduō 很多
Dutch: veel
French: beaucoup
German: viel
Italian: molto
Japanese: takusan no 沢山の
Korean: manŭn 많은
Portuguese: muito
Russian: mnógo много
Spanish: mucho
Swedish: många

1245. loud (noisy) [adj.]

Arabic: áali عالي
Chinese: dàshēng 大聲
Dutch: luid
French: bruyant
German: laut
Italian: rumoroso
Japanese: ōgoe no 大声の
Korean: shikkŭrŏun 시끄러운
Portuguese: barulhento
Russian: grómkiy громкий
Spanish: ruidoso
Swedish: ljudlig

1246. love [v.]

Arabic: hábba حب
Chinese: ài 愛
Dutch: beminnen
French: aimer
German: lieben
Italian: amare
Japanese: aisuru 愛する
Korean: saranghada 사랑하다
Portuguese: amar
Russian: lyubít' любить
Spanish: amar
Swedish: älska

1247. low [adj.]

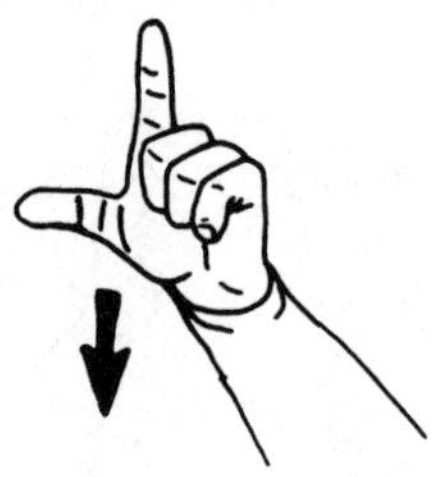

Arabic: munkháfed منخفض
Chinese: dīde 低的
Dutch: laag
French: bas
German: niedrig
Italian: basso
Japanese: hikui 低い
Korean: najŭn 낮은
Portuguese: baixo
Russian: nízkiy низкий
Spanish: bajo
Swedish: låg

1248. luck [n.]

Arabic: hadh حظ
Chinese: yùnqì 運氣
Dutch: geluk
French: chance
German: Glück
Italian: fortuna
Japanese: un 運
Korean: un 운
Portuguese: sorte
Russian: schást'ye счастье
Spanish: suerte
Swedish: lycka

1249. lucky [adj.]

Arabic: mahadhúdh محظوظ
Chinese: xìngyǜnde 幸運的
Dutch: boffend
French: fortuné
German: glücklich
Italian: fortunato
Japanese: un no yoi 運の良い
Korean: unsu johŭn 운수 좋은
Portuguese: sortudo
Russian: schastlívyy счастливый
Spanish: afortunado
Swedish: lycklig

1250. luggage [n.]

Arabic: amtiáa امتعة
Chinese: xínglǐ 行李
Dutch: bagage
French: bagage
German: Gepäck
Italian: bagaglio
Japanese: tenimotsu 手荷物
Korean: suhamul 수화물
Portuguese: bagagem
Russian: bagázh багаж
Spanish: equipaje
Swedish: bagage

1251. lumber [n.]

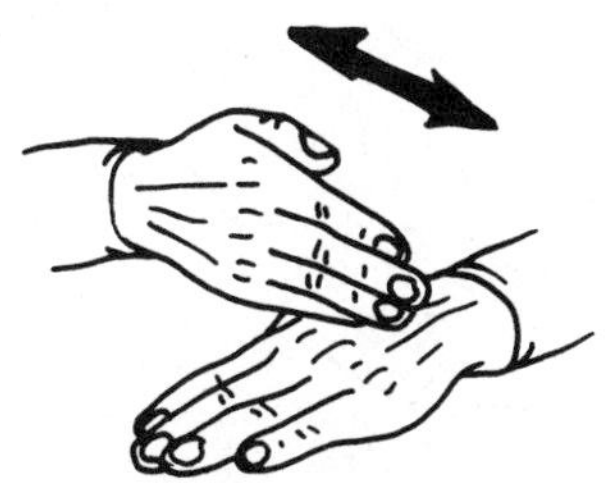

Arabic: kháshab خشب
Chinese: mùcái 木材
Dutch: timmerhout
French: bois de charpente
German: Bauholz
Italian: legname
Japanese: zaimoku 材木
Korean: jaemok 제목
Portuguese: madeira
Russian: pilomateriály пиломатериалы
Spanish: madera aserrada
Swedish: virke

1252. lunch [n.]

Arabic: ghedhá' غذاء
Chinese: wǔfàn 午飯
Dutch: lunch
French: déjeuner
German: Mittagessen
Italian: seconda colazione
Japanese: chūshoku 昼食
Korean: jŏmshim 점심
Portuguese: almôço
Russian: vtoróy závtrak второй завтрак
Spanish: almuerzo
Swedish: lunch

1253. machine [n.]

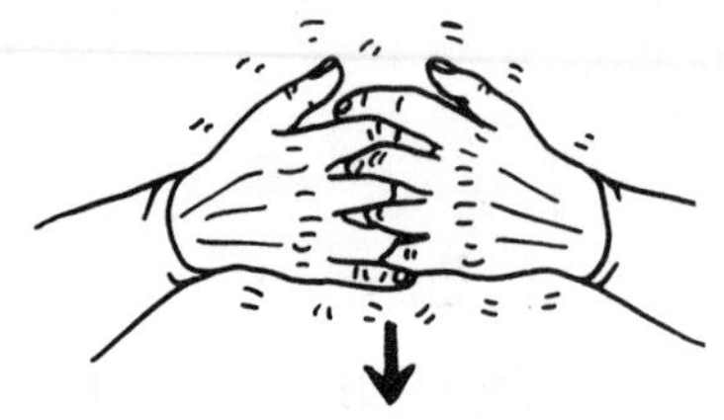

Arabic: ála آلة
Chinese: jīqì 機器
Dutch: machine
French: machine
German: Maschine
Italian: macchina
Japanese: kikai 機械
Korean: kigye 기계
Portuguese: máquina
Russian: mashína машина
Spanish: máquina
Swedish: maskin

1254. machinery [n.]

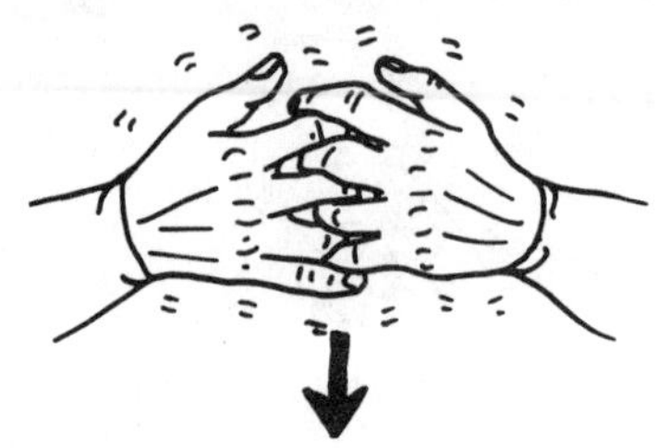

Arabic: al-aláat الالات
Chinese: jījiè 機械
Dutch: machinerie
French: mécanique
German: Maschinerie
Italian: macchinario
Japanese: kikairui 機械類
Korean: kigyeryu 기계류
Portuguese: maquinaria
Russian: mashíny машины
Spanish: maquinaria
Swedish: maskineri

1255. mad (insane) [adj.]

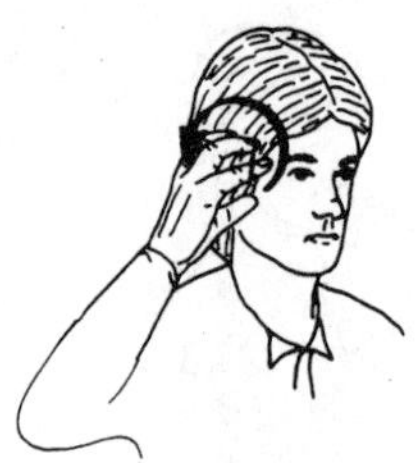

Arabic: majnún مجنون
Chinese: fēngkuángde 瘋狂的
Dutch: waanzinnig
French: fou
German: wahnsinnig
Italian: pazzo
Japanese: kiga kurutta 気が狂った
Korean: mich'in 미친
Portuguese: louco
Russian: sumasshédshiy сумасшедший
Spanish: loco
Swedish: vansinnig

1256. magazine [n.]

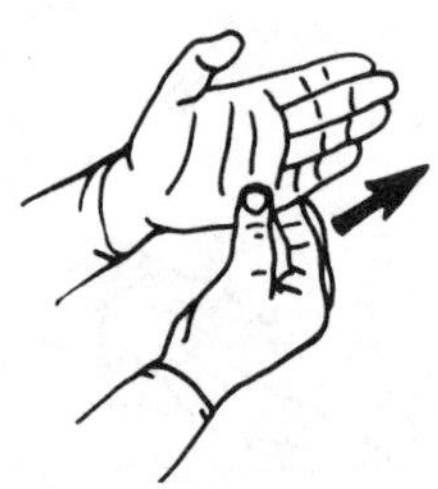

Arabic: majálla مجلة
Chinese: zázhì 雜誌
Dutch: tijdschrift
French: revue
German: Zeitschrift
Italian: rivista
Japanese: zasshi 雑誌
Korean: jabji 잡지
Portuguese: revista
Russian: zhurnál журнал
Spanish: revista
Swedish: tidskrift

1257. magic [n.]

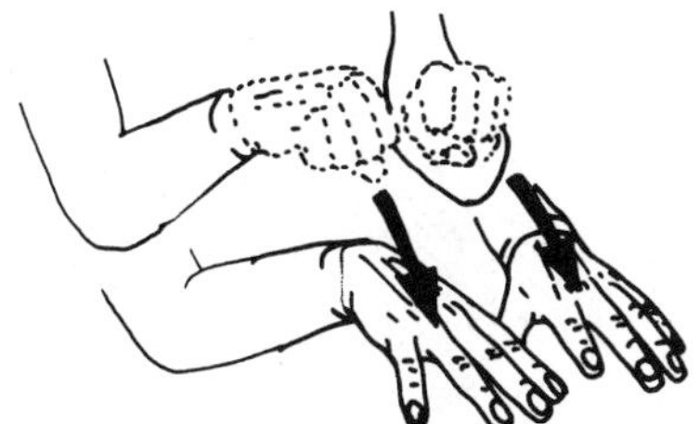

Arabic: séhir سحر
Chinese: mósù 魔術
Dutch: magie
French: magie
German: Magie
Italian: magia
Japanese: majutsu 魔術
Korean: yosul 요술
Portuguese: mágica
Russian: mágiya магия
Spanish: magia
Swedish: magi

1258. magnificent [adj.]

Arabic: aadhím عظيم
Chinese: tánghuángde 堂皇的
Dutch: prachtig
French: magnifique
German: prächtig
Italian: magnifico
Japanese: subarashii 素晴しい
Korean: jangŏmhan 장엄한
Portuguese: magnífico
Russian: velikolépnyy великолепный
Spanish: magnífico
Swedish: storartad

1259. maid (domestic servant) [n.]

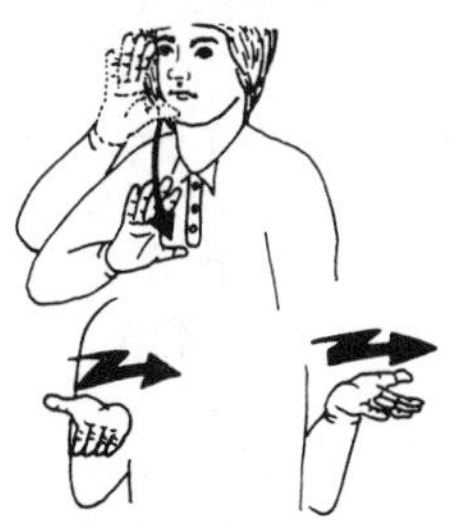

Arabic: khádema خادمة
Chinese: nǚpú 女僕
Dutch: dienstmeisje
French: domestique
German: Dienstmädchen
Italian: cameriera
Japanese: jochū 女中
Korean: hanyŏ 하녀
Portuguese: empregada
Russian: górnichnaya горничная
Spanish: criada
Swedish: hembiträde

1260. mail [n.]

Arabic: baríd بريد
Chinese: yóujiàn 郵件
Dutch: post
French: courrier
German: Post
Italian: posta
Japanese: yubin 郵便
Korean: up'yŏnmul 우편물
Portuguese: correio
Russian: póchta почта
Spanish: correo
Swedish: post

1261. main [adj.]

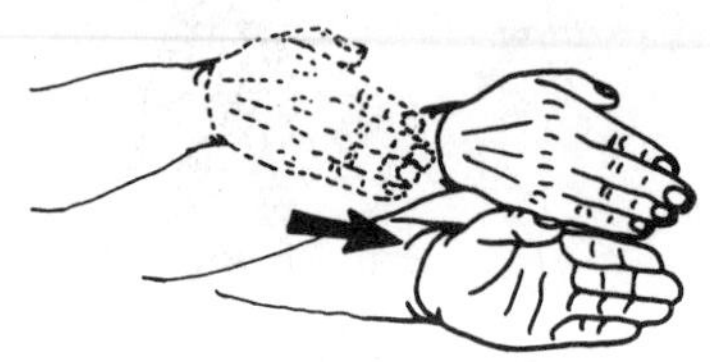

Arabic: ra'ísi رئيسي
Chinese: zhǔyàode 主要的
Dutch: voornaamste
French: principal
German: Haupt-
Italian: principale
Japanese: omona おもな
Korean: juyohan 주요한
Portuguese: principal
Russian: glávnyy главный
Spanish: principal
Swedish: huvud-

1262. mainly [adv.]

Arabic: gháliban غالباً
Chinese: zhǔyào 主要
Dutch: voornamelijk
French: surtout
German: hauptsächlich
Italian: principalmente
Japanese: omoni おもに
Korean: juro 주로
Portuguese: principalmente
Russian: glávnym óbrazom главным образом
Spanish: principalmente
Swedish: huvudsakligen

1263. maintain [v.]

Arabic: há'it حائط
Chinese: wéichí 維持
Dutch: handhaven
French: maintenir
German: unterhalten
Italian: mantenere
Japanese: hoji suru 保持する
Korean: yujihada 유지하다
Portuguese: manter
Russian: poddérzhivat' поддерживать
Spanish: mantener
Swedish: uppehålla

1264. majority [n.]

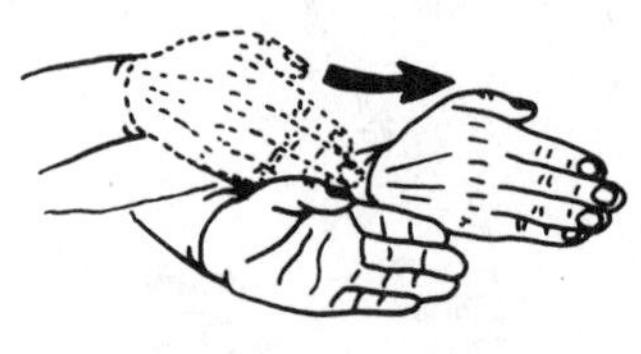

Arabic: ghalibíyya غالبية
Chinese: dàzhòng 大衆
Dutch: meerderheid
French: majorité
German: Mehrheit
Italian: maggioranza
Japanese: daitasū 大多数
Korean: daedasu 대다수
Portuguese: maioria
Russian: bol'shinstvó большинство
Spanish: mayoría
Swedish: majoritet

1265. make [v.]

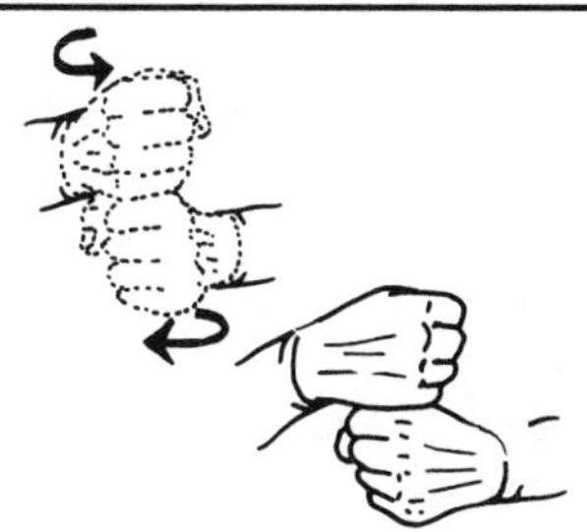

Arabic: fáala فعل
Chinese: zuò 做
Dutch: maken
French: faire
German: machen
Italian: fare
Japanese: tsukuru 作る
Korean: mandŭlda 만들다
Portuguese: fazer
Russian: délat' делать
Spanish: hacer
Swedish: göra

1266. man [n.]

Arabic: rájul رجل
Chinese: nán rén 男人
Dutch: man
French: homme
German: Mann
Italian: uomo
Japanese: otoko 男
Korean: namja 남자
Portuguese: homem
Russian: muzhchína мужчина
Spanish: hombre
Swedish: man

1267. manage [v.]

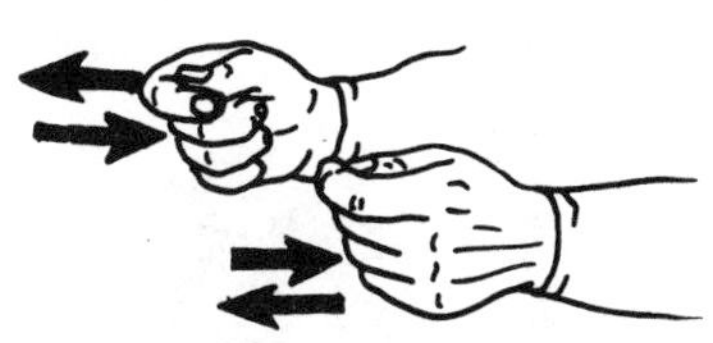

Arabic: adára ادار
Chinese: chŭlĭ 處理
Dutch: beheren
French: gérer
German: verwalten
Italian: dirigere
Japanese: kanri suru 管理する
Korean: kwallihada 관리하다
Portuguese: manejar
Russian: upravlyát' управлять
Spanish: manejar
Swedish: styra

1268. management [n.]

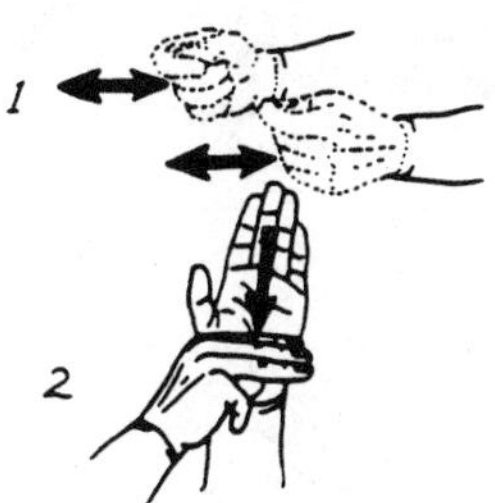

Arabic: idára ادارة
Chinese: jīngyíng 經營
Dutch: beheer
French: gestion
German: Verwaltung
Italian: direzione
Japanese: kanri 管理
Korean: kwalli 관리
Portuguese: administração
Russian: upravléniye управление
Spanish: administración
Swedish: styrelse

1269. manager [n.]

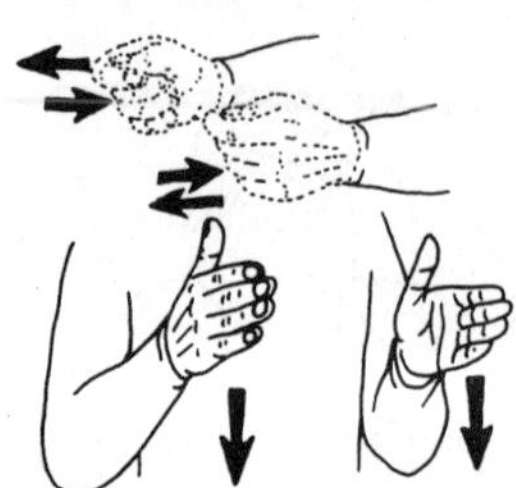

Arabic: mudír مدير
Chinese: jīnglǐ 經理
Dutch: directeur
French: gérant
German: Direktor
Italian: direttore
Japanese: shihainin 支配人
Korean: kwallija 관리자
Portuguese: gerente
Russian: upravlyáyushchiy управляющий
Spanish: gerente
Swedish: direktör

1270. manner (way of doing) [n.]

Arabic: uslúb اسلوب
Chinese: fāngshì 方式
Dutch: manier
French: manière
German: Manier
Italian: maniera
Japanese: yarikata やり方
Korean: t'aedo 태도
Portuguese: maneira
Russian: manéra манера
Spanish: manera
Swedish: sätt

1271. manual [n.]

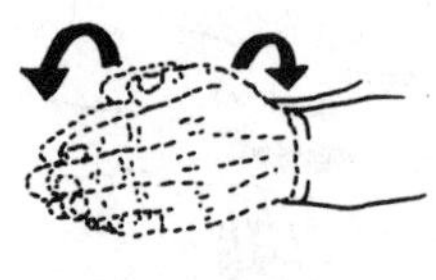

Arabic: kutáyyeb كتيب
Chinese: shǒucè 手册
Dutch: handboek
French: manuel
German: Handbuch
Italian: manuale
Japanese: tebiki 手引き
Korean: annaesŏ 안내서
Portuguese: manual
Russian: rukovódstvo руководство
Spanish: manual
Swedish: elementarbok

1272. manufacture [v.]

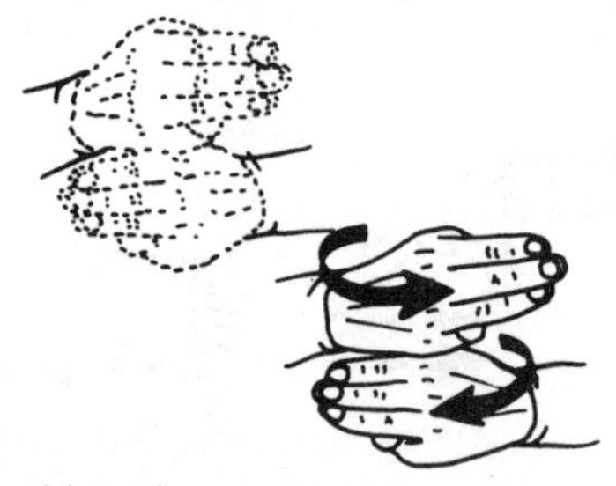

Arabic: sánnaa صنع
Chinese: zhìzào 製造
Dutch: vervaardigen
French: fabriquer
German: herstellen
Italian: fabbricare
Japanese: seizo suru 製造する
Korean: jejohada 제조하다
Portuguese: fabricar
Russian: izgotávlivat' изготавливать
Spanish: fabricar
Swedish: tillverka

1273. many [adj./adv.]

Arabic: kathír كثير
Chinese: hěnduō 很多
Dutch: veel
French: nombreux
German: viele
Italian: molti
Japanese: ōkuno 多くの
Korean: manŭn 많은
Portuguese: muitos
Russian: mnógo много
Spanish: muchos
Swedish: många

1274. map [n.]

Arabic: kharíta خريطة
Chinese: dìtú 地圖
Dutch: kaart
French: carte
German: Karte
Italian: mappa
Japanese: chizu 地図
Korean: jido 지도
Portuguese: mapa
Russian: kárta карта
Spanish: mapa
Swedish: karta

1275. March [n.]

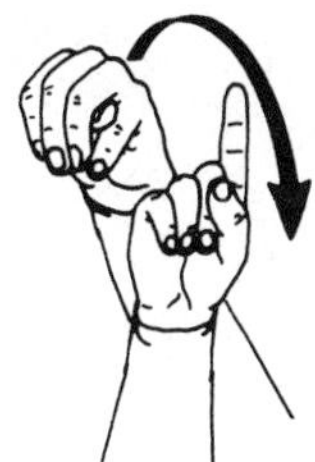

Arabic: máris مارس
Chinese: sānyuè 三月
Dutch: maart
French: mars
German: März
Italian: marzo
Japanese: sangatsu 三月
Korean: samwŏl 삼월
Portuguese: março
Russian: mart март
Spanish: marzo
Swedish: mars

1276. mark [v.]

Arabic: aaláma علامة
Chinese: biāojì 標記
Dutch: markeren
French: marquer
German: markieren
Italian: marcare
Japanese: shirushi o tsukeru 印をつける
Korean: p'yorŭlhada 표를 하다
Portuguese: marcar
Russian: markirovát' маркировать
Spanish: marcar
Swedish: märka

1277. market [n.]

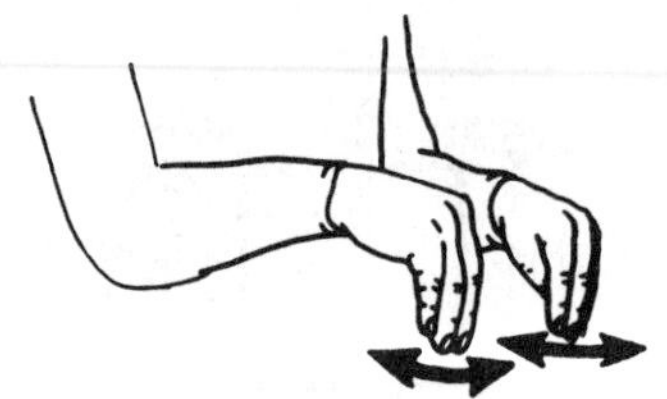

Arabic: suq سوق
Chinese: shìchǎng 市場
Dutch: markt
French: marché
German: Markt
Italian: mercato
Japanese: shijō 市場
Korean: shijang 시장
Portuguese: mercado
Russian: rýnok рынок
Spanish: mercado
Swedish: marknad

1278. marriage [n.]

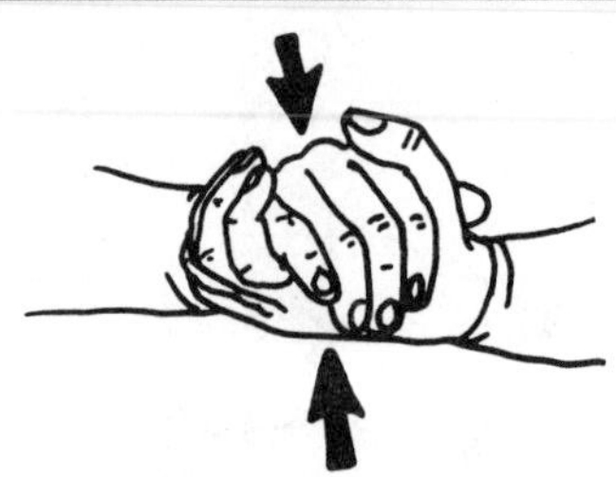

Arabic: zawáj زواج
Chinese: hūnyīn 婚姻
Dutch: huwelijk
French: mariage
German: Ehe
Italian: matrimonio
Japanese: kekkon 結婚
Korean: gyŏlhon 결혼
Portuguese: casamento
Russian: brak брак
Spanish: matrimonio
Swedish: äktenskap

1279. marvelous [adj.]

Arabic: múd-hish مدهش
Chinese: qímiào dě 奇妙的
Dutch: wonderbaar
French: merveilleux
German: wunderbar
Italian: meraviglioso
Japanese: odorokubeki 驚くべき
Korean: nollaun 놀라운
Portuguese: maravilhoso
Russian: izumítel'nyy изумительный
Spanish: maravilloso
Swedish: underbar

1280. master [n.]

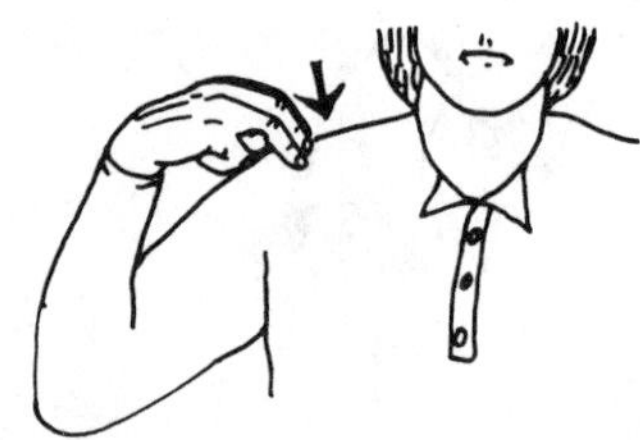

Arabic: séyyid سيد
Chinese: zhǔrén 主人
Dutch: meester
French: maître
German: Meister
Italian: padrone
Japanese: shujin 主人
Korean: juin 주인
Portuguese: mestre
Russian: khozyáin хозяин
Spanish: maestro
Swedish: mästare

1281. match (fire) [n.]

Arabic: kebríta كبريتة
Chinese: huŏchái 火柴
Dutch: lucifer
French: allumette
German: Streichholz
Italian: fiammifero
Japanese: matchi マッチ
Korean: sŏngnyang 성냥
Portuguese: fósforo
Russian: spíchka спичка
Spanish: fósforo
Swedish: tändsticka

1282. mathematics [n.]

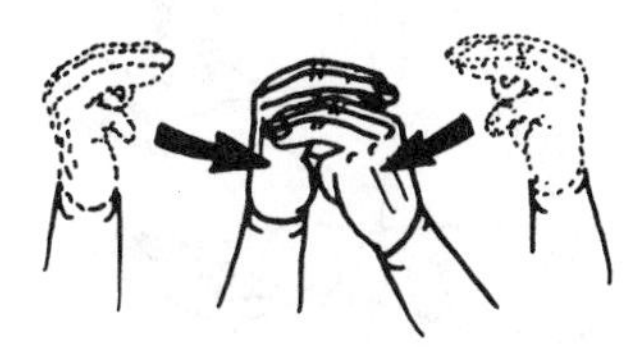

Arabic: riadhiát رياضيات
Chinese: shùxué 數學
Dutch: wiskunde
French: mathématiques
German: Mathematik
Italian: matematica
Japanese: sūgaku 数学
Korean: suhag 수학
Portuguese: matemática
Russian: matemátika математика
Spanish: matemáticas
Swedish: matematik

1283. matter (substance) [n.]

Arabic: mádda مادة
Chinese: shìwù 事物
Dutch: stof
French: matière
German: Stoff
Italian: materia
Japanese: busshitsu 物質
Korean: muljil 물질
Portuguese: matéria
Russian: veshchestvó вещество
Spanish: materia
Swedish: stoff

1284. May (month) [n.]

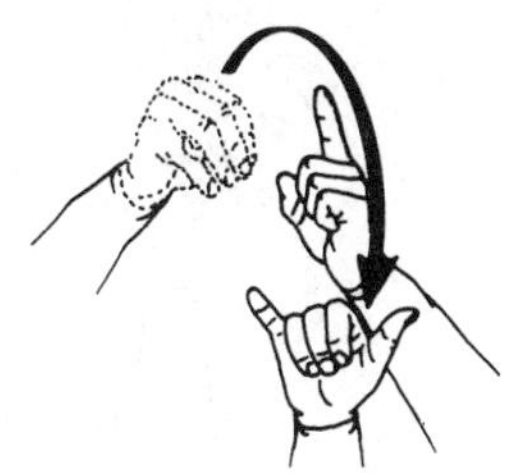

Arabic: máyu مايو
Chinese: wŭyuè 五月
Dutch: mei
French: mai
German: Mai
Italian: maggio
Japanese: gogatsu 五月
Korean: owŏl 오월
Portuguese: maio
Russian: maio маио
Spanish: mayo
Swedish: maj

1285. may [v.]

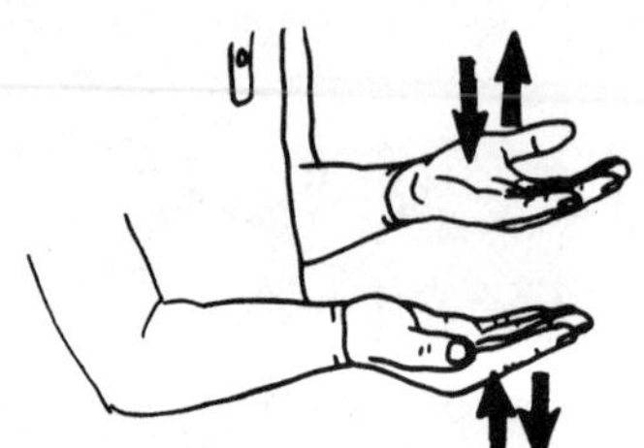

Arabic: istatá' استطاع
Chinese: kěyǐ 可以
Dutch: mogen
French: pouvoir
German: mögen
Italian: potere
Japanese:...kamo shirenai
…かも知れない
Korean: hal su it'da 할 수 있다
Portuguese: poder
Russian: moch' мочь
Spanish: poder
Swedish: kunna

1286. me [pron.]

Arabic: -ni ـني...
Chinese: wǒ 我
Dutch: mij
French: moi
German: mich
Italian: me/mi
Japanese: watakushi ni 私に
Korean: narŭl 나를
Portuguese: me/mim
Russian: menyá/mne/mnoy
меня/мне/мной
Spanish: me/mí
Swedish: mig

1287. meal (repast) [n.]

Arabic: wájba وجبة
Chinese: fàn 飯
Dutch: maaltijd
French: repas
German: Mahl
Italian: pasto
Japanese: shokuji 食事
Korean: shiksa 식사
Portuguese: refeição
Russian: yedá еда
Spanish: comida
Swedish: måltid

1288. mean [v.]

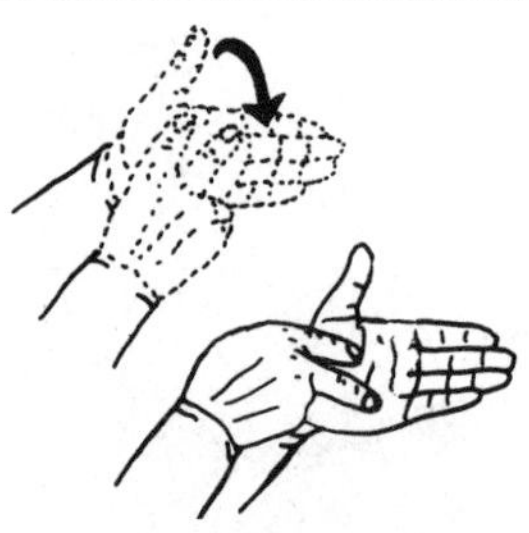

Arabic: áana عنى
Chinese: yìzhǐ 意指
Dutch: betekenen
French: signifier
German: bedeuten
Italian: significare
Japanese: imi suru 意味する
Korean: ŭimihada 의미하다
Portuguese: significar
Russian: znáchit' значить
Spanish: significar
Swedish: betyda

1289. meaning [n.]

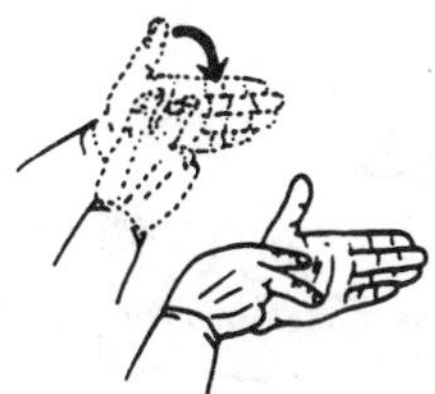

Arabic: máana معنى
Chinese: yìsī 意思
Dutch: betekenis
French: sens
German: Bedeutung
Italian: significato
Japanese: imi 意味
Korean: ttŭt 뜻
Portuguese: significado
Russian: znachéniye значение
Spanish: significado
Swedish: mening

1290. measure [v.]

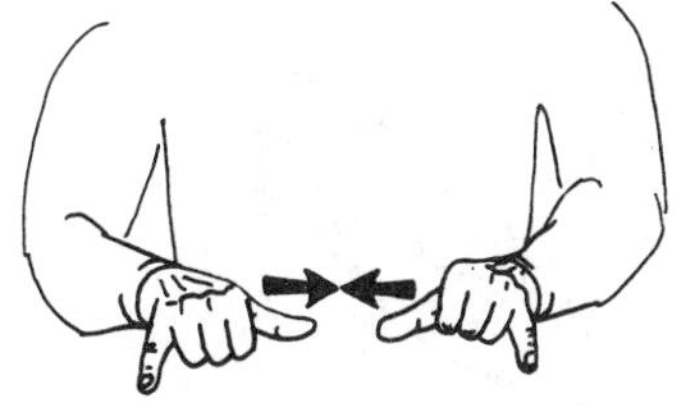

Arabic: qása قاس
Chinese: cèliáng 测量
Dutch: meten
French: mesurer
German: messen
Italian: misurare
Japanese: hakaru 計る
Korean: jaeda 재다
Portuguese: medir
Russian: izmeryát' измерять
Spanish: medir
Swedish: mäta

1291. meat [n.]

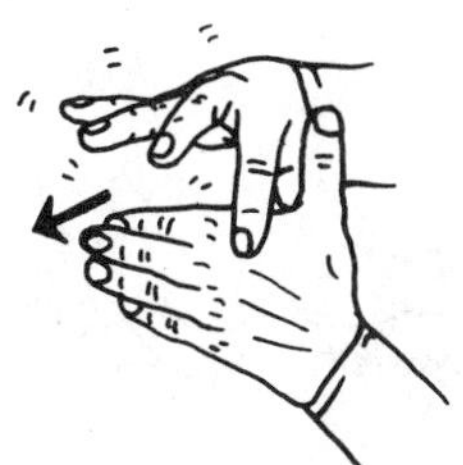

Arabic: láhem لحم
Chinese: ròu 肉
Dutch: vlees
French: viande
German: Fleisch
Italian: carne
Japanese: niku 肉
Korean: kogi 고기
Portuguese: carne
Russian: myáso мясо
Spanish: carne
Swedish: kött

1292. mechanic [n.]

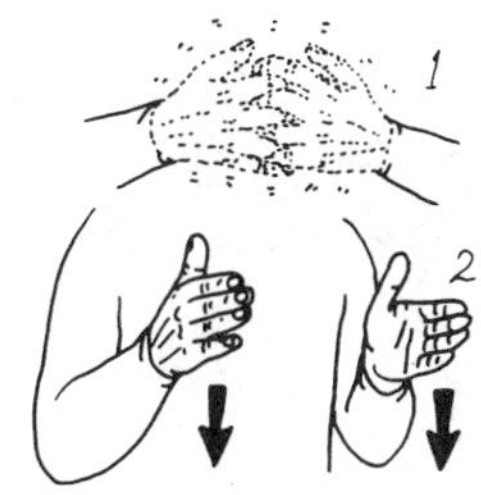

Arabic: mikaníki ميكانيكي
Chinese: jìgōng 技工
Dutch: werktuigkunde
French: mécanicien
German: Mechaniker
Italian: meccanico
Japanese: shūrikō 修理工
Korean: jikkong 직공
Portuguese: mecânico
Russian: mekhánik механик
Spanish: mecánico
Swedish: mekaniker

1293. medal [n.]

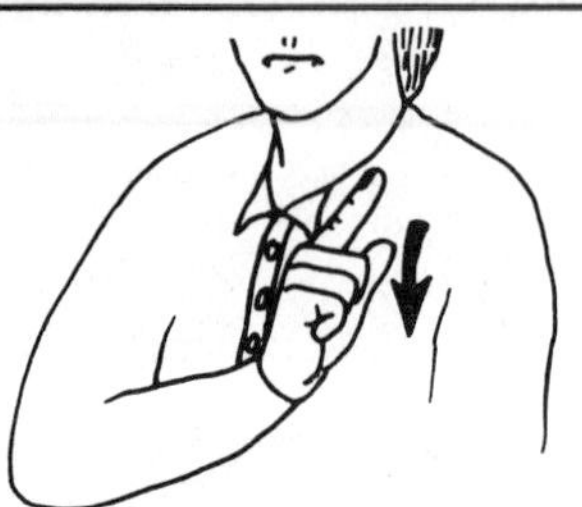

Arabic: midália مدالية
Chinese: jiǎngzhāng 獎章
Dutch: medaille
French: médaille
German: Medaille
Italian: medaglia
Japanese: kunshō 勲章
Korean: medal 메달
Portuguese: medalha
Russian: medál' медаль
Spanish: medalla
Swedish: medalj

1294. medicine [n.]

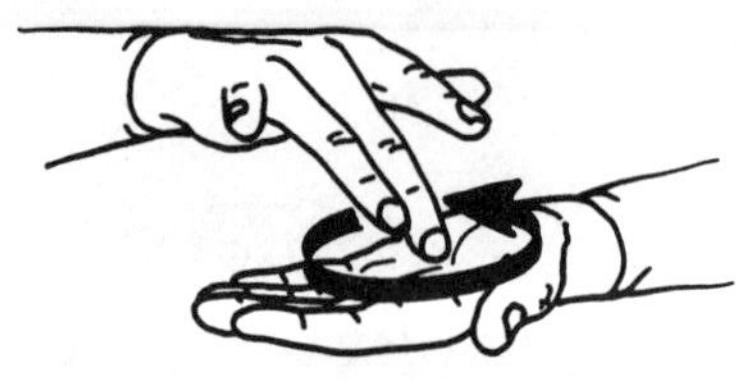

Arabic: dawá' دواء
Chinese: yào 藥
Dutch: medicijn
French: médicament
German: Medizin
Italian: medicina
Japanese: kusuri 薬
Korean: yak 약
Portuguese: medicina
Russian: lekárstvo лекарство
Spanish: medicina
Swedish: medicin

1295. meet (encounter) [v.]

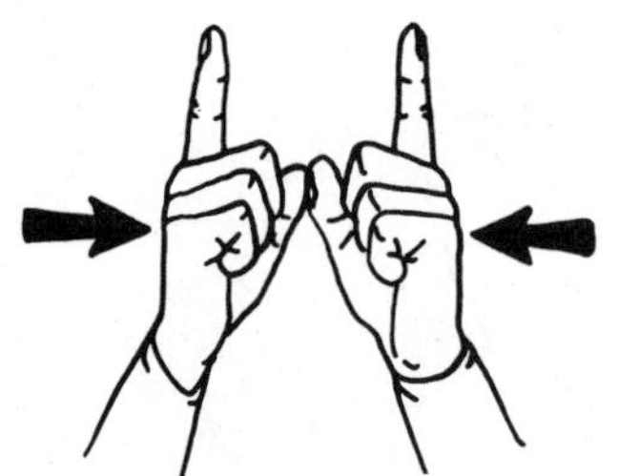

Arabic: láaqa لاقى
Chinese: yǜjiàn 遇見
Dutch: ontmoeten
French: rencontrer
German: begegnen
Italian: incontrare
Japanese: au 会う
Korean: mannada 만나다
Portuguese: encontrar
Russian: vstrechát' встречать
Spanish: encontrarse con
Swedish: möta

1296. meeting [n.]

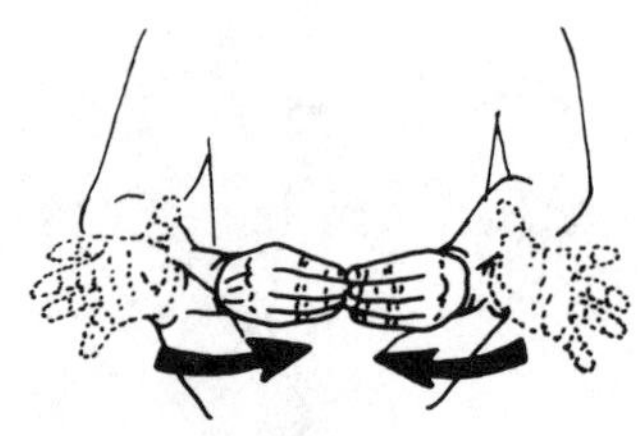

Arabic: ijteméaa اجتماع
Chinese: huìyì 會議
Dutch: bijeenkomst
French: réunion
German: Versammlung
Italian: riunione
Japanese: kaigō 会合
Korean: hoehap 회합
Portuguese: reunião
Russian: sobrániye собрание
Spanish: reunión
Swedish: möte

1297. melon [n.]

Arabic: shammám شمام
Chinese: guā 瓜
Dutch: meloen
French: melon
German: Melone
Italian: melone
Japanese: meron メロン
Korean: mellon 멜론
Portuguese: melão
Russian: dýnya дыня
Spanish: melón
Swedish: melon

1298. melt [v.]

Arabic: insáhara انصهر
Chinese: rónghuà 融化
Dutch: smelten
French: fondre
German: schmelzen
Italian: fondere
Japanese: tokeru 溶ける
Korean: nogta 녹다
Portuguese: derreter
Russian: táyat' таять
Spanish: derretir
Swedish: smälta

1299. member [n.]

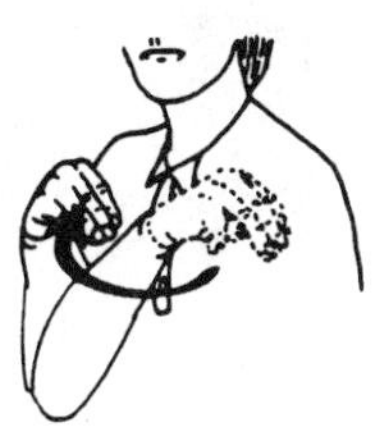

Arabic: ódu عضو
Chinese: huìyuán 會員
Dutch: lid
French: membre
German: Mitglied
Italian: membro
Japanese: kaiin 会員
Korean: hoewŏn 회원
Portuguese: membro
Russian: chlen член
Spanish: miembro
Swedish: medlem

1300. memorize [v.]

Arabic: tadhákara تذكر
Chinese: jìzhù 記住
Dutch: uit het hoofd leren
French: apprendre par coeur
German: auswendig lernen
Italian: imparare a memoria
Japanese: kioku suru 記憶する
Korean: kiŏghada 기억하다
Portuguese: decorar
Russian: zaúchivat' naizúst'
заучивать наизусть
Spanish: aprender de memoria
Swedish: lära sig utantill

1301. memory [n.]

Arabic: dhákira ذاكرة
Chinese: jìyì 記憶
Dutch: geheugen
French: mémoire
German: Gedächtnis
Italian: memoria
Japanese: kioku 記憶
Korean: kiŏg 기억
Portuguese: memória
Russian: pámyat' память
Spanish: memoria
Swedish: minne

1302. mend (repair) [v.]

Arabic: áslaha اصلح
Chinese: xiūzhèng 修正
Dutch: herstellen
French: réparer
German: reparieren
Italian: riparare
Japanese: naosu 直す
Korean: surihada 수리하다
Portuguese: reparar
Russian: ispravlyát' исправлять
Spanish: remendar
Swedish: reparera

1303. mental [adj.]

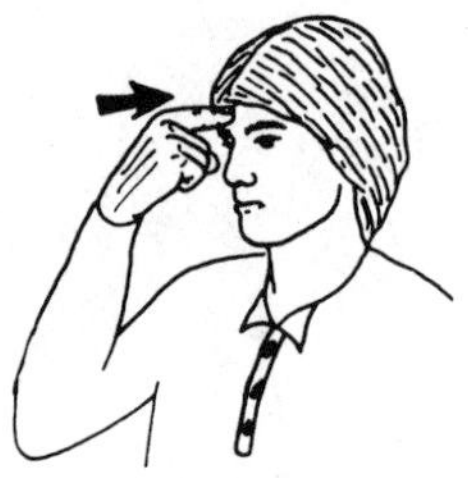

Arabic: áaqli عقلي
Chinese: jīngshénde 精神的
Dutch: geestelijk
French: mental
German: geistig
Italian: mentale
Japanese: seishin no 精神の
Korean: jŏngshinŭi 정신의
Portuguese: mental
Russian: úmstvennyy умственный
Spanish: mental
Swedish: själslig

1304. mention [v.]

Arabic: ashára íla اشار الى
Chinese: tídào 提到
Dutch: vermelden
French: mentionner
German: erwähnen
Italian: menzionare
Japanese: . . . ni tsuite hanasu …について話す
Korean: marhada 말하다
Portuguese: mencionar
Russian: upominát' упоминать
Spanish: mencionar
Swedish: nämna

1305. merchant [n.]

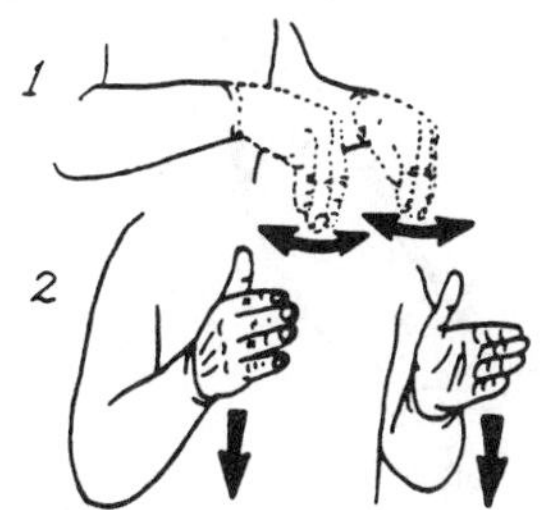

Arabic: tájir تاجر
Chinese: shāngrén 商人
Dutch: koopman
French: marchand
German: Kaufmann
Italian: commerciante
Japanese: shōnin 商人
Korean: sangin 상인
Portuguese: comerciante
Russian: torgóvets торговец
Spanish: comerciante
Swedish: köpman

1306. mercy [n.]

Arabic: ráhma رحمة
Chinese: réncí 仁慈
Dutch: barmhartigheid
French: miséricorde
German: Barmherzigkeit
Italian: misericordia
Japanese: nasake 情け
Korean: jabi 자비
Portuguese: misericórdia
Russian: milosérdiye милосердие
Spanish: misericordia
Swedish: barmhärtighet

1307. merge [v.]

Arabic: dámaja دمج
Chinese: hébìng 合併
Dutch: samengaan
French: amalgamer
German: verschmelzen
Italian: unirsi
Japanese: gōdō suru 合同する
Korean: haphada 합하다
Portuguese: convergir
Russian: slivát'sya сливаться
Spanish: convergir
Swedish: sammansmälta

1308. merit [n.]

Arabic: jadára جدارة
Chinese: gōnglaó 功勞
Dutch: verdienste
French: mérite
German: Verdienst
Italian: merito
Japanese: kachi 価値
Korean: jangchŏm 장점
Portuguese: mérito
Russian: zaslúga заслуга
Spanish: mérito
Swedish: förtjänst

1309. merry [adj.]

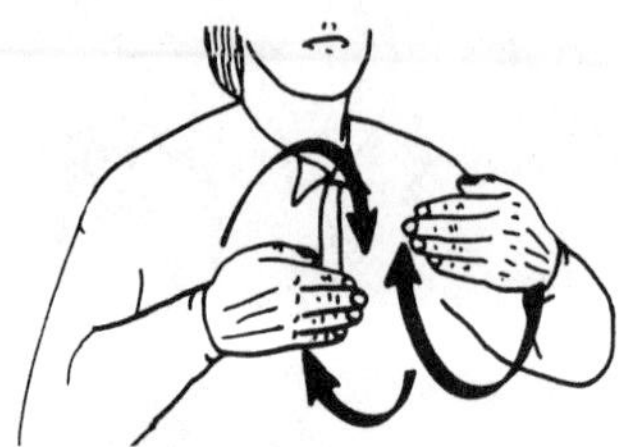

Arabic: márih مرح
Chinese: yúkuài 愉快
Dutch: vrolijk
French: joyeux
German: fröhlich
Italian: allegro
Japanese: yōki na 陽気な
Korean: jŭlgŏun 즐거운
Portuguese: alegre
Russian: vesyólyy весёлый
Spanish: alegre
Swedish: munter

1310. message [n.]

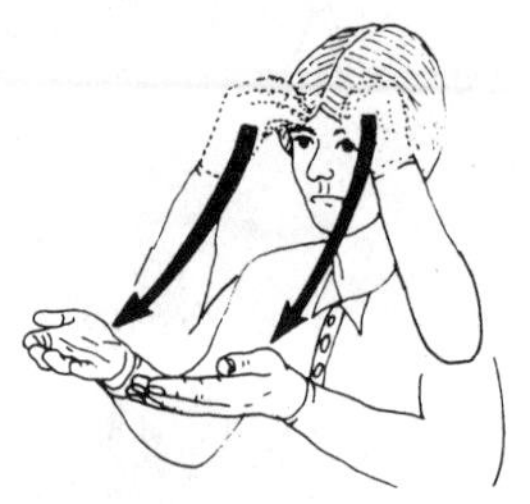

Arabic: resála رسالة
Chinese: xìnxí 信息
Dutch: boodschap
French: message
German: Botschaft
Italian: messaggio
Japanese: dengon 伝言
Korean: soshik 소식
Portuguese: mensagem
Russian: soobshchéniye сообщение
Spanish: mensaje
Swedish: meddelande

1311. metal [n.]

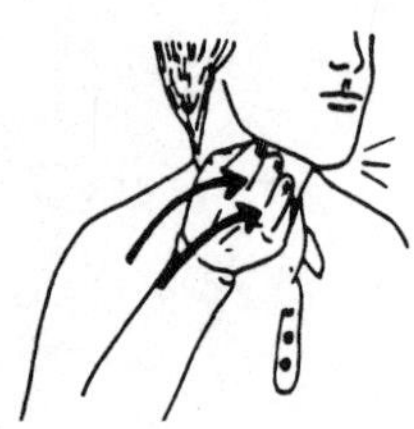

Arabic: máadan معدن
Chinese: jīnshǔ 金屬
Dutch: metaal
French: métal
German: Metall
Italian: metallo
Japanese: kinzoku 金属
Korean: kŭmsok 금속
Portuguese: metal
Russian: metáll металл
Spanish: metal
Swedish: metall

1312. meter (device) [n.]

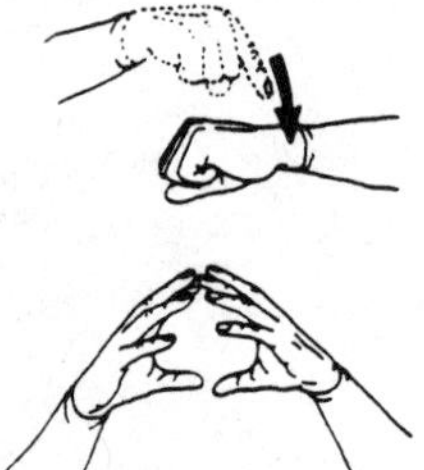

Arabic: aaddád عداد
Chinese: jìliàngbiǎo 計量表
Dutch: meter
French: compteur
German: Messgerät
Italian: contatore
Japanese: keiryōki 計量器
Korean: kyeryanggi 계량기
Portuguese: contador
Russian: schyótchik счётчик
Spanish: contador
Swedish: mätare

1313. meter (unit of measurement) [n.]

Arabic: mitr متر
Chinese: chǐ 尺
Dutch: meter
French: mètre
German: Meter
Italian: metro
Japanese: mētoru メートル
Korean: mit'ŏ 미터
Portuguese: metro
Russian: métr метр
Spanish: metro
Swedish: meter

1314. method [n.]

Arabic: taríqa طريقة
Chinese: fāngfǎ 方法
Dutch: methode
French: méthode
German: Methode
Italian: metodo
Japanese: hōhō 方法
Korean: bangbŏb 방법
Portuguese: método
Russian: métod метод
Spanish: método
Swedish: metod

1315. Mexico [n.]

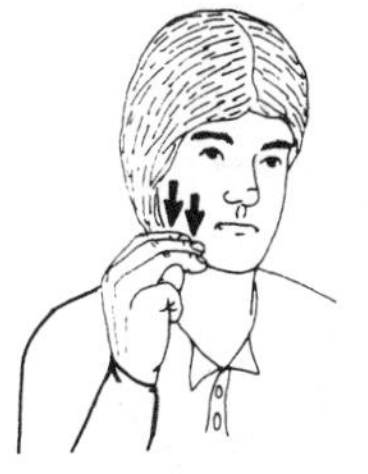

Arabic: al-maksík المكسيك
Chinese: mòxīgē 墨西哥
Dutch: Mexico
French: Mexique
German: Mexiko
Italian: Messico
Japanese: Mekishiko メキシコ
Korean: Mekshik'o 멕시코
Portuguese: México
Russian: Méksika Мексика
Spanish: México
Swedish: Mexiko

1316. middle [adj.]

Arabic: wásat وسط
Chinese: zhōngjiān 中間
Dutch: midden
French: milieu
German: mittlere
Italian: medio
Japanese: mannaka no 真中の
Korean: jungganŭi 중앙의
Portuguese: médio
Russian: srédniy средний
Spanish: medio
Swedish: mellerst

1317. midnight [n.]

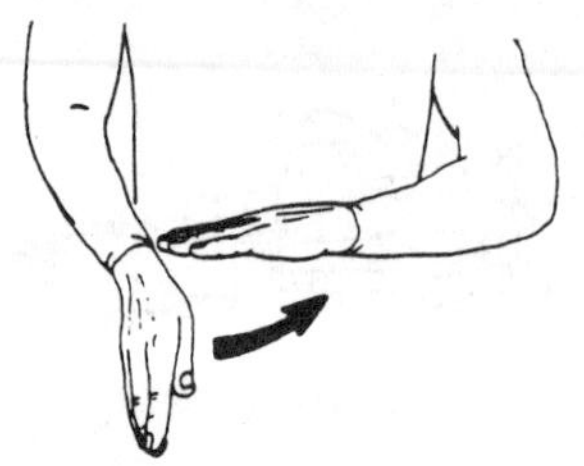

Arabic: muntásaf al-léyl منتصف الليل
Chinese: bànyiè 半夜
Dutch: middernacht
French: minuit
German: Mitternacht
Italian: mezzanotte
Japanese: mayonaka 夜中
Korean: hanbamchung 한밤중
Portuguese: meia-noite
Russian: pólnoch' полночь
Spanish: medianoche
Swedish: midnatt

1318. mighty [adj.]

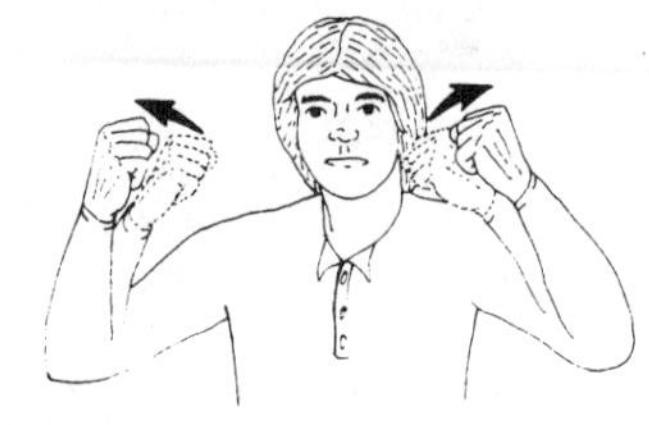

Arabic: qáwi قوي
Chinese: qiángdàde 強大的
Dutch: machtig
French: puissant
German: mächtig
Italian: potente
Japanese: kyodai na 強大な
Korean: himshen 힘센
Portuguese: poderoso
Russian: mogúshchestvennyy могущественный
Spanish: poderoso
Swedish: mäktig

1319. mile [n.]

Arabic: mil ميل
Chinese: lǐ 哩
Dutch: mijl
French: mille
German: Meile
Italian: miglio
Japanese: mairu マイル
Korean: mail 마일
Portuguese: milha
Russian: mílya миля
Spanish: milla
Swedish: mil

1320. military [adj.]

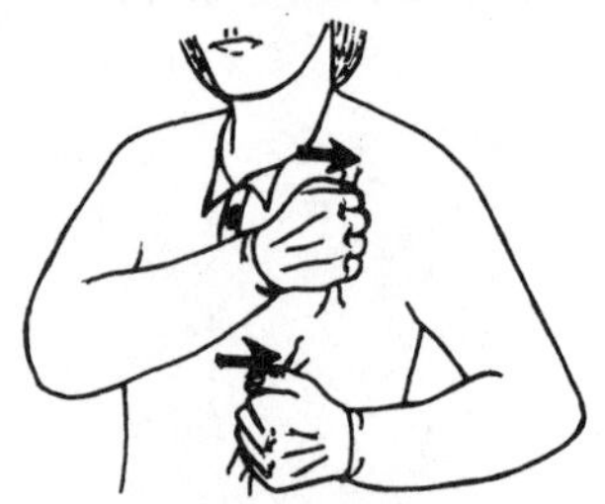

Arabic: áaskari عسكري
Chinese: jūnshì 軍事
Dutch: militair
French: militaire
German: militärisch
Italian: militare
Japanese: guntai no 軍隊の
Korean: gundaeŭi 군대의
Portuguese: militar
Russian: voyénnyy военный
Spanish: militar
Swedish: militär

1321. milk [n.]

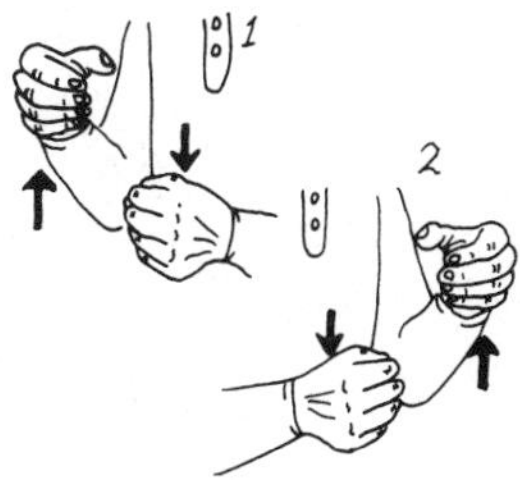

Arabic: halíb/lában لبن / حليب
Chinese: niúnǎi 牛奶
Dutch: melk
French: lait
German: Milch
Italian: latte
Japanese: miruku ミルク
Korean: uyu 우유
Portuguese: leite
Russian: molokó молоко
Spanish: leche
Swedish: mjölk

1322. mill [n.]

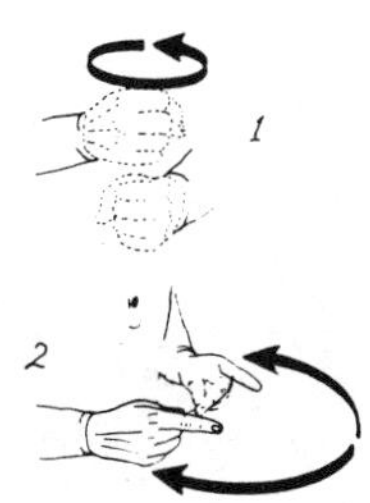

Arabic: mát-hana مطحنة
Chinese: mófǎng 磨坊
Dutch: molen
French: moulin
German: Mühle
Italian: mulino
Japanese: seifun jo 製粉所
Korean: mullebanga 물레방아
Portuguese: moinho
Russian: mél'nitsa мельница
Spanish: molino
Swedish: kvarn

1323. million [n.]

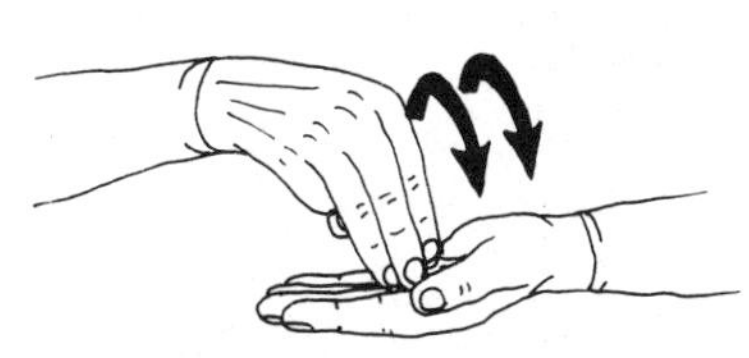

Arabic: milión مليون
Chinese: bǎiwàn 百萬
Dutch: miljoen
French: million
German: Million
Italian: milione
Japanese: hyaju-man 百万
Korean: baengman 백만
Portuguese: milhão
Russian: millión миллион
Spanish: millón
Swedish: million

1324. mind [n.]

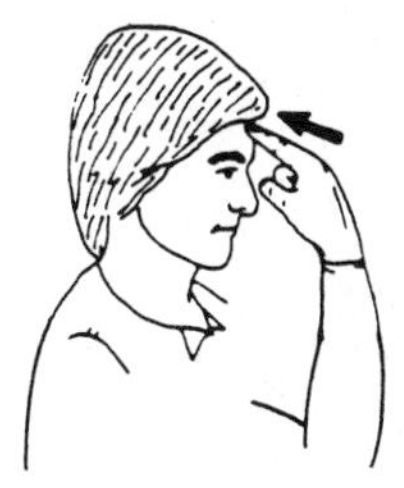

Arabic: áaqel عقل
Chinese: xīn 心
Dutch: verstand
French: esprit
German: Verstand
Italian: mente
Japanese: seishin 精神
Korean: maŭm 마음
Portuguese: mente
Russian: um ум
Spanish: mente
Swedish: förstånd

1325. mine [pron.]

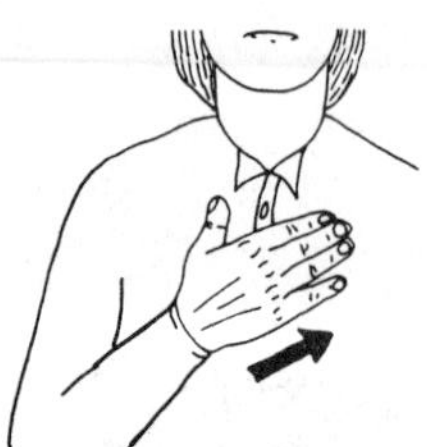

Arabic: li لي
Chinese: wǒde 我的
Dutch: mijn
French: mien
German: mein
Italian: mio
Japanese: watakushi no mono 私のもの
Korean: naegŏt 나의 것
Portuguese: meu
Russian: moy мой
Spanish: mío
Swedish: min

1326. minus [adj./prep.]

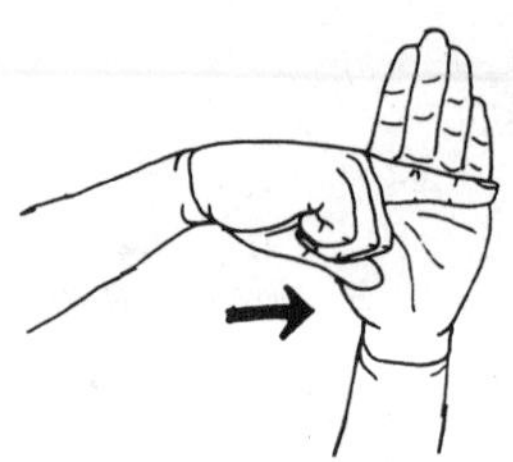

Arabic: náqas ناقص
Chinese: fù 負
Dutch: min
French: moins
German: minus
Italian: meno
Japanese: mainasu no マイナスの
Korean: bp'aeda 빼다
Portuguese: menos
Russian: mínus минус
Spanish: menos
Swedish: minus

1327. minute [n.]

Arabic: daqíqa دقيقة
Chinese: fēnzhōng 分鐘
Dutch: minuut
French: minute
German: Minute
Italian: minuto
Japanese: fun 分
Korean: bun 분
Portuguese: minuto
Russian: minúta минута
Spanish: minuto
Swedish: minut

1328. miracle [n.]

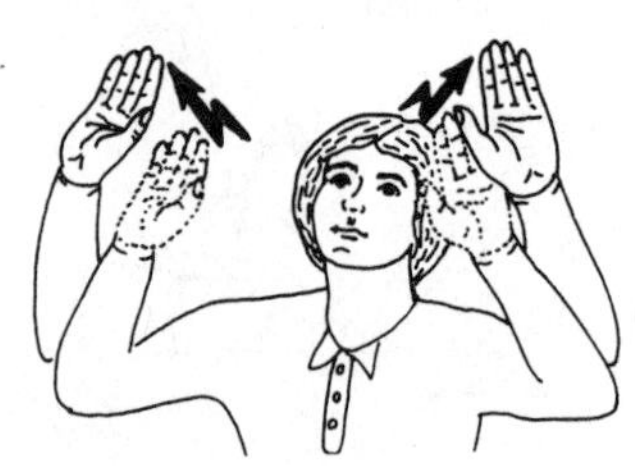

Arabic: móaajiza معجزة
Chinese: qíjī 奇蹟
Dutch: mirakel
French: miracle
German: Wunder
Italian: miracolo
Japanese: kiseki 奇跡
Korean: kijŏg 기적
Portuguese: milagre
Russian: chúdo чудо
Spanish: milagro
Swedish: mirakel

1329. mirror [n.]

Arabic: mir'áa مرآة
Chinese: jìngzi 鏡子
Dutch: spiegel
French: miroir
German: Spiegel
Italian: specchio
Japanese: kagami 鏡
Korean: kŏul 거울
Portuguese: espelho
Russian: zérkalo зеркало
Spanish: espejo
Swedish: spegel

1330. misfortune [n.]

Arabic: musíba مصيبة
Chinese: búxìng 不幸
Dutch: tegenslag
French: malchance
German: Unglück
Italian: disgrazia
Japanese: fukō 不幸
Korean: burun 불운
Portuguese: desgraça
Russian: neschást'ye несчастье
Spanish: desgracia
Swedish: olycka

1331. miss (fail to hit) [v.]

Arabic: ákhta'a اخطأ
Chinese: cuògùò 错過
Dutch: missen
French: manquer
German: verfehlen
Italian: mancare
Japanese: atesokonau 当てそこなう
Korean: noch'ida 놓치다
Portuguese: errar
Russian: ne popást' не попасть
Spanish: errar
Swedish: sakna

1332. missile [n.]

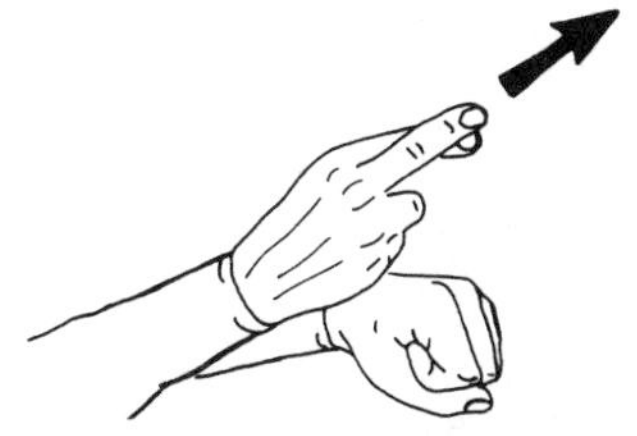

Arabic: sarúkh صاروخ
Chinese: fēidàn 飛弾
Dutch: raket
French: projectile
German: Rakete
Italian: missile
Japanese: misairu ミサイル
Korean: misail 미사일
Portuguese: míssil
Russian: rakéta ракета
Spanish: proyectil
Swedish: raket

1333. mistake [n.]

Arabic: kháta' خطأ
Chinese: cuòwù 錯誤
Dutch: fout
French: faute
German: Fehler
Italian: errore
Japanese: ayamachi 過ち
Korean: jalmot 잘 못
Portuguese: êrro
Russian: oshíbka ошибка
Spanish: error
Swedish: mistag

1334. misunderstand [v.]

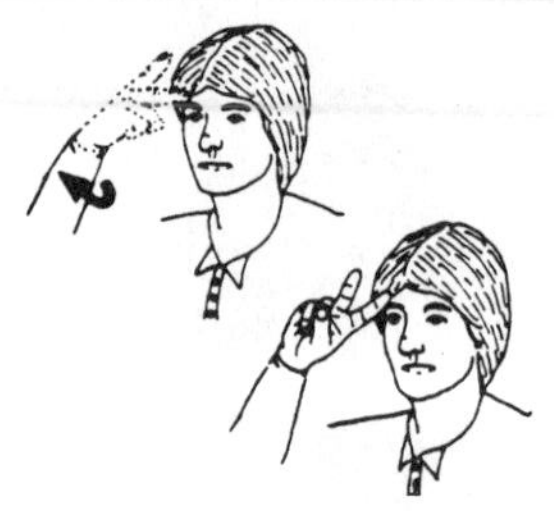

Arabic: asá' al-fáhem أساء الفهم
Chinese: wùjiě 誤解
Dutch: misverstaan
French: mal interpréter
German: mißverstehen
Italian: fraintendere
Japanese: gokai suru 誤解
Korean: ohaehada 오해하다
Portuguese: entender mal
Russian: neprávil'no ponimát' неправильно понимать
Spanish: entender mal
Swedish: missförstå

1335. mix [v.]

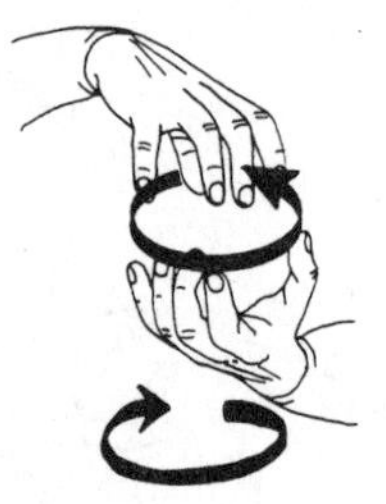

Arabic: khálata خلط
Chinese: hùnhé 混合
Dutch: mengen
French: mélanger
German: mischen
Italian: mischiare
Japanese: mazeru まぜる
Korean: sŏg'da 석다
Portuguese: misturar
Russian: sméshivat' смешивать
Spanish: mezclar
Swedish: blanda

1336. model (pattern) [n.]

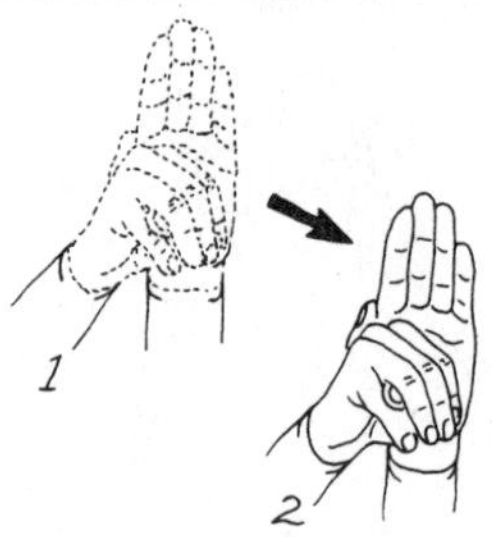

Arabic: namúdhaj نموذج
Chinese: móxíng 模型
Dutch: model
French: modèle
German: Modell
Italian: modello
Japanese: mohan 模範
Korean: mohyŏng 모형
Portuguese: modêlo
Russian: modél' модель
Spanish: modelo
Swedish: modell

1337. modern [adj.]

Arabic: áasri عصري
Chinese: xiàndàide 現代的
Dutch: modern
French: moderne
German: modern
Italian: moderno
Japanese: modan na モダンな
Korean: hyŏndaeŭi 현대의
Portuguese: moderno
Russian: sovreménnyy современный
Spanish: moderno
Swedish: modern

1338. moist [adj.]

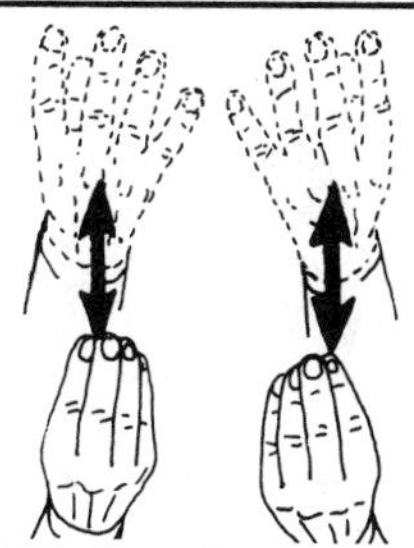

Arabic: ráteb رتب
Chinese: cháoshīde 潮濕的
Dutch: vochtig
French: humide
German: feucht
Italian: umido
Japanese: shimetta 湿った
Korean: ch'ugch'ug'han 축축한
Portuguese: úmido
Russian: vlázhnyy влажный
Spanish: húmedo
Swedish: fuktig

1339. moment [n.]

Arabic: láhadha لحظة
Chinese: shíhòu 時候
Dutch: moment
French: moment
German: Augenblick
Italian: momento
Japanese: shunkan 瞬間
Korean: sunkan 순간
Portuguese: momento
Russian: momént момент
Spanish: momento
Swedish: ögonblick

1340. Monday [n.]

Arabic: yum al-ithnéin يوم الاثنين
Chinese: xīngqí yī 星期一
Dutch: maandag
French: lundi
German: Montag
Italian: lunedì
Japanese: getsuyōbi 月曜日
Korean: wŏryoil 월요일
Portuguese: segunda-feira
Russian: ponedél'nik понедельник
Spanish: lunes
Swedish: måndag

1341. money [n.]

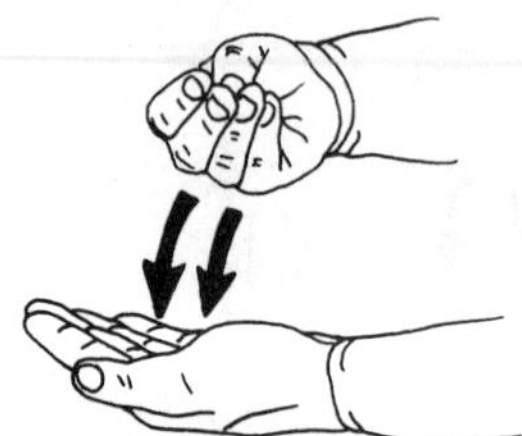

Arabic: noqúd نقود
Chinese: qián 錢
Dutch: geld
French: argent
German: Geld
Italian: danaro
Japanese: o-kane お金
Korean: don 돈
Portuguese: dinheiro
Russian: dén'gi деньги
Spanish: dinero
Swedish: pengar

1342. monkey [n.]

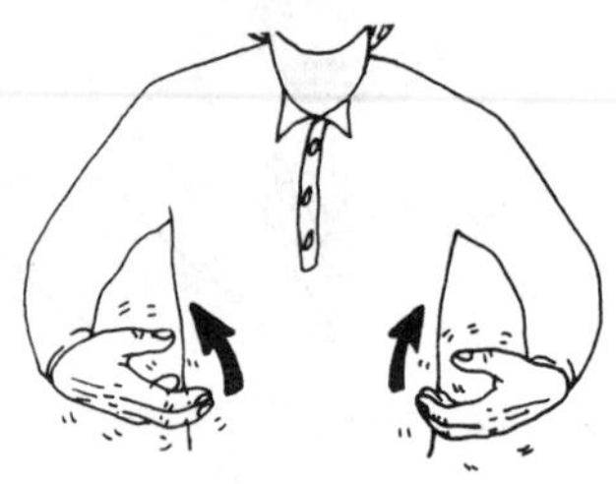

Arabic: qerd قرد
Chinese: hóuzi 猴子
Dutch: aap
French: singe
German: Affe
Italian: scimmia
Japanese: saru サル
Korean: wonsungi 원숭이
Portuguese: macaco
Russian: obez'yána обезьяна
Spanish: mono
Swedish: apa

1343. monotonous [adj.]

Arabic: mumíl ممل
Chinese: dāndiào 單調
Dutch: eentonig
French: monotone
German: monoton
Italian: monotono
Japanese: tanchō na 単調な
Korean: danjoroun 단조로운
Portuguese: monótono
Russian: monotónnyy монотонный
Spanish: monótono
Swedish: monoton

1344. month [n.]

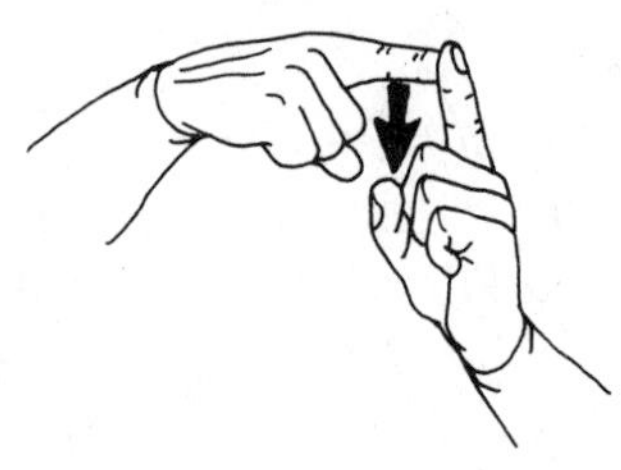

Arabic: sháher شهر
Chinese: yuè 月
Dutch: maand
French: mois
German: Monat
Italian: mese
Japanese: tsuki 月
Korean: dal 달
Portuguese: mês
Russian: mésyats месяц
Spanish: mes
Swedish: månad

1345. monthly [adj.]

Arabic: shahrían شهرياً
Chinese: měiyuède 每月的
Dutch: maandelijks
French: mensuel
German: monatlich
Italian: mensilmente
Japanese: maitsuki no 毎月の
Korean: maedarŭi 매달의
Portuguese: mensal
Russian: yezhemésyachnyy ежемесячный
Spanish: mensual
Swedish: månatlig

1346. mood [n.]

Arabic: mazáj مزاج
Chinese: xīnqíng 心情
Dutch: stemming
French: humeur
German: Stimmung
Italian: umore
Japanese: kibun 気分
Korean: kibun 기분
Portuguese: humor
Russian: nastroyéniye настроение
Spanish: humor
Swedish: stämning

1347. moon [n.]

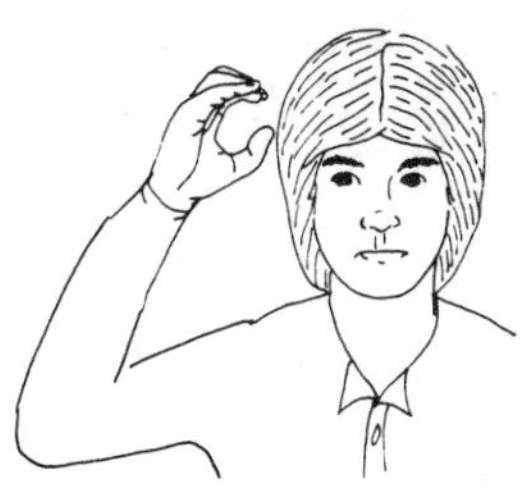

Arabic: qámar قمر
Chinese: yuèliàng 月亮
Dutch: maan
French: lune
German: Mond
Italian: luna
Japanese: tsuki 月
Korean: dal 달
Portuguese: lua
Russian: luná луна
Spanish: luna
Swedish: måne

1348. more [adj./adv.]

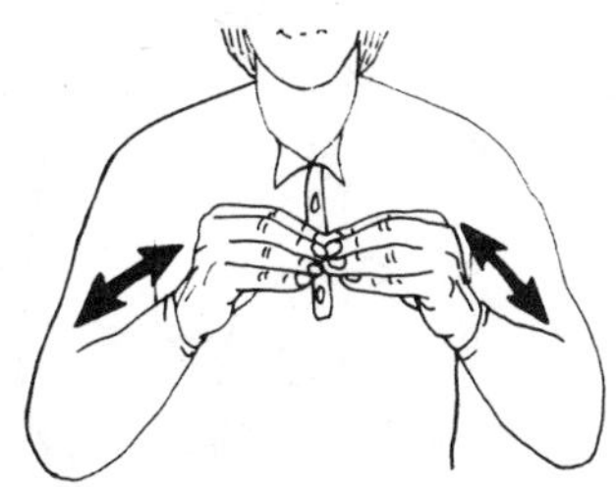

Arabic: ákther اكثر
Chinese: gèngduō 更多
Dutch: meer
French: plus
German: mehr
Italian: più
Japanese: motto もっと
Korean: dŏ manŭn 더 많은
Portuguese: mais
Russian: ból'shiy больший
Spanish: más
Swedish: mer

1349. moreover [adv.]

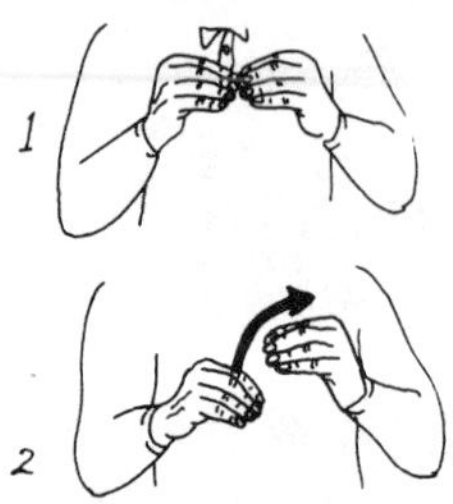

Arabic: áalawa áala dhálik
علاوة على ذلك
Chinese: kuàngqiě 況且
Dutch: bovendien
French: de plus
German: außerdem
Italian: inoltre
Japanese: sonoue その上
Korean: bbunmananira 뿐만 아니라
Portuguese: demais
Russian: króme tovó кроме того
Spanish: además
Swedish: dessutom

1350. morning [n.]

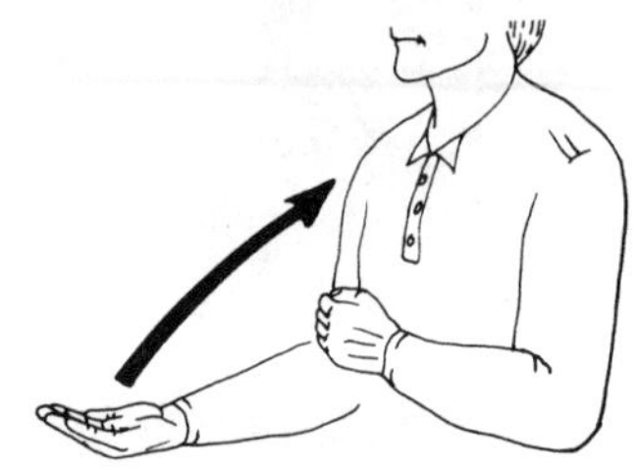

Arabic: sabáh صباح
Chinese: zǎoshàng 早上
Dutch: morgen
French: matin
German: Morgen
Italian: mattina
Japanese: asa 朝
Korean: ach'im 아침
Portuguese: manhã
Russian: útro утро
Spanish: mañana
Swedish: morgon

1351. most [adj./adv.]

Arabic: moáadham معظم
Chinese: zuìduō 最多
Dutch: meest
French: le plus
German: meist
Italian: il più
Japanese: mottomo ōku no
最も多くの
Korean: kajang manŭn 가장 많은
Portuguese: a mais
Russian: naiból'shiy наибольший
Spanish: la mayoría de
Swedish: mest

1352. mother [n.]

Arabic: um أم
Chinese: mǔqīn 母親
Dutch: moeder
French: mère
German: Mutter
Italian: madre
Japanese: haha 母
Korean: ŏmŏni 어머니
Portuguese: mãe
Russian: mat' мать
Spanish: madre
Swedish: mor

1353. motion (movement) [n.]

Arabic: háraka حركة
Chinese: dòngzuò 動作
Dutch: beweging
French: mouvement
German: Bewegung
Italian: movimento
Japanese: ugoki 動き
Korean: undong 운동
Portuguese: movimento
Russian: dvizhéniye движение
Spanish: movimiento
Swedish: rörelse

1354. motivate [v.]

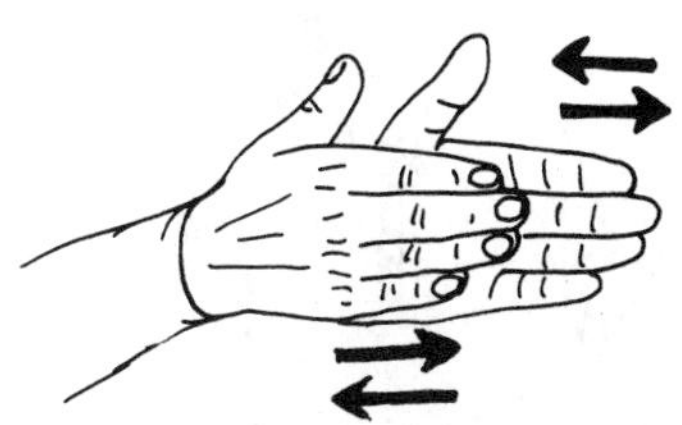

Arabic: háththa حث
Chinese: jīfā 激發
Dutch: motiveren
French: motiver
German: motivieren
Italian: motivare
Japanese: dōki o ataeru 動機を与える
Korean: jagŭgjuda 자극 주다
Portuguese: motivar
Russian: motivírovat' мотивировать
Spanish: motivar
Swedish: motivera

1355. motive [n.]

Arabic: háfez حافز
Chinese: dòngjī 動機
Dutch: motief
French: motif
German: Motiv
Italian: motivo
Japanese: dōki 動機
Korean: dongki 동기
Portuguese: motivo
Russian: motív мотив
Spanish: motivo
Swedish: motiv

1356. motor [n.]

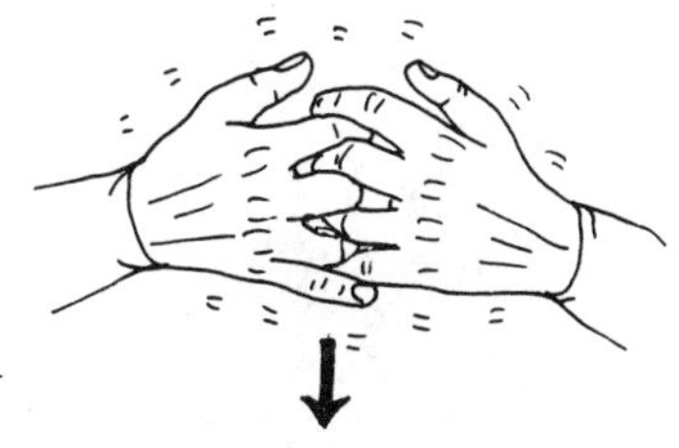

Arabic: muhárek محرك
Chinese: fādòngjī 發動機
Dutch: motor
French: moteur
German: Motor
Italian: motore
Japanese: mōtā モーター
Korean: mot'ŏ 모터
Portuguese: motor
Russian: motór мотор
Spanish: motor
Swedish: motor

1357. motorcycle [n.]

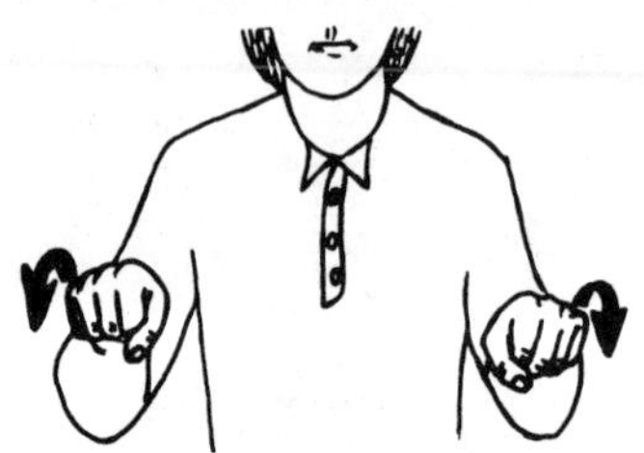

Arabic: motosíkel موتوسيكل
Chinese: mótuōchē 摩托車
Dutch: motorfiets
French: motocyclette
German: Motorrad
Italian: motocicletta
Japanese: ōtobai オートバイ
Korean: motŏsaikŭl 모터싸이클
Portuguese: motocicleta
Russian: mototsíkl мотоцикл
Spanish: motocicleta
Swedish: motorcykel

1358. mountain [n.]

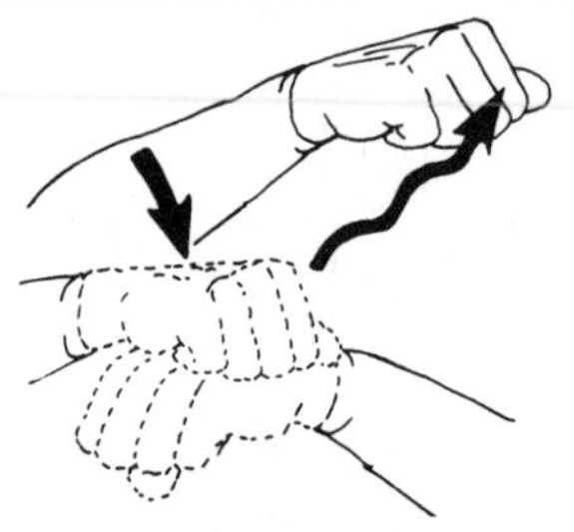

Arabic: jábal جبل
Chinese: shān 山
Dutch: berg
French: montagne
German: Berg
Italian: montagna
Japanese: yama 山
Korean: san 산
Portuguese: montanha
Russian: gorá гора
Spanish: montaña
Swedish: berg

1359. mourn [v.]

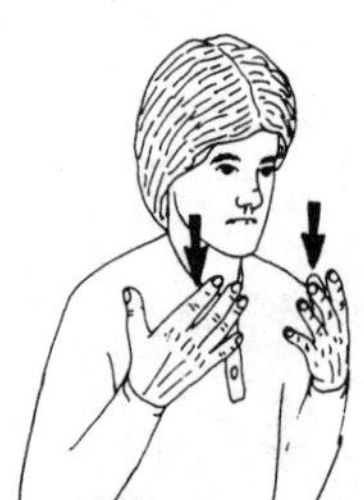

Arabic: nádaba ندب
Chinese: āidào 哀悼
Dutch: treuren
French: déplorer
German: trauern
Italian: rimpiangere
Japanese: kanashimu 悲しむ
Korean: sŭlp'ŏhada 슬퍼하다
Portuguese: lamentar
Russian: gorevát' горевать
Spanish: lamentar
Swedish: sörja

1360. mouse [n.]

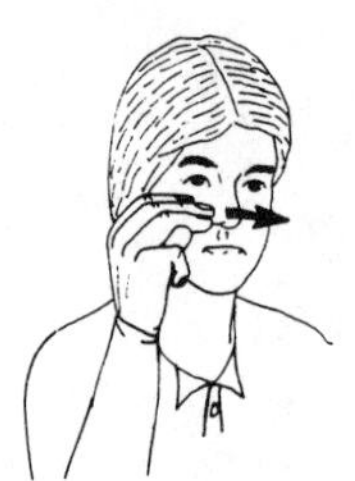

Arabic: fá'r فأر
Chinese: lǎoshǔ 老鼠
Dutch: muis
French: souris
German: Maus
Italian: topo
Japanese: nezumi ネズミ
Korean: saengjwi 생쥐
Portuguese: rato
Russian: mysh' мышь
Spanish: ratón
Swedish: mus

1361. moustache [n.]

Arabic: sháreb شارب
Chinese: xiǎo húzi 小鬍子
Dutch: snor
French: moustache
German: Schnurrbart
Italian: baffi
Japanese: kuchi-hige 口ひげ
Korean: k'otsuyŏm 콧수염
Portuguese: bigode
Russian: usý усы
Spanish: bigote
Swedish: mustasch

1362. mouth [n.]

Arabic: famm فم
Chinese: zuǐ 嘴
Dutch: mond
French: bouche
German: Mund
Italian: bocca
Japanese: kuchi 口
Korean: ip 입
Portuguese: boca
Russian: rot рот
Spanish: boca
Swedish: mun

1363. move [v.]

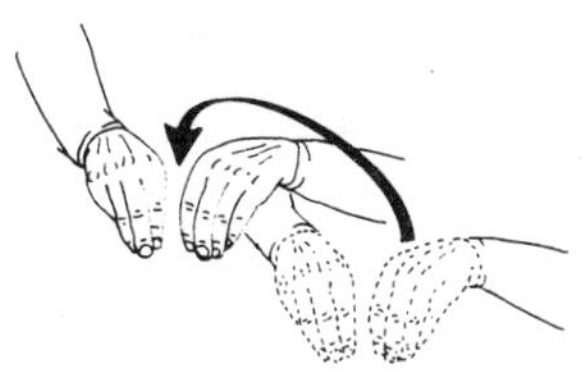

Arabic: tahárraka تحرك
Chinese: dòng 動
Dutch: bewegen
French: bouger
German: bewegen
Italian: muovere
Japanese: ugokasu 動かす
Korean: umjigida 움직이다
Portuguese: mover
Russian: dvígat' двигать
Spanish: mover
Swedish: röra

1364. movie(s) [n.]

Arabic: film فيلم
Chinese: diàngyǐng 電影
Dutch: bioscoop
French: cinéma
German: Film
Italian: cinema
Japanese: eiga 映画
Korean: yŏnghwa 영화
Portuguese: cinema
Russian: kinó кино
Spanish: cine
Swedish: bio

1365. much [adj./adv.]

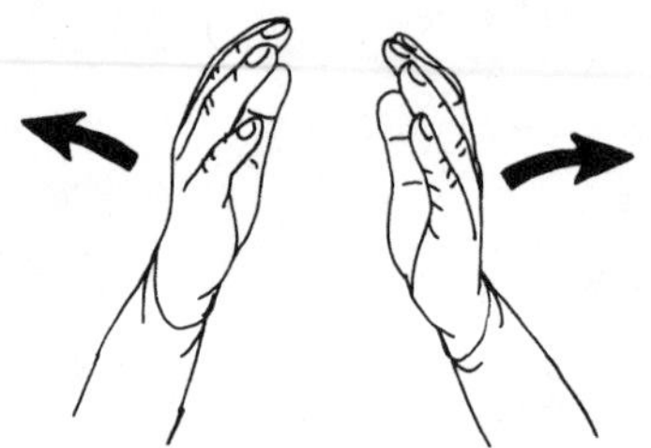

Arabic: kathíran كثيراً
Chinese: hěnduō 很多
Dutch: veel
French: beaucoup
German: viel
Italian: molto
Japanese: takusan no 沢山の
Korean: manŭn 많은
Portuguese: muito
Russian: mnógo много
Spanish: mucho
Swedish: mycket

1366. mud [n.]

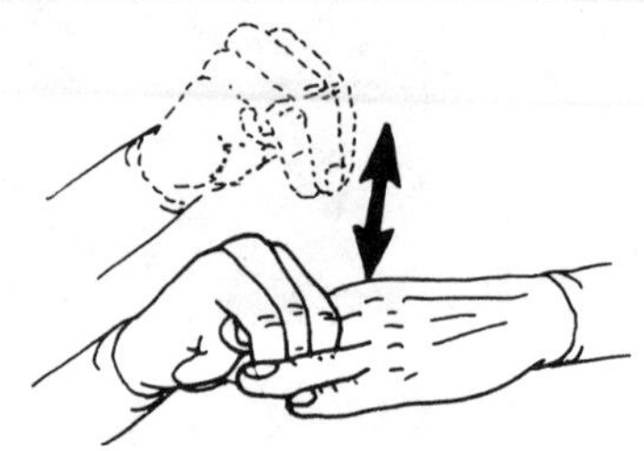

Arabic: tíen طين
Chinese: ní 泥
Dutch: modder
French: boue
German: Schlamm
Italian: fango
Japanese: doro 泥
Korean: jinhŭg 진흙
Portuguese: lama
Russian: gryáz' грязь
Spanish: lodo
Swedish: gyttja

1367. multiply [v.]

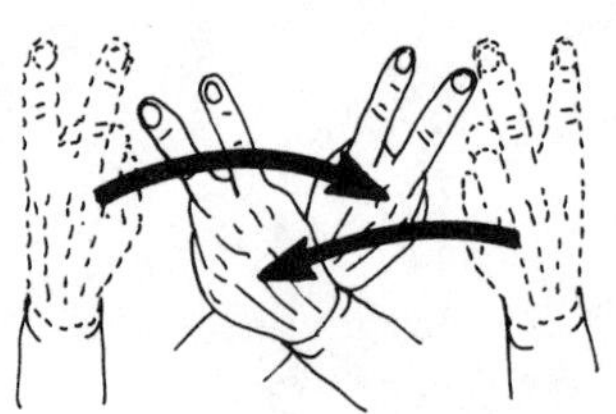

Arabic: dháafa ضاعف
Chinese: chéng 乘
Dutch: vermenigvuldigen
French: multiplier
German: multiplizieren
Italian: moltiplicare
Japanese: kakeru 掛ける
Korean: kop'hada 곱하다
Portuguese: multiplicar
Russian: umnozhát' умножать
Spanish: multiplicar
Swedish: multiplicera

1368. murder [n.]

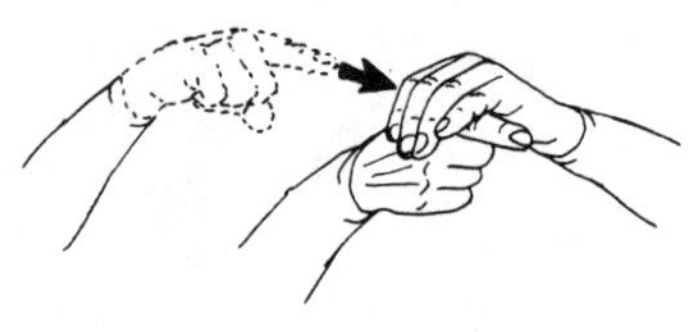

Arabic: qátela قاتل
Chinese: móshā 謀殺
Dutch: moord
French: meurtre
German: Mord
Italian: assassinio
Japanese: satsujin 殺人
Korean: sarin 살인
Portuguese: assassinato
Russian: ubíystvo убийство
Spanish: asesinato
Swedish: mord

1369. museum [n.]

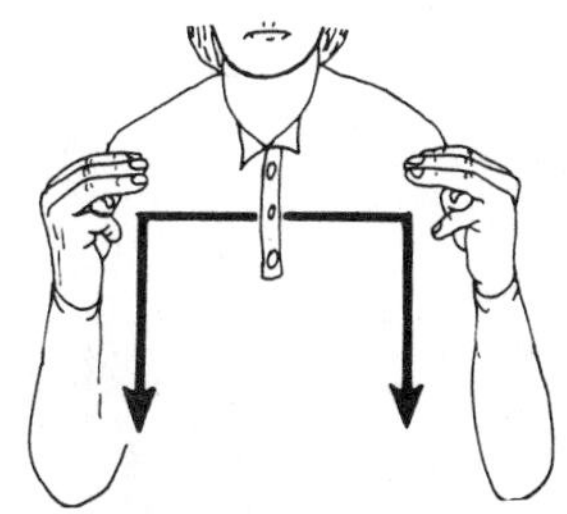

Arabic: mát-haf متحف
Chinese: bówùguǎn 博物館
Dutch: museum
French: musée
German: Museum
Italian: museo
Japanese: hakubutsu-kan 博物館
Korean: bangmulgwan 박물관
Portuguese: museu
Russian: muzéy музей
Spanish: museo
Swedish: museum

1370. mushroom(s) [n.]

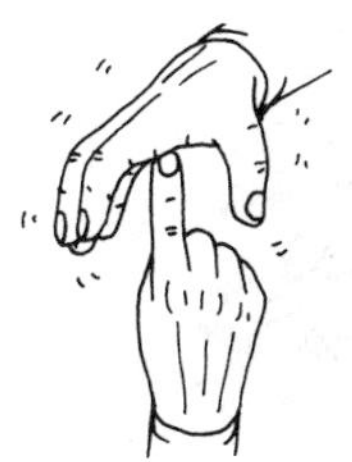

Arabic: futr فطر
Chinese: muógū 蘑菇
Dutch: paddestoel
French: champignon
German: Pilz
Italian: fungo
Japanese: kinoko キノコ
Korean: bŏsŏt 버섯
Portuguese: cogumelo
Russian: grib гриб
Spanish: hongo
Swedish: svamp

1371. music [n.]

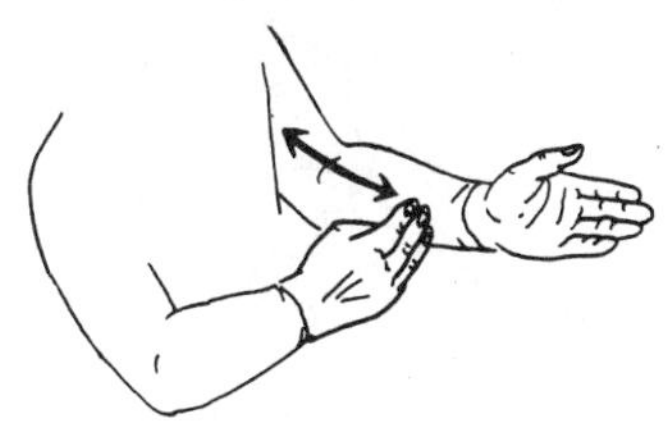

Arabic: musíeqa موسيقى
Chinese: yīnyuè 音樂
Dutch: muziek
French: musique
German: Musik
Italian: musica
Japanese: ongaku 音楽
Korean: umak 음악
Portuguese: música
Russian: múzyka музыка
Spanish: música
Swedish: musik

1372. must [v.]

Arabic: labúdda لابد
Chinese: bìxū 必須
Dutch: moeten
French: devoir
German: müssen
Italian: dovere
Japanese: . . . neba naranai
…ねばならない
Korean: haeyahanda 해야 한다
Portuguese: dever
Russian: dólzhen должен
Spanish: deber
Swedish: måste

1373. mutual [adj.]

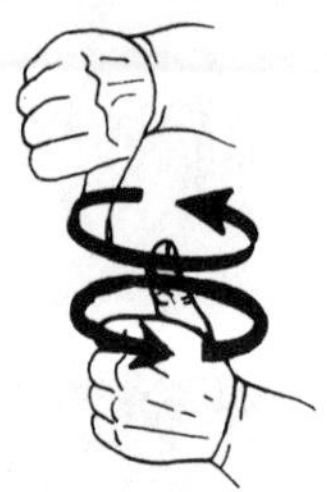

Arabic: mutabádal متبادل
Chinese: xiānghù 相互
Dutch: wederzijds
French: mutuel
German: gegenseitig
Italian: mutuo
Japanese: tagai no 互いの
Korean: sŏroŭi 서로의
Portuguese: mútuo
Russian: vzaímnyy взаимный
Spanish: mutuo
Swedish: ömsesidig

1374. my [pron.]

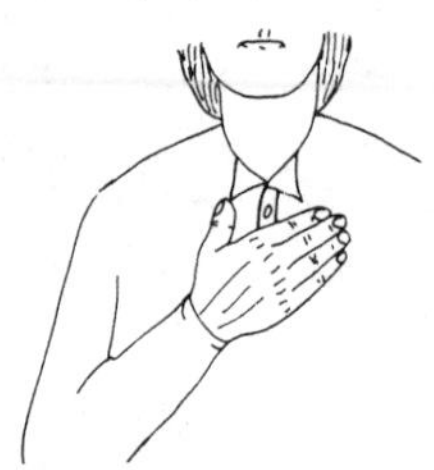

Arabic: li لي
Chinese: wŏde 我的
Dutch: mijn
French: mon
German: mein
Italian: mio
Japanese: watakushi no 私の
Korean: naŭi 나의
Portuguese: meu
Russian: moy мой
Spanish: mi
Swedish: min

1375. myself [pron.]

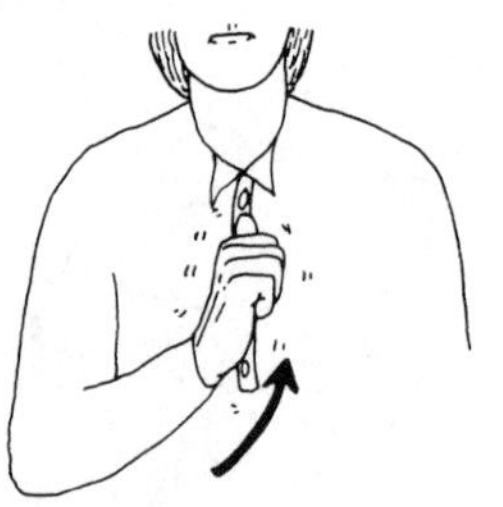

Arabic: nafsí نفسي
Chinese: wŏ zìjĭ 我自己
Dutch: mezelf
French: moi-même
German: ich selbst
Italian: me stesso
Japanese: watakushin jishin 私自身
Korean: na jashin 나 자신
Portuguese: eu mesmo
Russian: sebyá себя
Spanish: yo mismo
Swedish: mig själv

1376. mystery [n.]

Arabic: ser سر
Chinese: shénmì 神秘
Dutch: mysterie
French: mystère
German: Geheimnis
Italian: mistero
Japanese: misuterii ミステリー
Korean: shinbi 신비
Portuguese: mistério
Russian: táyna тайна
Spanish: misterio
Swedish: mysterium

1377. nail (hammer) [n.]

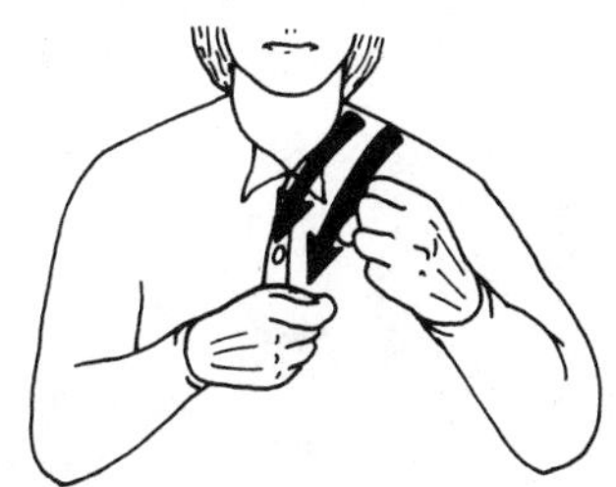

Arabic: mismár مسمار
Chinese: dīngzi 釘子
Dutch: nagel
French: clou
German: Nagel
Italian: chiodo
Japanese: kugi くぎ
Korean: mot 못
Portuguese: prego
Russian: gvózd' гвоздь
Spanish: clavo
Swedish: spik

1378. naked [adj.]

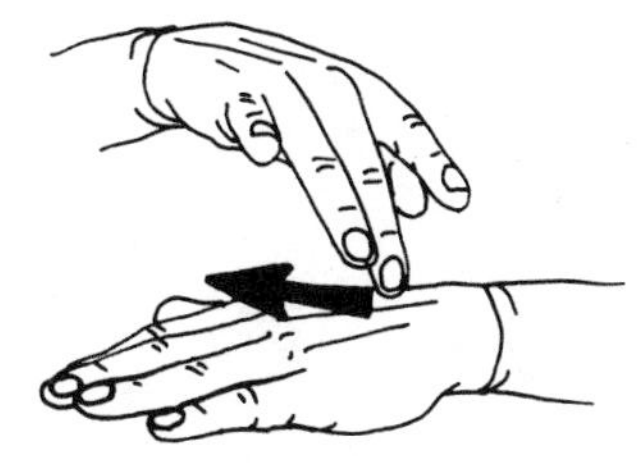

Arabic: áari عاري
Chinese: luǒ 裸
Dutch: naakt
French: nu
German: nackt
Italian: nudo
Japanese: hadaka no 裸の
Korean: bŏlgŏbŏsŭn 벌거벗은
Portuguese: nu
Russian: gólyy голый
Spanish: desnudo
Swedish: naken

1379. name [n.]

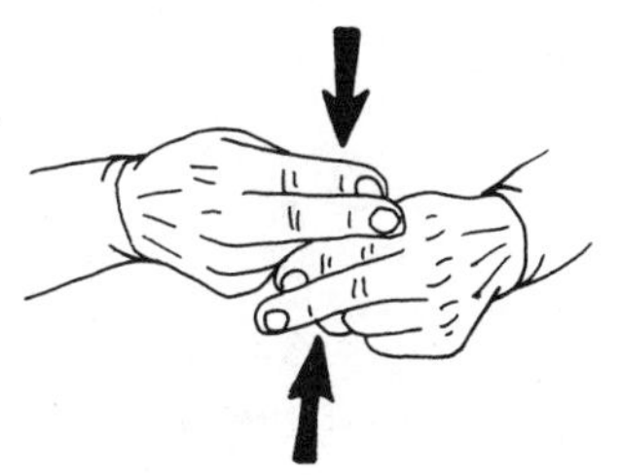

Arabic: ism اسم
Chinese: míngzì 名字
Dutch: naam
French: nom
German: Name
Italian: nome
Japanese: namae 名前
Korean: irŭm 이름
Portuguese: nome
Russian: ímya имя
Spanish: nombre
Swedish: namn

1380. napkin [n.]

Arabic: mandíl منديل
Chinese: zhǐjīn 紙巾
Dutch: servet
French: serviette
German: Serviette
Italian: tovagliolo
Japanese: napukin ナプキン
Korean: naepk'in 냅킨
Portuguese: guardanapo
Russian: salfétka салфетка
Spanish: servilleta
Swedish: servett

1381. narrate [v.]

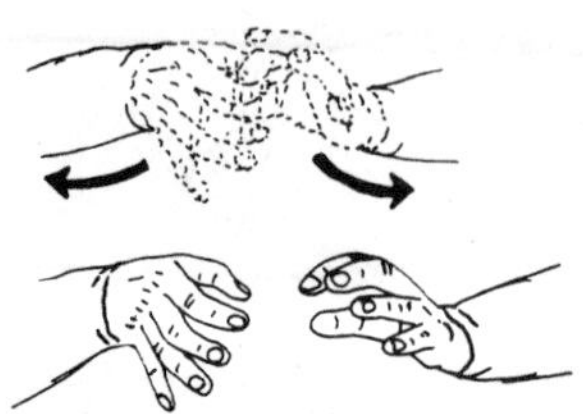

Arabic: háka حكى
Chinese: jiǎngshù 講述
Dutch: vertellen
French: raconter
German: erzählen
Italian: narrare
Japanese: monogataru 物語る
Korean: marhada 말하다
Portuguese: narrar
Russian: rasskázyvat' рассказывать
Spanish: narrar
Swedish: berätta

1382. narrow [adj.]

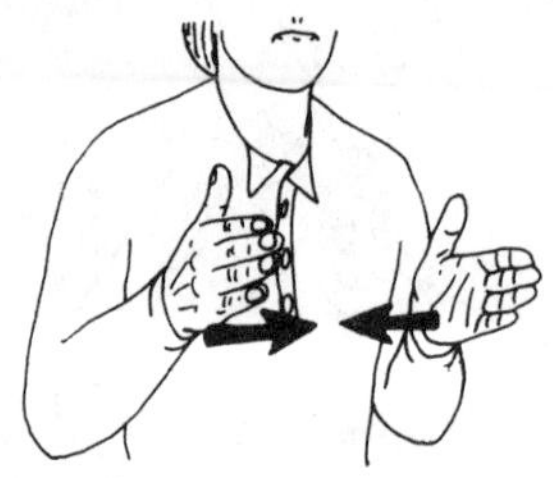

Arabic: dáyyeq ضيق
Chinese: zhǎide 窄的
Dutch: nauw
French: étroit
German: eng
Italian: stretto
Japanese: semai 狭い
Korean: jobŭn 좁은
Portuguese: estreito
Russian: úzkiy узкий
Spanish: estrecho
Swedish: trång

1383. nation [n.]

Arabic: úmma أمة
Chinese: guójiā 國家
Dutch: natie
French: nation
German: Nation
Italian: nazione
Japanese: kokka 国家
Korean: kungmin 국민
Portuguese: nação
Russian: nátsiya нация
Spanish: nación
Swedish: nation

1384. national [adj.]

Arabic: qáumi قومي
Chinese: guójiāde 國家的
Dutch: nationaal
French: national
German: national
Italian: nazionale
Japanese: kokka no 国家の
Korean: kungminŭi 국민의
Portuguese: nacional
Russian: natsionál'nyy национальный
Spanish: nacional
Swedish: nationell

1385. nationality [n.]

Arabic: jensía جنسية
Chinese: guójí 國籍
Dutch: nationaliteit
French: nationalité
German: Nationalität
Italian: nazionalità
Japanese: kokuseki 国籍
Korean: kugjŏg 국적
Portuguese: nacionalidade
Russian: natsionál'nost' национальность
Spanish: nacionalidad
Swedish: nationalitet

1386. native [adj.]

Arabic: aslí اصلي
Chinese: bĕndìde 本地的
Dutch: inheems
French: natif
German: einheimisch
Italian: nativo
Japanese: jikoku no 自国の
Korean: t'osanŭi 토산의
Portuguese: nativo
Russian: rodnóy родной
Spanish: nativo
Swedish: inhemsk

1387. natural [adj.]

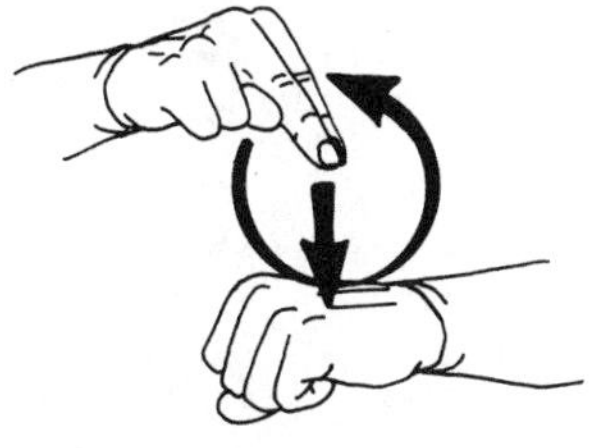

Arabic: futrí فطري
Chinese: zìránde 自然的
Dutch: natuurlijk
French: naturel
German: natürlich
Italian: naturale
Japanese: shizen no 自然の
Korean: jayŏnŭi 자연의
Portuguese: natural
Russian: yestéstvennyy естественный
Spanish: natural
Swedish: naturlig

1388. nature [n.]

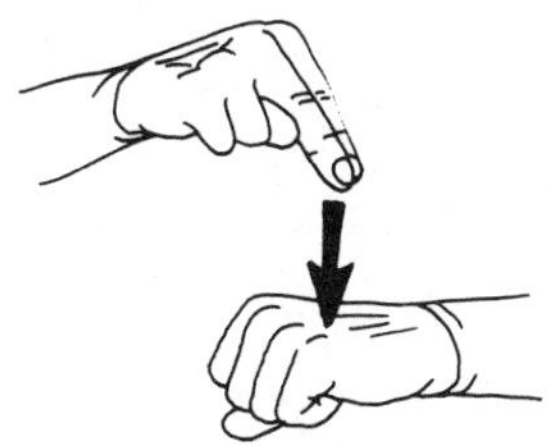

Arabic: tabíaa طبيعة
Chinese: zìrán 自然
Dutch: natuur
French: nature
German: Natur
Italian: natura
Japanese: shizen 自然
Korean: jayŏn 자연
Portuguese: natureza
Russian: priróda природа
Spanish: naturaleza
Swedish: natur

1389. naughty (mischievous) [adj.]

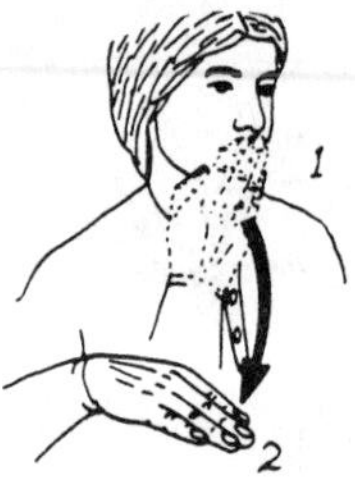

Arabic: sherír شرير
Chinese: wánpíde 頑皮的
Dutch: stout
French: méchant
German: unartig
Italian: birichino
Japanese: wampaku na わんぱくな
Korean: jangnankkurŏgiŭi 장난꾸러기의
Portuguese: travêsso
Russian: ozornóy озорной
Spanish: travieso
Swedish: stygg

1390. nausea [n.]

Arabic: duár al-báher دوار البحر
Chinese: ŏutù 嘔吐
Dutch: misselijkheid
French: nausée
German: Übelkeit
Italian: nausea
Japanese: hakike 吐き気
Korean: kuyŏkjil 구역질
Portuguese: náusea
Russian: toshnotá тошнота
Spanish: náusea
Swedish: illamående

1391. navy [n.]

Arabic: baharía بحرية
Chinese: hăijūn 海軍
Dutch: marine
French: marine
German: Marine
Italian: marina
Japanese: kaigun 海軍
Korean: haegun 해군
Portuguese: marinha
Russian: voyénno-morskóy flot военно-морской флот
Spanish: marina
Swedish: marin

1392. near [adj./adv.]

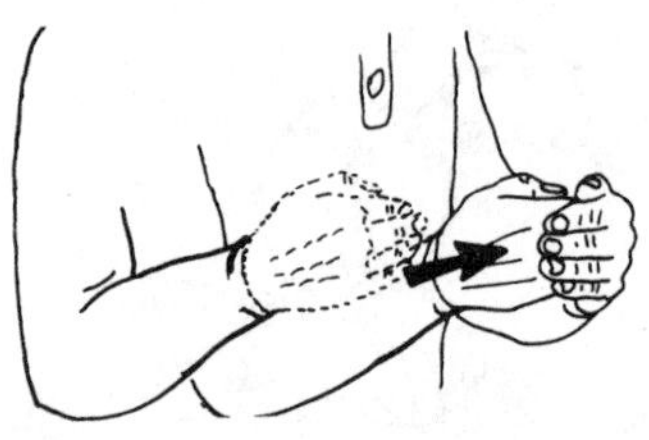

Arabic: qaríb قريب
Chinese: jìn 近
Dutch: nabij
French: près
German: nahe
Italian: vicino
Japanese: chikai 近い
Korean: kakkai 가까이
Portuguese: perto
Russian: blízkiy близкий
Spanish: cerca
Swedish: nära

1393. nearly [adv.]

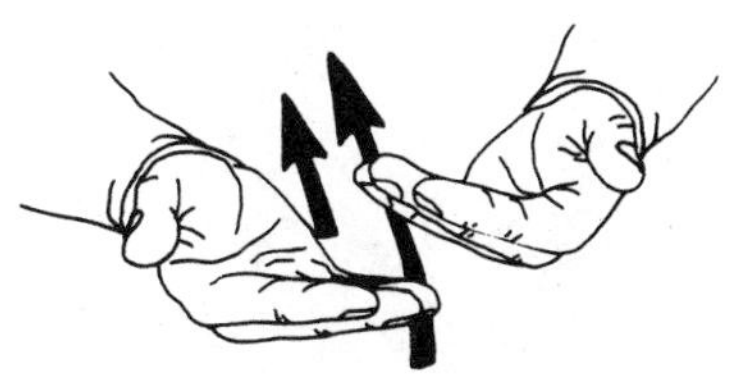

Arabic: taqríban تقريباً
Chinese: jīhū 幾乎
Dutch: bijna
French: presque
German: beinahe
Italian: quasi
Japanese: hotondo 殆ど
Korean: kŏŭi 거의
Portuguese: quase
Russian: ókolo около
Spanish: casi
Swedish: nästan

1394. neat (tidy) [adj.]

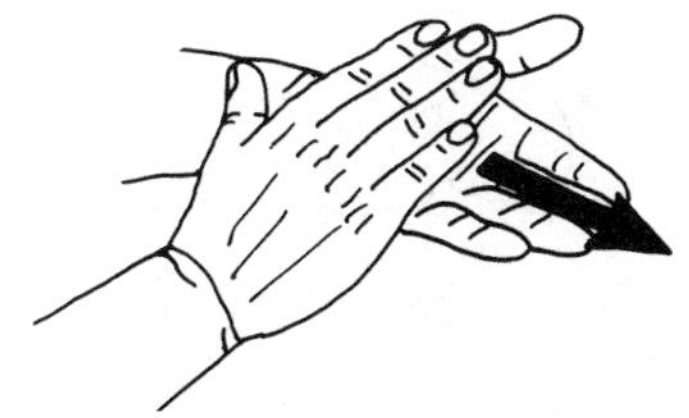

Arabic: aníeq انيق
Chinese: zhěngjiéde 整潔的
Dutch: net
French: net
German: nett
Italian: lindo
Japanese: kichin to shita きたんとした
Korean: tanjŏng'han 단정한
Portuguese: asseado
Russian: opryátnyy опрятный
Spanish: aseado
Swedish: prydlig

1395. necessary [adj.]

Arabic: daróri ضروري
Chinese: bìyàode 必要的
Dutch: noodzakelijk
French: nécessaire
German: notwendig
Italian: necessario
Japanese: hitsuyō na 必要
Korean: p'iryohan 필요한
Portuguese: necessário
Russian: neobkhodímyy необходимый
Spanish: necesario
Swedish: nödvändig

1396. neck [n.]

Arabic: ráqaba رقبة
Chinese: bózi 脖子
Dutch: hals
French: cou
German: Hals
Italian: collo
Japanese: kubi 首
Korean: mok 목
Portuguese: pescoço
Russian: shéya шея
Spanish: cuello
Swedish: hals

1397. need [n.]

Arabic: hája حاجة
Chinese: xūyào 需要
Dutch: behoefte
French: besoin
German: Notwendigkeit
Italian: bisogno
Japanese: hitsuyō 必要
Korean: p'iryo 필요
Portuguese: necessidade
Russian: nuzhdá нужда
Spanish: necesidad
Swedish: behov

1398. needle [n.]

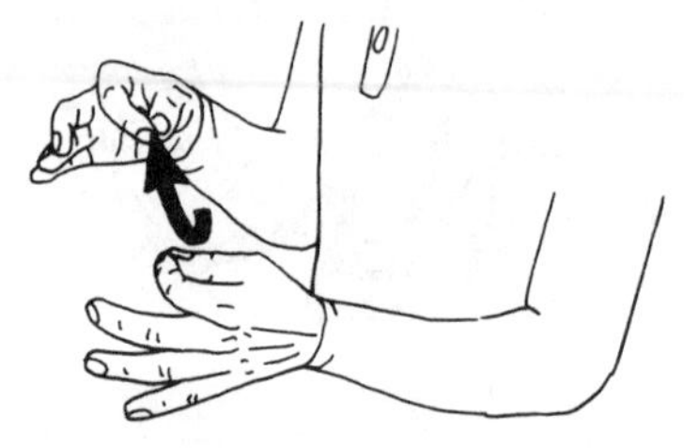

Arabic: ébra ابرة
Chinese: zhēn 針
Dutch: naald
French: aiguille
German: Nadel
Italian: ago
Japanese: hari 針
Korean: banŭl 바늘
Portuguese: agulha
Russian: igólka иголка
Spanish: aguja
Swedish: nål

1399. negative [adj.]

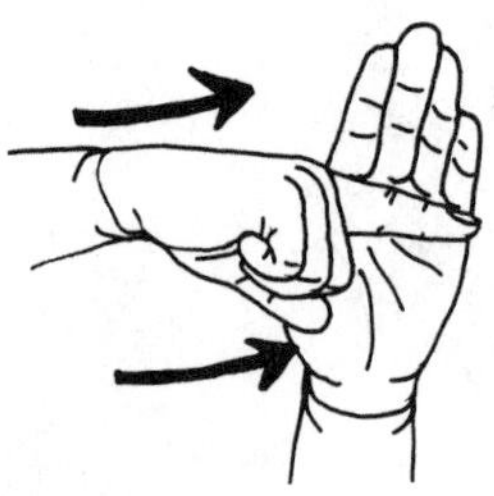

Arabic: sálbi سلبي
Chinese: fŏudìngde 否定的
Dutch: negatief
French: négatif
German: negativ
Italian: negativo
Japanese: hitei no 否定の
Korean: sogukchogin 소극적인
Portuguese: negativo
Russian: otritsátel'nyy отрицательный
Spanish: negativo
Swedish: negativ

1400. neglect [n.]

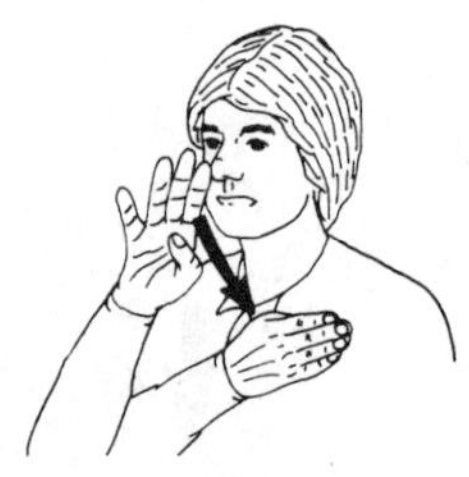

Arabic: ihmál اهمال
Chinese: hūshì 忽視
Dutch: verwaarlozing
French: négligence
German: Vernachlässigung
Italian: negligenza
Japanese: taiman 怠慢
Korean: t'aeman 태만
Portuguese: negligência
Russian: prenebrezhéniye пренебрежение
Spanish: negligencia
Swedish: försummelse

1401. negotiation(s) [n.]

Arabic: mufawadhát مفاوضات
Chinese: xiétiáo 協調
Dutch: onderhandeling
French: négociation
German: Verhandlung
Italian: negoziato
Japanese: kōshō 交渉
Korean: kyosŏp 교섭
Portuguese: negociação
Russian: peregovóry переговоры
Spanish: negociación
Swedish: underhandling

1402. neighbor [n.]

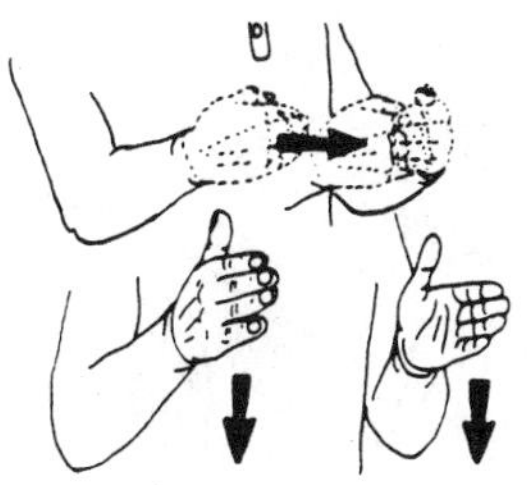

Arabic: jar جار
Chinese: línjū 鄰居
Dutch: buurman/buurvrouw
French: voisin
German: Nachbar
Italian: vicino
Japanese: rinjin 隣人
Korean: iutsaram 윗사람
Portuguese: vizinho
Russian: soséd сосед
Spanish: vecino
Swedish: granne

1403. neighborhood [n.]

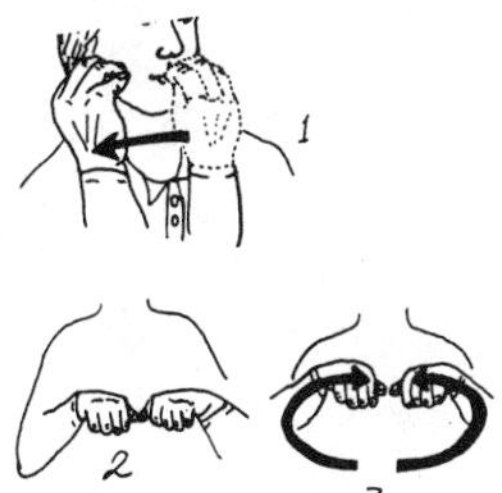

Arabic: al-juár الجوار
Chinese: fùjìn 附近
Dutch: buurt
French: voisinage
German: Nachbarschaft
Italian: vicinato
Japanese: kinjo 近所
Korean: kŭnch'ŏ 근처
Portuguese: vizinhança
Russian: sosédstvo соседство
Spanish: vecindad
Swedish: grannskap

1404. nephew [n.]

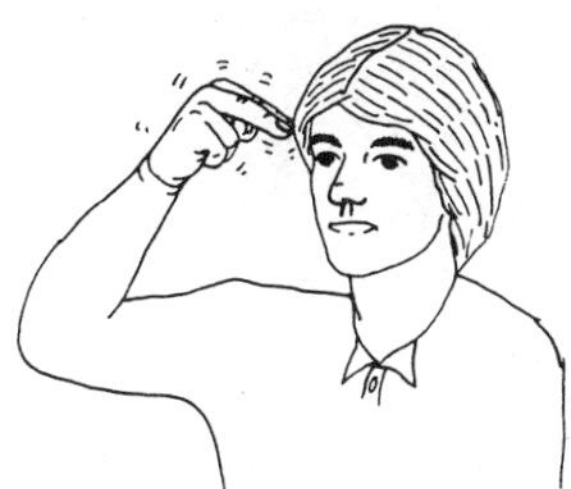

Arabic: íbnil-ákh/íbnil-úkht
ابن الاخ / ابن الاخت
Chinese: zhízi 姪子
Dutch: neef
French: neveu
German: Neffe
Italian: nipote
Japanese: oi 甥
Korean: jok'a 조카
Portuguese: sobrinho
Russian: plemyánnik племянник
Spanish: sobrino
Swedish: brorson/systerson

1405. nervous [adj.]

Arabic: áasabi عصبي
Chinese: jǐnzhāng 緊張
Dutch: nerveus
French: nerveux
German: nervös
Italian: nervoso
Japanese: shinkei no 神経の
Korean: hŭngbundoen 흥분된
Portuguese: nervoso
Russian: nérvnyy нервный
Spanish: nervioso
Swedish: nervös

1406. nest [n.]

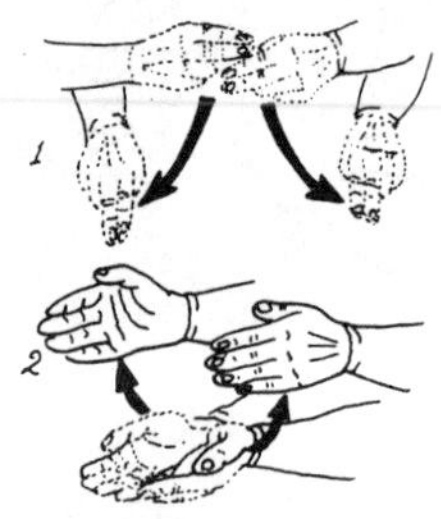

Arabic: óush عش
Chinese: cháo 巢
Dutch: nest
French: nid
German: Nest
Italian: nido
Japanese: su 巣
Korean: saejib 새집
Portuguese: ninho
Russian: gnezdó гнездо
Spanish: nido
Swedish: bo

1407. Netherlands [n.]

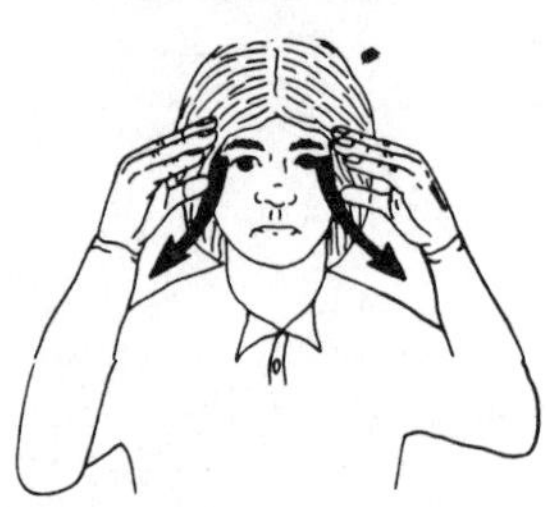

Arabic: holánda هولندا
Chinese: nídélán 尼德蘭
Dutch: Nederland
French: Pays-Bas
German: Niederlande
Italian: Paesi Bassi
Japanese: Oranda オランダ
Korean: Nedŏlaend 네델란드
Portuguese: Holanda
Russian: Niderlándy Нидерланды
Spanish: Países Bajos
Swedish: Nederländerna

1408. neutral [adj.]

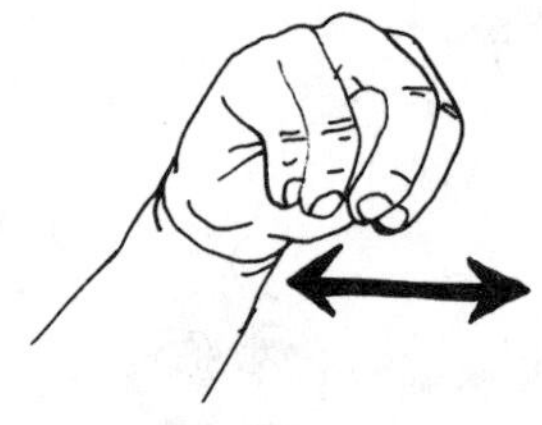

Arabic: muháyyed محايد
Chinese: zhōnglìde 中立的
Dutch: neutraal
French: neutre
German: neutral
Italian: neutrale
Japanese: chūritsu no 中立の
Korean: jungnibŭi 중립의
Portuguese: neutro
Russian: neytrál'nyy нейтральный
Spanish: neutral
Swedish: neutral

1409. never [adv.]

Arabic: ábadan أبداً
Chinese: cóngwèi 從未
Dutch: nooit
French: jamais
German: nie
Italian: mai
Japanese: keshite...shinai 決して…しない
Korean: kyŏlk'o...anida 결코 ~아니다
Portuguese: nunca
Russian: nikogdá никогда
Spanish: nunca
Swedish: aldrig

1410. nevertheless [adv.]

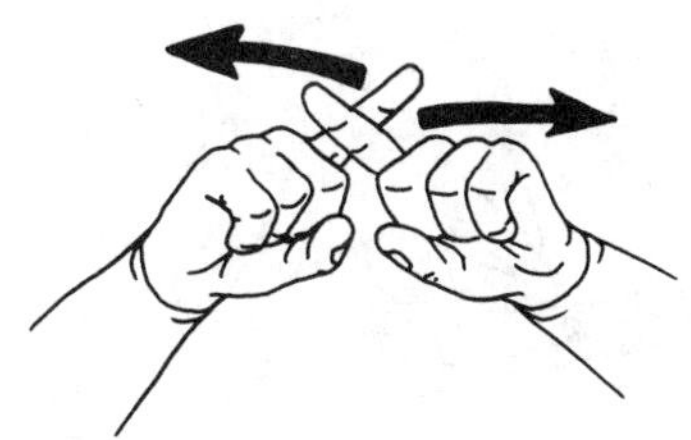

Arabic: wámaa dhálik ومع ذلك
Chinese: rán-ér 然而
Dutch: niettemin
French: néanmoins
German: nichtsdestoweniger
Italian: tuttavia
Japanese: soredemo yahari それでもやはり
Korean: gŭrŏch'iman 그렇치만
Portuguese: no entanto
Russian: tem ne méneye тем не менее
Spanish: no obstante
Swedish: icke dess mindre

1411. new [adj.]

Arabic: jadíd جديد
Chinese: xīnde 新的
Dutch: nieuw
French: nouveau
German: neu
Italian: nuovo
Japanese: atarashii 新しい
Korean: saeroun 새로운
Portuguese: nôvo
Russian: nóvyy новый
Spanish: nuevo
Swedish: ny

1412. news [n.]

Arabic: akhbár اخبار
Chinese: xīnwén 新聞
Dutch: nieuws
French: nouvelles
German: Nachrichten
Italian: notizia
Japanese: nyūsu ニュース
Korean: soshik 소식
Portuguese: notícias
Russian: nóvosti новости
Spanish: noticias
Swedish: nyhet

1413. newspaper [n.]

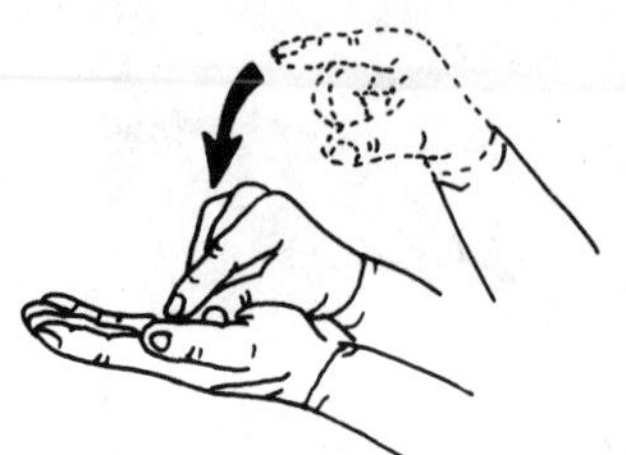

Arabic: jarída جريدة
Chinese: bàozhǐ 報紙
Dutch: krant
French: journal
German: Zeitung
Italian: giornale
Japanese: shimbun 新聞
Korean: shinmun 신문
Portuguese: jornal
Russian: gazéta газета
Spanish: periódico
Swedish: tidning

1414. New Zealand [n.]

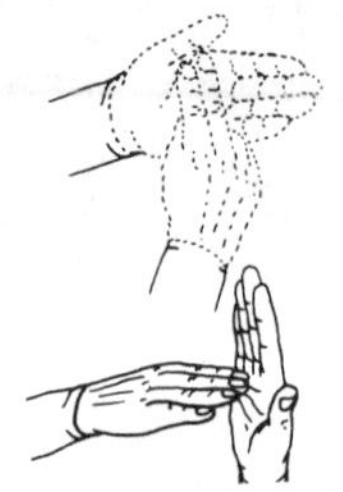

Arabic: niuzilánda نيوزيلاندا
Chinese: niǔxīlán 紐西蘭
Dutch: Nieuw Zeeland
French: Nouvelle-Zélande
German: Neuseeland
Italian: Nuova Zelandia
Japanese: Nyūjiirando ニュージーランド
Korean: Nyu Jilaend 뉴질렌드
Portuguese: Nova Zelândia
Russian: Nóvaya Zelándiya Новая Зеландия
Spanish: Nueva Zelanda
Swedish: Nya Zeeland

1415. next [adj.]

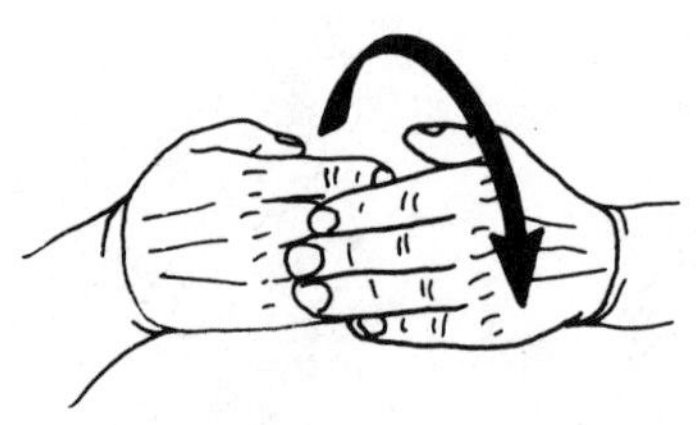

Arabic: táli تال
Chinese: xiàyígè 下一個
Dutch: naast
French: prochain
German: nächste
Italian: prossimo
Japanese: tsugi no 次の
Korean: daŭmŭi 다음의
Portuguese: próximo
Russian: sléduyushchiy следующий
Spanish: próximo
Swedish: näst

1416. nice [adj.]

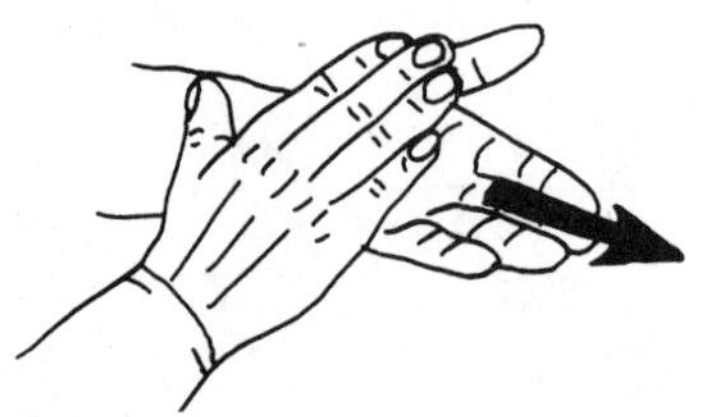

Arabic: hássan حسن
Chinese: měihǎode 美好的
Dutch: aardig
French: sympathique
German: sympathisch
Italian: simpatico
Japanese: yoi 良い
Korean: johŭn 좋은
Portuguese: simpático
Russian: mílyy милый
Spanish: simpático
Swedish: sympatisk

1417. niece [n.]

Arabic: bint il-ákh/bint il-úkht
بنت الاخ / بنت الاخت
Chinese: zhínǚ 姪女
Dutch: nicht
French: nièce
German: Nichte
Italian: nipote
Japanese: mei 姪
Korean: jok'attal 조카 딸
Portuguese: sobrinha
Russian: plemyánnitsa племянница
Spanish: sobrina
Swedish: brorsdotter/systerdotter

1418. night [n.]

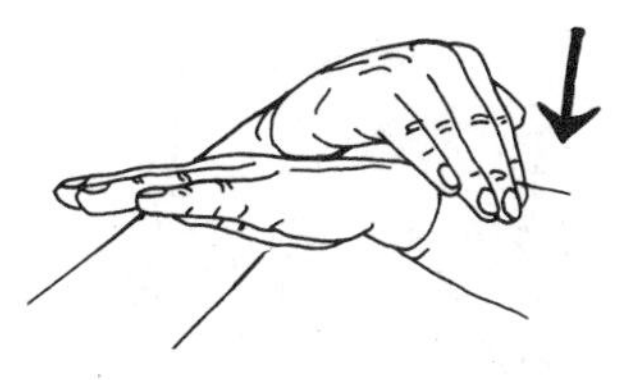

Arabic: léyl ليل
Chinese: wǎnshàng 晚上
Dutch: nacht
French: nuit
German: Nacht
Italian: notte
Japanese: yoru 夜
Korean: bam 밤
Portuguese: noite
Russian: noch' ночь
Spanish: noche
Swedish: natt

1419. nine [adj.]

Arabic: tisáa تسعة
Chinese: jiǔ 九
Dutch: negen
French: neuf
German: neun
Italian: nove
Japanese: kyū 九
Korean: ahop 아홉
Portuguese: nove
Russian: dévyat' девять
Spanish: nueve
Swedish: nio

1420. nineteen [adj.]

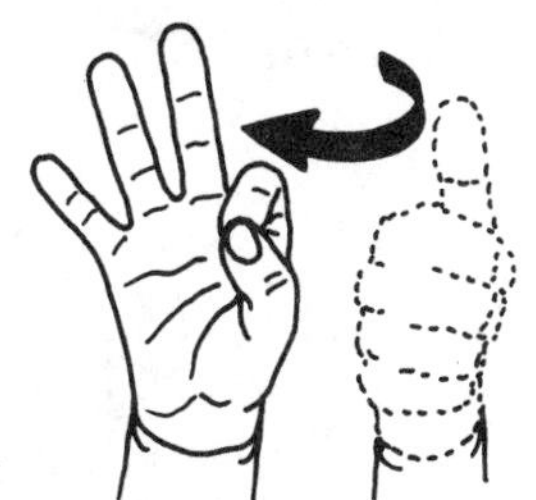

Arabic: tisáat áashar تسعة عشر
Chinese: shíjiǔ 十九
Dutch: negentien
French: dix-neuf
German: neunzehn
Italian: diciannove
Japanese: jūkyū 19
Korean: yŏrahop 열 아홉
Portuguese: dezenove
Russian: devyatnádtsat' девятнадцать
Spanish: diecinueve
Swedish: nitton

1421. ninety [adj.]

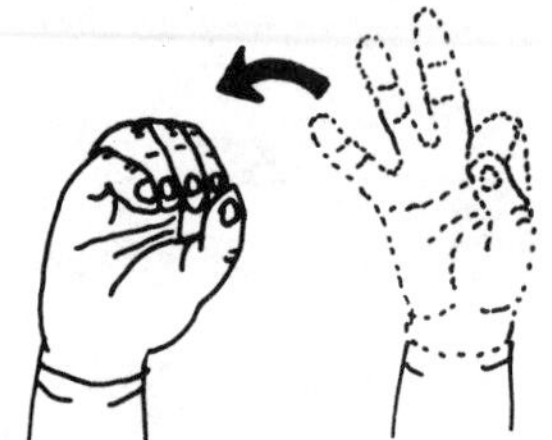

Arabic: tiséin تسعين
Chinese: jiǔshí 九十
Dutch: negentig
French: quatre-vingt-dix
German: neunzig
Italian: novanta
Japanese: kyūjū 90
Korean: ahŭn 아흔
Portuguese: noventa
Russian: devyanósto девяносто
Spanish: noventa
Swedish: nittio

1422. no [adv./interj.]

Arabic: la لا
Chinese: bù 不
Dutch: neen
French: non
German: kein/nein
Italian: no
Japanese: iie いいえ
Korean: aniyo 아니요
Portuguese: não
Russian: nyet нет
Spanish: no
Swedish: nej

1423. nobody (no one) [pron.]

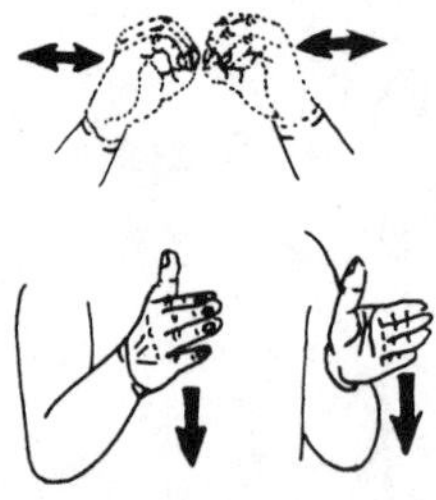

Arabic: la áhad لا احد
Chinese: méirén 沒人
Dutch: niemand
French: personne (ne)
German: niemand
Italian: nessuno
Japanese: daremo...nai 誰も…ない
Korean: amudo...anida
아무도 ~아니다
Portuguese: ninguém
Russian: niktó никто
Spanish: nadie
Swedish: ingen

1424. noise [n.]

Arabic: daudá' ضوضاء
Chinese: zàoyīn 噪音
Dutch: geluid
French: bruit
German: Lärm
Italian: rumore
Japanese: zatsuon 雑音
Korean: soŭm 소음
Portuguese: barulho
Russian: shum шум
Spanish: ruido
Swedish: ljud

1425. none [adj./adv./pron.]

Arabic: la áhad/la sháee
لا احد / لا شيء
Chinese: méiyǒu 沒有
Dutch: geen
French: aucun
German: keine
Italian: niente
Japanese: daremo . . . nai 誰も…ない
Korean: amudo . . . ant'a 아무도 ~않다
Portuguese: nenhum
Russian: nikakóy никакой
Spanish: ninguno
Swedish: ingen

1426. nonsense [n.]

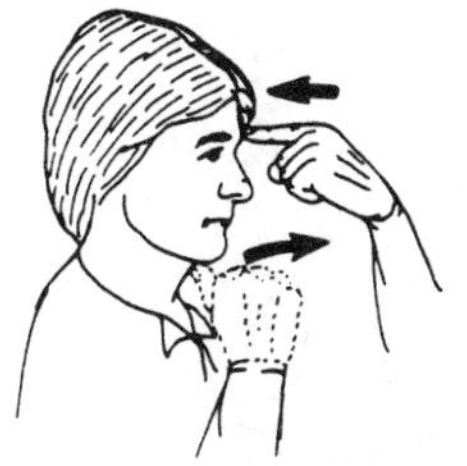

Arabic: herá' هراء
Chinese: fèihuà 廢話
Dutch: onzin
French: sottise
German: Unsinn
Italian: sciocchezza
Japanese: muimi 無意味
Korean: ŏrisŏgun sori 어리석은 소리
Portuguese: besteira
Russian: vzdór вздор
Spanish: tontería
Swedish: dumheter

1427. noon [n.]

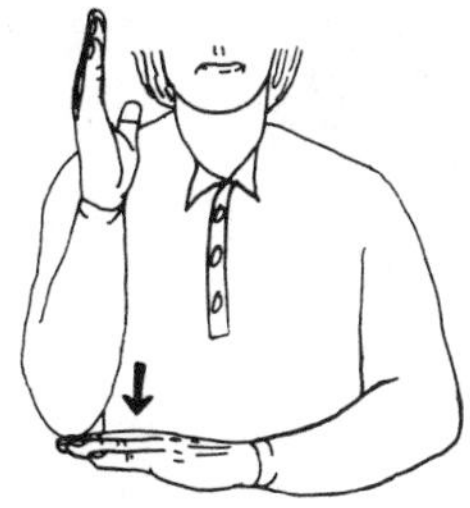

Arabic: dhóher ظهر
Chinese: zhōngwǔ 中午
Dutch: middag
French: midi
German: Mittag
Italian: mezzogiorno
Japanese: mahiru 真昼
Korean: jŏngo 정오
Portuguese: meio-dia
Russian: pólden' полдень
Spanish: mediodía
Swedish: middag

1428. normal [adj.]

Arabic: tabí'i طبيعي
Chinese: zhèngchángde 正常的
Dutch: normaal
French: normal
German: normal
Italian: normale
Japanese: futsūno 普通の
Korean: jŏngsangŭi 정상의
Portuguese: normal
Russian: normal'nyy нормальный
Spanish: normal
Swedish: normal

1429. north [n.]

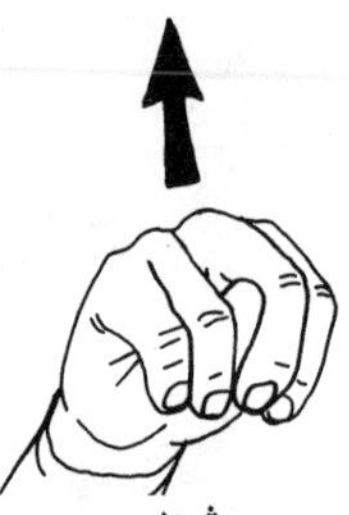

Arabic: shemál شمال
Chinese: běi 北
Dutch: noorden
French: nord
German: Norden
Italian: nord
Japanese: kita 北
Korean: bug 북
Portuguese: norte
Russian: séver север
Spanish: norte
Swedish: nord

1430. North America [n.]

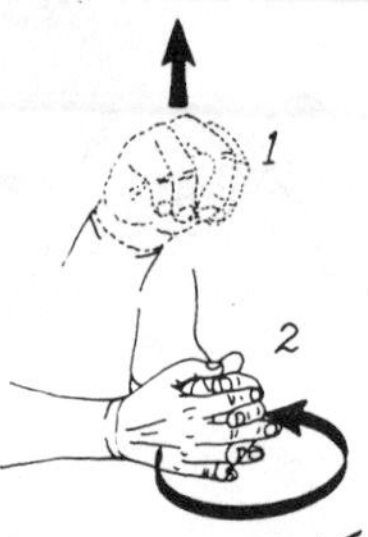

Arabic: shemál amríka شمال امريكا
Chinese: běi měizhōu 北美洲
Dutch: Noord Amerika
French: Amérique du Nord
German: Nordamerika
Italian: America del Nord
Japanese: Kita Amerika 北アメリカ
Korean: bug mi 북미
Portuguese: América do Norte
Russian: Sévernaya Amérika Северная Америка
Spanish: América del Norte
Swedish: Nordamerika

1431. Norway [n.]

Arabic: an-narwíj النرويج
Chinese: nuówēi 挪威
Dutch: Noorwegen
French: Norvège
German: Norwegen
Italian: Norvegia
Japanese: Noruwē ノルウエー
Korean: Norŭwei 놀웨이
Portuguese: Noruega
Russian: Norvégiya Норвегия
Spanish: Noruega
Swedish: Norge

1432. nose [n.]

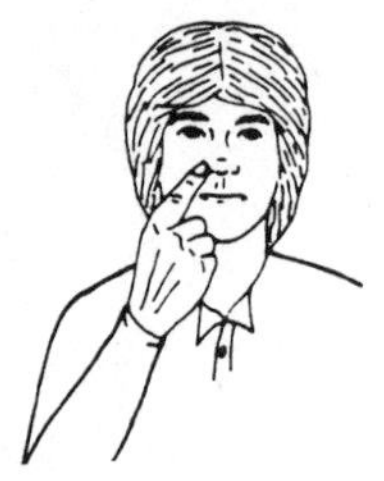

Arabic: anf انف
Chinese: bízi 鼻子
Dutch: neus
French: nez
German: Nase
Italian: naso
Japanese: hana 鼻
Korean: k'o 코
Portuguese: nariz
Russian: nos нос
Spanish: nariz
Swedish: näsa

1433. not [adv.]

Arabic: la لا
Chinese: bù 不
Dutch: niet
French: pas
German: nicht
Italian: non
Japanese: . . . de nai …でない
Korean: anida ~이 아니다
Portuguese: não
Russian: ne не
Spanish: no
Swedish: inte

1434. note [n.]

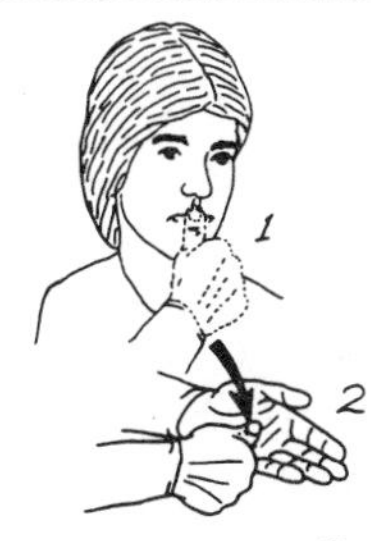

Arabic: mudhákkara مذكرة
Chinese: bǐjì 筆記
Dutch: aantekening
French: note
German: Notiz
Italian: nota
Japanese: memo メモ
Korean: girok 기록
Portuguese: nota
Russian: zapíska записка
Spanish: nota
Swedish: anteckning

1435. nothing [pron.]

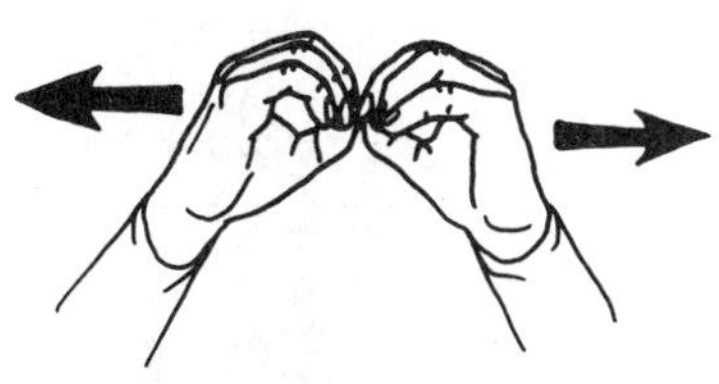

Arabic: la sháee لا شيء
Chinese: méishì 沒事
Dutch: niets
French: rien
German: nichts
Italian: niente
Japanese: nani mo nai 何もない
Korean: amugŏtto. . . ŏpda 아무것도 ~없다
Portuguese: nada
Russian: nichevó ничего
Spanish: nada
Swedish: ingenting

1436. notify (inform) [v.]

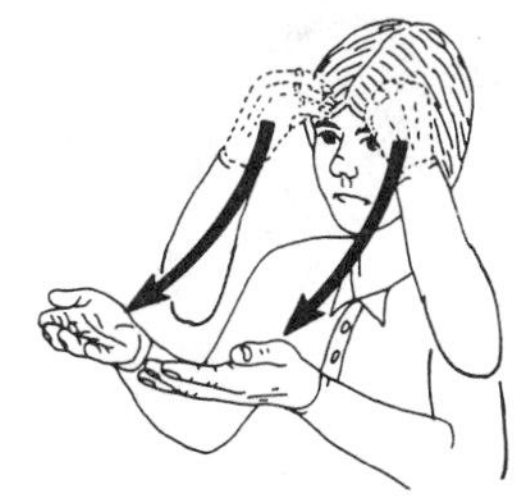

Arabic: ákhbara اخبر
Chinese: tōngzhī 通知
Dutch: mededelen
French: notifier
German: mitteilen
Italian: notificare
Japanese: tsūkoku suru 通告する
Korean: t'ongjihada 통지하다
Portuguese: informar
Russian: uvedomlyát' уведомлять
Spanish: notificar
Swedish: meddela

1437. noun [n.]

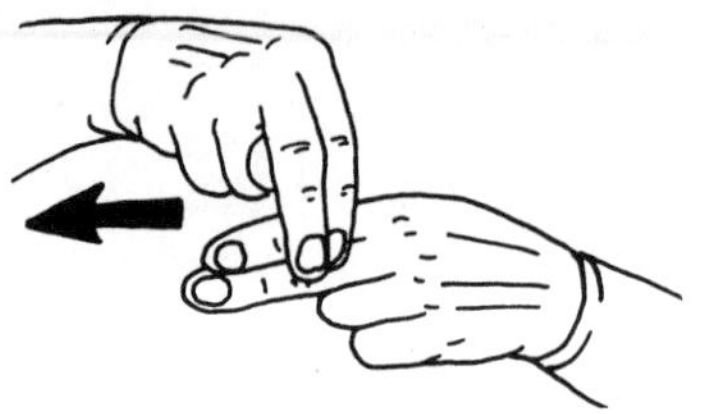

Arabic: ism اسم
Chinese: míngcí 名詞
Dutch: zelfstandig naamwoord
French: substantif
German: Hauptwort
Italian: sostantivo
Japanese: meishi 名詞
Korean: myŏngsa 명사
Portuguese: substantivo
Russian: ímya sushchestvítel'noye имя существительное
Spanish: sustantivo
Swedish: substantiv

1438. novelty [n.]

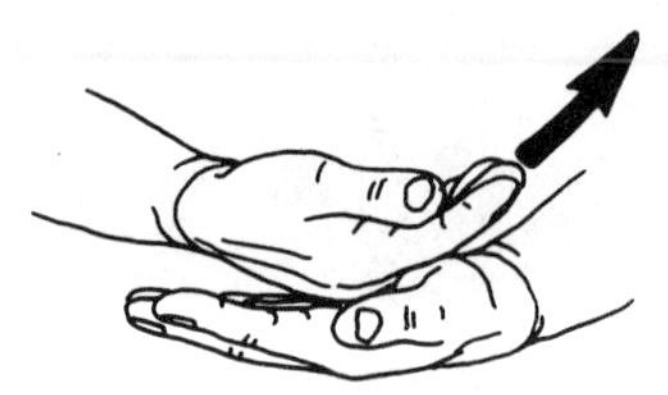

Arabic: shi' gher ma'lúf شيء غير مألوف
Chinese: xīnqí 新奇
Dutch: nieuwigheid
French: nouveauté
German: neuheit
Italian: novità
Japanese: mezurashisa 珍しさ
Korean: singiham 신기함
Portuguese: novidade
Russian: novizná новизна
Spanish: novedad
Swedish: ovanlighet

1439. November [n.]

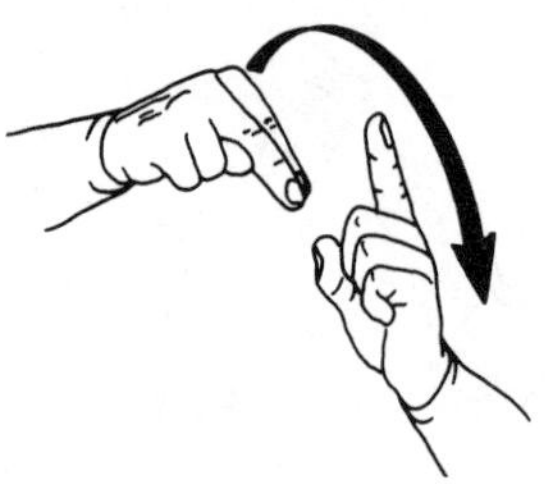

Arabic: novímber نوفمبر
Chinese: shíyīyuè 十一月
Dutch: november
French: novembre
German: November
Italian: novembre
Japanese: jūichigatsu 11月
Korean: shibirwŏl 십일월
Portuguese: novembro
Russian: noyábr' ноябрь
Spanish: noviembre
Swedish: november

1440. now [adv.]

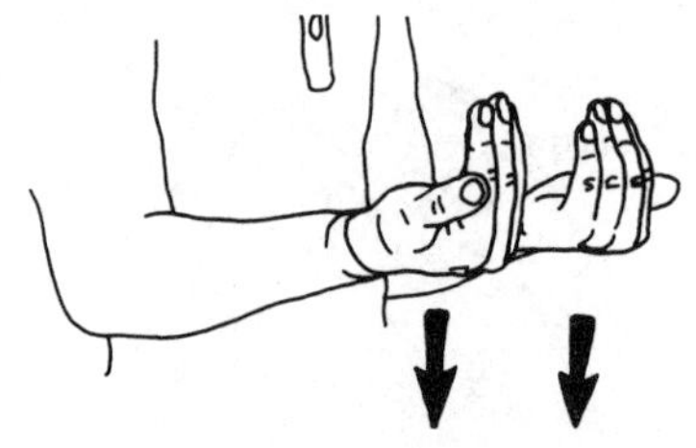

Arabic: al-áan الآن
Chinese: xiànzài 現在
Dutch: nu
French: maintenant
German: nun
Italian: adesso
Japanese: ima 今
Korean: jigŭm 지금
Portuguese: agora
Russian: seychás сейчас
Spanish: ahora
Swedish: nu

1441. number [n.]

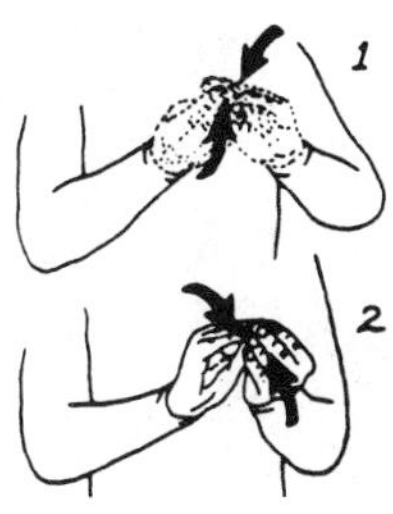

Arabic: ráqam رقم
Chinese: shùmù 數目
Dutch: nummer
French: nombre
German: Nummer
Italian: numero
Japanese: kazu 数
Korean: su 수
Portuguese: número
Russian: nómer номер
Spanish: número
Swedish: nummer

1442. numerous [adj.]

Arabic: aadíd عديد
Chinese: hěnduōde 很多的
Dutch: talrijk
French: nombreux
German: zahlreich
Italian: numeroso
Japanese: tasū no 多数の
Korean: sumanŭn 수많은
Portuguese: numeroso
Russian: mnogochíslennyy многочисленный
Spanish: numeroso
Swedish: talrik

1443. nurse [n.]

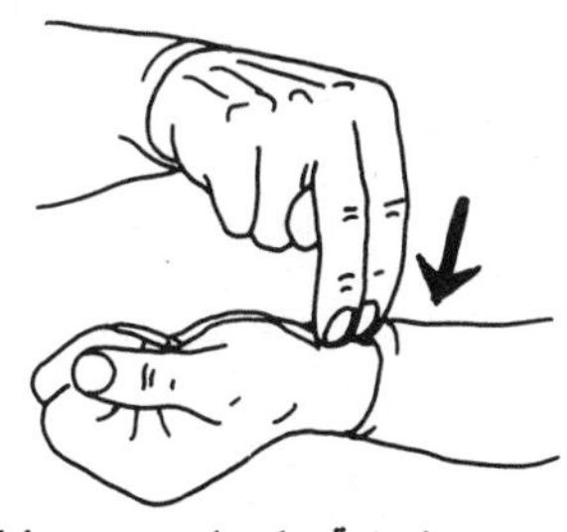

Arabic: mumáreda ممرضة
Chinese: hùshì 護士
Dutch: verpleegster
French: infirmière
German: Krankenschwester
Italian: infermiera
Japanese: kangofu 看護婦
Korean: kanhowŏn 간호원
Portuguese: enfermeira
Russian: medsestrá медсестра
Spanish: enfermera
Swedish: sjuksköterska

1444. nut [n.]

Arabic: mukassarát مكسرات
Chinese: jiānguǒ 堅果
Dutch: noot
French: noix
German: Nuß
Italian: noce
Japanese: konomi 木の実
Korean: hodu 호두
Portuguese: noz
Russian: orékh орех
Spanish: nuez
Swedish: nöt

1445. oath (pledge/vow) [n.]

Arabic: qásam قسم
Chinese: shìyuē 誓約
Dutch: eed
French: serment
German: Eid
Italian: giuramento
Japanese: chikai 誓い
Korean: maengse 맹세
Portuguese: juramento
Russian: klyátva клятва
Spanish: juramento
Swedish: ed

1446. obedience [n.]

Arabic: táa طاعة
Chinese: fúcóng 服從
Dutch: gehoorzaamheid
French: obéissance
German: Gehorsam
Italian: ubbidienza
Japanese: sunao na 素直な
Korean: bogjong 복종
Portuguese: obediência
Russian: poslushániye послушание
Spanish: obediencia
Swedish: lydnad

1447. object [n.]

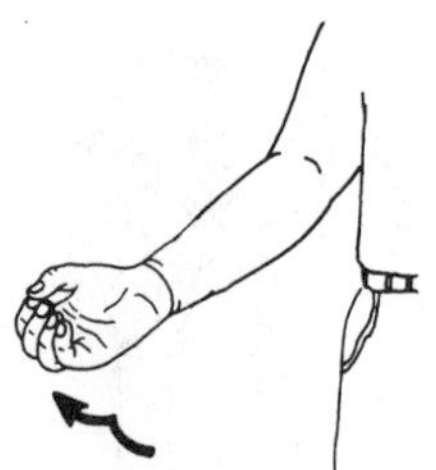

Arabic: hádaf هدف
Chinese: wùtǐ 物體
Dutch: voorwerp
French: objet
German: Objekt
Italian: oggetto
Japanese: mono 物
Korean: mulgŏn 물건
Portuguese: objeto
Russian: ob''yékt объект
Spanish: objeto
Swedish: objekt

1448. objection [n.]

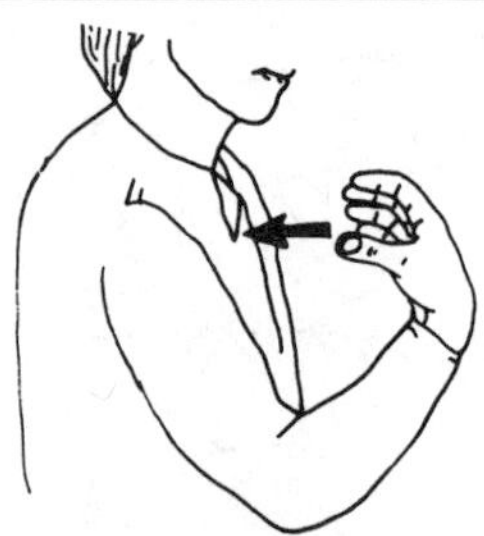

Arabic: iaatarád اعتراض
Chinese: fănduì 反對
Dutch: tegenwerping
French: objection
German: Einwand
Italian: obbiezione
Japanese: hantai 反対
Korean: bandae 반대
Portuguese: objeção
Russian: vozrazhéniye возражение
Spanish: objeción
Swedish: invändning

1449. objective [n.]

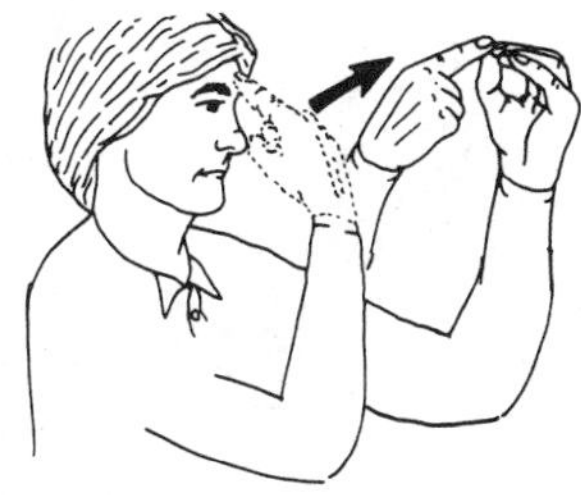

Arabic: hádaf هدف
Chinese: mùbiāo 目標
Dutch: objectief
French: objectif
German: Ziel
Italian: obbiettivo
Japanese: mokuteki 目的
Korean: mogjŏk 목적
Portuguese: objetivo
Russian: tsel' цель
Spanish: objetivo
Swedish: objektiv

1450. obligation [n.]

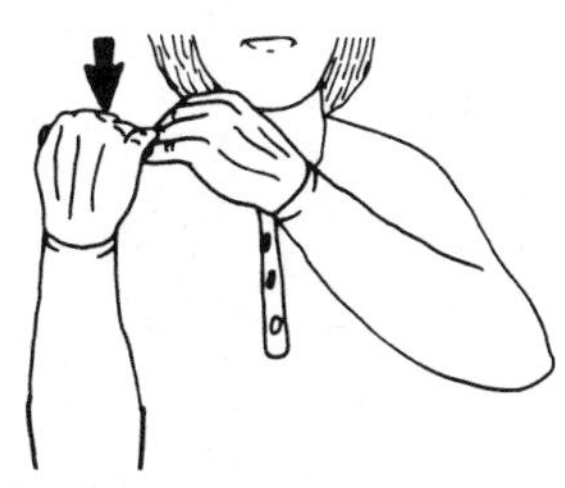

Arabic: wájib واجب
Chinese: yìwù 義務
Dutch: verplichting
French: obligation
German: Verpflichtung
Italian: obbligo
Japanese: gimu 義務
Korean: ŭimu 의무
Portuguese: obrigação
Russian: obyazátel'stvo обязательство
Spanish: obligación
Swedish: skyldighet

1451. obscure [adj.]

Arabic: múdhlim مظلم
Chinese: bùqīngchŭde 不清楚的
Dutch: duister
French: obscur
German: obskur
Italian: oscuro
Japanese: mōrō to shita もうろうとした
Korean: aemaehan 애매한
Portuguese: obscuro
Russian: tyómnyy тёмный
Spanish: obscuro
Swedish: mörk

1452. observe [v.]

Arabic: láhadha لاحظ
Chinese: guānchá 觀察
Dutch: observeren
French: observer
German: beobachten
Italian: osservare
Japanese: kansatsu suru 観察する
Korean: gwanch'arhada 관찰하다
Portuguese: observar
Russian: nablyudát' наблюдать
Spanish: observar
Swedish: observera

1453. obstacle [n.]

Arabic: áaqaba عقبة
Chinese: zhàngài 障礙
Dutch: hindernis
French: obstacle
German: Hindernis
Italian: ostacolo
Japanese: shōga 障害
Korean: bang'haemul 방해물
Portuguese: obstáculo
Russian: prepyátstviye препятствие
Spanish: obstáculo
Swedish: hinder

1454. obtain (get/procure) [v.]

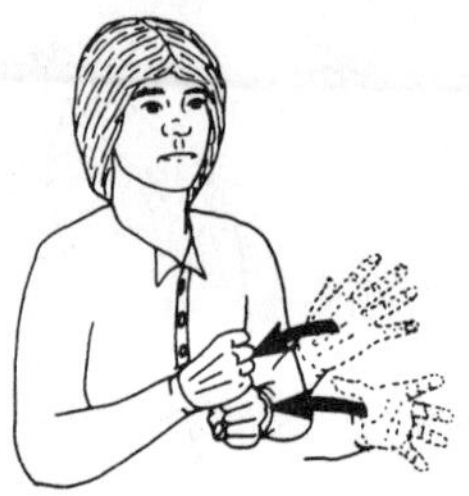

Arabic: hasála áala حصل على
Chinese: huòdé 獲得
Dutch: verkrijgen
French: obtenir
German: erlangen
Italian: ottenere
Japanese: te ni ireru 手に入れる
Korean: ŏtta 얻다
Portuguese: obter
Russian: dobyvát' добывать
Spanish: obtener
Swedish: erhålla

1455. obvious [adj.]

Arabic: wádeh واضح
Chinese: míngxiănde 明顯的
Dutch: duidelijk
French: évident
German: offensichtlich
Italian: ovvio
Japanese: akiraka na 明らかな
Korean: bunmyŏnghan 분명한
Portuguese: obvio
Russian: ochevídnyy очевидный
Spanish: obvio
Swedish: tydlig

1456. occasion [n.]

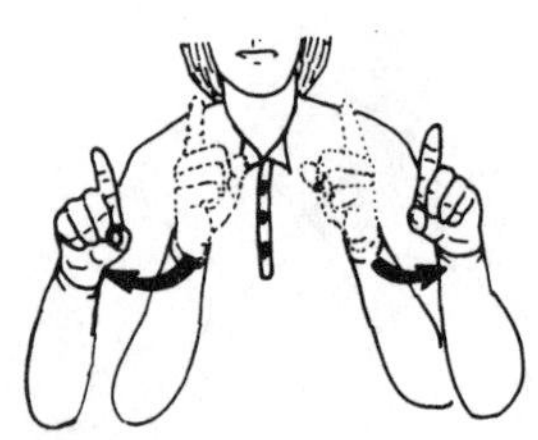

Arabic: fúrsa/munásaba فرصة / مناسبة
Chinese: chănghé 場合
Dutch: gelegenheid
French: occasion
German: Gelegenheit
Italian: occasione
Japanese: baai 場合
Korean: kihoe 기회
Portuguese: ocasião
Russian: slúchay случай
Spanish: ocasión
Swedish: tillfälle

1457. occasional [adj.]

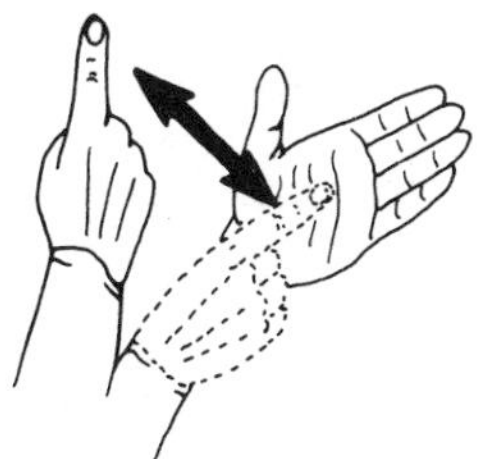

Arabic: áaradhi عرضي
Chinese: ǒu er 偶而
Dutch: toevallig
French: occasionnel
German: gelegentlich
Italian: occasionale
Japanese: tokiori no 時折りの
Korean: gakkŭm hanŭn 가끔하는
Portuguese: ocasional
Russian: slucháynyy случайный
Spanish: ocasional
Swedish: tillfällig

1458. occupation [n.]

Arabic: wadhífa وظيفة
Chinese: zhíyè 職業
Dutch: bezigheid
French: occupation
German: Beruf
Italian: occupazione
Japanese: shokugyō 職業
Korean: jigŏb 직업
Portuguese: ocupação
Russian: zanyátiye занятие
Spanish: ocupación
Swedish: sysselsättning

1459. occurrence [n.]

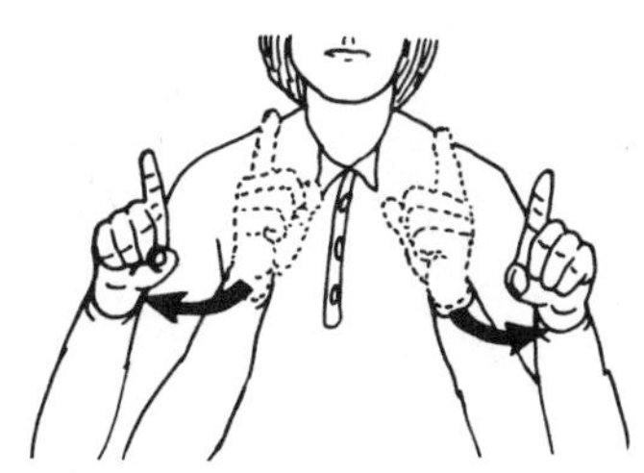

Arabic: hádatha حدث
Chinese: chūxiàn 出現
Dutch: voorval
French: événement
German: Vorfall
Italian: occorrenza
Japanese: dekigoto 出来事
Korean: sakŏn 사건
Portuguese: ocorrência
Russian: proisshéstviye происшествие
Spanish: acontecimiento
Swedish: händelse

1460. ocean [n.]

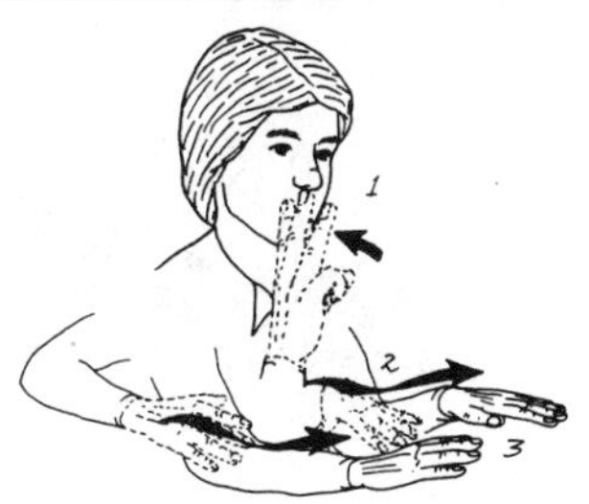

Arabic: muhíet محيط
Chinese: hǎiyáng 海洋
Dutch: oceaan
French: océan
German: Ozean
Italian: oceano
Japanese: taiyō 大洋
Korean: daeyang 대양
Portuguese: oceano
Russian: okeán океан
Spanish: océano
Swedish: ocean

1461. October [n.]

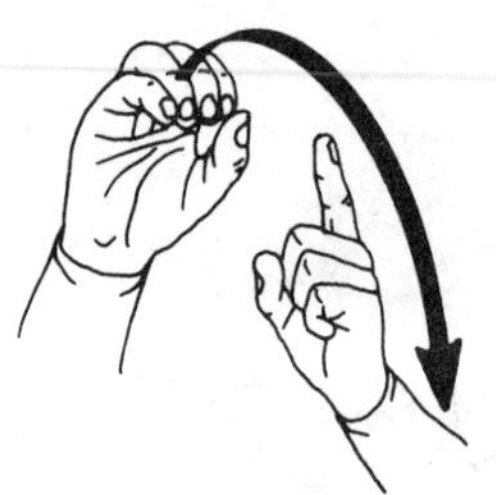

Arabic: október اكتوبر
Chinese: shíyuè 十月
Dutch: oktober
French: octobre
German: Oktober
Italian: ottobre
Japanese: jūgatsu 十月
Korean: shiwŏl 시월
Portuguese: outubro
Russian: oktyábr' октябрь
Spanish: octubre
Swedish: oktober

1462. odor [n.]

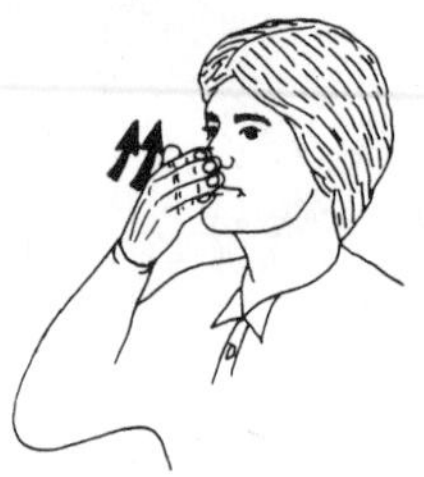

Arabic: ríha ريحة
Chinese: qìwèi 氣味
Dutch: reuk
French: odeur
German: Geruch
Italian: odore
Japanese: nioi 匂い
Korean: naemsae 냄새
Portuguese: odor
Russian: zápakh запах
Spanish: olor
Swedish: lukt

1463. offend [v.]

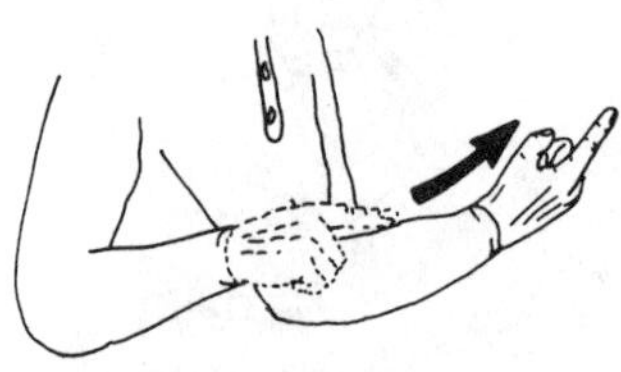

Arabic: dáyaqa ضايق
Chinese: màofàn 冒犯
Dutch: beledigen
French: offenser
German: beleidigen
Italian: offendere
Japanese: okoraseru 怒らせる
Korean: nohage hada 노하게하다
Portuguese: ofender
Russian: obizhát' обижать
Spanish: ofender
Swedish: såra

1464. offer (propose/suggest) [v.]

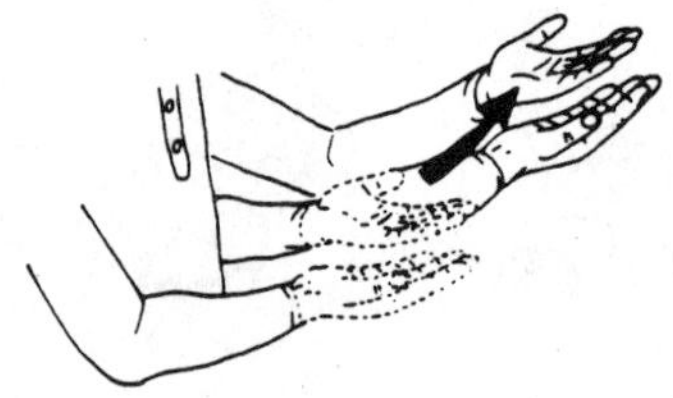

Arabic: iqtáraha اقترح
Chinese: tígòng 提供
Dutch: aanbieden
French: offrir
German: anbieten
Italian: offrire
Japanese: mōshideru 申し出る
Korean: jeŭihada 제의하다
Portuguese: oferecer
Russian: predlagát' предлагать
Spanish: ofrecer
Swedish: erbjuda

1465. office (room) [n.]

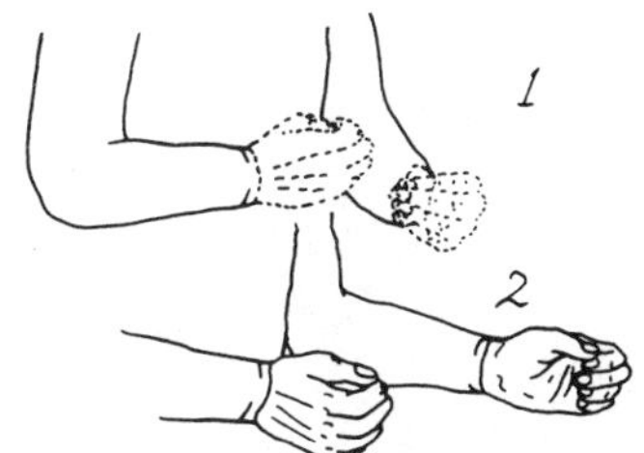

Arabic: máktab مكتب
Chinese: bàngōngshì 辦公室
Dutch: kantoor
French: bureau
German: Büro
Italian: ufficio
Japanese: jimusho 事務所
Korean: samuso 사무소
Portuguese: escritório
Russian: kontóra контора
Spanish: oficina
Swedish: kontor

1466. officer [n.]

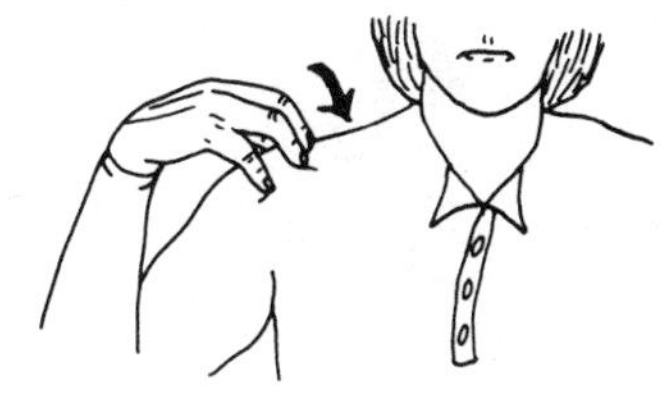

Arabic: dhábet ضابط
Chinese: guānyuán 官員
Dutch: officier
French: officier
German: Offizier
Italian: ufficiale
Japanese: yakunin 役人
Korean: janggyo 장교
Portuguese: oficial
Russian: ofitsér офицер
Spanish: oficial
Swedish: officer

1467. often [adv.]

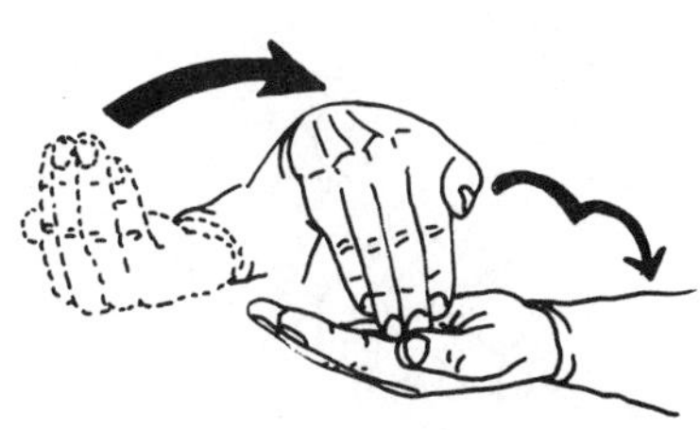

Arabic: kathíran كثيراً
Chinese: shícháng 時常
Dutch: vaak
French: souvent
German: oft
Italian: spesso
Japanese: shiba shiba しばしば
Korean: jaju 자주
Portuguese: frequentemente
Russian: chásto часто
Spanish: frecuentemente
Swedish: ofta

1468. oil (cooking/petroleum) [n.]

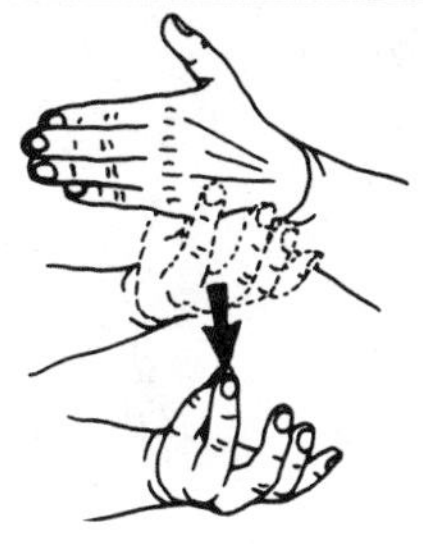

Arabic: zeyt زيت
Chinese: yóu/shíyóu 油/石油
Dutch: olie/petroleum
French: huile/pétrole
German: Öl
Italian: olio/petrolio
Japanese: abura/sekiyu 石油
Korean: kirŭm/sŏgyu 기름/석유
Portuguese: óleo/petróleo
Russian: máslo/néft' масло/нефть
Spanish: aceite/petróleo
Swedish: olja/bergolja

1469. old [adj.]

Arabic: qadím قديم
Chinese: lǎode 老的
Dutch: oud
French: vieux
German: alt
Italian: vecchio
Japanese: furui 古い
Korean: nŭlgŭn 늙은
Portuguese: velho
Russian: stáryy старый
Spanish: viejo
Swedish: gammal

1470. Olympic Games [n.]

Arabic: al-mubárayat al-olombía
المباريات الاولمبية
Chinese: àolínpīkèbǐsaì 奧林匹克比賽
Dutch: Olympische Spelen
French: Jeux Olympiques
German: Olympische Spiele
Italian: Giuochi Olimpici
Japanese: Gēmu Orimpikku
オリンピックゲーム
Korean: Ollimp'ik Gyŏnggi
올림픽 경기
Portuguese: Jogos Olímpicos
Russian: Olimpíyskiye ígry
Олимпийские игры
Spanish: Juegos Olímpicos
Swedish: Olympiska Spel

1471. omission [n.]

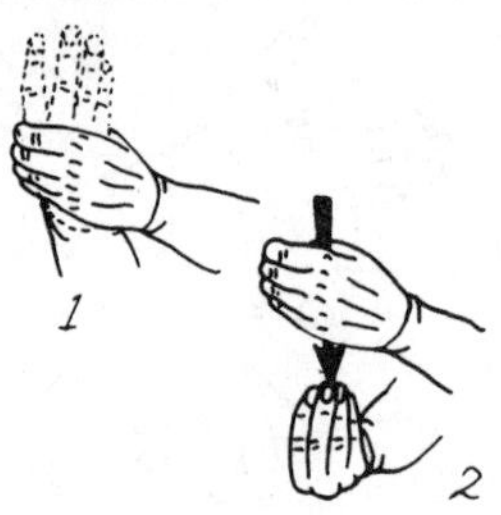

Arabic: eghfál اغفال
Chinese: shěnglüè 省略
Dutch: omissie
French: omission
German: Unterlassung
Italian: omissione
Japanese: shōryaku 省略
Korean: saengnyak 생략
Portuguese: omissão
Russian: upushchéniye упущение
Spanish: omisión
Swedish: utelämnande

1472. on [prep.]

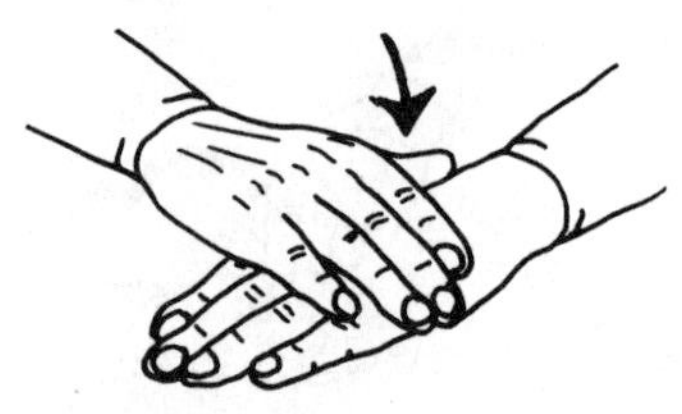

Arabic: áala على
Chinese: zài 在
Dutch: op
French: sur
German: auf
Italian: su
Japanese: . . .no ue ni …の上に
Korean: . . .wi e ~위의
Portuguese: sôbre
Russian: na на
Spanish: sobre
Swedish: på

1473. once [adv.]

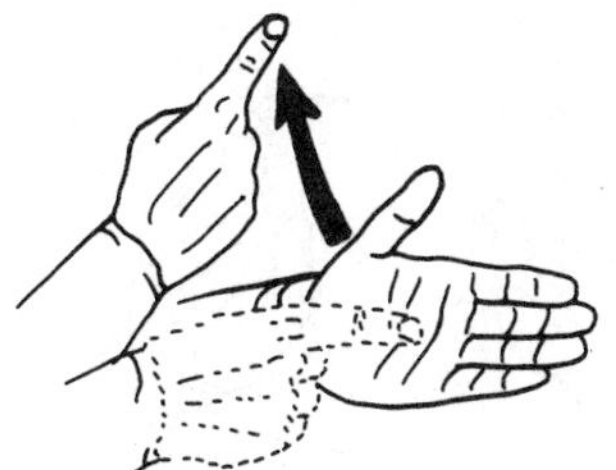

Arabic: márra مرة
Chinese: yīcì 一次
Dutch: eens
French: une fois
German: einmal
Italian: una volta
Japanese: ichido 一度
Korean: han bŏn 한번
Portuguese: uma vez
Russian: raz раз
Spanish: una vez
Swedish: en gång

1474. one [adj.]

Arabic: wáhed واحد
Chinese: yī 一
Dutch: één
French: un
German: ein
Italian: uno
Japanese: ichi 一つ
Korean: hana 하나
Portuguese: um
Russian: odín один
Spanish: uno
Swedish: en

1475. onion [n.]

Arabic: básal بصل
Chinese: yángcōng 洋葱
Dutch: ui
French: oignon
German: Zwiebel
Italian: cipolla
Japanese: tamanegi タマネギ
Korean: yangp'a 양파
Portuguese: cebola
Russian: luk лук
Spanish: cebolla
Swedish: lök

1476. only [adj./adv.]

Arabic: fáqat فقط
Chinese: zhǐyǒu 只有
Dutch: alleen
French: seulement
German: nur
Italian: solamente
Japanese: . . . dake …だけ
Korean: yuirhan 유일한
Portuguese: somente
Russian: tól'ko только
Spanish: solamente
Swedish: endast

1477. onward(s) [adv.]

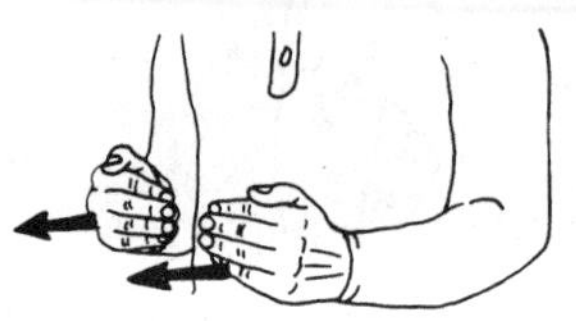

Arabic: ílal-amám الى الامام
Chinese: xiàngqián 向前
Dutch: vooruit
French: en avant
German: vorwärts
Italian: in avanti
Japanese: mae e 前へ
Korean: ap'ŭro 앞으로
Portuguese: para diante
Russian: vperyód вперёд
Spanish: para adelante
Swedish: framåt

1478. open [v.]

Arabic: fátaha فتح
Chinese: kāi 開
Dutch: openen
French: ouvrir
German: öffnen
Italian: aprire
Japanese: akeru 開ける
Korean: yŏlda 열다
Portuguese: abrir
Russian: otkryvát' открывать
Spanish: abrir
Swedish: öppna

1479. operate (manage/run) [v.]

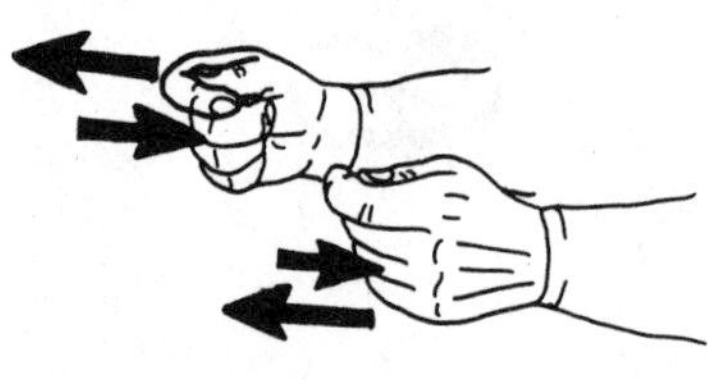

Arabic: shághghala شغل
Chinese: cāozuò 操作
Dutch: opereren
French: opérer
German: operieren
Italian: operare
Japanese: unei suru 運営する
Korean: kyŏngyŏnghada 경영하다
Portuguese: operar
Russian: operírovat' оперировать
Spanish: operar
Swedish: operera

1480. operation(action/function)[n.]

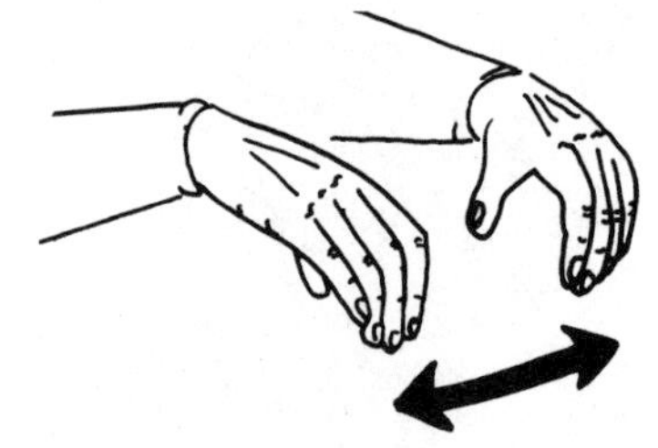

Arabic: aamalía عملية
Chinese: shŏushù 手術
Dutch: operatie
French: opération
German: Operation
Italian: operazione
Japanese: sagyō 作業
Korean: jagyong 작용
Portuguese: operação
Russian: operátsiya операция
Spanish: operación
Swedish: operation

1481. opinion [n.]

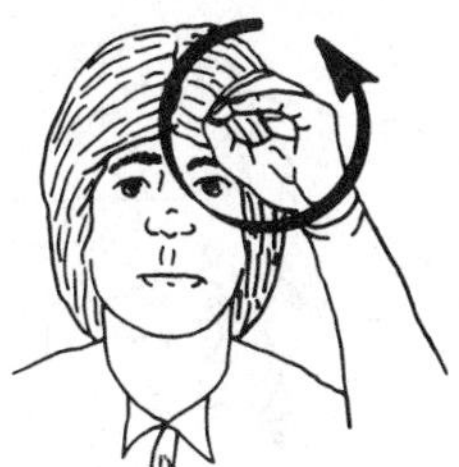

Arabic: rá'i رأي
Chinese: yìjiàn 意見
Dutch: mening
French: opinion
German: Meinung
Italian: opinione
Japanese: iken 意見
Korean: uikyŏn 의견
Portuguese: opinião
Russian: mnéniye мнение
Spanish: opinión
Swedish: mening

1482. opportunity [n.]

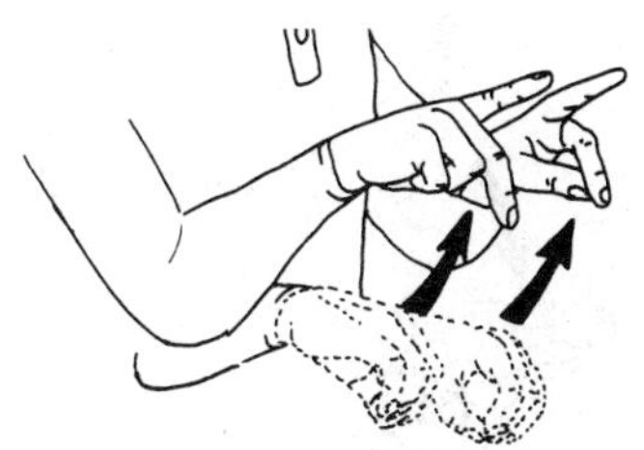

Arabic: fúrsa فرصة
Chinese: jīhuì 機會
Dutch: kans
French: occasion
German: Gelegenheit
Italian: occasione
Japanese: kikai 機会
Korean: kihoe 기회
Portuguese: oportunidade
Russian: vozmózhnost' возможность
Spanish: oportunidad
Swedish: tillfälle

1483. oppose [v.]

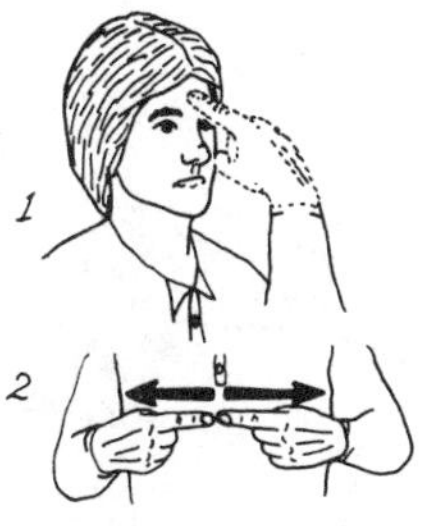

Arabic: iaatárada اعترض
Chinese: fǎnduì 反對
Dutch: weerstaan
French: opposer
German: widerstehen
Italian: opporre
Japanese: hantai suru 反対する
Korean: bandaehada 반대하다
Portuguese: opor
Russian: protivopostavlyát' противопоставлять
Spanish: oponer
Swedish: opponera

1484. opposite [adj.]

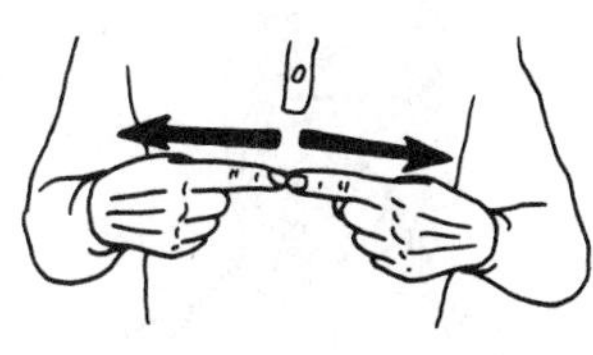

Arabic: dud ضد
Chinese: duìmiànde 對面的
Dutch: tegenovergesteld
French: opposé
German: gegenüberliegend
Italian: opposto
Japanese: gyaku no 逆くの
Korean: bandaeŭi 반대의
Portuguese: oposto
Russian: protivopolózhnyy противоположный
Spanish: opuesto
Swedish: motsatt

1485. oppress [v.]

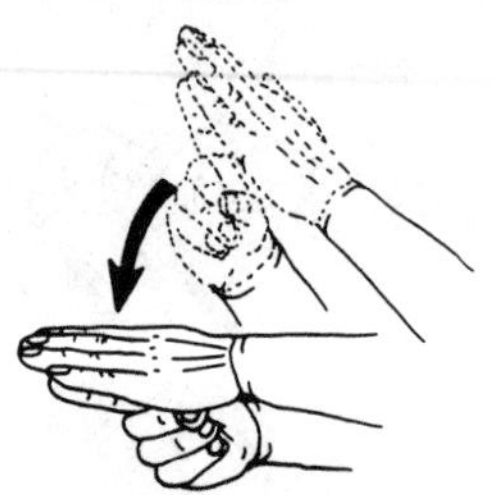

Arabic: ákhmada اخمد
Chinese: yāyì 壓抑
Dutch: onderdrukken
French: opprimer
German: unterdrücken
Italian: opprimere
Japanese: appaku suru 圧迫する
Korean: abbag'hada 압박하다
Portuguese: oprimir
Russian: pritesnyát' притеснять
Spanish: oprimir
Swedish: nedtrycka

1486. or [conj.]

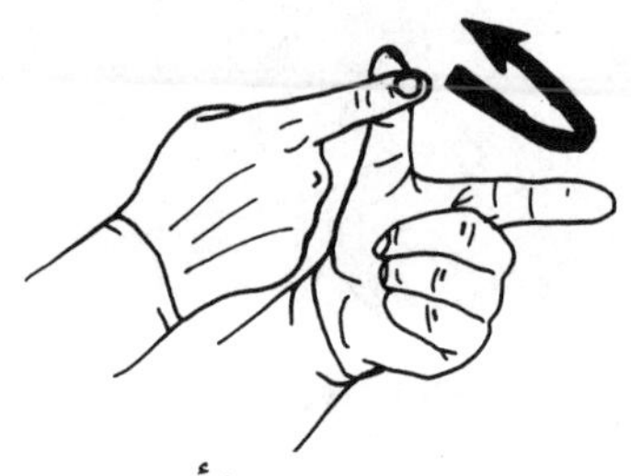

Arabic: áo أو
Chinese: huòzhě 或者
Dutch: of
French: ou
German: oder
Italian: o
Japanese: mata wa 又は
Korean: ttonŭn 또는
Portuguese: ou
Russian: íli или
Spanish: o
Swedish: eller

1487. oral [adj.]

Arabic: sháfahi شفهي
Chinese: kǒutóude 口頭的
Dutch: mondelijk
French: oral
German: mündlich
Italian: orale
Japanese: kōtō no 口頭の
Korean: kudu ŭi 구두의
Portuguese: oral
Russian: ústnyy устный
Spanish: oral
Swedish: muntlig

1488. orange [adj.]

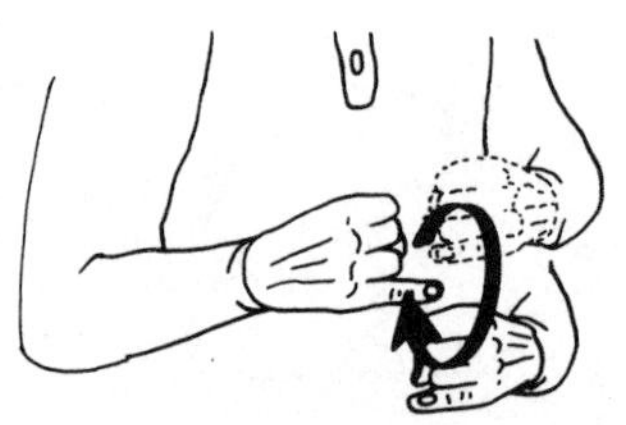

Arabic: burtuqáli برتقالي
Chinese: júsède 橘色的
Dutch: oranje
French: orange
German: orange
Italian: arancione
Japanese: orenji-iro no オレンジ色の
Korean: orenji saegŭi 오렌지색의
Portuguese: alaranjado
Russian: oránzhevyy оранжевый
Spanish: anaranjado
Swedish: apelsin-färgard

1489. orange [n.]

Arabic: burtuqál برتقال
Chinese: júzi 橘子
Dutch: sinaasappel
French: orange
German: Apfelsine
Italian: arancia
Japanese: orenji オレンジ
Korean: orenji 오렌지
Portuguese: laranja
Russian: apel'sín апельсин
Spanish: naranja
Swedish: apelsin

1490. orbit [n.]

Arabic: madár مدار
Chinese: guǐdào 軌道
Dutch: baan
French: orbite
German: Umlaufbahn
Italian: orbita
Japanese: kidō 軌道
Korean: kwedo 궤도
Portuguese: órbita
Russian: orbíta орбита
Spanish: órbita
Swedish: omloppsbana

1491. orchestra [n.]

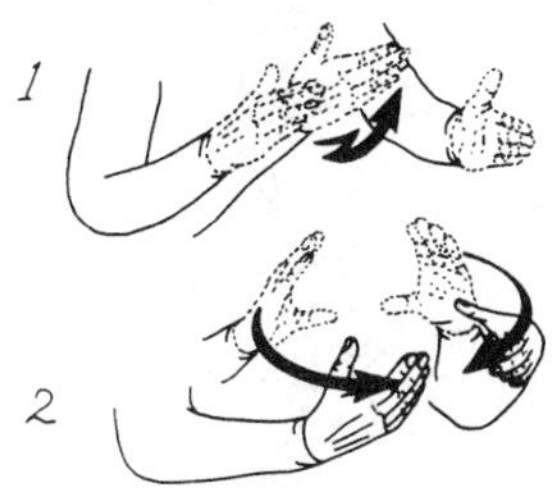

Arabic: órkestra اوركسترة
Chinese: guǎnxiányuètuán 交響樂團
Dutch: orkest
French: orchestre
German: Orchester
Italian: orchestra
Japanese: ōkesutora オーケストラ
Korean: ok'esŭt'ŭra 오케스트라
Portuguese: orquestra
Russian: orkéstr оркестр
Spanish: orquesta
Swedish: orkester

1492. order (command) [n.]

Arabic: amr أمر
Chinese: mìnglìng 命令
Dutch: bevel
French: ordre
German: Befehl
Italian: ordine
Japanese: meirei 命令
Korean: myŏngnyŏng 명령
Portuguese: ordem
Russian: prikáz приказ
Spanish: orden
Swedish: befallning

1493. order (arrangement) [n.]

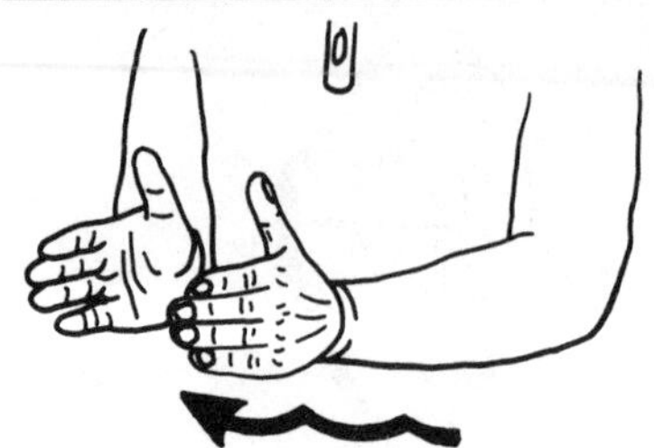

Arabic: tartíb ترتيب
Chinese: cìxù 次序
Dutch: orde
French: ordre
German: Ordnung
Italian: ordine
Japanese: junjo 順序
Korean: jilsŏ 질서
Portuguese: ordem
Russian: poryádok порядок
Spanish: orden
Swedish: ordning

1494. ordinary (usual) [adj.]

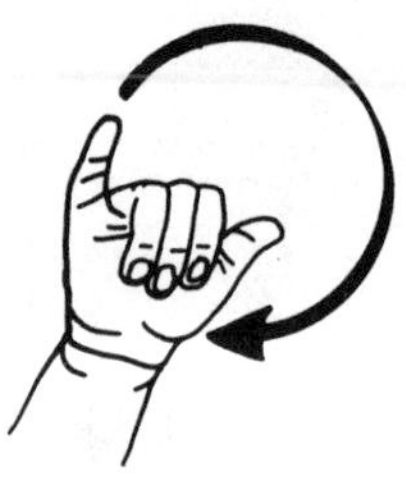

Arabic: áadi عادي
Chinese: píngcháng 平常
Dutch: gewoon
French: ordinaire
German: gewöhnlich
Italian: ordinario
Japanese: futsū no 普通の
Korean: bot'ongŭi 보통의
Portuguese: ordinário
Russian: obyknovénnyy обыкновенный
Spanish: ordinario
Swedish: vanlig

1495. organization [n.]

Arabic: munádhdhama منظمة
Chinese: zǔzhī 組織
Dutch: organizatie
French: organisation
German: Organisation
Italian: organizzazione
Japanese: soshiki 組織
Korean: jojig 조직
Portuguese: organização
Russian: organizátsiya организация
Spanish: organización
Swedish: organisation

1496. orientation [n.]

Arabic: taujíh توجيه
Chinese: dìng xiàng 定向
Dutch: oriëntatie
French: orientation
German: Orientierung
Italian: orientamento
Japanese: annai-shidō 案内指導
Korean: orienteishŏn 익숙케 함
Portuguese: orientação
Russian: orientátsiya ориентация
Spanish: orientación
Swedish: orientering

1497. origin [n.]

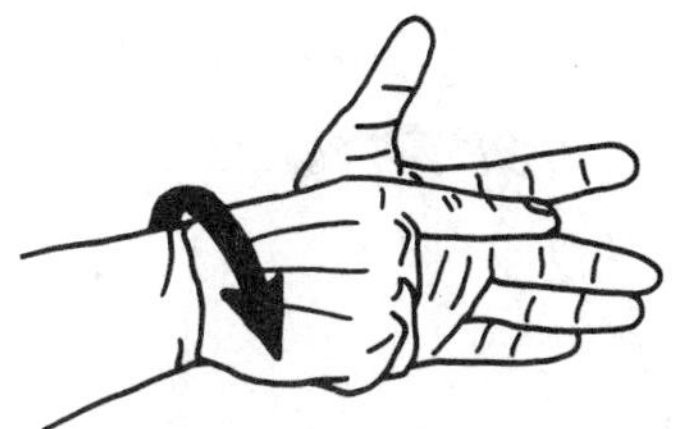

Arabic: asl اصل
Chinese: běnyuán 本源
Dutch: oorsprong
French: origine
German: Ursprung
Italian: origine
Japanese: genin 原因
Korean: kŭnwŏn 근원
Portuguese: origem
Russian: proiskhozhdéniye происхождение
Spanish: origen
Swedish: ursprung

1498. original [adj.]

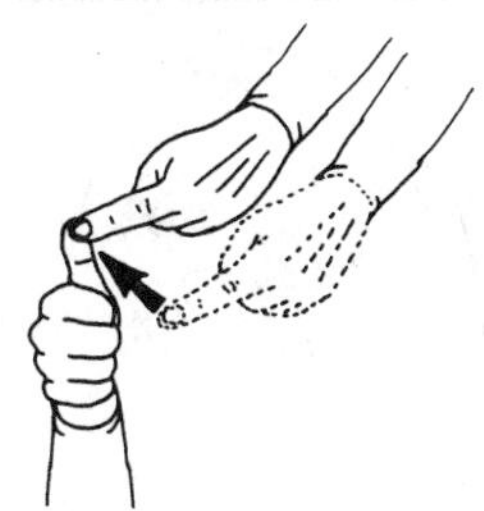

Arabic: aslí اصلي
Chinese: qǐchūdě 起初的
Dutch: origineel
French: original
German: original
Italian: originale
Japanese: honrai no 本来の
Korean: ch'oech'oŭi 최초의
Portuguese: original
Russian: originál'nyy оригинальный
Spanish: original
Swedish: originell

1499. other [adj.]

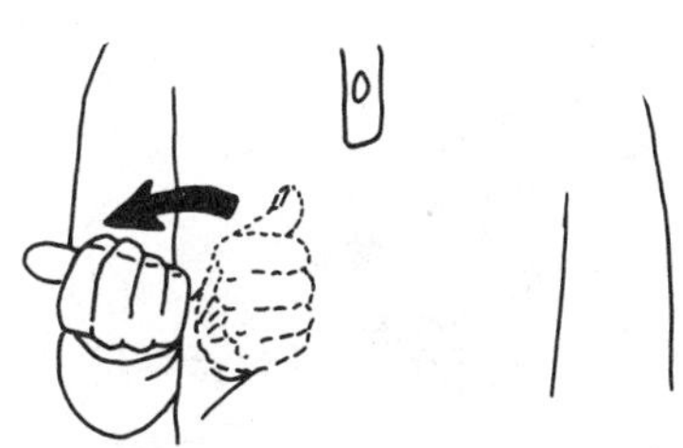

Arabic: akharín اخرين
Chinese: biéde 别的
Dutch: ander
French: autre
German: andere
Italian: altro
Japanese: hoka no 他の
Korean: darŭn 다른
Portuguese: outro
Russian: drugóy другой
Spanish: otro
Swedish: annan

1500. ounce [n.]

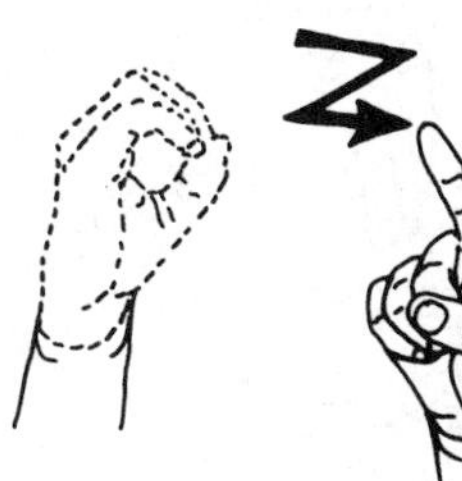

Arabic: auns اونس
Chinese: āngsī 盎司
Dutch: ons
French: once
German: Unze
Italian: oncia
Japanese: onsu オンス
Korean: onsŭ 온스
Portuguese: onça
Russian: úntsiya унция
Spanish: onza
Swedish: uns

1501. our [pron.]

Arabic: lána لنا
Chinese: wǒménde 我們的
Dutch: ons
French: notre
German: unser
Italian: nostro
Japanese: ware-ware no 我々の
Korean: uriŭi 우리의
Portuguese: nosso
Russian: nash наш
Spanish: nuestro
Swedish: vår

1502. ourselves [pron.]

Arabic: anfúsana انفسنا
Chinese: wǒménzìji 我們自己
Dutch: onszelf
French: nous-mêmes
German: wir selbst
Italian: noi stessi
Japanese: ware-ware jishin 我々自身
Korean: uri jashin 우리 자신
Portuguese: nós mesmos
Russian: sebyá себя
Spanish: nosotros mismos
Swedish: vi själva

1503. out [adv./prep.]

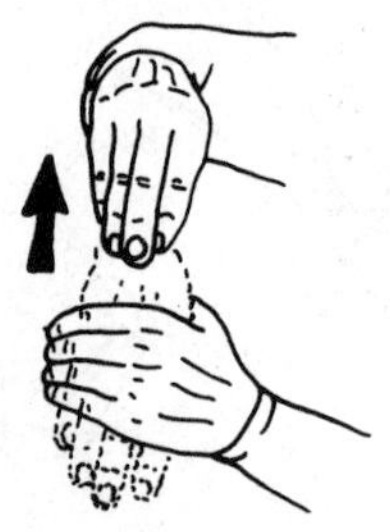

Arabic: khárij خارج
Chinese: chūqù 出去
Dutch: uit
French: hors
German: hinaus
Italian: fuori
Japanese: soto e 外へ
Korean: bakkŭro 밖으로
Portuguese: fora
Russian: iz из
Spanish: fuera
Swedish: ut

1504. over [adv./prep.]

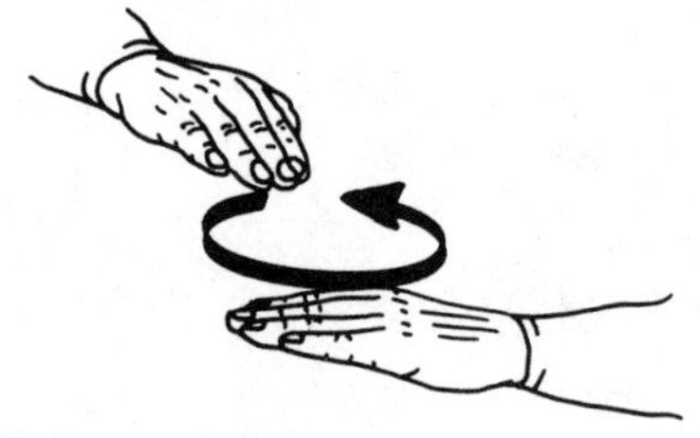

Arabic: fauq فوق
Chinese: zài...zhīshàng 在…之上
Dutch: over
French: sur
German: über
Italian: sopra
Japanese: ueni …の上に
Korean: wie 위
Portuguese: sôbre
Russian: nad над
Spanish: sobre
Swedish: över

1505. overcome [v.]

Arabic: házama هزم
Chinese: kèfú 克服
Dutch: overwinnen
French: vaincre
German: überwinden
Italian: vincere
Japanese: seifuku suru 征服する
Korean: igyŏnaeda 이겨내다
Portuguese: vencer
Russian: preodolevát' преодолевать
Spanish: vencer
Swedish: övervinna

1506. owe [v.]

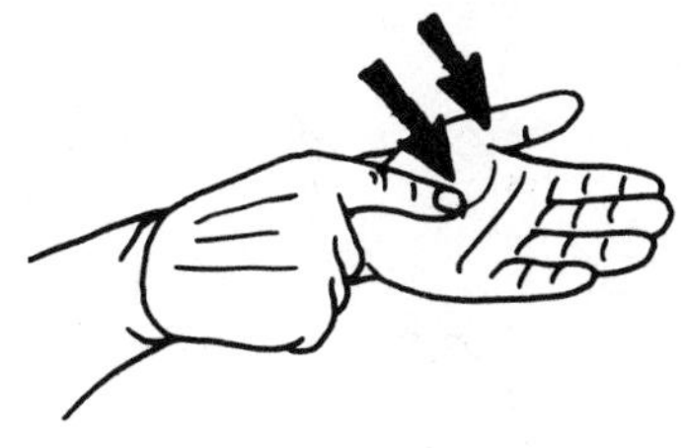

Arabic: yakún madínan láhu
يكون مديناً له
Chinese: qiànzhài 欠債
Dutch: schuldig zijn
French: devoir
German: schulden
Italian: dovere
Japanese: kari ga aru 借りがある
Korean: bit'jida 빚지다
Portuguese: dever
Russian: byt' dólzhnym быть должным
Spanish: deber
Swedish: vara skyldig

1507. own [adj.]

Arabic: milk ملك
Chinese: zìjǐde 自己的
Dutch: eigen
French: propre
German: eigen
Italian: proprio
Japanese: jishin no 自身の
Korean: jagiŭi 자기의
Portuguese: próprio
Russian: svoy свой
Spanish: propio
Swedish: egen

1508. own (possess) [v.]

Arabic: málaka ملك
Chinese: yŏngyŏu 擁有
Dutch: bezitten
French: posséder
German: besitzen
Italian: possedere
Japanese: shoyū suru 所有する
Korean: soyuhada 소유하다
Portuguese: possuir
Russian: vladét' владеть
Spanish: poseer
Swedish: äga

1509. owner [n.]

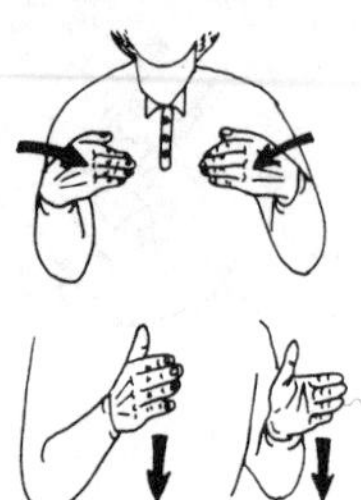

Arabic: málik مالك
Chinese: suŏyŏurén 所有人
Dutch: eigenaar
French: propriétaire
German: Besitzer
Italian: proprietario
Japanese: mochi-nushi 持主
Korean: soyuja 소유자
Portuguese: proprietário
Russian: vladélets владелец
Spanish: propietario
Swedish: ägare

1510. package [n.]

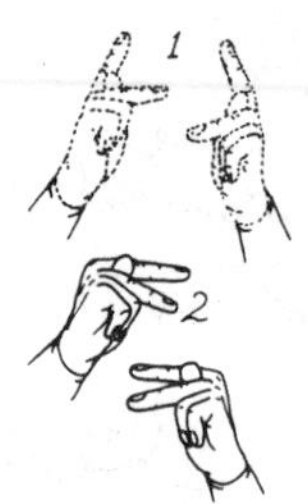

Arabic: súrra صرة
Chinese: baōguŏ 包裹
Dutch: pak
French: paquet
German: Paket
Italian: pacco
Japanese: tsutsumi 包み
Korean: sop'o 소포
Portuguese: pacote
Russian: posýlka посылка
Spanish: paquete
Swedish: paket

1511. page [n.]

Arabic: sáfha صفحة
Chinese: yè 頁
Dutch: pagina
French: page
German: Seite
Italian: pagina
Japanese: pēji ページ
Korean: p'eiji 페이지
Portuguese: página
Russian: stranítsa страница
Spanish: página
Swedish: sida

1512. pain [n.]

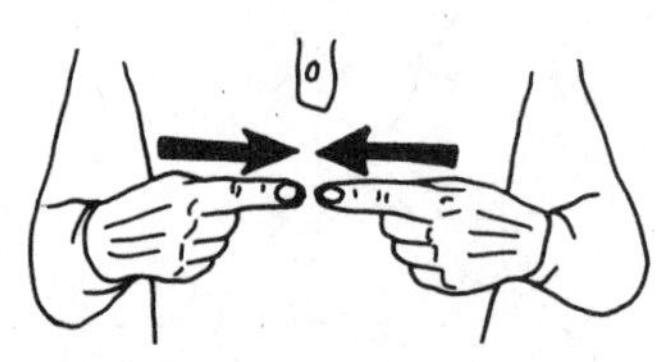

Arabic: aalám ألم
Chinese: tòngkŭ 痛苦
Dutch: pijn
French: douleur
German: Schmerz
Italian: dolore
Japanese: itami 痛み
Korean: ap'ŭm 아픔
Portuguese: dor
Russian: bol' боль
Spanish: dolor
Swedish: smärta

1513. paint [n.]

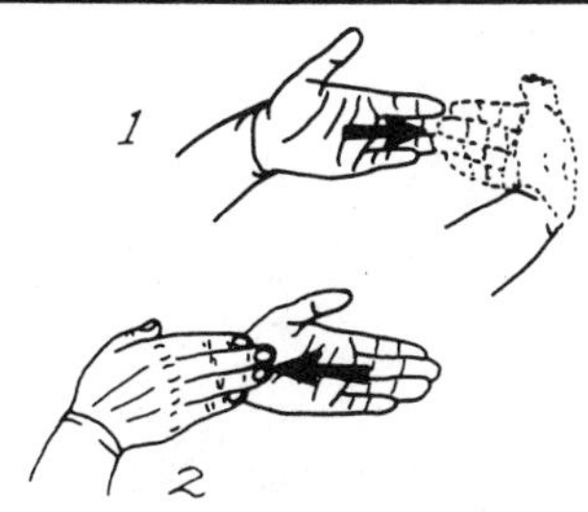

Arabic: dihán دهان
Chinese: yóuqī 油漆
Dutch: verf
French: peinture
German: Farbe
Italian: vernice
Japanese: penki ペンキ
Korean: p'eint'ŭ 페인트
Portuguese: tinta
Russian: kráska краска
Spanish: pintura
Swedish: färg

1514. painter (artist) [n.]

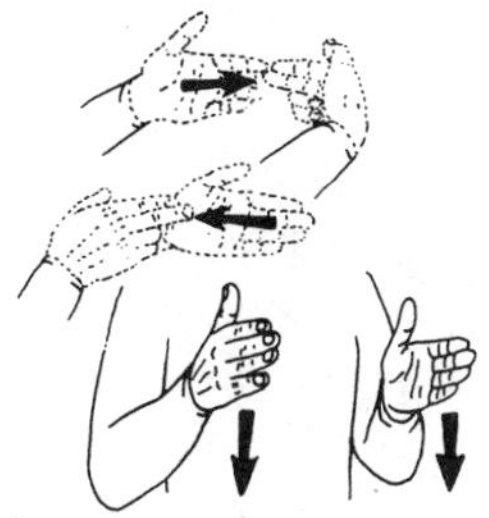

Arabic: ar-rassám الرسام
Chinese: huàjiā 畫家
Dutch: schilder
French: peintre
German: Maler
Italian: pittore
Japanese: gaka 画家
Korean: hwaga 화가
Portuguese: pintor
Russian: khudózhnik художник
Spanish: pintor
Swedish: målare

1515. pair [n.]

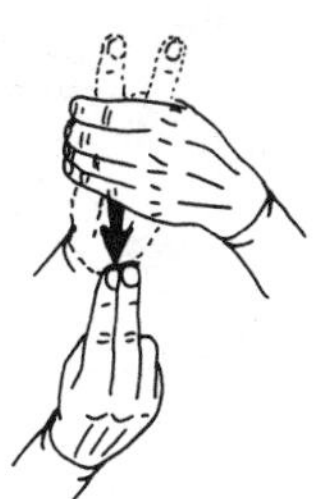

Arabic: zauj زوج
Chinese: shuāng 雙
Dutch: paar
French: paire
German: Paar
Italian: paio
Japanese: hitokumi 一組
Korean: ḥanssang 한쌍
Portuguese: par
Russian: pára пара
Spanish: par
Swedish: par

1516. palace [n.]

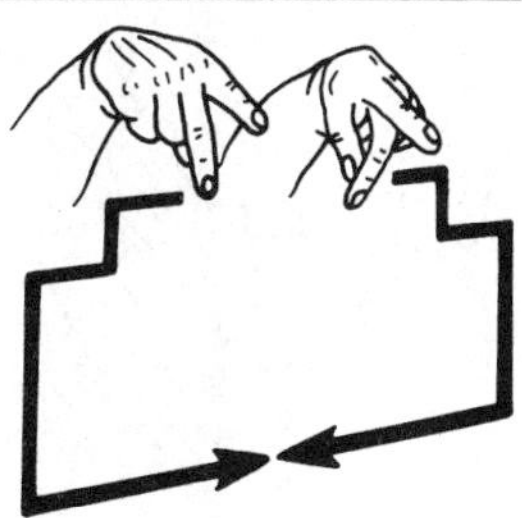

Arabic: qasr قصر
Chinese: huánggōng 皇宮
Dutch: paleis
French: palais
German: Palast
Italian: palazzo
Japanese: kyūden 宮殿
Korean: kungjŏn 궁전
Portuguese: palácio
Russian: dvoréts дворец
Spanish: palacio
Swedish: palats

1517. pale [adj.]

Arabic: báhet باهت
Chinese: cāngbái 蒼白
Dutch: bleek
French: pâle
German: blaß
Italian: pallido
Japanese: aozameta 青ざめた
Korean: ch'angbaek'han 창백한
Portuguese: pálido
Russian: blédnyy бледный
Spanish: pálido
Swedish: blek

1518. pancake(s) [n.]

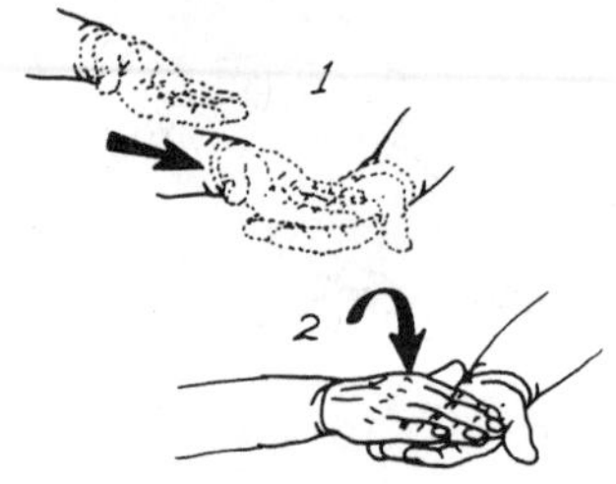

Arabic: fatíra فطيرة
Chinese: bójiānbǐng 薄煎餅
Dutch: pannekoek
French: crêpe
German: Pfannkuchen
Italian: frittella
Japanese: pankēki パンケーキ
Korean: pankeiki 팬케이크
Portuguese: panqueca
Russian: bliný блины
Spanish: panqueque
Swedish: pannkaka

1519. pants (trousers) [n.]

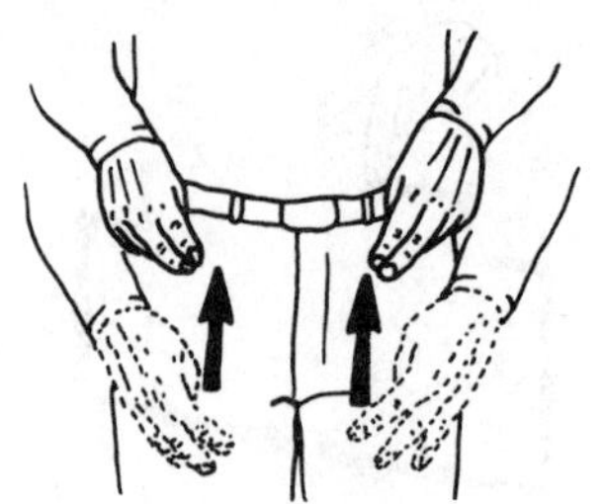

Arabic: bantalón بنطلون
Chinese: chángkù 長褲
Dutch: broek
French: pantalon
German: Hosen
Italian: calzoni
Japanese: zubon ズボン
Korean: baji 바지
Portuguese: calças
Russian: bryúki брюки
Spanish: pantalones
Swedish: byxor

1520. paper [n.]

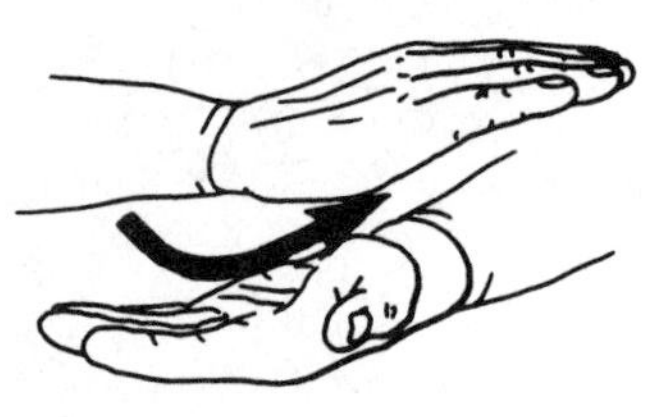

Arabic: wáraqa ورقة
Chinese: zhǐ 紙
Dutch: papier
French: papier
German: Papier
Italian: carta
Japanese: kami 紙
Korean: jongi 종이
Portuguese: papel
Russian: bumága бумага
Spanish: papel
Swedish: papper

1521. parade [n.]

Arabic: istaarád استعرض
Chinese: yóuxíng 遊行
Dutch: parade
French: parade
German: Parade
Italian: parata
Japanese: kōshin 行進
Korean: haengnyŏl 행렬
Portuguese: parada
Russian: parád парад
Spanish: desfile
Swedish: parad

1522. parallel [adj.]

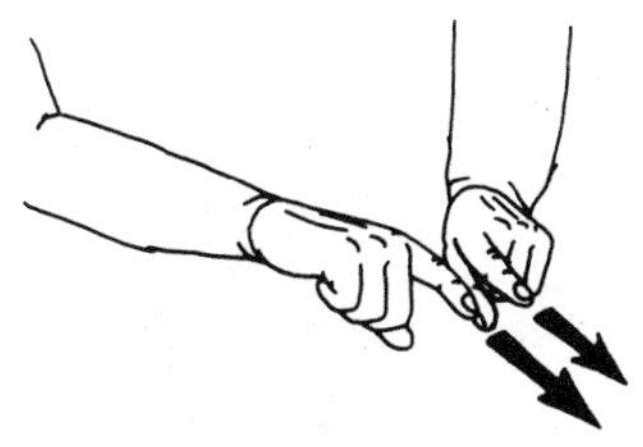

Arabic: muwázi موازي
Chinese: píngxíng 平行
Dutch: parallel
French: parallèle
German: parallel
Italian: parallelo
Japanese: heikō no 平行の
Korean: p'yŏnghaengŭi 평행의
Portuguese: paralelo
Russian: parallél'nyy параллельный
Spanish: paralelo
Swedish: parallell

1523. pardon me [interj.]

Arabic: áafwan عفواً
Chinese: duìbùqǐ 對不起
Dutch: pardon
French: excusez-moi
German: Entschuldigung
Italian: scusami
Japanese: gomen nasai 御免なさい
Korean: yong'sŏ hashipshiyo 용서하십시요
Portuguese: desculpe-me
Russian: prostíte простите
Spanish: discúlpeme
Swedish: ursäkta mig

1524. parents [n.]

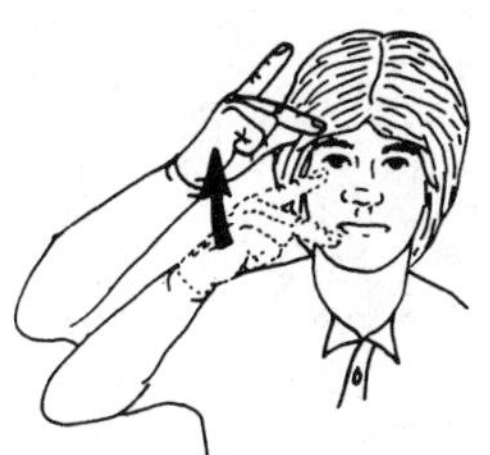

Arabic: walidéin والدين
Chinese: fùmǔ 父母
Dutch: ouders
French: parents
German: Eltern
Italian: genitori
Japanese: ryōshin 両親
Korean: bumo 부모
Portuguese: país
Russian: rodíteli родители
Spanish: padres
Swedish: föräldrar

1525. park [n.]

Arabic: hadíeqa حديقة
Chinese: gōnggyuán 公園
Dutch: park
French: parc
German: Park
Italian: parco
Japanese: kōen 公園
Korean: kongwŏn 공원
Portuguese: parque
Russian: park парк
Spanish: parque
Swedish: park

1526. park (vehicles) [v.]

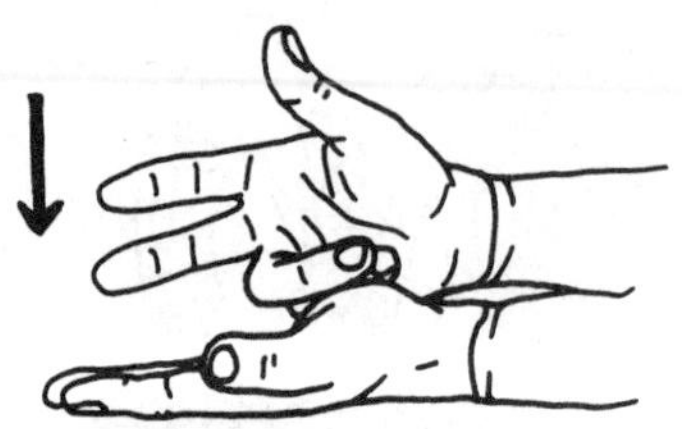

Arabic: máuqef موقف
Chinese: tíng 停
Dutch: parkeren
French: garer
German: parken
Italian: parcheggiare
Japanese: chūsha suru 駐車する
Korean: chuch'ahada 주차하다
Portuguese: estacionar
Russian: stávit' na stoyánku ставить на стоянку
Spanish: estacionar
Swedish: parkera

1527. part (section) [n.]

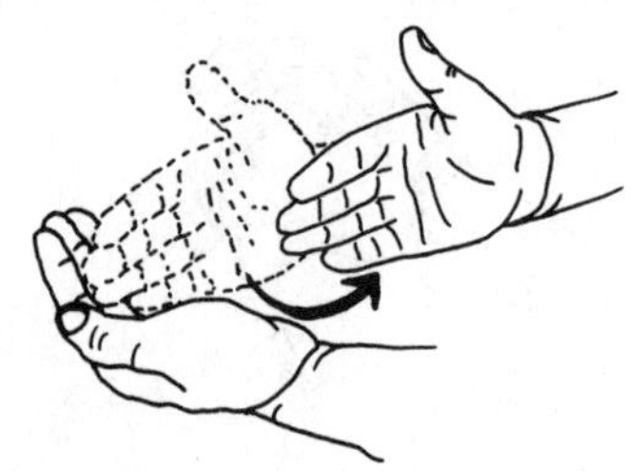

Arabic: júza' جزء
Chinese: bùfèn 部分
Dutch: deel
French: partie
German: Teil
Italian: parte
Japanese: bubun 部分
Korean: bubun 부분
Portuguese: parte
Russian: chast' часть
Spanish: parte
Swedish: del

1528. participate [v.]

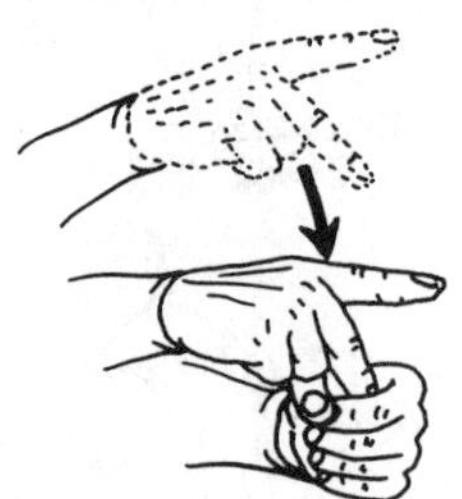

Arabic: shároka شارك
Chinese: cānjiā 參加
Dutch: deelnemen
French: participer
German: teilnehmen
Italian: participare
Japanese: sanka suru 参加する
Korean: chamgahada 참가하다
Portuguese: participar
Russian: uchástvovat' участвовать
Spanish: participar
Swedish: deltaga

1529. party (political) [n.]

Arabic: hezb حزب
Chinese: dǎng 黨
Dutch: partij
French: parti
German: Partei
Italian: partito
Japanese: seitō 政党
Korean: jŏngdang 정당
Portuguese: partido
Russian: pártiya партия
Spanish: partido
Swedish: parti

1530. pass (go by/through) [v.]

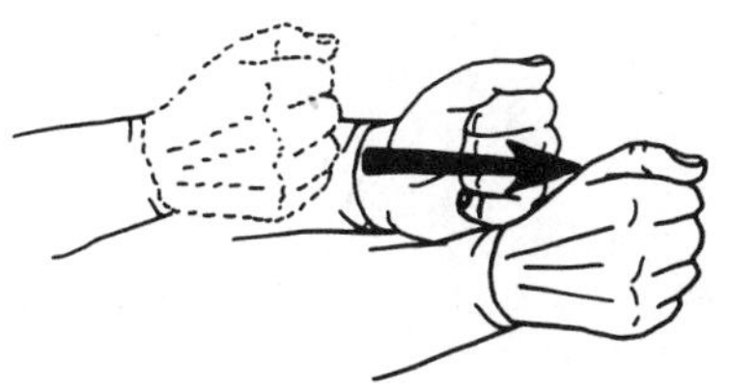

Arabic: márra مر
Chinese: guò 過
Dutch: voorbijgaan
French: passer
German: vorbeigehen
Italian: passare
Japanese: sugiru 過ぎる
Korean: chinagada 지나가다
Portuguese: passar
Russian: prokhodít' проходить
Spanish: pasar
Swedish: förflytta

1531. passenger [n.]

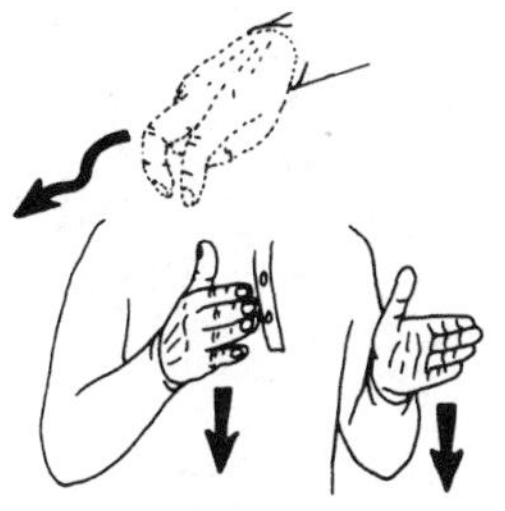

Arabic: musáfer مسافر
Chinese: chéngkè 乘客
Dutch: passagier
French: passager
German: Passagier
Italian: passeggero
Japanese: jōkyaku 乗客
Korean: sŭnggaek 승객
Portuguese: passageiro
Russian: passazhír пассажир
Spanish: pasajero
Swedish: passagerare

1532. passport [n.]

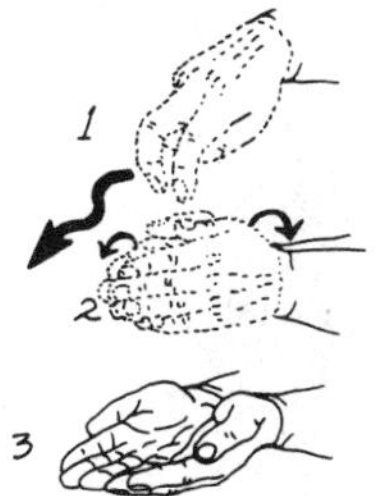

Arabic: jawáz sáfar جواز سفر
Chinese: hùzhào 護照
Dutch: paspoort
French: passeport
German: Paß
Italian: passaporto
Japanese: pasupōto パスポート
Korean: yŏkwŏn 여권
Portuguese: passaporte
Russian: pásport паспорт
Spanish: pasaporte
Swedish: pass

1533. past [n.]

Arabic: mádhi ماضي
Chinese: guòqù 過去
Dutch: verleden
French: passé
German: Vergangenheit
Italian: passato
Japanese: kako 過去
Korean: kwagŏ 과거
Portuguese: passado
Russian: próshloye прошлое
Spanish: pasado
Swedish: förflutna

1534. path [n.]

Arabic: taríeq طريق
Chinese: lùjìng 路徑
Dutch: pad
French: sentier
German: Pfad
Italian: sentiero
Japanese: komichi 小道
Korean: gil 길
Portuguese: trilha
Russian: tropínka тропинка
Spanish: senda
Swedish: stig

1535. patience [n.]

Arabic: sabr صبر
Chinese: nàixīng 耐心
Dutch: geduld
French: patience
German: Geduld
Italian: pazienza
Japanese: shimbō 辛抱
Korean: ch'amŭlsŏng 참을성
Portuguese: paciência
Russian: terpéniye терпение
Spanish: paciencia
Swedish: tålamod

1536. patient [n.]

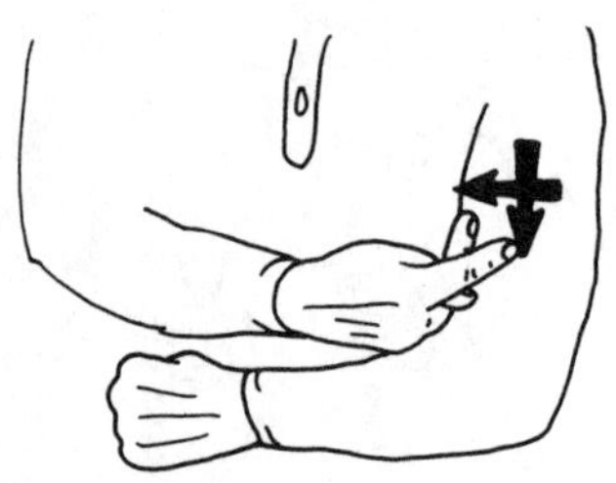

Arabic: maríd مريض
Chinese: bìnghuàn 病患
Dutch: patiënt
French: patient
German: Patient
Italian: paziente
Japanese: kanja 患者
Korean: hwanja 환자
Portuguese: paciente
Russian: patsiént пациент
Spanish: paciente
Swedish: patient

1537. pause [n.]

Arabic: tawáqquf توقف
Chinese: zhàngtíng 暂停
Dutch: pause
French: pause
German: Pause
Italian: pausa
Japanese: kyūshi 休止
Korean: mŏmch'um 멈춤
Portuguese: pausa
Russian: páuza пауза
Spanish: pausa
Swedish: paus

1538. pay [v.]

Arabic: dáfaa دفع
Chinese: fù 付
Dutch: betalen
French: payer
German: bezahlen
Italian: pagare
Japanese: harau 払う
Korean: jiburhada 지불하다
Portuguese: pagar
Russian: platít' платить
Spanish: pagar
Swedish: betala

1539. peace [n.]

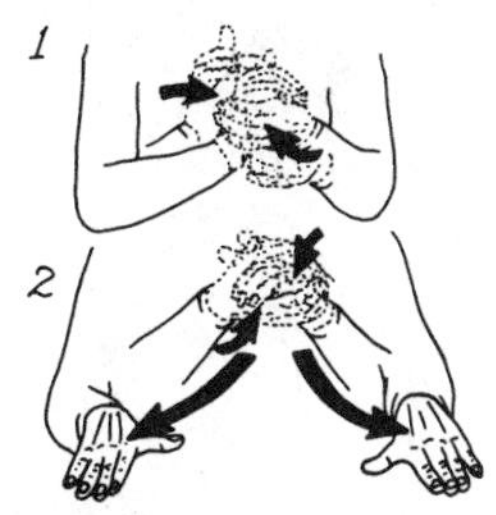

Arabic: salám سلام
Chinese: hépíng 和平
Dutch: vrede
French: paix
German: Friede
Italian: pace
Japanese: heiwa 平和
Korean: p'yŏnghwa 평화
Portuguese: paz
Russian: mir мир
Spanish: paz
Swedish: fred

1540. peak (summit) [n.]

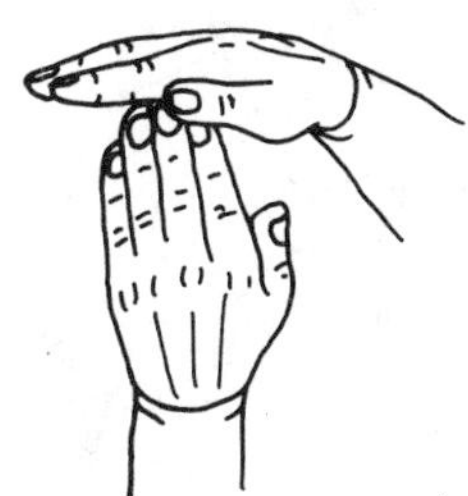

Arabic: qémma قمة
Chinese: jiānfēng 尖峰
Dutch: piek
French: cime
German: Gipfel
Italian: cima
Japanese: sanchō 山頂
Korean: sankkogtaegi 산꼭대기
Portuguese: pico
Russian: vershína вершина
Spanish: cima
Swedish: spets

1541. peel [n.]

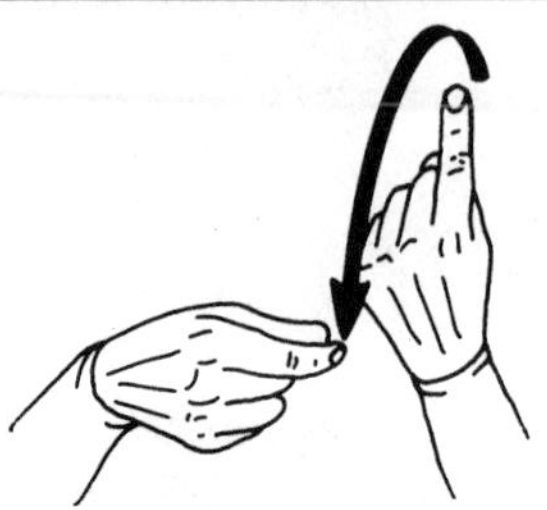

Arabic: qíshra قشرة
Chinese: guǒpí 果皮
Dutch: schil
French: pelure
German: Schale
Italian: buccia
Japanese: kawa 皮
Korean: kkŏpjil 껍질
Portuguese: casca
Russian: kórka корка
Spanish: cáscara
Swedish: skal

1542. pen (writing) [n.]

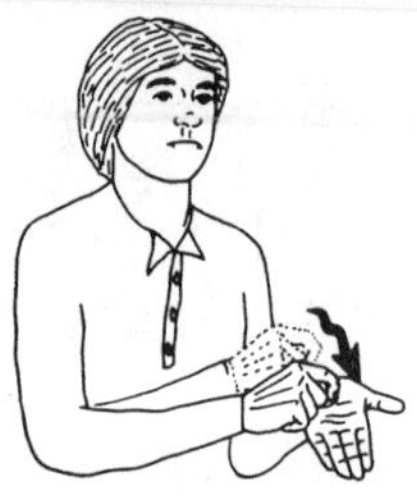

Arabic: qálam hebr قلم حبر
Chinese: bǐ 筆
Dutch: pen
French: plume
German: Füllhalter
Italian: penna
Japanese: pen ペン
Korean: p'en 펜
Portuguese: caneta
Russian: avtorúchka авторучка
Spanish: pluma
Swedish: penna

1543. penalty [n.]

Arabic: jazá' جزاء
Chinese: chěngfá 懲罰
Dutch: straf
French: peine
German: Strafe
Italian: penalità
Japanese: batsu 罰
Korean: hyŏngbŏl 형벌
Portuguese: penalidade
Russian: shtraf штраф
Spanish: castigo
Swedish: straff

1544. pencil [n.]

Arabic: qálam rasás قلم رصاص
Chinese: qiānbǐ 鉛筆
Dutch: potlood
French: crayon
German: Bleistift
Italian: matita
Japanese: empitsu 鉛筆
Korean: yŏnp'il 연필
Portuguese: lápis
Russian: karandásh карандаш
Spanish: lápiz
Swedish: blyertspenna

1545. penetrate [v.]

Arabic: ikhtáraqa اخترق
Chinese: sènrù 渗透
Dutch: doordringen
French: pénétrer
German: durchdringen
Italian: penetrare
Japanese: kantsū suru 貫通する
Korean: chimtuhada 침투하다
Portuguese: penetrar
Russian: pronikát' проникать
Spanish: penetrar
Swedish: genomtränga

1546. peninsula [n.]

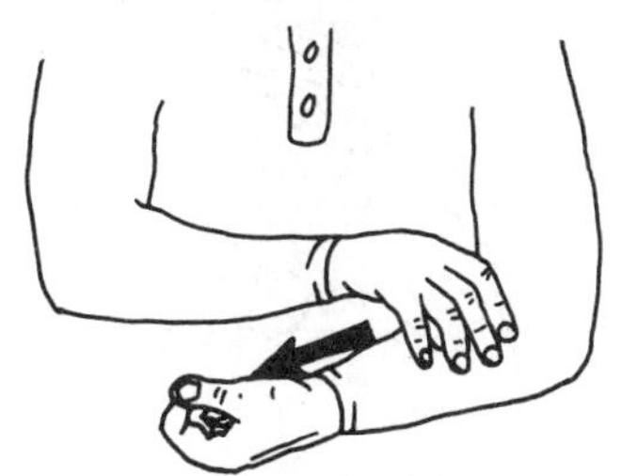

Arabic: jazíra جزيرة
Chinese: bàndǎo 半島
Dutch: schiereiland
French: péninsule
German: Halbinsel
Italian: penisola
Japanese: hantō 半島
Korean: bando 반도
Portuguese: península
Russian: poluóstrov полуостров
Spanish: península
Swedish: halvö

1547. penny (cent) [n.]

Arabic: al-bins البنس
Chinese: biànshì 辨士
Dutch: penny
French: penny
German: Penny
Italian: centesimo
Japanese: penii ペニー
Korean: iljŏn 일전
Portuguese: centavo
Russian: pénni пенни
Spanish: centavo
Swedish: penny

1548. people [n.]

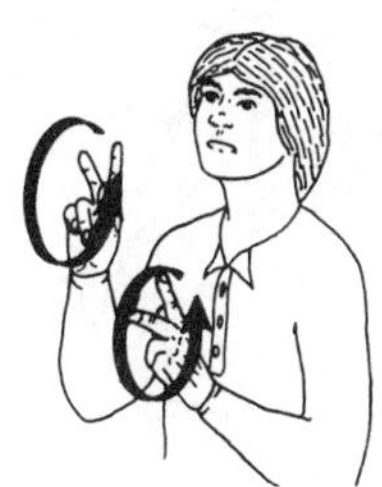

Arabic: nas ناس
Chinese: rénmen 人們
Dutch: mensen
French: gens
German: Leute
Italian: gente
Japanese: hitobito 人々
Korean: saramdŭl 사람들
Portuguese: gente
Russian: lyúdi люди
Spanish: gente
Swedish: folk

1549. pepper [n.]

Arabic: fílfil فلفل
Chinese: hújiāo 胡椒
Dutch: peper
French: poivre
German: Pfeffer
Italian: pepe
Japanese: koshō 胡椒
Korean: huch'u 후추
Portuguese: pimenta
Russian: pérets перец
Spanish: pimienta
Swedish: peppar

1550. percent [n.]

Arabic: fil-mí'a في المئة
Chinese: bǎifēnbǐ 百分比
Dutch: percent
French: pour cent
German: Prozent
Italian: per cento
Japanese: pāsento パーセント
Korean: pŏsentŭ 퍼센트
Portuguese: porcento
Russian: protsént процент
Spanish: por ciento
Swedish: procent

1551. perfect [adj.]

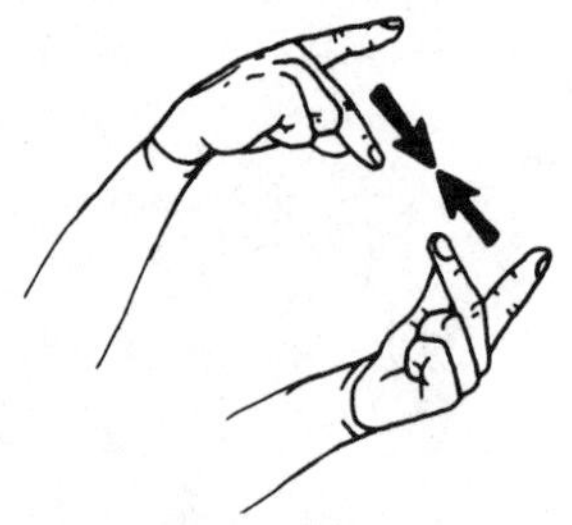

Arabic: kámil كامل
Chinese: wánměide 完美的
Dutch: perfect
French: parfait
German: perfekt
Italian: perfetto
Japanese: kampeki na 完全な
Korean: wanjŏnhan 완전한
Portuguese: perfeito
Russian: sovershénnyy совершенный
Spanish: perfecto
Swedish: perfekt

1552. performance (theater) [n.]

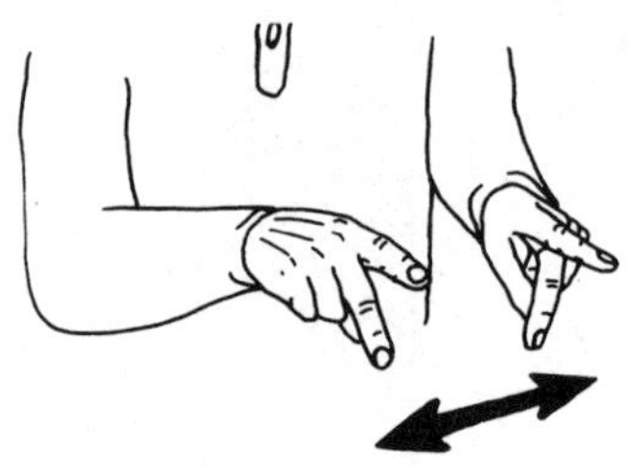

Arabic: tamthíl تمثيل
Chinese: biǎoyǎn 表演
Dutch: voorstelling
French: représentation
German: Aufführung
Italian: rappresentazione
Japanese: engeki 演劇
Korean: kongyŏn 공연
Portuguese: representação
Russian: ispolnéniye исполнение
Spanish: representación
Swedish: föreställning

1553. perhaps [adv.]

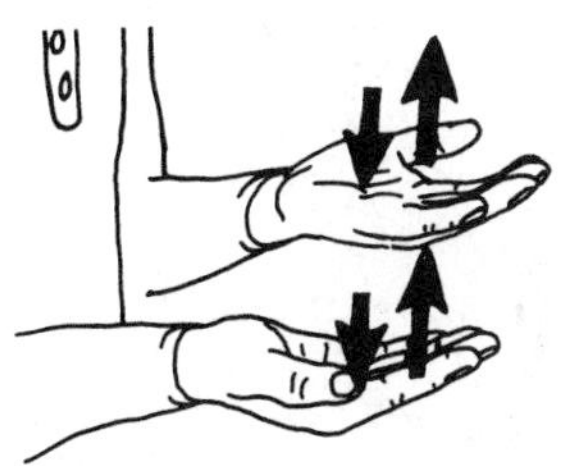

Arabic: rúbbama ربما
Chinese: yěxǔ 也許
Dutch: misschien
French: peut-être
German: vielleicht
Italian: forse
Japanese: osoraku おそらく
Korean: ama 아마
Portuguese: talvez
Russian: mózhet byt' может быть
Spanish: tal vez
Swedish: kanske

1554. period (punctuation) [n.]

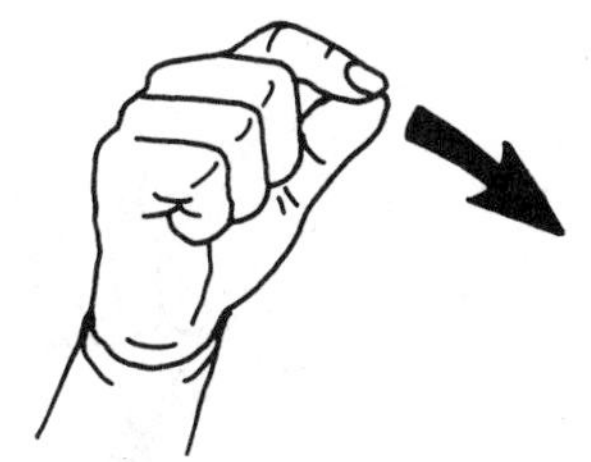

Arabic: núqta نقطة
Chinese: jùhào 句號
Dutch: punt
French: point
German: Punkt
Italian: punto
Japanese: kutōten 句読点
Korean: jongjibu 종지부
Portuguese: ponto
Russian: tóchka точка
Spanish: punto
Swedish: punkt

1555. period (time) [n.]

Arabic: fátra فترة
Chinese: shíqí 時期
Dutch: periode
French: période
German: Zeitraum
Italian: periodo
Japanese: jidai 時代
Korean: shigi 시기
Portuguese: período
Russian: períod период
Spanish: período
Swedish: period

1556. perish [v.]

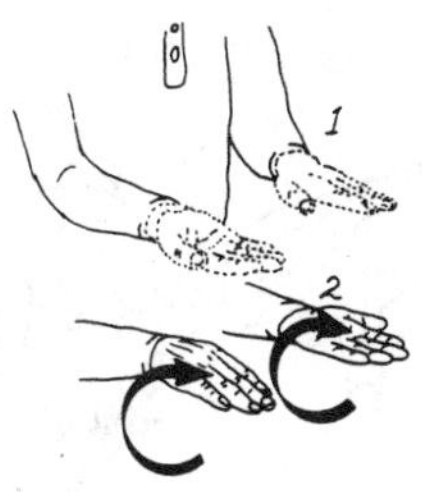

Arabic: áhlaka اهلك
Chinese: kūwěi 枯萎
Dutch: omkomen
French: périr
German: umkommen
Italian: perire
Japanese: horobiru 滅びる
Korean: sang'hada 상하다
Portuguese: perecer
Russian: pogibát' погибать
Spanish: perecer
Swedish: omkomma

1557. permanent [adj.]

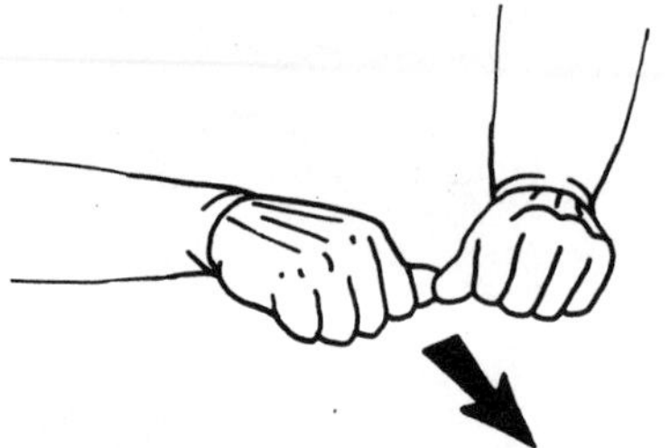

Arabic: dá'im دائم
Chinese: yǒngjiǔ 永久
Dutch: bestendig
French: permanent
German: beständig
Italian: permanente
Japanese: eikyū no 永久の
Korean: yǒnggujǒg'in 영구적인
Portuguese: permanente
Russian: postoyánnyy постоянный
Spanish: permanente
Swedish: ständig

1558. permission [n.]

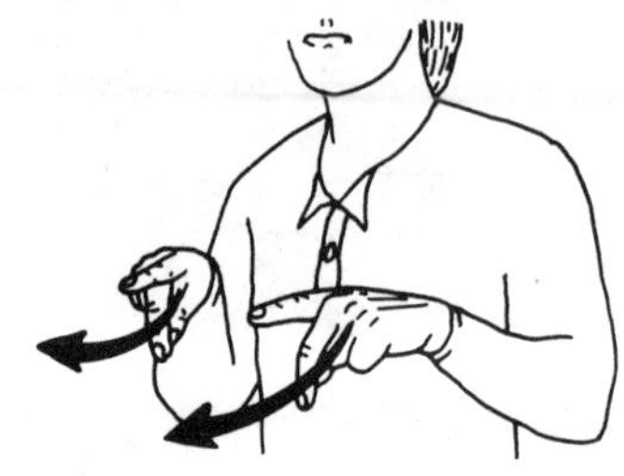

Arabic: tasríh تصريح
Chinese: xǔkě 許可
Dutch: toestemming
French: permission
German: Erlaubnis
Italian: permesso
Japanese: kyoka 許可
Korean: hǒga 허가
Portuguese: permissão
Russian: razreshéniye разрешение
Spanish: permiso
Swedish: tillåtelse

1559. perseverance [n.]

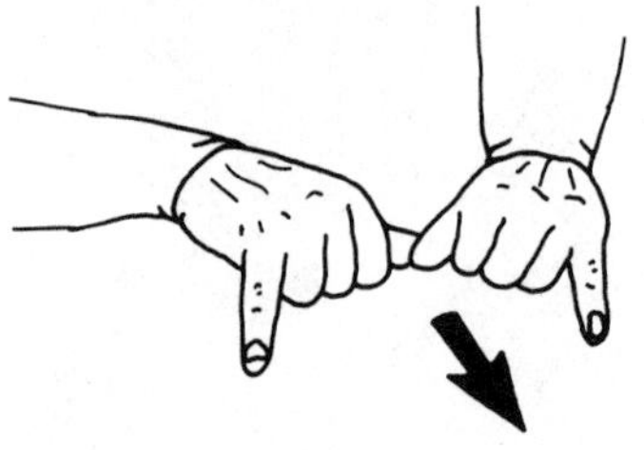

Arabic: muthábara مثابرة
Chinese: jiāndìng 堅定
Dutch: volharding
French: persévérance
German: Beharrlichkeit
Italian: perseveranza
Japanese: nintai 忍耐
Korean: innae 인내
Portuguese: perseverança
Russian: upórstvo упорство
Spanish: perseverancia
Swedish: ihärdighet

1560. persist [v.]

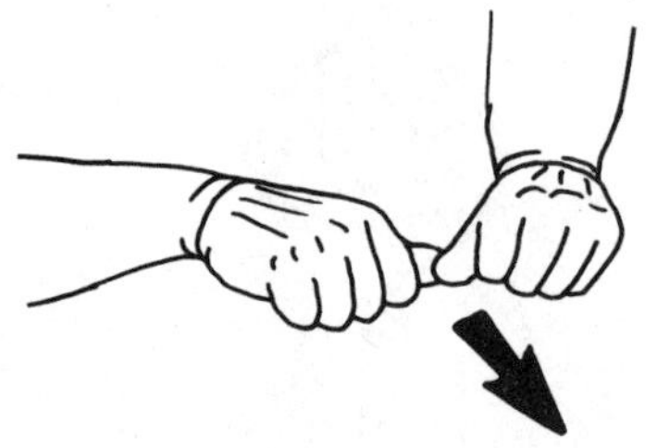

Arabic: thábara ثابر
Chinese: jiānchí 堅持
Dutch: volharden
French: persister
German: beharren
Italian: persistere
Japanese: shuchō suru 主張する
Korean: kojiphada 고집하다
Portuguese: persistir
Russian: upórstvovat' упорствовать
Spanish: persistir
Swedish: framhärda

1561. person [n.]

Arabic: shakhs شخص
Chinese: rén 人
Dutch: persoon
French: personne
German: Person
Italian: persona
Japanese: hito 人
Korean: saram 사람
Portuguese: pessoa
Russian: chelovék человек
Spanish: persona
Swedish: person

1562. personal [adj.]

Arabic: shákhsi شخصي
Chinese: sīrénde 私人的
Dutch: persoonlijk
French: personnel
German: persönlich
Italian: personale
Japanese: kojin no 個人の
Korean: gaeinŭi 개인의
Portuguese: pessoal
Russian: líchnyy личный
Spanish: personal
Swedish: personlig

1563. personality [n.]

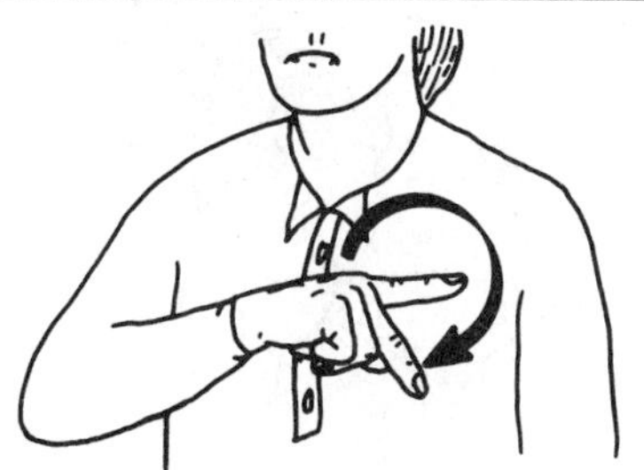

Arabic: shakhsíyya شخصية
Chinese: gèxìng 個性
Dutch: persoonlijkheid
French: personnalité
German: Persönlichkeit
Italian: personalità
Japanese: jinkaku 人格
Korean: inkyŏk 인격
Portuguese: personalidade
Russian: líchnost' личность
Spanish: personalidad
Swedish: personlighet

1564. perspiration [n.]

Arabic: áaraq عرق
Chinese: chūhàn 出汗
Dutch: zweet
French: transpiration
German: Schweiß
Italian: sudore
Japanese: ase 汗
Korean: ttam 땀
Portuguese: suor
Russian: pot пот
Spanish: sudor
Swedish: svett

1565. persuade [v.]

Arabic: áqnaa اقنع
Chinese: shuìfú 說服
Dutch: overtuigen
French: persuader
German: überreden
Italian: persuadere
Japanese: settoku suru 説得する
Korean: sŏldŭg'hada 설득하다
Portuguese: persuadir
Russian: ubezhdát' убеждать
Spanish: persuadir
Swedish: övertyga

1566. Peru [n.]

Arabic: bíro بيرة
Chinese: mìlŭ 秘魯
Dutch: Peru
French: Pérou
German: Peru
Italian: Perù
Japanese: Perū ペルー
Korean: Peru 페루
Portuguese: Peru
Russian: Péru Перу
Spanish: Perú
Swedish: Peru

1567. Philippines [n.]

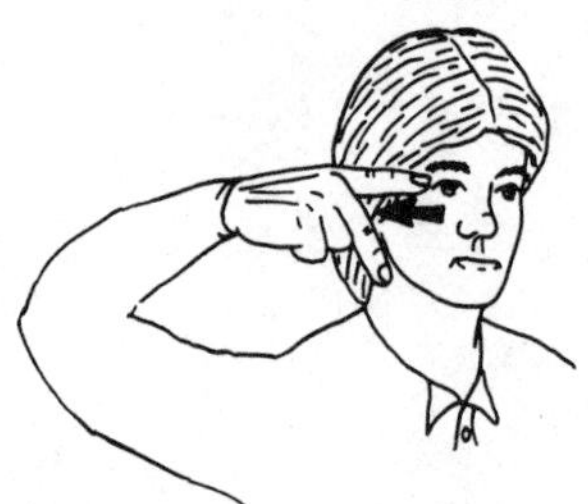

Arabic: al-filibín الفلبين
Chinese: fēilǜbīn 菲律賓
Dutch: Filippijnen
French: Philippines
German: Philippinen
Italian: Filippine
Japanese: Firipin フィリピン
Korean: Biyul'bin 비율빈
Portuguese: Filipinas
Russian: Filippíny Филиппины
Spanish: Filipinas
Swedish: Filippinerna

1568. philosophy [n.]

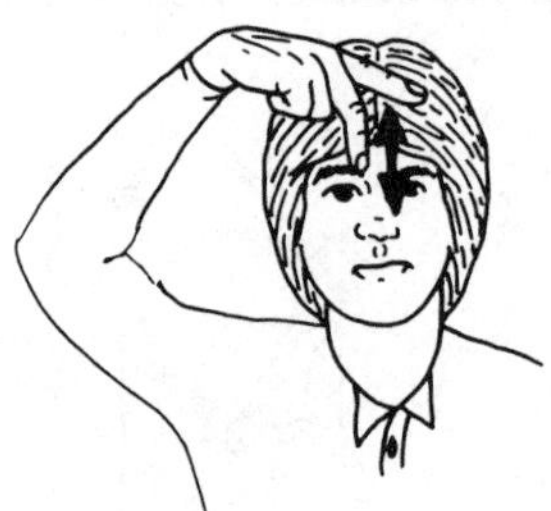

Arabic: fálsafa فلسفة
Chinese: zéxué 哲學
Dutch: filosofie
French: philosophie
German: Philosophie
Italian: filosofia
Japanese: tetsugaku 哲学
Korean: chŏrhak 철학
Portuguese: filosofia
Russian: filosófiya философия
Spanish: filosofía
Swedish: filosofi

1569. photograph [n.]

Arabic: súra صورة
Chinese: xiànpiàn 相片
Dutch: fotografie
French: photographie
German: Fotografie
Italian: fotografia
Japanese: shashin 写真
Korean: sajin 사진
Portuguese: fotografia
Russian: fotográfiya фотография
Spanish: fotografía
Swedish: fotografi

1570. physical [adj.]

Arabic: máddi مادي
Chinese: shēntǐde 身體的
Dutch: fysiek
French: physique
German: physisch
Italian: fisico
Japanese: nikutai no 肉体の
Korean: yukchejŏk 육체적
Portuguese: físico
Russian: fizícheskiy физический
Spanish: físico
Swedish: fysisk

1571. physician [n.]

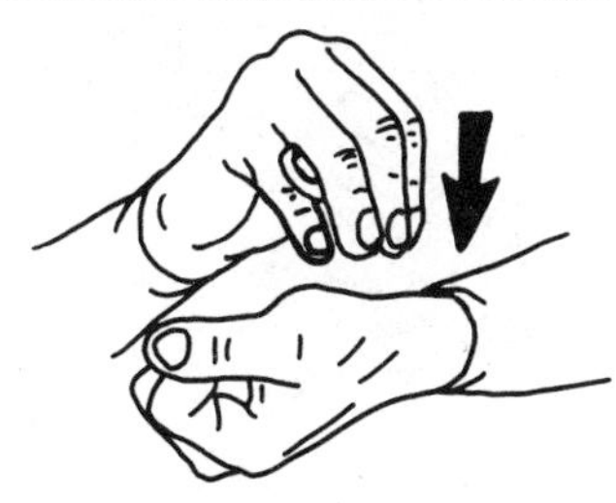

Arabic: tabíb طبيب
Chinese: yīshēng 醫生
Dutch: dokter
French: médecin
German: Arzt
Italian: medico
Japanese: ishi 医師
Korean: ŭisa 의사
Portuguese: médico
Russian: vrach врач
Spanish: médico
Swedish: läkare

1572. physics [n.]

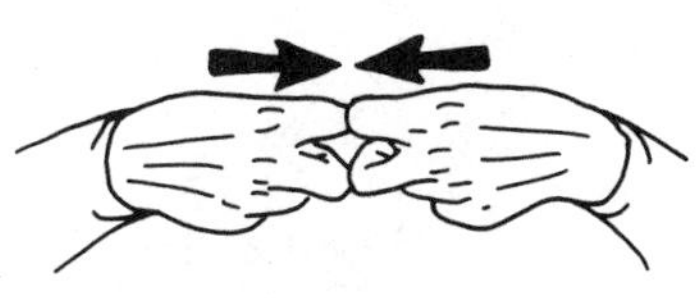

Arabic: fízia' فيزياء
Chinese: wùlǐ 物理
Dutch: natuurkunde
French: physique
German: Physik
Italian: fisica
Japanese: butsuri 物理
Korean: mulli hak 물리학
Portuguese: física
Russian: fízika физика
Spanish: física
Swedish: fysik

1573. piano [n.]

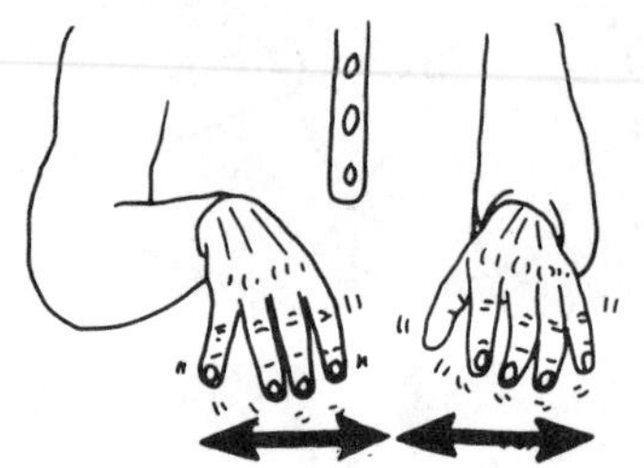

Arabic: biáno بيانو
Chinese: gāngqín 鋼琴
Dutch: piano
French: piano
German: Klavier
Italian: pianoforte
Japanese: piano ピアノ
Korean: pi'ano 피아노
Portuguese: piano
Russian: pianíno пианино
Spanish: piano
Swedish: piano

1574. picture [n.]

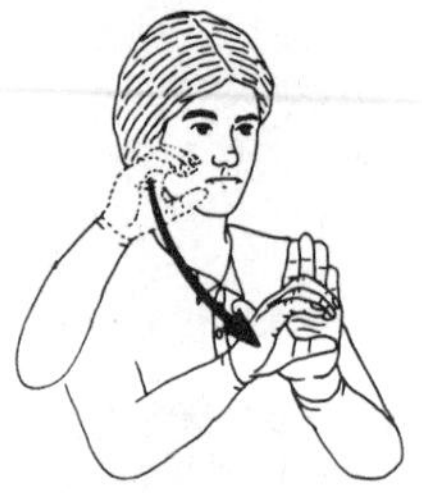

Arabic: súra صورة
Chinese: túhuà 圖畫
Dutch: afbeelding
French: image
German: Bild
Italian: quadro
Japanese: e 絵
Korean: kŭrim 그림
Portuguese: quadro
Russian: kartína картина
Spanish: cuadro
Swedish: tavla

1575. pie [n.]

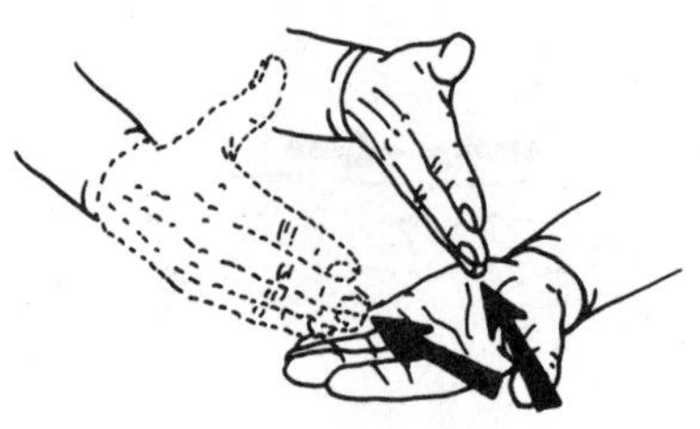

Arabic: fatíra فطيرة
Chinese: xiànbǐng 餡餅
Dutch: taart
French: tarte
German: Torte
Italian: torta
Japanese: pai パイ
Korean: p'ai 파이
Portuguese: torta
Russian: piróg пирог
Spanish: pastel
Swedish: paj

1576. piece [n.]

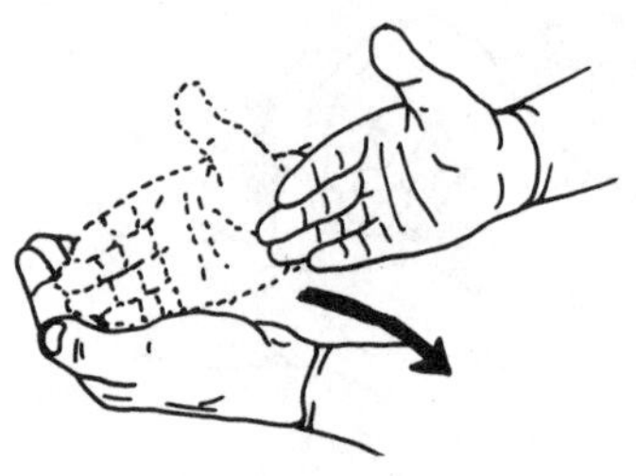

Arabic: qútaa قطعة
Chinese: piàn 片
Dutch: stuk
French: morceau
German: Stück
Italian: pezzo
Japanese: hitokire 一切れ
Korean: hanchogak 한조각
Portuguese: peça
Russian: kusók кусок
Spanish: pieza
Swedish: stycke

1577. pig [n.]

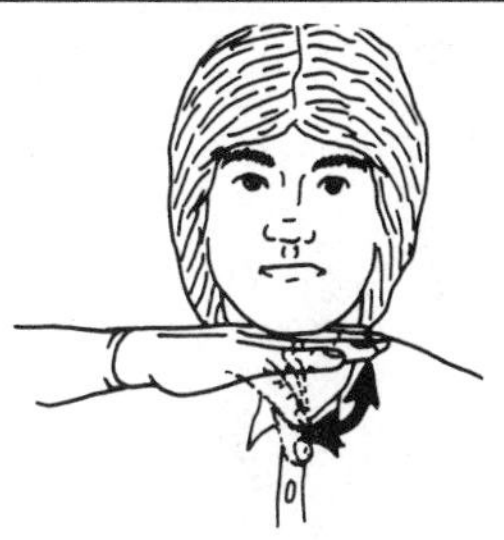

Arabic: khenzír خنزير
Chinese: zhū 豬
Dutch: varken
French: cochon
German: Schwein
Italian: porco
Japanese: buta 豚
Korean: dwaeji 돼지
Portuguese: porco
Russian: svin'yá свинья
Spanish: puerco
Swedish: gris

1578. pigeon [n.]

Arabic: hamáma حمامة
Chinese: gēzi 鴿子
Dutch: duif
French: pigeon
German: Taube
Italian: piccione
Japanese: hato ハト
Korean: bidŭlgi 비둘기
Portuguese: pomba
Russian: gólub' голубь
Spanish: paloma
Swedish: duva

1579. pile [n.]

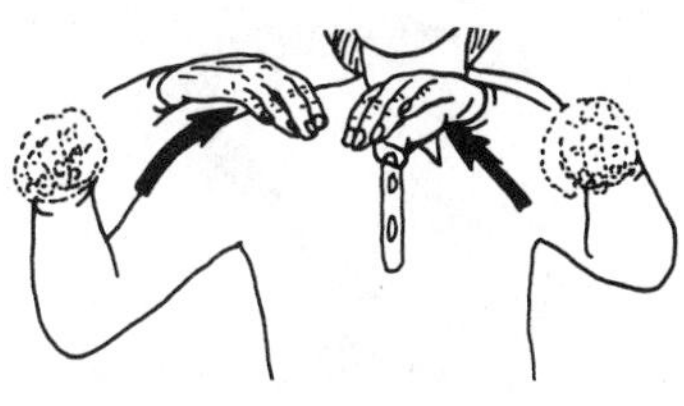

Arabic: kaum كوم
Chinese: duī 堆
Dutch: stapel
French: monceau
German: Haufen
Italian: mucchio
Japanese: tsumikasane 積み重ね
Korean: mudŏgi 무더기
Portuguese: pilha
Russian: kúcha куча
Spanish: montón
Swedish: hög

1580. pill [n.]

Arabic: hábbet dawá' حبة دواء
Chinese: yàowán 藥丸
Dutch: pil
French: pilule
German: Pille
Italian: pillola
Japanese: ganyaku 丸薬
Korean: allyak 알약
Portuguese: pílula
Russian: pilyúlya пилюля
Spanish: píldora
Swedish: piller

1581. pilot [n.]

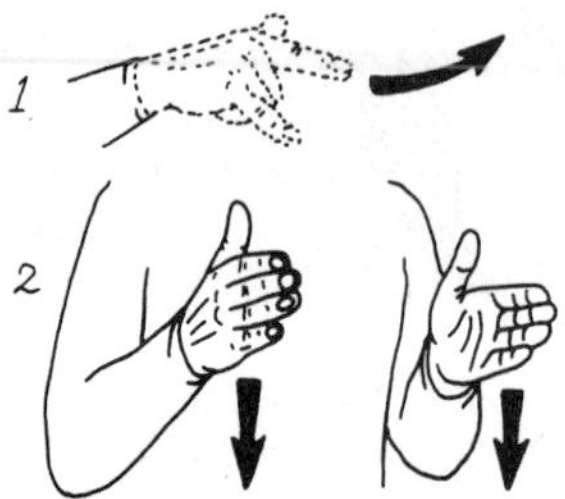

Arabic: tayyár طيار
Chinese: fēixíngyuán 飛行員
Dutch: piloot
French: pilote
German: Pilot
Italian: pilota
Japanese: pairotto パイロット
Korean: jojongsa 조종사
Portuguese: piloto
Russian: pilót пилот
Spanish: piloto
Swedish: pilot

1582. pin (needle) [n.]

Arabic: dabús دبوس
Chinese: biézhēn 別針
Dutch: speld
French: épingle
German: Stecknadel
Italian: spillo
Japanese: pin ピン
Korean: p'in 핀
Portuguese: alfinete
Russian: bulávka булавка
Spanish: alfiler
Swedish: knappnål

1583. pink [adj.]

Arabic: záhari زهري
Chinese: fěnhóng 粉紅
Dutch: rose
French: rose
German: rosa
Italian: rosa
Japanese: pinku-iro no ピンク色の
Korean: bunhongbit 분홍빛
Portuguese: côr-de-rosa
Russian: rózovyy розовый
Spanish: color rosa
Swedish: skär

1584. pipe (conduit) [n.]

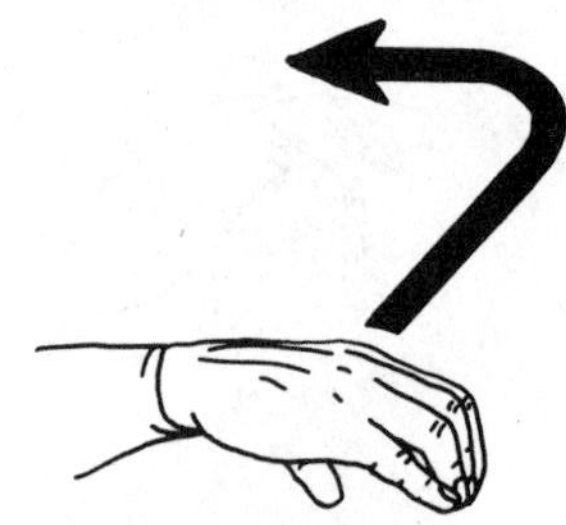

Arabic: masúra ماسورة
Chinese: guănzì 管子
Dutch: buis
French: conduit
German: Rohr
Italian: tubo
Japanese: paipu パイプ
Korean: p'aip'ŭ 파이프
Portuguese: tubo
Russian: trubá труба
Spanish: tubo
Swedish: rör

1585. pipe (smoking) [n.]

Arabic: ghaliún غليون
Chinese: yāndǒu 煙斗
Dutch: pijp
French: pipe
German: Pfeife
Italian: pipa
Japanese: paipu パイプ
Korean: dambaettae 담뱃대
Portuguese: cachimbo
Russian: trúbka трубка
Spanish: pipa
Swedish: pipa

1586. pity [n.]

Arabic: sháfaqa شفقة
Chinese: liánmín 憐憫
Dutch: medelijden
French: compassion
German: Mitleid
Italian: pietà
Japanese: awaremi 憐れみ
Korean: dongjŏng 동정
Portuguese: compaixão
Russian: zhálost' жалость
Spanish: compasión
Swedish: medlidande

1587. place [n.]

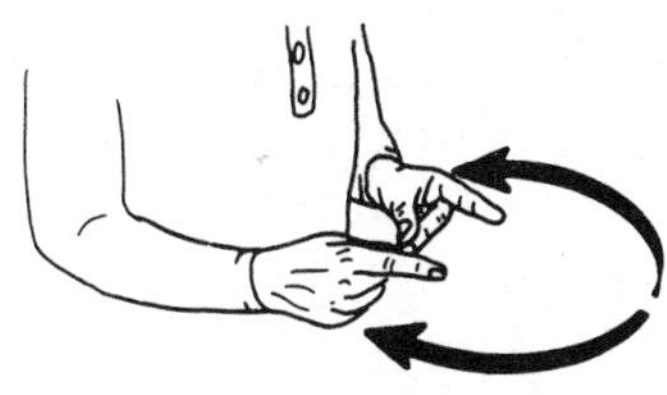

Arabic: makán مكان
Chinese: dìfāng 地方
Dutch: plaats
French: lieu
German: Platz
Italian: luogo
Japanese: basho 場所
Korean: jangso 장소
Portuguese: lugar
Russian: mésto место
Spanish: lugar
Swedish: plats

1588. place (put) [v.]

Arabic: wádaa وضع
Chinese: fàng 放
Dutch: plaatsen
French: placer
German: stellen
Italian: collocare
Japanese: oku 置く
Korean: duda 두다
Portuguese: colocar
Russian: klast'/stávit' класть/ставить
Spanish: colocar
Swedish: placera

1589. plain (simple) [adj.]

Arabic: basíet بسيط
Chinese: píngde 平的
Dutch: eenvoudig
French: simple
German: schlicht
Italian: semplice
Japanese: shisso na 質素な
Korean: sobak'han 소박한
Portuguese: simples
Russian: prostóy простой
Spanish: sencillo
Swedish: vanlig

1590. plan [n.]

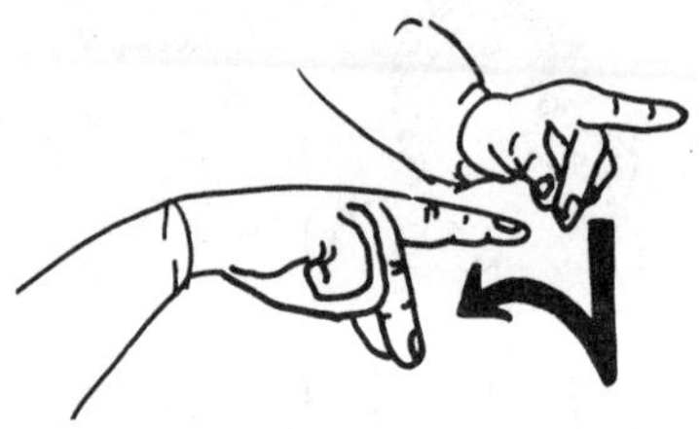

Arabic: khétta خطة
Chinese: jìhuà 計劃
Dutch: plan
French: plan
German: Plan
Italian: piano
Japanese: keikaku 計画
Korean: kyehoek 계획
Portuguese: plano
Russian: plan план
Spanish: plan
Swedish: plan

1591. plan [v.]

Arabic: kháttata خطط
Chinese: jìhuà 計劃
Dutch: ontwerpen
French: projeter
German: planen
Italian: progettare
Japanese: keikaku suru 計画する
Korean: kyehoek'hada 계획하다
Portuguese: planejar
Russian: planírovat' планировать
Spanish: planear
Swedish: planera

1592. planet [n.]

Arabic: káukab كوكب
Chinese: xíngxīng 行星
Dutch: planeet
French: planète
German: Planet
Italian: pianeta
Japanese: wakusei 惑星
Korean: wisŏng 위성
Portuguese: planeta
Russian: planéta планета
Spanish: planeta
Swedish: planet

1593. plant (organic) [n.]

Arabic: nabát نبات
Chinese: zhíwù 植物
Dutch: plant
French: plante
German: Pflanze
Italian: pianta
Japanese: shokubutsu 植物
Korean: shingmul 식물
Portuguese: planta
Russian: rasténiye растение
Spanish: planta
Swedish: planta

1594. plant [v.]

Arabic: záraa زرع
Chinese: zhòngzhí 種植
Dutch: planten
French: planter
German: pflanzen
Italian: piantare
Japanese: ueru 免
Korean: shimda 심다
Portuguese: plantar
Russian: sazhát' сажать
Spanish: plantar
Swedish: plantera

1595. plate (dish) [n.]

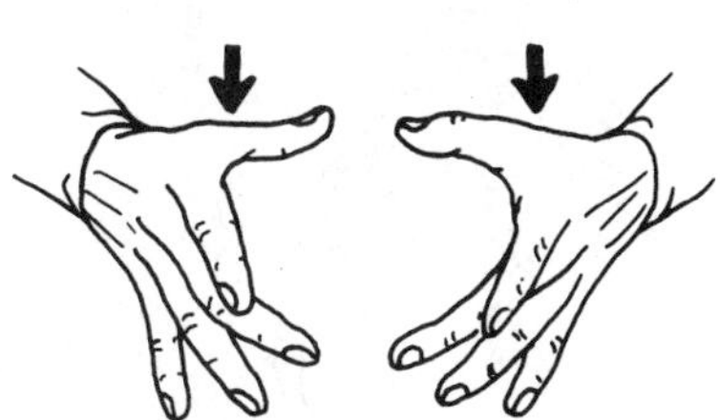

Arabic: tábaq طبق
Chinese: pánzi 盤子
Dutch: bord
French: assiette
German: Teller
Italian: piatto
Japanese: sara 皿
Korean: jŏpshi 접시
Portuguese: prato
Russian: tarélka тарелка
Spanish: plato
Swedish: tallrik

1596. platform [n.]

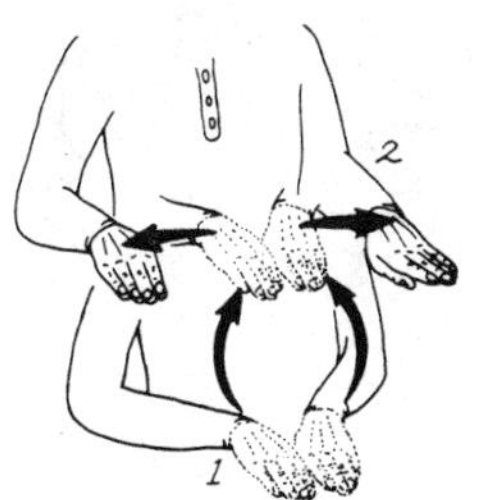

Arabic: manássa منصة
Chinese: tái 台
Dutch: platform
French: plate-forme
German: Plattform
Italian: piattaforma
Japanese: dai 台
Korean: dan 단
Portuguese: plataforma
Russian: platfórma платформа
Spanish: plataforma
Swedish: plattform

1597. play (theater) [n.]

Arabic: masrahíyya مسرحية
Chinese: huàjù 話劇
Dutch: toneelstuk
French: pièce
German: Schauspiel
Italian: dramma
Japanese: engeki 演劇
Korean: yŏngŭk 연극
Portuguese: peça
Russian: p'yésa пьеса
Spanish: obra teatral
Swedish: pjäs

1598. play [v.]

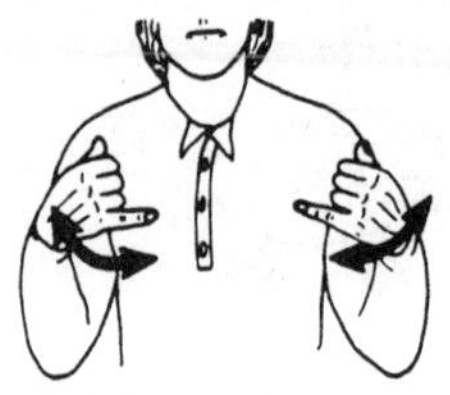

Arabic: láaiba لعب
Chinese: wán 玩
Dutch: spelen
French: défense
German: spielen
Italian: giocare
Japanese: asobu 遊ぶ
Korean: nolda 놀다
Portuguese: jogar
Russian: igrát' играть
Spanish: jugar
Swedish: spela

1599. plea [n.]

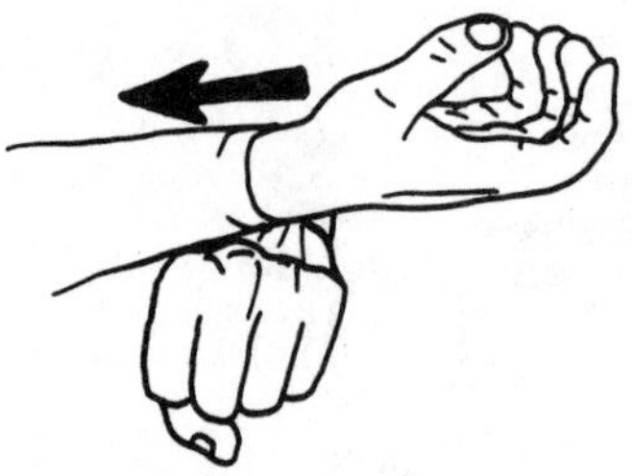

Arabic: dáawa qada'ía دعوى قضائية
Chinese: qǐngqiú 請求
Dutch: smeking
French: supplication
German: Plädoyer
Italian: supplica
Japanese: benkai 弁解
Korean: kanch'ŏng 간청
Portuguese: súplica
Russian: opravdániye оправдание
Spanish: súplica
Swedish: försvar

1600. pleasant [adj.]

Arabic: sáar سار
Chinese: yúkuài 愉快
Dutch: aangenaam
French: agréable
German: angenehm
Italian: piacevole
Japanese: yukai na 愉快な
Korean: kibun johŭn 기분 좋은
Portuguese: agradável
Russian: priyátnyy приятный
Spanish: agradable
Swedish: angenäm

1601. please [interj.]

Arabic: min fádlak من فضلك
Chinese: qǐng 請
Dutch: alstublieft
French: s'il vous plaît
German: bitte
Italian: per favore
Japanese: dōzo どうぞ
Korean: chebal 제발
Portuguese: por favor
Russian: pozháluysta пожалуйста
Spanish: por favor
Swedish: var så god

1602. please [v.]

Arabic: radá رضى
Chinese: tǎohǎo 討好
Dutch: bevallen
French: plaire
German: gefallen
Italian: accontentare
Japanese: yorokobasu 喜ばす
Korean: kibbuge hada 기쁘게 하다
Portuguese: agradar
Russian: nrávit'sya нравиться
Spanish: agradar
Swedish: behaga

1603. pledge [n.]

Arabic: dhamán ضمان
Chinese: shìyuē 誓約
Dutch: pand
French: gage
German: Pfand
Italian: pegno
Japanese: teitō 抵当
Korean: sŏyak 서약
Portuguese: penhor
Russian: zalóg залог
Spanish: promesa solemne
Swedish: underpant

1604. plenty [n.]

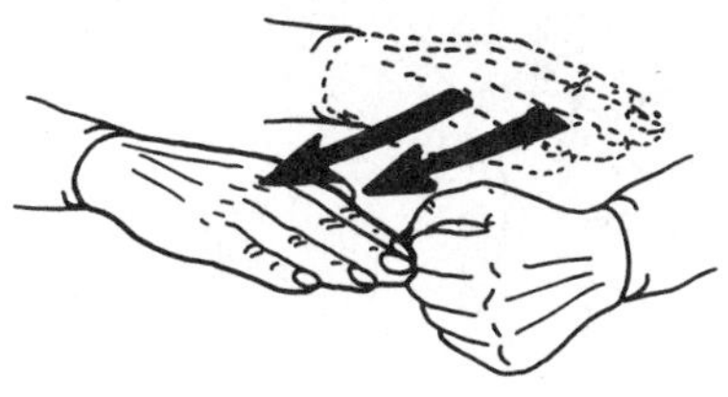

Arabic: kathír كثير
Chinese: fēngfù 豐富
Dutch: overvloed
French: abondance
German: Fülle
Italian: abbondanza
Japanese: takusan 沢山
Korean: manŭm 많음
Portuguese: abundância
Russian: izobíliye изобилие
Spanish: abundancia
Swedish: riklighet

1605. plow [v.]

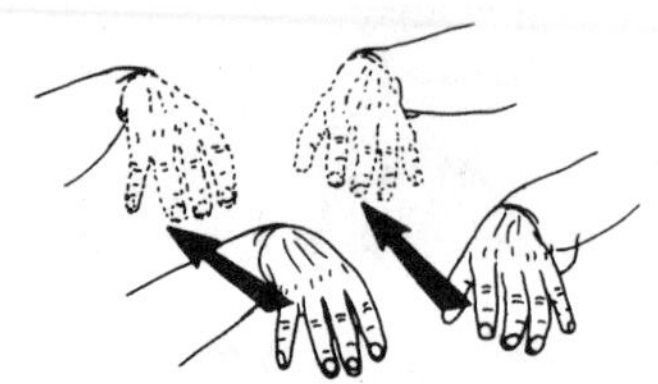

Arabic: háratha حرث
Chinese: gēng 耕
Dutch: ploegen
French: labourer
German: pflügen
Italian: arare
Japanese: tagayasu 耕す
Korean: jaenggijilhada 쟁기질하다
Portuguese: arar
Russian: pakhát' пахать
Spanish: arar
Swedish: ploja

1606. plus [prep.]

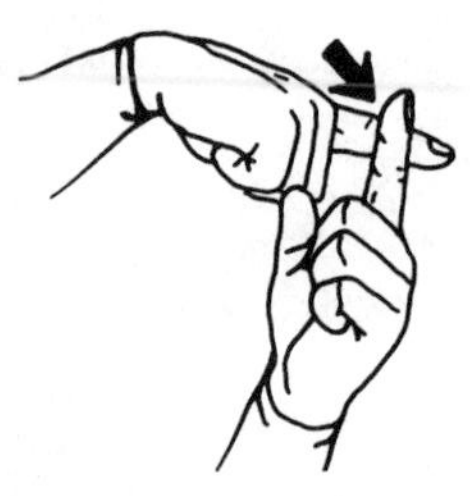

Arabic: zá'ed زائد
Chinese: jiā 加
Dutch: plus
French: plus
German: plus
Italian: più
Japanese: . . . o kuwaete …を加えて
Korean: . . . ŭl dŏhayŏ ~을 더하여
Portuguese: mais
Russian: plyús плюс
Spanish: más
Swedish: plus

1607. pocket [n.]

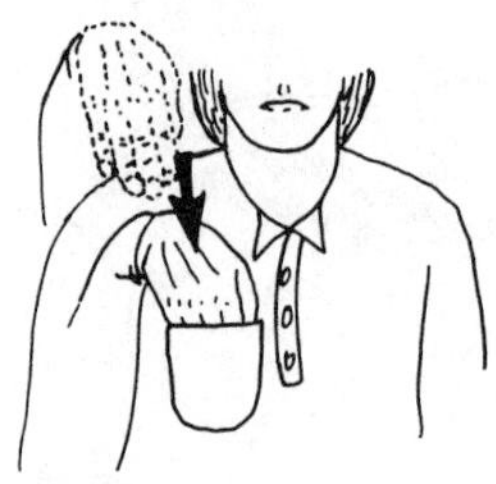

Arabic: jéb جيب
Chinese: kŏudài 口袋
Dutch: zak
French: poche
German: Tasche
Italian: tasca
Japanese: poketto ポケット
Korean: hojumŏni 호주머니
Portuguese: bolso
Russian: karmán карман
Spanish: bolsillo
Swedish: ficka

1608. poem [n.]

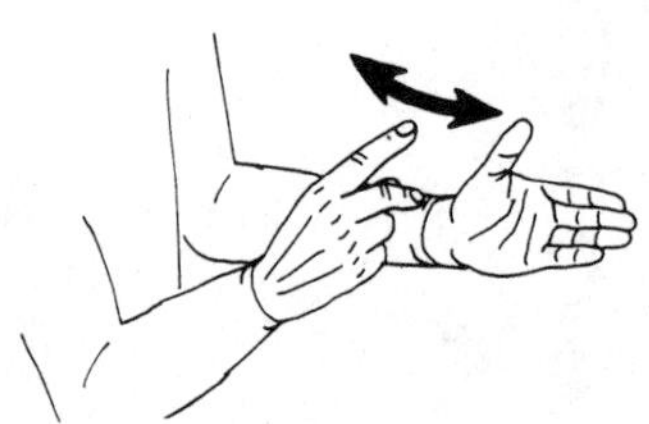

Arabic: qasída قصيدة
Chinese: shī 詩
Dutch: gedicht
French: poème
German: Gedicht
Italian: poema
Japanese: shi 詩
Korean: shi 시
Portuguese: poema
Russian: stikhotvoréniye стихотворение
Spanish: poema
Swedish: dikt

1609. point [n.]

Arabic: núqta نقطة
Chinese: diǎn 點
Dutch: punt
French: point
German: Punkt
Italian: punto
Japanese: saki 先
Korean: jŏm 점
Portuguese: ponto
Russian: punkt пункт
Spanish: punto
Swedish: punkt

1610. poison [n.]

Arabic: summ سم
Chinese: dúyaò 毒藥
Dutch: vergif
French: poison
German: Gift
Italian: veleno
Japanese: doku 毒
Korean: dog 독
Portuguese: veneno
Russian: yad яд
Spanish: veneno
Swedish: gift

1611. Poland [n.]

Arabic: bolánda بولندا
Chinese: pōlán 波蘭
Dutch: Polen
French: Pologne
German: Polen
Italian: Polonia
Japanese: Pōrando ポーランド
Korean: P'olaend 폴란드
Portuguese: Polônia
Russian: Pol'sha Польша
Spanish: Polonia
Swedish: Polen

1612. police [n.]

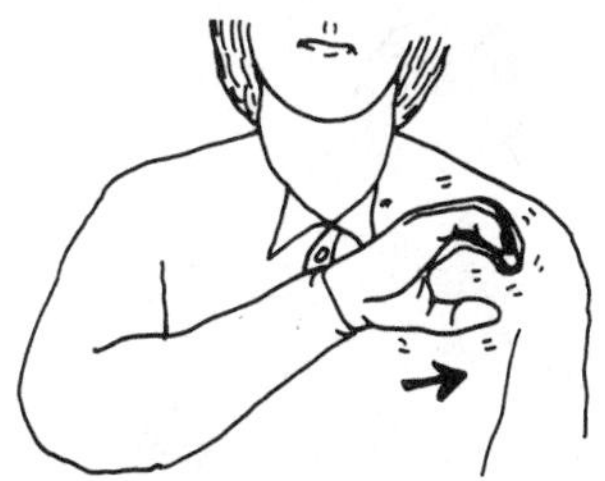

Arabic: shórta شرطة
Chinese: jǐngchá 警察
Dutch: politie
French: police
German: Polizei
Italian: polizia
Japanese: keisatsu 警察
Korean: kyŏngch'al 경찰
Portuguese: polícia
Russian: polítsiya полиция
Spanish: policía
Swedish: polis

1613. policy [n.]

Arabic: siyása سياسة
Chinese: zhèngchè 政策
Dutch: beleid
French: politique
German: Politik
Italian: politica
Japanese: seisaku 政策
Korean: jŏngch'aek 정책
Portuguese: política
Russian: polítika политика
Spanish: norma
Swedish: politik

1614. polish [v.]

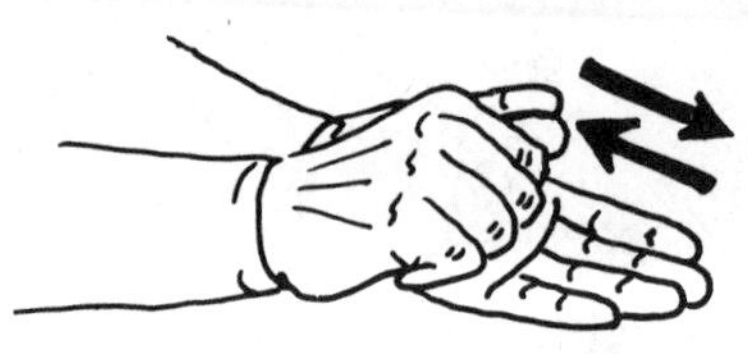

Arabic: lámaa لمع
Chinese: cāliàng 擦亮
Dutch: poetsen
French: polir
German: polieren
Italian: pulire
Japanese: migaku 磨く
Korean: dakda 닦다
Portuguese: polir
Russian: polirovát' полировать
Spanish: pulir
Swedish: polera

1615. polite [adj.]

Arabic: moáaddab مؤدب
Chinese: yǒu lǐmào 有禮貌
Dutch: beleefd
French: poli
German: höflich
Italian: cortese
Japanese: teinei na 丁寧な
Korean: kongsonhan 겸손한
Portuguese: cortês
Russian: vézhlivyy вежливый
Spanish: cortés
Swedish: artig

1616. politics [n.]

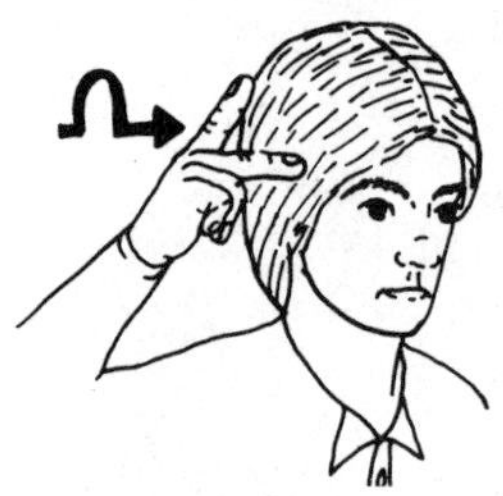

Arabic: siyása سياسة
Chinese: zhèngzhì 政治
Dutch: politiek
French: politique
German: Politik
Italian: politica
Japanese: seiji 政治
Korean: jŏngch'i 정치
Portuguese: política
Russian: polítika политика
Spanish: política
Swedish: politik

1617. pond [n.]

Arabic: bírka بركة
Chinese: chítáng 池塘
Dutch: vijver
French: étang
German: Teich
Italian: stagno
Japanese: ike 池
Korean: mot 못
Portuguese: tanque
Russian: prud пруд
Spanish: estanque
Swedish: damm

1618. pool (swimming) [n.]

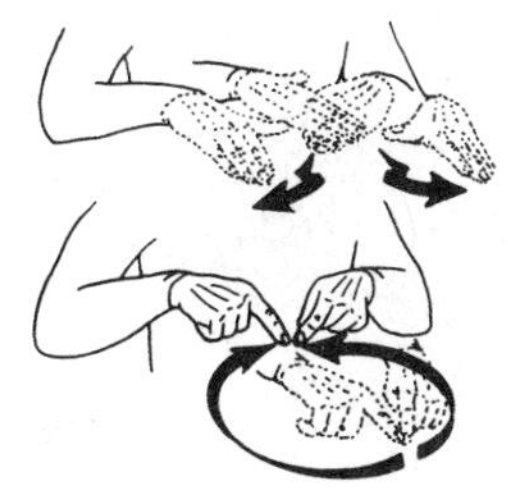

Arabic: hamám síbaha حمام سباحة
Chinese: yúyǒngchí 游泳池
Dutch: zwembad
French: piscine
German: Schwimmbad
Italian: piscina
Japanese: pūru プール
Korean: p'ul 풀
Portuguese: piscina
Russian: basséyn бассейн
Spanish: piscina
Swedish: simbassäng

1619. poor [adj.]

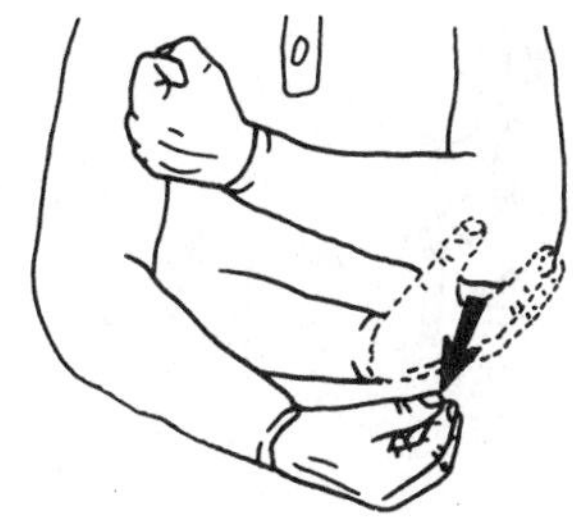

Arabic: faqír فقير
Chinese: qióng 窮
Dutch: arm
French: pauvre
German: arm
Italian: povero
Japanese: bimbō na 貧乏な
Korean: kananhan 가난한
Portuguese: pobre
Russian: bédnyy бедный
Spanish: pobre
Swedish: fattig

1620. popular [adj.]

Arabic: sháabi شعبي
Chinese: shòuhuānyíng 受歡迎
Dutch: in trek
French: populaire
German: beliebt
Italian: popolare
Japanese: ninki no aru 人気のある
Korean: inki innŭn 인기있는
Portuguese: popular
Russian: populyárnyy популярный
Spanish: popular
Swedish: populär

1621. population [n.]

Arabic: sukán سكان
Chinese: rénkǒu 人口
Dutch: bevolking
French: population
German: Bevölkerung
Italian: popolazione
Japanese: jinkō 人口
Korean: ingu 인구
Portuguese: população
Russian: naseléniye население
Spanish: población
Swedish: befolkning

1622. port [n.]

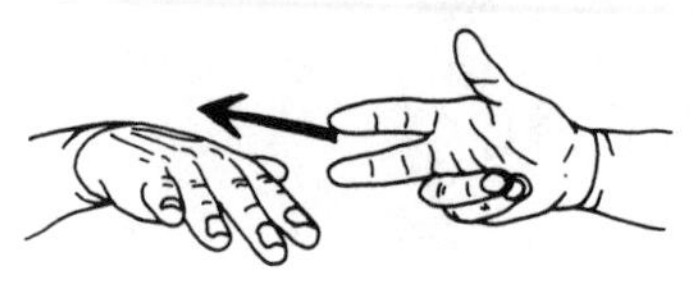

Arabic: mína' ميناء
Chinese: gǎng 港
Dutch: haven
French: port
German: Hafen
Italian: porto
Japanese: minato 港
Korean: hanggu 항구
Portuguese: porto
Russian: port порт
Spanish: puerto
Swedish: hamn

1623. portion [n.]

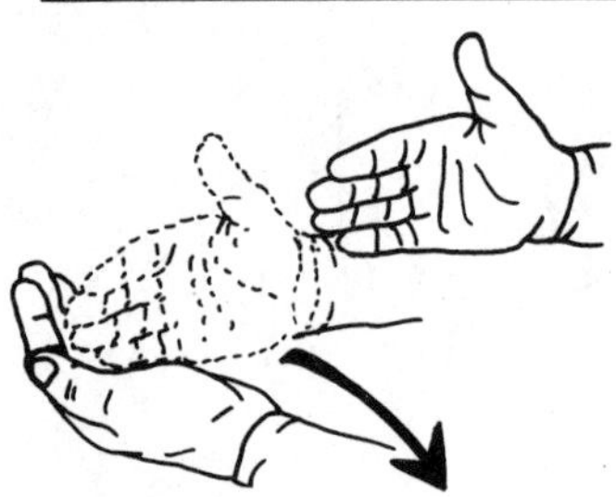

Arabic: júzu' جزء
Chinese: yí bùfèn 一部份
Dutch: deel
French: portion
German: Teil
Italian: porzione
Japanese: bubun 部分
Korean: ilbu 일부
Portuguese: porção
Russian: dólya доля
Spanish: porción
Swedish: portion

1624. Portugal [n.]

Arabic: al-burtughál البرتغال
Chinese: pútáoyá 葡萄牙
Dutch: Portugal
French: Portugal
German: Portugal
Italian: Portogallo
Japanese: Porutogaru ポルトガル
Korean: P'orŭt'ugal 포르투갈
Portuguese: Portugal
Russian: Portugáliya Португалия
Spanish: Portugal
Swedish: Portugal

1625. position [n.]

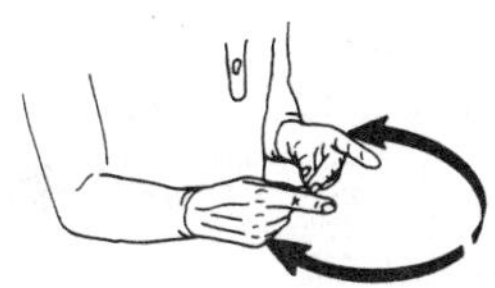

Arabic: máuqef موقف
Chinese: wèizhì 位置
Dutch: positie
French: position
German: Stellung
Italian: posizione
Japanese: ichi 位置
Korean: jiwi 지위
Portuguese: posição
Russian: polozhéniye положение
Spanish: posición
Swedish: position

1626. positive [adj.]

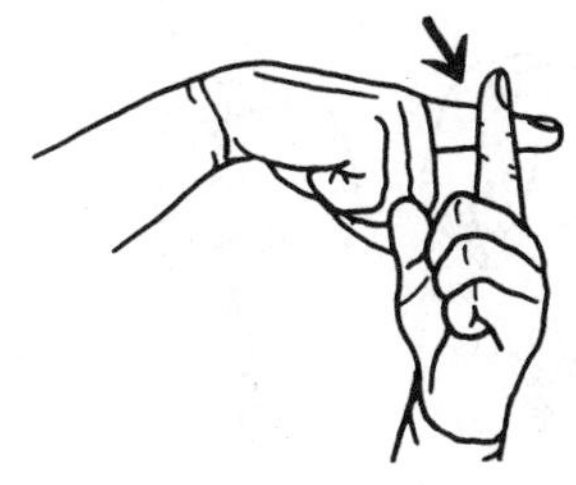

Arabic: ijábi ايجابي
Chinese: quèdìngde 確定的
Dutch: positief
French: positif
German: positiv
Italian: positivo
Japanese: meikaku na 明確な
Korean: hwakshirhan 확실한
Portuguese: positivo
Russian: polozhítel'nyy положительный
Spanish: positivo
Swedish: positiv

1627. possess [v.]

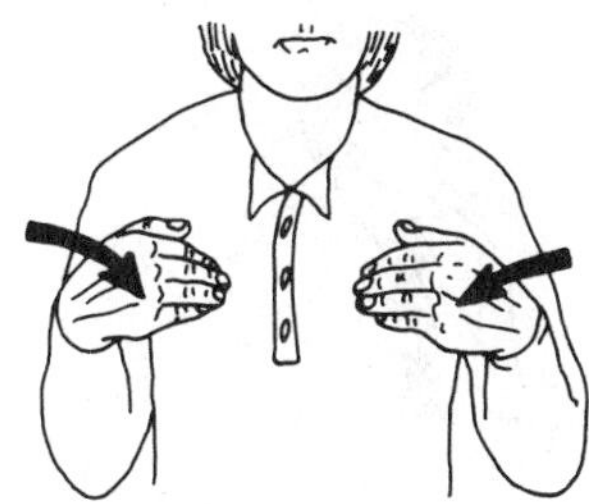

Arabic: málaka ملك
Chinese: yǒngyǒu 擁有
Dutch: bezitten
French: posséder
German: besitzen
Italian: possedere
Japanese: senyū suru 占有する
Korean: kajida 가지다
Portuguese: possuir
Russian: obladát' обладать
Spanish: poseer
Swedish: äga

1628. possibility [n.]

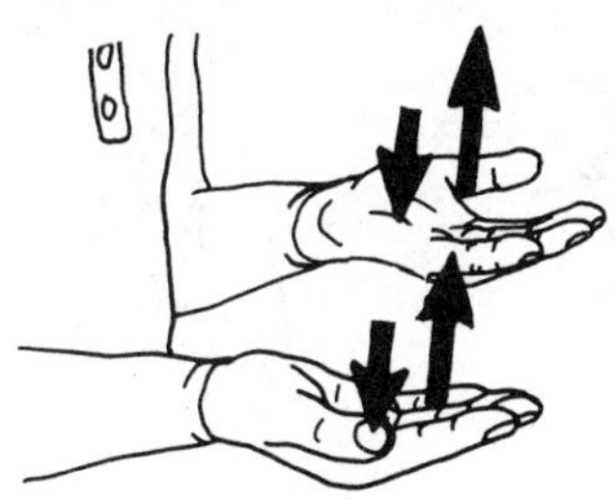

Arabic: ihtimál احتمال
Chinese: kěnéngxìng 可能性
Dutch: mogelijkheid
French: possibilité
German: Möglichkeit
Italian: possibilità
Japanese: kanō sei 可能性
Korean: kanŭngsŏng 가능성
Portuguese: possibilidade
Russian: vozmózhnost' возможность
Spanish: posibilidad
Swedish: möglighet

1629. possible [adj.]

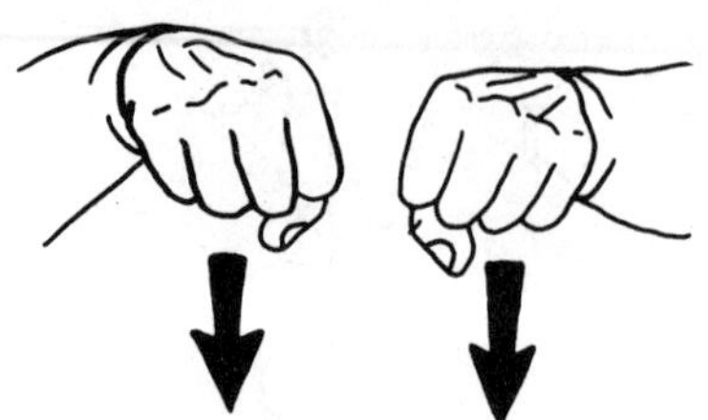

Arabic: múmkin ممكن
Chinese: kěnéng 可能
Dutch: mogelijk
French: possible
German: möglich
Italian: possibile
Japanese: kanō na 可能な
Korean: kanŭnghan 가능한
Portuguese: possível
Russian: vozmózhnyy возможный
Spanish: posible
Swedish: möjlig

1630. postpone [v.]

Arabic: ájjala اجل
Chinese: yánhuǎn 延緩
Dutch: uitstellen
French: ajourner
German: verschieben
Italian: rimandare
Japanese: enki suru 延期する
Korean: yŏnkihada 연기하다
Portuguese: adiar
Russian: otkládyvat' откладывать
Spanish: aplazar
Swedish: uppskjuta

1631. post office [n.]

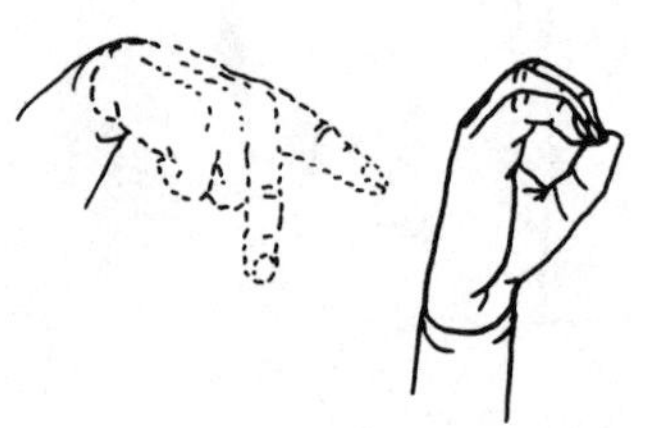

Arabic: máktab al-baríd مكتب البريد
Chinese: yóujú 郵局
Dutch: postkantoor
French: bureau de poste
German: Postamt
Italian: ufficio postale
Japanese: yūbinkyoku 郵便局
Korean: uch'eguk 우체국
Portuguese: correio
Russian: póchta почта
Spanish: casa de correos
Swedish: postkontor

1632. pot [n.]

Arabic: qedr قدر
Chinese: guō 鍋
Dutch: pot
French: pot
German: Topf
Italian: pentola
Japanese: nabe 鍋
Korean: danji 단지
Portuguese: pote
Russian: gorshók горшок
Spanish: olla
Swedish: gryta

1633. potato(es) [n.]

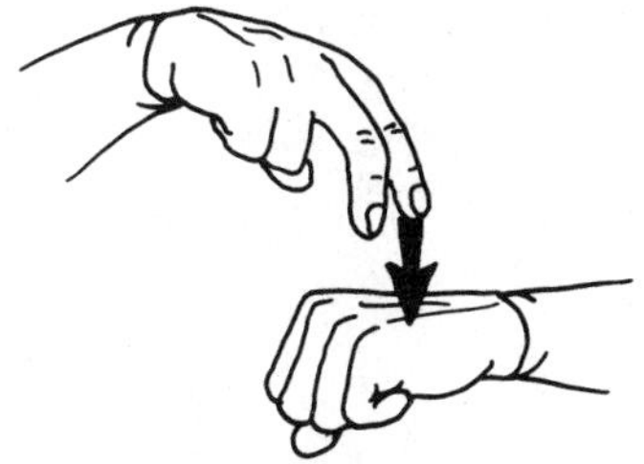

Arabic: batáta بطاطا
Chinese: mǎlíng shǔ 馬鈴薯
Dutch: aardappel
French: pomme de terre
German: Kartoffel
Italian: patata
Japanese: jagaimo ジャガイモ
Korean: kamja 감자
Portuguese: batata
Russian: kartófel' картофель
Spanish: patata
Swedish: pottis

1634. pound (weight) [n.]

Arabic: baund باوند
Chinese: yīngbàng 英磅
Dutch: pond
French: livre
German: Pfund
Italian: libbra
Japanese: pondo ポンド
Korean: p'aundŭ 파운드
Portuguese: libra
Russian: funt фунт
Spanish: libra
Swedish: pund

1635. pour [v.]

Arabic: sákaba سكب
Chinese: dào 倒
Dutch: gieten
French: verser
German: gießen
Italian: versare
Japanese: sosogu 注ぐ
Korean: butta 붓다
Portuguese: despejar
Russian: lit' лить
Spanish: verter
Swedish: hälla

1636. poverty [n.]

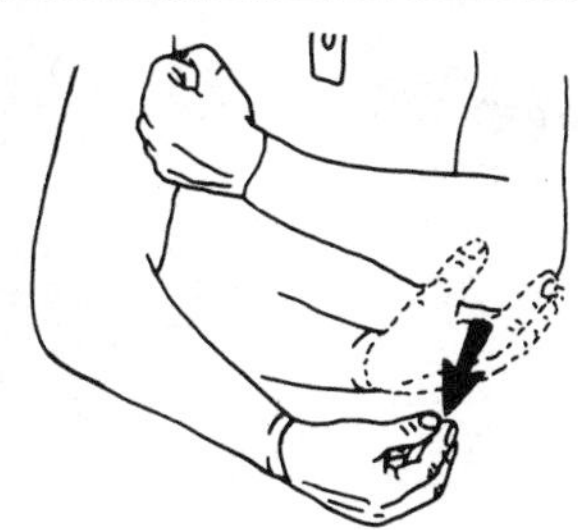

Arabic: faqr فقر
Chinese: pínqióng 貧窮
Dutch: armoede
French: pauvreté
German: Armut
Italian: povertà
Japanese: bimbō 貧乏
Korean: kanan 가난
Portuguese: pobreza
Russian: bédnost' бедность
Spanish: pobreza
Swedish: fattigdom

1637. powder [n.]

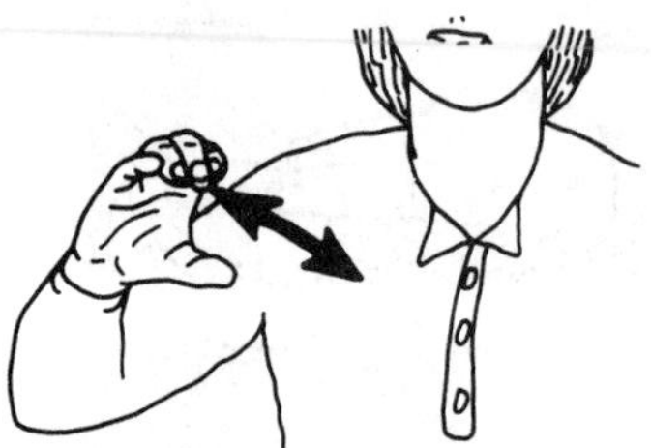

Arabic: mas-húq مسحوق
Chinese: fěn 粉
Dutch: poeder
French: poudre
German: Puder
Italian: polvere
Japanese: kona 粉
Korean: karu 가루
Portuguese: pó
Russian: poroshók порошок
Spanish: polvo
Swedish: puder

1638. power [n.]

Arabic: qúwwa قوة
Chinese: lìliàng 力量
Dutch: macht
French: pouvoir
German: Macht
Italian: potere
Japanese: chikara 力
Korean: him 힘
Portuguese: poder
Russian: síla сила
Spanish: poder
Swedish: makt

1639. practice [n.]

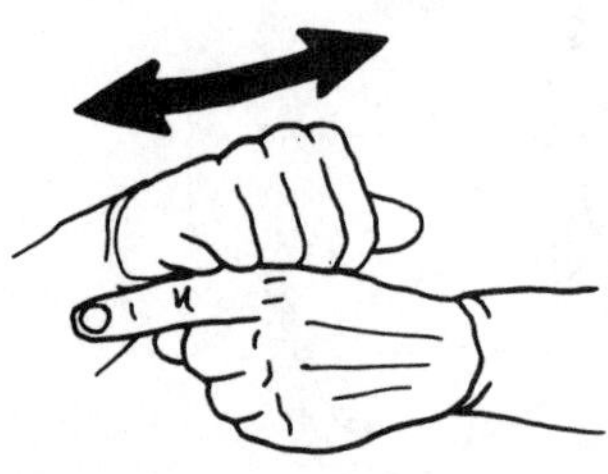

Arabic: tadríb تدريب
Chinese: liànxí 練習
Dutch: praktijk
French: pratique
German: Praxis
Italian: pratica
Japanese: renshū 練習
Korean: yŏnsŭp 연습
Portuguese: prática
Russian: práktika практика
Spanish: práctica
Swedish: praktik

1640. praise [v.]

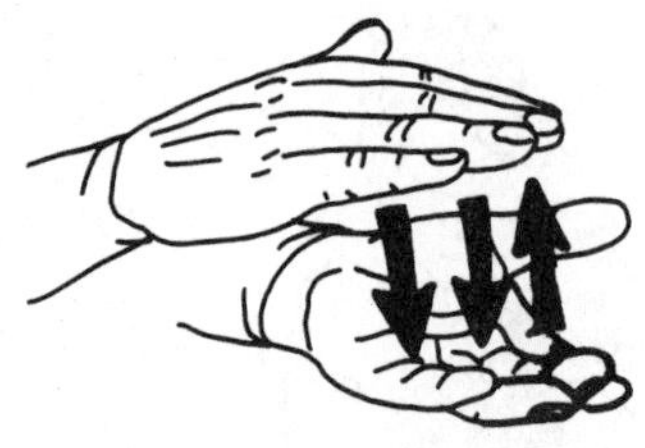

Arabic: mádaha مدح
Chinese: chēngzàn 稱贊
Dutch: loven
French: louer
German: loben
Italian: lodare
Japanese: homeru ほめる
Korean: ch'ingch'anhada 칭찬하다
Portuguese: louvar
Russian: khvalít' хвалить
Spanish: alabar
Swedish: lova

1641. pray [v.]

Arabic: sál-la صلى
Chinese: qídăo 祈禱
Dutch: bidden
French: prier
German: beten
Italian: pregare
Japanese: inoru 祈る
Korean: bilda 빌다
Portuguese: orar
Russian: molít'sya молиться
Spanish: rogar
Swedish: bedja

1642. precious [adj.]

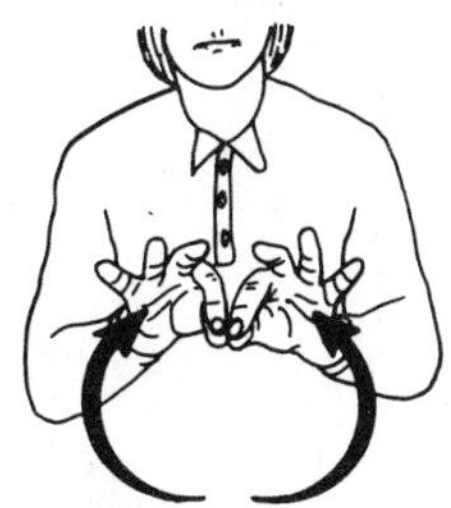

Arabic: thamín ثمين
Chinese: baŏguì 寶貴
Dutch: kostbaar
French: précieux
German: kostbar
Italian: prezioso
Japanese: taisetsu na 大切な
Korean: kwijung'han 귀중한
Portuguese: precioso
Russian: dragotsénnyy драгоценный
Spanish: precioso
Swedish: dyrbar

1643. precise [adj.]

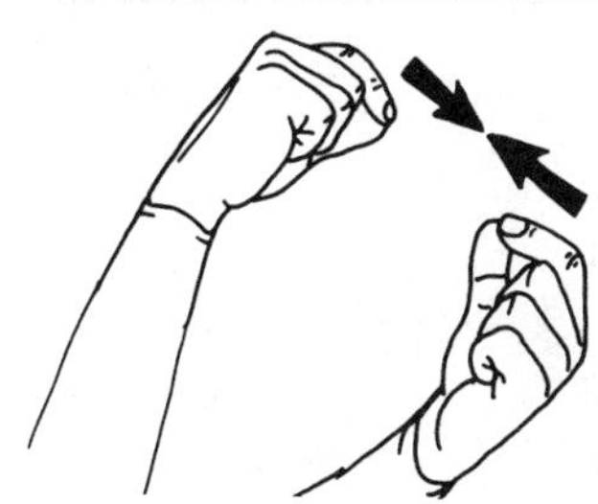

Arabic: madbút مضبوط
Chinese: quèshí 確實
Dutch: precies
French: précis
German: genau
Italian: preciso
Japanese: seikaku na 正確な
Korean: jŏnghwak'han 정확한
Portuguese: preciso
Russian: tóchnyy точный
Spanish: preciso
Swedish: precis

1644. predict [v.]

Arabic: tanábba 'a تنبأ
Chinese: yùcè 預測
Dutch: voorspellen
French: prédire
German: vorhersagen
Italian: predire
Japanese: yogen suru 予言する
Korean: yeŏnhada 예언하다
Portuguese: predizer
Russian: predskázyvat' предсказывать
Spanish: predecir
Swedish: förutsäga

1645. prefer [v.]

Arabic: fáddala فضل
Chinese: piānhào 偏好
Dutch: de voorkeur geven
French: préférer
German: vorziehen
Italian: preferire
Japanese: ...no hō o konomu
―…の方を好む
Korean: dŏ choahada 더 좋아하다
Portuguese: preferir
Russian: predpochitát' предпочитать
Spanish: preferir
Swedish: föredraga

1646. prepare [v.]

Arabic: jáhhaza جهز
Chinese: zhǔnbèi 準備
Dutch: voorbereiden
French: préparer
German: vorbereiten
Italian: preparare
Japanese: jumbi suru 準備する
Korean: maryŏnhada 마련하다
Portuguese: preparar
Russian: gotóvit' готовить
Spanish: preparar
Swedish: förbereda

1647. prescription (medical) [n.]

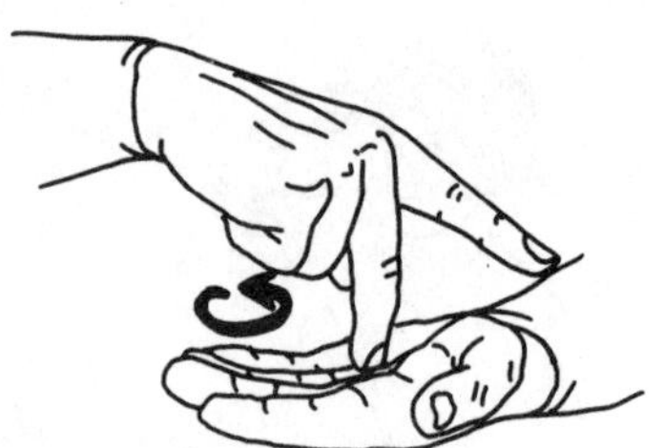

Arabic: wásfa tabíyya وصفة طبية
Chinese: yàofāng 藥方
Dutch: voorschrift
French: ordonnance
German: Rezept
Italian: ricetta
Japanese: shohō 処方
Korean: ch'ŏbang 처방
Portuguese: receita
Russian: predpisániye предписание
Spanish: receta
Swedish: recept

1648. presence [n.]

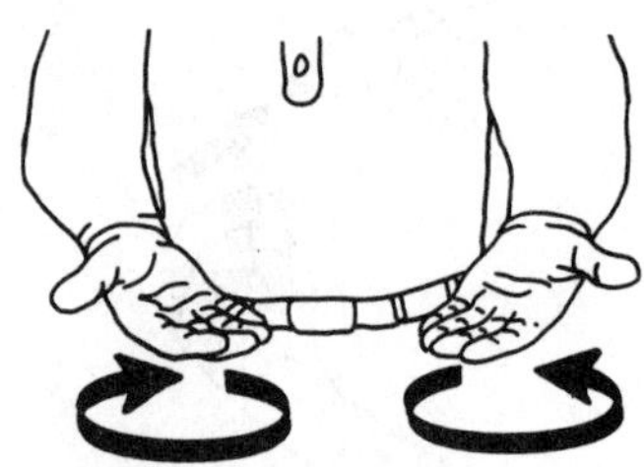

Arabic: hodúr حضور
Chinese: chūxí 出席
Dutch: aanwezigheid
French: présence
German: Anwesenheit
Italian: presenza
Japanese: sonzai 存在
Korean: ch'ulsŏk 출석
Portuguese: presença
Russian: prisútstviye присутствие
Spanish: presencia
Swedish: närvaro

1649. present (time) [adj.]

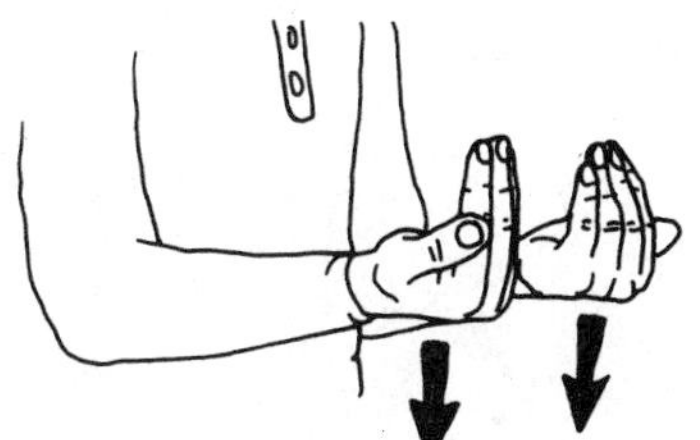

Arabic: háli حالي
Chinese: xiànzàide 現在的
Dutch: tegenwoordig
French: présent
German: gegenwärtig
Italian: presente
Japanese: genzaino 現在の
Korean: hyŏnjaeŭi 현재의
Portuguese: presente
Russian: nýneshniye нынешние
Spanish: presente
Swedish: nuvarande

1650. present (time) [n.]

Arabic: az-zamán الزمان
Chinese: xiànzài 現在
Dutch: heden
French: présent
German: Gegenwart
Italian: presente
Japanese: genzai 現在
Korean: hyŏnjae 현재
Portuguese: presente
Russian: nastoyáshcheye vrémya настоящее время
Spanish: actual
Swedish: nutid

1651. present [v.]

Arabic: qáddama قدم
Chinese: tíchū 提出
Dutch: voorstellen
French: présenter
German: präsentieren
Italian: presentare
Japanese: shintei suru 進呈する
Korean: sŏnsahada 선사하다
Portuguese: presentear
Russian: predstavlyát' представлять
Spanish: presentar
Swedish: presentera

1652. president [n.]

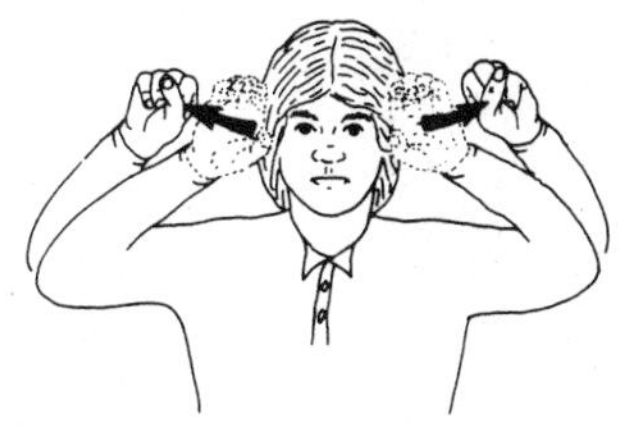

Arabic: ra'ís رئيس
Chinese: zŏngtŏng 總統
Dutch: president
French: président
German: Präsident
Italian: presidente
Japanese: daitōryō 大統領
Korean: daet'ongnyŏng 대통령
Portuguese: presidente
Russian: prezidént президент
Spanish: presidente
Swedish: president

1653. press (push) [v.]

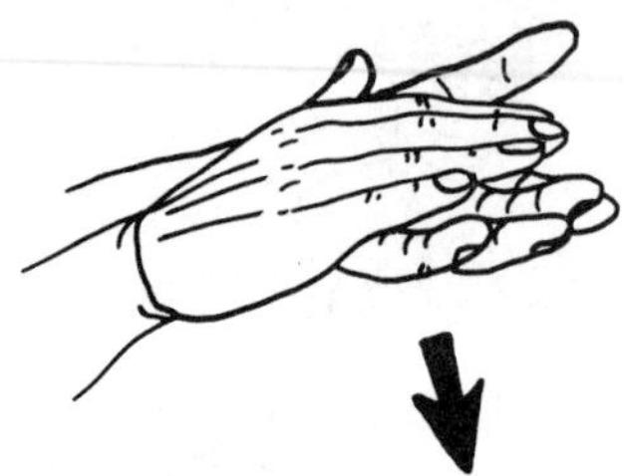

Arabic: dághata ضَغَطَ
Chinese: yā 壓
Dutch: drukken
French: presser
German: drücken
Italian: premere
Japanese: osu 押す
Korean: nurŭda 누르다
Portuguese: pressionar
Russian: nazhimát' нажимать
Spanish: presionar
Swedish: trycka

1654. pressure [n.]

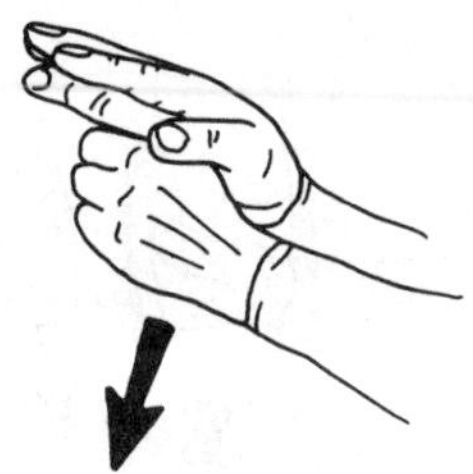

Arabic: dághat ضَغْط
Chinese: yālì 壓力
Dutch: druk
French: tension
German: Druck
Italian: pressione
Japanese: atsuryoku 圧力
Korean: amnyŏk 압력
Portuguese: pressão
Russian: davléniye давление
Spanish: presión
Swedish: tryck

1655. pretend [v.]

Arabic: idháa إدعى
Chinese: jiǎzhuāng 假裝
Dutch: voorwenden
French: feindre
German: vorgeben
Italian: fingere
Japanese: furi o suru 振りをする
Korean: . . .in ch'ehada ~인체하다
Portuguese: fingir
Russian: pritvoryát'sya притворяться
Spanish: fingir
Swedish: låtsa

1656. pretty [adj.]

Arabic: jamíl جميل
Chinese: piàoliàng 漂亮
Dutch: mooi
French: joli
German: hübsch
Italian: grazioso
Japanese: kirei na 綺麗な
Korean: yeppŭn 예쁜
Portuguese: bonito
Russian: khoróshen'kiy хорошенький
Spanish: bonito
Swedish: vacker

1657. prevent [v.]

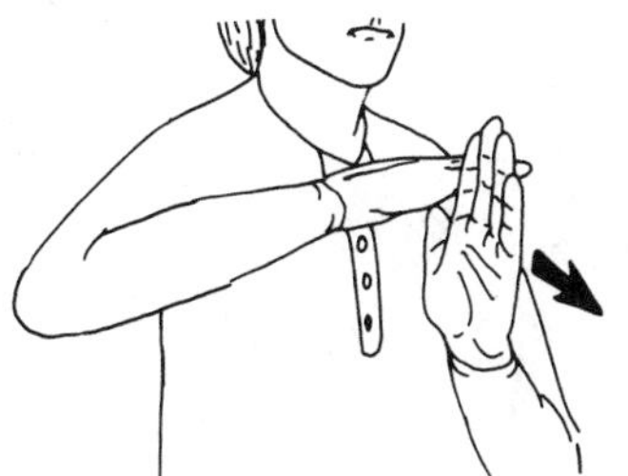

Arabic: mánaa منع
Chinese: yùfáng 預防
Dutch: verhinderen
French: empêcher
German: verhindern
Italian: impedire
Japanese: yobō suru 予防する
Korean: bang'haehada 방해하다
Portuguese: impedir
Russian: predotvrashchát' предотвращать
Spanish: impedir
Swedish: förhindra

1658. previous [adj.]

Arabic: sábaq سابق
Chinese: yǐqiánde 以前的
Dutch: voorafgaand
French: préalable
German: vorhergehend
Italian: previo
Japanese: mae no 前の
Korean: ijŏnŭi 이전의
Portuguese: prévio
Russian: predydúshchiy предыдущий
Spanish: previo
Swedish: föregående

1659. price [n.]

Arabic: tháman ثمن
Chinese: jiàgé 價格
Dutch: prijs
French: prix
German: Preis
Italian: prezzo
Japanese: nedan 値段
Korean: kagyŏk 가격
Portuguese: preço
Russian: tsená цена
Spanish: precio
Swedish: pris

1660. pride [n.]

Arabic: fakhr فخر
Chinese: jiāoào 驕傲
Dutch: trots
French: fierté
German: Stolz
Italian: orgoglio
Japanese: hokori 誇り
Korean: jarang 자랑
Portuguese: orgulho
Russian: górdost' гордость
Spanish: orgullo
Swedish: stolthet

1661. priest [n.]

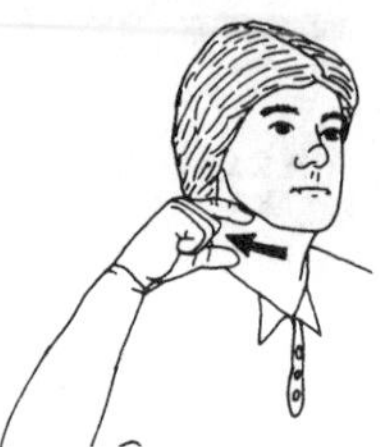

Arabic: qesís قسيس
Chinese: jiàoshì 教士
Dutch: priester
French: prêtre
German: Priester
Italian: prete
Japanese: bokushi 牧師
Korean: sinbu 신부
Portuguese: padre
Russian: svyashchénnik священник
Spanish: sacerdote
Swedish: präst

1662. primary [adj.]

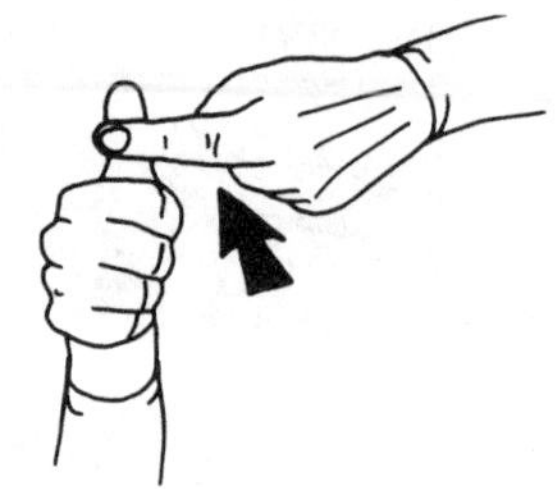

Arabic: áwwali اولي
Chinese: dìyīde 第一的
Dutch: voornaamste
French: principal
German: primär
Italian: primario
Japanese: saisho no 最初の
Korean: bollaeŭi 본래의
Portuguese: primário
Russian: pervíchnyy первичный
Spanish: primario
Swedish: primär

1663. principal [adj.]

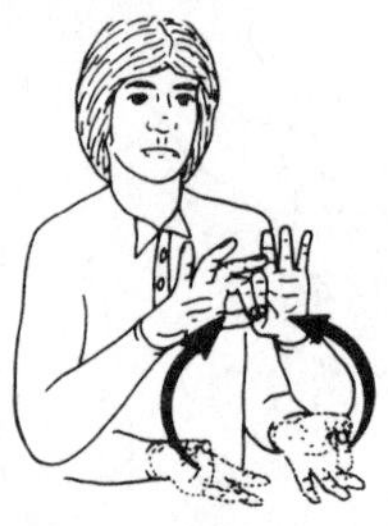

Arabic: ra'ísi رئيسي
Chinese: zhǔyàode 主要的
Dutch: voornaamste
French: principal
German: hauptsächlich
Italian: principale
Japanese: shuyō na 主要な
Korean: juyohan 주요한
Portuguese: principal
Russian: osnovnóy основной
Spanish: principal
Swedish: huvudsaklig

1664. principle [n.]

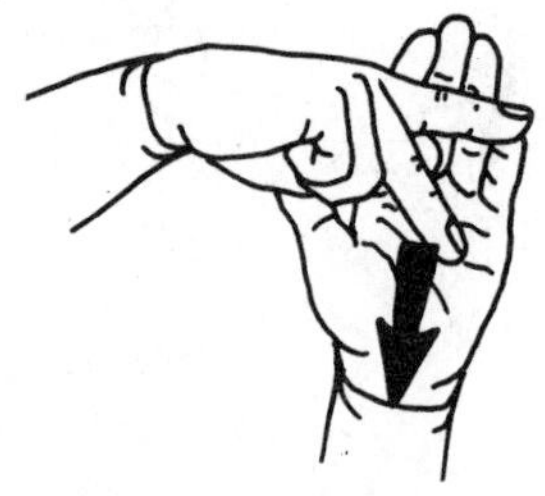

Arabic: mábda' مبدأ
Chinese: yuánzé 原則
Dutch: principe
French: principe
German: Prinzip
Italian: principio
Japanese: shugi 主義
Korean: gyojang 원리
Portuguese: princípio
Russian: príntsip принцип
Spanish: principio
Swedish: princip

1665. print [v.]

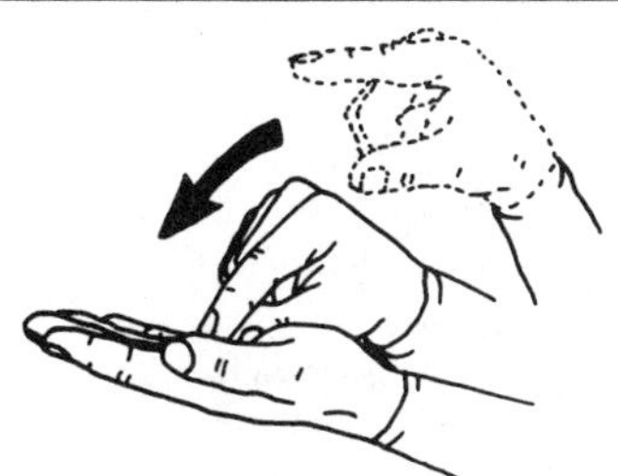

Arabic: tábaa طبع
Chinese: yìnshuā 印刷
Dutch: drukken
French: imprimer
German: drucken
Italian: stampare
Japanese: insatsu suru 印刷する
Korean: inswaehada 인쇄하다
Portuguese: imprimir
Russian: pechátat' печатать
Spanish: imprimir
Swedish: trycka

1666. prison [n.]

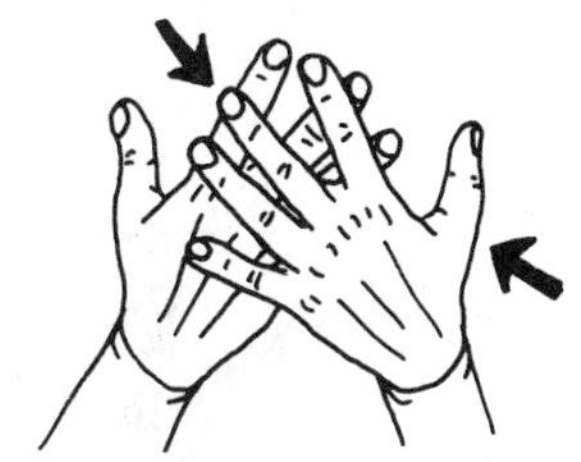

Arabic: sijn سجن
Chinese: jiānyǜ 監獄
Dutch: gevangenis
French: prison
German: Gefängnis
Italian: prigione
Japanese: keimusho 刑務所
Korean: kyodoso 교도소
Portuguese: prisão
Russian: tyur'má тюрьма
Spanish: prisión
Swedish: fängelse

1667. privacy [n.]

Arabic: seríyya سرية
Chinese: yǐnsī 隱私
Dutch: afzondering
French: intimité
German: Zurückgezogenheit
Italian: intimità
Japanese: puraibashii プライバシー
Korean: sasaenghwal 사생활
Portuguese: intimidade
Russian: uyedinéniye уединение
Spanish: intimidad
Swedish: avskildhet

1668. private [adj.]

Arabic: khas خاص
Chinese: sīrénde 私人的
Dutch: privaat
French: privé
German: privat
Italian: privato
Japanese: kojin-no 個人の
Korean: sachŏgin 사적인
Portuguese: privado
Russian: chástnyy частный
Spanish: privado
Swedish: privat

1669. privilege [n.]

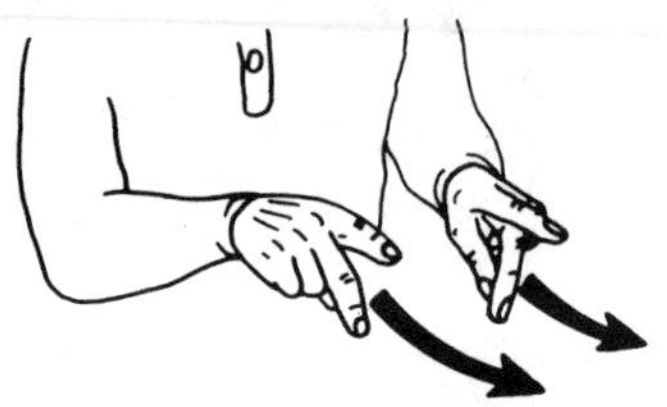

Arabic: imtiáz امتياز
Chinese: tèquán 特權
Dutch: voorrecht
French: privilège
German: Privileg
Italian: privilegio
Japanese: tokken 特権
Korean: t'ŭkkwŏn 특권
Portuguese: privilégio
Russian: privilégiya привилегия
Spanish: privilegio
Swedish: privilegium

1670. prize [n.]

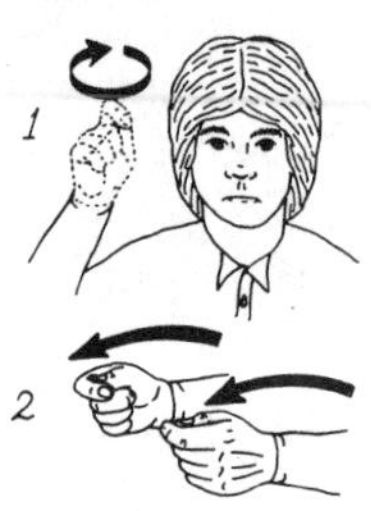

Arabic: já'iza جائزة
Chinese: jiǎngpǐn 獎品
Dutch: prijs
French: prix
German: Preis
Italian: premio
Japanese: shō 賞
Korean: sang 상
Portuguese: prêmio
Russian: prémiya премия
Spanish: premio
Swedish: pris

1671. probably [adv.]

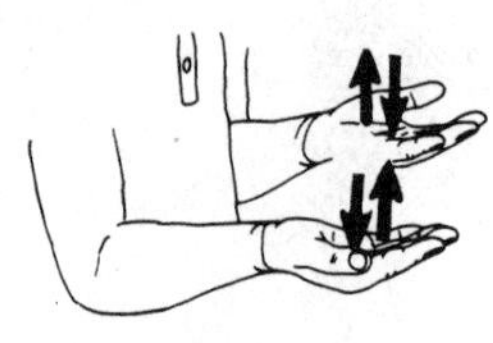

Arabic: min al-muhtámal من المحتمل
Chinese: dàgài 大概
Dutch: waarschijnlijk
French: probablement
German: wahrscheinlich
Italian: probabilmente
Japanese: tabun たぶん
Korean: ama 아마
Portuguese: provavelmente
Russian: veroyátno вероятно
Spanish: probablemente
Swedish: sannolikt

1672. problem [n.]

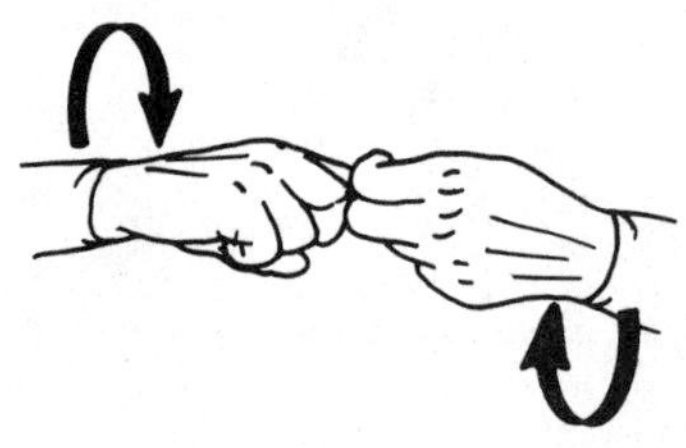

Arabic: múshkila مشكلة
Chinese: wèntí 問題
Dutch: probleem
French: problème
German: Problem
Italian: problema
Japanese: mondai 問題
Korean: munje 문제
Portuguese: problema
Russian: probléma проблема
Spanish: problema
Swedish: problem

1673. procedure [n.]

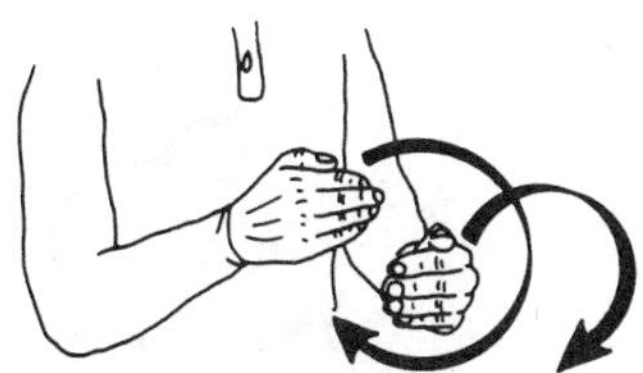

Arabic: ijráa اجراء
Chinese: chéngxù 程序
Dutch: procedure
French: procédure
German: Prozedur
Italian: procedimento
Japanese: tetsuzuki 手続
Korean: jŏlch'a 절차
Portuguese: procedimento
Russian: protsedúra процедура
Spanish: procedimiento
Swedish: procedur

1674. produce [v.]

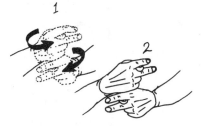

Arabic: ántaja انتج
Chinese: zhìzào 製造
Dutch: produceren
French: produire
German: produzieren
Italian: produrre
Japanese: seisan suru 生産する
Korean: mandŭlda 만들다
Portuguese: produzir
Russian: proizvodít' производить
Spanish: producir
Swedish: framställa

1675. profession [n.]

Arabic: míhna مهنة
Chinese: zhíyè 職業
Dutch: beroep
French: profession
German: Beruf
Italian: professione
Japanese: shokugyō 専門職業
Korean: jig'ŏp 직업
Portuguese: profissão
Russian: proféssiya профессия
Spanish: profesión
Swedish: yrke

1676. profit (gain) [n.]

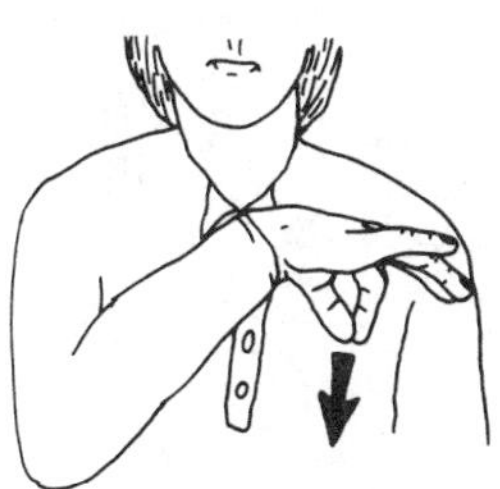

Arabic: máksab مكسب
Chinese: lìrùn 利潤
Dutch: winst
French: profit
German: Gewinn
Italian: profitto
Japanese: rieki 利益
Korean: iik 이익
Portuguese: lucro
Russian: príbyl' прибыль
Spanish: ganancia
Swedish: vinst

1677. program [n.]

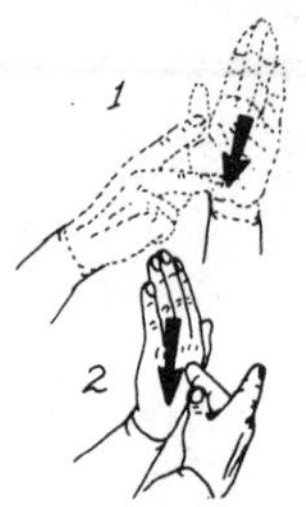

Arabic: barnámij برنامج
Chinese: jiémù 節目
Dutch: programma
French: programme
German: Programm
Italian: programma
Japanese: bangumi 番組
Korean: p'ŭrogŭraem 프로그람
Portuguese: programa
Russian: prográmma программа
Spanish: programa
Swedish: program

1678. progress [n.]

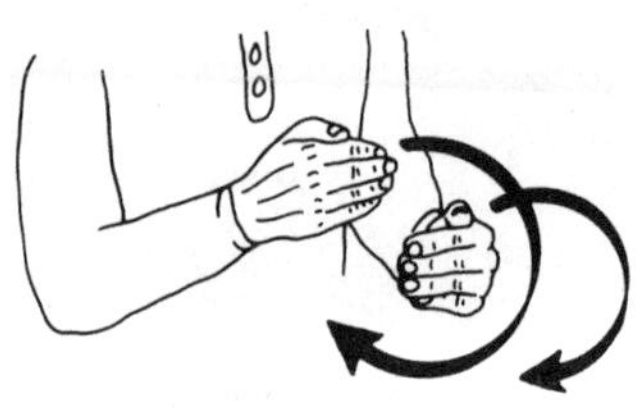

Arabic: taqáddum تقدم
Chinese: jìnbù 進步
Dutch: vooruitgang
French: progrès
German: Fortschritt
Italian: progresso
Japanese: shimpo 進歩
Korean: jŏnjin 전진
Portuguese: progresso
Russian: progréss прогресс
Spanish: progreso
Swedish: framsteg

1679. prohibit [v.]

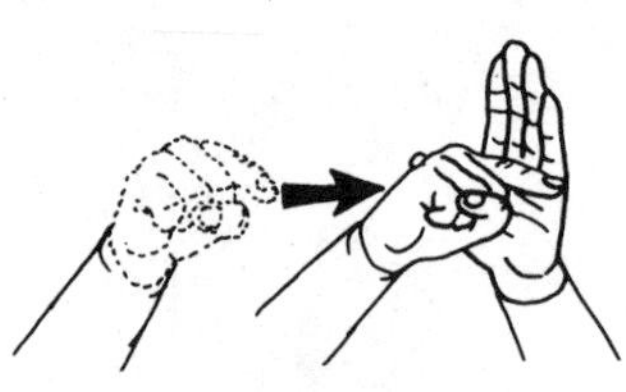

Arabic: mánaa منع
Chinese: jìnzhǐ 禁止
Dutch: verbieden
French: prohiber
German: verbieten
Italian: proibire
Japanese: kinjiru 禁じる
Korean: kŭmhada 금하다
Portuguese: proibir
Russian: zapreshchát' запрещать
Spanish: prohibir
Swedish: förbjuda

1680. project [n.]

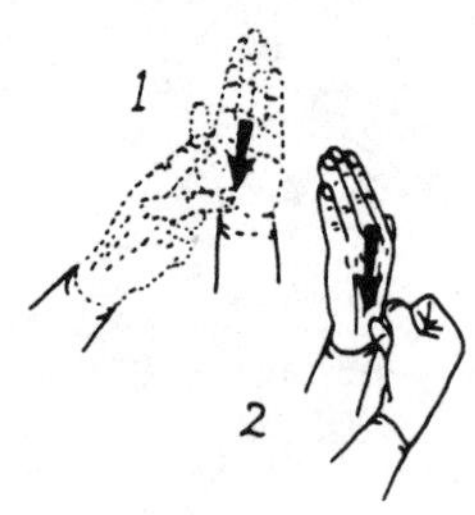

Arabic: mashrúaa مشروع
Chinese: fāngàn 方案
Dutch: project
French: projet
German: Projekt
Italian: progetto
Japanese: keikaku 計画
Korean: kyehoek 계획
Portuguese: projeto
Russian: proyékt проект
Spanish: proyecto
Swedish: projekt

1681. prominent (well-known)[adj.]

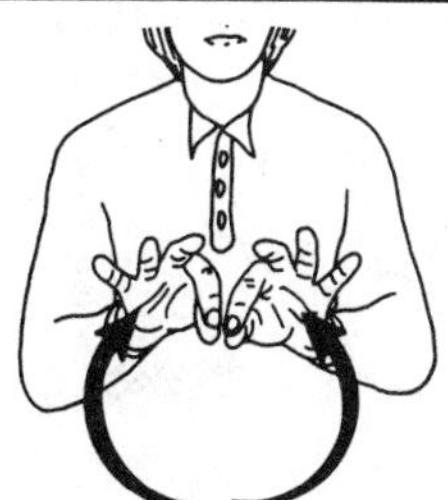

Arabic: shahír شهير
Chinese: jiéchūde 傑出的
Dutch: prominent
French: proéminent
German: prominent
Italian: prominente
Japanese: chomei na 著名な
Korean: jŏmyŏng'han 저명한
Portuguese: conhecido
Russian: vystupáyushchiy выступающий
Spanish: prominente
Swedish: framstående

1682. promise [n.]

Arabic: wáad وعد
Chinese: nuòyán 諾言
Dutch: belofte
French: promesse
German: Versprechen
Italian: promessa
Japanese: yakusoku 約束
Korean: yaksok 약속
Portuguese: promessa
Russian: obeshchániye обещание
Spanish: promesa
Swedish: löfte

1683. promote [v.]

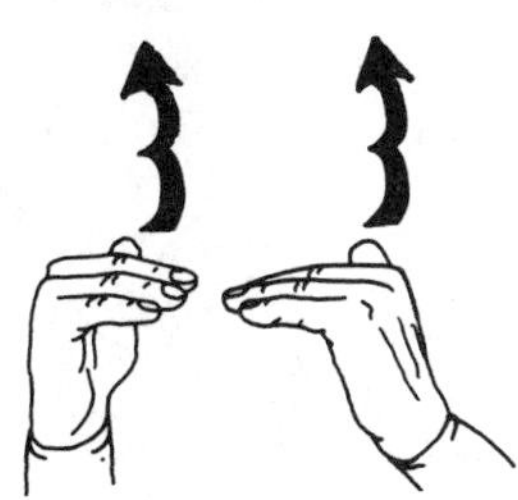

Arabic: ráqqa رقى
Chinese: zēngjìn 增進
Dutch: bevorderen
French: promouvoir
German: befördern
Italian: promuovere
Japanese: zōshin saseru 増進させる
Korean: jingŭpshik'ida 진급시키다
Portuguese: promover
Russian: sposóbstvovat' способствовать
Spanish: promover
Swedish: befordra

1684. pronounce [v.]

Arabic: láfadha لفظ
Chinese: fāyīn 發音
Dutch: uitspreken
French: prononcer
German: aussprechen
Italian: pronunziare
Japanese: hatsuon suru 発音する
Korean: barŭmhada 발음하다
Portuguese: pronunciar
Russian: proiznosít' произносить
Spanish: pronunciar
Swedish: uttala

1685. proof [n.]

Arabic: burhán برهان
Chinese: zhèngjǜ 證據
Dutch: bewijs
French: preuve
German: Beweis
Italian: prova
Japanese: shōko 証拠
Korean: jŭnggŏ 증거
Portuguese: prova
Russian: dokazátel'stvo доказательство
Spanish: prueba
Swedish: bevis

1686. proper (appropriate) [adj.]

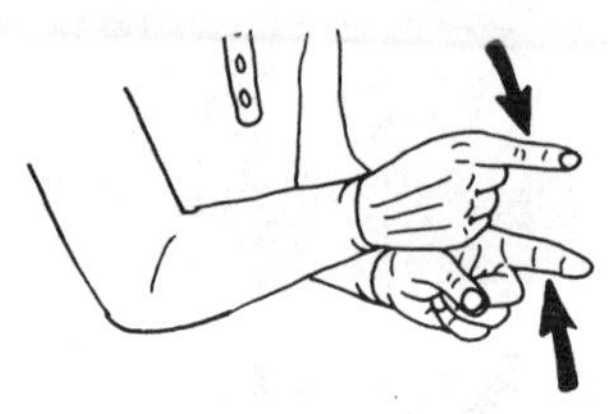

Arabic: munáseb مناسب
Chinese: qiàdàng 恰當
Dutch: gepast
French: propre
German: richtig
Italian: proprio
Japanese: tekitō na 適当な
Korean: jŏgdanghan 정당한
Portuguese: próprio
Russian: podkhodyáshchiy подходящий
Spanish: propio
Swedish: egentlig

1687. property [n.]

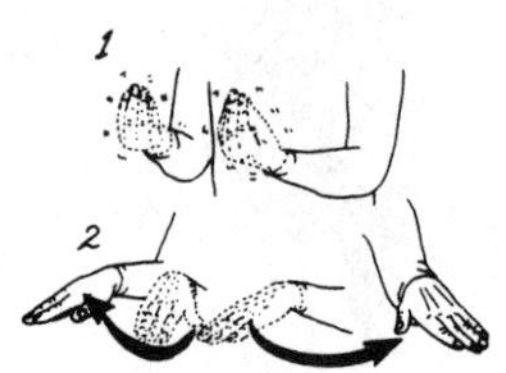

Arabic: milk ملك
Chinese: cáichǎn 財產
Dutch: eigendom
French: propriété
German: Eigentum
Italian: proprietà
Japanese: zaisan 財産
Korean: jaesan 재산
Portuguese: propriedade
Russian: imúshchestvo имущество
Spanish: propiedad
Swedish: egendom

1688. propose [v.]

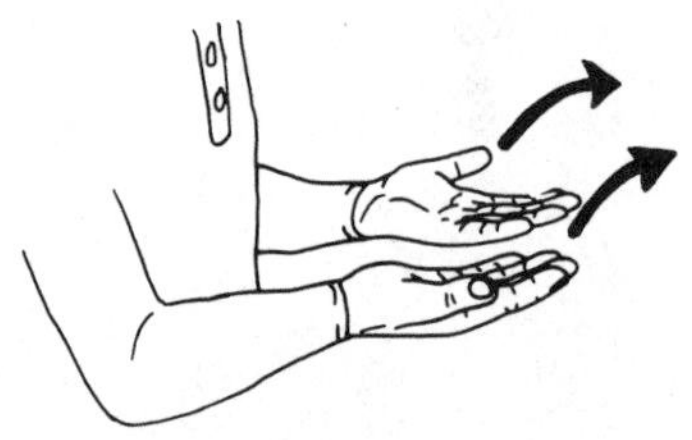

Arabic: iqtáraha اقترح
Chinese: tíyì 提議
Dutch: voorstellen
French: proposer
German: vorschlagen
Italian: proporre
Japanese: mōshikomu 申し込む
Korean: jeanhada 제안하다
Portuguese: propor
Russian: predlagát' предлагать
Spanish: proponer
Swedish: föreslå

1689. protect [v.]

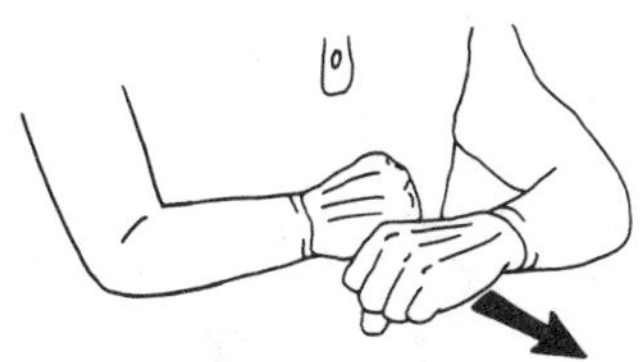

Arabic: háma حمى
Chinese: bǎohù 保護
Dutch: beschermen
French: protéger
German: schützen
Italian: proteggere
Japanese: hogo suru 保護する
Korean: bohohada 보호하다
Portuguese: proteger
Russian: zashchishchát' защищать
Spanish: proteger
Swedish: skydda

1690. protest [v.]

Arabic: iaatárada اعترض
Chinese: kàngyì 抗議
Dutch: protesteren
French: protester
German: protestieren
Italian: protestare
Japanese: kōgi suru 抗議する
Korean: hangŭihada 항의하다
Portuguese: protestar
Russian: protestovát' протестовать
Spanish: protestar
Swedish: protestera

1691. protestant [n.]

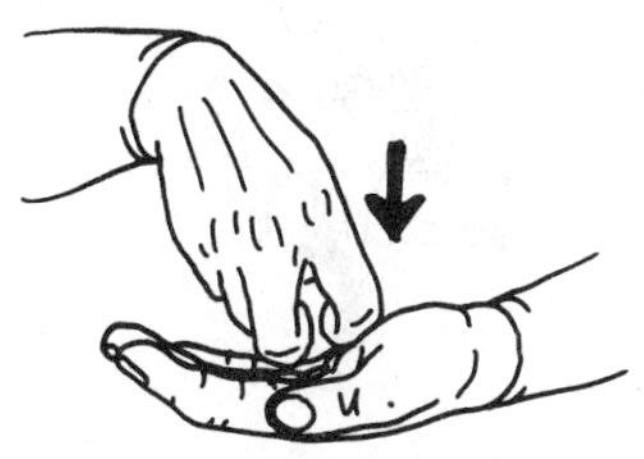

Arabic: al-brotustánti البروتستانتي
Chinese: xīnjiàotú 新教徒
Dutch: protestant
French: protestant
German: Protestant
Italian: protestante
Japanese: shinkyōto 新教徒
Korean: shinkyodo 신교도
Portuguese: protestante
Russian: protestánt протестант
Spanish: protestante
Swedish: protestant

1692. proud [adj.]

Arabic: fakhór فخور
Chinese: jiāo ào de 驕傲的
Dutch: trots
French: fier
German: stolz
Italian: orgoglioso
Japanese: hokori to suru 誇りとする
Korean: jarangsŭrŏun 자랑스러운
Portuguese: orgulhoso
Russian: górdyy гордый
Spanish: orgulloso
Swedish: stolt

1693. provide [v.]

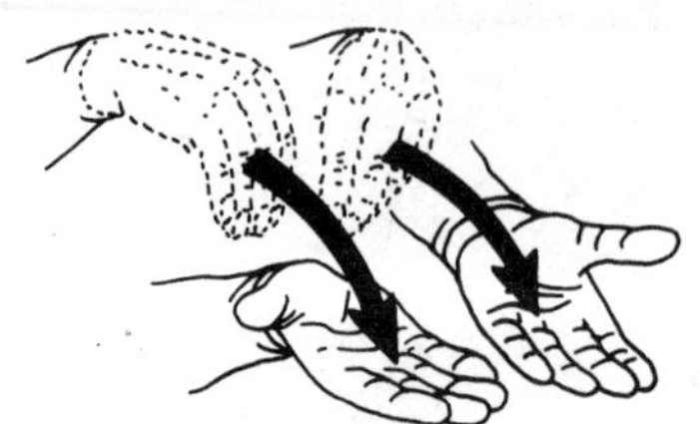

Arabic: záwwada زود
Chinese: gōngjǐ 供給
Dutch: voorzien
French: pourvoir
German: versehen
Italian: provvedere
Japanese: kyōkyū suru 供給する
Korean: konggŭp'hada 공급하다
Portuguese: prover
Russian: obespéchivat' обеспечивать
Spanish: proveer
Swedish: förse

1694. psychiatrist [n.]

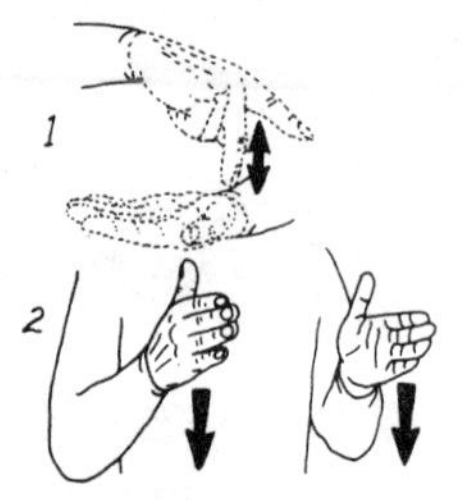

Arabic: tabíb nafsáni طبيب نفساني
Chinese: xīnlǐyīshēng 心理醫生
Dutch: psychiater
French: psychiatre
German: Psychiater
Italian: psichiatra
Japanese: seishimbyōi 精神病医
Korean: shimnihakja 심리학자
Portuguese: psiquiatra
Russian: psikhiátr психиатр
Spanish: psiquiatra
Swedish: psykiater

1695. psychology [n.]

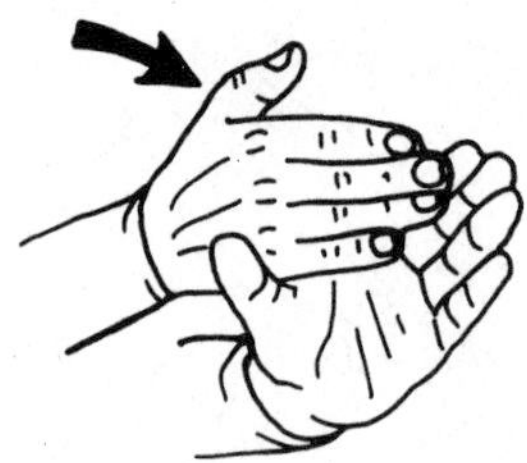

Arabic: áalm an-náfs علم النفس
Chinese: xīnlǐxué 心理學
Dutch: psychologie
French: psychologie
German: Psychologie
Italian: psicologia
Japanese: shinrigaku 心理学
Korean: shimnihak 심리학
Portuguese: psicologia
Russian: psikhológiya психология
Spanish: psicología
Swedish: psykologi

1696. public [adj.]

Arabic: áam عامْ
Chinese: gōnggòng 公共
Dutch: publiek
French: public
German: öffentlich
Italian: pubblico
Japanese: kōshū no 公衆の
Korean: kongjungŭi 공중의
Portuguese: público
Russian: obshchéstvennyy общественный
Spanish: público
Swedish: offentlig

1697. publish [v.]

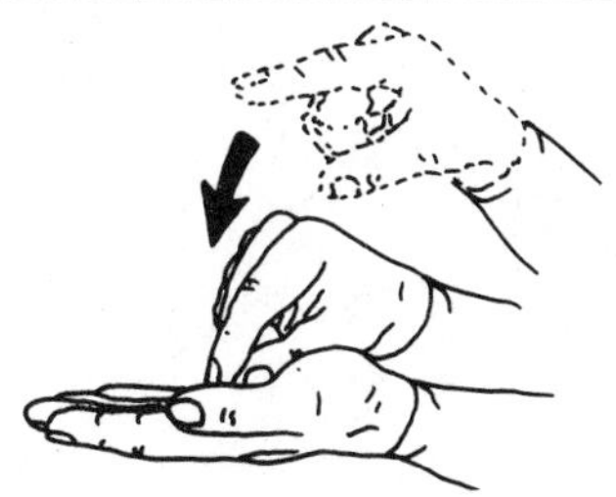

Arabic: náshara نشر
Chinese: chūbǎn 出版
Dutch: publiceren
French: publier
German: veröffentlichen
Italian: pubblicare
Japanese: shuppan suru 出版する
Korean: ch'ulp'anhada 출판하다
Portuguese: publicar
Russian: izdavát' издавать
Spanish: publicar
Swedish: offentliggöra

1698. pull [v.]

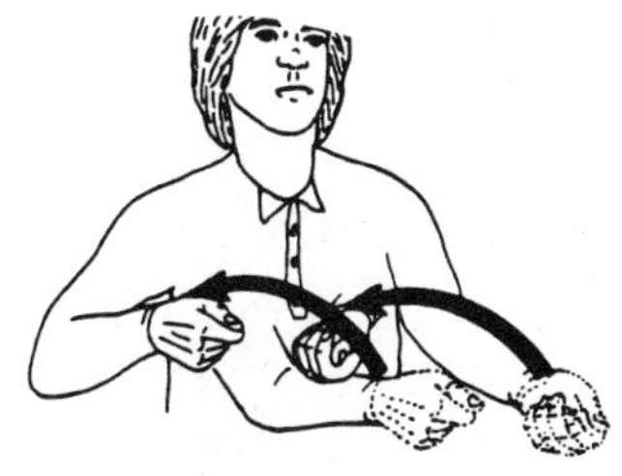

Arabic: járra جر
Chinese: tuōlā 拖拉
Dutch: trekken
French: tirer
German: ziehen
Italian: tirare
Japanese: hiku 引く
Korean: kkŭlda 끌다
Portuguese: puxar
Russian: tyanút' тянуть
Spanish: tirar
Swedish: draga

1699. pulse [n.]

Arabic: nábdha نبضة
Chinese: màibó 脈搏
Dutch: pols
French: pouls
German: Puls
Italian: polso
Japanese: myakuhaku 脈搏
Korean: maekbak 맥박
Portuguese: pulso
Russian: pul's пульс
Spanish: pulso
Swedish: puls

1700. pump [n.]

Arabic: mádakhkha مضخة
Chinese: jítǒng 唧筒
Dutch: pomp
French: pompe
German: Pumpe
Italian: pompa
Japanese: pompu ポンプ
Korean: p'ŏmp'u 펌프
Portuguese: bomba
Russian: nasós насос
Spanish: bomba
Swedish: pump

1701. punish [v.]

Arabic: áaqaba عاقب
Chinese: chŭfá 處罰
Dutch: straffen
French: punir
German: bestrafen
Italian: punire
Japanese: bassuru 罰する
Korean: bŏl juda 벌주다
Portuguese: castigar
Russian: nakázyvat' наказывать
Spanish: castigar
Swedish: straffa

1702. pure [adj.]

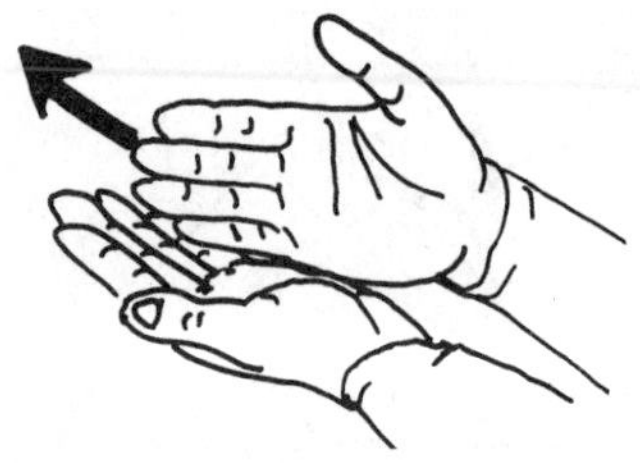

Arabic: sáafi صافي
Chinese: chúnde 純的
Dutch: puur
French: pur
German: rein
Italian: puro
Japanese: junsui na 純粋な
Korean: sunsuhan 순수한
Portuguese: puro
Russian: chístyy чистый
Spanish: puro
Swedish: ren

1703. purpose [n.]

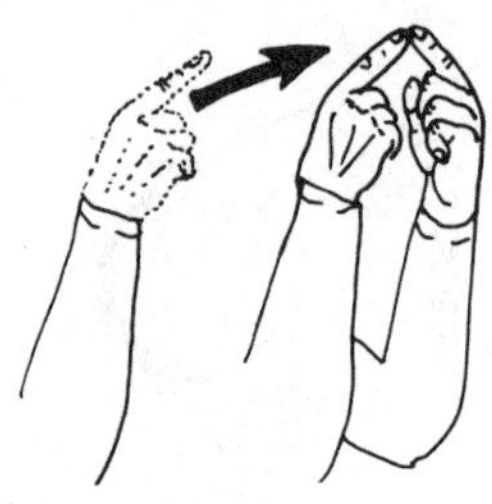

Arabic: sábab سبب
Chinese: mùdì 目的
Dutch: doel
French: but
German: Zweck
Italian: proposito
Japanese: mokuteki 目的
Korean: mokjŏg 목적
Portuguese: propósito
Russian: tsel' цель
Spanish: propósito
Swedish: avsikt

1704. purse (handbag) [n.]

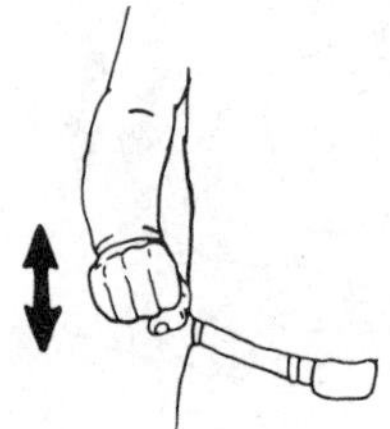

Arabic: jezdán جزدان
Chinese: qiánbāo 錢包
Dutch: handtas
French: sac à main
German: Handtasche
Italian: borsa
Japanese: saifu 財布
Korean: jikap 지갑
Portuguese: bolsa
Russian: súmka сумка
Spanish: bolsa
Swedish: handväska

1705. pursue [v.]

Arabic: láheq لاحق
Chinese: zhuīqiú 追求
Dutch: achtervolgen
French: poursuivre
German: verfolgen
Italian: perseguire
Japanese: tsuiseki suru 追跡する
Korean: dwitchotda 뒤쫓다
Portuguese: perseguir
Russian: preslédovat' преследовать
Spanish: perseguir
Swedish: förfölja

1706. push [v.]

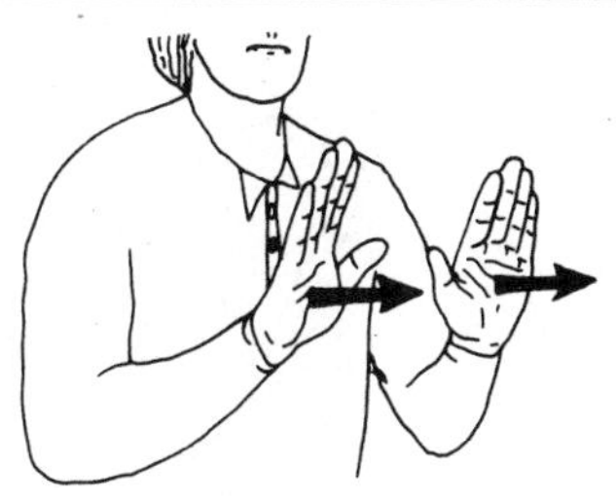

Arabic: dáfaa دفع
Chinese: tuī 推
Dutch: duwen
French: pousser
German: schieben
Italian: spingere
Japanese: osu 押す
Korean: milda 밀다
Portuguese: empurrar
Russian: tolkát' толкать
Spanish: empujar
Swedish: skjuta på

1707. put [v.]

Arabic: wádaa وضع
Chinese: fàng 放
Dutch: plaatsen
French: mettre
German: setzen/stellen
Italian: mettere
Japanese: oku 置く
Korean: duda 두다
Portuguese: colocar
Russian: klast'/stávit' класть/ставить
Spanish: poner
Swedish: lägga

1708. puzzle (enigma) [n.]

Arabic: lughz لغز
Chinese: míhuò 迷惑
Dutch: raadsel
French: énigme
German: Rätsel
Italian: enigma
Japanese: nazo 謎
Korean: susukkeki 수수께끼
Portuguese: enigma
Russian: zagádka загадка
Spanish: enigma
Swedish: huvudbry

1709. quality [n.]

Arabic: nawaaía نوعية
Chinese: pǐnzhí 品質
Dutch: kwaliteit
French: qualité
German: Qualität
Italian: qualità
Japanese: hinshitsu 品質
Korean: p'umjil 품질
Portuguese: qualidade
Russian: káchestvo качество
Spanish: calidad
Swedish: kvalitet

1710. quantity [n.]

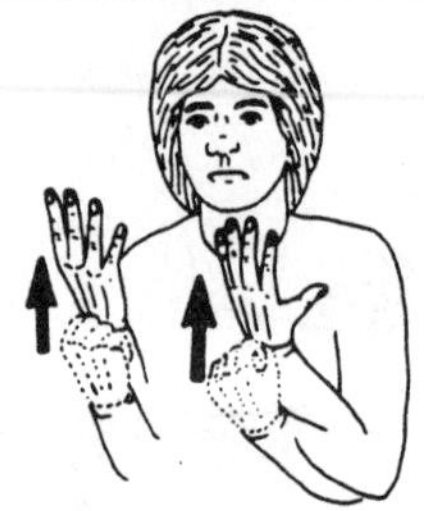

Arabic: méqdar مقدار
Chinese: shùliàng 數量
Dutch: hoeveelheid
French: quantité
German: Quantität
Italian: quantità
Japanese: ryō 量
Korean: bullyang 분량
Portuguese: quantidade
Russian: kolíchestvo количество
Spanish: cantidad
Swedish: kvantitet

1711. quarrel [v.]

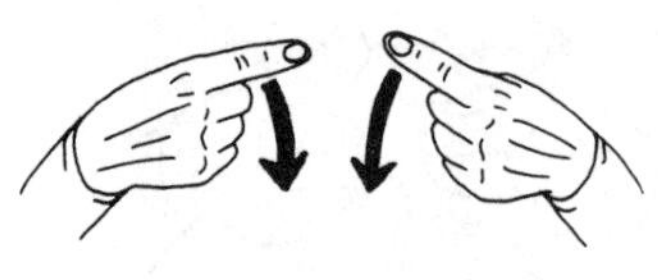

Arabic: takhássama تخاصم
Chinese: chǎojià 吵架
Dutch: ruzie maken
French: se quereller
German: streiten
Italian: litigare
Japanese: kenka suru 喧嘩する
Korean: ssauda 싸우다
Portuguese: disputar
Russian: ssórit'sya ссориться
Spanish: disputar
Swedish: gräla

1712. quarter (one-fourth) [n.]

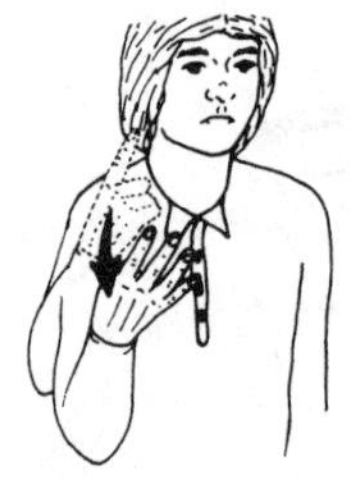

Arabic: rúbaa ربع
Chinese: sìfēnzhīyī 四分之一
Dutch: kwart
French: quart
German: Viertel
Italian: quarto
Japanese: yombun no ichi 四分の一
Korean: sabunui il 사분의 일
Portuguese: quarto
Russian: chétvert' четверть
Spanish: cuarto
Swedish: kvart

1713. queen [n.]

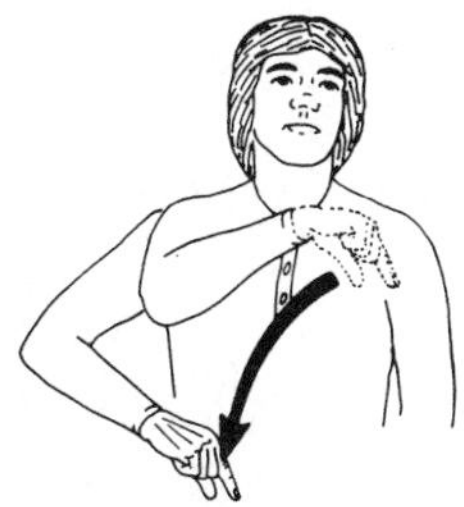

Arabic: málika ملكة
Chinese: huánghòu 皇后
Dutch: koningin
French: reine
German: Königin
Italian: regina
Japanese: jo-ō 女王
Korean: yŏwang 여왕
Portuguese: rainha
Russian: koroléva королева
Spanish: reina
Swedish: drottning

1714. question [n.]

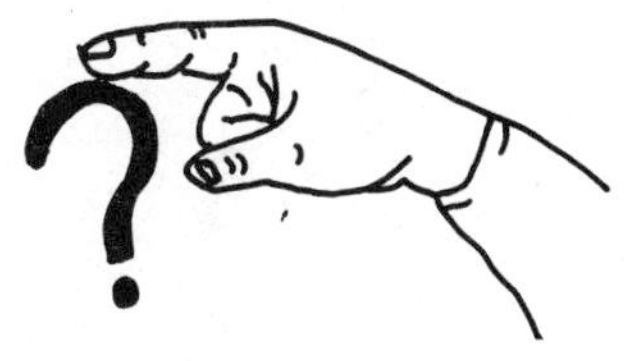

Arabic: su'ál سؤال
Chinese: wèntí 問題
Dutch: vraag
French: question
German: Frage
Italian: domanda
Japanese: shitsumon 質問
Korean: jilmun 질문
Portuguese: pergunta
Russian: voprós вопрос
Spanish: pregunta
Swedish: fråga

1715. quick [adj.]

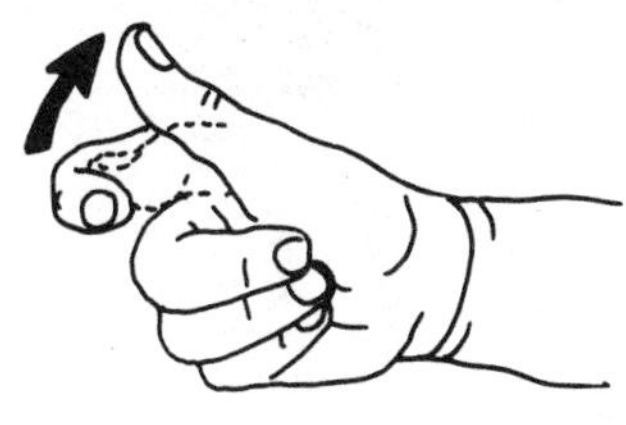

Arabic: saríaa سريع
Chinese: kuài 快
Dutch: vlug
French: rapide
German: schnell
Italian: rapido
Japanese: hayai 速い
Korean: pparŭn 빠른
Portuguese: rápido
Russian: býstryy быстрый
Spanish: rápido
Swedish: kvick

1716. quiet [adj.]

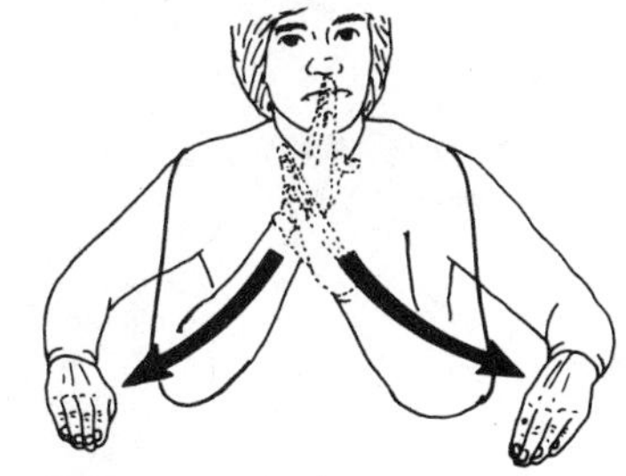

Arabic: hádi هادئ
Chinese: ānjìng 安靜
Dutch: stil
French: calme
German: still
Italian: quieto
Japanese: shizukana 静かな
Korean: joyong'han 조용한
Portuguese: quieto
Russian: spokóynyy спокойный
Spanish: quieto
Swedish: stilla

1717. quit [v.]

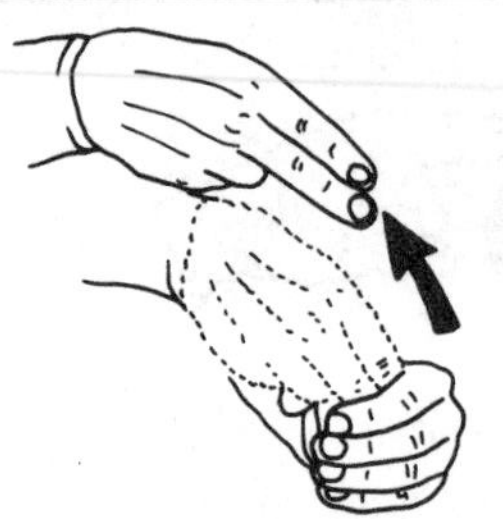

Arabic: takhálla aan تخلى عن
Chinese: fàngqì 放棄
Dutch: ophouden
French: abandonner
German: aufhören
Italian: lasciare
Japanese: yameru 止める
Korean: kŭmanduda 그만두다
Portuguese: largar
Russian: brosát' бросать
Spanish: abandonar
Swedish: upphöra

1718. quotation [n.]

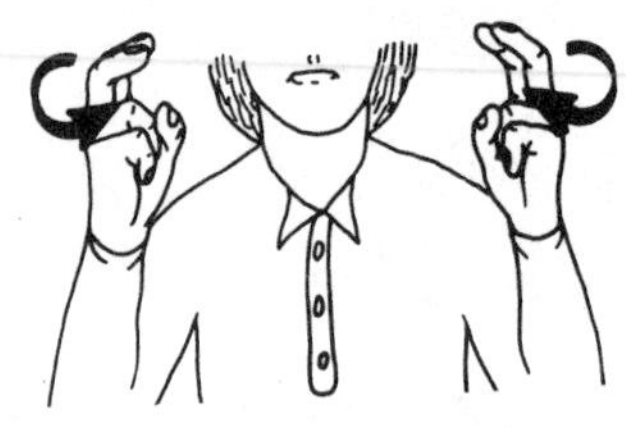

Arabic: iqtibás اقتباس
Chinese: yǐnwén 引文
Dutch: citaat
French: citation
German: Zitat
Italian: citazione
Japanese: inyō 引用
Korean: inyong 인용
Portuguese: citação
Russian: tsitáta цитата
Spanish: cita
Swedish: citat

1719. rabbit [n.]

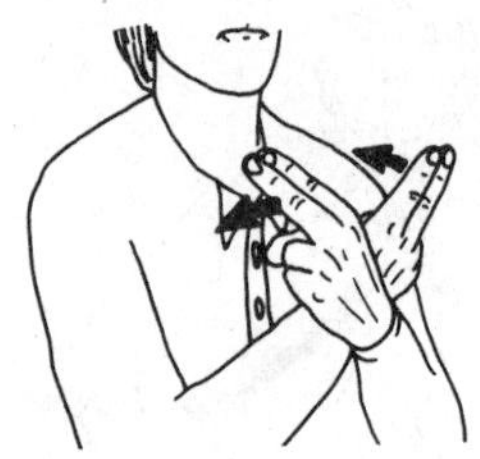

Arabic: árnab ارنب
Chinese: tùzi 兔子
Dutch: konijn
French: lapin
German: Kaninchen
Italian: coniglio
Japanese: usagi 兎
Korean: t'okki 토끼
Portuguese: coelho
Russian: królik кролик
Spanish: conejo
Swedish: kanin

1720. race (contest) [n.]

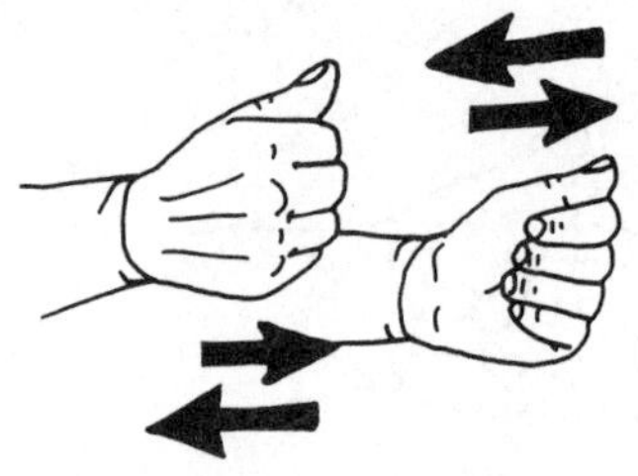

Arabic: síbaaq سباق
Chinese: jìngsài 競賽
Dutch: wedloop
French: course
German: Rennen
Italian: corsa
Japanese: kyōsō 競争
Korean: kyŏngju 경주
Portuguese: corrida
Russian: gónki гонки
Spanish: carrera
Swedish: kapplöpning

1721. radio [n.]

Arabic: rádio راديو
Chinese: shóuyīnjī 收音機
Dutch: radio
French: radio
German: Radio
Italian: radio
Japanese: rajio ラジオ
Korean: radio 라디오
Portuguese: rádio
Russian: rádio радио
Spanish: radio
Swedish: radio

1722. railroad [n.]

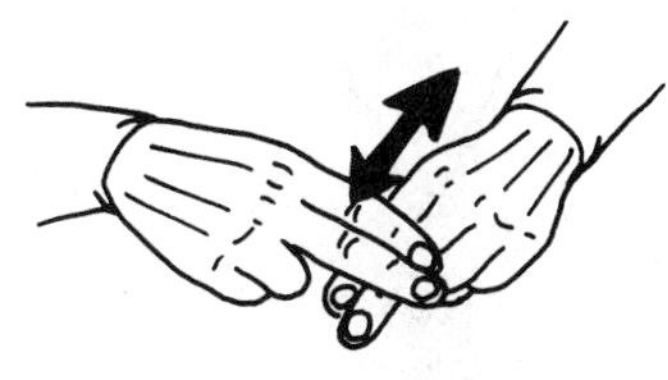

Arabic: síket al-hadíd سكة الحديد
Chinese: tiělù 鐵路
Dutch: spoorweg
French: chemin de fer
German: Eisenbahn
Italian: ferrovia
Japanese: tetsudō 鉄道
Korean: ch'ŏldo 철도
Portuguese: estrada de ferro
Russian: zheléznaya doróga железная дорога
Spanish: ferrocarril
Swedish: järnväg

1723. rain [n.]

Arabic: mátar مطر
Chinese: yǔ 雨
Dutch: regen
French: pluie
German: Regen
Italian: pioggia
Japanese: ame 雨
Korean: bi 비
Portuguese: chuva
Russian: dozhd' дождь
Spanish: lluvia
Swedish: regn

1724. raise (lift) [v.]

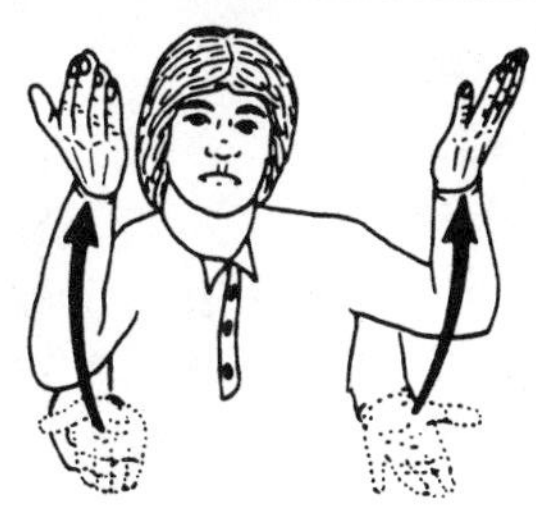

Arabic: ráfaa رفع
Chinese: táigāo 擡高
Dutch: opheffen
French: élever
German: heben
Italian: alzare
Japanese: ageru 上げる
Korean: ollida 올리다
Portuguese: levantar
Russian: podnimát' поднимать
Spanish: levantar
Swedish: höja

1725. rapid [adj.]

Arabic: saríaa سريع
Chinese: xùnsù 迅速
Dutch: snel
French: rapide
German: schnell
Italian: rapido
Japanese: hayai 速い
Korean: pparŭn 빠른
Portuguese: rápido
Russian: skóryy скорый
Spanish: rápido
Swedish: hastig

1726. rare (scarce) [adj.]

Arabic: náder نادر
Chinese: xīshǎo 稀少
Dutch: zeldzaam
French: rare
German: selten
Italian: raro
Japanese: mezurashii 珍しい
Korean: tŭmŭn 드문
Portuguese: raro
Russian: rédkiy редкий
Spanish: escaso
Swedish: sällsynt

1727. rat [n.]

Arabic: fa'r فأر
Chinese: laŏshŭ 老鼠
Dutch: rat
French: rat
German: Ratte
Italian: ratto
Japanese: nezumi ネズミ
Korean: jwi 쥐
Portuguese: rato
Russian: krýsa крыса
Spanish: rata
Swedish: råtta

1728. rate (ratio) [n.]

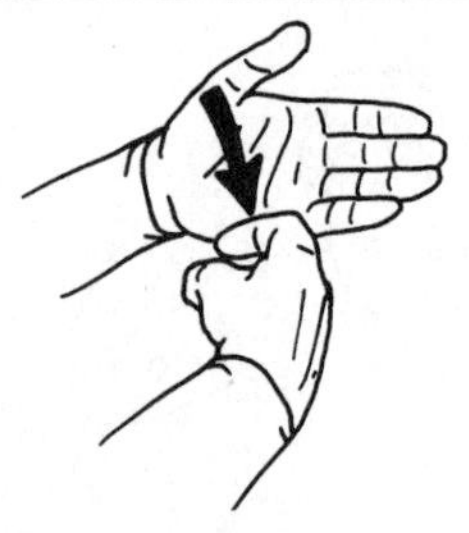

Arabic: moáaddal معدل
Chinese: bǐlǜ 比率
Dutch: verhouding
French: proportion
German: Verhältnis
Italian: proporzione
Japanese: wariai 割合
Korean: biyul 비율
Portuguese: razão
Russian: propórtsiya пропорция
Spanish: proporción
Swedish: proportion

1729. raw (uncooked) [adj.]

Arabic: náee نيء
Chinese: shēngde 生的
Dutch: rauw
French: cru
German: roh
Italian: crudo
Japanese: nama no 生の
Korean: nalgŏsŭi 날것의
Portuguese: cru
Russian: syróy сырой
Spanish: crudo
Swedish: rå

1730. ray [n.]

Arabic: sho'a' شعاع
Chinese: shèxiàn 射線
Dutch: straal
French: rayon
German: Strahl
Italian: raggio
Japanese: kōsen 光線
Korean: kwangsŏn 광선
Portuguese: raio
Russian: luch луч
Spanish: rayo
Swedish: stråle

1731. razor [n.]

Arabic: mus al-hiláqa موسى الحلاقة
Chinese: tìdāo 剃刀
Dutch: scheermes
French: rasoir
German: Rasierapparat
Italian: rasoio
Japanese: kamisori かみそり
Korean: myŏndok'al 면도칼
Portuguese: navalha
Russian: brítva бритва
Spanish: navaja de afeitar
Swedish: rakkniv

1732. reach (attain) [v.]

Arabic: nála نال
Chinese: dádào 達到
Dutch: bereiken
French: atteindre
German: erreichen
Italian: raggiungere
Japanese: tassuru 達する
Korean: doch'ag'hada 도착하다
Portuguese: alcançar
Russian: dostigát' достигать
Spanish: alcanzar
Swedish: uppnå

1733. reaction [n.]

Arabic: rad al-feáal رد الفعل
Chinese: fǎnyìng 反應
Dutch: reactie
French: réaction
German: Reaktion
Italian: reazione
Japanese: hannō 反応
Korean: bandong 반동
Portuguese: reação
Russian: reáktsiya реакция
Spanish: reacción
Swedish: reaktion

1734. read [v.]

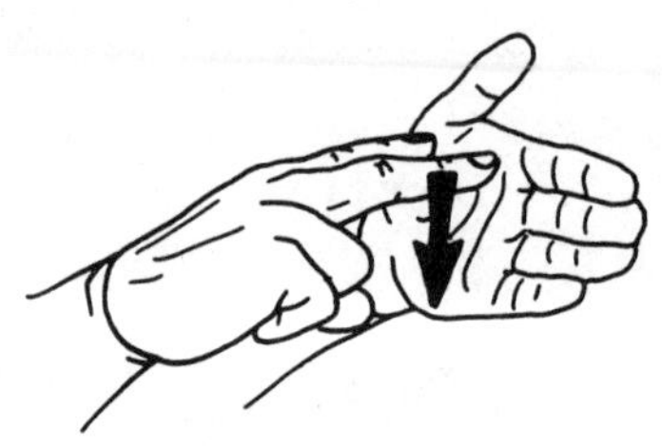

Arabic: qára'a قرأ
Chinese: dú 讀
Dutch: lezen
French: lire
German: lesen
Italian: leggere
Japanese: yomu 読む
Korean: ikda 읽다
Portuguese: ler
Russian: chitát' читать
Spanish: leer
Swedish: läsa

1735. ready (prepared) [adj.]

Arabic: jáhez جاهز
Chinese: zhǔnbèihǎode 準備好的
Dutch: gereed
French: prêt
German: bereit
Italian: preparato
Japanese: yoi no dekita 用意の出来た
Korean: junbidoen 준비된
Portuguese: preparado
Russian: gotóvyy готовый
Spanish: preparado
Swedish: beredd

1736. real [adj.]

Arabic: haqíeqi حقيقي
Chinese: zhēnde 真的
Dutch: echt
French: réel
German: wirklich
Italian: reale
Japanese: genjitsu no 現実の
Korean: shiljeŭi 실제의
Portuguese: real
Russian: nastoyáshchiy настоящий
Spanish: real
Swedish: verklig

1737. realize [v.]

Arabic: ádraka ادرك
Chinese: tǐhuì 體會
Dutch: realizeren
French: réaliser
German: realisieren
Italian: rendersi conto
Japanese: satoru 悟る
Korean: shirhyŏnhada 실현하다
Portuguese: realizar
Russian: realizovát' реализовать
Spanish: realizar
Swedish: realisera

1738. really [adv.]

Arabic: háqqan حقاً
Chinese: zhēnde 真的
Dutch: werkelijk
French: vraiment
German: wirklich
Italian: veramente
Japanese: hontō ni 本当に
Korean: jŏngmallo 정말로
Portuguese: realmente
Russian: deystvítel'no действительно
Spanish: verdaderamente
Swedish: verkligen

1739. rear [adj.]

Arabic: náder نادر
Chinese: hòumiàn 後面
Dutch: achterkant
French: arrière
German: hinter
Italian: posteriore
Japanese: ushiro no 後ろの
Korean: baehuŭi 배후의
Portuguese: posterior
Russian: zádniy задний
Spanish: posterior
Swedish: baksides

1740. reason (cause) [n.]

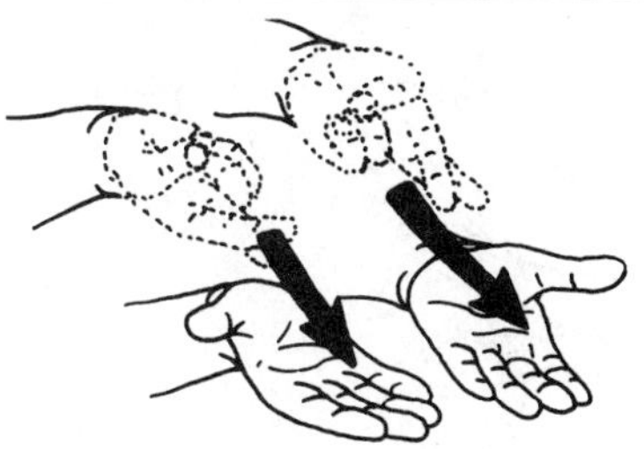

Arabic: sábab سبب
Chinese: yuányīn 原因
Dutch: oorzaak
French: cause
German: Ursache
Italian: causa
Japanese: riyū 理由
Korean: iyu 이유
Portuguese: causa
Russian: prichína причина
Spanish: causa
Swedish: orsak

1741. reason (intelligence) [n.]

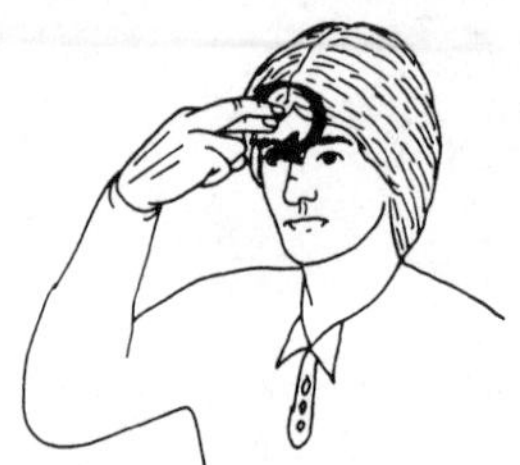

Arabic: áaql عقل
Chinese: lǐzhì 理智
Dutch: rede
French: raison
German: Verstand
Italian: ragione
Japanese: shiryo 思慮
Korean: isŏng 이성
Portuguese: razão
Russian: rázum разум
Spanish: razón
Swedish: förstånd

1742. rebellion [n.]

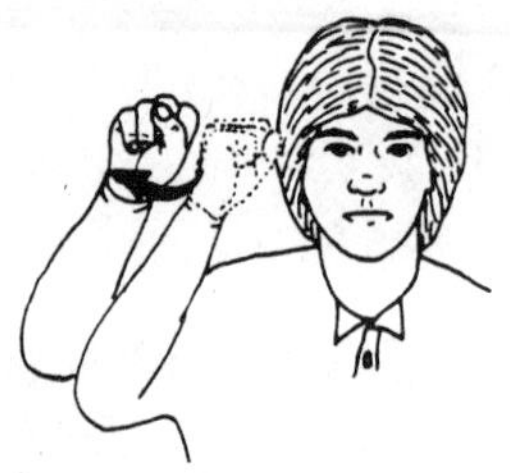

Arabic: tháura ثورة
Chinese: fǎnpàn 反叛
Dutch: oproer
French: rébellion
German: Aufstand
Italian: ribellione
Japanese: hankō 反抗
Korean: ballan 반란
Portuguese: rebelião
Russian: vosstániye восстание
Spanish: rebelión
Swedish: uppror

1743. receipt [n.]

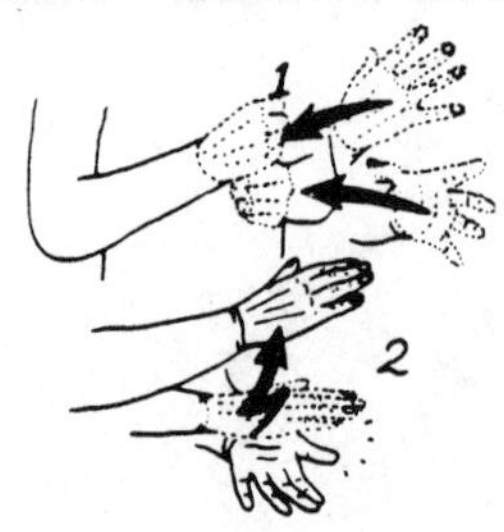

Arabic: ísal ايصال
Chinese: shōujù 收據
Dutch: ontvangsbewijs
French: reçu
German: Quittung
Italian: quietanza
Japanese: ryōshū sho 領収書
Korean: yŏngsujŭng 영수증
Portuguese: recibo
Russian: kvitántsiya квитанция
Spanish: recibo
Swedish: kvitto

1744. receive [v.]

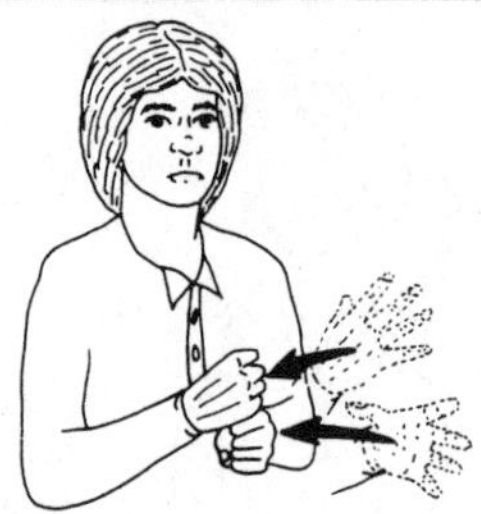

Arabic: istálama استلم
Chinese: shōu 收
Dutch: ontvangen
French: recevoir
German: empfangen
Italian: ricevere
Japanese: uketoru 受け取る
Korean: batta 받다
Portuguese: receber
Russian: poluchát' получать
Spanish: recibir
Swedish: mottaga

1745. recent [adj.]

Arabic: jadíd جديد
Chinese: jìnláide 近來的
Dutch: recent
French: récent
German: jüngst
Italian: recente
Japanese: chikagoro no 近頃の
Korean: ch'oekŭnŭi 최근의
Portuguese: recente
Russian: nedávniy недавний
Spanish: reciente
Swedish: ny

1746. reception (social) [n.]

Arabic: isteqbál استقبال
Chinese: jiēdàihuì 接待會
Dutch: receptie
French: accueil
German: Empfang
Italian: ricevimento
Japanese: settai 接待
Korean: hwanyŏnghoe 환영회
Portuguese: recepção
Russian: priyóm приём
Spanish: recibimiento
Swedish: mottagande

1747. recognize [v.]

Arabic: taárrafa تعرف
Chinese: rènchū 認出
Dutch: herkennen
French: reconnaître
German: erkennen
Italian: riconoscere
Japanese: mitomeru 認める
Korean: araboda 알아보다
Portuguese: reconhecer
Russian: uznavát' узнавать
Spanish: reconocer
Swedish: erkänna

1748. recommend [v.]

Arabic: áosa اوصى
Chinese: tuījiàn 推薦
Dutch: aanbevelen
French: recommander
German: empfehlen
Italian: raccomandare
Japanese: suisen suru 推薦する
Korean: ch'uch'ŏnhada 추천하다
Portuguese: recomendar
Russian: rekomendovát' рекомендовать
Spanish: recomendar
Swedish: rekommendera

1749. record [v.]

Arabic: sájjala سجل
Chinese: lù 錄
Dutch: optekenen
French: enregistrer
German: eintragen
Italian: registrare
Japanese: kiroku suru 記録する
Korean: kirokhada 기록하다
Portuguese: registrar
Russian: zapísyvat' записывать
Spanish: registrar
Swedish: anteckna

1750. record (sports) [n.]

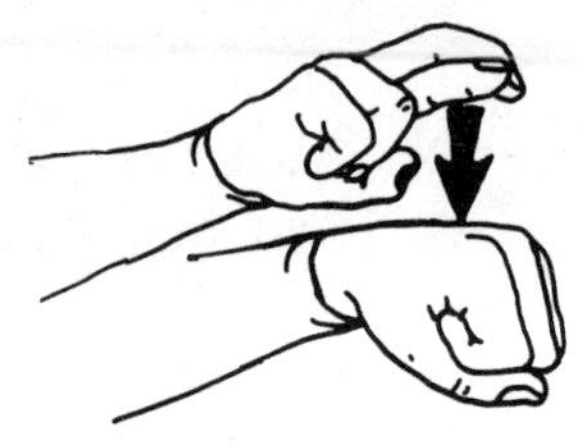

Arabic: ráqam qeási رقم قياسي
Chinese: jìlù 記錄
Dutch: record
French: record
German: Rekord
Italian: primato
Japanese: saikō kiroku 最高記録
Korean: kirok 기록
Portuguese: recorde
Russian: rekórd рекорд
Spanish: récord
Swedish: rekord

1751. recreation [n.]

Arabic: istijmám استجمام
Chinese: yúlè 娛樂
Dutch: ontspanning
French: récréation
German: Erholung
Italian: ricreazione
Japanese: goraku 娯楽
Korean: orak 오락
Portuguese: recreação
Russian: razvlechéniye развлечение
Spanish: recreación
Swedish: förströelse

1752. red [adj.]

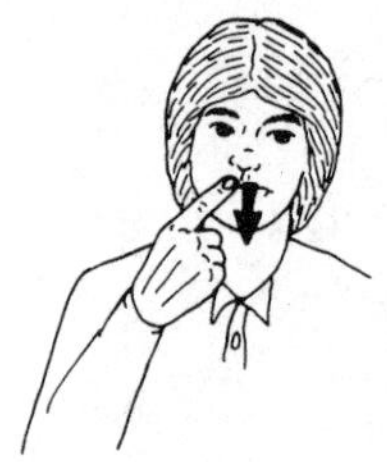

Arabic: áhmar احمر
Chinese: hóng 紅
Dutch: rood
French: rouge
German: rot
Italian: rosso
Japanese: akai 赤
Korean: ppalgan 빨간
Portuguese: vermelho
Russian: krásnyy красный
Spanish: rojo
Swedish: röd

1753. reduce [v.]

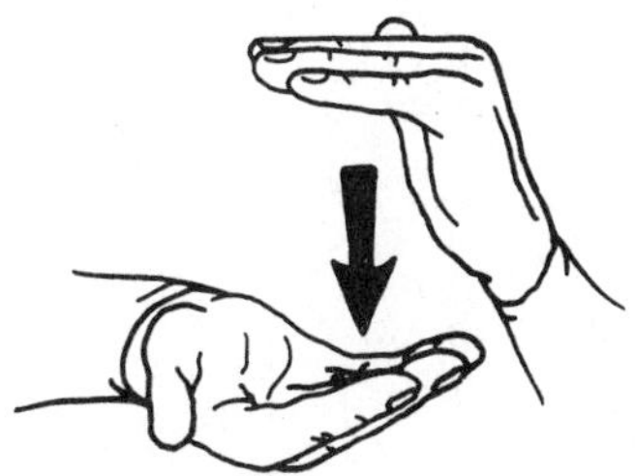

Arabic: ánqasa انقص
Chinese: suōjiăn 縮減
Dutch: verminderen
French: réduire
German: vermindern
Italian: ridurre
Japanese: herasu 減らす
Korean: jurida 줄이다
Portuguese: reduzir
Russian: ponizhát' понижать
Spanish: reducir
Swedish: reducera

1754. refer (to) [v.]

Arabic: ashára íla اشار الى
Chinese: tíjí 提及
Dutch: verwijzen
French: référer
German: verweisen
Italian: riferire
Japanese: toiawaseru 問い合わせる
Korean: ŏngŭb'hada 언급하다
Portuguese: referir
Russian: otnosít' относить
Spanish: referir
Swedish: hänvisa

1755. reflect (image) [v.]

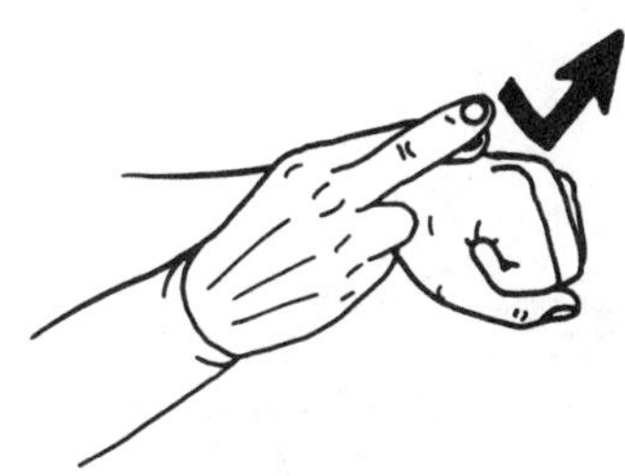

Arabic: áakasa عكس
Chinese: fănshè 反射
Dutch: weerkaatsen
French: refléter
German: widerspiegeln
Italian: riflettere
Japanese: utsu su 写す
Korean: bansahada 반사하다
Portuguese: refletir
Russian: otrazhát' отражать
Spanish: reflejar
Swedish: återkasta

1756. refresh [v.]

Arabic: jáddada جدد
Chinese: tíshén 提神
Dutch: verfrissen
French: rafraîchir
German: erfrischen
Italian: rinfrescare
Japanese: sawayaka ni suru
爽やかにする
Korean: saerobgehada 새롭게 하다
Portuguese: refrescar
Russian: osvezhát' освежать
Spanish: refrescar
Swedish: uppfriska

1757. refrigerator [n.]

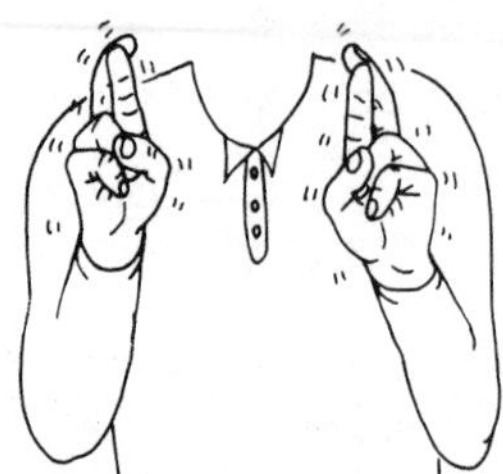

Arabic: thallája ثلاجة
Chinese: bīngxiāng 冰箱
Dutch: koelkast
French: réfrigérateur
German: Kühlschrank
Italian: frigorifero
Japanese: reizōko 冷蔵庫
Korean: naengjanggo 냉장고
Portuguese: refrigerador
Russian: kholodíl'nik холодильник
Spanish: refrigerador
Swedish: kylskåp

1758. refuse [v.]

Arabic: ráfada رفض
Chinese: jùjué 拒絶
Dutch: weigeren
French: refuser
German: verweigern
Italian: rifiutare
Japanese: kotowaru 断わる
Korean: gŏjŏrhada 거절하다
Portuguese: recusar
Russian: otkázyvat' отказывать
Spanish: rehusar
Swedish: vägra

1759. region [n.]

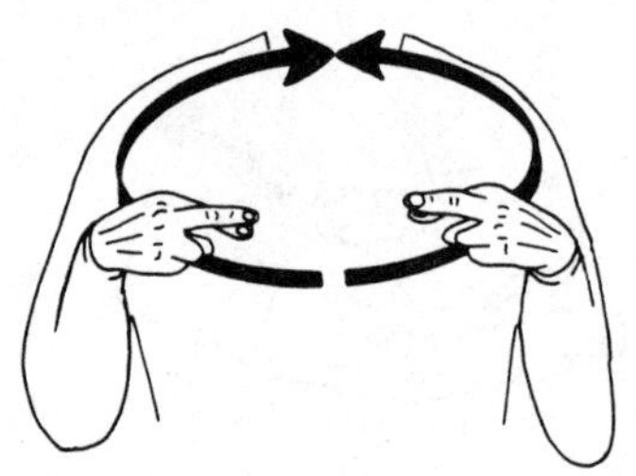

Arabic: mánteqa منطقة
Chinese: dìqū 地區
Dutch: streek
French: région
German: Gegend
Italian: regione
Japanese: chihō 地方
Korean: jiyŏk 지역
Portuguese: região
Russian: rayón район
Spanish: región
Swedish: trakt

1760. register [v.]

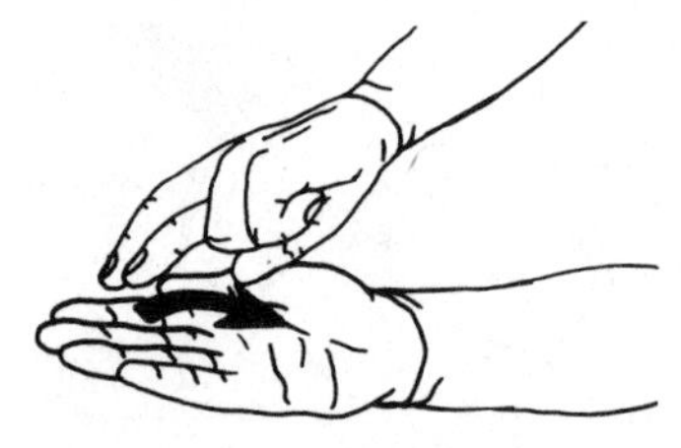

Arabic: sajjála سجل
Chinese: dēngjì 登記
Dutch: registreren
French: enregistrer
German: registrieren
Italian: registrare
Japanese: tōroku suru 登録する
Korean: dŭngnok'hada 등록하다
Portuguese: registrar
Russian: registrírovat' регистрировать
Spanish: registrar
Swedish: registrera

1761. regret [v.]

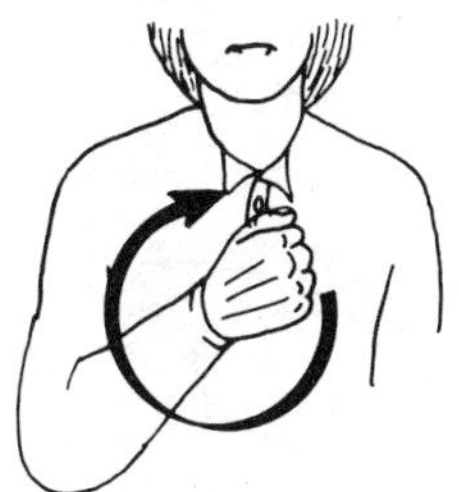

Arabic: tanáddama áala تندم على
Chinese: hoùhuǐ 後悔
Dutch: betreuren
French: regretter
German: bedauern
Italian: rimpiangere
Japanese: zannen ni omou 残念に思う
Korean: huhoehada 후회하다
Portuguese: sentir
Russian: sozhalét' сожалеть
Spanish: lamentar
Swedish: beklaga

1762. regular [adj.]

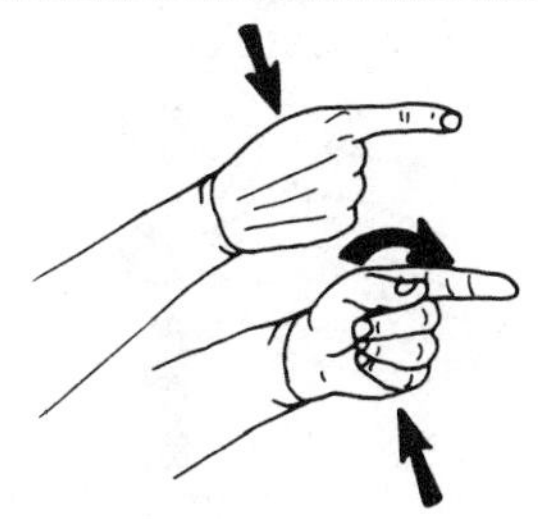

Arabic: áadi عادي
Chinese: píngcháng 平常
Dutch: regelmatig
French: régulier
German: regelmaßig
Italian: regolare
Japanese: kisokuteki na 規則的な
Korean: jŏngshikŭi 정식의
Portuguese: regular
Russian: regulyárnyy регулярный
Spanish: regular
Swedish: regelbunden

1763. regulate [v.]

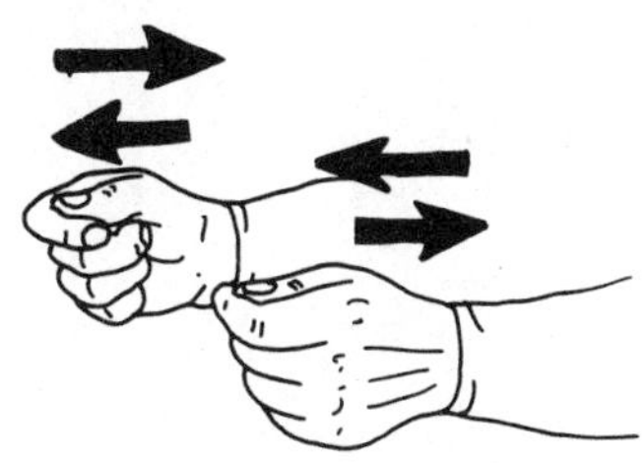

Arabic: nádhdhama نظم
Chinese: guǎnzhì 管制
Dutch: regelen
French: régler
German: regeln
Italian: regolare
Japanese: chōsetsu suru 調節する
Korean: kyujŏnghada 규정하다
Portuguese: regular
Russian: regulírovat' регулировать
Spanish: regular
Swedish: reglera

1764. regulation(s) [n.]

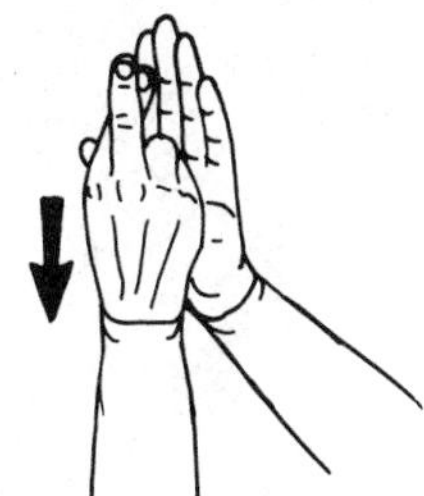

Arabic: tandhím تنظيم
Chinese: guīzé 規則
Dutch: regeling
French: règlement
German: Regelung
Italian: regolamento
Japanese: kisoku 規則
Korean: kyuch'ik 규칙
Portuguese: regulamento
Russian: ustáv устав
Spanish: reglamento
Swedish: reglering

1765. reinforce [v.]

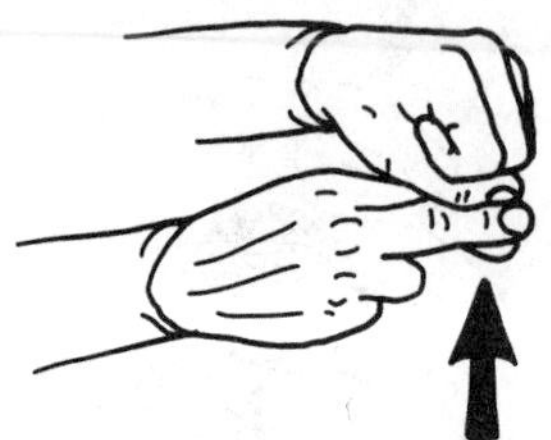

Arabic: qáwwa قوي
Chinese: jiāqiáng 加強
Dutch: versterken
French: renforcer
German: verstärken
Italian: rinforzare
Japanese: hokyō suru 補強する
Korean: boganghada 보강하다
Portuguese: reforçar
Russian: podkreplyát' подкреплять
Spanish: reforzar
Swedish: förstärka

1766. reject [v.]

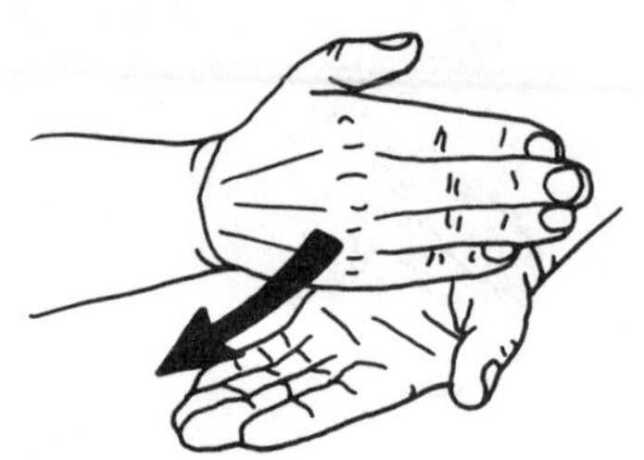

Arabic: ráfada رفض
Chinese: jùjué 拒絶
Dutch: verwerpen
French: rejeter
German: verwerfen
Italian: respingere
Japanese: kyozetsu suru 拒絶する
Korean: bŏrida 버리다
Portuguese: rejeitar
Russian: otvergát' отвергать
Spanish: rechazar
Swedish: avslå

1767. relationship (connection) [n.]

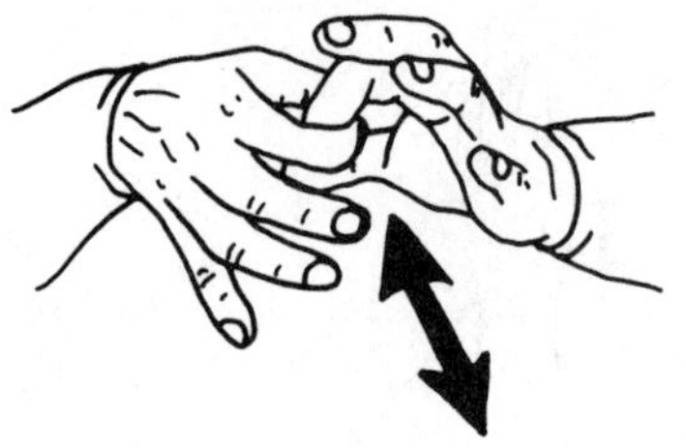

Arabic: aaláqa علاقة
Chinese: guānxì 關係
Dutch: verwantschap
French: rapport
German: Verwandtschaft
Italian: rapporto
Japanese: kankei 関係
Korean: kwangye 관계
Portuguese: relacionamento
Russian: otnoshéniye отношение
Spanish: relación
Swedish: släktskap

1768. relative [n.]

Arabic: qarîb قريب
Chinese: qīnqì 親戚
Dutch: familielid
French: parent
German: Verwandter
Italian: parente
Japanese: shinseki 親戚
Korean: ch'inch'ŏk 친척
Portuguese: parente
Russian: ródstvennik родственник
Spanish: pariente
Swedish: släkting

1769. relax [v.]

Arabic: istérkha استرخى
Chinese: fàngsōng 放鬆
Dutch: zich ontspannen
French: se détendre
German: entspannen
Italian: rilassare
Japanese: yurumeru ゆるめる
Korean: nŭtch'uda 늦추다
Portuguese: relaxar
Russian: oslablyát' ослаблять
Spanish: relajar
Swedish: slappna av

1770. release [v.]

Arabic: hárrara حرر
Chinese: fàngchū 放出
Dutch: vrijlaten
French: libérer
German: freilassen
Italian: liberare
Japanese: hanasu 放す
Korean: sŏkpanghada 석방하다
Portuguese: soltar
Russian: otpuskát' отпускать
Spanish: soltar
Swedish: lössläppa

1771. relief [n.]

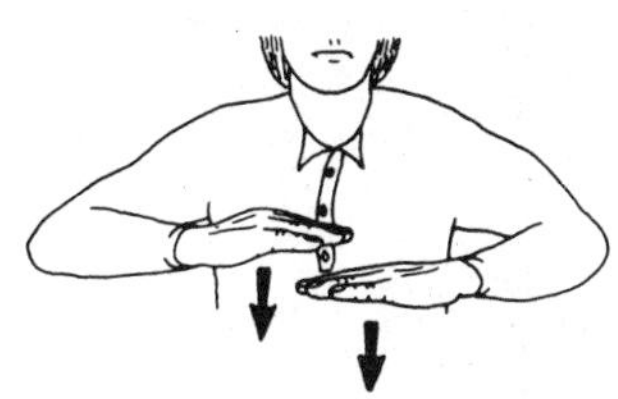

Arabic: ráha راحة
Chinese: jiěchú 解除
Dutch: opluchting
French: soulagement
German: Erleichterung
Italian: sollievo
Japanese: anshin 安心
Korean: jegŏ 제거
Portuguese: alívio
Russian: oblegchéniye облегчение
Spanish: alivio
Swedish: lättnad

1772. religion [n.]

Arabic: diána ديانة
Chinese: zōngjiào 宗教
Dutch: godsdienst
French: religion
German: Religion
Italian: religione
Japanese: shūkyō 宗教
Korean: jongkyo 종교
Portuguese: religião
Russian: relígiya религия
Spanish: religión
Swedish: religion

1773. rely (on) [v.]

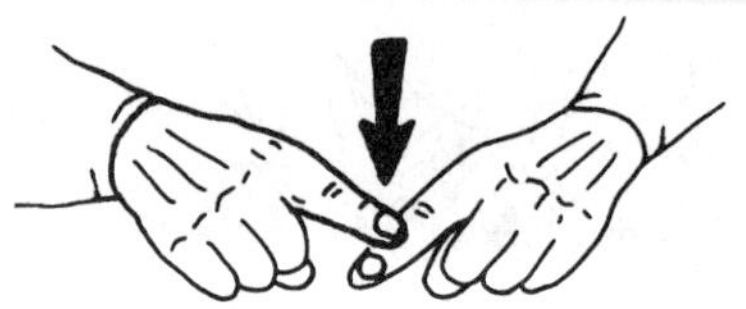

Arabic: iaatámada áala اعتمد على
Chinese: yīlài 依賴
Dutch: rekenen op
French: compter sur
German: verlassen auf
Italian: contare su
Japanese: ate ni suru あてにする
Korean: ŭijihada 의지하다
Portuguese: contar com
Russian: polagát'sya na полагаться на
Spanish: contar con
Swedish: lita på

1774. remain (stay) [v.]

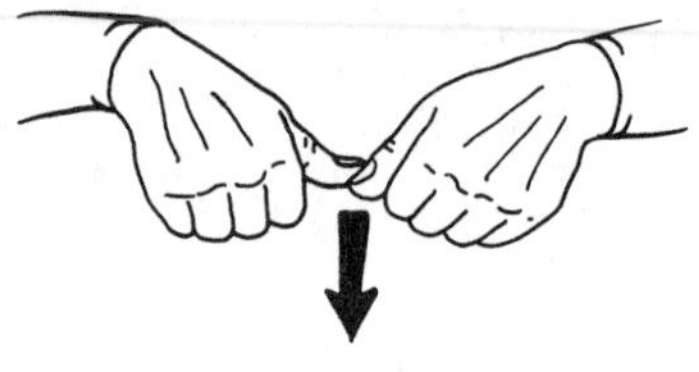

Arabic: báqaa بقى
Chinese: dòuliú 逗留
Dutch: blijven
French: rester
German: bleiben
Italian: rimanere
Japanese: nokoru 残る
Korean: mŏmurŭda 머무르다
Portuguese: permanecer
Russian: ostavát'sya оставаться
Spanish: permanecer
Swedish: återstå

1775. remainder [n.]

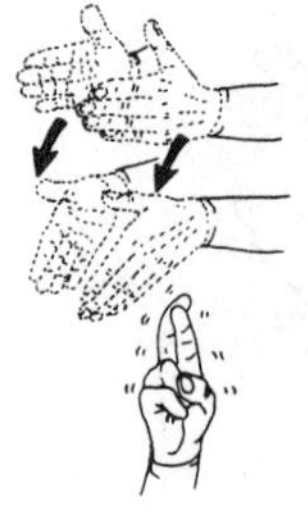

Arabic: al-báaqi الباقي
Chinese: shèngyü 剩余
Dutch: rest
French: reste
German: Rest
Italian: resto
Japanese: nokori 残り
Korean: namŏji 나머지
Portuguese: resto
Russian: ostátok остаток
Spanish: resto
Swedish: rest

1776. remark [n.]

Arabic: muláhadha ملاحظة
Chinese: pínglùn 評論
Dutch: opmerking
French: remarque
German: Bemerkung
Italian: osservazione
Japanese: chui 注意
Korean: nonp'yŏng 논평
Portuguese: observação
Russian: zamechániye замечание
Spanish: observación
Swedish: anmärkning

1777. remember [v.]

Arabic: tadhákkara تذكر
Chinese: jìdé 記得
Dutch: zich herinneren
French: se rappeler
German: sich erinnern
Italian: ricordarsi
Japanese: omoidasu 思い出す
Korean: kiŏk'hada 기억하다
Portuguese: recordar-se
Russian: pómnit' помнить
Spanish: acordarse
Swedish: minnas

1778. remind [v.]

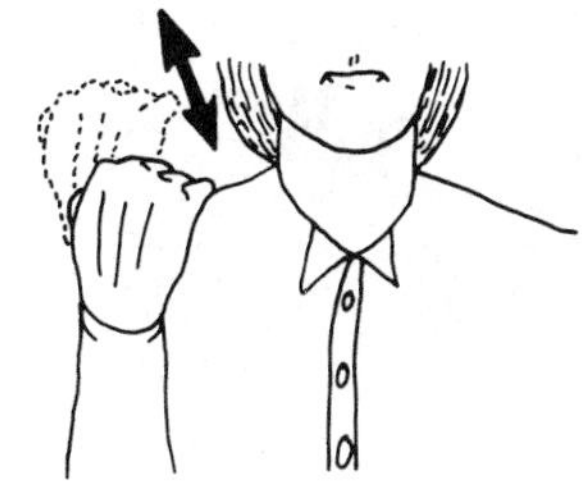

Arabic: dháakkara ذكر
Chinese: tíxǐng 提醒
Dutch: herinneren
French: rappeler à
German: erinnern
Italian: rammentare
Japanese: omoidasaseru 思い出させる
Korean: saenggangnagehada 생각나게하다
Portuguese: recordar
Russian: napominát' напоминать
Spanish: recordar
Swedish: påminna

1779. remote [adj.]

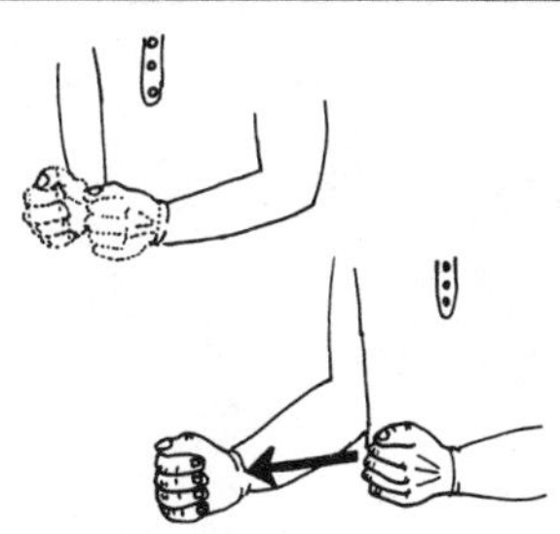

Arabic: baa-íd بعيد
Chinese: yiáo yuǎn 遥遠
Dutch: afgelegen
French: distant
German: abgelegen
Italian: remoto
Japanese: hempi na へきそん
Korean: mŏn 먼
Portuguese: remoto
Russian: otdalyónnyy отдалённый
Spanish: remoto
Swedish: avlägsen

1780. remove [v.]

Arabic: náqala نقل
Chinese: yíkāi 移開
Dutch: verwijderen
French: enlever
German: entfernen
Italian: togliere
Japanese: utsusu 移す
Korean: ch'iuda 치우다
Portuguese: remover
Russian: ustranyát' устранять
Spanish: quitar
Swedish: avlägsna

1781. rent [v.]

Arabic: istá'jara استأجر
Chinese: zū 租
Dutch: huren
French: louer
German: mieten
Italian: affittare
Japanese: chinshaku suru 賃借する
Korean: billyŏjuda 빌려주다
Portuguese: alugar
Russian: nanimát' нанимать
Spanish: alquilar
Swedish: hyra

1782. repair [v.]

Arabic: áslaha اصلح
Chinese: xiūlǐ 修理
Dutch: herstellen
French: réparer
German: reparieren
Italian: riparare
Japanese: shūri suru 修理する
Korean: koch'ida 고치다
Portuguese: reparar
Russian: remontírovat' ремонтировать
Spanish: reparar
Swedish: reparera

1783. repair(s) [n.]

Arabic: isláah اصلاح
Chinese: xiūfù 修復
Dutch: herstelling
French: réparation
German: Reparatur
Italian: riparazione
Japanese: shūri 修理
Korean: suri 수리
Portuguese: conserto
Russian: remónt ремонт
Spanish: reparación
Swedish: reparation

1784. repeat [v.]

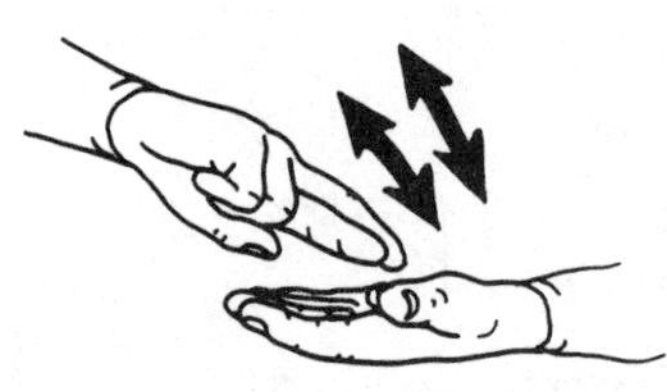

Arabic: kárrara كرر
Chinese: chóngfù 重復
Dutch: herhalen
French: répéter
German: wiederholen
Italian: ripetere
Japanese: kurikaesu 繰り返す
Korean: doep'uri marhada 되풀이하다
Portuguese: repetir
Russian: povtoryát' повторять
Spanish: repetir
Swedish: upprepa

1785. replace (substitute) [v.]

Arabic: istábdala استبدل
Chinese: qǔdài 取代
Dutch: vervangen
French: remplacer
German: ersetzen
Italian: sostituire
Japanese: torikaeru 取り換える
Korean: daech'ihada 대치하다
Portuguese: substituir
Russian: zamenyát' заменять
Spanish: reemplazar
Swedish: ersätta

1786. reply [v.]

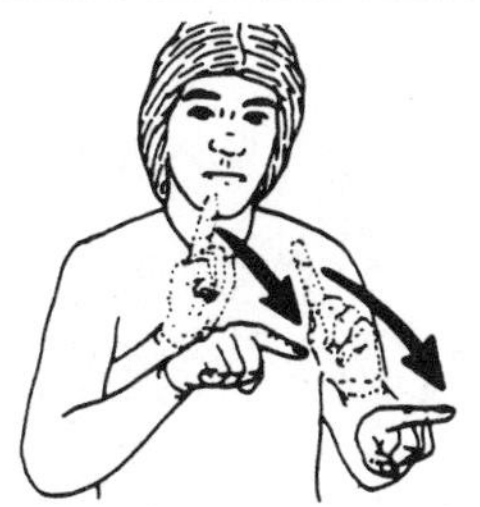

Arabic: ajáaba اجاب
Chinese: dáfù 答覆
Dutch: antwoorden
French: répondre
German: antworten
Italian: rispondere
Japanese: henji o suru 返事をする
Korean: daedap'hada 대답하다
Portuguese: responder
Russian: otvechát' отвечать
Spanish: responder
Swedish: svara

1787. report [n.]

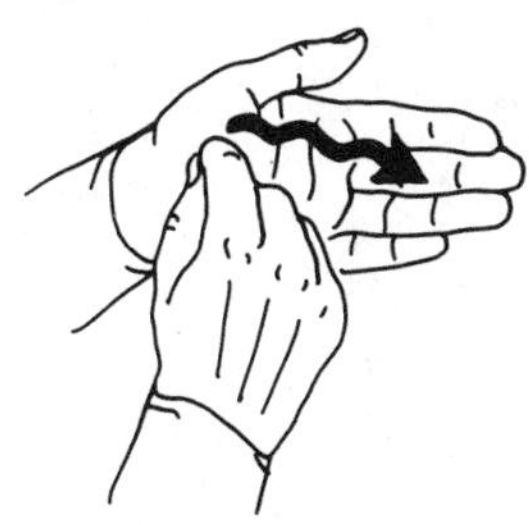

Arabic: taqrír تقرير
Chinese: bàogào 報告
Dutch: verslag
French: rapport
German: Bericht
Italian: rapporto
Japanese: hōkoku 報告
Korean: bogo 보고
Portuguese: relatório
Russian: doklád доклад
Spanish: informe
Swedish: rapport

1788. report [v.]

Arabic: wásafa وصف
Chinese: bàogào 報告
Dutch: rapporteren
French: rapporter
German: berichten
Italian: riferire
Japanese: hōkoku suru 報告する
Korean: bogohada 보고하다
Portuguese: relatar
Russian: soobshchát' сообщать
Spanish: informar
Swedish: rapportera

1789. represent [v.]

Arabic: máththala مثّل
Chinese: dàibiǎo 代表
Dutch: vertegenwoordigen
French: représenter
German: darstellen
Italian: rappresentare
Japanese: daihyō suru 代表する
Korean: daep'yohada 대표하다
Portuguese: representar
Russian: predstavlyát' представлять
Spanish: representar
Swedish: representera

1790. representative [n.]

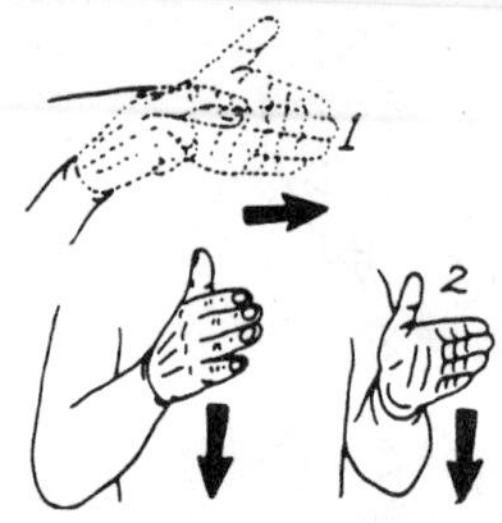

Arabic: mumáththil ممثّل
Chinese: dàibiǎo 代表
Dutch: vertegenwoordiger
French: représentant
German: Repräsentant
Italian: rappresentante
Japanese: daihyōsha 代表者
Korean: daep'yo 대표
Portuguese: representante
Russian: predstavítel' представитель
Spanish: representante
Swedish: representant

1791. request [n.]

Arabic: tálab طلب
Chinese: qǐngqiú 請求
Dutch: verzoek
French: requête
German: Bitte
Italian: richiesta
Japanese: irai 依頼
Korean: yoku 요구
Portuguese: pedido
Russian: prós'ba просьба
Spanish: solicitud
Swedish: begäran

1792. requirement [n.]

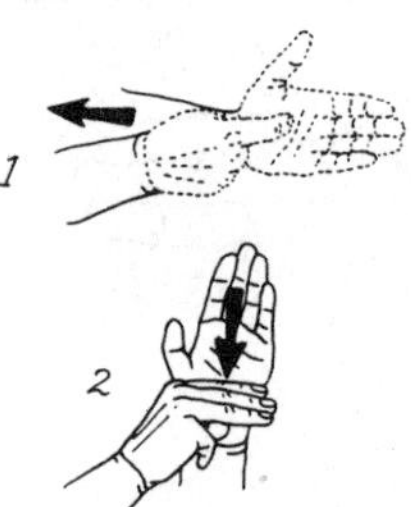

Arabic: mátlab مطلب
Chinese: yāoqiú 要求
Dutch: vereiste
French: exigence
German: Anforderung
Italian: requisito
Japanese: yōkyū 要求
Korean: yogu 요구
Portuguese: exigência
Russian: trébovaniye требование
Spanish: exigencia
Swedish: krav

1793. rescue [v.]

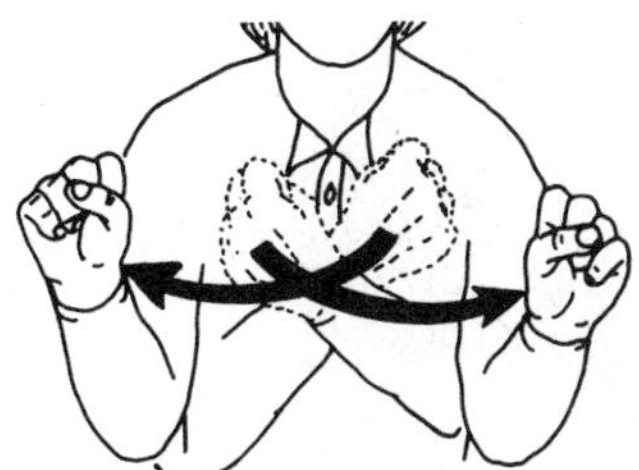

Arabic: ánqadha انقذ
Chinese: jiù 救
Dutch: redden
French: sauver
German: retten
Italian: salvare
Japanese: sukuidasu 救い出す
Korean: kuch'urhada 구출하다
Portuguese: salvar
Russian: spasát' спасать
Spanish: rescatar
Swedish: rädda

1794. research [n.]

Arabic: báheth بحث
Chinese: yánjiù 研究
Dutch: onderzoek
French: recherche
German: Forschung
Italian: ricerca
Japanese: kenkyū 研究
Korean: yŏnku 연구
Portuguese: investigação
Russian: isslédovaniye исследование
Spanish: investigación
Swedish: forskning

1795. resemble [v.]

Arabic: shábbaha شبه
Chinese: lèisì 類似
Dutch: gelijken op
French: ressembler à
German: gleichen
Italian: rassomigliare
Japanese: nite iru 似ている
Korean: bisŭt 비슷하다
Portuguese: assemelhar-se a
Russian: pokhodít' na походить на
Spanish: asemejarse a
Swedish: likna

1796. reserve [n.]

Arabic: hajz حجز
Chinese: cúcáng 貯藏
Dutch: reserve
French: réserve
German: Reserve
Italian: riserva
Japanese: yobi 予備
Korean: yebi 예비
Portuguese: reserva
Russian: rezérv резерв
Spanish: reserva
Swedish: reserv

1797. reserve [v.]

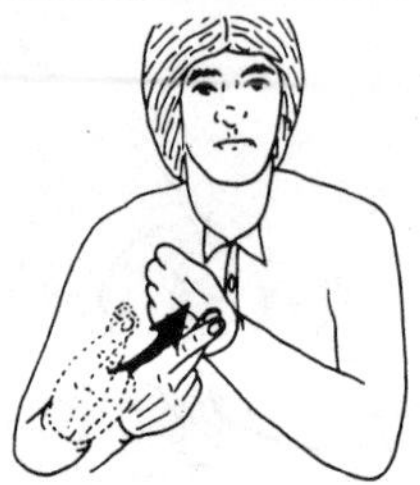

Arabic: hájaza حجز
Chinese: bǎoliú 保留
Dutch: reserveren
French: réserver
German: reservieren
Italian: riservare
Japanese: yoyaku suru 予約する
Korean: yeyak'hada 예약하다
Portuguese: reservar
Russian: rezervírovat' резервировать
Spanish: reservar
Swedish: reservera

1798. residence [n.]

Arabic: máskan مسكن
Chinese: jūmín 居民
Dutch: woonplaats
French: résidence
German: Wohnsitz
Italian: residenza
Japanese: jūtaku 住宅
Korean: juso 주소
Portuguese: residência
Russian: mestozhítel'stvo местожительство
Spanish: residencia
Swedish: bostad

1799. resign [v.]

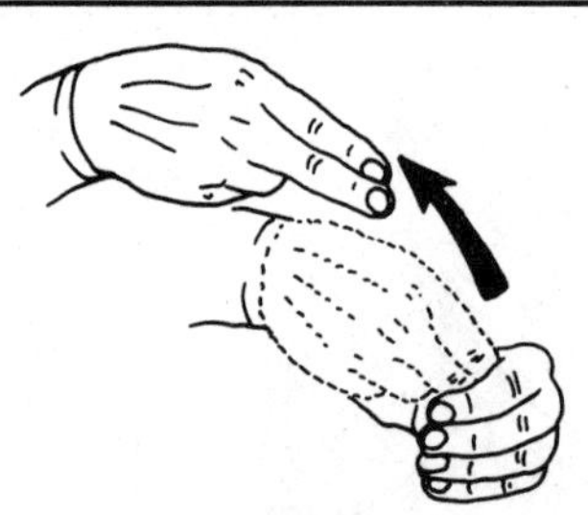

Arabic: istáqbala استقبل
Chinese: cízhí 辭職
Dutch: ontslag nemen
French: démissionner
German: zurücktreten
Italian: dimettersi
Japanese: jinin suru 辞任する
Korean: saimhada 사임하다
Portuguese: demitir-se
Russian: otkázyvat'sya ot dólzhnosti отказываться от должности
Spanish: renunciar
Swedish: avgå

1800. resistance [n.]

Arabic: muqáwwama مقاومة
Chinese: dǐkàng 抵抗
Dutch: weerstand
French: résistance
German: Widerstand
Italian: resistenza
Japanese: teikō 抵抗
Korean: banhang 반항
Portuguese: resistência
Russian: soprotivléniye сопротивление
Spanish: resistencia
Swedish: motstånd

1801. resolve (solve) [v.]

Arabic: hálla حل
Chinese: jiějué 解决
Dutch: oplossen
French: résoudre
German: auflösen
Italian: risolvere
Japanese: kaiketsu suru 解決する
Korean: haekyŏlhada 해결하다
Portuguese: resolver
Russian: reshát' решать
Spanish: resolver
Swedish: upplösa

1802. resource [n.]

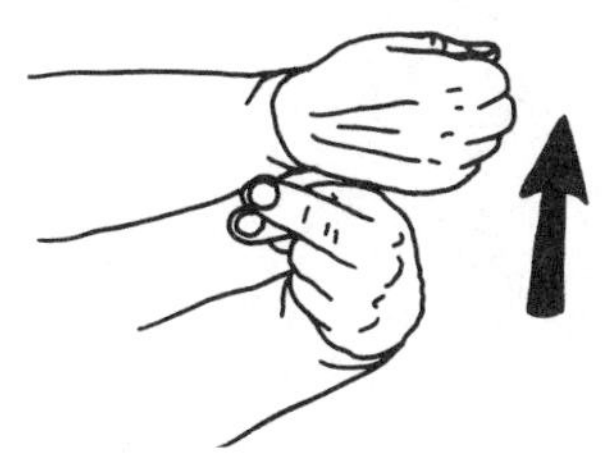

Arabic: másdar مصدر
Chinese: zīyuán 资源
Dutch: hulpbron
French: ressource
German: Hilfsmittel
Italian: risorsa
Japanese: kyōkyūgen 供給源
Korean: jawŏn 자원
Portuguese: recurso
Russian: resúrs ресурс
Spanish: recurso
Swedish: resurs

1803. respect (esteem) [n.]

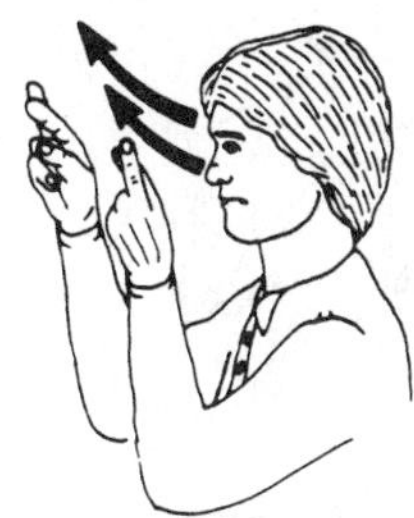

Arabic: ehtirám احترم
Chinese: zūnzhòng 尊重
Dutch: achting
French: respect
German: Achtung
Italian: rispetto
Japanese: sonkei 尊敬
Korean: jonjung 존중
Portuguese: respeito
Russian: uvazhéniye уважение
Spanish: respeto
Swedish: aktning

1804. responsibility [n.]

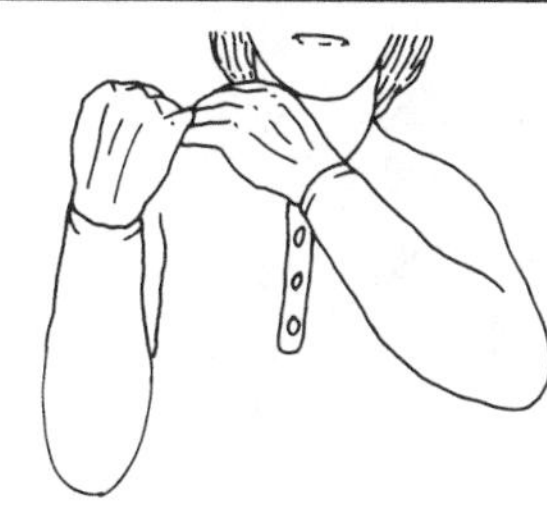

Arabic: mas uulíyya مسئولية
Chinese: zérèn 責任
Dutch: verantwoordelijkheid
French: responsabilité
German: Verantwortlichkeit
Italian: responsabilità
Japanese: sekinin 責任
Korean: ch'aegim 책임
Portuguese: responsabilidade
Russian: otvétstvennost' ответственность
Spanish: responsabilidad
Swedish: ansvar

1805. rest [v.]

Arabic: istaráha استراح
Chinese: xiūxí 休息
Dutch: rusten
French: se reposer
German: ruhen
Italian: riposarsi
Japanese: yasumu 休む
Korean: shwida 쉬다
Portuguese: descansar
Russian: otdykhát' отдыхать
Spanish: descansar
Swedish: vila

1806. restaurant [n.]

Arabic: mátaam مطعم
Chinese: cāngguǎn 餐館
Dutch: restaurant
French: restaurant
German: Restaurant
Italian: ristorante
Japanese: restoran レストラン
Korean: shig'dang 식당
Portuguese: restaurante
Russian: restorán ресторан
Spanish: restaurante
Swedish: restaurang

1807. restrict [v.]

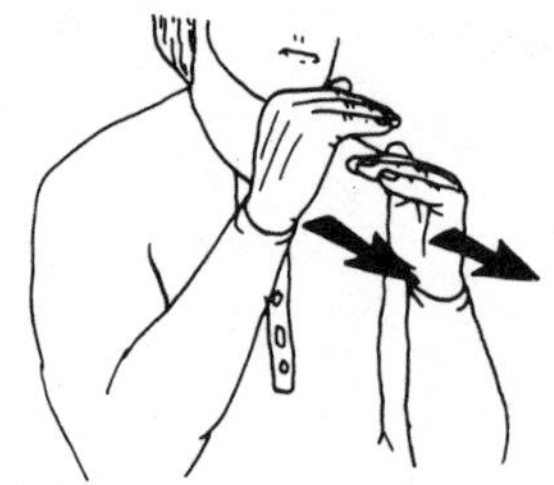

Arabic: háddada حدد
Chinese: xiànzhì 限制
Dutch: beperken
French: restreindre
German: beschränken
Italian: restringere
Japanese: seigen suru 制限する
Korean: jehanhada 제한하다
Portuguese: restringir
Russian: ograníchivat' ограничивать
Spanish: restringir
Swedish: inskränka

1808. result [n.]

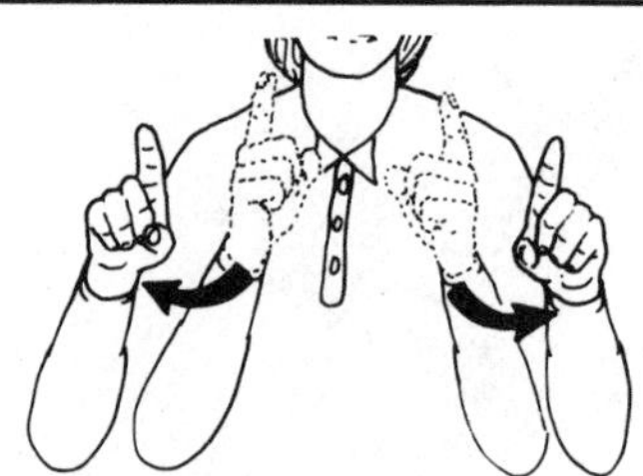

Arabic: natíja نتيجة
Chinese: jiéguǒ 結果
Dutch: resultaat
French: résultat
German: Resultat
Italian: risultato
Japanese: kekka 結果
Korean: kyŏlgwa 결과
Portuguese: resultado
Russian: rezul'tát результат
Spanish: resultado
Swedish: resultat

1809. retreat [v.]

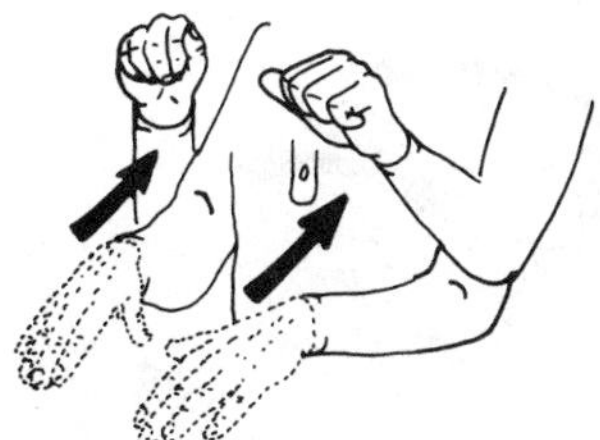

Arabic: tarájaa تراجع
Chinese: yǐntuì 引退
Dutch: zich terugtrekken
French: se retirer
German: sich zurückziehen
Italian: ritirarsi
Japanese: taikyaku suru 退却
Korean: hut'oehada 후퇴하다
Portuguese: retirar-se
Russian: otstupát' отступать
Spanish: retirarse
Swedish: retirera

1810. return [v.]

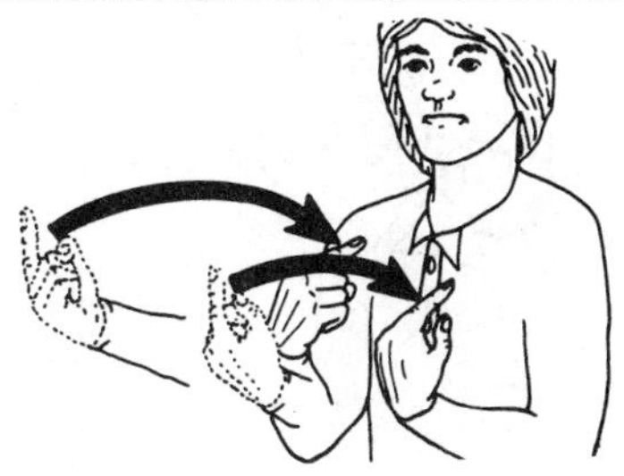

Arabic: áada عاد
Chinese: huí 回
Dutch: terugkomen
French: revenir
German: zurückkehren
Italian: restituire
Japanese: kaeru 帰る
Korean: doraoda 돌아오다
Portuguese: voltar
Russian: vozvrashchát' возвращать
Spanish: devolver
Swedish: återvända

1811. reveal [v.]

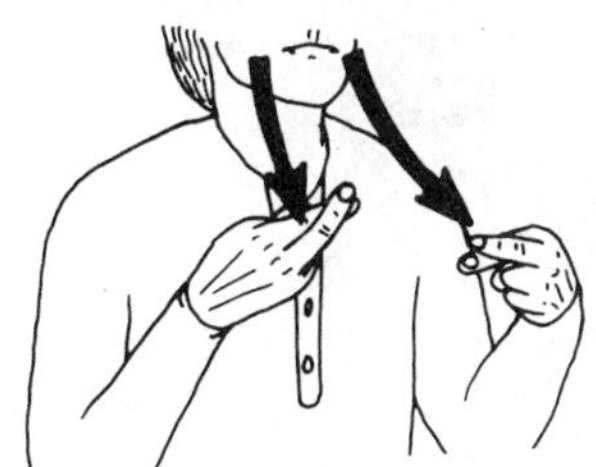

Arabic: káshafa كشف
Chinese: xiǎnxiàn 顯現
Dutch: onthullen
French: révéler
German: enthüllen
Italian: rivelare
Japanese: arawasu 現す
Korean: nat'anaeda 나타나다
Portuguese: revelar
Russian: vyyavlyát' выявлять
Spanish: revelar
Swedish: uppenbara

1812. revenge [n.]

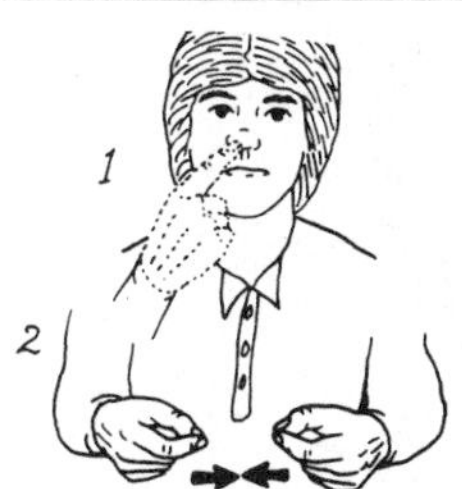

Arabic: thá'r ثأر
Chinese: fùchóu 復仇
Dutch: wraak
French: vengeance
German: Rache
Italian: vendetta
Japanese: fukushū 復讐
Korean: boksu 복수
Portuguese: vingança
Russian: revánsh реванш
Spanish: venganza
Swedish: hämnd

1813. revolution (political) [n.]

Arabic: tháura ثورة
Chinese: gémìng 革命
Dutch: revolutie
French: révolution
German: Revolution
Italian: rivoluzione
Japanese: kakumei 革命
Korean: hyŏngmyŏng 혁명
Portuguese: revolução
Russian: revolyútsiya революция
Spanish: revolución
Swedish: revolution

1814. reward [n.]

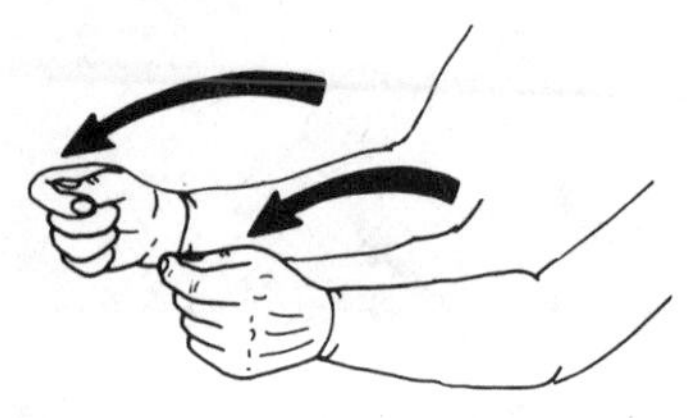

Arabic: mukáfa'a مكافأة
Chinese: bàochóu 報酬
Dutch: beloning
French: récompense
German: Belohnung
Italian: ricompensa
Japanese: hōshū 報酬
Korean: bosu 보수
Portuguese: recompensa
Russian: nagráda награда
Spanish: recompensa
Swedish: belöning

1815. rice [n.]

Arabic: aróz الرز
Chinese: mǐfàn 米飯
Dutch: rijst
French: riz
German: Reis
Italian: riso
Japanese: kome 米
Korean: ssal 쌀
Portuguese: arroz
Russian: ris рис
Spanish: arroz
Swedish: ris

1816. rich [adj.]

Arabic: gháni غني
Chinese: fùyòu 富裕
Dutch: rijk
French: riche
German: reich
Italian: ricco
Japanese: kanemochi no 金持の
Korean: p'ungbuhan 풍부한
Portuguese: rico
Russian: bogátyy богатый
Spanish: rico
Swedish: rik

1817. ride (vehicle) [v.]

Arabic: rákeba ركب
Chinese: dāchéng 搭乘
Dutch: rijden
French: monter (en, à)
German: fahren
Italian: andare in macchina
Japanese: noru 乗る
Korean: t'ada 타다
Portuguese: andar de automóvel
Russian: yékhat' ехать
Spanish: pasear en coche
Swedish: akå

1818. ridiculous [adj.]

Arabic: sakhíf سخيف
Chinese: kěxiào 可笑
Dutch: belachelijk
French: ridicule
German: lächerlich
Italian: ridicolo
Japanese: bakarashii 馬鹿らしい
Korean: usŭun 웃으운
Portuguese: ridículo
Russian: nelépyy нелепый
Spanish: ridículo
Swedish: löjlig

1819. rifle [n.]

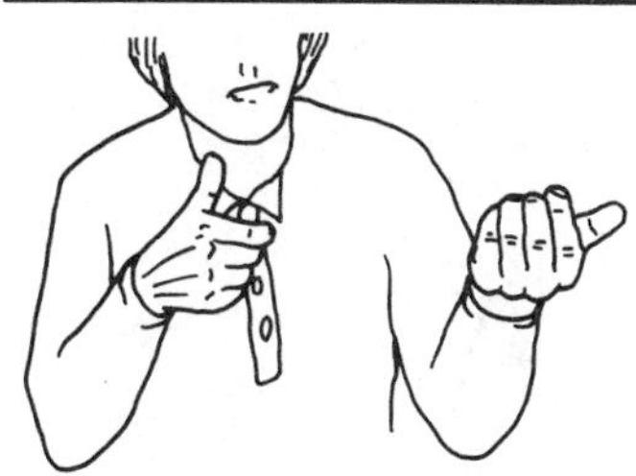

Arabic: bunduqía بندقية
Chinese: bùqiāng 步鎗
Dutch: geweer
French: fusil
German: Gewehr
Italian: fucile
Japanese: shōjū 小銃
Korean: soch'ong 소총
Portuguese: rifle
Russian: vintóvka винтовка
Spanish: rifle
Swedish: gevär

1820. right (correct) [adj.]

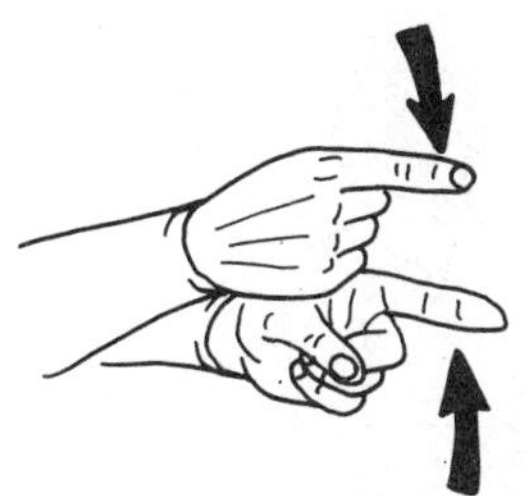

Arabic: sahíh صحيح
Chinese: zhèngquè 正確
Dutch: juist
French: correct
German: richtig
Italian: corretto
Japanese: tadashii 正しい
Korean: jŏnghwak'han 정확한
Portuguese: correto
Russian: právil'nyy правильный
Spanish: correcto
Swedish: riktig

1821. right (direction) [adj.]

Arabic: yamín يمين
Chinese: yòu 右
Dutch: rechts
French: droit
German: rechts
Italian: destra
Japanese: migi 右
Korean: orŭntchogŭi 오른쪽의
Portuguese: direita
Russian: právyy правый
Spanish: derecha
Swedish: höger

1822. right (privilege) [n.]

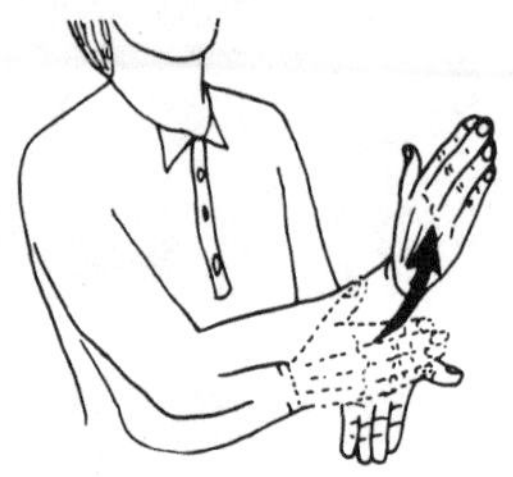

Arabic: haq حق
Chinese: quánlì 權利
Dutch: recht
French: droit
German: Recht
Italian: diritto
Japanese: kenri 権利
Korean: kwŏlli 권리
Portuguese: direito
Russian: právo право
Spanish: derecho
Swedish: rätt

1823. ring (finger) [n.]

Arabic: khátim خاتم
Chinese: jièzhǐ 戒指
Dutch: ring
French: bague
German: Ring
Italian: anello
Japanese: yubiwa 指輪
Korean: banji 반지
Portuguese: anel
Russian: kol'tsó кольцо
Spanish: anillo
Swedish: ring

1824. ring (sound) [v.]

Arabic: yátrok aj-járas يطرق الجرس
Chinese: ànlíng 按鈴
Dutch: klinken
French: sonner
German: klingeln
Italian: suonare
Japanese: naru 鳴る
Korean: ullida 울리다
Portuguese: tocar
Russian: zvonít' звонить
Spanish: sonar
Swedish: ringa

1825. ripe [adj.]

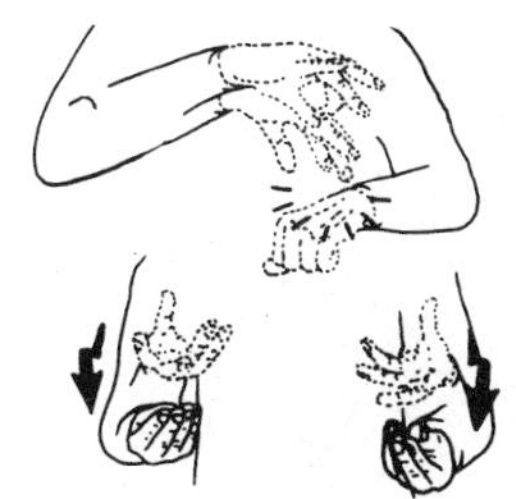

Arabic: nádej ناضج
Chinese: shóude 熟的
Dutch: rijp
French: mûr
German: reif
Italian: maturo
Japanese: jukushita 熟した
Korean: igŭn 익은
Portuguese: maduro
Russian: zrélyy зрелый
Spanish: maduro
Swedish: mogen

1826. rise (ascend) [v.]

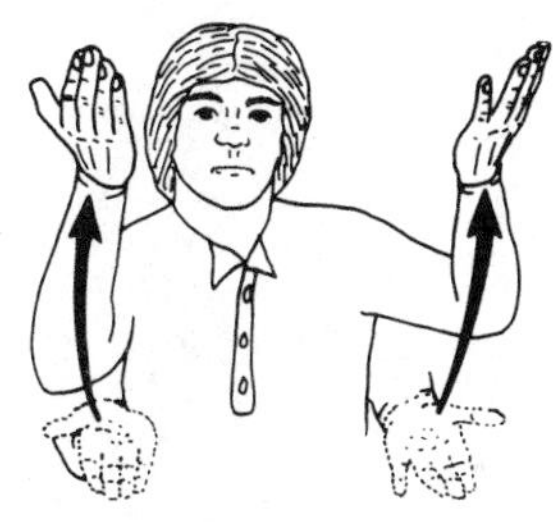

Arabic: irtáfaa ارتفع
Chinese: shàngshēng 上升
Dutch: opstijgen
French: monter
German: aufsteigen
Italian: salire
Japanese: noboru 登る
Korean: orŭda 오르다
Portuguese: subir
Russian: podnimát'sya подниматься
Spanish: subir
Swedish: stiga upp

1827. river [n.]

Arabic: nahr نهر
Chinese: hé 河
Dutch: stroom
French: fleuve
German: Fluß
Italian: fiume
Japanese: kawa 川
Korean: kang 강
Portuguese: rio
Russian: reká река
Spanish: río
Swedish: flod

1828. road [n.]

Arabic: taríq طريق
Chinese: lù 路
Dutch: weg
French: route
German: Straße
Italian: strada
Japanese: michi 道
Korean: kil 길
Portuguese: estrada
Russian: doróga дорога
Spanish: camino
Swedish: väg

1829. rob [v.]

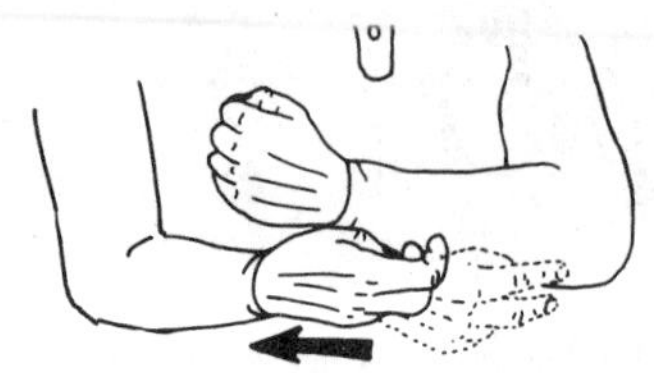

Arabic: sáraqa سرق
Chinese: qiǎng 搶
Dutch: roven
French: voler
German: rauben
Italian: derubare
Japanese: nusumu 盗む
Korean: ppaeatta 빼앗다
Portuguese: roubar
Russian: grábit' грабить
Spanish: robar
Swedish: röva

1830. rock [n.]

Arabic: sákhra صخرة
Chinese: shítóu 石頭
Dutch: rots
French: rocher
German: Felsen
Italian: roccia
Japanese: iwa 岩
Korean: bawi 바위
Portuguese: rocha
Russian: skalá скала
Spanish: roca
Swedish: klippa

1831. rocket [n.]

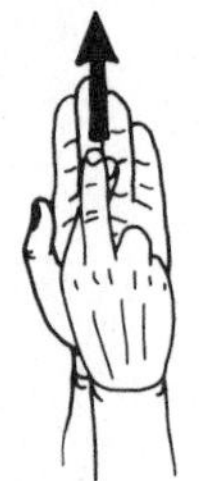

Arabic: sarúkh صاروخ
Chinese: huǒjiàn 火箭
Dutch: raket
French: fusée
German: Rakete
Italian: razzo
Japanese: roketto ロケット
Korean: roketŭ 로켓트
Portuguese: foguete
Russian: rakéta ракета
Spanish: cohete
Swedish: raket

1832. roll [v.]

Arabic: dáhraja دحرج
Chinese: gǔndòng 滾動
Dutch: rollen
French: rouler
German: rollen
Italian: arrotolare
Japanese: korogasu 転がす
Korean: kurŭda 굴르다
Portuguese: rolar
Russian: katít' катить
Spanish: rodar
Swedish: rulla

1833. Romania [n.]

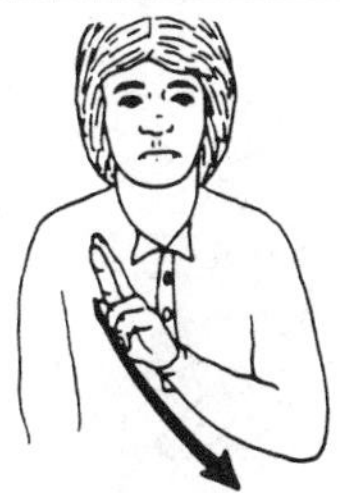

Arabic: rumánia رومانيا
Chinese: luómǎníyǎ 羅馬尼亞
Dutch: Roemenië
French: Roumanie
German: Rumänien
Italian: Romania
Japanese: Rūmania ルーマニア
Korean: Rumania 루마니아
Portuguese: Romênia
Russian: Rumýniya Румыния
Spanish: Rumania
Swedish: Rumänien

1834. roof [n.]

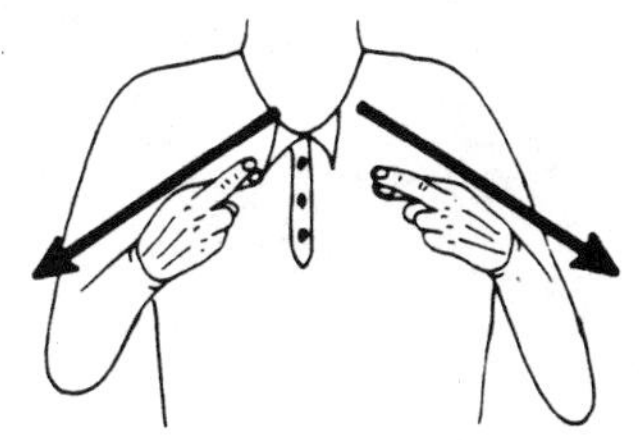

Arabic: saqf سقف
Chinese: wūdǐng 屋頂
Dutch: dak
French: toit
German: Dach
Italian: tetto
Japanese: yane 屋根
Korean: jibung 지붕
Portuguese: telhado
Russian: krýsha крыша
Spanish: techo
Swedish: tak

1835. room (building) [n.]

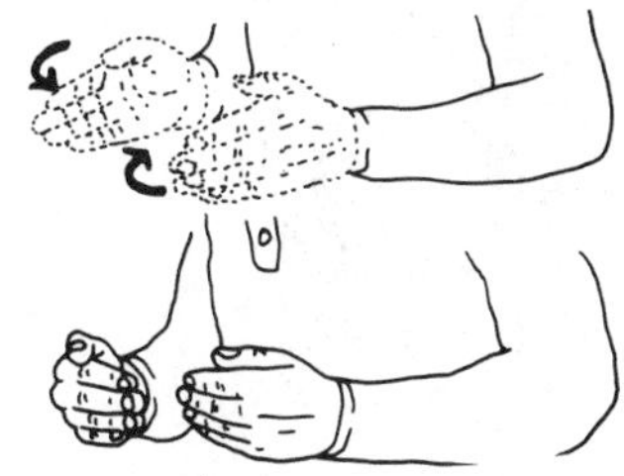

Arabic: ghórfa غرفة
Chinese: wūzi 屋子
Dutch: kamer
French: chambre
German: Zimmer
Italian: camera
Japanese: heya 部屋
Korean: bang 방
Portuguese: quarto
Russian: kómnata комната
Spanish: cuarto
Swedish: rum

1836. root [n.]

Arabic: jadhr جذر
Chinese: gēn 根
Dutch: wortel
French: racine
German: Wurzel
Italian: radice
Japanese: ne 根
Korean: ppuri 뿌리
Portuguese: raiz
Russian: kóren' корень
Spanish: raíz
Swedish: rot

1837. rope [n.]

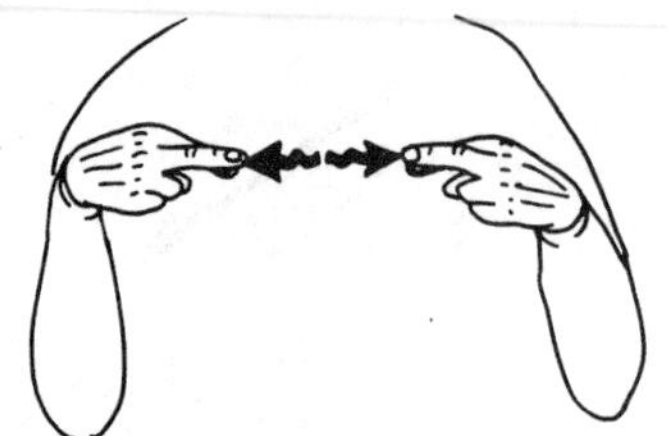

Arabic: hábl حبل
Chinese: shéngzi 繩子
Dutch: touw
French: corde
German: Seil
Italian: corda
Japanese: nawa なわ
Korean: batjul 밧줄
Portuguese: corda
Russian: veryóvka верёвка
Spanish: soga
Swedish: rep

1838. rough (not smooth) [adj.]

Arabic: kháshen خشن
Chinese: cūzào 粗糙
Dutch: ruw
French: rude
German: rauh
Italian: ruvido
Japanese: dekobokona でこぼこな
Korean: gŏch'in 거친
Portuguese: áspero
Russian: sherokhovátyy шероховатый
Spanish: áspero
Swedish: ojämn

1839. round [adj.]

Arabic: mustadír مستدير
Chinese: yuán 圓
Dutch: rond
French: rond
German: rund
Italian: rotondo
Japanese: marui 丸い
Korean: dunggŭn 둥근
Portuguese: redondo
Russian: krúglyy круглый
Spanish: redondo
Swedish: rund

1840. row (file/line) [n.]

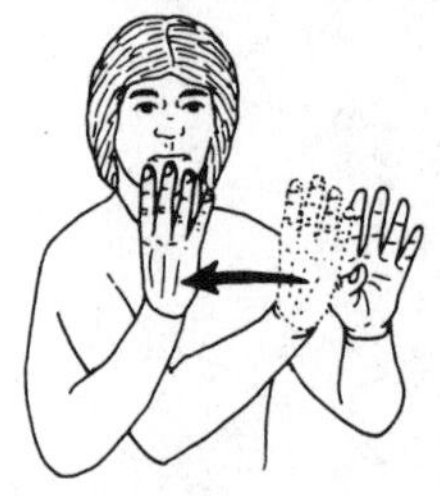

Arabic: saff صف
Chinese: pái 排
Dutch: rij
French: rang
German: Reihe
Italian: fila
Japanese: retsu 列
Korean: jul 줄
Portuguese: fila
Russian: ryad ряд
Spanish: fila
Swedish: rad

1841. rub [v.]

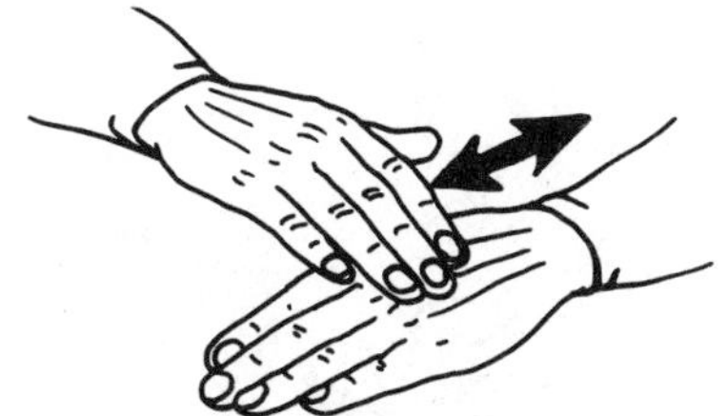

Arabic: hákka حك
Chinese: cā 擦
Dutch: wrijven
French: frotter
German: reiben
Italian: strofinare
Japanese: kosuru こする
Korean: bibida 비비다
Portuguese: esfregar
Russian: terét' тереть
Spanish: frotar
Swedish: gnida

1842. rubber (material) [n.]

Arabic: mattát مطاط
Chinese: xiàngjiāo 橡膠
Dutch: rubber
French: caoutchouc
German: Gummi
Italian: gomma
Japanese: gomu ゴム
Korean: gomu 고무
Portuguese: borracha
Russian: rezína резина
Spanish: goma
Swedish: gummi

1843. rude [adj.]

Arabic: gher muhádhdheb غير مهذب
Chinese: cūbàode 粗暴的
Dutch: grof
French: impoli
German: grob
Italian: rude
Japanese: burei na 無礼な
Korean: bŏrŭt'ŏmnŭn 버릇없는
Portuguese: rude
Russian: grúbyy грубый
Spanish: rudo
Swedish: ohövlig

1844. ruin (destruction) [n.]

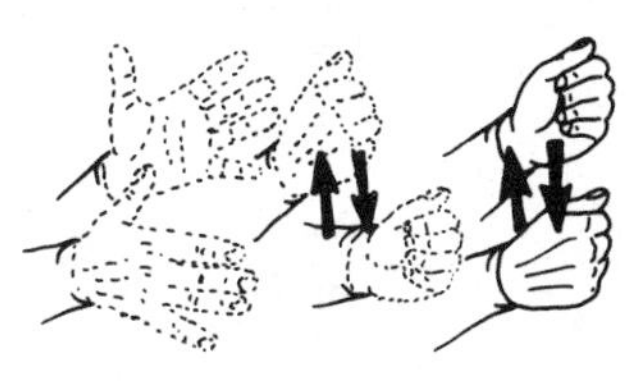

Arabic: kharáb خراب
Chinese: huǐmiè 毀滅
Dutch: ruïne
French: ruine
German: Ruine
Italian: rovina
Japanese: hakai 破壊
Korean: bunggoe 붕괴
Portuguese: ruína
Russian: gíbel' гибель
Spanish: ruina
Swedish: ruin

1845. rule (regulation) [n.]

Arabic: qanún قانون
Chinese: guīzé 規則
Dutch: regel
French: règle
German: Regel
Italian: regola
Japanese: kisoku 規則
Korean: kyuch'ik 규칙
Portuguese: regra
Russian: právilo правило
Spanish: regla
Swedish: regel

1846. run (move swiftly) [v.]

Arabic: rákada ركد
Chinese: pǎo 跑
Dutch: lopen
French: courir
German: rennen
Italian: correre
Japanese: hashiru 走る
Korean: dallida 달리다
Portuguese: correr
Russian: bégat' бегать
Spanish: correr
Swedish: springa

1847. Russia [n.]

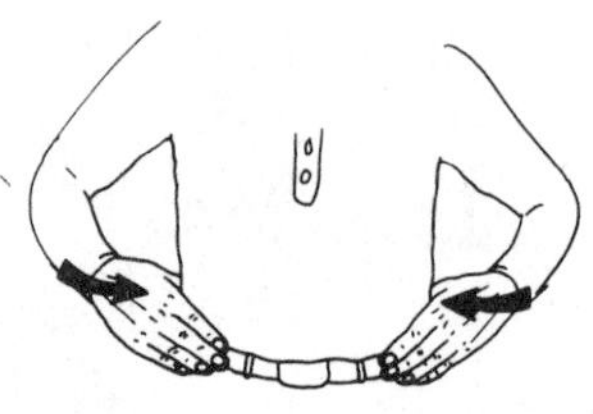

Arabic: rúsia روسيا
Chinese: èrguó 俄國
Dutch: Rusland
French: Russie
German: Russland
Italian: Russia
Japanese: Roshia ロシア
Korean: Rŏshia 러시아
Portuguese: Rússia
Russian: Rossíya Россия
Spanish: Rusia
Swedish: Ryssland

1848. Russian [adj.]

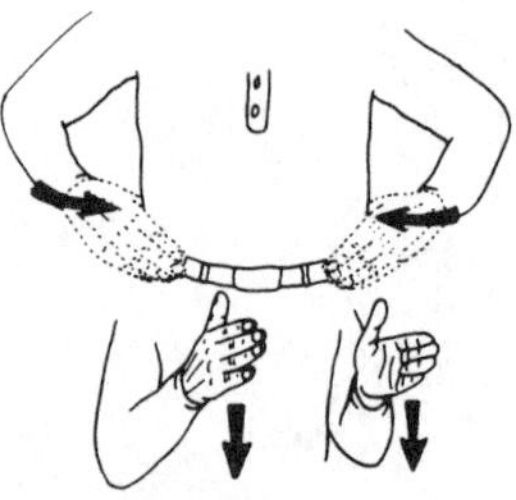

Arabic: rúsi روسي
Chinese: èrguóde 俄國的
Dutch: russisch
French: russe
German: russisch
Italian: russo
Japanese: Roshia no ロシアの
Korean: Rŏshiaŭi 러시안의
Portuguese: russo
Russian: rússkiy русский
Spanish: ruso
Swedish: rysk

1849. sacrifice [n.]

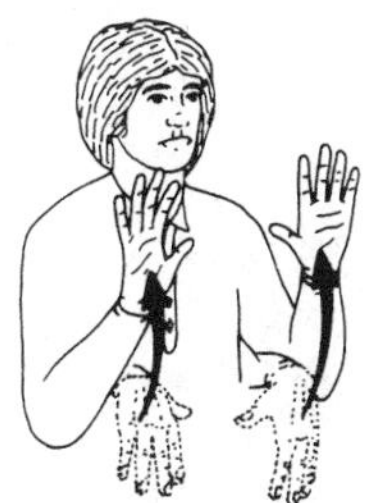

Arabic: tad-héa تضحية
Chinese: xīshēng 犧牲
Dutch: offer
French: sacrifice
German: Opfer
Italian: sacrificio
Japanese: gisei 犠牲
Korean: huisaeng 희생
Portuguese: sacrificio
Russian: zhértva жертва
Spanish: sacrificio
Swedish: offer

1850. sad [adj.]

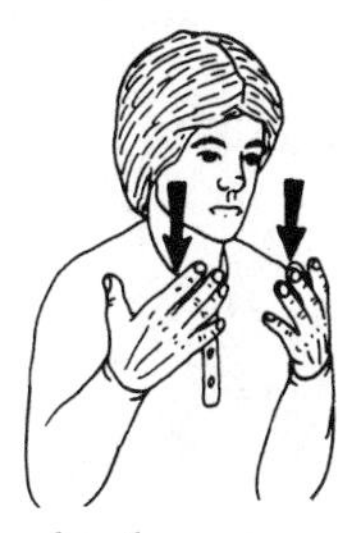

Arabic: hazín حزين
Chinese: bēishāngde 悲傷的
Dutch: bedroefd
French: triste
German: traurig
Italian: triste
Japanese: kanashii 悲しい
Korean: sŭlpŭn 슬픈
Portuguese: triste
Russian: pechál'nyy печальный
Spanish: triste
Swedish: sorgsen

1851. safe [adj.]

Arabic: salím سليم
Chinese: ānquán 安全
Dutch: veilig
French: sûr
German: sicher
Italian: sicuro
Japanese: anzen na 安心な
Korean: anjŏnhan 안전한
Portuguese: seguro
Russian: bezopásnyy безопасный
Spanish: seguro
Swedish: säker

1852. sailing [n.]

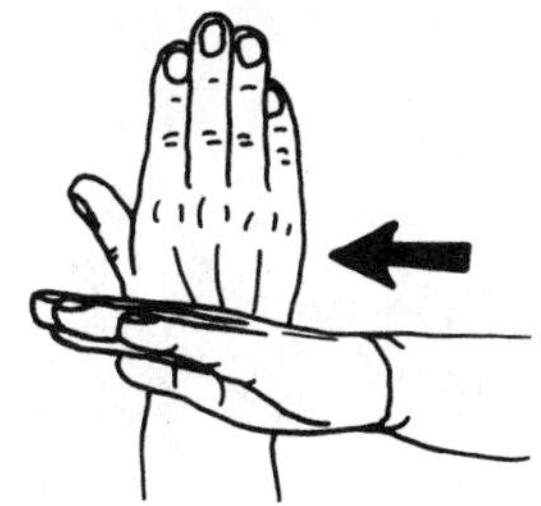

Arabic: íbhar ابحار
Chinese: hángxíng 航行
Dutch: zeilen
French: navigation
German: Segeln
Italian: navigazione
Japanese: hansō 帆走
Korean: hang'hae 항해
Portuguese: navegação
Russian: párusnyy sport парусный спорт
Spanish: navegación
Swedish: segling

1853. sailor [n.]

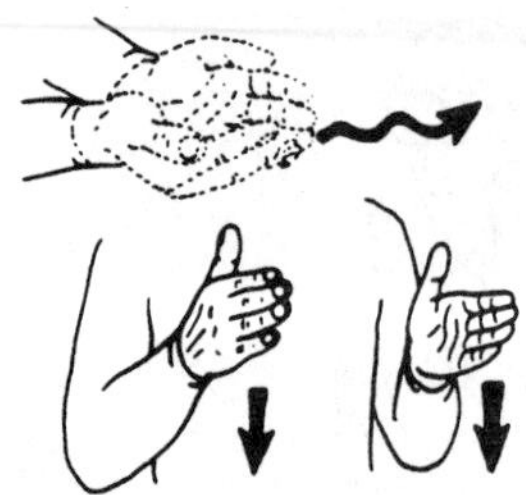

Arabic: báhhar بحار
Chinese: hǎiyuán 海員
Dutch: matroos
French: marin
German: Matrose
Italian: marinaio
Japanese: suihei 水兵
Korean: sŏnwŏn 선원
Portuguese: marinheiro
Russian: moryák моряк
Spanish: marinero
Swedish: sjöman

1854. salad [n.]

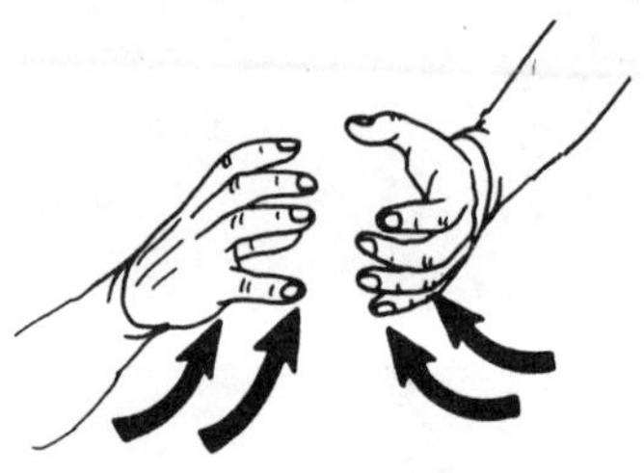

Arabic: sálata سلطة
Chinese: shēngcài 生菜
Dutch: salade
French: salade
German: Salat
Italian: insalata
Japanese: sarada サラダ
Korean: saellŏdŭ 샐러드
Portuguese: salada
Russian: salát салат
Spanish: ensalada
Swedish: sallad

1855. salary [n.]

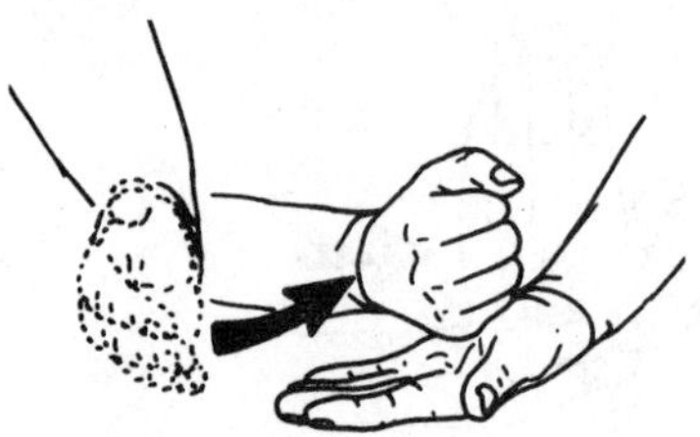

Arabic: ráteb راتب
Chinese: xīnshuǐ 薪水
Dutch: salaris
French: salaire
German: Gehalt
Italian: salario
Japanese: kyūryō 給料
Korean: bonggŭp 봉급
Portuguese: salário
Russian: zhálovan'ye жалованье
Spanish: salario
Swedish: lön

1856. sale [n.]

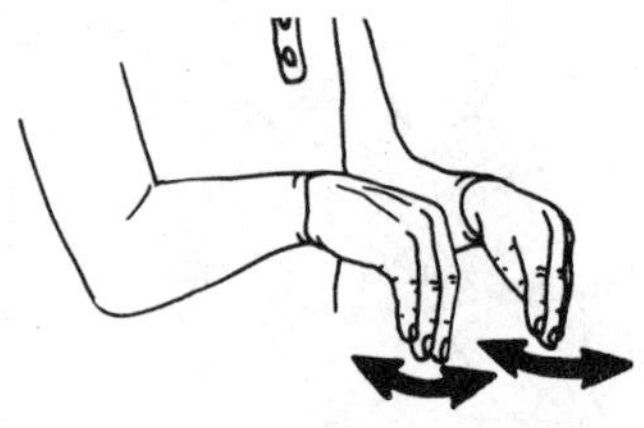

Arabic: béyaa بيع
Chinese: pāimài 拍賣
Dutch: verkoop
French: vente
German: Verkauf
Italian: vendita
Japanese: hambai 販売
Korean: p'anmae 판매
Portuguese: venda
Russian: prodázha продажа
Spanish: venta
Swedish: försäljning

1857. salesperson [n.]

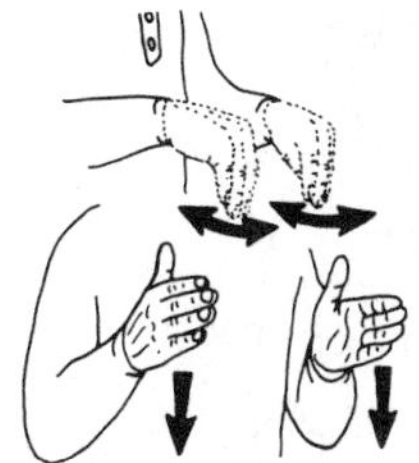

Arabic: beyáa بياع
Chinese: tuīxiāoyuán 推銷員
Dutch: verkoper
French: vendeur
German: Verkäufer
Italian: venditore
Japanese: ten-in 店員
Korean: p'anmaewŏn 판매원
Portuguese: vendedor
Russian: prodavéts продавец
Spanish: vendedor
Swedish: försäljare

1858. salt [n.]

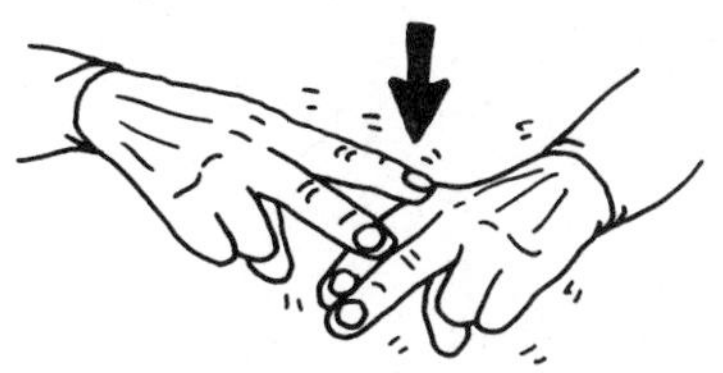

Arabic: milh ملح
Chinese: yán 鹽
Dutch: zout
French: sel
German: Salz
Italian: sale
Japanese: shio 塩
Korean: sogŭm 소금
Portuguese: sal
Russian: sol' соль
Spanish: sal
Swedish: salt

1859. same [adj.]

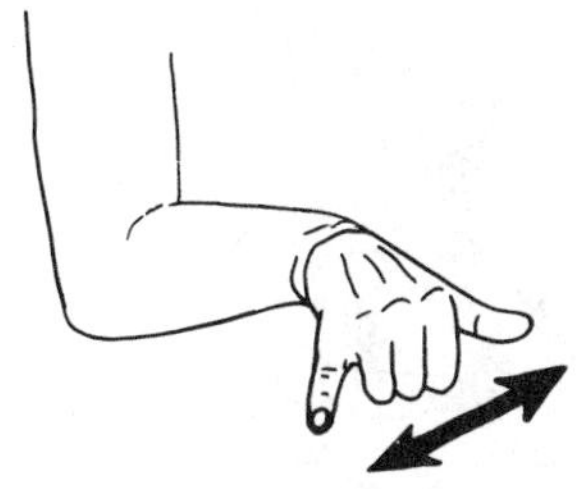

Arabic: nafs نفس
Chinese: xiānftóng 相同
Dutch: dezelfde/hetzelfde
French: même
German: derselbe
Italian: stesso
Japanese: onaji 同じ
Korean: kat'ŭn 같은
Portuguese: mesmo
Russian: tot zhe sámyy
тот же самый
Spanish: mismo
Swedish: samma

1860. sample [n.]

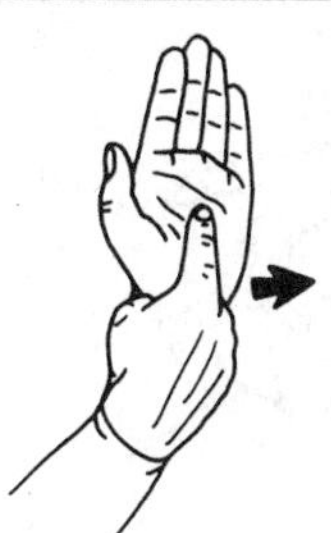

Arabic: aaína عينة
Chinese: yàngpǐn 様品
Dutch: monster
French: échantillon
German: Probe
Italian: campione
Japanese: mihon 見本
Korean: kyŏnbon 견본
Portuguese: amostra
Russian: obrazéts образец
Spanish: muestra
Swedish: provbit

1861. sand [n.]

Arabic: rámil رمل
Chinese: shā 沙
Dutch: zand
French: sable
German: Sand
Italian: sabbia
Japanese: suna 砂
Korean: morae 모래
Portuguese: areia
Russian: pesók песок
Spanish: arena
Swedish: sand

1862. sandwich [n.]

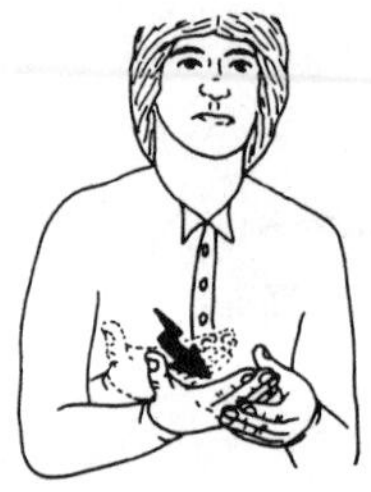

Arabic: sándwich ساندويتش
Chinese: sānmínzhì 三明治
Dutch: sandwich
French: sandwich
German: belegtes Brot
Italian: panino imbottito
Japanese: sandoitchi サンドイッチ
Korean: saendŭwitch 샌드위치
Portuguese: sanduiche
Russian: sándvich сандвич
Spanish: sandwich
Swedish: smörgås

1863. satellite [n.]

Arabic: tábeaa تابع
Chinese: wèixīng 衛星
Dutch: satelliet
French: satellite
German: Satellit
Italian: satellite
Japanese: eisei 衛星
Korean: wisŏng 위성
Portuguese: satélite
Russian: spútnik спутник
Spanish: satélite
Swedish: satellit

1864. satisfaction [n.]

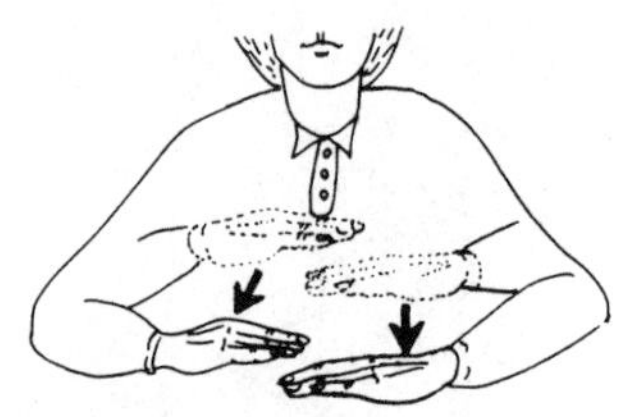

Arabic: rída رضا
Chinese: mǎnzú 滿足
Dutch: voldoening
French: satisfaction
German: Befriedigung
Italian: soddisfazione
Japanese: manzoku 満足
Korean: manjok 만족
Portuguese: satisfação
Russian: udovletvoréniye удовлетворение
Spanish: satisfacción
Swedish: tillfredsställning

1865. Saturday [n.]

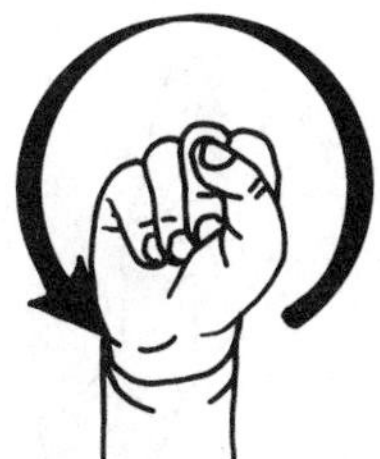

Arabic: as-sábt السبت
Chinese: xīngqí liù 星期六
Dutch: zaterdag
French: samedi
German: Samstag
Italian: sabato
Japanese: doyōbi 土曜日
Korean: t'oyoil 토요일
Portuguese: sábado
Russian: subbóta суббота
Spanish: sábado
Swedish: lördag

1866. sausage [n.]

Arabic: sújuq سجق
Chinese: xiāngcháng 香腸
Dutch: worst
French: saucisse
German: Wurst
Italian: salsiccia
Japanese: sōsēji ソーセージ
Korean: ssoseiji 쏘세지
Portuguese: salsicha
Russian: kolbasá колбаса
Spanish: salchicha
Swedish: korv

1867. save (lives) [v.]

Arabic: ánqadha انقذ
Chinese: zhěngjiù 拯救
Dutch: redden
French: sauver
German: retten
Italian: salvare
Japanese: sukuu 救う
Korean: kuhae naeda 구해내다
Portuguese: salvar
Russian: spasát' спасать
Spanish: salvar
Swedish: rädda

1868. saw [n.]

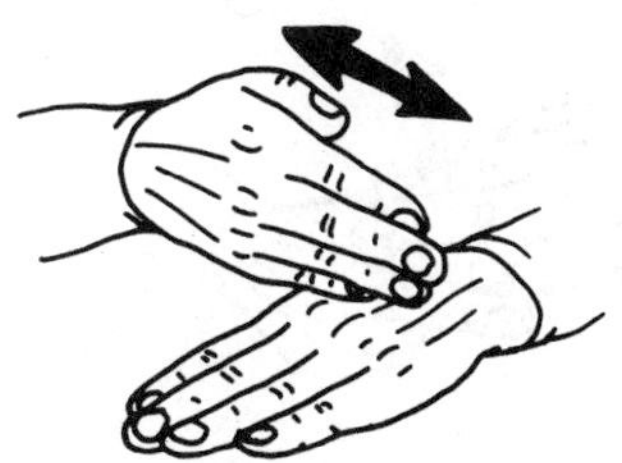

Arabic: minshár منشار
Chinese: jǜzi 鋸子
Dutch: zaag
French: scie
German: Säge
Italian: sega
Japanese: nokogiri 鋸
Korean: t'op 톱
Portuguese: serra
Russian: pilá пила
Spanish: sierra
Swedish: såg

1869. say [v.]

Arabic: qála قال
Chinese: shuō 說
Dutch: zeggen
French: dire
German: sagen
Italian: dire
Japanese: iu 言う
Korean: marhada 말하다
Portuguese: dizer
Russian: govorít' говорить
Spanish: decir
Swedish: säga

1870. scale (degree) [n.]

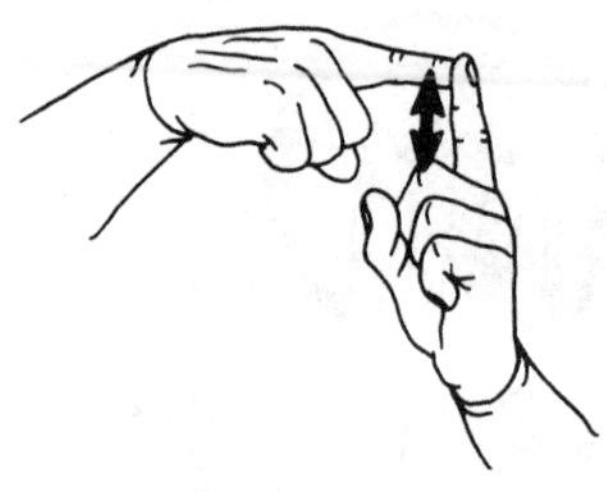

Arabic: mizán ميزان
Chinese: biāodù 標度
Dutch: schaal
French: échelle
German: Maßstab
Italian: scala
Japanese: memori 目盛り
Korean: jŏngdo 정도
Portuguese: escala
Russian: masshtáb масштаб
Spanish: escala
Swedish: måttstock

1871. scale(s) (weight) [n.]

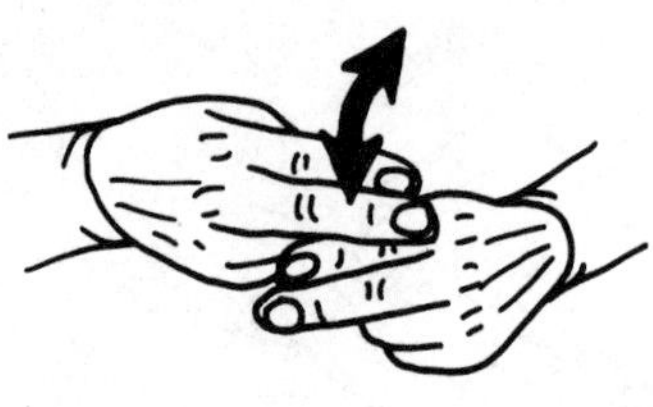

Arabic: mizán ميزان
Chinese: bàngcèng 磅稱
Dutch: weegschaal
French: balance
German: Waage
Italian: bilancia
Japanese: hakari 秤り
Korean: jŏul 저울
Portuguese: balança
Russian: vesý весы
Spanish: balanza
Swedish: våg

1872. scarce [adj.]

Arabic: náder نادر
Chinese: quēfá 缺乏
Dutch: schaars
French: rare
German: spärlich
Italian: scarso
Japanese: marena 稀な
Korean: dŭmun 드문
Portuguese: escasso
Russian: skúdnyy скудный
Spanish: escaso
Swedish: knapp

1873. scare [v.]

Arabic: áfzaa افزع
Chinese: pà 怕
Dutch: schrikken
French: effrayer
German: erschrecken
Italian: spaventare
Japanese: odokasu 驚かす
Korean: nollagehada 놀라게하다
Portuguese: assustar
Russian: pugát' пугать
Spanish: asustar
Swedish: skrämma

1874. scatter [v.]

Arabic: náthara نثر
Chinese: sànbù 散佈
Dutch: verstrooien
French: disperser
German: zerstreuen
Italian: sparpagliare
Japanese: chirabaru 散らばる
Korean: ppurida 뿌리다
Portuguese: espalhar
Russian: razbrásyvat' разбрасывать
Spanish: esparcir
Swedish: beströ

1875. scene [n.]

Arabic: mándhar منظر
Chinese: jǐngsèi 景色
Dutch: scene
French: scène
German: Szene
Italian: scena
Japanese: gemba 現場
Korean: jangmyŏn 장면
Portuguese: cena
Russian: stséna сцена
Spanish: escena
Swedish: scen

1876. scent (smell) [n.]

Arabic: as-shám الشم
Chinese: qìwèi 氣味
Dutch: geur
French: odeur
German: Geruch
Italian: odore
Japanese: nioi 匂い
Korean: naemsae 냄새
Portuguese: cheiro
Russian: zápakh запах
Spanish: olor
Swedish: lukt

1877. scheme (plan) [n.]

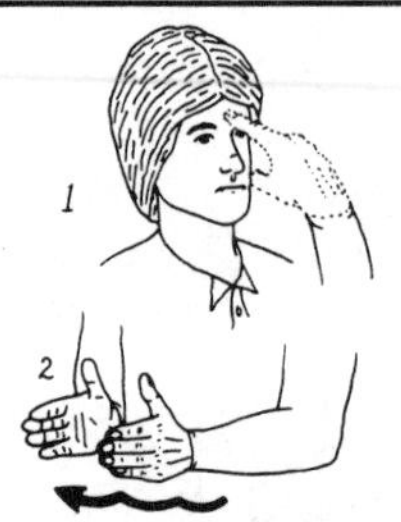

Arabic: mukháttat مخطط
Chinese: fāngàn 方案
Dutch: schema
French: système
German: Schema
Italian: schema
Japanese: keikaku 計画
Korean: kyehoek 계획
Portuguese: esquema
Russian: skhéma схема
Spanish: esquema
Swedish: schema

1878. school [n.]

Arabic: mádrasa مدرسة
Chinese: xuéxiào 學校
Dutch: school
French: école
German: Schule
Italian: scuola
Japanese: gakkō 学校
Korean: hakkyo 학교
Portuguese: escola
Russian: shkóla школа
Spanish: escuela
Swedish: skola

1879. science [n.]

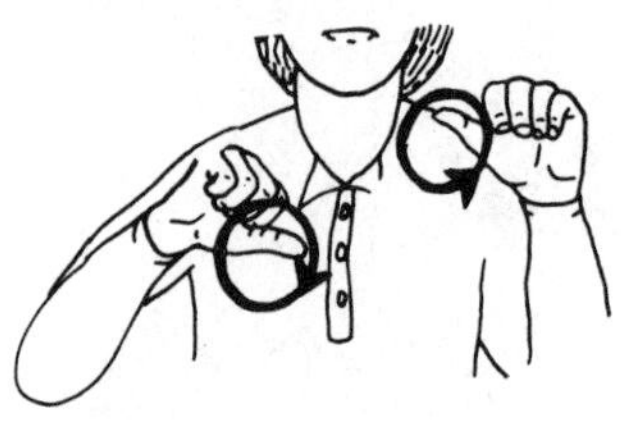

Arabic: elm علم
Chinese: kēxué 科學
Dutch: wetenschap
French: science
German: Wissenschaft
Italian: scienza
Japanese: kagaku 科学
Korean: kwahak 과학
Portuguese: ciência
Russian: naúka наука
Spanish: ciencia
Swedish: vetenskap

1880. scissors [n.]

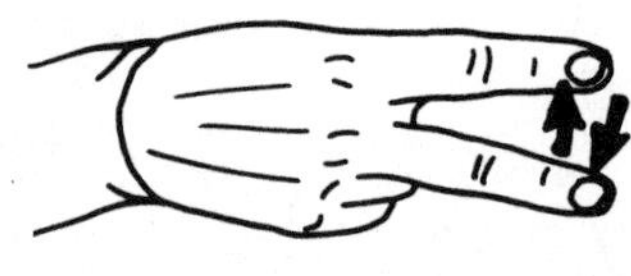

Arabic: máqas مقص
Chinese: jiǎndāo 剪刀
Dutch: schaar
French: ciseaux
German: Schere
Italian: forbici
Japanese: hasami 鋏
Korean: kawi 가위
Portuguese: tesoura
Russian: nózhnitsy ножницы
Spanish: tijeras
Swedish: sax

1881. scold [v.]

Arabic: wábbakha وبخ
Chinese: mà 罵
Dutch: bekijven
French: gronder
German: beschimpfen
Italian: sgridare
Japanese: shikaru 叱る
Korean: kkujitta 꾸짖다
Portuguese: ralhar
Russian: braníť бранить
Spanish: regañar
Swedish: gräla på

1882. score (game) [n.]

Arabic: isába اصابة
Chinese: défēn 得分
Dutch: stand
French: nombre de points
German: Spielergebnis
Italian: punteggio
Japanese: sukoā スコア
Korean: dŭkjŏm 득점
Portuguese: marcador
Russian: schyót счёт
Spanish: tantos
Swedish: poängsumma

1883. Scotland [n.]

Arabic: iskutlánda اسكتلندا
Chinese: sūgélán 蘇格蘭
Dutch: Schotland
French: Écosse
German: Schottland
Italian: Scozia
Japanese: Sukottorando スコットランド
Korean: Sŭk'ot'ŭllaendŭ 스코트랜드
Portuguese: Escócia
Russian: Shotlándiya Шотландия
Spanish: Escocia
Swedish: Skottland

1884. scratch [v.]

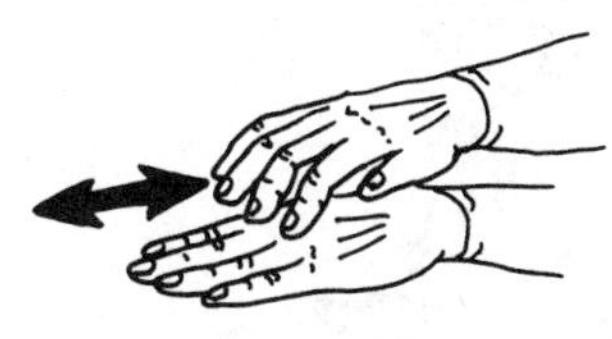

Arabic: khárbasha خربش
Chinese: zhuā 抓
Dutch: krassen
French: gratter
German: kratzen
Italian: grattare
Japanese: hikkaku 引っ掻く
Korean: halk'wida 할키다
Portuguese: arranhar
Russian: tsarápat' царапать
Spanish: arañar
Swedish: klösa

1885. scream [v.]

Arabic: sárakha صرخ
Chinese: jiānjiào 尖叫
Dutch: schreeuwen
French: crier
German: schreien
Italian: gridare
Japanese: himei o ageru 悲鳴をあげる
Korean: sorijirŭda 소리지르다
Portuguese: gritar
Russian: krichát' кричать
Spanish: gritar
Swedish: skrika

1886. sculpture [n.]

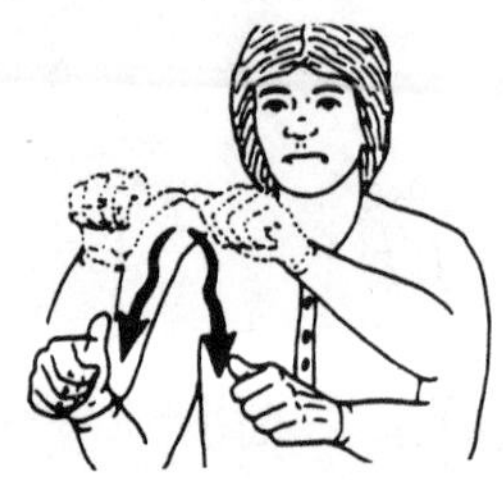

Arabic: timthál تمثال
Chinese: diāoxiàng 雕像
Dutch: beeldhouwwerk
French: sculpture
German: Skulptur
Italian: scultura
Japanese: chōkoku 彫刻
Korean: jogak 조각
Portuguese: escultura
Russian: skul'ptúra скульптура
Spanish: escultura
Swedish: skulptur

1887. sea [n.]

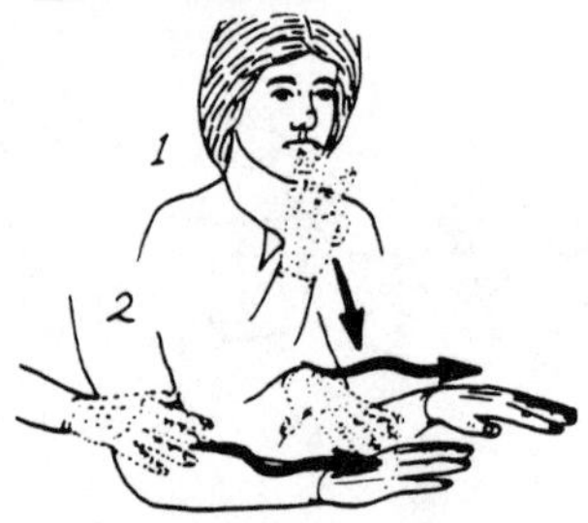

Arabic: báhar بحر
Chinese: hǎi 海
Dutch: zee
French: mer
German: Meer
Italian: mare
Japanese: umi 海
Korean: bada 바다
Portuguese: mar
Russian: móre море
Spanish: mar
Swedish: hav

1888. seal (stamp) [n.]

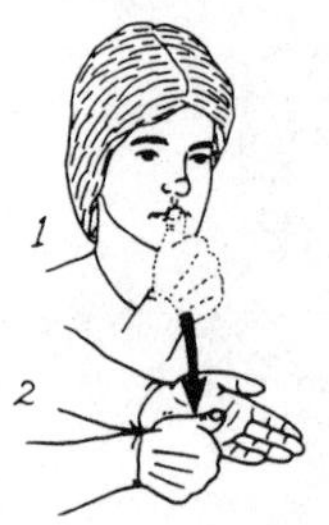

Arabic: khatm ختم
Chinese: yìnzhāng 印章
Dutch: zegel
French: timbre
German: Siegel
Italian: sigillo
Japanese: fūin 封印
Korean: dojang 도장
Portuguese: sêlo
Russian: pechát' печать
Spanish: sello
Swedish: sigill

1889. search [v.]

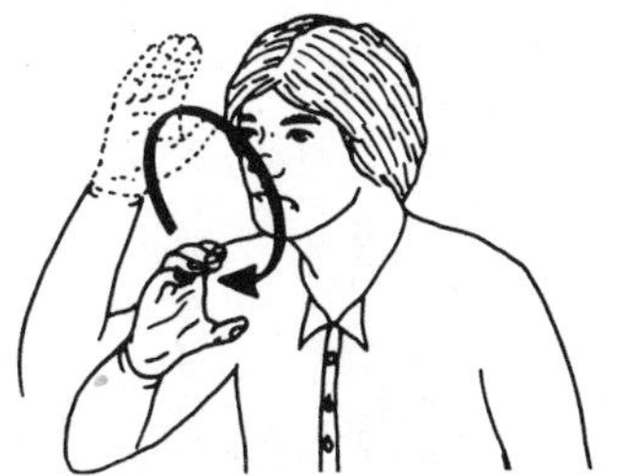

Arabic: báhatha بحث
Chinese: sōuchá 搜查
Dutch: zoeken
French: chercher
German: suchen
Italian: cercare
Japanese: sagasu 捜す
Korean: ch'atta 찾다
Portuguese: buscar
Russian: obýskivat' обыскивать
Spanish: buscar
Swedish: söka

1890. season [n.]

Arabic: fasl فصل
Chinese: jìjié 季節
Dutch: jaargetijde
French: saison
German: Jahreszeit
Italian: stagione
Japanese: kisetsu 季節
Korean: kyejŏl 계절
Portuguese: estação
Russian: sezón сезон
Spanish: estación
Swedish: årstrid

1891. seat [n.]

Arabic: máqaad مقعد
Chinese: zuòwèi 座位
Dutch: zitplaats
French: siège
German: Sitzplatz
Italian: sedile
Japanese: seki 席
Korean: jwasŏk 좌석
Portuguese: assento
Russian: mésto место
Spanish: asiento
Swedish: sittplats

1892. second (time) [n.]

Arabic: tháni ثاني
Chinese: miǎo 秒
Dutch: seconde
French: seconde
German: Sekunde
Italian: secondo
Japanese: byō 秒
Korean: ch'o 초
Portuguese: segundo
Russian: sekúnda секунда
Spanish: segundo
Swedish: sekund

1893. secret [n.]

Arabic: sirr سر
Chinese: mìmì 秘密
Dutch: geheim
French: secret
German: Geheimnis
Italian: segreto
Japanese: himitsu 秘密
Korean: bimil 비밀
Portuguese: segrêdo
Russian: táyna тайна
Spanish: secreto
Swedish: hemlighet

1894. secretary [n.]

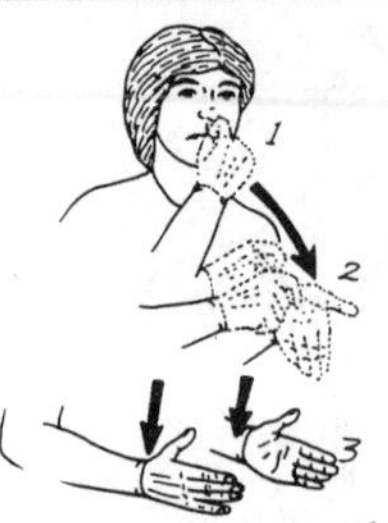

Arabic: sekretér سكرتير
Chinese: mìshū 秘書
Dutch: secretaresse
French: secrétaire
German: Sekretär
Italian: segretario
Japanese: hisho 秘書
Korean: bisŏ 비서
Portuguese: secretário
Russian: sekretár' секретарь
Spanish: secretaria
Swedish: sekreterare

1895. see [v.]

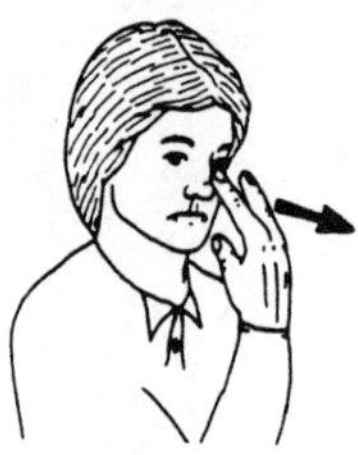

Arabic: ra'a رآى
Chinese: kàn 看
Dutch: zien
French: voir
German: sehen
Italian: vedere
Japanese: miru 見る
Korean: boda 보다
Portuguese: ver
Russian: vídet' видеть
Spanish: ver
Swedish: se

1896. seed [n.]

Arabic: bédhra بذرة
Chinese: zhŏngzi 種子
Dutch: zaad
French: semence
German: Samen
Italian: seme
Japanese: tane 種
Korean: ssi 씨
Portuguese: semente
Russian: sémya семя
Spanish: semilla
Swedish: frö

1897. seem [v.]

Arabic: yábdu يبدو
Chinese: haŏxiàng 好像
Dutch: lijken
French: sembler
German: scheinen
Italian: sembrare
Japanese: . . .rashii …らしい
Korean: boida 보이다
Portuguese: parecer
Russian: kazát'sya казаться
Spanish: parecer
Swedish: förefalla

1898. seize [v.]

Arabic: istáula áala استولى على
Chinese: bŭzhuā 捕抓
Dutch: grijpen
French: saisir
German: ergreifen
Italian: prendere
Japanese: toraeru 捕える
Korean: butjabda 붙잡다
Portuguese: agarrar
Russian: zakhvátyvat' захватывать
Spanish: agarrar
Swedish: gripa

1899. seldom [adv.]

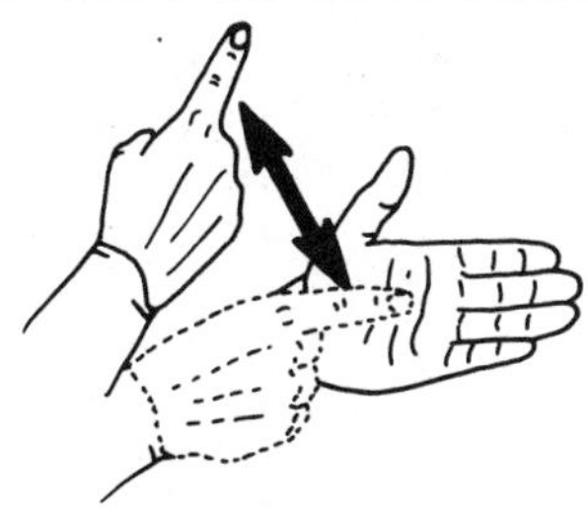

Arabic: nádiran نادراً
Chinese: hĕnshăo 很少
Dutch: zelden
French: rarement
German: selten
Italian: raramente
Japanese: mare ni 稀に
Korean: jomch'ŏrŏm. . .haji ant'a
좀처럼 ~하지 않다
Portuguese: raramente
Russian: rédko редко
Spanish: raramente
Swedish: sällan

1900. select [v.]

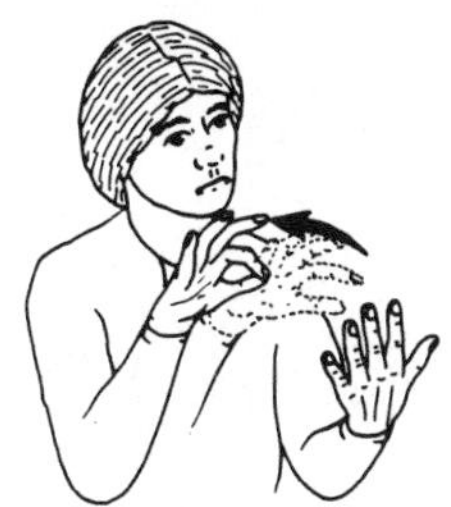

Arabic: ikhtára اختار
Chinese: xuăn 選
Dutch: uitkiezen
French: choisir
German: auswählen
Italian: scegliere
Japanese: erabu 選ぶ
Korean: korŭda 고르다
Portuguese: selecionar
Russian: otbirát' отбирать
Spanish: seleccionar
Swedish: utvälja

1901. selfish [adj.]

Arabic: anáni اناني
Chinese: zìsī 自私
Dutch: zelfzuchtig
French: égoïste
German: selbstsüchtig
Italian: egoistico
Japanese: wagamama na 我がままな
Korean: igichŏk 이기적
Portuguese: egoísta
Russian: egoistíchnyy эгоистичный
Spanish: egoísta
Swedish: självisk

1902. sell [v.]

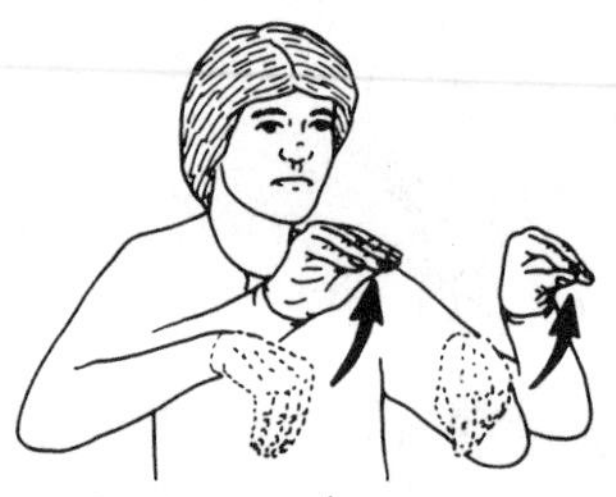

Arabic: bá-aa باع
Chinese: mài 賣
Dutch: verkopen
French: vendre
German: verkaufen
Italian: vendere
Japanese: uru 売る
Korean: p'alda 팔다
Portuguese: vender
Russian: prodavát' продавать
Spanish: vender
Swedish: sälja

1903. send [v.]

Arabic: ársala ارسل
Chinese: sòng 送
Dutch: zenden
French: envoyer
German: senden
Italian: inviare
Japanese: okuru 送る
Korean: bonaeda 보내다
Portuguese: enviar
Russian: posylát' посылать
Spanish: enviar
Swedish: sända

1904. sense (feeling) [n.]

Arabic: ehsás إحساس
Chinese: gănjué 感覺
Dutch: gevoel
French: sens
German: Sinn
Italian: senso
Japanese: kankaku 感覚
Korean: gamgak 감각
Portuguese: sentido
Russian: chúvstvo чувство
Spanish: sentido
Swedish: sinne

1905. sense (meaning) [n.]

Arabic: máana معنى
Chinese: yìyì 意義
Dutch: betekenis
French: sens
German: Bedeutung
Italian: senso
Japanese: imi 意味
Korean: kamgak 감각
Portuguese: sentido
Russian: smysl смысл
Spanish: significado
Swedish: betydelse

1906. sensitive [adj.]

Arabic: hassás حساس
Chinese: mǐngǎn 敏感
Dutch: gevoelig
French: sensible
German: empfindlich
Italian: sensibile
Japanese: binkan na 敏感な
Korean: min'gamhan 민감한
Portuguese: sensível
Russian: chuvstvítel'nyy чувствительный
Spanish: sensible
Swedish: känslig

1907. sentence (grammar) [n.]

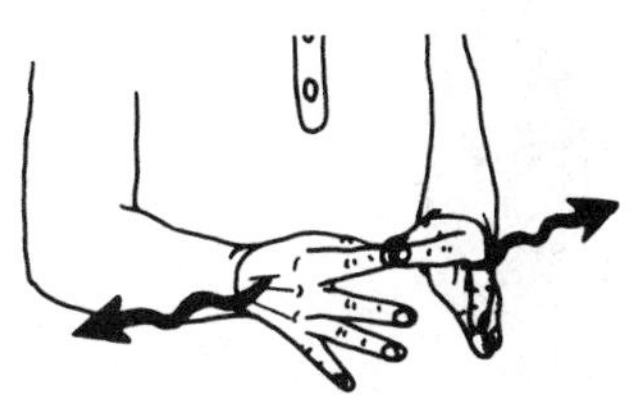

Arabic: júmla جملة
Chinese: jùzi 句子
Dutch: zin
French: phrase
German: Satz
Italian: frase
Japanese: bun 文
Korean: munjang 문장
Portuguese: frase
Russian: fráza фраза
Spanish: frase
Swedish: mening

1908. sentence (legal) [n.]

Arabic: hukm حكم
Chinese: pànxíng 判刑
Dutch: vonnis
French: jugement
German: Urteil
Italian: condanna
Japanese: hanketsu 判決
Korean: p'angyŏl 판결
Portuguese: sentença
Russian: prigovór приговор
Spanish: sentencia
Swedish: dom

1909. separate [adj.]

Arabic: munfásel منفصل
Chinese: fēnkāi 分開
Dutch: afzonderlijk
French: séparé
German: getrennt
Italian: separato
Japanese: wakareta 分れた
Korean: kaegaeŭi 개개의
Portuguese: separado
Russian: otdél'nyy отдельный
Spanish: separado
Swedish: avskild

1910. separate [v.]

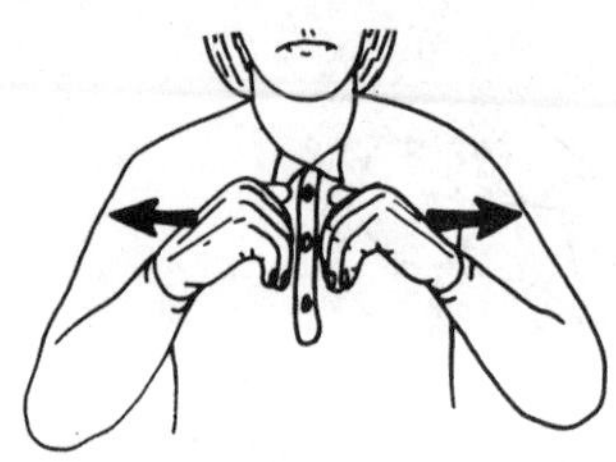

Arabic: fasl فصل
Chinese: fēnlí 分離
Dutch: scheiden
French: séparer
German: trennen
Italian: separare
Japanese: wakareru 分れる
Korean: bullihada 분리하다
Portuguese: separar
Russian: otdelyát' отделять
Spanish: separar
Swedish: avskilja

1911. September [n.]

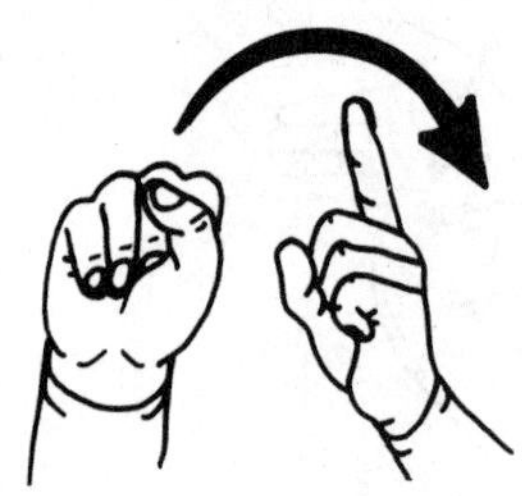

Arabic: sebtémber سبتمبر
Chinese: jiŭyuè 九月
Dutch: september
French: septembre
German: September
Italian: settembre
Japanese: kugatsu 九月
Korean: kuwŏl 구월
Portuguese: setembro
Russian: sentyábr' сентябрь
Spanish: septiembre
Swedish: september

1912. serious [adj.]

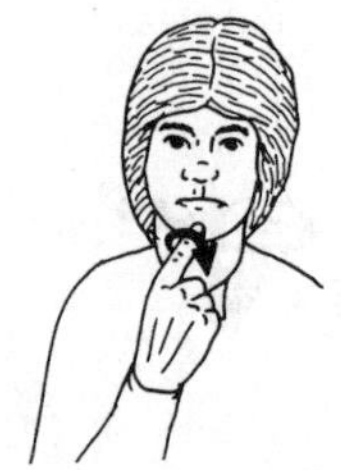

Arabic: jéddi جدي
Chinese: yánzhòngde 嚴重的
Dutch: ernstig
French: sérieux
German: ernsthaft
Italian: serio
Japanese: majimena 真面目な
Korean: shimgak'han 심각한
Portuguese: sério
Russian: ser'yóznyy серьёзный
Spanish: serio
Swedish: seriös

1913. servant [n.]

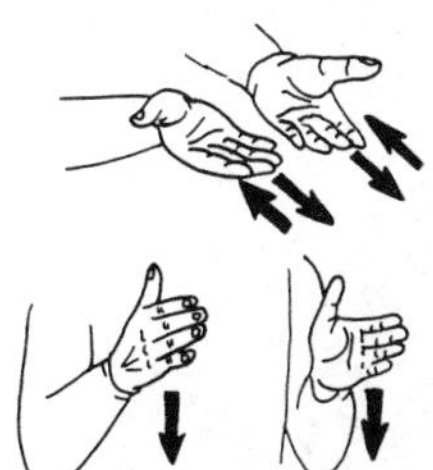

Arabic: khádim/khádima خادم / خادمة
Chinese: púrén 僕人
Dutch: bediende
French: domestique
German: Diener
Italian: servitore
Japanese: meshitsukai 召使い
Korean: hain 하인
Portuguese: servente
Russian: slugá слуга
Spanish: criado
Swedish: betjänt

1914. service (work) [n.]

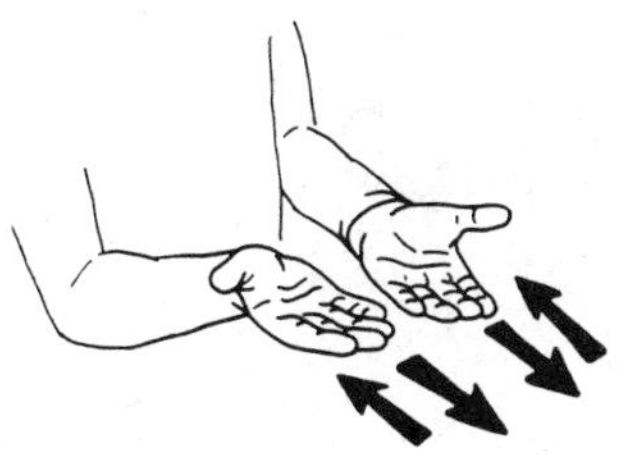

Arabic: khídma خدمة
Chinese: fúwù 服務
Dutch: dienst
French: service
German: Dienst
Italian: servizio
Japanese: tsutome 務め
Korean: bongsa 봉사
Portuguese: serviço
Russian: slúzhba служба
Spanish: servicio
Swedish: tjänst

1915. service (maintenance) [n.]

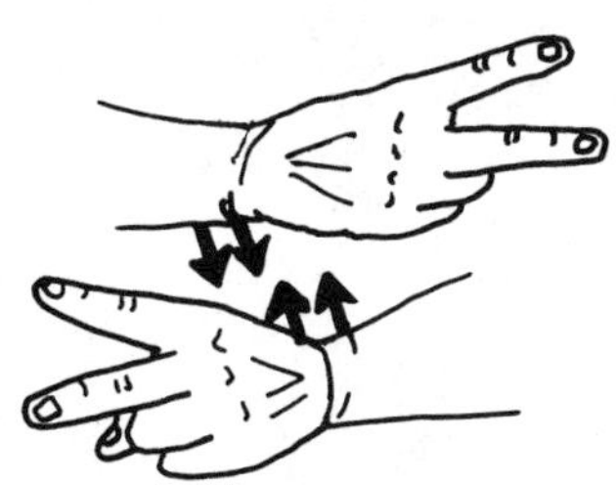

Arabic: siána صيانة
Chinese: baŏyǎng 保養
Dutch: onderhoud
French: entretien
German: Instandhaltung
Italian: manutenzione
Japanese: teire 手入れ
Korean: bojon 보존
Portuguese: manutenção
Russian: obslúzhivaniye обслуживание
Spanish: mantenimiento
Swedish: underhåll

1916. seven [adj.]

Arabic: sábaa سبعة
Chinese: qī 七
Dutch: zeven
French: sept
German: sieben
Italian: sette
Japanese: nana 七
Korean: ilgop 일곱
Portuguese: sete
Russian: sem' семь
Spanish: siete
Swedish: sju

1917. seventeen [adj.]

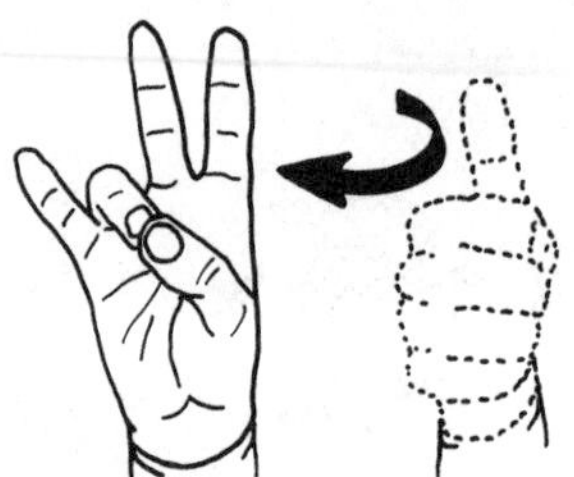

Arabic: sábaat áashar سبعة عشر
Chinese: shíqī 十七
Dutch: zeventien
French: dix-sept
German: siebzehn
Italian: diciassette
Japanese: jūnana 17
Korean: yŏl ilgop 열 일곱
Portuguese: dezessete
Russian: semnádtsat' семнадцать
Spanish: diecisiete
Swedish: sjutton

1918. seventy [adj.]

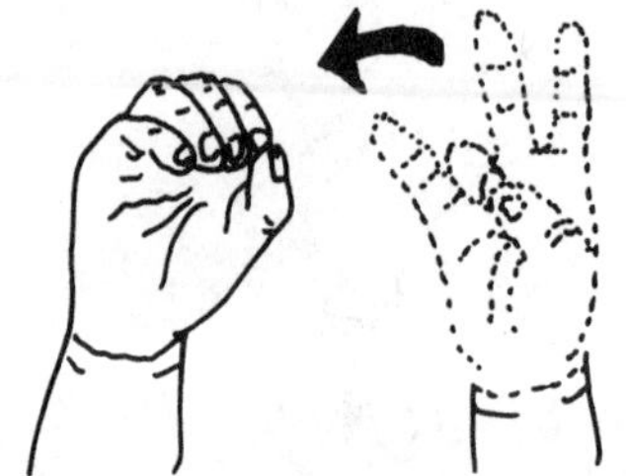

Arabic: sabaeín سبعين
Chinese: qīshí 七十
Dutch: zeventig
French: soixante-dix
German: siebzig
Italian: settanta
Japanese: nanajū 70
Korean: irhŭn 일흔
Portuguese: setenta
Russian: sém'desyat семьдесят
Spanish: setenta
Swedish: sjuttio

1919. several [adj.]

Arabic: aadíd عديد
Chinese: yìxie 一些
Dutch: verscheidene
French: plusieurs
German: verschiedene
Italian: parecchi
Japanese: sūko no 数個の
Korean: yŏrŏsŭi 여럿의
Portuguese: vários
Russian: néskol'ko несколько
Spanish: varios
Swedish: enskild

1920. severe [adj.]

Arabic: qási قاس
Chinese: yánzhòng 嚴重
Dutch: streng
French: sévère
German: streng
Italian: severo
Japanese: kibishii 厳しい
Korean: ŏmkyŏk'han 엄격한
Portuguese: severo
Russian: suróvyy суровый
Spanish: severo
Swedish: sträng

1921. sew [v.]

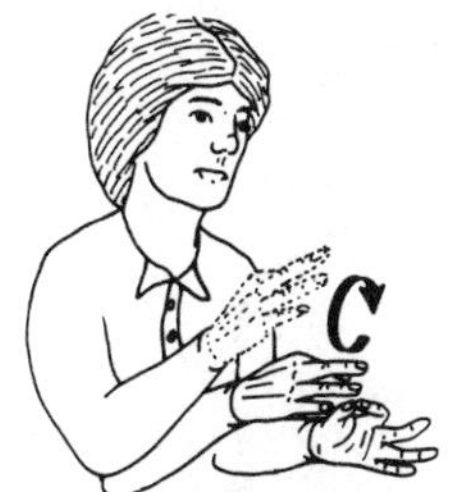

Arabic: khéyyata خيط
Chinese: féng 縫
Dutch: naaien
French: coudre
German: nähen
Italian: cucire
Japanese: nuu 縫う
Korean: kkwemaeda 꿰메다
Portuguese: costurar
Russian: shit' шить
Spanish: coser
Swedish: sy

1922. sex [n.]

Arabic: jins جنس
Chinese: xìng 性
Dutch: geslacht
French: sexe
German: Geschlecht
Italian: sesso
Japanese: sei 性
Korean: sŏng 성
Portuguese: sexo
Russian: pol пол
Spanish: sexo
Swedish: kön

1923. shadow [n.]

Arabic: dhill ظل
Chinese: yǐngzi 影子
Dutch: schaduw
French: ombre
German: Schatten
Italian: ombra
Japanese: kage 影
Korean: kŭrimja 그림자
Portuguese: sombra
Russian: ten' тень
Spanish: sombra
Swedish: skugga

1924. shake [v.]

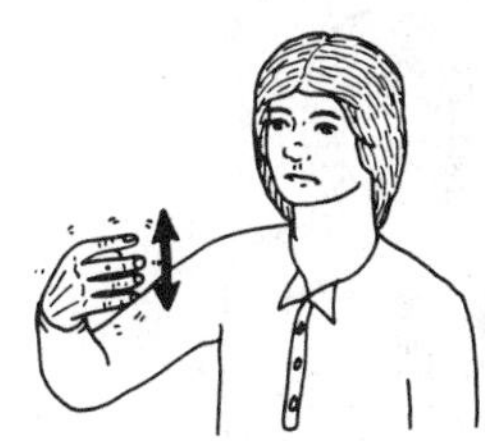

Arabic: házza هز
Chinese: yáo 摇
Dutch: schudden
French: secouer
German: schütteln
Italian: scuotere
Japanese: yureru 揺れる
Korean: ttŏlda 떨다
Portuguese: sacudir
Russian: tryastí трясти
Spanish: sacudir
Swedish: skaka

1925. shallow [adj.]

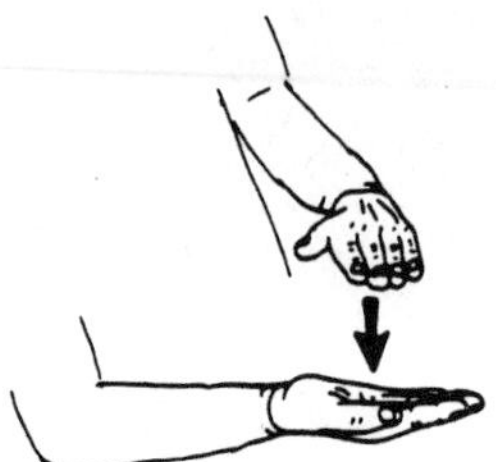

Arabic: dháhel ضحل
Chinese: qiǎn 浅
Dutch: ondiep
French: peu profond
German: seicht
Italian: poco profondo
Japanese: asai 浅い
Korean: yat'hŭn 얕은
Portuguese: pouco profundo
Russian: mélkiy мелкий
Spanish: poco profundo
Swedish: grund

1926. shame [n.]

Arabic: khájal خجل
Chinese: chǐrù 耻辱
Dutch: schaamte
French: honte
German: Scham
Italian: vergogna
Japanese: haji 恥
Korean: ch'angp'i 창피
Portuguese: vergonha
Russian: styd стыд
Spanish: vergüenza
Swedish: skam

1927. shape [n.]

Arabic: shákl شكل
Chinese: xíngzhuàng 形状
Dutch: vorm
French: forme
German: Form
Italian: forma
Japanese: katachi 形
Korean: moyang 모양
Portuguese: forma
Russian: fórma форма
Spanish: forma
Swedish: form

1928. share [n.]

Arabic: nasíb نصيب
Chinese: bùfèn 部分
Dutch: deel
French: part
German: Teil
Italian: parte
Japanese: buntan 分担
Korean: mok 몫
Portuguese: parte
Russian: dólya доля
Spanish: participación
Swedish: del

1929. sharp (knife) [adj.]

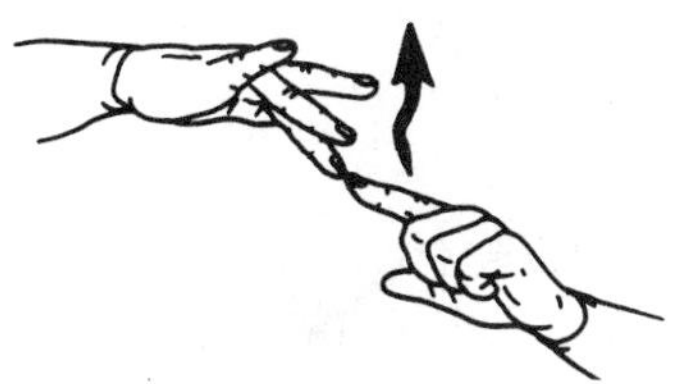

Arabic: háad حاد
Chinese: ruìlì 鋭利
Dutch: scherp
French: affilé
German: scharf
Italian: affilato
Japanese: surudoi 鋭い
Korean: nalk'aroun 날카로운
Portuguese: afiado
Russian: óstryy острый
Spanish: afilado
Swedish: vass

1930. shave [v.]

Arabic: hálaqa حلق
Chinese: tì 剃
Dutch: zich scheren
French: se raser
German: sich rasieren
Italian: radere
Japanese: soru そる
Korean: myŏndohada 면도하다
Portuguese: barbear-se
Russian: brít'sya бриться
Spanish: afeitar(se)
Swedish: raka sig

1931. she [pron.]

Arabic: híyya هي
Chinese: tā 她
Dutch: zij
French: elle
German: sie
Italian: ella
Japanese: kanojo wa 彼女は
Korean: kuyŏja 그 여자
Portuguese: ela
Russian: oná она
Spanish: ella
Swedish: hon

1932. sheep [n.]

Arabic: kharúf خروف
Chinese: yáng 羊
Dutch: schaap
French: mouton
German: Schaf
Italian: pecora
Japanese: hitsuji 羊
Korean: yang 양
Portuguese: carneiro
Russian: ovtsá овца
Spanish: oveja
Swedish: får

1933. shelf [n.]

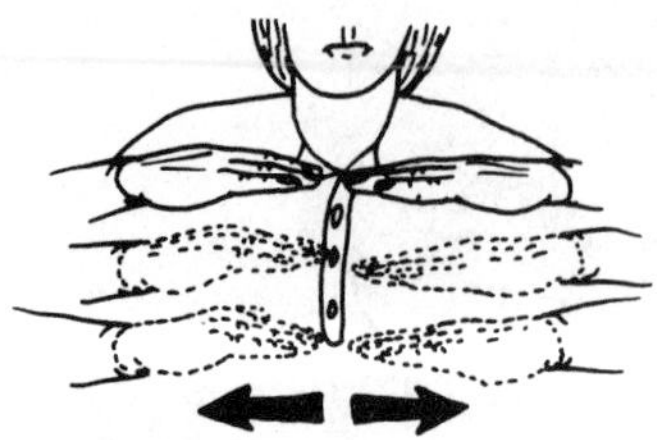

Arabic: raff رف
Chinese: jiàzi 架子
Dutch: plank
French: étagère
German: Regal
Italian: scaffale
Japanese: tana 棚
Korean: sŏnban 선반
Portuguese: prateleira
Russian: pólka полка
Spanish: estante
Swedish: hylla

1934. shine [v.]

Arabic: lámaa لمع
Chinese: fāliàng 發亮
Dutch: schijnen
French: briller
German: scheinen
Italian: brillare
Japanese: hikaru 光る
Korean: bit'nada 빛나다
Portuguese: brilhar
Russian: svetít' светить
Spanish: brillar
Swedish: skina

1935. ship [n.]

Arabic: safína سفينة
Chinese: chuán 船
Dutch: schip
French: navire
German: Schiff
Italian: nave
Japanese: fune 船
Korean: bae 배
Portuguese: navio
Russian: korábl' корабль
Spanish: barco
Swedish: skepp

1936. shirt [n.]

Arabic: qamís قميص
Chinese: chènyī 襯衣
Dutch: hemd
French: chemise
German: Hemd
Italian: camicia
Japanese: shatsu シャツ
Korean: syassŭ 샤쓰
Portuguese: camisa
Russian: rubáshka рубашка
Spanish: camisa
Swedish: skjorta

1937. shock [n.]

Arabic: sádma صدمة
Chinese: zhènjīng 震驚
Dutch: schok
French: choc
German: Schock
Italian: scossa
Japanese: shōgeki 衝撃
Korean: ch'unggyŏk 충격
Portuguese: choque
Russian: shok шок
Spanish: choque
Swedish: chock

1938. shoe(s) [n.]

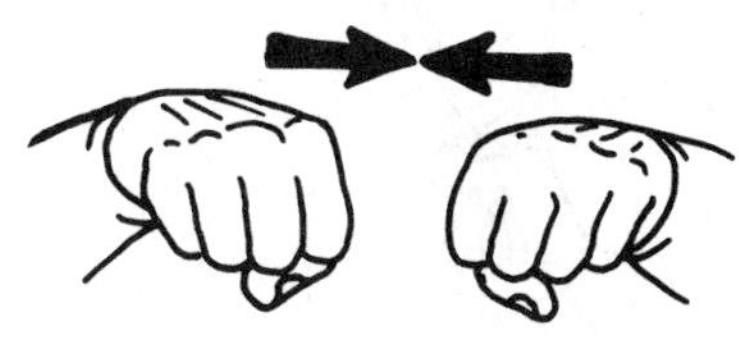

Arabic: hidhá' حذاء
Chinese: xiézi 鞋子
Dutch: schoen
French: chaussure
German: Schuh
Italian: scarpa
Japanese: kutsu 靴
Korean: kudu 구두
Portuguese: sapato
Russian: bashmák башмак
Spanish: zapato
Swedish: sko

1939. shoot [v.]

Arabic: sáwwaba صوب
Chinese: shè 射
Dutch: schieten
French: tirer
German: schießen
Italian: sparare
Japanese: utsu 撃つ
Korean: ssoda 쏘다
Portuguese: atirar
Russian: strelyát' стрелять
Spanish: disparar
Swedish: skjuta

1940. shore [n.]

Arabic: sháti' شاطئ
Chinese: àn 岸
Dutch: kust
French: rivage
German: Ufer
Italian: riva
Japanese: kishi 岸
Korean: badatka 바닷가
Portuguese: praia
Russian: béreg берег
Spanish: orilla
Swedish: strand

1941. short [adj.]

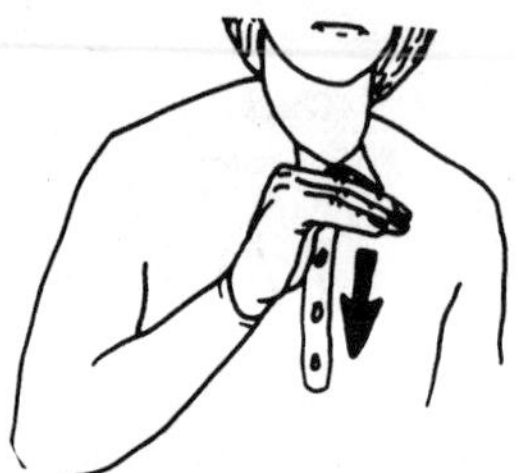

Arabic: qasír قصير
Chinese: duǎn 短
Dutch: kort
French: court
German: kurz
Italian: corto
Japanese: mijikai 短い
Korean: jjalbun 짧은
Portuguese: curto
Russian: korótkiy короткий
Spanish: corto
Swedish: kort

1942. shoulder [n.]

Arabic: kátef كتف
Chinese: jiān 肩
Dutch: schoulder
French: épaule
German: Schulter
Italian: spalla
Japanese: kata 肩
Korean: ŏkkae 어깨
Portuguese: ombro
Russian: plechó плечо
Spanish: hombro
Swedish: axel

1943. shout [v.]

Arabic: sárakha صرخ
Chinese: hǒu 吼
Dutch: schreeuwen
French: crier
German: schreien
Italian: gridare
Japanese: sakebu 叫ぶ
Korean: oech'ida 외치다
Portuguese: gritar
Russian: krichát' кричать
Spanish: gritar
Swedish: skrika

1944. shovel [n.]

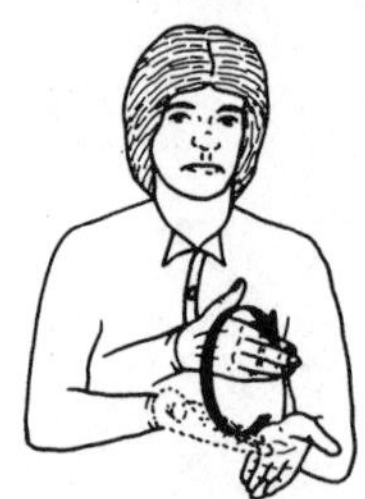

Arabic: míjrafa مجرفة
Chinese: chǎngzi 鏟子
Dutch: schop
French: pelle
German: Schaufel
Italian: pala
Japanese: shaberu シャベル
Korean: sap 삽
Portuguese: pá
Russian: lopáta лопата
Spanish: pala
Swedish: skovel

1945. show [v.]

Arabic: áarada عرض
Chinese: zhǎnshì 展示
Dutch: tonen
French: montrer
German: zeigen
Italian: mostrare
Japanese: miseru 見せる
Korean: karik'ida 가리키다
Portuguese: mostrar
Russian: pokázyvat' показывать
Spanish: mostrar
Swedish: visa

1946. shy [adj.]

Arabic: khajúl خجول
Chinese: hàixiū 害羞
Dutch: schuw
French: timide
German: schüchtern
Italian: timido
Japanese: hanikanda はにかんだ
Korean: sujubŭn 수줍은
Portuguese: tímido
Russian: zasténchivyy застенчивый
Spanish: tímido
Swedish: blyg

1947. sick [adj.]

Arabic: maríd مريض
Chinese: bìng 病
Dutch: ziek
French: malade
German: krank
Italian: ammalato
Japanese: byōkino 病気の
Korean: byŏngnan 병난
Portuguese: doente
Russian: bol'nóy больной
Spanish: enfermo
Swedish: sjuk

1948. side [n.]

Arabic: jáneb جانب
Chinese: biāng 邊
Dutch: kant
French: côté
German: Seite
Italian: lato
Japanese: sokumen 側面
Korean: jjok 쪽
Portuguese: lado
Russian: storoná сторона
Spanish: lado
Swedish: sida

1949. sign [n.]

Arabic: ishára اشارة
Chinese: biǎozhì 標誌
Dutch: teken
French: signe
German: Zeichen
Italian: segno
Japanese: shirushi 印
Korean: shinho 신호
Portuguese: sinal
Russian: znak знак
Spanish: signo
Swedish: tecken

1950. significance [n.]

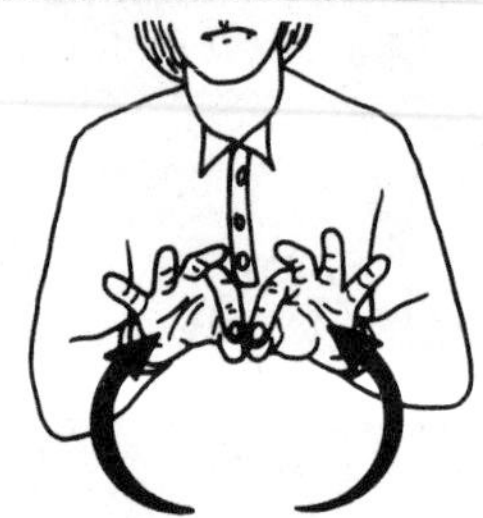

Arabic: máana معنى
Chinese: zhòngyàoxìng 重要性
Dutch: betekenis
French: signification
German: Bedeutung
Italian: significato
Japanese: jūyōsei 重要性
Korean: jungyosŏng 중요성
Portuguese: significação
Russian: znachéniye значение
Spanish: significado
Swedish: betydelse

1951. silence [n.]

Arabic: samt صمت
Chinese: chénmò 沈默
Dutch: stilte
French: silence
German: Stille
Italian: silenzio
Japanese: chimmoku 沈黙
Korean: ch'immuk 침묵
Portuguese: silêncio
Russian: molchániye молчание
Spanish: silencio
Swedish: tystnad

1952. silver [n.]

Arabic: fédhdha فضة
Chinese: yín 銀
Dutch: zilver
French: argent
German: Silber
Italian: argento
Japanese: gin 銀
Korean: ŭn 은
Portuguese: prata
Russian: serebró серебро
Spanish: plata
Swedish: silver

1953. similar [adj.]

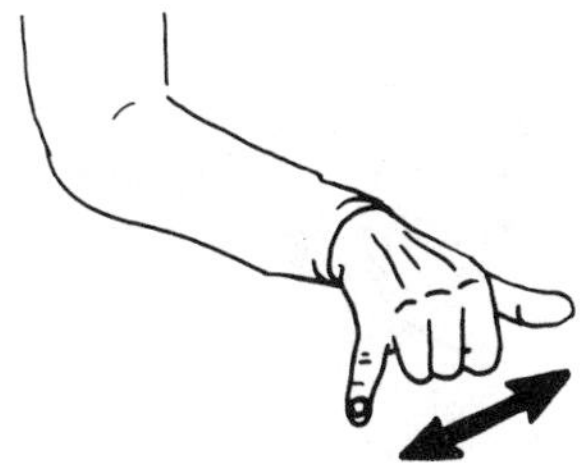

Arabic: momáthil مماثل
Chinese: lèisì 類似
Dutch: gelijkend
French: similaire
German: ähnlich
Italian: simile
Japanese: nite iru 似ている
Korean: bisŭt'han 비슷한
Portuguese: semelhante
Russian: podóbnyy подобный
Spanish: similar
Swedish: lik

1954. simple [adj.]

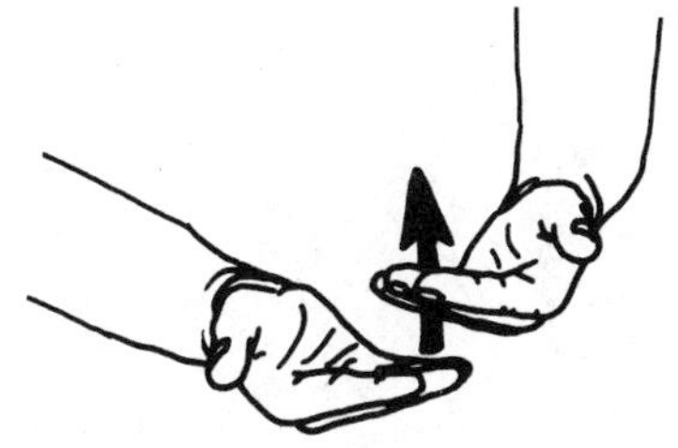

Arabic: basíet بسيط
Chinese: jiǎndān 簡單
Dutch: eenvoudig
French: simple
German: einfach
Italian: semplice
Japanese: tanjun na 単純な
Korean: kandanhan 간단한
Portuguese: simples
Russian: prostóy простой
Spanish: simple
Swedish: enkel

1955. simultaneous(ly) [adj./adv.]

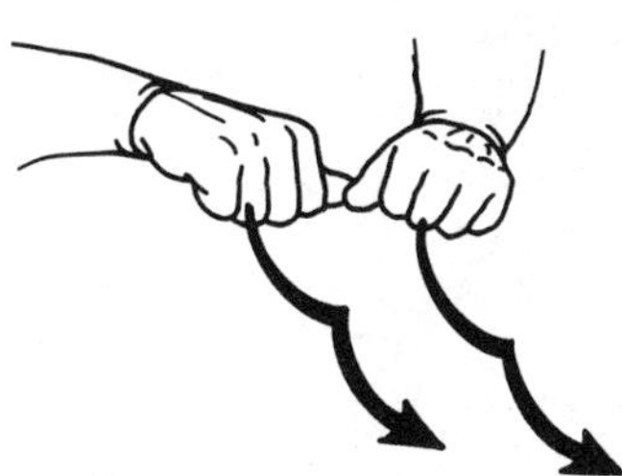

Arabic: máan معاً
Chinese: tóngshí 同時
Dutch: tegelijkertijd
French: simultanément
German: gleichzeitig
Italian: simultaneamente
Japanese: dōji no 同じの (に)
Korean: dongshie 동시의
Portuguese: simultaneamente
Russian: odnovrémenno одновременно
Spanish: simultáneamente
Swedish: samtidigt

1956. sin [n.]

Arabic: ithm اثم
Chinese: zuì 罪
Dutch: zonde
French: péché
German: Sünde
Italian: peccato
Japanese: tsumi 罪
Korean: joe 죄
Portuguese: pecado
Russian: grekh грех
Spanish: pecado
Swedish: synd

1957. sincere [adj.]

Arabic: múkhlas مخلص
Chinese: zhēnchéng 真誠
Dutch: oprecht
French: sincère
German: aufrichtig
Italian: sincero
Japanese: seijitsu na 誠実な
Korean: jinshirhan 진실한
Portuguese: sincero
Russian: ískrenniy искренний
Spanish: sincero
Swedish: uppriktig

1958. sing [v.]

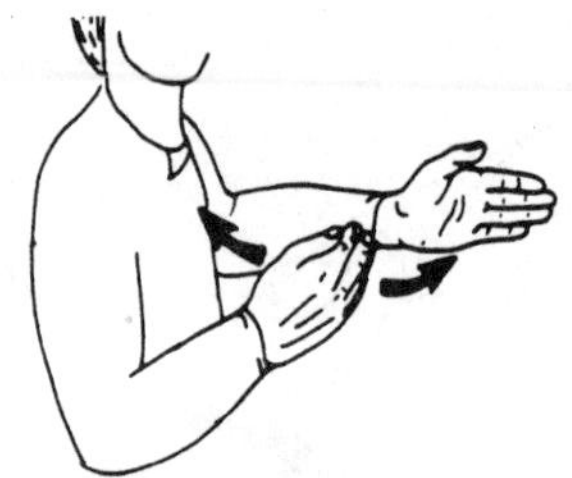

Arabic: ghánna غنى
Chinese: chàng 唱
Dutch: zingen
French: chanter
German: singen
Italian: cantare
Japanese: utau 歌う
Korean: noraehada 노래하다
Portuguese: cantar
Russian: pet' петь
Spanish: cantar
Swedish: sjunga

1959. sink [v.]

Arabic: ghráriqa غرق
Chinese: chén 沈
Dutch: zinken
French: s'enfoncer
German: sinken
Italian: affondare
Japanese: shizumu 沈む
Korean: karaanta 가라앉다
Portuguese: afundar
Russian: tonút' тонуть
Spanish: hundir
Swedish: sjunka

1960. sister [n.]

Arabic: ukht اخت
Chinese: jiěmèi 姐妹
Dutch: zuster
French: soeur
German: Schwester
Italian: sorella
Japanese: ane 姉
Korean: jamae 자매
Portuguese: irmã
Russian: sestrá сестра
Spanish: hermana
Swedish: syster

1961. sit (down) [v.]

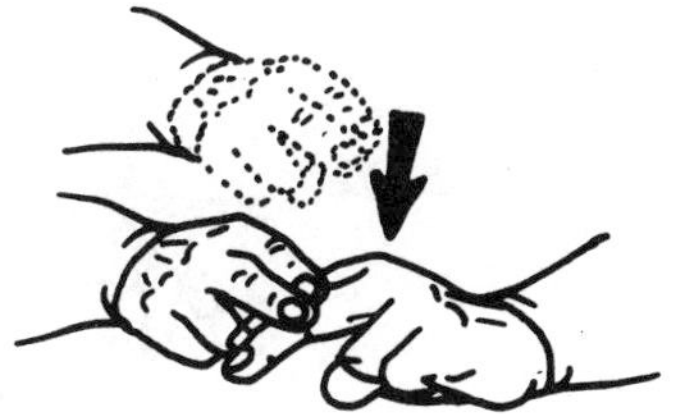

Arabic: jálasa جلس
Chinese: zuò 坐
Dutch: gaan zitten
French: s'asseoir
German: sich setzen
Italian: sedersi
Japanese: suwaru 座る
Korean: anta 앉다
Portuguese: sentar-se
Russian: sadít'sya садиться
Spanish: sentarse
Swedish: sätta sig

1962. situation [n.]

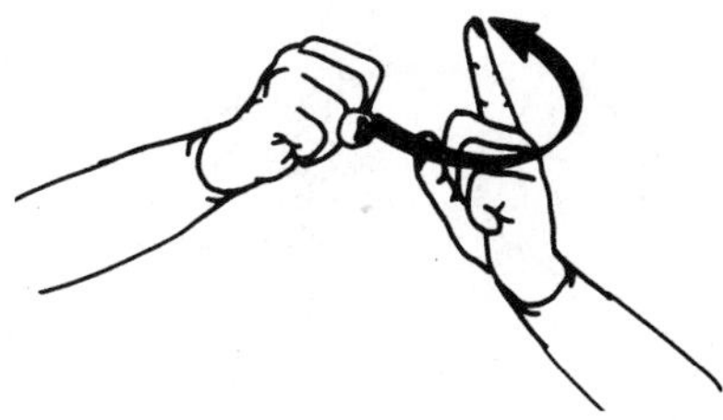

Arabic: hála حالة
Chinese: qíngkuàng 情况
Dutch: situatie
French: situation
German: Situation
Italian: situazione
Japanese: jitai 事態
Korean: ch'ŏji 처지
Portuguese: situação
Russian: situátsiya ситуация
Spanish: situación
Swedish: situation

1963. six [adj.]

Arabic: sítta ستة
Chinese: liù 六
Dutch: zes
French: six
German: sechs
Italian: sei
Japanese: roku 六
Korean: yŏsŏt 여섯
Portuguese: seis
Russian: shest' шесть
Spanish: seis
Swedish: sex

1964. sixteen [adj.]

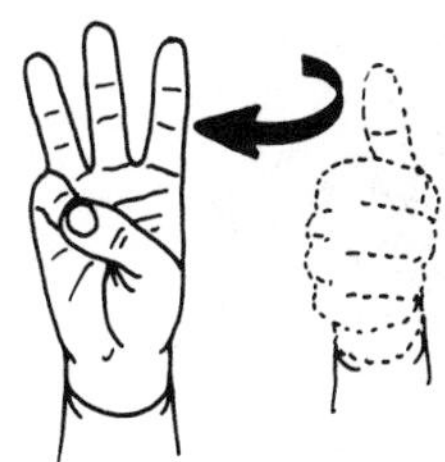

Arabic: síttat áashar ستة عشر
Chinese: shíliù 十六
Dutch: zestien
French: seize
German: sechzehn
Italian: sedici
Japanese: jūroku 16
Korean: yŏl yŏsŏt 열 여섯
Portuguese: dezesseis
Russian: shestnádtsat' шестнадцать
Spanish: dieciseis
Swedish: sexton

1965. sixty [adj.]

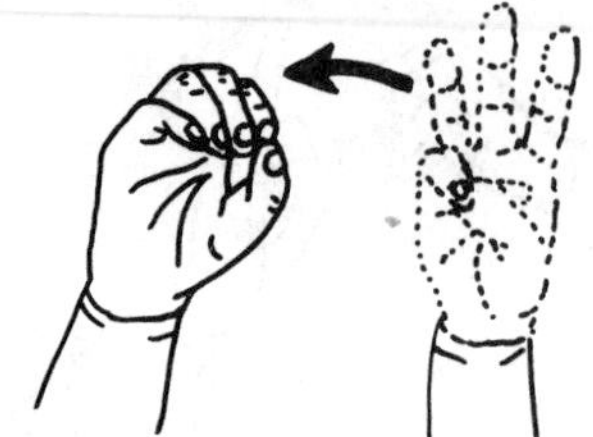

Arabic: sitún ستون
Chinese: liùshí 六十
Dutch: zestig
French: soixante
German: sechzig
Italian: sessanta
Japanese: rokujū 60
Korean: yesun 예순
Portuguese: sessenta
Russian: shest'desyát шестьдесят
Spanish: sesenta
Swedish: sextio

1966. size [n.]

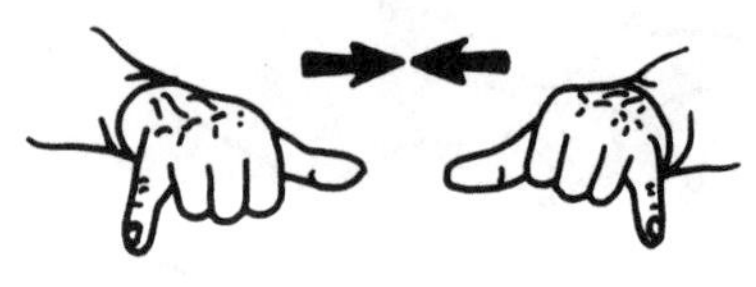

Arabic: hájem حجم
Chinese: chǐcùn 尺寸
Dutch: grootte
French: taille
German: Größe
Italian: misura
Japanese: ōkisa 大きさ
Korean: k'ŭgi 크기
Portuguese: tamanho
Russian: razmér размер
Spanish: tamaño
Swedish: storlek

1967. skill [n.]

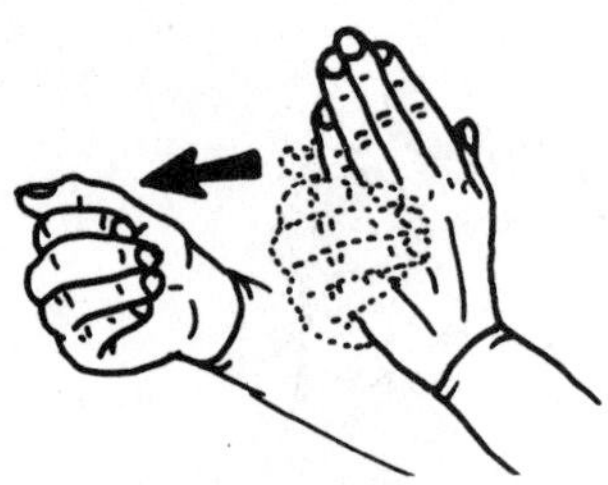

Arabic: mahára مهارة
Chinese: jìqiǎo 技巧
Dutch: bekwaamheid
French: habileté
German: Geschicklichkeit
Italian: abilità
Japanese: gijutsu 技術
Korean: kisul 기술
Portuguese: habilidade
Russian: kvalifikátsiya квалификация
Spanish: habilidad
Swedish: skicklighet

1968. skin (human) [n.]

Arabic: jild جلد
Chinese: pífū 皮肤
Dutch: huid
French: peau
German: Haut
Italian: pelle
Japanese: hifu 皮膚
Korean: p'ibu 피부
Portuguese: pele
Russian: kózha кожа
Spanish: piel
Swedish: hud

1969. sky [n.]

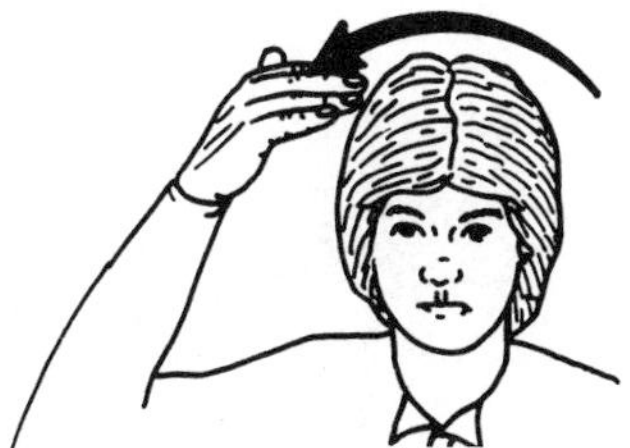

Arabic: sámaa' سماء
Chinese: tiānkōng 天空
Dutch: hemel
French: ciel
German: Himmel
Italian: cielo
Japanese: sora 空
Korean: hanŭl 하늘
Portuguese: céu
Russian: nébo небо
Spanish: firmamento
Swedish: himmel

1970. sleep [v.]

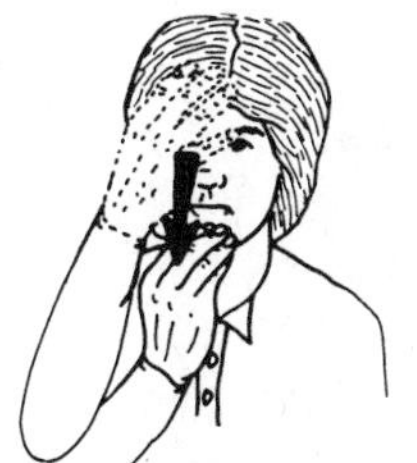

Arabic: ná'im نائم
Chinese: shuìjiào 睡覺
Dutch: slapen
French: dormir
German: schlafen
Italian: dormire
Japanese: nemuru 眠る
Korean: jamjada 잠자다
Portuguese: dormir
Russian: spat' спать
Spanish: dormir
Swedish: sova

1971. slender (people) [adj.]

Arabic: nahíf نحيف
Chinese: miáotiáo 苗條
Dutch: slank
French: svelte
German: schlank
Italian: snello
Japanese: hossori shita ほっそりした
Korean: nalssinhan 날씬한
Portuguese: esbelto
Russian: tónkiy тонкий
Spanish: esbelto
Swedish: slank

1972. slide [v.]

Arabic: inzálaqa انزلق
Chinese: huá 滑
Dutch: glijden
French: glisser
German: gleiten
Italian: scivolare
Japanese: suberu 滑る
Korean: mikkŭrŏjida 미끄러지다
Portuguese: deslizar
Russian: skol'zít' скользить
Spanish: deslizar
Swedish: glida

1973. slight (insignificant) [adj.]

Arabic: tafíf طفيف
Chinese: qīngwéide 輕微的
Dutch: onbeduidend
French: insignifiant
German: geringfügig
Italian: insignificante
Japanese: sukoshi no 少しの
Korean: yakkanŭi 약간의
Portuguese: insignificante
Russian: neznachítel'nyy незначительный
Spanish: insignificante
Swedish: obetydlig

1974. slow [adj.]

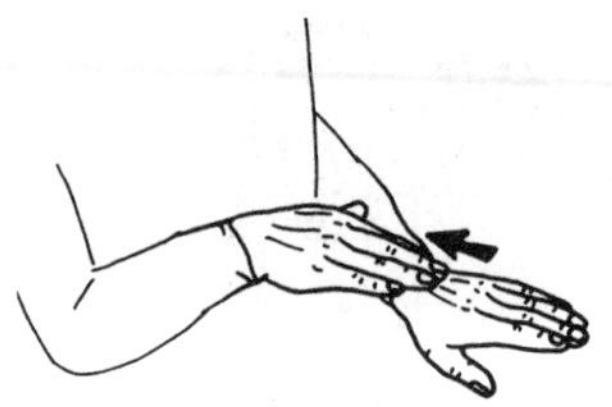

Arabic: batí' بطيء
Chinese: màn 慢
Dutch: langzaam
French: lent
German: langsam
Italian: lento
Japanese: osoi 遅い
Korean: nŭrin 느린
Portuguese: lento
Russian: médlennyy медленный
Spanish: lento
Swedish: långsam

1975. sly [adj.]

Arabic: hakím حكيم
Chinese: jiǎohuá 狡猾
Dutch: listig
French: rusé
German: listig
Italian: scaltro
Japanese: zurui ずるい
Korean: kyohwarhan 교활한
Portuguese: astuto
Russian: khítryy хитрый
Spanish: astuto
Swedish: listig

1976. small [adj.]

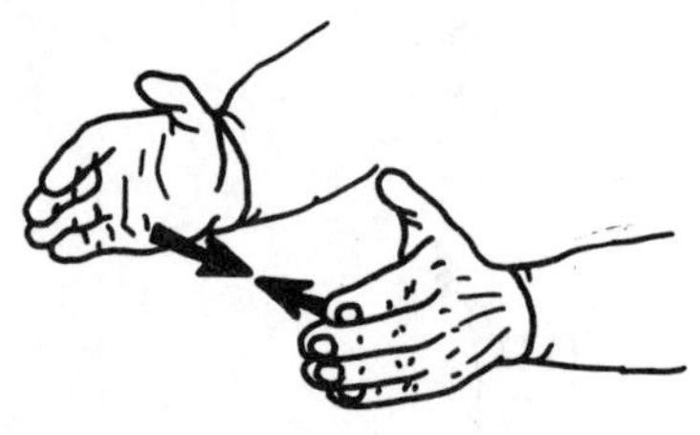

Arabic: saghír صغير
Chinese: xiǎo 小
Dutch: klein
French: petit
German: klein
Italian: piccolo
Japanese: chiisai 小さい
Korean: jagŭn 작은
Portuguese: pequeno
Russian: málen'kiy маленький
Spanish: pequeño
Swedish: liten

1977. smell [v.]

Arabic: shámma شم
Chinese: wén 聞
Dutch: ruiken
French: sentir
German: riechen
Italian: fiutare
Japanese: niou 匂う
Korean: naemsaerŭl madta 냄새를 맡다
Portuguese: cheirar
Russian: obonyát' обонять
Spanish: oler
Swedish: lukta

1978. smile [n.]

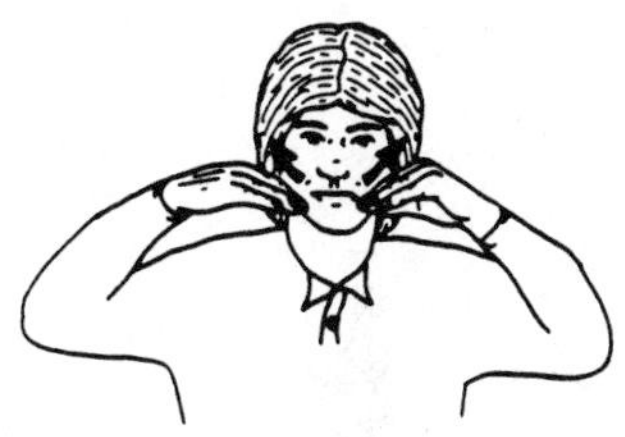

Arabic: tabássama تبسم
Chinese: wéixiào 微笑
Dutch: glimlach
French: sourire
German: lächeln
Italian: sorriso
Japanese: hohoemi 微笑み
Korean: miso 미소
Portuguese: sorriso
Russian: ulýbka улыбка
Spanish: sonrisa
Swedish: leende

1979. smoke [n.]

Arabic: dukhán دخان
Chinese: yān 煙
Dutch: rook
French: fumée
German: Rauch
Italian: fumo
Japanese: kemuri 煙
Korean: yŏnki 연기
Portuguese: fumaça
Russian: dym дым
Spanish: humo
Swedish: rök

1980. smoke [v.]

Arabic: dákhkhana دخن
Chinese: xīyān 吸煙
Dutch: roken
French: fumer
German: rauchen
Italian: fumare
Japanese: kemuru 煙る
Korean: yŏnkirŭl naeda 연기를 내다
Portuguese: fumar
Russian: kurít' курить
Spanish: fumar
Swedish: röka

1981. smooth [adj.]

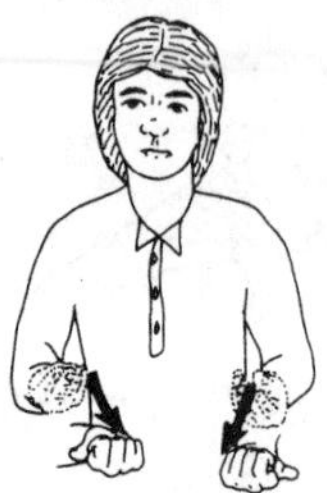

Arabic: náaem ناعم
Chinese: pīnghuá 平滑的
Dutch: glad
French: lisse
German: glatt
Italian: liscio
Japanese: nameraka na 滑らかな
Korean: maekkŭrŏun 매끄러운
Portuguese: liso
Russian: gládkiy гладкий
Spanish: liso
Swedish: jämn

1982. snake [n.]

Arabic: thoaabán ثعبان
Chinese: shé 蛇
Dutch: slang
French: serpent
German: Schlange
Italian: serpente
Japanese: hebi へび
Korean: baem 뱀
Portuguese: cobra
Russian: zmeyá змея
Spanish: culebra
Swedish: orm

1983. sneeze [v.]

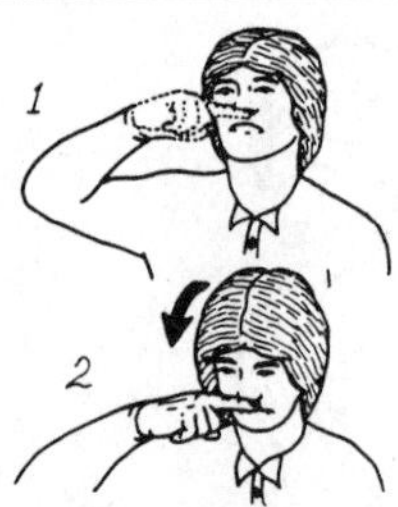

Arabic: áatasa عطس
Chinese: dăpēntì 打噴嚏
Dutch: niezen
French: éternuer
German: niesen
Italian: starnutire
Japanese: kushami o suru くしゃみをする
Korean: jaech'aegihada 재채기하다
Portuguese: espirrar
Russian: chikhát' чихать
Spanish: estornudar
Swedish: nysa

1984. snow [n.]

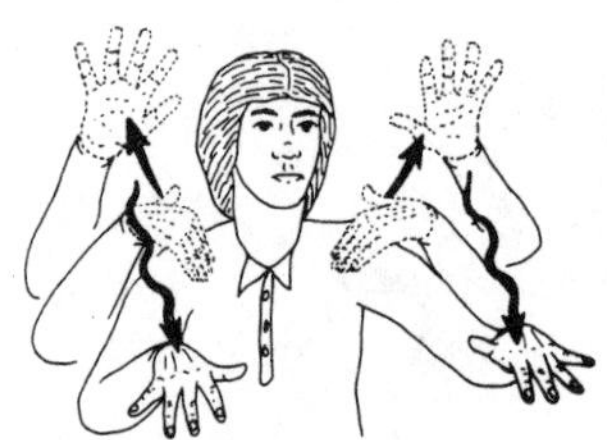

Arabic: thalj ثلج
Chinese: xuě 雪
Dutch: sneeuw
French: neige
German: Schnee
Italian: neve
Japanese: yuki 雪
Korean: nun 눈
Portuguese: neve
Russian: sneg снег
Spanish: nieve
Swedish: snö

1985. soap [n.]

Arabic: sabún صابون
Chinese: féizào 肥皂
Dutch: zeep
French: savon
German: Seife
Italian: sapone
Japanese: sekken 石けん
Korean: binu 비누
Portuguese: sabão
Russian: mýlo мыло
Spanish: jabón
Swedish: tvål

1986. soccer [n.]

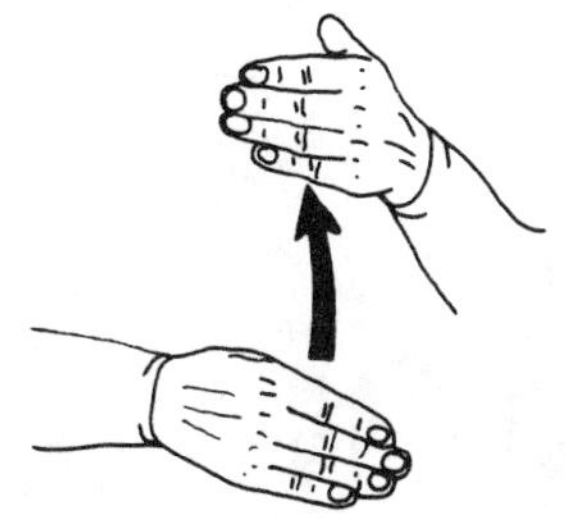

Arabic: kórat al-qádam كرة القدم
Chinese: zúqiú 足球
Dutch: voetbal
French: football
German: Fußball
Italian: calcio
Japanese: sakkā サッカー
Korean: ch'ukku 축구
Portuguese: futebol
Russian: futból футбол
Spanish: fútbol
Swedish: fotboll

1987. socialism [n.]

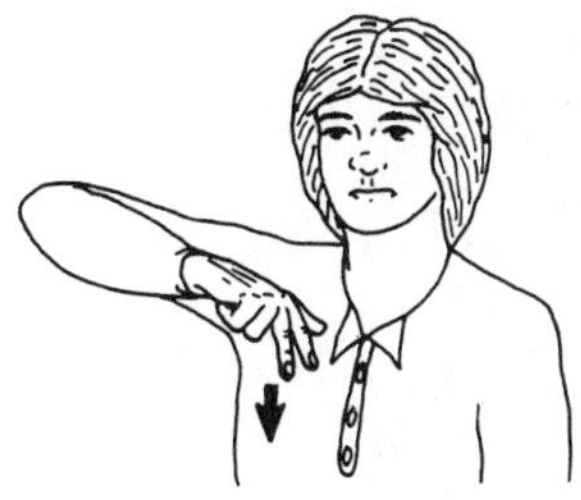

Arabic: ishterakía اشتراكية
Chinese: shèhuì zhǔyì 社會主義
Dutch: socialisme
French: socialisme
German: Sozialismus
Italian: socialismo
Japanese: shakai shugi 社会主義
Korean: sahoejuŭi 사회주의
Portuguese: socialismo
Russian: sotsialízm социализм
Spanish: socialismo
Swedish: socialism

1988. society [n.]

Arabic: mujtámaa مجتمع
Chinese: shèhuì 社會
Dutch: maatschappij
French: société
German: Gesellschaft
Italian: società
Japanese: shakai 社会
Korean: sahoe 사회
Portuguese: sociedade
Russian: óbshchestvo общество
Spanish: sociedad
Swedish: samhället

1989. sock(s) [n.]

Arabic: jawárib جوارب
Chinese: wàzi 襪子
Dutch: sok
French: chaussette
German: Socke
Italian: calza
Japanese: kutsushita 靴下
Korean: yangmal 양말
Portuguese: meia
Russian: nosók носок
Spanish: calcetín
Swedish: socka

1990. soft [adj.]

Arabic: náaem ناعم
Chinese: ruǎn 軟
Dutch: zacht
French: doux
German: weich
Italian: morbido
Japanese: yawarakai 柔わらかい
Korean: budŭrŏun 부드러운
Portuguese: mole
Russian: myágkiy мягкий
Spanish: blando
Swedish: mjuk

1991. soil [n.]

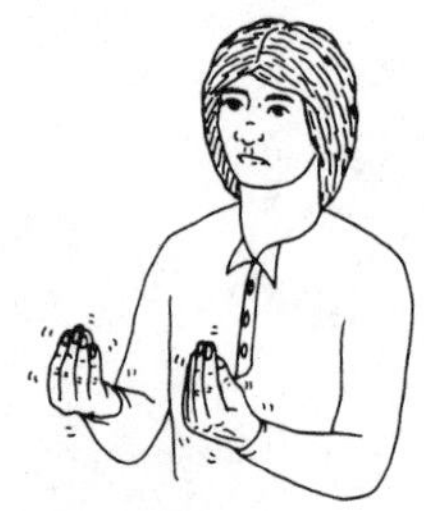

Arabic: túrba تربة
Chinese: tǔ 土
Dutch: aarde
French: terre
German: Erde
Italian: suolo
Japanese: tsuchi 土
Korean: hŭk 흙
Portuguese: terra
Russian: póchva почва
Spanish: tierra
Swedish: jord

1992. soldier [n.]

Arabic: júndi جندي
Chinese: jūnrén 軍人
Dutch: soldaat
French: soldat
German: Soldat
Italian: soldato
Japanese: gunjin 軍人
Korean: kunin 군인
Portuguese: soldado
Russian: soldát солдат
Spanish: soldado
Swedish: soldat

1993. solid [adj.]

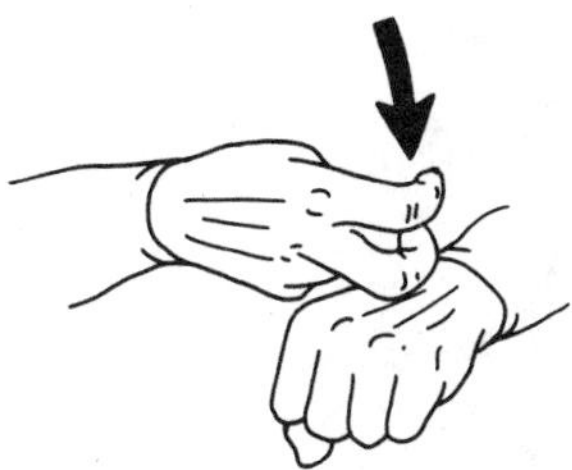

Arabic: salb صلب
Chinese: jiēshí 堅實
Dutch: stevig
French: solide
German: fest
Italian: solido
Japanese: kotai no 個体の
Korean: ttanttanhan 딴딴한
Portuguese: sólido
Russian: tvyórdyy твёрдый
Spanish: sólido
Swedish: fast

1994. some [adj.]

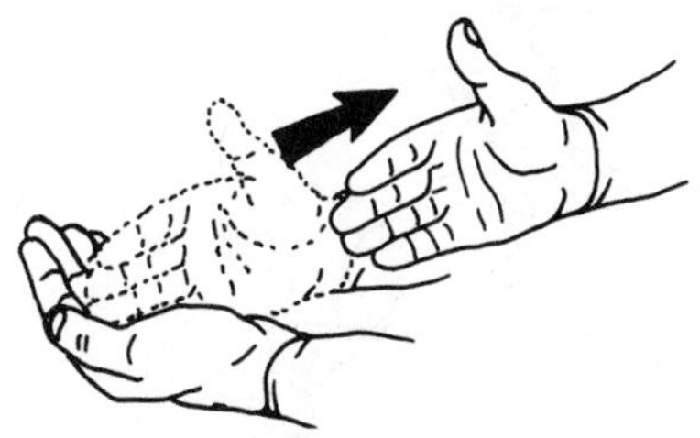

Arabic: báadh بعض
Chinese: yìxiē 一些
Dutch: enkele
French: quelque
German: einige
Italian: qualche
Japanese: ikuraka no いくらかの
Korean: ŏttŏn 어떤
Portuguese: algum
Russian: nékotoryy некоторый
Spanish: algún
Swedish: några

1995. someone (somebody) [pron.]

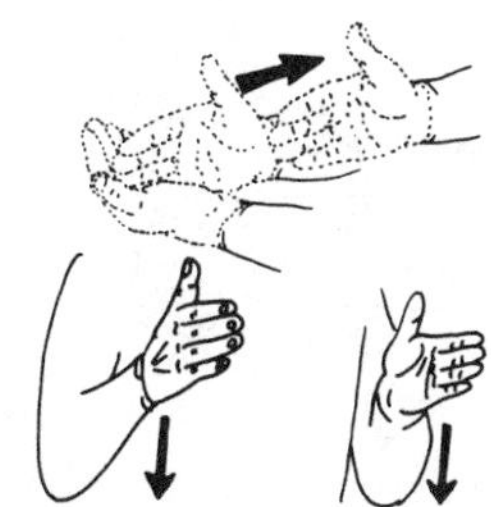

Arabic: áhad احد
Chinese: yǒu rén 有人
Dutch: iemand
French: quelqu'un
German: jemand
Italian: qualcuno
Japanese: dareka 誰か
Korean: nugunga 누군가
Portuguese: alguém
Russian: któ-to кто-то
Spanish: alguien
Swedish: någon

1996. something [pron.]

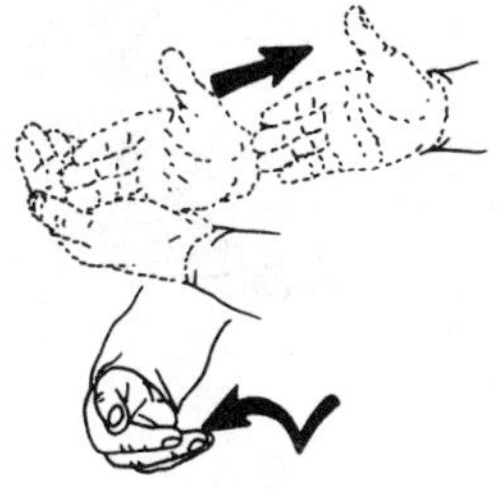

Arabic: sháee' شيء
Chinese: mǒu shì 某些
Dutch: iets
French: quelque chose
German: etwas
Italian: qualcosa
Japanese: nanika なにか
Korean: muŏshinga 무엇인가
Portuguese: alguma coisa
Russian: chtó-to что-то
Spanish: alguna cosa
Swedish: något

1997. sometimes [adv.]

Arabic: ahiánan احياناً
Chinese: yǒushí 有時
Dutch: soms
French: quelquefois
German: manchmal
Italian: qualche volta
Japanese: tokidoki 時々
Korean: ttaettaero 때때로
Portuguese: às vezes
Russian: inogdá иногда
Spanish: a veces
Swedish: ibland

1998. son [n.]

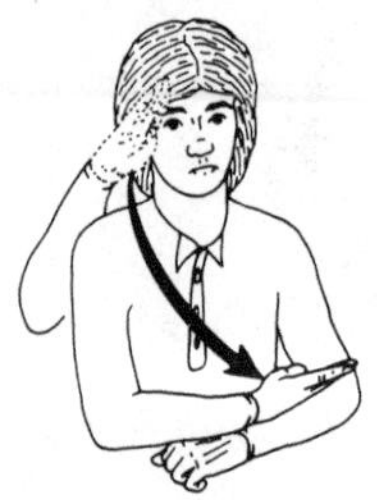

Arabic: ibn ابن
Chinese: érzi 兒子
Dutch: zoon
French: fils
German: Sohn
Italian: figlio
Japanese: musuko 息子
Korean: adŭl 아들
Portuguese: filho
Russian: syn сын
Spanish: hijo
Swedish: son

1999. song [n.]

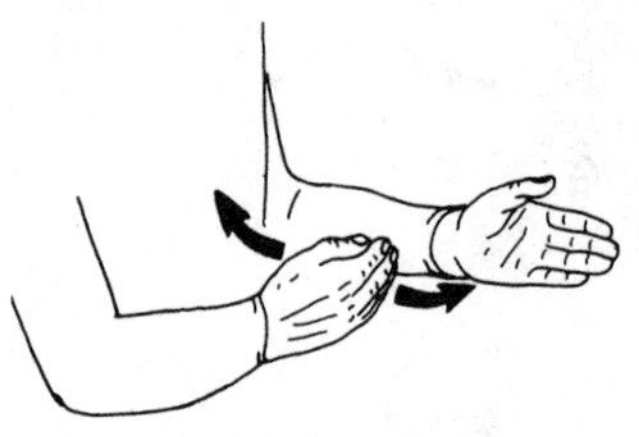

Arabic: ughníyya اغنية
Chinese: gē 歌
Dutch: lied
French: chanson
German: Lied
Italian: canzone
Japanese: uta 歌
Korean: norae 노래
Portuguese: canção
Russian: pésnya песня
Spanish: canción
Swedish: sång

2000. soon [adv.]

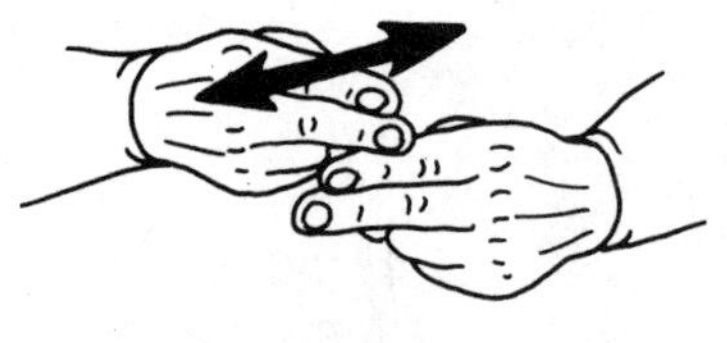

Arabic: qaríban قريباً
Chinese: bùjiǔ 不久
Dutch: spoedig
French: bientôt
German: bald
Italian: presto
Japanese: sugu ni すぐに
Korean: kot 곧
Portuguese: logo
Russian: skóro скоро
Spanish: pronto
Swedish: snart

2001. sorrow (grief) [n.]

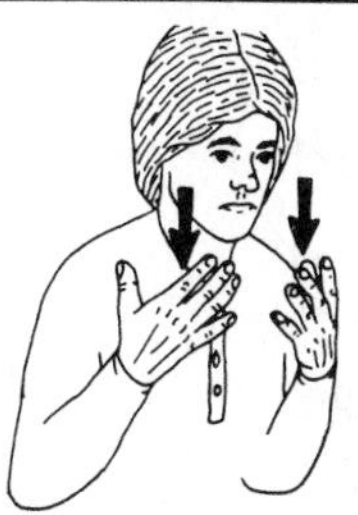

Arabic: huzn حزن
Chinese: bēishāng 悲傷
Dutch: smart
French: peine
German: Kummer
Italian: dolore
Japanese: kanashimi 悲しみ
Korean: sŭlpŭm 슬픔
Portuguese: dor
Russian: góre горе
Spanish: aflicción
Swedish: sorg

2002. soul [n.]

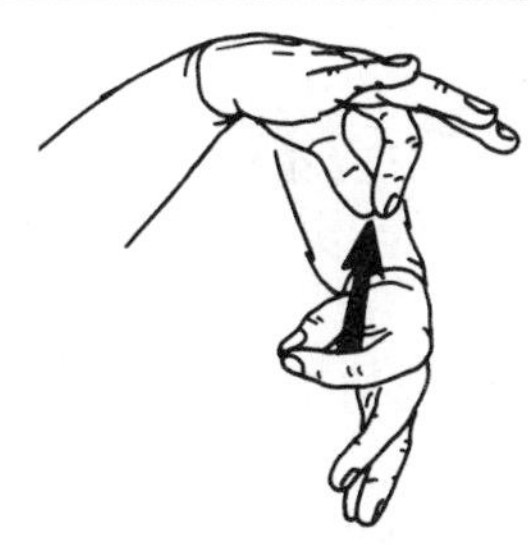

Arabic: rúah روح
Chinese: línghún 靈魂
Dutch: ziel
French: âme
German: Seele
Italian: anima
Japanese: tamashii 魂
Korean: yŏng'hon 영혼
Portuguese: alma
Russian: dushá душа
Spanish: alma
Swedish: själ

2003. sound [n.]

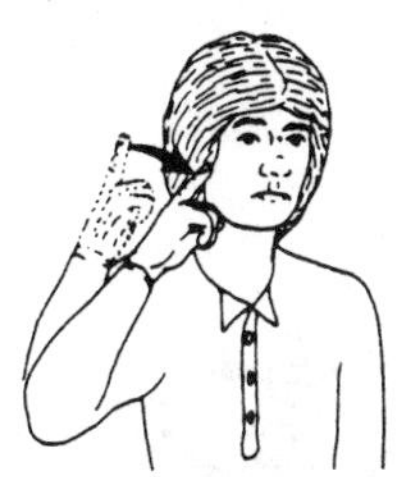

Arabic: saut صوت
Chinese: shēngyīn 聲音
Dutch: geluid
French: son
German: Schall
Italian: suono
Japanese: oto 音
Korean: sori 소리
Portuguese: som
Russian: zvuk звук
Spanish: sonido
Swedish: ljud

2004. soup [n.]

Arabic: shúraba شوربة
Chinese: tāng 湯
Dutch: soep
French: soupe
German: Suppe
Italian: minestra
Japanese: sūpu スープ
Korean: kuk 국
Portuguese: sopa
Russian: sup суп
Spanish: sopa
Swedish: soppa

2005. sour [adj.]

Arabic: hámedh حامض
Chinese: suān 酸
Dutch: zuur
French: aigre
German: sauer
Italian: agro
Japanese: suppai 酸っぱい
Korean: shin 신
Portuguese: azêdo
Russian: kíslyy кислый
Spanish: agrio
Swedish: sur

2006. south [n.]

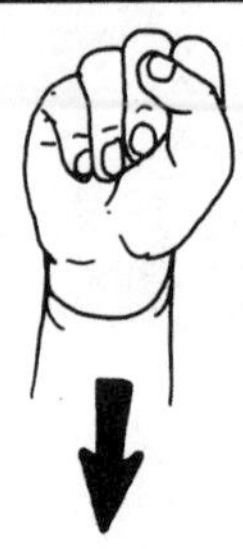

Arabic: janúb جنوب
Chinese: nán 南
Dutch: zuiden
French: sud
German: Süden
Italian: sud
Japanese: minami 南
Korean: namtchok 남쪽
Portuguese: sul
Russian: yug юг
Spanish: sur
Swedish: söder

2007. South Africa [n.]

Arabic: janúb afríqia جنوب افريقيا
Chinese: nánfēi 南非
Dutch: Zuid Afrika
French: Afrique du Sud
German: Südafrika
Italian: Africa del Sud
Japanese: Minami Afurika 南アフリカ
Korean: Nam Apŭrika 남아프리카
Portuguese: África do Sul
Russian: Yúzhnaya Áfrika Южная Африка
Spanish: África del Sur
Swedish: Sydafrika

2008. South America [n.]

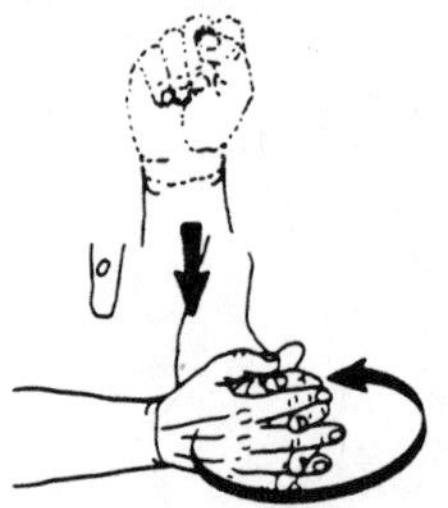

Arabic: amríkal-janubíyya امريكا الجنوبية
Chinese: nánměizhōu 南美洲
Dutch: Zuid Amerika
French: Amérique du Sud
German: Südamerika
Italian: America del Sud
Japanese: Minami Amerika 南アメリカ
Korean: Nammi 남미
Portuguese: América do Sul
Russian: Yúzhnaya Amérika Южная Америка
Spanish: América del Sur
Swedish: Sydamerika

2009. Soviet Union [n.]

Arabic: al-itihád al-sufiáti الاتحاد السوفيتي
Chinese: sūlián 蘇聯
Dutch: Sovjetunie
French: Union Soviétique
German: Sowjetunion
Italian: Unione Sovietica
Japanese: Sobieto Rempō ソビエト連邦
Korean: Soryŏn 쏘련
Portuguese: União Soviética
Russian: Sovétskiy Soyúz Советский Союз
Spanish: Unión Soviética
Swedish: Sovjetunionen

2010. sow [v.]

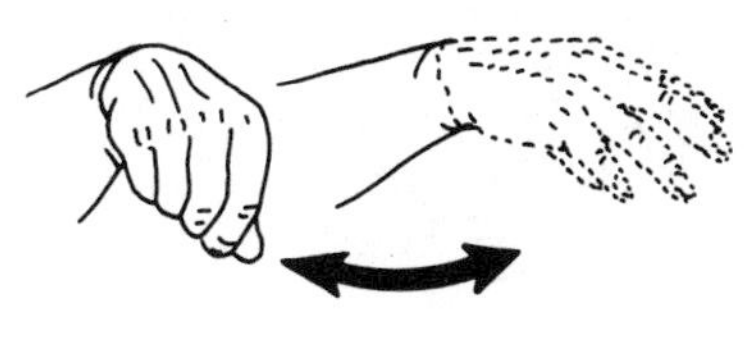

Arabic: záraa زرع
Chinese: bòzhòng 播種
Dutch: zaaien
French: semer
German: säen
Italian: seminare
Japanese: maku 種をまく
Korean: ppurida 뿌리다
Portuguese: semear
Russian: séyat' сеять
Spanish: sembrar
Swedish: så

2011. space [n.]

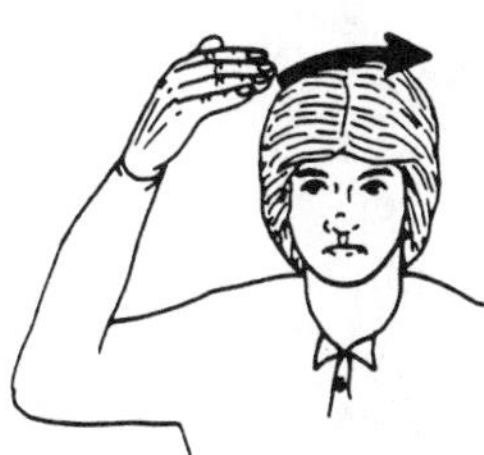

Arabic: farágh فراغ
Chinese: kōngjiān 空間
Dutch: ruimte
French: espace
German: Raum
Italian: spazio
Japanese: kūkan 空間
Korean: konggan 공간
Portuguese: espaço
Russian: prostránstvo пространство
Spanish: espacio
Swedish: rum

2012. spacecraft [n.]

Arabic: as-safínal-fada'ía السفينة الفضائية
Chinese: tàikōngchuán 太空船
Dutch: ruimtevaartuig
French: vaisseau spatial
German: Raumschiff
Italian: astronave
Japanese: uchūryokōsen 宇宙飛行船
Korean: ujusŏn 우주선
Portuguese: astronave
Russian: kosmícheskiy korábl' космический корабль
Spanish: astronave
Swedish: rumfartyg

2013. Spain [n.]

Arabic: isbánia اسبانيا
Chinese: xībānyá 西班牙
Dutch: Spanje
French: Espagne
German: Spanien
Italian: Spagna
Japanese: Supein スペイン
Korean: Sŭp'ein 스페인
Portuguese: Espanha
Russian: Ispániya Испания
Spanish: España
Swedish: Spanien

2014. spark [n.]

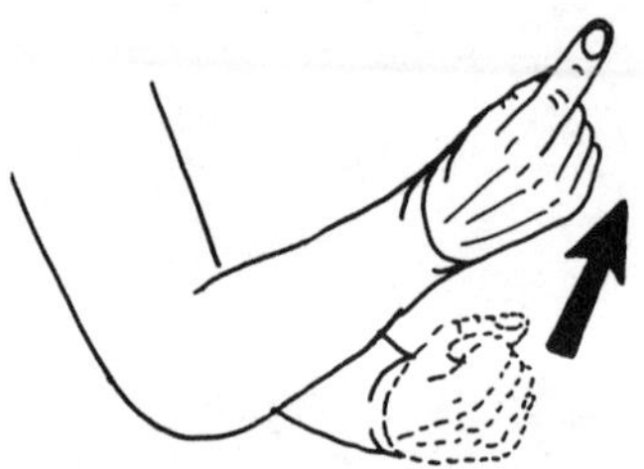

Arabic: sharára شرارة
Chinese: huǒhuā 火花
Dutch: vonk
French: étincelle
German: Funken
Italian: scintilla
Japanese: hibana 火花
Korean: bulkkot 불꽃
Portuguese: faísca
Russian: ískra искра
Spanish: chispa
Swedish: gnista

2015. speak [v.]

Arabic: taháddatha تحدث
Chinese: shuō 說
Dutch: spreken
French: parler
German: sprechen
Italian: parlare
Japanese: hanasu 話す
Korean: marhada 말하다
Portuguese: falar
Russian: govorít' говорить
Spanish: hablar
Swedish: tala

2016. special [adj.]

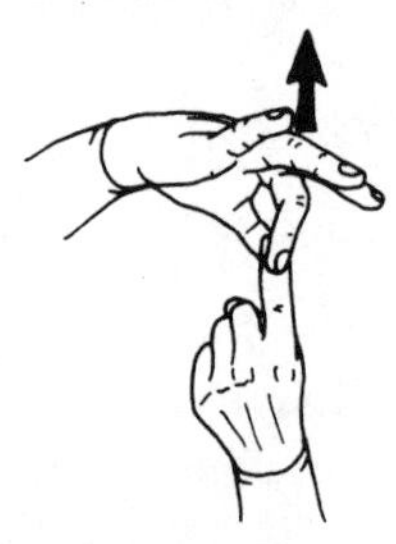

Arabic: khaas خاص
Chinese: tèbié 特別
Dutch: speciaal
French: spécial
German: speziell
Italian: speciale
Japanese: tokubetsu no 特別の
Korean: t'ŭkbyŏrhan 특별한
Portuguese: especial
Russian: spetsiál'nyy специальный
Spanish: especial
Swedish: speciell

2017. specialty [n.]

Arabic: ikhtisás إختصاص
Chinese: shàncháng 擅長
Dutch: specialiteit
French: spécialité
German: Spezialität
Italian: specialità
Japanese: semmon 専門
Korean: t'ŭksanmul 특산물
Portuguese: especialidade
Russian: spetsiál'nost' специальность
Spanish: especialidad
Swedish: specialitet

2018. specific [adj.]

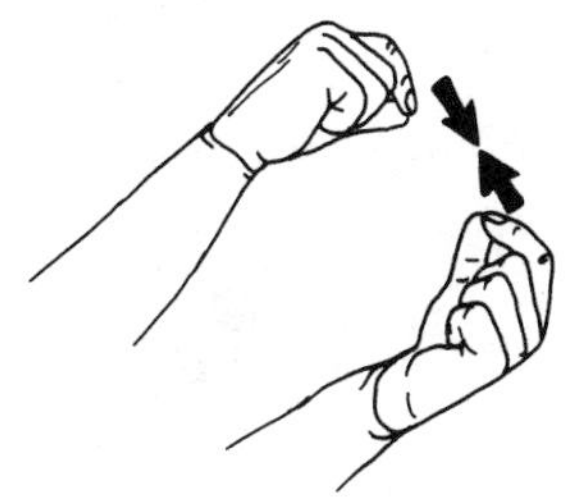

Arabic: moáaian معين
Chinese: tèdìngde 特定的
Dutch: specifiek
French: spécifique
German: spezifisch
Italian: specifico
Japanese: tokushu na 特殊な
Korean: t'ŭkjŏng'han 특정한
Portuguese: específico
Russian: konkrétnyy конкретный
Spanish: específico
Swedish: specifik

2019. speech [n.]

Arabic: khútba خطبة
Chinese: yǎnshuō 演説
Dutch: toespraak
French: discours
German: Rede
Italian: discorso
Japanese: enzetsu 演説
Korean: yŏnsŏl 연설
Portuguese: discurso
Russian: rech' речь
Spanish: discurso
Swedish: tal

2020. speed [n.]

Arabic: súraa سرعة
Chinese: sùdù 速度
Dutch: snelheid
French: vitesse
German: Geschwindigkeit
Italian: velocità
Japanese: hayasa 速さ
Korean: sokdo 속도
Portuguese: velocidade
Russian: skórost' скорость
Spanish: velocidad
Swedish: hastighet

2021. spell [v.]

Arabic: tahájja' تهجى
Chinese: pīn 拼
Dutch: spellen
French: épeler
German: buchstabieren
Italian: sillabare
Japanese: tsuzuru つづる
Korean: ch'ŏljahada 철자하다
Portuguese: soletrar
Russian: proiznosít' po búkvam произносить по буквам
Spanish: deletrear
Swedish: stava

2022. spend (money) [v.]

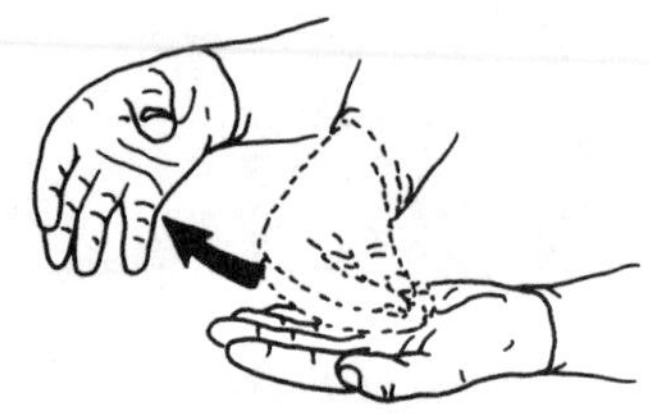

Arabic: sárafa صرف
Chinese: huā 花
Dutch: uitgeven
French: dépenser
German: ausgeben
Italian: spendere
Japanese: tsukau 使う
Korean: sobihada 소비하다
Portuguese: gastar
Russian: trátit' тратить
Spanish: gastar
Swedish: ge ut

2023. spider [n.]

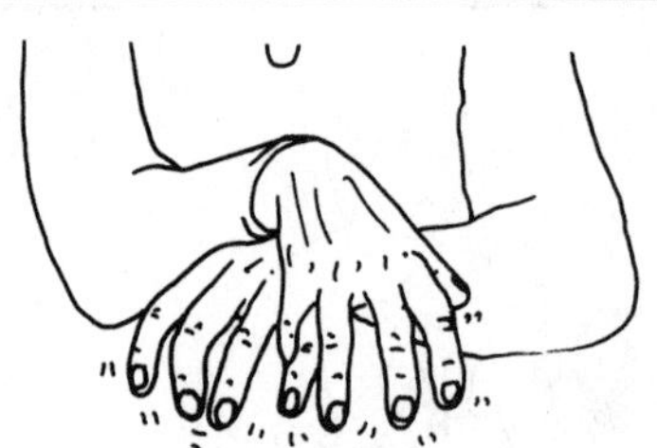

Arabic: áankabut عنكبوت
Chinese: zhizhū 蜘蛛
Dutch: spin
French: araignée
German: Spinne
Italian: ragno
Japanese: kumo クモ
Korean: kŏmi 거미
Portuguese: aranha
Russian: paúk паук
Spanish: araña
Swedish: spindel

2024. spirit [n.]

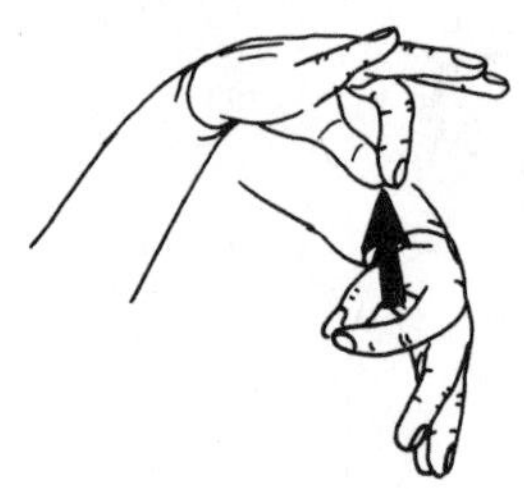

Arabic: rúah روح
Chinese: jingshén 精神
Dutch: geest
French: esprit
German: Geist
Italian: spirito
Japanese: seishin 精神
Korean: jŏngshin 정신
Portuguese: espírito
Russian: dukh дух
Spanish: espíritu
Swedish: ande

2025. splendid [adj.]

Arabic: múshreq مشرق
Chinese: huīhuángde 輝煌的
Dutch: schitterend
French: splendide
German: glänzend
Italian: splendido
Japanese: migoto na 見事な
Korean: jangŏmhan 장엄한
Portuguese: esplêndido
Russian: velikolépnyy великолепный
Spanish: espléndido
Swedish: glänsande

2026. spoiled [adj.]

Arabic: mudállal مدلل
Chinese: fŭbài 腐敗
Dutch: bedorven
French: gâté
German: verdorben
Italian: guastato
Japanese: kusatta 腐った
Korean: ssŏgŭn 썩은
Portuguese: estragado
Russian: ispórchennyy испорченный
Spanish: estropeado
Swedish: förstörd

2027. spoon [n.]

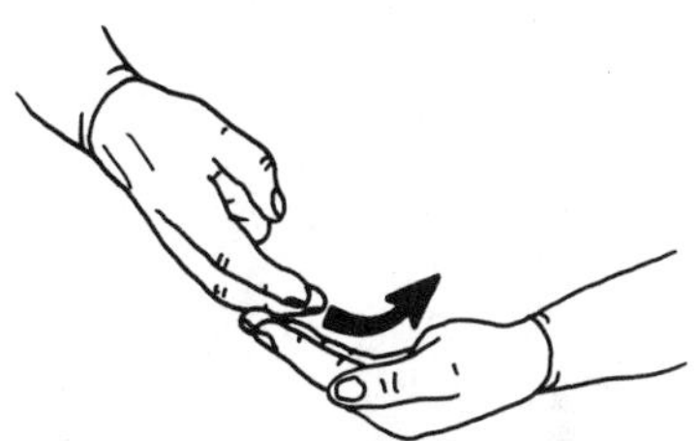

Arabic: milaáqa ملعقة
Chinese: tāng chí 湯匙
Dutch: lepel
French: cuillère
German: Löffel
Italian: cucchiaio
Japanese: supūn スプーン
Korean: sutkarag 숟가락
Portuguese: colher
Russian: lózhka ложка
Spanish: cuchara
Swedish: sked

2028. sport [n.]

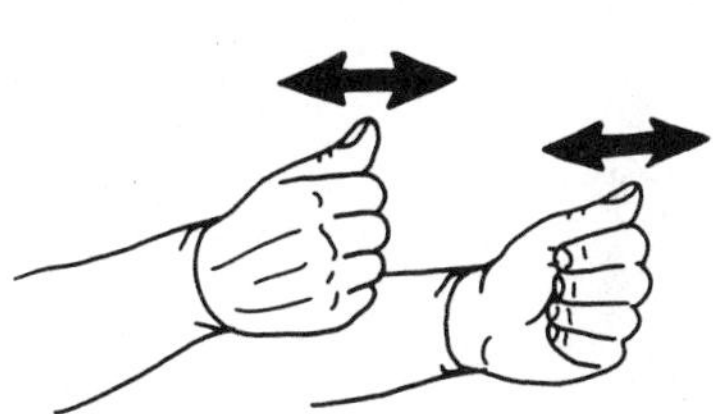

Arabic: riádha رياضة
Chinese: yùndòng 運動
Dutch: sport
French: sport
German: Sport
Italian: sport
Japanese: undō 運動
Korean: sup'och'ŭ 스포츠
Portuguese: esporte
Russian: sport спорт
Spanish: deporte
Swedish: sport

2029. spot (stain) [n.]

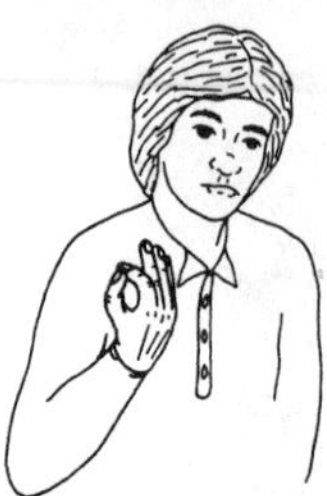

Arabic: búqaa بقعة
Chinese: bāndiǎn 斑點
Dutch: vlek
French: tache
German: Fleck
Italian: macchia
Japanese: oten 汚点
Korean: jŏm 점
Portuguese: mancha
Russian: pyatnó пятно
Spanish: mancha
Swedish: fläck

2030. spread [v.]

Arabic: fárada فرد
Chinese: sànkāi 散開
Dutch: spreiden
French: étendre
German: ausbreiten
Italian: stendere
Japanese: hirogeru 広げる
Korean: p'yŏda 펴다
Portuguese: espalhar
Russian: rasprostranyát' распространять
Spanish: extender
Swedish: sprida

2031. spring (season [n.]

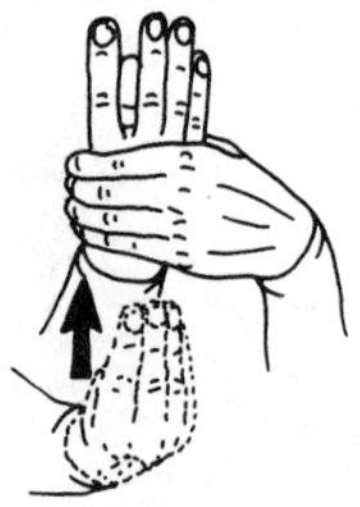

Arabic: rabíaa ربيع
Chinese: chūntiān 春天
Dutch: lente
French: printemps
German: Frühling
Italian: primavera
Japanese: haru 春
Korean: bom 봄
Portuguese: primavera
Russian: vesná весна
Spanish: primavera
Swedish: vår

2032. spy [n.]

Arabic: jasús جاسوس
Chinese: jiàndié 間諜
Dutch: spion
French: espion
German: Spion
Italian: spia
Japanese: supai スパイ
Korean: sŭp'ai 스파이
Portuguese: espião
Russian: shpión шпион
Spanish: espía
Swedish: spion

2033. square (shape) [n.]

Arabic: murábbaa مربع
Chinese: zhèngfāng 正方
Dutch: vierkant
French: carré
German: Quadrat
Italian: quadrato
Japanese: shikaku 四角
Korean: jŏngsagak'yŏng 정사각형
Portuguese: quadrado
Russian: kvadrát квадрат
Spanish: cuadrado
Swedish: kvadrat

2034. squeeze [v.]

Arabic: áasara عصر
Chinese: jǐ 挤
Dutch: knijpen
French: serrer
German: quetschen
Italian: spremere
Japanese: shimetsukeru 締めつける
Korean: joeda 조이다
Portuguese: espremer
Russian: szhimát' сжимать
Spanish: exprimir
Swedish: krama ur

2035. stage (theater) [n.]

Arabic: munássa منصة
Chinese: wǔ tái 舞台
Dutch: toneel
French: scène
German: Bühne
Italian: scena
Japanese: butai 舞台
Korean: mudae 무대
Portuguese: cena
Russian: stséna сцена
Spanish: escenario
Swedish: platform

2036. stairs [n.]

Arabic: salálem سلالم
Chinese: lóutī 楼梯
Dutch: trap
French: escalier
German: Treppe
Italian: scala
Japanese: kaidan 階段
Korean: kyedan 계단
Portuguese: escada
Russian: léstnitsa лестница
Spanish: escalera
Swedish: trappa

2037. stamp (postage) [n.]

Arabic: tábeaa طابع
Chinese: yóupiào 郵票
Dutch: postzegel
French: timbre-poste
German: Briefmarke
Italian: francobollo
Japanese: kitt 切手
Korean: up'yo 우표
Portuguese: sêlo
Russian: márka марка
Spanish: estampilla
Swedish: frimärke

2038. stand (on one's feet) [v.]

Arabic: wáqafa وقف
Chinese: zhàn 站
Dutch: staan
French: se tenir debout
German: stehen
Italian: stare in piedi
Japanese: tatsu 立つ
Korean: sŏda 서다
Portuguese: estar de pé
Russian: stoyát' стоять
Spanish: estar de pie
Swedish: stå

2039. star [n.]

Arabic: níjma نجمة
Chinese: xīngxīng 星星
Dutch: ster
French: étoile
German: Stern
Italian: stella
Japanese: hoshi 星
Korean: byŏl 별
Portuguese: estrêla
Russian: zvezdá звезда
Spanish: estrella
Swedish: stjärna

2040. starvation [n.]

Arabic: júa' جوع
Chinese: jī èr 饑餓
Dutch: uithongering
French: inanition
German: Verhungern
Italian: fame
Japanese: kiga 飢餓
Korean: kikŭn 기근
Portuguese: inanição
Russian: golodániye голодание
Spanish: inanición
Swedish: svältning

2041. state (political entity) [n.]

Arabic: weláya ولاية
Chinese: zhōu 州
Dutch: staat
French: état
German: Staat
Italian: stato
Japanese: kokka 国家
Korean: kukka 국가
Portuguese: estado
Russian: gosudárstvo государство
Spanish: estado
Swedish: stat

2042. state [v.]

Arabic: qárara قرر
Chinese: chénshù 陳述
Dutch: verklaren
French: déclarer
German: erklären
Italian: dichiarare
Japanese: noberu 述べる
Korean: marhada 말하다
Portuguese: declarar
Russian: zayavlyát' заявлять
Spanish: declarar
Swedish: förklara

2043. statement [n.]

Arabic: tasríh تصريح
Chinese: shēngmíng 聲明
Dutch: verklaring
French: déclaration
German: Erklärung
Italian: dichiarazione
Japanese: hōkokusho 報告書
Korean: jinsul 진술
Portuguese: declaração
Russian: zayavléniye заявление
Spanish: declaración
Swedish: uttalande

2044. station [n.]

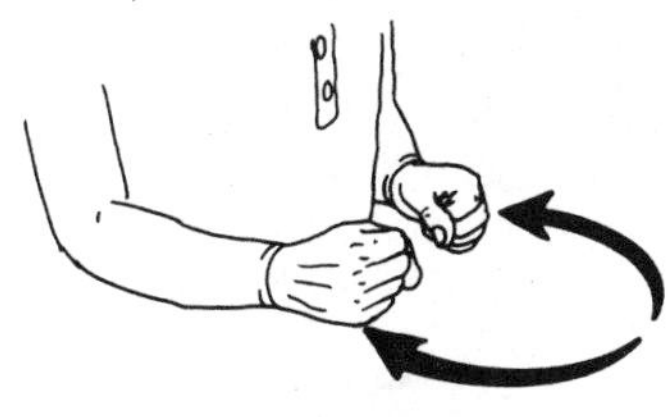

Arabic: muhátta محطة
Chinese: zhàn 站
Dutch: station
French: station
German: Station
Italian: stazione
Japanese: eki 馬天
Korean: jŏnggŏjang 정거장
Portuguese: estação
Russian: stántsiya станция
Spanish: estación
Swedish: station

2045. statistics [n.]

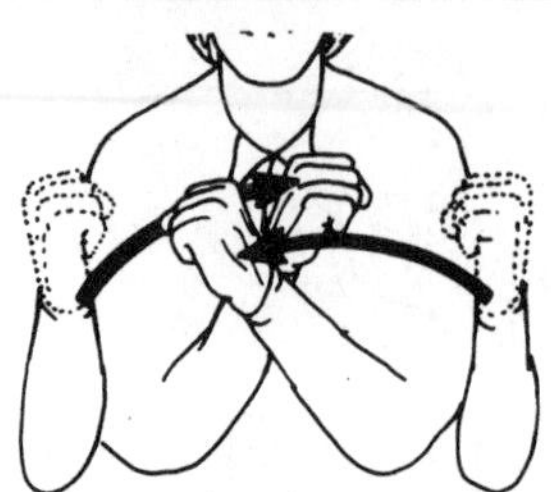

Arabic: elm al-ihsá' علم الاحصاء
Chinese: tǒngjì 統計
Dutch: statistiek
French: statistique
German: Statistik
Italian: statistica
Japanese: tōkei 統計
Korean: t'onggye 통계
Portuguese: estatística
Russian: statístika статистика
Spanish: estadística
Swedish: statistik

2046. statue [n.]

Arabic: timthál تمثال
Chinese: diāoxiàng 雕像
Dutch: standbeeld
French: statue
German: Statue
Italian: statua
Japanese: zō 像
Korean: josang 조상
Portuguese: estátua
Russian: státuya статуя
Spanish: estatua
Swedish: staty

2047. steal [v.]

Arabic: sáraqa سرق
Chinese: tōu 偷
Dutch: stelen
French: voler
German: stehlen
Italian: rubare
Japanese: nusumu 盗む
Korean: humch'ida 훔치다
Portuguese: roubar
Russian: krast' красть
Spanish: robar
Swedish: stjäla

2048. steam [n.]

Arabic: bukhár بخار
Chinese: zhēngqì 蒸汽
Dutch: stoom
French: vapeur
German: Dampf
Italian: vapore
Japanese: jōki 蒸気
Korean: jŭnggi 증기
Portuguese: vapor
Russian: par пар
Spanish: vapor
Swedish: ånga

2049. steel [n.]

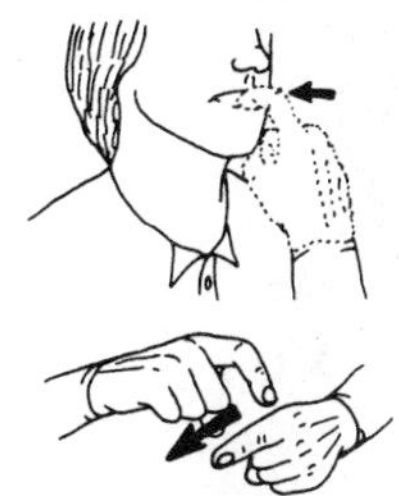

Arabic: salb صلب
Chinese: gāng 鋼
Dutch: staal
French: acier
German: Stahl
Italian: acciaio
Japanese: kōtetsu 鋼鉄
Korean: kangch'ŏl 강철
Portuguese: aço
Russian: stal' сталь
Spanish: acero
Swedish: stål

2050. step (pace) [n.]

Arabic: khútwa خطوة
Chinese: bù 步
Dutch: stap
French: pas
German: Schritt
Italian: passo
Japanese: ayumi 歩み
Korean: kŏrŭm 걸음
Portuguese: passo
Russian: shag шаг
Spanish: paso
Swedish: steg

2051. stick [n.]

Arabic: aása عصا
Chinese: gùn 桿
Dutch: stok
French: bâton
German: Stock
Italian: bastone
Japanese: bō 棒
Korean: makdaegi 막대기
Portuguese: pau
Russian: pálka палка
Spanish: palo
Swedish: käpp

2052. stingy (miserly) [adj.]

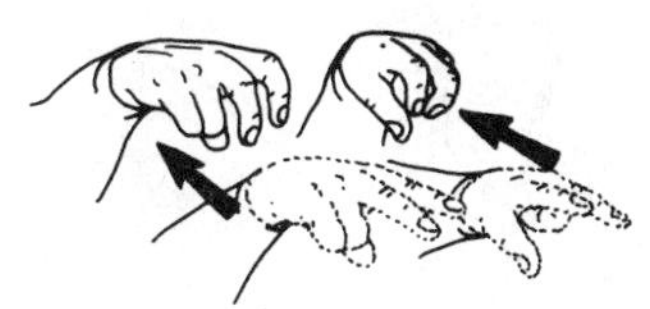

Arabic: bakhíl بخيل
Chinese: xiǎoqì 小氣
Dutch: gierig
French: avare
German: geizig
Italian: tirchio
Japanese: kechina けちな
Korean: insaek'han 인색한
Portuguese: ávaro
Russian: skupóy скупой
Spanish: tacaño
Swedish: girig

2053. stir [v.]

Arabic: mázaja مزج
Chinese: jiǎo 攪
Dutch: roeren
French: remuer
German: rühren
Italian: mescolare
Japanese: kakimazeru 掻き混ぜる
Korean: hwijŏtta 휘젓다
Portuguese: mexer
Russian: razméshivat' размешивать
Spanish: revolver
Swedish: röra

2054. stocking(s) [n.]

Arabic: jáurab جورب
Chinese: cháng wà 長襪
Dutch: kous(en)
French: bas
German: Strumpf
Italian: calza
Japanese: sutokkingu ストッキング
Korean: yangmal 양말
Portuguese: meia
Russian: chulók чулок
Spanish: media
Swedish: strumpa

2055. stomach [n.]

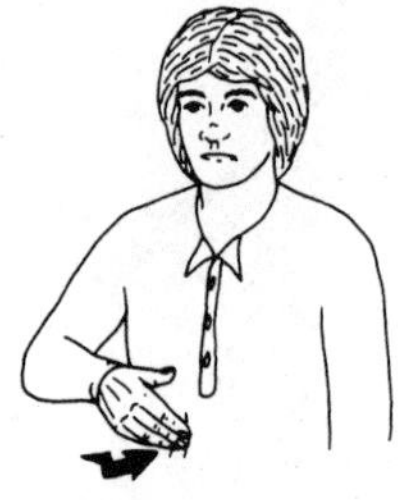

Arabic: máadha معدة
Chinese: wèi 胃
Dutch: maag
French: estomac
German: Magen
Italian: stomaco
Japanese: i 胃
Korean: wi 위
Portuguese: estômago
Russian: zhivót живот
Spanish: estómago
Swedish: mage

2056. stop [v.]

Arabic: tawáqafa توقف
Chinese: tíng 停
Dutch: stoppen
French: arrêter
German: halten
Italian: fermare
Japanese: yameru 止める
Korean: mŏmch'uda 멈추다
Portuguese: parar
Russian: ostanávlivat' останавливать
Spanish: parar
Swedish: stoppa

2057. store (shop) [n.]

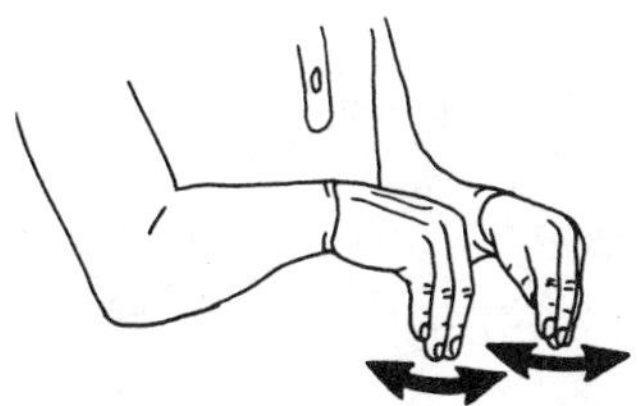

Arabic: dukán دكان
Chinese: shāngdiàn 商店
Dutch: winkel
French: magasin
German: Geschäft
Italian: magazzino
Japanese: mise 店
Korean: kage 가게
Portuguese: loja
Russian: magazín магазин
Spanish: tienda
Swedish: magasin

2058. storm [n.]

Arabic: iaasár اعصار
Chinese: bàofēngyǔ 暴風雨
Dutch: storm
French: tempête
German: Sturm
Italian: tempesta
Japanese: arashi 嵐
Korean: p'okp'ungu 폭풍우
Portuguese: tempestade
Russian: búrya буря
Spanish: tempestad
Swedish: storm

2059. story (floor) [n.]

Arabic: tábeq طابق
Chinese: lóu 樓
Dutch: verdieping
French: étage
German: Stockwerk
Italian: piano
Japanese: kai 階
Korean: ch'ŭng 층
Portuguese: andar
Russian: etázh этаж
Spanish: piso
Swedish: våning

2060. story (tale) [n.]

Arabic: qéssa قصة
Chinese: gùshì 故事
Dutch: verhaal
French: histoire
German: Erzählung
Italian: racconto
Japanese: monogatari 物語
Korean: iyagi 이야기
Portuguese: história
Russian: rasskáz рассказ
Spanish: cuento
Swedish: historia

2061. stove (cooking) [n.]

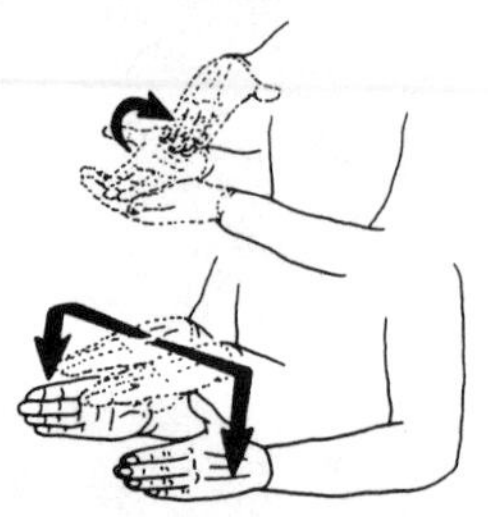

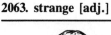

Arabic: máuqed موقد
Chinese: lúzi 爐子
Dutch: kachel
French: fourneau
German: Ofen
Italian: stufa
Japanese: sutōbu ストーブ
Korean: sŭt'obu 스토브
Portuguese: fogão
Russian: pech' печь
Spanish: estufa
Swedish: ugn

2062. straight [adj.]

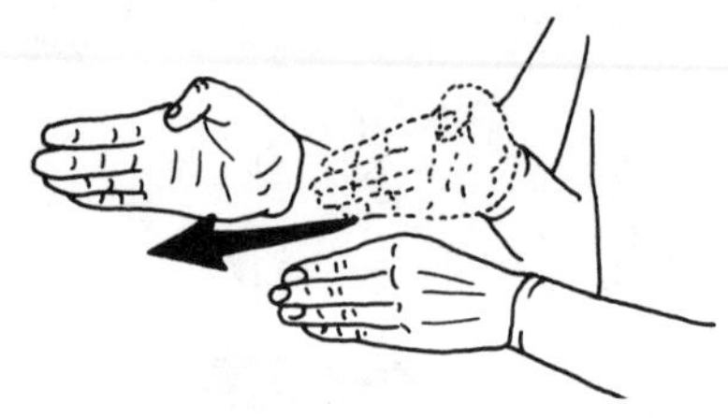

Arabic: mustaqím مستقيم
Chinese: zhí 直
Dutch: recht
French: droit
German: gerade
Italian: diritto
Japanese: massuguna 真直ぐな
Korean: ttok'barŭn 똑바른
Portuguese: direto
Russian: pryamóy прямой
Spanish: derecho
Swedish: rak

2063. strange [adj.]

Arabic: gharíb غريب
Chinese: qíguài 奇怪
Dutch: vreemd
French: étrange
German: fremd
Italian: strano
Japanese: kimyōna 奇妙な
Korean: isang'han 이상한
Portuguese: estranho
Russian: stránnyy странный
Spanish: extraño
Swedish: främmande

2064. stream (current) [n.]

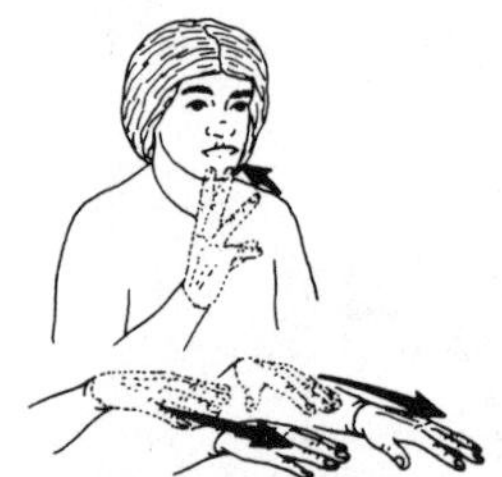

Arabic: jádwal جدول
Chinese: shuĭliú 水流
Dutch: stroom
French: courant
German: Strom
Italian: corrente
Japanese: nagare 流れ
Korean: sinae 시내
Portuguese: corrente
Russian: potók поток
Spanish: corriente
Swedish: ström

2065. street [n.]

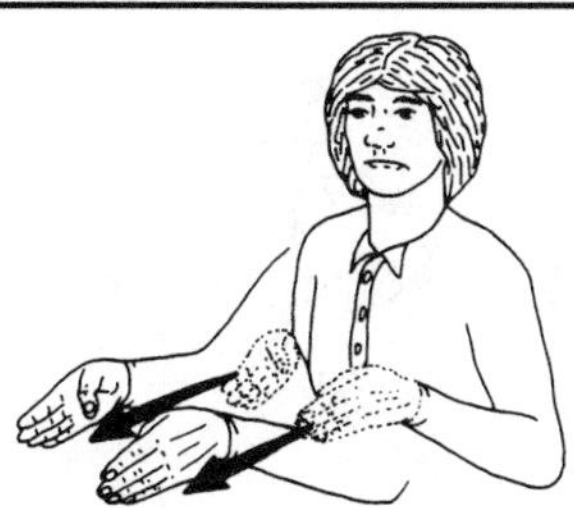

Arabic: sháreaa شارع
Chinese: jiē 街
Dutch: straat
French: rue
German: Straße
Italian: via
Japanese: tōri 通り
Korean: kŏri 거리
Portuguese: rua
Russian: úlitsa улица
Spanish: calle
Swedish: gata

2066. strength [n.]

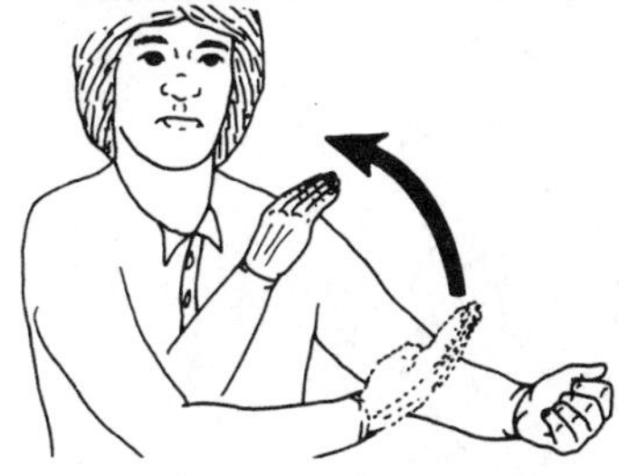

Arabic: qúwwa قوة
Chinese: lìqì 力氣
Dutch: sterkte
French: force
German: Stärke
Italian: forza
Japanese: chikara 力
Korean: him 힘
Portuguese: força
Russian: síla сила
Spanish: fuerza
Swedish: styrka

2067. stress (tension) [n.]

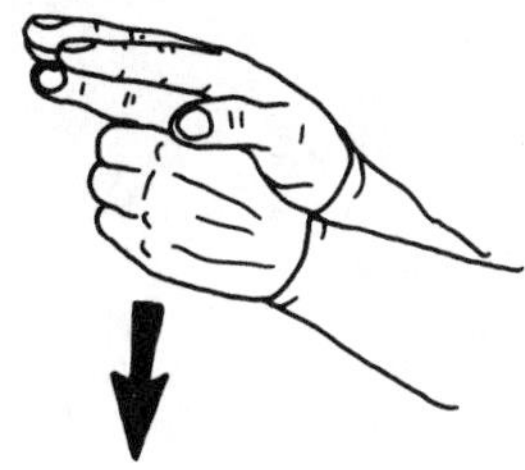

Arabic: ijhád اجهاد
Chinese: yālì 壓力
Dutch: spanning
French: tension
German: Spannung
Italian: tensione
Japanese: sutoresu ストレス
Korean: ap'bag 압박
Portuguese: tensão
Russian: napryazhéniye напряжение
Spanish: tensión
Swedish: spänning

2068. stretch [v.]

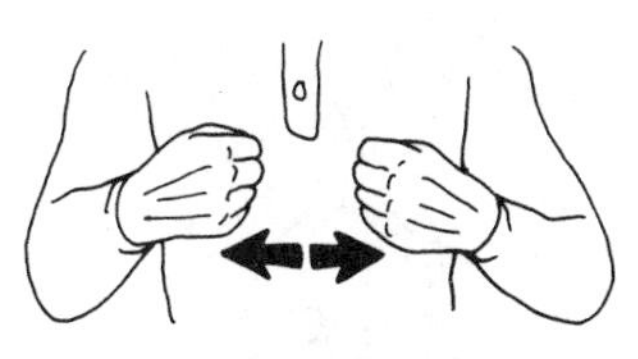

Arabic: tamáddada تمدد
Chinese: shēnzhang 伸張
Dutch: strekken
French: étendre
German: strecken
Italian: tendere
Japanese: nobasu 伸ばす
Korean: p'yŏda 펴다
Portuguese: esticar
Russian: vytyágivat' вытягивать
Spanish: estirar
Swedish: sträcka

2069. strict [adj.]

Arabic: sárem صارم
Chinese: yángé 嚴格
Dutch: streng
French: strict
German: streng
Italian: severo
Japanese: kibishii 厳しい
Korean: ŏmkyŏg'han 엄격한
Portuguese: severo
Russian: strógiy строгий
Spanish: estricto
Swedish: sträng

2070. strike (labor) [n.]

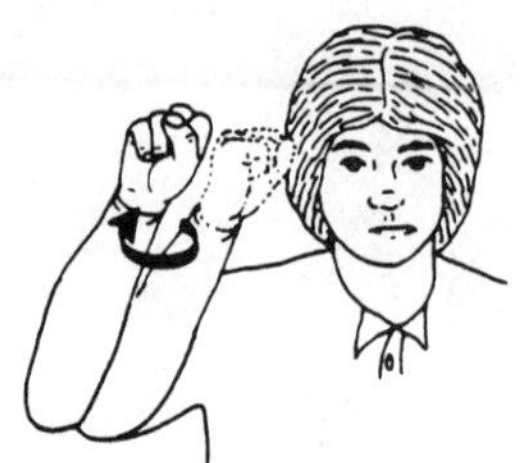

Arabic: idráb اضراب
Chinese: bàgōng 罷工
Dutch: staking
French: grève
German: Streik
Italian: sciopero
Japanese: sutoraiki ストライキ
Korean: p'aŏp 파업
Portuguese: greve
Russian: zabastóvka забастовка
Spanish: huelga
Swedish: strejk

2071. string [n.]

Arabic: wátar وتر
Chinese: xiàn 線
Dutch: draad
French: ficelle
German: Schnur
Italian: spago
Japanese: himo 紐
Korean: kkŭn 끈
Portuguese: barbante
Russian: bechyóvka бечёвка
Spanish: cuerda
Swedish: snöre

2072. strong [adj.]

Arabic: qawí قوي
Chinese: qiángde 強的
Dutch: sterk
French: fort
German: stark
Italian: forte
Japanese: tsuyoi 強い
Korean: kang'han 강한
Portuguese: forte
Russian: síl'nyy сильный
Spanish: fuerte
Swedish: stark

2073. struggle [n.]

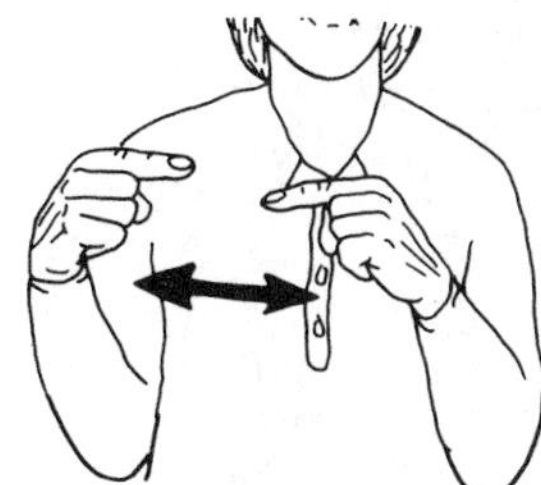

Arabic: kefáh كفاح
Chinese: zhēngzhá 掙扎
Dutch: gevecht
French: lutte
German: Kampf
Italian: lotta
Japanese: funtō 奮闘
Korean: t'ujaeng 투쟁
Portuguese: luta
Russian: bor'bá борьба
Spanish: lucha
Swedish: kamp

2074. stubborn [adj.]

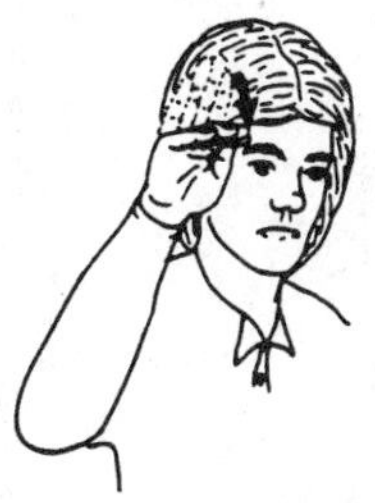

Arabic: aaníd عنيد
Chinese: wángùde 頑固的
Dutch: hardnekkig
French: têtu
German: hartnäckig
Italian: cocciuto
Japanese: ganko na 頑固な
Korean: kojip'sen 고집센
Portuguese: teimoso
Russian: upórnyy упорный
Spanish: obstinado
Swedish: hardnackad

2075. student [n.]

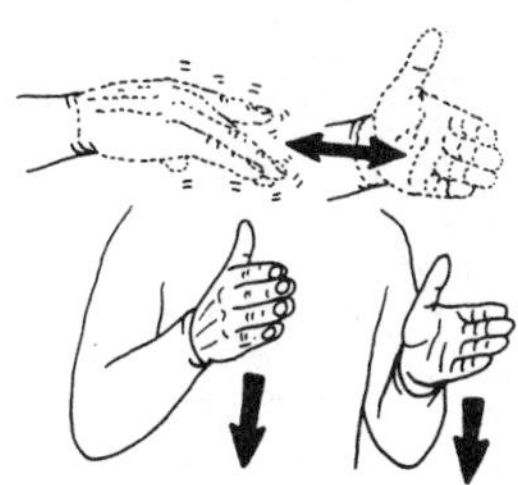

Arabic: táleb طالب
Chinese: xuéshēng 學生
Dutch: student
French: étudiant
German: Student
Italian: studente
Japanese: gakusei 学生
Korean: hak'saeng 학생
Portuguese: estudante
Russian: studént студент
Spanish: estudiante
Swedish: student

2076. study [v.]

Arabic: dárasa درس
Chinese: xuéxí 學習
Dutch: studeren
French: étudier
German: studieren
Italian: studiare
Japanese: benkyō suru 勉強する
Korean: kongbuhada 공부하다
Portuguese: estudar
Russian: izuchát' изучать
Spanish: estudiar
Swedish: studera

2077. stupid [adj.]

Arabic: ghábi غبي
Chinese: bèn 笨
Dutch: dom
French: stupide
German: dumm
Italian: stupido
Japanese: bakana 馬鹿な
Korean: ŏrisŏgun 어리석은
Portuguese: estúpido
Russian: glúpyy глупый
Spanish: estúpido
Swedish: dum

2078. subject [n.]

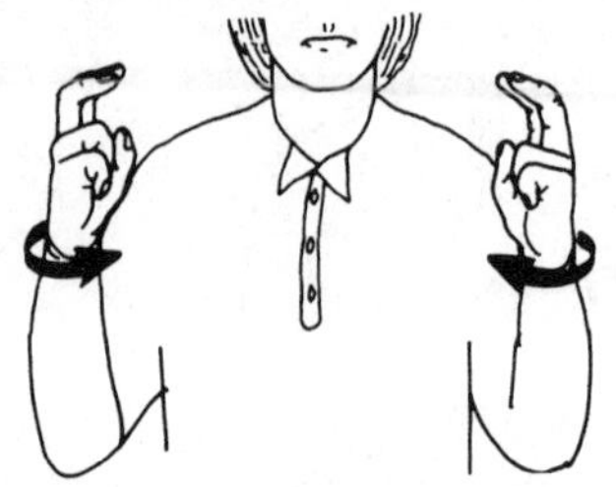

Arabic: maudúaa موضوع
Chinese: zhǔtí 主題
Dutch: onderwerp
French: sujet
German: Subjekt
Italian: soggetto
Japanese: shudai 主題
Korean: jemok 제목
Portuguese: sujeito
Russian: predmét предмет
Spanish: sujeto
Swedish: subjekt

2079. submit (present) [v.]

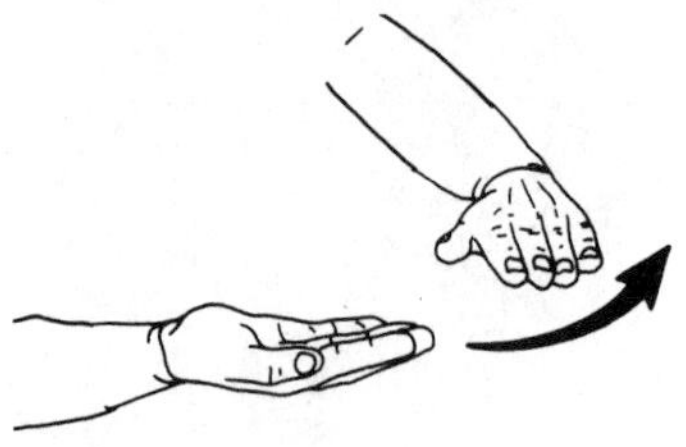

Arabic: qáddama قدم
Chinese: chéngjiāo 呈交
Dutch: voorleggen
French: présenter
German: vorlegen
Italian: presentare
Japanese: teishutsu suru 提出する
Korean: jech'urhada 제출하다
Portuguese: apresentar
Russian: predstavlyát' представлять
Spanish: presentar
Swedish: framlägga

2080. subscribe (newspaper) [v.]

Arabic: ishtáraka اشترك
Chinese: dìngyuè 訂閱
Dutch: abonneren
French: s'abonner
German: abonnieren
Italian: abbonarsi
Japanese: kōdoku suru 購読する
Korean: kudok'hada 구독하다
Portuguese: assinar
Russian: podpísyvat'sya подписываться
Spanish: subscribirse
Swedish: underteckna

2081. subsequent [adj.]

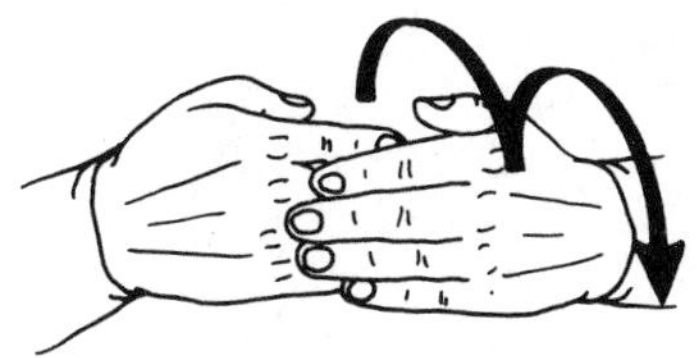

Arabic: láhaq لاحق
Chinese: suíhoù 隨後
Dutch: volgend
French: subséquent
German: folgend
Italian: susseguente
Japanese: kekkato shite okoru 結果として起こる
Korean: gyŏlgwaŭi 결과의
Portuguese: subseqüente
Russian: posléduyushchiy последующий
Spanish: subsiguiente
Swedish: följande

2082. substance (matter) [n.]

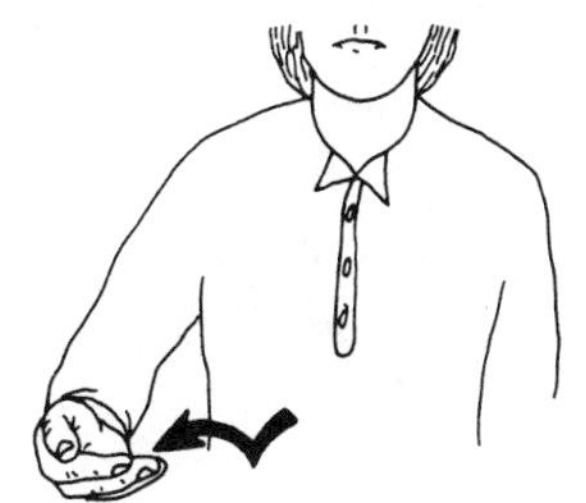

Arabic: mádda مادة
Chinese: běnzhí 本旨
Dutch: substantie
French: substance
German: Substanz
Italian: sostanza
Japanese: busshitsu 物質
Korean: bonjil 본질
Portuguese: substância
Russian: veshchestvó вещество
Spanish: substancia
Swedish: substans

2083. substantial [adj.]

Arabic: haqíeqi حقيقي
Chinese: shíjì 實際
Dutch: substantieel
French: substantiel
German: wesentlich
Italian: sostanziale
Japanese: jisshitsuteki na 実質的な
Korean: shilchaehanŭn 실재하는
Portuguese: substancial
Russian: sushchéstvennyy существенный
Spanish: substancial
Swedish: väsentlig

2084. substitute [v.]

Arabic: istábdala استبدل
Chinese: dàitì 代替
Dutch: vervangen
French: substituer
German: ersetzen
Italian: sostituire
Japanese: daiyō suru 代用する
Korean: daeyong'hada 대용하다
Portuguese: substituir
Russian: zamenyát' заменять
Spanish: substituir
Swedish: ersätta

2085. subtract [v.]

Arabic: khasáma خصم
Chinese: kòuchú 扣除
Dutch: aftrekken
French: soustraire
German: subtrahieren
Italian: sottrarre
Japanese: hiku 引く
Korean: ppaeda 빼다
Portuguese: subtrair
Russian: vychitát' вычитать
Spanish: substraer
Swedish: subtrahera

2086. success [n.]

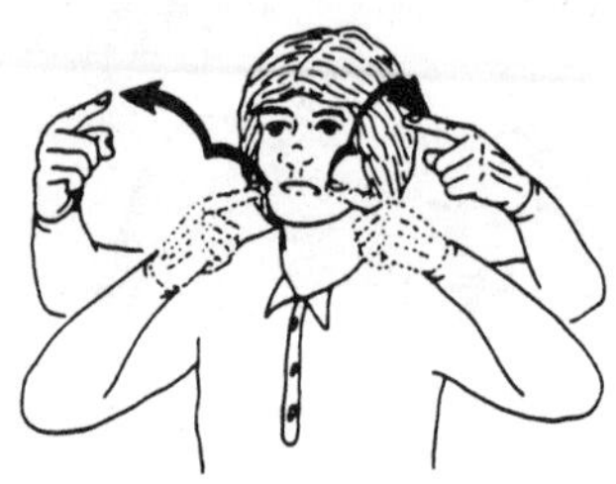

Arabic: naják نجاح
Chinese: chénggōng 成功
Dutch: succes
French: succès
German: Erfolg
Italian: successo
Japanese: seikō 成功
Korean: sŏnggong 성공
Portuguese: sucesso
Russian: uspékh успех
Spanish: éxito
Swedish: succé

2087. suddenly [adv.]

Arabic: fáj'a فجأة
Chinese: túrán 突然
Dutch: plotseling
French: soudain
German: plötzlich
Italian: improvvisamente
Japanese: kyūni 突然に
Korean: kapchagi 갑자기
Portuguese: repentinamente
Russian: vdrug вдруг
Spanish: de repente
Swedish: plötsligt

2088. suffer [v.]

Arabic: ta'állama تألم
Chinese: shòukǔ 受苦
Dutch: lijden
French: souffrir
German: leiden
Italian: soffrire
Japanese: kurushimu 苦しむ
Korean: koerowahada 괴로와하다
Portuguese: sofrer
Russian: stradát' страдать
Spanish: sufrir
Swedish: lida

2089. sufficient [adj.]

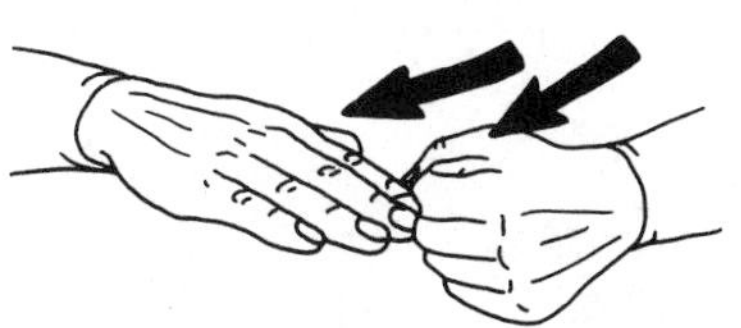

Arabic: káfi كافي
Chinese: zúgòu 足夠
Dutch: voldoende
French: suffisant
German: genügend
Italian: sufficiente
Japanese: jūbun na 充分な
Korean: ch'ungbunhan 충분한
Portuguese: suficiente
Russian: dostátochnyy достаточный
Spanish: suficiente
Swedish: tillräcklig

2090. sugar [n.]

Arabic: as-súkar السكر
Chinese: táng 糖
Dutch: suiker
French: sucre
German: Zucker
Italian: zucchero
Japanese: satō 砂糖
Korean: sŏlt'ang 설탕
Portuguese: açucar
Russian: sákhar caxap
Spanish: azúcar
Swedish: socker

2091. suggest [v.]

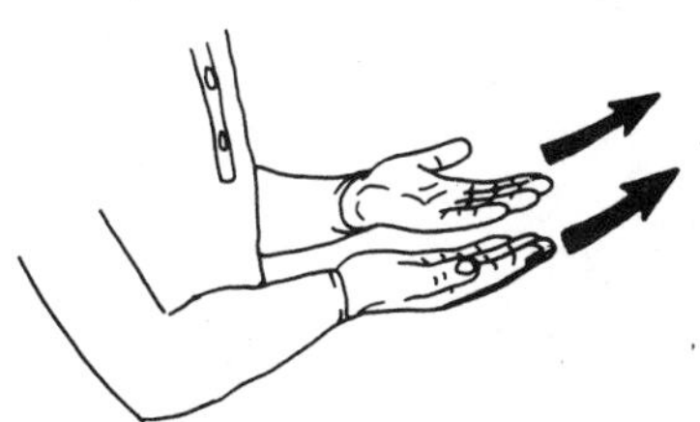

Arabic: iqtáraha اقترح
Chinese: jiànyì 建議
Dutch: voorstellen
French: suggérer
German: vorschlagen
Italian: suggerire
Japanese: teian suru 提案する
Korean: amshihada 암시하다
Portuguese: sugerir
Russian: predlagát' предлагать
Spanish: sugerir
Swedish: föreslå

2092. suicide [n.]

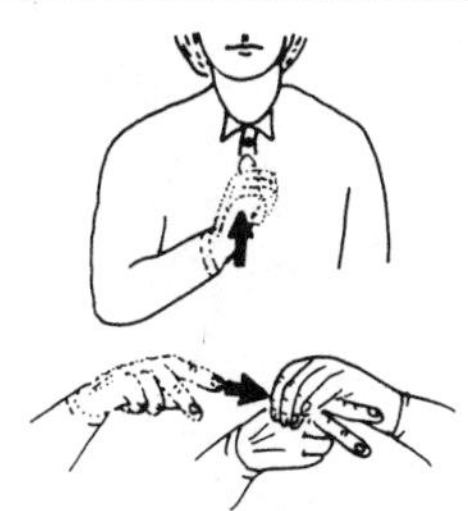

Arabic: intehár انتحار
Chinese: zìshā 自殺
Dutch: zelfmoord
French: suicide
German: Selbstmord
Italian: suicida
Japanese: jisatsu 自殺
Korean: jasal 자살
Portuguese: suicídio
Russian: samoubíystvo самоубийство
Spanish: suicidio
Swedish: självmord

2093. suit (clothes) [n.]

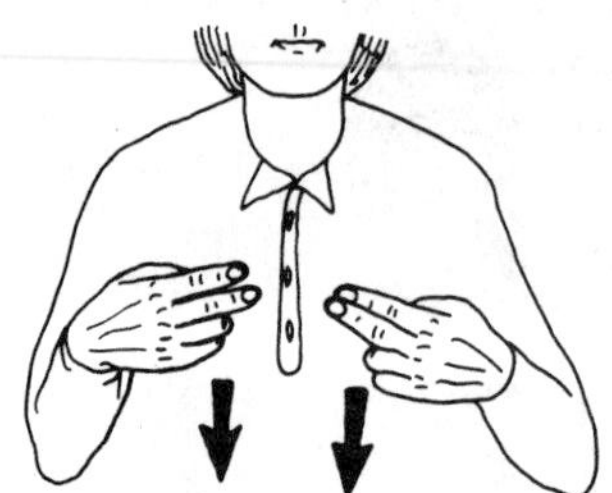

Arabic: bádla بدلة
Chinese: tàozhuāng 套裝
Dutch: kostuum
French: complet
German: Anzug
Italian: vestito
Japanese: yōfuku hitosoroi 洋服一そろい
Korean: yangbok 양복
Portuguese: terno
Russian: kostyúm костюм
Spanish: traje
Swedish: kostym

2094. suitcase [n.]

Arabic: haqíbet as-sáfar حقيبة السفر
Chinese: shǒutíxiāng 手提箱
Dutch: valies
French: valise
German: Koffer
Italian: valigia
Japanese: sūtsukēsu スーツケース
Korean: yŏhaeng kabang 여행가방
Portuguese: mala
Russian: chemodán чемодан
Spanish: maleta
Swedish: resväska

2095. sum [n.]

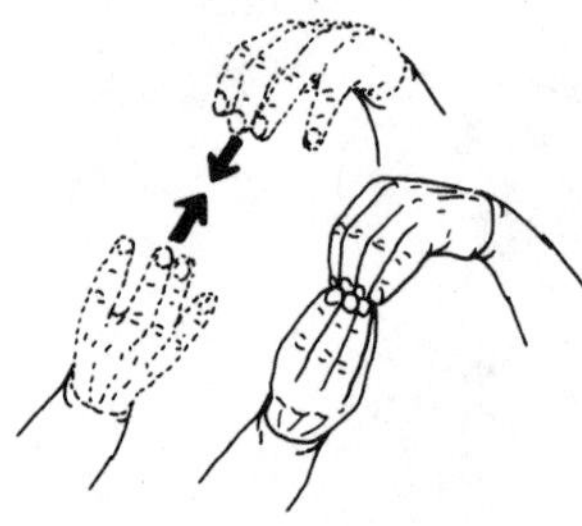

Arabic: majmúaa مجموع
Chinese: zǒngshù 總數
Dutch: som
French: somme
German: Summe
Italian: somma
Japanese: sōgaku 総額
Korean: hapkye 합계
Portuguese: soma
Russian: súmma сумма
Spanish: suma
Swedish: summa

2096. summarize [v.]

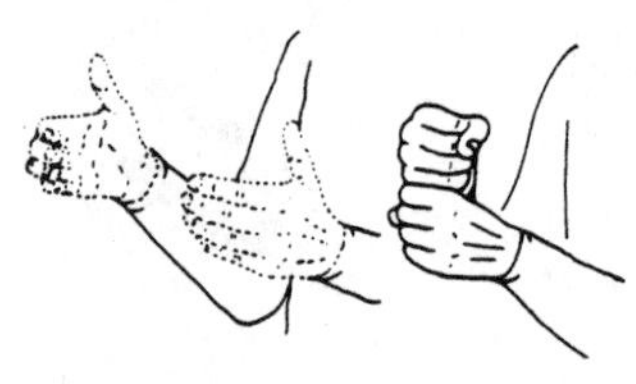

Arabic: ikhtásara إختصر
Chinese: zǒngguā 總括
Dutch: opsommen
French: résumer
German: zusammenfassen
Italian: riassumere
Japanese: yōyaku suru 要約
Korean: yoyak'hada 요약하다
Portuguese: resumir
Russian: obobshchát' обобщать
Spanish: resumir
Swedish: sammanfatta

2097. summer [n.]

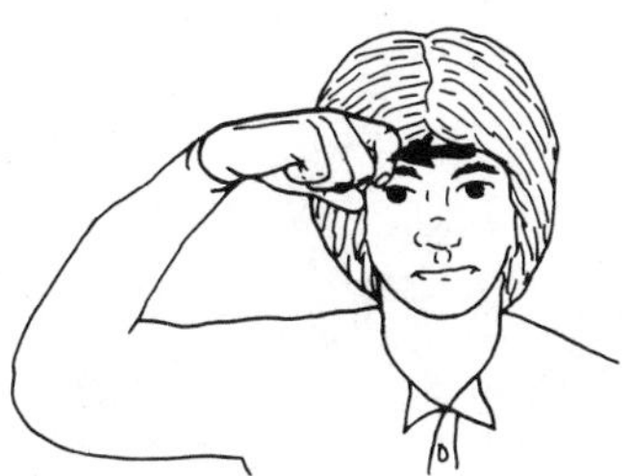

Arabic: sáif صيف
Chinese: xiàtiān 夏天
Dutch: zomer
French: été
German: Sommer
Italian: estate
Japanese: natsu 夏
Korean: yŏrŭm 여름
Portuguese: verão
Russian: léto лето
Spanish: verano
Swedish: sommar

2098. summon (call) [v.]

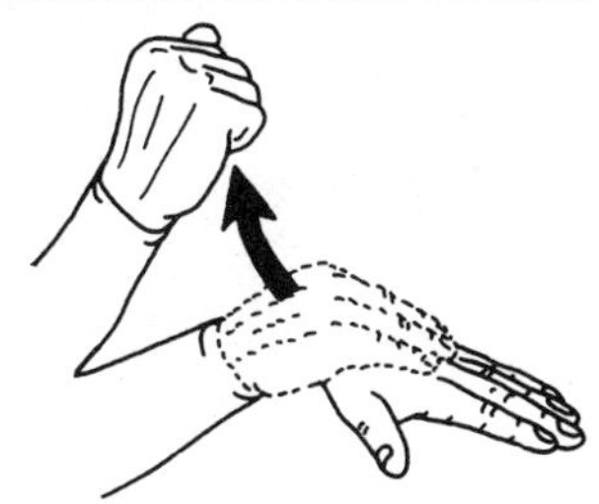

Arabic: dáa دعى
Chinese: zhàohuàn 召喚
Dutch: ontbieden
French: convoquer
German: vorladen
Italian: convocare
Japanese: shōshū suru 召集する
Korean: sojip'hada 소집하다
Portuguese: convocar
Russian: vyzyvát' вызывать
Spanish: convocar
Swedish: sammankalla

2099. sun [n.]

Arabic: shams شمس
Chinese: tàiyáng 太陽
Dutch: zon
French: soleil
German: Sonne
Italian: sole
Japanese: taiyō 太陽
Korean: hae 해
Portuguese: sol
Russian: sólntse солнце
Spanish: sol
Swedish: sol

2100. Sunday [n.]

Arabic: al-áhad الاحد
Chinese: xīngqí rì 星期日
Dutch: zondag
French: dimanche
German: Sonntag
Italian: domenica
Japanese: nichiyōbi 日曜日
Korean: iryoil 일요일
Portuguese: domingo
Russian: voskresén'ye воскресенье
Spanish: domingo
Swedish: söndag

2101. sunrise [n.]

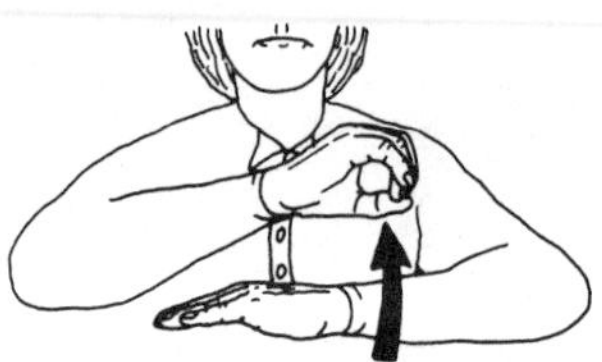

Arabic: shurúq as-shams شروق الشمس
Chinese: rìchū 日出
Dutch: zonsopgang
French: lever du soleil
German: Sonnenaufgang
Italian: levata del sole
Japanese: hinode 日の出
Korean: haedoji 해돋이
Portuguese: nascer do sol
Russian: voskhód sólntsa восход солнца
Spanish: salida del sol
Swedish: soluppgång

2102. sunset [n.]

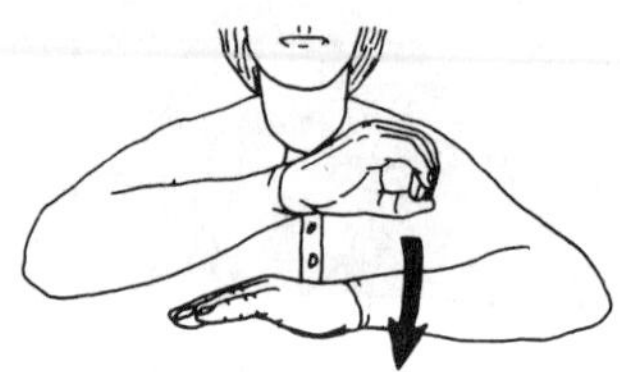

Arabic: ghurúb as-shams غروب الشمس
Chinese: rìluò 日落
Dutch: zonsondergang
French: coucher du soleil
German: Sonnenuntergang
Italian: tramonto del sole
Japanese: nichibotsu 日没
Korean: ilmol 일몰
Portuguese: pôr do sol
Russian: zakhód sólntsa заход солнца
Spanish: puesta del sol
Swedish: solnedgång

2103. superior [adj.]

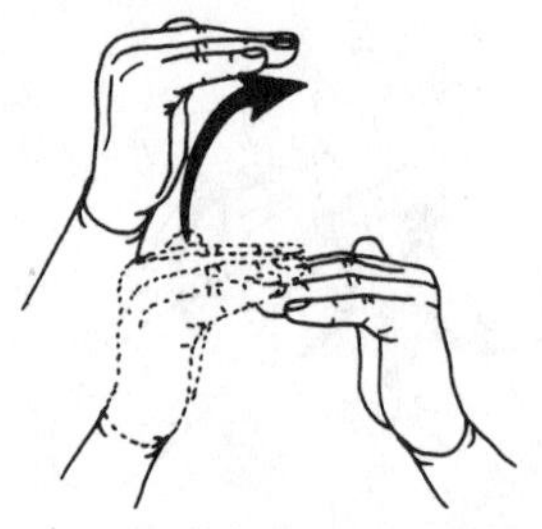

Arabic: ájdar اجدر
Chinese: yōuyuède 優越的
Dutch: superieur
French: supérieur
German: höher
Italian: superiore
Japanese: sugureta 〔より〕勝れた
Korean: usuhan 우수한
Portuguese: superior
Russian: výsshiy высший
Spanish: superior
Swedish: överlägsen

2104. supper (evening meal) [n.]

Arabic: áasha' عشاء
Chinese: wǎncān 晚餐
Dutch: avondeten
French: souper
German: Abendessen
Italian: cena
Japanese: yūshoku 夕食
Korean: jŏnyŏk shiksa 저녁식사
Portuguese: jantar
Russian: úzhin ужин
Spanish: cena
Swedish: kvällsmat

2105. supply (provide) [v.]

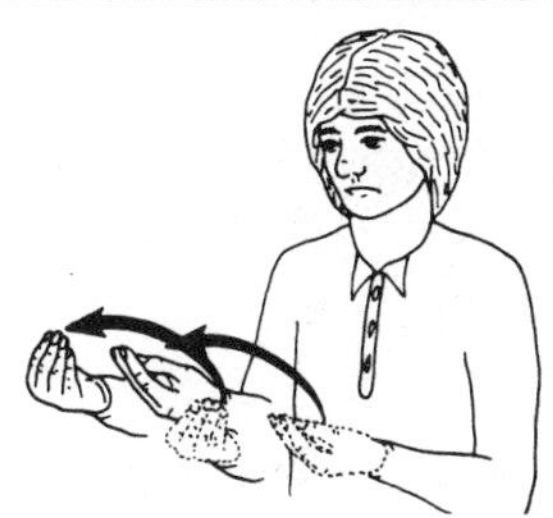

Arabic: záwwada زود
Chinese: gōngjǐ 供給
Dutch: leveren
French: fournir
German: liefern
Italian: fornire
Japanese: kyōkyū suru 供給する
Korean: konggŭp'hada 공급하다
Portuguese: fornecer
Russian: snabzhát' снабжать
Spanish: suministrar
Swedish: leverera

2106. support [n.]

Arabic: ta'íd تأييد
Chinese: zhīchí 支持
Dutch: steun
French: soutien
German: Unterstützung
Italian: sostegno
Japanese: enjo 援助
Korean: jiji 지지
Portuguese: apoio
Russian: poddérzhka поддержка
Spanish: apoyo
Swedish: understöd

2107. suppose [v.]

Arabic: iftáradha افترض
Chinese: jiǎdìng 假定
Dutch: veronderstellen
French: supposer
German: vermuten
Italian: supporre
Japanese: . . .to katei suru …と仮定する
Korean: sangsanghada 상상하다
Portuguese: supor
Russian: polagát' полагать
Spanish: suponer
Swedish: förmoda

2108. suppress [v.]

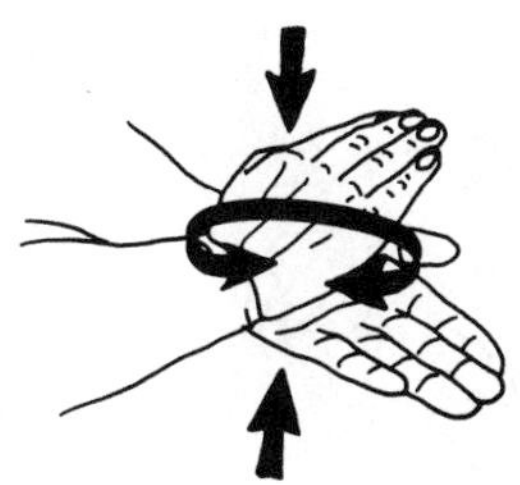

Arabic: qámaa قمع
Chinese: yāyì 壓抑
Dutch: onderdrukken
French: supprimer
German: unterdrücken
Italian: sopprimere
Japanese: osaeru 抑える
Korean: jinap'hada 진압하다
Portuguese: suprimir
Russian: podavlyát' подавлять
Spanish: suprimir
Swedish: undertrycka

2109. sure [adj.]

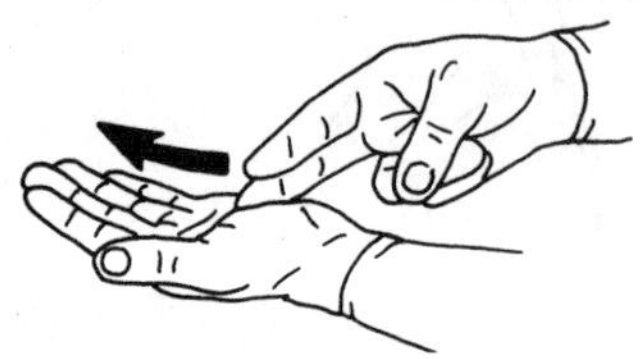

Arabic: akíd اكيد
Chinese: quèdìng 確定
Dutch: zeker
French: sûr
German: sicher
Italian: sicuro
Japanese: tashika na 確かな
Korean: hwakshirhan 확신하다
Portuguese: certo
Russian: uvérennyy уверенный
Spanish: seguro
Swedish: säker

2110. surely [adv.]

Arabic: bit-takíd بالتأكيد
Chinese: yídìng 一定
Dutch: zeker
French: sûrement
German: sicherlich
Italian: sicuramente
Japanese: tashika ni 確かに
Korean: hwakshirhi 확실히
Portuguese: certamente
Russian: konéchno конечно
Spanish: seguramente
Swedish: säkerligen

2111. surface [n.]

Arabic: sat-h سطح
Chinese: biǎomiàn 表面
Dutch: oppervlakte
French: surface
German: Oberfläche
Italian: superficie
Japanese: hyōmen 表面
Korean: p'yomyŏn 표면
Portuguese: superfície
Russian: povérkhnost' поверхность
Spanish: superficie
Swedish: yta

2112. surgery [n.]

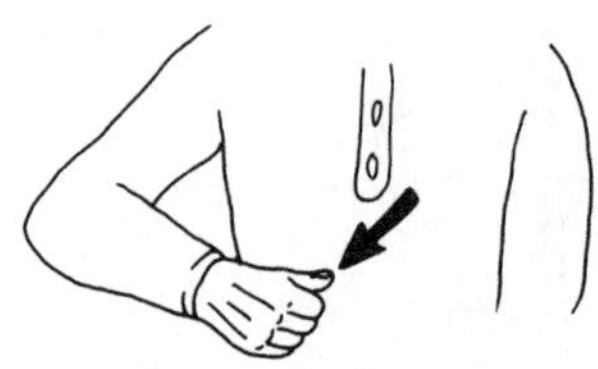

Arabic: jiráha جراحة
Chinese: shǒushù 手術
Dutch: chirurgie
French: chirurgie
German: Chirurgie
Italian: chirurgia
Japanese: shujutsu 手術
Korean: oekwa 외과
Portuguese: cirurgia
Russian: khirurgíya хирургия
Spanish: cirugía
Swedish: kirurgi

2113. surprise [n.]

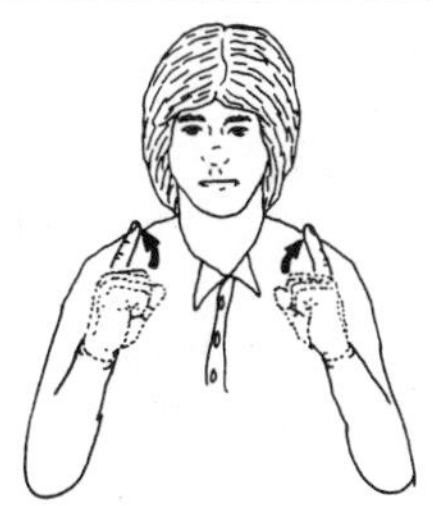

Arabic: mufája'a مفاجئة
Chinese: jīngqí 驚奇
Dutch: verrassing
French: surprise
German: Überraschung
Italian: sorpresa
Japanese: odoroki 驚き
Korean: nollam 놀람
Portuguese: surpresa
Russian: syurpríz сюрприз
Spanish: sorpresa
Swedish: överraskning

2114. surprise [v.]

Arabic: yufáji' يفاجئ
Chinese: chījīng 吃驚
Dutch: verrassen
French: étonner
German: überraschen
Italian: sorprendere
Japanese: odorokaseru 驚かす
Korean: nollage hada 놀라게 하다
Portuguese: surpreender
Russian: udivlyát' удивлять
Spanish: sorprender
Swedish: överraska

2115. surrender [v.]

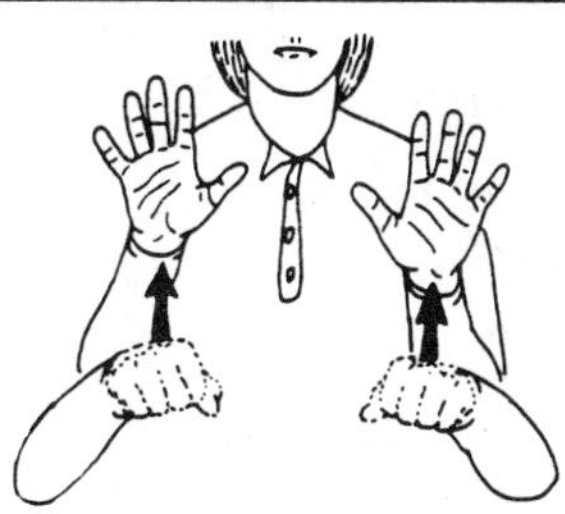

Arabic: istáslama استسلم
Chinese: tóuxiáng 投降
Dutch: zich overgeven
French: se rendre
German: sich ergeben
Italian: arrendersi
Japanese: kōfuku suru 降服する
Korean: hangbok'hada 항복하다
Portuguese: render-se
Russian: sdavát'sya сдаваться
Spanish: rendirse
Swedish: ge sig

2116. surround [v.]

Arabic: aháta احاط
Chinese: bāowéi 包圍
Dutch: omringen
French: entourer
German: umringen
Italian: circondare
Japanese: kakomu 囲む
Korean: dullŏssada 둘러싸다
Portuguese: cercar
Russian: okruzhát' окружать
Spanish: cercar
Swedish: omringa

2117. suspect [v.]

Arabic: ishtábaha bi اشتبه ب
Chinese: huáiyí 懷疑
Dutch: verdenken
French: soupçonner
German: verdächtigen
Italian: sospettare
Japanese: utagau 疑う
Korean: ŭishimhada 의심하는
Portuguese: suspeitar
Russian: podozreváť подозревать
Spanish: sospechar
Swedish: misstänka

2118. suspicion [n.]

Arabic: ishtibá اشتباه
Chinese: huáiyí 懷疑
Dutch: verdenking
French: soupçon
German: Verdacht
Italian: sospetto
Japanese: utagai 疑い
Korean: ŭishim 의심
Portuguese: suspeita
Russian: podozréniye подозрение
Spanish: sospecha
Swedish: misstanke

2119. swallow [v.]

Arabic: járaa جرع
Chinese: tūn 吞
Dutch: slikken
French: avaler
German: schlucken
Italian: inghiottire
Japanese: nomikomu 飲み込む
Korean: samk'ida 삼키다
Portuguese: engolir
Russian: glotát' глотать
Spanish: tragar
Swedish: svälja

2120. swear (oath) [v.]

Arabic: hálafa حلف
Chinese: fāshì 發誓
Dutch: zweren
French: jurer
German: schwören
Italian: giurare
Japanese: chikau 誓う
Korean: maengsehada 맹세하는
Portuguese: jurar
Russian: klyást'sya клясться
Spanish: jurar
Swedish: svärja

2121. Sweden [n.]

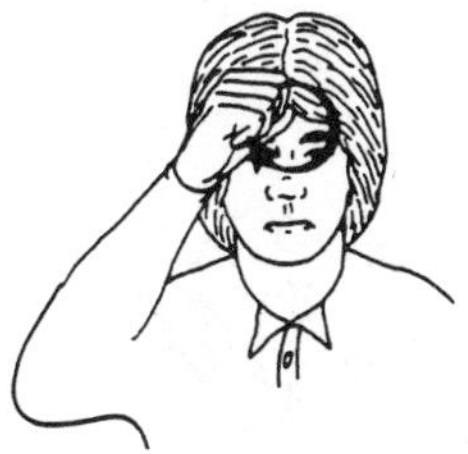

Arabic: as-suwéid السويد
Chinese: ruìdiǎn 瑞典
Dutch: Zweden
French: Suède
German: Schweden
Italian: Svezia
Japanese: Suēden スウェーデン
Korean: Sǔweden 스웨덴
Portuguese: Suécia
Russian: Shvétsiya Швеция
Spanish: Suecia
Swedish: Sverige

2122. sweet [adj.]

Arabic: hélu حلو
Chinese: tián 甜
Dutch: zoet
French: doux
German: süß
Italian: dolce
Japanese: amai 甘い
Korean: dan 단
Portuguese: doce
Russian: sládkiy сладкий
Spanish: dulce
Swedish: söt

2123. swim [v.]

Arabic: sábaha سبح
Chinese: yóuyǒng 游泳
Dutch: zwemmen
French: nager
German: schwimmen
Italian: nuotare
Japanese: oyogu 泳ぐ
Korean: suyǒnghada 수영하다
Portuguese: nadar
Russian: plávat' плавать
Spanish: nadar
Swedish: simma

2124. swing [v.]

Arabic: ta'árjaha تأرجح
Chinese: yáobǎi 摇摆
Dutch: zwaaien
French: balancer
German: schwingen
Italian: dondolare
Japanese: yureru 揺れる
Korean: hǔndǔllida 흔들리다
Portuguese: balançar
Russian: kachát' качать
Spanish: oscilar
Swedish: svänga

2125. Switzerland [n.]

Arabic: suísra سويسرا
Chinese: ruìshì 瑞士
Dutch: Zwitserland
French: Suisse
German: Schweiz
Italian: Svizzera
Japanese: Suisu スイス
Korean: Sŭwisŭ 스위스
Portuguese: Suíça
Russian: Shveytsáriya Швейцария
Spanish: Suiza
Swedish: Schweiz

2126. sword [n.]

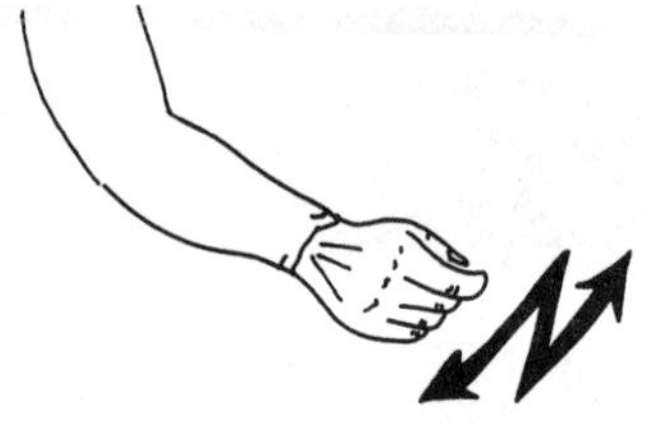

Arabic: sáif سيف
Chinese: jiàn 劍
Dutch: zwaard
French: épée
German: Schwert
Italian: spada
Japanese: katana 刀
Korean: k'al 칼
Portuguese: espada
Russian: shpága шпага
Spanish: espada
Swedish: svärd

2127. sympathy [n.]

Arabic: taátafa تعاطف
Chinese: tóngqíng 同情
Dutch: medelijden
French: compassion
German: Mitgefühl
Italian: compassione
Japanese: dōjō 同情
Korean: dongjŏng 동정
Portuguese: compaixão
Russian: sochúvstviye сочувствие
Spanish: compasión
Swedish: medkänsla

2128. system [n.]

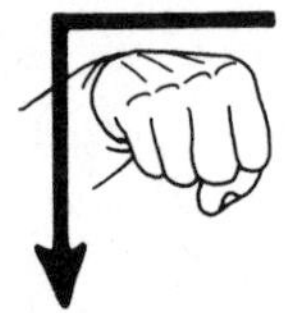
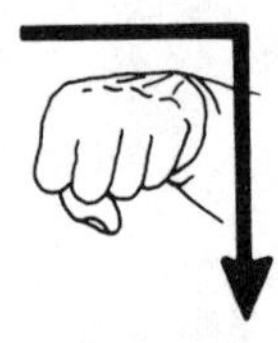

Arabic: nedhám نظام
Chinese: xìtŏng 系統
Dutch: systeem
French: système
German: System
Italian: sistema
Japanese: seido 制度
Korean: jedo 제도
Portuguese: sistema
Russian: sistéma система
Spanish: sistema
Swedish: system

2129. table [n.]

Arabic: jádwal جدول
Chinese: zhuōzi 桌子
Dutch: tafel
French: table
German: Tisch
Italian: tavola
Japanese: tēburu テーブル
Korean: t'eibul 테이블
Portuguese: mesa
Russian: stol стол
Spanish: mesa
Swedish: bord

2130. tail [n.]

Arabic: dhanb ذنب
Chinese: wěibā 尾巴
Dutch: staart
French: queue
German: Schwanz
Italian: coda
Japanese: shippo 尻尾
Korean: kkori 꼬리
Portuguese: cauda
Russian: khvost хвост
Spanish: cola
Swedish: svans

2131. take [v.]

Arabic: ákhadha اخذ
Chinese: ná 拿
Dutch: nemen
French: prendre
German: nehmen
Italian: prendere
Japanese: toru 取る
Korean: jabda 잡다
Portuguese: tomar
Russian: brat' брать
Spanish: tomar
Swedish: ta

2132. talent [n.]

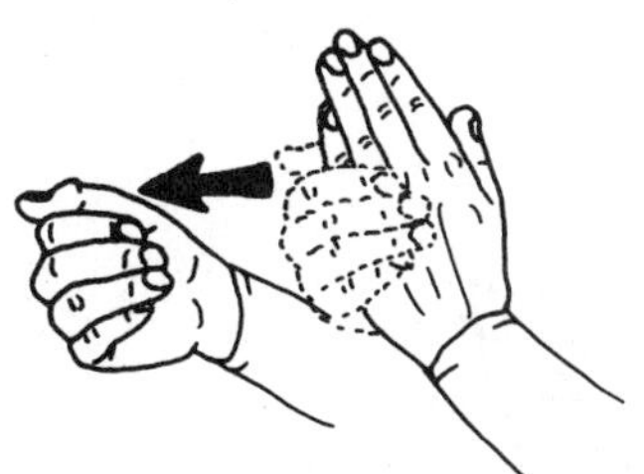

Arabic: máuhiba موهبة
Chinese: cáinéng 才能
Dutch: talent
French: talent
German: Talent
Italian: talento
Japanese: sainō 才能
Korean: jaenŭng 재능
Portuguese: talento
Russian: talánt талант
Spanish: talento
Swedish: talang

2133. talk [v.]

Arabic: takállama تكلم
Chinese: shuōhuà 說話
Dutch: spreken
French: parler
German: reden
Italian: parlare
Japanese: hanasu 話す
Korean: marhada 말하다
Portuguese: falar
Russian: govorít' говорить
Spanish: hablar
Swedish: tala

2134. tall [adj.]

Arabic: tawíl طويل
Chinese: gāode 高的
Dutch: hoog
French: haut
German: hoch
Italian: alto
Japanese: takai 高い
Korean: nop'ŭn 높은
Portuguese: alto
Russian: vysókiy высокий
Spanish: alto
Swedish: hög

2135. tame (domesticated) [adj.]

Arabic: alíf اليف
Chinese: xúnfúde 馴服的
Dutch: tam
French: domestique
German: zahm
Italian: addomesticato
Japanese: nareta なれた
Korean: gildŭrin 길 들인
Portuguese: domesticado
Russian: priruchyónnyy приручённый
Spanish: domesticado
Swedish: tam

2136. tape [n.]

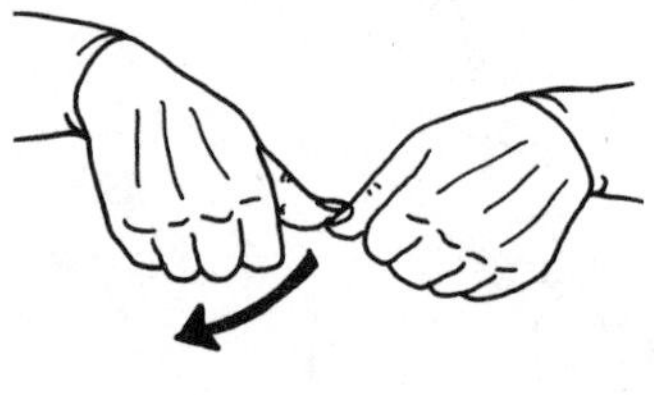

Arabic: sharíet شريط
Chinese: lùyīndài 錄音帶
Dutch: band
French: bande
German: Band
Italian: nastro
Japanese: tēpu テープ
Korean: t'eip'ŭ 테이프
Portuguese: fita
Russian: lénta лента
Spanish: cinta
Swedish: band

2137. tape recorder [n.]

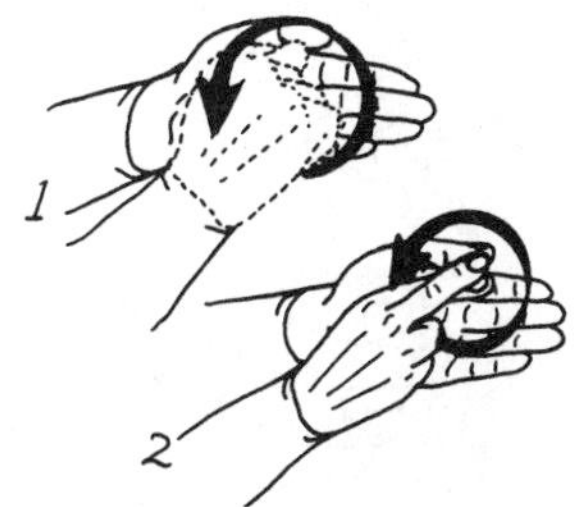

Arabic: musájjil مسجل
Chinese: lùyīnjī 錄音機
Dutch: bandopnemer
French: magnétophone
German: Tonbandgerät
Italian: registratore a nastro
Japanese: tēpu rekōdā
テープレコーダー
Korean: nogŭmki 녹음기
Portuguese: gravador
Russian: magnitofón магнитофон
Spanish: grabadora
Swedish: kassettbandspelare

2138. task [n.]

Arabic: múhimma مهمة
Chinese: rènwù 任務
Dutch: taak
French: tâche
German: Aufgabe
Italian: compito
Japanese: shigoto 仕事
Korean: il 일
Portuguese: tarefa
Russian: zadácha задача
Spanish: tarea
Swedish: uppgift

2139. taste [n.]

Arabic: táam طعم
Chinese: wèidào 味道
Dutch: smaak
French: goût
German: Geschmack
Italian: gusto
Japanese: aji 味
Korean: mat 맛
Portuguese: gosto
Russian: vkus вкус
Spanish: gusto
Swedish: smak

2140. tax [n.]

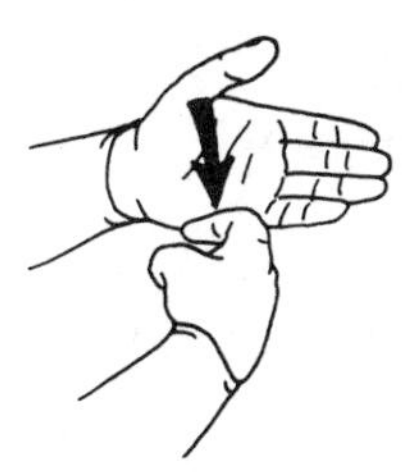

Arabic: dharíba ضريبة
Chinese: shuì 稅
Dutch: belasting
French: impôt
German: Steuer
Italian: tassa
Japanese: zeikin 税金
Korean: segŭm 세금
Portuguese: imposto
Russian: nalóg налог
Spanish: impuesto
Swedish: skatt

2141. taxi [n.]

Arabic: táksi تاكسي
Chinese: jìchéngchē 計程車
Dutch: taxi
French: taxi
German: Taxi
Italian: tassi
Japanese: takushii タクシー
Korean: t'aekshi 택시
Portuguese: táxi
Russian: taksí такси
Spanish: taxi
Swedish: taxi

2142. tea [n.]

Arabic: sháee شاي
Chinese: chá 茶
Dutch: thee
French: thé
German: Tee
Italian: tè
Japanese: ocha お茶
Korean: ch'a 차
Portuguese: chá
Russian: chay чай
Spanish: té
Swedish: te

2143. teach [v.]

Arabic: áallama علم
Chinese: jiāo 教
Dutch: onderwijzen
French: enseigner
German: lehren
Italian: insegnare
Japanese: oshieru 教える
Korean: karŭch'ida 가르치다
Portuguese: ensinar
Russian: uchít' учить
Spanish: enseñar
Swedish: lära

2144. teacher [n.]

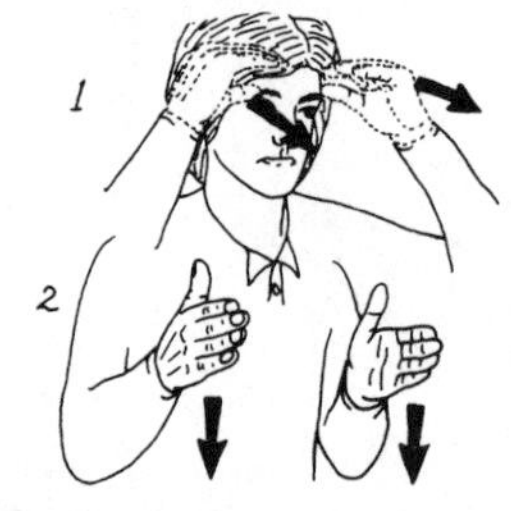

Arabic: moáalim معلم
Chinese: laŏshī 老師
Dutch: onderwijzer
French: maître d'école
German: Lehrer
Italian: insegnante
Japanese: sensei 先生
Korean: sŏnsaeng 선생
Portuguese: mestre
Russian: uchítel' учитель
Spanish: maestro
Swedish: lärare

2145. team [n.]

Arabic: faríeq فريق
Chinese: duì 隊
Dutch: ploeg
French: équipe
German: Mannschaft
Italian: squadra
Japanese: chiimu チーム
Korean: t'im 팀
Portuguese: equipe
Russian: kománda команда
Spanish: equipo
Swedish: lag

2146. tear [v.]

Arabic: mázzaqa مزق
Chinese: sī 撕
Dutch: scheuren
French: déchirer
German: reißen
Italian: strappare
Japanese: yabuku 破る
Korean: tchitta 찢다
Portuguese: rasgar
Russian: rvat' рвать
Spanish: rasgar
Swedish: riva

2147. tease [v.]

Arabic: dáiaqa ضايق
Chinese: xìnòng 戲弄
Dutch: plagen
French: taquiner
German: necken
Italian: stuzzicare
Japanese: karakau からかう
Korean: jipjŏkkŏrida 찍접거리다
Portuguese: aborrecer
Russian: draznít' дразнить
Spanish: embromar
Swedish: reta

2148. teeth [n.]

Arabic: asnán أسنان
Chinese: yáchǐ 牙齒
Dutch: tanden
French: dents
German: Zähne
Italian: denti
Japanese: ha 歯
Korean: i 이
Portuguese: dentes
Russian: zúby зубы
Spanish: dientes
Swedish: tand

2149. telegram [n.]

Arabic: barqíyya برقية
Chinese: diànbào 電報
Dutch: telegram
French: télégramme
German: Telegramm
Italian: telegramma
Japanese: dempō 電報
Korean: jŏnbo 전보
Portuguese: telegrama
Russian: telegrámma телеграмма
Spanish: telegrama
Swedish: telegram

2150. telephone [n.]

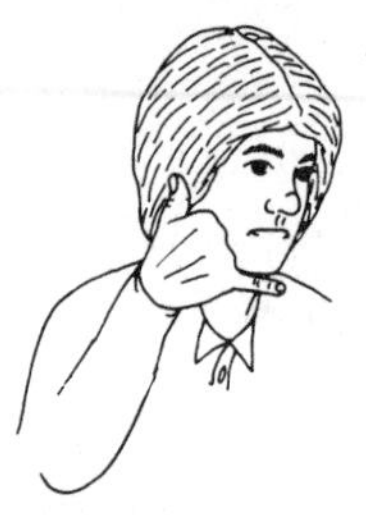

Arabic: hátef هاتف
Chinese: diànhuà 電話
Dutch: telefoon
French: téléphone
German: Telefon
Italian: telefono
Japanese: denwa 電話
Korean: jŏnhwa 전화
Portuguese: telefone
Russian: telefón телефон
Spanish: teléfono
Swedish: telefon

2151. television [n.]

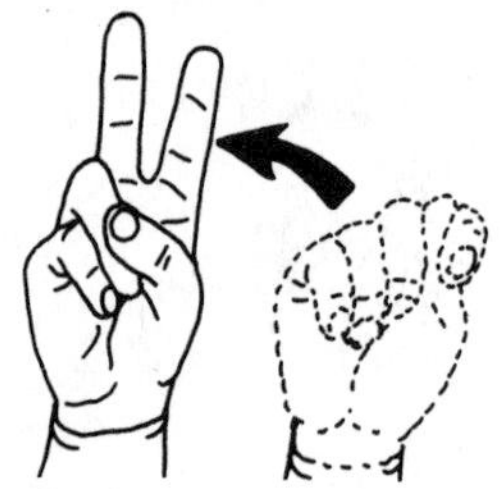

Arabic: telefizión تلفزيون
Chinese: diànshì 電視
Dutch: televisie
French: télévision
German: Fernsehen
Italian: televisione
Japanese: terebi テレビ
Korean: t'ellebijŏn 텔레비젼
Portuguese: televisão
Russian: televízor телевизор
Spanish: televisión
Swedish: television

2152. tell [v.]

Arabic: ákhbara اخبر
Chinese: gàosù 告訴
Dutch: vertellen
French: raconter
German: erzählen
Italian: dire
Japanese: noberu 述べる
Korean: marhada 말하다
Portuguese: dizer
Russian: skazát' сказать
Spanish: decir
Swedish: tala om

2153. temperature [n.]

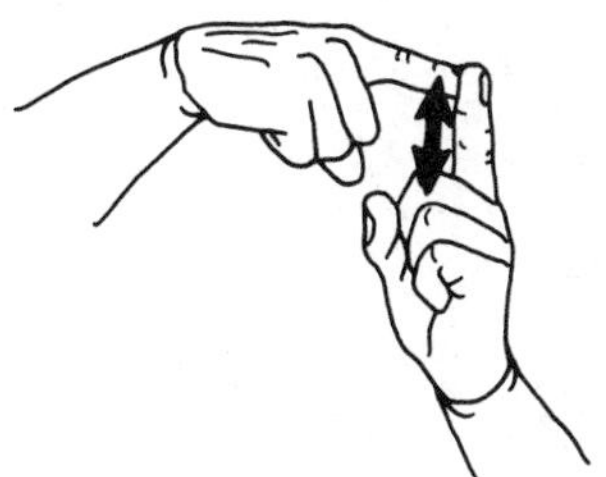

Arabic: dárajet al-harára درجة الحرارة
Chinese: wēndù 温度
Dutch: temperatuur
French: température
German: Temperatur
Italian: temperatura
Japanese: ondo 温度
Korean: ondo 온도
Portuguese: temperatura
Russian: temperatúra температура
Spanish: temperatura
Swedish: temperatur

2154. temporary [adj.]

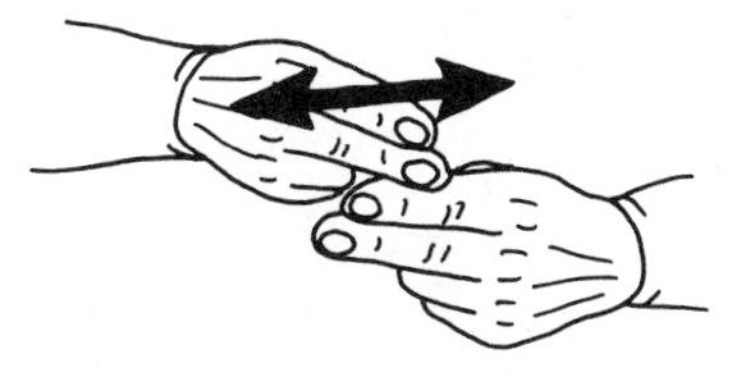

Arabic: moáaqatan مؤقتاً
Chinese: zhànshí 暫時
Dutch: tijdelijk
French: temporaire
German: zeitweilig
Italian: temporaneo
Japanese: rinji no 臨時の
Korean: ilshijŏkŭi 일시적인
Portuguese: temporário
Russian: vrémennyy временный
Spanish: temporario
Swedish: tillfällig

2155. temptation [n.]

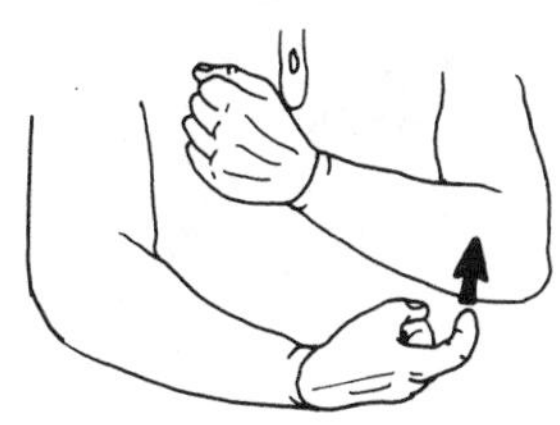

Arabic: ighrá' اغراء
Chinese: yòuhuò 誘惑
Dutch: verleiding
French: tentation
German: Versuchung
Italian: tentazione
Japanese: yūwaku 誘惑
Korean: yuhok 유혹
Portuguese: tentação
Russian: iskushéniye искушение
Spanish: tentación
Swedish: frestelse

2156. ten [adj.]

Arabic: áashra عشرة
Chinese: shí 十
Dutch: tien
French: dix
German: zehn
Italian: dieci
Japanese: jū 10
Korean: yŏl 열
Portuguese: dez
Russian: désyat' десять
Spanish: diez
Swedish: tio

2157. tendency [n.]

Arabic: méil ميل
Chinese: qūshì 趨勢
Dutch: neiging
French: tendance
German: Tendenz
Italian: tendenza
Japanese: keikō 傾向
Korean: kyŏng'hyang 경향
Portuguese: tendência
Russian: tendéntsiya тенденция
Spanish: tendencia
Swedish: tendens

2158. tender [adj.]

Arabic: ghadd غض
Chinese: nènde 嫩的
Dutch: teder
French: tendre
German: zart
Italian: tenero
Japanese: yawarakana 柔らかな
Korean: yŏnhan 연한
Portuguese: tenro
Russian: nézhnyy нежный
Spanish: tierno
Swedish: öm

2159. tennis [n.]

Arabic: ténis تنس
Chinese: wǎngqiú 網球
Dutch: tennis
French: tennis
German: Tennis
Italian: tennis
Japanese: tenisu テニス
Korean: t'enisŭ 테니스
Portuguese: tênis
Russian: ténnis теннис
Spanish: tenis
Swedish: tennis

2160. tent [n.]

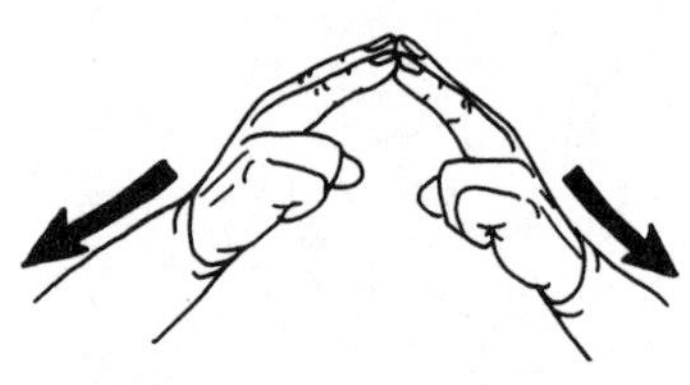

Arabic: kháyma خيمة
Chinese: zhàngpéng 帳篷
Dutch: tent
French: tente
German: Zelt
Italian: tenda
Japanese: tento テント
Korean: t'ent'ŭ 텐트
Portuguese: tenda
Russian: palátka палатка
Spanish: tienda de campaña
Swedish: tält

2161. terrible [adj.]

Arabic: fadhía' فظيع
Chinese: kĕpà 可怕
Dutch: vreselijk
French: terrible
German: schrecklich
Italian: terribile
Japanese: hidoi ひどい
Korean: mushimushihan 무시무시한
Portuguese: terrível
Russian: uzhásnyy ужасный
Spanish: terrible
Swedish: förfärlig

2162. terror [n.]

Arabic: rú'ab رعب
Chinese: kŏngbù 恐怖
Dutch: verschrikking
French: terreur
German: Schrecken
Italian: terrore
Japanese: kyōfu 恐怖
Korean: gongp'o 공포
Portuguese: terror
Russian: úzhas ужас
Spanish: terror
Swedish: skräck

2163. test (examination) [n.]

Arabic: imtihán امتحان
Chinese: kăoshì 考試
Dutch: examen
French: examen
German: Examen
Italian: esame
Japanese: shiken 試験
Korean: shihŏm 시험
Portuguese: exame
Russian: ekzámen экзамен
Spanish: examen
Swedish: prov

2164. test (proof/trial) [n.]

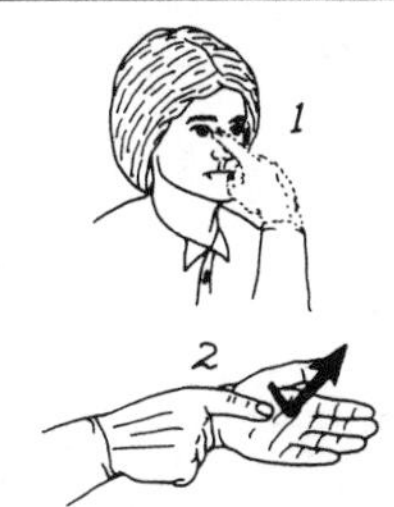

Arabic: ikhtibár اختبار
Chinese: shìyàn 試驗
Dutch: proef
French: épreuve
German: Probe
Italian: prova
Japanese: jikken 実験
Korean: kŏmsa 검사
Portuguese: prova
Russian: próba проба
Spanish: prueba
Swedish: prov

2165. testimony [n.]

Arabic: shaháda شهادة
Chinese: zhèngyán 證言
Dutch: getuigenis
French: témoignage
German: Zeugnis
Italian: testimonianza
Japanese: shōgen 証言
Korean: jŭngŏn 증언
Portuguese: testemunho
Russian: pokazániye показание
Spanish: testimonio
Swedish: vittnesmål

2166. textbook [n.]

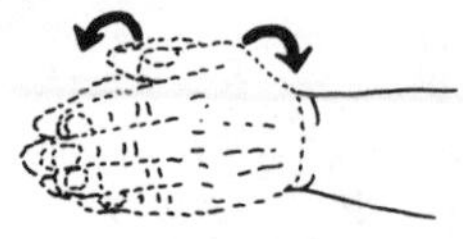

Arabic: márjea' مرجع
Chinese: jiàokēshū 教科書
Dutch: studieboek
French: livre de classe
German: Lehrbuch
Italian: libro di testo
Japanese: kyōkasho 教科書
Korean: kyokwasŏ 교과서
Portuguese: compêndio
Russian: uchébnik учебник
Spanish: libro de texto
Swedish: lärobok

2167. than [conj.]

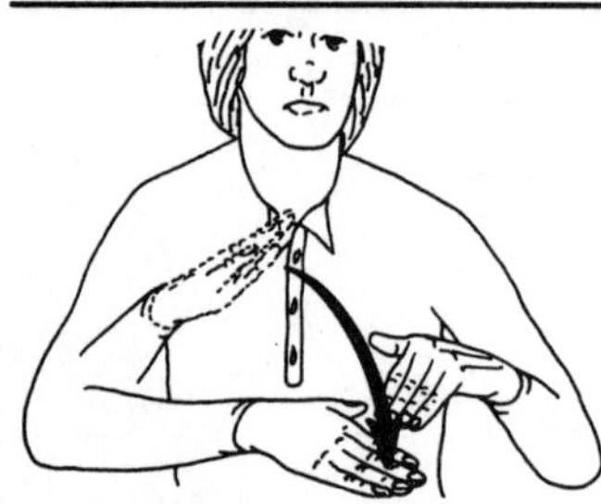

Arabic: min من
Chinese: bǐ 比
Dutch: dan
French: que
German: als
Italian: che
Japanese: . . . yori …よりも
Korean: boda ~보다
Portuguese: que
Russian: chem чем
Spanish: que
Swedish: än

2168. thank you [interj.]

Arabic: shúkran شكراً
Chinese: xièxie 謝謝
Dutch: dank u
French: merci
German: danke schön
Italian: grazie
Japanese: arigatō 有り難とう
Korean: kamsahamnida 감사 합니다
Portuguese: obrigado
Russian: spasíbo спасибо
Spanish: gracias
Swedish: tack

2169. that [pron.]

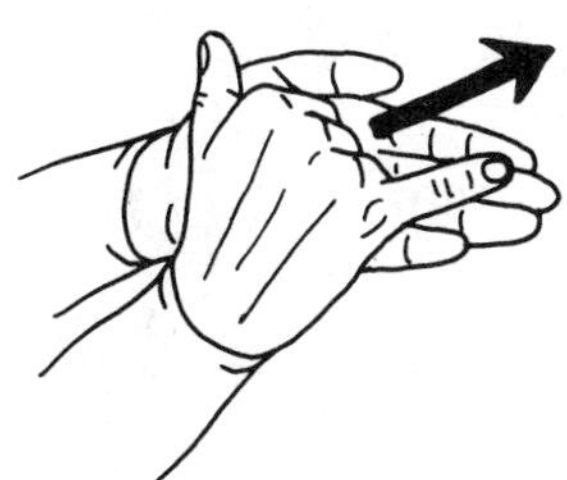

Arabic: dhálika ذلك
Chinese: nàge 那個
Dutch: die/dat
French: celui-là
German: das
Italian: quello
Japanese: sore それ
Korean: jŏgŏt 그것
Portuguese: aquele
Russian: tot тот
Spanish: aquél
Swedish: den

2170. theater (drama) [n.]

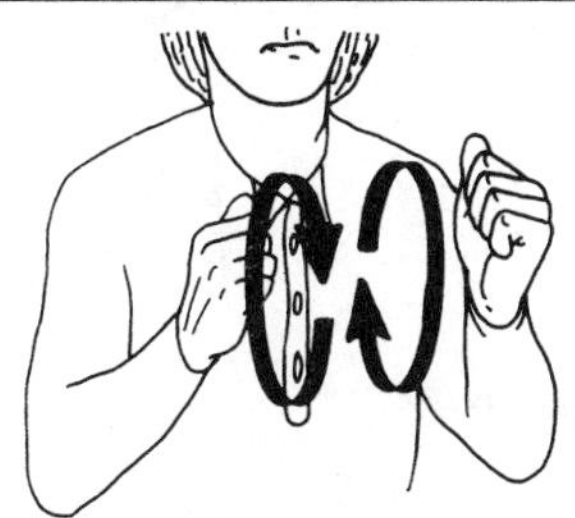

Arabic: másrah مسرح
Chinese: jùcháng 劇場
Dutch: theater
French: théâtre
German: Theater
Italian: teatro
Japanese: gekijo 劇場
Korean: gŭgjang 극장
Portuguese: teatro
Russian: teátr театр
Spanish: teatro
Swedish: teater

2171. theft [n.]

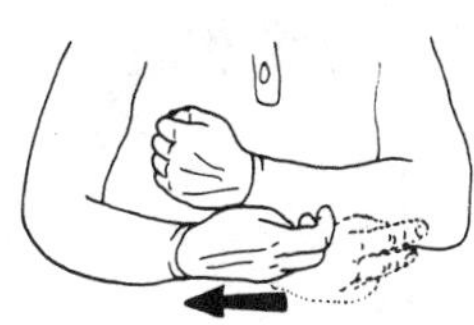

Arabic: sárieqa سرقة
Chinese: dàoqiè 盜竊
Dutch: diefstal
French: vol
German: Diebstahl
Italian: furto
Japanese: nusumi 盗み
Korean: jŏldo 도둑질
Portuguese: roubo
Russian: krázha кража
Spanish: robo
Swedish: stöld

2172. their(s) [adj./pron.]

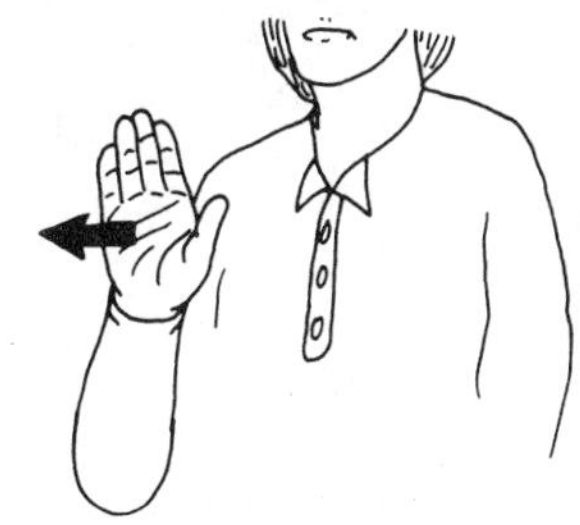

Arabic: láhum لهم
Chinese: tāmende 他們的
Dutch: hun
French: leur
German: ihr
Italian: il loro
Japanese: karera no 彼らの
Korean: gŭ saramdurŭi gŏt
그 사람들의 것
Portuguese: seu
Russian: ikh их
Spanish: su
Swedish: deras

2173. them [pron.]

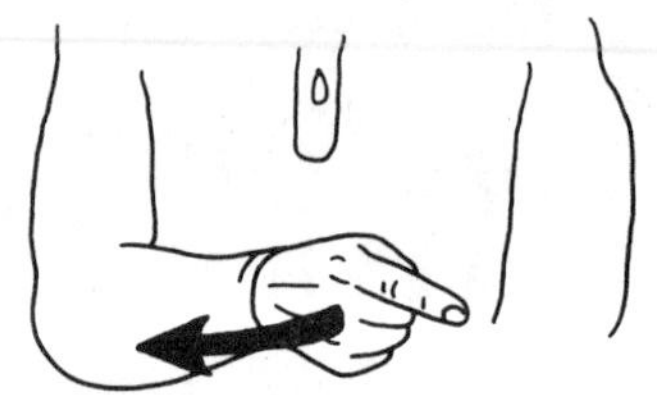

Arabic: hum هم
Chinese: tāmen 他們
Dutch: hen/hun
French: les/leur
German: sie/ihnen
Italian: li/loro
Japanese: karerao 彼らを
Korean: gŭdŭrŭl/gudurege
그들／그들에게
Portuguese: os/lhes
Russian: ikh/im/imi их/им/ими
Spanish: les
Swedish: dem

2174. theme [n.]

Arabic: maudúa' موضوع
Chinese: zhŭtí 主題
Dutch: thema
French: thème
German: Thema
Italian: tema
Japanese: shudai 主題
Korean: juje 주제
Portuguese: tema
Russian: téma тема
Spanish: tema
Swedish: tema

2175. themselves [pron.]

Arabic: anfúsahum انفسهم
Chinese: tāmen zìjĭ 他們自己
Dutch: zichzelf
French: eux-mêmes
German: sich selber
Italian: essi stessi
Japanese: karerajishin 彼ら自身の
Korean: gŭdŭl jashin 그들 자신
Portuguese: eles mesmos
Russian: sebyá себя
Spanish: ellos mismos
Swedish: sig själva

2176. then [adv.]

Arabic: thúmma ثم
Chinese: ránér 然而
Dutch: toen
French: alors
German: dann
Italian: allora
Japanese: soshite そして
Korean: gŭttae 그때
Portuguese: então
Russian: togdá тогда
Spanish: entonces
Swedish: då

2177. theory [n.]

Arabic: nadharía نظرية
Chinese: lǐlùn 理論
Dutch: theorie
French: théorie
German: Theorie
Italian: teoria
Japanese: riron 理論
Korean: iron 이론
Portuguese: teoria
Russian: teóriya теория
Spanish: teoría
Swedish: teori

2178. there [adv.]

Arabic: hunáka هناك
Chinese: nàli 那裡
Dutch: daar
French: là
German: dort
Italian: là
Japanese: sokoni そこに
Korean: kŏgie 거기
Portuguese: ali
Russian: tam там
Spanish: allí
Swedish: där

2179. therefore [adv.]

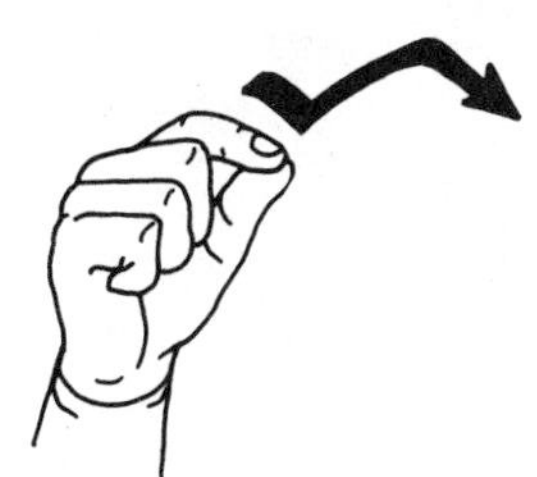

Arabic: lidhálika لذلك
Chinese: yīncǐ 因此
Dutch: daarom
French: donc
German: darum
Italian: quindi
Japanese: dakara だから
Korean: kŭrŏmŭro 그러므로
Portuguese: portanto
Russian: poétomu поэтому
Spanish: por consiguiente
Swedish: därför

2180. thermometer [n.]

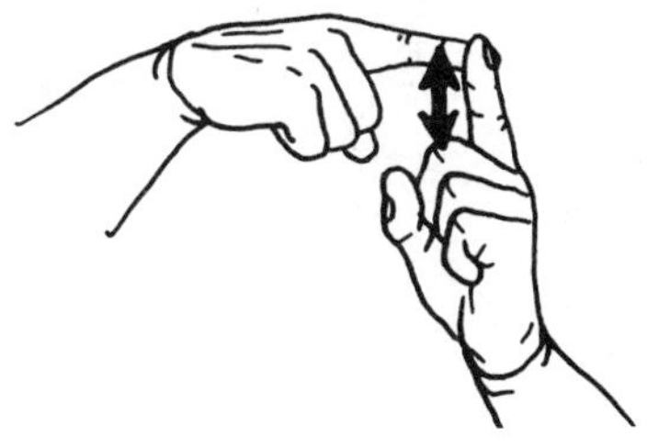

Arabic: termométr تيرمومتر
Chinese: wēndùjì 温度計
Dutch: thermometer
French: thermomètre
German: Thermometer
Italian: termometro
Japanese: ondokei 温度計
Korean: ondogye 온도계
Portuguese: termômetro
Russian: termómetr термометр
Spanish: termómetro
Swedish: termometer

2181. these [adj./pron.]

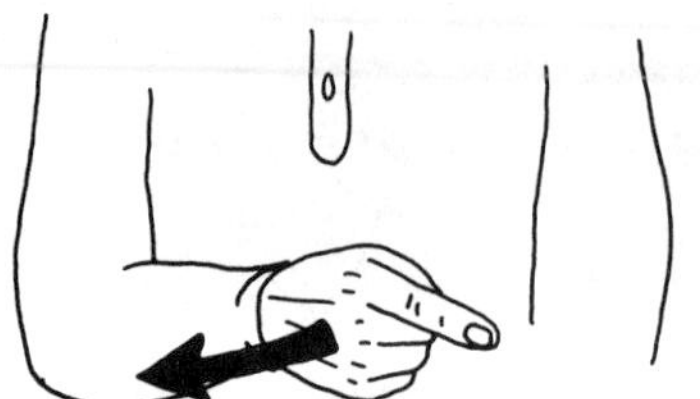

Arabic: hadhíhi هذه
Chinese: zhèxiē 這些
Dutch: deze
French: ces
German: diese
Italian: questi
Japanese: korera これら
Korean: igŏtdŭl 이것들
Portuguese: estes
Russian: éti эти
Spanish: estos
Swedish: dessa

2182. they [pron.]

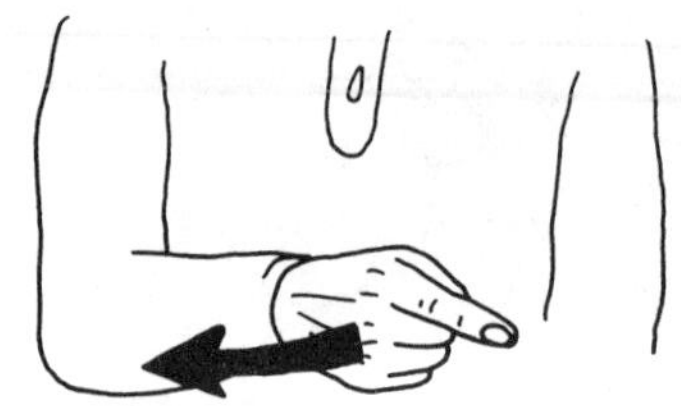

Arabic: hum هم
Chinese: tāmen 他們
Dutch: zij
French: ils
German: sie
Italian: essi
Japanese: karera 彼ら
Korean: gŭdŭl 그들
Portuguese: eles
Russian: oní они
Spanish: ellos
Swedish: de

2183. thick [adj.]

Arabic: samík سميك
Chinese: nóng 濃
Dutch: dik
French: épais
German: dick
Italian: spesso
Japanese: atsui 厚い
Korean: dukkŏun 두꺼운
Portuguese: espêsso
Russian: tólstyy толстый
Spanish: espeso
Swedish: tjock

2184. thief [n.]

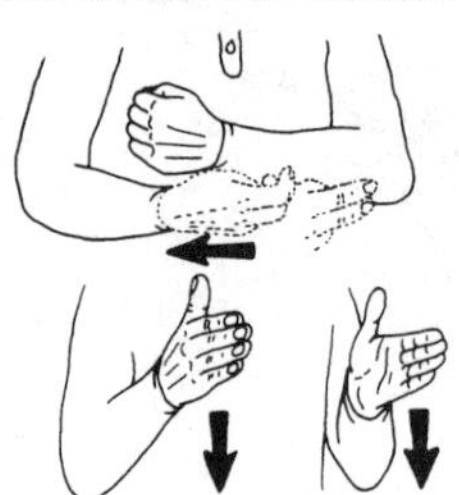

Arabic: loss لص
Chinese: zéi 賊
Dutch: dief
French: voleur
German: Dieb
Italian: ladro
Japanese: dorobō 泥棒
Korean: doduk 도둑
Portuguese: ladrão
Russian: vor вор
Spanish: ladrón
Swedish: tjuv

2185. thin [adj.]

Arabic: raqíeq رقيق
Chinese: shòu 瘦
Dutch: dun
French: mince
German: dünn
Italian: sottile
Japanese: usui 薄い
Korean: yalbŭn 얇은
Portuguese: delgado
Russian: tónkiy тонкий
Spanish: delgado
Swedish: tunn

2186. thing [n.]

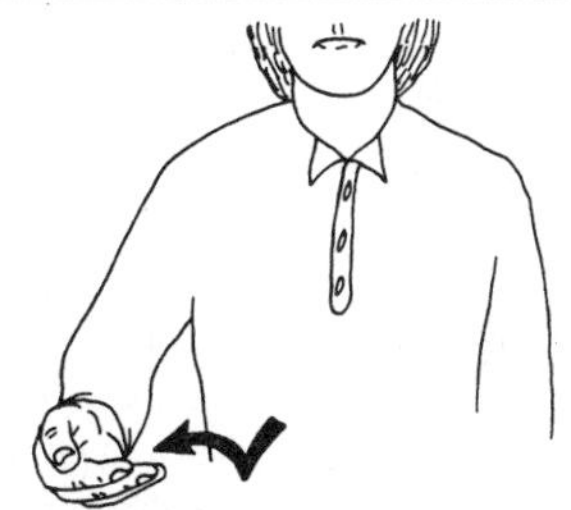

Arabic: sháee' شيء
Chinese: dōngxi 東西
Dutch: ding
French: chose
German: Ding
Italian: cosa
Japanese: mono 物
Korean: mulgŏn 물건
Portuguese: coisa
Russian: véshch' вещь
Spanish: cosa
Swedish: sak

2187. think [v.]

Arabic: fákkara فكر
Chinese: xiǎng 想
Dutch: denken
French: penser
German: denken
Italian: pensare
Japanese: kangaeru 考える
Korean: saenggak'hada 생각하다
Portuguese: pensar
Russian: dúmat' думать
Spanish: pensar
Swedish: tänka

2188. thirst [n.]

Arabic: áatash عطش
Chinese: kǒukě 口渇
Dutch: dorst
French: soif
German: Durst
Italian: sete
Japanese: nodo no kawaki 喉のかわき
Korean: mongmarŭm 목마른
Portuguese: sêde
Russian: zházhda жажда
Spanish: sed
Swedish: törst

2189. thirteen [adj.]

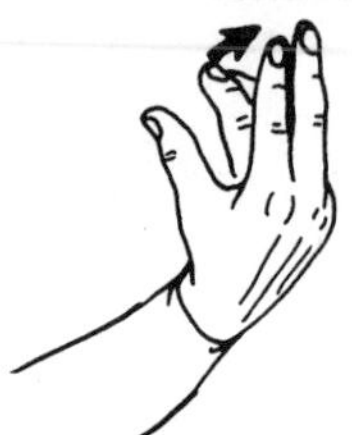

Arabic: thaláthat áashar ثلاثة عشر
Chinese: shísān 十三
Dutch: dertien
French: treize
German: dreizehn
Italian: tredici
Japanese: jūsan 13
Korean: yŏl set 열 셋
Portuguese: treze
Russian: trinádtsat' тринадцать
Spanish: trece
Swedish: tretton

2190. thirty [adj.]

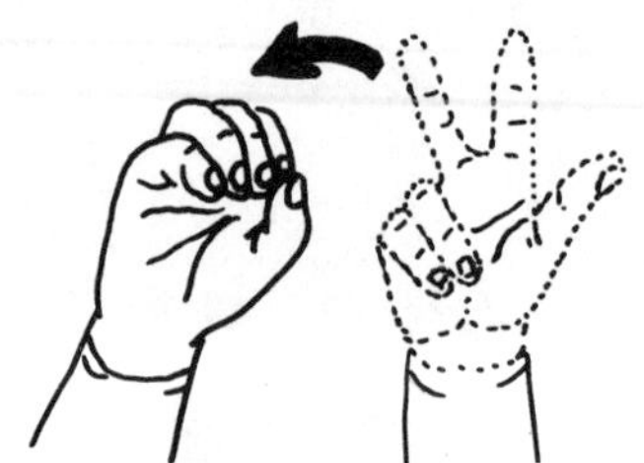

Arabic: thalathín ثلاثين
Chinese: sānshí 三十
Dutch: dertig
French: trente
German: dreißig
Italian: trenta
Japanese: sanjū 30
Korean: sŏrŭn 서른
Portuguese: trinta
Russian: trídtsat' тридцать
Spanish: treinta
Swedish: trettio

2191. this [adj./pron.]

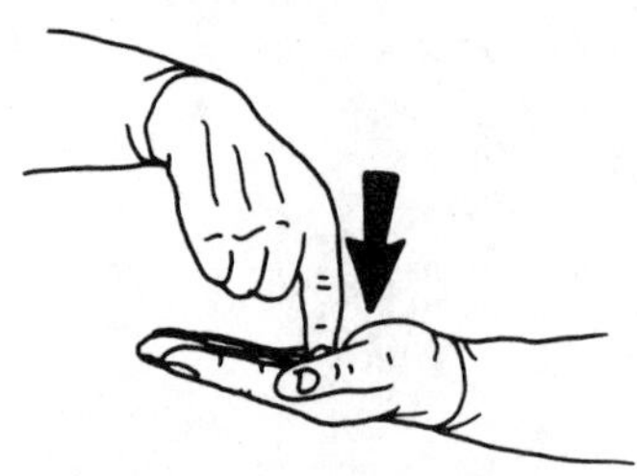

Arabic: hádha هذا
Chinese: zhè 這
Dutch: deze
French: ce
German: dies
Italian: questo
Japanese: kore これ
Korean: igŏt 이것
Portuguese: este
Russian: éto это
Spanish: este
Swedish: detta

2192. thought [n.]

Arabic: fíkra فكرة
Chinese: sīxiǎng 思想
Dutch: gedachte
French: pensée
German: Gedanke
Italian: pensiero
Japanese: kangae 考え
Korean: saenggak 생각
Portuguese: pensamento
Russian: mysl' мысль
Spanish: pensamiento
Swedish: tanke

2193. thousand [n.]

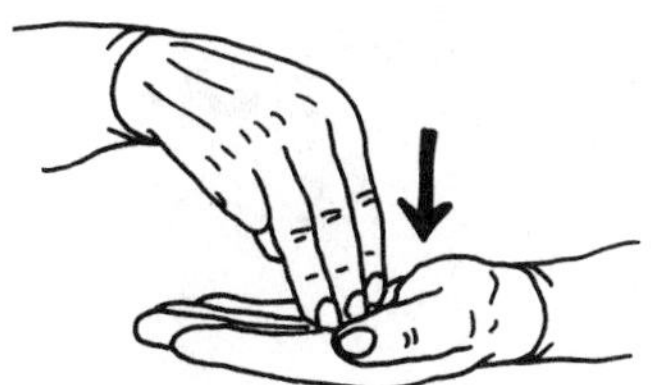

Arabic: alf ألف
Chinese: qiān 千
Dutch: duizend
French: mille
German: tausend
Italian: mille
Japanese: sen 千
Korean: ch'ŏn 천
Portuguese: mil
Russian: týsyacha тысяча
Spanish: mil
Swedish: tusen

2194. thread [n.]

Arabic: kháyet خيط
Chinese: xiàn 線
Dutch: draad
French: fil
German: Faden
Italian: filo
Japanese: ito 糸
Korean: shil 실
Portuguese: fio
Russian: nit' нить
Spanish: hilo
Swedish: tråd

2195. threat [n.]

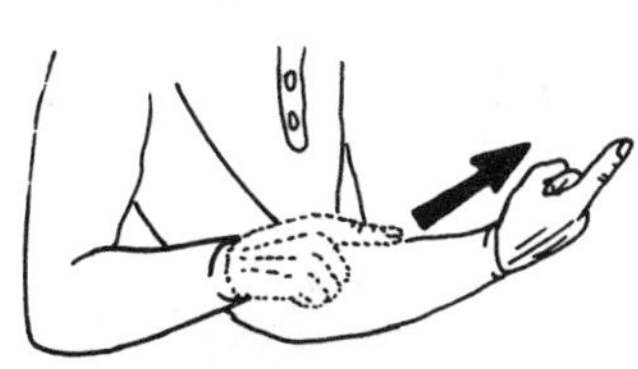

Arabic: tahdíd تهديد
Chinese: wēixié 威脅
Dutch: dreiging
French: menace
German: Drohung
Italian: minaccia
Japanese: kyōhaku 脅迫
Korean: hyobbak 협박
Portuguese: ameaça
Russian: ugróza угроза
Spanish: amenaza
Swedish: hot

2196. three [adj.]

Arabic: thalátha ثلاثة
Chinese: sān 三
Dutch: drie
French: trois
German: drei
Italian: tre
Japanese: san 三
Korean: set 셋
Portuguese: três
Russian: tri три
Spanish: tres
Swedish: tre

2197. throat [n.]

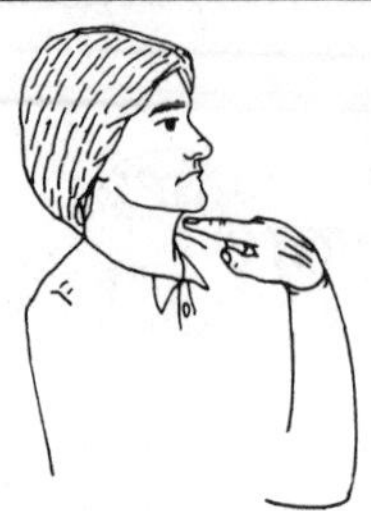

Arabic: húnjura حنجرة
Chinese: hóulóng 喉嚨
Dutch: keel
French: gorge
German: Kehle
Italian: gola
Japanese: nodo 喉
Korean: mokkumŏng 목구멍
Portuguese: garganta
Russian: górlo горло
Spanish: garganta
Swedish: strupe

2198. through [prep.]

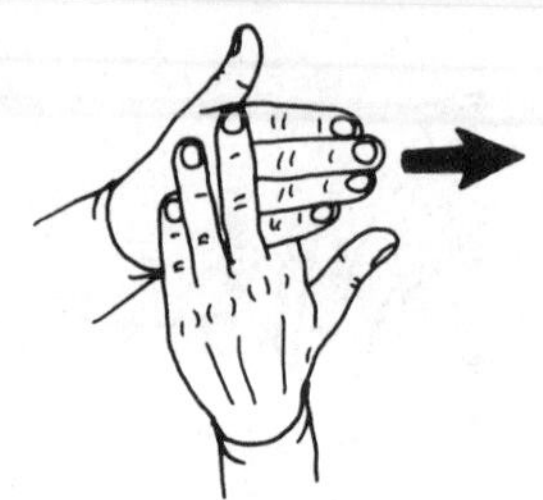

Arabic: khilál خلال
Chinese: tōngguò 通過
Dutch: door
French: par
German: durch
Italian: attraverso
Japanese: . . . o tōshite …を通して
Korean: t'onghayŏ ___ 통하여
Portuguese: por
Russian: chérez через
Spanish: a través de
Swedish: genom

2199. throw [v.]

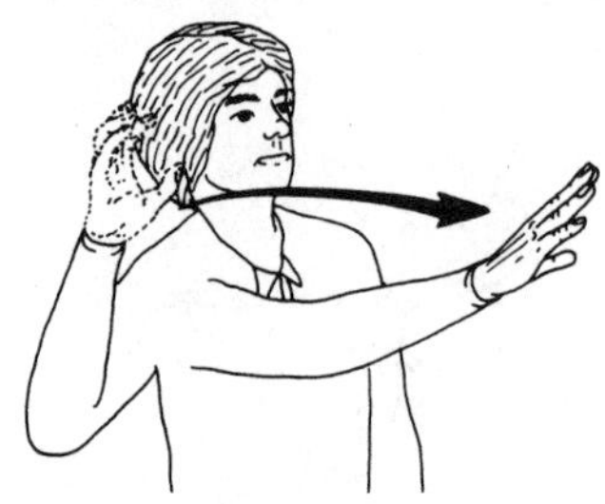

Arabic: rámma رمى
Chinese: diū 丢
Dutch: werpen
French: jeter
German: werfen
Italian: gettare
Japanese: nageru 投げる
Korean: dŏnjida 던지다
Portuguese: atirar
Russian: brosát' бросать
Spanish: arrojar
Swedish: kasta

2200. thunder [n.]

Arabic: ráad رعد
Chinese: léi 雷
Dutch: donder
French: tonnerre
German: Donner
Italian: tuono
Japanese: kaminari 雷
Korean: uroe 우뢰
Portuguese: trovão
Russian: grom гром
Spanish: trueno
Swedish: åska

2201. Thursday [n.]

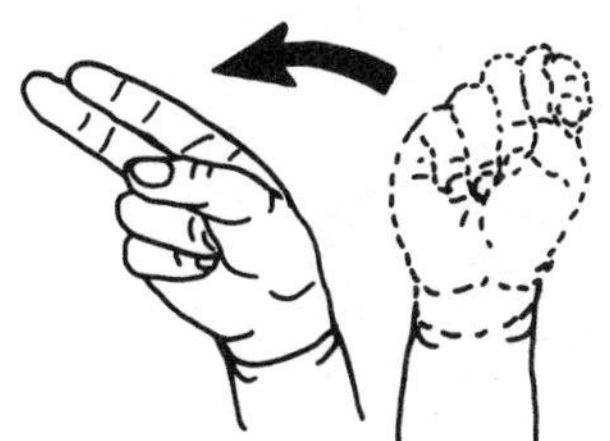

Arabic: al-khamís الخميس
Chinese: xīngqísì 星期四
Dutch: donderdag
French: jeudi
German: Donnerstag
Italian: giovedì
Japanese: mokuyōbi 木曜日
Korean: mogyoil 목요일
Portuguese: quinta-feira
Russian: chetvérg четверг
Spanish: jueves
Swedish: torsdag

2202. thus [adv.]

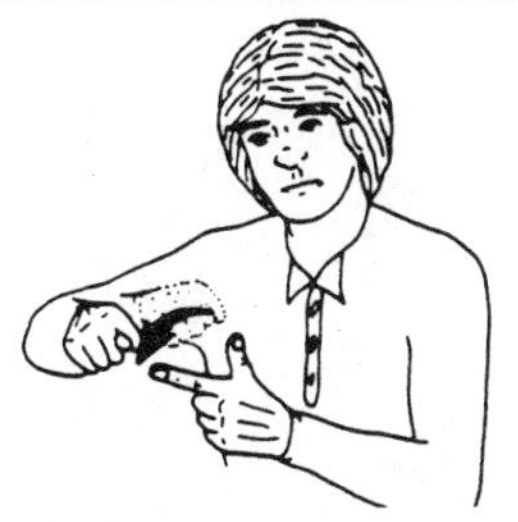

Arabic: hakádha هكذا
Chinese: rúcǐ 如此
Dutch: zo
French: ainsi
German: so
Italian: così
Japanese: sore dakara それだから
Korean: gŭraesŏ 그래서
Portuguese: assim
Russian: tak так
Spanish: así
Swedish: således

2203. ticket [n.]

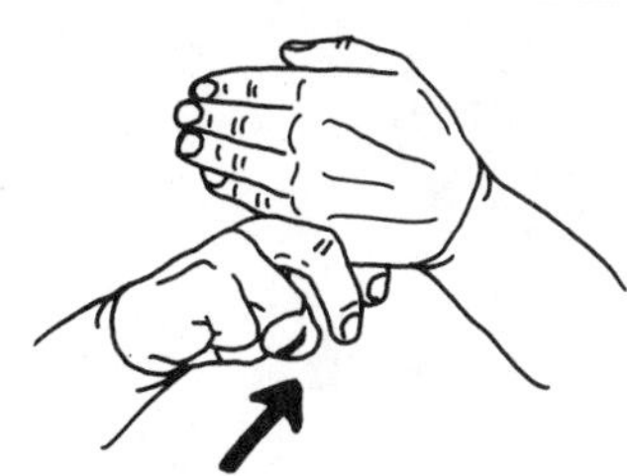

Arabic: tádhkara تذكرة
Chinese: piào 票
Dutch: toegangsbewijs
French: billet
German: Eintrittskarte
Italian: biglietto
Japanese: kippu 切符
Korean: p'yo 표
Portuguese: bilhete
Russian: bilét билет
Spanish: boleto
Swedish: biljett

2204. tie (bond) [n.]

Arabic: rabt ربط
Chinese: liánjié 連結
Dutch: band
French: lien
German: Verbindung
Italian: vincolo
Japanese: musubi 結び
Korean: udae 유대
Portuguese: vínculo
Russian: svyáz' связь
Spanish: vínculo
Swedish: band

2205. tie (necktie) [n.]

Arabic: rebát al-ónoq رباط العنق
Chinese: lǐngdài 領帶
Dutch: das
French: cravate
German: Krawatte
Italian: cravatta
Japanese: nekutai ネクタイ
Korean: nekt'ai 넥타이
Portuguese: gravata
Russian: gálstuk галстук
Spanish: corbata
Swedish: slips

2206. tie (bind) [v.]

Arabic: rábata رباط
Chinese: bǎng 綁
Dutch: binden
French: lier
German: binden
Italian: legare
Japanese: musubu 結ぶ
Korean: mukda 묶다
Portuguese: atar
Russian: svyázyvat' связывать
Spanish: atar
Swedish: binda

2207. time [n.]

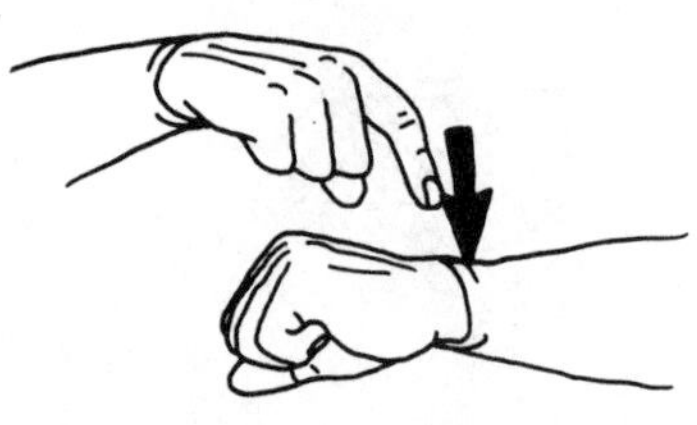

Arabic: waqt وقت
Chinese: shíjiān 時間
Dutch: tijd
French: temps
German: Zeit
Italian: tempo
Japanese: jikan 時間
Korean: shigan 시간
Portuguese: tempo
Russian: vrémya время
Spanish: tiempo
Swedish: tid

2208. timid [adj.]

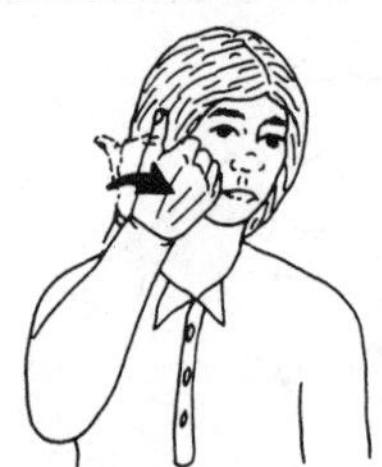

Arabic: jabán جبان
Chinese: dǎn xiǎo 膽小
Dutch: schuchter
French: timide
German: furchtsam
Italian: timido
Japanese: okubyōna 臆病な
Korean: kŏpmanŭn 겁 많은
Portuguese: tímido
Russian: róbkiy робкий
Spanish: tímido
Swedish: blyg

2209. tire [n.]

Arabic: itár اطار
Chinese: lúntāi 輪胎
Dutch: band
French: pneu
German: Reifen
Italian: pneumatico
Japanese: taiya タイヤ
Korean: t'aiŏ 타이어
Portuguese: pneu
Russian: shína шина
Spanish: neumático
Swedish: däck

2210. tired [adj.]

Arabic: mútaab متعب
Chinese: lèi 累
Dutch: vermoeid
French: fatigué
German: müde
Italian: stanco
Japanese: tsukareta 疲れた
Korean: p'igonhan 피곤한
Portuguese: cansado
Russian: ustályy усталый
Spanish: cansado
Swedish: trött

2211. title [n.]

Arabic: láqab لقب
Chinese: biāotí 標題
Dutch: titel
French: titre
German: Titel
Italian: titolo
Japanese: hyōdai 標題
Korean: ch'ing'ho 칭호
Portuguese: título
Russian: zagláviye заглавие
Spanish: título
Swedish: titel

2212. to [prep.]

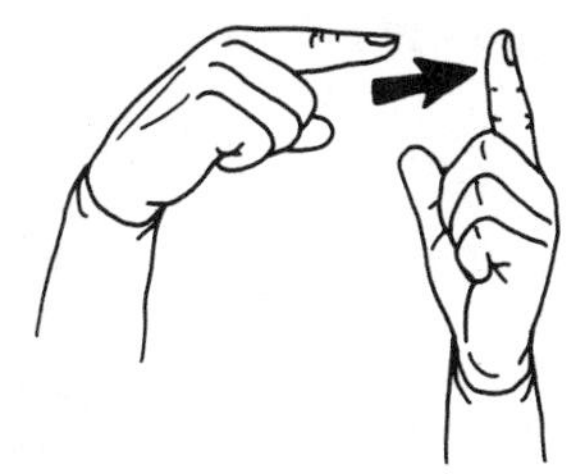

Arabic: íla الى
Chinese: dào 到
Dutch: naar
French: à
German: zu
Italian: a
Japanese: . . . ni …に
Korean: ŭro ~으로
Portuguese: a
Russian: v/na/k в/на/к
Spanish: a
Swedish: till

2213. today [adv.]

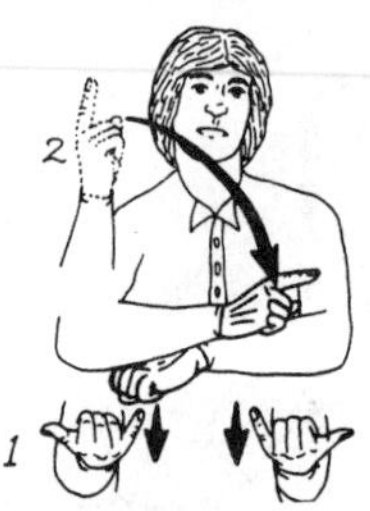

Arabic: al-yáum اليوم
Chinese: jīntiān 今天
Dutch: vandaag
French: aujourd'hui
German: heute
Italian: oggi
Japanese: kyō 今日
Korean: onŭl 오늘
Portuguese: hoje
Russian: sevódnya сегодня
Spanish: hoy
Swedish: i dag

2214. together [adv.]

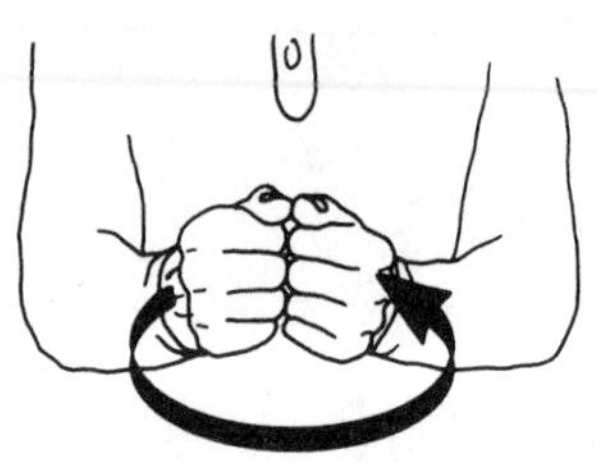

Arabic: maan معاً
Chinese: yìqǐ 一起
Dutch: samen
French: ensemble
German: zusammen
Italian: insieme
Japanese: isshoni 一緒に
Korean: gach'i 같이
Portuguese: juntos
Russian: vméste вместе
Spanish: juntos
Swedish: tillsammans

2215. toilet [n.]

Arabic: merhád مرحاض
Chinese: xǐshǒujiān 洗手間
Dutch: toilet
French: toilette
German: Toilette
Italian: toletta
Japanese: benjo 便所
Korean: byŏnso 변소
Portuguese: toalete
Russian: tualét туалет
Spanish: retrete
Swedish: toalett

2216. tolerate [v.]

Arabic: ihtámala احتمل
Chinese: rěnshòu 忍受
Dutch: verdragen
French: tolérer
German: dulden
Italian: tollerare
Japanese: mokunin suru 黙認する
Korean: ch'amnŭnda 참는다
Portuguese: tolerar
Russian: dopuskát' допускать
Spanish: tolerar
Swedish: tolerera

2217. tomato(es) [n.]

Arabic: bandóra بندورة
Chinese: fānqié/xīhóngshì 蕃茄，西紅柿
Dutch: tomaat
French: tomate
German: Tomate
Italian: pomodoro
Japanese: tomato トマト
Korean: tomato 토마토
Portuguese: tomate
Russian: pomidór помидор
Spanish: tomate
Swedish: tomat

2218. tomorrow [adv.]

Arabic: ghádhan غداً
Chinese: míngtiān 明天
Dutch: morgen
French: demain
German: morgen
Italian: domani
Japanese: ashita 明日
Korean: naeil 내일
Portuguese: amanhã
Russian: závtra завтра
Spanish: mañana
Swedish: i morgon

2219. ton [n.]

Arabic: ton طن
Chinese: dùn 噸
Dutch: ton
French: tonne
German: Tonne
Italian: tonnellata
Japanese: ton トン
Korean: t'on 톤
Portuguese: tonelada
Russian: tónna тонна
Spanish: tonelada
Swedish: ton

2220. tongue [n.]

Arabic: lissán لسان
Chinese: shétóu 舌頭
Dutch: tong
French: langue
German: Zunge
Italian: lingua
Japanese: shita 舌
Korean: hyŏ 혀
Portuguese: língua
Russian: yazýk язык
Spanish: lengua
Swedish: tunga

2221. tonight [adv.]

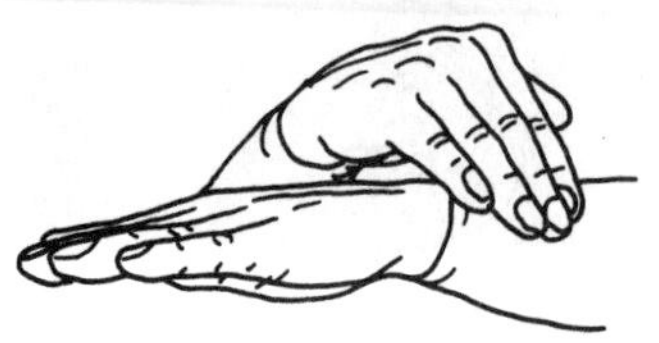

Arabic: al-léila الليلة
Chinese: jīn wǎn 今晚
Dutch: vanavond
French: ce soir
German: heute abend
Italian: stanotte
Japanese: komban 今晩
Korean: onŭl jŏnyŏk 오늘저녁
Portuguese: esta noite
Russian: sevódnya vécherom сегодня вечером
Spanish: esta noche
Swedish: i natt

2222. tool (implement) [n.]

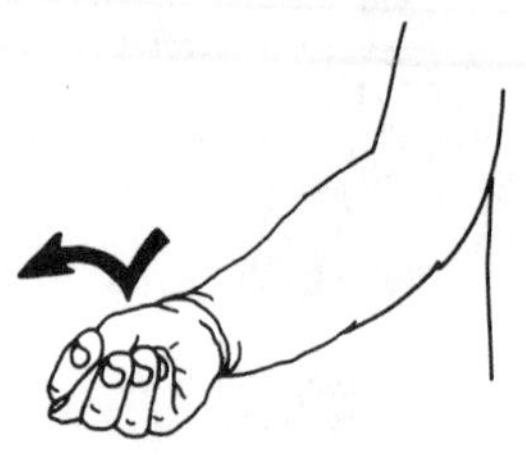

Arabic: aadá اداة
Chinese: gōngjù 工具
Dutch: werktuig
French: outil
German: Werkzeug
Italian: arnese
Japanese: dōgu 道具
Korean: yŏnjang 연장
Portuguese: ferramenta
Russian: instrumént инструмент
Spanish: herramienta
Swedish: verktyg

2223. tooth [n.]

Arabic: sin سن
Chinese: yáchǐ 牙齒
Dutch: tand
French: dent
German: Zahn
Italian: dente
Japanese: ha 歯
Korean: i 이
Portuguese: dente
Russian: zub зуб
Spanish: diente
Swedish: tand

2224. top [n.]

Arabic: qímma قمة
Chinese: dǐng 頂
Dutch: top
French: sommet
German: Oberteil
Italian: cima
Japanese: chōjō 頂上
Korean: kkogdaegi 꼭대기
Portuguese: tôpo
Russian: vershína вершина
Spanish: cima
Swedish: topp

2225. topic [n.]

Arabic: maudúa' موضوع
Chinese: zhǔtí 主題
Dutch: onderwerp
French: sujet
German: Thema
Italian: tema
Japanese: wadai 話題
Korean: hwaje 화제
Portuguese: tópico
Russian: predmét предмет
Spanish: tema
Swedish: samtalsämne

2226. tornado [n.]

Arabic: iaasár اعصار
Chinese: lǒngjuǎnfēng 龍捲風
Dutch: tornado
French: tornade
German: Wirbelsturm
Italian: turbine
Japanese: tatsumaki 竜巻
Korean: pok'pung 폭풍
Portuguese: tornado
Russian: tornádo торнадо
Spanish: tornado
Swedish: tornado

2227. total [n.]

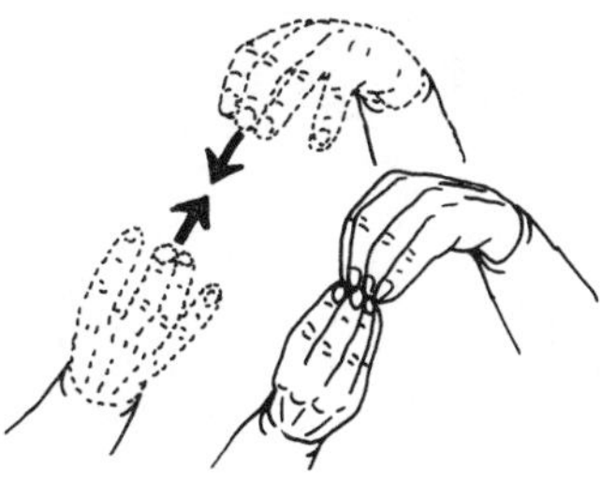

Arabic: majmúaa مجموع
Chinese: zǒngjì 總計
Dutch: totaal
French: total
German: Gesamtsumme
Italian: totale
Japanese: sōkei 総計
Korean: hap'kye 합계
Portuguese: total
Russian: itóg итог
Spanish: total
Swedish: summa

2228. touch [v.]

Arabic: lámasa لمس
Chinese: jiēchù 接觸
Dutch: aanraken
French: toucher
German: berühren
Italian: toccare
Japanese: sawaru 触る
Korean: manjida 만지다
Portuguese: tocar
Russian: trógat' трогать
Spanish: tocar
Swedish: beröra

2229. towel [n.]

Arabic: mánshafa منشفة
Chinese: máojīn 毛巾
Dutch: handdoek
French: serviette de bain
German: Handtuch
Italian: asciugamano
Japanese: taoru タオル
Korean: t'awŏl 타월
Portuguese: toalha
Russian: polotēntse полотенце
Spanish: toalla
Swedish: handduk

2230. tower [n.]

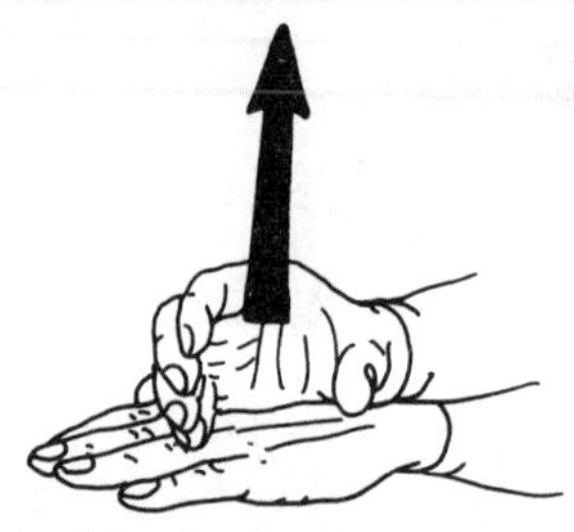

Arabic: burj برج
Chinese: tǎ 塔
Dutch: toren
French: tour
German: Turm
Italian: torre
Japanese: tō 塔
Korean: t'ap 탑
Portuguese: tôrre
Russian: výshka вышка
Spanish: torre
Swedish: torn

2231. town [n.]

Arabic: madína مدينة
Chinese: chéng 城
Dutch: stad
French: ville
German: Stadt
Italian: città
Japanese: machi 町
Korean: ŭp 읍
Portuguese: cidade
Russian: górod город
Spanish: ciudad
Swedish: stad

2232. toy [n.]

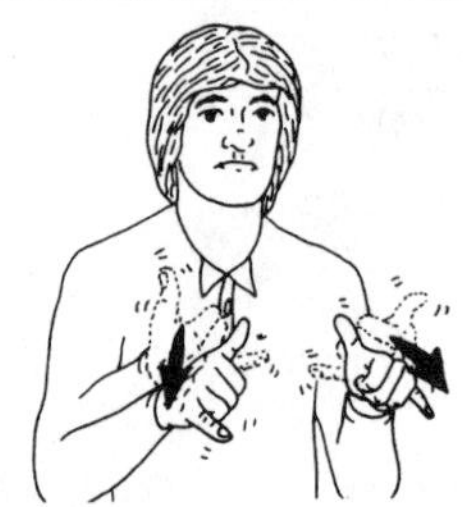

Arabic: lúaaba لعبة
Chinese: wánjǜ 玩具
Dutch: speelgoed
French: jouet
German: Spielzeug
Italian: giocattolo
Japanese: omocha おもちゃ
Korean: changnangam 장난감
Portuguese: brinquedo
Russian: igrúshka игрушка
Spanish: juguete
Swedish: leksak

2233. tractor [n.]

Arabic: jarár جرار
Chinese: tuōlājī 拖拉機
Dutch: tractor
French: tracteur
German: Traktor
Italian: trattore
Japanese: torakutā トラクター
Korean: t'uraekt'ŏ 트랙터
Portuguese: trator
Russian: tráktor трактор
Spanish: tractor
Swedish: traktor

2234. trade [n.]

Arabic: tijára تجارة
Chinese: jiāoyì 交易
Dutch: handel
French: commerce
German: Handel
Italian: commercio
Japanese: bōeki 貿易
Korean: muyŏk 무역
Portuguese: comércio
Russian: torgóvlya торговля
Spanish: comercio
Swedish: handel

2235. tradition [n.]

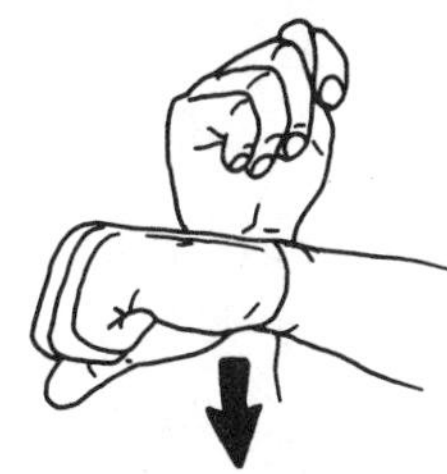

Arabic: taqalíd تقاليد
Chinese: chuántŏng 傳統
Dutch: traditie
French: tradition
German: Tradition
Italian: tradizione
Japanese: dento 伝統
Korean: jŏnt'ong 전통
Portuguese: tradição
Russian: tradítsiya традиция
Spanish: tradición
Swedish: tradition

2236. traffic (vehicle) [n.]

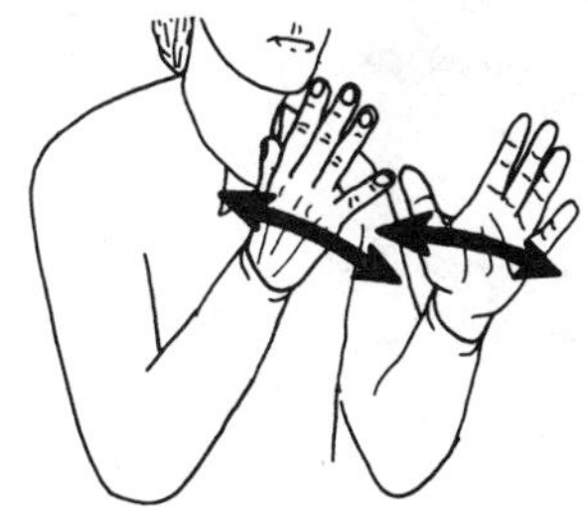

Arabic: murúr مرور
Chinese: jiāotōng 交通
Dutch: verkeer
French: circulation
German: Verkehr
Italian: traffico
Japanese: kōtsu 交通
Korean: kyot'ong 교통
Portuguese: tráfego
Russian: dvizhéniye движение
Spanish: tráfico
Swedish: trafik

2237. tragedy [n.]

Arabic: ma'sá مأساة
Chinese: bēijù 悲劇
Dutch: tragedie
French: tragédie
German: Tragödie
Italian: tragedia
Japanese: higeki 悲劇
Korean: bigŭg 비극
Portuguese: tragédia
Russian: tragédiya трагедия
Spanish: tragedia
Swedish: tragedi

2238. train [n.]

Arabic: qetár قطار
Chinese: hŭochē 火車
Dutch: trein
French: train
German: Zug
Italian: treno
Japanese: kisha 汽車
Korean: kich'a 기차
Portuguese: trem
Russian: póyezd поезд
Spanish: tren
Swedish: tåg

2239. training [n.]

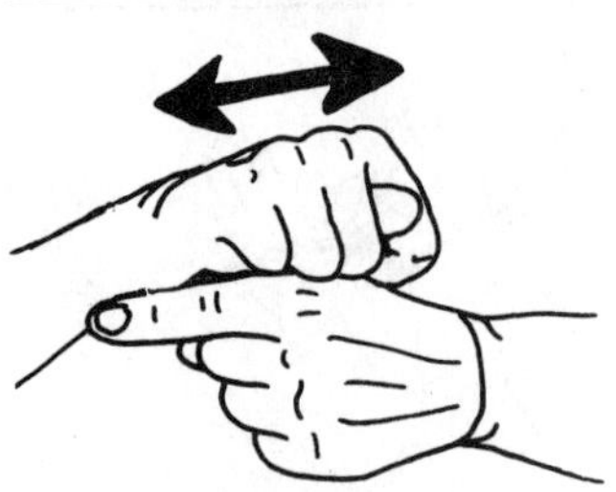

Arabic: tadríb تدريب
Chinese: xùnliàn 訓練
Dutch: training
French: entraînement
German: Ausbildung
Italian: addestramento
Japanese: kunren 訓練
Korean: hullyŏn 훈련
Portuguese: treinamento
Russian: treniróvka тренировка
Spanish: capacitación
Swedish: träning

2240. transfer [v.]

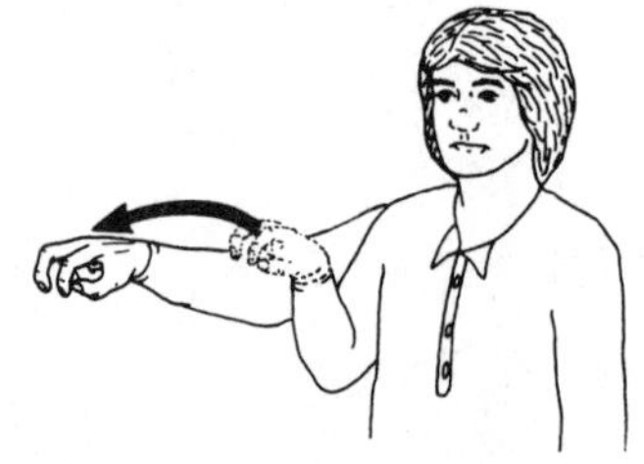

Arabic: háwwala حول
Chinese: zhuănyí 轉移
Dutch: overplaatsen
French: transférer
German: übertragen
Italian: trasferire
Japanese: utsusu 移す
Korean: omgida 옮기다
Portuguese: transferir
Russian: perenosít' переносить
Spanish: transferir
Swedish: överföra

2241. translate [v.]

Arabic: tárjama ترجم
Chinese: fānyì 翻譯
Dutch: vertalen
French: traduire
German: übersetzen
Italian: tradurre
Japanese: honyaku suru 翻訳する
Korean: bŏnyŏk'hada 번역하다
Portuguese: traduzir
Russian: perevodít' переводить
Spanish: traducir
Swedish: översätta

2242. transport [v.]

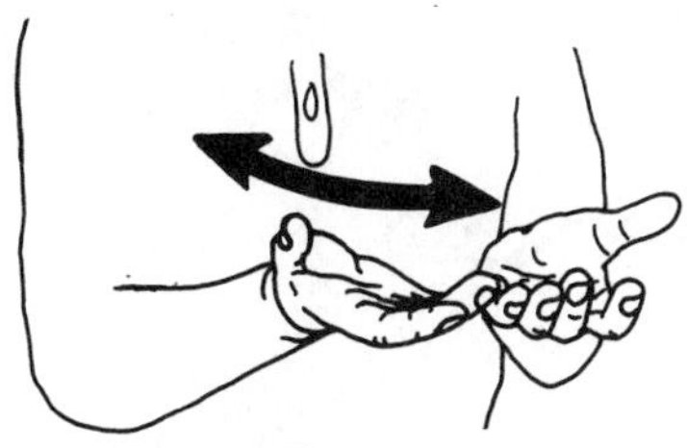

Arabic: náqala نقل
Chinese: shūsòng 輸送
Dutch: vervoeren
French: transporter
German: transportieren
Italian: trasportare
Japanese: unsō suru 運送する
Korean: susonghada 수송하다
Portuguese: transportar
Russian: perevozít' перевозить
Spanish: transportar
Swedish: transportera

2243. transportation [n.]

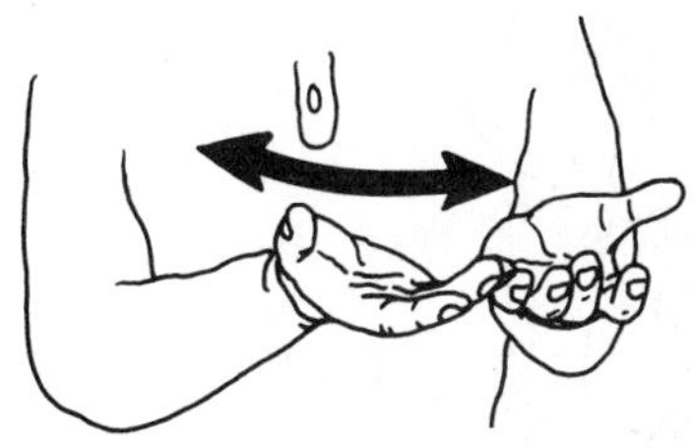

Arabic: naql نقل
Chinese: yùnshū 運輸
Dutch: vervoer
French: transport
German: Beförderung
Italian: trasporto
Japanese: yusōkikan 輸送機関
Korean: susong 수송
Portuguese: transporte
Russian: tránsport транспорт
Spanish: transporte
Swedish: transport

2244. trap [n.]

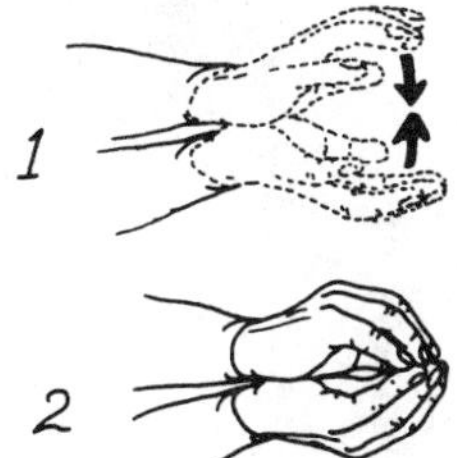

Arabic: fakh فخ
Chinese: xiànjǐng 陷阱
Dutch: val
French: piège
German: Falle
Italian: trappola
Japanese: wana わな
Korean: olgami 올가미
Portuguese: armadilha
Russian: zapadnyá западня
Spanish: trampa
Swedish: fälla

2245. travel [v.]

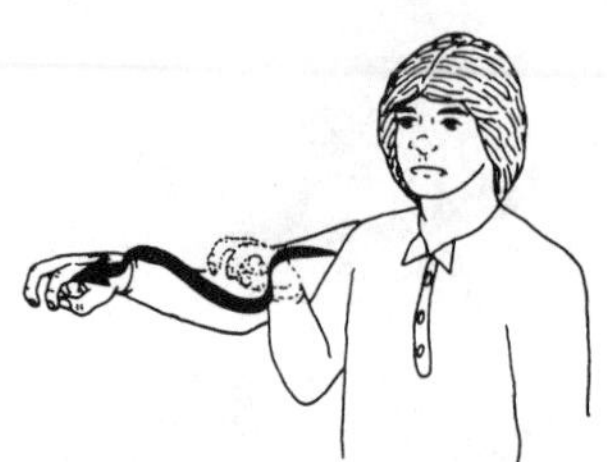

Arabic: sáfara سافر
Chinese: lǚxíng 旅行
Dutch: reizen
French: voyager
German: reisen
Italian: viaggiare
Japanese: ryokō suru 旅行する
Korean: yŏhaeng'hada 여행하다
Portuguese: viajar
Russian: puteshéstvovat' путешествовать
Spanish: viajar
Swedish: resa

2246. treasure [n.]

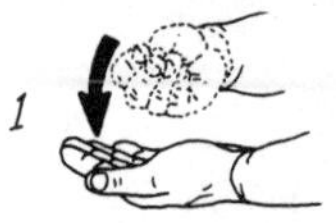

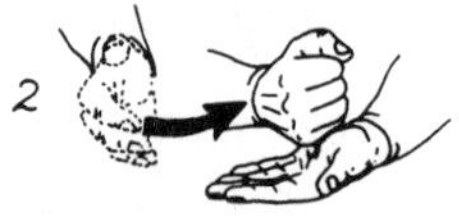

Arabic: thárwa ثروة
Chinese: bǎozàng 寶藏
Dutch: schat
French: trésor
German: Schatz
Italian: tesoro
Japanese: takara 宝
Korean: pobae 보배
Portuguese: tesouro
Russian: sokróvishche сокровище
Spanish: tesoro
Swedish: rikedom

2247. treasurer [n.]

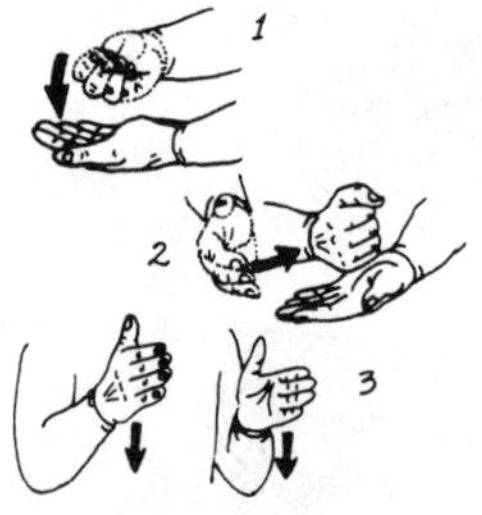

Arabic: amín as-sandúq امين الصندوق
Chinese: sīkù 司庫
Dutch: schatmeester
French: trésorier
German: Schatzmeister
Italian: tesoriere
Japanese: kaikei gakari 会計係
Korean: jaemukwan 재무관
Portuguese: tesoureiro
Russian: kaznachéy казначей
Spanish: tesorero
Swedish: finansmästare

2248. tree [n.]

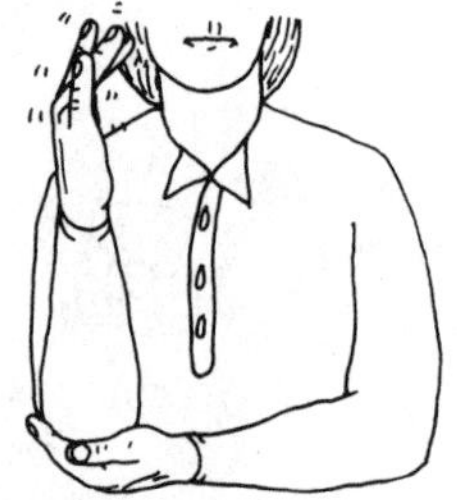

Arabic: shájara شجرة
Chinese: shù 樹
Dutch: boom
French: arbre
German: Baum
Italian: albero
Japanese: ki 木
Korean: namu 나무
Portuguese: árvore
Russian: dérevo дерево
Spanish: árbol
Swedish: träd

2249. triangle [n.]

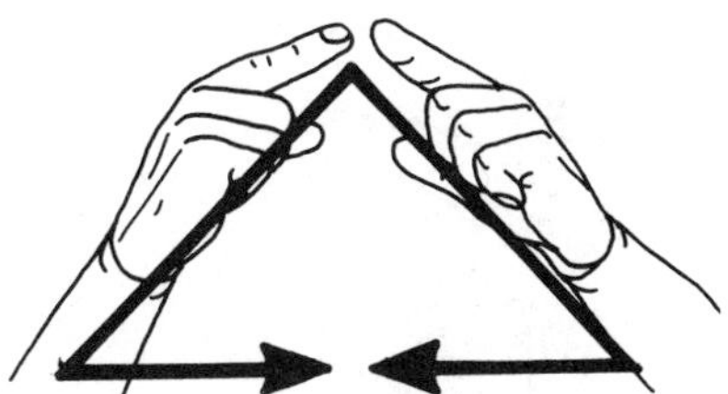

Arabic: muthállath مثلث
Chinese: sānjiăo 三角
Dutch: driehoek
French: triangle
German: Dreieck
Italian: triangolo
Japanese: sankakukei 三角形
Korean: samgak'hyong 삼각형
Portuguese: triângulo
Russian: treugól'nik треугольник
Spanish: triángulo
Swedish: triangel

2250. trip [n.]

Arabic: réhla رحلة
Chinese: lǚxíng 旅行
Dutch: tocht
French: voyage
German: Reise
Italian: viaggio
Japanese: ryokō 旅行
Korean: yŏhaeng 여행
Portuguese: viagem
Russian: poyézdka поездка
Spanish: viaje
Swedish: resa

2251. triumph [n.]

Arabic: nasr نصر
Chinese: kăixuán 凯旋
Dutch: triomf
French: triomphe
German: Triumph
Italian: trionfo
Japanese: daishōri 大勝利
Korean: sŭngni 승리
Portuguese: triunfo
Russian: triúmf триумф
Spanish: triunfo
Swedish: triumf

2252. trivial [adj.]

Arabic: táfi تافه
Chinese: suŏsuì 琐碎
Dutch: onbeduidend
French: trivial
German: trivial
Italian: banale
Japanese: tsumaranai つまらない
Korean: sasohan 사소한
Portuguese: trivial
Russian: triviál'nyy тривиальный
Spanish: trivial
Swedish: bagatelle

2253. trouble [n.]

Arabic: idtiráb اضطراب
Chinese: máfán 麻煩
Dutch: zorg
French: souci
German: Sorge
Italian: disturbo
Japanese: shimpai 心配
Korean: gŏkjŏng 걱정
Portuguese: preocupação
Russian: bespokóystvo беспокойство
Spanish: preocupación
Swedish: besvär

2254. trousers [n.]

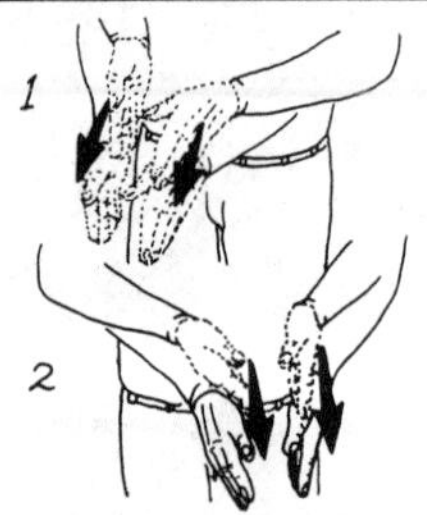

Arabic: bantalunát بنطلونات
Chinese: kùzi 褲子
Dutch: broek
French: pantalon
German: Hosen
Italian: calzoni
Japanese: zubon ズボン
Korean: baji 바지
Portuguese: calças
Russian: bryúki брюки
Spanish: pantalones
Swedish: byxor

2255. truck [n.]

Arabic: sháhina شاحنة
Chinese: huòchē 貨車
Dutch: vrachtwagen
French: camion
German: Lastwagen
Italian: camion
Japanese: torakku トラック
Korean: t'ŭrŏk 트럭
Portuguese: caminhão
Russian: gruzovík грузовик
Spanish: camión
Swedish: lastbil

2256. true [adj.]

Arabic: sahíeh صحيح
Chinese: zhēnde 真的
Dutch: waar
French: vrai
German: wahr
Italian: vero
Japanese: shinjitsu no 真実の
Korean: ch'amdoen 참된
Portuguese: verdadeiro
Russian: vérnyy верный
Spanish: verdadero
Swedish: sannt

2257. trunk (storage) [n.]

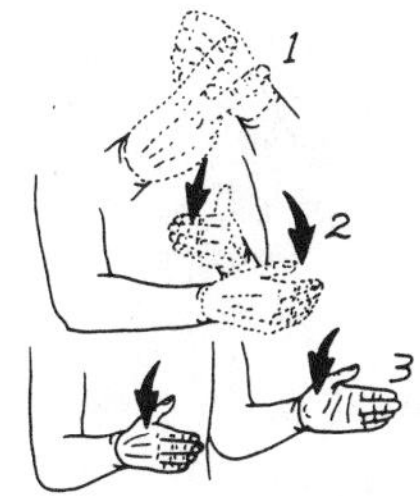

Arabic: sandúq صندوق
Chinese: xínglǐxiāng 行李箱
Dutch: koffer
French: malle
German: Koffer
Italian: baule
Japanese: toranku トランク
Korean: t'ŭrŏngk'ŭ 트렁크
Portuguese: baú
Russian: sundúk сундук
Spanish: baúl
Swedish: koffert

2258. truth [n.]

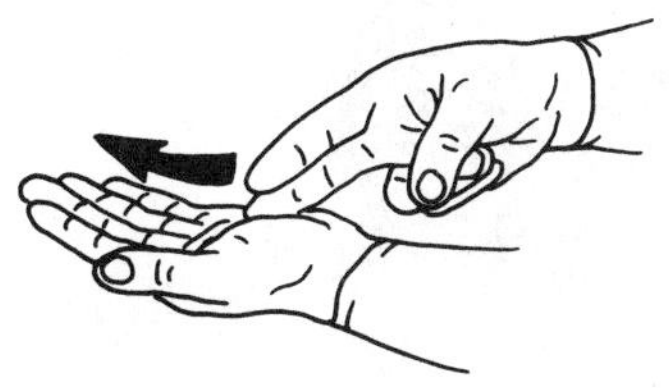

Arabic: sedq صدق
Chinese: shìshí 事實
Dutch: waarheid
French: vérité
German: Wahrheit
Italian: verità
Japanese: shinjitsu 真実
Korean: jinshil 진실
Portuguese: verdade
Russian: právda правда
Spanish: verdad
Swedish: sanning

2259. try (attempt) [v.]

Arabic: háwala حاول
Chinese: shì 試
Dutch: proberen
French: tenter
German: versuchen
Italian: tentare
Japanese: kokoromiru 試みる
Korean: haeboda 해보다
Portuguese: tentar
Russian: pytát'sya пытаться
Spanish: intentar
Swedish: försöka

2260. Tuesday [n.]

Arabic: ath-thalathá' الثلاثاء
Chinese: xīngqí èr 星期二
Dutch: dinsdag
French: mardi
German: Dienstag
Italian: martedì
Japanese: kayōbi 火曜日
Korean: hwayoil 화요일
Portuguese: terça-feira
Russian: vtórnik вторник
Spanish: martes
Swedish: tisdag

2261. Turkey (country) [n.]

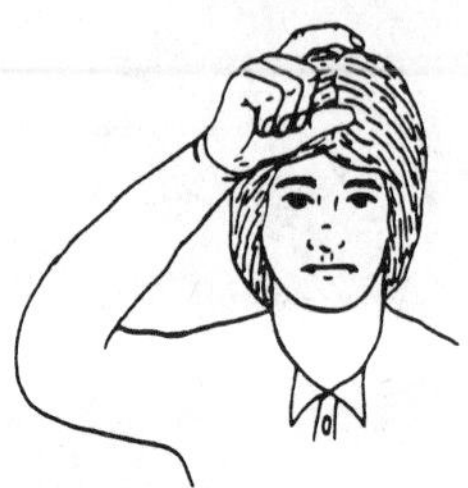

Arabic: turkíyya تركيا
Chinese: tǔěrqí 土耳其
Dutch: Turkije
French: Turquie
German: Türkei
Italian: Turchia
Japanese: Toruko トルコ
Korean: T'ŏk'i 터키
Portuguese: Turquia
Russian: Túrtsiya Турция
Spanish: Turquía
Swedish: Turkiet

2262. turn [v.]

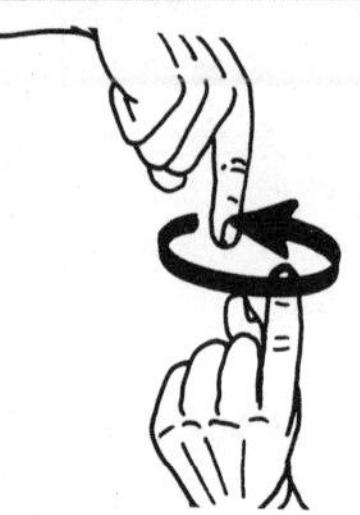

Arabic: láffa لف
Chinese: zhuǎndòng 轉動
Dutch: draaien
French: tourner
German: drehen
Italian: girare
Japanese: magaru 曲る
Korean: dolda 돌다
Portuguese: girar
Russian: vrashchát' вращать
Spanish: girar
Swedish: vända

2263. twelve [adj.]

Arabic: íthna áashar اثنى عشر
Chinese: shíèr 十二
Dutch: twaalf
French: douze
German: zwölf
Italian: dodici
Japanese: jūni 12
Korean: yŏl tul 열 둘
Portuguese: doze
Russian: dvenádtsat' двенадцать
Spanish: doce
Swedish: tolv

2264. twenty [adj.]

Arabic: ishrín عشرين
Chinese: èrshí 二十
Dutch: twintig
French: vingt
German: zwanzig
Italian: venti
Japanese: nijū 20
Korean: sŭmul 스물
Portuguese: vinte
Russian: dvádtsat' двадцать
Spanish: veinte
Swedish: tjugo

2265. twice [adv.]

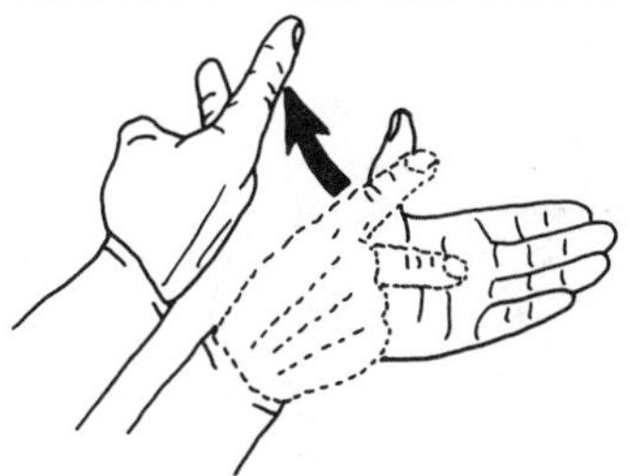

Arabic: maratéin مرتين
Chinese: liǎngcì 兩次
Dutch: tweemaal
French: deux fois
German: zweimal
Italian: due volte
Japanese: nido 二度
Korean: du bŏn 두번
Portuguese: duas vezes
Russian: dvázhdy дважды
Spanish: dos veces
Swedish: två gånger

2266. twilight [n.]

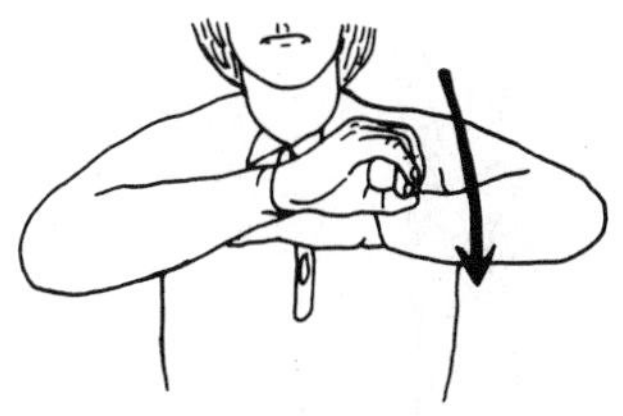

Arabic: ash-sháfaq الشفق
Chinese: límíng 黎明
Dutch: schemering
French: crépuscule
German: Halbdunkel
Italian: crepuscolo
Japanese: yūguredoki 夕暮れ時
Korean: hwang'hon 황혼
Portuguese: crepúsculo
Russian: súmerki сумерки
Spanish: crepúsculo
Swedish: skymning

2267. twin(s) [n.]

Arabic: táu'am توئم
Chinese: shuāngbāotāi 雙胞胎
Dutch: tweeling
French: jumeau
German: Zwilling
Italian: gemello
Japanese: futago no hitori 双子の一人
Korean: ssangdongi 쌍둥이
Portuguese: gêmeo
Russian: bliznéts близнец
Spanish: gemelo
Swedish: tvilling

2268. twist [v.]

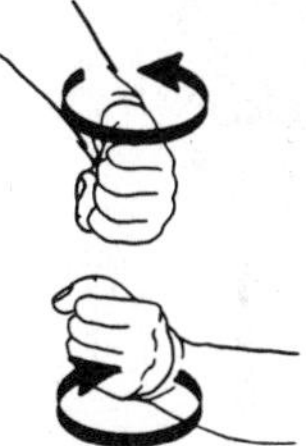

Arabic: bárama برم
Chinese: niǔ 扭
Dutch: draaien
French: tordre
German: drehen
Italian: torcere
Japanese: hineru ひねる
Korean: bit'ŭlda 비틀다
Portuguese: torcer
Russian: skrúchivat' скручивать
Spanish: torcer
Swedish: vrida

2269. two [adj.]

Arabic: ithnéin اثنين
Chinese: èr 二
Dutch: twee
French: deux
German: zwei
Italian: due
Japanese: ni 二つ
Korean: dul 둘
Portuguese: dois
Russian: dva два
Spanish: dos
Swedish: två

2270. type [v.]

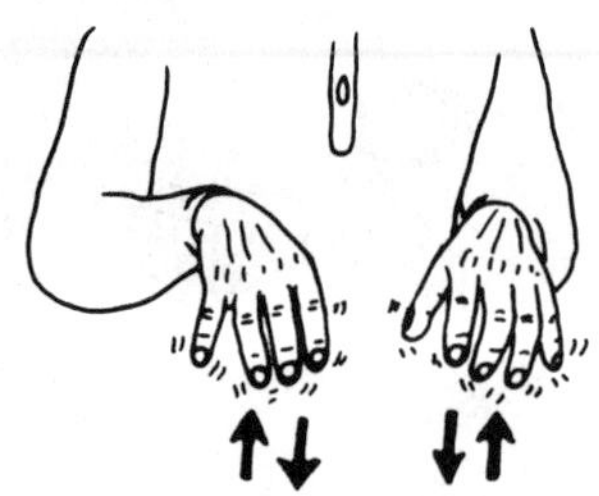

Arabic: tábaa طبع
Chinese: dǎzì 打字
Dutch: typen
French: dactylographier
German: tippen
Italian: dattilografare
Japanese: taipu タイプ
Korean: t'ajahada 타자하다
Portuguese: datilografar
Russian: pisát' na mashínke писать на машинке
Spanish: mecanografiar
Swedish: maskinskriva

2271. ugly [adj.]

Arabic: qabíeh قبيح
Chinese: chǒu 醜
Dutch: lelijk
French: laid
German: häßlich
Italian: brutto
Japanese: minikui 醜い
Korean: ch'uhan 추한
Portuguese: feio
Russian: bezobráznyy безобразный
Spanish: feo
Swedish: ful

2272. umbrella [n.]

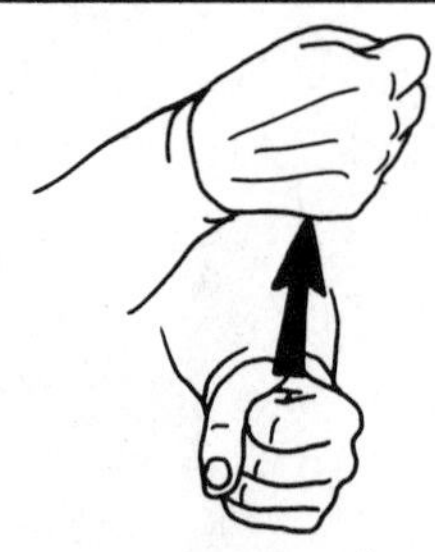

Arabic: madhálla مظلة
Chinese: yǔsǎn 雨伞
Dutch: paraplu
French: parapluie
German: Schirm
Italian: ombrello
Japanese: kasa 傘
Korean: usan 우산
Portuguese: guarda-chuva
Russian: zóntik зонтик
Spanish: paraguas
Swedish: paraply

2273. uncle [n.]

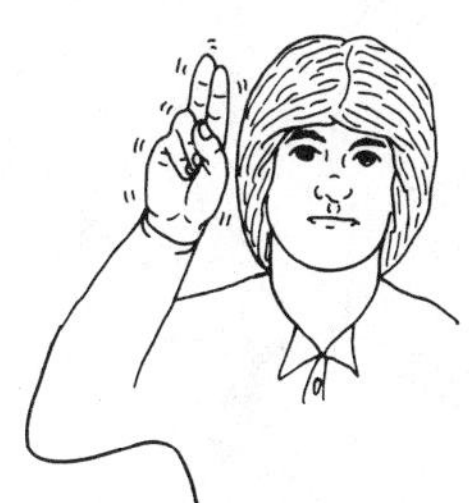

Arabic: áam/khal خال / عم
Chinese: shúfù 叔父 · 伯父
Dutch: oom
French: oncle
German: Onkel
Italian: zio
Japanese: oji 伯父
Korean: ajŏssi 아저씨
Portuguese: tio
Russian: dyádya дядя
Spanish: tío
Swedish: farbror/morbror

2274. under [adv./prep.]

Arabic: taht تحت
Chinese: zài...xiàmiàn 在下面
Dutch: onder
French: sous
German: unter
Italian: sotto
Japanese: shitani 下に
Korean: araee 아래에
Portuguese: debaixo
Russian: pod под
Spanish: bajo
Swedish: under

2275. understand [v.]

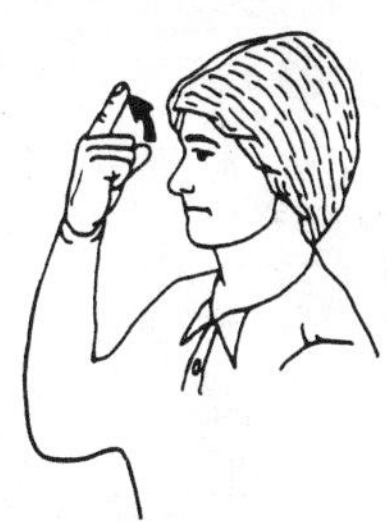

Arabic: fáhima فهم
Chinese: míngbái 明白
Dutch: verstaan
French: comprendre
German: verstehen
Italian: capire
Japanese: wakaru 分かる
Korean: ihaehada 이해하다
Portuguese: compreender
Russian: ponimát' понимать
Spanish: entender
Swedish: förstå

2276. undress [v.]

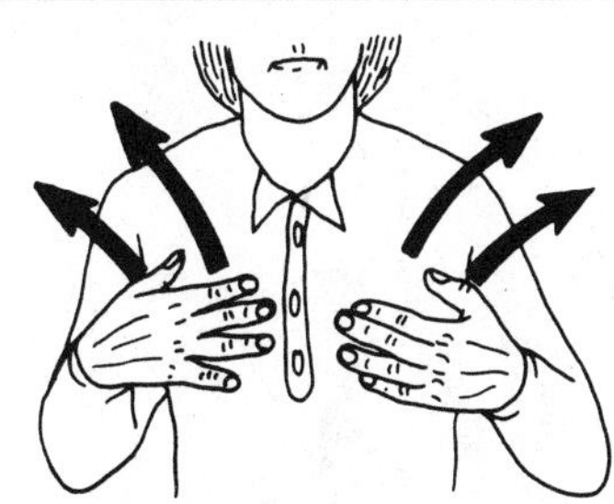

Arabic: taárra تعرى
Chinese: tuōyī 脱衣
Dutch: uitkleden
French: se déshabiller
German: sich ausziehen
Italian: svestirsi
Japanese: kimono o nugu 着物を脱ぐ
Korean: osŭl bŏtta 옷을 벗다
Portuguese: despir-se
Russian: razdevát'sya раздеваться
Spanish: desnudarse
Swedish: klä av sig

2277. unemployment [n.]

Arabic: betála بطالة
Chinese: shīyè 失業
Dutch: werkloosheid
French: chômage
German: Arbeitslosigkeit
Italian: disoccupazione
Japanese: shitsugyō 失業
Korean: shirŏp 실업
Portuguese: desemprego
Russian: bezrabótitsa безработица
Spanish: desempleo
Swedish: arbetslöshet

2278. uniform [adj.]

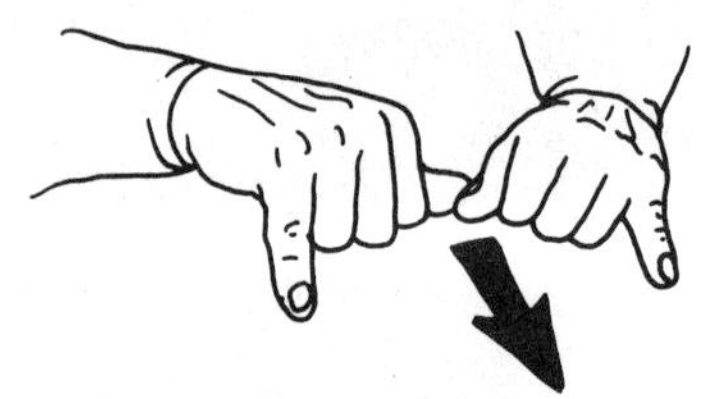

Arabic: muntádham منتظم
Chinese: zhěngqí 整齊
Dutch: uniform
French: uniforme
German: gleichförmig
Italian: uniforme
Japanese: ittei no 一定の
Korean: kat'ŭn 같은
Portuguese: uniforme
Russian: odnoobráznyy однообразный
Spanish: uniforme
Swedish: likformig

2279. uniform [n.]

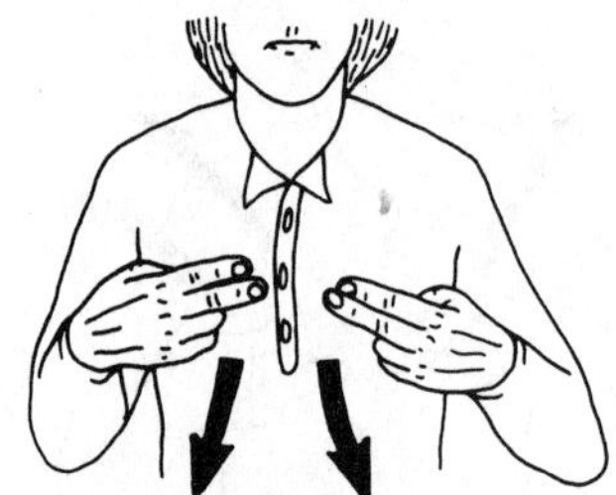

Arabic: zéy زي
Chinese: zhìfú 制服
Dutch: uniform
French: uniforme
German: Uniform
Italian: uniforme
Japanese: seifuku 制服
Korean: jebok 제복
Portuguese: uniforme
Russian: fórma форма
Spanish: uniforme
Swedish: uniform

2280. union (joined together) [n.]

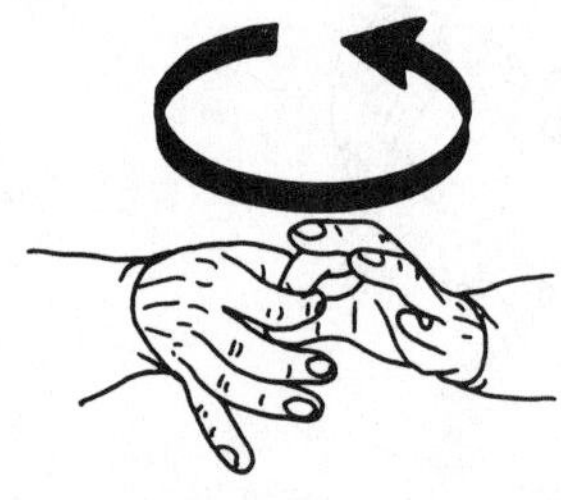

Arabic: itehád اتحاد
Chinese: liánhé 聯合
Dutch: unie
French: union
German: Union
Italian: unione
Japanese: dōmei 同盟
Korean: yŏnmaeng 연맹
Portuguese: união
Russian: soyúz союз
Spanish: unión
Swedish: union

2281. unit [n.]

Arabic: wéhda وحدة
Chinese: dānwèi 單位
Dutch: eenheid
French: unité
German: Einheit
Italian: unità
Japanese: tani 単位
Korean: danwi 단위
Portuguese: unidade
Russian: yedinítsa единица
Spanish: unidad
Swedish: enhet

2282. unite [v.]

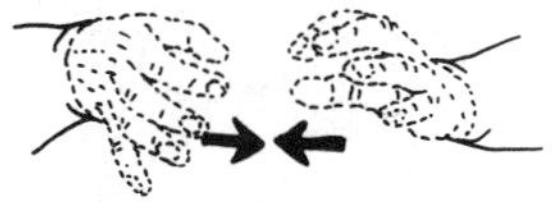

Arabic: itáhada اتحد
Chinese: jiéhé 結合
Dutch: verenigen
French: unir
German: vereinen
Italian: unire
Japanese: ketsugō suru 結合する
Korean: kyŏrhap'hada 교합하다
Portuguese: unir
Russian: ob''yedinyát' объединять
Spanish: unir
Swedish: förena

2283. united [adj.]

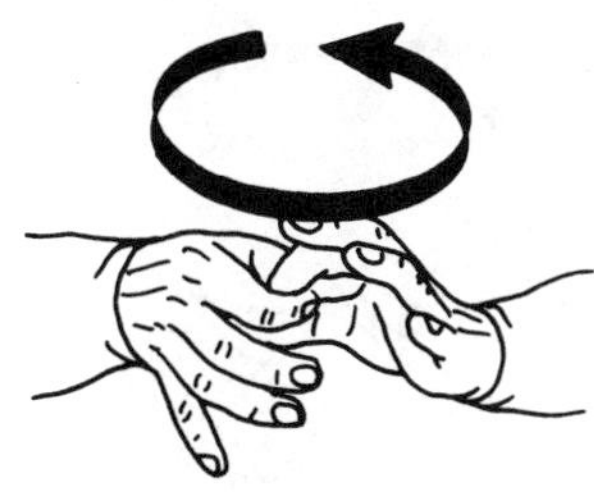

Arabic: mutáhed متحد
Chinese: liánhé 聯合
Dutch: verenigd
French: unis
German: vereinigt
Italian: unito
Japanese: rengō shita 連合した
Korean: hapch'in 합친
Portuguese: unido
Russian: ob''yedinyónnyy объединённый
Spanish: unido
Swedish: förenade

2284. United Kingdom [n.]

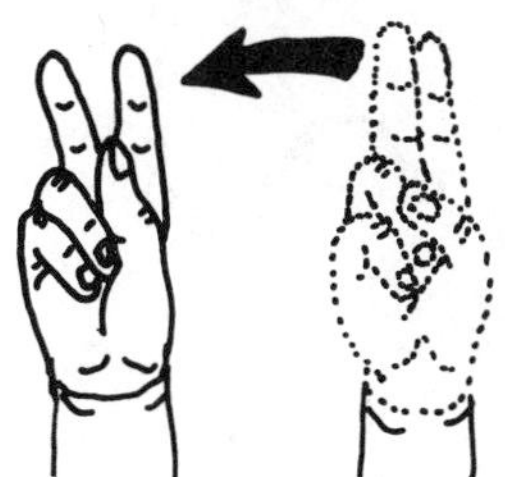

Arabic: al-mámlaka al-mutáheda المملكة المتحدة
Chinese: liánhéwángguó 聯合王國
Dutch: Verenigd Koninkrijk
French: Royaume-Uni
German: Vereinigtes Königreich
Italian: Regno Unito
Japanese: Rengō Okoku 連合王国
Korean: Yŏngguk 영국
Portuguese: Reino Unido
Russian: Soyedinyónnoye Korolévstvo Соединённое Королевство
Spanish: Reino Unido
Swedish: Storbritannien

2285. United Nations [n.]

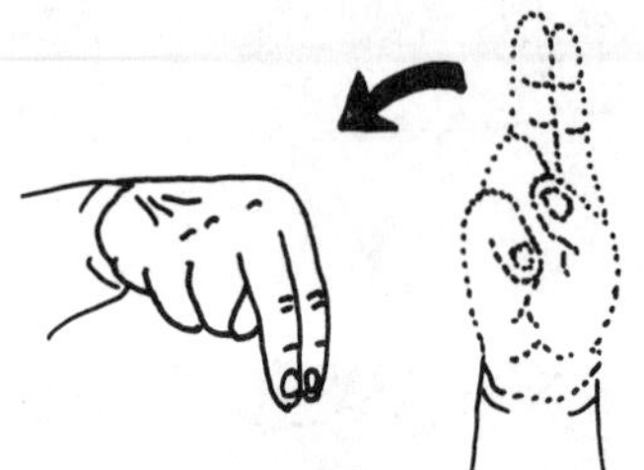

Arabic: al-úmam al-mutáheda
الامم المتحدة
Chinese: liánhéguó 聯合國
Dutch: Verenigde Naties
French: Nations Unies
German: Vereinte Nationen
Italian: Nazioni Unite
Japanese: Kokusairengō 国際連合
Korean: Yŏnhapkuk 연합국
Portuguese: Nações Unidas
Russian: Organizátsiya ob"yedinyónnykh nátsiy
Организация объединённых наций
Spanish: Naciones Unidas
Swedish: Förenta nationerna

2286. United States [n.]

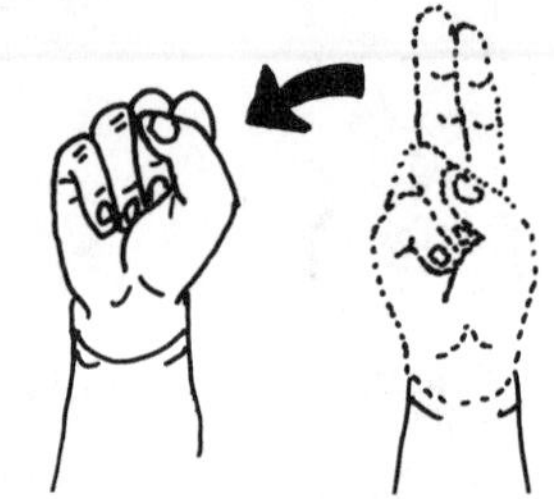

Arabic: al-wilayát al-mutáheda
الولايات المتحدة
Chinese: meǐlijiān hézhòngguó
美利堅合衆國
Dutch: Verenigde Staten
French: États-Unis
German: Vereinigte Staaten
Italian: Stati Uniti d'America
Japanese: Amerika Gasshūkoku
アメリカ合衆国
Korean: Amerik'a hapchungguk
아메리카 합중국
Portuguese: Estados Unidos
Russian: Soyedinyónnyye Shtáty Amériki
Соединённые Штаты Америки
Spanish: Estados Unidos
Swedish: Förenta staterna

2287. universal [adj.]

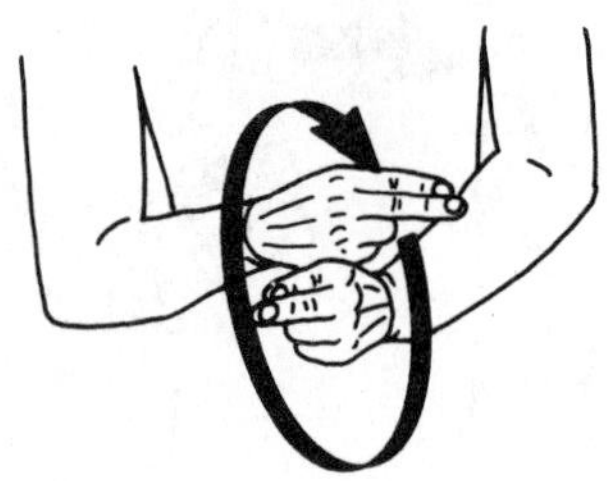

Arabic: áalami عالمي
Chinese: quánshìjiède 全世界
Dutch: universeel
French: universel
German: allgemein
Italian: universale
Japanese: zensekai no 全世界の
Korean: jŏnsegyeŭi 전 세계의
Portuguese: universal
Russian: universál'nyy
универсальный
Spanish: universal
Swedish: universell

2288. university [n.]

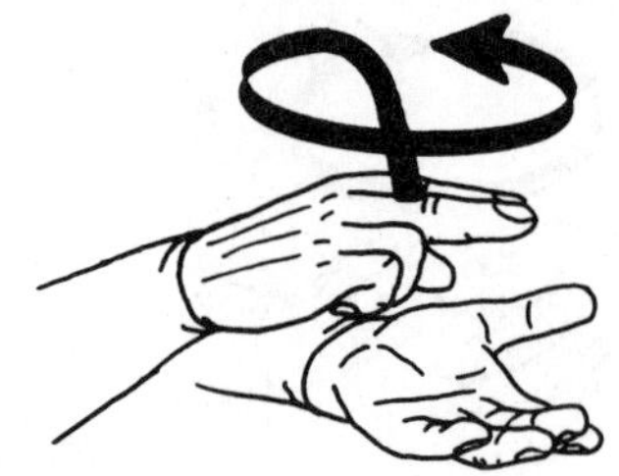

Arabic: jámiaa جامعة
Chinese: dàxué 大學
Dutch: universiteit
French: université
German: Universität
Italian: università
Japanese: daigaku 大学
Korean: daehakkyo 대학교
Portuguese: universidade
Russian: universitét университет
Spanish: universidad
Swedish: universitet

2289. unjust [adj.]

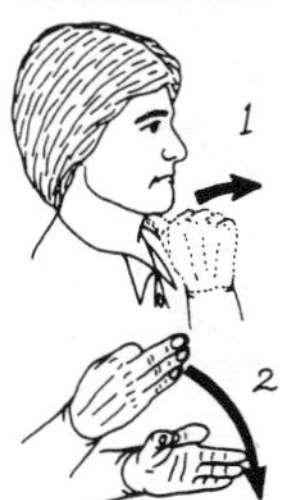

Arabic: dhálim ظالم
Chinese: bùgōngzhèng 不公正
Dutch: onrechtvaardig
French: injuste
German: ungerecht
Italian: ingiusto
Japanese: fusei na 不正な
Korean: olch'i anŭn 옳지 않은
Portuguese: injusto
Russian: nespravedlívyy несправедливый
Spanish: injusto
Swedish: orättvis

2290. unless [conj.]

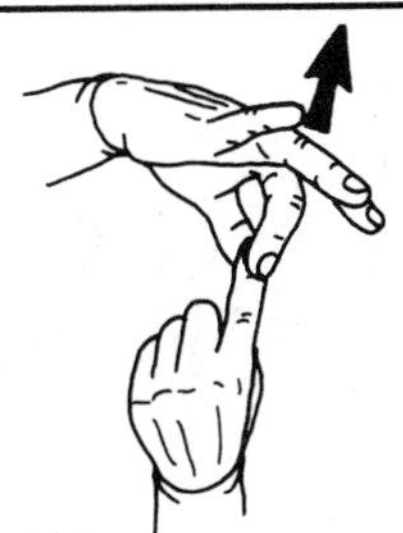

Arabic: ílla الا
Chinese: chúfēi 除非
Dutch: tenzij
French: à moins que
German: wenn nicht
Italian: a meno che
Japanese: moshi. . .de nakereba ____ もし…でなければ
Korean: . . .i animyŏn ~이 아니면
Portuguese: a menos que
Russian: yésli ne если не
Spanish: a menos que
Swedish: såvida ej

2291. unnecessary [adj.]

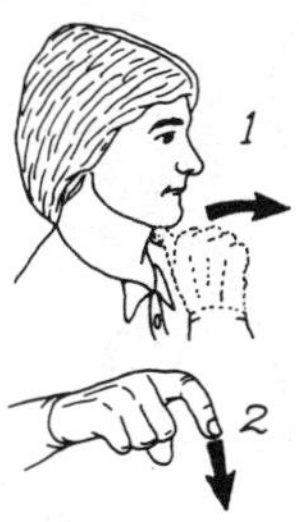

Arabic: gher dharúri غير ضروري
Chinese: bù bìyào 不必要
Dutch: onnodig
French: inutile
German: unnötig
Italian: superfluo
Japanese: fuhitsuyō na 不必要な
Korean: bulp'iryohan 불 필요한
Portuguese: desnecessario
Russian: nenúzhnyy ненужный
Spanish: innecesario
Swedish: onödig

2292. until [prep.]

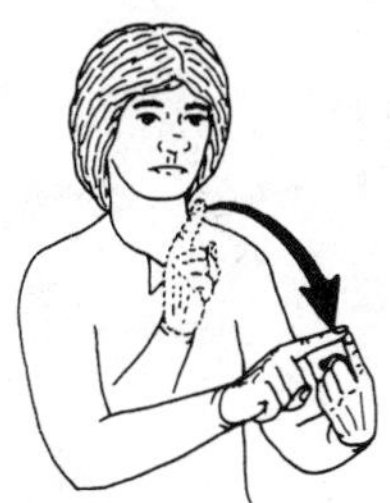

Arabic: hátta حتى
Chinese: zhídào 直到
Dutch: tot
French: jusqu'à
German: bis
Italian: fino a
Japanese: . . .made …まで
Korean: . . .kkaji ~까지
Portuguese: até
Russian: do до
Spanish: hasta
Swedish: tills

2293. up [adv./prep.]

Arabic: fauq فوق
Chinese: xiàngshàng 向上
Dutch: opwaarts
French: en haut
German: aufwärts
Italian: in su
Japanese: ue ni 上に
Korean: wiro 위로
Portuguese: para cima
Russian: navérkh наверх
Spanish: hacia arriba
Swedish: uppåt

2294. upper [adj.]

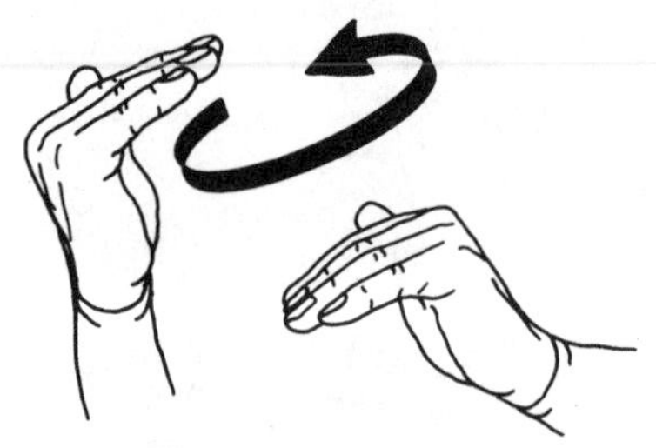

Arabic: áala اعلى
Chinese: shàngbiānde 上邊的
Dutch: hoger
French: supérieur
German: obere
Italian: superiore
Japanese: ue no 上の
Korean: witchogŭi 위쪽의
Portuguese: superior
Russian: vérkhniy верхний
Spanish: superior
Swedish: övre

2295. urge (exhort) [v.]

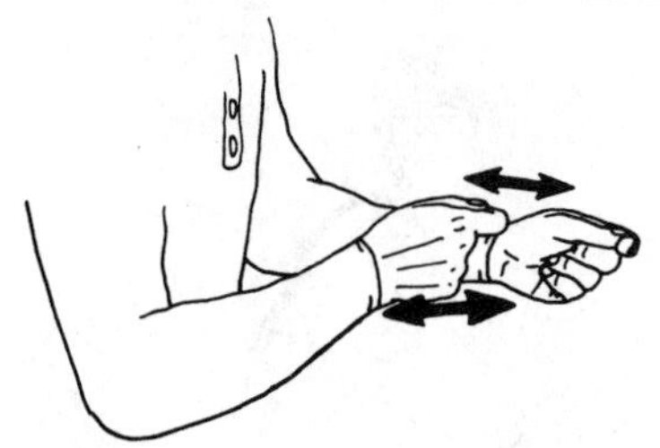

Arabic: háththa حث
Chinese: cuīcù 催促
Dutch: aansporen
French: presser
German: drängen
Italian: esortare
Japanese: saisoku suru 催促する
Korean: jaech'og'hada 재촉하다
Portuguese: apressar
Russian: podgonyát' подгонять
Spanish: urgir
Swedish: uppmana

2296. urgent [adj.]

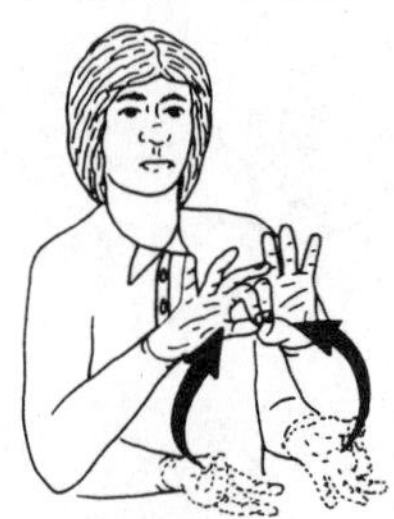

Arabic: mustaájel مستعجل
Chinese: jĭnjí 緊急
Dutch: dringend
French: urgent
German: dringend
Italian: urgente
Japanese: kinkyū no 緊急の
Korean: kinkŭp'han 긴급한
Portuguese: urgente
Russian: sróchnyy срочный
Spanish: urgente
Swedish: brådskande

2297. Uruguay [n.]

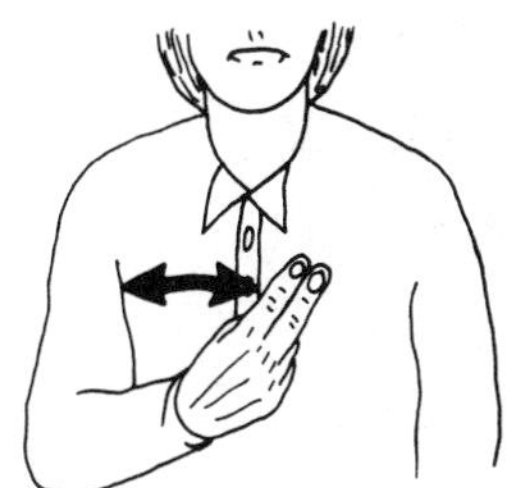

Arabic: urugwáy اورجواي
Chinese: ūlāguī 烏拉圭
Dutch: Uruguay
French: Uruguay
German: Uruguay
Italian: Uruguay
Japanese: Uruguai ウルグアイ
Korean: Urugwai 우루과이
Portuguese: Uruguai
Russian: Urugváy Уругвай
Spanish: Uruguay
Swedish: Uruguay

2298. us [pron.]

Arabic: naa نا
Chinese: wǒmen 我們
Dutch: ons
French: nous
German: uns
Italian: noi
Japanese: wareware ni 我々に
Korean: uriege 우리에게
Portuguese: nós
Russian: nas/nam/nami нас/нам/нами
Spanish: nosotros
Swedish: oss

2299. use [v.]

Arabic: istáamala استعمل
Chinese: yòng 用
Dutch: gebruiken
French: utiliser
German: gebrauchen
Italian: usare
Japanese: tsukau 使う
Korean: sayonghada 사용하다
Portuguese: usar
Russian: upotreblyát' употреблять
Spanish: usar
Swedish: använda

2300. useful [adj.]

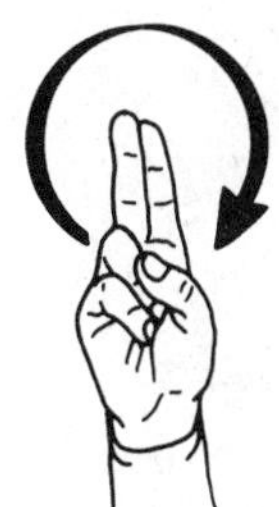

Arabic: mufíd مفيد
Chinese: yǒuyòng 有用
Dutch: nuttig
French: utile
German: nützlich
Italian: utile
Japanese: benrina 便利な
Korean: yuyong'han 유용한
Portuguese: útil
Russian: poléznyy полезный
Spanish: útil
Swedish: användbar

2301. usual [adj.]

Arabic: áadi عادي
Chinese: tōngcháng 通常
Dutch: gewoon
French: habituel
German: gewöhnlich
Italian: usuale
Japanese: itsumono いつもの
Korean: bot'ongŭi 보통의
Portuguese: usual
Russian: obyknovénnyy обыкновенный
Spanish: usual
Swedish: vanlig

2302. vacant [adj.]

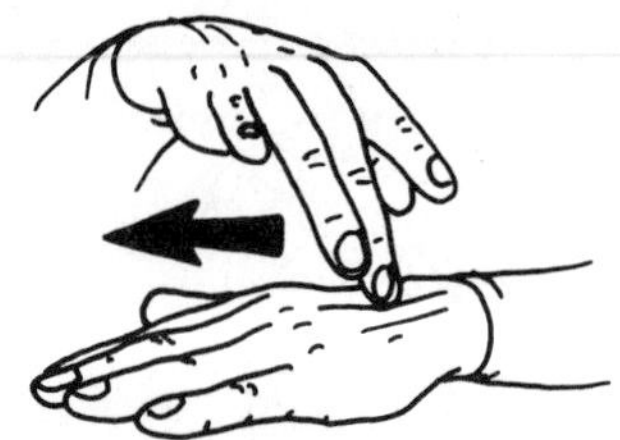

Arabic: kháli خالي
Chinese: kòng 空
Dutch: leeg
French: vide
German: frei
Italian: vacante
Japanese: kara no 空の（からの）
Korean: t'ŏng bin 텅빈
Portuguese: vago
Russian: svobódnyy свободный
Spanish: vacante
Swedish: ledig

2303. vacation (holidays) [n.]

Arabic: ótla عطلة
Chinese: jiàqí 假期
Dutch: vakantie
French: vacances
German: Ferien
Italian: vacanza
Japanese: kyūka 休暇
Korean: hyuga 휴가
Portuguese: férias
Russian: kaníkuly каникулы
Spanish: vacaciones
Swedish: semester

2304. vague [adj.]

Arabic: ghámed غامض
Chinese: hánhú 含糊
Dutch: vaag
French: vague
German: unbestimmt
Italian: vago
Japanese: aimai na 曖昧な
Korean: magyŏnhan 막연한
Portuguese: vago
Russian: neopredelyónnyy неопределённый
Spanish: vago
Swedish: obestämd

2305. (in) vain [adj.]

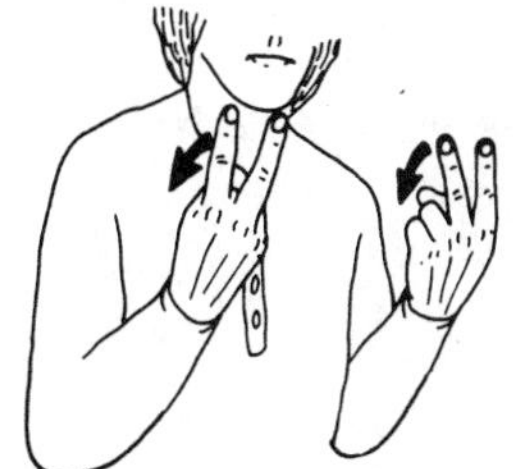

Arabic: áabathan عبثاً
Chinese: túrán 徒然
Dutch: tevergeefs
French: en vain
German: vergebens
Italian: invano
Japanese: mueki no 無益の
Korean: hŏtdoe 헛되이
Portuguese: em vão
Russian: naprásno напрасно
Spanish: en vano
Swedish: förgäves

2306. valid [adj.]

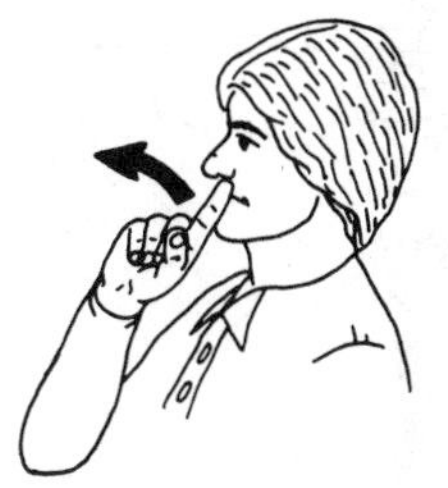

Arabic: sháraai شرعي
Chinese: yǒuxiào 有效
Dutch: geldig
French: valide
German: gültig
Italian: valido
Japanese: yūkō na 有効な
Korean: yuhyohan 유효한
Portuguese: válido
Russian: deystvítel'nyy действительный
Spanish: válido
Swedish: giltig

2307. valley [n.]

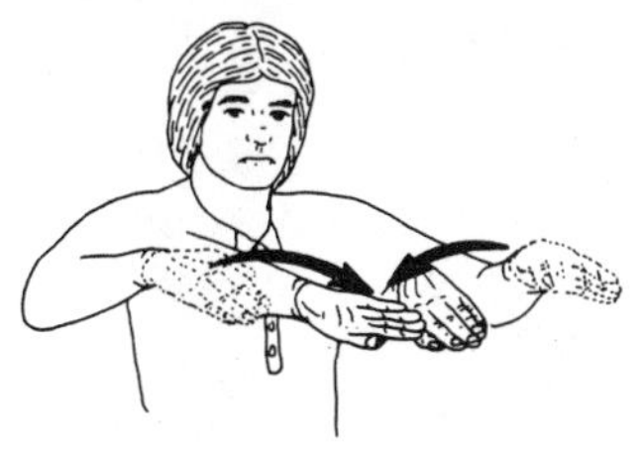

Arabic: wádi وادي
Chinese: shāngǔ 山谷
Dutch: vallei
French: vallée
German: Tal
Italian: valle
Japanese: tani 谷
Korean: kyegok 계곡
Portuguese: vale
Russian: dolína долина
Spanish: valle
Swedish: dal

2308. valuable [adj.]

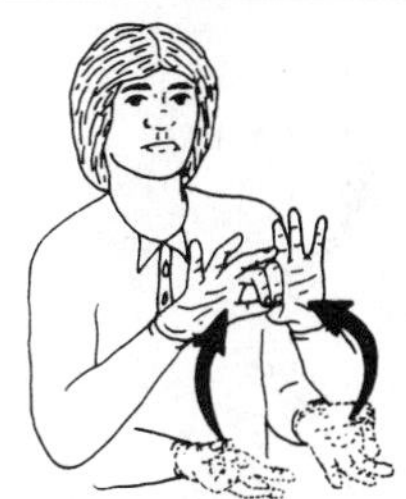

Arabic: thamín ثمين
Chinese: yǒu jiàzhí 有價值
Dutch: waardevol
French: précieux
German: wertvoll
Italian: prezioso
Japanese: kichō na 貴重な
Korean: kapbissan 값 비싼
Portuguese: valioso
Russian: tsénnyy ценный
Spanish: valioso
Swedish: värdefull

2309. vanish [v.]

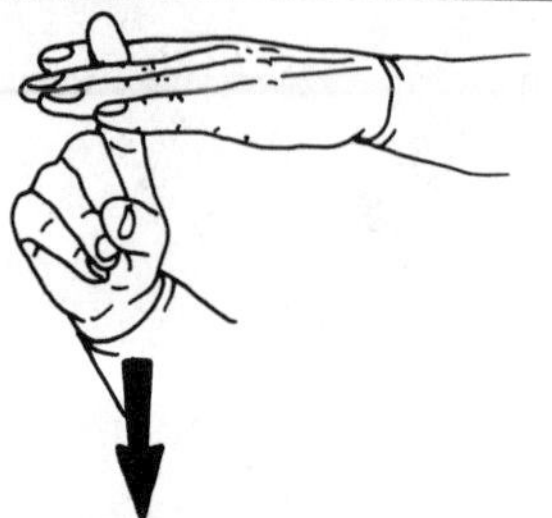

Arabic: ikhtáfa اختفى
Chinese: xiāoshī 消失
Dutch: verdwijnen
French: disparaître
German: verschwinden
Italian: svanire
Japanese: kieru 消える
Korean: sarajida 사라지다
Portuguese: desaparecer
Russian: ischezát' исчезать
Spanish: desvanecerse
Swedish: försvinna

2310. various [adj.]

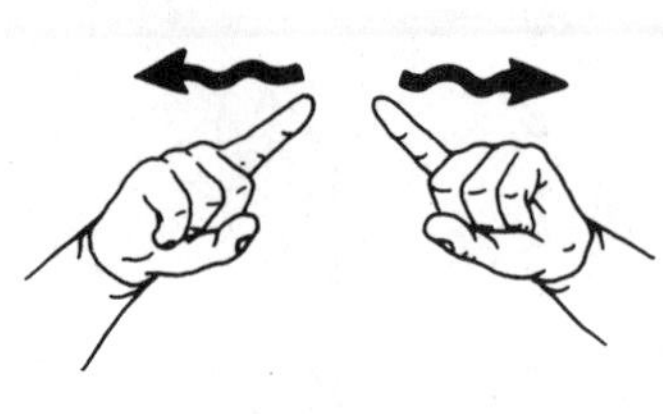

Arabic: mutanáwwa متنوع
Chinese: gèzhŏngde 各種的
Dutch: verscheiden
French: divers
German: verschiedene
Italian: vario
Japanese: iroiro na いろいろな
Korean: yŏrŏ kajiŭi 여러가지의
Portuguese: vários
Russian: ráznyy разный
Spanish: varios
Swedish: olika

2311. vegetable(s) [n.]

Arabic: khudár خضار
Chinese: shūcài 蔬菜
Dutch: groente(n)
French: légumes
German: Gemüse
Italian: legumi
Japanese: yasai 野菜
Korean: ch'aeso 채소
Portuguese: legumes
Russian: óvoshchi овощи
Spanish: legumbres
Swedish: grönsaker

2312. Venezuela [n.]

Arabic: fenzewélla فنزويلا
Chinese: wĕinèiruìlā 委內瑞拉
Dutch: Venezuela
French: Venezuela
German: Venezuela
Italian: Venezuela
Japanese: Benezuera ベネズエラ
Korean: Benejuella 베네주엘라
Portuguese: Venezuela
Russian: Venesuéla Венесуэла
Spanish: Venezuela
Swedish: Venezuela

2313. verb [n.]

Arabic: féaal فعل
Chinese: dòngcí 動詞
Dutch: werkwoord
French: verbe
German: Verb
Italian: verbo
Japanese: dōshi 動詞
Korean: dongsa 동사
Portuguese: verbo
Russian: glagól глагол
Spanish: verbo
Swedish: verb

2314. very [adv.]

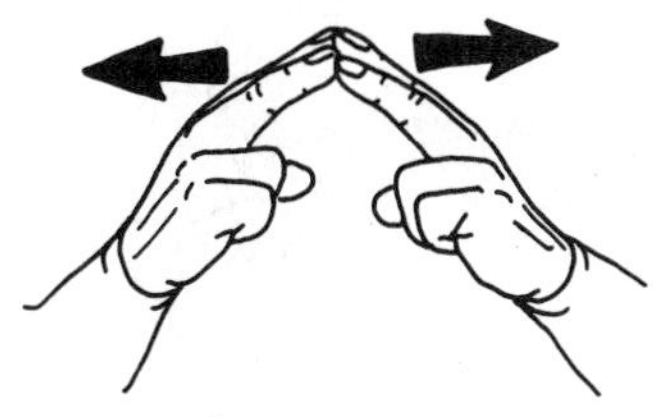

Arabic: jíddan جداً
Chinese: hěn 很
Dutch: zeer
French: très
German: sehr
Italian: molto
Japanese: totemo とても
Korean: maeu 매우
Portuguese: muito
Russian: óchen' очень
Spanish: muy
Swedish: mycket

2315. victory [n.]

Arabic: intisár انتصار
Chinese: shènglì 勝利
Dutch: overwinning
French: victoire
German: Sieg
Italian: vittoria
Japanese: shōri 勝利
Korean: sŭngni 승리
Portuguese: vitória
Russian: pobéda победа
Spanish: victoria
Swedish: seger

2316. Vietnam [n.]

Arabic: fitnám فيتنام
Chinese: yuènán 越南
Dutch: Viëtnam
French: Vietnam
German: Vietnam
Italian: Vietnam
Japanese: Betonamu ベトナム
Korean: Wŏllam 월남
Portuguese: Vietnã
Russian: V'yetnám Вьетнам
Spanish: Vietnam
Swedish: Vietnam

2317. view [n.]

Arabic: mándhar منظر
Chinese: guāndiǎn 觀點
Dutch: zicht
French: vue
German: Anblick
Italian: veduta
Japanese: keshiki 景色
Korean: kyŏngch'i 경치
Portuguese: vista
Russian: vid вид
Spanish: vista
Swedish: utsikt

2318. village [n.]

Arabic: qária قرية
Chinese: chūn 村
Dutch: dorp
French: village
German: Dorf
Italian: villaggio
Japanese: mura 村
Korean: maŭl 마을
Portuguese: aldeia
Russian: derévnya деревня
Spanish: aldea
Swedish: by

2319. vinegar [n.]

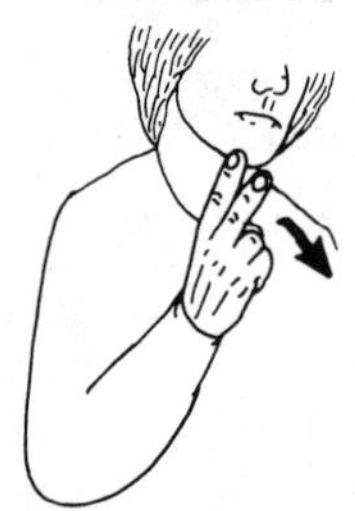

Arabic: khal خل
Chinese: cù 醋
Dutch: azijn
French: vinaigre
German: Essig
Italian: aceto
Japanese: su 酢
Korean: shikcho 식초
Portuguese: vinagre
Russian: úksus уксус
Spanish: vinagre
Swedish: ättika

2320. violation [n.]

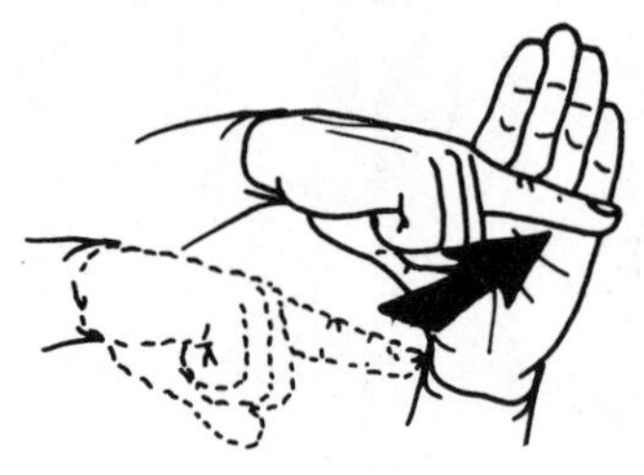

Arabic: intihák انتهاك
Chinese: wéiguī 違規
Dutch: overtreding
French: infraction
German: Verletzung
Italian: violazione
Japanese: ihan 違反
Korean: wiban 위반
Portuguese: violação
Russian: narushéniye нарушение
Spanish: violación
Swedish: kränkning

2321. visible [adj.]

Arabic: mandhúr منظور
Chinese: kàn de jiàn 看得見
Dutch: zichtbaar
French: visible
German: sichtbar
Italian: visibile
Japanese: mieru 見える
Korean: nune boinŭn 눈에 보이는
Portuguese: visível
Russian: vídimyy видимый
Spanish: visible
Swedish: synlig

2322. visit [v.]

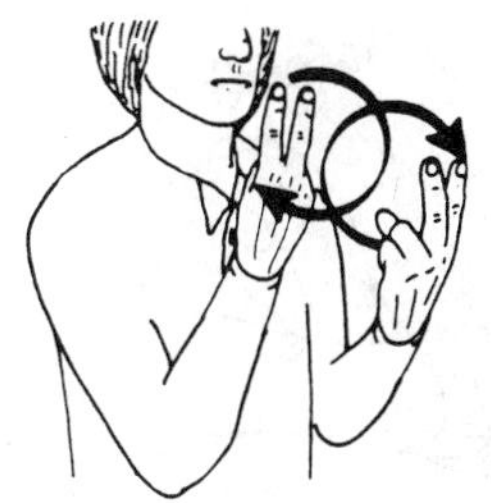

Arabic: ziáda زيادة
Chinese: făngwèn 訪問
Dutch: bezoeken
French: visiter
German: besuchen
Italian: visitare
Japanese: tazuneru 訪ねる
Korean: bangmunhada 방문하다
Portuguese: visitar
Russian: poseshchát' посещать
Spanish: visitar
Swedish: besöka

2323. vital [adj.]

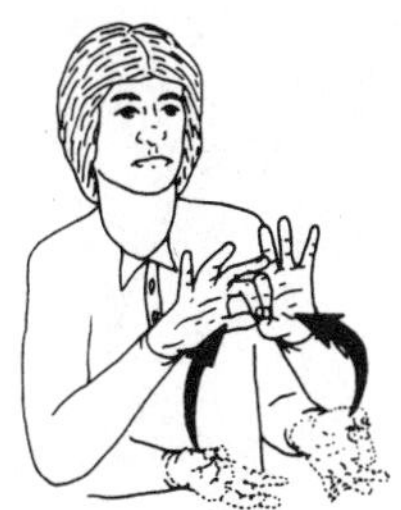

Arabic: asási اساسي
Chinese: shēngmìngde 生命的
Dutch: essentieel
French: vital
German: lebenswichtig
Italian: vitale
Japanese: zettai ni hitsuyō na 絶対に必要な
Korean: saengmyŏngŭi 생명의
Portuguese: vital
Russian: zhíznennyy жизненный
Spanish: vital
Swedish: livsviktig

2324. vocabulary [n.]

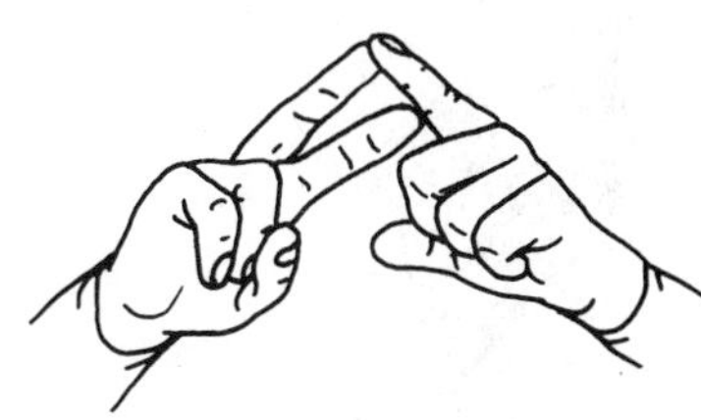

Arabic: talíeq al-lisán طليق اللسان
Chinese: zìhuì 字彙
Dutch: woordenschat
French: vocabulaire
German: Wortschatz
Italian: vocabolario
Japanese: yōgohani 用語範囲
Korean: ŏhwi 단어집
Portuguese: vocabulário
Russian: zapás slov запас слов
Spanish: vocabulario
Swedish: ordlista

2325. vocation [n.]

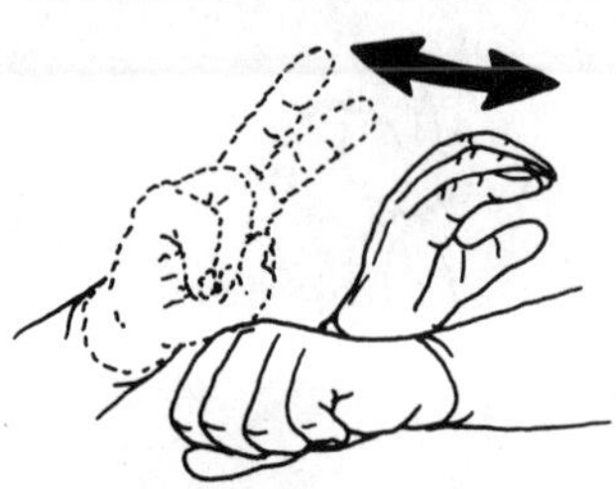

Arabic: méhna مهنة
Chinese: zhíyè 職業
Dutch: roeping
French: vocation
German: Berufung
Italian: vocazione
Japanese: shokugyō 職業
Korean: jigŏp 직업
Portuguese: vocação
Russian: prizvániye призвание
Spanish: vocación
Swedish: kallelse

2326. voice [n.]

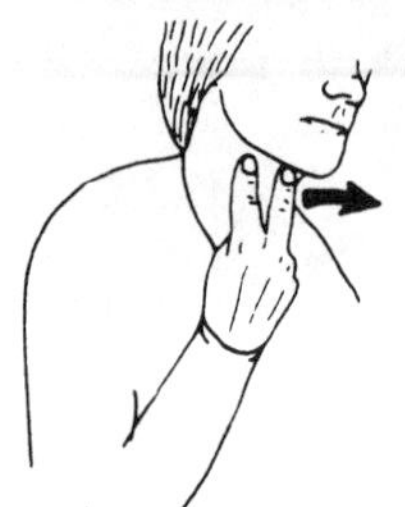

Arabic: saut صوت
Chinese: shēngyīn 聲音
Dutch: stem
French: voix
German: Stimme
Italian: voce
Japanese: koe 声
Korean: moksori 목소리
Portuguese: voz
Russian: gólos голос
Spanish: voz
Swedish: röst

2327. volcano [n.]

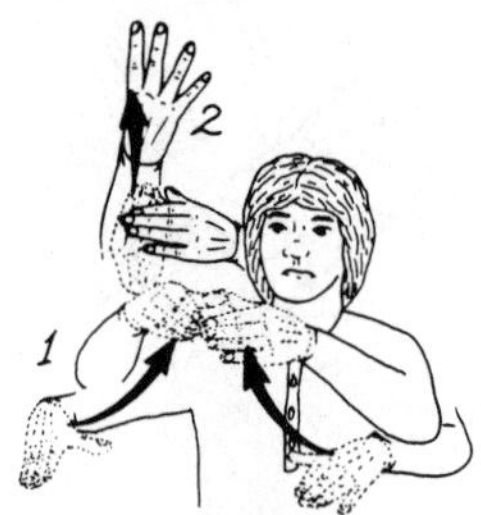

Arabic: burkán بركان
Chinese: huŏshān 火山
Dutch: vulkaan
French: volcan
German: Vulkan
Italian: vulcano
Japanese: kazan 火山
Korean: hwasan 화산
Portuguese: vulcão
Russian: vulkán вулкан
Spanish: volcán
Swedish: vulkan

2328. volleyball [n.]

Arabic: kúrat al-yád كرة اليد
Chinese: páiqiú 排球
Dutch: volleyball
French: volley-ball
German: Volleyball
Italian: palla a volo
Japanese: barēboru バレーボール
Korean: baeku 배구
Portuguese: voleibol
Russian: voleyból волейбол
Spanish: voleibol
Swedish: volleyboll

2329. volunteer [n.]

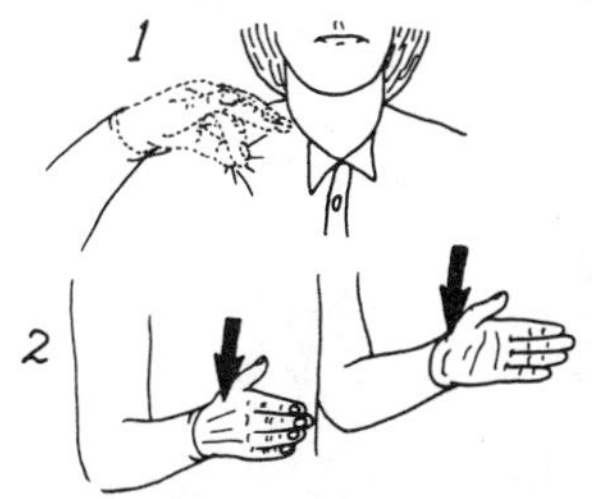

Arabic: mutatáwwaa متطوع
Chinese: zhìyuànzhě 志願者
Dutch: vrijwilliger
French: volontaire
German: Freiwilliger
Italian: volontario
Japanese: shigansha 志願者
Korean: jiwŏnja 지원자
Portuguese: voluntário
Russian: dobrovólets доброволец
Spanish: voluntario
Swedish: frivillig

2330. vote [v.]

Arabic: sáwwata صوت
Chinese: tóupiào 投票
Dutch: stemmen
French: voter
German: wählen
Italian: votare
Japanese: tōhyō suru 投票する
Korean: t'up'yohada 투표하다
Portuguese: votar
Russian: golosovát' голосовать
Spanish: votar
Swedish: rösta

2331. wage(s) [v.]

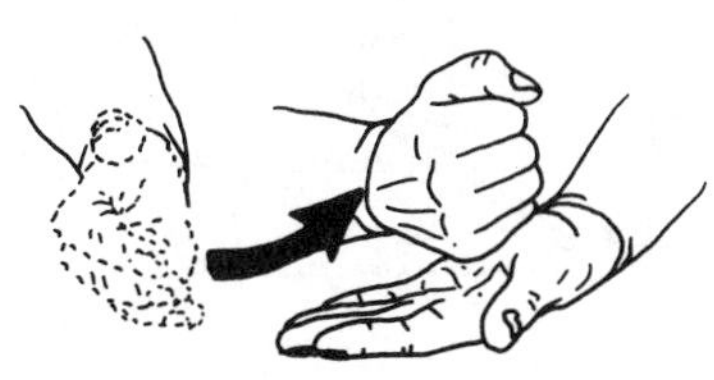

Arabic: áajr اجر
Chinese: gōngzī 工資
Dutch: loon
French: salaire
German: Lohn
Italian: salario
Japanese: kyūryō 給料
Korean: imgŭm 임금
Portuguese: salário
Russian: zarpláta зарплата
Spanish: salario
Swedish: lon

2332. wagon (cart) [n.]

Arabic: áaraba عربة
Chinese: yùnhuòmǎchē 運貨馬車
Dutch: wagen
French: charrette
German: Wagen
Italian: carro
Japanese: nibasha 荷馬車
Korean: jimmach'a 짐마차
Portuguese: carro
Russian: teléga телега
Spanish: carro
Swedish: vagn

2333. waist [n.]

Arabic: khasr خصر
Chinese: yāo 腰
Dutch: middel
French: taille
German: Taille
Italian: cintura
Japanese: dō no kubire 胴のくびれ
Korean: hŏri 허리
Portuguese: cintura
Russian: táliya талия
Spanish: cintura
Swedish: midja

2334. wait [v.]

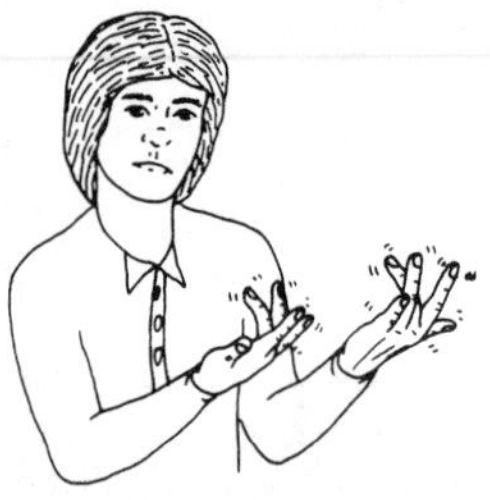

Arabic: intádhara انتظر
Chinese: děng 等
Dutch: wachten
French: attendre
German: warten
Italian: aspettare
Japanese: matsu 待つ
Korean: gidarida 기다리다
Portuguese: esperar
Russian: zhdat' ждать
Spanish: esperar
Swedish: vänta

2335. waiter [n.]

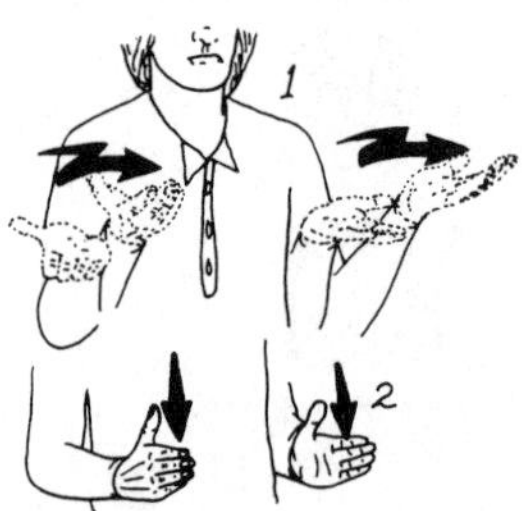

Arabic: an-nádil النادل
Chinese: fúwùyuán 服務員
Dutch: kelner
French: garçon
German: Ober
Italian: cameriere
Japanese: weitā ウェーター
Korean: weit'ŏ 웨이터
Portuguese: garçom
Russian: ofitsiánt официант
Spanish: camarero
Swedish: kypare

2336. walk [v.]

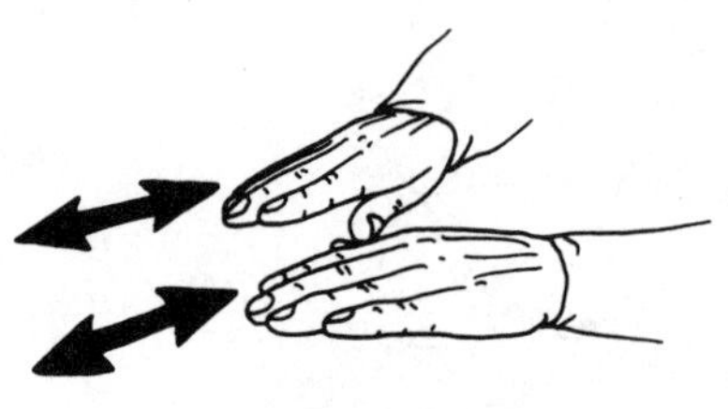

Arabic: másha مشى
Chinese: zǒu 走
Dutch: wandelen
French: promener
German: gehen
Italian: camminare
Japanese: aruku 歩く
Korean: kŏtta 걷다
Portuguese: andar
Russian: idtí идти
Spanish: andar
Swedish: gå

2337. wall [n.]

Arabic: há'it حائط
Chinese: qiáng 牆
Dutch: muur
French: mur
German: Mauer
Italian: muro
Japanese: kabe 壁
Korean: byŏk 벽
Portuguese: muro
Russian: stená стена
Spanish: pared
Swedish: mur

2338. wander [v.]

Arabic: tajáwwala تجول
Chinese: páihuí 徘徊
Dutch: zwerven
French: errer
German: wandern
Italian: vagare
Japanese: samayou さまよう
Korean: doradanida 돌아다니다
Portuguese: vaguear
Russian: brodít' бродить
Spanish: vagar
Swedish: vandra

2339. want [v.]

Arabic: aráda اراد
Chinese: yào 要
Dutch: willen
French: vouloir
German: wollen
Italian: volere
Japanese: hoshii 欲しい
Korean: wonhada 원하다
Portuguese: querer
Russian: khotét' хотеть
Spanish: querer
Swedish: vilja

2340. war [n.]

Arabic: harb حرب
Chinese: zhànzhēng 戰爭
Dutch: oorlog
French: guerre
German: Krieg
Italian: guerra
Japanese: sensō 戦争
Korean: jŏnjaeng 전쟁
Portuguese: guerra
Russian: voyná война
Spanish: guerra
Swedish: krig

2341. warm [adj.]

Arabic: dáfi' دافئ
Chinese: nuǎnhuo 暖和
Dutch: warm
French: chaud
German: warm
Italian: caldo
Japanese: atatakai 暖かい
Korean: ttattut'han 따뜻한
Portuguese: quente
Russian: tyóplyy тёплый
Spanish: tibio
Swedish: varm

2342. warn [v.]

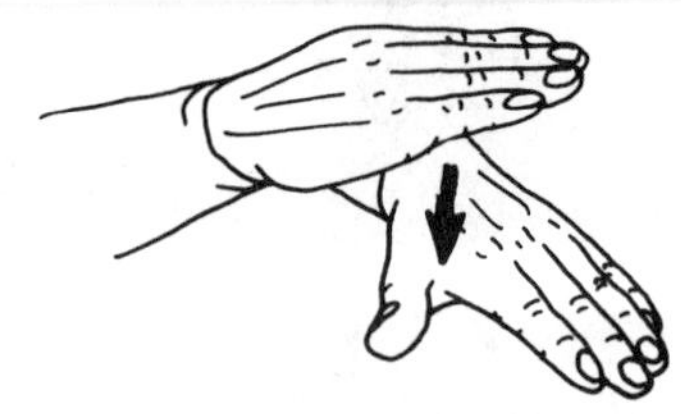

Arabic: hádhdhara حذر
Chinese: jǐnggào 警告
Dutch: waarschuwen
French: avertir
German: warnen
Italian: avvertire
Japanese: chūkoku suru 警告する
Korean: kyŏnggohada 경고하다
Portuguese: avisar
Russian: preduprezhdát' предупреждать
Spanish: advertir
Swedish: varna

2343. wash [v.]

Arabic: ghásala غسل
Chinese: xǐ 洗
Dutch: wassen
French: laver
German: waschen
Italian: lavare
Japanese: arau 洗う
Korean: set'ak'hada 세탁하다
Portuguese: lavar
Russian: myt' мыть
Spanish: lavar
Swedish: tvätta

2344. waste [v.]

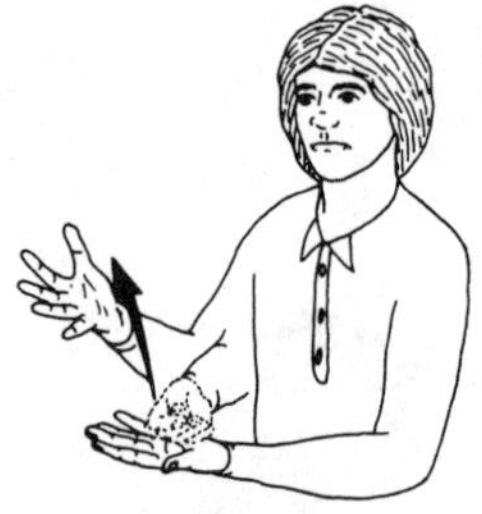

Arabic: áfsada افسد
Chinese: làngfèi 浪費
Dutch: verspillen
French: gaspiller
German: verschwenden
Italian: sprecare
Japanese: muda ni suru 無駄にする
Korean: nangbihada 낭비하다
Portuguese: desperdiçar
Russian: rastochát' расточать
Spanish: malgastar
Swedish: förslösa

2345. watch (timepiece) [n.]

Arabic: sá-aa ساعة
Chinese: biǎo 錶
Dutch: horloge
French: montre
German: Uhr
Italian: orologio
Japanese: tokē 時計
Korean: shigye 시계
Portuguese: relógio
Russian: chasý часы
Spanish: reloj
Swedish: klocka

2346. watch (observe) [v.]

Arabic: ráqaba راقب
Chinese: guānkàn 觀看
Dutch: gadeslaan
French: observer
German: beobachten
Italian: osservare
Japanese: keikai suru 警戒する
Korean: kwanch'arhada 관찰하다
Portuguese: observar
Russian: nablyudát' наблюдать
Spanish: observar
Swedish: iaktta

2347. water [n.]

Arabic: ma' ماء
Chinese: shuǐ 水
Dutch: water
French: eau
German: Wasser
Italian: acqua
Japanese: mizu 水
Korean: mul 물
Portuguese: água
Russian: vodá вода
Spanish: agua
Swedish: vatten

2348. wave [v.]

Arabic: rafráfa رفرف
Chinese: zhāoshǒu 招手
Dutch: zwaaien
French: faire signe de la main
German: winken
Italian: agitare la mano
Japanese: furi ugokasu 振り動かす
Korean: hŭndŭlda 흔들다
Portuguese: acenar com a mão
Russian: makhát' махать
Spanish: hacer señal
Swedish: vinka

2349. way (road) [n.]

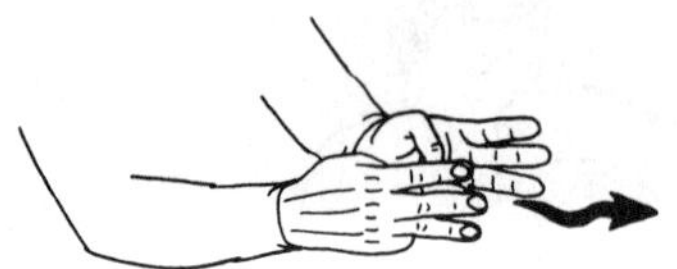

Arabic: taríeq طريق
Chinese: lù 路
Dutch: weg
French: chemin
German: Weg
Italian: via
Japanese: michi 道
Korean: gil 길
Portuguese: caminho
Russian: put' путь
Spanish: camino
Swedish: väg

2350. way (method) [n.]

Arabic: taríeqa طريقة
Chinese: fāngfǎ 方法
Dutch: manier
French: manière
German: Weise
Italian: maniera
Japanese: hōhō 方法
Korean: bangbŏp 방법
Portuguese: maneira
Russian: spósob способ
Spanish: manera
Swedish: vis

2351. we [pron.]

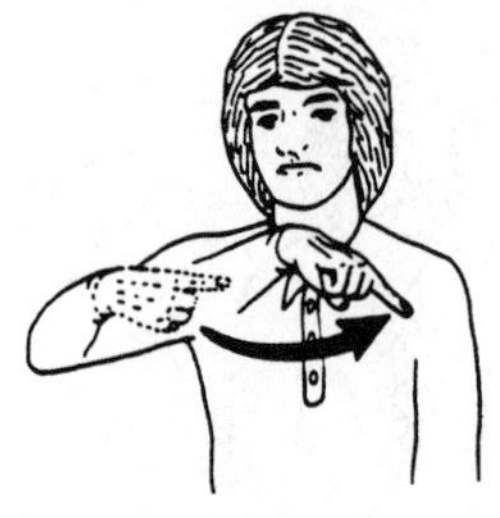

Arabic: náhnu نحن
Chinese: wǒmen 我們
Dutch: wij
French: nous
German: wir
Italian: noi
Japanese: warewarewa 我々は
Korean: uri 우리
Portuguese: nós
Russian: my мы
Spanish: nosotros
Swedish: vi

2352. weak [adj.]

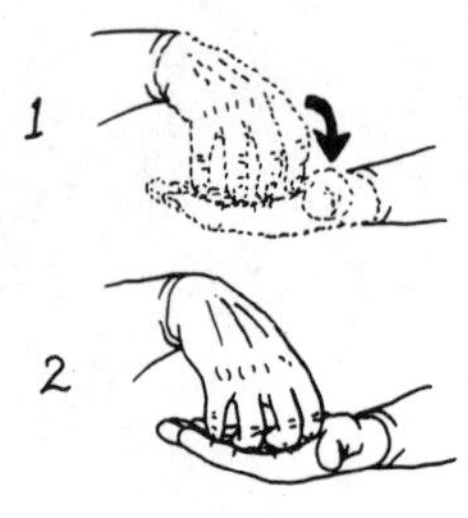

Arabic: dhaaíf ضعيف
Chinese: ruò 弱
Dutch: zwak
French: faible
German: schwach
Italian: debole
Japanese: yowai 弱い
Korean: yak'han 약한
Portuguese: fraco
Russian: slábyy слабый
Spanish: débil
Swedish: svag

2353. wealth [n.]

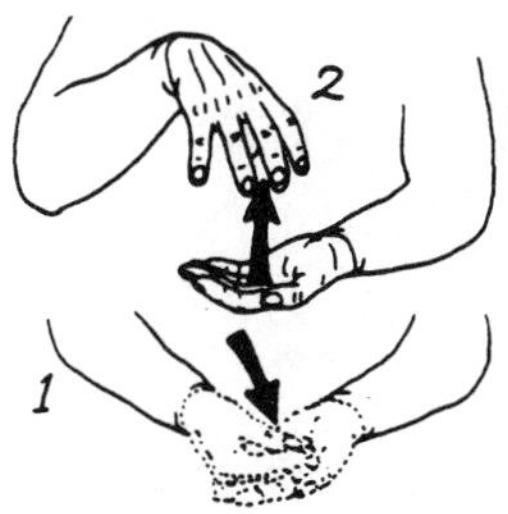

Arabic: thárwa ثروة
Chinese: cáifù 財富
Dutch: weelde
French: richesse
German: Reichtum
Italian: ricchezza
Japanese: zaisan 財産
Korean: jaesan 재산
Portuguese: riqueza
Russian: bogátstvo богатство
Spanish: riqueza
Swedish: rikedom

2354. wear [v.]

Arabic: lábisa لبس
Chinese: chuān 穿
Dutch: dragen
French: porter
German: tragen
Italian: indossare
Japanese: kiru 着る
Korean: ipda 입다
Portuguese: trazer
Russian: nosít' носить
Spanish: llevar
Swedish: bära

2355. weary [adj.]

Arabic: múrhaq مرهق
Chinese: píjuànde 疲倦的
Dutch: vermoeid
French: fatigué
German: müde
Italian: stanco
Japanese: tsukareta 疲れた
Korean: jich'in 지친
Portuguese: cansado
Russian: utomlyónnyy утомлённый
Spanish: cansado
Swedish: trött

2356. weather [n.]

Arabic: taqs طقس
Chinese: tiānqì 天氣
Dutch: weder
French: temps
German: Wetter
Italian: tempo
Japanese: tenki 天気
Korean: nalssi 날씨
Portuguese: tempo
Russian: pogóda погода
Spanish: tiempo
Swedish: väder

2357. wedding [n.]

Arabic: zawáj زواج
Chinese: hūnlǐ 婚禮
Dutch: bruiloft
French: noces
German: Hochzeit
Italian: sposalizio
Japanese: kekkonshiki 結婚式
Korean: kyŏrhon 결혼
Portuguese: casamento
Russian: svád'ba свадьба
Spanish: boda
Swedish: bröllop

2358. Wednesday [n.]

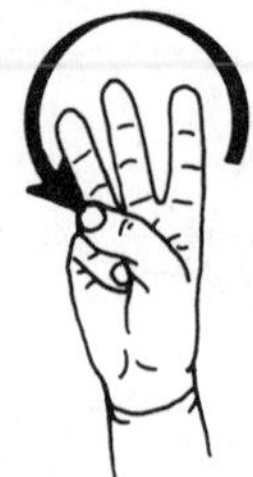

Arabic: al-árbaa الاربعاء
Chinese: xīngqí sān 星期三
Dutch: woensdag
French: mercredi
German: Mittwoch
Italian: mercoledì
Japanese: suiyōbi 水曜日
Korean: suyoil 수요일
Portuguese: quarta-feira
Russian: sredá среда
Spanish: miércoles
Swedish: onsdag

2359. week [n.]

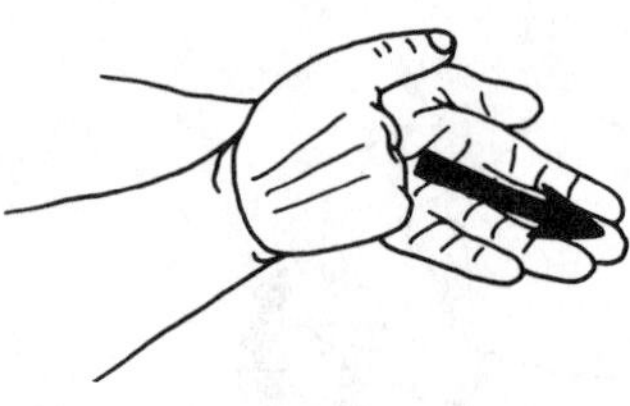

Arabic: usbúaa اسبوع
Chinese: xīngqí 星期
Dutch: week
French: semaine
German: Woche
Italian: settimana
Japanese: shū 週
Korean: ju 주
Portuguese: semana
Russian: nedélya неделя
Spanish: semana
Swedish: vecka

2360. weekly [adj.]

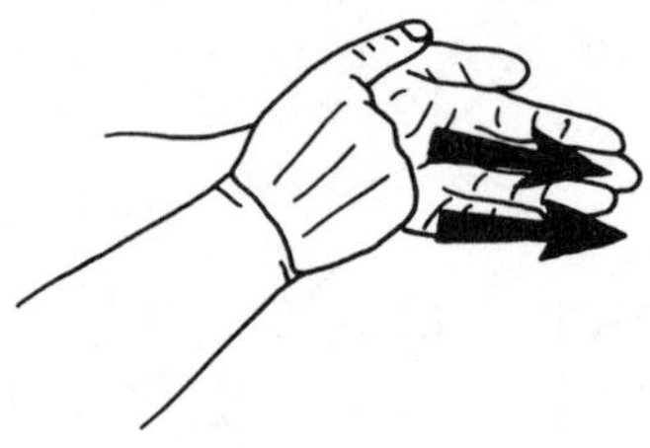

Arabic: usbuaaían اسبوعياً
Chinese: měizhōu 每週
Dutch: wekelijks
French: hebdomadaire
German: wöchentlich
Italian: settimanale
Japanese: maishū no 毎週の
Korean: maejuŭi 매주의
Portuguese: semanal
Russian: yezhenedél'nyy еженедельный
Spanish: semanal
Swedish: veckans

2361. weep [v.]

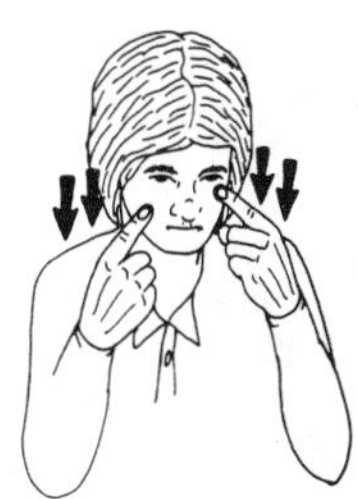

Arabic: báka بكى
Chinese: kū 哭
Dutch: wenen
French: pleurer
German: weinen
Italian: piangere
Japanese: naku 泣く
Korean: ulda 울다
Portuguese: chorar
Russian: plákat' плакать
Spanish: llorar
Swedish: gråta

2362. weigh [v.]

Arabic: wázana وزن
Chinese: chèng 稱
Dutch: wegen
French: peser
German: wiegen
Italian: pesare
Japanese: omosa o hakaru 重さを計る
Korean: mugerŭl dalda 무게를 달다
Portuguese: pesar
Russian: vzvéshivat' взвешивать
Spanish: pesar
Swedish: väga

2363. welcome! [interj.]

Arabic: áhlan wa sáhlan اهلاً وسهلاً
Chinese: huānyíng 歡迎
Dutch: welkom
French: bienvenue
German: Willkommen
Italian: benvenuto
Japanese: yōkoso ようこそ！
Korean: ŏsŏ oshipshiyo 어서 오십시오
Portuguese: bem-vindo
Russian: dobró pozhálovat'
добро пожаловать
Spanish: bienvenido
Swedish: välkommen

2364. well [adv.]

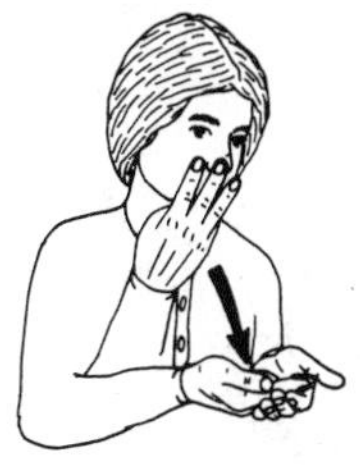

Arabic: hásanan حسناً
Chinese: hǎo 好
Dutch: wel
French: bien
German: gut
Italian: bene
Japanese: yoku 良く
Korean: joŭn 좋은
Portuguese: bem
Russian: khoroshó хорошо
Spanish: bien
Swedish: bra

2365. west [n.]

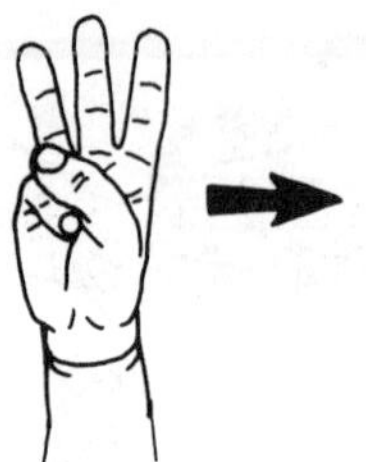

Arabic: ghárban غرباً
Chinese: xīfāng 西方
Dutch: westen
French: ouest
German: Westen
Italian: ovest
Japanese: nishi 西
Korean: sŏtchok 서쪽
Portuguese: oeste
Russian: západ запад
Spanish: oeste
Swedish: väster

2366. wet [adj.]

Arabic: mablúl مبلول
Chinese: shī 濕
Dutch: nat
French: mouillé
German: naß
Italian: molle
Japanese: nureta 濡れた
Korean: jŏjŭn 젖은
Portuguese: molhado
Russian: mókryy мокрый
Spanish: mojado
Swedish: vat

2367. what [pron.]

Arabic: mádha ماذا
Chinese: shénmo 什麽
Dutch: wat
French: quoi
German: was
Italian: che
Japanese: nani なに
Korean: muŏt 무엇
Portuguese: quê
Russian: chto что
Spanish: que
Swedish: vad

2368. wheat [n.]

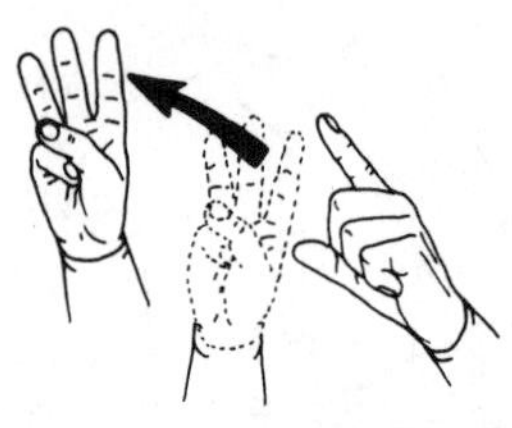

Arabic: qamh قمح
Chinese: mài 麥
Dutch: tarwe
French: blé
German: Weizen
Italian: frumento
Japanese: mugi 麦
Korean: mil 밀
Portuguese: trigo
Russian: pshenítsa пшеница
Spanish: trigo
Swedish: vete

2369. wheel [n.]

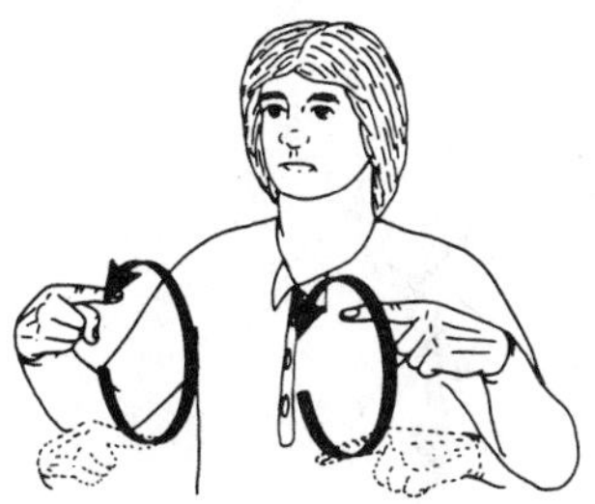

Arabic: áajala عجلة
Chinese: lúnzi 輪子
Dutch: wiel
French: roue
German: Rad
Italian: ruota
Japanese: sharin 車輪
Korean: bak'wi 바퀴
Portuguese: roda
Russian: kolesó колесо
Spanish: rueda
Swedish: hjul

2370. when [adv.]

Arabic: máta متى
Chinese: shénmo shíhòu 什麼時候
Dutch: wanneer
French: quand
German: wann
Italian: quando
Japanese: itsu いつ
Korean: ŏnje 언제
Portuguese: quando
Russian: kogdá когда
Spanish: cuando
Swedish: när

2371. whenever [conj.]

Arabic: kúllama كلما
Chinese: wúlùn héshí 無論何時
Dutch: wanneer ook
French: n'importe quand
German: wann immer
Italian: ogni volta che
Japanese: itsudemo いつでも
Korean: ŏnjena 언제나
Portuguese: sempre que
Russian: kogdá by ni когда бы ни
Spanish: siempre que
Swedish: när. . .än

2372. where/where to [adv.]

Arabic: éina/íla éina اين / الى اين
Chinese: nǎr 那兒
Dutch: waar/waartoe
French: où/vers où
German: wo
Italian: dove
Japanese: doko どこへ
Korean: ŏdisŏ 어디서
Portuguese: onde
Russian: gde/kudá где/куда
Spanish: donde
Swedish: var

2373. whether [conj.]

Arabic: sawá' سواء
Chinese: shìfǒu 是否
Dutch: of
French: soit
German: ob
Italian: se
Japanese: . . . ka dō ka …かどらか
Korean: . . . inji ŏttŏnji ~인지, 어떤지
Portuguese: se
Russian: li ли
Spanish: si
Swedish: om

2374. which [pron.]

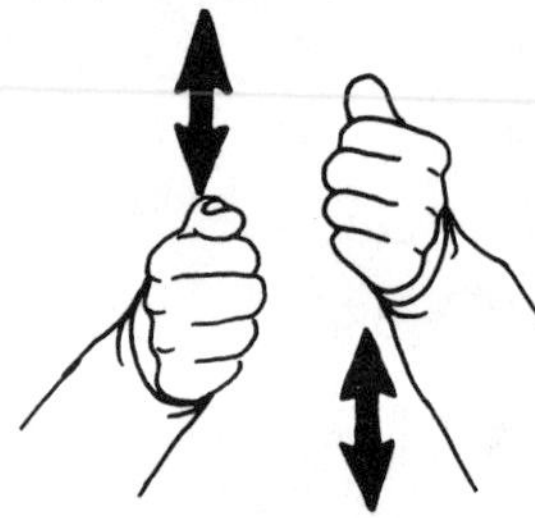

Arabic: áee اي
Chinese: nǎge 那個
Dutch: welk
French: qui
German: welcher
Italian: il quale
Japanese: dochira どちら
Korean: ŏnŭ gŏt 어느것
Portuguese: qual
Russian: kotóryy который
Spanish: cual
Swedish: vilken

2375. while [conj./prep.]

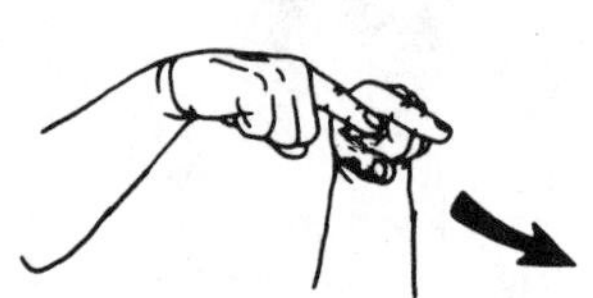

Arabic: beináma بينما
Chinese: dāng 當
Dutch: terwijl
French: pendant que
German: während
Italian: mentre
Japanese: aida ni 間に
Korean: hanŭn dongan 하는 동안
Portuguese: enquanto
Russian: poká пока
Spanish: mientras
Swedish: medan

2376. whiskey [n.]

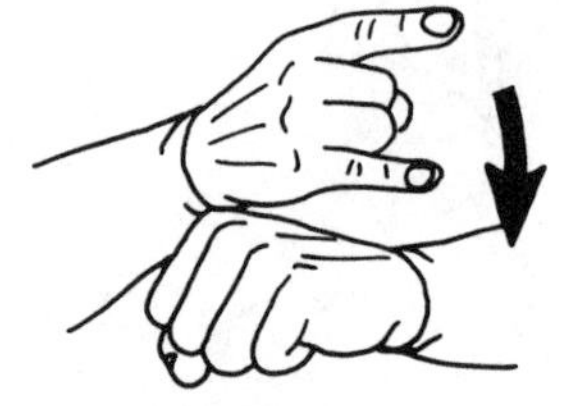

Arabic: wíski ويسكي
Chinese: wēishìjì 威士忌
Dutch: whisky
French: whisky
German: Whisky
Italian: whisky
Japanese: uisukii ウイスキー
Korean: wisŭk'i 위스키
Portuguese: uísque
Russian: víski виски
Spanish: whisky
Swedish: visky

2377. whisper [v.]

Arabic: hámasa همس
Chinese: ěryǔ 耳語
Dutch: fluisteren
French: chuchoter
German: flüstern
Italian: sussurrare
Japanese: sasayaku こっそり話す
Korean: soksagida 속삭이다
Portuguese: sussurrar
Russian: sheptát' шептать
Spanish: susurrar
Swedish: viska

2378. whistle [n.]

Arabic: sufára صفارة
Chinese: kǒushào 口哨
Dutch: fluit
French: sifflet
German: Pfeife
Italian: fischio
Japanese: kuchibue 口笛
Korean: horurugi 호르라기
Portuguese: apito
Russian: svistók свисток
Spanish: silbato
Swedish: visselpipa

2379. white [adj.]

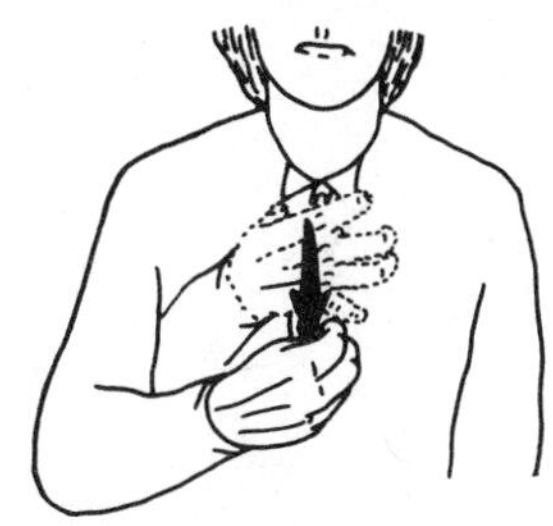

Arabic: ábyadh ابيض
Chinese: bái 白
Dutch: wit
French: blanc
German: weiß
Italian: bianco
Japanese: shiroi 白い
Korean: hŭin 흰
Portuguese: branco
Russian: bélyy белый
Spanish: blanco
Swedish: vit

2380. who [pron.]

Arabic: man من
Chinese: shuí 誰
Dutch: wie
French: qui
German: wer
Italian: chi
Japanese: dare 誰
Korean: nugu 누구
Portuguese: quem
Russian: kto кто
Spanish: quien
Swedish: vem

2381. whole [adj.]

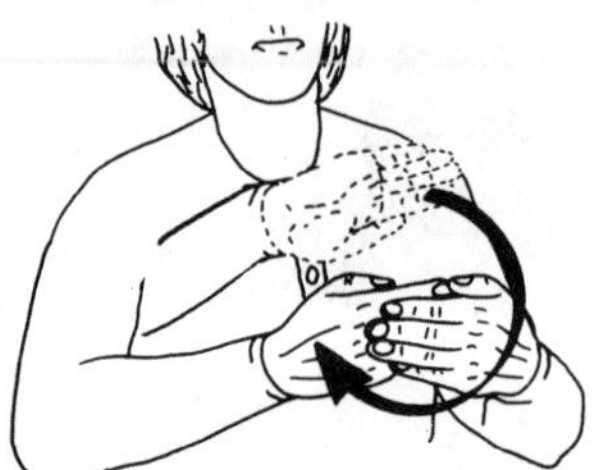

Arabic: kull/kámil كل / كامل
Chinese: zhěnggè 整個
Dutch: heel
French: entier
German: ganz
Italian: intero
Japanese: zentai no 全体の
Korean: jŏn 전
Portuguese: inteiro
Russian: tsélyy целый
Spanish: entero
Swedish: hel

2382. whose [pron.]

Arabic: líman لمن
Chinese: shuíde 誰的
Dutch: van wie
French: dont
German: wessen
Italian: di chi
Japanese: dare no 誰の
Korean: nuguŭi 누구의
Portuguese: de quem
Russian: chey чей
Spanish: de quién
Swedish: vems

2383. why [adv.]

Arabic: limádha لماذا
Chinese: wèishénmo 為什麼
Dutch: waarom
French: pourquoi
German: warum
Italian: perchè
Japanese: naze なぜ
Korean: wae 왜
Portuguese: por quê
Russian: pochemú почему
Spanish: por qué
Swedish: varför

2384. wicked [adj.]

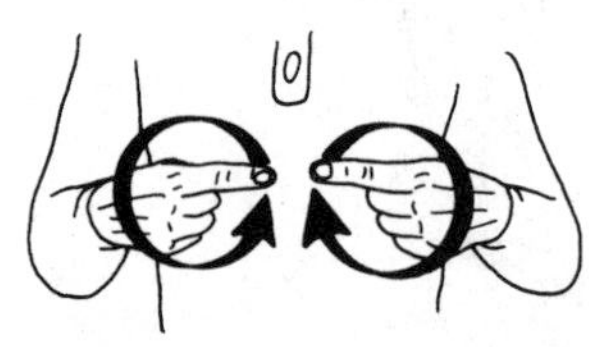

Arabic: shirír شرير
Chinese: xiéèr 邪惡
Dutch: kwaadaardig
French: méchant
German: böse
Italian: malvagio
Japanese: ijiwarui 意地の悪い
Korean: nappŭn 나쁜
Portuguese: mau
Russian: zloy злой
Spanish: malvado
Swedish: syndig

2385. wide [adj.]

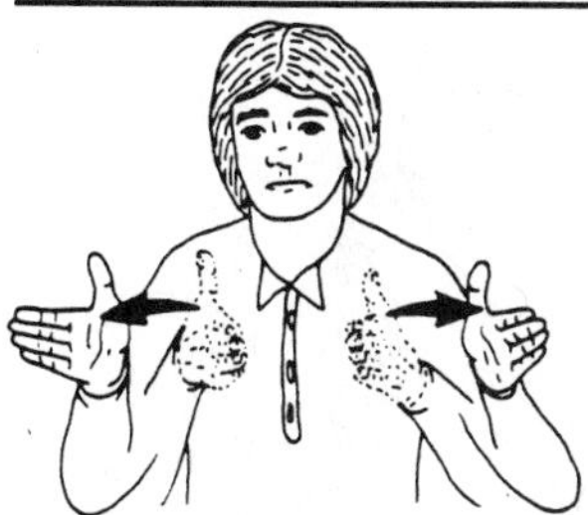

Arabic: wáseaa واسع
Chinese: kuān 寬
Dutch: wijd
French: large
German: breit
Italian: largo
Japanese: hiroi 広い
Korean: nŏlbŭn 넓은
Portuguese: largo
Russian: shirókiy широкий
Spanish: ancho
Swedish: vid

2386. widow [n.]

Arabic: ármala ارملة
Chinese: guǎfù 寡婦
Dutch: weduwe
French: veuve
German: Witwe
Italian: vedova
Japanese: mibōjin 未亡人
Korean: kwabu 과부
Portuguese: viúva
Russian: vdová вдова
Spanish: viuda
Swedish: änka

2387. wife [n.]

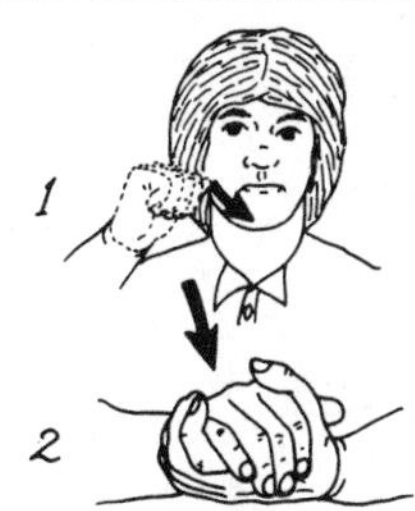

Arabic: záuja زوجة
Chinese: qīzi 妻子
Dutch: echtgenote
French: épouse
German: Frau
Italian: moglie
Japanese: tsuma 妻
Korean: anae 아내
Portuguese: esposa
Russian: zhená жена
Spanish: esposa
Swedish: fru

2388. wild [adj.]

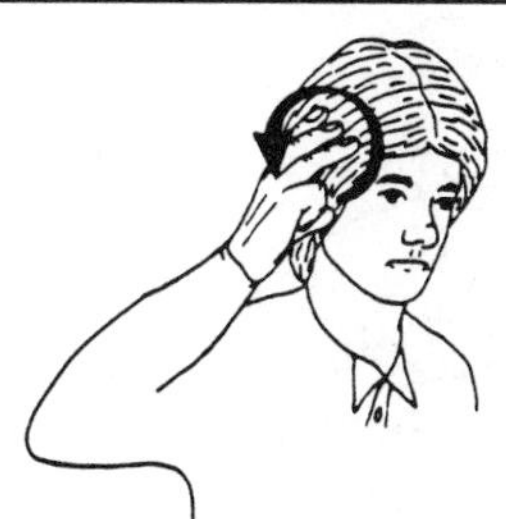

Arabic: mutawáhhesh متوحش
Chinese: yěshēngde 野生的
Dutch: wild
French: sauvage
German: wild
Italian: selvaggio
Japanese: yasei no 野生の
Korean: yasaengŭi 야생의
Portuguese: selvagem
Russian: díkiy дикий
Spanish: salvaje
Swedish: vild

2389. willingly [adv.]

Arabic: bi-rághba برغبة
Chinese: lèyì 樂意
Dutch: graag
French: volontiers
German: gern
Italian: volontariamente
Japanese: susunde 進んで
Korean: kikkŏi 기꺼이
Portuguese: de boa vontade
Russian: okhótno охотно
Spanish: de buena gana
Swedish: gärna

2390. win [v.]

Arabic: fáza فاز
Chinese: yíng 贏
Dutch: winnen
French: gagner
German: gewinnen
Italian: vincere
Japanese: katsu 勝つ
Korean: igida 이기다
Portuguese: ganhar
Russian: vyígryvat' выигрывать
Spanish: ganar
Swedish: vinna

2391. wind [n.]

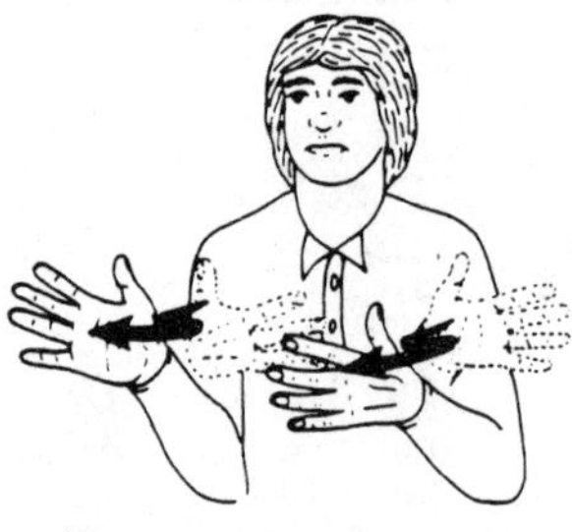

Arabic: ríh ريح
Chinese: fēng 風
Dutch: wind
French: vent
German: Wind
Italian: vento
Japanese: kaze 風
Korean: baram 바람
Portuguese: vento
Russian: véter ветер
Spanish: viento
Swedish: vind

2392. window [n.]

Arabic: shibbák شباك
Chinese: chuānghù 窗戶
Dutch: raam
French: fenêtre
German: Fenster
Italian: finestra
Japanese: mado 窓
Korean: ch'ang 창
Portuguese: janela
Russian: oknó окно
Spanish: ventana
Swedish: fönster

2393. wine [n.]

Arabic: nabídh نبيذ
Chinese: jiǔ 酒
Dutch: wijn
French: vin
German: Wein
Italian: vino
Japanese: budō shu ブドウ酒
Korean: p'odoju 포도주
Portuguese: vinho
Russian: vinó вино
Spanish: vino
Swedish: vin

2394. wing [n.]

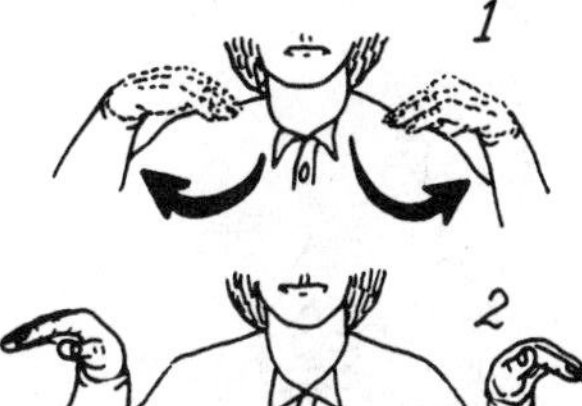

Arabic: janáh جناح
Chinese: chìbǎng 翅膀
Dutch: vleugel
French: aile
German: Flügel
Italian: ala
Japanese: tsubasa 翼
Korean: nalgae 날개
Portuguese: asa
Russian: kryló крыло
Spanish: ala
Swedish: vinge

2395. winter [n.]

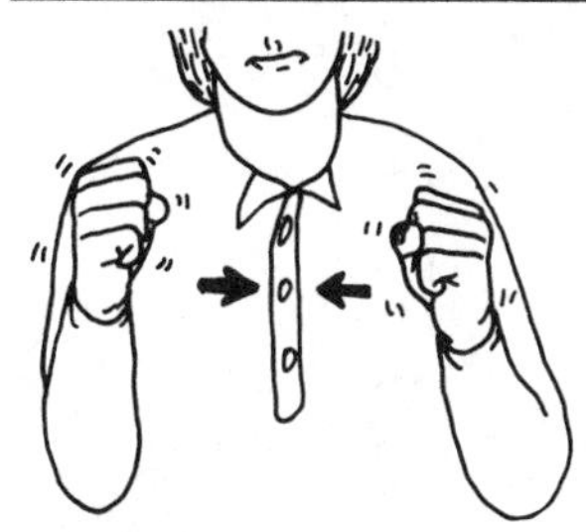

Arabic: shitá' شتاء
Chinese: dōngtiān 冬天
Dutch: winter
French: hiver
German: Winter
Italian: inverno
Japanese: fuyu 冬
Korean: kyŏul 겨울
Portuguese: inverno
Russian: zimá зима
Spanish: invierno
Swedish: vinter

2396. wipe [v.]

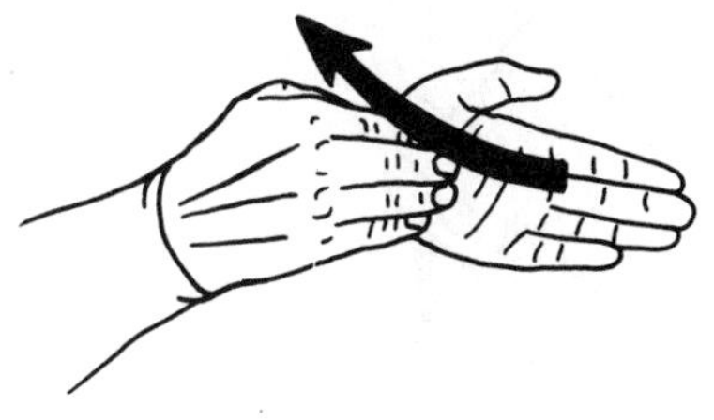

Arabic: másaha مسح
Chinese: cā 擦
Dutch: vegen
French: essuyer
German: wischen
Italian: asciugare
Japanese: fuku 拭く
Korean: dakda 닦다
Portuguese: limpar
Russian: vytirát' вытирать
Spanish: enjugar
Swedish: torka av

2397. wire [n.]

Arabic: silk سلك
Chinese: tiěsī 鐵絲
Dutch: draad
French: fil métallique
German: Draht
Italian: filo metallico
Japanese: harigane 針金
Korean: ch'ŏlsa 철사
Portuguese: fio de metal
Russian: próvoloka проволока
Spanish: alambre
Swedish: metalltråd

2398. wisdom [n.]

Arabic: híkma حكمة
Chinese: zhìhuì 智慧
Dutch: wijsheid
French: sagesse
German: Weisheit
Italian: saggezza
Japanese: chie 知恵
Korean: ch'ongmyŏng 총명
Portuguese: sabedoria
Russian: múdrost' мудрость
Spanish: sabiduría
Swedish: visdom

2399. wish [n.]

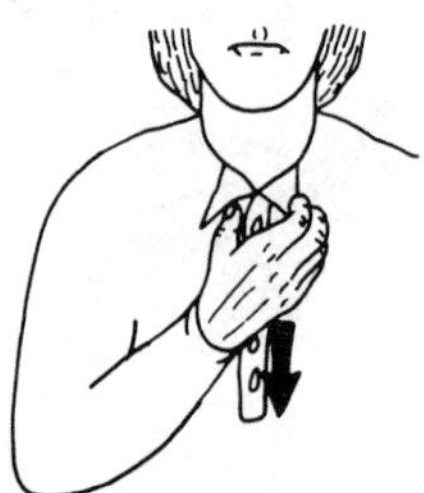

Arabic: rágheba رغبة
Chinese: yuànwàng 願望
Dutch: wens
French: souhait
German: Wunsch
Italian: desiderio
Japanese: negai 願い
Korean: sowŏn 소원
Portuguese: desejo
Russian: zhelániye желание
Spanish: deseo
Swedish: önskan

2400. with [prep.]

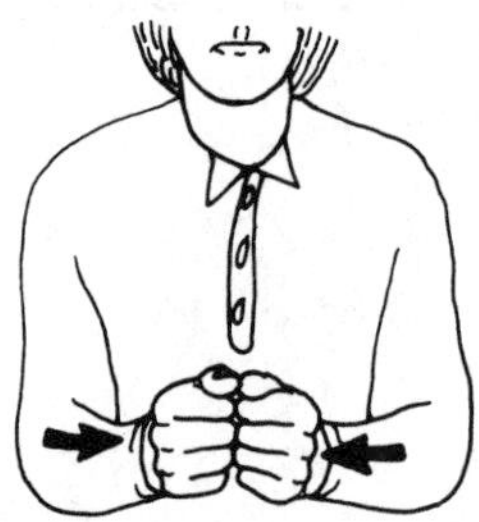

Arabic: máa مع
Chinese: gēn 跟
Dutch: met
French: avec
German: mit
Italian: con
Japanese: . . . to …と
Korean: . . . wa hamkke ~와 함께
Portuguese: com
Russian: s/so с/со
Spanish: con
Swedish: med

2401. within [adv./prep.]

Arabic: dákhel داخل
Chinese: zàilǐmiàn 在…裏面
Dutch: binnenin
French: dans
German: innerhalb
Italian: dentro
Japanese: . . .no nakani …の中に
Korean: . . .ŭi soge ~의 속에
Portuguese: dentro
Russian: vnutrí внутри
Spanish: dentro
Swedish: inuti

2402. without [prep.]

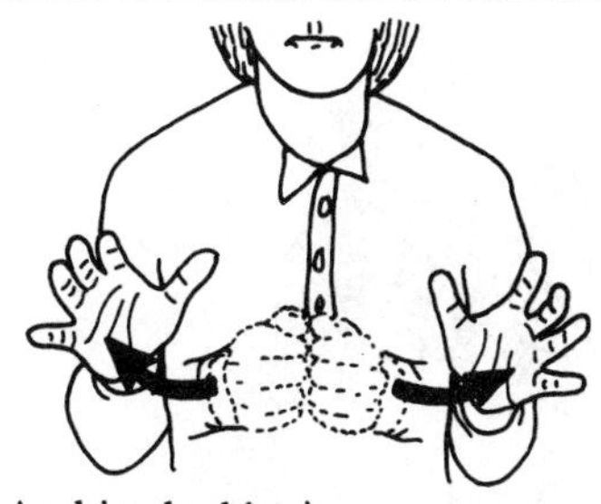

Arabic: bedún بدون
Chinese: méiyǒu 沒有
Dutch: zonder
French: sans
German: ohne
Italian: senza
Japanese: . . .nashi ni …なしに
Korean: . . .ŏpshi ~없이
Portuguese: sem
Russian: bez без
Spanish: sin
Swedish: utan

2403. witness (person) [n.]

Arabic: sháhed شاهد
Chinese: zhèngrén 證人
Dutch: getuige
French: témoin
German: Zeuge
Italian: testimone
Japanese: shōnin 証人
Korean: jŭngin 증인
Portuguese: testemunha
Russian: svidétel' свидетель
Spanish: testigo
Swedish: vittne

2404. wolf [n.]

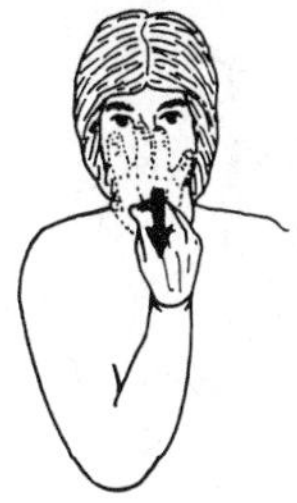

Arabic: thi'b ذئب
Chinese: láng 狼
Dutch: wolf
French: loup
German: Wolf
Italian: lupo
Japanese: ōkami オオカミ
Korean: iri 이리
Portuguese: lobo
Russian: volk волк
Spanish: lobo
Swedish: varg

2405. woman [n.]

Arabic: ímra'a امرأة
Chinese: nǚren 女人
Dutch: vrouw
French: femme
German: Frau
Italian: donna
Japanese: onna 女
Korean: yŏja 여자
Portuguese: mulher
Russian: zhénshchina женщина
Spanish: mujer
Swedish: kvinna

2406. wonder (marvel) [n.]

Arabic: áajab عجب
Chinese: qíguài 奇怪
Dutch: wonder
French: merveille
German: Wunder
Italian: meraviglia
Japanese: kyōtan 驚嘆
Korean: nollaum 놀라움
Portuguese: maravilha
Russian: chúdo чудо
Spanish: maravilla
Swedish: under

2407. wonderful [adj.]

Arabic: aajíb عجيب
Chinese: qí miào 奇妙
Dutch: fantastisch
French: merveilleux
German: wunderbar
Italian: meraviglioso
Japanese: subarashii 素晴しい
Korean: nollaun 놀라운
Portuguese: maravilhoso
Russian: zamechátel'nyy замечательный
Spanish: maravilloso
Swedish: underbar

2408. wood [n.]

Arabic: kháshab خشب
Chinese: mùtóu 木頭
Dutch: hout
French: bois
German: Holz
Italian: legno
Japanese: mokuzai 木材
Korean: namu 나무
Portuguese: madeira
Russian: dérevo дерево
Spanish: madera
Swedish: trä

2409. wool [n.]

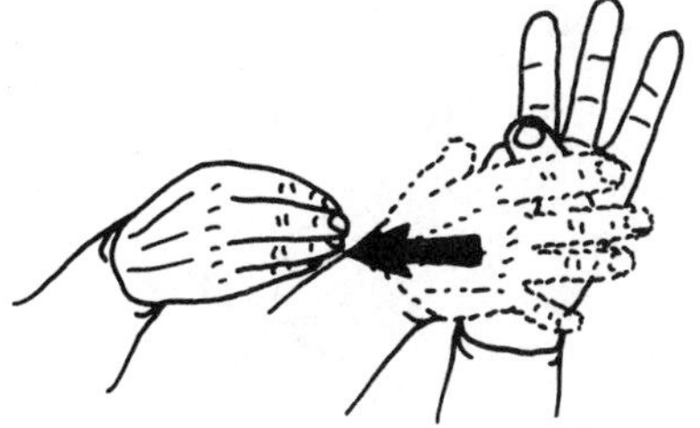

Arabic: suf صوف
Chinese: yángmáo 羊毛
Dutch: wol
French: laine
German: Wolle
Italian: lana
Japanese: yōmō 羊毛
Korean: t'ŏlshil 털실
Portuguese: lã
Russian: sherst' шерсть
Spanish: lana
Swedish: ull

2410. word [n.]

Arabic: kálima كلمة
Chinese: cì 字
Dutch: woord
French: mot
German: Wort
Italian: parola
Japanese: kotoba 言葉
Korean: mal 말
Portuguese: palavra
Russian: slóvo слово
Spanish: palabra
Swedish: ord

2411. work [n.]

Arabic: áamal عَمَلْ
Chinese: gōngzuò 工作
Dutch: werk
French: travail
German: Arbeit
Italian: lavoro
Japanese: shigoto 仕事
Korean: il 일
Portuguese: trabalho
Russian: rabóta работа
Spanish: trabajo
Swedish: arbete

2412. work [v.]

Arabic: áamila عَمِلَ
Chinese: gōngzuò 工作
Dutch: werken
French: travailler
German: arbeiten
Italian: lavorare
Japanese: hataraku 働く
Korean: irhada 일하다
Portuguese: trabalhar
Russian: rabótat' работать
Spanish: trabajar
Swedish: arbeta

2413. worker [n.]

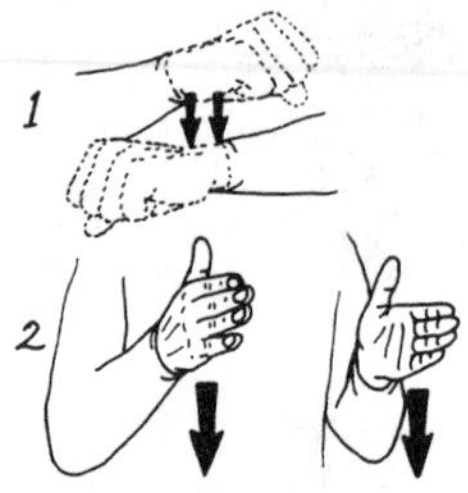

Arabic: áamel عامل
Chinese: gōngrén 工人
Dutch: arbeider
French: travailleur
German: Arbeiter
Italian: lavoratore
Japanese: hataraku hito 働く人
Korean: nodongja 노동자
Portuguese: trabalhador
Russian: rabótnik работник
Spanish: trabajador
Swedish: arbetare

2414. world [n.]

Arabic: áalam عالم
Chinese: shìjiè 世界
Dutch: wereld
French: monde
German: Welt
Italian: mondo
Japanese: sekai 世界
Korean: segye 세계
Portuguese: mundo
Russian: mir мир
Spanish: mundo
Swedish: värld

2415. worm [n.]

Arabic: dúda دودة
Chinese: chóng 蟲
Dutch: worm
French: ver
German: Wurm
Italian: verme
Japanese: mushi 足のない虫
Korean: bŏlle 벌레
Portuguese: verme
Russian: cherv' червь
Spanish: gusano
Swedish: mask

2416. worry [v.]

Arabic: qáliqa قلق
Chinese: dānxīn 擔心
Dutch: zich zorgen maken
French: se préoccuper
German: sich sorgen
Italian: preoccuparsi
Japanese: shimpai suru 心配する
Korean: gŏkjŏng'hada 걱정하다
Portuguese: preocupar-se
Russian: bespokóit'sya беспокоиться
Spanish: preocuparse
Swedish: oroa sig

2417. worse [adj./adv.]

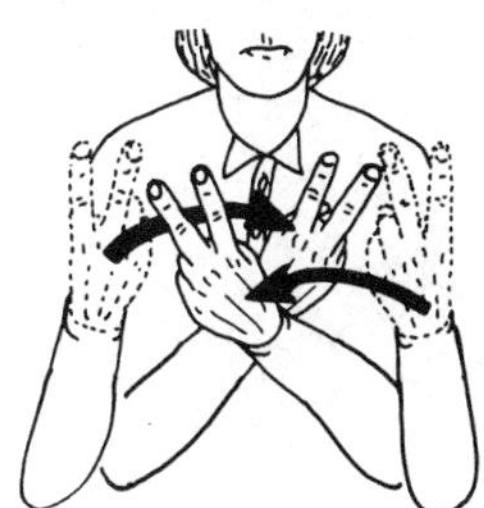

Arabic: áswa' أسوأ
Chinese: jiàochā 較差
Dutch: slechter
French: pire
German: schlechter
Italian: peggiore
Japanese: sara ni warui さらに…悪い
Korean: dŏuk nappun 더 나쁜
Portuguese: pior
Russian: khúdshiy худший
Spanish: peor
Swedish: värre

2418. worst [adj./adv.]

Arabic: al-áswa' الأسوأ
Chinese: zuìchā 最差
Dutch: slechtst
French: le pire
German: schlechtest
Italian: il peggiore
Japanese: saiaku na 最悪な
Korean: gajang nappun 가장 나쁜
Portuguese: o pior
Russian: naikhúdshiy наихудший
Spanish: lo peor
Swedish: värst

2419. worth [n.]

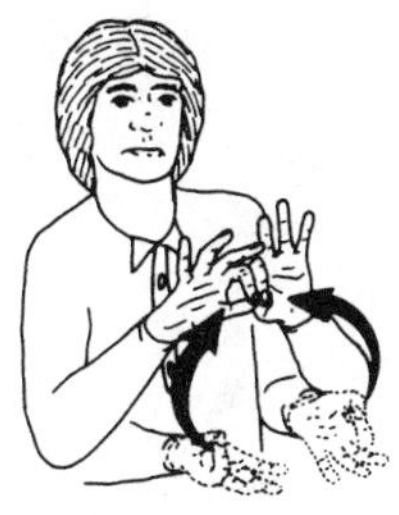

Arabic: qíma قيمة
Chinese: jiàzhí 價值
Dutch: waarde
French: valeur
German: Wert
Italian: valore
Japanese: kachi 価値
Korean: kach'i 가치
Portuguese: valor
Russian: tsená цена
Spanish: valor
Swedish: värde

2420. worthless [adj.]

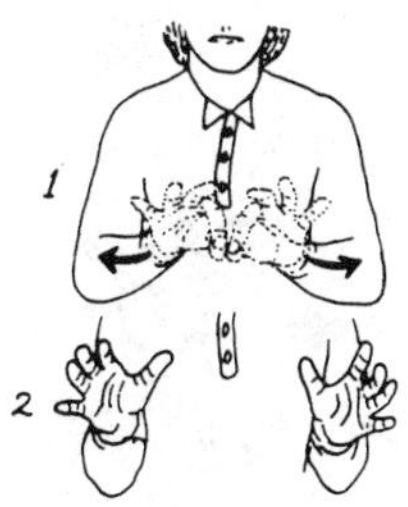

Arabic: la qímata láhu لا قيمة له
Chinese: méijiàzhí 沒價值
Dutch: waardeloos
French: sans valeur
German: wertlos
Italian: privo di valore
Japanese: kachi no nai 価値のない
Korean: kach'i ŏmnŭn 가치 없는
Portuguese: sem valor
Russian: nichevó ne stóyashchiy ничего не стоящий
Spanish: sin valor
Swedish: värdelös

2421. wound [n.]

Arabic: jorh جُرْح
Chinese: shangkǒu 傷口
Dutch: wonde
French: blessure
German: Wunde
Italian: ferita
Japanese: kizu 傷
Korean: sangch'ŏ 상처
Portuguese: ferida
Russian: rána рана
Spanish: herida
Swedish: sår

2422. wrap [v.]

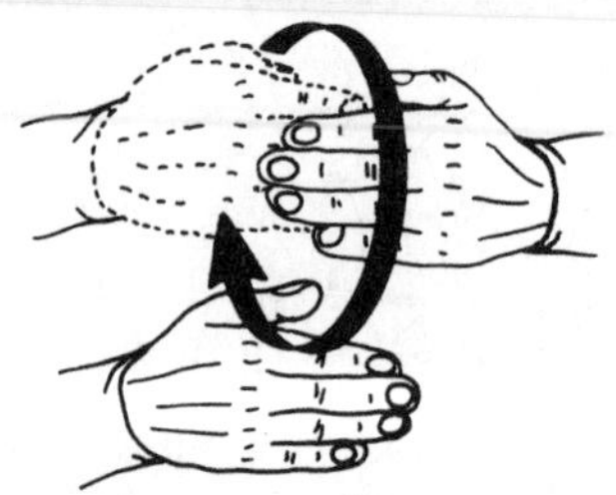

Arabic: ghállafa غلّف
Chinese: bāo 包
Dutch: wikkelen
French: envelopper
German: einwickeln
Italian: avvolgere
Japanese: tsutsumu 包む
Korean: ssada 싸다
Portuguese: envolver
Russian: zavyórtyvat' завёртывать
Spanish: envolver
Swedish: svepa in

2423. wreck (collision) [n.]

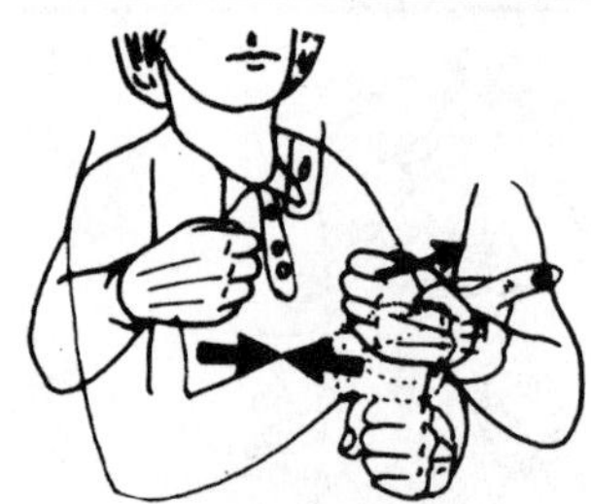

Arabic: tasáddum تصادم
Chinese: pèngzhuàng 碰撞
Dutch: botsing
French: collision
German: Zusammenstoß
Italian: collisione
Japanese: zangai 残がい
Korean: ch'ungdol 충돌
Portuguese: choque
Russian: avárіya авария
Spanish: choque
Swedish: sammanstötning

2424. wrestling [n.]

Arabic: séraa صراع
Chinese: shuāijiāo 摔角
Dutch: worsteling
French: lutte
German: Ringkampf
Italian: lotta
Japanese: resuringu レスリング
Korean: resŭlling 레슬링
Portuguese: luta
Russian: bor'bá борьба
Spanish: lucha libre
Swedish: brottning

2425. write [v.]

Arabic: kátaba كتب
Chinese: xiě 寫
Dutch: schrijven
French: écrire
German: schreiben
Italian: scrivere
Japanese: kaku 書く
Korean: ssŭda 쓰다
Portuguese: escrever
Russian: pisát' писать
Spanish: escribir
Swedish: skriva

2426. writer [n.]

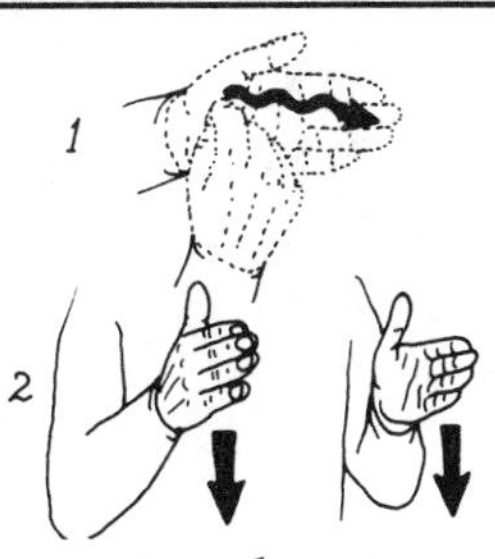

Arabic: kátib كاتب
Chinese: zuòjiā 作家
Dutch: schrijver
French: écrivain
German: Schreiber
Italian: scrittore
Japanese: sakka 作家
Korean: jakka 작가
Portuguese: escritor
Russian: pisátel' писатель
Spanish: escritor
Swedish: skrivare

2427. wrong (erroneous) [adj.]

Arabic: ghálat غلط
Chinese: cuò 錯
Dutch: verkeerd
French: erroné
German: falsch
Italian: erroneo
Japanese: machigatta 間違った
Korean: tŭllin 틀린
Portuguese: errado
Russian: neprávil'nyy неправильный
Spanish: erróneo
Swedish: orätt

2428. yard (enclosure) [n.]

Arabic: hadíeqa حديقة
Chinese: yuànzi 院子
Dutch: erf
French: cour
German: Hof
Italian: cortile
Japanese: niwa 庭
Korean: madang 마당
Portuguese: cercado
Russian: dvor двор
Spanish: patio
Swedish: gård

2429. yawn [v.]

Arabic: tathá'aba تثاءب
Chinese: dǎ hēqiàn 打哈欠
Dutch: geeuwen
French: bailler
German: gähnen
Italian: sbadigliare
Japanese: akubisuru あくびする
Korean: hap'umhada 하품하다
Portuguese: bocejar
Russian: zevát' зевать
Spanish: bostezar
Swedish: gäspa

2430. year [n.]

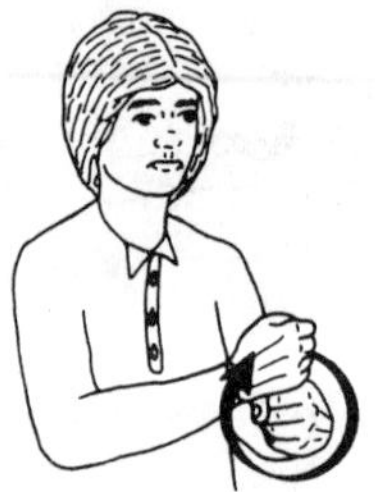

Arabic: sána سنة
Chinese: nián 年
Dutch: jaar
French: an
German: Jahr
Italian: anno
Japanese: toshi 年
Korean: hae 해
Portuguese: ano
Russian: god год
Spanish: año
Swedish: år

2431. yearly [adj.]

Arabic: sanawían سنوياً
Chinese: měi nián de 每年的
Dutch: jaarlijks
French: annuel
German: jährlich
Italian: annuale
Japanese: maitoshi 毎年
Korean: maenyŏnŭi 매년의
Portuguese: anual
Russian: yezhegódnyy ежегодный
Spanish: anualmente
Swedish: årlig

2432. yellow [adj.]

Arabic: ásfar اصفر
Chinese: huáng 黄
Dutch: geel
French: jaune
German: gelb
Italian: giallo
Japanese: kiiroi 黄色い
Korean: noran 노란
Portuguese: amarelo
Russian: zhyóltyy жёлтый
Spanish: amarillo
Swedish: gul

2433. yes [interj.]

Arabic: náam نعم
Chinese: duì 對
Dutch: ja
French: oui
German: ja
Italian: si
Japanese: hai はい
Korean: ye 예
Portuguese: sim
Russian: da да
Spanish: sí
Swedish: ja

2434. yesterday [n.]

Arabic: ams امس
Chinese: zuótiān 昨天
Dutch: gisteren
French: hier
German: gestern
Italian: ieri
Japanese: kinō 昨日
Korean: ŏje 어제
Portuguese: ontem
Russian: vcherá вчера
Spanish: ayer
Swedish: i går

2435. yet [adv.]

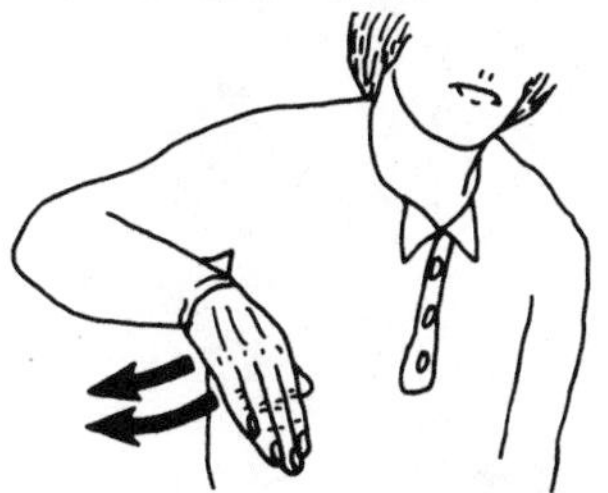

Arabic: hátta al-an حتى الان
Chinese: hái 還
Dutch: nog
French: encore
German: noch
Italian: ancora
Japanese: mada まだ
Korean: ajik 아직
Portuguese: todavia
Russian: yeshchyó ещё
Spanish: todavía
Swedish: ännu

2436. yield (give up) [v.]

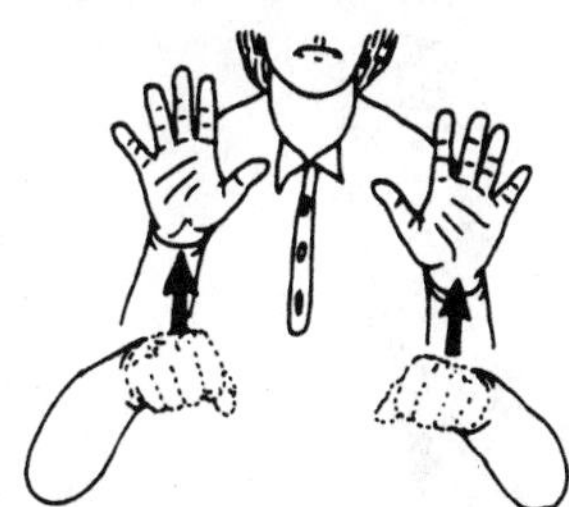

Arabic: istáslama استسلم
Chinese:ràngyǔ 讓與
Dutch: overgeven
French: céder
German: nachgeben
Italian: cedere
Japanese: yuzuru 譲る
Korean: yangbo'hada 산출하다
Portuguese: ceder
Russian: ustupát' уступать
Spanish: ceder
Swedish: ge vika

2437. you [pron.]

Arabic: ínta/ínti أنتَ / أنتِ
Chinese: nǐ 你
Dutch: je/u
French: tu/vous
German: du/Sie
Italian: tu/voi
Japanese: anata あなた
Korean: dangshin/dangshindul
당신／당신들
Portuguese: tu/vos
Russian: ty/tebyá/vy/vas
ты/тебя/вы/вас
Spanish: tú/usted
Swedish: du/ni

2438. young [adj.]

Arabic: saghír صغير
Chinese: niánqīng 年輕
Dutch: jong
French: jeune
German: jung
Italian: giovane
Japanese: wakai 若い
Korean: jŏlmun 젊은
Portuguese: jovem
Russian: molodóy молодой
Spanish: joven
Swedish: ung

2439. your(s) [adj./pron.]

Arabic: láka لك
Chinese: nǐde 你的
Dutch: jouw/uw
French: ton/votre
German: dein/Ihr
Italian: tuo/vostro
Japanese: anata no あなたの
Korean: dangshinŭi/dangshindŭrŭi
당신의／당신들의
Portuguese: teu/vosso
Russian: tvoy/vash твой/ваш
Spanish: tuyo/suyo
Swedish: din/er

2440. you're welcome! [interj.]

Arabic: áafwan عفواً
Chinese: búxiè 不謝
Dutch: graag gedaan
French: de rien
German: gern geschehen
Italian: prego
Japanese: dō itashimashite
どう致しまして！
Korean: ch'ŏnmanŭi malssŭm
천만의 말씀！
Portuguese: de nada
Russian: pozháluysta пожалуйста
Spanish: de nada
Swedish: ingen orsak

2441. youth (youthhood) [n.]

Arabic: shabáb شباب
Chinese: qīngchūn 青春
Dutch: jeugd
French: jeunesse
German: Jugend
Italian: gioventù
Japanese: seinenjidai 青年時代
Korean: ch'ŏngnyŏn 청년
Portuguese: juventude
Russian: mólodost' молодость
Spanish: juventud
Swedish: ungdom

2442. Yugoslavia [n.]

Arabic: yughosláfia يوغوسلافيا
Chinese: nánsīlāfū 南斯拉夫
Dutch: Joegoslavië
French: Yougoslavie
German: Jugoslawien
Italian: Yugoslavia
Japanese: Yūgosurabia ユーゴスラビア
Korean: Yugosŭlabia 유고슬라비아
Portuguese: Jugoslávia
Russian: Yugosláviya Югославия
Spanish: Yugoeslavia
Swedish: Jugoslavien

2443. Zambia [n.]

Arabic: zámbia زامبيا
Chinese: sānbǐyà 尚比亞
Dutch: Zambia
French: Zambie
German: Zambia
Italian: Zambia
Japanese: Zambia サンビア
Korean: Jambia 잠비아
Portuguese: Zâmbia
Russian: Zámbiya Замбия
Spanish: Zambia
Swedish: Zambia

2444. zeal [n.]

Arabic: hamás حماس
Chinese: rèchéng 熱誠
Dutch: ijver
French: zèle
German: Eifer
Italian: zelo
Japanese: nekkyō 熱狂
Korean: yŏlshim 열심
Portuguese: zêlo
Russian: usérdiye усердие
Spanish: celo
Swedish: iver

2445. zero [n.]

Arabic: sifr صفر
Chinese: líng 零
Dutch: nul
French: zéro
German: null
Italian: zero
Japanese: zero ゼロ
Korean: jero 제로
Portuguese: zero
Russian: nul' нуль
Spanish: cero
Swedish: noll

2446. zoo [n.]

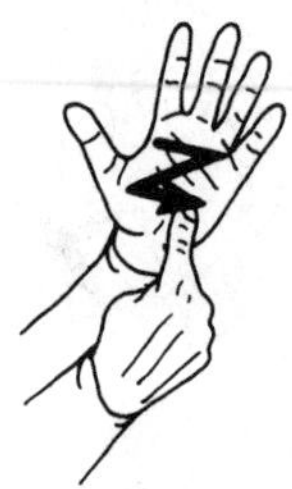

Arabic: hadíeqat al-hayawanát
حديقة الحيوانات
Chinese: dòngwùyuán 動物園
Dutch: dierentuin
French: zoo
German: Tiergarten
Italian: giardino zoologico
Japanese: dōbutsuen 動物園
Korean: dongmurwŏn 동물원
Portuguese: jardim zoológico
Russian: zoopárk зоопарк
Spanish: zoológico
Swedish: djurpark

Cross Index

ي

ش

أ

七畫

九畫

十二畫

十三畫

A

aanbevelen 447, 1748
aanbieden 1464
aanbrengen 109
aandringen 1097
aanduiden 1085
aangenaam 1600
aankleden (zich) 656
aankomst 128
aankondigen 92
aanmoedigen 702
aannemen 142
aanraken 2228
aansporen 2295
aanstellen 110
aantekening 1434
aantrekkelijk 153
aantrekken 152
aanval 148
aanwennen 18
aanwezigheid 1648
aap 1342
aardappel 1633
aardbeving 678
aardbol 929
aarde 677, 1991
aardig 1416
aarzelen 1019
abonneren 2080
absurd 9
accepteren 10
acht 687
achter 219
achterblijven 1176
achtergrond 175
achterkant 1739
achteruit 176
achtervolgen 381, 1705
achting 1803
achttien 688
acteur 27
actrice 28
adem 289
administratie 32
adres 31
advertentie 38
advies 39
adviseren 40
advocaat 1188
afbeelding 1574
afdeling 585
afgelegen 1779
afhangen 586
afkorten 2
afleveren 578
Afrika 43
Afrika (Zuid) 2007
afschaffen 4
afscheid 785
afspraak 111
afstand 635
aftrekken 2085
afwezigheid 8
afwijken 601
afzondering 1667
afzonderlijk 102, 1909
aktief 25
aktiviteit 26
al 71
alarm 59
Albanië 60
alfabet 70
algemeen 449
alleen 68, 1238, 1476
allen 64
alles 737
als 133
alstublieft 1601
altijd 74
altijd (voor) 859
ambassadeur 76
ambitie 77
ambulance 78
Amerika 79
Amerika (Noord) 1430
Amerika (Zuid) 2008
amerikaans 80
analyseren 84
ander 1499
ander (een) 95
angst 798
annuleren 335
antwoord 96
antwoorden 1786
appartement 103
appel 108
applaudisseren 107
april 116
arbeider 2413
Argentinië 118
arm 121, 1619
armoede 1636
arresteren 127
artiest 132
artikel 130
assisteren 140
associeren 141
atleet 146
attentie 150
audiëntie 154
augustus 155
Australië 157
auteur 159
auto 346
autoriteit 160
avond 733
avondeten 2104
avontuur 37
Azië 135
azijn 2319

B

baan 1490
baard 205
baby 172
bad 199
bagage 179, 1250
bakken 180, 893
baksteen 292
bal 183
banaan 184
band 2136, 2204, 2209
bandopnemer 2137
bang 42
bank 186, 226
barmhartigheid 1306
barsten 312
basis 193, 196, 867
basketbal 198
bed 210
bedekken 516
bediende 1913
bedorven 2026
bedrag 82
bedriegen 384
bedroefd 1850
bedrog 560
beeld 1068
beeldhouwwerk 1886
been 266, 1201
beetje (een) 1231
begeleiden 12
begerig 672
beginnen 217
begraafplaats 364
begrafenis 899
begraven 313
begrip 466
behalve 748
beheer 1268
beheren 1267
behoefte 1397
beide 272
beide (één van) 690
beïnvloeden 41
bekennen 473
bekijven 1881
bekwaam 340
bekwaamheid 1967
bel 222
belachelijk 1818
belangrijk 1073
belasting 2140
beledigen 1463
belediging 1105
beleefd 1615
beleid 1613
België 220
belofte 1682
beloning 1814
beminnen 1246
benadrukken 699
beneden 224, 651
benzine 911
bepalen 572, 598
beperken 1807
bereiken 1732
berekenen 325
berg 1358
beroep 700, 1675
beroven 588
bes 230
beschaamd 134
beschermen 1689
beschrijven 591
beschuldigen 17, 251
beslissen 562
bespreken 623
bestaan 755
beste 233
bestendig 1557
betalen 1538
betekenen 1288
betekenis 1289, 1905, 1950
beter 236
betreffende 5

R

S

baril 192
bas 1247
bas (le) 2054
base 193, 196, 867
baseball 194
basketball 198
bataille 200
bateau 261
bâtir 487
bâton 2051
battre 206
battre (se) 815
bavarder 382
beau 207, 985
beaucoup 1244, 1365
bébé 172
Belgique 220
besoin 1397
bétail 359
beurre 319
Bible 239
bibliothèque 1213
bicyclette 240
bidon 332
bien 2364
bien aimer 1221
bientôt 2000
bienveillant 1160
bienvenue 2363
bière 214
billet 2203
blanc 2379
blé 2368
blesser 1092
blessure 2421
bleu 258
bloc 254
bocal 1136
boeuf 213
boire 657
bois 2408
bois de charpente 1251
boîte 278
boiteux 1178
bol 277
Bolivie 265
bon 940
bonbon 338
bonheur 988
bonjour 1013
bonnet 339
botte 268
bouche 1362
boue 1366
bouger 1363
bougie 337
bouillir 263
bouteille 274
bouton 321
boxe 279
branche 282
bras 121
bref 296
Brésil 284
brillant 297
briller 1934
brique 292
brise 290
brosse 320
brouillard 845
broyer 966
bruit 1424
brûler 311
brun 301
brutal 812
bruyant 1245
bûche 1236
buisson 315
Bulgarie 306
bulletin 309
bureau 1465
bureau de poste 1631
but 935, 1703

C

cacher 1020
cadeau 924
cadre 872
café 431
calculer 325
calendrier 326
calme 329, 1716
camion 2255
camp 331
Canada 334
canard 665
candidat 336
caoutchouc 1842
capable 340
capacité 3
capacité 341
capitaine 344
capitale 342
capitaliste 343
capturer 345
caractère 380
carnaval 351
carré 2033
carte 347, 1274
catalogue 356
catholique 358
cause 1740
causer 360
ce 1128, 2191
ce soir 2221
céder 2436
ceinture 225
célébrer 363
célibataire 173
celui-là 2169
cent 1052
centime 365
centimètre 367
centre 366
cependant 1045
cercle 410
cerf 568
cerise 389
certain 369
certificat 370
cerveau 281
ces 2181
cesser 362
chaîne 371
chaise 372
chaleur 1007
chambre 1835
chambre à coucher 211
champ 811
champignon 1370
champion 376
chance 1248
changer 378
chanson 1999
chanter 1958
chapeau 995
chapitre 379
chaque 671
charbon 428
charge 310
charrette 354, 2332
chasse 1055
chasser 381
chat 355
chaud 2341
chaussette 1989
chaussure 1938
chauve 182
chef 394
chemin 2349
chemin de fer 1722
cheminée 399
chemise 1936
cher 556
chercher 1889
cheval 1038
cheveu 979
chèvre 936
chien 644
Chili 397
Chine 401
chirurgie 2112
choc 1937
chocolat 402
choisir 405
choisir 1900
choix 403
chômage 2277
chose 2186
chou 323
chrétien 406
chuchoter 2377
ciel 1008, 1969
cigarette 409
cime 1540
cimetière 364
cinéma 1364
cinq 829
cinquante 814
circulation 2236
cirque 411
ciseaux 1880
citation 1718
citoyen 412
citron 1203
civil 414
clair 418
classe 415
clé 1155
client 542
cloche 222
clôture 806
clou 1377
club 426
cochon 1577
coeur 1006
coiffeur 189

Q

R

S

A
Abend 733
Abendessen 2104
Abenteuer 37
aber 318
abgelegen 1779
abhängen 586
Abkömmling 590
abkürzen 2
abnehmen 565
abonnieren 2080
absagen 335
abschaffen 4
abschätzen 731
Abschied 785
absurd 9
Abteilung 585
abweichen 601
Abwesenheit 8
acht 687
Achtung 150, 1803
achtzehn 688
achtzig 689
Adresse 31
Affe 1342
Afrika 43
Ägypten 686
ähnlich 1953
aktiv 25
akzeptieren 10
Alarm 59
Albanien 60
alkoholisches Getränk 1227
alle 64
Allee 162
allein 68
alles 737
alles in allem 73
allgemein 449, 2287
Alphabet 70
als 2167
alt 1469
Alter 48
Amerika 79
amerikanisch 80
amüsant 83
an 145
analysieren 84
anbieten 1464
Anblick 2317
andere 1499
anderer, ein 95
anerkennen 114
anfangen 217
Anforderung 1792
angeln 828
angenehm 1600
Angriff 148
Angst 798
ängstlich 42
ankleiden (sich) 656
ankündigen 92
Ankunft 128
Anleihe 1233
annehmen 142
ansammeln 15
anscheinend 105
anstatt 1101
Anstellung 700
Anstrengung 684
antik 86
Antwort 96
antworten 1786
Anwesenheit 1648
Anzeige 38
anzeigen 1085
anziehen 152
anziehend 153
Anzug 2093
Apfel 108
Apfelsine 1489
applaudieren 107
April 116
Arbeit 1141, 1172, 2411
arbeiten 2412
Arbeiter 2413
Arbeitslosigkeit 2277
Argentinien 118
ärgern 93
arm 1619
Arm 121
Armee 123
Armut 1636
arrangieren 126
Arzt 1571
Asien 135
Astronaut 144
Atem 289
Äthiopien 729
Athlet 146
auch 72
auf 1472
auf Wiedersehen 941
Aufführung 1552
Aufgabe 2138
aufhören 362, 1717
auflösen 634, 1801
aufmerksam machen 61
aufrichtig 1957
aufrütteln 125
Aufstand 1742
aufsteigen 1826
aufteilen 639
auftragen 109
aufwärts 2293
Auge 770
Augenblick 1339
August 155
Ausbildung 2239
ausbreiten 2030
ausdehnen 769
Ausdruck 768
Ausgang 756
ausgeben 2022
ausgezeichnet 747
Ausland, im 7
ausradieren 722
ausschließen 751
außer 748
außerdem 232, 1349
aussprechen 1684
Ausstattung 721
ausstellen 632
Australien 157
auswählen 1900
auswendig lernen 1300
ausziehen (sich) 2276
Auto 346
Autor 159
Autorität 160
Axt 171

B
Baby 172
backen 180
Bad 199
bald 2000
Ball 183
Banane 184
Band 2136
Bank (Bänke) 186
Bank (Banken) 226
Bankett 187
Barmherzigkeit 1306
Bart 205
Baseball 194
Basis 196
Basketball 198
bauen 304
Bauer 787
Bauernhof 786
Bauholz 1251
Baum 2248
Baumwolle 508
beabsichtigen 1108
bedauern 1761
bedecken 516
bedeuten 1288
Bedeutung 1289, 1905, 1950
beeilen (sich) 1056
Beerdigung 899
Beere 230
Befehl 446, 1492
befördern 1683
Beförderung 2243
befreien 875
Befriedigung 1864
begegnen 1295
Begeisterung 714
begleiten 12
begraben 313
begreifen 464
Begriff 466
beharren 1560
Beharrlichkeit 1559
bei 145
beide 272
Bein 1201
beinahe 1393
Beispiel 745
beißen 247
beistehen 140
beitragen 495
Bekanntmachung 309
bekennen 473
beklagen (sich) 458
bekommen 921
belegtes Brot 1862
beleidigen 1463
Beleidigung 1105
Belgien 220
beliebt 1620
belobigen 447
Belohnung 1814
Bemerkung 1776

E

echt 918
Ecke 505
Ehe 1278
Ehemann 1058
Ehre 1035
Ehrgeiz 77
ehrlich 1034
Ei 685
Eid 1445
Eifer 2444
eifersüchtig 1137
eifrig 672
eigen 1507
Eigentum 1687
ein 1474
ein anderer 95
ein bißchen 1231
ein jeder 99
Einbildung 1069
Eindruck 1075
einer von beiden 690
einfach 1954
einfangen 345
Einfluß 1087
Eingang 716
eingeschlafen 137
eingreifen 1111
einheimisch 1386
Einheit 2281
einige 1994
Einkommen 1080
einladen 1120
einmal 1473
einsam 1239
einschließen 1079
eintragen 1749
eintreten 713
Eintrittskarte 2203
Einwand 1448
einwickeln 2422
einzeln 1238
Eis 1060
Eisen 1124
Eisenbahn 1722
Eiskreme 1061
Eitelkeit 463
Ekel 625
Elefant 693
elektrisch 692
elf 695
eliminieren 696
Eltern 1524
Empfang 1746
empfangen 1744
empfehlen 1748
empfindlich 1906
Ende 703
enden 823
eng 1382
Engel 88
England 708
englisch 709
Enkel 952
Enkelin 949
enorm 711
Entäuschung 892
entdecken 597, 622
Ente 665
entfernen 1780
Entfernung 635
enthüllen 1811
entkommen 724
entlang 69
entlassen 629
entmutigen 621
entscheiden 562
entschuldigen 752
entschuldigen (sich) 104
Entschuldigung 1523
entspannen 1769
entstehen 120
enttäuschen 619
entwicklen 599
Entwicklung 600
Entzücken 577
er 1000
er selbst 1025
erbauen 487
Erbschaft 1090
Erdball 929
Erdbeben 678
Erde 677, 1991
Ereignis 734
Erfahrung 762
erfinden 1118
Erfolg 2086
Erfordernis 579
erfrischen 1756
ergeben (sich) 2115
ergreifen 1898
Erholung 1751
erinnern 1778
erinnern (sich) 1777
erkennen 1747
erklären 563, 765, 2042
Erklärung 2043
erlangen 1454
erlauben 65
Erlaubnis 1558
Erleichterung 1771
ermutigen 702
ernennen 110
ernst 676
ernsthaft 1912
Ernte 993
erregen 750
erreichen 20, 1732
erröten 259
erschaffen 524
erscheinen 106
erschöpfen 754
erschrecken 1873
ersetzen 1785, 2084
erst 826
erstaunen 75, 143
ersticken 404
ertragen 704
ertrinken 660
erwägen 484
erwähnen 1304
erwarten 758
erweitern 757
erwerben 21
erzählen 1381, 2152
Erzählung 2060
es 1128
Esel 647
essen 681
Essig 2319
etwas 1996
etwas, irgend 100
Europa 730
Examen 743, 2163
existieren 755
Experiment 763
explodieren 766

F

Fabrik 773
Fachmann 764
Faden 2194
fähig 340
Fähigkeit 3
fahren 658, 1817
Fahrrad 240
Fahrstuhl 694
Falle 2244
fallen 780
fallen lassen 659
falsch 781, 2427
falten 846
Familie 783
fangen 357
Farbe 440, 1513
Faß 192
fast 67
faulen 559
Faulheit 1190
Februar 799
Fehler 723, 1333
feiern 363
Feiertag 1030
Feigling 518
fein 821
Feind 705
Feld 811
Felsen 1830
Fenster 2392
Ferien 2303
fern 784
Fernsehen 2151
fest 1993
Fest 807
festmachen 147, 791, 830
feststellen 727
fett 792
Fett 959
feucht 547, 1338
Feuer 825
Fieber 808
Figur 816
Film 818, 1364
finden 820
Finger 822
Finnland 824
Firma 453
Fisch 827
flach 835
Flagge 831
Flamme 832
Flasche 274
Fleck 2029
Fleisch 1291
Fleiß 609
fliegen 844
fliehen 837

fließen 842
Flügel 2394
Flughafen 57
Flugzeug 56
Fluß 1827
Flüssigkeit 1226
flüstern 2377
Flut 839
folgen 847
folgend 2081
Fonds 898
Football 853
Form 1927
formen 863
Forschung 1794
Fortschritt 1678
Fotografie 1569
Frage 1714
fragen 136
Frankreich 873
französisch 878
Frau (Gattin) 2387
Frau (Weib) 2405
frei 2302
Freiheit 876, 1212
freilassen 1770
freimütig 874
Freitag 881
Freiwilliger 2329
fremd 857, 2063
Freude 1146
Freund 882
freundlich 883
Friede 1539
Friedhof 364
frieren 877
frisch 880
Friseur 189
froh 927
fröhlich 387, 1309
Frosch 885
Frost 888
Frucht 891
früh 674
Frühling 2031
Frühstück 287
Fuchs 870
führen 1191
Führer 974, 1192
Fülle 1604
füllen 817
Füllhalter 1542
Fundament 867
fünf 829
fünfzehn 813
fünfzig 814
Funken 2014
Funktion 897
für 854
für immer 859
furchtsam 2208
Fuß 851, 852
Fußball 1986
Fußboden 840
Füße 804
füttern 802

G

Gabel 862
gähnen 2429
Gallone 906
Gans 942
ganz 715, 2381
garantieren 970
Garten 909
Gas 910
Gast 973
Gebäude 305
geben 926
Gebiet 117
geboren 270
gebrauchen 2299
Geburt 245
Geburtstag 246
Gedächtnis 1301
Gedanke 2192
Gedicht 1608
Gedränge 529
Geduld 1535
Gefahr 549
gefallen 1602
Gefängnis 1132, 1666
gefroren 890
Gefühl 803
gegen 47
Gegend 1759
gegenseitig 1373
Gegenstand 130
gegenüberliegend 1484
Gegenwart 1650
gegenwärtig 538, 1649
Gehalt 1855
Geheimnis 1376, 1893
gehen 934, 2336
Gehirn 281
Gehör 1005
gehorchen, nicht 630
gehören 223
Gehorsam 1446
Geist 922, 2024
geistig 1303
geizig 2052
Gelächter 1186
gelb 2432
Geld 1341
Geld spielen, um 907
Gelegenheit 377, 1456, 1482
gelegentlich 1457
Gemeinschaft 452
Gemüse 2311
genau 16, 741, 741
Generation 914
genießen 710
genug 712
genügend 2089
Geographie 919
Gepäck 179, 1250
gerade 2062
gerecht 777
Gerechtigkeit 1153
Gericht 514
geringfügig 1973
geringst 1196
gern 2389
gern geschehen 2440
gern mögen 1221
gerne haben, nicht 628
Geruch 1462, 1876
Gesamtsumme 2227
Geschäft 316, 2057
geschäftig 317
geschehen 987
geschehen, gern 2440
Geschenk 924
Geschichte 1026
Geschicklichkeit 1967
Geschirr 626
Geschlecht 1922
Geschmack 2139
Geschwätz 943
Geschwindigkeit 2020
Gesellschaft 1988
Gesetz 1187
gesetzlich 1202
Gesicht 772
Gespräch 498
gestern 2434
Gesundheit 1003
Getreide 946
getrennt 102, 1909
Gewehr 976, 1819
Gewinn 1676
gewinnen 905, 2390
Gewissen 481
gewöhnen 18
Gewohnheit 977
gewöhnlich 1494, 2301
gießen 1635
Gift 1610
Gipfel 1540
glänzend 2025
Glas 928
glatt 1981
Glaube 221, 778
gleich 62, 720, 1220
gleichen 1795
gleichförmig 2278
Gleichgewicht 181
Gleichgültigkeit 1086
gleichzeitig 1955
gleiten 1972
Glocke 222
Glück 988, 1248
glücklich 989, 1249
Gold 938
Golf 939
Gott 937
Grab 957
graben 608
Grad 573
Graduierter 945
Grammatik 947
Gras 955
gratulieren 477
grau 958
grausam 531
Grenze 1222
Griechenland 962
grob 1843
groß 241, 960, 1181
großartig 948
Großbritannien 961
Größe 1966
großmütig 915
Großmutter 951
Großvater 950

T

Tag 553
täglich 545
Taille 2333
Tal 2307
Talent 2132
Tante 156
tanzen 548
tapfer 283
Tasche 1607
Taschenlampe 834
Taschentuch 984
Tasse 534
Tat 566
Tat, in der 1082
Tätigkeit 26
tatsächlich 29
taub 555
Taube 1578
tauchen 638
Taufe 188
tausend 2193
Taxi 2141
Tee 2142
Teich 1617
Teil 1527, 1623, 1928
teilnehmen 1528
Telefon 2150
Telegramm 2149
Teller 1595
Temperatur 2153
Tendenz 2157
Tennis 2159
teuer 761
Teufel 602
Theater 2170
Thema 2174, 2225
Theorie 2177
Thermometer 2180
tief 567
Tier 91
Tiergarten 2446
Tinte 1093
tippen 2270
Tisch 2129
Tischler 352
Titel 2211
Tochter 552
Tod 557
Toilette 2215
Tomate 2217
Tonbandgerät 2137
Tonne 2219
Topf 1632
Tor 912
töricht 850
Torte 1575
tot 554
töten 1157
Tradition 2235
tragen 204, 353, 2354
Tragödie 2237
Traktor 2233
transportieren 2242
trauern 1359
Traum 655
traurig 1850
trennen 1910
Treppe 2036
treu 779
trinken 657
Triumph 2251
trivial 2252
trocken 664
Trommel 662
trotz 595
Tschechoslowakei 544
Tuch 423
tun 642
Tür 648
Türkei 2261
Turm 2230

U

Übel 740
Übelkeit 1390
über 6, 1504
überall 738
übereinstimmen 50
übereinstimmen, nicht 617
überraschen 2114
Überraschung 2113
überreden 1565
überschreiten 746
übersetzen 2241
übertragen 2240
übertreiben 742
überwinden 1505
überzeugen 499
Übung 753
Ufer 1940
Uhr 421, 2345
um 5
umarmen 698
Umgebung 719
umkommen 1556
Umlaufbahn 1490
umringen 2116
Unabhängigkeit 1083
unartig 1389
unbestimmt 2304
und 87
unehrlich 627
Unfall 11
Ungarn 1053
ungefähr 115
ungerecht 2289
ungeschickt 170, 427
ungesetzlich 1066
Unglück 1330
Uniform 2279
Union 2280
Universität 2288
unmöglich 1074
unnötig 2291
Unordnung 631
uns 2298
Unschuld 1094
unser 1501
Unsinn 1426
unten 224
unter 228, 2274
unterbrechen 1114
unterdrücken 1485, 2108
unterhalten 1263
Unterlassung 1471
unterrichten 1103
Unterschied 606
Unterstützung 2106
untersuchen 744, 767, 1119
unverantwortlich 1125
unverzüglich 1071
unwissend 1065
Unze 1500
Unzufriedenheit 633
Ursache 1740
Ursprung 1497
Urteil 1908
Uruguay 2297

V

Vater 794
Venezuela 2312
Verabredung 111
verachten 594
Verachtung 489
verändern 378
Verantwortlichkeit 1804
Verb 2313
Verband 185
verbergen 1020
verbessern 1076
verbeugen (sich) 276
verbieten 855, 1679
verbinden 1142
Verbindung 479, 2204
Verbrechen 525
Verbündeter 66
Verdacht 2118
verdächtigen 2117
verdienen 592, 675
Verdienst 1308
verdorben 2026
vereinen 2282
vereinigen 141
vereinigt 2283
Vereinigte Staaten 2286
Vereinigtes Königreich 2284
Vereinte Nationen 2285
Verfassung 486
verfehlen 1331
verfolgen 1705
Vergangenheit 1533
vergeben 861
vergebens 2305
vergessen 860
vergleichen 454
verhaften 127
Verhältnis 1728
Verhandlung 1401
verhindern 1657
Verhungern 2040
Verkauf 1856
verkaufen 1902
Verkäufer 1857
Verkehr 2236
Verlangen 593
verlassen 1
verlassen auf 1773
Verlauf 513
verlegen machen 697
verletzen 1092
Verletzung 2320
verlieren 1243

W

Z

A

a 145, 2212
a meno che 2290
a parte 102
abbandonare 1
abbastanza 712
abbonarsi 2080
abbondanza 1604
abbracciare 698
abbreviare 2
abile 419
abilità 1967
abituare 18
abitudine 977
abolire 4
accadere 987
accampamento 331
accanto a 231
accettare 10
acciaio 2049
accigliarsi 889
accompagnare 12
accontentare 490, 1602
accordarsi 50
accumulare 15
accusare 17
aceto 2319
acqua 2347
acquistare 21
addestramento 2239
addio 785
addomesticato 2135
addormentato 137
adesso 1440
aeroplano 56
aeroplano a reazione 1139
aeroporto 57
affare 316
afferrare 357
affilato 1929
affittare 1781
afflizione 965
affondare 1959
affrettarsi 1056
Africa 43
Africa del Sud 2007
aggiungere 30
agire 23
agitare la mano 2348
ago 1398
agosto 155
agricoltura 51
agro 2005
aiutare 140, 1014
al di là 238
ala 2394
Albania 60
albergo 1041
albero 2248
alfabeto 70
alimentare 802
all'estero 7
allarmare 61
allarme 59
alleato 66
allegro 387, 1309
allora 2176
altezza 1010
altezzoso 997
alto 1021, 2134
altro 1499
altro, l'uno o l' 690
altro, un 95
alzare 1724
amare 1246
amare, non 628
amaro 248
ambasciatore 76
ambedue 272
ambiente 719
ambizione 77
ambulanza 78
America 79
America del Nord 1430
America del Sud 2008
americano 80
amichevole 883
amico 882
ammalato 1947
ammettere 34
amministrazione 32
ammirare 33
analizzare 84
anche 72
ancora 2435
andare 934
andare in macchina 1817
anello 1823
angelo 88
angolo 505
anima 2002
animale 91
anitra 665
annegare 660
anno 2430
annuale 94, 2431
annullare 335
annunciare 92
ansia 97
antenato 85
antico 86
ape 212
apparentemente 105
apparire 106
appartamento 103
appartenere 223
appendere 986
applaudire 107
applicare 109
apprezzare 112
approssimativamente 115
approvare 114
appuntamento 111
aprile 116
aprire 1478
arancia 1489
arancione 1488
arare 1605
Argentina 118
argento 1952
aria 55
armamento 122
arnese 2222
arrabbiato 90
arrampicarsi 420
arrendersi 2115
arrestare 127
arricciare 537
arrivederci 941
arrivo 128
arrossire 259
arrotolare 1832
arte 129
articolo 130
artificiale 131
artista 132
ascensore 694
asciugamano 2229
asciugare 2396
ascoltare 1229
Asia 135
asino 647
aspettare 2334
aspirare 138
assassinio 1368
assenza 8
assicurazione 1106
associare 141
assurdo 9
astronauta 144
astronave 2012
atleta 146
attaccare 147
attacco 148
attento 349
attenzione 150
attitudine 151
attività 26
attivo 25
attore 27
attraente 153
attrarre 152
attraversare 528
attraverso 22, 2198
attrice 28
aula 416
aumentare 1081
Australia 157
Austria 158
auto 346
autobus 314
autore 159
autorità 160
autunno 161
avanti 52, 866
avanti, in 1477
avanzare 35
avere 998
avido 963
avventura 37
avvertire 2342
avvicinarsi 113
avvocato 1188
avvolgere 2422
azione 24

B

bacca 230
baciare 1164
baffi 1361
bagaglio 179, 1250
bagno 199
ballare 548
bambini 396
bambino 172, 395
bambola 645
banale 2252

dissolvere 634
distanza 635
distribuire 636
distruggere 596
disturbare 637
disturbo 2253
dito 822
divenire 209
divertente 83, 900
divertimento 896
dividere 639
divorzio 640
dizionario 604
dodici 2263
dolce 2122
dolere 1057
dollaro 646
dolore 19, 1512, 2001
domanda 1714
domandare 136
domani 2218
domenica 2100
dondolare 2124
donna 2405
dono (per corrompere) 291
dopo 44
doppio 649
dormire 1970
dorso 174
dove 2372
dovere 670, 1372, 1506
dovunque 101, 738
dramma 1597
dubbio 650
due 2269
due volte 2265
durante 669
duro 991

E

e 87
ebreismo 1147
eccedere 746
eccellente 747
eccetto 748
eccitare 750
economico 383
edificio 305
educazione 682
effetto 683
Egitto 686
egli 1000
egoistico 1901
elefante 693
eleggere 691
elettrico 692
elicottero 1011
eliminare 696
ella 1931
enigma 1708
enorme 711, 1047
entrare 713
entrata 716
entusiasmo 714
eppure 1045
equilibrio 181
equipaggiamento 721
erba 955
eredità 1090
eroe 1017
erroneo 2427
errore 723, 1333
esagerare 742
esame 743, 2163
esaminare 744
esatto 16, 741
esaurire 754
escludere 751
esempio 745
esercito 123
esercizio 753
esibire 632
esigenza 579
esistere 755
esitare 1019
esortare 2295
espandere 757
espellere 759
esperienza 762
esperimento 763
esperto 764
esplodere 766
esplorare 767
espressione 768
essa/la 1128
essenziale 726
essere 201
essere umano 1048
essi 2182
essi stessi 2175
esso 1128
est 679
estate 2097
estendere 769
età 48
Etiopia 729
Europa 730
evento 734
evitare 164

F

fa (tempo) 49
fabbrica 773
fabbricare 1272
faccia 772
facciata 887
facile 680
fagiolo 203
falegname 352
falso 781
fama 782
fame 1054, 2040
famiglia 783
fango 1366
fantasma 922
far cadere 659
fardello 310
fare 642, 1265
farfalla 320
farina 841
fato 793
fatto 566
fattoria 786
favore 796
favore, per 1601
favorito 797
fazzoletto 984
febbraio 799
febbre 808
fede 221, 778
fedele 779
felice 989
felicità 988
femmina 805
ferire 1092
ferita 2421
fermare 830, 2056
feroce 812
ferro 1124
ferrovia 1722
festa 1030
festival 807
fiamma 832
fiammifero 1281
fiducia 474
fieno 999
figlia 552
figlio 1998
figura 816
fila 1840
Filippine 1567
filo 2194
filo metallico 2397
filosofia 1568
finale 819
fine 703
finestra 2392
fingere 1655
finire 823
Finlandia 824
fino a 2292
finzione 810
fiore 256, 843
fischio 2378
fisica 1572
fisico 1570
fissare 791
fiume 1827
fiutare 1977
foglia 1193
folla 529
fondazione 867
fondere 1298
fondo 275, 898
forbici 1880
forchetta 862
foresta 858
forma 863, 1927
formaggio 388
fornire 2105
forse 1553
forte 2072
fortuna 1248
fortunato 1249
forza 2066
forza aerea 58
fotografia 1569
fra 81, 237
fragrante 871
fraintendere 1334
francese 878
Francia 873
franco 874
francobollo 2037
frase 1907

fratello 300
freddo 398, 434
frequente 879
fresco 501, 880
fretta 994
friggere 893
frigorifero 1757
frittella 1518
frumento 2368
frustrazione 892
frutta 891
fucile 976, 1819
fuggire 724, 837
fulmine 1219
fumare 1980
fumo 1979
funerale 899
fungo 1370
funzione 897
fuoco 825
fuori 1503
furto 2171
futuro 904

G

galleggiare 838
gallone 906
gamba 1201
gancio 1036
garantire 970
gas 910
gatto 355
gelato 1061
gelo 888
geloso 1137
gemello 2267
generazione 914
genere 1161
generoso 915
genitori 1524
gennaio 1134
gente 1548
gentile 916, 1160
gentiluomo 917
genuino 918
geografia 919
Germania 920
gesso 374
Gesù 1138
gettare 2199
ghiaccio 1060
già 71
giallo 2432
Giappone 1135
giardino 909
giardino zoologico 2446
gigante 923
giocare 1598
giocare d'azzardo 907
giocattolo 2232
gioco 908
gioia 1146
gioiello 1140
giornale 1413
giornalista 1144
giorno 553
giovane 2438
giovedì 2201
gioventù 2441
girare 2262
giù 651
giudicare 1148
giugno 1152
Giuochi Olimpici 1470
giuramento 1445
giurare 2120
giustizia 1153
giusto 777
globo 929
gloria 931
godere 710
goffo 170, 427
gola 2197
golf 939
gomma 1842
governo 944
grado 573
grammatica 947
Gran Bretagna 961
granaio 191
grande 241, 948, 960
grandine 978
grano 946
granoturco 504
grasso 792, 959
grato 956
grattare 1884
grazie 2168
grazioso 1656
Grecia 962
gridare 1885, 1943
grigio 958
grosso 1181
gruppo 968
guadagnare 675, 905
guanto 932
guardare 1241
guardia 971
guastato 2026
guerra 2340
guida 974
guidare 658, 1191
gusto 2139

I

idea 1062
ieri 2434
ignorante 1065
il loro 2172
il peggiore 2418
il più 1351
il quale 2374
illegale 1066
imbarazzare 697
imitare 1070
immaginazione 1069
immagine 1068
immediatamente 1072
immediato 1071
imparare 1195
imparare a memoria 1300
impaziente 672
impedire 1657
impiego 700
importante 1073
impossible 1074
impressione 1075
improvvisamente 2087
imputridire 559
in 145, 1077, 1116
in avanti 1477
in luogo di 1101
in su 2293
inchinarsi 276
inchiostro 1093
incidente 11
includere 1079
incontrare 1295
incoraggiare 702
India 1084
indicare 1085
indifferenza 1086
indipendenza 1083
indirizzo 31
indossare 2354
infermiera 1443
inferno 1012
influenza 1087
influire su 41
informare 1088
informazione 1089
ingannare 384
inganno 560
ingegnere 707
Inghilterra 708
inghiottire 2119
inginocchiarsi 1166
ingiusto 2289
inglese 709
iniezione 1091
innocenza 1094
inoltre 232, 1349
inondazione 839
insalata 1854
insegnante 2144
insegnare 2143
inseguire 381
inserzione pubblicitaria 38
insetto 303, 1095
insieme 2214
insieme, tutti 73
insignificante 1973
insistere 1097
installare 1100
insulto 1105
intelligente 1107
intendere 1108
intensità 1109
interesse 1110
interferire 1111
internazionale 1112
intero 715, 2381
interpretare 1113
interrompere 1114
intervallo 1115
intimità 1667
intorno a 124
invano 2305
inventare 1118
inverno 2395
investigare 1119
inviare 1903
invidioso 718
invitare 1120
io 1059

mondo 2414
moneta 432
monotono 1343
montagna 1358
morbido 1990
mordere 247
morire 605
morte 557
morto 554
mostrare 1945
motivare 1354
motivo 1355
motocicletta 1357
motore 706, 1356
movimento 1353
mucchio 1579
mulino 1322
muovere 1363
muro 2337
museo 1369
musica 1371
mutuo 1373

N

narcotico 661
narrare 1381
nascere 270
nascita 245
nascondere 1020
naso 1432
nastro 2136
Natale 407
nativo 1386
natura 1388
naturale 1387
nausea 1390
nave 1935
navigazione 1852
nazionale 1384
nazionalità 1385
nazione 1383
Nazioni Unite 2285
nebbia 845
necessario 1395
negare 584
negativo 1399
negligente 350
negligenza 1400
negoziato 1401
nemico 705
nero 249
nervoso 1405
nessuno 1423
neutrale 1408
neve 1984
nido 1406
niente 1425, 1435
nipote 949, 952, 1404, 1417
no 1422
noce 1444
nodo 1169
noi 2298, 2351
noi stessi 1502
noioso 269
nome 1379
nominare 110
non 1433
nonna 951
nonno 950
nord 1429
normale 1428
Norvegia 1431
nostro 1501
nota 1434
notificare 1436
notizia 1412
notte 1418
novanta 1421
nove 1419
novembre 1439
novità 1438
nudo 190, 1378
numero 1441
numeroso 1442
nuotare 2123
Nuova Zelandia 1414
nuovo 1411
nuovo, di 46
nuvola 425

O

o 1486
obbiettivo 1449
obbiezione 1448
obbligo 1450
oca 942
occasionale 1457
occasione 377, 1456
occasione 1482
occhiali 771
occhio 770
occorrenza 1459
occupato 317
occupazione 1458
oceano 1460
odiare 996
odore 1462, 1876
offendere 1463
offrire 1464
oggetto 1447
oggi 2213
ogni 671, 735
ogni volta che 2371
Olanda 1031
olio 1468
ombra 1923
ombrello 2272
omissione 1471
oncia 1500
onesto 1034
onorario 800
onore 1035
operare 1479
operazione 1480
opinione 1481
opporre 1483
opposto 1484
opprimere 1485
ora 1042
orale 1487
orbita 1490
orchestra 1491
ordinario 1494
ordine 446, 1492, 1493
orecchio 673
organizzazione 1495
orgoglio 1660
orgoglioso 1692
orientamento 1496
originale 1498
origine 1497
oro 938
orologio 421, 2345
oscurità 930
oscuro 550, 1451
ospedale 1039
ospite 973
osservare 1452, 2346
osservazione 1776
osso 266
ostacolo 1453
ottanta 689
ottenere 921, 1454
otto 687
ottobre 1461
ovest 2365
ovvio 1455
ozioso 1063

P

pacco 1510
pace 1539
padre 794
padrone 1280
paese 511
Paesi Bassi 1407
pagare 1538
pagina 1511
paio 1515
pala 1944
palazzo 1516
palla 183
palla a volo 2328
pallacanestro 198
pallido 1517
pallone 853
pallottola 308
pane 285
paniere 197
panino imbottito 1862
panna 523
parallelo 1522
parata 1521
parcheggiare 1526
parco 1525
parecchi 1919
parente 1768
parlare 2015, 2133
parola 2410
parte 1527, 1928
parte, a 102
participare 1528
partire 1198
partito 1529
passaporto 1532
passare 1530
passato 1533
passeggero 1531
passo 2050
pasto 1287
patata 1633
paura 798
pausa 1537
pavimento 840

paziente 1536
pazienza 1535
pazzo 522, 1255
peccato 1956
pecora 1932
peggiore 2417
peggiore, il 2418
pegno 1603
pelle 1968
pelliccia 901
pellicola 818
penalità 1543
penetrare 1545
penisola 1546
penna 1542
pensare 2187
pensiero 2192
pentola 1632
pepe 1549
per 854
per cento 1550
per favore 1601
per sempre 859
perchè 208
perchè? 2383
perdere 1194, 1243
perdonare 861
perfetto 1551
pericolo 549
periodo 1555
perire 1556
permanente 1557
permesso 1558
permettere 65
perseguire 1705
perseveranza 1559
persistere 1560
persona 1561
personale 1562
personalità 1563
persuadere 1565
Perù 1566
pesante 1009
pesare 2362
pescare 828
pesce 827
petrolio 1468
pettegolezzo 943
pettine 441
petto 391
pezzo 1576
piacere 1221
piacevole 1600
pianeta 1592
piangere 532, 2361
piano 835, 2059
piano (il) 1590
pianoforte 1573
pianta 1593
piantare 1594
piattaforma 1596
piatto 626, 1595
piccione 1578
piccolo 1231, 1976
piede 851, 852
piedi 804
piegare 227, 846
pieno 895
pietà 1586
pigrizia 1190
pillola 1580
pilota 1581
pioggia 1723
pipa 1585
piscina 1618
pittore 1514
più 1348, 1606
più, il 1351
più lontano 788
più lontano 903
più tardi 1184
pneumatico 2209
pochi 809
poco profondo 1925
poema 1608
politica 1613, 1616
polizia 1612
pollice 1078
pollo 393
Polonia 1611
polso 1699
polvere 1637
pomeriggio 45
pomodoro 2217
pompa 1700
ponte 295
popolare 1620
popolazione 1621
porco 1577
porta 648
portare 204, 298, 353
porto 990, 1622
Portogallo 1624
porzione 1623
positivo 1626
posizione 1234, 1625
possedere 1508, 1627
possibile 1629
possibilità 1628
posta 1260
posteriore 1739
potente 1318
potere 333, 1285, 1638
povero 1619
povertà 1636
pranzo 610
pratica 1639
precedentemente 864
preciso 1643
predire 1644
preferire 1645
pregare 216, 1641
prego 2440
premere 1653
premio 166, 1670
prendere 1898, 2131
prendere a prestito 271
preoccuparsi 2416
preoccupazione 467
preparare 1646
preparato 1735
presentare 1117, 1651, 2079
presente 1649
presente (il) 1650
presenza 1648
presidente 373, 1652
pressione 1654
prestito 1233
presto 2000
presumere 758
presunzione 463
prete 1661
previo 1658
prezioso 1642, 2308
prezzo 1659
prigione 1666
prima 215
prima colazione 287
primario 1662
primato 1750
primavera 2031
primo 826
principale 1261, 1663
principalmente 1262
principio 1664
privare 588
privato 1668
privilegio 1669
privo di valore 2420
probabilmente 1671
problema 1672
procedimento 1673
produrre 1674
professione 1675
profitto 1676
profondo 567
profondo, poco 1925
progettare 1591
progetto 1680
programma 1677
progresso 1678
proibire 855, 1679
promessa 1682
prominente 1681
promuovere 1683
pronunziare 1684
proporre 1688
proporzione 1728
proposito 1703
proprietà 1687
proprietario 1509
proprio 1507, 1686
prossimo 1415
proteggere 1689
protestante 1691
protestare 1690
prova 739, 1685, 2164
provvedere 1693
psichiatra 1694
psicologia 1695
pubblicare 1697
pubblicitario 38
pubblico 1696
pugilato 279
pulire 1614
pulito 417
punire 1701
puntare 54
punteggio 1882
punto 1554, 1609
puro 1702

Q

quadrato 2033
quadro 1574
qualche 98, 1994
qualche volta 1997

scrivere 2425
scultura 1886
scuola 1878
scuotere 1924
scure 171
scusami 1523
scusare 752
scusarsi 104
se 1064, 2373
se stesso 1131
secco 664
secolo 368
seconda colazione 1252
secondo 1892
sedersi 1961
sedia 372
sedici 1964
sedile 1891
sega 1868
segno 1949
segretario 1894
segreto 1893
seguire 847
sei 1963
selvaggio 2388
sembrare 1897
seme 1896
seminare 2010
semplice 1589, 1954
sempre 74
sempre, per 859
seno 288
sensibile 1906
senso 1904, 1905
sentiero 1534
sentimento 803
sentire 1004
senza 2402
separare 1910
separato 1909
sera 733
serio 676, 1912
serpente 1982
serrare 1235
servitore 1913
servizio 1914
sessanta 1965
sesso 1922
sete 2188
settanta 1918
sette 1916
settembre 1911
settimana 2359
settimanale 2360
severo 1920, 2069
sfida 375
sfondo 175
sforzo 684
sgridare 1881
si 2433
sicuramente 2110
sicuro 1851, 2109
sigaretta 409
sigillo 1888
significare 1288
significato 1289, 1950
signora 1175
silenzio 1951
sillabare 2021
simile 1220, 1953
simpatico 1416
simultaneamente 1955
sincero 1957
sinistro 1200
sistema 2128
situazione 1962
smussato 667
snello 1971
soccorso 53
socialismo 1987
società 1988
soddisfazione 1864
soffiare 257
soffocare 404
soffrire 2088
soggetto 2078
sogno 655
solamente 1476
soldato 1992
sole 2099
solido 1993
solitario 1239
sollecito 674
sollievo 1771
solo 68, 1238
somma 2095
sopportare 704
sopprimere 2108
sopra 6, 1504
sordo 555
sorella 1960
sorgere 120
sorprendere 2114
sorpresa 2113
sorriso 1978
sospettare 2117
sospetto 2118
sostantivo 1437
sostanza 2082
sostanziale 2083
sostegno 2106
sostituire 1785, 2084
sotterrare 313
sottile 2185
sotto 224, 228, 2274
sottrarre 2085
spada 2126
Spagna 2013
spago 2071
spalla 1942
sparare 1939
sparire 618
sparpagliare 1874
spaventare 1873
spaventato 42
spavento 884
spazio 2011
spazzola 302
specchio 1329
speciale 2016
specialità 2017
specialmente 725
specifico 2018
spendere 2022
speranza 1037
spesa 760
spesso 1467, 2183
spia 2032
spiaggia 202
spiegare 765
spillo 1582
spingere 1706
spirito 2024
splendido 2025
sport 2028
sposa 293
sposalizio 2357
sposo 294
sprecare 2344
spremere 2034
squadra 2145
stabilire 727
stagione 1890
stagno 1617
stampare 1665
stanco 2210, 2355
stanotte 2221
stare in piedi 2038
starnutire 1983
Stati Uniti d'America 2286
statistica 2045
stato 2041
statua 2046
stazione 2044
stella 2039
stendere 2030
stesso 1859
stivale 268
stoffa 423
stomaco 2055
storia 1026
strada 1828
strada maestra 1022
straniero 857
strano 2063
strappare 2146
strato 1189
stretto 1382
strisciare 521
strofinare 1841
strumento 1104
studente 2075
studiare 2076
stufa 2061
stupido 668, 2077
stupire 143
stuzzicare 2147
su 1472
sua 1130
successo 2086
succo 1149
sud 2006
sudicio 616
sudiciume 615
sudore 1564
sufficiente 2089
suggerire 2091
suicida 2092
suo 1130
suolo 1991
suonare 1824
suono 2003
superficie 2111
superfluo 2291
superiore 2103, 2294
supplica 1599
supporre 142, 2107

susseguente 2081
sussurrare 2377
svago 1203
svanire 2309
svegliare 125, 165
svenire 776
svestirsi 2276
Svezia 2121
sviluppare 599
sviluppo 600
Svizzera 2125

T

tagliare 543
talento 2132
tamburo 662
tardi 1183
tardi, più 1184
tasca 1607
tassa 2140
tassi 2141
tavola 2129
tazza 534
tè 2142
teatro 2170
telefono 2150
telegramma 2149
televisione 2151
tema 2174, 2225
temerario 264
temperatura 2153
tempesta 2058
tempo 2356
tempo (ora) 2207
temporaneo 2154
tenda 2160
tendenza 2157
tendere 2068
tenere 1028, 1154
tenero 2158
tennis 2159
tensione 2067
tentare 149, 2259
tentazione 2155
teoria 2177
termometro 2180
terra 677, 967, 1179
terremoto 678
terribile 169, 654, 2161
terrore 2162
tesoriere 2247
tesoro 2246
tessera 347
testimone 2403
testimonianza 2165
tetto 1834
timido 195, 1946, 2208
tirare 1698
tirchio 2052
titolo 2211
toccare 2228
togliere 1780
toletta 2215
tollerare 2216
tomba 957
tonnellata 2219
topo 1360
torcere 2268
toro 307
torre 2230
torta 324, 1575
tosse 509
totale 2227
tovagliolo 1380
tradire 235
tradizione 2235
tradurre 2241
traffico 2236
tragedia 2237
tramonto del sole 2102
trappola 2244
trascinare 652
trasferire 2240
trasportare 2242
trasporto 2243
trattore 2233
tre 2196
tredici 2189
treno 2238
trenta 2190
triangolo 2249
tribunale 514
trionfo 2251
triste 1850
trovare 820
tu 2437
tubo 1584
tuffare 638
tuo 2439
tuono 2200
turbine 2226
Turchia 2261
tuttavia 1410
tutti 736
tutti insieme 73
tutto 64, 737

U

ubbidienza 1446
ubriaco 663
uccello 244
uccidere 1157
udienza 154
udito 1005
ufficiale 1466
ufficio 1465
ufficio postale 1631
uguale 62, 720, 732
ultimo 1182
umanità 1049
umido 547, 1338
umile 1050
umore 1051, 1346
una volta 1473
undici 695
Ungheria 1053
uniforme 2278, 2279
unione 2280
Unione Sovietica 2009
unire 1142, 2282
unirsi 1307
unità 2281
unito 2283
universale 2287
università 2288
uno 1474
uomo 1266
uovo 685
urgente 2296
Uruguay 2297
usare 2299
uscita 756
usuale 2301
utile 2300
uva 954

V

vacante 2302
vacanza 2303
vacca 517
vagare 2338
vago 2304
valido 2306
valigia 2094
valle 2307
valore 2419
valore, privo di 2420
valutare 731
valutazione 728
vantaggio 36
vantarsi 260
vapore 2048
vario 2310
vaso 1136
vecchio 1469
vedere 1895
vedova 2386
veduta 2317
veleno 1610
veloce 790
velocità 2020
vendere 1902
vendetta 1812
vendita 1856
venditore 1857
venerdì 881
Venezuela 2312
venire 444
venti 2264
vento 2391
veramente 1082, 1738
verbo 2313
verde 964
vergogna 1926
vergognoso 134
verifica 385
verificare 386
verità 2258
verme 2415
vernice 1513
vero 2256
versare 1635
vertiginoso 641
vestirsi 656
vestiti 424
vestito 2093
via 168, 2065, 2349
viaggiare 2245
viaggio 1145, 2250
viale 162
vicinato 1403
vicino 1392, 1402
Vietnam 2316
villaggio 2318
vincere 1505, 2390

あ

い

う

え

ベネズエラ　2312
へび　1982
部屋　1835
減らす　1753
ヘリコプター　1011
ペルー　1566
ベルギー　220
ベルト　225
ペン　1542
弁解　1599
ペンキ　1513
勉強する　2076
弁護士　1188
便所　2215
返事をする　1786
ベンチ　226
便利な　497,2300
へきそん　1779

ほ

棒　2051
貿易　2234
崩壊する　435,596
方角　613
冒険　37
報告　1787
報告書　2043
報告する　1788
帽子　339,995
報酬　800,1814
宝石　1140
包帯　185
方法　1314,2350
法律　1187
法律の　1202
他の　1499
補強する　1765
牧師　1661
ポケット　1607
保険　1106
保護する　1689
ほこり　615
誇り　1660
誇りとする　1692
星　2039
欲しい　2339
干し草　999
保持する　1263
保証する　970
ボタン　321
墓地　364
ほっそりした　1971
ホテル　1041
ボート　261
殆ど　67,1393
骨　266
骨組み　872
炎　832
微笑み　1978
ほめる　1640
ポーランド　1611
ボリビア　265
掘る　608
ポルトガル　1624
滅びる　1556
本　267
本質的な　726
ポンド　1634
本当に　1738
ポンプ　1700
本物の　918
翻訳する　2241
本来の　1498

ま

毎週の　2360
埋葬する　313
毎月の　1345
マイナスの　1326
毎日の　545
毎年　2431
マイル　1319
前に　215
前の　1658
前へ　1477
負かす　569
曲がった　527
曲る　2262
巻きこむ　1121
巻く　537
まく　**2010**
曲げる　227
孫(男の)　952
孫娘　949
真面目な　1912
魔術　1257
まぜる　1335
また　72
まだ　2435
又は　1486
町　2231
間違った　2427
待つ　2334
真直ぐな　2062
全く　73,1082
マッチ　1281
祭り　807
…まで　2292
窓　2392
学ぶ　1195
真似る　1070
豆　203
真昼　1427
守る　570
麻薬　**61**
丸い　1839
丸太　1236
稀な　1872
稀に　1899
まわりに　124
満足　1864
満足する　490
真中の　1316

み

実　230
見えなくなる　618
見える　2321
磨く　1614
右　1821
見事な　2025
ミサイル　1332
短い　1941
水　2347
湖　1177
ミステリー　1376
見捨てる　1
店　2057
見せる　1945
満たす　817
道　1828,2349
見つける　820
ミツバチ　212
見積もり　728
認める　34,1747
緑の　964
港　990,1622
南　2006
南アメリカ　2008
南アフリカ　2007
醜い　2271
見張り　971
未亡人　2386
見本　745,1860
目まいがする　641
耳　673
脈搏　1699
見破る　597
魅力のある　153
見る　1241,1895
ミルク　1321
民主主義　580

む

無意味　1426
無益の　2305
無関心　1086
麦　2368
虫　303
無邪気　1094
むずかしい　607
息子　1998
結び　2204
結び目　1169
結ぶ　**2206**
娘　552
無責任な　1125
無駄にする　2344
無知な　1065
胸　288,391
村　2318
無理にさせる　856

め

目　770
姪　1417
明確な　1626
名詞　1437
命じる　110
名声　782
明白な　105
名誉　931,1035
命令　446,1492
眼鏡　771
メキシコ　1315
めくらの　253
召使い　1913
珍しい　1726
珍しさ　1438
メートル　1313
目まいがする　641
メモ　1434
目盛り　1870
メロン　1297
目をさまさせる　165
綿　508
免許　1214

を

가

가까이 1392
가게 2057
가격 1659
가공 810
가구 902
가끔하는 1457
가난 1636
가난한 1619
가난한 1954
가능성 1628
가능한 1629
가다 934
가득찬 895
가라앉다 1959
가루 841
가루 1637
가르치다 1103
가르치다 2143
가리키다 612
가리키다 1945
까만 249
가스 910
가슴 391
가슴 288
가운데 81
가을 161
가위 1880
가짜의 781
가장 나쁜 2418
가장 많은 1351
가장 적은 1196
가장 좋은 233
가정하다 142
가져오다 298
가족 783
가죽 1197 1197
가지 282
~까지 2292
가지다 998
가지다 1627
가축 359
가치 2419
가치가 있다 592
가치 없는 2420
깡통 332
깨끗한 417
각각의 671
깨뜨리다 286
껍질 1541
꼬리 2130
꼬매다 1921
꼭대기 2224
꼭 필요한 726
꽃 256
꽃 843
꾸부리다 227
꿈 655
끈 2071
끌다 152
끌다 652
끌다 1698
끓이다 263
간격 1115
간단한 296
간선도로 1022
간섭하다 1111
간여하다 1121
간청 1599
간호원 1443
갈다 966
갈론 906
갈색의 301
갈쿠리 1036
감각 803
감각 1904
감각 1905
감사하는 956
감사하다 112
감사합니다 2168
감옥 1132
감자 1633
감추다 1020
감탄하다 33
갑자기 2087
값 507
값 비싼 2308
강 1827
강요하다 455
강요하다 856
강의 1199
강조하다 699
강철 2049
강한 2072
같은 1859
같은 2278
같이 2214
개 644
개개의 1909
개구리 885
개념 466
개량하다 1076
개인의 1562
거기 2178
거대한 711
거대한 1047
거리 635
거리 2065
거미 2023
거울 1329
거위 942
거의 67
거의 1393
거인 923
거절하다 1758
거짓말 1215
거짓말쟁이 1211
거친 1838
걱정 348
걱정 2253
걱정하다 2416
건강 1003
건너가다 528
건너서 22
건물 305
건초 999
걷다 2336
걸음 2050
검사 385
검사 2164
검사하다 1098
겁 많은 2208
겁쟁이 518
게으른 1063
게으름 1190
겨냥하다 54
겨울 2395
격려하다 702
격렬 1109
견디다 704
견본 1860
견적 728
결과 483
결과 683
결과 1808
결과의 2081
결백 1094
결심하다 598
결정하다 562
결코 ~아니다 1409
결핍 1173
결함 571
결합하다 1142
결혼 1278
결혼 2357
겸손한 1050
겸손한 1615
경계하다 61
경고하다 2342
경멸하다 594
경영하다 1479
경쟁하다 456
경주 1720
경찰 1612
경치 2317
경향 2157
경험 762
곁에 231
계곡 2307
계단 2036
계도 1490
계량기 1312
계산서 14
계산한다 325

나

다

라

마

바

사

아

오스트렐리아 *157*
오스트리아 *158*
오월 *1284*
오케스트라 *1491*
오해하다 *1334*
오후 *45*
옥수수 *504*
온도 *2153*
온도계 *2180*
올가미 *2244*
올리다 *1724*
올림픽 경기 *1470*
옳지 않은 *2289*
옮기다 *2240*
옷 *424*
옷을 벗다 *2276*
와 *87*
~와 함께 *2400*
완성하다 *459*
완전한 *1551*
왕 *1162*
왕국 *1163*
왕관 *530*
왜 *2383*
외과 *2112*
외국의 *857*
~외에 *232*
외치다 *1943*
왼쪽의 *1200*
요구 *1792*
요구 *579*
요구 *1791*
요리하다 *500*
요술 *1257*
요약하다 *2096*
욕심 많은 *963*
용감한 *283*
용기 *512*
용서하다 *861*
용서하다 *752*
용서하십시요 *1523*
우둔한 *668*
우뢰 *2200*
우루과이 *2297*
우리 *2351*
우리에게 *2298*
우리의 *1501*
우리자신 *1502*
우박 *978*
우산 *2272*
우수한 *1818*
우수한 *2103*
우수한 *747*
우스운 *900*
우승자 *376*
우울 *930*
우유 *1321*
우주선 *2012*
우주인 *144*
우체국 *1631*
우편물 *1260*
우표 *2037*
운 *1248*
운동 *1353*
운동 *753*
운동가 *146*
운명 *793*
운반하다 *353*
운수 좋은 *1249*
운전하다 *658*
울다 *532*
울다 *2361*
울리다 *1824*
울타리 *806*
움직이다 *1363*
웃다 *1185*
웃음 *1186*
웅대한 *948*
위 *1504*
위 *2055*
위대한 *960*
위로 *2293*
위반 *2320*
위성 *1592*
위성 *1863*
위스키 *2376*
위원회 *448*
~위의 *1472*
위쪽의 *2294*
위치 *1234*
위하여 *854*
위험 *549*
원 *410*
원리 *1664*
원숭이 *1342*
원조 *53*
원하다 *2339*
월남 *2316*
월요일 *1340*
웨이터 *2335*
윗사람 *1402*
유고슬라비아 *2442*
유대 *2204*
유령 *922*
유럽 *730*
유모 *1051*
유용한 *2300*
유월 *1152*
유일한 *1476*
유죄의 *975*
유지하다 *1263*
유태교 *1147*
유행 *789*
유혹 *2155*
유요한 *2306*
육군 *123*
육체적 *1570*
~으로 *2212*
은 *1952*
은행 *186*
~을 더하여 *1606*
음식 *848*
음악 *1371*
읍 *2231*
의견 *1062*
의견 *1481*
의무 *670*
의무 *1450*
의미하다 *1288*
의사 *1571*
의사 *643*
~의 속에 *2401*
의식하는 *482*
의심 *650*
의심 *2118*
의심하는 *2117*
의자 *372*
의장 *373*
의존하다 *586*
의지하다 *1773*
이 *2223*
이 *2148*
이것 *2191*
이것들 *2181*
이겨내다 *1505*
이기다 *2390*
이기적 *1901*
이란 *1122*
이론 *2177*
이르키다 *360*
이른 *674*
이름 *1379*
이리 *2404*
이발사 *189*
이상한 *2063*
이성 *1741*
이스라엘 *1127*
~이 아니다 *1433*
~이 아니면 *2290*
이야기 *2060*
이월 *799*
이유 *1740*
이익 *36*
이익 *229*
이익 *1676*
이전의 *264*
이전의 *1658*
이집트 *686*
이태리 *1129*
이티오피아 *729*
이해하다 *2275*
이혼 *640*
익숙케 함 *1496*
익숙하다 *18*
익은 *1825*
인간 *1048*

자

카

타

틈 519
팀 2145

파

파괴하다 596
파다 608
파란 258
파업 2070
파운드 1634
파이 1575
파이프 1584
판결 1908
판매 1856
판매원 1857
팔 121
팔다 1902
팔월 155
팬케이크 1518
퍼센트 1550
펌프 1700
페루 1566
페이지 1511
페인트 1513
펜 1542
펴다 2030
펴다 2068
편리한 497
편안 445
편지 1208
평가하다 731
평균 163
평등한 732
평탄한 835
평행의 1522
평화 1539
포기하다 4
포도 954
포도주 2393
포옹하다 698
포함하다 1079
폭발하다 766
폭풍 2226
폭풍우 2058
폴란드 1611
폴투갈 1624
풀 955
풀 1618
풀다 257
품다 464
품질 1709
풍부한 1816
표 2203
표를 하다 1276
표면 2111
표현 768
프로그람 1677
피 255
피곤한 2210
피부 1968
피아노 1573
피하다 164
피해 546
피 1582
필름 818
필요 1397
필요한 1395

하

하나 1474
하녀 1259
하느님 937
하는 동안 2375
하늘 1008
하늘 1969
하다 642
하인 1913
하품하다 2429
학교 1878
학생 2075
학회 1102
학회 1102
한국 1171
한밤중 1317
한번 1473
한쌍 1515
한조각 1576
할머니 951
할 수 있다 333
할 수 있다 1285
할아버지 950
할 작정이다 1108
할키다 1884
함께 하다 12
합계 2227
합계 2095
합법적인 1202
합치다 443
합친 2283
합하다 1307
항가리 1053
항구 990
항구 1622
항복하다 2115
항아리 1136
항의하다 1690
항해 1852
해 2430
해 2099
해결하다 1881
해고하다 629
해군 1391
해돋이 2101
해변 202
해변 429
해보다 2259
해야한다 1372
해외 7
행동 26
행동 218
행동하다 471
행렬 1521
행복 988
행복한 989
행위 24
행위 566
행정 32
행하다 23
향기로운 871
허가 1558
허락하다 65
허락하다 953
허리 2333
헌법 486
헐거운 1242
헛되이 2305
헬리콥터 1011
혀 2220
혁명 1813
현대의 1337
현재 1650
현재의 1649
현재의 538
협력하다 502
협박 2195
형벌 1543
형제 300
호기심이 강한 536
호두 1444
호르라기 2378
호수 1177
호주머니 1607
호텔 1041
혼란 476
흘 981
흘로 68
홍수 839
화가 1514
화산 2327
화요일 2260
화제 2225
확신 474
확신하다 2109
확실한 369
확실한 1626
확실히 2110
확인 475
확인하다 386
확장하다 757
환경 719
환영회 1746
환자 1536

A

a 145, 2212
a mais 1351
a menos que 2290
à parte 102
à volta de 124
abaixo 224, 651
abandonar 1
abelha 212
abolir 4
aborrecer 93, 273, 2147
abraçar 698
abreviar 2
abril 116
abrir 1478
absurdo 9
abundância 1604
acabar 823
acampamento 331
ação 24, 566
aceitar 10
acenar com a mão 2348
acidente 11
aço 2049
acompanhar 12
aconselhar 40
acontecer 987
acontecimento 734
acordar 165
acostumar 18
açucar 2090
acumular 15
acusar 17
adeus 941
adiante 52, 866
adiante, mais 903
adiar 1630
adicionar 30
administração 32, 1268
admirar 33
admitir 34
adormecido 137
adquirir 21
advogado 1188
aeroporto 57
afetar 41
afiado 1929
aflição 965
afogar 660
África 43
África do Sul 2007
afundar 1959
agarrar 357
agarrar 1898
agir 23
agora 1440
agôsto 155
agradar 1602
agradável 1600
agricultura 51
água 2347
agulha 1398
ajoelhar-se 1166
ajudar 140, 1014
alaranjado 1488
alarme 59
Albânia 60
alcançar 20, 1732
aldeia 2318
alegre 387, 927, 1309
alegria 1146
além 238
além de 232
Alemanha 920
alertar 61
alfabeto 70
alface 1209
alfinete 1582
algodão 508
alguém 1995
algum 1994
alguma coisa 1996
ali 2178
aliado 66
alimentar 802
alívio 1771
alma 2002
almôço 610, 1252
alto 1021, 2134
altura 1010
alugar 1781
amanhã 2218
amar 1246
amarelo 2432
amargo 248
ambição 77
ambos 272
ambulância 78
ameaça 2195
América 79
América do Norte 1430
América do Sul 2008
americano 80
amigável 883
amigo 882
amostra 1860
analisar 84
andar 2059, 2336
andar de automóvel 1817
anel 1823
animal 91
aniversário 246
anjo 88
ano 2430
ansiedade 97
antepassado 85
antes 215
antigamente 864
antigo 86
anual 94, 2431
anunciar 92
anúncio 38
ao lado de 231
apagar 722
aparecer 106
aparentemente 105
apartamento 103
apesar de 595
apito 2378
aplaudir 107
aplicar 109
apodrecer 559
apoio 2106
apontar 54
aposta 234
apreciar 112
aprender 1195
apresentar 1117, 2079
apressar 2295
apressar-se 1056
aprovar 114
aproveitar 710
aproximadamente 115
aproximar-se 113
aquele 2169
aqui 1016
ar 55
aranha 2023
arar 1605
arbusto 315
areia 1861
Argentina 118
armadilha 2244
armamento 122
arranhar 1884
arranjar 126
arrastar 652
arroz 1815
arte 129
artificial 131
artigo 130
artista 132
árvore 2248
às vezes 1997
asa 2394
Ásia 135
áspero 1838
aspirar 138
assassinato 1368
asseado 1394
assemelhar-se a 1795
assento 1891
assim 2202
assinar 2080
associar 141
assustar 1873
astronauta 144
astronave 2012
astuto 1975
ataque 148
atar 2206
até 2292
atenção 150
atirar 1939, 2199
atitude 151
atividade 26
ativo 25
atleta 146
ator 27
atraente 153
atrair 152
atrás 219
atrasar 574
através de 22
atravessar 528
atrevido 264
atriz 28
audiência 154
aumentar 1081
ausência 8
Austrália 157
Áustria 158
autor 159
autoridade 160
avaliar 731
avançar 35
ávaro 2052
avenida 162

aventura 37
avião 56
avião a jato 1139
avisar 2342
avô 950
avó 951
azêdo 2005
azul 258

B

baga 230
bagagem 179, 1250
baixo 1247
bala 308
balança 1871
balançar 2124
banana 184
banco 186, 226
bandagem 185
bandeira 831
banho 199
banquête 187
barato 383
barba 205
barbante 2071
barbear-se 1930
barbeiro 189
barco 261
barril 192
barulhento 1245
barulho 1424
base 193, 196
basquetebol 198
bastante 712
batalha 200
batata 1633
bater 206, 1027, 1168
batismo 188
baú 2257
bêbado 663
bebê 172
beber 657
bebidas alcoólicas 1227
beijar 1164
beisebol 194
Bélgica 220
belo 207
bem 2364
bem-vindo 2363
benefício 229
besteira 1426
Bíblia 239
biblioteca 1213
bicicleta 240
bigode 1361
bilhão 242
bilhete 2203
bloco 254
boca 1362
bocejar 2429
bola 183
boletim 309
Bolívia 265
bôlo 324
bolsa 1704
bolso 1607
bom 940
bom dia 1013
bomba 1700
bombom 338
bondoso 1160
boneca 645
bonito 985, 1656
borboleta 320
borracha 1842
bota 268
botão 321
boxe 279
braço 121
branco 2379
Brasil 284
breve 296
brilhante 297
brilhar 1934
brinquedo 2232
brisa 290
Bulgária 306
buraco 1029
burro 647
buscar 1889

C

cabeça 1001
cabelo 979
cabra 936
caça 1055
caçar 381
cachimbo 1585
cada 671, 735
cadeia 371
cadeira 372
café 431
café da manhã 287
cair 780
cair, deixar 659
caixa 278
calças 1519, 2254
calcular 325
calendário 326
calmo 329
calor 1007
cama 210
camada 1189
caminhão 2255
caminho 2349
camisa 1936
campainha 222
campeão 376
campo 811
Canadá 334
canção 1999
cancelar 335
candidato 336
caneta 1542
cansado 2210, 2355
cantar 1958
cão 644
capacidade 3, 341
capaz 340
capital 342
capitalista 343
capitão 344
capítulo 379
capturar 345
cara 772
caráter 380
careca 182
carência 1173
carnaval 351
carne 1291
carne de vaca 213
carneiro 1932
caro 556, 761
carpinteiro 352
carregar 204, 353
carreta 354
carro 346, 2332
carta 1208
cartão 347
carvão 428
casa 1043
casaco 430
casamento 1278, 2357
casca 1541
castanho 301
castigar 1701
catálogo 356
católico 358
catorze 869
cauda 2130
causa 1740
causar 360
cautela 361
cavalheiro 917
cavalo 1038
cavar 608
cebola 1475
ceder 2436
cedo 674
cego 253
celebrar 363
celeiro 191
cem 1052
cemitério 364
cena 1875, 2035
centavo 365, 1547
centímetro 367
centro 366
cêrca 806
cercado 2428
cercar 2116
cérebro 281
cereja 389
certamente 2110
certificado 370
certo 369, 2109
cerveja 214
cessar 362
cêsto 197
céu 1008, 1969
chá 2142
chama 832
chamar 328
chaminé 399
chão 840
chapéu 995
chave 1155
Checoslováquia 544
chefe 394
chegada 128
cheio 895
cheirar 1977
cheiro 1876
Chile 397
China 401
chocar 439

D

delicioso 576
demais 1349
demitir-se 1799
democracia 580
demonstrar 581
dente 2223
dentes 2148
dentista 583
dentro 1096, 2401
dentro de 1116
departamento 585
depender 586
depois 44
depositar 587
derreter 1298
derrotar 569
desafio 375
desagrado 633
desajeitado 170, 427
desanimar 621
desaparacer 618, 2309
desapontar 619
desbotar 774
descansar 1805
descendente 590
descender 589
descobrir 622
descrever 591
descuidado 350
desculpar 752
desculpar-se 104
desculpe-me 1523
desejo 593, 2399
desejoso 672
desemprego 2277
desenhar 653
desenvolver 599
desenvolvimento 600
desgostar 628
desgôsto 625
desgraça 1330
deslizar 1972
desmaiar 776
desmoronar-se 435
desnecessario 2291
desobedecer 630
desonesto 627
desordem 631
despedida 785
despejar 1635
desperdiçar 2344
despertar 125
despesa 760
despir-se 2276
desprezar 594
desprêzo 489
destino 793
destruir 596
desviar-se 601
detectar 597
determinar 598
Deus 937
dever 670, 1372, 1506
devido 666
dez 2156
dezembro 561
dezenove 1420
dezesseis 1964
dezessete 1917
dezoito 688
dia 553
diabo 602
diamante 603
diante, para 1477
diário 545
dicionário 604
diferença 606
difícil 607
diminuir 565
Dinamarca 582
dinheiro 1341
diploma 611
direção 613
direita 1821
direito 1822
direto 2062
diretor 614
dirigir 612, 658
disciplina 620
discordar 617
discurso 2019
discutir 623
disputar 119, 1711
dissolver 634
distância 635
distribuir 636
divertido 83
divertimento 896
dívida 558
dividir 639
divórcio 640
dizer 1869, 2152
dobrar 227
dobrar 846
doce 2122
doença 624, 1067
doente 1947
doer 1057
dois 2269
dólar 646
domesticado 2135
domingo 2100
dor 19, 1512, 2001
dor de cabeça 1002
dormir 1970
doze 2263
droga 661
duas vezes 2265
duplo 649
durante 669
duro 991
dúvida 650

E

e 87
edifício 305
educação 682
efeito 683
Egito 686
egoísta 1901
ela 1015, 1128, 1931
ela mesma 1018
ele 1000, 1024, 1128
ele mesmo 1025
elefante 693
eleger 691
eles 2182
eles mesmos 2175
elétrico 692
elevador 694
eliminar 696
elogiar 447
em 145, 1077
em vão 2305
em vez de 1101
embaixador 76
embaraçar 697
empregada 1259
emprêgo 700
empréstimo 1233
empurrar 1706
encaracolar 537
encher 817
encontrar 820, 1295
encontro marcado 111
encorajar 702
endereço 31
enfadonho 667
enfatizar 699
enfermeira 1443
enganar 384
engano 560
engatinhar 521
engenheiro 707
engolir 2119
engraçado 900
enigma 1708
enorme 711, 1047
enquanto 2375
ensinar 2143
entanto, no 1410
então 2176
entender mal 1334
enterrar 313
entrada 716
entrar 713
entre 81, 237
entregar 578
entusiasmo 714
envelope 717
envergonhado 134
enviar 1903
envolver 1121, 2422
equilíbrio 181
equipamento 721
equipe 2145
errado 2427
errar 1331
êrro 723, 1333
esbelto 1971
escada 1174, 2036
escala 1870
escapar 724
escasso 1872
Escócia 1883
escola 1878
escolha 403
escolher 405
esconder 1020
escôva 302
escrever 2425
escritor 2426
escritório 1465
escultura 1886
escuro 550
escutar 1229
esfôrço 684

esfregar 1841
esgotar 754
espaço 2011
espada 2126
espalhar 1874, 2030
Espanha 2013
espantar 75, 143
espanto 884
especial 2016
especialidade 2017
especialmente 725
específico 2018
espelho 1329
esperança 1037
esperar 758, 2334
esperto 419
espêsso 2183
espião 2032
espingarda 976
espírito 2024
espirrar 1983
esplêndido 2025
esporte 2028
esposa 2387
espremer 2034
esquecer 860
esquema 1877
esquerdo 1200
esquina 505
essencial 726
esta noite 2221
estabelecer 727
estação 1890, 2044
estacionar 1526
estado 2041
Estados Unidos 2286
estar de pé 2038
estatística 2045
estátua 2046
este (leste) 679
este 2191
estender 769
estes 2181
esticar 2068
estimativa 728
estômago 2055
estrada 1022, 1828
estrada de ferro 1 722
estragado 2026
estrangeiro, no 7
estranho 857, 2063
estreito 1382
estrêla 2039
estudante 2075
estudar 2076
estúpido 668, 2077
Etiópia 729
eu 1059
eu mesmo 1375
Europa 730
evitar 164
exagerar 742
exame 743, 2163
examinar 744
exato 16, 741
exceder 746
excelente 747
exceto 748
excitar 750
excluir 751
exemplo 745
exercício 753
exército 123
exibir 632
exigência 579, 1792
existir 755
expandir 757
experiência 762, 763
explicar 765
explodir 766
explorar 767
expressão 768
expulsar 759

F

fábrica 773
fabricar 1272
faca 1167
fácil 680
faísca 2014
falar 2015, 2133
falso 781
fama 782
família 783
fantasma 922
fardo 310
farinha 841
favor 796
favor, por 1601
favorito 797
fazenda 786
fazendeiro 787
fazer 642, 1265
fé 778
febre 808
fechadura 1235
fechar 422
feijão 203
feio 2271
felicidade 988
feliz 989
fêmea 805
fenda 519
feno 999
feriado 1030
férias 2303
ferida 2421
ferir 1092
feroz 812
ferramenta 2222
ferro 1124
ferver 263
festival 807
fevereiro 799
ficar atrás 1176
ficção 810
fiel 779
figura 816
fila 1840
filha 552
filho 1998
Filipinas 1567
filme 818
filosofia 1568
fim 703
final 819
fingir 1655
Finlândia 824
fino 821
fio 2194
fio de metal 2397
física 1572
físico 1570
fita 2136
fixar 791, 830
flor 256, 843
floresta 858
fluir 842
flutuar 838
fofoca 943
fogão 2061
fogo 825
foguete 1831
folha 1193
fome 1054
fora 168, 1503
força 2066
força aérea 58
forçar 856
forma 1927
formar 863
fornecer 2105
forte 2072
fósforo 1281
fotografia 1569
fracassar 775
fraco 801, 2352
fragrante 871
França 873
francês 878
franco 874
frango 393
franzir as sobrancelhas 889
frase 1907
frente 887
frequente 879
frequentemente 1467
fresco 501, 880
frio 434
friorento 398
fritar 893
frustração 892
fruta 891
fugir 837
fumaça 1979
fumar 1980
função 897
fundação 867
fundo 175, 275
fundos 898
funeral 899
futebol (americano) 853
futebol 1986
futuro 904

G

gabar-se 260
gado 359
galão 906
ganancioso 963
gancho 1036
ganhar 675, 905, 2390
ganso 942
garantir 970
garçom 2335

garfo 862
garganta 2197
garrafa 274
gás 910
gasolina 911
gastar 2022
gato 355
geada 888
geléia 1133
gelo 1060
gêmeo 2267
gênero 1161
generoso 915
gente 1548
geografia 919
geração 914
gerente 1269
gigante 923
girar 2262
giz 374
globo 929
glória 931
golfe 939
gordo 792
gordura 959
gôrro 339
gostar de 1221
gosto 2139
govêrno 944
Grã-Bretanha 961
graduado 945
grama 955
gramática 947
grande 241, 960, 1181
grandioso 948
granizo 978
grão 946
grato 956
grau 573
gravador 2137
gravata 2205
Grécia 962
greve 2070
gritar 1885, 1943
grupo 968
guarda 971
guarda-chuva 2272
guardanapo 1380
guerra 2340
guia 974
guiar 1191

H

há (tempo) 49
habilidade 1967
hábito 977
helicóptero 1011
herança 1090
herói 1017
hesitar 1019
história 1026, 2060
hoje 2213
Holanda 1031, 1407
homem 1266
honesto 1034
honorário 800
honra 1035
hora 1042
hóspede 973
hospital 1039
hotel 1041
humanidade 1049
humilde 1050
humor 1051, 1346
Hungria 1053

I

idade 48
idéia 1062
ignorante 1065
igreja 408
igual 62, 720
ilegal 1066
ilha 1126
imagem 1068
imaginação 1069
imediatamente 1072
imediato 1071
imitar 1070
impedir 1657
importante 1073
impossível 1074
imposto 2140
impressão 1075
imprimir 1665
inanição 2040
incluir 1079
incomodar 637
independência 1083
India 1084
indicar 1085
indiferença 1086
inferno 1012
influência 1087
informação 1089
informar 1088, 1436
Inglaterra 708
inglês 709
inimigo 705
injeção 1091
injusto 2289
inocência 1094
inseto 303, 1095
insignificante 1973
insistir 1097
inspecionar 1098
inspiração 1099
instalar 1100
instituto 1102
instruir 1103
instrumento 1104
insulto 1105
inteiramente 73
inteiro 715, 2381
inteligente 1107
intencionar 1108
intensidade 1109
interêsse 1110
interferir 1111
internacional 1112
interpretar 1113
interromper 1114
intervalo 1115
intimidade 1667
inundação 839
invejoso 718
inventar 1118
inverno 2395
investigação 1794
investigar 1119
ir 934
Irã 1122
Irlanda 1123
irmã 1960
irmão 300
irresponsável 1125
Israel 1127
Itália 1129

J

já 71
janeiro 1134
janela 2392
jantar 2104
Japão 1135
jardim 909
jardim zoológico 2446
jarra 1136
Jesus 1138
jogar 1598
jogar à dinheiro 907
jôgo 908
Jogos Olímpicos 1470
jóia 1140
jornal 1413
jornalista 1144
jovem 2438
judaísmo 1147
Jugoslávia 2442
julgar 1148
julho 1150
junho 1152
juntar 243, 1142
juntos 2214
juramento 1445
jurar 2120
justiça 1153
justo 777
juventude 2441

L

lã 2409
lábio 1225
lado 1948
lado (ao...de) 231
ladrão 2184
lago 1177
lama 1366
lamentar 1359
lanterna 834
lápis 1544
lar 1033
laranja 1489
largar 1717
largo 299, 2385
lata 332
lavar 2343
leão 1224
legal 1202
legumes 2311
lei 1187
leite 1321
lenço 984
lenha 1236
lento 1974

ler 1734
leste 679
levantar 1724
lhe 1015, 1024
lhes 2173
liberdade 876, 1212
libertar 875
libra 1634
lição 1206
licença 1214
líder 1192
limão 1204
limite 1222
limpar 2396
limpo 417
língua 1180, 2220
linha 1223
líquido 1226
liso 1981
lisonjear 836
lista 1228
litro 1230
livro 267
lobo 2404
localização 1234
lógica 1237
logo 2000
loja 2057
longe 784
longe, mais 788
longo 1240
longo (ao. . .de) 69
louco 522, 1255
louvar 1640
lua 1347
lucro 1676
lugar 1587
luta 2073, 2424
lutar 815
luva 932
luz 1218

M

maçã 108
macaco 1342
maçante 269
machado 171
madeira 1251, 2408
maduro 1825
mãe 1352
mágica 1257
magnífico 1258
maio 1284
maioria 1264
mais 1348, 1606
mais adiante 903
mais longe 788
mais tarde 1184
mal 740
mala 2094
mancha 2029
maneira 1270, 2350
manejar 1267
manhã 1350
manteiga 319
manter 1028, 1154, 1263
manual 1271
manutenção 1915
mão 983
mapa 1274
máquina 1253
máquina fotográfica 330
maquinaria 1254
mar 1887
maravilha 2406
maravilhoso 1279, 2407
marcador 1882
marcar 1276
março 1275
marido 1058
marinha 1391
marinheiro 1853
martelo 982
mas 318
mastigar 392
matar 1157
matemática 1282
matéria 1283
mau 177, 2384
me 1286
mecânico 1292
medalha 1293
medicina 1294
médico 643, 1571
médio 163, 1316
medir 1290
mêdo 798
mêdo, com 42
meia 1989, 2054
meia-noite 1317
meio ambiente 719
meio-dia 1427
melão 1297
melhor 236
melhor, o 233
melhorar 1076
membro 1299
memória 1301
mencionar 1304
menos 1205, 1326
menos (a. . .que) 2290
mensagem 1310
mensal 1345
mental 1303
mente 1324
mentira 1215
mentiroso 1211
mercado 1277
merecer 592
mergulhar 638
mérito 1308
mês 1344
mesa 2129
mesmo 1859
mestre 1280, 2144
meta 935
metade 980
metal 1311
método 1314
metro 1313
meu 1325, 1374
mexer 2053
México 1315
mil 2193
milagre 1328
milha 1319
milhão 1323
milho 504
militar 1320
mim 1286
mínimo, o 1196
minuto 1327
misericórdia 1306
míssil 1332
mistério 1376
misturar 1335
mobília 902
môça 925
môço 280
moda 789
modêlo 1336
moderno 1337
moeda 432
moer 966
moinho 1322
moldura 872
mole 1990
molhado 2366
momento 1339
monótono 1343
montanha 1358
morder 247
morrer 605
morte 557
morto 554
mostrar 1945
motivar 1354
motivo 1355
motocicleta 1357
motor 706, 1356
mover 1363
movimento 1353
mudar 378
muito 1244, 1365, 2314
muitos 1273
mulher 2405
multidão 529
multiplicar 1367
mundo 2414
muro 2337
museu 1369
música 1371
mútuo 1373

N

nação 1383
nacional 1384
nacionalidade 1385
Nações Unidas 2285
nada 1435
nadar 2123
não 1422, 1433
nariz 1432
narrar 1381
nascer 270
nascer do sol 2101
nascimento 245
nata 523
Natal 407
nativo 1386
natural 1387
natureza 1388
náusea 1390
navalha 1731
navegação 1852
navio 1935

necessário 1395
necessidade 1397
negar 584
negativo 1399
negligência 1400
negociação 1401
negócio 316
nenhum 1425
nervoso 1405
neta 949
neto 952
neutro 1408
neve 1984
nevoeiro 845
ninguém 1423
ninho 1406
nível 1210
nó 1169
no entanto 1410
noite 733, 1418
noiva 293
noivo 294
nome 1379
nomear 110
normal 1428
norte 1429
Noruega 1431
nós 2298, 2351
nós mesmos 1502
nosso 1501
nota 1434
notícias 1412
Nova Zelândia 1414
nove 1419
novembro 1439
noventa 1421
novidade 1438
nôvo 1411
noz 1444
nu 190, 1378
número 1441
numeroso 1442
nunca 1409
nuvem 425

O

o melhor 233
o mínimo 1196
o pior 2418
obediência 1446
objeção 1448
objetivo 1449
objeto 1447
obrigação 1450
obrigado 2168
obscuridade 930
obscuro 1451
observação 1776
observar 1452, 2346
obstáculo 1453
obter 921, 1454
obvio 1455
ocasião 377, 1456
ocasional 1457
oceano 1460
ócio 1203
ocioso 1063
ocorrência 1459
óculos 771
ocupação 1458
ocupado 317
odiar 996
odor 1462
oeste 2365
ofender 1463
oferecer 1464
oficial 1466
oitenta 689
oito 687
óleo 1468
olhar 1241
olho 770
ombro 1942
omissão 1471
onça 1500
onde 2372
ônibus 314
ontem 2434
onze 695
operação 1480
operar 1479
opinião 1481
opor 1483
oportunidade 1482
oposto 1484
oprimir 1485
oral 1487
orar 1641
órbita 1490
ordem 446, 1492, 1493
ordinário 1494
orelha 673
organização 1495
orgulho 1660
orgulhoso 1692
orientação 1496
origem 1497
original 1498
orquestra 1491
os 2173
osso 266
ou 1486
ouro 938
outono 161
outra vez 46
outro 1499
outro, um 95
outro, um ou 690
outubro 1461
ouvido 1005
ouvir 1004
ovo 685

P

pá 1944
paciência 1535
paciente 1536
pacote 1510
padre 1661
pagar 1538
página 1511
pai 794
país 511, 1524
palácio 1516
palavra 2410
pálido 1517
pano 423
panqueca 1518
pão 285
papel 1520
par 1515
para 854
para cima 2293
para diante 1477
para sempre 859
para trás 176
parabenizar 477
parada 1521
paralelo 1522
parar 2056
parecer 1897
parente 1768
parque 1525
parte 1527, 1928
parte, à 102
participar 1528
partido 1529
partir 1198
passado 1533
passageiro 1531
passaporte 1532
passar 1530
pássaro 244
passo 2050
pato 665
pau 2051
pausa 1537
paz 1539
pé 851, 852
peça 1576, 1597
pecado 1956
pedido 1791
pedir 216
pedir emprestado 271
peito 391
peixe 827
pele 901, 1968
penalidade 1543
pendurar 986
penetrar 1545
penhor 1603
península 1546
pensamento 2192
pensar 2187
pente 441
pequeno 1976
perder 1243
perdoar 861
perecer 1556
perfeito 1551
pergunta 1714
perguntar 136
perigo 549
período 1555
perito 764
permanecer 1774
permanente 1557
permissão 1558
permitir 65
perna 1201
perseguir 1705
perseverança 1559
persistir 1560
personalidade 1563
persuadir 1565
pertencer 223

perto 1392
Peru 1566
pés 804
pesado 1009
pesar 2362
pescar 828
pescoço 1396
pessoa 1561
pessoal 1562
petróleo 1468
piada 1143
piano 1573
pico 1540
pilha 1579
piloto 1581
pílula 1580
pimenta 1549
pintor 1514
pior 2417
pior, o 2418
piscina 1618
planejar 1591
planeta 1592
plano 732, 835
plano, o 1590
planta 1593
plantar 1594
plataforma 1596
pneu 2209
pó 1637
pobre 1619
pobreza 1636
poder 333, 1285, 1638
poderoso 1318
poema 1608
polegada 1078
polícia 1612
polir 1614
política 1613, 1616
Polônia 1611
pomba 1578
pontapés, dar 1156
ponte 295
ponto 1554, 1609
população 1621
popular 1620
por 854, 2198
pôr do sol 2102
por favor 1601
por quê 2383
por tôda parte 738
porção 1623
porcento 1550
porco 1577
porque 208
porta 648
portanto 2179
portão 912
porto 990, 1622
Portugal 1624
posição 1625
positivo 1626
possibilidade 1628
possível 1629
possuir 1508, 1627
posterior 1739
pote 1632
pouco 1231
pouco profundo 1925
poucos 809
praia 202, 1940
prata 1952
prateleira 1933
prática 1639
prato 626, 1595
precioso 1642
preciso 1643
preço 1659
predizer 1644
preferir 1645
prego 1377
preguiça 1190
prêmio 166, 1670
prender 127, 147
preocupação 467, 2253
preocupar-se 2416
preparado 1735
preparar 1646
presença 1648
presente 1649
presente, o 924
presente (tempo) 1650
presentear 1651
presidente 373, 1652
pressa 994
pressão 1654
pressionar 1653
preto 249
prévio 1658
primário 1662
primavera 2031
primeiro 826
primo 515
principal 1261, 1663
principalmente 1262
princípio 1664
prisão 1132, 1666
privado 1668
privar 588
privilégio 1669
problema 1672
procedimento 1673
produzir 1674
profissão 1675
profundo 567
profundo, pouco 1925
programa 1677
progresso 1678
proibir 855, 1679
projeto 1680
promessa 1682
promover 1683
pronunciar 1684
propor 1688
propósito 1703
propriedade 1687
proprietário 1509
próprio 1507, 1686
proteger 1689
protestante 1691
protestar 1690
prova 739, 1685, 2164
provavelmente 1671
prover 1693
próximo 1415
psicologia 1695
psiquiatra 1694
publicar 1697
público 1696
pular 1151
pulso 1699
puro 1702
puxar 1698

Q

quadrado 2033
quadro 1574
quadro negro 250
qual 2374
qualidade 1709
qualquer 98
qualquer coisa 100
qualquer parte 101
qualquer pessoa 99
quando 2370
quantidade 82, 1710
quanto 1046
quarenta 865
quarta-feira 2358
quarto 1712, 1835
quarto de dormir 211
quase 67, 1393
quatro 868
que 2167
quê 2367
queijo 388
queimar 311
queixo 400
quem 2380
quem, de 2382
quente 1040, 2341
querer 2339
quieto 1716
quilograma 1158
quilômetro 1159
quinta-feira 2201
quinze 813

R

rã 885
rádio 1721
rainha 1713
raio 1730
raiva 89
raiz 1836
ralhar 1881
ramo 282
rápido 790, 1715, 1725
rapôsa 870
raramente 1899
raro 1726
rasgar 2146
rato 1360, 1727
razão 1728, 1741
reação 1733
real 29, 1736
realizar 13, 1737
realmente 1082, 1738
rebelião 1742
rebentar 312
receber 1744
receita 1647
recente 1745
recepção 1746
recibo 1743
reclamar 458

substantivo 1437
substituir 1785, 2084
subtrair 2085
sucesso 2086
suco 1149
Suécia 2121
suficiente 2089
sufocar 404
sugerir 2091
Suíça 2125
suicídio 2092
sujeira 615
sujeito 2078
sujo 616
sul 2006
suor 1564
superfície 2111
superior 2103, 2294
súplica 1599
supor 142, 2107
suportar 704
suprimir 2108
surdo 555
surgir 120
surpreender 2114
surpresa 2113
suspeita 2118
suspeitar 2117
sussurrar 2377

T

taça 534
talento 2132
talvez 1553
tamanho 1966
também 72
tambor 662
tanque 1617
tarde 45
tarde, mais 1184
tardio 1183
tarefa 2138
táxi 2141
teatro 2170
teimoso 2074
telefone 2150
telegrama 2149
televisão 2151
telhado 1834
tema 2174
temperatura 2153
tempestade 2058
tempo 2356
tempo (hora) 2207
temporário 2154
tenda 2160
tendência 2157
tênis 2159
tenro 2158
tensão 2067
tentação 2155
tentar 149, 2259
teoria 2177
ter 998
terça-feira 2260
termômetro 2180
terno 2093
terra 677, 967, 1179, 1991
terremoto 678
terrível 169, 654, 2161
terror 2162
tesoura 1880
tesoureiro 2247
tesouro 2246
testemunha 2403
testemunho 2165
teu 2439
tia 156
tijela 277
tijolo 292
tímido 195, 1946, 2208
tinta 1093, 1513
tio 2273
título 2211
toalete 2215
toalha 2229
tocar 1824, 2228
tôda parte, por 738
todavia 2435
tôdo 64
todos 736
tolerar 2216
tolice 850
tolo 849
tomar 2131
tomate 2217
tonelada 2219
tópico 2225
tôpo 2224
torcer 2268
tornado 2226
tornar-se 209
tôrre 2230
torta 1575
tosse 509
total 2227
touro 307
trabalhador 2413
trabalhar 2412
trabalho 1141, 1172, 2411
tradição 2235
traduzir 2241
tráfego 2236
tragédia 2237
trair 235
transferir 2240
transportar 2242
transporte 2243
trás, para 176
trator 2233
travêsso 1389
trazer 298, 2354
treinamento 2239
trem 2238
trepar 420
três 2196
treze 2189
triângulo 2249
tribunal 514
trigo 2368
trilha 1534
trinta 2190
triste 1850
triunfo 2251
trivial 2252
trocar 749
trovão 2200
tu 2437
tubo 1584
tudo 737
Turquia 2261

U

uísque 2376
último 1182
um 1474
um ou outro 690
um outro 95
uma vez 1473
úmido 547, 1338
união 2280
União Soviética 2009
unidade 2281
unido 2283
uniforme 2278, 2279
unir 2282
universal 2287
universidade 2288
urgente 2296
Uruguai 2297
usar 2299
usual 2301
útil 2300
uvas 954

V

vaca 517
vago 2302, 2304
vaguear 2338
vaidade 463
vale 2307
válido 2306
valioso 2308
valor 2419
valor, sem 2420
vantagem 36
vão, em 2305
vapor 2048
vários 1919, 2310
vazar 1194
vazio 701
veado 568
vela 337
velho 1469
velocidade 2020
vencer 1505
venda 1856
vendedor 1857
vender 1902
veneno 1610
Venezuela 2312
vento 2391
ver 1895
verão 2097
verbo 2313
verdade 2258
verdadeiro 918, 2256
verde 964
vergonha 1926
verificação 385
verificar 386
verme 2415
vermelho 1752
vertiginoso 641
vestir-se 656

А

Б

В

Е

Ж

З

зеркало 1329
зерно 946
зима 2395
злой 740, 2384
змея 1982
знак 1949
знать 1170
значение 1289, 1950
значить 1288
золото 938
зонтик 2272
зоопарк 2446
зрелый 1825
зуб 2223
зубной врач 583
зубы 2148
зябкий 398

И

и 87
иголка 1398
игра 908
играть 1598
играть в азартные игры 907
игрушка 2232
идея 1062
идти 934, 2336
из 1503
избегать 164
избирать 691
известность 782
извинять 752
извиняться 104
изгиб 540
изготавливать 1272
издавать 1697
излечивать 535
измерять 1290
изменять 378
изобилие 1604
изобретать 1118
Израиль 1127
изумительный 1279
изумлять 75
изучать 2076
Иисус 1138
или 1486
им (он) 1024
им (они) 2173
иметь 998
ими 2173
имущество 1687
имя 1379
имя существительное 1437
Индия 1084
инженер 707
иногда 1997
иностранный 857
институт 1102
инструмент 1104, 2222
интенсивность 1109
интервал 1115
интерес 1110
информация 1089
информировать 1088
инъекция 1091
Иран 1122
Ирландия 1123
исключать 751, 759
искра 2014
искренний 874, 1957
искусственный 131
искусство 129
искушение 2155
Испания 2013
исполнение 1552
испорченный 2026
исповедовать 473
исправлять 506, 1302
испуг 884
испуганный 42
исследование 1794
исследовать 767
история 1026
истощать 754
исчезать 618, 2309
Италия 1129
итог 2227
иудаизм 1147
их 2172, 2173
июль 1150
июнь 1152

К

к 2212
каждый 671, 735
казаться 1897
казначей 2247
как 133, 1044
календарь 326
Канада 334
кандидат 336
каникулы 2303
капиталист 343
капитан 344
капуста 323
карандаш 1544
карета скорой помощи 78
карман 1607
карманный фонарь 834
карнавал 351
карта 347, 1274
картина 1574
картофель 1633
каталог 356
катить 1832
католик 358
качать 2124
качество 1709
кашель 509
квадрат 2033
квалификация 1967
квартира 103
квитанция 1743
кепка 339
килограмм 1158
километр 1159
кино 1364
кипеть 263
кирпич 292
кислый 2005
Китай 401
кладбище 364
кланяться 276
класс 415, 416
класть 587, 1588, 1707
клей 933
клуб 426
ключ 1155
клясться 2120
клятва 1445
книга 267
когда 2370
когда бы ни 2371
кожа 1197, 1968
козёл 936
колбаса 1866
колебаться 1019
колесо 2369
количество 82, 1710
колледж 438
колокол 222
кольцо 1823
команда 446, 2145
комитет 448
коммунизм 451
комната 1835
компетентный 457
компьютер 462
комфорт 445
конверт 717
конгресс 478
конец 703
конечно 2110
конкретный 2018
конкурировать 456
конституция 486
контакт 488
континент 492
контора 1465
контроль 496
конференция 472
конфета 338
кончать 823
копаться 608
копия 503
корабль 1935
корень 1836
Корея 1171
корзина 197
коричневый 301
корка 1541
королева 1713
королевство 1163
король 1162
коробка 278
корова 517
короткий 1941
космический корабль 2012
космонавт 144
кость 266
костюм 2093
который 2374
кофе 431
кошка 355
кража 2171
красивый 207, 985
краска 1513
краснеть 259
красный 1752
красть 2047

краткий 296
крещение 188
кривой 527
критика 526
кричать 1885, 1943
кровать 210
кровь 255
кролик 1719
кроме 232, 748
кроме того 1349
круг 410
круглый 1839
крыло 2394
крыса 1727
крыша 1834
крюк 1036
кто 2380
кто-нибудь 99
кто-то 1995
Куба 533
куда 2372
куда-нибудь 101
кузен 515
кукла 645
кукуруза 504
курить 1980
курица 393
курс 513
кусать 247
кусок 1576
куст 315
кухня 1165
куча 1579

Л

лагерь 331
лгун 1211
лев 1224
левый 1200
лёгкий 680
лёд 1060
лекарство 1294
лекция 1199
лента 2136
лень 1190
лес 858
лестница 1174, 2036
летать 844
лето 2097
ли 2373
лимон 1204
линия 1223
лиса 870
лист 1193
литр 1230
лить 1635
лифт 694
лицензия 1214
лицо 772
личность 1563
личный 1562
лишать 588
ловить 357
ловить рыбу 828
логика 1237
лодка 261
ложиться 1216
ложка 2027
ложный 781
ложь 1215
ломать 286
лопата 1944
лошадь 1038
лук 1475
луна 1347
луч 1730
лучше 236
лучший 233
лысый 182
льстить 836
любимый 797
любить 1221, 1246
любить, не 628
любоваться 33
любопытный 536
люди 1548
лягушка 885

М

магазин 2057
магия 1257
магнитофон 2137
май 1284
маленький 1976
мальчик 280
манера 1270
марка 2037
маркировать 1276
март 1275
масло 319, 1468
масштаб 1870
математика 1282
мать 1352
махать 2348
машина 346, 1253
машины 1254
мебель 902
медаль 1293
медленный 1974
медсестра 1443
между 237
международный 1112
Мексика 1315
мел 374
мелкий 1925
мелькать 833
мельница 1322
меньший 1205
меня 1286
мёртвый 554
место 1587, 1891
местожительство 1798
местонахождение 1234
месяц 1344
металл 1311
метод 1314
метр 1313
мех 901
механик 1292
мешок 178
миллиард 242
миллион 1323
милосердие 1306
милость 796
милый 1416
миля 1319
минус 1326
минута 1327
мир 1539, 2414
мне 1286
мнение 1481
много 1244, 1273, 1365
многочисленный 1442
мной 1286
могила 957
могущественный 1318
мода 789
модель 1336
может быть 1553
мозг 281
мой 1325, 1374
мокрый 2366
молиться 1641
молния 1219
молодой 2438
молодость 2441
молоко 1321
молоток 982
молоть 966
молчание 1951
момент 1339
монета 432
монотонный 1343
море 1887
мороженое 1061
мороз 888
моряк 1853
мост 295
мотив 1355
мотивировать 1354
мотор 1356
мотоцикл 1357
мочь 333, 1285
мрак 930
мудрость 2398
муж 1058
мужество 512
мужчина 1266
музей 1369
музыка 1371
мука 841
мы 2351
мыло 1985
мысль 2192
мыть 2343
мышь 1360
мягкий 916, 1990
мясо 1291
мяч 183

Н

на 145, 1077, 1116, 1472, 2212
наблюдать 1452, 2346
наверх 2293
наводнение 839
навсегда 859
нагибать 227
награда 166, 1814
над 6, 1504
надежда 1037
надоедать 273
нажимать 1653
назад 176
назначать 110

О

Р

Т

A

a 145, 2212
a menos que 2290
a veces 1997
abajo 224, 651
abandonar 1, 1717
abeja 212
abogado 1188
abolir 4
abrazar 698
abreviar 2
abrigo 430
abril 116
abrir 1478
absurdo 9
abuela 951
abuelo 950
abundancia 1604
aburrido 269
acabar 823
accidente 11
acción 24
aceite 1468
acentuar 699
aceptar 10
acercarse 113
acero 2049
acompañar 12
aconsejar 40
acontecimiento 734, 1459
acordarse 1777
acostarse 1216
acostumbrar 18
actitud 151
actividad 26
activo 25
actor 27
actriz 28
actual 1650
acumular 15
acusar 17
adelante 866
adelante, para 1477
además 232, 1349
adiós 941
administración 32, 1268
admirar 33
admitir 34
adquirir 21
advertencia 361
advertir 2342
aeropuerto 57
afectar 41
afeitar(se) 1930
afilado 1929
aflicción 965, 2001
afortunado 1249
África 43
África del Sur 2007
agarrar 1898
agosto 155
agotar 754
agradable 1600
agradar 1602
agradecido 956
agricultura 51
agrio 2005
agua 2347
aguantar 704
aguja 1398
agujero 1029
ahogar 404, 660
ahora 1440
aire 55
ajedrez 390
ala 2394
alabar 1640
alambre 2397
alarma 59
Albania 60
alcanzar 1732
alcoba 211
aldea 2318
alegre 387, 927, 1309
alegría 1146
Alemania 920
alertar 61
alfabeto 70
alfiler 1582
algodón 508
alguien 1995
algún 1994
alguna cosa 1996
aliado 66
aliento 289
alimentar 802
alivio 1771
alma 2002
almuerzo 610, 1252
alquilar 1781
alrededor de 124
altivo 997
alto 1021, 2134
altura 1010
allí 2178
amar 1246
amargo 248
amarillo 2432
ambición 77
ambiente 719
ambos 272
ambulancia 78
amenaza 2195
América 79
América del Norte 1430
América del Sur 2008
americano 80
amigo 882
amistoso 883
ampliar 757
analizar 84
anaranjado 1488
añadir 30
ancho 299, 2385
andar 2336
ángel 87
anillo 1823
animal 90
animar 702
año 2430
ansiedad 97
anteojos 771
antepasado 85
anteriormente 864
antes 215
antiguo 86
anual 94
anualmente 2431
anunciar 91
anuncio 38
aparecer 106
aparentemente 105
apartamento 103
aparte 102
aplaudir 107
aplazar 1630
aplicar 109
apoyo 2106
apreciar 112
aprender 1195
aprender de memoria 1300
apresurarse 1056
aprobar 114
aproximadamente 115
apuesta 234
apuntar 54
aquél 2169
aquí 1016
araña 2023
arañar 1884
arar 1605
árbol 2248
arbusto 315
arena 1861
Argentina 118
armamento 122
arte 129
artículo 130
artificial 131
artista 132
arrastrar 652
arrastrarse 521
arrestar 127
arrodillarse 1166
arrojar 2199
arroz 1815
ascensor 694
aseado 1394
asemejarse a 1795
asesinato 1368
así 2202
Asia 135
asiento 1891
asociar 141
asombrar 75, 143
áspero 1838
aspirar 138
astronauta 144
astronave 2012
astuto 1975
asustar 1873
ataque 148
atar 2206
atención 150
atleta 146
atractivo 153
atraer 152
atrevido 264
audiencia 154
aula 416
aumentar 1081
ausencia 8
Australia 157
Austria 158
autobús 314
autor 159
autoridad 160

avanzar 35
avenida 162
aventura 37
avergonzado 134
avergonzar 697
ávido 672
avión 56
avión a reacción 1139
ayer 2434
ayuda 53
ayudar 140, 1014
azúcar 2090
azul 258

B

bailar 548
bajo 1247, 2274
bala 308
balanza 1871
baloncesto 198
banana 184
banco 186, 226
bandera 831
baño 199
banquete 187
barato 383
barba 205
barbero 189
barbilla 400
barco 261, 1935
barril 192
base 193, 196
bastante 712
batalla 200
batir 206
baúl 2257
bautismo 188
baya 230
bebé 172
beber 657
béisbol 194
Bélgica 220
bello 207
beneficio 229
berza 323
besar 1164
Biblia 239
biblioteca 1213
bicicleta 240
bien 2364
bienvenido 2363
bigote 1361
blanco 2379
blando 1990
bloque 254
boca 1362
boda 2357
boletín 309
boleto 2203
Bolivia 265
bolsa 178, 1704
bolsillo 1607
bomba 1700
bombón 338
bondadosa 1160
bonito 1656
borracho 663
borrar 722
bosque 858
bostezar 2429
bota 268
botella 274
botón 321
boxeo 279
Brasil 284
brazo 121
breve 296
brillante 297
brillar 1934
brisa 290
bucear 638
bueno 940
buenos días 1013
Bulgaria 306
burro 647
buscar 1889

C

caballero 917
caballo 1038
cabeza 1001
cabra 936
cada 671, 735
cadena 371
caer 780
café 431
caja 278
calcetín 1989
calcular 325
calendario 326
calidad 1709
caliente 1040
calmado 329
calor 1007
calvo 182
calle 2065
cama 210
cámara fotográfica 330
camarero 2335
cambiar 378, 749
camino 1828, 2349
camión 2255
camisa 1936
campamento 331
campana 222
campeón 376
campo 811
Canadá 334
cancelar 335
canción 1999
candidato 336
cansado 2210, 2355
cantar 1958
cantidad 82, 1710
capa 1189
capacidad 341
capacitación 2239
capaz 340
capital 342
capitalista 343
capitán 344
capítulo 379
capturar 345
cara 772
carácter 380
carbón 428
cárcel 1132
carencia 1173
carga 310
carnaval 351
carne 1291
carne de res 213
caro 761
carpintero 352
carta 1208
carrera 1720
carreta 354
carretera 1022
carro 2332
casa 1033, 1043
cáscara 1541
casi 67, 1393
castaño 301
castigar 1701
castigo 1543
catálogo 356
católico 358
catorce 869
causa 1740
causar 360
cavar 608
caza 1055
cebolla 1475
ceder 2436
celebrar 363
celo 2444
celoso 1137
cementerio 364
cena 2104
centavo 365, 1547
centímetro 367
centro 366
cepillo 302
cerca 806, 1392
cercar 2116
cerebro 281
cereza 389
cero 2445
certificado 370
cerveza 214
cerradura 1235
cerrar 422
cesar 362
césped 955
cesto 197
ciego 253
cielo 1008
ciencia 1879
ciento 1052
ciento, por 1550
cierto 369
ciervo 568
cigarrillo 409
cima 1540, 2224
cinco 829
cincuenta 814
cine 1364
cinta 2136
cintura 2333
cinturón 225
circo 411
círculo 410
cirugía 2112
cita 111, 1718
ciudad 413, 2231
ciudadano 412

civil 414
claro 418
clase 415
clavo 1377
cliente 542
club 426
cobarde 518
cocer al horno 180
cocina 1165
cocinar 500
coche 346
codicioso 963
coger 357
cohete 1831
coincidir 433
cojo 1178
cola 933, 2130
colgar 986
colina 1023
colocar 1588
color 440
color rosa 1583
collar 436
combate 442
combinar 443
combustible 894
comenzar 217
comer 681
comerciante 1305
comercio 2234
cómico 900
comida 848, 1287
comité 448
como 133
cómo 1044
comodidad 445
compañía 453
comparar 454
compasión 1586, 2127
compeler 455
competente 457
competir 456
completar 459
complicar 460
componer 461
comportamiento 218
comprar 322
computadora 462
común 449
comunicación 450
comunidad 452
comunismo 451
con 2400
concebir 464
conceder 953
concentrar 465
concepto 466
conciencia 481
conclusión 468
condenar 469
condición 470
conducir 471, 658
conejo 1719
conexión 479
conferencia 472, 1199
confesar 473
confidencia 474
confirmación 475
confusión 476
congelado 890
congelar 877
congreso 478
conjetura 972
conquistar 480
consciente 482
consciente de 167
consecuencia 483
consejo 39
considerar 484
constante 485
constitución 486
construir 304, 487
contacto 488
contador 1312
contar 510
contar con 1773
contenido 491
contentar 490
continente 492
continuar 493
contra 47
contradecir 494
contribuir 495
control 496
convencer 499
conveniente 497
convenir 50
convergir 1307
conversación 498
convocar 2098
cooperar 502
copia 503
corazón 1006
corbata 2205
Corea 1171
corona 530
cortar 543
cortés 1615
cortina 539
corto 1941
correcto 1820
corregir 506
correo 1260
correos, casa de 1631
correr 1846
corriente 538, 2064
cosa 2186
cosecha 993
coser 1921
costa 429
costo 507
costumbre 541
crear 524
crecer 969
creencia 221
crepúsculo 2266
criada 1259
criado 1913
crimen 525
cristiano 406
crítica 526
crudo 1729
cruel 531
cruzar 528
cuadrado 2033
cuadro 1574
cual 2374
cualquier 98
cualquier cosa 100
cualquiera 99
cualquiera de los dos 690
cuando 2370
cuánto 1046
cuarenta 865
cuarto 1712, 1835
cuatro 868
Cuba 533
cubrir 516
cuchara 2027
cuchillo 1167
cuello 1396
cuenta 14
cuento 2060
cuerda 2071
cuero 1197
cuerpo 262
cuidado 348
cuidadoso 349
culebra 1982
culpa 795
culpable 975
culpar 251
cumpleaños 246
curar 535
curioso 536
curso 513
curva 540

Ch

charlar 382
Checoslovaquia 544
Chile 397
chimenea 399
China 401
chismes 943
chispa 2014
chiste 1143
chocar 439
chocolate 402
choque 520, 1937, 2423

D

daño 546, 992
dar 926
dar una patada 1156
de 886
de nada 2440
de buena gana 2389
debajo 228
deber 670, 1372, 1506
debido 666
débil 801, 2352
decepcionar 619
decidir 562
decir 1869, 2152
declaración 2043
declarar 563, 2042
decorar 564
dedo 822
defender 570
deficiencia 571
definir 572
dejar 1207
dejar caer 659
delante 52
deleite 577

deletrear 2021
delgado 2185
delicado 575
delicioso 576
democracia 580
demostrar 581
dentista 583
dentro 1096, 2401
dentro de 1116
departamento 585
depender 586
deporte 2028
depositar 587
derecha 1821
derecho (el) 1822
derecho 2062
derretir 1298
derrotar 569
desafío 375
desagradar 628
desanimar 621
desaparecer 618
desarrollar 599
desarrollo 600
desayuno 287
descansar 1805
descender 589
descendiente 590
descontento 633
describir 591
descubrir 622
descuidado 350
desempleo 2277
deseo 593, 2399
desfile 1521
desgracia 1330
deshonesto 627
deslizar 1972
desmayarse 776
desnudarse 2276
desnudo 190, 1378
desobedecer 630
desorden 631
despedida 785
despedir 629
despertar 165
desplomarse 435
despreciar 594
desprecio 489
después 44
destellar 833
desteñirse 774
destino 793
destruir 596
desvanecerse 2309
desviar 601
detectar 597
determinar 598
detrás de 219
deuda 558
devolver 1810
día 553
día festivo 1030
diablo 602
diamante 603
diario 545
dibujar 653
diccionario 604
diciembre 561
diecinueve 1420
dieciocho 688
dieciséis 1964
diecisiete 1917
diente 2223
dientes 2148
diez 2156
diferencia 606
difícil 607
diligencia 609
Dinamarca 582
dinero 1341
Dios 937
diploma 611
dirección 31, 613
director 614
dirigir 612
disciplina 620
discordar 617
disculparse 104
discúlpeme 1523
discurso 2019
discutir 623
disgusto 625
disminuir 565
disolver 634
disparar 1939
disponer 126
disputar 119, 1711
distancia 635
distribuir 636
diversión 896
divertido 83
dividir 639
divorcio 640
doblar 227, 846
doble 649
doce 2263
dólar 646
doler 1057
dolor 19, 1512
dolor de cabeza 1002
domesticado 2135
domingo 2100
donde 2372
donde, a 2372
dondequiera 101
dormido 137
dormir 1970
dos 2269
dos veces 2265
duda 650
dulce 2122
durante 669
duro 991

E

edad 48
edificio 305
educación 682
efecto 683
Egipto 686
egoísta 1901
ejemplo 745
ejercicio 753
ejército 123
él 1000, 1024
él mismo 1025
eléctrico 692
elefante 693
elegir 691
eliminar 696
ella 1015, 1931
ella misma 1018
ello 1128
ellos 2182
ellos mismos 2175
embajador 76
embotado 667
embromar 2147
empleo 700
empujar 1706
en 145, 1077
en vez de 1101
encomendar 447
encontrar 820
encontrarse con 1295
enemigo 705
enero 1134
enfermedad 624, 1067
enfermera 1443
enfermo 1947
engaño 560
enigma 1708
enjugar 2396
enojado 89
enojo 88
enorme 711, 1047
ensalada 1854
enseñar 2143
entender 2275
entender mal 1334
enteramente 73
entero 715, 2381
enterrar 313
entonces 2176
entrada 716
entrar 713
entre 81, 237
entregar 578
entusiasmo 714
enviar 1903
envidioso 718
envolver 1121, 2422
equilibrio 181
equipaje 179, 1250
equipo 721, 2145
errar 1331
erróneo 2427
error 723, 1333
esbelto 1971
escala 1870
escalera 1174, 2036
escapar 724
escarcha 888
escaso 1726, 1872
escena 1875
escenario 2035
Escocia 1883
escoger 405
esconder 1020
escribir 2425
escritor 2426
escuchar 1229
escuela 1878
escultura 1886
esencial 726
esfuerzo 684

espacio 2011
espada 2126
espalda 174
España 2013
esparcir 1874
especial 2016
especialidad 2017
especialmente 725
específico 2018
espejo 1329
esperanza 1037
esperar 758, 2334
espeso 2183
espía 2032
espíritu 2024
espléndido 2025
esposa 2387
esposo 1058
esquema 1877
esquina 505
establecer 727
establo 191
estación 1890, 2044
estacionar 1526
estadística 2045
estado 2041
Estados Unidos 2286
estafar 384
estampilla 2037
estanque 1617
estante 1933
estar 201
estatua 2046
este (el) 679
este 2191
estimación 728
estirar 2068
estómago 2055
estornudar 1983
estos 2181
estrecho 1382
estrella 2039
estricto 2069
estropeado 2026
estudiante 2075
estudiar 2076
estufa 2061
estúpido 668, 2077
Etiopía 729
Europa 730
evaluar 731
evitar 164
exacto 16, 741
exagerar 742
examen 743, 2163
examinar 744
exceder 746
excelente 747
excepto 748
excitar 125, 750
excluir 751
excusar 752
exhibir 632
exigencia 579, 1792
existir 755
éxito 2086
experiencia 762
experimento 763
experto 764
explicar 765
explorar 767
explotar 766
expresión 768
exprimir 2034
expulsar 759
extender 769, 2030
extranjero 857
extranjero, al 7
extraño 2063

F

fábrica 773
fabricar 1272
fácil 680
falso 781
fama 782
familia 783
fantasma 922
fastidiar 93
favor 796
favor, por 1601
favorito 797
fe 778
febrero 799
fecha 551
felicidad 988
felicitar 477
feliz 989
feo 2271
feroz 812
ferrocarril 1722
ficción 810
fiebre 808
fiel 779
fiesta 807
figura 816
fijar 791, 830
fila 1840
Filipinas 1567
filosofía 1568
fin 703
final 819
fingir 1655
Finlandia 824
fino 821
firmamento 1969
física 1572
físico 1570
flor 256, 843
flotar 838
fluir 842
fondo 175, 275
fondos 898
forma 863, 1927
forzar 856
fósforo 1281
fotografía 1569
fracasar 775
fragante 871
francés 878
Francia 873
franco 874
frasco 1136
frase 1907
frecuente 879
frecuentemente 1467
freír 893
frente 887
fresco 398, 501, 880
frijol 203
frío 434
frotar 1841
fruncir 889
frustración 892
fruta 891
fuego 825
fuera 1503
fuerte 2072
fuerza aérea 58
fuerza 2066
fumar 1980
función 897
fundamento 867
funeral 899
fusil 976
fútbol 1986
fútbol americano 853
futuro 904

G

galón 906
ganado 359
ganancia 1676
ganar 675, 905, 2390
gancho 1036
ganso 942
garantizar 970
garganta 2197
gas 910
gasolina 911
gastar 2022
gasto 760
gato 355
gemelo 2267
generación 914
género 1161
generoso 915
gente 1548
genuino 918
geografía 919
gerente 1269
gigante 923
girar 2262
globo 929
gloria 931
gobierno 944
golf 939
golpear 1027, 1168
goma 1842
gordo 792
gorra 339
gotear 1194
gozar 710
grabadora 2137
gracias 2168
grado 573
graduado 945
gramática 947
Gran Bretaña 961
grande 241, 960, 1181
grandioso 948
granizo 978
granja 786
granjero 787
grano 946
grasa 959

nariz 1432
narrar 1381
nata 523
nativo 1386
natural 1387
naturaleza 1388
náusea 1390
navaja de afeitar 1731
navegación 1852
Navidad 407
necesario 1395
necesidad 1397
negar 584
negativo 1399
negligencia 1400
negociación 1401
negocio 316
negro 249
nervioso 1405
neumático 2209
neutral 1408
nido 1406
niebla 845
nieta 949
nieto 952
nieve 1984
ninguno 1425
niño 395
niños 396
nivel 1210
no 1422, 1433
noche 1418
noche, esta 2221
nombrar 110
nombre 1379
norma 1613
normal 1428
norte 1429
Noruega 1431
nosotros mismos 1502
nosotros 2298, 2351
nota 1434
noticias 1412
notificar 1436
novedad 1438
noventa 1421
novia 293
noviembre 1439
novio 294
nube 425
nudo 1169
nuestro 1501
Nueva Zelanda 1414
nueve 1419
nuevo 1411
nuez 1444
número 1441
numeroso 1442
nunca 1409

O

o 1486
obediencia 1446
objeción 1448
objetivo 1449
objeto 1447
obligación 1450
obra teatral 1597
obrar 23
obscuridad 930
obscuro 550, 1451
observación 1776
observar 1452, 2346
obstáculo 1453
obstante, no 1410
obstinado 2074
obtener 921, 1454
obvio 1455
ocasión 1456
ocasional 1457
océano 1460
ocio 1203
ocioso 1063
octubre 1461
ocupación 1458
ocupado 317
ochenta 689
ocho 687
odiar 996
oeste 2365
ofender 1463
oficial 1466
oficina 1465
ofrecer 1464
oído 1005
oír 1004
ojo 770
oler 1977
olor 1462, 1876
olvidar 860
olla 1632
omisión 1471
once 695
onza 1500
operación 1480
operar 1479
opinión 1481
oponer 1483
oportunidad 377, 1482
oprimir 1485
opuesto 1484
oral 1487
órbita 1490
orden 446, 1492, 1493
ordinario 1494
oreja 673
organización 1495
orgullo 1660
orgulloso 1692
orientación 1496
origen 1497
original 1498
orilla 1940
oro 938
orquesta 1491
oscilar 2124
otoño 161
otra vez 46
otro 95, 1499
oveja 1932

P

paciencia 1535
paciente 1536
padre 794
padres 1524
pagar 1538
página 1511
país 511
Países Bajos 1407
pájaro 244
pala 1944
palabra 2410
palacio 1516
pálido 1517
palo 2051
paloma 1578
pan 285
paño 423
panqueque 1518
pantalones 1519, 2254
pañuelo 984
papel 1520
paquete 1510
par 1515
para 854
paraguas 2272
paralelo 1522
parar 2056
parecer 1897
pared 2337
pariente 1768
parque 1525
parte 1527
participación 1928
participar 1528
partido 1529
partir 1198
pasado 1533
pasajero 1531
pasaporte 1532
pasar 1530
pasear en coche 1817
paso 2050
pastel 1575
patata 1633
patio 2428
pato 665
pausa 1537
paz 1539
pecado 1956
pecho 391
pedir 216
pedir prestado 271
peine 441
película 818
peligro 549
pelo 979
pelota 183
penetrar 1545
península 1546
pensamiento 2192
pensar 2187
peor 2417
peor, lo 2418
pequeño 1976
perder 1243
perdonar 861
perecer 1556
pereza 1190
perfecto 1551
periódico 1413
periodista 1144
período 1555
permanecer 1774
permanente 1557

Q

R

A

absurd 9
acceptera 10
ackumulera 15
aderton 688
adjö 941
administration 32
adress 31
advokat 1188
affärer 316
Afrika 43
aktiv 25
aktivitet 26
aktning 1803
akå 1817
alarm 59
alarmera 61
Albanien 60
aldrig 1409
alfabet 70
all 64
alla 736
allmän 449
alltid 74
alltid, för 859
allting 737
allvarlig 676
ambassadör 76
ambition 77
ambulans 78
Amerika 79
amerikansk 80
analysera 84
anda 289
ande 2024
anfall 148
anförtro 447
angenäm 1600
anka 665
anklaga 17
ankomst 128
anmärkning 1776
annan 1499
annan, en 95
annons 38
annullera 335
ansikte 772
ansträngning 684
anställning 700
ansvar 1804
antaga 142
anteckna 1749
anteckning 1434
använda 2299
användbar 2300
apa 1342
apelsin 1489
apelsin-färgard 1488
applådera 107
april 116
arbeta 2412
arbetare 2413
arbete 1172, 2411
arbetslöshet 2277
Argentina 118
arm 121
armé 123
arrestera 127
artig 1615
artikel 130
arv 1090
Asien 135
ask 278
associera 141
astronaut 144
atlet 146
augusti 155
Australien 157
autoritet 160
avbryta 1114
avdelning 585
aveny 162
avfatta 464
avgå 1799
avkomling 590
avlägsen 1779
avlägsna 1780
avlägsnare 903
avresa 1198
avsikt 1703
avskaffa 4
avskild 1909
avskildhet 1667
avskilja 1910
avskräcka 621
avsluta 823
avslå 1766
avsmak 625
avstånd 635
avtalat möte 111
avundsjuk 718
avvika 601
axel 1942

B

baby 172
backe 1023
bad 199
bagage 179, 1250
bagatelle 2252
baka 180
bakgrund 175
bakom 219
baksides 1739
bakåt 176
banan 184
band 2136, 2204
bank 186
bankett 187
barmhärtighet 1306
barn 395, 396
bas 193
baseboll 194
basis 196
basketboll 198
be om ursäkt 104
bedja 1641
bedrägeri 560
bedrövelse 965
befallning 446, 1492
befolkning 1621
befordra 1683
befria 875
begrava 313
begravning 899
begrepp 466
begära 216
begäran 1791
behaga 1602
behov 1397
beklaga 1761
beklaga sig 458
bekräftelse 475
bekväm 497
bekymmer 348, 467
bekänna 473
Belgien 220
belopp 82
belåten 490
belöning 1814
ben 266, 1201
bensin 911
beredd 1735
berg 1358
bergolja 1468
beroende, vara 586
berusad 663
beräkna 325
beräkning 728
berätta 1381
berömmelse 782
beröra 2228
beröva 588
besegra 569
beskriva 591
beströ 1874
bestämma 562, 598
beständig 485
besvika 619
besvär 2253
besvära 273
besöka 2322
betala 1538
betjänt 1913
betona 699
betyda 1288
betydelse 1905, 1950
betäcka 516
beundra 33
bevilja 953
bevis 739, 1685
bi 212
Bibel 239
bibliotek 1213
bidraga 495
bil 346
bild 1068
biljett 2203
billig 383
binda 243, 2206
bio 1364
bita 247
bitter 248
bland 81
blanda 1335
blek 1517
bli 209
bli efter 1176
blind 253
blixt 1219
blixtra 833
block 254
blod 255
blomma 256, 843
blyertspenna 1544
blyg 195, 1946, 2208
blå 258
blåsa 257

bläck 1093
bo 1406
bok 267
Bolivia 265
boll 183
bomull 508
bord 2129
borgare 412
borste 302
bort 168
bortom 238
boskap 359
bostad 1798
botten 275
boxning 279
bra 2364
Brasilien 284
bred 299
bredvid 231
brev 1208
bris 290
brist 1173
brista 312
bristfällighet 571
bro 295
broder 300
brorsdotter 1417
brorson 1404
brost 391
brott 525
brottning 2424
brud 293
brudgum 294
brun 301
bryta 286
brådskande 2296
bränna 311
bränsle 894
bröd 285
bröllop 2357
bröst 288
buga 276
Bulgarien 306
bulletin 309
bundsförvant 66
burk 332
buske 315
buss 314
by 2318
bygga 304
byggnad 305
byxor 1519, 2254
båda 272
båt 261
bälte 225
bänk 226
bär 230
bära 204, 353, 2354
bäst 233
bättre 236
böja 227
böna 203
börda 310
börja 217

C

cent 365
center 366
centimeter 367
certifikat 370
chef 394
Chile 397
chock 1937
choklad 402
cigarrett 409
cirkel 410
cirkus 411
citat 1718
citron 1204
college 438
cykel 240

D

dag 553
dag, i 2213
daglig 545
dal 2307
dam 1175
damm 1617
Danmark 582
dansa 548
data-maskin 462
datum 551
de 2182
december 561
definiera 572
dekorera 564
del 1527, 1928
dela 639
deltaga 1528
dem 2173
demokrati 580
demonstrera 581
den 1128, 2169
deponera 587
deras 2172
dessa 2181
dessutom 232, 1349
det 1128
detta 2191
diamant 603
dikt 1608
dimma 845
din 2439
diplom 611
direktör 614, 1269
disciplin 620
diskutera 623
djup 567
djur 91
djurpark 2446
djärv 264
djävul 602
docka 645
doftande 871
doktor 643
dollar 646
dom 1908
domstol 514
dop 188
dotter 552
dotterdotter 949
dotterson 952
draga 1698
dricka 657
driva ut 759
drottning 1713
drunkna 660
dröm 655
du 2437
dubbel 649
duglig 340
dum 668, 2077
dumheter 1426
duva 1578
dyka 638
dyr 761
dyrbar 1642
dysterhet 930
då 2176
dålig 177
dåre 849
däck 2209
där 2178
därför 2179
därför att 208
dö 605
död 554, 557
döda 1157
döma 1148
dörr 648
döv 555

E

ed 1445
effekt 683
efter 44
eftermiddag 45
egen 1507
egendom 1687
egentlig 1686
Egypten 686
eld 825
elefant 693
elektriskt 692
elementarbok 1271
eliminera 696
eller 1486
elva 695
emellertid 1045
emot 47
en 1474
en annan 95
en gång 1473
endast 1476
endera 690
engelsk 709
England 708
enhet 2281
enkel 1954
enorm 711
ensam 68, 1238, 1239
enskild 1919
entusiasm 714
er 2439
erbjuda 1464
erfarenhet 762
erhålla 1454
erkänna 1747
ersätta 1785, 2084
erövra 480
etablera 727
Etiopien 729
Europa 730
evaluera 731

exakt 741
examen 743
exempel 745
exercis 753
existera 755
experiment 763
expert 764
explodera 766

F

fabrik 773
fader 794
faktisk 29
falla 659, 780
falsk 781
familj 783
fara 549
farbror 2273
farfar 950
farmor 951
farväl 785
fast 1993
fat 626
fattig 1619
fattigdom 1636
favorit 797
feber 808
februari 799
feg 518
fel 723
fem 829
femtio 814
femton 813
festival 807
fet 792
fett 959
ficka 1607
ficklampa 834
fiende 705
figur 816
Filippinerna 1567
film 818
filosofi 1568
filt 252
fin 575, 821
finansmästare 2247
finger 822
Finland 824
finna 820
fira 363
fisk 827
fiska 828
fjorton 869
fjäril 320
flagga 831
flaska 274
flicka 925
flintskalllig 182
flit 609
flod 839, 1827
fly 724, 837
flyga 844
flygplan 56
flygplats 57
flygvapen 58
flyta 838, 842
fläck 2029
folk 1548
folkmassa 529
fonder 898
form 1927
forma 863
forntids 86
forskning 1794
fortsätta 493
fot 851, 852
fotboll 853
fotboll 1986
fotografi 1569
framhärda 1560
framlägga 2079
framsida 887
framsteg 1678
framstående 1681
framställa 1674
framtid 904
framträda 106
framtvinga 455
framåt 866, 1477
Frankrike 873
fransk 878
fred 1539
fredag 881
frestelse 2155
frihet 876, 1212
frimärke 2037
frivillig 2329
frost 888
fru 2387
frukost 287
frukt 891
fruktan 798
fruktsanvärd 169
frusen 890
frysa 877
fråga 136, 1714
från 886
frånvaro 8
främmande 2063
frö 1896
fuktig 547, 1338
ful 2271
full 895
fullborda 13
funktion 897
fuska 384
fylla 817
fyra 868
fyrtio 865
fysik 1572
fysisk 1570
få 809, 921
fågel 244
fånga 357
får 1932
fälla 2244
fält 811
fängelse 1132, 1666
färg 440, 1513
färsk 880
fästa 147, 791
född 270
födelse 245
födelsedag 246
följa 12, 847
följande 2081
följd 483
fönster 2392
för 854
för alltid 859
för. . .sedan 49
föra 471
förakt 489
förakta 594
förarga 93
förband 185
förbereda 1646
förbindelse 479
förbjuda 855, 1679
förbättra 1076
fördel 36, 229
fördröja 574
fördöma 469
före 52, 215
föredraga 1645
förefalla 1897
föregående 1658
föreläsning 1199
förena 1142, 2282
förenade 2283
Förenta nationerna 2285
Förenta staterna 2286
föreslå 1688, 2091
föreställning 1552
förfader 85
författare 159
förflutna 1533
förflytta 1530
förfärlig 2161
förfölja 1705
förgäves 2305
förhindra 1657
förklara 765, 2042
förkorta 2
förlora 1243
förlåta 861
förlänga 769
förminska 565
förmoda 2107
förmåga 3
förneka 584
förolämpning 1105
förr 864
förråda 235
förse 1693
försiktig 349
försiktighet 361
förskräcklig 654
förslösa 2344
förstå 826
förströelse 1751
förstå 2275
förstånd 1324
förstånd 1741
förstärka 1765
förstöra 596
förstörd 2026
försummelse 1400
försvar 1599
försvara 570
försvinna 618, 2309
försäkring 1106
försäljare 1857
försäljning 1856
försöka 149, 2259
förtjäna 592
förtjänst 1308

förtroende 474
förutsäga 1644
förvirring 476
förvåna 75, 143
förvänta 758
föräldrar 1524
förändra 378
fötter 804

G

gaffel 862
galen 522
gallon 906
gammal 1469
garantera 970
gardin 539
gas 910
gata 2065
ge 926
ge sig 2115
ge ut 2022
ge vika 2436
gemenskap 452
genast 1072
genera 697
generation 914
generös 915
genom 2198
genomsnittlig 163
genomtränga 1545
geografi 919
get 936
gevär 976, 1819
gift 1610
gilla 114
giltig 2306
girig 963, 2052
gissning 972
glad 387, 927
glas 928
glass 1061
glasögon 771
glida 1972
glob 929
glädje 577, 1146
glänsande 297, 2025
glömma 860
gnida 1841
gnista 2014
god 940
god dag 1013
golf 939
golv 840
grad 573
graduerad 945
grammatik 947
granne 1402
grannskap 1403
gratulera 477
grav 957
Grekland 962
gren 282
gripa 1898
gris 1577
groda 885
grund 967, 1925
grupp 968
grym 531
gryta 1632
grå 958
gråta 532, 2361
grädde 523
gräla 119, 1711
gräla på 1881
gräns 1222
gräs 955
gräva 608
grön 964
grönsaker 2311
Gud 937
gul 2432
guld 938
gummi 1842
gyttja 1366
gå 934, 2336
gå ned 589
går, i 2434
gård 2428
gås 942
gåva 924
gäckande 892
gärna 2389
gärning 566
gäspa 2429
gäst 973
gömma 1020
göra 642, 1265
göra framsteg 35

H

ha 998
hagel 978
haka 400
hall 981
hals 1396
halvö 1546
hammare 982
hamn 990, 1622
han 1000
hand 983
handduk 2229
handel 2234
handla 23
handling 24
handskar 932
handväska 1704
hardnackad 2074
hast 994
hastig 1725
hastighet 2020
hata 996
hatt 995
hav 1887
hel 715, 2381
helgdag 1030
helig 1032
helikopter 1011
helt och hållet 73
helvete 1012
hembiträde 1259
hemlighet 1893
henne 1015
henne själv 1018
herre 917
herrfrisör 189
het 1040
hetta 1007
himmel 1008, 1969
hinder 1453
hiss 694
historia 1026, 2060
hjort 568
hjul 2369
hjälp 53
hjälpa 140, 1014
hjälte 1017
hjärna 281
hjärta 1006
Holland 1031
hon 1931
hona 805
honom 1024
honom själv 1025
honorer 800
hopp 1037
hoppa 1151
hos 145
hosta 509
hot 2195
hotell 1041
hud 1968
humör 1051
hund 644
hundra 1052
hunger 1054
hur 1044
hur mycket 1046
hur många 1046
hus 1033, 1043
huvud 1001
huvud- 1261
huvudbry 1708
huvudsaklig 1663
huvudsakligen 1262
huvudstad 342
huvudvärk 1002
hylla 1933
hyra 1781
hål 1029
hålla 1028, 1154
hållning 151
hår 979
hård 991
hälft 980
hälla 1635
hälsa 1003
hämnd 1812
hända 987
händelse 734, 1459
hänga 986
hänvisa 1754
här 1016
häst 1038
hö 999
hög 1021, 1579, 2134
högdragen 997
höger 1821
höja 1724
höjd 1010
höra 1004
hörn 505
hörsel 1005
höst 161

I

i 145, 1077
i dag 2213
i går 2434
i morgon 2218
i natt 2221
i stället för 1101
iaktta 2346
ibland 1997
icke dess mindre 1410
idé 1062
igen 46
ihärdighet 1559
illamående 1390
ilska 89
imitera 1070
in 1077
in i 1116
inbillning 1069
inbilskhet 463
inbjuda 1120
Indien 1084
inflytande 1087
information 1089
informera 1088
ingen 1423, 1425
ingen orsak 2440
ingenjör 707
ingenting 1435
ingripa 1111
ingäng 716
inhemsk 1386
injektion 1091
inkomst 1080
innehåll 491
insekt 1095
insistera 1097
inskränka 1807
inspektera 1098
inspiration 1099
installera 1100
institut 1102
instruera 1103
instrument 1104
instämma 50
inte 1433
intelligent 1107
intensitet 1109
internationell 1112
intervall 1115
intresse 1110
intryck 1075
inträda 713
inuti 1096, 2401
inveckla 1121
inverka 41
invändning 1448
Iran 1122
Irland 1123
is 1060
Israel 1127
isär 102
Italien 1129
iver 2444
ivrig 672

J

ja 2433
jag 1059
jaga 381
jakt 1055
januari 1134
Japan 1135
Jesus 1138
jet 1139
jobb 1141
jord 677, 1991
jordbruk 51
jordbävning 678
journalist 1144
Judendom 1147
Jugoslavien 2442
Jul 407
juli 1150
juni 1152
just 777
juvel 1140
jämföra 454
jämn 732, 835, 1981
jämvikt 181
järn 1124
järnväg 1722
jätte 923

K

kaffe 431
kaka 324
kalender 326
kall 434
kallelse 2325
kalv 327
kamera 330
kamm 441
kamp 442, 2073
Kanada 334
kandidat 336
kanin 1719
kanske 1553
kapacitet 341
kapitalist 343
kapitel 379
kapplöpning 1720
kapten 344
karaktär 380
karneval 351
karta 1274
kassettbandspelare 2137
kasta 2199
katalog 356
katolik 358
katt 355
kedja 371
kilogram 1158
kilometer 1159
Kina 401
kirurgi 2112
klandra 251
klar 418
klass 415
klassrum 416
klippa 1830
klocka 222, 2345
klubb 426
klumpig 170, 427
klä av sig 2276
klä sig 656
kläder 424
klättra 420
klösa 1884
knacka 1168
knapp 321, 1872
knappnål 1582
kniv 1167
knut 1169
knäböja 1166
ko 517
koffert 2257
koka 263, 500
kol 428
kollapsa 435
kollidera 439
kollision 520
kombinera 443
komfort 445
komma 444
kommitté 448
kommunism 451
kompetent 457
komplettera 459
komplicera 460
koncentrera 465
konfekt 338
konferens 472
kongress 478
konst 129
konstgjord 131
konstitution 486
konstruera 487
kontakt 488
kontinent 492
konto 14
kontor 1465
kontroll 385, 496
kontrollera 386
kontsnär 132
konversation 498
kopia 503
kopp 534
Korea 1171
korg 197
korn 946
korrigera 506
korsa 528
kort 296, 347, 1941
korv 1866
kostym 2093
krage 436
krama ur 2034
krav 579, 1792
krig 2340
kristen 406
krita 374
kritik 526
krok 1036
krokig 527
krona 530
kropp 262
kruka 1136
kräla 521
kränkning 2320
Kuba 533
kula 308
kund 542
kung 1162
kungarike 1163
kunna 333, 1285

kurs 513
kurva 540
kusin 515
kust 429
kuvert 717
kvadrat 2033
kvalitet 1709
kvantitet 1710
kvarn 1322
kvart 1712
kvick 1715
kvinna 2405
kvitto 1743
kväll 733
kvällsmat 2104
kyckling 393
kylig 398
kylskåp 1757
kypare 2335
kyrka 408
kyrkogård 364
kyssa 1164
kål 323
känsla 803
känslig 1906
käpp 2051
kär 556
kärra 354
kök 1165
kön 1922
köpa 322
köpman 1305
köra 658
körsbär 389
kött 1291

L

lada 191
lag 1187, 2145
laga 830
lager 1189
laglig 1202
lam 1178
land 511, 1179
lantbruk 786
lantbrukare 787
lastbil 2255
leda 1191
ledare 974, 1192
ledig 2302
ledighet 1203
leende 1978
lejon 1224
leksak 2232
lektion 1206
leva 1232
levande 63
leverera 578, 2105
licens 1214
lida 2088
lik 62, 1220, 1953
lika 720
likformig 2278
likgiltighet 1086
likna 1795
lim 933
lina 1223
lista 1228
listig 1975
lita på 1773
liten 1231, 1976
liter 1230
liv 1217
livsviktig 2323
ljud 1424, 2003
ljudlig 1245
ljus 1218
locka 537
logik 1237
lon 2331
lova 1640
luft 55
lugn 329
lukt 1462, 1876
lukta 1977
lunch 1252
lustig 83, 900
lycka 988, 1248
lycklig 989, 1249
lydnad 1446
lyssna 1229
låg 1247
låga 832
lån 1233
låna 271
lång 1240
långsam 1974
långt 784
lås 1235
låta 1207
låtsa 1655
läcka 1194
läcker 576
läder 1197
läge 1234
lägenhet 103
läger 331
lägga 1707
lägga sig 1216
läka 535
läkare 1571
längre 788
längs 69
läpp 1225
lära 2143
lära sig utantill 1300
lära sig 1195
lärare 2144
lärobok 2166
läsa 1734
lätt 680
lättja 1190
lättnad 1771
löfte 1682
lögn 1215
lögnare 1211
löjlig 850, 1818
lök 1475
lön 1855
lördag 1865
lös 1242
lössläppa 1770
löv 1193

M

magasin 2057
mage 2055
magi 1257
maj 1284
majoritet 1264
majs 504
makt 1638
mala 966
man 1266
marin 1391
marknad 1277
marmelad 1133
mars 1275
mask 2415
maskin 1253
maskineri 1254
maskinskriva 2270
mat 848
mata 802
matematik 1282
med 2400
medalj 1293
medan 2375
medborgerlig 414
meddela 1436
meddelande 450, 1310
medföra 298
medicin 1294
medkänsla 2127
medlem 1299
medlidande 1586
medveten 482
medveten om 167
mekaniker 1292
mellan 237
mellerst 1316
melon 1297
men 318
mening 1289, 1481, 1907
mer 1348
mest 1351
metall 1311
metalltråd 2397
meter 1313
metod 1314
Mexiko 1315
middag 610, 1427
midja 2333
midnatt 1317
mig 1286
mig själv 1375
mil 1319
mild 916
militär 1320
miljard 242
million 1323
min 1325, 1374
mindre 1205
minnas 1777
minne 1301
minst 1196
minus 1326
minut 1327
mirakel 1328
missförstå 1334
misslyckas 775
missnöje 633
misstanke 2118
misstänka 2117
mistag 1333
mjuk 1990

segling 1852
sekel 368
sekreterare 1894
sekund 1892
semester 2303
sen 1183
senare 1184
september 1911
seriös 1912
servett 1380
sex 1963
sextio 1965
sexton 1964
sida 1511, 1948
sig själva 2175
sigill 1888
sigsjälvt 1131
sikta 54
silver 1952
simbassäng 1618
simma 2123
sinn 1130
sinne 1904
sist 1182
sittplats 1891
situation 1962
sju 1916
sjuk 1947
sjukdom 624, 1067
sjukhus 1039
sjuksköterska 1443
sjunga 1958
sjunka 1959
sjuttio 1918
sjutton 1917
själ 2002
själslig 1303
självisk 1901
självmord 2092
självständighet 1083
sjö 1177
sjöman 1853
skada 546, 992, 1092
skaffa sig 21
skaka 1924
skal 1541
skam 1926
skamsen 134
skapa 524
skatt 2140
sked 2027
skepp 1935
skicka bort 629
skicklig 419
skicklighet 1967
skillnad 606
skilsmässa 640
skina 1934
skjorta 1936
skjuta 1939
skjuta på 1706
sko 1938
skog 858
skola 1878
skonliteratur 810
skorsten 399
Skottland 1883
skovel 1944
skratt 1186
skratta 1185
skrika 1885, 1943
skriva 2425
skrivare 2426
skryta 260
skräck 884, 2162
skrämma 1873
skugga 1923
skuld 558, 795
skulptur 1886
skvaller 943
skydda 1689
skyldig 666, 975
skyldig, vara 1506
skyldighet 1450
skymning 2266
skynda sig 1056
skådespelare 27
skådespelerska 28
skål 277
skägg 205
skämt 1143
skär 1583
skära 543
skörd 993
slag 200
slank 1971
slappna av 1769
slips 2205
slut 703
sluta 422
slutlig 819
slutsats 468
slå 206, 1027
släkting 1768
släktskap 1767
släpa 652
släppa in 34
slö 667
smak 2139
smickra 836
smuts 615
smutsig 616
smälta 1298
smärta 1512
smör 319
smörgås 1862
snabb 790
snart 2000
snickare 352
snö 1984
snöre 2071
socialism 1987
socka 1989
socker 2090
sol 2099
soldat 1992
solnedgång 2102
soluppgång 2101
sommar 2097
son 1998
sondotter 949
sonson 952
soppa 2004
sorg 2001
sorgsen 1850
sort 1161
sova 1970
sovande 137
Sovjetunionen 2009
sovrum 211
Spanien 2013
sparka 1156
specialitet 2017
speciell 2016
specifik 2018
spegel 1329
spel 908
spela 907, 1598
spets 1540
spik 1377
spindel 2023
spion 2032
sport 2028
spricka 519
sprida 2030
springa 1846
sprit 1227
språk 1180
spänning 2067
spöke 922
stad 413, 2231
stark 2072
stat 2041
station 2044
statistik 2045
staty 2046
stava 2021
stearinljus 337
steg 2050
stege 1174
steka 893
stiftelse 867
stig 1534
stiga upp 1826
stilla 1716
stjäla 2047
stjärna 2039
stock 1236
stoff 1283
stol 372
stolt 1692
stolthet 1660
stoppa 2056
stor 241, 960, 1181
storartad 948, 1258
Storbritannien 961, 2284
storlek 1966
storm 2058
straff 1543
straffa 1701
strand 202, 1940
strejk 2070
strida 815
strumpa 2054
strupe 2197
strypa 404
stråle 1730
sträcka 2068
sträng 1920, 2069
sträva 138
ström 2064
student 2075
studera 2076
stycke 1576
stygg 1389
styra 1267
styrelse 1268
styrka 2066

stå 2038
stål 2049
stället, i...för 1101
stämning 1346
ständig 1557
stängsel 806
stöld 2171
störa 637
stövel 268
subjekt 2078
substans 2082
substantiv 1437
subtrahera 2085
succé 2086
summa 2095, 2227
sur 2005
svag 801, 2352
sval 501
svamp 1370
svans 2130
svar 96
svara 1786
svart 249
svart tavla 250
svartsjuk 1137
svepa in 2422
Sverige 2121
svett 1564
svimma 776
svår 607
svälja 2119
svältning 2040
svänga 2124
svärd 2126
svärja 2120
sy 1921
Sydafrika 2007
Sydamerika 2008
sympatisk 1416
synd 1956
syndig 2384
synlig 2321
sysselsättning 1458
system 2128
syster 1960
systerdotter 1417
systerson 1404
så 133, 2010
såg 1868
således 2202
sång 1999
sår 2421
såra 1463
såvida ej 2290
säga 1869
säker 369, 1851, 2109
säkerligen 2110
sälja 1902
sällan 1899
sällskap 453
sällsynt 1726
sända 1903
säng 210
särsjuktsynnerhet 725
sätt 1270
sätta sig 1961
söder 2006
söka 1889
söndag 2100
sörja 1359
söt 2122

T

ta 2131
tack 2168
tacksam 956
tak 1834
tal 2019
tala 2015, 2133
tala om 2152
talang 2132
tallrik 1595
talrik 1442
tam 2135
tand 2148, 2223
tandläkare 583
tanke 2192
tant 156
tapper 283
tavla 1574
taxi 2141
te 2142
teater 2170
tecken 1949
tegelsten 292
telefon 2150
telegram 2149
television 2151
tema 2174
temperatur 2153
tendens 2157
tennis 2159
teori 2177
termometer 2180
tid 2207
tidig 674
tidning 1413
tidskrift 1256
till 2212
tilldra sig 152
tilldragande 153
tillfredsställning 1864
tillfångata 345
tillfälle 1456, 1482
tillfällig 1457, 2154
tillfällighet 377
tillhöra 223
tillkännage 92
tillräcklig 712, 2089
tills 2292
tillsammans 2214
tillverka 1272
tillåta 65
tillåtelse 1558
tillägga 30
tillämpa 109
timme 1042
tio 2156
tisdag 2260
titel 2211
titta 1241
Tjeckoslovakien 544
tjock 2183
tjugo 2264
tjur 307
tjuv 2184
tjäna 675
tjänst 796, 1914
toalett 2215
tolerera 2216
tolka 1113
tolv 2263
tom 701
tomat 2217
ton 2219
topp 2224
torka av 2396
torn 2230
tornado 2226
torr 664
torsdag 2201
tradition 2235
trafik 2236
tragedi 2237
trakt 1759
traktor 2233
transport 2243
transportera 2242
trappa 2036
tre 2196
trettio 2190
tretton 2189
triangel 2249
triumf 2251
tro 221, 778
trogen 779
trots 595
trumma 662
tryck 1654
trycka 1653, 1665
tråd 2194
tråkig 269
trång 1382
trä 2408
träd 2248
trädgård 909
träning 2239
trött 2210, 2355
tugga 392
tum 1078
tung 1009
tunga 2220
tunn 2185
tunna 192
Turkiet 2261
tusen 2193
tveka 1019
tvilling 2267
tvinga 856
tvivel 650
två 2269
två gånger 2265
tvål 1985
tvärs över 22
tvätta 2343
tycka illa om 628
tycka om 1221
tydlig 1455
tydligen 105
tyg 423
Tyskland 920
tystnad 1951
tåg 2238
tålamod 1535
tält 2160
tändsticka 1281
tänka 2187